STEPS IN THE ACCOUNTING CYCLE

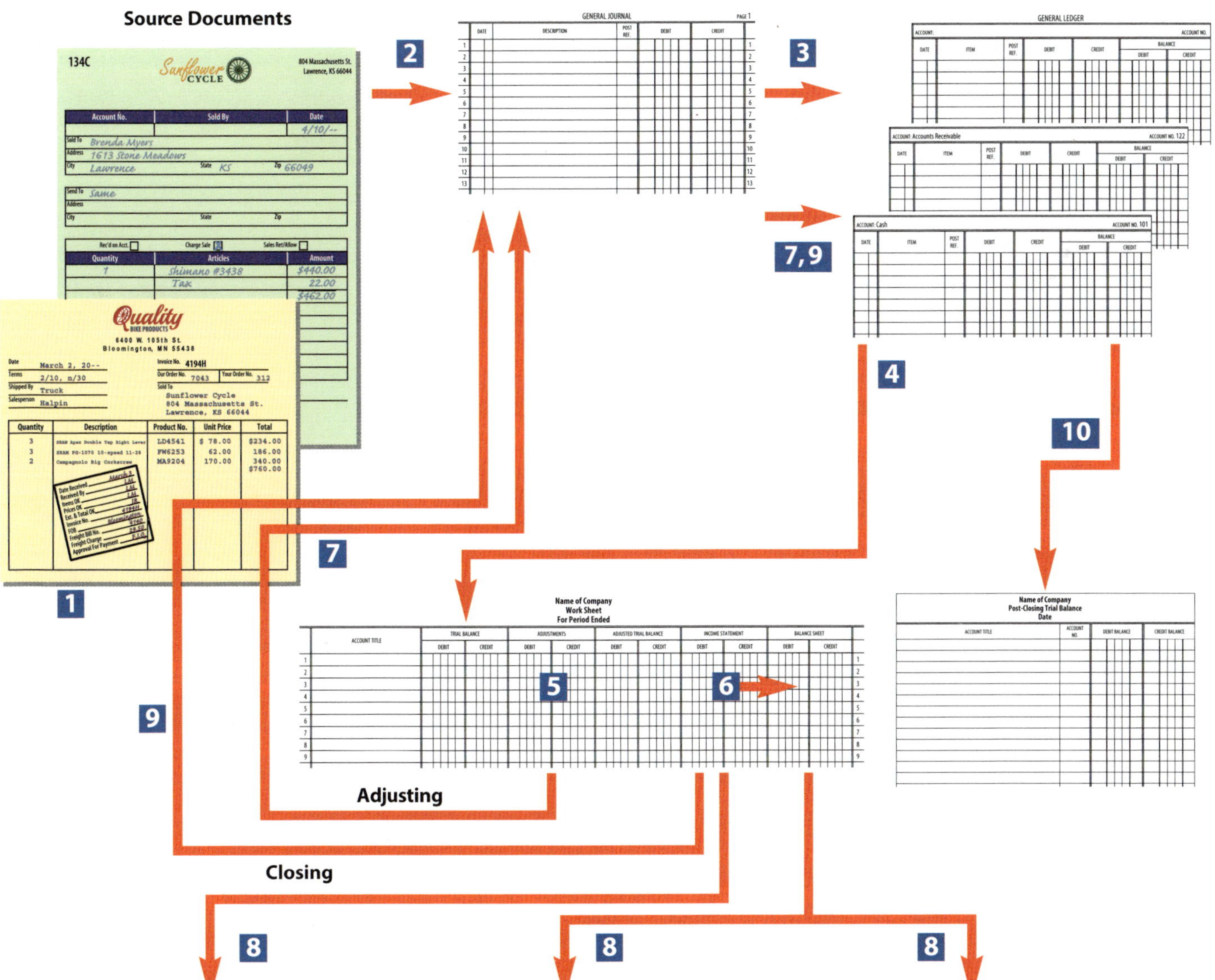

Mitchell's Campus Delivery Income Statement For Month Ended June 30, 20 --		
Revenues:		
Delivery fees		$2,150
Expenses:		
Wages expense	$650	
Rent expense	200	
Phone expense	50	
Total expenses		900
Net income		$1,250

Mitchell's Campus Delivery Statement of Owner's Equity For Month Ended June 30, 20 --		
Mitchell Williams, capital, June 1, 20--		$ —
Investments during June		2,000
Total investment		$2,000
Net income for June	$1,250	
Less: withdrawals for June	150	
Increase in capital		1,100
Mitchell Williams, capital, June 30, 20--		$3,100

Mitchell's Campus Delivery Balance Sheet June 30, 20 --			
Assets		Liabilities	
Cash	$ 370	Accounts payable	$1,800
Accounts receivable	650		
Supplies	80	Owner's Equity	
Prepaid insurance	200	Mitchell Williams, capital	3,100
Delivery equipment	3,600		
		Total liabilities and	
Total assets	$4,900	owner's equity	$4,900

Steps in the Accounting Cycle

During Accounting Period:

1. Analyze source documents.
2. Journalize the transactions.
3. Post to the ledger accounts.

End of Accounting Period:

4. Prepare a trial balance.
5. Determine and prepare the needed adjustments on the work sheet.
6. Complete an end-of-period work sheet.
7. Journalize and post the adjusting entries.
8. Prepare an income statement, statement of owner's equity, and balance sheet.
9. Journalize and post the closing entries.
10. Prepare a post-closing trial balance.

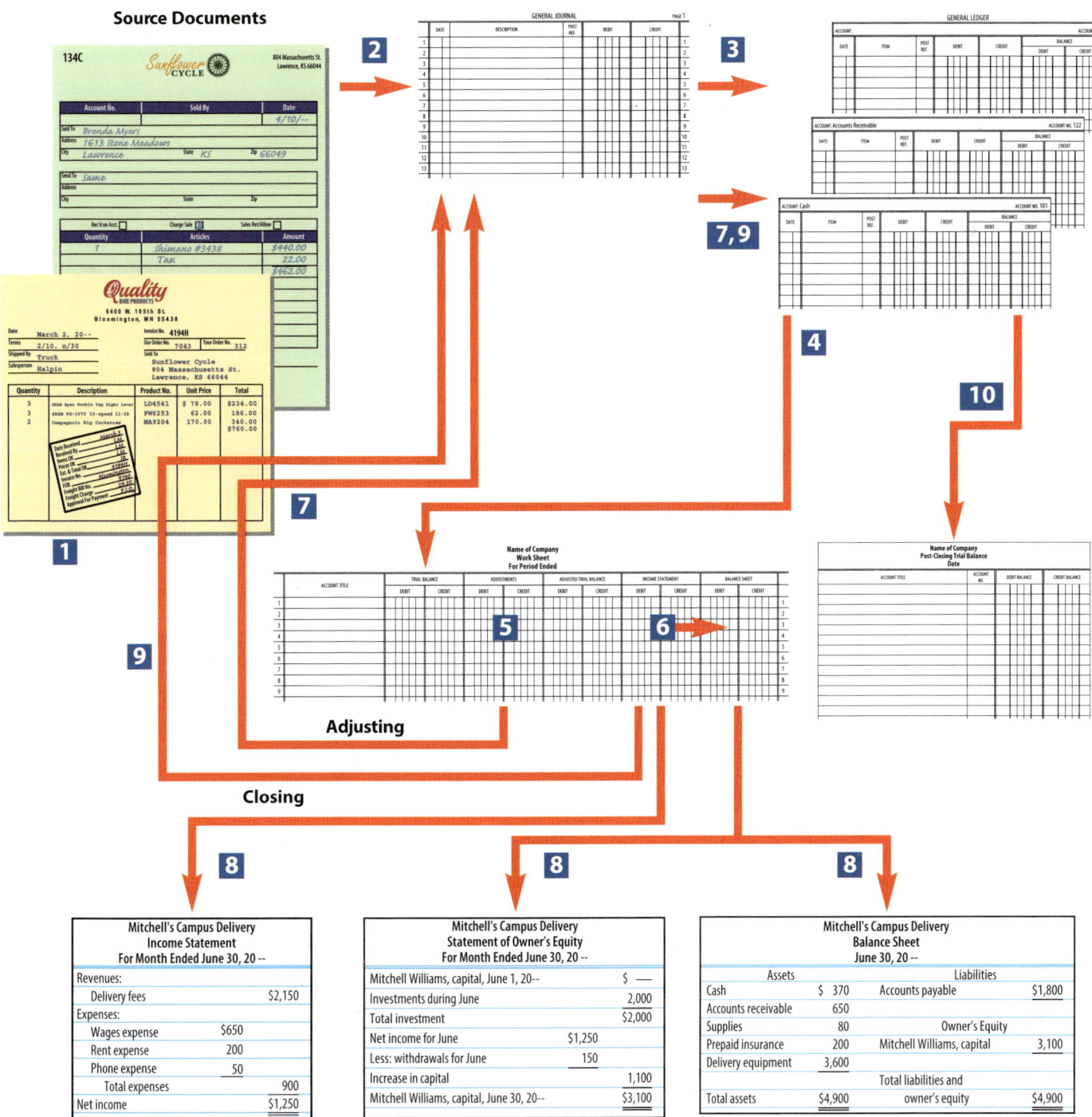

23e

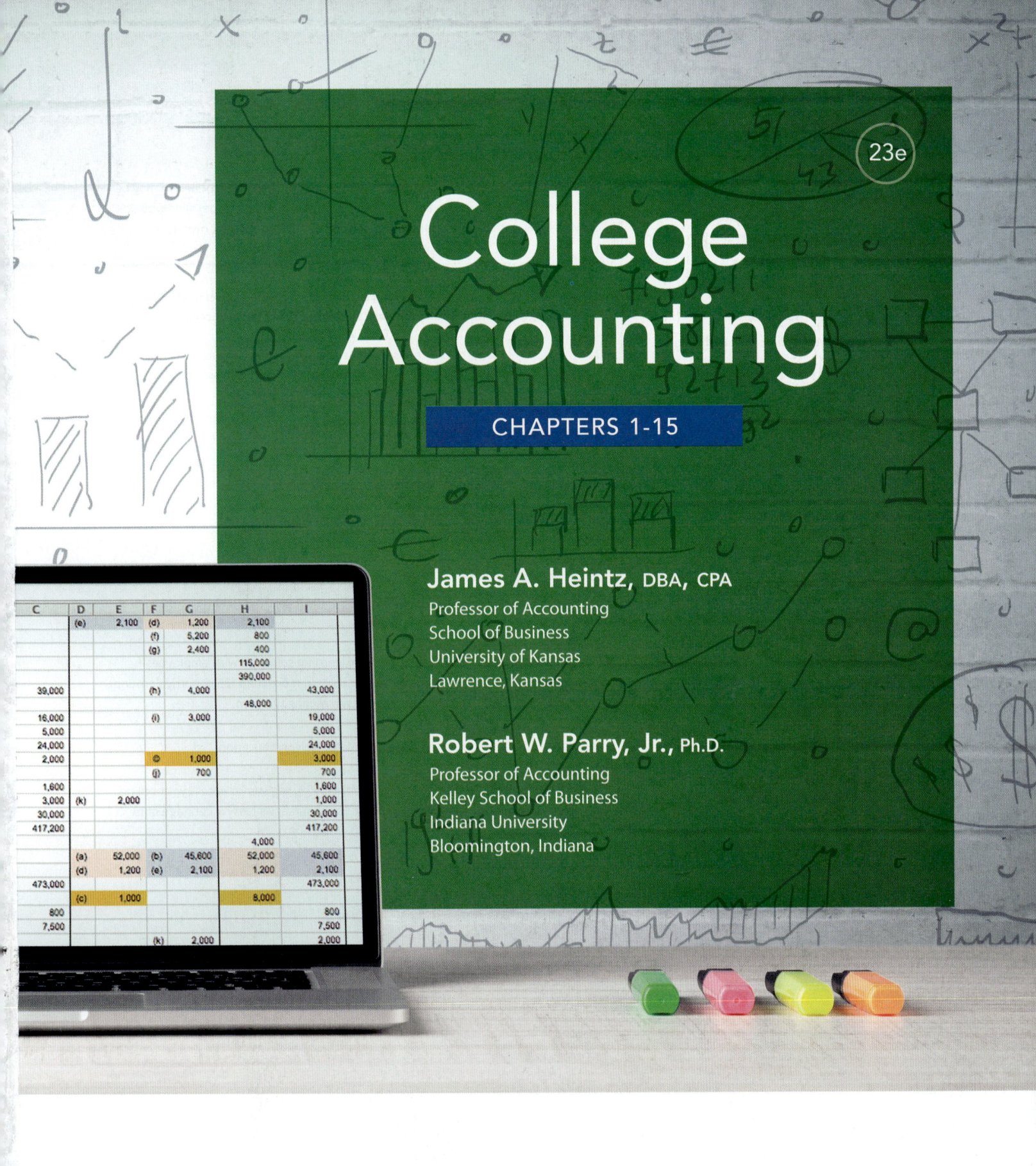

College Accounting

CHAPTERS 1-15

James A. Heintz, DBA, CPA
Professor of Accounting
School of Business
University of Kansas
Lawrence, Kansas

Robert W. Parry, Jr., Ph.D.
Professor of Accounting
Kelley School of Business
Indiana University
Bloomington, Indiana

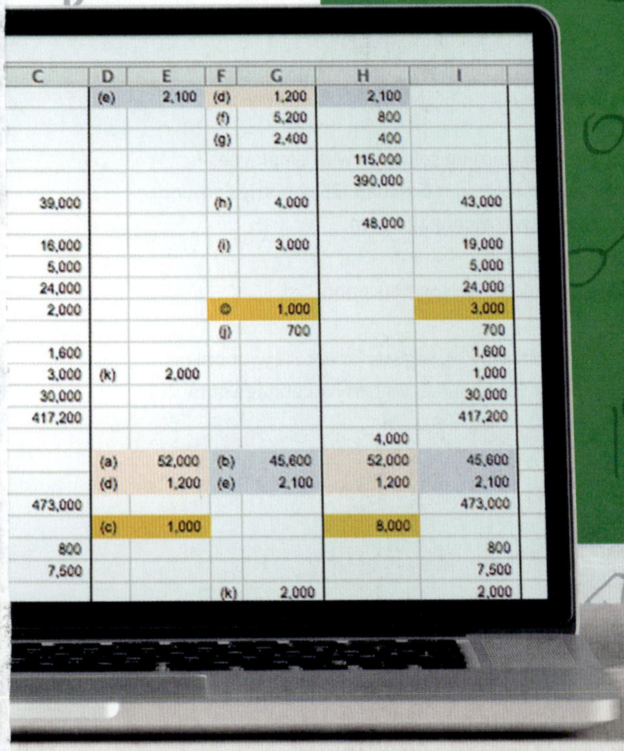

CENGAGE

Australia • Brazil • Mexico • Singapore • United Kingdom • United States

CENGAGE

College Accounting, **23rd Edition, Chapters 1-15**
James A. Heintz and Robert W. Parry

Senior Vice President, Higher Ed Product, Content, and Market Development: Erin Joyner

Product Director: Jason Fremder

Product Manager: Christopher Rader

Learning Designer: Kristen Meere

Senior Digital Delivery Leads: Sally Nieman and Tim Ross

Senior Content Manager: Tim Bailey

Product Assistant: Aiyana Moore

Executive Marketing Manager: Nathan Anderson

Production Service/Composition: SPi Global

Senior Designer: Bethany Bourgeois

Cover and Internal Designer: Ke Design/Ted Knapke

Cover Image: iStock.com/cifotart

Design Images:

"A Broader View" Feature: Johannes Kornelius/Shutterstock.com

"Your Perspective" Feature: leungchopan/Shutterstock.com

Theme image used on title page, front and back matter tabs, and part openers: ra2studio/Shutterstock.com

Intellectual Property Analyst: Reba Frederics

Intellectual Property Project Manager: Carly Belcher

Library of Congress Control Number: 2018956464

ISBN: 978-1-337-79476-3

Cengage
20 Channel Center Street
Boston, MA 02210
USA

Cengage is a leading provider of customized learning solutions with employees residing in nearly 40 different countries and sales in more than 125 countries around the world. Find your local representative at **www.cengage.com**.

Cengage products are represented in Canada by Nelson Education, Ltd.

To learn more about Cengage platforms and services, register or access your online learning solution, or purchase materials for your course, visit **www.cengage.com**.

Printed in the United States of America
Print Number: 01 Print Year: 2018

ABOUT THE AUTHORS

James A. Heintz

James A. Heintz was a Professor of Accounting for 15 years, including 13 years as the Director of Accounting and Information Systems, in the School of Business at the University of Kansas. He is now Professor Emeritus at Kansas. Prior to joining the University of Kansas, he was Accounting Department Head at the University of Connecticut for eight years, and Assistant, Associate, and Full Professor at Indiana University for 20 years. He also taught for many years for the University of Kansas and the University of Iowa in a study abroad program in Northern Italy. His doctorate is from Washington University in St. Louis, and he is a CPA. He was Price Waterhouse Faculty Fellow at Indiana, Arthur Andersen Faculty Fellow at Connecticut, and Deloitte & Touche Faculty Fellow at Kansas. Professor Heintz has won numerous school and university teaching awards, including five teaching awards from Doctoral Student Associations. He has served in various capacities on 27 doctoral dissertation committees. Professor Heintz has published numerous articles in accounting and business journals, such as *The Accounting Review; Auditing: A Journal of Practice and Theory; Accounting Horizons; Accounting and Business Research; Journal of Business Finance and Accounting;* and *International Journal of Accounting Education and Research*. He served on the editorial board of *Auditing: A Journal of Practice and Theory* for seven years and was president of the Accounting Programs Leadership Group of the AAA. He also has participated in external reviews of accounting programs at 12 major universities.

Robert W. Parry

Robert W. Parry is Professor Emeritus of Accounting at Indiana University's Kelley School of Business in Bloomington, Indiana. An accomplished teacher, Professor Parry has taught accounting at virtually all levels. While earning his MBA, he taught accounting at Bishop Klonowski High School in Scranton, Pennsylvania. While earning his Ph.D., he taught introductory financial and managerial accounting at Northampton County Community College and Lehigh University. At Indiana, he taught in the Undergraduate, MBA, MBA in Accounting, Master of Science in Accounting, the online Kelley Direct MBA Program, and Ph.D. Programs. In addition, he has taught accounting in the Consortium of Universities for International Studies in Asolo, Italy. During his 35 years at Indiana University, he won or was nominated for a total of 27 teaching excellence awards, including recognition twice by *Business Week* as one of the country's Outstanding MBA Faculty. In addition, he was awarded the Indiana University Distinguished Service Award for his efforts in planning and deploying a new, integrated MBA Core Program. He also received the Kelley School of Business Innovative Teaching Award for his role in designing and implementing the curriculum for the Master of Science in Accounting Program.

Parry has conducted research in the areas of public finance, governmental accounting, and accounting education. His work has been published in many journals, including *Public Finance Quarterly*, *Public Budgeting and Financial Management*, *Financial Analysts Journal*, *Accounting Horizons*, *Management Accounting*, *Research in Accounting Regulation*, *Research in Governmental and Non-Profit Accounting*, *Issues in Accounting Education*, and *Journal of Accounting Education*. Professor Parry was a lead author on the *Service Efforts and Accomplishments* research report published by the Governmental Accounting Standards Board. He also served on many committees of the American Accounting Association, including President of the Government and Nonprofit Accounting Section.

Rob and his wife, Jane, enjoy golf, ballroom dancing, hiking, kayaking, travel, and working in the yard. They have two children, Mitchell and Jessica, and four grandchildren, Anya Catrin Parry, Rohan Macsen Parry, Damon Robert Williams, and Mitchell David Williams.

Where *Accounting Education* and the *Real World* Meet

As the leading choice in college accounting, Heintz & Parry's ***College Accounting 23e*** combines a proven, step-by-step approach and excellent examples with a tightly integrated online homework tool that makes accounting understandable to every student, regardless of their accounting background or business experience. The Heintz & Parry program, well-known for its quality, consistency, and technology, focuses on the practical skills students need to transition from the classroom to the workplace. With even more practice opportunities and independent study resources than ever before, the 23rd edition delivers the tools students need to succeed.

As the authors of *College Accounting 23e*, we are excited about this new edition and the enhancements made to the CengageNOWv2 online homework system. We believe that a truly integrated textbook and online homework system that serves as an extension of the classroom will help students be more successful in the college accounting course and better prepared for the real world.

Many of the end-of-chapter exercises and problems in CNOWv2 have "Show Me How" videos. If you are having difficulty with an assignment, a video icon indicates that additional help is available in CengageNOWv2. There, you can click on the icon. A voice-over, PowerPoint video presentation will pop up with an explanation of how to solve a similar exercise. We think these videos are similar to a quick visit to our offices. Hope you find them helpful.

Throughout the revision process, we spent much of our time participating in the CengageNOWv2 development. We viewed it as essential to clearly connect CengageNOWv2 with the *College Accounting 23e* text by ensuring consistent terminology use, meaningful feedback for the students, and examples consistent with those in the textbook.

We hope this preface will serve as a guide to help you gain the most knowledge from this text and its supporting materials.

Sincerely,

Jim Heintz and Rob Parry

Chapters 1–27: 9781337794756
Chapters 1–15: 9781337794763
Chapters 1–9: 9781337794787

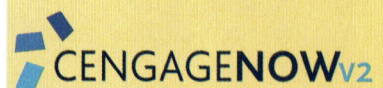

CENGAGE**NOW**v2

Where *Accounting Education* and Digital Learning Meet

College Accounting 23e combined with CengageNOWv2 elevates student thinking with unique content that addresses each phase of the learning process. The text combined with the digital content in **CengageNOWv2** offers students clearly defined tools to optimize their learning experience. Included are many proven resources including algorithmic activities, test bank, course management tools, reporting and assessment options, and much more.

Recent CengageNOWv2 Enhancements

- Refreshed Design: This refreshed look will help you and your students focus easily and quickly on what is important, while maintaining the same functionality that CengageNOW users know and love.
- Integration with Popular Learning Management Systems: Single login, deep linking, and grade return! (Check with your local Learning Consultant for more details!)
- Upload Files Capability: You can now upload files in CengageNOWv2 for student use—including videos, Excel files, Word files, and more.
- Email Instructor Feature: Students can now send you a screenshot of the question they are working on directly through CengageNOWv2 and ask specific questions about where they are stuck.
- Better Date Management: When modifying assignment due dates for a whole course, the system will now automatically adjust due dates based on a new start date, making it easier to reuse a course from one term to the next and adjust for snow days.
- Streamlined Assignment Creation Process: A simplified and streamlined Assignment Creation process allows instructors to quickly set up and manage assignments from a single page!
- New Report Options: New reporting options allow you to get better reports on your students' progress.
- New Student Registration Process: When you create a course, a URL will be generated that will automatically take students right into the instructor's course without them having to enter the course key!

CENGAGENOWv2

Blank Sheet of Paper Experience A less-leading Blank Sheet of Paper Experience discourages overreliance on the system.

- The use of drop down menus and Smart Entry (type-ahead) has been eliminated.
- Students must refer to the Chart of Accounts and decide for themselves which account is impacted.
- The number of accounts in each transaction is not given away.
- Whether the account should be debited or credited is not given away.
- Transactions may be entered in any order (as long as the entries are correct).
- Check My Work feedback only reports on what students have actually attempted, which prevents students from "guessing" their way through the assignment.

"Jim and I love the "Blank Sheet of Paper Experience" for the Mastery Problems and select end-of-chapter problems. This addition in CengageNOWv2 gives students the chance to complete the problems online without the technology giving away the correct responses."

Where *Accounting Education* and Digital Learning Meet

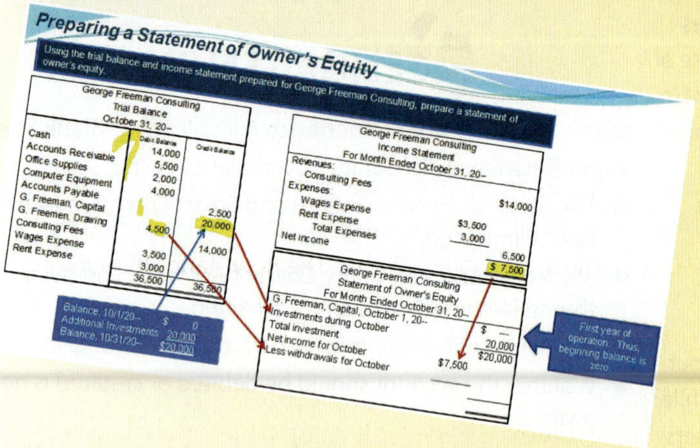

Mastery Problems available in Blank Sheet of Paper offer students a real-world opportunity to test their expertise in each chapter's content. Check My Work feedback provides truly helpful guidance to assist in the completion of a question before the student submits the assignment for grading. This feature can be turned on or off by the instructor.

- **Easy-to-use course management options** offer flexibility and continuity from one semester to the next.
- The most **robust** and **flexible assignment options** in the industry.
- **Cengage Learning Testing Powered by Cognero** is a flexible, online system that allows you to:
  - author, edit, and manage test bank content from multiple Cengage Learning solutions
  - create multiple test versions in an instant
  - deliver tests from your LMS, your classroom, or wherever you want
- Each problem is tagged by topic, learning objectives, level of difficulty, Bloom's Taxonomy, AICPA, ACBSP, and general business program standards allowing you to **analyze student work from the gradebook and generate reports on learning outcomes**.

> "If a student needs help with end-of-chapter materials, in Show Me How videos, Rob and I show students how to solve sample problems and exercises."
>
> Jim Heintz

Where *Accounting Education* and Digital Learning Meet

A Note to Faculty Colleagues on Revenue Recognition and Spreadsheets

Revenue Recognition

In this edition, we have expanded our discussion of sales returns and allowances to address the new revenue recognition standard issued by the FASB and IASB. This standard emphasizes the concept of recognizing revenue once the "performance obligation" has been satisfied. Of course, if a customer has the right to return merchandise, the performance obligation has not been fully satisfied at the time of the initial sale. Businesses have always recorded the *actual* returns and allowances and reported the related impact on the financial statements. The new standard requires firms to account for *actual and expected* returns and allowances: those that were returned this year and those expected to be returned next year as a result of this year's sales. We illustrate this process under the periodic and perpetual inventory systems. Here, let us share our approach to addressing this issue.

Periodic Inventory System—Under the periodic inventory system, Merchandise Inventory is not updated for inventory transactions during the year. We simply make an adjustment to the account at the end of the year. We make the same assumption for Estimated Returns Inventory and Customer Refunds Payable, new accounts introduced in this edition to address the new revenue recognition standard. No entries are made to these accounts during the year. Further, we assume Estimated Returns Inventory is adjusted the same way we have always adjusted Merchandise Inventory, by first removing the old inventory and then entering the new inventory in a two-step process. Customer Refunds Payable is also adjusted (up or down) at the end of each year to properly reflect the estimated refunds to be granted next year as a result of this year's sales.

Perpetual Inventory System—Under the perpetual inventory system, entries are made to Merchandise Inventory throughout the year. Thus, assuming no shrinkage, the balance of this account should reflect the merchandise inventory held by the business at any point in time. We make the same assumption for Estimated Returns Inventory. At the end of each year, this account is adjusted to reflect an estimate of the cost of the inventory sold this year, but expected to be returned next year. This is done by debiting Estimated Returns Inventory and crediting Cost of Goods Sold. When customers return inventory sold in the prior year we debit Merchandise Inventory and credit Estimated Returns Inventory.

Similarly, we adjust Customer Refunds Payable at the end of each year to reflect the customer refunds expected to be paid next year as a result of this year's sales. This is done by debiting Sales Returns and Allowances and crediting Customer Refunds Payable. When customers return inventory sold in the prior year, we debit Customer Refunds Payable and credit Cash.

New Six-Column Spreadsheet

In Chapters 5 and 6 you will see the familiar 10-column work sheet. However, in Chapter 14, we introduce a new six-column spreadsheet. This is done to recognize the important role computer spreadsheets play in accounting. We have eliminated the Income Statement and Balance Sheet columns and rely on the Adjusted Trial Balance columns for the preparation of financial statements. Further, we illustrate how net income can be calculated using the Adjusted Trial Balance Columns on the spreadsheet.

Where *Accounting Education*, the *Classroom*, and the *Workplace* Meet

Real-World Examples, bringing accounting concepts to life.

College Accounting, 23e maintains its dedication to its proven step-by-step style, clear explanations, excellent examples, and a relevant approach. Practical learning aids and fine-tuned pedagogy highlight and build upon key content to reinforce the accounting principles.

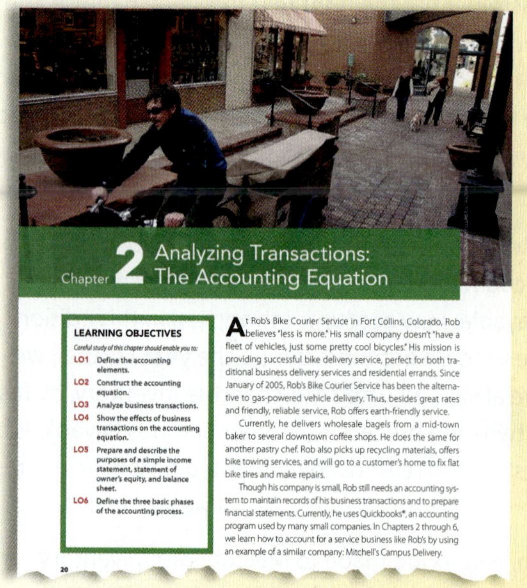

Chapter 2 Analyzing Transactions: The Accounting Equation

LEARNING OBJECTIVES

Careful study of this chapter should enable you to:

- LO1 Define the accounting elements.
- LO2 Construct the accounting equation.
- LO3 Analyze business transactions.
- LO4 Show the effects of business transactions on the accounting equation.
- LO5 Prepare and describe the purposes of a simple income statement, statement of owner's equity, and balance sheet.
- LO6 Define the three basic phases of the accounting process.

At Rob's Bike Courier Service in Fort Collins, Colorado, Rob believes "less is more." His small company doesn't "have a fleet of vehicles, just some pretty cool bicycles." His mission is providing successful bike delivery service, perfect for both traditional business delivery services and residential errands. Since January of 2005, Rob's Bike Courier Service has been the alternative to gas-powered vehicle delivery. Thus, besides great rates and friendly, reliable service, Rob offers earth-friendly service.

Currently, he delivers wholesale bagels from a mid-town baker to several downtown coffee shops. He does the same for another pastry chef. Rob also picks up recycling materials, offers bike towing services, and will go to a customer's home to fix flat bike tires and make repairs.

Though his company is small, Rob still needs an accounting system to maintain records of his business transactions and to prepare financial statements. Currently, he uses Quickbooks®, an accounting program used by many small companies. In Chapters 2 through 6, we learn how to account for a service business like Rob's by using an example of a similar company: Mitchell's Campus Delivery.

20

- **Chapter openers** feature small companies from throughout the United States, setting the stage for why each chapter's content is relevant and important in the business world.

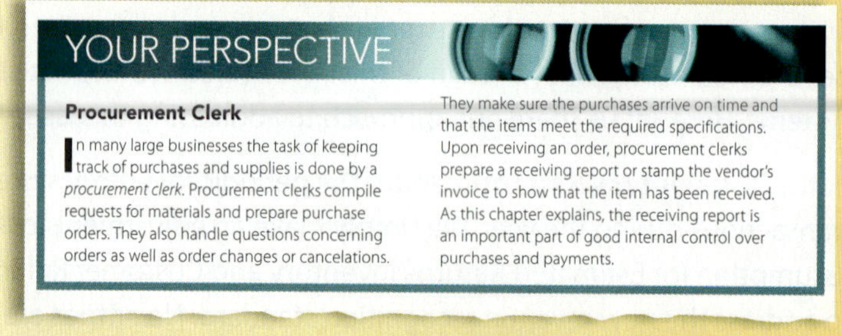

YOUR PERSPECTIVE

Procurement Clerk

In many large businesses the task of keeping track of purchases and supplies is done by a *procurement clerk*. Procurement clerks compile requests for materials and prepare purchase orders. They also handle questions concerning orders as well as order changes or cancelations. They make sure the purchases arrive on time and that the items meet the required specifications. Upon receiving an order, procurement clerks prepare a receiving report or stamp the vendor's invoice to show that the item has been received. As this chapter explains, the receiving report is an important part of good internal control over purchases and payments.

- **Your Perspective** showcases everyday student jobs, such as a procurement clerk, cashier, or lodging manager to illustrate how accounting relates to tasks that students encounter on a daily basis. The jobs highlighted in the "Your Perspective" features throughout this textbook are described in detail in the *U.S. Bureau of Labor Statistics' Occupational Outlook Handbook* (OOH). For more information about each job, type the job title in the "Search Handbook" box in the OOH website.

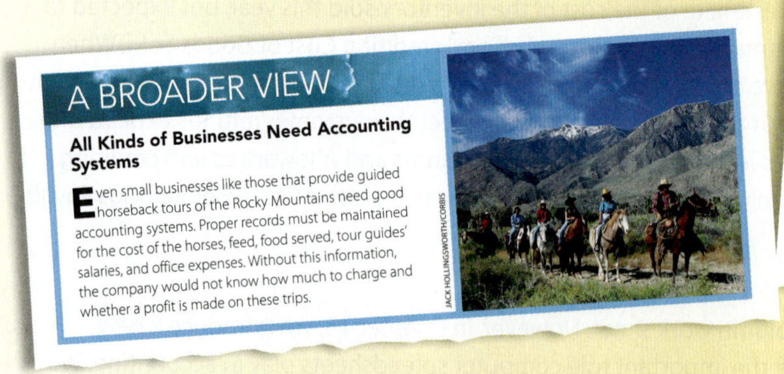

A BROADER VIEW

All Kinds of Businesses Need Accounting Systems

Even small businesses like those that provide guided horseback tours of the Rocky Mountains need good accounting systems. Proper records must be maintained for the cost of the horses, feed, food served, tour guides' salaries, and office expenses. Without this information, the company would not know how much to charge and whether a profit is made on these trips.

JACK HOLLINGSWORTH/CORBIS

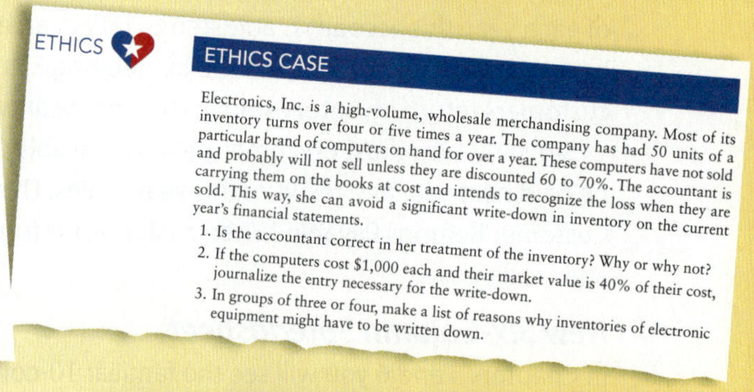

ETHICS

ETHICS CASE

Electronics, Inc. is a high-volume, wholesale merchandising company. Most of its inventory turns over four or five times a year. The company has had 50 units of a particular brand of computers on hand for over a year. These computers have not sold and probably will not sell unless they are discounted 60 to 70%. The accountant is carrying them on the books at cost and intends to recognize the loss when they are sold. This way, she can avoid a significant write-down in inventory on the current year's financial statements.

1. Is the accountant correct in her treatment of the inventory? Why or why not?
2. If the computers cost $1,000 each and their market value is 40% of their cost, journalize the entry necessary for the write-down.
3. In groups of three or four, make a list of reasons why inventories of electronic equipment might have to be written down.

- **A Broader View** feature provides captivating examples of actual business events or situations that relate to each chapter's accounting topics. Students more easily retain topics when they understand the connection to the business world.

- **Ethics Cases** provide future business leaders with a clear understanding of the important ethical implications in modern accounting procedures and decisions. These cases highlight work-related ethical dilemmas and invite further analysis by the student independently or through classroom discussions.

Where *Accounting Education*, the *Classroom*, and the *Workplace* Meet

Superior Pedagogy, designed to keep students on track and truly help them succeed.

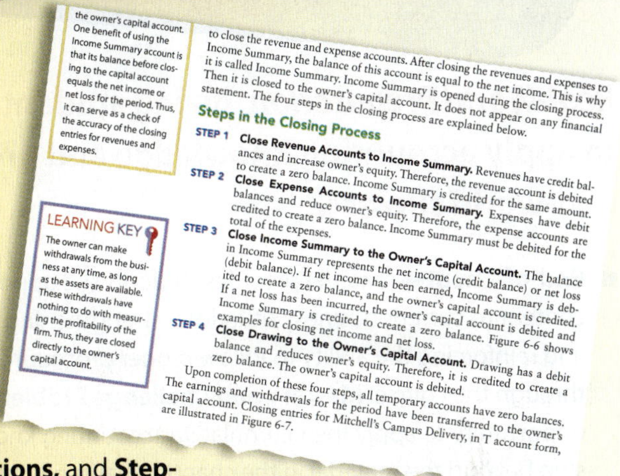

the owner's capital account. One benefit of using the Income Summary account is that its balance before closing to the capital account equals the net income or net loss for the period. Thus, it can serve as a check of the accuracy of the closing entries for revenues and expenses.

to close the revenue and expense accounts. After closing the revenues and expenses to Income Summary, the balance of this account is equal to the net income. This is why it is called Income Summary. Income Summary is opened during the closing process. Then it is closed to the owner's capital account. It does not appear on any financial statement. The four steps in the closing process are explained below.

Steps in the Closing Process

STEP 1 **Close Revenue Accounts to Income Summary.** Revenues have credit balances and increase owner's equity. Therefore, the revenue account is debited to create a zero balance. Income Summary is credited for the same amount.

STEP 2 **Close Expense Accounts to Income Summary.** Expenses have debit balances and reduce owner's equity. Therefore, the expense accounts are credited to create a zero balance. Income Summary must be debited for the total of the expenses.

STEP 3 **Close Income Summary to the Owner's Capital Account.** The balance in Income Summary represents the net income (credit balance) or net loss (debit balance). If net income has been earned, Income Summary is debited to create a zero balance, and the owner's capital account is credited. If a net loss has been incurred, the owner's capital account is debited and Income Summary is credited to create a zero balance. Figure 6-6 shows examples for closing net income and net loss.

STEP 4 **Close Drawing to the Owner's Capital Account.** Drawing has a debit balance and reduces owner's equity. Therefore, it is credited to create a zero balance. The owner's capital account is debited.

Upon completion of these four steps, all temporary accounts have zero balances. The earnings and withdrawals for the period have been transferred to the owner's capital account. Closing entries for Mitchell's Campus Delivery, in T account form, are illustrated in Figure 6-7.

LEARNING KEY The owner can make withdrawals from the business at any time, as long as the assets are available. These withdrawals have nothing to do with measuring the profitability of the firm. Thus, they are closed directly to the owner's capital account.

- **Learning Objectives** connect the chapter coverage from beginning to end.

  Problems in CengageNOWv2 are linked to the eBook, by Learning Objective, to guide students as they complete their homework.

CENGAGENOWv2

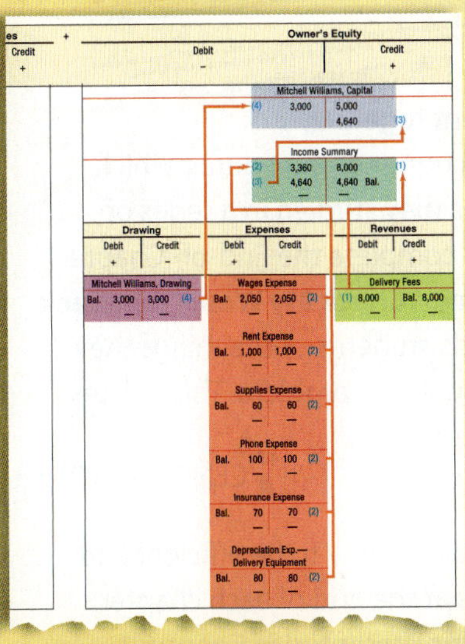

- **Excellent Examples, Clear Illustrations,** and **Step-by-Step Instructions** guide students visually through the steps of learning accounting. Heintz & Parry are well known for thorough, relevant, and visually simple examples.
- **Color-Coding System** helps students understand how accounts are classified and assists them with following the key transactions presented, clarifying the impact of transactions on the accounting equation.

CHECKPOINT ✓

Complete Checkpoint-2 on page 305 to test your basic understanding of LO4.

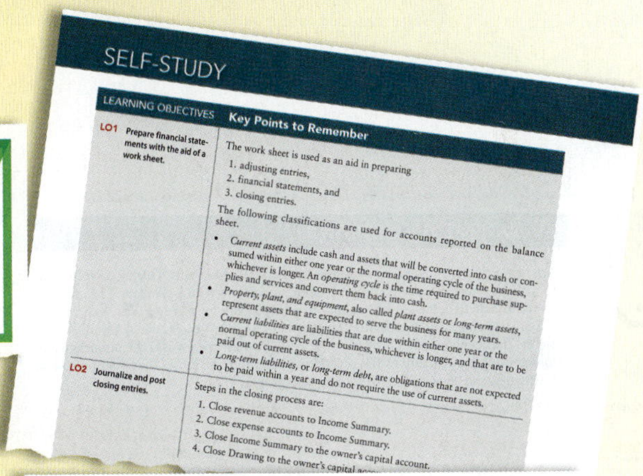

SELF-STUDY

LEARNING OBJECTIVES	Key Points to Remember
LO1 Prepare financial statements with the aid of a work sheet.	The work sheet is used as an aid in preparing 1. adjusting entries, 2. financial statements, and 3. closing entries. The following classifications are used for accounts reported on the balance sheet. • *Current assets* include cash and assets that will be converted into cash or consumed within either one year or the normal operating cycle of the business, whichever is longer. An *operating cycle* is the time required to purchase supplies and services and convert them back into cash. • *Property, plant, and equipment*, also called *plant assets* or *long-term assets*, represent assets that are expected to serve the business for many years. • *Current liabilities* are liabilities that are due within either one year or the normal operating cycle of the business, whichever is longer, and that are to be paid out of current assets. • *Long-term liabilities*, or *long-term debt*, are obligations that are not expected to be paid within a year and do not require the use of current assets.
LO2 Journalize and post closing entries.	Steps in the closing process are: 1. Close revenue accounts to Income Summary. 2. Close expense accounts to Income Summary. 3. Close Income Summary to the owner's capital account. 4. Close Drawing to the owner's capital account.

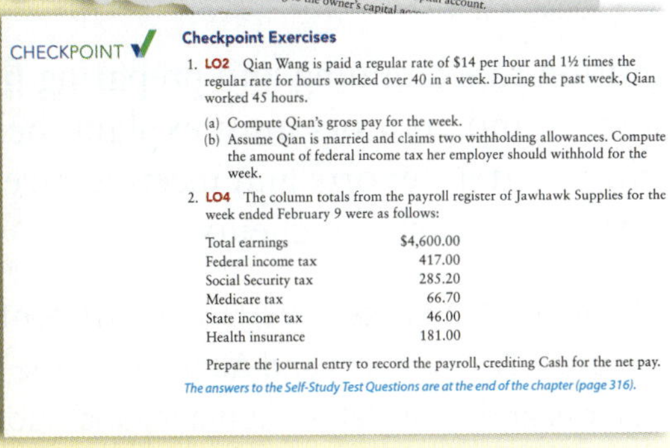

CHECKPOINT ✓ **Checkpoint Exercises**

1. **LO2** Qian Wang is paid a regular rate of $14 per hour and 1½ times the regular rate for hours worked over 40 in a week. During the past week, Qian worked 45 hours.
   (a) Compute Qian's gross pay for the week.
   (b) Assume Qian is married and claims two withholding allowances. Compute the amount of federal income tax her employer should withhold for the week.
2. **LO4** The column totals from the payroll register of Jawhawk Supplies for the week ended February 9 were as follows:

Total earnings	$4,600.00
Federal income tax	417.00
Social Security tax	285.20
Medicare tax	66.70
State income tax	46.00
Health insurance	181.00

Prepare the journal entry to record the payroll, crediting Cash for the net pay.

The answers to the Self-Study Test Questions are at the end of the chapter (page 316).

- **Self-Study featuring Checkpoint Exercises** offers the best in ongoing, self-review. These end-of-chapter summaries provide a strong framework for study, recap chapter content, emphasize **Key Points to Remember**, and provide **Demonstration Problems** and solutions. Checkpoint call-outs, at the end of each learning objective, direct students to the **Self-Study Test Questions and Checkpoint Exercises**, allowing students to check their understanding of each learning objective.
- **The Adaptive Study Plan within CengageNOWv2** allows students to focus their study on the areas they are weakest. First, students take a **quiz** to assess where they are now. An **Adaptive Study Plan** will be crafted based on their results. After working through the study plan resources, students can take **another quiz** to see how they improved.

CENGAGENOWv2

Where *Accounting Education*, the *Classroom*, and the *Workplace* Meet

Real-World Preparation, giving students the experience to apply accounting knowledge and prepare them for real-world success.

- **End-of-Chapter** material provides students the opportunity to apply chapter content to current business situations, strengthening decision-making skills, and reinforcing the ability to follow proper procedures as they progress through the course. **Mastery and Challenge Problems** give students the opportunity to apply their cumulative accounting knowledge and move a step beyond the material in the chapter, sharpening their problem solving and critical thinking skills.

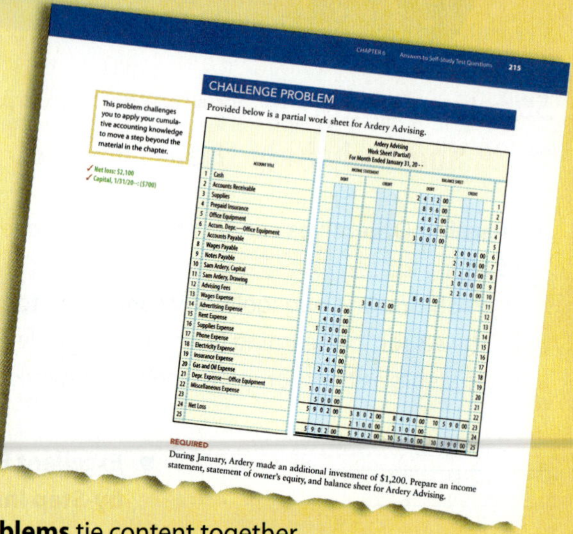

- **Comprehensive Problems** tie content together, giving students a chance to apply accounting procedures, which helps them understand the processes they studied in a series of chapters (1–6 and 7–15). As students complete the End-of- Chapter Material and Comprehensive Problems, **"Check My Work" feedback** (available in CengageNOWv2) reminds students of the things they need to consider when thinking through the problem. This creates an online instructional tool to help students reach deeper understanding.

CENGAGENOWv2

CHECK LIST
- Managing
- Planning
- Drafting
- Break
- Revising
- Managing

MANAGING YOUR WRITING

You are a public accountant with many small business clients. During a recent visit to a client's business, the bookkeeper approached you with a problem. The columns of the trial balance were not equal. You helped the bookkeeper find and correct the error, but believe you should go one step further. Write a memo to all of your clients that explains the purpose of the double-entry framework, the importance of maintaining the equality of the accounting equation, the errors that might cause an inequality, and suggestions for finding the errors.

- **Managing Your Writing** teaches students how to be efficient and effective writers. Writing assignments at the end of each chapter are accompanied by a **Checklist of tips** presented in Chapter 1, serving as a reminder to students to seek the additional help as they complete their assignment.

"In addition to examining and preparing financial documentation, accountants and auditors must explain their findings. This includes preparing written reports and meeting face-to-face with organization managers and individual clients."

Bureau of Labor Statistics, U.S. Department of Labor, Occupational Outlook Handbook, Accountants and Auditors, on the Internet at https://www.bls.gov/ooh/business-and-financial/accountants-and-auditors.htm (visited June 11, 2018).

Where *Accounting Education*, the *Classroom*, and the *Workplace* Meet

Real-World Technology, providing students the employability skills and confidence needed for workplace success.

- **Excel Online** Cengage and Microsoft have partnered in CNOWv2 to provide students with a uniform, authentic Excel experience. It provides instant feedback, built-in video tips, and easily accessible spreadsheet work. These features allow you to spend more time teaching college accounting applications, and less time troubleshooting Excel.

  These new algorithmic activities offer pre-populated data directly in Microsoft Excel Online. Each student receives their own version of the problem to perform the necessary data calculations in Excel Online. Their work is constantly saved in Cengage cloud storage as a part of homework assignments in CNOWv2. It's easily retrievable so students can review their answers without cumbersome file management and numerous downloads/uploads.

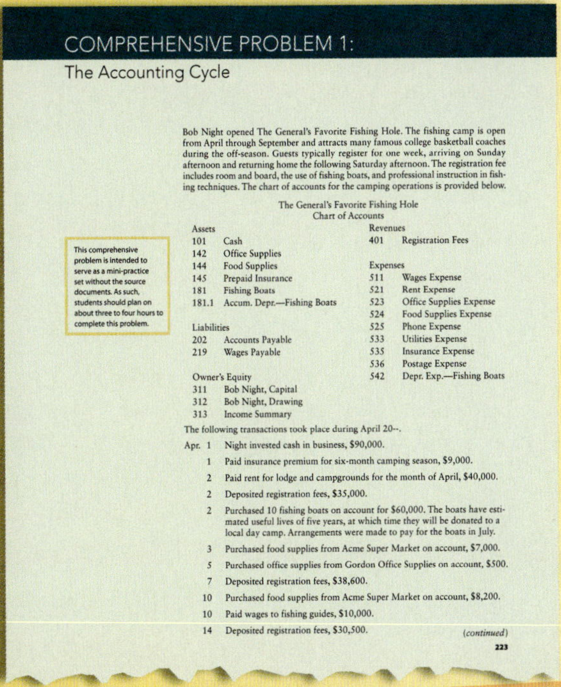

COMPREHENSIVE PROBLEM 1:

The Accounting Cycle

This comprehensive problem is intended to serve as a mini-practice set without the source documents. As such, students should plan on about three to four hours to complete this problem.

Bob Night opened The General's Favorite Fishing Hole. The fishing camp is open from April through September and attracts many famous college basketball coaches during the off-season. Guests typically register for one week, arriving on Sunday afternoon and returning home the following Saturday afternoon. The registration fee includes room and board, the use of fishing boats, and professional instruction in fishing techniques. The chart of accounts for the camping operations is provided below.

The General's Favorite Fishing Hole
Chart of Accounts

Assets		Revenues	
101	Cash	401	Registration Fees
142	Office Supplies		
144	Food Supplies	Expenses	
145	Prepaid Insurance	511	Wages Expense
181	Fishing Boats	521	Rent Expense
181.1	Accum. Depr.—Fishing Boats	523	Office Supplies Expense
		524	Food Supplies Expense
Liabilities		525	Phone Expense
202	Accounts Payable	533	Utilities Expense
219	Wages Payable	535	Insurance Expense
		536	Postage Expense
Owner's Equity		542	Depr. Exp.—Fishing Boats
311	Bob Night, Capital		
312	Bob Night, Drawing		
313	Income Summary		

The following transactions took place during April 20--.

Apr.	1	Night invested cash in business, $90,000.
	1	Paid insurance premium for six-month camping season, $9,000.
	2	Paid rent for lodge and campgrounds for the month of April, $40,000.
	2	Deposited registration fees, $35,000.
	2	Purchased 10 fishing boats on account for $60,000. The boats have estimated useful lives of five years, at which time they will be donated to a local day camp. Arrangements were made to pay for the boats in July.
	3	Purchased food supplies from Acme Super Market on account, $7,000.
	5	Purchased office supplies from Gordon Office Supplies on account, $500.
	7	Deposited registration fees, $38,600.
	10	Purchased food supplies from Acme Super Market on account, $8,200.
	10	Paid wages to fishing guides, $10,000.
	14	Deposited registration fees, $30,500.

(continued)

223

- **Comprehensive Problems are available to be solved using QuickBooks®**, as well as using the manual method.

- **Excel templates** are provided for selected exercises and problems. To help students stay on track, certain cells are coded to display a red asterisk when an incorrect answer is entered.

> "Employment of accountants and auditors is expected to grow 10% from 2016 to 2026 … with about 139,900 new jobs expected over the projections decade."
>
> Bureau of Labor Statistics, National Employment Matrix as of January 30, 2018.

CHAPTER-BY-CHAPTER ENHANCEMENTS

Many of the end-of-chapter exercises and problems have "Show Me How" videos in CNOWv2. If the student is having difficulty with an assignment, the video icon indicates that additional help is available in CengageNOWv2. There, the student can click on the icon. A voice-over, PowerPoint video presentation will pop up with an explanation of how to solve a similar exercise. We think these videos are similar to a quick office visit.

Chapter 1: Introduction to Accounting

- Updated Jets.com opener.
- Updated statistics on job opportunities for Figures 1-6 and 1-7.
- Updated accounting position descriptions and salary information.

Chapter 2: Analyzing Transactions: The Accounting Equation

- Updated "A Broader View" on AT&T.
- Updated transactions for Mitchell's Campus Delivery.
- New margin note on revenue recognition.
- Updated financial statements to reflect revised transactions.

Chapter 3: The Double-Entry Framework

- Updated information on AppRiver opener.
- Updated transactions for Mitchell's Campus Delivery.
- Updated financial statements to reflect revised transactions.

Chapter 4: Journalizing and Posting Transactions

- Revised entries for Mitchell's Campus Delivery.
- Enhanced discussion on making corrections in the accounting system.

Chapter 5: Adjusting Entries and the Work Sheet

- Updated chapter opener on Floyd's 99 Barbershop.
- Enhanced discussion of the revenue recognition principle to reflect new accounting standard.
- Updated adjustments and adjusting entries for Mitchell's Campus Delivery.
- Enhanced discussion of the accrual basis of accounting.
- New work sheet illustrations in Figures 5-16, 5-17, and 5-18.

Chapter 6: Financial Statements and the Closing Process

- Updated financial statement to reflect revised transactions for Mitchell's Campus Delivery.
- Updated closing entries and post-closing trial balance for Mitchell's Campus Delivery.

Chapter 7: Accounting for Cash

- Updated chapter opener on H20Audio.
- Increased coverage of electronic banking and security issues.
- Revised "Your Perspective" regarding cashier.
- Updated "A Broader View" with new fraud information.

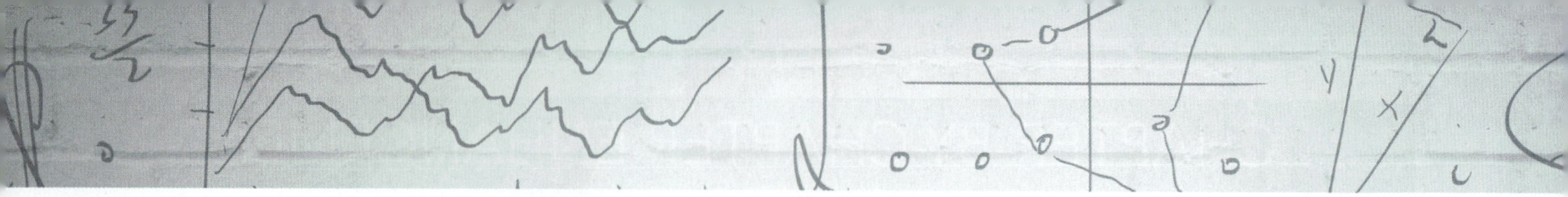

Chapter 8: Payroll Accounting: Employee Earnings and Deductions

- Updated chapter opener on Intechra Group.
- Updated text and end-of-chapter materials for new FIT withholding tables and Social Security maximum.
- Increased wage and salary amounts to more current pay scales.

Chapter 9: Payroll Accounting: Employer Taxes and Reports

- Emphasized IRS preference for electronic filing and payment of taxes.
- Provided full explanation and new illustration of lookback period for tax deposits.
- Provided new Form 941.

Chapter 10: Accounting for Sales and Cash Receipts

- Provided new chapter opener on Kalso Earth Shoes.
- Explained and illustrated new accounts, transactions, and adjustments for new FASB revenue standard.
- Provided new "Your Perspective" regarding Financial Clerk.

Chapter 11: Accounting for Purchases and Cash Payments

- Updated chapter opener on Innovar Environmental.
- Added description of use of voucher system for internal control over purchases and cash payments.

Chapter 12: Special Journals

- Revised chapter opener on Nutra Planet.
- Explained and illustrated alternative form of purchases journal.

Chapter 13: Accounting for Merchandise Inventory

- Updated opening story on Marsh Supermarkets.
- New margin note on returned merchandise inventory account.
- New foreshadowing of adjustment for inventory expected to be returned in the next accounting period.

Chapter 14: Adjustments for a Merchandising Business

- Revised learning objectives, LO3 and LO5.
- Revised introduction to the chapter to alert reader to the use of a new spreadsheet to assist in the adjusting process and preparation of financial statements.
- New discussion of end-of-period adjustments for customer refunds expected to be paid next period as a result of sales made in the current period under the periodic inventory system (FASB ASC 606).
- New discussion of end-of-period adjustments for the estimated cost of merchandise inventory sold this year, but expected to be returned next year under the periodic inventory system (FASB ASC 606).
- New accounts introduced: Estimated Returns Inventory and Customer Refunds Payable.

- New spreadsheet, six column format, for preparing adjustments.
- New discussion of end-of-period adjustments for customer refunds expected to be paid next period as a result of sales made in the current period under the perpetual inventory system (FASB ASC 606).
- New discussion of end-of-period adjustments for the estimated cost of merchandise inventory sold this year, but expected to be returned next year under the perpetual inventory system (FASB ASC 606).
- New, or heavily revised, end of chapter assignments that address new revenue recognition standard:
  - Demonstration Problem.
  - Multiple Choice Questions: 1, 2, 3, and 5.
  - Review Questions: 6 and 7.
  - Exercises: 14-2A/B, 14-4A/B, 14-7A/B, 14-8A/B, and 14-11A/B.
  - Problems: 14-13A/B and 14-14A/B.
  - Mastery Problem.

Chapter 15: Financial Statements and Year-End Accounting for a Merchandising Business

- New use of Adjusted Trial Balance columns in a six-column spreadsheet to prepare financial statements.
- Revised spreadsheet, financial statements, closing entries, post-closing trial balance, and discussion of reversing entries for Sunflower Cycle to include new accounts (Estimated Returns Inventory and Customer Refunds Payable) and to address new revenue recognition standard.
- New, or heavily revised, end of chapter assignments that address new revenue recognition standard:
  - Demonstration Problem.
  - Checkpoint Exercises: 1, 2, 3, 4, and 5.
  - Exercises: 15-2A/B, 15-3A/B, 15-4A/B, and 15-5A/B.
  - Problems: 15-8A/B, 15-9A/B, and 15-10A/B.
  - Mastery Problem.

STUDENT AND INSTRUCTOR RESOURCES

Student Supplements and Resources

QuickBooks Data Files for Comprehensive Problems

These data sets allow you to complete the requirements of the Comprehensive Problems using QuickBooks software. Al templates can be downloaded for free from the student website located at Cengage.com.

Excel Templates

These templates are provided for selected end-of-chapter exercises and problems, designated by an icon in the text. They are designed to help you set up and work the assignment. To help you stay on track, certain cells are coded to display a red asterisk when an incorrect answer is entered. Your instructor may ask you to use the template for homework assignments. All templates can be downloaded for free from the student website located at Cengage.com.

Student Website

Now, mastering accounting concepts is easier than ever with the rich array of learning resources at the Heintz & Parry student website found at Cengage.com. Designed specifically to help you learn the most from your course and earn the grade you want, this website's interactive study center features chapter-by-chapter PowerPoint® student slides, online quizzes, flashcards, outlines, key terms, and a final exam, as well as links to accounting resources and more.

Study Guide and Working Papers

The study guide and working papers for the text assignments are provided together in one resource for your convenience. Written by the text authors to ensure accuracy and consistent quality, this resource provides chapter outlines linked to learning objectives and a set of "C" assignments that include review questions, exercises, and problems to enhance your learning experience. Students can purchase the study guide and working papers at Cengage.com.
Chapters 1–15: (ISBN: 978-1-337-91356-0)

Trey's Fast Cleaning Service Practice Set

This practice set features a sole proprietorship service business simulation. It reviews the accounting cycle and accounting for cash. This practice set includes access to relevant online data files (appropriate for use after Chapter 7). Students can purchase this practice set through Cengage.com.

Coolspring Furniture Practice Set

Practice your accounting success, including working with payroll taxes, within this sole proprietorship merchandising business. This practice set includes access to online data files to complete the practice set (appropriate for use after Chapter 12). Students can purchase this practice set through Cengage.com.

Using QuickBooks Accountant for Accounting

This book teaches fundamental accounting concepts and principles while developing students' proficiency with the market-leading accounting software, QuickBooks Accountant by Intuit. This well-organized and concise text teaches the technology and application of accounting skills by illustrating how accounting information is created and used.
2018 edition: (ISBN: 978-0-357-04207-6)

Instructor Supplements

CengageNOWv2

CengageNOWv2 is a powerful course management and online homework resource that provides control and customization to optimize the student learning experience. Included are many proven resources including algorithmic activities, test bank, course management tools, reporting and assessment options, and much more.

Instructor Resource Guide

The Instructor Resource Guide is available in electronic format and contains a correlation grid with changes from the 22nd edition to the 23rd edition, enhanced chapter outlines with teaching tips, suggested in-class exercises, figure references, and homework suggestions.

Solutions Manual

The Solutions Manual is prepared by the text authors. It is available in electronic format and contains carefully verified solutions for all text assignments, including Review Questions, all Exercises and Problem sets, Challenge and Mastery problems, Comprehensive Problems 1 and 2, as well as suggested answers to the Ethics Cases and the Managing Your Writing exercises.

Test Bank

The Test Bank has been revised and verified and tagging standards have been added including level of difficulty, learning objectives, Bloom's Taxonomy, AICPA, ACBSP, and general business program standards (BUSPROG) to allow greater guidance in developing assessments and evaluating student progress. The Test Bank is available in electronic format on the Instructor Website.

Cognero Information Testing Software

Cengage Learning Testing powered by Cognero is a flexible, online system that allows you to author, edit, and manage test bank content from multiple Cengage Learning solutions, create multiple test versions in an instant, and deliver tests from your LMS, your classroom, or wherever you want.

(ISBN: 978-1-337-91350-8)

Study Guide and Working Papers

Written by the text authors to ensure accuracy and quality consistent with the text, the study guide and the working papers for the text assignments are provided together in one convenient resource. Students can reinforce their learning experience with chapter outlines that are linked to learning objectives and a set of "C" assignments that include review questions, exercises, and problems. The working papers are tailored to the text's end-of-chapter assignments. (Solutions for the working papers are included in the Solutions Manual. Solutions for study guide assignments are available on the Instructor Website.)

Chapters 1–15: (ISBN: 978-1-337-91356-0)

Study Guide Solutions

Solutions to all Study Guide set "C" assignments are available on the Instructor Website.

Trey's Fast Cleaning Service Practice Set

Put your students to work within a sole proprietorship business in this dynamic simulation for use after text Chapter 7. Students will review the basics of accrual accounting, including the accounting cycle and accounting for cash.

Coolspring Furniture Practice Set

This practice set features a sole proprietorship merchandising business and can be completed using either the general journal alone or special journals. The practice set is appropriate for use after Chapter 12 of the text and covers the topic of payroll.

Instructor Website

Instructors can log into the password-protected website through http://login.cengage.com. This site places all the teaching resources in one place. It includes the Instructor's Resource Guide, PowerPoint® lecture presentations, Test Bank in PDF format, Solutions to the spreadsheet templates, Study Guide Solutions in Word format, and the Solutions Manual in Word format.

DEDICATION

We are grateful to our wives, Celia Heintz and Jane Parry, and our children, Andrea Heintz Tangari, John Heintz, Jessica Parry, and Mitch Parry, for their love, support, and assistance during the preparation of the 23rd edition. We especially want to thank Jessica Parry and Chris Williams for granting permission to use Professor Parry's grandson's name, Mitchell Williams throughout the first six chapters.

ACKNOWLEDGEMENTS

We thank the following individuals for their helpful contributions to this revision of *College Accounting*.

Abe Qastin, *Lakeland College*
Adam Baker, *Minnesota State Community and Technical College*
Alex Gialanella, *Manhattanville College*
Alyson Crow, *Temple College*
Amanda Hardin, *Mississippi Delta Community College*
Amy Chataginer, *Mississippi Gulf Coast Community College*
Amy Smith, *Pearl River Community College*
Anna Boulware, *St. Charles Community College*
Anne Bikofsky, *College of Westchester*
Anne Borsellino, *McLennan Community College*
Barbara L. Squires, *Corning Community College*
Barbara Prince, *Anoka Ramsey Community College, Cambridge*
Barbara Squires, *Corning Community College*
Belinda Chastain, *Spartanburg Community College*
Beth Berry, *Glendale Community College*
Bhaskar Singh, *College of Menominee Nation*
Bob Urell, *Irvine Valley College*
Bonnie Hopson, *Athens Technical College*
Brad Davis, *Santa Rosa Junior College*
Brian Fink, *Danville Area Community College*
Britt Blackwell, *Central Community College*
Carol Ann Kirby, *Portland Community College*
Carol Ottaway, *Chemeketa Community College*
Cheryl Corke, *Genesee Community College*
Christy Chauvin, *Delgado Community College*
Chuck Smith, *Iowa Western Community College*
Cynthia E. Moody-Paige, *Erwin Technical Center*
Dale Walker, *Arkansas State University—Little Rock Air Force Base*
Daniel J. Kerch, *Pennsylvania Highlands Community College*
Dawn Stevens, *Northwest Mississippi Community College*
Deanna Knight, *Daytona State College*
Debbie Adkins, *University of Phoenix*
Diana Sullivan, *Portland Community College*
Dianne Henline, *Texarkana College*
Dmitriy Kalyagin, *Chabot College*
Dominique Svarc, *Harper College*
Don Williams, *Feather River College*
Eilene LePelley, *Lane Community College*
Ellen Orr, *Seminole State College of Florida*
Eric Stadnik, *Santa Rosa Junior College*
Eugene Schneider, *ASA Institute of Business and Technology*
George Holder, *Cloud County Community College*

Glenn Pate, *Palm Beach State College*
Gloria Sanchez, *Mt. San Jacinto College*
Greg Lauer, *North Iowa Area Community College*
H. Gin Chong, *Prairie View A&M University*
Jackie Marshall, *Ohio Business College*
James M. Emig, *Villanova University*
Jan Hogue, *Laurel Technical Institute*
Jean Rodgers, *Wenatchee Valley College*
Jeanette Milius, *Iowa Western Community College*
Jeff Hsu, *St. Louis Community College at Meramec*
Jennifer Garcia, *Blinn College*
Jim Bauer, *Archbishop Moeller High School*
Jody Dunaway, *Herzing University*
Joe Adamo, *Cazenovia College*
John Allen Fortner, *Daytona State College*
John Fasler, *Whatcom Community College*
John Fortner, *Daytona State College*
John Nader, *Davenport University*
John Seilo, *Orange Coast College*
Johnny Howard, *Arkansas State University—Mountain Home*
Jolena Grande, *Cypress College*
Joseph M. Nicassio, *Westmoreland County Community College*
Judith Toland, *Bucks County Community College*
Judy Boozer, *Lane Community College*
Judy Hurtt, *East Central Community College*
Julia Angel, *North Arkansas College*
June Hanson, *Upper Iowa University*
Junnae Landry, *Pratt Community College*
Karen Alexander, *College of The Albemarle*
Karen M. Kydd, *Husson University*
Karen Welch, *Tennessee College of Applied Technology—Jackson*
Kathleen Fratianne, *Blackhawk Technical College*
Kathleen Smith, *Tennessee College of Applied Technology*
Kathy Beith, *Milan Institute*
Kathy Bowen, *Murray State College*
Keith Blankenship, *South College-Asheville*
Kerry Stager, *Lake Area Technical Institute*
Kim Anderson, *Elgin Community College*
Kim Hurt, *Central Community College*
Kim Potts, *North Arkansas College*
Kippi Harraid, *Trinity Valley Community College*
Kirk Canzano, *Long Beach City College*
La Vonda Ramey, *Schoolcraft College*
Laurie Gambrell, *Copiah-Lincoln Community College*
Lawrence A. Roman, *Cuyahoga Community College*
Leonia Houston, *Holmes Community College*
Leslie Schmidt, *Front Range Community College*
Linda Arndt, *LCO College*
Lingling Zhang, *American River College*
Lisa Briggs, *Columbus State Community College*
Lisa Nash, *Vincennes University*
Lisa Novak, *Mott Community College*
Lori Grady, *Bucks County Community College*
Lorna Hofer, *Lake Area Technical Institute*
Luis Plascencia, *Harold Washington College*
M. Jeff Quinlan, *Madison Area Technical College*
Mabel Machin, *Valencia College*
Marcia Shulman, *New York University*
Marilyn St. Clair, *Weatherford College*
Marina Grau, *Houston Community College*
Mark Gale, *Cosumnes River College*
Mark Wells, *Big Sandy Community and Technical College*
Meg Costello Lambert, *Oakland Community College-Auburn Hills Campus*
Melvin Williams, *College of the Mainland*
Michael Dole, *Marquette University*
Michele Wehrle, *Community College of Allegheny County*
Mike Belleman, *St Clair County Community College*
Mike Boren, *Tooele Applied Technology College*
Molly McFadden-May, *Tulsa Community College—Metro*
Monica Quattlebaum, *Phillips Community College of the University of Arkansas*
Morgan Rockett, *Moberly Area Community College*
Nancy Lee Howard, *Mt. Hood Community College*
Nelly Cintron Lorenzo, *Valencia College-West Campus*
Norma Cerpa, *Custom Training Solutions*
Nova Randolph, *Shawnee Community College*
Pam Perry, *Hinds Community College*
Patricia Worsham, *Norco College*
Patrick Borja, *Citrus College*
Perry Sellers, *Lone Star College System*
R. Stephen Holman, *Elizabethtown Community and Technical College*
Richard J. Pettit, *Mountain View College*
Rick Street, *Spokane Community College*
Robert Brooks, *San Bernardino Valley College*
Robert Derstine, *West Chester University*

Robin Fuller, *Mississippi Gulf Coast Community College*
Roger McMillian, *Mineral Area College*
Ronald Edward Camp, *Trinity Valley Community College*
Ronald Pearson, *Bay College*
Rosemary C. Garcia, *New Mexico State University, Doña Ana Community College*
Rosemary Nurre, *College Of San Mateo*
Ruth Gregory, *East Central Community College*
Sandra Sturdy, *Bay College*
Scott Birk, *Portland Community College*
Scott Wallace, *Blue Mountain Community College*
Sharon R. Morgan, *Western Nevada College*
Shawn Abbott, *College of the Siskiyous*
Sherry Laskie, *Milan Institute*
Shirley A. Montagne, *Community College of Vermont*
Sonora White, *Caddo Kiowa Technology Center*
Spencer Miller, *Eastern Idaho Technical College*
Stella Sorovigas, *Lansing Community College*
Stephanie Cox, *Louisiana Delta Community College*
Steven Ernest, *Baton Rouge Community College*
Sue Sandblom, *Scottsdale Community College*
Sue Savino, *Copiah Lincoln Community College*
Sueann Hely, *West Kentucky Community and Technical College*
Susan Davis, *Green River Community College*
Susan Greene, *Cloud County Community College*
Susan Mundy, *City University of Seattle*
Tatyana Pashnyak, *Bainbridge State College*
Teresa Worthy, *Gaston College*
Therese Rice, *North Hennepin Community College*
Thomas Gross, *Herzing University*
Tilda A. Woody, *Navajo Technical University*
Tim Green, *North Georgia Technical College*
Tim Whited, *American National University*
Tom Snare, *South Hills School of Business and Technology*
Toni Hartley, *Laurel Business Institute*
Tricia Popowsky, *Redlands Community College*
Tynia Kessler, *Lake Land College*
Vickie Boeder, *Madison Area Technical College—Watertown*
Vicky Lassiter, *Wayne Community College*
Wayne Corlis, *Mid Michigan Community College*
Wendy Eismont, *South Hills School of Business and Technology*
Whit Hunt, *South Plains College*

Special recognition goes to the following supplemental preparers for their revision work on the instructor and student materials:

Mark D. Sears
Alice Sineath, *Forsyth Technical Community College*
Domenic Tavella, *Carlow University*

We would like to thank the following individuals for their detailed verification of the homework:

Robin Browning
Alice Sineath, *Forsyth Technical Community College*
Erin Dischler, *Milwaukee Area Technical College*
Domenic Tavella, *Carlow University*
Brenda McVey, *Green River Community College*

We are honored to serve as the authors of the all-time and current best-selling college accounting text. As has been true for almost three decades, we are delighted with the editorial and marketing support provided by Cengage. Without their support and the constructive comments and suggestions made by our loyal friends using our text, this success would not have been possible. We are anxious to receive your comments on this edition, because we want to make the next one even better.

James A. Heintz
jheintz@ku.edu

Rob Parry
parry@indiana.edu

BRIEF CONTENTS

1 Accounting for a Service Business

Chapter 1 Introduction to Accounting 3

Chapter 2 Analyzing Transactions: The Accounting Equation 20

Chapter 3 The Double-Entry Framework 50

Chapter 4 Journalizing and Posting Transactions 85

Chapter 5 Adjusting Entries and the Work Sheet 130

Chapter 6 Financial Statements and the Closing Process 184

Comprehensive Problem 1: The Accounting Cycle 223

Comprehensive Problem 1, Period 2: The Accounting Cycle 225

2 Accounting for Cash and Payroll

Chapter 7 Accounting for Cash 231

Chapter 8 Payroll Accounting: Employee Earnings and Deductions 282

Chapter 9 Payroll Accounting: Employer Taxes and Reports 317

3 Accounting for a Merchandising Business

Chapter 10 Accounting for Sales and Cash Receipts 355

Chapter 11 Accounting for Purchases and Cash Payments 399

Chapter 12 Special Journals 441

Chapter 13 Accounting for Merchandise Inventory 488

Chapter 14 Adjustments for a Merchandising Business 525

Chapter 15 Financial Statements and Year-End Accounting for a Merchandising Business 566

Comprehensive Problem 2: Accounting Cycle with Subsidiary Ledgers: Part 1 614

Comprehensive Problem 2: Accounting Cycle with Subsidiary Ledgers: Part 2 616

Index 619

Module: Accounting for a Professional Service Business: The Combination Journal. *Module available online only at Cengage.com*

CONTENTS

Part 1 Accounting for a Service Business

CHAPTER 1
Introduction to Accounting 3

The Purpose of Accounting 4
The Accounting Process 4
Generally Accepted Accounting Principles (GAAP) 5
Three Types of Ownership Structures 6
Sole Proprietorship 6; Partnership 7; Corporation 7
Types of Businesses 7
A BROADER VIEW 7
Career Opportunities in Accounting 8
Accounting Clerks 8; Bookkeepers and Para-Accountants 8; Accountants 8; Job Opportunities 10
YOUR PERSPECTIVE 12
Managing Your Writing 13
Self-Study 16
Key Points to Remember 16
Key Terms 16
Applying Your Knowledge 18
Review Questions 18
Series A Exercises 19
Series B Exercises 19
Managing Your Writing 19

CHAPTER 2
Analyzing Transactions: The Accounting Equation 20

The Accounting Elements 21
Assets 21; Liabilities 21; Owner's Equity 21
A BROADER VIEW 22
The Accounting Equation 22
Analyzing Business Transactions 23
Effect of Transactions on the Accounting Equation 23
Expanding the Accounting Equation: Revenues, Expenses, and Withdrawals 25; Effect of Revenue, Expense, and Withdrawal Transactions on the Accounting Equation 26
Financial Statements 32
The Income Statement 32; The Statement of Owner's Equity 34; The Balance Sheet 34
Overview of the Accounting Process 35
Self-Study 35
Key Points to Remember 35
Demonstration Problem 36
Key Terms 38
Self-Study Test Questions 40
CHECKPOINT EXERCISES 41
Applying Your Knowledge 42
Review Questions 42
Series A Exercises and Problems 42
Series B Exercises and Problems 45
Managing Your Writing 47
Mastery Problem 48
Challenge Problem 48
Answers to Self-Study Test Questions 49
CHECKPOINT EXERCISES 49

CHAPTER 3
The Double-Entry Framework 50

The T Account 51
Balancing a T Account 51
Debits and Credits 52
Assets 52; Liabilities and Owner's Equity 53; The Owner's Equity Umbrella 53; Owner's Capital 53; Revenues 53; Expenses 54; Drawing 54; Normal Balances 54
Transaction Analysis 54
Debits and Credits: Asset, Liability, and Owner's Equity Accounts 55; Debits and Credits: Including Revenues, Expenses, and Drawing 57
A BROADER VIEW 61
Summary of Transactions 65
The Trial Balance 66
Self-Study 68
Key Points to Remember 68
Demonstration Problem 70

Key Terms 72
Self-Study Test Questions 73
CHECKPOINT EXERCISES 74
Applying Your Knowledge 74
Review Questions 74
Series A Exercises and Problems 74
Series B Exercises and Problems 78
Managing Your Writing 82
Mastery Problem 82
Challenge Problem 84
Answers to Self-Study Test Questions 84
CHECKPOINT EXERCISES 84

CHAPTER 4
Journalizing and Posting Transactions 85

Flow of Data 86
Source Documents 86
A BROADER VIEW 87
The Chart of Accounts 88
The General Journal 89
Journalizing 89
The General Ledger 93
General Ledger Account 94; Posting to the General Ledger 95; The Trial Balance 101
Finding and Correcting Errors in the Trial Balance 102
Correcting Entries 102
Self-Study 104
Key Points to Remember 104
Demonstration Problem 105
Key Terms 111
Self-Study Test Questions 112
CHECKPOINT EXERCISES 113
Applying Your Knowledge 114
Review Questions 114
Series A Exercises and Problems 114
Series B Exercises and Problems 120
Managing Your Writing 125
Mastery Problem 125
Challenge Problem 127
Answers to Self-Study Test Questions 128
CHECKPOINT EXERCISES 128

CHAPTER 5
Adjusting Entries and the Work Sheet 130

End-of-Period Adjustments 131
A BROADER VIEW 132
Supplies 132; Prepaid Insurance 133; Wages Expense 135; Depreciation Expense 136; Expanded Chart of Accounts 138
Posting Adjusting Entries 138
The Work Sheet 140
The 10-Column Work Sheet 140; Preparing the Work Sheet 142
Finding Errors on the Work Sheet 147
Journalizing Adjusting Entries from the Work Sheet 147
Methods of Accounting: Cash, Modified Cash, and Accrual 149
Self-Study 152
Key Points to Remember 152
Demonstration Problem 153
Key Terms 156
Self-Study Test Questions 157
CHECKPOINT EXERCISES 158
Applying Your Knowledge 159
Review Questions 159
Series A Exercises and Problems 160
Series B Exercises and Problems 166
Managing Your Writing 173
Mastery Problem 175
Challenge Problem 176
Answers to Self-Study Test Questions 177
CHECKPOINT EXERCISES 178
APPENDIX: DEPRECIATION METHODS 179
Straight-Line Method 179
Sum-of-the-Years'-Digits 180
Double-Declining-Balance Method 181
Modified Accelerated Cost Recovery System 181
Key Points to Remember 182
Key Terms 182
Review Questions 183
Series A Exercises 183
Series B Exercises 183

CHAPTER **6**

Financial Statements and the Closing Process 184

The Financial Statements 185

The Income Statement 185; The Statement of Owner's Equity 185; The Balance Sheet 186; Additional Investments by the Owner (Revisited) 188

The Closing Process 189

Steps in the Closing Process 190; Journalize Closing Entries 192; Post the Closing Entries 192

YOUR PERSPECTIVE 193

Post-Closing Trial Balance 194

A BROADER VIEW 195

The Accounting Cycle 195

Steps in the Accounting Cycle 195

Self-Study 196

- Key Points to Remember 196
- Demonstration Problem 197
- Key Terms 200
- Self-Study Test Questions 201

CHECKPOINT EXERCISES 202

Applying Your Knowledge 202

- Review Questions 202
- Series A Exercises and Problems 203
- Series B Exercises and Problems 208
- Managing Your Writing 213
- Mastery Problem 213
- Challenge Problem 215

Answers to Self-Study Test Questions 215

CHECKPOINT EXERCISES 216

APPENDIX: STATEMENT OF CASH FLOWS 218

Types of Business Activities 218

Preparing the Statement of Cash Flows 219

Key Points to Remember 221

Key Terms 221

Review Questions 222

Series A Exercise and Problem 222

Series B Exercise and Problem 222

Comprehensive Problem 1: The Accounting Cycle 223

Comprehensive Problem 1, Period 2: The Accounting Cycle 225

Part 2 Accounting for Cash and Payroll

CHAPTER **7**

Accounting for Cash 231

Checking Account 232

Opening a Checking Account 232; Making Deposits 232; Endorsements 232; Automated Teller Machines 234; Writing Checks 235; Bank Statement 235

Reconciling the Bank Statement 236

Deposits 236; Cash Payments 237; Reasons for Differences Between Bank and Book Balances 238; Steps in Preparing the Bank Reconciliation 238; Illustration of a Bank Reconciliation 239; Journal Entries 241; Electronic Banking 242

A BROADER VIEW 243

The Petty Cash Fund 243

Establishing a Petty Cash Fund 243; Making Payments from a Petty Cash Fund 244; Petty Cash Payments Record 244; Replenishing the Petty Cash Fund 246

The Change Fund and Cash Short and Over 246

Establishing and Operating the Change Fund 246; Cash Short and Over 247

YOUR PERSPECTIVE 248

Self-Study 248

- Key Points to Remember 248
- Demonstration Problem 249
- Key Terms 251
- Self-Study Test Questions 253

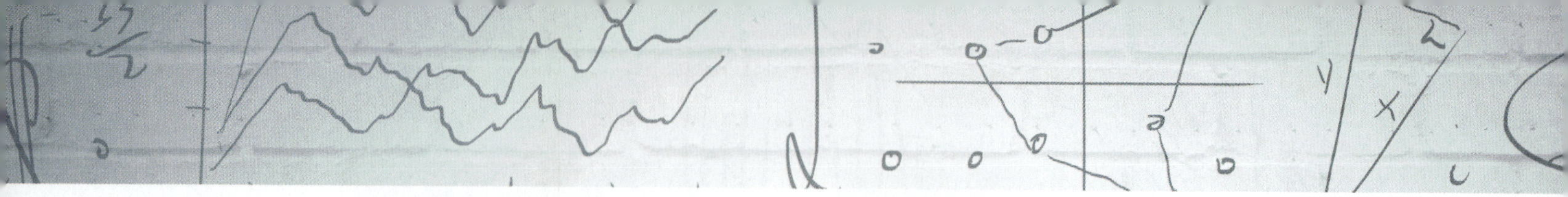

CHECKPOINT EXERCISES 253

Applying Your Knowledge 254

- Review Questions 254
- Series A Exercises and Problems 255
- Series B Exercises and Problems 259
- Managing Your Writing 263
- Ethics Case 263
- Mastery Problem 264
- Challenge Problem 265

Answers to Self-Study Test Questions 266

CHECKPOINT EXERCISES 266

APPENDIX: INTERNAL CONTROLS 267

Importance of Internal Control 267

Key Components of Internal Control 268

Control Environment 268; Risk Assessment 269; Control Activities 269; Information and Communication System 270; Monitoring Processes 270

Internal Controls Over Cash Receipts 271

Internal Controls Over Cash Payments 272

Voucher System 273; The Purchasing Process 273; The Payment Process 275

Key Points to Remember 277

Key Terms 277

Review Questions 278

Series A Exercises and Problems 278

Series B Exercises and Problems 279

CHAPTER 8
Payroll Accounting: Employee Earnings and Deductions 282

Employees and Independent Contractors 283

Employee Earnings and Deductions 283

Salaries and Wages 283; Computing Total Earnings 284; Deductions from Total Earnings 286; Computing Net Pay 290

Payroll Records 291

Payroll Register 291; Paying Employees 292; Employee Earnings Record 294

Accounting for Employee Earnings and Deductions 294

Journalizing Payroll Transactions 294

A BROADER VIEW 295

Wages and Salaries Expense 297; Employee Federal Income Tax Payable 297; Social Security and Medicare Taxes Payable 298; Other Deductions 298

Payroll Record-Keeping Methods 298

Self-Study 299

- Key Points to Remember 299
- Demonstration Problem 300
- Key Terms 304
- Self-Study Test Questions 304

CHECKPOINT EXERCISES 305

Applying Your Knowledge 306

- Review Questions 306
- Series A Exercises and Problems 306
- Series B Exercises and Problems 310
- Managing Your Writing 313
- Ethics Case 313
- Mastery Problem 314
- Challenge Problem 315

Answers to Self-Study Test Questions 316

CHECKPOINT EXERCISES 316

CHAPTER 9
Payroll Accounting: Employer Taxes and Reports 317

Employer Payroll Taxes 318

Employer FICA Taxes 318; Self-Employment Tax 319; Employer FUTA Tax 320; SUTA Tax 320

Accounting for Employer Payroll Taxes 321

Journalizing Employer Payroll Taxes 321; Payroll Taxes Expense 322; Social Security and Medicare Taxes Payable 322; FUTA Tax Payable 323; SUTA Tax Payable 323; Total Payroll Cost of an Employee 323

Reporting and Payment Responsibilities 323

Federal Income Tax Withholding and Social Security and Medicare Taxes 324; FUTA Taxes 325; SUTA Taxes 329; Employee Wage and Tax Statement 330; Summary of Employee Wages and Taxes 331; Employment Eligibility Verification 332; Summary of Taxes, Reports, and Payments 332

Workers' Compensation Insurance 333

A BROADER VIEW 334

Self-Study 336

- Key Points to Remember 336
- Demonstration Problem 337
- Key Terms 339
- Self-Study Test Questions 339

CHECKPOINT EXERCISES 340

Applying Your Knowledge 341
- Review Questions 341
- Series A Exercises and Problems 342
- Series B Exercises and Problems 346
- Managing Your Writing 349
- Ethics Case 350
- Mastery Problem 350
- Challenge Problem 351

Answers to Self-Study Test Questions 351

CHECKPOINT EXERCISES 351

Part 3 Accounting for a Merchandising Business

CHAPTER 10 Accounting for Sales and Cash Receipts 355

Merchandise Sales Transactions 356
- *Retailer 356; Wholesaler 357; Credit Memorandum 358*

Merchandise Sales Accounts 359
- *Sales Account 359; Sales Tax Payable Account 360; Sales Returns and Allowances Account 361; Sales Discounts Account 362*

Journalizing and Posting Sales and Cash Receipts Transactions 364
- *Journalizing Sales 364; Posting Sales to the General Ledger 364; Posting Sales to the Accounts Receivable Ledger 365; Sales Returns and Allowances 368; Cash Receipts 368*

YOUR PERSPECTIVE 368

A BROADER VIEW 370
- *Journalizing Cash Receipts 370; Posting Cash Receipts to the General Ledger and Accounts Receivable Ledger 371*

Schedule of Accounts Receivable 372

Self-Study 374
- Key Points to Remember 374
- Demonstration Problem 375
- Key Terms 381
- Self-Study Test Questions 382

CHECKPOINT EXERCISES 383

Applying Your Knowledge 384
- Review Questions 384
- Series A Exercises and Problems 384
- Series B Exercises and Problems 389
- Managing Your Writing 394
- Ethics Case 394
- Mastery Problem 394
- Challenge Problem 397

Answers to Self-Study Test Questions 397

CHECKPOINT EXERCISES 397

CHAPTER 11 Accounting for Purchases and Cash Payments 399

Merchandise Purchases Transactions 400
- *Purchase Requisition 400; Purchase Order 400; Receiving Report and Purchase Invoice 400*

YOUR PERSPECTIVE 401
- *Voucher System 402; Cash and Trade Discounts 402*

Merchandise Purchases Accounts 404
- *Purchases Account 404; Purchases Returns and Allowances Account 405; Purchases Discounts Account 406; Freight-In Account 406*

A BROADER VIEW 407
- *Computation of Gross Profit 408*

Journalizing and Posting Purchases and Cash Payments Transactions 409
- *Purchases 409; Posting Purchases to the General Ledger 410; Posting Purchases to the Accounts Payable Ledger 411; Purchases Returns and Allowances 412; Cash Payments 413; Posting Cash Payments to the General Ledger and Accounts Payable Ledger 414*

Schedule of Accounts Payable 415

Self-Study 416
- Key Points to Remember 416
- Demonstration Problem 418

Key Terms 422
Self-Study Test Questions 423
CHECKPOINT EXERCISES 423
Applying Your Knowledge 424
Review Questions 424
Series A Exercises and Problems 425
Series B Exercises and Problems 429
Managing Your Writing 434
Ethics Case 434
Mastery Problem 434
Challenge Problem 436
Answers to Self-Study Test Questions 436
CHECKPOINT EXERCISES 436
APPENDIX: THE NET-PRICE METHOD OF RECORDING PURCHASES 438
Net-Price Method 438
Recording with the Net-Price Method 438
Key Points to Remember 439
Key Terms 439
Review Questions 440
Series A Exercise 440
Series B Exercise 440

CHAPTER **12**
Special Journals 441

Special Journals 442
Sales Journal 443
Posting from the Sales Journal 444
Cash Receipts Journal 447
Posting from the Cash Receipts Journal 448
A BROADER VIEW 452
Purchases Journal 452
Posting from the Purchases Journal 453
Cash Payments Journal 456
Posting from the Cash Payments Journal 457
Self-Study 460
Key Points to Remember 460
Demonstration Problem 464
Key Terms 469
Self-Study Test Questions 470
CHECKPOINT EXERCISES 470
Applying Your Knowledge 471
Review Questions 471
Series A Exercises and Problems 472
Series B Exercises and Problems 477
Managing Your Writing 483
Ethics Case 483
Mastery Problem 484
Challenge Problem 485
Answers to Self-Study Test Questions 486
CHECKPOINT EXERCISES 487

CHAPTER **13**
Accounting for Merchandise Inventory 488

The Impact of Merchandise Inventory on Financial Statements 489
YOUR PERSPECTIVE 490
Types of Inventory Systems: Periodic and Perpetual 491
Assigning Costs to Inventory and Cost of Goods Sold 492
Taking a Physical Inventory 492
A BROADER VIEW 493
The Periodic Inventory System 494; The Perpetual Inventory System 498; Lower-of-Cost-or-Market Method of Inventory Valuation 498
Estimating Ending Inventory and Cost of Goods Sold 500
Gross Profit Method of Estimating Inventory 500; Retail Method of Estimating Inventory 501
Self-Study 502
Key Points to Remember 502
Demonstration Problem 503
Key Terms 506
Self-Study Test Questions 507
CHECKPOINT EXERCISES 508
Applying Your Knowledge 509
Review Questions 509
Series A Exercises and Problems 509
Series B Exercises and Problems 513
Managing Your Writing 516
Ethics Case 517
Mastery Problem 517
Challenge Problem 518
Answers to Self-Study Test Questions 518
CHECKPOINT EXERCISES 519
APPENDIX: PERPETUAL INVENTORY METHOD: LIFO AND MOVING-AVERAGE METHODS 520

Perpetual LIFO 520
Perpetual Moving-Average 521
Key Points to Remember 522
Key Terms 523
Review Question 523
Series A Exercise and Problem 523
Series B Exercise and Problem 524

CHAPTER 14 Adjustments for a Merchandising Business 525

Adjustments for Merchandise Inventory: Periodic Inventory System 526
YOUR PERSPECTIVE 528
Adjustment for Unearned Revenue 530
Expanded Chart of Accounts 531
A BROADER VIEW 533
Adjustments for a Merchandising Business 533
Adjusting Entries 536
Adjusting Entries Under the Perpetual Inventory System 537
Adjustments for Expected Sales Returns and Allowances 538; Adjustments for Inventory Shrinkage 539
Self-Study 540
Key Points to Remember 540
Demonstration Problem 541
Key Terms 545
Self-Study Test Questions 545
CHECKPOINT EXERCISES 546
Applying Your Knowledge 547
Review Questions 547
Series A Exercises and Problems 548
Series B Exercises and Problems 554
Managing Your Writing 560
Ethics Case 560
Mastery Problem 560
Challenge Problem 561
Answers to Self-Study Test Questions 562
CHECKPOINT EXERCISES 562
APPENDIX: EXPENSE METHOD OF ACCOUNTING FOR PREPAID EXPENSES 563
The Expense Method 563
Adjusting Entries Under the Expense Method 563
Key Points to Remember 564
Key Terms 565
Series A Exercise 565
Series B Exercise 565

CHAPTER 15 Financial Statements and Year-End Accounting for a Merchandising Business 566

The Income Statement 567
The Statement of Owner's Equity 570
Balance Sheet 571
Current Assets 571; Property, Plant, and Equipment 572; Current Liabilities 573; Long-Term Liabilities 573; Owner's Equity 573
Financial Statement Analysis 573
Balance Sheet Analysis 573; Interstatement Analysis 574
Closing Entries 576
Post-Closing Trial Balance 577
A BROADER VIEW 578
Reversing Entries 579
Self-Study 582
Key Points to Remember 582
Demonstration Problem 584
Key Terms 590
Self-Study Test Questions 591
CHECKPOINT EXERCISES 592
Applying Your Knowledge 594
Review Questions 594
Series A Exercises and Problems 594
Series B Exercises and Problems 602
Managing Your Writing 608
Ethics Case 609
Mastery Problem 609
Challenge Problem 611
Answers to Self-Study Test Questions 611
CHECKPOINT EXERCISES 612

Comprehensive Problem 2: Accounting Cycle with Subsidiary Ledgers, Part 1 614

Comprehensive Problem 2: Accounting Cycle with Subsidiary Ledgers, Part 2 616

Index 619

Module: Accounting for a Professional Service Business: The Combination Journal. *Module available online only at Cengage.com*

The Modified Cash and Accrual Bases of Accounting M-1
Accounting for a Professional Service Business M-3
The Combination Journal M-3
Journalizing in a Combination Journal M-6
General Columns M-6; General and Special Accounts M-6; Special Accounts M-6; Description Column M-6
Proving the Combination Journal M-7
Posting from the Combination Journal M-7
Determining the Cash Balance M-9
Performing End-of-Period Work for a Professional Service Business M-9
Preparing the Work Sheet M-9; Preparing Financial Statements M-9; Preparing Adjusting and Closing Entries M-13
Self-Study M-14
Key Points to Remember M-14
Demonstration Problem M-15
Key Terms M-19
Self-Study Test Questions M-19
CHECKPOINT EXERCISES M-20
Applying Your Knowledge M-21
Review Questions M-21
Series A Exercises and Problems M-21
Series B Exercises and Problems M-26
Managing Your Writing M-29
Ethics Case M-30
Mastery Problem M-30
Challenge Problem M-32
Answers to Self-Study Test Questions M-32
CHECKPOINT EXERCISES M-32

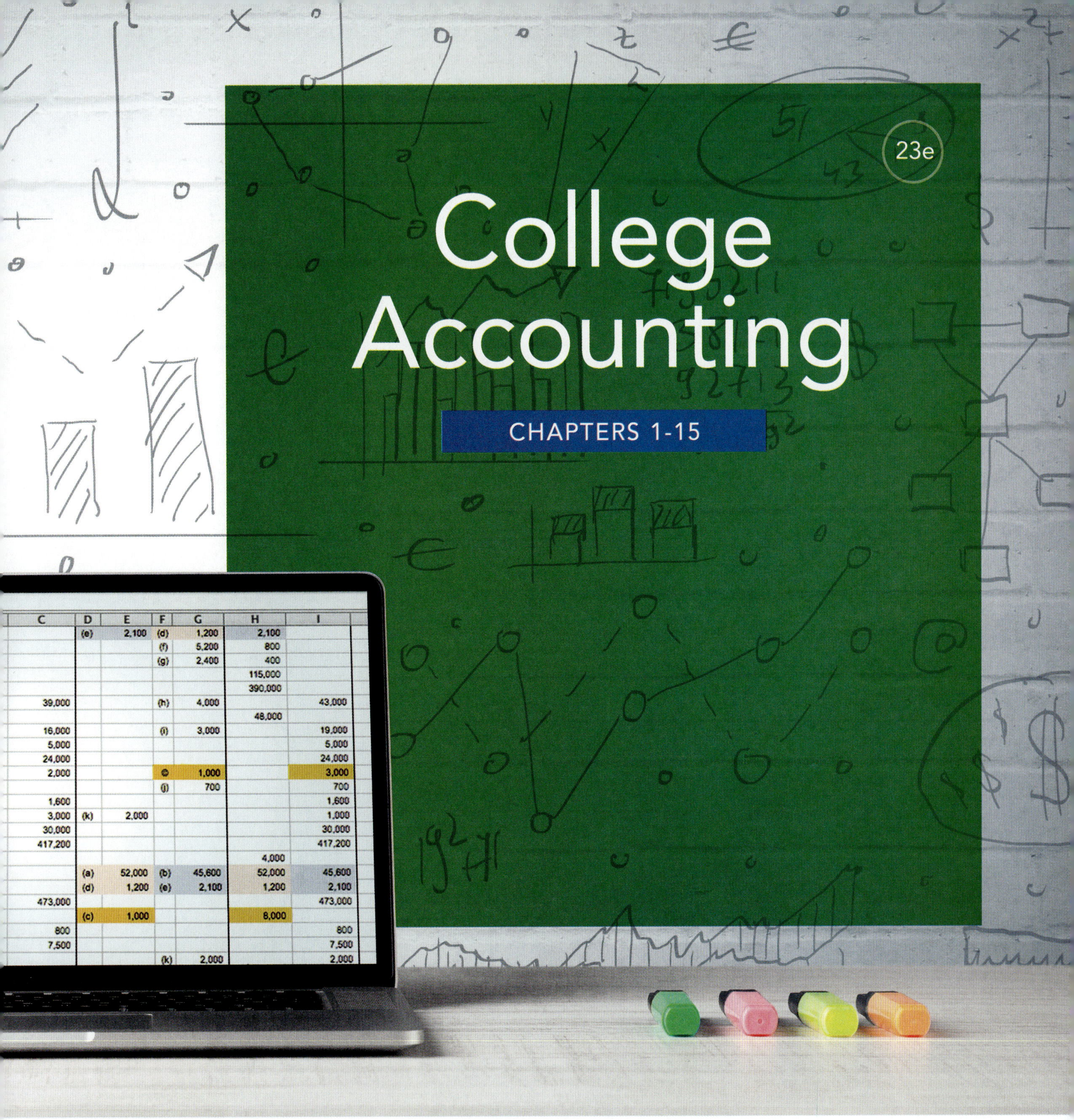
23e
College Accounting
CHAPTERS 1-15

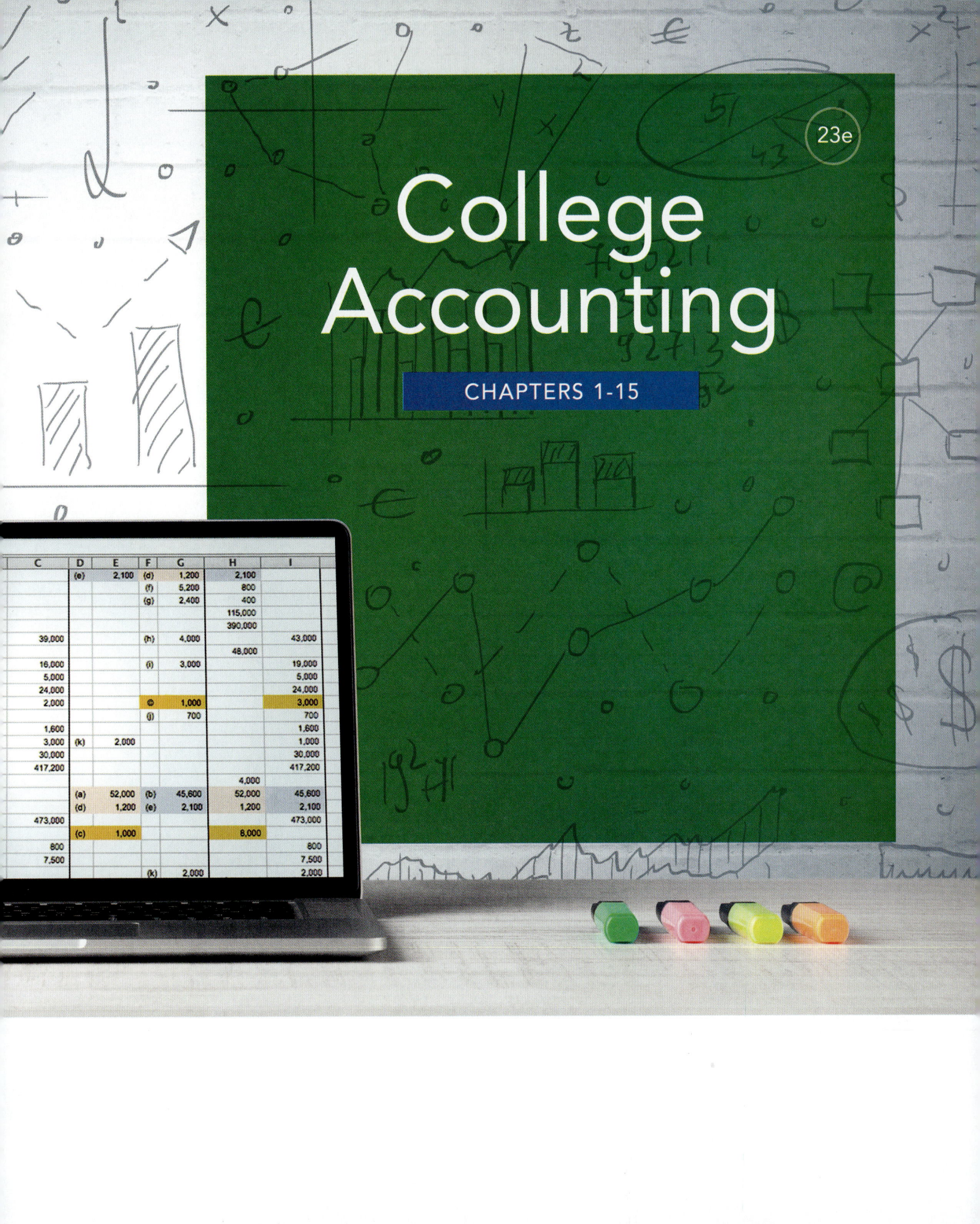

1 Accounting for a Service Business

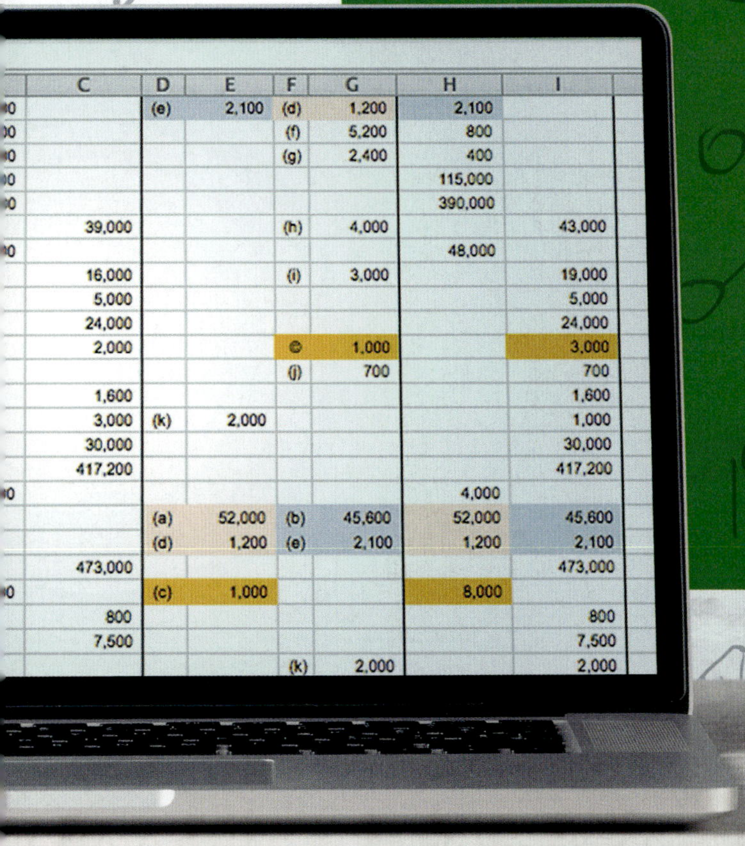

1 Introduction to Accounting
2 Analyzing Transactions: The Accounting Equation
3 The Double-Entry Framework
4 Journalizing and Posting Transactions
5 Adjusting Entries and the Work Sheet
6 Financial Statements and the Closing Process

Add some color to your learning!

Throughout the text, you will be introduced to many important terms and types of accounts. To help you learn the different terms and types of accounts, we have coded many of them using the following color key in Part 1:

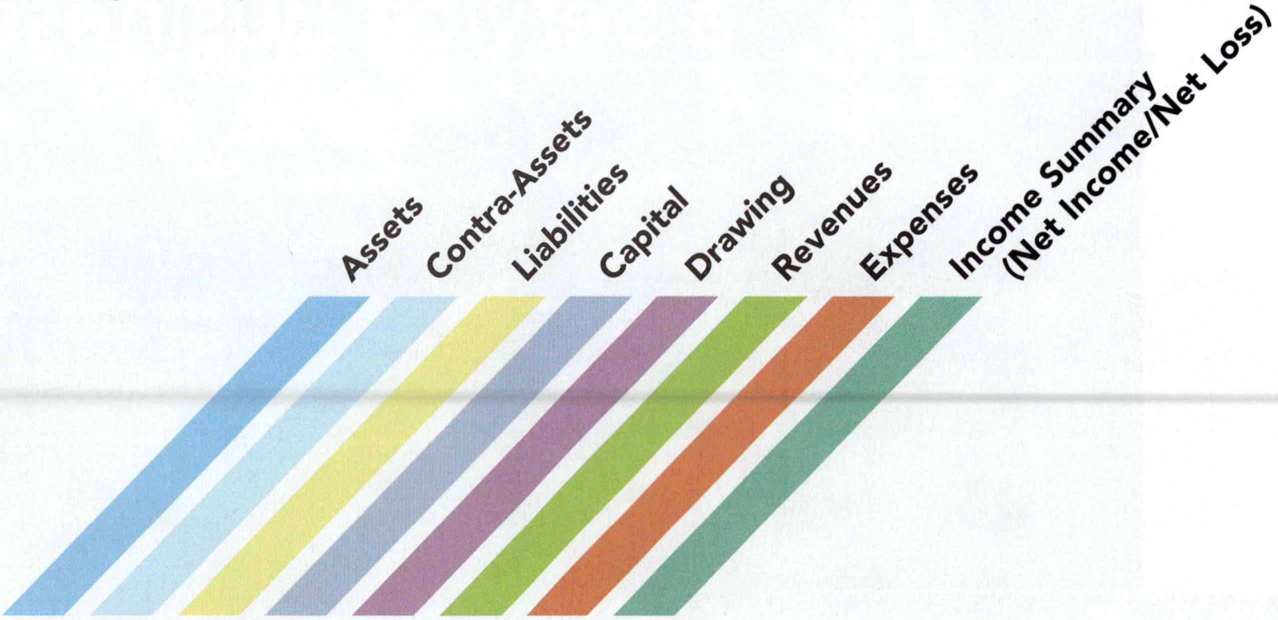

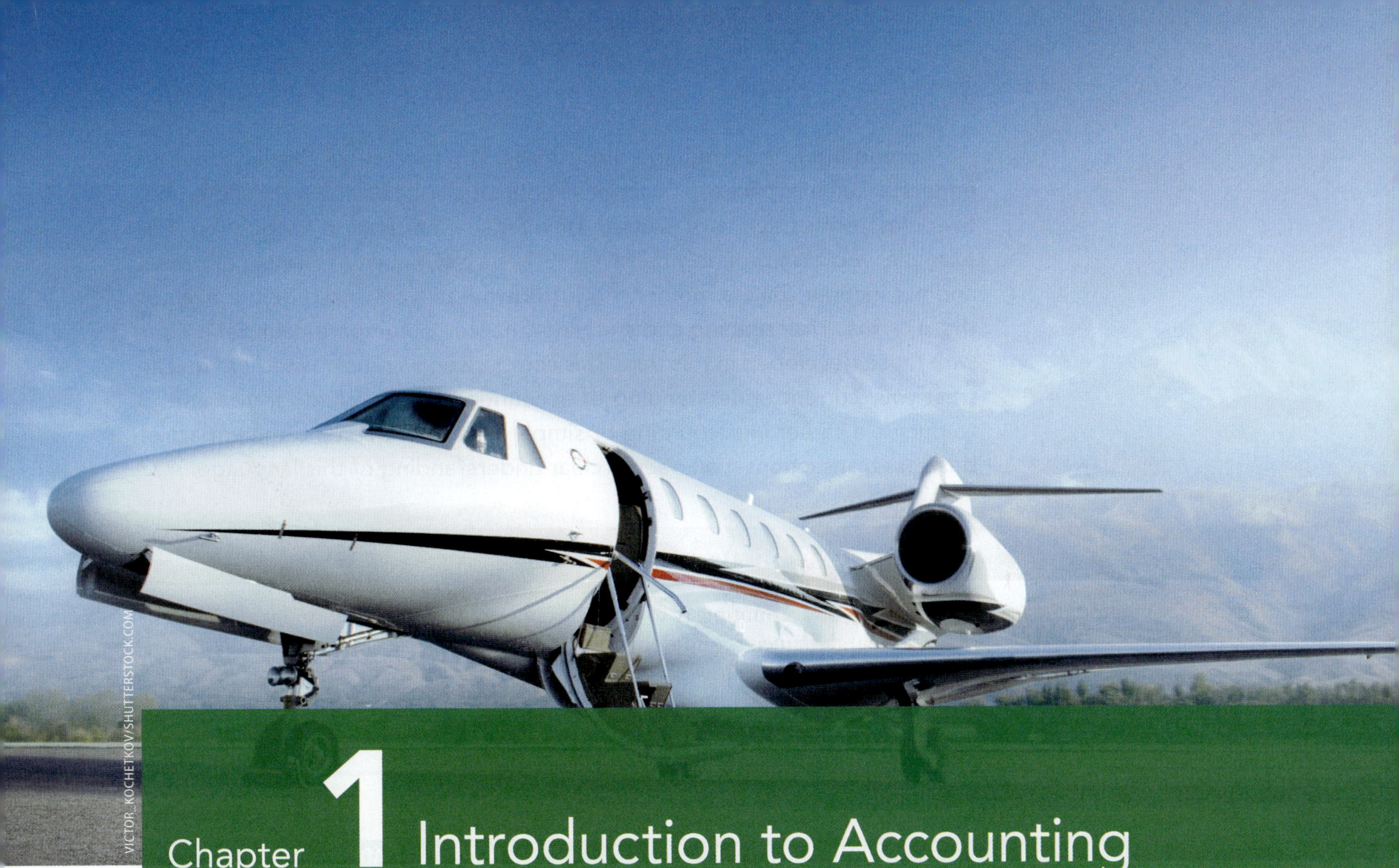

VICTOR_KOCHETKOV/SHUTTERSTOCK.COM

Chapter 1 Introduction to Accounting

Need a private jet to get away for the weekend, attend a business meeting, or visit Mom? Call Jets.com. Established in 1999, Jets.com serves as a broker for private jet services. Call or go online, and its technology will automatically send your trip request/itinerary to a network of approved operators who will locate available aircraft. Operators will competitively bid for your business, resulting in significant savings and increased aircraft options for you.

In addition to a system that links customers with private jet service, Jets.com needs a system to account for its business transactions. Thus, it employs accounting professionals who understand the accounting process and generally accepted accounting principles.

Welcome to the world of accounting. We are delighted that you have decided to join us. A solid foundation in accounting concepts and techniques will serve you well. This is true whether you accept a professional position in accounting, work for or own a business, or simply seek a better understanding of your personal finances.

Oh, and what does it cost to take a private jet to the Super Bowl? Rates run from $5,500 to $15,000 per hour on one of the busiest weekends of the year.

LEARNING OBJECTIVES

Careful study of this chapter should enable you to:

LO1 **Describe the purpose of accounting.**

LO2 **Describe the accounting process.**

LO3 **Define GAAP and describe the process used by FASB to develop these principles.**

LO4 **Define three types of business ownership structures.**

LO5 **Classify different types of businesses by activities.**

LO6 **Identify career opportunities in accounting.**

Accounting is the language of business. You must learn this language to understand the impact of economic events on a specific company. Common, everyday terms have very precise meanings when used in accounting. For example, you have probably heard terms like asset, liability, revenue, expense, and net income. Take a moment to jot down how you would define each of these terms. After reading and studying Chapter 2, compare your definitions with those developed in this text. This comparison will show whether you can trust your current understanding of accounting terms. Whether you intend to pursue a career in accounting or simply wish to understand the impact of business transactions, you need a clear understanding of this language.

LO1 The Purpose of Accounting

Describe the purpose of accounting.

The purpose of accounting is to provide financial information about the current operations and financial condition of a business to individuals, agencies, and organizations. As shown in Figure 1-1, owners, managers, creditors, and government agencies all need accounting information. Other users of accounting information include customers, clients, labor unions, stock exchanges, and financial analysts.

FIGURE 1-1 Users of Accounting Information

USER	INFORMATION NEEDED	DECISIONS MADE BY USERS
Owners—Present and future	Company's profitability and current financial condition.	If business is good, owners may consider making additional investments for growth. If business is poor, they may want to talk to management to find out why and may consider closing the business.
Managers—May or may not own business	Detailed measures of business performance.	Managers need to make operating decisions. How much and what kinds of inventory should be carried? Is business strong enough to support higher wages for employees?
Creditors—Present and future	Company's profitability, debt outstanding, and assets that could be used to secure debt.	Should a loan be granted to this business? If so, what amount of debt can the business support, and what interest rate should be charged?
Government Agencies—National, state, and local	Company's profitability, cash flows, and overall financial condition.	The IRS enforces U.S. tax laws to determine how much income tax the business must pay. Local governments may be willing to adjust property taxes paid by the business to encourage it to stay in town.

LO2 The Accounting Process

Describe the accounting process.

Accounting is a system of gathering financial information about a business and reporting this information to users. The six major steps of the accounting process are analyzing, recording, classifying, summarizing, reporting, and interpreting (Figure 1-2). Computers are often used in the recording, classifying, summarizing, and reporting steps. Whether or not computers are used, the accounting concepts and techniques are the same. Information entered into the computer system must reflect a proper application of these concepts. Otherwise, the output will be meaningless.

FIGURE 1-2 The Accounting Process

- **Analyzing** is looking at events that have taken place and thinking about how they affect the business. This first step in the accounting process usually occurs when the business receives some type of information, such as a bill, that needs to be properly entered into the business's records. This first step also involves deciding if the piece of information should result in an accounting entry or not.
- **Recording** is entering financial information about events into the accounting system. Although this can be done with paper and pencil, most businesses use computers to perform routine record-keeping operations.
- **Classifying** is sorting and grouping similar items together rather than merely keeping a simple, diary-like record of numerous events.
- **Summarizing** is the aggregation of many similar events to provide information that is easy to understand. For example, a firm may buy and sell baseballs during the year. Summarizing provides information on the total baseballs bought and sold and the change in the number of baseballs held from the beginning to the end of the period.
- **Reporting** is telling the results. In accounting, it is common to use tables of numbers to report results.
- **Interpreting** is deciding the meaning and importance of the information in various reports. This may include ratio analysis to help explain how pieces of information relate to one another.

LO3

Generally Accepted Accounting Principles (GAAP)

Define GAAP and describe the process used by FASB to develop these principles.

Soon after the stock market crash of 1929, the federal government established the Securities and Exchange Commission (SEC). The purpose of this government agency is to help develop standards for reporting financial information to stockholders. The SEC currently has authority over companies publicly traded on the major stock exchanges (New York and NASDAQ). It has the power to require these firms to follow certain rules when preparing their financial statements. These rules are referred to as **generally accepted accounting principles (GAAP).**

Rather than developing GAAP on its own, the SEC encouraged the creation of a private standard-setting body. It did so because it believed the private sector had better access to the resources and talent necessary to develop these standards. Since 1973, the Financial Accounting Standards Board (FASB) has filled this role. In developing accounting standards, FASB follows a specific process and relies on the advice of many organizations. When an accounting issue is identified, the following steps are followed:

1. The issue is placed on FASB's agenda. This lets everyone know that the Board plans to develop a standard addressing this issue.
2. After researching an issue, FASB issues a **Preliminary Views** document. This document identifies the pros and cons of various accounting treatments for an event and invites others to comment.
3. To gather additional views on the issue, the Board will often hold **public hearings** around the country. Interested parties are invited to express their opinions at these hearings.

SOURCE: FINANCIAL ACCOUNTING STANDARDS BOARD

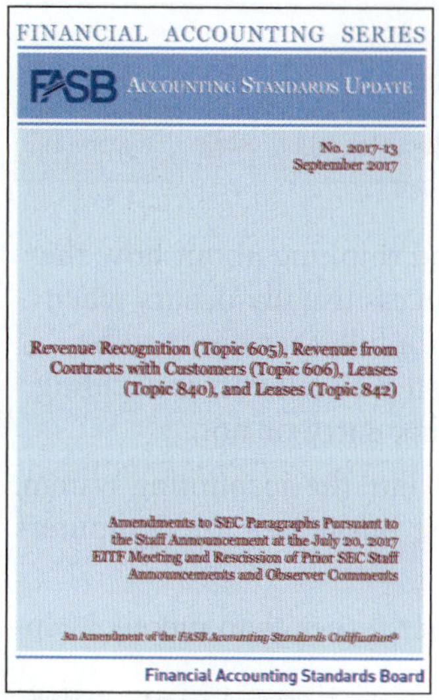
FINANCIAL ACCOUNTING SERIES

FASB ACCOUNTING STANDARDS UPDATE

No. 2017-13
September 2017

Revenue Recognition (Topic 605), Revenue from Contracts with Customers (Topic 606), Leases (Topic 840), and Leases (Topic 842)

Amendments to SEC Paragraphs Pursuant to the Staff Announcement at the July 20, 2017 EITF Meeting and Rescission of Prior SEC Staff Announcements and Observer Comments

An Amendment of the FASB Accounting Standards Codification®

Financial Accounting Standards Board

SOURCE: FINANCIAL ACCOUNTING STANDARDS BOARD

4. Following these hearings, the Board issues an **Exposure Draft.** This document explains the rules that FASB believes firms should follow in accounting for this event.
5. After considering feedback on the Exposure Draft, the Board issues a final **Accounting Standards Update** which amends the **Financial Accounting Standards Board Accounting Standards Codification.** This Codification is an electronic database that provides one authoritative source for the standards that must be followed by U.S. companies.

Throughout this process, many parties participate by testifying at public hearings or by sending letters to the Board explaining why they agree or disagree with the proposed standard. These parties include the American Institute of Certified Public Accountants (AICPA), the American Accounting Association (AAA), the Institute of Management Accountants (IMA), Financial Executives International (FEI), corporate executives and accountants, representatives from the investment community, analysts, bankers, industry associations, and the SEC and other government agencies. Clearly, FASB considers the views of a wide range of parties. By doing so, it maximizes the likelihood of developing and gaining acceptance of the most appropriate accounting and disclosure requirements.

The International Accounting Standards Board (IASB) issues accounting standards followed by many firms in countries outside the United States. These are called International Financial Reporting Standards (IFRS). In recent years, the IASB and FASB have worked together to try to minimize the differences in these standards. These standards may eventually converge into one set of standards used around the world.

LO4 Three Types of Ownership Structures

Define three types of business ownership structures.

One or more persons may own a business. Businesses are classified according to who owns them and the specific way they are organized. Three types of ownership structures are (1) sole proprietorship, (2) partnership, and (3) corporation (Figure 1-3). Accountants provide information to owners of all three types of ownership structures.

FIGURE 1-3 Types of Ownership Structures—Advantages and Disadvantages

TYPES OF OWNERSHIP STRUCTURES		
Sole Proprietorship	**Partnership**	**Corporation**
• One owner • Owner assumes all risk • Owner makes all decisions	• Two or more partners • Partners share risks • Partners may disagree on how to run business	• Stockholders • Stockholders have limited risk • Stockholders may have little influence on business decisions

Most businesses in the United States operate as sole proprietorships or partnerships. However, corporations earn the highest amount of revenue.

Sole Proprietorship

A **sole proprietorship** is owned by one person. The owner is usually called a proprietor. The proprietor often manages the business. The owner assumes all risks for the business, and personal assets can be taken to pay creditors. The advantage of a sole proprietorship is that the owner can make all decisions.

Partnership

A **partnership** is owned by more than one person. One or more partners may manage the business. Like proprietors, partners assume the risks for the business, and their assets may be taken to pay creditors. An advantage of a partnership is that owners share risks and decision making. A disadvantage is that partners may disagree about the best way to run the business.

Corporation

The largest corporations in the United States are known as the "Fortune 500."

A **corporation** is owned by stockholders (or shareholders). Corporations may have many owners, and they usually employ professional managers. The owners' risk is usually limited to their initial investment, and they often have very little influence on the business decisions.

LO5 Types of Businesses

Classify different types of businesses by activities.

Businesses are classified according to the type of service or product provided. Some businesses provide a service. Others sell a product. A business that provides a service is called a **service business**. A business that buys a product from another business to sell to customers is called a **merchandising business**. A business that makes a product to sell is called a **manufacturing business**. You will learn about all three types of businesses in this book. Figure 1-4 lists examples of types of businesses organized by activity.

FIGURE 1-4 Types and Examples of Businesses Organized by Activities

SERVICE	MERCHANDISING	MANUFACTURING
Travel Agency	Department Store	Automobile Manufacturer
Computer Consultant	Pharmacy	Furniture Maker
Physician	Grocery Store	Toy Factory

A BROADER VIEW

All Kinds of Businesses Need Accounting Systems

Even small businesses like those that provide guided horseback tours of the Rocky Mountains need good accounting systems. Proper records must be maintained for the cost of the horses, feed, food served, tour guides' salaries, and office expenses. Without this information, the company would not know how much to charge and whether a profit is made on these trips.

JACK HOLLINGSWORTH/CORBIS

LO6 Career Opportunities in Accounting

Identify career opportunities in accounting.

Accounting offers many career opportunities. The positions described below require varying amounts of education, experience, and technological skill.

Accounting Clerks

Businesses with large quantities of accounting tasks to perform daily often employ **accounting clerks** to record, sort, and file accounting information. Often, accounting clerks will specialize in cash, payroll, accounts receivable, accounts payable, inventory, or purchases. As a result, they are involved with only a small portion of the total accounting responsibilities for the firm. Accounting clerks usually have at least one year of accounting education.

Bookkeepers and Para-Accountants

Bookkeepers generally supervise the work of accounting clerks, help with daily accounting work, and summarize accounting information. In small-to-medium-sized businesses, the bookkeeper may also help managers and owners interpret the accounting information. Bookkeepers usually have one to two years of accounting education and experience as an accounting clerk.

Para-accountants provide many accounting, auditing, or tax services under the direct supervision of an accountant. A typical para-accountant has a two-year degree or significant accounting and bookkeeping experience.

Accountants

The difference between accountants and bookkeepers is not always clear, particularly in smaller companies where bookkeepers also help interpret the accounting information. In large companies, the distinction is clearer. Bookkeepers focus on the processing of accounting data. **Accountants** design the accounting information system and focus on analyzing and interpreting information. They also look for important trends in the data and study the impact of alternative decisions.

Most accountants enter the field with a college degree in accounting. In fact, since many states require 150 credit hours to sit for the CPA exam, many students are also earning a master's degree in accounting before entering the profession. Accountants are employed in public accounting, private (managerial) accounting, and governmental and not-for-profit accounting (Figure 1-5).

FIGURE 1-5 Accounting Careers

ACCOUNTING CAREERS		
Public Accounting • Auditing • Taxation • Management Advisory Services	**Private Accounting** • Accounting Information Systems • Financial Accounting • Cost Accounting • Budgeting • Tax Accounting • Internal Auditing	**Governmental and Not-for-Profit Accounting**

Public Accounting

Public accountants offer services in much the same way as doctors and lawyers. The public accountant can achieve professional recognition as a **Certified Public Accountant (CPA)**. This is done by meeting certain educational and experience requirements as determined by each state and passing a uniform examination prepared by the American Institute of Certified Public Accountants.

Many CPAs work alone, while others work for local, regional, national, or international accounting firms that vary in scope and size. The largest public accounting firms in the United States are known as the "Big Four." They are Deloitte, Ernst & Young, KPMG, and PricewaterhouseCoopers.

Services offered by public accountants are listed below.

- **Auditing.** Auditing involves the application of standard review and testing procedures to be certain that proper accounting policies and practices have been followed. The purpose of the audit is to provide an independent opinion that the financial information about a business is fairly presented in a manner consistent with generally accepted accounting principles.
- **Taxation.** Tax specialists advise on tax planning, prepare tax returns, and represent clients before governmental agencies such as the Internal Revenue Service.
- **Management Advisory Services.** Given the financial training and business experience of public accountants, many businesses seek their advice on a wide variety of managerial issues. Often, accounting firms are involved in designing computerized accounting systems.
- **Forensic Accounting.** Forensic accounting is a rapidly growing segment of accounting practice. It includes fraud detection, fraud prevention, litigation support, business valuations, expert witness services, and other investigative activities. Public accounting firms offer forensic accounting services, but forensic accountants also work for insurance companies, banks, law enforcement agencies, and other organizations. By meeting certain requirements, and passing the Certified Fraud Examiner exam, a forensic accountant may earn a **Certified Fraud Examiner (CFE)** designation.

In 2002, the **Sarbanes-Oxley Act (SOX)** was passed by Congress to help improve reporting practices of public companies. The act was in response to accounting scandals at firms like Enron, WorldCom, Cendant, Xerox, and others. Key provisions of SOX are listed below.

- The Public Company Accounting Oversight Board (PCAOB) was created to enforce SOX rules and regulations. The PCAOB also has authority to set auditing standards for public company audits and to perform inspections of auditing firms.
- For the largest companies, external auditors are required to report on the effectiveness of a public company's accounting procedures.
- Auditing firms are prohibited from offering many nonaudit services to their public audit clients.
- Auditing firms must rotate lead audit partners off audit engagements every five years.
- The CEO and CFO must personally certify that the financial statements are accurate.

It is difficult to guarantee that information provided in financial statements is always complete and accurate. These measures are a step in the right direction. If our economy and financial markets are to function properly, information provided in financial statements must be reliable.

Private (Managerial) Accounting

Many accountants are employees of private business firms. The **controller** oversees the entire accounting process and is the principal accounting officer of the company. Private or managerial accountants perform a wide variety of services for the business. These services are listed below.

- **Accounting Information Systems.** Accountants in this area design and implement manual and computerized accounting systems.
- **Financial Accounting.** Based on the accounting data prepared by the bookkeepers and accounting clerks, accountants prepare various reports and financial statements and help in analyzing operating, investing, and financing decisions.
- **Cost Accounting.** The cost of producing specific products or providing services must be measured. Further analysis is also done to determine whether the products are produced and services are provided in the most cost-effective manner.
- **Budgeting.** In the budgeting process, accountants help managers develop a financial plan.
- **Tax Accounting.** Instead of hiring a public accountant, a company may have its own accountants. They focus on tax planning, preparation of tax returns, and dealing with the Internal Revenue Service and other governmental agencies.
- **Internal Auditing.** Internal auditors review the operating and accounting control procedures adopted by management to make sure the controls are adequate and are being followed. They also monitor the accuracy and timeliness of the reports provided to management and to external parties.

A managerial accountant can achieve professional status as a **Certified Management Accountant (CMA)**. This is done by passing a uniform examination offered by the Institute of Management Accountants. An internal auditor can achieve professional recognition as a **Certified Internal Auditor (CIA)** by passing the uniform examination offered by the Institute of Internal Auditors.

Governmental and Not-for-Profit Accounting

Thousands of governmental and not-for-profit organizations (states, cities, schools, churches, and hospitals) gather and report financial information. These organizations employ a large number of accountants. Since these entities are not profit oriented, the rules are somewhat different for governmental and not-for-profit organizations. However, many accounting procedures are similar to those found in profit-seeking enterprises.

Job Opportunities

Job growth in some areas will be much greater than in others. Employment advertisements often indicate that accountants and accounting clerks are expected to have computer skills. Computer skills definitely increase the opportunities available to you in your career. Almost every business needs accountants, accounting clerks, and bookkeepers. Figure 1-6 shows the expected growth for different industry sectors. Notice that growth will be greatest in health care services. Chapters 2 through 9 introduce accounting skills that you will need to work in a service business, like health care. Chapter 10 begins the discussion of merchandising businesses. Accounting for manufacturing businesses is addressed in the last chapters of the book.

Figure 1-7 shows an overall increase in projected demand for accounting skills. Demand for billing and posting clerks, accountants and auditors, and budget analysts is expected to increase by 14.1%, 10.0%, and 6.5% respectively from 2016 to 2026. Demand for bookkeepers, accounting, and auditing clerks is projected to dip by 1.5%.

Figure 1-8 provides various job descriptions in the accounting profession along with the range of salaries paid.

FIGURE 1-6 Expected Job Growth by Industry 2016–2026 (in thousands)

The growth in the number of new jobs from 2016 to 2026 will vary according to industry. As shown above, health care industries are expected to account for a large portion of the new jobs projected through 2026. Other industries are shown for comparison purposes. Note that professional and business services also appear to provide good opportunities. Total employment for all industry sectors is projected to grow by 7.4% over the decade, resulting in 11.5 million new jobs.

Source: Bureau of Labor Statistics News Release, January 30, 2018: Employment Projections—2016–2026. *(https://www.bls.gov/news.release/pdf/ecopro.pdf)*

FIGURE 1-7 Expected Demand

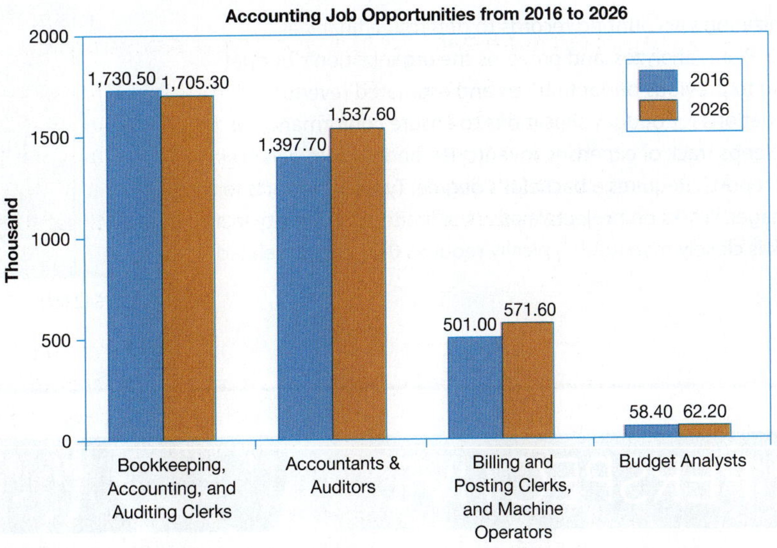

The highest number of jobs available is expected to be for bookkeepers, accounting and auditing clerks, though a 1.5 percent dip in these jobs over the decade is projected. As shown below, jobs for accountants and auditors are expected to increase by 10 percent. The projected growth, or decline, for each area from 2016 to 2026 is shown below.

	Thousands	Percentage
Accountants and auditors	139.9	10.0%
Budget analysts	3.8	6.5%
Bookkeeping, accounting, and auditing clerks	−25.2	−1.5%
Billing and posting clerks, and machine operators	70.6	14.1%

Source: Bureau of Labor Statistics, National Employment Matrix as of January 30, 2018. *(https://www.bls.gov/emp/ep_table_102.htm)*

FIGURE 1-8 **Accounting Positions according to Salary.com, 2018**

Accounting Clerk I

Performs routine accounting activities such as maintenance of the general ledger, preparation of various accounting statements and financial reports. Posts journal entries and verifies billings, invoices and checks. Assists in completing moderately complex calculations. Reconciles accounts and bank statements. Has a basic understanding of bookkeeping and accounting principles. Is proficient with spreadsheets and other software tools. Typically requires a high school diploma. Typically reports to a supervisor or manager. Possesses a moderate understanding of general aspects of the job. Works under the close direction of senior personnel in the functional area. May require 0-1 year of general work experience.

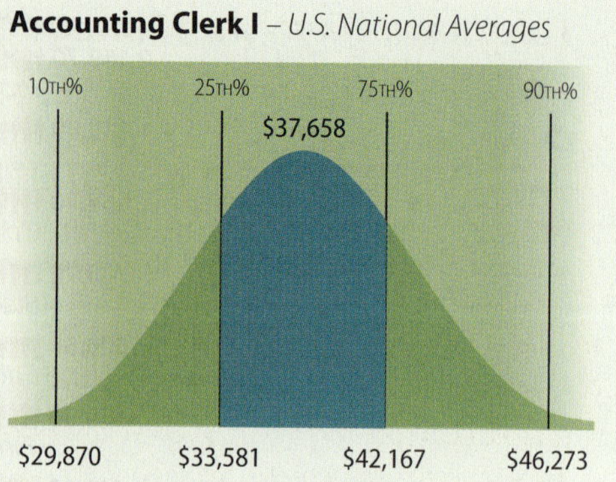

Bookkeeper

Maintains and records a complete and systematic set of business transactions. Balances ledgers, reconciles accounts, and prepares reports to show receipts, expenditures, accounts receivable, and payable. Follows bookkeeping procedures established by the organization. May require an associate's degree or its equivalent. Typically reports to a supervisor or a manager. Gaining or has attained full proficiency in a specific area of discipline. Works under moderate supervision. Typically requires 1-3 years of related experience.

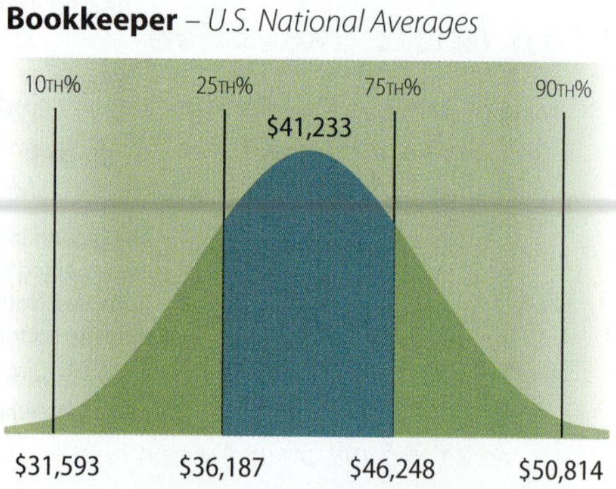

Budet Analyst I

Analyzes an organization's accounting records to determine financial resources required. Plans, analyzes, and prepares the organization's budget activities according to previous budget figures and estimated revenue. Makes recommendations for budget allocations to ensure conformance to budgetary limits. Keeps track of expenses, inventories, and budget balances. Prepares financial reports. Requires a bachelor's degree. Typically reports to a supervisor or manager. Works on projects/matters of limited complexity in a support role. Work is closely managed. Typically requires 0-2 years of related experience.

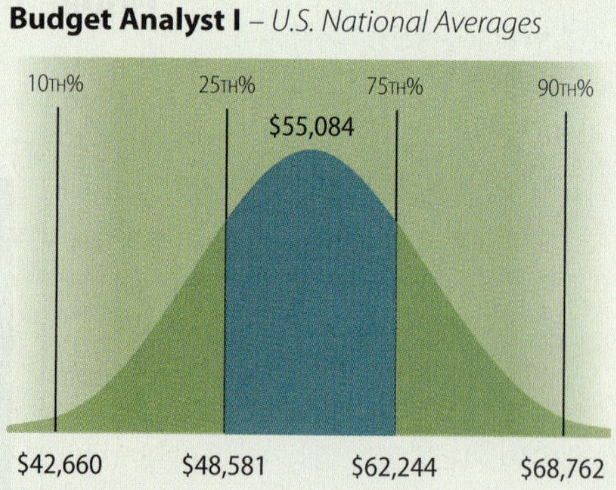

YOUR PERSPECTIVE

Industrial Engineering Technician

Accounting is the language of business and the eyes and ears of management. No matter the job, it likely provides accounting information that management uses to make important operating decisions. Even a technology-oriented job, such as *industrial engineering technician*, involves accounting. These technicians assist engineers in devising systems that make products or provide services. They also perform duties that provide accounting information such as analyzing production costs and managing supply chain costs to control inventory.

Accounts Payable Manager

Manages all activities in the accounts payable function. Ensures timely payments of vendor invoices and expense vouchers and maintains accurate records and control reports. Reviews applicable accounting reports and accounts payable register to ensure accuracy. Typically requires a bachelor's degree. Typically reports to a head of a unit/department. Manages subordinate staff in the day-to-day performance of their jobs. True first level manager. Ensures that project/department milestones/goals are met and adhering to approved budgets. Has full authority for personnel actions. Extensive knowledge of department processes. Typically requires 5 years experience in the related area as an individual contributor. 1 to 3 years supervisory experience may be required.

Accounts Payable manager – *U.S. National Averages*

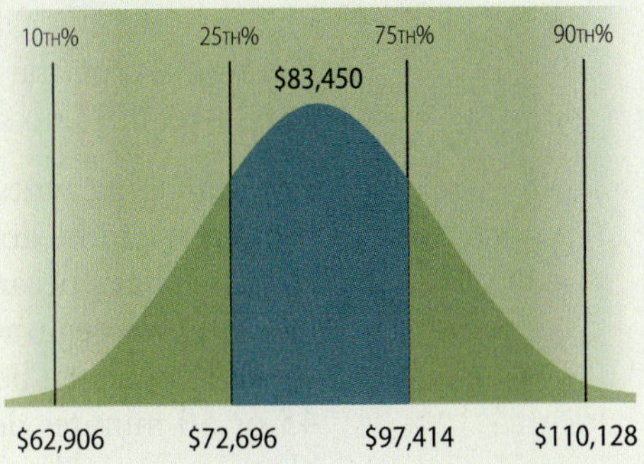

Top Audit Executive

Oversees all aspects of an organization's auditing function. Plans and directs all accounting and financial data. Designs internal auditing procedures and ensures they are followed. Monitors procedures for effectiveness and provides recommendations for improvement. Requires a bachelor's degree. Typically reports to top management. Manages a business unit, division, or corporate function with major organizational impact. Establishes overall direction and strategic initiatives for the given major function or line of business. Has acquired the business acumen and leadership experience to become a top function or division head.

Top Audit Executive – *U.S. National Averages*

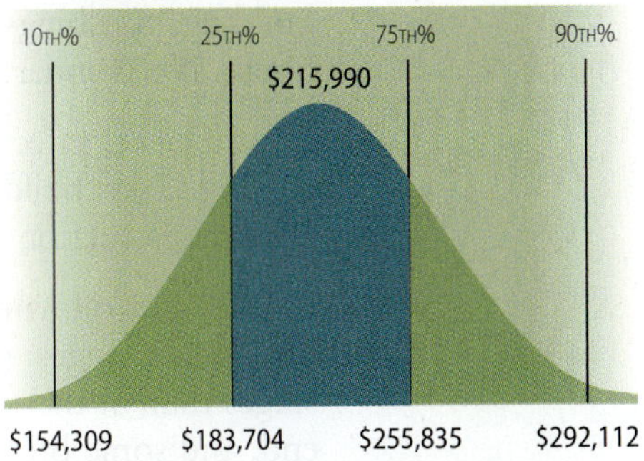

Controller

Leads and directs an organization's accounting functions. Establishes and maintains the organization's overall accounting systems, procedures, and policies. Directs all analysis and reporting of financial information including budgets, planning, and required filings and reports. Presents findings and recommendations to management. Requires a bachelor's degree of accounting or finance. Typically reports to Chief Financial Officer (CFO). Typically requires CPA. Manages a departmental function within a broader corporate function. Develops major goals to support broad functional objectives. Approves policies developed within various sub-functions and departments. Comprehensive knowledge of the overall departmental function. Typically requires 8+ years of managerial experience.

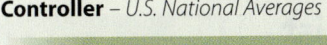

Controller – *U.S. National Averages*

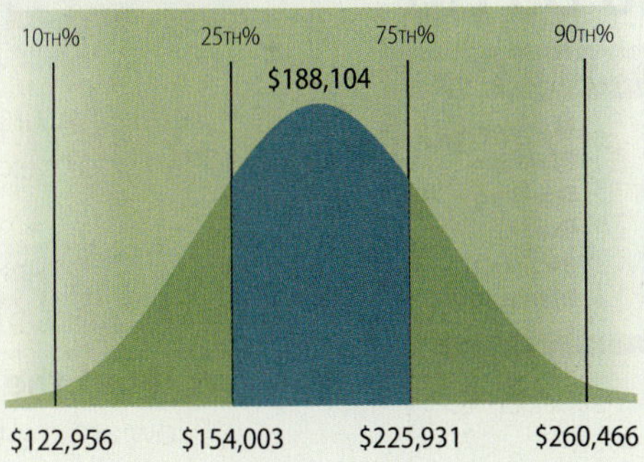

Source: Salary.com, March 2018.

Managing Your Writing

Regardless of the type of career you desire, writing skills are important in business and your personal life. Becoming a good writer requires practice and a strategy for the process used to prepare memos, letters, and other documents. On pages 14 and 15, Ken Davis, *Professor Emeritus of English at Indiana University*, offers an excellent approach to managing your writing. Take a moment to read Ken's tips. Then, practice his approach by completing the writing assignments as you finish each chapter.

From: Ken Davis
Subject: Managing Your Writing
To: Accounting Students

Here's a secret: the business writing that you and I do—the writing that gets the world's work done—requires no special gift. It can be managed, like any other business process.

Managing writing is largely a matter of managing time. Writing is a process, and like any process it can be done efficiently or inefficiently. Unfortunately, most of us are pretty inefficient writers. That's because we try to get each word, each sentence, right the first time. Given a letter to write, we begin with the first sentence. We think about that sentence, write it, revise it, even check its spelling, before going on to the second sentence. In an hour of writing, we might spend 45 or 50 minutes doing this kind of detailed drafting. We spend only a few minutes on overall planning at the beginning and only a few minutes on overall revising at the end.

That approach to writing is like building a house by starting with the front door: planning, building, finishing—even washing the windows—before doing anything with the rest of the house. No wonder most of us have so much trouble writing.

Efficient, effective writers take better charge of their writing time. They *manage* their writing. Like building contractors, they spend time planning before they start construction. Once construction has started, they don't try to do all of the finishing touches as they go.

As the following illustration shows, many good writers break their writing process into three main stages: planning, drafting, and revising. They spend more time at the first and third stages than at the second. They also build in some "management" time at the beginning and the end, and some break time in the middle. To manage *your* writing time, try the following steps.

To Do List

CHECK LIST
- ☐ Managing
- ☐ Planning
- ☐ Drafting
- ☐ Break
- ☐ Revising
- ☐ Managing

☐ At the **Managing Stage** *(perhaps two or three minutes for a one-hour writing job):*

Remind yourself that writing *can* be managed and that it's largely a matter of managing time. Plan your next hour.

☐ At the **Planning Stage** *(perhaps 20 minutes out of the hour):*

1. Find the "we." Define the community to which you and your reader belong. Then ask, "How are my reader and I alike and different?"—in knowledge, attitudes, and circumstances.

2. Define your purpose. Remember the advice a consultant once gave Stanley Tool executives: "You're not in the business of making drills: you're in the business of making holes." Too many of us lose sight of the difference between making drills and making holes when we write letters and memos. We focus on the piece of writing—the tool itself—not its purpose. The result: our writing often misses the chance to be as effective as it could be. When you're still at the planning stage, focus on the outcome you want, not on the means you will use to achieve it.

3. Get your stuff together. Learn from those times when you've turned a one-hour home-improvement project into a three- or four-hour job by having to make repeated trips to the hardware store for tools or parts. Before you start the drafting stage of writing, collect the information you need.

4. Get your ducks in a row. Decide on the main points you want to make. Then, make a list or rough outline placing your points in the most logical order.

At the **Drafting Stage** *(perhaps 5 minutes out of the hour):*

5. Do it wrong the first time. Do a "quick and dirty" draft, without editing. Think of your draft as a "prototype," written not for the end user but for your own testing and improvement. Stopping to edit while you draft breaks your train of thought and keeps you from being a good writer. (*Hint:* If you are writing at a computer, try turning off the monitor during the drafting stage.)

At the **Break Stage** *(perhaps 5 minutes):*

6. Take a break and change hats. Get away from your draft, even if for only a few minutes. Come back with a fresh perspective—the reader's perspective.

At the **Revising Stage** *(perhaps 25 minutes):*

7. Signal your turns. Just as if you were driving a car, you're leading your reader through new territory. Use "turn signals"—*and, in addition, but, however, or, therefore, because, for example*—to guide your reader from sentence to sentence.

8. Say what you mean. Put the point of your sentences in the subjects and verbs. For example, revise "There are drawbacks to using this accounting method" to "This accounting method has some drawbacks." You'll be saying what you mean, and you'll be a more effective communicator.

9. Pay by the word. Reading your memo requires work. If your sentences are wordy and you are slow to get to the point, the reader may decide that it is not worth the effort. Pretend you are paying the reader by the word to read your memo. Then, revise your memo to make it as short and to the point as possible.

10. Translate into English. Keep your words simple. (Lee Iacocca put both these tips in one "commandment of good management": "Say it in English and keep it short.") Remember that you write to express, not impress.

11. Finish the job. Check your spelling, punctuation, and mechanics.

Finally, at the **Managing Stage** *(2 to 3 minutes):*

12. Evaluate your writing process. Figure out how to improve it next time.

By following these 12 steps, you can take charge of your writing time. Begin today to *manage your writing*. As a United Technologies Corporation advertisement in *The Wall Street Journal* admonished, "If you want to manage somebody, manage yourself. Do that well and you'll be ready to stop managing and start leading."

Dr. Kenneth W. Davis is Professor Emeritus of English at Indiana University, and a writing trainer and coach.

LEARNING OBJECTIVES		Key Points to Remember
LO1	**Describe the purpose of accounting.**	The purpose of accounting is to provide financial information about a business to individuals and organizations.
LO2	**Describe the accounting process.**	The six major steps of the accounting process are analyzing, recording, classifying, summarizing, reporting, and interpreting.
LO3	**Define GAAP and describe the process used by FASB to develop these principles.**	Generally accepted accounting principles (GAAP) are the rules that businesses must follow when preparing financial statements. FASB takes the following steps to develop an accounting standard: 1. The issue is placed on the Board's agenda. 2. After researching the issue, a Preliminary Views document is issued. 3. Public hearings are held. 4. An Exposure Draft is issued. 5. The Board issues an Accounting Standards Update which amends the FASB Accounting Standards Codification.
LO4	**Define three types of business ownership structures.**	Three types of business ownership structures are the sole proprietorship, the partnership, and the corporation.
LO5	**Classify different types of businesses by activities.**	Different types of businesses classified by activities are a service business, a merchandising business, and a manufacturing business.
LO6	**Identify career opportunities in accounting.**	Career opportunities in accounting include work in public accounting, private accounting, and governmental and not-for-profit accounting.

KEY TERMS

accountant (8) Designs the accounting information system and focuses on analyzing and interpreting information.

accounting (4) A system of gathering financial information about a business and reporting this information to users.

accounting clerk (8) Records, sorts, and files accounting information.

accounting information systems (10) Accountants in this area design and implement manual and computerized accounting systems.

Accounting Standards Update (6) A standard issued by the Financial Accounting Standards Board. These standards must be followed when preparing financial statements. The updates are included in the FASB Accounting Standards Codification.

analyzing (5) Looking at events that have taken place and thinking about how they affect the business.

auditing (9) Reviewing and testing to be certain that proper accounting policies and practices have been followed.

bookkeeper (8) Generally supervises the work of accounting clerks, helps with daily accounting work, and summarizes accounting information.

budgeting (10) The process in which accountants help managers develop a financial plan.

Certified Fraud Examiner (CFE) (9) A forensic accountant who has passed the exam offered by the Association of Certified Fraud Examiners.

Certified Internal Auditor (CIA) (10) An internal auditor who has achieved professional recognition by passing the uniform examination offered by the Institute of Internal Auditors.

Certified Management Accountant (CMA) (10) An accountant who has passed an examination offered by the Institute of Management Accountants.

Certified Public Accountant (CPA) (9) A public accountant who has met certain educational and experience requirements and has passed an examination prepared by the American Institute of Certified Public Accountants.

classifying (5) Sorting and grouping similar items together rather than merely keeping a simple, diary-like record of numerous events.

Controller (10) The accountant who oversees the entire accounting process and is the principal accounting officer of a company.

corporation (7) A type of ownership structure in which stockholders own the business. The owners' risk is usually limited to their initial investment, and they usually have very little influence on the business decisions.

cost accounting (10) Determining the cost of producing specific products or providing services and analyzing for cost effectiveness.

Exposure Draft (6) This document explains the rules that FASB believes firms should follow in accounting for a particular event. Based on the responses to the Exposure Draft, the Board will decide if any changes are necessary before issuing a final standard.

financial accounting (10) Includes preparing various reports and financial statements and analyzing operating, investing, and financing decisions.

Financial Accounting Standards Board Accounting Standards Codification (6) This Codification is an electronic database that provides one authoritative source for the standards which must be followed by U.S. companies.

forensic accounting (9) A specialized field that combines fraud detection, fraud prevention, litigation support, expert witnessing, business valuations, and other investigative activities.

generally accepted accounting principles (GAAP) (5) Procedures and guidelines developed by the Financial Accounting Standards Board to be followed in the accounting and reporting process.

internal auditing (10) Reviewing the operating and accounting control procedures adopted by management to make sure the controls are adequate and being followed; assuring that accurate and timely information is provided.

interpreting (5) Deciding the meaning and importance of the information in various reports.

management advisory services (9) Providing advice to businesses on a wide variety of managerial issues.

manufacturing business (7) A business that makes a product to sell.

merchandising business (7) A business that buys products to sell.

para-accountant (8) A paraprofessional who provides many accounting, auditing, or tax services under the direct supervision of an accountant.

partnership (7) A type of ownership structure in which more than one person owns the business.

Preliminary Views (5) The first document issued by FASB when developing an accounting standard. This document identifies the pros and cons of various accounting treatments for an event and invites others to comment.

public hearing (5) Following the issuance of a discussion memorandum, public meetings are often held by FASB to gather opinions on the accounting issue.

recording (5) Entering financial information about events affecting the company into the accounting system.

reporting (5) Telling the results of the financial information.

Sarbanes-Oxley Act (SOX) (9) An act passed by Congress to help improve reporting practices of public companies.

service business (7) A business that provides a service.

sole proprietorship (6) A type of ownership structure in which one person owns the business.

summarizing (5) Bringing the various items of information together to determine a result.

tax accounting (10) Services focused on tax planning, preparing tax returns, and dealing with the Internal Revenue Service and other governmental agencies.

taxation (9) See tax accounting.

APPLYING YOUR KNOWLEDGE

CengageNowv2 provides "Show Me How" videos for selected exercises and problems. Additional resources, such as Excel templates for completing selected exercises and problems, are available for download from the companion website at Cengage.com.

REVIEW QUESTIONS

LO1 1. What is the purpose of accounting?

LO1 2. Identify four user groups normally interested in financial information about a business.

LO2 3. Identify the six major steps of the accounting process and explain each step.

LO3 4. What are generally accepted accounting principles (GAAP)?

LO3 5. Describe the steps followed by the Financial Accounting Standards Board when developing an accounting standard.

LO3 6. What is the name of the organization that issues accounting standards followed by many firms in countries outside the United States?

LO4 7. Identify the three types of ownership structures and discuss the advantages and disadvantages of each.

LO5 8. Identify three types of businesses according to activities.

LO6 9. What are the main functions of an accounting clerk?

LO6 10. Name and describe four areas of specialization for a public accountant.

LO6 11. What is the purpose of the Sarbanes-Oxley Act?

LO6 12. Name and describe six areas of specialization for a managerial accountant.

SERIES A EXERCISES

E 1-1A (LO1)

PURPOSE OF ACCOUNTING Match the following users with the information needed.

1. Owners
2. Managers
3. Creditors
4. Government agencies

a. Whether the firm can pay its bills on time
b. Detailed, up-to-date information to measure business performance (and plan for future operations)
c. To determine taxes to be paid and whether other regulations are met
d. The firm's current financial condition

E 1-2A (LO2)

ACCOUNTING PROCESS List the six major steps of the accounting process in order (1–6) and define each.

_______ Recording 2
_______ Summarizing 4
_______ Reporting 5
_______ Analyzing 1
_______ Interpreting 6
_______ Classifying 3

SERIES B EXERCISES

E 1-1B (LO1)

PURPOSE OF ACCOUNTING Describe the kind of information needed by the users listed.

Owners (present and future)
Managers
Creditors (present and future)
Government agencies

E 1-2B (LO2)

ACCOUNTING PROCESS Match the following steps of the accounting process with their definitions.

Analyzing
Recording
Classifying
Summarizing
Reporting
Interpreting

a. Telling the results
b. Looking at events that have taken place and thinking about how they affect the business
c. Deciding the importance of the various reports
d. Aggregating many similar events to provide information that is easy to understand
e. Sorting and grouping like items together
f. Entering financial information into the accounting system

CHECK LIST
- ☐ **Managing**
- ☐ **Planning**
- ☐ **Drafting**
- ☐ **Break**
- ☐ **Revising**
- ☐ **Managing**

MANAGING YOUR WRITING

Take a moment to think about what it would be like to run your own business. If you started a business, what would it be? Prepare a one-page memo that describes the type of business you would enjoy the most. Would it be a service, merchandising, or manufacturing business? Explain what form of ownership you would prefer and why.

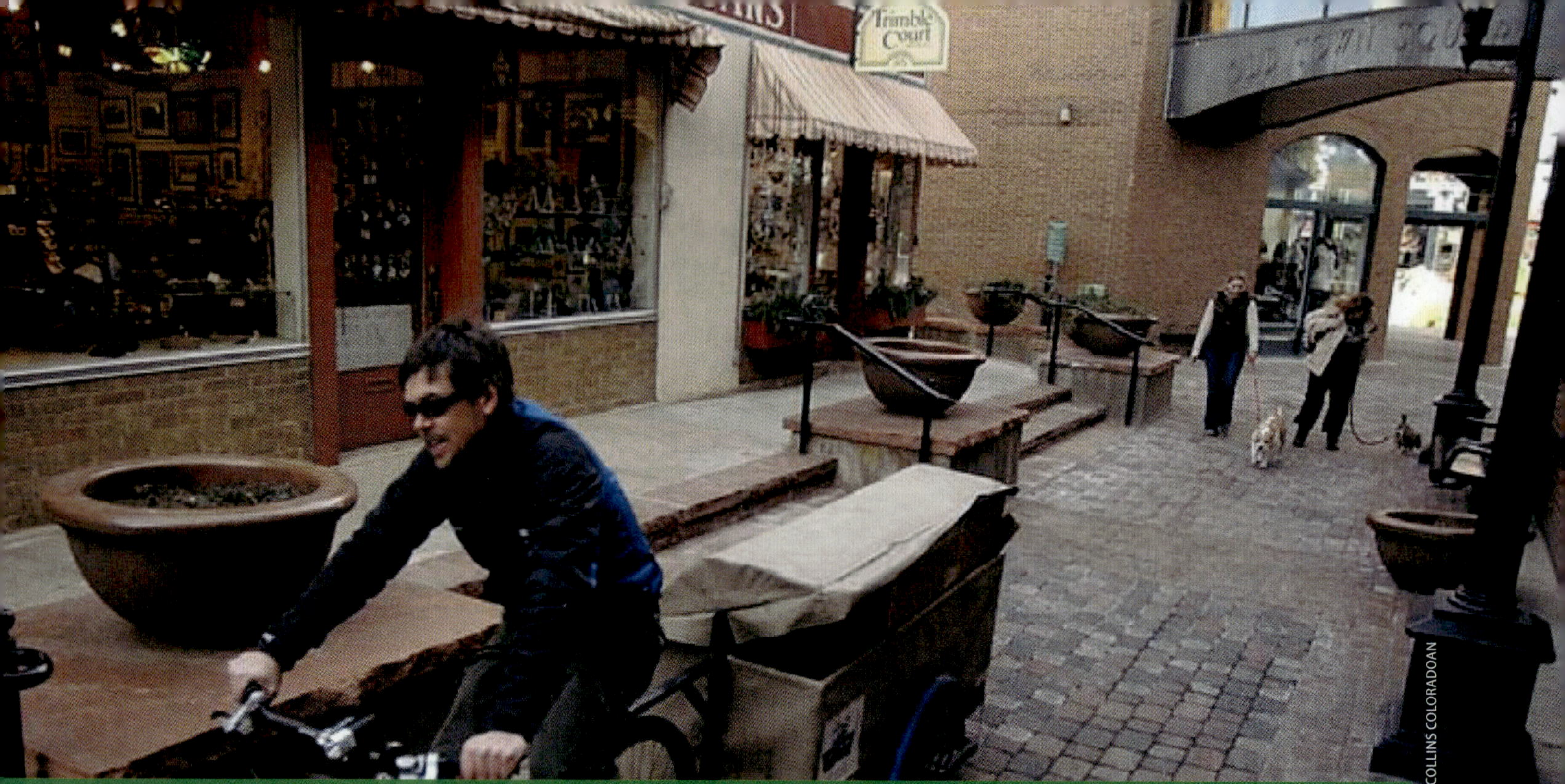

RICH ABRAHAMSON/FORT COLLINS COLORADOAN

Chapter 2 Analyzing Transactions: The Accounting Equation

LEARNING OBJECTIVES

Careful study of this chapter should enable you to:

- **LO1** Define the accounting elements.
- **LO2** Construct the accounting equation.
- **LO3** Analyze business transactions.
- **LO4** Show the effects of business transactions on the accounting equation.
- **LO5** Prepare and describe the purposes of a simple income statement, statement of owner's equity, and balance sheet.
- **LO6** Define the three basic phases of the accounting process.

At Rob's Bike Courier Service in Fort Collins, Colorado, Rob believes "less is more." His small company doesn't "have a fleet of vehicles, just some pretty cool bicycles." His mission is providing successful bike delivery service, perfect for both traditional business delivery services and residential errands. Since January of 2005, Rob's Bike Courier Service has been the alternative to gas-powered vehicle delivery. Thus, besides great rates and friendly, reliable service, Rob offers earth-friendly service.

Currently, he delivers wholesale bagels from a mid-town baker to several downtown coffee shops. He does the same for another pastry chef. Rob also picks up recycling materials, offers bike towing services, and will go to a customer's home to fix flat bike tires and make repairs.

Though his company is small, Rob still needs an accounting system to maintain records of his business transactions and to prepare financial statements. Currently, he uses Quickbooks®, an accounting program used by many small companies. In Chapters 2 through 6, we learn how to account for a service business like Rob's by using an example of a similar company: Mitchell's Campus Delivery.

The entire accounting process is based on one simple equation, called the accounting equation. In this chapter, you will learn how to use this equation to analyze business transactions. You will also learn how to prepare financial statements that report the effect of these transactions on the financial condition of a business.

LO1 The Accounting Elements

Define the accounting elements.

Before the accounting process can begin, the entity to be accounted for must be defined. A **business entity** is an individual, association, or organization that engages in economic activities and controls specific economic resources. This definition allows the personal and business finances of an owner to be accounted for separately.

Three basic accounting elements exist for every business entity: assets, liabilities, and owner's equity. These elements are defined below.

Assets

LEARNING KEY
Pay close attention to the definitions for the basic accounting elements. A clear understanding of these definitions will help you analyze even the most complex business transactions.

Assets are items that are owned by a business and will provide future benefits. Examples of assets include cash, merchandise, furniture, fixtures, machinery, buildings, and land. Businesses may also have an asset called **accounts receivable**. This asset represents the amount of money owed to the business by its customers as a result of making sales "on account," or "on credit." Making sales on account simply means that the customers have promised to pay sometime in the future.

Liabilities

Liabilities represent something owed to another business entity. The amount owed represents a probable future outflow of assets as a result of a past event or transaction. Liabilities are debts or obligations of the business that can be paid with cash, goods, or services.

The most common liabilities are accounts payable and notes payable. An **account payable** is an unwritten promise to pay a supplier for assets purchased or services received. Acquiring assets or services by promising to make payments in the future is referred to as making a purchase "on account," or "on credit." Formal written promises to pay suppliers or lenders specified sums of money at definite future times are known as **notes payable**.

Owner's Equity

LEARNING KEY
The business entity's assets and liabilities are separate from the owner's nonbusiness assets and liabilities.

CHECKPOINT
Complete Checkpoint-1 on page 41 to test your basic understanding of LO1.

Owner's equity is the amount by which the business assets exceed the business liabilities. Other terms used for owner's equity include **net worth** and **capital**. If there are no business liabilities, the owner's equity is equal to the total assets.

The owner of a business may have business assets and liabilities as well as nonbusiness assets and liabilities. For example, the business owner probably owns a home, clothing, and a car, and perhaps owes the dentist for dental service. These are personal, nonbusiness assets and liabilities. According to the **business entity concept**, nonbusiness assets and liabilities are not included in the business entity's accounting records.

If the owner invests money or other assets in the business, the item invested is reclassified from a nonbusiness asset to a business asset. If the owner withdraws money or other assets from the business for personal use, the item withdrawn is reclassified from a business asset to a nonbusiness asset. These distinctions are important and allow the owner to make decisions based on the financial condition and results of the business apart from nonbusiness activities.

CHAMPIOFOTO/SHUTTERSTOCK.COM

A BROADER VIEW

Assets and the Cost of Products We Buy

Next time you buy something, think of all the assets a company needs to produce that product. If the product comes from a capital-intensive industry, one that requires heavy investments in assets, the company must price the product high enough to cover the cost of using the assets and replacing them when they wear out. For example, AT&T recently reported that the cost of property, plant, and equipment used for operating purposes came to over $319 billion.

LO2 The Accounting Equation

Construct the accounting equation.

The relationship between the three basic accounting elements—assets, liabilities, and owner's equity—can be expressed in the form of a simple equation known as the **accounting equation**.

Assets	=	Liabilities	+	Owner's Equity

This equation reflects the fact that both outsiders and insiders have an interest in the assets of a business.

- Liabilities represent the outside interests of creditors.
- Owner's equity represents the inside interests of owners.

Or, viewed another way,

The left side of the equation shows the assets. *The right side of the equation shows where the money came from to buy the assets.*

When two elements are known, the third can always be calculated. For example, assume that assets on December 31 total $60,400. On that same day, the business liabilities consist of $5,400 owed for equipment. Owner's equity is calculated by subtracting total liabilities from total assets, $60,400 − $5,400 = $55,000.

LEARNING KEY

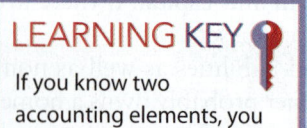

If you know two accounting elements, you can calculate the third element.

Total assets	$60,400
Total liabilities	−5,400
Owner's equity	$55,000

Assets	=	Liabilities	+	Owner's Equity
$60,400	=	$5,400	+	$55,000
$60,400	=	**$60,400**		

If during the next accounting period, assets increased by $10,000 and liabilities increased by $3,000, owner's equity must have increased by $7,000 ($10,000 − $3,000) as shown on the next page.

	Assets	=	Liabilities	+	Owner's Equity
BB	$60,400		$5,400		$55,000
	+10,000	=	+3,000	+	+7,000
EB	$70,400	=	$8,400	+	$62,000
	$70,400	=	**$70,400**		

BB: Beginning balance
EB: Ending balance

CHECKPOINT

Complete Checkpoint-2 on page 41 to test your basic understanding of LO2.

Note also that after computing the ending balances for assets, liabilities, and owner's equity, the accounting equation remains in balance.

LO3 Analyzing Business Transactions

Analyze business transactions.

A **business transaction** is an economic event that has a direct impact on the business. A business transaction almost always requires an exchange between the business and another outside entity. We must be able to measure this exchange in dollars. Examples of business transactions include buying goods and services, selling goods and services, buying and selling assets, making loans, and borrowing money.

All business transactions affect the accounting equation through specific accounts. An **account** is a separate record used to summarize changes in each asset, liability, and the owner's equity of a business. **Account titles** provide a description of the particular type of asset, liability, or owner's equity affected by a transaction.

Three basic questions must be answered when analyzing the effects of a business transaction on the accounting equation. These questions help address the steps in the accounting process discussed in Chapter 1.

1. What happened?
   - Make certain you understand the event that has taken place.
2. Which accounts are affected?
   - Identify the accounts that are affected.
   - Classify these accounts as assets, liabilities, or owner's equity.
3. How is the accounting equation affected?
   - Determine which accounts have increased or decreased.
   - Make certain that the accounting equation remains in balance after the transaction has been entered.

LO4 Effect of Transactions on the Accounting Equation

Show the effects of business transactions on the accounting equation.

In Chapters 2 through 6, we will focus on learning how to account for a business similar to Rob's Bike Courier Service, discussed in the chapter opener. In these chapters, we will focus on Mitchell's Campus Delivery. By studying Mitchell's business transactions and accounting techniques, you will learn about business and accounting. A major advantage of studying accounting is that it helps you learn a great deal about business.

As explained earlier, we must first understand the economic substance of events. Then, we must determine how that information is entered into the accounting system. *If Mitch does not understand the economic events affecting his delivery business and their impact on the accounting equation, the events will not be correctly entered into the accounting system.*

Each transaction affects at least two accounts and one or more of the three basic accounting elements. A transaction increases or decreases specific asset, liability, or owner's equity accounts. Assume that the following transactions occurred during June 20--, the first month of operations for Mitchell's Campus Delivery.

Remember, capital does not mean cash. The cash is shown in the cash account.

Transaction (a): Investment by owner

An Increase in an Asset Offset by an Increase in Owner's Equity. Mitch Williams opened a bank account with a deposit of $5,000 for his business. The new business now has $5,000 of the asset Cash. Since Mitch contributed the asset, the owner's equity element, Mitchell Williams, Capital, increases by the same amount.

Assets (Items Owned)	=	**Liabilities** (Amounts Owed)	+	**Owner's Equity** (Owner's Investment)
Cash	=			Mitchell Williams, Capital
(a) **$5,000**	=			**$5,000**

Transaction (b): Purchase of an asset for cash

An Increase in an Asset Offset by a Decrease in Another Asset. Mitch decided that the fastest and easiest way to get around campus and find parking is on a motor scooter. Thus, he bought a motor scooter (delivery equipment) for $2,000 cash. Mitch exchanged one asset, cash, for another, delivery equipment. This transaction reduces Cash and creates a new asset, Delivery Equipment.

LEARNING KEY

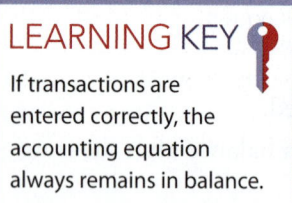

If transactions are entered correctly, the accounting equation always remains in balance.

	Assets (Items Owned)			=	**Liabilities** (Amounts Owed)	+	**Owner's Equity** (Owner's Investment)
	Cash	+	Delivery Equipment	=			Mitch Williams, Capital
	$5,000						$5,000
(b)	**−2,000**		**+$2,000**				
	$3,000	+	$2,000	=			$5,000
	$5,000			=			**$5,000**

Transaction (c): Purchase of an asset on account

An Increase in an Asset Offset by an Increase in a Liability. Mitch hired a friend to work for him, which meant that a second scooter would be needed. Given Mitch's limited cash, he bought a secondhand model for $1,800. The seller agreed to allow Mitch to spread the payments over the next three months. This transaction increased an asset, Delivery Equipment, by $1,800 and increased the liability, Accounts Payable, by an equal amount.

	Assets (Items Owned)			=	Liabilities (Amounts Owed)	+	Owner's Equity (Owner's Investment)
	Cash	+	Delivery Equipment	=	Accounts Payable	+	Mitchell Williams, Capital
	$3,000		$2,000				$5,000
(c)			+1,800		+$1,800		
	$3,000	+	$3,800	=	$1,800	+	$5,000
	$6,800			=	$6,800		

Transaction (d): Payment on a loan

A Decrease in an Asset Offset by a Decrease in a Liability. Mitch paid the first installment on the scooter of $600 [see transaction (c)]. This payment decreased the asset, Cash, and the liability, Accounts Payable, by $600.

	Assets (Items Owned)			=	Liabilities (Amounts Owed)	+	Owner's Equity (Owner's Investment)
	Cash	+	Delivery Equipment	=	Accounts Payable	+	Mitchell Williams, Capital
	$3,000		$3,800		$1,800		$5,000
(d)	−600				−600		
	$2,400	+	$3,800	=	$1,200	+	$5,000
	$6,200			=	$6,200		

Expanding the Accounting Equation: Revenues, Expenses, and Withdrawals

In the preceding sections, three key accounting elements of every business entity were defined and explained: assets, liabilities, and owner's equity. To complete the explanation of the accounting process, three additional elements must be added to the discussion: revenues, expenses, and withdrawals.

Revenues

More precisely, revenue is recognized when a "performance obligation" is satisfied. We will address the details of revenue recognition later in the text.

Revenues represent the amount a business charges customers for products sold or services performed. Customers generally pay with cash or a credit card, or they promise to pay at a later date. Most businesses recognize revenues when earned, even if cash has not yet been received. Separate accounts are used to recognize different types of revenue. Examples include Delivery Fees; Consulting Fees; Rent Revenue, if the business rents space to others; Interest Revenue, for interest earned on bank deposits; and Sales, for sales of merchandise. *Revenues increase both assets and owner's equity.*

Expenses

Expenses represent the *decrease* in assets (or *increase* in liabilities) as a result of a company's efforts to produce revenues. Common examples of expenses are rent, salaries, supplies consumed, and taxes. As with revenues, separate accounts are used to keep the accounting records for each different type of expense. Expenses are "incurred" as

- assets are consumed (such as supplies), or
- services are provided (by employees, for example) to the business.

> **LEARNING KEY**
>
> It is important to remember that expenses do not always reduce cash and revenues do not always increase cash right away.

The two main purposes of recognizing an expense are (a) to keep track of the amount and types of expenses incurred and (b) to show the reduction in owner's equity. Again, an expense can cause a reduction in assets or an increase in liabilities. Wages earned by employees is a good example.

- If paid, the expense reduces owner's equity and an asset, Cash.
- If not paid, the expense reduces owner's equity and increases a liability, Wages Payable.

Either way, owner's equity is reduced. If total revenues are greater than total expenses for the period, the excess is the **net income**, or net profit, for the period. On the other hand, if total expenses are greater than total revenues for the period, the excess is a **net loss** for the period.

Revenues	$9,000	Revenues	$ 3,000
Expenses	5,000	Expenses	5,000
Net income	$4,000	Net loss	$(2,000)

The owner can determine the time period used in the measurement of net income or net loss. It may be a month, a quarter (three months), a year, or some other time period. The concept that income determination can be made on a periodic basis is known as the **accounting period concept**. Any accounting period of 12 months is called a **fiscal year**. The fiscal year frequently coincides with the calendar year.

> **LEARNING KEY**
>
> Owner's Equity
>
> | Decrease | Increase |
> |---|---|
> | Expenses | Revenues |
> | Drawing | Owner's Investments |

Withdrawals

Withdrawals, or **drawing**, reduce owner's equity as a result of the owner taking cash or other assets out of the business for personal use. Since earnings are expected to offset withdrawals, this reduction is viewed as temporary.

The accounting equation is expanded to include revenues, expenses, and withdrawals. Note that revenues increase owner's equity, while expenses and drawing reduce owner's equity.

	Assets (Items Owned)			=	Liabilities (Amounts Owed)	+	Owner's Equity (Owner's Investment)			+	(Earnings)		
	Cash	+	Delivery Equipment	=	Accounts Payable	+	Mitchell Williams, Capital	−	Mitchell Williams, Drawing	+	Revenues	−	Expenses
Balance	$2,400	+	$3,800	=	$1,200	+	$5,000						
			$6,200	=			$6,200						

Effect of Revenue, Expense, and Withdrawal Transactions on the Accounting Equation

To show the effects of revenue, expense, and withdrawal transactions, the example of Mitchell's Campus Delivery will be continued. Assume that the following transactions took place in Mitchell's business during June 20--.

Transaction (e): Delivery revenues earned in cash

An Increase in an Asset Offset by an Increase in Owner's Equity Resulting from Revenue. Mitch received $2,100 cash from clients for delivery services. This transaction increased the asset, Cash, and increased owner's equity by $2,100. The increase in owner's equity is shown by increasing the revenue account, Delivery Fees, by $2,100.

	Assets (Items Owned)			=	Liabilities (Amounts Owed)	+	Owner's Equity (Owner's Investment)			+	(Earnings)			
	Cash	+	Delivery Equipment	=	Accounts Payable	+	Mitchell Williams, Capital	−	Mitchell Williams, Drawing	+	Revenues	−	Expenses	Description
	$2,400		$3,800		$1,200		$5,000							
(e)	+2,100										+$2,100			Deliv. Fees
	$4,500	+	$3,800	=	$1,200	+	$5,000			+	$2,100			
	$8,300			=	$8,300									

Transaction (f): Paid rent for month

A Decrease in an Asset Offset by a Decrease in Owner's Equity Resulting from an Expense. Mitch rents a small office near campus. He paid $1,000 for office rent for June. This transaction decreased both Cash and owner's equity by $1,000. The decrease in owner's equity is shown by increasing an expense called Rent Expense by $1,000. An increase in an expense decreases owner's equity.

	Assets (Items Owned)			=	Liabilities (Amounts Owed)	+	Owner's Equity (Owner's Investment)			+	(Earnings)			
	Cash	+	Delivery Equipment	=	Accounts Payable	+	Mitchell Williams, Capital	−	Mitchell Williams, Drawing	+	Revenues	−	Expenses	Description
	$4,500	+	$3,800		$1,200		$5,000				$2,100			
(f)	−1,000												+$1,000	Rent Exp.
	$3,500	+	$3,800	=	$1,200	+	$5,000			+	$2,100	−	$1,000	
	$7,300			=	$7,300									

Transaction (g): Paid phone bill

A Decrease in an Asset Offset by a Decrease in Owner's Equity Resulting from an Expense. Mitch paid $100 in cash for phone service. This transaction, like the previous one, decreased both Cash and owner's equity. This decrease in owner's equity is shown by increasing an expense called Phone Expense by $100.

	Assets (Items Owned)			=	Liabilities (Amounts Owed)	+	Owner's Equity (Owner's Investment)			+	(Earnings)			
	Cash	+	Delivery Equipment	=	Accounts Payable	+	Mitchell Williams, Capital	−	Mitchell Williams, Drawing	+	Revenues	−	Expenses	Description
	$3,500		$3,800		$1,200		$5,000				$2,100		$1,000	
(g)	−100												+100	Phone Expense
	$3,400	+	$3,800	=	$1,200	+	$5,000			+	$2,100	−	$1,100	
	$7,200			=	$7,200									

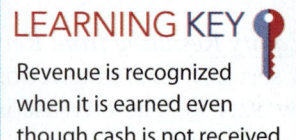

> **LEARNING KEY**
>
> Revenue is recognized when it is earned even though cash is not received.

Transaction (h): Delivery revenues earned on account

An Increase in an Asset Offset by an Increase in Owner's Equity Resulting from Revenue. Mitch extends credit to regular customers. Often, delivery services are performed for which payment will be received later. Since revenues are recognized when earned, an increase in owner's equity must be reported by increasing the revenue account. Since no cash is received at this time, Cash cannot be increased. Instead, an increase is reported for another asset, Accounts Receivable. *The total of Accounts Receivable at any point in time reflects the amount owed to Mitch by his customers.* Deliveries made on account amounted to $2,400. Accounts Receivable and Delivery Fees are increased.

	Assets (Items Owned)			=	**Liabilities** (Amounts Owed)	+	**Owner's Equity** (Owner's Investment)		+	(Earnings)		
	Cash +	Accounts Receivable	+ Delivery Equipment	=	Accounts Payable	+	Mitchell Williams, Capital	− Mitchell Williams, Drawing	+	Revenues	− Expenses	Description
	$3,400		$3,800		$1,200		$5,000			$2,100	$1,100	
(h)		**+$2,400**								**+2,400**		**Deliv. Fees**
	$3,400 +	$2,400	+ $3,800	=	$1,200	+	$5,000		+	$4,500	− $1,100	
		$9,600		=				**$9,600**				

Transaction (i): Purchase of supplies

An Increase in an Asset Offset by a Decrease in an Asset. Mitch bought pens, paper, delivery envelopes, and other supplies for $80 cash. These supplies should last for several months. Since they will generate future benefits, the supplies should be recorded as an asset. The accounting equation will show an increase in an asset, Supplies, and a decrease in Cash.

	Assets (Items Owned)				=	**Liabilities** (Amounts Owed)	+	**Owner's Equity** (Owner's Investment)		+	(Earnings)		
	Cash	+ Accounts Receivable	+ Supplies	+ Delivery Equipment	=	Accounts Payable	+	Mitchell Williams, Capital	− Mitchell Williams, Drawing	+	Revenues	− Expenses	Description
	$3,400	$2,400		$3,800		$1,200		$5,000			$4,500	$1,100	
(i)	**−80**		**+$80**										
	$3,320	+ $2,400	+ $80	+ $3,800	=	$1,200	+	$5,000		+	$4,500	− $1,100	
			$9,600		=			**$9,600**					

> As shown in transactions (i) and (j), transactions do not always affect both sides of the accounting equation.

Transaction (j): Cash receipts from prior sales on account

An Increase in an Asset Offset by a Decrease in an Asset. Mitch received $1,900 in cash for delivery services performed for customers earlier in the month [see transaction (h)]. Receipt of this cash increases the cash account and reduces the amount due from customers reported in the accounts receivable account. *Notice that owner's equity is not affected in this transaction. Owner's equity increased in transaction (h) when revenue was recognized as it was earned, rather than now when cash is received.*

Assets (Items Owned)							=	Liabilities (Amounts Owed)	+	Owner's Equity (Owner's Investment)			+	(Earnings)			
Cash	+	Accounts Receivable	+	Supplies	+	Delivery Equipment	=	Accounts Payable	+	Mitchell Williams, Capital	−	Mitchell Williams, Drawing	+	Revenues	−	Expenses	Description
$3,320		$2,400		$80		$3,800		$1,200		$5,000				$4,500		$1,100	
(j) **+1,900**		**−1,900**															
$5,220	+	$ 500	+	$80	+	$3,800	=	$1,200	+	$5,000			+	$4,500	−	$1,100	
$9,600							=	**$9,600**									

Transaction (k): Purchase of an asset on account making a partial payment

An Increase in an Asset Offset by a Decrease in an Asset and an Increase in a Liability. With business increasing, Mitch hired a second employee and bought a third motor scooter. The scooter cost $1,000. Mitch paid $300 in cash and will spread the remaining payments over the next four months. The asset Delivery Equipment increases by $1,000, Cash decreases by $300, and the liability Accounts Payable increases by $700. *Note that this transaction changes three accounts. Even so, the accounting equation remains in balance.*

Assets (Items Owned)							=	Liabilities (Amounts Owed)	+	Owner's Equity (Owner's Investment)			+	(Earnings)			
Cash	+	Accounts Receivable	+	Supplies	+	Delivery Equipment	=	Accounts Payable	+	Mitchell Williams, Capital	−	Mitchell Williams, Drawing	+	Revenues	−	Expenses	Description
$5,220		$500		$80		$3,800		$1,200		$5,000				$4,500		$1,100	
(k) **−300**						**+1,000**		**+700**									
$4,920	+	$500	+	$80	+	$4,800	=	$1,900	+	$5,000			+	$4,500	−	$1,100	
$10,300							=	**$10,300**									

> **LEARNING KEY**
> Both supplies and insurance are recorded as assets because they will provide benefits for several months.

Transaction (l): Payment of insurance premium

An Increase in an Asset Offset by a Decrease in an Asset. Since Mitch plans to graduate and sell the business next January, he paid $700 for a seven-month liability insurance policy. Insurance is paid in advance and will provide future benefits. Thus, it is treated as an asset. We must expand the equation to include another asset, Prepaid Insurance, and show that Cash has been reduced.

Assets (Items Owned)									=	Liabilities (Amounts Owed)	+	Owner's Equity (Owner's Investment)			+	(Earnings)			
Cash	+	Accounts Receivable	+	Supplies	+	Prepaid Insurance	+	Delivery Equipment	=	Accounts Payable	+	Mitchell Williams, Capital	−	Mitchell Williams, Drawing	+	Revenues	−	Expenses	Description
$4,920		$500		$80				$4,800		$1,900		$5,000				$4,500		$1,100	
(l) **−700**						**$700**													
$4,220	+	$500	+	$80	+	$700	+	$4,800	=	$1,900	+	$5,000			+	$4,500	−	$1,100	
$10,300									=	**$10,300**									

Transaction (m): Payment of wages

A Decrease in an Asset Offset by a Decrease in Owner's Equity Resulting from an Expense. Mitch paid his part-time employees $1,650 in wages. This represents an additional business expense. As with other expenses, Cash is reduced and owner's equity is reduced by increasing an expense.

	Assets (Items Owned)					=	Liabilities (Amounts Owed)	+	Owner's Equity (Owner's Investment) +		(Earnings)		
	Cash +	Accounts Receivable +	Supplies +	Prepaid Insurance +	Delivery Equipment	=	Accounts Payable	+	Mitchell Williams, Capital –	Mitchell Williams, Drawing +	Revenues –	Expenses	Description
	$4,220	$500	$80	$700	$4,800		$1,900		$5,000		$4,500	$1,100	
(m)	–1,650											+1,650	Wages Exp.
	$2,570 +	$500 +	$80 +	$700 +	$4,800	=	$1,900	+	$5,000	+	$4,500 –	$2,750	
	$8,650					=	**$8,650**						

Transaction (n): Deliveries made for cash and on account

An Increase in Two Assets Offset by an Increase in Owner's Equity. Total delivery fees for the remainder of the month amounted to $3,500: $900 in cash and $2,600 on account. Since all of these delivery fees have been earned, the revenue account increases by $3,500. Also, Cash increases by $900 and Accounts Receivable increases by $2,600. Thus, revenues increase assets and owner's equity. Note, once again, that recording these revenues impacts three accounts while the equation remains in balance.

	Assets (Items Owned)					=	Liabilities (Amounts Owed)	+	Owner's Equity (Owner's Investment) +		(Earnings)		
	Cash +	Accounts Receivable +	Supplies +	Prepaid Insurance +	Delivery Equipment	=	Accounts Payable	+	Mitchell Williams, Capital –	Mitchell Williams, Drawing +	Revenues –	Expenses	Description
	$2,570	$ 500	$80	$700	$4,800		$1,900		$5,000		$4,500	$2,750	
(n)	+900	+2,600									+3,500		Deliv. Fees
	$3,470 +	$3,100 +	$80 +	$700 +	$4,800	=	$1,900	+	$5,000	+	$8,000 –	$2,750	
	$12,150					=	**$12,150**						

LEARNING KEY

Withdrawals by the owner are reported in the drawing account. Withdrawals are the opposite of investments by the owner.

Transaction (o): Withdrawal of cash from business

A Decrease in an Asset Offset by a Decrease in Owner's Equity Resulting from a Withdrawal by the Owner. At the end of the month, Mitch took $3,000 in cash from the business to pay for textbooks, extra class fees, and living expenses. Since these expenditures are not related to his delivery business, this is a withdrawal. Withdrawals can be viewed as the opposite of investments by the owner. Both owner's equity and Cash decrease.

	Assets (Items Owned)					=	Liabilities (Amounts Owed)	+	Owner's Equity (Owner's Investment) +		(Earnings)		
	Cash +	Accounts Receivable +	Supplies +	Prepaid Insurance +	Delivery Equipment	=	Accounts Payable	+	Mitchell Williams, Capital –	Mitchell Williams, Drawing +	Revenues –	Expenses	Description
	$3,470	$3,100	$80	$700	$4,800		$1,900		$5,000		$8,000	$2,750	
(o)	–3,000									+$3,000			
	$ 470 +	$3,100 +	$80 +	$700 +	$4,800	=	$1,900	+	$5,000 –	$3,000 +	$8,000 –	$2,750	
	$9,150					=	**$9,150**						

FIGURE 2-1 Summary of Transactions Illustrated

	Assets (Items Owned)					= Liabilities (Amounts Owed)	+ Owner's Equity (Owner's Investment) +		(Earnings)		
Trans-action	Cash	+ Accounts Receivable	+ Supplies	+ Prepaid Insurance	+ Delivery Equipment	= Accounts Payable	+ Mitchell Williams, Capital	− Mitchell Williams, Drawing	+ Revenues	− Expenses	Description
Balance											
(a)	5,000						5,000				
Balance	5,000						5,000				
(b)	(2,000)				2,000						
Balance	3,000				2,000		5,000				
(c)					1,800	1,800					
Balance	3,000				3,800	1,800	5,000				
(d)	(600)					(600)					
Balance	2,400				3,800	1,200	5,000				
(e)	2,100								2,100		Deliv. Fees
Balance	4,500				3,800	1,200	5,000		2,100		
(f)	(1,000)									1,000	Rent Exp.
Balance	3,500				3,800	1,200	5,000		2,100	1,000	
(g)	(100)									100	Phone Exp.
Balance	3,400				3,800	1,200	5,000		2,100	1,100	
(h)		2,400							2,400		Deliv. Fees
Balance	3,400	2,400			3,800	1,200	5,000		4,500	1,100	
(i)	(80)		80								
Balance	3,320	2,400	80		3,800	1,200	5,000		4,500	1,100	
(j)	1,900	(1,900)									
Balance	5,220	500	80		3,800	1,200	5,000		4,500	1,100	
(k)	(300)				1,000	700					
Balance	4,920	500	80		4,800	1,900	5,000		4,500	1,100	
(l)	(700)			700							
Balance	4,220	500	80	700	4,800	1,900	5,000		4,500	1,100	
(m)	(1,650)									1,650	Wages Exp.
Balance	2,570	500	80	700	4,800	1,900	5,000		4,500	2,750	
(n)	900	2,600							3,500		Deliv. Fees
Balance	3,470	3,100	80	700	4,800	1,900	5,000		8,000	2,750	
(o)	(3,000)							3,000			
Balance	**470**	+ **3,100**	+ **80**	+ **700**	+ **4,800**	= **1,900**	+ **5,000**	− **3,000**	+ **8,000**	− **2,750**	

Cash	$ 470	Accounts Payable	$1,900
Accounts Receivable	3,100	Mitchell Williams, Capital	5,000
Supplies	80	Mitchell Williams, Drawing	(3,000)
Prepaid Insurance	700	Delivery Fees	8,000
Delivery Equipment	4,800	Rent Expense	(1,000)
Total Assets	$9,150	Phone Expense	(100)
		Wages Expense	(1,650)
		Total Liabilities and Owner's Equity	$9,150

Amounts in ( ) are subtracted

As with the running totals in the table, the listing immediately below the table provides proof that the accounting equation is in balance.

CHECKPOINT

Complete Checkpoint-3 on page 41 to test your basic understanding of LO3/4.

Figure 2-1 shows a summary of the transactions. Use this summary to test your understanding of transaction analysis by describing the economic event represented by each transaction. At the bottom of Figure 2-1, the asset accounts and their totals are compared with the liability and owner's equity accounts and their totals.

LO5

Financial Statements

Prepare and describe the purposes of a simple income statement, statement of owner's equity, and balance sheet.

Three financial statements commonly prepared by a business entity are the income statement, statement of owner's equity, and balance sheet. The transaction information gathered and summarized in the accounting equation may be used to prepare these financial statements. Figure 2-2 shows the following:

1. A summary of the specific revenue and expense transactions and the ending totals for the asset, liability, capital, and drawing accounts from the accounting equation
2. The financial statements and their linkages with the accounting equation and each other

Note that each of the financial statements in Figure 2-2 has a heading consisting of the following:

HEADING FOR FINANCIAL STATEMENTS	
1. The name of the company	Mitchell's Campus Delivery
2. The title of the statement	Income Statement, Statement of Owner's Equity, or Balance Sheet
3. The time period covered or the date of the statement	For Month Ended June 30, 20--, or June 30, 20--

The income statement and statement of owner's equity provide information concerning events covering a period of time, in this case, *the month ended* June 30, 20--. The balance sheet, on the other hand, offers a picture of the business on *a specific date*, June 30, 20--.

GUIDELINES FOR PREPARING FINANCIAL STATEMENTS

1. Financial statements are prepared primarily for users not associated with the company. To make a good impression and enhance understanding, financial statements must follow a standard form with careful attention to placement, spacing, and indentations.
2. All statements have a heading with the name of the company, name of the statement, and accounting period or date.
3. Single rules (underlines) indicate that the numbers above the line have been added or subtracted. Double rules (double underlines) indicate a total.
4. Dollar signs are used at the top of columns and for the first amount entered in a column beneath a ruling.
5. On the income statement, some companies list expenses from highest to lowest dollar amount, with miscellaneous expense listed last.
6. On the balance sheet, assets are listed from most liquid to least liquid. **Liquidity** measures the ease with which the asset will be converted to cash. Liabilities are listed from most current to least current.

The Income Statement

The **income statement**, sometimes called the **profit and loss statement** or **operating statement**, reports the profitability of business operations for a specific period of time. Mitchell's income statement shows the revenues earned for the month of June.

FIGURE 2-2 Summary and Financial Statements

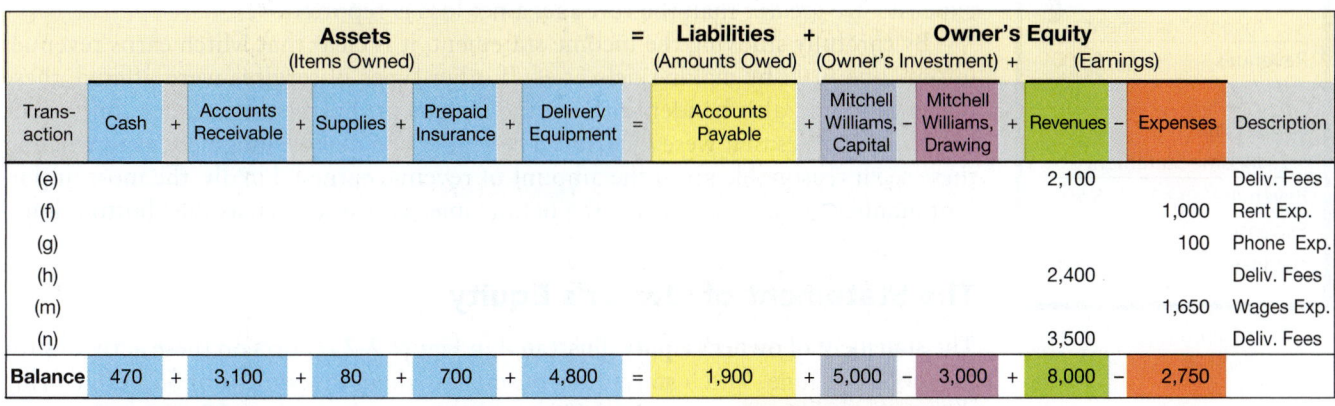

	Assets (Items Owned)					=	Liabilities (Amounts Owed)	+	Owner's Equity (Owner's Investment) +			(Earnings)			
Trans-action	Cash	+ Accounts Receivable	+ Supplies	+ Prepaid Insurance	+ Delivery Equipment	=	Accounts Payable	+	Mitchell Williams, Capital	−	Mitchell Williams, Drawing	+ Revenues	−	Expenses	Description
(e)												2,100			Deliv. Fees
(f)														1,000	Rent Exp.
(g)														100	Phone Exp.
(h)												2,400			Deliv. Fees
(m)														1,650	Wages Exp.
(n)												3,500			Deliv. Fees
Balance	470	+ 3,100	+ 80	+ 700	+ 4,800	=	1,900	+	5,000	−	3,000	+ 8,000	−	2,750	

Mitchell's Campus Delivery
Income Statement
For Month Ended June 30, 20 --

Revenues:		
Delivery fees		$8,000
Expenses:		
Wages expense	$1,650	
Rent expense	1,000	
Phone expense	100	
Total expenses		2,750
Net income		$5,250

$ at top of columns.

Expenses are listed in the first column and totaled in the second column under the revenues.

Underline to show numbers above have been added or subtracted.

Double underline totals.

Mitchell's Campus Delivery
Statement of Owner's Equity
For Month Ended June 30, 20 --

Mitchell Williams, capital, June 1, 20 --		$ —
Investments during June		5,000
Total investment		$5,000
Net Income for June	$5,250	
Less Withdrawals for June	3,000	
Increase in capital		2,250
Mitchell Williams, capital, June 30, 20 --		$7,250

Many companies use a dash (—) to represent a zero on financial statements.

Withdrawals are deducted from net income in the first column. The net increase in capital is reported in the second column.

$ for first number under a ruling.

$ on total and under rulings.

Mitchell's Campus Delivery
Balance Sheet
June 30, 20 --

Assets		Liabilities	
Cash	$ 470	Accounts payable	$1,900
Accounts receivable	3,100		
Supplies	80	Owner's Equity	
Prepaid insurance	700	Mitchell Williams, capital	7,250
Delivery equipment	4,800		
		Total liabilities and	
Total assets	$9,150	owner's equity	$9,150

Double underline totals.

LEARNING KEY

Income Statement	
Revenues	$ 500
Expenses	400
Net income	$ 100

Income Statement	
Revenues	$ 500
Expenses	700
Net loss	$(200)

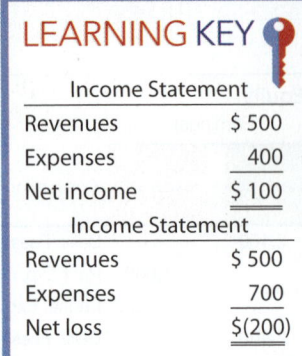

Next, the expenses incurred as a result of the efforts made to earn these revenues are deducted. If the revenues are greater than the expenses, net income is reported. If the expenses are greater than the revenue, a net loss is reported.

By carefully studying the income statement, it is clear that Mitch earns revenues in only one way: by making deliveries. If other types of services were offered, these revenues would also be identified on the statement. Further, the reader can see the kinds of expenses that were incurred. The reader can make a judgment as to whether these seem reasonable given the amount of revenue earned. Finally, the most important number on the statement is the net income. This is known as the "bottom line."

The Statement of Owner's Equity

The **statement of owner's equity** illustrated in Figure 2-2 reports on these activities for the month of June. Mitch started his business with an investment of $5,000. During the month of June, he earned $5,250 in net income and withdrew $3,000 for personal expenses. Mitch's $5,000 original investment, plus the net increase of $2,250, results in his ending capital of $7,250.

Note that Mitchell's original investment and later withdrawal are taken from the accounting equation. *The net income figure could have been computed from information in the accounting equation. However, it is easier to simply transfer net income as reported on the income statement to the statement of owner's equity.* This is an important linkage between the income statement and statement of owner's equity.

If Mitch had a net loss of $500 for the month, the statement of owner's equity would be prepared as shown in Figure 2-3.

FIGURE 2-3 Statement of Owner's Equity with Net Loss

Mitchell's Campus Delivery Statement of Owner's Equity For Month Ended June 30, 20 --		
Mitchell Williams, capital, June 1, 20 --		$ —
Investments during June		5,000
Total investment		$5,000
Less: Net loss for June	$500	
Withdrawals for June	3,000	
Decrease in capital		(3,500)
Mitchell Williams, capital, June 30, 20 --		$1,500

Most firms also prepare a statement of cash flows. Given the complexity of this statement, we will postpone its discussion until later in this text.

CHECKPOINT

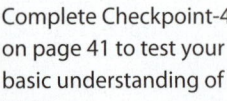

Complete Checkpoint-4 on page 41 to test your basic understanding of LO5.

The Balance Sheet

The **balance sheet** reports a firm's assets, liabilities, and owner's equity on a specific date. It is called a balance sheet because it confirms that the accounting equation has remained in balance. It is also referred to as a **statement of financial position** or **statement of financial condition.**

As illustrated in Figure 2-2, the asset and liability accounts are taken from the accounting equation and reported on the balance sheet. *The total of Mitchell's capital account on June 30 could have been computed from the owner's equity accounts in the accounting equation ($5,000 − $3,000 + $8,000 − $2,750 = $7,250). However, it is simpler to take the June 30, 20--, capital as computed on the statement of owner's equity and transfer it to the balance sheet.* This is an important linkage between these two statements.

LO6 Overview of the Accounting Process

Define the three basic phases of the accounting process.

Figure 2-4 shows the three basic phases of the accounting process in terms of input, processing, and output.

- **Input.** Business transactions provide the necessary *input*.
- **Processing.** Recognizing the effect of these transactions on the assets, liabilities, owner's equity, revenues, and expenses of a business is the *processing* function.
- **Output.** The financial statements are the *output*.

FIGURE 2-4 Input, Processing, and Output

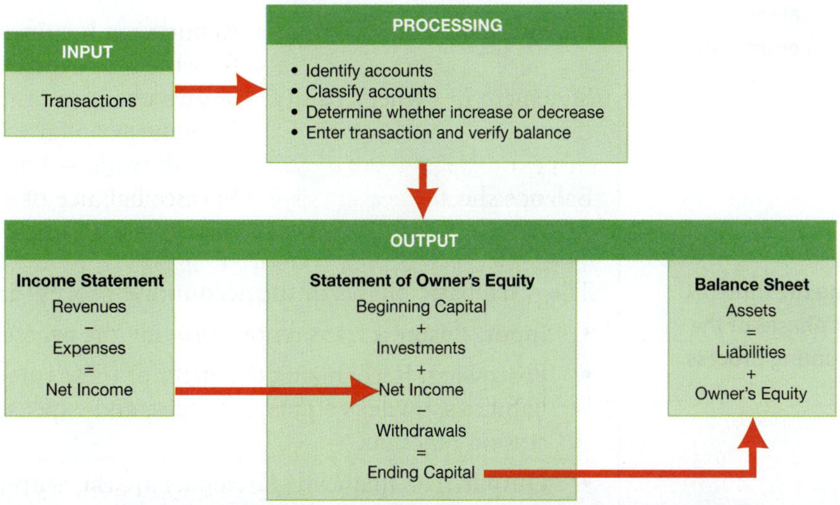

SELF-STUDY

LEARNING OBJECTIVES	Key Points to Remember
LO1 Define the accounting elements.	The three key accounting elements are assets, liabilities, and owner's equity. Owner's equity is expanded in LO4 to include revenues, expenses, and drawing.
LO2 Construct the accounting equation.	The accounting equation is Assets = Liabilities + Owner's Equity
LO3 Analyze business transactions.	Three questions must be answered in analyzing business transactions: 1. What happened? 2. Which accounts are affected? 3. How is the accounting equation affected?
LO4 Show the effects of business transactions on the accounting equation.	Each transaction affects at least two accounts and one or more of the three basic accounting elements. The transactions described in this chapter can be classified into five groups: 1. Increase in an asset offset by an increase in owner's equity. 2. Increase in an asset offset by a decrease in another asset.

(*continued*)

LEARNING OBJECTIVES	Key Points to Remember
LO4 (concluded)	3. Increase in an asset offset by an increase in a liability. 4. Decrease in an asset offset by a decrease in a liability. 5. Decrease in an asset offset by a decrease in owner's equity.
LO5 Prepare and describe the purposes of a simple income statement, statement of owner's equity, and balance sheet.	The purposes of the income statement, statement of owner's equity, and balance sheet can be summarized as follows: STATEMENT — PURPOSE Income statement — Reports net income or loss Revenues − Expenses = Net Income or Loss Statement of owner's equity — Shows changes in the owner's capital account Beginning Capital + Investments + Net Income − Withdrawals = Ending Capital Balance sheet — Verifies balance of accounting equation Assets = Liabilities + Owner's Equity
LO6 Define the three basic phases of the accounting process.	The three basic phases of the accounting process are shown below. • **Input.** Business transactions provide the necessary input. • **Processing.** Recognizing the effect of these transactions on the assets, liabilities, owner's equity, revenues, and expenses of a business is the processing function. • **Output.** The financial statements are the output.

DEMONSTRATION PROBLEM

Kenny Young has started his own business, Home and Away Inspections. He inspects property for buyers and sellers of real estate. Young rents office space and has a part-time assistant to answer the phone and help with inspections. The transactions for the month of September are as follows:

(a) On the first day of the month, Young invested cash by making a deposit in a bank account for the business, $15,000.
(b) Paid rent for September, $300.
(c) Bought a used truck for cash, $8,000.
(d) Purchased tools on account from Crafty Tools, $3,000.
(e) Paid electricity bill, $50.
(f) Paid two-year premium for liability insurance on truck, $600.
(g) Received cash from clients for services performed, $2,000.
(h) Paid part-time assistant (wages) for first half of month, $200.
(i) Performed inspection services for clients on account, $1,000.
(j) Paid phone bill, $35.
(k) Bought office supplies costing $300. Paid $100 cash and will pay the balance next month, $200.
(l) Received cash from clients for inspections performed on account in (i), $300.
(m) Paid part-time assistant (wages) for last half of month, $250.
(n) Made partial payment on tools bought in (d), $1,000.

(o) Earned additional revenues amounting to $2,000: $1,400 in cash and $600 on account.

(p) Young withdrew cash at the end of the month for personal expenses, $500.

REQUIRED

1. Enter the transactions in an accounting equation similar to the one illustrated below.

Assets (Items Owned)						=	Liabilities (Amounts Owed)	+	Owner's Equity (Owner's Investment) +		(Earnings)		
Cash +	Accounts Receivable +	Supplies +	Prepaid Insurance +	Tools +	Truck	=	Accounts Payable	+	Kenny Young, Capital –	Kenny Young, Drawing	+ Revenues –	Expenses	Description

2. Compute the ending balances for all accounts.
3. Prepare an income statement for Home and Away Inspections for the month of September 20--.
4. Prepare a statement of owner's equity for Home and Away Inspections for the month of September 20--.
5. Prepare a balance sheet for Home and Away Inspections as of September 30, 20--.

SOLUTION 1, 2.

	Assets (Items Owned)						Liabilities (Amounts Owed)	Owner's Equity (Owner's Investment) +		(Earnings)		
	Cash +	Accounts Receivable +	Supplies +	Prepaid Insurance +	Tools +	Truck =	Accounts Payable +	Kenny Young, Capital –	Kenny Young, Drawing +	Revenues –	Expenses	Description
(a)	15,000							15,000				
(b)	(300)										300	Rent Exp.
(c)	(8,000)					8,000						
(d)					3,000		3,000					
(e)	(50)										50	Utilities Exp.
(f)	(600)			600								
(g)	2,000									2,000		Inspect. Fees
(h)	(200)										200	Wages Exp.
(i)		1,000								1,000		Inspect. Fees
(j)	(35)										35	Phone Exp.
(k)	(100)		300				200					
(l)	300	(300)										
(m)	(250)										250	Wages Exp.
(n)	(1,000)						(1,000)					
(o)	1,400	600								2,000		Inspect. Fees
(p)	(500)								500			
Bal.	**7,665** +	**1,300** +	**300** +	**600** +	**3,000** +	**8,000** =	**2,200** +	**15,000** –	**500** +	**5,000** –	**835**	

SOLUTION 3.

Home and Away Inspections
Income Statement
For Month Ended September 30, 20 --

Revenues:		
Inspection fees		$ 5,000
Expenses:		
Wages expense	$450	
Rent expense	300	
Utilities expense	50	
Phone expense	35	
Total expenses		835
Net income		$ 4,165

SOLUTION 4.

Home and Away Inspections
Statement of Owner's Equity
For Month Ended September 30, 20 - -

Kenny Young, capital, September 1, 20 - -		$ —
Investment during September		15,000
Total investment		$15,000
Net income for September	$4,165	
Less withdrawals for September	500	
Increase in capital		3,665
Kenny Young, capital, September 30, 20 - -		$18,665

SOLUTION 5.

Home and Away Inspections
Balance Sheet
September 30, 20 --

Assets		Liabilities	
Cash	$ 7,665	Accounts payable	$ 2,200
Accounts receivable	1,300		
Supplies	300	Owner's Equity	
Prepaid insurance	600	Kenny Young, capital	18,665
Tools	3,000		
Truck	8,000		
		Total liabilities and	
Total assets	$20,865	owner's equity	$20,865

KEY TERMS

account (23) A separate record used to summarize changes in each asset, liability, and owner's equity of a business.

account title (23) Provides a description of the particular type of asset, liability, owner's equity, revenue, or expense.

accounting equation (22) The accounting equation consists of the three basic accounting elements: Assets = Liabilities + Owner's Equity.

accounting period concept (26) The concept that income determination can be made on a periodic basis.

accounts payable (21) An unwritten promise to pay a supplier for assets purchased or services received.

accounts receivable (21) An amount owed to a business by its customers as a result of the sale of goods or services.

asset (21) An item that is owned by a business and will provide future benefits.

balance sheet (34) Reports assets, liabilities, and owner's equity on a specific date. It is called a balance sheet because it confirms that the accounting equation is in balance.

business entity (21) An individual, association, or organization that engages in economic activities and controls specific economic resources.

business entity concept (21) The concept that nonbusiness assets and liabilities are not included in the business entity's accounting records.

business transaction (23) An economic event that has a direct impact on the business.

capital (21) Another term for owner's equity, the amount by which the business assets exceed the business liabilities.

drawing (26) Withdrawals that reduce owner's equity as a result of the owner taking cash or other assets out of the business for personal use.

expenses (25) The decrease in assets (or increase in liabilities) as a result of efforts to produce revenues.

fiscal year (26) Any accounting period of 12 months' duration.

income statement (32) Reports the profitability of business operations for a specific period of time.

input (35) Business transactions provide the necessary input for the accounting information system.

liability (21) Something owed to another business entity.

liquidity (32) A measure of the ease with which an asset will be converted to cash.

net income (26) The excess of total revenues over total expenses for the period.

net loss (26) The excess of total expenses over total revenues for the period.

net worth (21) Another term for owner's equity, the amount by which the business assets exceed the business liabilities.

notes payable (21) A formal written promise to pay a supplier or lender a specified sum of money at a definite future time.

operating statement (32) Another name for the income statement, which reports the profitability of business operations for a specific period of time.

output (35) The financial statements are the output of the accounting information system.

owner's equity (21) The amount by which the business assets exceed the business liabilities.

processing (35) Recognizing the effect of transactions on the assets, liabilities, owner's equity, revenues, and expenses of a business.

profit and loss statement (32) Another name for the income statement, which reports the profitability of business operations for a specific period of time.

revenues (25) The amount a business charges customers for products sold or services performed.

statement of financial condition (34) Another name for the balance sheet, which reports assets, liabilities, and owner's equity on a specific date.

statement of financial position (34) Another name for the balance sheet, which reports assets, liabilities, and owner's equity on a specific date.

statement of owner's equity (34) Reports beginning capital plus net income less withdrawals to compute ending capital.

withdrawals (26) Reduce owner's equity as a result of the owner taking cash or other assets out of the business for personal use.

SELF-STUDY TEST QUESTIONS

True/False

1. **LO1** Assets are items that are owned by the business and are expected to provide future benefits.
2. **LO1** Accounts Payable is an example of an asset account.
3. **LO1** According to the business entity concept, nonbusiness assets and liabilities are not included in the business's accounting records.
4. **LO2** The accounting equation (Assets = Liabilities + Owner's Equity) must always be in balance.
5. **LO2** When an asset increases, a liability must also increase.
6. **LO3** Expenses represent outflows of assets or increases in liabilities as a result of efforts to produce revenues.
7. **LO5** When total revenues exceed total expenses, the difference is called net loss.

Multiple Choice

1. **LO4** An increase to which of these accounts will increase owner's equity?
   (a) Accounts Payable
   (b) Drawing
   (c) Client Fees
   (d) Rent Expense
2. **LO4** When delivery revenue is earned in cash, which accounts increase or decrease?
   (a) Cash increases; Revenue increases.
   (b) Cash decreases; Revenue increases.
   (c) Cash decreases; Revenue decreases.
   (d) Cash does not change; owner's equity increases.

3. **LO4** When delivery revenue is earned on account, which accounts increase or decrease?
   (a) Cash increases; Revenue increases.
   (b) Accounts Receivable increases; Revenue increases.
   (c) Accounts Receivable increases; Revenue decreases.
   (d) Accounts Receivable decreases; Revenue decreases.

4. **LO4** When payment is made on an existing debt, which accounts increase or decrease?
   (a) Cash increases; Accounts Receivable increases.
   (b) Cash decreases; Accounts Payable increases.
   (c) Cash increases; Accounts Payable increases.
   (d) Cash decreases; Accounts Payable decreases.

5. **LO5** Which of the following accounts does not appear on the income statement?
   (a) Delivery Fees
   (b) Wages Expense
   (c) Drawing
   (d) Rent Expense

CHECKPOINT ✓

Checkpoint Exercises

1. **LO1** Label each of the following accounts as an asset (A), a liability (L), or owner's equity (OE), using the following format:

Account	Classification
Accounts Receivable	________
Accounts Payable	________
Judy Smith, Capital	________

2. **LO2** What is missing from the accounting equation below?

   ____?____ = Liabilities + Owner's Equity

3. **LO3/4** What are the effects of the following transactions on the accounting equation? Indicate an increase (+) or decrease (−) under the affected asset, liability, and owner's equity headings.

Transaction	Assets	Liabilities	Owner's Equity
a. Purchase of an asset on account.	______	______	______
b. Made payment on account for transaction (a).	______	______	______

4. **LO5** Classify the following accounts as assets (A), liabilities (L), owner's equity (OE), revenue (R), or expense (E). Indicate the financial statement on which the account belongs—income statement (IS), statement of owner's equity (SOE), or balance sheet (BS).

Account	Classification	Financial Statement
Accounts Payable	________	________
Peggy Welsch, Drawing	________	________
Rent Expense	________	________
Sales	________	________
Equipment	________	________

The answers to the Self-Study Test Questions are at the end of the chapter (page 49).

APPLYING YOUR KNOWLEDGE

CengageNowv2 provides "Show Me How" videos for selected exercises and problems. Additional resources, such as Excel templates for completing selected exercises and problems, are available for download from the companion website at Cengage.com.

REVIEW QUESTIONS

LO1 1. Why is it necessary to distinguish between business assets and liabilities and nonbusiness assets and liabilities of a single proprietor?

LO1/4 2. Name and define the six major elements of the accounting equation.

LO3 3. List the three basic questions that must be answered when analyzing the effects of a business transaction on the accounting equation.

LO5 4. What is the function of an income statement?

LO5 5. What is the function of a statement of owner's equity?

LO5 6. What is the function of a balance sheet?

LO6 7. What are the three basic phases of the accounting process?

SERIES A EXERCISES

E 2-1A (LO1)

ACCOUNTING ELEMENTS Label each of the following accounts as an asset (A), a liability (L), or owner's equity (OE), using the following format:

Item	Account	Classification
Money in bank	Cash	
Office supplies	Supplies	
Money owed	Accounts Payable	
Office chairs	Office Furniture	
Net worth of owner	John Smith, Capital	
Money withdrawn by owner	John Smith, Drawing	
Money owed by customers	Accounts Receivable	

E 2-2A (LO2)

THE ACCOUNTING EQUATION Using the accounting equation, compute the missing elements.

Assets	=	Liabilities	+	Owner's Equity
______	=	$27,000	+	$17,000
$32,000	=	$18,000	+	______
$27,000	=	______	+	$20,000

E 2-3A (LO3/4)

✓ Assets following (d): $32,200

EFFECTS OF TRANSACTIONS (BALANCE SHEET ACCOUNTS) John Sullivan started a business. During the first month (February 20--), the following transactions occurred. Show the effect of each transaction on the accounting equation: *Assets = Liabilities + Owner's Equity*. After each transaction, show the new totals.

(a) Invested cash in the business, $27,000.

(b) Bought office equipment on account, $7,500.

(c) Bought office equipment for cash, $1,600.

(d) Paid cash on account to supplier in transaction (b), $2,300.

E 2-4A (LO3/4)
✓ Assets following (k): $31,586

EFFECTS OF TRANSACTIONS (REVENUE, EXPENSE, WITHDRAWALS) This exercise is an extension of Exercise 2-3A. Let's assume John Sullivan completed the following additional transactions during February. Show the effect of each transaction on the basic elements of the expanded accounting equation: *Assets = Liabilities + Owner's Equity (Capital − Drawing + Revenues − Expenses)*. After transaction (k), report the totals for each element. Demonstrate that the accounting equation has remained in balance.

(e) Received cash from a client for professional services, $1,500.
(f) Paid office rent for February, $600.
(g) Paid February phone bill, $64.
(h) Withdrew cash for personal use, $1,000.
(i) Performed services for clients on account, $750.
(j) Paid wages to part-time employee, $1,200.
(k) Received cash for services performed on account in transaction (i), $400.

E 2-5A (LO1/5)

FINANCIAL STATEMENT ACCOUNTS Label each of the following accounts as an asset (A), liability (L), owner's equity (OE), revenue (R), or expense (E). Indicate the financial statement on which the account belongs—income statement (IS), statement of owner's equity (SOE), or balance sheet (BS)—in a format similar to the following.

Account	Classification	Financial Statement
Cash		
Rent Expense		
Accounts Payable		
Service Fees		
Supplies		
Wages Expense		
Ramon Martinez, Drawing		
Ramon Martinez, Capital		
Prepaid Insurance		
Accounts Receivable		

E 2-6A (LO5)
✓ Capital, 6/30: $22,000

STATEMENT OF OWNER'S EQUITY REPORTING NET INCOME Betsy Ray started an accounting service on June 1, 20--, by investing $20,000. Her net income for the month was $10,000, and she withdrew $8,000. Prepare a statement of owner's equity for the month of June.

E 2-7A (LO5)
✓ Capital, 6/30: $9,000

STATEMENT OF OWNER'S EQUITY REPORTING NET LOSS Based on the information provided in Exercise 2-6A, prepare a statement of owner's equity assuming Ray had a net loss of $3,000.

SERIES A PROBLEMS

P 2-8A (LO1/2)
✓ 3: $32,040 = $12,910 + $19,130

THE ACCOUNTING EQUATION Dr. John Salvaggi is a chiropractor. As of December 31, he owned the following property that related to his professional practice.

Cash	$ 3,500
Office Equipment	6,400
X-ray Equipment	10,220
Laboratory Equipment	6,840

He also owes the following business suppliers:

Chateau Gas Company	$ 3,430
Aloe Medical Supply Company	4,120

REQUIRED

1. From the preceding information, compute the accounting elements and enter them in the accounting equation shown as follows.

Assets	=	Liabilities	+	Owner's Equity
________	=	________	+	________

2. During January, the assets increase by $8,540, and the liabilities increase by $3,360. Compute the resulting accounting equation.
3. During February, the assets decrease by $3,460, and the liabilities increase by $2,000. Compute the resulting accounting equation.

P 2-9A (LO3/4)
✓ Total cash following (g): $12,950

EFFECT OF TRANSACTIONS ON ACCOUNTING EQUATION Jay Pembroke started a business. During the first month (April 20--), the following transactions occurred.

(a) Invested cash in business, $18,000.
(b) Bought office supplies for $4,600: $2,000 in cash and $2,600 on account.
(c) Paid one-year insurance premium, $1,200.
(d) Earned revenues totaling $3,300: $1,300 in cash and $2,000 on account.
(e) Paid cash on account to the company that supplied the office supplies in transaction (b), $2,300.
(f) Paid office rent for the month, $750.
(g) Withdrew cash for personal use, $100.

REQUIRED

Show the effect of each transaction on the individual accounts of the expanded accounting equation: *Assets = Liabilities + Owner's Equity (Capital − Drawing + Revenues − Expenses)*. After transaction (g), report the totals for each element. Demonstrate that the accounting equation has remained in balance.

P 2-10A (LO5)
✓ Net income: $2,550

INCOME STATEMENT Based on Problem 2-9A, prepare an income statement for Jay Pembroke for the month of April 20--.

P 2-11A (LO5)
✓ Capital, 4/30: $20,450

STATEMENT OF OWNER'S EQUITY Based on Problem 2-9A, prepare a statement of owner's equity for Jay Pembroke for the month of April 20--.

P 2-12A (LO5)
✓ Total assets, 4/30: $20,750

BALANCE SHEET Based on Problem 2-9A, prepare a balance sheet for Jay Pembroke as of April 30, 20--.

SERIES B EXERCISES

E 2-1B (LO1)

ACCOUNTING ELEMENTS Label each of the following accounts as an asset (A), liability (L), or owner's equity (OE) using the following format.

Account	Classification
Cash	
Accounts Payable	
Supplies	
Bill Jones, Drawing	
Prepaid Insurance	
Accounts Receivable	
Bill Jones, Capital	

E 2-2B (LO2)

THE ACCOUNTING EQUATION Using the accounting equation, compute the missing elements.

Assets	=	Liabilities	+	Owner's Equity
______	=	$20,000	+	$ 5,000
$30,000	=	$15,000	+	______
$20,000	=	______	+	$10,000

E 2-3B (LO3/4)
✓ Assets following (d): $32,500

EFFECTS OF TRANSACTIONS (BALANCE SHEET ACCOUNTS) Jon Wallace started a business. During the first month (March 20--), the following transactions occurred. Show the effect of each transaction on the accounting equation: *Assets = Liabilities + Owner's Equity*. After each transaction, show the new account totals.

(a) Invested cash in the business, $30,000.
(b) Bought office equipment on account, $4,500.
(c) Bought office equipment for cash, $1,600.
(d) Paid cash on account to supplier in transaction (b), $2,000.

E 2-4B (LO3/4)
✓ Assets following (k): $34,032

EFFECTS OF TRANSACTIONS (REVENUE, EXPENSE, WITHDRAWALS) This exercise is an extension of Exercise 2-3B. Let's assume Jon Wallace completed the following additional transactions during March. Show the effect of each transaction on the basic elements of the expanded accounting equation: *Assets = Liabilities + Owner's Equity (Capital − Drawing + Revenues − Expenses)*. After transaction (k), report the totals for each element. Demonstrate that the accounting equation has remained in balance.

(e) Performed services and received cash, $3,000.
(f) Paid rent for March, $1,000.
(g) Paid March phone bill, $68.

(continued)

(h) Jon Wallace withdrew cash for personal use, $800.
(i) Performed services for clients on account, $900.
(j) Paid wages to part-time employee, $500.
(k) Received cash for services performed on account in transaction (i), $500.

E 2-5B (LO1/5)

FINANCIAL STATEMENT ACCOUNTS Label each of the following accounts as an asset (A), liability (L), owner's equity (OE), revenue (R), or expense (E). Indicate the financial statement on which the account belongs—income statement (IS), statement of owner's equity (SOE), or balance sheet (BS)—in a format similar to the following.

Account	Classification	Financial Statement
Cash		
Rent Expense		
Accounts Payable		
Service Fees		
Supplies		
Wages Expense		
Amanda Wong, Drawing		
Amanda Wong, Capital		
Prepaid Insurance		
Accounts Receivable		

E 2-6B (LO5)
✓ Capital, 6/30: $14,000

STATEMENT OF OWNER'S EQUITY REPORTING NET INCOME Efran Lopez started a financial consulting service on June 1, 20--, by investing $15,000. His net income for the month was $6,000, and he withdrew $7,000 for personal use. Prepare a statement of owner's equity for the month of June.

E 2-7B (LO5)
✓ Capital, 6/30: $6,000

STATEMENT OF OWNER'S EQUITY REPORTING NET LOSS Based on the information provided in Exercise 2-6B, prepare a statement of owner's equity assuming Lopez had a net loss of $2,000.

SERIES B PROBLEMS

P 2-8B (LO1/2)
✓ 3: $25,235 = $10,165 + $15,070

THE ACCOUNTING EQUATION Dr. Patricia Parsons is a dentist. As of January 31, Parsons owned the following property that related to her professional practice:

Cash	$3,560
Office Equipment	4,600
X-ray Equipment	8,760
Laboratory Equipment	5,940

She also owes the following business suppliers:

Cupples Gas Company	$1,815
Swan Dental Lab	2,790

REQUIRED

1. From the preceding information, compute the accounting elements and enter them in the accounting equation as shown below.

Assets	=	Liabilities	+	Owner's Equity
________	=	________	+	________

2. During February, the assets increase by $4,565, and the liabilities increase by $3,910. Compute the resulting accounting equation.
3. During March, the assets decrease by $2,190, and the liabilities increase by $1,650. Compute the resulting accounting equation.

P 2-9B (LO3/4)
✓ Total cash following (g): $11,300

EFFECT OF TRANSACTIONS ON ACCOUNTING EQUATION David Segal started a business. During the first month (October 20--), the following transactions occurred.

(a) Invested cash in the business, $15,000.
(b) Bought office supplies for $3,800: $1,800 in cash and $2,000 on account.
(c) Paid one-year insurance premium, $1,000.
(d) Earned revenues amounting to $2,700: $1,700 in cash and $1,000 on account.
(e) Paid cash on account to the company that supplied the office supplies in transaction (b), $1,800.
(f) Paid office rent for the month, $650.
(g) Withdrew cash for personal use, $150.

REQUIRED

Show the effect of each transaction on the individual accounts of the expanded accounting equation: *Assets = Liabilities + Owner's Equity (Capital − Drawing + Revenues − Expenses)*. After transaction (g), report the totals for each element. Demonstrate that the accounting equation has remained in balance.

P 2-10B (LO5)
✓ Net income: $2,050

INCOME STATEMENT Based on Problem 2-9B, prepare an income statement for David Segal for the month of October 20--.

P 2-11B (LO5)
✓ Capital, 10/31: $16,900

STATEMENT OF OWNER'S EQUITY Based on Problem 2-9B, prepare a statement of owner's equity for David Segal for the month of October 20--.

P 2-12B (LO5)
✓ Total assets, 10/31: $17,100

BALANCE SHEET Based on Problem 2-9B, prepare a balance sheet for David Segal as of October 31, 20--.

CHECK LIST
- ☐ Managing
- ☐ Planning
- ☐ Drafting
- ☐ Break
- ☐ Revising
- ☐ Managing

MANAGING YOUR WRITING

Write a brief memo that explains the differences and similarities between expenses and withdrawals.

MASTERY PROBLEM

✓ Cash following (p): $3,105
✓ Revenue following (p): $2,100

Lisa Vozniak started her own business, We Do Windows. She offers interior and exterior window cleaning for local area residents. Lisa rents a garage to store her tools and cleaning supplies and has a part-time assistant to answer the phone and handle third-story work. (Lisa is afraid of heights.) The transactions for the month of July are as follows:

(a) Lisa invested cash by making a deposit in a bank account for the business, $8,000.
(b) Paid rent for July, $150.
(c) Purchased a used van for cash, $5,000.
(d) Purchased tools on account from Clean Tools, $600.
(e) Purchased cleaning supplies that cost $300. Paid $200 cash and will pay the balance next month, $100.
(f) Paid part-time assistant (wages) for first half of month, $100.
(g) Paid for advertising, $75.
(h) Paid two-year premium for liability insurance on van, $480.
(i) Received cash from clients for services performed, $800.
(j) Performed cleaning services for clients on account, $500.
(k) Paid phone bill, $40.
(l) Received cash from clients for window cleaning performed on account in transaction (j), $200.
(m) Paid part-time assistant (wages) for last half of month, $150.
(n) Made partial payment on tools purchased in transaction (d), $200.
(o) Earned additional revenues amounting to $800: $600 in cash and $200 on account.
(p) Vozniak withdrew cash at the end of the month for personal expenses, $100.

REQUIRED

1. Enter the above transactions in an accounting equation similar to the one illustrated below.

Assets (Items Owned)						=	Liabilities (Amounts Owed)	+	Owner's Equity (Owner's Investment)		+	(Earnings)		
Cash +	Accounts Receivable +	Supplies +	Prepaid Insurance +	Tools +	Van	=	Accounts Payable	+	Lisa Vozniak, Capital −	Lisa Vozniak, Drawing	+	Revenues −	Expenses	Description

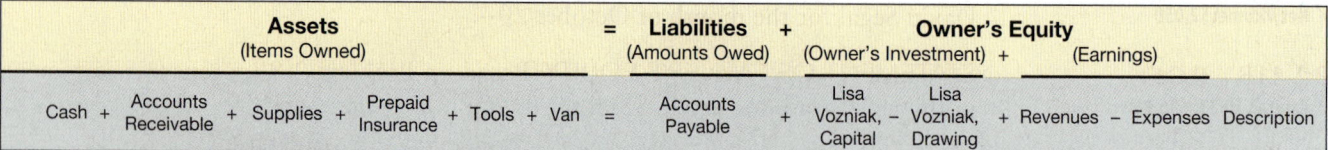

2. After transaction (p), compute the balance of each account.
3. Prepare an income statement for We Do Windows for the month of July 20--.
4. Prepare a statement of owner's equity for We Do Windows for the month of July 20--.
5. Prepare a balance sheet for We Do Windows as of July 31, 20--.

This problem challenges you to apply your cumulative accounting knowledge to move a step beyond the material in the chapter.

CHALLENGE PROBLEM

✓ Cash difference: $2,165

In this chapter, you learned about three important financial statements: the income statement, statement of owner's equity, and balance sheet. As mentioned in the margin note on page 34, most firms also prepare a statement of cash flows. Part of this statement reports the cash received from customers and cash paid for goods and services.

REQUIRED

Take another look at the Demonstration Problem for Kenny Young's "Home and Away Inspections." Note that when revenues are measured based on the amount earned, and expenses are measured based on the amount incurred, net income for the period was $4,165. Now, compute the difference between cash received from customers and cash paid to suppliers of goods and services by completing the form provided below. Are these measures different? Which provides a better measure of profitability?

Cash from customers		______
Cash paid for wages	______	
Cash paid for rent	______	
Cash paid for utilities	______	
Cash paid for insurance	______	
Cash paid for supplies	______	
Cash paid for phone	______	
Total cash paid for operating items		______
Difference between cash received from customers and cash paid for goods and services		______

ANSWERS TO SELF-STUDY TEST QUESTIONS

True/False

1. T
2. F (Accounts Payable is a liability.)
3. T
4. T
5. F (Other changes could occur: capital could increase, revenue could increase, etc.)
6. T
7. F (net income)

Multiple Choice

1. c 2. a 3. b 4. d 5. c

Checkpoint Exercises

1.

Account	Classification
Accounts Receivable	A
Accounts Payable	L
Judy Smith, Capital	OE

2. Assets = Liabilities + Owner's Equity

3.

Transaction	Assets	Liabilities	Owner's Equity
a. Purchase of an asset on account.	+	+	
b. Made payment on account for transaction (a).	–	–	

4.

Account	Classification	Financial Statement
Accounts Payable	L	BS
Peggy Welsch, Drawing	OE	SOE
Rent Expense	E	IS
Sales	R	IS
Equipment	A	BS

SILVANO AUDISIO/SHUTTERSTOCK.COM

Chapter 3 The Double-Entry Framework

LEARNING OBJECTIVES

Careful study of this chapter should enable you to:

LO1 **Define the parts of a T account.**

LO2 **Foot and balance a T account.**

LO3 **Describe the effects of debits and credits on specific types of accounts.**

LO4 **Use T accounts to analyze transactions.**

LO5 **Prepare a trial balance and explain its purposes and linkages with the financial statements.**

Tired of receiving spam e-mail messages? Or, are you worried about your computer picking up a virus, or being hacked? Businesses have the same concerns. In response to demand for email and web security, AppRiver was founded in April of 2002 to provide simple, yet powerful protection from Internet-based threats to businesses of any size. The company is based in Gulf Breeze, Florida, and maintains multiple data centers at secure locations in the United States, Europe, and Asia. AppRiver's 200 employees protect more than 60,000 companies around the world by providing spam and virus protection, email encryption, and web security.

Just as internet security is important to you in your personal life and to businesses, the same can be said about accounting. A solid understanding of financial accounting will help you manage your personal finances and help you understand business transactions in your professional life. In this chapter, you will learn about the double-entry framework used by businesses to enter transactions into an accounting system. You could use the same concepts for your personal transactions or for a business you might start.

The terms asset, liability, owner's equity, revenue, and expense were explained in Chapter 2. Examples showed how individual business transactions change one or more of these basic accounting elements. Each transaction had a dual effect. An increase or decrease in any asset, liability, owner's equity, revenue, or expense was *always* accompanied by an offsetting change within the basic accounting elements. The fact that each transaction has a dual effect upon the accounting elements provides the basis for what is called double-entry accounting. To understand double-entry accounting, it is important to learn how T accounts work and the role of debits and credits in accounting.

LO1 The T Account

Define the parts of a T account.

The assets of a business may consist of a number of items, such as cash, accounts receivable, equipment, buildings, and land. The liabilities may consist of one or more items, such as accounts payable and notes payable. Similarly, owner's equity may consist of the owner's investments and various revenue and expense items. A separate account is used to record the increases and decreases in each type of asset, liability, owner's equity, revenue, and expense.

The T account gets its name from the fact that it resembles the letter T. The three major parts of an account are as follows:

LEARNING KEY
Debit means left and credit means right.

1. the title,
2. the debit, or left side, and
3. the credit, or right side.

Title	
Debit = Left	Credit = Right

The debit side is always on the left, and the credit side is always on the right. This is true for all types of asset, liability, owner's equity, revenue, and expense accounts.

Sometimes new accounting students think that a debit is bad because it sounds like "debt." Similarly, credit sounds like a good thing, especially when the bank says they will credit your account. Please clear your mind of these thoughts. ***In accounting, debit simply means left and credit means right.***

LO2 Balancing a T Account

Foot and balance a T account.

To determine the balance of a T account at any time, simply total the dollar amounts on the debit and credit sides. These totals are known as footings. The difference between the footings is called the balance of the account. This amount is then written on the side with the larger footing.

In Chapter 2, the accounting equation was used to analyze business transactions. This required columns in which to record the increases and decreases in various accounts. Let's compare this approach with the use of a T account for the transactions affecting cash. When a T account is used, increases in cash are recorded on the debit side and decreases are recorded on the credit side. Transactions for Mitchell's Campus Delivery are shown in Figure 3-1.

FIGURE 3-1 Cash T Account

COLUMNAR SUMMARY (From Chapter 2, page 31)

Transaction	Cash
(a)	5,000
(b)	(2,000)
(d)	(600)
(e)	2,100
(f)	(1,000)
(g)	(100)
(i)	(80)
(j)	1,900
(k)	(300)
(l)	(700)
(m)	(1,650)
(n)	900
(o)	(3,000)
Balance	470

T ACCOUNT FORM

Cash

	(a)	5,000	(b)	2,000	
	(e)	2,100	(d)	600	
	(j)	1,900	(f)	1,000	
	(n)	900	(g)	100	
footing →		**9,900**	(i)	80	
			(k)	300	
			(l)	700	
			(m)	1,650	
			(o)	3,000	
Balance →		470		**9,430**	← footing

CHECKPOINT

Complete Checkpoint-1 on page 74 to test your basic understanding of LO2.

LO3 Debits and Credits

Describe the effects of debits and credits on specific types of accounts.

To **debit** an account means to enter an amount on the left or debit side of the account. To **credit** an account means to enter an amount on the right or credit side of the account. *Debits may increase or decrease the balances of specific accounts. This is also true for credits. To learn how to use debits and credits, it is best to focus on the accounting equation.*

Abbreviations: Often debit and credit are abbreviated as: Dr. = Debit, Cr. = Credit (based on the Latin terms "debere" and "credere")

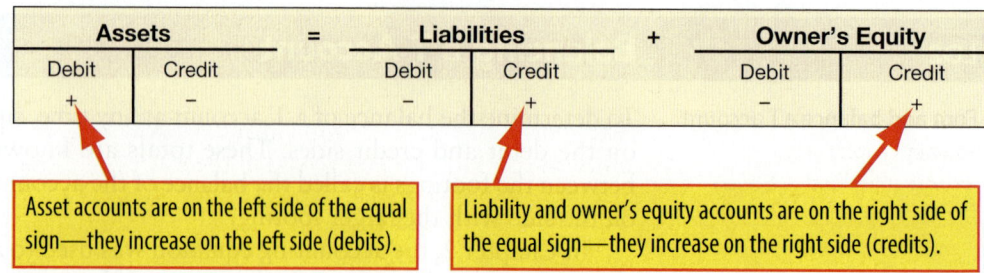

Assets		=	Liabilities		+	Owner's Equity	
Debit	Credit		Debit	Credit		Debit	Credit
+	−		−	+		−	+

Asset accounts are on the left side of the equal sign—they increase on the left side (debits).

Liability and owner's equity accounts are on the right side of the equal sign—they increase on the right side (credits).

Assets

Assets are on the left side of the accounting equation. Therefore, increases are entered on the left (debit) side of an asset account, and decreases are entered on the right (credit) side.

Liabilities and Owner's Equity

Liabilities and owner's equity are on the right side of the equation. Therefore, increases are entered on the right (credit) side, and decreases are entered on the left (debit) side.

The Owner's Equity Umbrella

Owner's equity includes four types of accounts: Owner's Capital, Revenues, Expenses, and Drawing. Expanding the accounting equation helps illustrate the use of debits and credits. Since these accounts affect owner's equity, they are shown under the "umbrella" of owner's equity in the accounting equation in Figure 3-2. It is helpful to think of the Owner's Capital account as hovering over the revenue, expense, and drawing accounts like an umbrella. Since revenues increase Owner's Capital, the revenue account is shown under the credit side of Owner's Capital. Since expenses and drawing reduce Owner's Capital, they are shown under the debit side of Owner's Capital.

FIGURE 3-2 The Accounting Equation and the Owner's Equity Umbrella

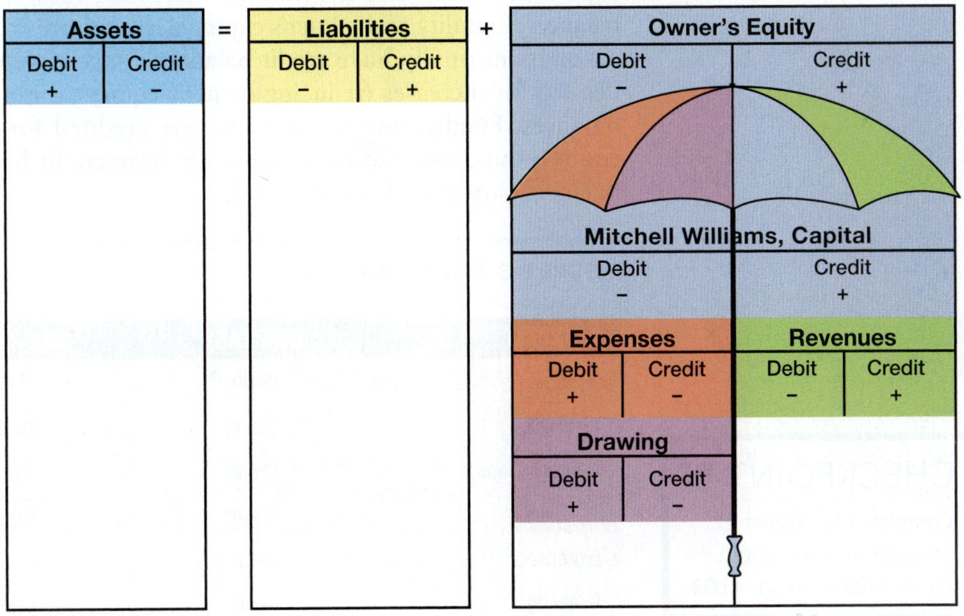

LEARNING KEY

You could credit the owner's capital account for revenues and debit the capital account for expenses and withdrawals. However, this is not a good idea. Using specific accounts provides additional information about why owner's equity increased or decreased.

Owner's Capital

The owner's capital account, Mitchell Williams, Capital, in Figure 3-2 reports the amount the owner has invested in the business. These investments increase the owner's equity and are credited to the owner's capital account.

Revenues

Revenues increase owner's equity. Revenues could be recorded directly on the credit side of the owner's capital account. However, readers of financial statements are interested in the specific types of revenues earned. Therefore, specific revenue accounts, like Delivery Fees, Sales, and Service Fees, are used. These specific accounts are credited when revenue is earned.

Remember: An increase in an expense decreases owner's equity.

Expenses

Expenses decrease owner's equity. Expenses could be recorded on the debit side of the owner's capital account. However, readers of financial statements want to see the types of expenses incurred during the accounting period. Thus, specific expense accounts are maintained for items like rent, wages, advertising, and utilities. These specific accounts are debited as expenses are incurred.

Drawing

Withdrawals of cash and other assets by the owner for personal reasons decrease owner's equity. Withdrawals could be debited directly to the owner's capital account. However, readers of financial statements want to know the amount of withdrawals for the accounting period. Thus, as shown in Figure 3-2, withdrawals are debited to a separate account, Drawing.

Normal Balances

A **normal balance** is the side of an account that is used to increase the account. Thus, the normal balances for the accounts illustrated in Figure 3-2 are shown with a "+" sign. Since assets are debited for increases, these accounts normally have **debit balances**. Liability and owner's capital accounts are credited for increases; thus, these accounts normally have **credit balances**. Since expense and drawing accounts are debited for increases (reducing owner's equity), these accounts normally have debit balances. Finally, revenue accounts are credited for increases (increasing owner's equity); thus, these accounts normally have credit balances. A summary of normal balances is provided in Figure 3-3.

FIGURE 3-3 Normal Balances

ACCOUNT	INCREASE	DECREASE	NORMAL BALANCE
Assets	Debit	Credit	Debit
Liabilities	Credit	Debit	Credit
Owner's Capital	Credit	Debit	Credit
Revenues	Credit	Debit	Credit
Expenses	Debit	Credit	Debit
Drawing	Debit	Credit	Debit

CHECKPOINT

Complete Checkpoint-2 on page 74 to test your basic understanding of LO3.

LO4

Transaction Analysis

Use T accounts to analyze transactions.

In Chapter 2, you learned how to analyze transactions by using the accounting equation. Here, we continue to use the accounting equation, but add debits and credits by using T accounts. As shown in Figure 3-4, the three basic questions that must be answered when analyzing a transaction are essentially the same but are expanded slightly to address the use of the owner's equity umbrella and T accounts. You must determine the location of the account within the accounting equation and/or the owner's equity umbrella. You must also determine whether the accounts should be debited or credited.

LEARNING KEY

Since the accounting equation must stay in balance, there must be at least one debit and at least one credit for each transaction.

FIGURE 3-4 Steps in Transaction Analysis

1. **What happened?**
   Be sure you understand the event that has taken place.

2. **Which accounts are affected?**
   Once you understand what happened, you must:
   - Identify the accounts that are affected.
   - Classify these accounts as assets, liabilities, owner's equity, revenues, or expenses.
   - Identify the location of the accounts in the accounting equation and/or the owner's equity umbrella—left or right.

3. **How is the accounting equation affected?**
   - Determine whether the accounts have increased or decreased.
   - Determine whether the accounts should be debited or credited.
   - Make certain the accounting equation remains in balance after the transaction has been entered.
     (1) Assets = Liabilities + Owner's Equity
     (2) Debits = Credits for every transaction

Debits and Credits: Asset, Liability, and Owner's Equity Accounts

Transactions (a) through (d) from Mitchell's Campus Delivery (Chapter 2) demonstrate the double-entry process for transactions affecting asset, liability, and owner's equity accounts.

As you study each transaction, answer the three questions: (1) What happened? (2) Which accounts are affected? and (3) How is the accounting equation affected? The transaction statement tells you what happened. The analysis tells which accounts are affected. The illustration shows you how the accounting equation is affected.

Transaction (a): Investment by owner

Mitchell Williams, opened a bank account with a deposit of $5,000 for his business (Figure 3-5).

Analysis. As a result of this transaction, the business acquired an asset, Cash. In exchange for the asset, the business gave Mitchell Williams, owner's equity. The owner's equity account is called Mitchell Williams, Capital. The transaction is entered as an increase in an asset and an increase in owner's equity. Debit Cash and credit Mitchell Williams, Capital for $5,000.

FIGURE 3-5 Transaction (a): Investment by Owner

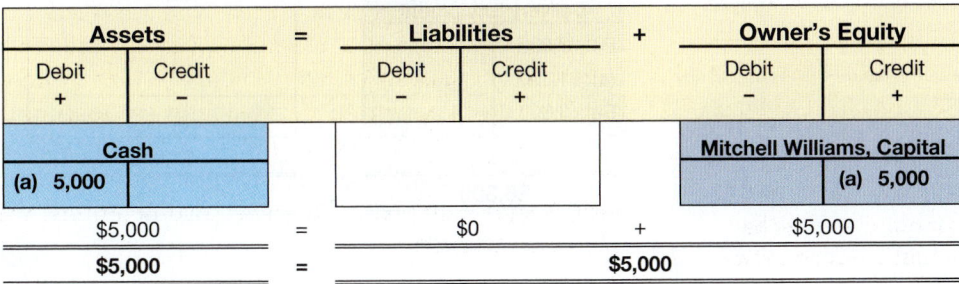

Assets		=	Liabilities		+	Owner's Equity	
Debit +	Credit −		Debit −	Credit +		Debit −	Credit +
Cash						Mitchell Williams, Capital	
(a) 5,000							(a) 5,000
$5,000		=	$0		+	$5,000	
$5,000		=	**$5,000**				

Transaction (b): Purchase of an asset for cash

Mitch bought a motor scooter (delivery equipment) for $2,000 cash (Figure 3-6).

Analysis. Mitch exchanged one asset, Cash, for another, Delivery Equipment. Debit Delivery Equipment and credit Cash for $2,000. Notice that the total assets are still $5,000 as they were following transaction (a). Transaction (b) shifted assets from cash to delivery equipment, but total assets remained the same.

FIGURE 3-6 Transaction (b): Purchase of an Asset for Cash

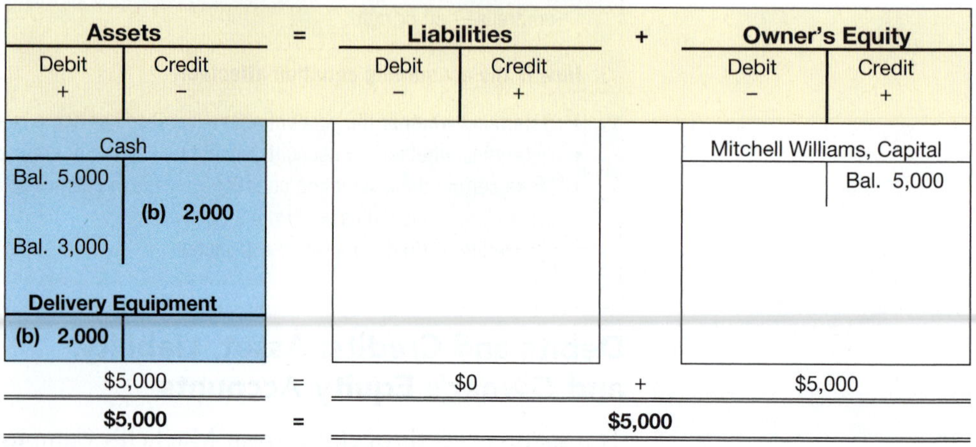

Transaction (c): Purchase of an asset on account

Mitch bought a second motor scooter on account for $1,800 (Figure 3-7). Recall from Chapter 2 that "on account" means Mitch will pay for the asset later.

Analysis. The asset, Delivery Equipment, increases by $1,800 and the liability, Accounts Payable, increases by the same amount. Thus, debit Delivery Equipment and credit Accounts Payable for $1,800.

FIGURE 3-7 Transaction (c): Purchase of an Asset on Account

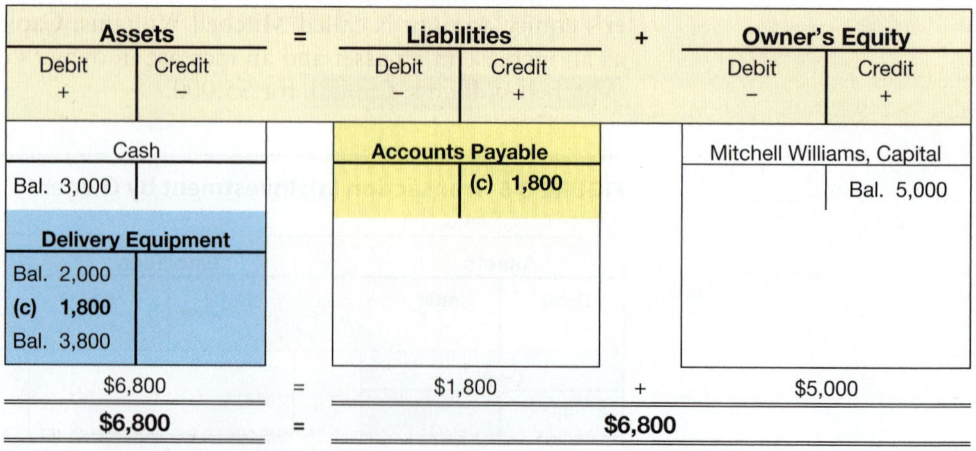

Transaction (d): Payment on account

Mitch made the first $600 payment on the scooter purchased in transaction (c) (Figure 3-8).

Analysis. This payment decreases the asset, Cash, and decreases the liability, Accounts Payable. Debit Accounts Payable and credit Cash for $600.

FIGURE 3-8 Transaction (d): Payment on Account

Assets		=	Liabilities		+	Owner's Equity	
Debit +	Credit −		Debit −	Credit +		Debit −	Credit +
Cash			**Accounts Payable**			Mitchell Williams, Capital	
Bal. 3,000				Bal. 1,800			Bal. 5,000
	(d) 600		**(d) 600**				
Bal. 2,400				Bal. 1,200			
Delivery Equipment							
Bal. 3,800							
$6,200		=	$1,200		+	$5,000	
$6,200		=			**$6,200**		

> **LEARNING KEY**
> Credits increase the capital account. Revenues increase capital. Thus, revenues are shown under the credit side of owner's equity and the capital account. Debits decrease the capital account. Expenses and drawing reduce the capital account. Thus, they are shown under the debit side of owner's equity and the capital account.

Notice that for transactions (a) through (d), the debits equal credits and the accounting equation is in balance. Review transactions (a) through (d). Again, identify the accounts that were affected and how they were classified (assets, liabilities, or owner's equity). Finally, note each account's location within the accounting equation.

Debits and Credits: Including Revenues, Expenses, and Drawing

Transactions (a) through (d) involved only assets, liabilities, and the owner's capital account. To complete the illustration of Mitchell's Campus Delivery, the equation is expanded to include revenues, expenses, and drawing. Remember, revenues increase owner's equity and are shown under the credit side of the capital account. Expenses and drawing decrease owner's equity and are shown under the debit side of the capital account. The expanded equation is shown in Figure 3-9.

FIGURE 3-9 The Expanded Accounting Equation

Assets		=	Liabilities		+	Owner's Equity					
Debit +	Credit −		Debit −	Credit +		Debit −				Credit +	
						Drawing		**Expenses**		**Revenues**	
						Debit +	Credit −	Debit +	Credit −	Debit −	Credit +

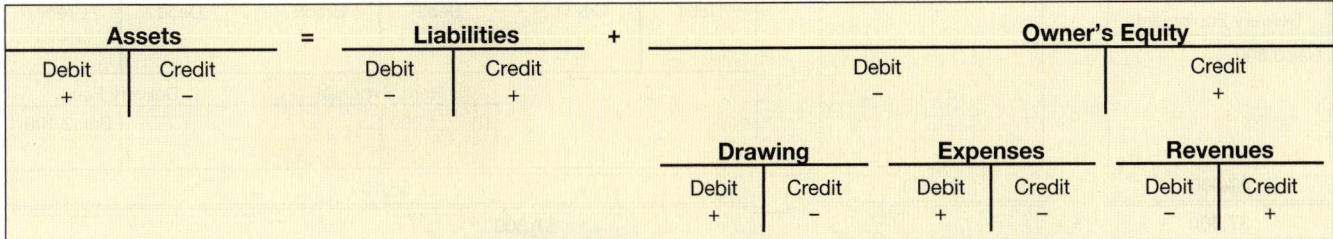

Transaction (e): Delivery revenues earned in cash

Mitch made deliveries and received $2,100 cash from clients (Figure 3-10).

Analysis. The asset, Cash, and the revenue, Delivery Fees, increase. Debit Cash and credit Delivery Fees for $2,100.

FIGURE 3-10 Transaction (e): Delivery Revenues Earned in Cash

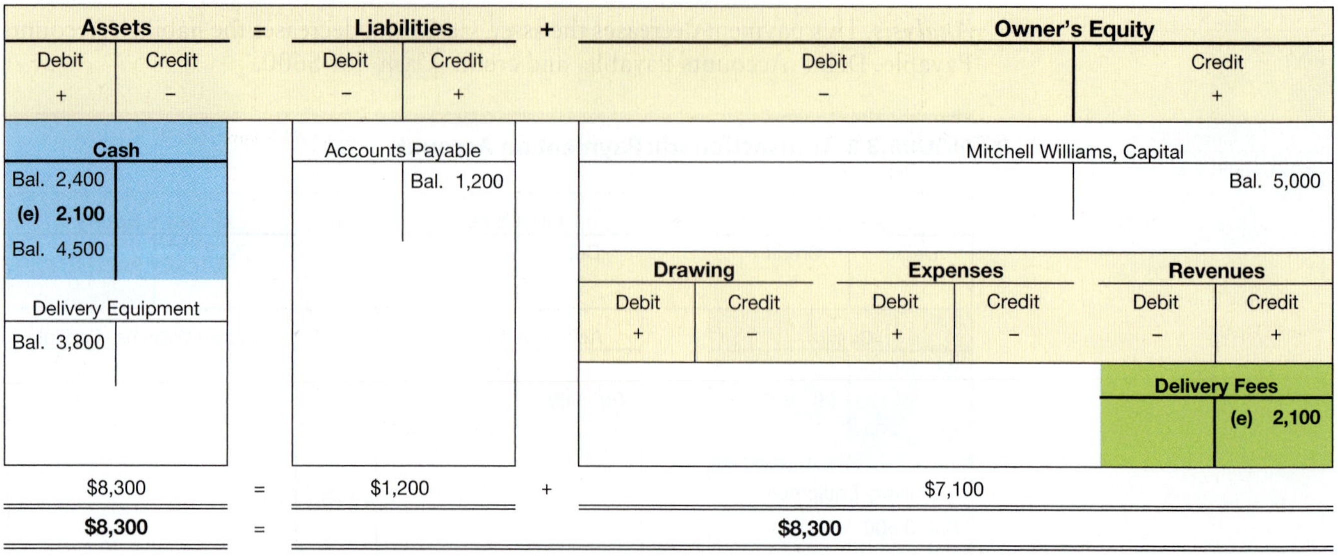

Transaction (f): Paid rent for month

Mitch paid $1,000 for office rent for June (Figure 3-11).

Analysis. Rent Expense increases and Cash decreases. Debit Rent Expense and credit Cash for $1,000.

A debit to an expense account *increases* that expense and *decreases* owner's equity. Notice that the placement of the plus and minus signs for expenses is opposite the placement of the signs for owner's equity. Note also that expenses are located on the left (debit) side of the owner's equity umbrella.

FIGURE 3-11 Transaction (f): Paid Rent for Month

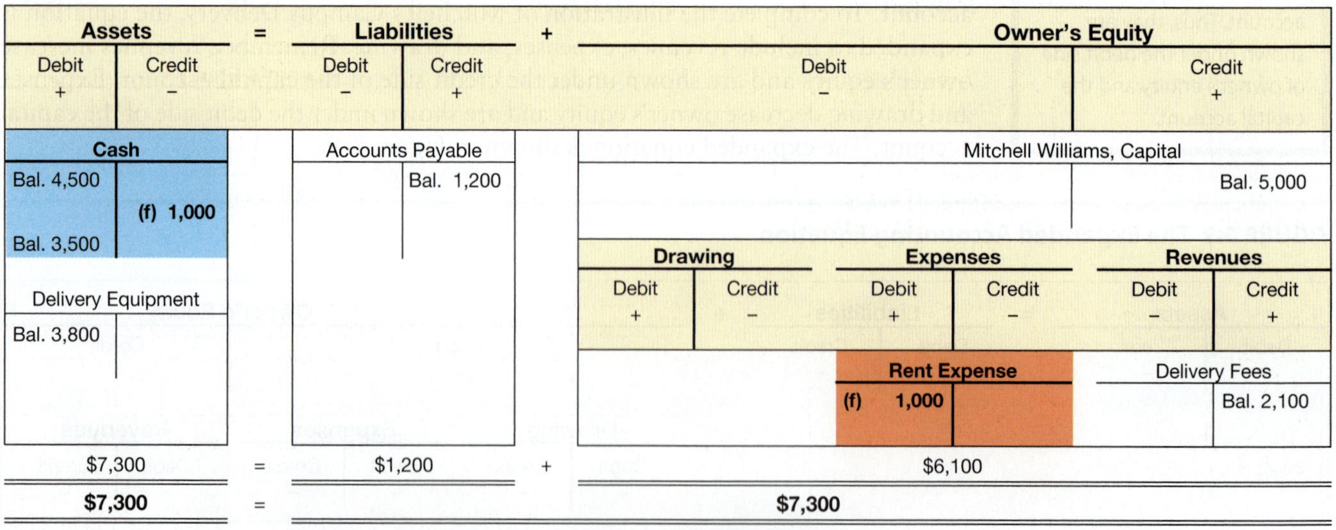

Transaction (g): Paid phone bill

Mitch paid for phone service, $100 (Figure 3-12).

Analysis. This transaction, like the previous one, increases an expense and decreases an asset. Debit Phone Expense and credit Cash for $100.

FIGURE 3-12 **Transaction (g): Paid Phone Bill**

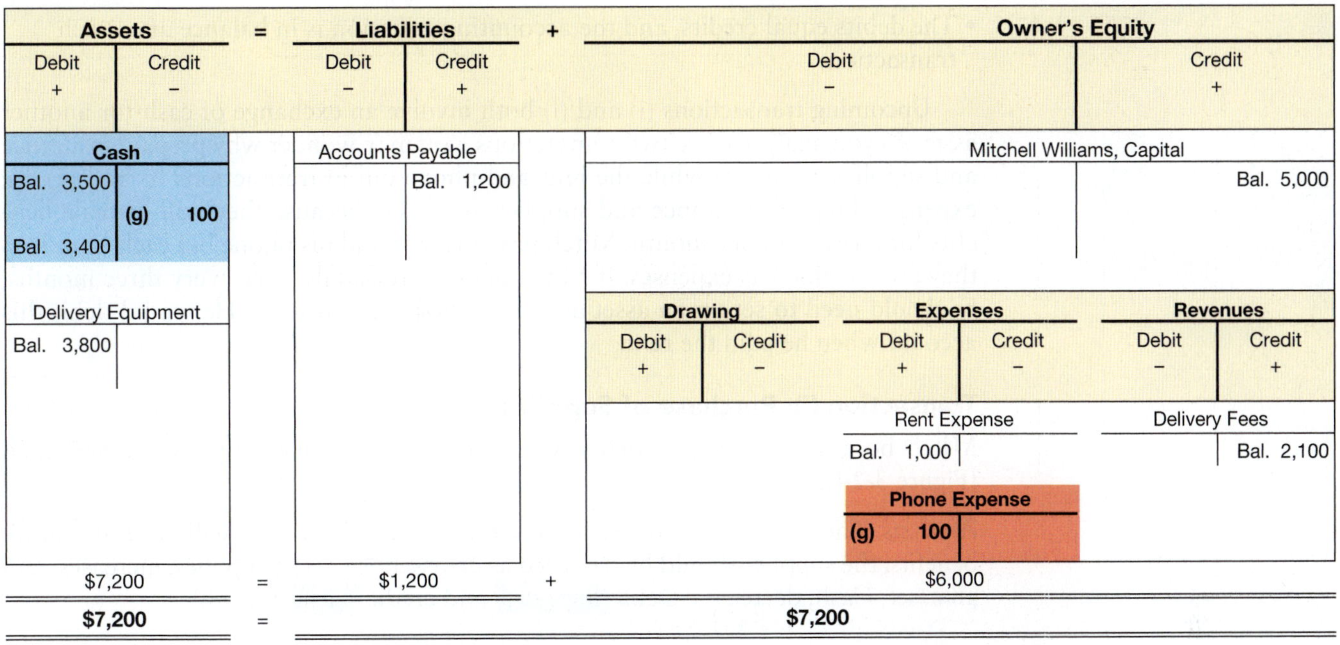

Transaction (h): Delivery revenues earned on account

Mitch made deliveries on account for $2,400 (Figure 3-13).

Analysis. As discussed in Chapter 2, delivery services are performed for which payment will be received later. This is called offering services "on account" or "on credit." Instead of receiving cash, Mitch receives a promise that his customers will pay cash in the future. Therefore, the asset, Accounts Receivable, increases. Since revenues are recognized when earned, the revenue account, Delivery Fees, also increases. Debit Accounts Receivable and credit Delivery Fees for $2,400.

FIGURE 3-13 **Transaction (h): Delivery Revenues Earned on Account**

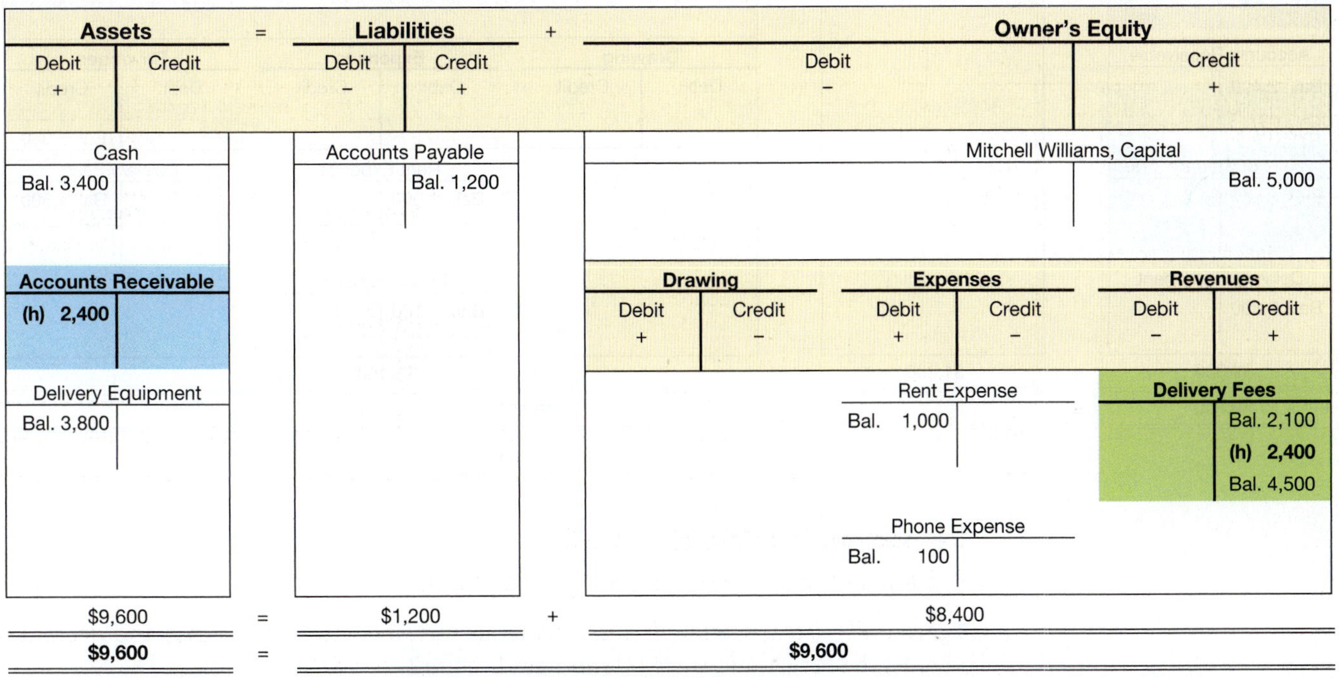

Review transactions (e) through (h). Note the following:

- Expense and revenue transactions do not always affect cash.
- The debits equal credits, and the accounting equation is in balance after each transaction.

Upcoming transactions (i) and (l) both involve an exchange of cash for another asset. As you analyze these two transactions, you may wonder why prepaid insurance and supplies are assets while the rent and phone bill in transactions (f) and (g) are expenses. Prepaid insurance and supplies are assets because they will provide benefits for more than one month. Mitch pays his rent and his phone bill each month so they are classified as expenses. If Mitch paid his rent only once every three months, he would need to set up an asset account called Prepaid Rent. He would debit this account when he paid the rent.

Transaction (i): Purchase of Supplies

Mitch bought pens, paper, delivery envelopes, and other supplies for $80 cash (Figure 3-14).

Analysis. These supplies will last for several months. Since they will generate future benefits, the supplies should be recorded as an asset. An asset, Supplies, increases, and an asset, Cash, decreases. Debit Supplies and credit Cash for $80.

FIGURE 3-14 Transaction (i): Purchase of Supplies

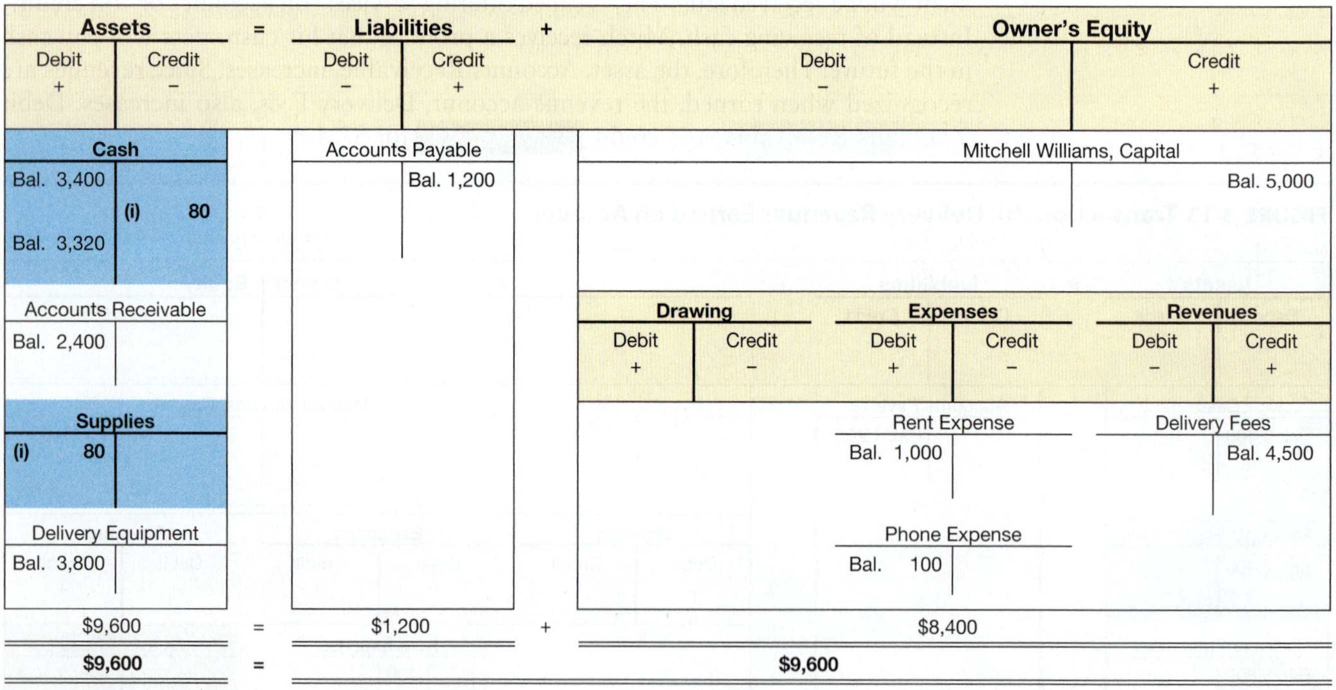

A BROADER VIEW

Supplies—Asset or Expense?

When businesses buy office supplies from Staples or other suppliers, the supplies are initially recorded as assets. This is done because the supplies will provide future benefits. Those still remaining in inventory at the end of the accounting period are reported on the balance sheet as assets. Supplies actually used during the period are recognized as an expense on the income statement. We will discuss how to account for the expense in Chapter 5.

BAI-BUA'S DAD/SHUTTERSTOCK.COM

Transaction (j): Cash receipts from prior sales on account

Mitch received $1,900 in cash for delivery services performed for customers earlier in the month [see transaction (h)] (Figure 3-15).

Analysis. This transaction increases Cash and reduces the amount due from customers reported in Accounts Receivable. Debit Cash and credit Accounts Receivable $1,900.

As you analyze transaction (j), notice which accounts are affected and the location of these accounts in the accounting equation. Mitch received cash, but this transaction did not affect revenue. The revenue was recorded in transaction (h). Transaction (j) is an exchange of one asset (Accounts Receivable) for another asset (Cash).

FIGURE 3-15 Transaction (j): Cash Receipts from Prior Sales on Account

Assets		=	Liabilities		+	Owner's Equity	
Debit +	Credit −		Debit −	Credit +		Debit −	Credit +

Assets

Cash	
Bal. 3,320	
(j) 1,900	
Bal. 5,220	

Accounts Receivable	
Bal. 2,400	
	(j) 1,900
Bal. 500	

Supplies	
Bal. 80	

Delivery Equipment	
Bal. 3,800	

Liabilities

Accounts Payable	
	Bal. 1,200

Owner's Equity

Mitchell Williams, Capital	
	Bal. 5,000

Drawing		Expenses		Revenues	
Debit +	Credit −	Debit +	Credit −	Debit −	Credit +

Rent Expense	
Bal. 1,000	

Phone Expense	
Bal. 100	

Delivery Fees	
	Bal. 4,500

Assets		Liabilities		Owner's Equity
$9,600	=	$1,200	+	$8,400
$9,600	=	**$9,600**		

As you analyze transactions (k) through (o), make certain that you understand what has happened in each transaction. Identify the accounts that are affected and the locations of these accounts within the accounting equation. Notice that the accounting equation remains in balance after every transaction and debits equal credits for each transaction.

Transaction (k): Purchase of an asset on credit making a partial payment

Mitch bought a third motor scooter for $1,000. Mitch made a down payment of $300 and spread the remaining payments over the next four months (Figure 3-16).

Analysis. The asset, Delivery Equipment, increases by $1,000, Cash decreases by $300, and the liability, Accounts Payable, increases by $700. Thus, debit Delivery Equipment for $1,000, credit Cash for $300, and credit Accounts Payable for $700. This transaction requires one debit and two credits. Even so, total debits ($1,000) equal the total credits ($700 + $300) and the accounting equation remains in balance.

FIGURE 3-16 Transaction (k): Purchase of an Asset on Credit Making a Partial Payment

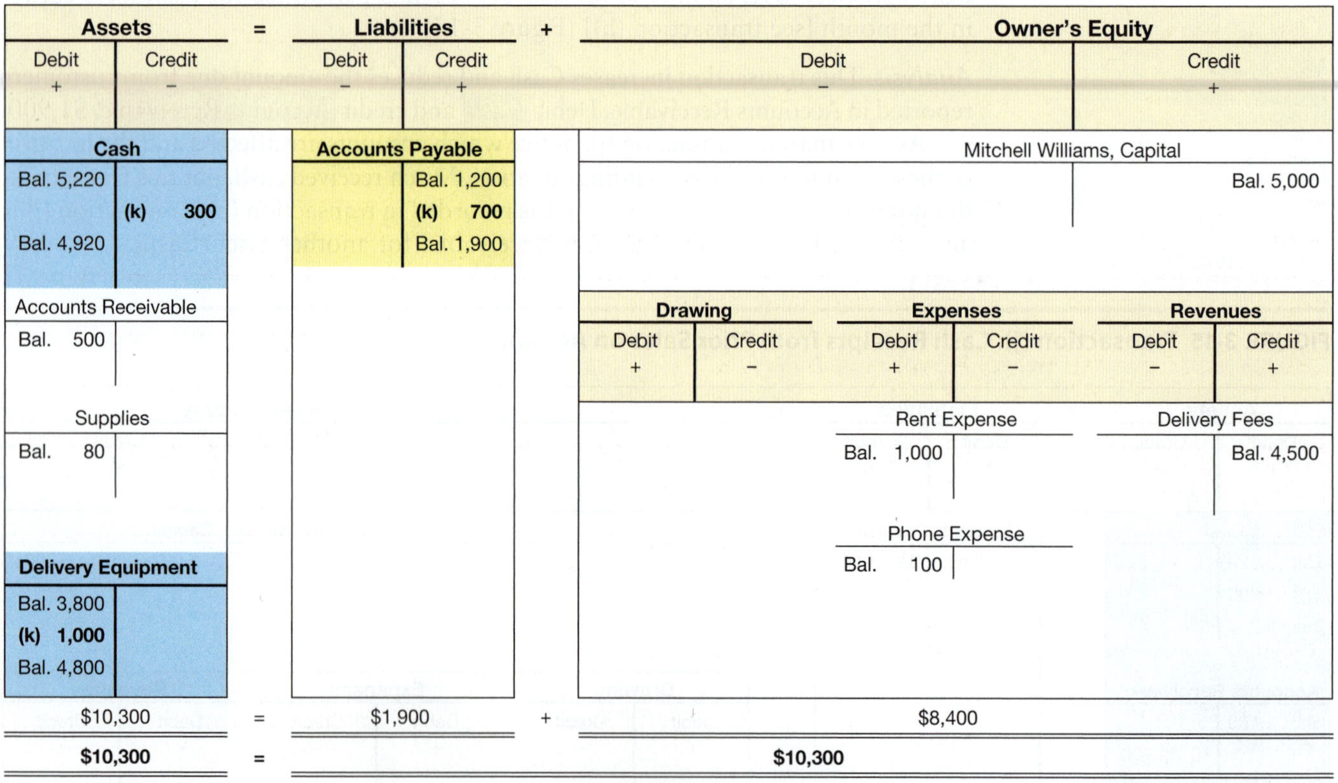

Transaction (l): Payment of insurance premium

Mitch paid $700 for an eight-month liability insurance policy (Figure 3-17).

Analysis. Since insurance is paid in advance and will provide future benefits, it is treated as an asset. Therefore, one asset, Prepaid Insurance, increases and another, Cash, decreases. Debit Prepaid Insurance and credit Cash for $700.

Transaction (m): Payment of wages

Mitch paid his part-time employees $1,650 in wages (Figure 3-18).

Analysis. This is an additional business expense. Wages Expense increases and Cash decreases. Debit Wages Expense and credit Cash for $1,650.

FIGURE 3-17 Transaction (l): Payment of Insurance Premium

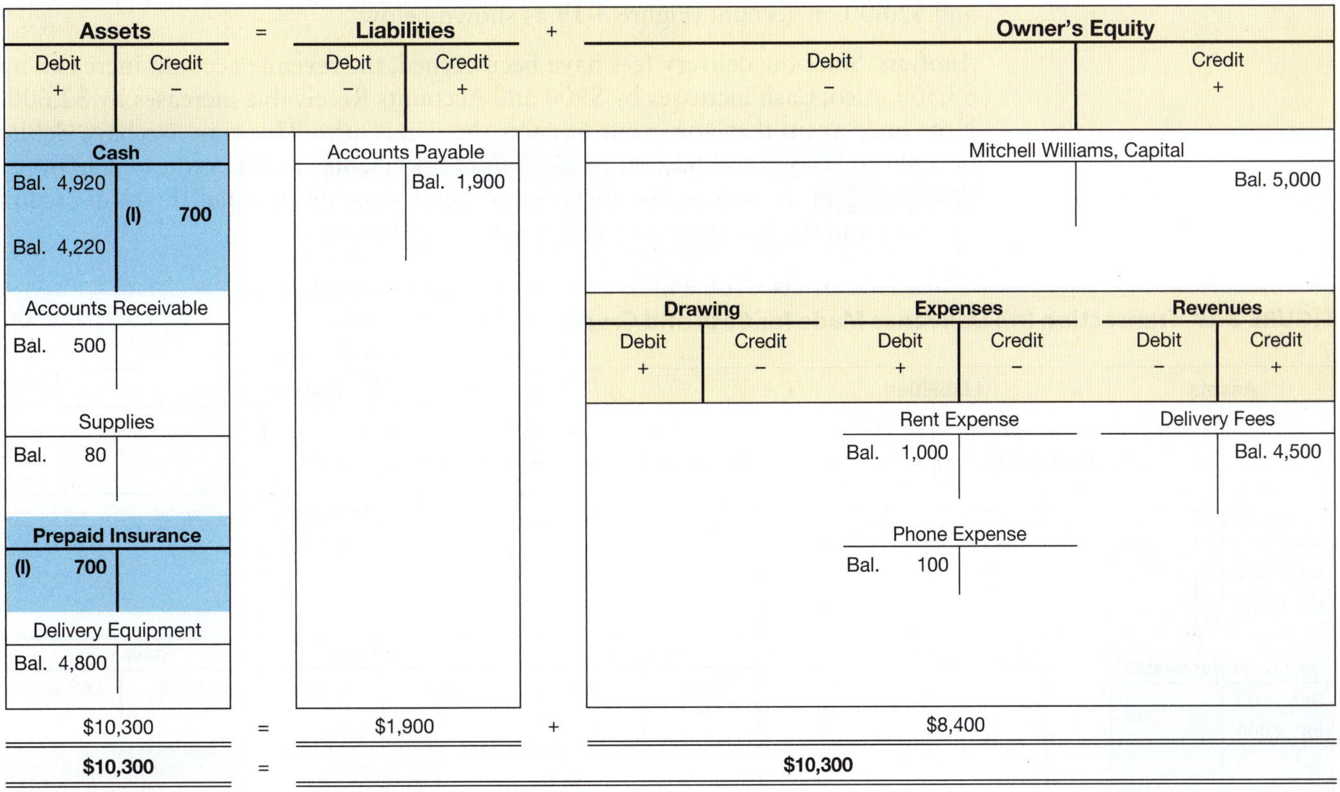

FIGURE 3-18 Transaction (m): Payment of Wages

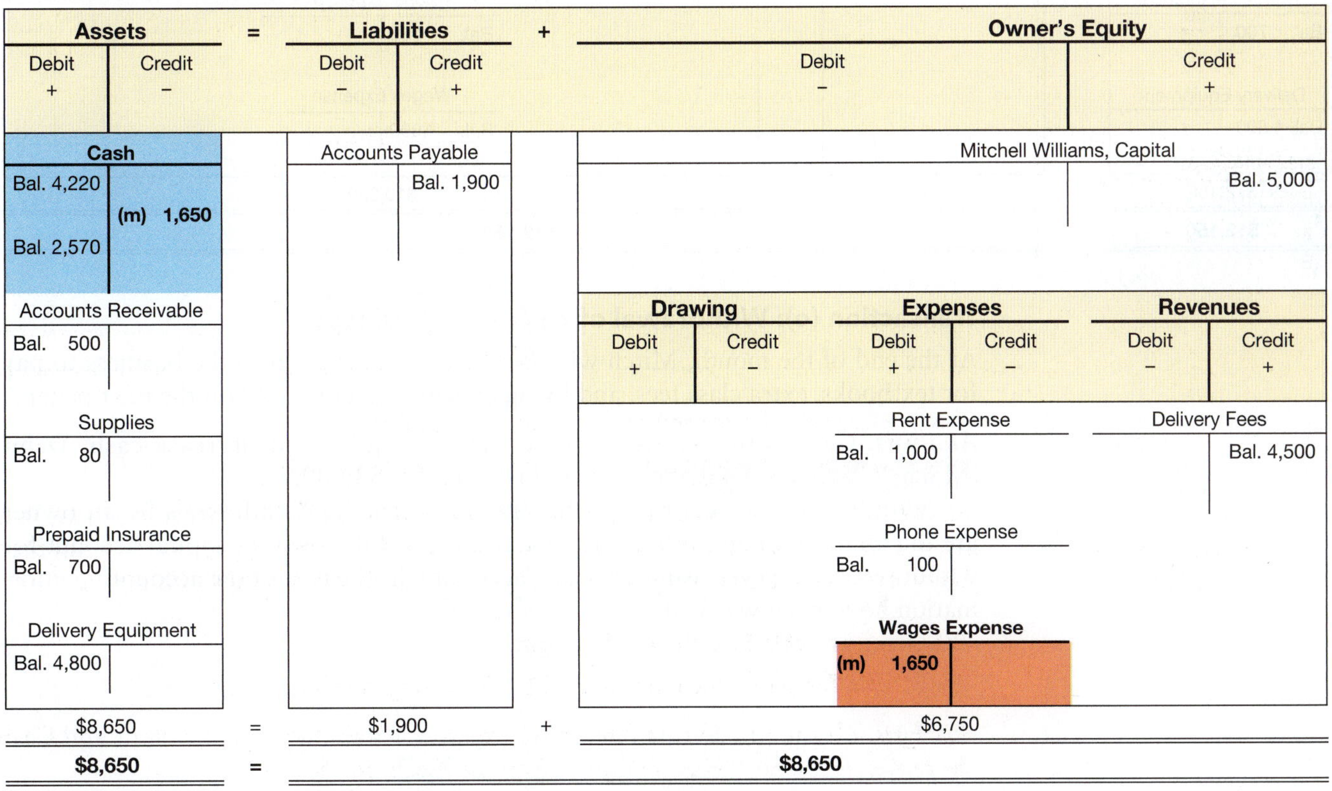

Transaction (n): Deliveries made for cash and credit

Total delivery fees for the remainder of the month amounted to $3,500: $900 in cash and $2,600 on account (Figure 3-19 as shown below).

Analysis. Since the delivery fees have been earned, the revenue account increases by $3,500. Also, Cash increases by $900 and Accounts Receivable increases by $2,600. Note once again that one event impacts three accounts. This time we have debits of $900 to Cash and $2,600 to Accounts Receivable and a credit of $3,500 to Delivery Fees. As before, the total debits ($900 + $2,600) equal the total credits ($3,500) and the accounting equation remains in balance.

FIGURE 3-19 Transaction (n): Deliveries Made for Cash and Credit

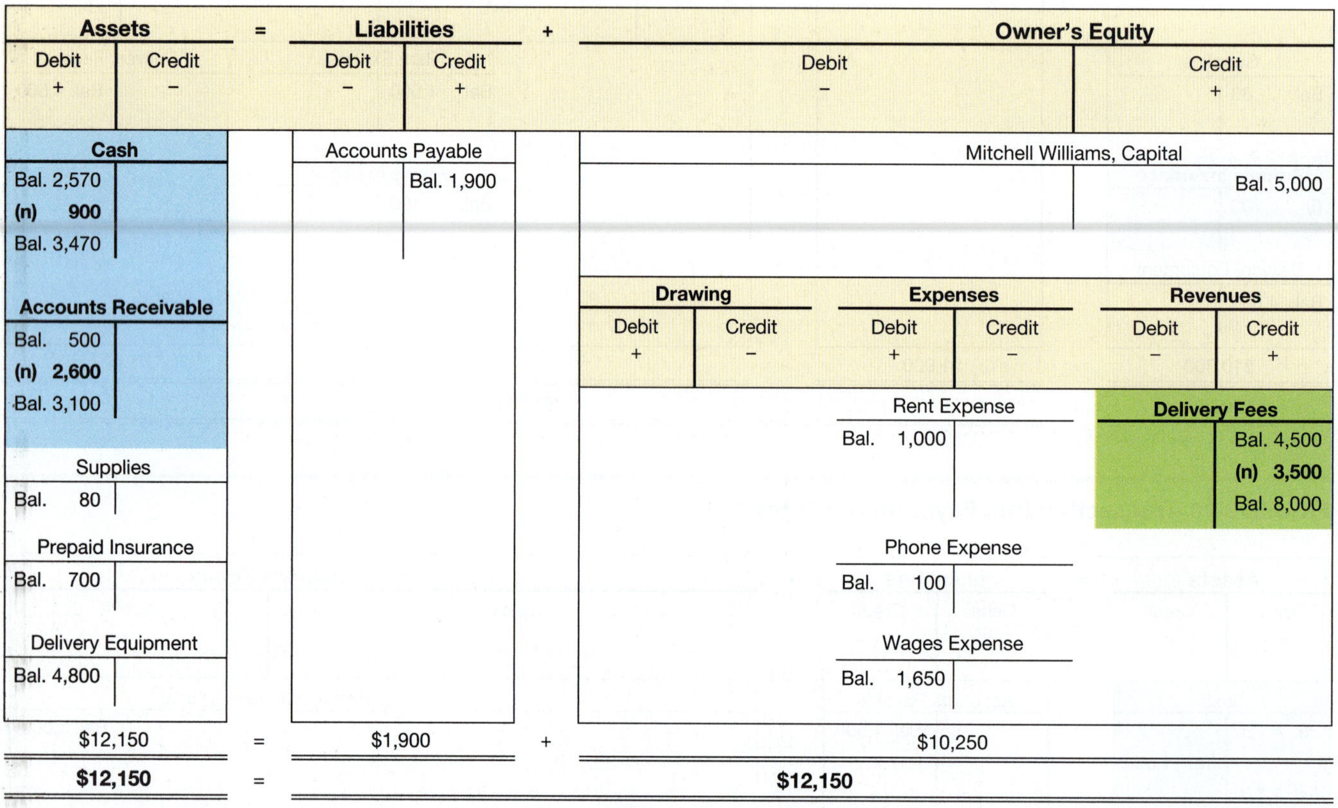

Transaction (o): Withdrawal of cash from business

At the end of the month, Mitch withdrew $3,000 in cash from the business to pay for textbooks, extra class fees, and living expenses (Figure 3-20 on the next page).

Analysis. Cash withdrawals decrease owner's equity and decrease cash. Debit Mitchell Williams, Drawing and credit Cash for $3,000.

Withdrawals are reported in the drawing account. Withdrawals by an owner are the opposite of an investment. You could debit the owner's capital account for withdrawals. However, using a specific account tells the user of the accounting information how much was withdrawn for the period.

FIGURE 3-20 Transaction (o): Withdrawal of Cash from Business

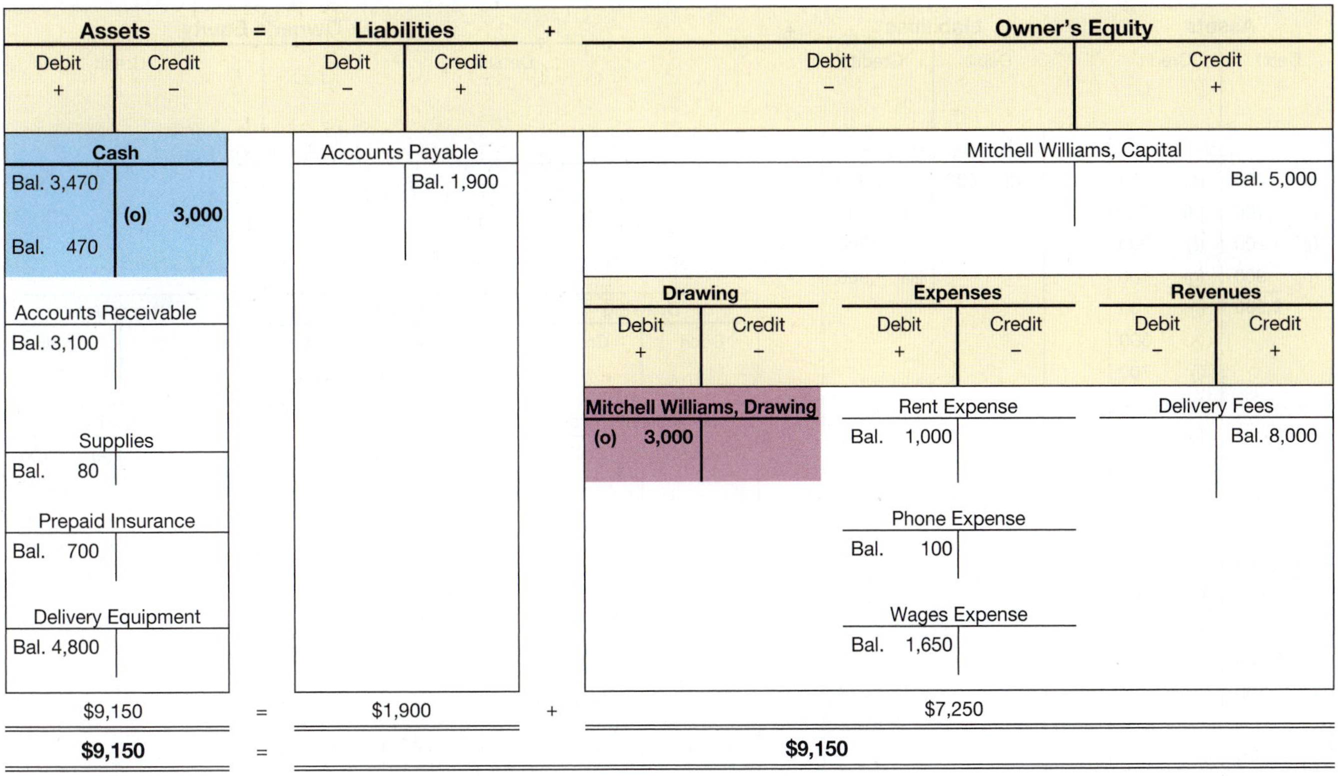

Summary of Transactions

In illustrating transactions (a) through (o), each T account for Mitchell's Campus Delivery shows a balance before and after each transaction. To focus your attention on the transaction being explained, only a single entry was shown. In practice, this is not done. Instead, each account gathers all transactions for a period. Mitchell's accounts, with all transactions listed, are shown in Figure 3-21. Note the following four items:

1. The footings are directly under the debit (left) and credit (right) sides of the T account for those accounts with more than one debit or credit.
2. The balance is shown on the side with the larger footing.
3. The footing serves as the balance for accounts with entries on only one side of the account.
4. If an account has only a single entry, it is not necessary to enter a footing or balance.

CHECKPOINT

Complete Checkpoint-3 on page 74 to test your basic understanding of LO4.

FIGURE 3-21 Summary of Transactions (a) Through (o)

Assets		=	Liabilities		+	Owner's Equity	
Debit +	Credit −		Debit −	Credit +		Debit −	Credit +

Assets

Cash	
(a) 5,000	(b) 2,000
(e) 2,100	(d) 600
(j) 1,900	(f) 1,000
(n) 900	(g) 100
9,900	(i) 80
	(k) 300
	(l) 700
	(m) 1,650
	(o) 3,000
	9,430
Bal. 470	

Accounts Receivable	
(h) 2,400	(j) 1,900
(n) 2,600	
5,000	
Bal. 3,100	

Supplies	
(i) 80	

Prepaid Insurance	
(l) 700	

Delivery Equipment	
(b) 2,000	
(c) 1,800	
(k) 1,000	
Bal. 4,800	

Liabilities

Accounts Payable	
(d) 600	(c) 1,800
	(k) 700
	2,500
	Bal. 1,900

Owner's Equity

Mitchell Williams, Capital	
	(a) 5,000

Drawing		Expenses		Revenues	
Debit +	Credit −	Debit +	Credit −	Debit −	Credit +

Mitchell Williams, Drawing	
(o) 3,000	

Rent Expense	
(f) 1,000	

Phone Expense	
(g) 100	

Wages Expense	
(m) 1,650	

Delivery Fees	
	(e) 2,100
	(h) 2,400
	(n) 3,500
	Bal. 8,000

Assets		Liabilities		Owner's Equity
$9,150	=	$1,900	+	$7,250
$9,150	=	**$9,150**		

LO5 The Trial Balance

Prepare a trial balance and explain its purposes and linkages with the financial statements.

Recall the following two very important rules in double-entry accounting:

1. The sum of the debits must equal the sum of the credits.

   At least two accounts are affected by each transaction. This rule is so important that many computer accounting programs will not permit a transaction to be entered into the accounting system unless the debits equal the credits.

2. The accounting equation must remain in balance.

In illustrating the transactions for Mitchell's Campus Delivery, the equality of the accounting equation was verified after each transaction. Because of the large

> **LEARNING KEY**
>
> A trial balance provides proof that total debits equal total credits and shows that the accounting equation is in balance.

number of transactions entered each day, this is not done in practice. Instead, a trial balance is prepared periodically to determine the equality of the debits and credits. A **trial balance** is a list of all accounts showing the title and balance of each account. By totaling the debits and credits, their equality can be tested.

A trial balance of Mitchell's accounts, taken on June 30, 20--, is shown in Figure 3-22. This date is shown on the third line of the heading. The trial balance shows that the debit and credit totals are equal in amount. This is proof that (1) in entering transactions (a) through (o), the total of the debits was equal to the total of the credits, and (2) the accounting equation has remained in balance.

A trial balance is not a formal statement or report. Normally, only the accountant sees it. As shown in Figure 3-23, a trial balance can be used as an aid in preparing the financial statements.

> Since a trial balance is not a formal statement, dollar signs are not used. Formal statements include: Income Statement, Statement of Owner's Equity, Balance Sheet, and Statement of Cash Flows.

FIGURE 3-22 Trial Balance

Mitchell's Campus Delivery
Trial Balance
June 30, 20--

ACCOUNT TITLE	DEBIT BALANCE	CREDIT BALANCE
Cash	470 00	
Accounts Receivable	3100 00	
Supplies	80 00	
Prepaid Insurance	700 00	
Delivery Equipment	4800 00	
Accounts Payable		1900 00
Mitchell Williams, Capital		5000 00
Mitchell Williams, Drawing	3000 00	
Delivery Fees		8000 00
Rent Expense	1000 00	
Phone Expense	100 00	
Wages Expense	1650 00	
	14900 00	14900 00

FIGURE 3-23 Linkages Between the Trial Balance and Financial Statements

Mitchell's Campus Delivery
Trial Balance
June 30, 20--

ACCOUNT TITLE	DEBIT BALANCE	CREDIT BALANCE
Cash	470 00	
Accounts Receivable	3100 00	
Supplies	80 00	
Prepaid Insurance	700 00	
Delivery Equipment	4800 00	
Accounts Payable		1900 00
Mitchell Williams, Capital		5000 00
Mitchell Williams, Drawing	3000 00	
Delivery Fees		8000 00
Rent Expense	1000 00	
Phone Expense	100 00	
Wages Expense	1650 00	
	14900 00	14900 00

(*continued*)

If the beginning capital balance was $5,000 and Mitch made no additional investments, the statement would be prepared as follows:

Mitchell's Campus Delivery Statement of Owner's Equity For Month Ended June 30, 20 --		
Mitchell Williams, capital, June 1, 20 --		$5,000
Net income for 20 --	$5,250	
Less withdrawals for 20 --	3,000	
Increase in capital		2,250
Mitchell Williams, capital, June 30, 20 --		$7,250

FIGURE 3-23 Linkages Between the Trial Balance and Financial Statements (*concluded*)

Mitchell's Campus Delivery Income Statement For Month Ended June 30, 20 --		
Revenue:		
Delivery fees		$8,000
Expenses:		
Wages expense	$1,650	
Rent expense	1,000	
Phone expense	100	
Total expenses		2,750
Net income		$5,250

Mitchell's Campus Delivery Statement of Owner's Equity For Month Ended June 30, 20 --		
Mitchell Williams, capital, June 1, 20 --		$ —
Investments during June		5,000
Total investment		$5,000
Net income for 20 --	$5,250	
Less withdrawals for 20 --	3,000	
Increase in capital		2,250
Mitchell Williams, capital, June 30, 20 --		$7,250

Mitchell's Campus Delivery Balance Sheet June 30, 20 --			
Assets		Liabilities	
Cash	$ 470	Accounts payable	$1,900
Accounts receivable	3,100		
Supplies	80	Owner's Equity	
Prepaid insurance	700	Mitchell Williams, capital	7,250
Delivery equipment	4,800		
Total assets	$9,150	Total liabilities and owner's equity	$9,150

CHECKPOINT

Complete Checkpoint-4 on page 74 to test your basic understanding of LO5.

SELF-STUDY

LEARNING OBJECTIVES	Key Points to Remember
LO1 Define the parts of a T account.	The parts of a T account are 1. the title, 2. the debit, or left side, and 3. the credit, or right side.

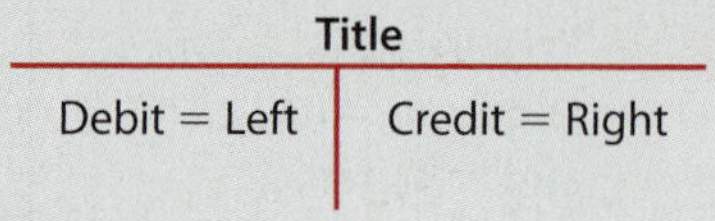

LEARNING OBJECTIVES — Key Points to Remember

LO2 Foot and balance a T account.

Rules for footing and balancing T accounts are:

1. The footings are directly under the debit (left) and credit (right) sides of the T account for those accounts with more than one debit or credit.
2. The balance is shown on the side with the larger footing.
3. The footing serves as the balance for accounts with entries on only one side of the account.
4. If an account has only a single entry, it is not necessary to enter a footing or balance.

LO3 Describe the effects of debits and credits on specific types of accounts.

Rules for debits and credits. (See illustration below.)

1. Assets are on the left side of the accounting equation. Therefore, increases are entered on the left (debit) side of an asset account and decreases are entered on the right (credit) side.
2. Liabilities and owner's equity are on the right side of the accounting equation. Therefore, increases are entered on the right (credit) side and decreases are entered on the left (debit) side.
3. Revenues increase owner's equity. Therefore, increases are entered on the right (credit) side and decreases are entered on the left (debit) side.
4. Expenses and drawing decrease owner's equity. Therefore, increases are entered on the left (debit) side and decreases are entered on the right (credit) side.

Accounting Equation with Owner's Equity Umbrella

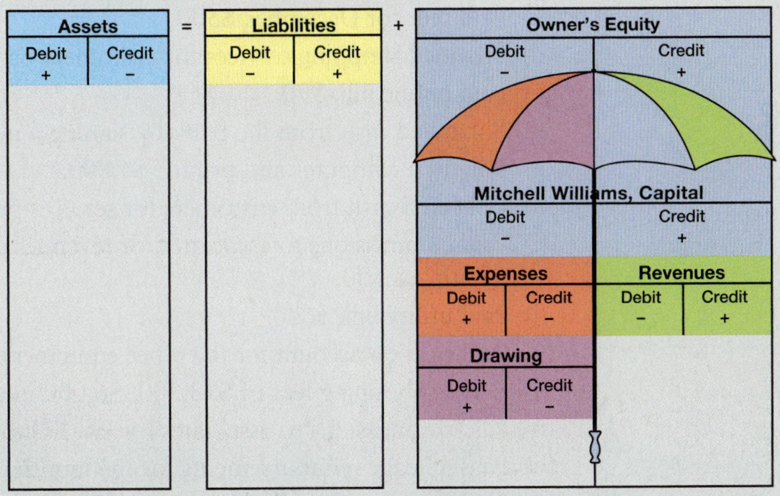

LO4 Use T accounts to analyze transactions.

Picture the accounting equation in your mind as you analyze transactions. When entering transactions in T accounts:

1. The sum of the debits must equal the sum of the credits.
2. At least two accounts are affected by each transaction.
3. When finished, the accounting equation must remain in balance.

LO5 Prepare a trial balance and explain its purposes and linkages with the financial statements.

A trial balance shows that the debit and credit totals are equal. A trial balance also can be used in preparing the financial statements.

DEMONSTRATION PROBLEM

Celia Pints opened We-Buy, You-Pay Shopping Services. For a fee that is based on the amount of research and shopping time required, Pints and her associates will shop for almost anything from groceries to home furnishings. Business is particularly heavy around Christmas and in early summer. The business operates from a rented store front. The associates receive a commission based on the revenues they produce and a mileage reimbursement for the use of their personal automobiles for shopping trips. Pints decided to use the following accounts to record transactions.

Assets	Owner's Equity
Cash	Celia Pints, Capital
Accounts Receivable	Celia Pints, Drawing
Office Equipment	Revenue
Computer Equipment	Shopping Fees
Liabilities	Expenses
Accounts Payable	Rent Expense
Notes Payable	Phone Expense
	Commissions Expense
	Utilities Expense
	Travel Expense

The following transactions are for the month of December 20--.

(a) Pints invested cash in the business, $30,000.
(b) Bought office equipment for $10,000. Paid $2,000 in cash and promised to pay the balance over the next four months.
(c) Paid rent for December, $500.
(d) Provided shopping services for customers on account, $5,200.
(e) Paid phone bill, $90.
(f) Borrowed cash from the bank by signing a note payable, $5,000.
(g) Bought a computer and printer, $4,800.
(h) Collected cash from customers for services performed on account, $4,000.
(i) Paid commissions to associates for revenues generated during the first half of the month, $3,500.
(j) Paid utility bill, $600.
(k) Paid cash on account for the office equipment purchased in transaction (b), $2,000.
(l) Earned shopping fees of $13,200: $6,000 in cash and $7,200 on account.
(m) Paid commissions to associates for last half of month, $7,000.
(n) Paid mileage reimbursements for the month, $1,500.
(o) Paid cash on note payable to bank, $1,000.
(p) Pints withdrew cash for personal use, $2,000.

REQUIRED

1. Enter the transactions for December in T accounts. Use the accounting equation as a guide for setting up the T accounts.
2. Foot the T accounts and determine their balances as necessary.
3. Prepare a trial balance of the accounts as of December 31 of the current year.
4. Prepare an income statement for the month ended December 31 of the current year.
5. Prepare a statement of owner's equity for the month ended December 31 of the current year.
6. Prepare a balance sheet as of December 31 of the current year.

SOLUTION 1, 2.

Assets		=	Liabilities		+	Owner's Equity	
Debit +	Credit −		Debit −	Credit +		Debit −	Credit +

Assets

Cash

Debit	Credit
(a) 30,000	(b) 2,000
(f) 5,000	(c) 500
(h) 4,000	(e) 90
(l) 6,000	(g) 4,800
45,000	(i) 3,500
	(j) 600
	(k) 2,000
	(m) 7,000
	(n) 1,500
	(o) 1,000
	(p) 2,000
	24,990
Bal. 20,010	

Accounts Receivable

Debit	Credit
(d) 5,200	(h) 4,000
(l) 7,200	
12,400	
Bal. 8,400	

Office Equipment

Debit	Credit
(b) 10,000	

Computer Equipment

Debit	Credit
(g) 4,800	

Liabilities

Accounts Payable

Debit	Credit
(k) 2,000	(b) 8,000
	Bal. 6,000

Notes Payable

Debit	Credit
(o) 1,000	(f) 5,000
	Bal. 4,000

Owner's Equity

Celia Pints, Capital

Debit	Credit
	(a) 30,000

Drawing		Expenses		Revenues	
Debit +	Credit −	Debit +	Credit −	Debit −	Credit +

Celia Pints, Drawing

Debit	Credit
(p) 2,000	

Rent Expense

Debit	Credit
(c) 500	

Phone Expense

Debit	Credit
(e) 90	

Commissions Expense

Debit	Credit
(i) 3,500	
(m) 7,000	
Bal. 10,500	

Utilities Expense

Debit	Credit
(j) 600	

Travel Expense

Debit	Credit
(n) 1,500	

Shopping Fees

Debit	Credit
	(d) 5,200
	(l) 13,200
	Bal. 18,400

$43,210 = $10,000 + $33,210

$43,210 = **$43,210**

SOLUTION 3.

We-Buy, You-Pay Shopping Services
Trial Balance
December 31, 20 --

ACCOUNT TITLE	DEBIT BALANCE	CREDIT BALANCE
Cash	20,010.00	
Accounts Receivable	8,400.00	
Office Equipment	10,000.00	
Computer Equipment	4,800.00	
Accounts Payable		6,000.00
Notes Payable		4,000.00
Celia Pints, Capital		30,000.00
Celia Pints, Drawing	2,000.00	
Shopping Fees		18,400.00
Rent Expense	500.00	
Phone Expense	90.00	
Commissions Expense	10,500.00	
Utilities Expense	600.00	
Travel Expense	1,500.00	
	58,400.00	58,400.00

SOLUTION 4.

We-Buy, You-Pay Shopping Services
Income Statement
For Month Ended December 31, 20 --

Revenue:		
Shopping fees		$18,400
Expenses:		
Commissions expense	$10,500	
Travel expense	1,500	
Utilities expense	600	
Rent expense	500	
Phone expense	90	
Total expenses		13,190
Net income		$ 5,210

SOLUTION 5.

We-Buy, You-Pay Shopping Services
Statement of Owner's Equity
For Month Ended December 31, 20 --

Celia Pints, capital, December 1, 20 --		$ —
Investments during December		30,000
Total investment		$30,000
Net income for December	$5,210	
Less withdrawals for December	2,000	
Increase in capital		3,210
Celia Pints, capital, December 31, 20 --		$33,210

SOLUTION 6.

We-Buy, You-Pay Shopping Services
Balance Sheet
December 31, 20 --

Assets		Liabilities	
Cash	$20,010	Accounts payable	$ 6,000
Accounts receivable	8,400	Notes payable	4,000
Office equipment	10,000	Total liabilities	$10,000
Computer equipment	4,800		
		Owner's Equity	
		Celia Pints, capital	33,210
Total assets	$43,210	Total liabilities and owner's equity	$43,210

KEY TERMS

balance (51) The difference between the footings of an account.

credit (52) To enter an amount on the right side of an account.

credit balance (54) The normal balance of liability, owner's equity, and revenue accounts.

debit (52) To enter an amount on the left side of an account.

debit balance (54) The normal balance of asset, expense, and drawing accounts.

double-entry accounting (51) A system in which each transaction has a dual effect on the accounting elements.

footings (51) The total dollar amounts on the debit and credit sides of an account.

normal balance (54) The side of an account that is increased.

trial balance (67) A list of all accounts, showing the title and balance of each account, used to prove that the sum of the debits equals the sum of the credits.

SELF-STUDY TEST QUESTIONS

True/False

1. **LO3** To debit an account is to enter an amount on the left side of the account.
2. **LO3** Liability accounts normally have debit balances.
3. **LO3** Increases in owner's equity are entered as credits.
4. **LO3** Revenue accounts normally have debit balances.
5. **LO3** To credit an account is to enter an amount on the right side of the account.
6. **LO3** A debit to an asset account will decrease it.

Multiple Choice

1. **LO3** A common example of an asset is
   (a) Professional Fees.
   (b) Rent Expense.
   (c) Accounts Receivable.
   (d) Accounts Payable.
2. **LO3** The accounting equation may be expressed as
   (a) Assets = Liabilities − Owner's Equity.
   (b) Assets = Liabilities + Owner's Equity.
   (c) Liabilities = Owner's Equity − Assets.
   (d) all of the above.
3. **LO3** Liability, owner's equity, and revenue accounts normally have
   (a) debit balances.
   (b) large balances.
   (c) negative balances.
   (d) credit balances.
4. **LO4** To record the payment of rent expense, an accountant would
   (a) debit Cash; credit Rent Expense.
   (b) debit Rent Expense; debit Cash.
   (c) debit Rent Expense; credit Cash.
   (d) credit Rent Expense; credit Cash.
5. **LO4** An investment of cash by the owner will
   (a) increase assets and owner's equity.
   (b) increase assets and liabilities.
   (c) increase liabilities and owner's equity.
   (d) increase owner's equity and decrease liabilities.

CHECKPOINT ✓

Checkpoint Exercises

1. **LO2** Foot and balance the accounts receivable T account shown below.

Accounts Receivable

Debit	Credit
100	50
200	30

2. **LO3** Complete the following questions using either "debit" or "credit":

   (a) The asset account Supplies is increased with a __________.
   (b) The owner's capital account is increased with a __________.
   (c) The rent expense account is increased with a __________.

3. **LO4** Analyze the following transaction using the T accounts provided below. Robb Todd purchased equipment for $300 cash.

Cash

Equipment

4. **LO5** The following accounts have normal balances. Prepare a trial balance. Accounts Payable, $20; Accounts Receivable, $90; Capital, $40; Sales, $200; Cash, $100; Rent Expense, $70.

The answers to the Self-Study Test Questions are at the end of the chapter (page 84).

APPLYING YOUR KNOWLEDGE

CengageNowv2 provides "Show Me How" videos for selected exercises and problems. Additional resources, such as Excel templates for completing selected exercises and problems, are available for download from the companion website at Cengage.com.

REVIEW QUESTIONS

LO1 1. What are the three major parts of a T account?

LO1 2. What is the left side of the T account called? the right side?

LO2 3. What is a footing?

LO3 4. What is the relationship between the revenue and expense accounts and the owner's equity account?

LO5 5. What is the function of the trial balance?

SERIES A EXERCISES

E 3-1A (LO2)
✓ Cash bal.: $1,200 (Dr.)

FOOT AND BALANCE A T ACCOUNT Foot and balance the cash T account shown below.

Cash

Debit	Credit
500	100
400	200
600	

E 3-2A (LO3)

DEBIT AND CREDIT ANALYSIS Complete the following statements using either "debit" or "credit":

(a) The cash account is increased with a ______________.
(b) The owner's capital account is increased with a ______________.
(c) The delivery equipment account is increased with a ______________.
(d) The cash account is decreased with a ______________.
(e) The liability account Accounts Payable is increased with a ______________.
(f) The revenue account Delivery Fees is increased with a ______________.
(g) The asset account Accounts Receivable is increased with a ______________.
(h) The rent expense account is increased with a ______________.
(i) The owner's drawing account is increased with a ______________.

E 3-3A (LO2/3/4)
✓ Cash bal. after (c): $3,100 (Dr.)

ANALYSIS OF T ACCOUNTS Richard Gibbs began a business called Richard's Shoe Repair.

1. Create T accounts for Cash; Supplies; Richard Gibbs, Capital; and Utilities Expense. Identify the following transactions by letter and place them on the proper side of the T accounts:
   (a) Invested cash in the business, $6,500.
   (b) Purchased supplies for cash, $700.
   (c) Paid utility bill, $2,700.
2. Foot the T account for cash and enter the ending balance.

E 3-4A (LO3)

NORMAL BALANCE OF ACCOUNT Indicate the normal balance (debit or credit) for each of the following accounts:

1. Cash
2. Wages Expense
3. Accounts Payable
4. Owner's Drawing
5. Supplies
6. Owner's Capital
7. Equipment

E 3-5A (LO4)

TRANSACTION ANALYSIS Linda Kipp started a business on May 1, 20--. Analyze the following transactions for the first month of business using T accounts. Label each T account with the title of the account affected and then place the transaction letter and the dollar amount on the debit or credit side.

(a) Invested cash in the business, $5,000.
(b) Bought equipment for cash, $700.
(c) Bought equipment on account, $600.
(d) Paid cash on account for equipment purchased in transaction (c), $400.
(e) Withdrew cash for personal use, $900.

E 3-6A (LO2)
✓ Cash bal. after (e): $3,000 (Dr.)

FOOT AND BALANCE T ACCOUNTS Foot and balance the T accounts prepared in Exercise 3-5A if necessary.

E 3-7A (LO2/4)
✓ Cash bal. after (k): $24,400 (Dr.)

ANALYSIS OF TRANSACTIONS Charles Chadwick opened a business called Charlie's Detective Service in January 20--. Set up T accounts for the following accounts: Cash; Accounts Receivable; Office Supplies; Computer Equipment; Office Furniture; Accounts Payable; Charles Chadwick, Capital; Charles Chadwick, Drawing; Professional Fees; Rent Expense; and Utilities Expense.

The following transactions occurred during the first month of business. Record these transactions in T accounts. After all transactions are recorded, foot and balance the accounts if necessary.

(a) Invested cash in the business, $30,000.
(b) Bought office supplies for cash, $300.
(c) Bought office furniture for cash, $5,000.
(d) Purchased computer and printer on account, $8,000.
(e) Received cash from clients for services, $3,000.
(f) Paid cash on account for computer and printer purchased in transaction (d), $4,000.
(g) Earned professional fees on account during the month, $9,000.
(h) Paid cash for office rent for January, $1,500.
(i) Paid utility bills for the month, $800.
(j) Received cash from clients billed in transaction (g), $6,000.
(k) Withdrew cash for personal use, $3,000.

E 3-8A (LO5)
✓ Trial bal. total debits: $46,000

TRIAL BALANCE Based on the transactions recorded in Exercise 3-7A, prepare a trial balance for Charlie's Detective Service as of January 31, 20--.

E 3-9A (LO5)
✓ Trial bal. total debits: $42,800

TRIAL BALANCE The following accounts have normal balances. Prepare a trial balance for Kenny's Lawn Service as of September 30, 20--.

Cash	$10,000
Accounts Receivable	6,000
Supplies	1,600
Prepaid Insurance	1,200
Mowing Equipment	16,000
Accounts Payable	4,000
Kenny Young, Capital	20,000
Kenny Young, Drawing	2,000
Mowing Fees	18,800
Wages Expense	4,200
Rent Expense	1,800

E 3-10A, E 3-11A, E 3-12A

Provided below is a trial balance for Juanita's Delivery Service. **Use this trial balance for Exercises 3-10A, 3-11A, and 3-12A.**

Juanita's Delivery Service
Trial Balance
September 30, 20 --

ACCOUNT TITLE	DEBIT BALANCE	CREDIT BALANCE
Cash	5 000 00	
Accounts Receivable	3 000 00	
Supplies	800 00	
Prepaid Insurance	600 00	
Delivery Equipment	8 000 00	
Accounts Payable		2 000 00
Juanita Raye, Capital		10 000 00
Juanita Raye, Drawing	1 000 00	
Delivery Fees		9 400 00
Wages Expense	2 100 00	
Rent Expense	900 00	
	21 400 00	21 400 00

E 3-10A (LO5)
✓ Net income: $6,400

INCOME STATEMENT From the information in the trial balance presented above, prepare an income statement for Juanita's Delivery Service for the month ended September 30, 20--.

E 3-11A (LO5)
✓ Capital, 9/30: $15,400

STATEMENT OF OWNER'S EQUITY From the information in the trial balance presented above, prepare a statement of owner's equity for Juanita's Delivery Service for the month ended September 30, 20--. Assume this is not the first month of operations and the owner did not invest in the business during September.

E 3-12A (LO5)
✓ Total assets, 9/30: $17,400

BALANCE SHEET From the information in the trial balance presented for Juanita's Delivery Service on page 76, prepare a balance sheet for Juanita's Delivery Service as of September 30, 20--.

SERIES A PROBLEMS

P 3-13A (LO2/4/5)
✓ Cash bal. after (p): $21,805 (Dr.)
✓ Trial bal. total debits: $44,900

T ACCOUNTS AND TRIAL BALANCE Wilhelm Kohl started a business in May 20-- called Kohl's Home Repair. Kohl hired a part-time college student as an assistant. Kohl has decided to use the following accounts for recording transactions:

Assets
- Cash
- Accounts Receivable
- Office Supplies
- Prepaid Insurance
- Equipment
- Van

Liabilities
- Accounts Payable

Owner's Equity
- Wilhelm Kohl, Capital
- Wilhelm Kohl, Drawing

Revenue
- Service Fees

Expenses
- Rent Expense
- Wages Expense
- Phone Expense
- Gas and Oil Expense

The following transactions occurred during May:

(a) Invested cash in the business, $25,000.
(b) Purchased a used van for cash, $6,000.
(c) Purchased equipment on account, $4,000.
(d) Received cash for services rendered, $7,500.
(e) Paid cash on account owed from transaction (c), $2,300.
(f) Paid rent for the month, $850.
(g) Paid phone bill, $230.
(h) Earned revenue on account, $4,500.
(i) Purchased office supplies for cash, $160.
(j) Paid wages to an assistant, $800.
(k) Purchased a one-year insurance policy, $1,100.
(l) Received cash from services performed in transaction (h), $3,400.
(m) Paid cash for gas and oil expense on the van, $155.
(n) Purchased additional equipment for $4,200, paying $1,500 cash and spreading the remaining payments over the next 10 months.
(o) Earned service fees for the remainder of the month of $3,500: $1,900 in cash and $1,600 on account.
(p) Withdrew cash at the end of the month, $2,900.

REQUIRED

1. Enter the transactions in T accounts, identifying each transaction with its corresponding letter.
2. Foot and balance the accounts where necessary.
3. Prepare a trial balance as of May 31, 20--.

P 3-14A (LO5)
✓ Net income: $13,465
✓ Owner's equity, 5/31: $35,565
✓ Total assets, 5/31: $39,965

NET INCOME AND CHANGE IN OWNER'S EQUITY Refer to the trial balance of Kohl's Home Repair in Problem 3-13A to determine the following information. Use the format provided below.

1. a. Total revenue for the month ________
   b. Total expenses for the month ________
   c. Net income for the month ________
2. a. Wilhelm Kohl's original investment in the business ________
   + Net income for the month ________
   − Owner's drawing ________
   Increase (decrease) in capital ________
   = Ending owner's equity ________
   b. End of month accounting equation:

Assets	=	Liabilities	+	Owner's Equity
________	=	________	+	________

P 3-15A (LO5)
✓ NI: $13,465
✓ Capital, 5/31/20--: $35,565
✓ Total assets 5/31/20--: $39,965

FINANCIAL STATEMENTS Refer to the trial balance in Problem 3-13A and to the analysis of the change in owner's equity in Problem 3-14A.

REQUIRED

1. Prepare an income statement for Kohl's Home Repair for the month ended May 31, 20--.
2. Prepare a statement of owner's equity for Kohl's Home Repair for the month ended May 31, 20--.
3. Prepare a balance sheet for Kohl's Home Repair as of May 31, 20--.

SERIES B EXERCISES

E 3-1B (LO2)
✓ Accts. Pay: $400 (Cr.)

FOOT AND BALANCE A T ACCOUNT Foot and balance the accounts payable T account shown below.

Accounts Payable	
300	450
250	350
	150

E 3-2B (LO3)

DEBIT AND CREDIT ANALYSIS Complete the following statements using either "debit" or "credit":

(a) The asset account Prepaid Insurance is increased with a ________.
(b) The owner's drawing account is increased with a ________.

(c) The asset account Accounts Receivable is decreased with a ________.
(d) The liability account Accounts Payable is decreased with a ________.
(e) The owner's capital account is increased with a ________.
(f) The revenue account Professional Fees is increased with a ________.
(g) The expense account Repair Expense is increased with a ________.
(h) The asset account Cash is decreased with a ________.
(i) The asset account Delivery Equipment is decreased with a ________.

E 3-3B (LO2/3/4)
✓ Cash bal. after (c): $3,900 (Dr.)

ANALYSIS OF T ACCOUNTS Roberto Alvarez began a business called Roberto's Fix-It Shop.

1. Create T accounts for Cash; Supplies; Roberto Alvarez, Capital; and Utilities Expense. Identify the following transactions by letter and place them on the proper side of the T accounts:
   (a) Invested cash in the business, $6,000.
   (b) Purchased supplies for cash, $1,200.
   (c) Paid utility bill, $900.
2. Foot the T account for cash and enter the ending balance.

E 3-4B (LO3)

NORMAL BALANCE OF ACCOUNT Indicate the normal balance (debit or credit) for each of the following accounts:

1. Cash
2. Rent Expense
3. Notes Payable
4. Owner's Drawing
5. Accounts Receivable
6. Owner's Capital
7. Tools

E 3-5B (LO4)

TRANSACTION ANALYSIS George Atlas started a business on June 1, 20--. Analyze the following transactions for the first month of business using T accounts. Label each T account with the title of the account affected and then place the transaction letter and the dollar amount on the debit or credit side.

(a) Invested cash in the business, $7,000.
(b) Purchased equipment for cash, $900.
(c) Purchased equipment on account, $1,500.
(d) Paid cash on account for equipment purchased in transaction (c), $800.
(e) Withdrew cash for personal use, $1,100.

E 3-6B (LO2)
✓ Cash bal. after (e): $4,200 (Dr.)

FOOT AND BALANCE T ACCOUNTS Foot and balance the T accounts prepared in Exercise 3-5B if necessary.

E 3-7B (LO2/4)
✓ Cash bal. after (k): $9,000 (Dr.)

ANALYSIS OF TRANSACTIONS Nicole Lawrence opened a business called Nickie's Neat Ideas in January 20--. Set up T accounts for the following accounts: Cash; Accounts Receivable; Office Supplies; Computer Equipment; Office Furniture; Accounts Payable; Nicole Lawrence, Capital; Nicole Lawrence, Drawing; Professional Fees; Rent Expense; and Utilities Expense.

The following transactions occurred during the first month of business. Record these transactions in T accounts. After all transactions have been recorded, foot and balance the accounts if necessary.

(a) Invested cash in the business, $18,000.
(b) Purchased office supplies for cash, $500.
(c) Purchased office furniture for cash, $8,000.
(d) Purchased computer and printer on account, $5,000.
(e) Received cash from clients for services, $4,000.
(f) Paid cash on account for computer and printer purchased in transaction (d), $2,000.
(g) Earned professional fees on account during the month, $7,000.
(h) Paid office rent for January, $900.
(i) Paid utility bills for the month, $600.
(j) Received cash from clients that were billed previously in transaction (g), $3,000.
(k) Withdrew cash for personal use, $4,000.

E 3-8B (LO5)
✓ Trial bal. total debits: $32,000

TRIAL BALANCE Based on the transactions recorded in Exercise 3-7B, prepare a trial balance for Nickie's Neat Ideas as of January 31, 20--.

E 3-9B (LO5)
✓ Trial bal. total debits: $55,000

TRIAL BALANCE The following accounts have normal balances. Prepare a trial balance for Betty's Cleaning Service as of September 30, 20--.

Cash	$14,000	Betty Par, Capital	$24,000
Accounts Receivable	8,000	Betty Par, Drawing	4,000
Supplies	1,200	Cleaning Fees	25,000
Prepaid Insurance	1,800	Wages Expense	6,000
Cleaning Equipment	18,000	Rent Expense	2,000
Accounts Payable	6,000		

E 3-10B, E 3-11B, E 3-12B

Provided below is a trial balance for Bill's Delivery Service. **Use this trial balance for Exercises 3-10B, 3-11B, and 3-12B.**

Bill's Delivery Service
Trial Balance
September 30, 20 --

ACCOUNT TITLE	DEBIT BALANCE	CREDIT BALANCE
Cash	7 0 0 0 00	
Accounts Receivable	4 0 0 0 00	
Supplies	6 0 0 00	
Prepaid Insurance	9 0 0 00	
Delivery Equipment	9 0 0 0 00	
Accounts Payable		3 0 0 0 00
Bill Swift, Capital		12 0 0 0 00
Bill Swift, Drawing	2 0 0 0 00	
Delivery Fees		12 5 0 0 00
Wages Expense	3 0 0 0 00	
Rent Expense	1 0 0 0 00	
	27 5 0 0 00	27 5 0 0 00

E 3-10B (LO5)
✓ Net income: $8,500

INCOME STATEMENT From the information in the trial balance presented above, prepare an income statement for Bill's Delivery Service for the month ended September 30, 20--.

3-11B (LO5)
✓ Capital, 9/30: $18,500

STATEMENT OF OWNER'S EQUITY From the information in the trial balance presented above, prepare a statement of owner's equity for Bill's Delivery Service for the month ended September 30, 20--. Assume this is not the first month of operations and the owner did not invest in the business during September.

E 3-12B (LO5)
✓ Total assets, 9/30: $21,500

BALANCE SHEET From the information in the trial balance presented for Bill's Delivery Service on page 80, prepare a balance sheet for Bill's Delivery Service as of September 30, 20--.

SERIES B PROBLEMS

P 3-13B (LO2/4/5)
✓ Cash bal. after (p): $20,200 (Dr.)
✓ Trial bal. total debits: $44,300

T ACCOUNTS AND TRIAL BALANCE Sue Jantz started a business in August 20-- called Jantz Plumbing Service. Jantz hired a part-time college student as an administrative assistant. Jantz has decided to use the following accounts:

Assets	Owner's Equity
Cash	Sue Jantz, Capital
Accounts Receivable	Sue Jantz, Drawing
Office Supplies	Revenue
Prepaid Insurance	Service Fees
Plumbing Equipment	Expenses
Van	Rent Expense
Liabilities	Wages Expense
Accounts Payable	Phone Expense
	Advertising Expense

The following transactions occurred during August:

(a) Invested cash in the business, $30,000.
(b) Purchased a used van for cash, $8,000.
(c) Purchased plumbing equipment on account, $4,000.
(d) Received cash for services rendered, $3,000.
(e) Paid cash on account owed from transaction (c), $1,000.
(f) Paid rent for the month, $700.
(g) Paid phone bill, $100.
(h) Earned revenue on account, $4,000.
(i) Purchased office supplies for cash, $300.
(j) Paid wages to student, $500.
(k) Purchased a one-year insurance policy, $800.
(l) Received cash from services performed in transaction (h), $3,000.
(m) Paid cash for advertising expense, $2,000.
(n) Purchased additional plumbing equipment for $2,000, paying $500 cash and spreading the remaining payments over the next six months.
(o) Earned revenue from services for the remainder of the month of $2,800: $1,100 in cash and $1,700 on account.
(p) Withdrew cash at the end of the month, $3,000.

REQUIRED

1. Enter the transactions in T accounts, identifying each transaction with its corresponding letter.
2. Foot and balance the accounts where necessary.
3. Prepare a trial balance as of August 31, 20--.

P 3-14B (LO5)
✓ Net income: $6,500
✓ Owner's equity, 8/31: $33,500
✓ Total assets, 8/31: $38,000

NET INCOME AND CHANGE IN OWNER'S EQUITY Refer to the trial balance of Jantz Plumbing Service in Problem 3-13B to determine the following information. Use the format provided below.

1. a. Total revenue for the month		______
b. Total expenses for the month		______
c. Net income for the month		______
2. a. Sue Jantz's original investment in the business		______
+ Net income for the month	______	
− Owner's drawing	______	
Increase (decrease) in capital		______
= Ending owner's equity		______

b. End of month accounting equation:

Assets	=	Liabilities	+	Owner's Equity
______	=	______	+	______

P 3-15B (LO5)
✓ NI: $6,500
✓ Capital, 8/31/20--: $33,500
✓ Total assets, 8/31/20--: $38,000

FINANCIAL STATEMENTS Refer to the trial balance in Problem 3-13B and to the analysis of the change in owner's equity in Problem 3-14B.

REQUIRED

1. Prepare an income statement for Jantz Plumbing Service for the month ended August 31, 20--.
2. Prepare a statement of owner's equity for Jantz Plumbing Service for the month ended August 31, 20--.
3. Prepare a balance sheet for Jantz Plumbing Service as of August 31, 20--.

CHECK LIST
- ☐ Managing
- ☐ Planning
- ☐ Drafting
- ☐ Break
- ☐ Revising
- ☐ Managing

MANAGING YOUR WRITING

Write a one-page memo to your instructor explaining how you could use the double-entry system to maintain records of your personal finances. What types of accounts would you use for the accounting elements?

✓ Cash bal. after (p): $1,980 (Dr.)
✓ Trial bal. debit total: $5,840
✓ Net income: $500
✓ Total assets: $4,300

MASTERY PROBLEM

Craig Fisher started a lawn service called Craig's Quick Cut to earn money over the summer months. Fisher has decided to use the following accounts for recording transactions:

(continued)

Assets	Revenue
Cash	Lawn Fees
Accounts Receivable	Expenses
Mowing Equipment	Rent Expense
Lawn Tools	Wages Expense
Liabilities	Phone Expense
Accounts Payable	Gas and Oil Expense
Notes Payable	Transportation Expense
Owner's Equity	
Craig Fisher, Capital	
Craig Fisher, Drawing	

Transactions for the month of June are listed below.

(a) Invested cash in the business, $3,000.

(b) Bought mowing equipment for $1,000: paid $200 in cash and promised to pay the balance over the next four months.

(c) Paid garage rent for June, $50.

(d) Provided lawn services for customers on account, $520.

(e) Paid phone bill, $30.

(f) Borrowed cash from the bank by signing a note payable, $500.

(g) Bought lawn tools, $480.

(h) Collected cash from customers for services performed on account in transaction (d), $400.

(i) Paid associates for lawn work done during the first half of the month, $350.

(j) Paid for gas and oil for the equipment, $60.

(k) Paid cash on account for the mowing equipment purchased in transaction (b), $200.

(l) Earned lawn fees of $1,320: $600 in cash and $720 on account.

(m) Paid associates for last half of month, $700.

(n) Reimbursed associates for costs incurred using their own vehicles for transportation, $150.

(o) Paid on note payable to bank, $100.

(p) Withdrew cash for personal use, $200.

REQUIRED

1. Enter the transactions for June in T accounts. Use the accounting equation as a guide for setting up the T accounts.
2. Foot and balance the T accounts where necessary.
3. Prepare a trial balance of the accounts as of June 30, 20--.
4. Prepare an income statement for the month ended June 30, 20--.
5. Prepare a statement of owner's equity for the month ended June 30, 20--.
6. Prepare a balance sheet as of June 30, 20--.

This problem challenges you to apply your cumulative accounting knowledge to move a step beyond the material in the chapter.

✓ Capital, 8/31/20--: $600

CHALLENGE PROBLEM

Your friend Chris Stevick started a part-time business in June and has been keeping her own accounting records. She has been preparing monthly financial statements. At the end of August, she stopped by to show you her performance for the most recent month. She prepared the following income statement and balance sheet:

Income Statement		Balance Sheet	End of Month	Beginning of Month
Revenues	$500	Cash	$600	$400
Expenses	200	Capital	600	400
Net income	$300			

Chris has also heard that there is a statement of owner's equity, but she is not familiar with that statement. She asks if you can help her prepare one. After confirming that she has no assets other than cash, no liabilities, and made no additional investments in the business in August, you agree.

REQUIRED

1. Prepare the statement of owner's equity for your friend's most recent month.
2. What suggestions might you give to Chris that would make her income statement more useful?

ANSWERS TO SELF-STUDY TEST QUESTIONS

True/False

1. T
2. F (Liability accounts normally have credit balances.)
3. T
4. F (credit balances)
5. T
6. F (increase)

Multiple Choice

1. c 2. b 3. d 4. c 5. a

Checkpoint Exercises

1. Accounts Receivable

	Debit	Credit
	100	50
	200	30
	300	**80**
Bal.	220	

2. (a) The asset account Supplies is increased with a debit.
   (b) The owner's capital account is increased with a credit.
   (c) The rent expense account is increased with a debit.

3. Cash

Debit	Credit
	300

Equipment

Debit	Credit
300	

4. Trial Balance

Trial Balance		
Cash	100	
Accounts Receivable	90	
Accounts Payable		20
Capital		40
Sales		200
Rent Expense	70	
	260	260

Chapter 4 Journalizing and Posting Transactions

Campus Advantage (CA) provides a comprehensive range of student residential services in the following areas: management, development, acquisition, and consulting. It specializes in the creation of modern, full-service facilities that are secure, private, and equipped with all of the tools that today's students need for success. Its communities are no-hassle alternatives to dorm living with full dining service options. CA has facilities across the country, but each student residence reflects the unique identity of the school and community it serves. University Crossing, CA furnished, luxury, student apartments in Manhattan, Kansas, are just minutes from Kansas State University.

As with all businesses, CA relies on an accounting system to maintain a record of transactions from the source document through the preparation of the trial balance and financial statements. In this chapter, we discuss source documents, the chart of accounts, and the process used to journalize and post transactions. And, just in case an error is made, we address how to find and correct errors.

LEARNING OBJECTIVES

Careful study of this chapter should enable you to:

LO1 Describe the flow of data from source documents to the trial balance.

LO2 Describe and explain the purpose of source documents.

LO3 Describe the chart of accounts as a means of classifying financial information.

LO4 Journalize transactions.

LO5 Post to the general ledger and prepare a trial balance.

LO6 Explain how to find and correct errors.

The double-entry framework of accounting was explained and illustrated in Chapter 3. To demonstrate the use of debits and credits, business transactions were entered directly into T accounts. Now we will take a more detailed look at the procedures used to account for business transactions.

LO1

Flow of Data

Describe the flow of data from source documents to the trial balance.

This chapter traces the flow of financial data from the source documents through the accounting information system. This process includes the following steps:

1. Analyze what happened by using information from source documents and the firm's chart of accounts.
2. Enter business transactions in the general journal in the form of journal entries.
3. Post these journal entries to the accounts in the general ledger.
4. Prepare a trial balance.

The flow of data from the source documents through the preparation of a trial balance is shown in Figure 4-1.

FIGURE 4-1 Flow of Data from Source Documents through Trial Balance

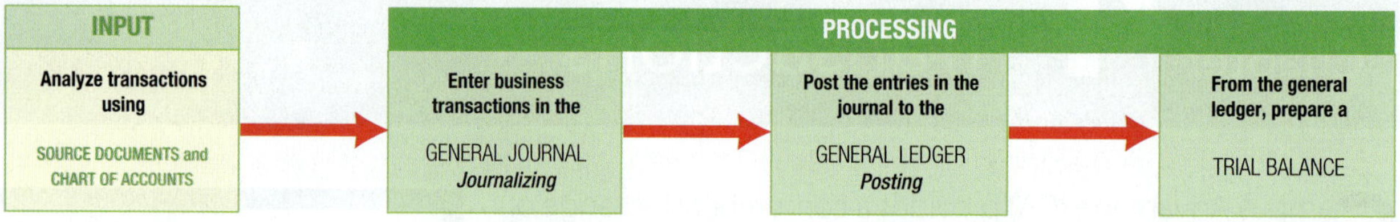

LO2

Source Documents

Describe and explain the purpose of source documents.

Almost any document that provides information about a business transaction can be called a **source document**. A source document triggers the analysis of what happened. It begins the process of entering transactions in the accounting system. Examples of source documents are shown in Figure 4-2. These source documents provide information that is useful in determining the effect of business transactions on specific accounts.

In addition to serving as input for transaction analysis, source documents serve as objective evidence of business transactions. If anyone questions the accounting records, these documents may be used as objective, verifiable evidence of the accuracy of the accounting records. For this reason, source documents are filed for possible future reference. *Having objective, verifiable evidence that a transaction occurred is an important accounting concept.*

FIGURE 4-2 Source Documents

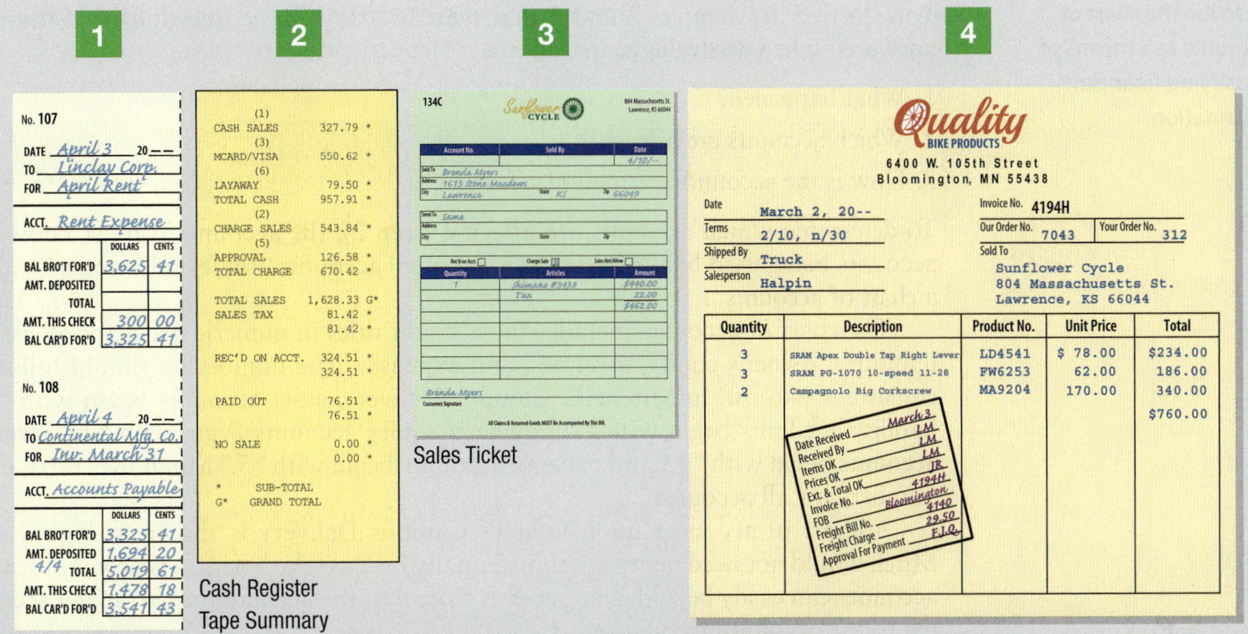

Check Stubs | Cash Register Tape Summary | Sales Ticket | Purchase Invoice

SOURCE DOCUMENTS	
Example	**Provides Information About**
1. Check stubs or copies of checks	Cash payments
2. Receipt stubs, copies of receipts, cash register tapes, or memos of cash register totals	Cash receipts
3. Copies of sales tickets or sales invoices issued to customers or clients	Sales of goods or services
4. Purchase invoices received from suppliers	Purchase of goods or services

A BROADER VIEW

Electronic Source Documents

With the ability to go shopping in cyberspace, more transactions are being initiated electronically. This means that more and more "source documents" will be in an electronic form.

SCOTT OLSON/GETTY IMAGES

CHECKPOINT

Complete Checkpoint-1 on page 113 to test your basic understanding of LO2.

LO3 The Chart of Accounts

Describe the chart of accounts as a means of classifying financial information.

You learned in Chapters 2 and 3 that there are three basic questions that must be answered when analyzing transactions.

1. What happened?
2. Which accounts are affected?
3. How is the accounting equation affected?

To determine which accounts are affected (step 2), the accountant must know the accounts being used by the business. A list of all accounts used by a business is called a **chart of accounts**.

The chart of accounts includes the account titles in numeric order for all assets, liabilities, owner's equity, revenues, and expenses. The numbering should follow a consistent pattern. In Mitchell's Campus Delivery, asset accounts begin with "1," liability accounts begin with "2," owner's equity accounts begin with "3," revenue accounts begin with "4," and expense accounts begin with "5." Mitch uses three-digit numbers for all accounts.

A chart of accounts for Mitchell's Campus Delivery is shown in Figure 4-3. Mitch would not need many accounts initially because the business is new. Additional accounts can easily be added as needed. Note that the accounts are arranged according to the accounting equation.

FIGURE 4-3 Chart of Accounts

MITCHELL'S CAMPUS DELIVERY
CHART OF ACCOUNTS

Assets	(100–199)	Revenues	(400–499)
101	Cash	401	Delivery Fees
122	Accounts Receivable		
141	Supplies	**Expenses**	**(500–599)**
145	Prepaid Insurance	511	Wages Expense
185	Delivery Equipment	521	Rent Expense
		525	Phone Expense
Liabilities	**(200–299)**		
202	Accounts Payable		
Owner's Equity	**(300–399)**		
311	Mitchell Williams, Capital		
312	Mitchell Williams, Drawing		

Assets begin with 1

Liabilities begin with 2

Owner's Equity begin with 3

Revenues begin with 4

Expenses begin with 5

LO4 The General Journal

Journalize transactions.

A day-by-day listing of the transactions of a business is called a **journal**. The purpose of a journal is to provide a record of all transactions completed by the business. The journal shows the date of each transaction, titles of the accounts to be debited and credited, and the amounts of the debits and credits.

A journal is commonly referred to as a **book of original entry** because it is here that the first formal accounting record of a transaction is made. Although many types of journals are used in business, the simplest journal form is a two-column general journal (Figure 4-4). Any kind of business transaction may be entered into a general journal.

A **two-column general journal** is so-named because it has only two amount columns, one for debit amounts and one for credit amounts. Journal pages are numbered in the upper right-hand corner. The five column numbers in Figure 4-4 are explained in Figure 4-5.

> **LEARNING KEY**
> A journal provides a day-by-day listing of all transactions completed by the business.

FIGURE 4-4 Two-Column General Journal

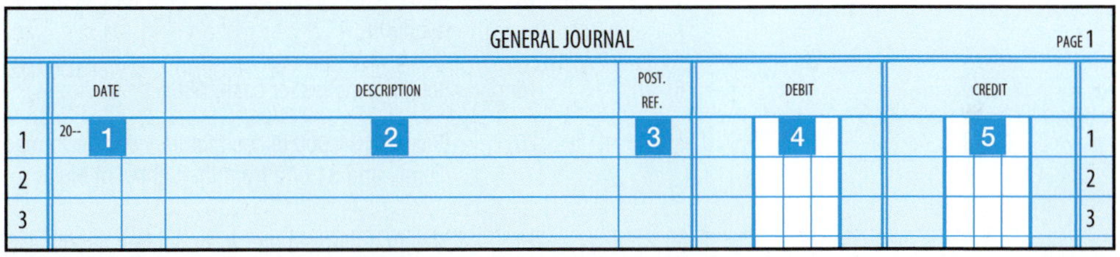

FIGURE 4-5 The Columns in a Two-Column General Journal

Column 1 Date	The year is entered in small figures at the top of the column immediately below the column heading. The year is repeated only at the top of each new page. The month is entered for the first entry on the page and for the first transaction of the month. The day of the month is recorded for every transaction, even if it is the same as the prior entry.
Column 2 Description	The *Description* or *Explanation* column is used to enter the titles of the accounts affected by each transaction and to provide a very brief description of the transaction. Each transaction affects two or more accounts. The account(s) to be debited are entered first at the extreme left of the column. The account(s) to be credited are listed after the debits and indented. The description should be entered immediately following the last credit entry with an additional indentation.
Column 3 Posting Reference	No entries are made in the *Posting Reference* column during journalizing. Entries are made in this column when the debits and credits are copied to the proper accounts in the ledger. This process will be explained in detail later in this chapter.
Column 4 Debit Amount	The *Debit amount column* is used to enter the amount to be debited to an account. The amount should be entered on the same line as the title of that account.
Column 5 Credit Amount	The *Credit amount column* is used to enter the amount to be credited to an account. The amount should be entered on the same line as the title of that account.

Journalizing

Entering the transactions day-by-day in a journal is called **journalizing**. For every transaction, the entry should include the date, the title of each account affected, the amounts, and a brief description.

To illustrate the journalizing process, transactions for the first month of operations of Mitchell's Campus Delivery will be journalized. The transactions are listed in Figure 4-6. Since you analyzed these transactions in Chapters 2 and 3, the journalizing process should be easier to understand. Let's start with a close look at the steps followed when journalizing the first transaction, Mitchell's initial investment of $5,000.

> **LEARNING KEY**
> When journalizing, the exact account titles shown in the chart of accounts must be used. Refer to the chart of accounts in Figure 4-3 as you review the entries for Mitchell's Campus Delivery.

FIGURE 4-6 Summary of Transactions

SUMMARY OF TRANSACTIONS
MITCHELL'S CAMPUS DELIVERY

Transaction		
(a)	June 1	Mitchell Williams invested cash in his business, $5,000.
(b)	3	Bought delivery equipment for cash, $2,000.
(c)	5	Bought delivery equipment on account from Big Red Scooters, $1,800.
(d)	6	Paid first installment from transaction (c) to Big Red Scooters, $600.
(e)	6	Received cash for delivery services rendered, $2,100.
(f)	7	Paid cash for June office rent, $1,000.
(g)	15	Paid phone bill, $100.
(h)	15	Made deliveries on account for a total of $2,400: Library ($400) and the School of Music ($2,000).
(i)	16	Bought supplies for cash, $80.
(j)	20	Received $1,900 in cash for services performed in transaction (h): $400 from the Library and $1,500 from the School of Music.
(k)	25	Bought a third scooter from Big Red Scooters, $1,000. Paid $300 cash, with the remaining payments expected over the next four months.
(l)	26	Paid cash for a seven-month liability insurance policy, $700. Coverage began on June 1.
(m)	27	Paid wages of part-time employees, $1,650.
(n)	30	Earned delivery fees for the remainder of the month amounting to $3,500. $900 in cash and $2,600 on account. Deliveries on account: Library ($250) and Athletic Ticket Office ($2,350).
(o)	30	Mitch withdrew cash for personal use, $3,000.

Transaction (a)

June 1 Mitchell Williams opened a bank account with a deposit of $5,000 for his business.

STEP 1 **Enter the date.** Since this is the first entry on the journal page, the year is entered on the first line of the Date column (in small print at the top of the line). The month and day are entered on the same line, below the year, in the Date column.

GENERAL JOURNAL — PAGE 1

	DATE		DESCRIPTION	POST. REF.	DEBIT	CREDIT	
1	20-- June	1					1
2							2

STEP 2 Enter the debit. Cash is entered on the first line at the extreme left of the Description column. The amount of the debit, $5,000, is entered on the same line in the Debit column. Since this is not a formal financial statement, dollar signs are not used.

In Chapter 3, we simply debited the T account.

Cash	
(a) 5,000	

GENERAL JOURNAL PAGE 1

	DATE		DESCRIPTION	POST. REF.	DEBIT	CREDIT	
1	20-- June	1	Cash		5 0 0 0 00		1
2							2

STEP 3 Enter the credit. The title of the account to be credited, Mitchell Williams, Capital, is entered on the second line, **indented one-half inch from the left side of the Description column.** The amount of the credit, $5,000, is entered on the same line in the Credit column.

In Chapter 3, we simply credited the T account.

Mitchell Williams, Capital	
	(a) 5,000

GENERAL JOURNAL PAGE 1

	DATE		DESCRIPTION	POST. REF.	DEBIT	CREDIT	
1	20-- June	1	Cash		5 0 0 0 00		1
2			Mitchell Williams, Capital			5 0 0 0 00	2

STEP 4 Enter the explanation. The explanation of the entry is entered on the next line, **indented an additional one-half inch.** The second line of the explanation, if needed, is also indented the same distance as the first.

GENERAL JOURNAL PAGE 1

	DATE		DESCRIPTION	POST. REF.	DEBIT	CREDIT	
1	20-- June	1	Cash		5 0 0 0 00		1
2			Mitchell Williams, Capital			5 0 0 0 00	2
3			Owner's original investment in				3
4			delivery business				4

Enter the next transaction. To enter transaction (b), the purchase of a motor scooter (delivery equipment) for $2,000 cash, we skip a line and follow the same four steps. Note that the month and year do not need to be repeated. The day of the month must, however, be entered.

GENERAL JOURNAL PAGE 1

	DATE		DESCRIPTION	POST. REF.	DEBIT	CREDIT	
1	20-- June	1	Cash		5 0 0 0 00		1
2			Mitchell Williams, Capital			5 0 0 0 00	2
3			Owner's original investment in				3
4			delivery business				4
5							5
6		3	Delivery Equipment		2 0 0 0 00		6
7			Cash			2 0 0 0 00	7
8			Purchased delivery equipment for cash				8

Skip a line → 5

The journal entries for the month of June are shown in Figure 4-7. Note that the entries on June 25 and June 30 affect more than two accounts. Entries requiring more than one debit and/or one credit are called **compound entries**. The entry on June 25 has two credits. The credits are listed after the debit, indented and listed one under the other. The entry on June 30 has two debits. They are aligned with the left margin of the Description column and listed one under the other. In both cases, the debits equal the credits.

FIGURE 4-7 General Journal Entries

List debits first.

List credits second and indented.

Explanation is third and indented.

Space to make entries easier to read. To prevent improper changes to entries, the extra spacing might not be used in practice.

GENERAL JOURNAL PAGE 1

DATE		DESCRIPTION	POST. REF.	DEBIT	CREDIT
20-- June	1	Cash		5 0 0 0 00	
		Mitchell Williams, Capital			5 0 0 0 00
		Owner's original investment in			
		delivery business			
	3	Delivery Equipment		2 0 0 0 00	
		Cash			2 0 0 0 00
		Purchased delivery equipment for cash			
	5	Delivery Equipment		1 8 0 0 00	
		Accounts Payable			1 8 0 0 00
		Purchased delivery equipment on account			
		from Big Red Scooters			
	6	Accounts Payable		6 0 0 00	
		Cash			6 0 0 00
		Made partial payment to Big Red Scooters			
	6	Cash		2 1 0 0 00	
		Delivery Fees			2 1 0 0 00
		Received cash for delivery services			
	7	Rent Expense		1 0 0 0 00	
		Cash			1 0 0 0 00
		Paid office rent for June			
	15	Phone Expense		1 0 0 00	
		Cash			1 0 0 00
		Paid phone bill for June			
	15	Accounts Receivable		2 4 0 0 00	
		Delivery Fees			2 4 0 0 00
		Deliveries made on account for			
		Library ($400) and School of Music ($2,000)			

(Continued)

FIGURE 4-7 General Journal Entries (*concluded*)

GENERAL JOURNAL PAGE 2

	DATE		DESCRIPTION	POST. REF.	DEBIT	CREDIT	
1	20-- June	16	Supplies		80 00		1
2			Cash			80 00	2
3			Purchased supplies for cash				3
4							4
5		20	Cash		1900 00		5
6			Accounts Receivable			1900 00	6
7			Received cash on account from				7
8			Library ($400) and School of Music ($1,500)				8
9							9
10		25	Delivery Equipment		1000 00		10
11			Accounts Payable			700 00	11
12			Cash			300 00	12
13			Purchased scooter with down payment;				13
14			balance on account with Big Red Scooters				14
15							15
16		26	Prepaid Insurance		700 00		16
17			Cash			700 00	17
18			Paid premium for seven-month				18
19			insurance policy				19
20							20
21		27	Wages Expense		1650 00		21
22			Cash			1650 00	22
23			Paid employees				23
24							24
25		30	Cash		900 00		25
26			Accounts Receivable		2600 00		26
27			Delivery Fees			3500 00	27
28			Deliveries made for cash and on account to				28
29			Library ($250) and				29
30			Athletic Ticket Office ($2,350)				30
31							31
32		30	Mitchell Williams, Drawing		3000 00		32
33			Cash			3000 00	33
34			Owner's withdrawal				34

Line up credits

Compound entry

Debits = Credits

Line up debits

Compound entry

Debits = Credits

CHECKPOINT

Complete Checkpoint-2 on page 113 to test your basic understanding of LO4.

LO5 The General Ledger

Post to the general ledger and prepare a trial balance.

The journal provides a day-by-day record of business transactions. To determine the current balance of specific accounts, however, the information in the journal must be transferred to accounts similar to the T accounts illustrated in Chapter 3. This process is called posting.

> **LEARNING KEY**
>
> While the *journal* provides a day-by-day record of business transactions, the *ledger* provides a record of the transactions entered in each account.

A complete set of all the accounts used by a business is known as the **general ledger**. The general ledger accumulates a complete record of the debits and credits made to each account as a result of entries made in the journal. The accounts are numbered and arranged in the same order as the chart of accounts. That is, accounts are numbered and grouped by classification: assets, liabilities, owner's equity, revenues, and expenses.

General Ledger Account

For purposes of illustration, the T account was introduced in Chapter 3. In practice, businesses are more likely to use a version of the account called the **general ledger account**. Figure 4-8 compares the cash T account from Chapter 3 for Mitchell's Campus Delivery and a general ledger account summarizing the same cash transactions.

> A three-column account with just one column for the normal balance also may be used.

A four-column general ledger account contains columns for the debit or credit transaction and columns for the debit or credit running balance. In addition, there are columns for the date, description of the item, and posting reference.

The Item column is used to provide descriptions of special entries. For example, "Balance" is written in this column when the balance of an account is transferred to a new page. In addition, "Correcting," "Adjusting," "Closing," or "Reversing" may be written in this column when these types of entries are made. Correcting entries are described later in the chapter. Adjusting, closing, and reversing entries are illustrated in Chapters 5, 6, and 15, respectively.

The Posting Reference (Post. Ref.) column is used to indicate the journal page from which an entry was posted, or a check mark (✓) is inserted to indicate that no posting was required.

As shown in Figure 4-8, the primary advantage of the T account is that the debit and credit sides of the account are easier to identify. Thus, for demonstration purposes

FIGURE 4-8 Comparison of T Account and General Ledger Account

Cash

Debit		Credit	
(a)	5,000	(b)	2,000
(e)	2,100	(d)	600
(j)	1,900	(f)	1,000
(n)	900	(g)	100
	9,900	(i)	80
		(k)	300
		(l)	700
		(m)	1,650
		(o)	3,000
Bal.	470		*9,430*

GENERAL LEDGER

ACCOUNT: Cash ACCOUNT NO. 101

DATE		ITEM	POST. REF.	DEBIT	CREDIT	BALANCE DEBIT	BALANCE CREDIT
20-- June	1			5,000.00		5,000.00	
	3				2,000.00	3,000.00	
	6				600.00	2,400.00	
	6			2,100.00		4,500.00	
	7				1,000.00	3,500.00	
	15				100.00	3,400.00	
	16				80.00	3,320.00	
	20			1,900.00		5,220.00	
	25				300.00	4,920.00	
	26				700.00	4,220.00	
	27				1,650.00	2,570.00	
	30			900.00		3,470.00	
	30				3,000.00	470.00	

Transaction Amount (Debit and Credit columns) — Running Balance (Balance columns)

LEARNING KEY

Although similar to a T account, the general ledger account keeps a running balance.

and analyzing what happened, T accounts are very helpful. However, computing the balance of a T account is cumbersome. The primary advantage of the general ledger account is that it maintains a running balance.

Note that the heading for the general ledger account has the account title and an account number. The account number is taken from the chart of accounts and is used in the posting process.

Posting to the General Ledger

LEARNING KEY

Posting is simply the process of copying the exact dates and dollar amounts from the journal to the correct ledger accounts.

The process of copying the debits and credits from the journal to the ledger accounts is known as **posting**. All amounts entered in the journal must be posted to the general ledger accounts. Posting from the journal to the ledger is done daily or at frequent intervals.

To illustrate the posting process, the first journal entry for Mitchell's Campus Delivery will be posted step by step. There are five steps in the process of posting each debit and credit. First, let's post the debit to Cash (Figure 4-9).

FIGURE 4-9 Posting a Debit

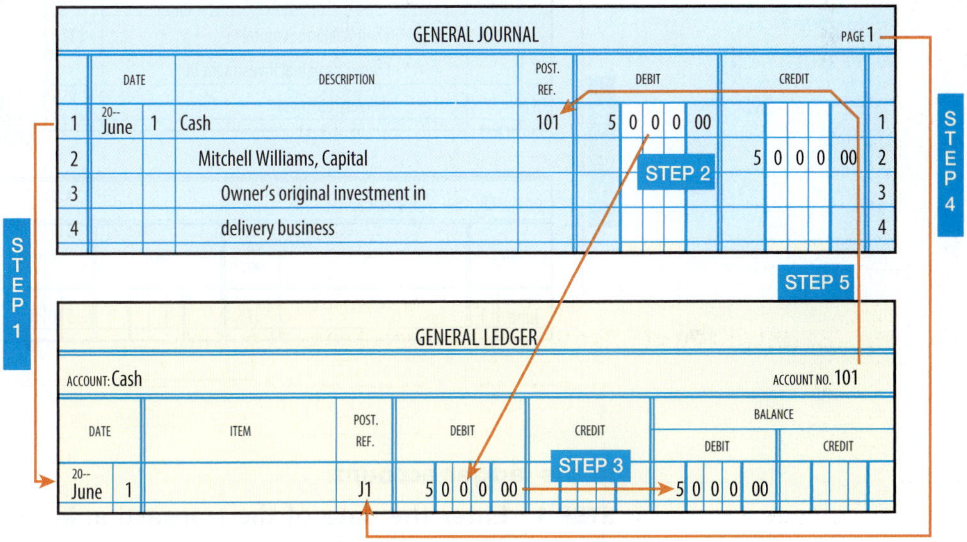

In the ledger account:

STEP 1 **Enter the date of the transaction in the Date column.** Enter the year, "20--," the month, "June," and the day, "1," in the Date column of the cash account.

STEP 2 **Enter the debit.** Copy the $5,000 debit to Cash in the journal to the Debit column of the ledger. Since this is not a formal financial statement, dollar signs are not used.

STEP 3 **Enter the balance of the account.** Enter the $5,000 balance in the Balance columns under Debit. (If the balance of the account is zero, draw a line through the Debit and Credit columns.)

STEP 4 **Enter the journal page in the Posting Reference column.** Enter "J1" in the Posting Reference column since the posting came from page 1 of the journal.

The Item column is left blank, except for special reasons such as indicating the beginning balance, adjusting, correcting, closing, or reversing entries.

LEARNING KEY

Posting references indicate that a journal entry has been posted to the general ledger.

In the journal:

STEP 5 Enter the ledger account number in the Posting Reference column. Enter the account number for Cash, 101 (see chart of accounts in Figure 4-3 on page 88), in the Posting Reference column of the journal on the same line as the debit to Cash for $5,000.

Step 5 is the last step in the posting process. After this step is completed, the posting references will indicate which journal entries have been posted to the ledger accounts. This is very helpful, particularly if you are interrupted during the posting process. The information in the Posting Reference columns of the journal and ledger provides a link between the journal and ledger known as a cross-reference.

Now let's post the credit portion of the first entry (Figure 4-10).

FIGURE 4-10 Posting a Credit

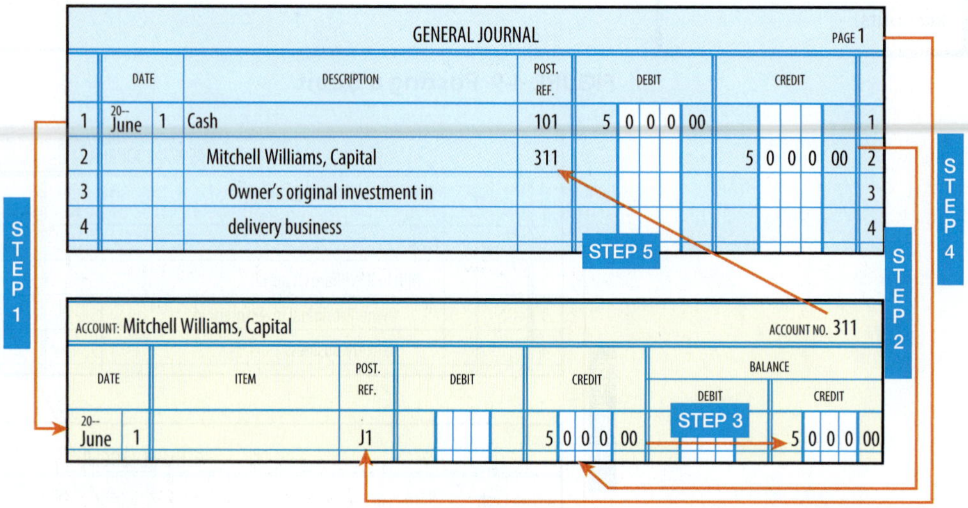

In the ledger account:

STEP 1 Enter the date of the transaction in the Date column. Enter the year, "20--," the month, "June," and the day, "1," in the Date column of the account Mitchell Williams, Capital.

STEP 2 Enter the credit. Copy the $5,000 credit to Mitchell Williams, Capital in the journal to the Credit column in the ledger.

STEP 3 Enter the balance of the account. Enter the $5,000 balance in the Balance columns under Credit. (If the balance of the account is zero, draw a line through the Debit and Credit columns.)

STEP 4 Enter the journal page in the Posting Reference column. Enter "J1" in the Posting Reference column since the posting came from page 1 of the journal.

The Item column is left blank, except for special reasons such as indicating the beginning balance, adjusting, correcting, closing, or reversing entries.

In the journal:

STEP 5 Enter the ledger account number in the Posting Reference column. Enter the account number for Mitchell Williams, Capital, 311, in the Posting Reference column. Again, this last step indicates that the credit has been posted to the general ledger.

After posting the journal entries for Mitchell's Campus Delivery for the month of June, the general journal and general ledger should appear as illustrated in Figures 4-11 and 4-12 on pages 97–100. *Note that the Posting Reference column of the journal has been filled in because the entries have been posted.*

FIGURE 4-11 General Journal After Posting

GENERAL JOURNAL PAGE 1

	DATE		DESCRIPTION	POST. REF.	DEBIT	CREDIT	
1	20-- June	1	Cash	101	5000 00		1
2			Mitchell Williams, Capital	311		5000 00	2
3			Owner's original investment in				3
4			delivery business				4
5							5
6		3	Delivery Equipment	185	2000 00		6
7			Cash	101		2000 00	7
8			Purchased delivery equipment for cash				8
9							9
10		5	Delivery Equipment	185	1800 00		10
11			Accounts Payable	202		1800 00	11
12			Purchased delivery equipment on account				12
13			from Big Red Scooters				13
14							14
15		6	Accounts Payable	202	600 00		15
16			Cash	101		600 00	16
17			Made partial payment to Big Red Scooters				17
18							18
19		6	Cash	101	2100 00		19
20			Delivery Fees	401		2100 00	20
21			Received cash for delivery services				21
22							22
23		7	Rent Expense	521	1000 00		23
24			Cash	101		1000 00	24
25			Paid office rent for June				25
26							26
27		15	Phone Expense	525	100 00		27
28			Cash	101		100 00	28
29			Paid phone bill for June				29
30							30
31		15	Accounts Receivable	122	2400 00		31
32			Delivery Fees	401		2400 00	32
33			Deliveries made on account for				33
34			Library ($400) and School of Music ($2,000)				34
35							35

FIGURE 4-11 General Journal After Posting (*concluded*)

GENERAL JOURNAL PAGE 2

DATE		DESCRIPTION	POST. REF.	DEBIT	CREDIT
20-- June	16	Supplies	141	80 00	
		Cash	101		80 00
		Purchased supplies for cash			
	20	Cash	101	1900 00	
		Accounts Receivable	122		1900 00
		Received cash on account from			
		Library ($400) and School of Music ($1,500)			
	25	Delivery Equipment	185	1000 00	
		Accounts Payable	202		700 00
		Cash	101		300 00
		Purchased scooter with down payment;			
		balance on account with Big Red Scooters			
	26	Prepaid Insurance	145	700 00	
		Cash	101		700 00
		Paid premium for seven-month			
		insurance policy			
	27	Wages Expense	511	1650 00	
		Cash	101		1650 00
		Paid employees			
	30	Cash	101	900 00	
		Accounts Receivable	122	2600 00	
		Delivery Fees	401		3500 00
		Deliveries made for cash and on account to			
		Library ($250) and			
		Athletic Ticket Office ($2,350)			
	30	Mitchell Williams, Drawing	312	3000 00	
		Cash	101		3000 00
		Owner's withdrawal			

FIGURE 4-12 General Ledger After Posting

GENERAL LEDGER

ACCOUNT: Cash ACCOUNT NO. 101

DATE		ITEM	POST. REF.	DEBIT	CREDIT	BALANCE DEBIT	BALANCE CREDIT
20-- June	1		J1	5,000.00		5,000.00	
	3		J1		2,000.00	3,000.00	
	6		J1		600.00	2,400.00	
	6		J1	2,100.00		4,500.00	
	7		J1		1,000.00	3,500.00	
	15		J1		100.00	3,400.00	
	16		J2		80.00	3,320.00	
	20		J2	1,900.00		5,220.00	
	25		J2		300.00	4,920.00	
	26		J2		700.00	4,220.00	
	27		J2		1,650.00	2,570.00	
	30		J2	900.00		3,470.00	
	30		J2		3,000.00	470.00	

For asset, expense, and drawing accounts, a running balance is maintained by adding the debit or subtracting the credit from the previous balance.

ACCOUNT: Accounts Receivable ACCOUNT NO. 122

DATE		ITEM	POST. REF.	DEBIT	CREDIT	BALANCE DEBIT	BALANCE CREDIT
20-- June	15		J1	2,400.00		2,400.00	
	20		J2		1,900.00	500.00	
	30		J2	2,600.00		3,100.00	

ACCOUNT: Supplies ACCOUNT NO. 141

DATE		ITEM	POST. REF.	DEBIT	CREDIT	BALANCE DEBIT	BALANCE CREDIT
20-- June	16		J2	80.00		80.00	

ACCOUNT: Prepaid Insurance ACCOUNT NO. 145

DATE		ITEM	POST. REF.	DEBIT	CREDIT	BALANCE DEBIT	BALANCE CREDIT
20-- June	26		J2	700.00		700.00	

ACCOUNT: Delivery Equipment ACCOUNT NO. 185

DATE		ITEM	POST. REF.	DEBIT	CREDIT	BALANCE DEBIT	BALANCE CREDIT
20-- June	3		J1	2,000.00		2,000.00	
	5		J1	1,800.00		3,800.00	
	25		J2	1,000.00		4,800.00	

FIGURE 4-12 General Ledger After Posting (*concluded*)

ACCOUNT: Accounts Payable — ACCOUNT NO. 202

DATE		ITEM	POST. REF.	DEBIT	CREDIT	BALANCE DEBIT	BALANCE CREDIT
20-- June	5		J1		1 8 0 0 00		1 8 0 0 00
	6		J1	6 0 0 00			1 2 0 0 00
	25		J2		7 0 0 00		1 9 0 0 00

For liability, revenue, and capital accounts, a running balance is maintained by adding the credit or subtracting the debit from the previous balance.

ACCOUNT: Mitchell Williams, Capital — ACCOUNT NO. 311

DATE		ITEM	POST. REF.	DEBIT	CREDIT	BALANCE DEBIT	BALANCE CREDIT
20-- June	1		J1		5 0 0 0 00		5 0 0 0 00

ACCOUNT: Mitchell Williams, Drawing — ACCOUNT NO. 312

DATE		ITEM	POST. REF.	DEBIT	CREDIT	BALANCE DEBIT	BALANCE CREDIT
20-- June	30		J2	3 0 0 0 00		3 0 0 0 00	

ACCOUNT: Delivery Fees — ACCOUNT NO. 401

DATE		ITEM	POST. REF.	DEBIT	CREDIT	BALANCE DEBIT	BALANCE CREDIT
20-- June	6		J1		2 1 0 0 00		2 1 0 0 00
	15		J1		2 4 0 0 00		4 5 0 0 00
	30		J2		3 5 0 0 00		8 0 0 0 00

ACCOUNT: Wages Expense — ACCOUNT NO. 511

DATE		ITEM	POST. REF.	DEBIT	CREDIT	BALANCE DEBIT	BALANCE CREDIT
20-- June	27		J2	1 6 5 0 00		1 6 5 0 00	

ACCOUNT: Rent Expense — ACCOUNT NO. 521

DATE		ITEM	POST. REF.	DEBIT	CREDIT	BALANCE DEBIT	BALANCE CREDIT
20-- June	7		J1	1 0 0 0 00		1 0 0 0 00	

ACCOUNT: Phone Expense — ACCOUNT NO. 525

DATE		ITEM	POST. REF.	DEBIT	CREDIT	BALANCE DEBIT	BALANCE CREDIT
20-- June	15		J1	1 0 0 00		1 0 0 00	

The Trial Balance

In Chapter 3, a **trial balance** was used to prove that the totals of the debit and credit balances in the T accounts were equal. In this chapter, a trial balance is used to prove the equality of the debits and credits in the ledger accounts. A trial balance can be prepared daily, weekly, monthly, or whenever desired. Before preparing a trial balance, all transactions should be journalized and posted so that the effect of all transactions will be reflected in the ledger accounts.

The trial balance for Mitchell's Campus Delivery shown in Figure 4-13 was prepared from the balances in the general ledger in Figure 4-12. The accounts are listed in the order used in the chart of accounts. This order is also often used when preparing financial statements. In Chapter 2, we pointed out that many firms list expenses from highest to lowest amounts. Some firms list expenses according to the chart of accounts, which is the method we will follow.

LEARNING KEY

The chart of accounts determines the order for listing accounts in the general ledger and trial balance. This order may also be used when preparing financial statements.

FIGURE 4-13 Trial Balance

Mitchell's Campus Delivery
Trial Balance
June 30, 20 - -

ACCOUNT TITLE	ACCOUNT NO.	DEBIT BALANCE	CREDIT BALANCE
Cash	101	470 00	
Accounts Receivable	122	3 100 00	
Supplies	141	80 00	
Prepaid Insurance	145	700 00	
Delivery Equipment	185	4 800 00	
Accounts Payable	202		1 900 00
Mitchell Williams, Capital	311		5 000 00
Mitchell Williams, Drawing	312	3 000 00	
Delivery Fees	401		8 000 00
Wages Expense	511	1 650 00	
Rent Expense	521	1 000 00	
Phone Expense	525	100 00	
		14 900 00	14 900 00

CHECKPOINT

Complete Checkpoint-3 on page 113 to test your basic understanding of LO5.

Even though the trial balance indicates that the ledger is in balance, the ledger can still contain errors. For example, if a journal entry was made debiting or crediting the wrong accounts, or if an item was posted to the wrong account, the ledger will still be in balance. It is important, therefore, to be very careful in preparing the journal entries and in posting them to the ledger accounts.

LO6 Finding and Correcting Errors in the Trial Balance

Explain how to find and correct errors.

Tips are available to help if your trial balance has an error. Figure 4-14 offers hints for finding the error when your trial balance does not balance.

FIGURE 4-14 Tips for Finding Errors in the Trial Balance

1. Double check your addition. Review balances to see if they are too large or small, relative to other accounts, or entered in the wrong column.
2. Find the difference between the debits and the credits.
   a. If the difference is equal to the amount of a specific transaction, perhaps you forgot to post the debit or credit portion of this transaction.
   b. Divide the difference by 2. If the difference is evenly divisible by 2, you may have posted two debits or two credits for a transaction. If a debit was posted as a credit, it would mean that one transaction had two credits and no debits. The difference between the total debits and credits would be twice the amount of the debit that was posted as a credit.
   c. Divide the difference by 9. If the difference is evenly divisible by 9, you may have committed a **slide error** or a **transposition error**. A slide occurs when debit or credit amounts "slide" a digit or two to the left or right when entered. For example, if *$250* was entered as *$25*:

\$250	−	\$25	=	\$225
\$225	÷	9	=	\$25

The difference is evenly divisible by 9.

A transposition occurs when two digits are reversed. For example, if *$250* was entered as *$520*:

\$520	−	\$250	=	\$270
\$270	÷	9	=	\$30

Again, the difference is evenly divisible by 9.

If the tips in Figure 4-14 don't work, you must retrace your steps through the accounting process. Double check your addition for the ledger accounts. Also trace all postings. Be patient as you search for your error. Use this process as an opportunity to reinforce your understanding of the flow of information through the accounting system. Much can be learned while looking for an error.

Once you have found an error, it is important to make the correction in a manner that is easy for others to observe and understand. Although you may want to erase when correcting your homework, this is not acceptable in practice. An erasure may suggest that you are trying to hide something. Instead, you should make a correcting entry.

Correcting Entries

If an incorrect entry has been journalized and posted to the wrong account, a **correcting entry** should be made. For example, assume that a $400 payment for Rent Expense was incorrectly debited to Repair Expense and correctly credited to

Cash. This requires a correcting entry and explanation as shown in Figure 4-15. Figure 4-16 shows the effects of the correcting entry on the ledger accounts. Generally, "Correcting" is written in the Item column of the general ledger account.

When using a computerized accounting system, the journal entries are automatically posted to the ledger. To correct an error, the correcting entry method should be used.

FIGURE 4-15 Correcting Entry Method

GENERAL JOURNAL — PAGE 6

	DATE		DESCRIPTION	POST. REF.	DEBIT	CREDIT	
1	20-- Sept.	25	Rent Expense	521	400 00		1
2			Repair Expense	537		400 00	2
3			To correct error in which payment for rent				3
4			was debited to Repair Expense				4
5							5

FIGURE 4-16 Effects of Correcting Entry on Ledger Accounts

GENERAL LEDGER

ACCOUNT: Rent Expense — ACCOUNT NO. 521

DATE		ITEM	POST. REF.	DEBIT	CREDIT	BALANCE DEBIT	BALANCE CREDIT
20-- Sept.	25	Correcting	J6	400 00		400 00	

ACCOUNT: Repair Expense — ACCOUNT NO. 537

DATE		ITEM	POST. REF.	DEBIT	CREDIT	BALANCE DEBIT	BALANCE CREDIT
20-- Sept.	10		J5	50 00		50 00	
	15		J5	400 00		450 00	
	25	Correcting	J6		400 00	50 00	

CHECKPOINT

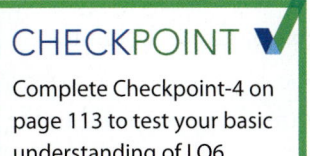

Complete Checkpoint-4 on page 113 to test your basic understanding of LO6.

SELF-STUDY

LEARNING OBJECTIVES	Key Points to Remember
LO1 Describe the flow of data from source documents to the trial balance.	The flow of data from the source documents to the trial balance is as follows: 1. Analyze business transactions. 2. Journalize transactions in the general journal. 3. Post journal entries to the general ledger. 4. Prepare a trial balance. 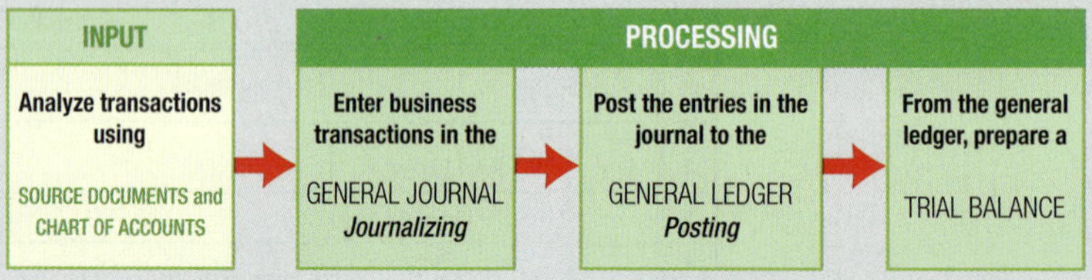
LO2 Describe and explain the purpose of source documents.	Source documents trigger the analysis of business transactions and the entries into the accounting system.
LO3 Describe the chart of accounts as a means of classifying financial information.	The chart of accounts includes the account titles in numerical order for all assets, liabilities, owner's equity, revenues, and expenses. The chart of accounts is used in classifying information about transactions.
LO4 Journalize transactions.	A journal provides a day-by-day listing of transactions. The journal shows the date, titles of the accounts to be debited or credited, and the amounts of the debits and credits. The steps in the journalizing process are as follows: 1. Enter the date. 2. Enter the debit. Accounts to be debited are entered first. 3. Enter the credit. Accounts to be credited are entered after the debits and are indented one-half inch. 4. Enter the explanation. A brief explanation of the transaction should be entered in the description column on the line following the last credit. The explanation should be indented an additional one-half inch.
LO5 Post to the general ledger and prepare a trial balance.	The general ledger is a complete set of all accounts used by the business. The steps in posting from the general journal to the general ledger are as follows: In the general ledger: 1. Enter the date of each transaction. 2. Enter the amount of each debit or credit in the Debit or Credit column. 3. Enter the new balance. 4. Enter the journal page number from which each transaction is posted in the Posting Reference column.

(*continued*)

LEARNING OBJECTIVES	Key Points to Remember
LO5 **(concluded)**	In the journal: 5. Enter the account number to which each transaction is posted in the Posting Reference column. The trial balance provides a check to make sure the total of all debit balances in the ledger accounts equals the total of all credit balances in the ledger accounts.
LO6 **Explain how to find and correct errors.**	Errors may be found by verifying your addition, by dividing the difference between the debits and credits by 2 or 9, and by retracing your steps through the accounting process. If an incorrect entry has been made and posted, a correcting entry must be made.

DEMONSTRATION PROBLEM

George Fielding is a financial planning consultant. He provides budgeting, estate planning, tax planning, and investing advice for professional golfers. He developed the following chart of accounts for his business:

Assets		Revenues	
101	Cash	401	Professional Fees
142	Office Supplies		
		Expenses	
Liabilities		511	Wages Expense
202	Accounts Payable	521	Rent Expense
		525	Phone Expense
Owner's Equity		533	Utilities Expense
311	George Fielding, Capital	534	Charitable Contributions Expense
312	George Fielding, Drawing	538	Automobile Expense

The following transactions took place during the month of December of the current year:

Dec.	1	Fielding invested cash to start the business, $20,000.
	3	Paid Bollhorst Real Estate for December office rent, $1,000.
	4	Received cash from Aaron Patton, a client, for services, $2,500.
	6	Paid T. Z. Anderson Electric for December heating and light, $75.
	7	Received cash from Andrew Conder, a client, for services, $2,000.
	12	Paid Fichter's Super Service for gasoline and oil purchases for the company car, $60.

(*continued*)

Dec. 14 Paid Hillenburg Staffing for temporary secretarial services during the past two weeks, $600.

17 Bought office supplies from Bowers Office Supply on account, $280.

20 Paid Mitchell Phone Co. for business calls during the past month, $100.

21 Fielding withdrew cash for personal use, $1,100.

24 Made donation to the National Multiple Sclerosis Society, $100.

27 Received cash from Billy Walters, a client, for services, $2,000.

28 Paid Hillenburg Staffing for temporary secretarial services during the past two weeks, $600.

29 Made payment on account to Bowers Office Supply, $100.

REQUIRED

1. Record the preceding transactions in a general journal.
2. Post the entries to the general ledger.
3. Prepare a trial balance.
4. Prepare an income statement, statement of owner's equity, and balance sheet for the month of December.

SOLUTION 1, 2.

GENERAL JOURNAL PAGE 1

	DATE		DESCRIPTION	POST. REF.	DEBIT	CREDIT	
1	20-- Dec.	1	Cash	101	20,000 00		1
2			George Fielding, Capital	311		20,000 00	2
3			Owner's original investment in				3
4			consulting business				4
5							5
6		3	Rent Expense	521	1,000 00		6
7			Cash	101		1,000 00	7
8			Paid rent for December				8
9							9
10		4	Cash	101	2,500 00		10
11			Professional Fees	401		2,500 00	11
12			Received cash for services rendered				12
13							13
14		6	Utilities Expense	533	75 00		14
15			Cash	101		75 00	15
16			Paid utilities				16
17							17
18		7	Cash	101	2,000 00		18
19			Professional Fees	401		2,000 00	19
20			Received cash for services rendered				20
21							21

(continued)

GENERAL JOURNAL PAGE 1

	DATE		DESCRIPTION	POST. REF.	DEBIT	CREDIT	
22	20-- Dec.	12	Automobile Expense	538	60 00		22
23			Cash	101		60 00	23
24			Paid for gas and oil				24
25							25
26		14	Wages Expense	511	600 00		26
27			Cash	101		600 00	27
28			Paid temporary secretaries				28
29							29
30		17	Office Supplies	142	280 00		30
31			Accounts Payable	202		280 00	31
32			Purchased office supplies on account from				32
33			Bowers Office Supply				33
34							34
35							35

GENERAL JOURNAL PAGE 2

	DATE		DESCRIPTION	POST. REF.	DEBIT	CREDIT	
1	20-- Dec.	20	Phone Expense	525	100 00		1
2			Cash	101		100 00	2
3			Paid phone bill				3
4							4
5		21	George Fielding, Drawing	312	1100 00		5
6			Cash	101		1100 00	6
7			Owner's withdrawal				7
8							8
9		24	Charitable Contributions Expense	534	100 00		9
10			Cash	101		100 00	10
11			Contribution to National Multiple				11
12			Sclerosis Society				12
13							13
14		27	Cash	101	2000 00		14
15			Professional Fees	401		2000 00	15
16			Received cash for services rendered				16
17							17
18		28	Wages Expense	511	600 00		18
19			Cash	101		600 00	19
20			Paid temporary secretaries				20
21							21
22		29	Accounts Payable	202	100 00		22
23			Cash	101		100 00	23
24			Payment on account to Bowers Office Supply				24

SOLUTION 2.

GENERAL LEDGER

ACCOUNT: Cash — ACCOUNT NO. 101

DATE		ITEM	POST. REF.	DEBIT	CREDIT	BALANCE DEBIT	BALANCE CREDIT
20-- Dec.	1		J1	20,000.00		20,000.00	
	3		J1		1,000.00	19,000.00	
	4		J1	2,500.00		21,500.00	
	6		J1		75.00	21,425.00	
	7		J1	2,000.00		23,425.00	
	12		J1		60.00	23,365.00	
	14		J1		600.00	22,765.00	
	20		J2		100.00	22,665.00	
	21		J2		1,100.00	21,565.00	
	24		J2		100.00	21,465.00	
	27		J2	2,000.00		23,465.00	
	28		J2		600.00	22,865.00	
	29		J2		100.00	22,765.00	

ACCOUNT: Office Supplies — ACCOUNT NO. 142

DATE		ITEM	POST. REF.	DEBIT	CREDIT	BALANCE DEBIT	BALANCE CREDIT
20-- Dec.	17		J1	280.00		280.00	

ACCOUNT: Accounts Payable — ACCOUNT NO. 202

DATE		ITEM	POST. REF.	DEBIT	CREDIT	BALANCE DEBIT	BALANCE CREDIT
20-- Dec.	17		J1		280.00		280.00
	29		J2	100.00			180.00

ACCOUNT: George Fielding, Capital — ACCOUNT NO. 311

DATE		ITEM	POST. REF.	DEBIT	CREDIT	BALANCE DEBIT	BALANCE CREDIT
20-- Dec.	1		J1		20,000.00		20,000.00

(continued)

ACCOUNT: George Fielding, Drawing — ACCOUNT NO. 312

DATE		ITEM	POST. REF.	DEBIT	CREDIT	BALANCE DEBIT	BALANCE CREDIT
20-- Dec.	21		J2	1,100.00		1,100.00	

ACCOUNT: Professional Fees — ACCOUNT NO. 401

DATE		ITEM	POST. REF.	DEBIT	CREDIT	BALANCE DEBIT	BALANCE CREDIT
20-- Dec.	4		J1		2,500.00		2,500.00
	7		J1		2,000.00		4,500.00
	27		J2		2,000.00		6,500.00

ACCOUNT: Wages Expense — ACCOUNT NO. 511

DATE		ITEM	POST. REF.	DEBIT	CREDIT	BALANCE DEBIT	BALANCE CREDIT
20-- Dec.	14		J1	600.00		600.00	
	28		J2	600.00		1,200.00	

ACCOUNT: Rent Expense — ACCOUNT NO. 521

DATE		ITEM	POST. REF.	DEBIT	CREDIT	BALANCE DEBIT	BALANCE CREDIT
20-- Dec.	3		J1	1,000.00		1,000.00	

ACCOUNT: Phone Expense — ACCOUNT NO. 525

DATE		ITEM	POST. REF.	DEBIT	CREDIT	BALANCE DEBIT	BALANCE CREDIT
20-- Dec.	20		J2	100.00		100.00	

ACCOUNT: Utilities Expense ACCOUNT NO. 533

DATE		ITEM	POST. REF.	DEBIT	CREDIT	BALANCE DEBIT	BALANCE CREDIT
20-- Dec.	6		J1	75 00		75 00	

ACCOUNT: Charitable Contributions Expense ACCOUNT NO. 534

DATE		ITEM	POST. REF.	DEBIT	CREDIT	BALANCE DEBIT	BALANCE CREDIT
20-- Dec.	24		J2	100 00		100 00	

ACCOUNT: Automobile Expense ACCOUNT NO. 538

DATE		ITEM	POST. REF.	DEBIT	CREDIT	BALANCE DEBIT	BALANCE CREDIT
20-- Dec.	12		J1	60 00		60 00	

SOLUTION 3.

George Fielding, Financial Planning Consultant
Trial Balance
December 31, 20 --

ACCOUNT TITLE	ACCOUNT NO.	DEBIT BALANCE	CREDIT BALANCE
Cash	101	22 765 00	
Office Supplies	142	280 00	
Accounts Payable	202		180 00
George Fielding, Capital	311		20 000 00
George Fielding, Drawing	312	1 100 00	
Professional Fees	401		6 500 00
Wages Expense	511	1 200 00	
Rent Expense	521	1 000 00	
Phone Expense	525	100 00	
Utilities Expense	533	75 00	
Charitable Contributions Expense	534	100 00	
Automobile Expense	538	60 00	
		26 680 00	26 680 00

(continued)

SOLUTION 4.

George Fielding, Financial Planning Consultant Income Statement For Month Ended December 31, 20 --		
Revenue:		
Professional fees		$6,500
Expenses:		
Wages expense	$1,200	
Rent expense	1,000	
Phone expense	100	
Utilities expense	75	
Charitable contributions expense	100	
Automobile expense	60	
Total expenses		2,535
Net income		$3,965

George Fielding, Financial Planning Consultant Statement of Owner's Equity For Month Ended December 31, 20 --		
George Fielding, capital, December 1, 20 --		$ —
Investments during December		20,000
Total investment		$20,000
Net income for December	$3,965	
Less withdrawals for December	1,100	
Increase in capital		2,865
George Fielding, Capital, December 31, 20 --		$22,865

George Fielding, Financial Planning Consultant Balance Sheet December 31, 20 --			
Assets		Liabilities	
Cash	$22,765	Accounts payable	$ 180
Office Supplies	280	Owner's equity	
		George Fielding, capital	22,865
Total assets	$23,045	Total liabilities and owner's equity	$23,045

KEY TERMS

book of original entry (89) The journal or the first formal accounting record of a transaction.

chart of accounts (88) A list of all accounts used by a business.

compound entry (92) A general journal entry that affects more than two accounts.

correcting entry (102) An entry to correct an incorrect entry that has been journalized and posted to the wrong account.

cross-reference (96) The information in the Posting Reference columns of the journal and ledger that provides a link between the journal and ledger.

general ledger (94) A complete set of all the accounts used by a business. The general ledger accumulates a complete record of the debits and credits made to each account as a result of entries made in the journal.

general ledger account (94) An account with columns for the debit or credit transaction and columns for the debit or credit running balance.

journal (89) A day-by-day listing of the transactions of a business.

journalizing (89) Entering the transactions in a journal.

posting (95) Copying the debits and credits from the journal to the ledger accounts.

slide error (102) An error that occurs when debit or credit amounts "slide" a digit or two to the left or right.

source document (86) Any document that provides information about a business transaction.

transposition error (102) An error that occurs when two digits are reversed.

trial balance (101) A list used to prove that the totals of the debit and credit balances in the ledger accounts are equal.

two-column general journal (89) A journal with only two amount columns, one for debit amounts and one for credit amounts.

SELF-STUDY TEST QUESTIONS

True/False

1. **LO2** Source documents serve as historical evidence of business transactions.
2. **LO3** The chart of accounts lists capital accounts first, followed by liabilities, assets, expenses, and revenue.
3. **LO4** No entries are made in the Posting Reference column at the time of journalizing.
4. **LO4** When entering the credit item in a general journal, it should be listed after all debits and indented.
5. **LO6** When an incorrect entry has been journalized and posted to the wrong account, a correcting entry should be made.

Multiple Choice

1. **LO2** Which of the following is not a source document?
   (a) Check stub
   (b) Cash register tape
   (c) Journal entry
   (d) Purchase invoice
2. **LO3** A revenue account will begin with the number ________ in the chart of accounts.
   (a) 1 (c) 3
   (b) 2 (d) 4

3. **LO4** To purchase an asset such as office equipment on account, you would credit which account?
   (a) Cash (c) Accounts Payable
   (b) Accounts Receivable (d) Capital

4. **LO4** When fees are earned and the customer promises to pay later, which account is debited?
   (a) Cash (c) Accounts Payable
   (b) Accounts Receivable (d) Capital

5. **LO6** When the correct numbers are used but are in the wrong order, the error is called a
   (a) transposition. (c) reversal.
   (b) slide. (d) correcting entry.

CHECKPOINT

Checkpoint Exercises

1. **LO2** A check stub serves as a source document for what kind of transaction?

2. **LO4** Indicate the information that would be entered for each of the lettered items in the general journal provided below.

GENERAL JOURNAL — PAGE

	DATE		DESCRIPTION	POST. REF.	DEBIT	CREDIT	
1	A B	C	D	G	H		1
2			E	J		I	2
3			F				3
4							4
5							5

3. **LO5** Indicate the information that would be entered for each of the lettered items in the general ledger account provided below.

GENERAL LEDGER

ACCOUNT: A — ACCOUNT NO. B

DATE		ITEM	POST. REF.	DEBIT	CREDIT	BALANCE DEBIT	BALANCE CREDIT
C D	E	F	G	H	I	J	K

4. **LO6** Dunkin Company made the following entry for the payment of $500 cash for rent expense:

Rent Expense	500	
Rent Payable		500

Prepare a correcting entry.

The answers to the Self-Study Test Questions are at the end of the chapter (pages 128–129).

APPLYING YOUR KNOWLEDGE

CengageNowv2 provides "Show Me How" videos for selected exercises and problems. Additional resources, such as Excel templates for completing selected exercises and problems, are available for download from the companion website at Cengage.com.

REVIEW QUESTIONS

LO1 1. Trace the flow of accounting information through the accounting system.

LO2 2. Name a source document that provides information about each of the following types of business transactions:

   a. Cash payment
   b. Cash receipt
   c. Sale of goods or services
   d. Purchase of goods or services

LO3 3. Explain the purpose of a chart of accounts.

LO3 4. Name the five types of financial statement classifications for which it is ordinarily desirable to keep separate accounts.

LO4 5. Where is the first formal accounting record of a business transaction usually made?

LO4 6. Describe the four steps required to journalize a business transaction in a general journal.

LO5 7. In what order are the accounts customarily placed in the ledger?

LO5 8. Explain the primary advantage of a general ledger account.

LO5 9. Explain the five steps required when posting the journal to the ledger.

LO5 10. What information is entered in the Posting Reference column of the journal as an amount is posted to the proper account in the ledger?

LO6 11. Explain why the ledger can still contain errors even though the trial balance is in balance. Give examples of two such types of errors.

LO6 12. What is a slide error?

LO6 13. What is a transposition error?

LO6 14. What is a correcting entry?

SERIES A EXERCISES

E 4-1A (LO2)

SOURCE DOCUMENTS Source documents trigger the analysis of events requiring an accounting entry. Match the following source documents with the type of information they provide.

1. Check stubs or check register	a. A good or service has been sold.
2. Purchase invoice from suppliers (vendors)	b. Cash has been received by the business.
3. Sales tickets or invoices to customers	c. Cash has been paid by the business.
4. Receipts or cash register tapes	d. Goods or services have been purchased by the business.

E 4-2A (LO4)

GENERAL JOURNAL ENTRIES For each of the following transactions, list the account to be debited and the account to be credited in the general journal.

1. Invested cash in the business, $5,000.
2. Paid office rent, $500.
3. Purchased office supplies on account, $300.
4. Received cash for services rendered (fees), $400.
5. Paid cash on account, $50.
6. Rendered services on account, $300.
7. Received cash for an amount owed by a customer, $100.

E 4-3A (LO5)
✓ Final Cash bal.: $4,950

GENERAL LEDGER ACCOUNTS Set up T accounts for each of the general ledger accounts needed for Exercise 4-2A and post debits and credits to the accounts. Foot the accounts and enter the balances. Prove that total debits equal total credits.

E 4-4A (LO4)

GENERAL JOURNAL ENTRIES Diane Bernick has opened Bernick's Consulting. Journalize the following transactions that occurred during January of the current year. Use the following journal pages: January 1–10, page 1; and January 11–29, page 2. Use the following chart of accounts:

Chart of Accounts

Assets
101 Cash
142 Office Supplies
181 Office Equipment

Liabilities
202 Accounts Payable

Owner's Equity
311 Diane Bernick, Capital
312 Diane Bernick, Drawing

Revenues
401 Consulting Fees

Expenses
511 Wages Expense
521 Rent Expense
525 Phone Expense
533 Utilities Expense
549 Miscellaneous Expense

Jan.	1	Bernick invested cash in the business, $12,000.
	2	Paid office rent, $750.
	3	Purchased office equipment on account, $1,300.
	5	Received cash for services rendered, $950.
	8	Paid phone bill, $85.
	10	Paid for a magazine subscription (miscellaneous expense), $20.
	11	Purchased office supplies on account, $250.
	15	Made a payment on account (see Jan. 3 transaction), $200.
	18	Paid part-time employee, $600.
	21	Received cash for services rendered, $800.
	25	Paid utilities bill, $105.
	27	Bernick withdrew cash for personal use, $400.
	29	Paid part-time employee, $600.

E 4-5A (LO5)
✓ Final Cash bal.: $10,990
✓ Trial bal. total debits: $15,100

GENERAL LEDGER ACCOUNTS; TRIAL BALANCE Set up general ledger accounts using the chart of accounts provided in Exercise 4-4A. Post the transactions from Exercise 4-4A to the general ledger accounts and prepare a trial balance.

E 4-6A (LO5)
✓ Total assets, Jan. 31: $12,540

FINANCIAL STATEMENTS From the information in Exercises 4-4A and 4-5A, prepare an income statement, a statement of owner's equity, and a balance sheet.

E 4-7A (LO5)
✓ Total assets, July 31: $7,100

FINANCIAL STATEMENTS From the following trial balance taken after one month of operation, prepare an income statement, a statement of owner's equity, and a balance sheet.

TJ's Paint Service
Trial Balance
July 31, 20--

ACCOUNT TITLE	ACCOUNT NO.	DEBIT BALANCE	CREDIT BALANCE
Cash	101	4300 00	
Accounts Receivable	122	1100 00	
Supplies	141	800 00	
Paint Equipment	183	900 00	
Accounts Payable	202		2150 00
TJ Ulza, Capital	311		3205 00
TJ Ulza, Drawing	312	500 00	
Painting Fees	401		3600 00
Wages Expense	511	900 00	
Rent Expense	521	250 00	
Phone Expense	525	50 00	
Transportation Expense	526	60 00	
Utilities Expense	533	70 00	
Miscellaneous Expense	549	25 00	
		8955 00	8955 00

E 4-8A (LO6)

FINDING AND CORRECTING ERRORS On May 25, after the transactions had been posted, Joe Adams discovered that the following entry contains an error. The cash received represents a collection on account, rather than new service fees. Correct the error in the general journal using a correcting entry.

22							22
23	20-- May	23	Cash	101	1000 00		23
24			Service Fees	401		1000 00	24
25			Received cash for services previously earned				25

SERIES A PROBLEMS

P 4-9A (LO4/5)
✓ Cash bal., Jan. 31: $10,021
✓ Trial bal. total debits: $13,460

JOURNALIZING AND POSTING TRANSACTIONS Annette Creighton opened Creighton Consulting. She rented a small office and paid a part-time worker to answer the phone and make deliveries. Her chart of accounts is as follows:

Chart of Accounts

Assets		Revenues	
101	Cash	401	Consulting Fees
142	Office Supplies		
181	Office Equipment	Expenses	
		511	Wages Expense
Liabilities		512	Advertising Expense
202	Accounts Payable	521	Rent Expense
		525	Phone Expense
Owner's Equity		526	Transportation Expense
311	Annette Creighton, Capital	533	Utilities Expense
312	Annette Creighton, Drawing	549	Miscellaneous Expense

Creighton's transactions for the first month of business are as follows:

Jan.	1	Creighton invested cash in the business, $10,000.
	1	Paid rent, $500.
	2	Purchased office supplies on account, $300.
	4	Purchased office equipment on account, $1,500.
	6	Received cash for services rendered, $580.
	7	Paid phone bill, $42.
	8	Paid utilities bill, $38.
	10	Received cash for services rendered, $360.
	12	Made payment on account, $50.
	13	Paid for car rental while visiting an out-of-town client (transportation expense), $150.
	15	Paid part-time worker, $360.
	17	Received cash for services rendered, $420.
	18	Creighton withdrew cash for personal use, $100.
	20	Paid for a newspaper ad, $26.
	22	Reimbursed part-time employee for cab fare incurred delivering materials to clients (transportation expense), $35.
	24	Paid for books on consulting practices (miscellaneous expense), $28.
	25	Received cash for services rendered, $320.
	27	Made payment on account for office equipment purchased, $150.
	29	Paid part-time worker, $360.
	30	Received cash for services rendered, $180.

(continued)

REQUIRED

1. Set up general ledger accounts from the chart of accounts.
2. Journalize the transactions for January in a two-column general journal. Use the following journal page numbers: January 1–10, page 1; January 12–24, page 2; January 25–30, page 3.
3. Post the transactions to the general ledger.
4. Prepare a trial balance.
5. Prepare an income statement and a statement of owner's equity for the month of January and a balance sheet as of January 31, 20--.

P 4-10A (LO4/5)
✓ Cash bal., June 30: $3,958
✓ Trial bal. total debits: $22,358

JOURNALIZING AND POSTING TRANSACTIONS Jim Andrews opened a delivery business in March. He rented a small office and has a part-time assistant. His trial balance shows accounts for the first three months of business.

Jim's Quick Delivery
Trial Balance
May 31, 20 - -

ACCOUNT TITLE	ACCOUNT NO.	DEBIT BALANCE	CREDIT BALANCE
Cash	101	3 8 2 6 00	
Accounts Receivable	122	1 2 1 2 00	
Office Supplies	142	6 4 8 00	
Office Equipment	181	2 1 0 0 00	
Delivery Truck	185	8 0 0 0 00	
Accounts Payable	202		6 0 0 0 00
Jim Andrews, Capital	311		4 4 7 8 00
Jim Andrews, Drawing	312	1 8 0 0 00	
Delivery Fees	401		9 8 8 0 00
Wages Expense	511	1 2 0 0 00	
Advertising Expense	512	9 0 00	
Rent Expense	521	9 0 0 00	
Phone Expense	525	1 2 6 00	
Electricity Expense	533	9 8 00	
Charitable Contributions Expense	534	6 0 00	
Gas and Oil Expense	538	1 8 6 00	
Miscellaneous Expense	549	1 1 2 00	
		20 3 5 8 00	20 3 5 8 00

Andrews' transactions for the month of June are as follows:

June 1 Paid rent, $300.
2 Performed delivery services for $300: $100 in cash and $200 on account.
4 Paid for newspaper advertising, $15.
6 Purchased office supplies on account, $180.
7 Received cash for delivery services rendered, $260.
9 Paid cash on account (truck payment), $200.
10 Purchased a copier (office equipment) for $700: paid $100 in cash and put $600 on account.

June 11	Made a contribution to the Red Cross (charitable contributions), $20.
12	Received cash for delivery services rendered, $380.
13	Received cash on account for services previously rendered, $100.
15	Paid a part-time worker, $200.
16	Paid electric bill, $36.
18	Paid phone bill, $46.
19	Received cash on account for services previously rendered, $100.
20	Andrews withdrew cash for personal use, $200.
21	Paid for gas and oil, $32.
22	Made payment on account (for office supplies), $40.
24	Received cash for services rendered, $340.
26	Paid for a magazine subscription (miscellaneous expense), $15.
27	Received cash for services rendered, $180.
27	Received cash on account for services previously rendered, $100.
29	Paid for gasoline, $24.
30	Paid a part-time worker, $200.

REQUIRED

1. Set up general ledger accounts by entering the balances as of June 1.
2. Journalize the transactions for June in a two-column general journal. Use the following journal pages: June 1–10, page 7; June 11–20, page 8; June 21–30, page 9.
3. Post the entries to the general ledger.
4. Prepare a trial balance.

P 4-11A (LO6)

CORRECTING ERRORS Assuming that all entries have been posted, prepare correcting entries for each of the following errors.

1. The following entry was made to record the purchase of $700 in supplies on account:

Supplies	142	700	
Cash	101		700

2. The following entry was made to record the payment of $450 in wages:

Rent Expense	521	450	
Cash	101		450

3. The following entry was made to record a $300 payment to a supplier on account:

Supplies	142	100	
Cash	101		100

SERIES B EXERCISES

E 4-1B (LO2)

SOURCE DOCUMENTS What type of information is found on each of the following source documents?

1. Cash register tape
2. Sales ticket (issued to customer)
3. Purchase invoice (received from supplier or vendor)
4. Check stub

E 4-2B (LO4)

GENERAL JOURNAL ENTRIES For each of the following transactions, list the account to be debited and the account to be credited in the general journal.

1. Invested cash in the business, $1,000.
2. Performed services on account, $200.
3. Purchased office equipment on account, $500.
4. Received cash on account for services previously rendered, $200.
5. Made a payment on account, $100.

E 4-3B (LO5)
✓ Final Cash bal.: $1,100

GENERAL LEDGER ACCOUNTS Set up T accounts for each of the general ledger accounts needed for Exercise 4-2B and post debits and credits to the accounts. Foot the accounts and enter the balances. Prove that total debits equal total credits.

E 4-4B (LO4)

GENERAL JOURNAL ENTRIES Sengel Moon opened The Bike Doctor. Journalize the following transactions that occurred during the month of October of the current year. Use the following journal pages: October 1–12, page 1; and October 14–29, page 2. Use the following chart of accounts:

Chart of Accounts

Assets
101 Cash
141 Bicycle Parts
142 Office Supplies

Liabilities
202 Accounts Payable

Owner's Equity
311 Sengel Moon, Capital
312 Sengel Moon, Drawing

Revenues
401 Repair Fees

Expenses
511 Wages Expense
521 Rent Expense
525 Phone Expense
533 Utilities Expense
549 Miscellaneous Expense

Oct.	1	Moon invested cash in the business, $15,000.
	2	Paid shop rental for the month, $300.
	3	Purchased bicycle parts on account, $2,000.
	5	Purchased office supplies on account, $250.
	8	Paid phone bill, $38.
	9	Received cash for services, $140.
	11	Paid a sports magazine subscription (miscellaneous expense), $15.

Oct. 12	Made payment on account (see Oct. 3 transaction), $100.
14	Paid part-time employee, $300.
15	Received cash for services, $350.
16	Paid utilities bill, $48.
19	Received cash for services, $250.
23	Moon withdrew cash for personal use, $50.
25	Made payment on account (see Oct. 5 transaction), $50.
29	Paid part-time employee, $300.

E 4-5B (LO5)
✓ Final Cash bal.: $14,539
✓ Trial bal. total debits: $17,840

GENERAL LEDGER ACCOUNTS; TRIAL BALANCE Set up general ledger accounts using the chart of accounts provided in Exercise 4-4B. Post the transactions from Exercise 4-4B to the general ledger accounts and prepare a trial balance.

E 4-6B (LO5)
✓ Total assets, Oct. 31: $16,789

FINANCIAL STATEMENTS From the information in Exercises 4-4B and 4-5B, prepare an income statement, a statement of owner's equity, and a balance sheet.

E 4-7B (LO5)
✓ Total assets, Mar. 31: $11,900

FINANCIAL STATEMENTS From the following trial balance taken after one month of operation, prepare an income statement, a statement of owner's equity, and a balance sheet.

AT Speaker's Bureau
Trial Balance
March 31, 20 - -

ACCOUNT TITLE	ACCOUNT NO.	DEBIT BALANCE	CREDIT BALANCE
Cash	101	6 6 0 0 00	
Accounts Receivable	122	2 8 0 0 00	
Office Supplies	142	1 0 0 0 00	
Office Equipment	181	1 5 0 0 00	
Accounts Payable	202		3 0 0 0 00
AT Speaker, Capital	311		6 0 9 8 00
AT Speaker, Drawing	312	8 0 0 00	
Speaking Fees	401		4 8 0 0 00
Wages Expense	511	4 0 0 00	
Rent Expense	521	2 0 0 00	
Phone Expense	525	3 5 00	
Travel Expense	526	4 5 0 00	
Utilities Expense	533	8 8 00	
Miscellaneous Expense	549	2 5 00	
		13 8 9 8 00	13 8 9 8 00

E 4-8B (LO6)

FINDING AND CORRECTING ERRORS On April 25, after the transactions had been posted, Mary Smith discovered the following entry contains an error. When her customer received services, Cash was debited, but the service was provided on account. Correct the error in the journal using a correcting entry.

27							27
28	20-- Apr.	21	Cash	101	3 0 0 00		28
29			Service Fees	401		3 0 0 00	29
30			Revenue earned from services				30
31			previously rendered				31

SERIES B PROBLEMS

P 4-9B (LO4/5)
✓ Cash bal., May 31: $4,500
✓ Trial bal. total debits: $8,790

JOURNALIZING AND POSTING TRANSACTIONS Benito Mendez opened Mendez Appraisals. He rented office space and has a part-time secretary to answer the phone and make appraisal appointments. His chart of accounts is as follows:

Chart of Accounts

Assets		Revenues	
101	Cash	401	Appraisal Fees
122	Accounts Receivable		
142	Office Supplies	Expenses	
181	Office Equipment	511	Wages Expense
		512	Advertising Expense
Liabilities		521	Rent Expense
202	Accounts Payable	525	Phone Expense
		526	Transportation Expense
Owner's Equity		533	Electricity Expense
311	Benito Mendez, Capital	549	Miscellaneous Expense
312	Benito Mendez, Drawing		

Mendez's transactions for the first month of business are as follows:

May	1	Mendez invested cash in the business, $5,000.
	2	Paid rent, $500.
	3	Purchased office supplies, $100.
	4	Purchased office equipment on account, $2,000.
	5	Received cash for services rendered, $280.
	8	Paid phone bill, $38.
	9	Paid electric bill, $42.
	10	Received cash for services rendered, $310.
	13	Paid part-time employee, $500.
	14	Paid car rental for out-of-town trip, $200.
	15	Paid for newspaper ad, $30.
	18	Received cash for services rendered, $620.
	19	Paid mileage reimbursement for part-time employee's use of personal car for business deliveries (transportation expense), $22.
	21	Mendez withdrew cash for personal use, $50.
	23	Made payment on account for office equipment purchased earlier, $200.

May 24 Earned appraisal fee, which will be paid in a week, $500.
26 Paid for newspaper ad, $30.
27 Paid for local softball team sponsorship (miscellaneous expense), $15.
28 Paid part-time employee, $500.
29 Received cash on account, $250.
30 Received cash for services rendered, $280.
31 Paid cab fare (transportation expense), $13.

REQUIRED

1. Set up general ledger accounts from the chart of accounts.
2. Journalize the transactions for May in a two-column general journal. Use the following journal page numbers: May 1–10, page 1; May 13–24, page 2; May 26–31, page 3.
3. Post the transactions to the general ledger.
4. Prepare a trial balance.
5. Prepare an income statement and a statement of owner's equity for the month of May, and a balance sheet as of May 31, 20--.

P 4-10B (LO4/5)
✓ Cash bal., Nov. 30: $7,012
✓ Trial bal. total debits: $16,105

JOURNALIZING AND POSTING TRANSACTIONS Ann Taylor owns a suit tailoring shop. She opened business in September. She rented a small work space and has an assistant to receive job orders and process claim tickets. Her trial balance shows her account balances for the first two months of business.

Taylor Tailoring
Trial Balance
October 31, 20 --

ACCOUNT TITLE	ACCOUNT NO.	DEBIT BALANCE	CREDIT BALANCE
Cash	101	6,211.00	
Accounts Receivable	122	484.00	
Tailoring Supplies	141	1,000.00	
Tailoring Equipment	183	3,800.00	
Accounts Payable	202		4,125.00
Ann Taylor, Capital	311		6,130.00
Ann Taylor, Drawing	312	800.00	
Tailoring Fees	401		3,600.00
Wages Expense	511	800.00	
Advertising Expense	512	34.00	
Rent Expense	521	600.00	
Phone Expense	525	60.00	
Electricity Expense	533	44.00	
Miscellaneous Expense	549	22.00	
		13,855.00	13,855.00

(continued)

Taylor's transactions for November are as follows:

Nov.	1	Paid rent, $300.
	2	Purchased tailoring supplies on account, $150.
	3	Purchased a new button hole machine on account, $300.
	5	Earned first week's revenue, $400: $100 in cash and $300 on account.
	8	Paid for newspaper advertising, $13.
	9	Paid phone bill, $28.
	10	Paid electric bill, $21.
	11	Received cash on account from customers, $200.
	12	Earned second week's revenue, $450: $200 in cash and $250 on account.
	15	Paid assistant, $400.
	16	Made payment on account, $100.
	17	Paid for magazine subscription (miscellaneous expense), $12.
	19	Earned third week's revenue, $450: $300 in cash, $150 on account.
	23	Received cash on account from customers, $300.
	24	Paid for newspaper advertising, $13.
	26	Paid for postage (miscellaneous expense), $12.
	27	Earned fourth week's revenue, $600: $200 in cash and $400 on account.
	30	Received cash on account from customers, $400.

REQUIRED

1. Set up general ledger accounts by entering the balances as of November 1, 20--.
2. Journalize the transactions for November in a two-column general journal. Use the following journal page numbers: November 1–11, page 7; November 12–24, page 8; November 26–30, page 9.
3. Post the entries to the general ledger.
4. Prepare a trial balance.

P 4-11B (LO6)

CORRECTING ERRORS Assuming that all entries have been posted, prepare correcting entries for each of the following errors.

1. The following entry was made to record the purchase of $400 in equipment on account:

Supplies	142	400	
Cash	101		400

2. The following entry was made to record the payment of $200 for advertising:

Repair Expense	537	200	
Cash	101		200

3. The following entry was made to record a $600 payment to a supplier on account:

Prepaid Insurance	145	400	
Cash	101		400

CHECK LIST
- ☐ Managing
- ☐ Planning
- ☐ Drafting
- ☐ Break
- ☐ Revising
- ☐ Managing

MANAGING YOUR WRITING

You are a public accountant with many small business clients. During a recent visit to a client's business, the bookkeeper approached you with a problem. The columns of the trial balance were not equal. You helped the bookkeeper find and correct the error, but believe you should go one step further. Write a memo to all of your clients that explains the purpose of the double-entry framework, the importance of maintaining the equality of the accounting equation, the errors that might cause an inequality, and suggestions for finding the errors.

MASTERY PROBLEM

✓ Cash bal., June 30: $45,495
✓ Trial bal. total debits: $96,200

Barry Bird opened the Barry Bird Basketball Camp for children ages 10 through 18. Campers typically register for one week in June or July, arriving on Sunday and returning home the following Saturday. College players serve as cabin counselors and assist the local college and high school coaches who run the practice sessions. The registration fee includes a room, meals at a nearby restaurant, and basketball instruction. In the off-season, the facilities are used for weekend retreats and coaching clinics. Bird developed the following chart of accounts for his service business:

Chart of Accounts

Assets
- 101 Cash
- 142 Office Supplies
- 183 Athletic Equipment
- 184 Basketball Facilities

Liabilities
- 202 Accounts Payable

Owner's Equity
- 311 Barry Bird, Capital
- 312 Barry Bird, Drawing

Revenues
- 401 Registration Fees

Expenses
- 511 Wages Expense
- 512 Advertising Expense
- 524 Food Expense
- 525 Phone Expense
- 533 Utilities Expense
- 536 Postage Expense

(continued)

The following transactions took place during the month of June:

June 1	Bird invested cash in the business, $10,000.
1	Purchased basketballs and other athletic equipment, $3,000.
2	Paid Hite Advertising for flyers that had been mailed to prospective campers, $5,000.
2	Collected registration fees, $15,000.
2	Rogers Construction completed work on a new basketball court that cost $12,000. Arrangements were made to pay the bill in July.
5	Purchased office supplies on account from Gordon Office Supplies, $300.
6	Received bill from Magic's Restaurant for meals served to campers on account, $5,800.
7	Collected registration fees, $16,200.
10	Paid wages to camp counselors, $500.
14	Collected registration fees, $13,500.
14	Received bill from Magic's Restaurant for meals served to campers on account, $6,200.
17	Paid wages to camp counselors, $500.
18	Paid postage, $85.
21	Collected registration fees, $15,200.
22	Received bill from Magic's Restaurant for meals served to campers on account, $6,500.
24	Paid wages to camp counselors, $500.
28	Collected registration fees, $14,000.
30	Received bill from Magic's Restaurant for meals served to campers on account, $7,200.
30	Paid wages to camp counselors, $500.
30	Paid Magic's Restaurant on account, $25,700.
30	Paid utility bill, $500.
30	Paid phone bill, $120.
30	Bird withdrew cash for personal use, $2,000.

REQUIRED

1. Enter the transactions in a general journal. Use the following journal pages: June 1–6, page 1; June 7–22, page 2; June 24–30, page 3.
2. Post the entries to the general ledger.
3. Prepare a trial balance.

CHALLENGE PROBLEM

This problem challenges you to apply your cumulative accounting knowledge to move a step beyond the material in the chapter.

✓ **Total debits: $19,150**

Journal entries and a trial balance for Fred Phaler Consulting follow. As you will note, the trial balance does not balance, suggesting that there are errors. Recall that the chapter offers tips on identifying individual posting errors. These techniques are not as effective when there are two or more errors. Thus, you will need to first carefully inspect the trial balance to see if you can identify any obvious errors due to amounts that either look out of proportion or are simply reported in the wrong place. Then, you will need to carefully evaluate the other amounts by using the techniques offered in the text, or tracing the journal entries to the amounts reported on the trial balance. (*Hint:* Four errors were made in the posting process and preparation of the trial balance.)

GENERAL JOURNAL PAGE 1

	DATE		DESCRIPTION	POST. REF.	DEBIT	CREDIT	
1	20-- June	1	Cash	101	10,000.00		1
2			Fred Phaler, Capital	311		10,000.00	2
3							3
4		2	Rent Expense	521	500.00		4
5			Cash	101		500.00	5
6							6
7		3	Cash	101	4,000.00		7
8			Professional Fees	401		4,000.00	8
9							9
10		4	Utilities Expense	533	100.00		10
11			Cash	101		100.00	11
12							12
13		7	Cash	101	3,000.00		13
14			Professional Fees	401		3,000.00	14
15							15
16		12	Automobile Expense	526	50.00		16
17			Cash	101		50.00	17
18							18
19		14	Wages Expense	511	500.00		19
20			Cash	101		500.00	20
21							21
22		14	Office Supplies	142	250.00		22
23			Accounts Payable	202		250.00	23
24							24
25		20	Phone Expense	525	100.00		25
26			Cash	101		100.00	26
27							27
28		21	Fred Phaler, Drawing	312	1,200.00		28
29			Cash	101		1,200.00	29
30							30
31		24	Accounts Receivable	122	2,000.00		31
32			Professional Fees	401		2,000.00	32
33							33
34		25	Accounts Payable	202	100.00		34
35			Cash	101		100.00	35
36							36
37		30	Wages Expense	511	300.00		37
38			Cash	101		300.00	38

(continued)

Fred Phaler Consulting
Trial Balance
June 30, 20 - -

ACCOUNT TITLE	ACCOUNT NO.	DEBIT BALANCE	CREDIT BALANCE
Cash	101		13,900.00
Accounts Receivable	122	2,000.00	
Office Supplies	142	250.00	
Accounts Payable	202	100.00	
Fred Phaler, Capital	311		10,000.00
Fred Phaler, Drawing	312	2,100.00	
Professional Fees	401		9,000.00
Wages Expense	511	800.00	
Rent Expense	521	500.00	
Phone Expense	525	100.00	
Automobile Expense	526	50,000.00	
Utilities Expense	533	100.00	
		55,950.00	32,900.00

REQUIRED

1. Find the errors.
2. Explain what caused the errors.
3. Prepare a corrected trial balance.

ANSWERS TO SELF-STUDY TEST QUESTIONS

True/False

1. T
2. F (A, L, OE, R, E)
3. T
4. T
5. T

Multiple Choice

1. c 2. d 3. c 4. b 5. a

Checkpoint Exercises

1. A cash payment.
2. A Year in which entry was made. (Needed for first transaction on this page.)

B Month in which entry was made. (Needed for first transaction on this page.)

C Day of the month entry was made. (Needed for every transaction.)

D Account debited.

E Account credited.

F Description of transaction.

G Account number for account debited to indicate the debit has been posted.

H Amount for account debited.

I Amount for account credited.

J Account number for account credited to indicate the credit has been posted.

3. A Account title.
   B Account number.
   C Year of transaction. (Needed for first transaction on this page.)
   D Month of transaction. (Needed for first transaction on this page.)
   E Day of month transaction was made. (Needed for every transaction.)
   F Generally left blank, except for special reasons such as indicating the beginning balance, adjusting, correcting, closing, or reversing entries.
   G Journal page from which entry was posted.
   H Dollar amount of debit.
   I Dollar amount of credit.
   J Balance if account has a debit balance.
   K Balance if account has a credit balance.

4.

GENERAL JOURNAL PAGE 1

	DATE		DESCRIPTION	POST. REF.	DEBIT	CREDIT	
1			Rent Payable		500 00		1
2			Cash			500 00	2
3			To correct error in which payment for rent				3
4			was credited to Rent Payable rather than Cash.				4
5							5

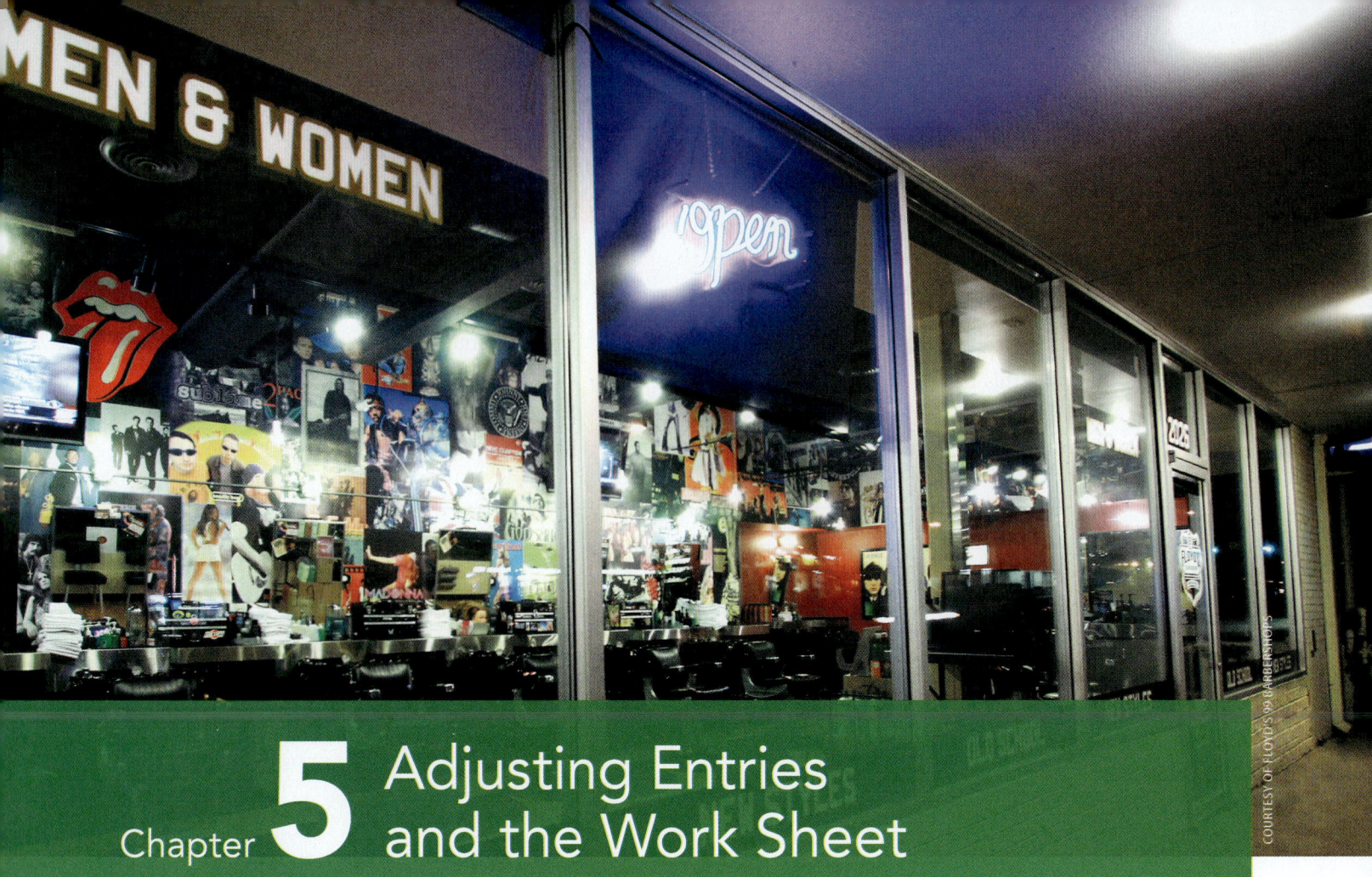

Chapter 5 Adjusting Entries and the Work Sheet

LEARNING OBJECTIVES

Careful study of this chapter should enable you to:

LO1 Prepare end-of-period adjustments.

LO2 Post adjusting entries to the general ledger.

LO3 Prepare a work sheet.

LO4 Describe methods for finding errors on the work sheet.

LO5 Journalize adjusting entries from the work sheet.

LO6 Explain the cash, modified cash, and accrual bases of accounting.

Floyd's 99 Barbershop, founded in 2001, is a contemporary full-service barbershop/hair-care concept offering haircuts, coloring, styling, and shaves. In a setting where *Hard Rock* meets haircuts, customers listen to custom designed Floyd's 99 Radio, watch TV, surf the Internet, and get a signature shoulder massage and hot lather neck shave all as a part of their overall haircut experience. As they like to say, "Floyd's 99 is NOT your grandfather's barbershop." Headquartered in Greenwood Village, Colorado, Floyd's 99 has 113 shops in 13 states, primarily Colorado, California, Texas, Illinois, and Maryland.

As a rapidly growing company, Floyd's 99 uses the accrual basis of accounting, which requires making end-of-period adjusting entries. In this chapter, you will learn why adjusting entries are important, how they are made, and how they affect the financial statements. In addition, you will learn how to use a work sheet to help in the preparation of adjusting entries and the financial statements.

Up to this point, you have learned how to journalize business transactions, post to the ledger, and prepare a trial balance. Now it is time to learn how to make end-of-period adjustments to the accounts listed in the trial balance. This chapter explains the need for adjustments and illustrates how they are made with or without the use of a work sheet.

LO1 End-of-Period Adjustments

Prepare end-of-period adjustments.

Throughout the accounting period, business transactions are entered in the accounting system. These transactions are based on exchanges between the business and other companies and individuals. During the accounting period, other changes occur that affect the business's financial condition. For example, equipment is wearing out, prepaid insurance and supplies are being used up, and employees are earning wages that have not yet been paid. Since these events have not been entered into the accounting system, **adjusting entries** must be made prior to the preparation of financial statements.

> **LEARNING KEY**
> Transactions are entered as they occur throughout the year. Adjustments are made at the end of the accounting period for items that do not involve exchanges with an outside party.

These adjustments are guided by three important principles. The **revenue recognition principle** states that revenues should be recognized when earned, regardless of when cash is received from the customer. Revenues are considered earned when a service has been provided or a product has been sold. Similarly, the **expense recognition principle** states that expenses should be recognized when incurred, regardless of when cash is paid. Expenses are generally considered incurred when services are received or assets are consumed as a result of efforts made to generate revenues. The proper matching of revenues earned during an accounting period with the expenses incurred to produce the revenues is often referred to as the **matching principle**. This approach offers the best measure of net income. The income statement reports earnings for a specific period of time, and the balance sheet reports the assets, liabilities, and owner's equity on a specific date. Thus, to follow these three principles, the accounts must be brought up to date before financial statements are prepared. This requires adjusting some of the accounts listed in the trial balance. Figure 5-1 lists reasons to adjust the trial balance.

FIGURE 5-1 Reasons to Adjust the Trial Balance

1. To report all revenues earned during the accounting period.
2. To report all expenses incurred to produce the revenues earned in the accounting period.
3. To accurately report the assets on the balance sheet date. Some assets may have been used up during the accounting period.
4. To accurately report the liabilities on the balance sheet date. Expenses may have been incurred but not yet paid.

> **LEARNING KEY**
> Matching revenues earned with expenses incurred to produce those revenues offers the best measure of net income.

Generally, adjustments are made and financial statements prepared at the end of a 12-month period called a **fiscal year**. This period does not need to be the same as a calendar year. In fact, many businesses schedule their fiscal year-end for a time when business is slow. In this chapter, we continue the illustration of Mitchell's Campus Delivery and will prepare adjustments at the end of the first month of operations. We will focus on the following accounts: Supplies, Prepaid Insurance, Wages Expense, and Delivery Equipment.

CC/DREAMSTIME.COM

A BROADER VIEW

Adjusting Entries

Are adjusting entries important? The Walt Disney Company and Mattel, Inc. probably think so. The Walt Disney Company granted Mattel the right to make and sell toys based on Disney characters. In return, Mattel agreed to make payments to Disney as the toys were sold. One of the issues in a court case was whether Mattel should have made an adjusting entry when it fell behind on these payments. The entry would have been:

Royalty Expense	17,000,000	
Accounts Payable (Disney)		17,000,000

This adjusting entry would have reduced Mattel's fourth-quarter earnings for that year by more than 15%. Following an investigation by the Securities and Exchange Commission, Mattel eventually agreed to make an adjustment to later financial statements.

Supplies

During June, Mitch purchased supplies consisting of paper, pens, and delivery envelopes for $80. *Since these supplies were expected to provide future benefits, Supplies, an asset, was debited at the time of the purchase.* No other entries were made to the supplies account during June. As reported on the trial balance in Figure 5-2, the $80 balance remains in the supplies account at the end of the month.

FIGURE 5-2 Trial Balance

Mitchell's Campus Delivery
Trial Balance
June 30, 20 - -

ACCOUNT TITLE	ACCOUNT NO.	DEBIT BALANCE	CREDIT BALANCE
Cash	101	470 00	
Accounts Receivable	122	3,100 00	
Supplies	141	80 00	
Prepaid Insurance	145	700 00	
Delivery Equipment	185	4,800 00	
Accounts Payable	202		1,900 00
Mitchell Williams, Capital	311		5,000 00
Mitchell Williams, Drawing	312	3,000 00	
Delivery Fees	401		8,000 00
Wages Expense	511	1,650 00	
Rent Expense	521	1,000 00	
Phone Expense	525	100 00	
		14,900 00	14,900 00

LEARNING KEY Since it is not practical to make a journal entry for supplies expense each time supplies are used, one adjusting entry is made at the end of the accounting period.

As supplies are used, an expense is incurred. However, it is not practical to make a journal entry to recognize this expense and the reduction in the supplies account every time someone uses an envelope. It is more efficient to wait until the end of the accounting period to make one adjusting entry to reflect the expense incurred for the use of supplies for the entire month.

> **LEARNING KEY**
> By making an adjusting entry that debits Supplies Expense and credits Supplies, you are taking the amount of supplies used out of Supplies and putting it in Supplies Expense.

At the end of the month, an inventory, or physical count, of the remaining supplies is taken. The inventory shows that supplies costing $20 were still unused at the end of June. Since Mitch bought supplies costing $80, and only $20 worth remain, supplies costing $60 must have been used ($80 – $20 = $60). Thus, supplies expense for the month is $60.

Since $60 worth of supplies have been used, Supplies Expense is debited and Supplies (asset) is credited for $60. This entry is illustrated in Figure 5-3 in T account and general journal form. Thus, as shown in Figure 5-4, supplies with a cost of $20 will be reported as an asset on the balance sheet and a supplies expense of $60 will be reported on the income statement. The adjusting entry affected an income statement account (Supplies Expense) and a balance sheet account (Supplies).

FIGURE 5-3 Adjustment for Supplies

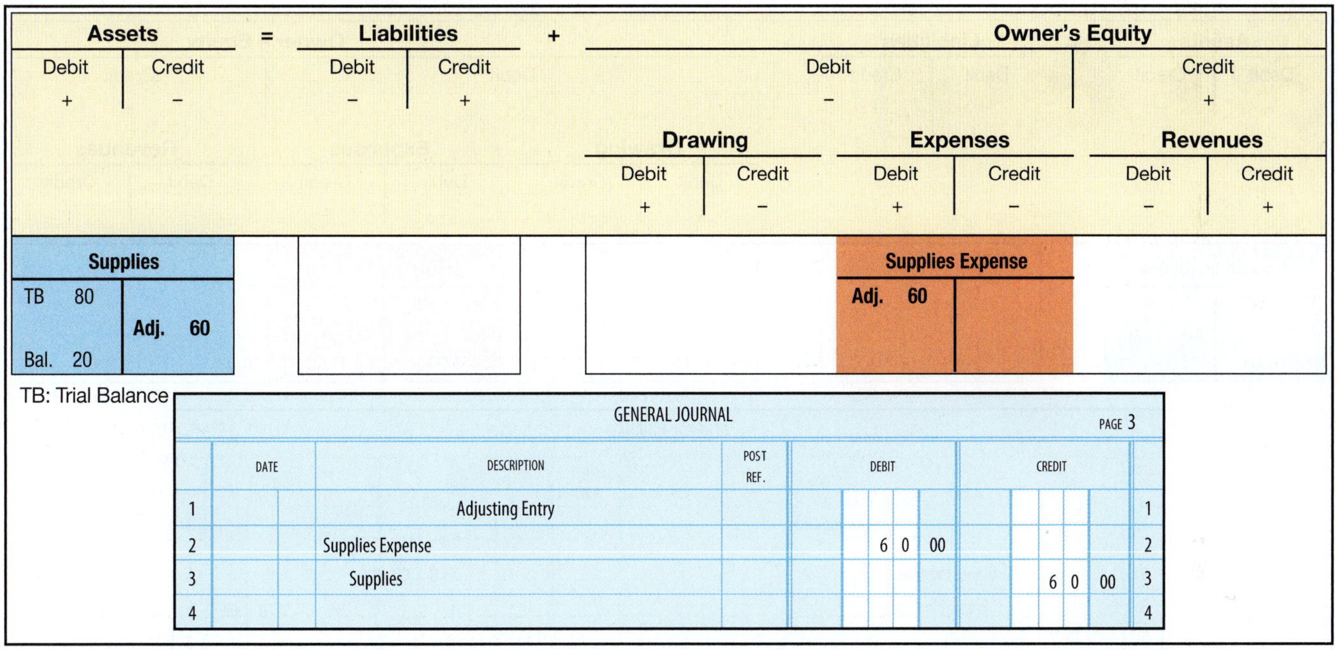

FIGURE 5-4 Effect of Adjusting Entry for Supplies on Financial Statements

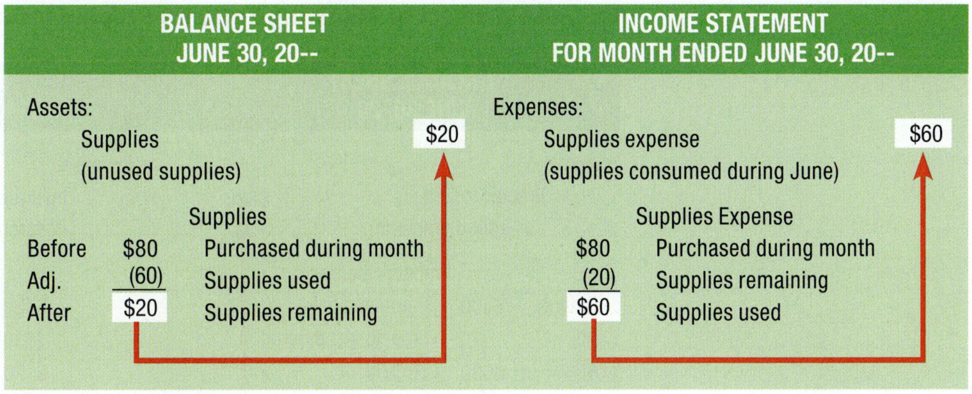

Prepaid Insurance

On June 18, Mitch paid $700 for a ten-month liability insurance policy with coverage beginning on June 1. *Prepaid Insurance, an asset, was debited because the insurance policy is expected to provide future benefits in the form of insurance coverage, or a cash refund if the policy is canceled.* The $700 balance is reported on the trial balance. As the insurance policy expires with the passage of time, the asset should be reduced and an expense recognized.

Since the $700 premium covers ten months, the cost of the expired coverage for June is $70 ($700 ÷ 10 months). As shown in Figure 5-5, the adjusting entry is to debit Insurance Expense for $70 and credit Prepaid Insurance for $70. Figure 5-6 shows that the unexpired portion of the insurance premium will be reported on the balance sheet as Prepaid Insurance of $630. The expired portion will be reported on the income statement as Insurance Expense of $70.

FIGURE 5-5 Adjustment for Expired Insurance

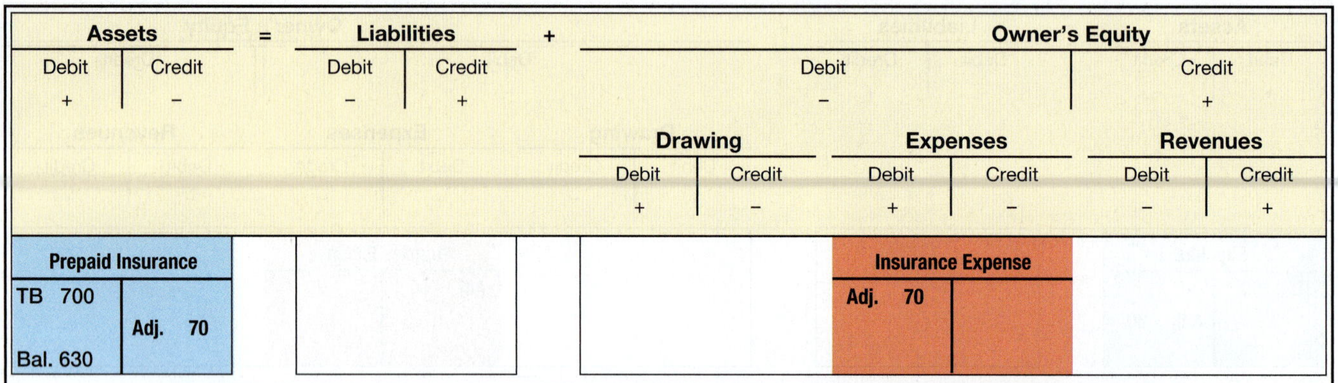

GENERAL JOURNAL PAGE 3

	DATE		DESCRIPTION	POST REF.	DEBIT	CREDIT	
1			Adjusting Entry				1
5			Insurance Expense		70 00		5
6			Prepaid Insurance			70 00	6
7							7

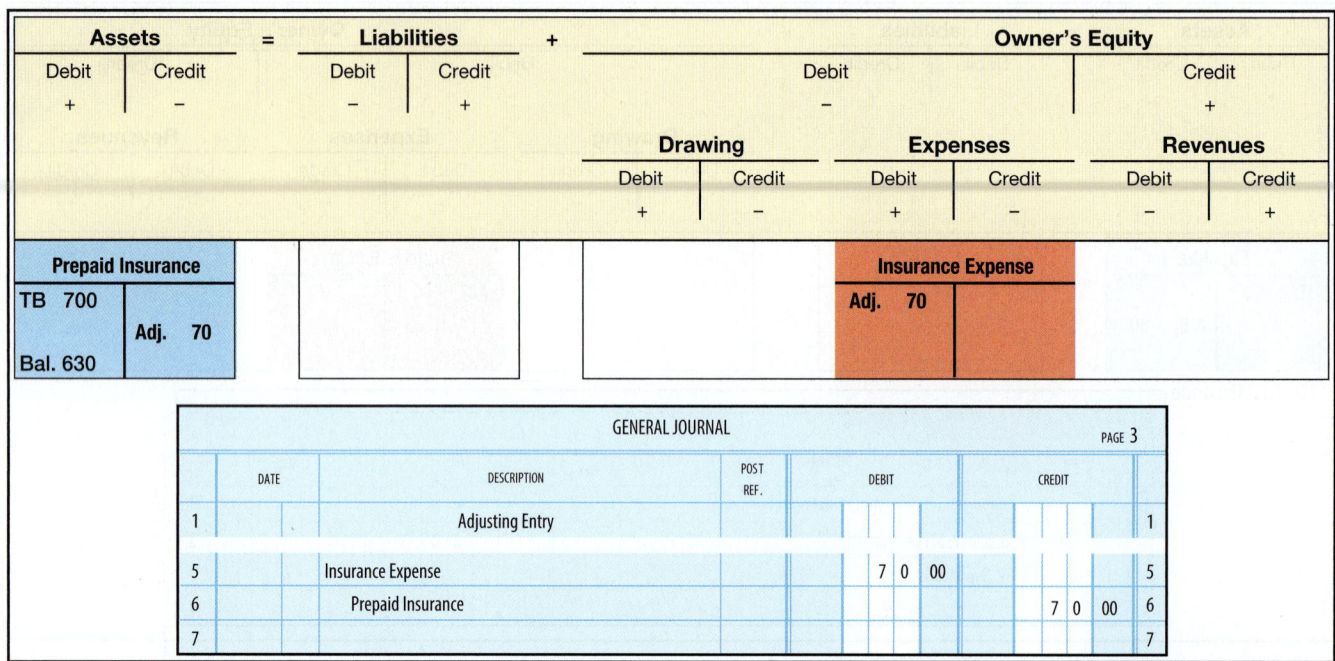

FIGURE 5-6 Effect of Adjusting Entry for Prepaid Insurance on Financial Statements

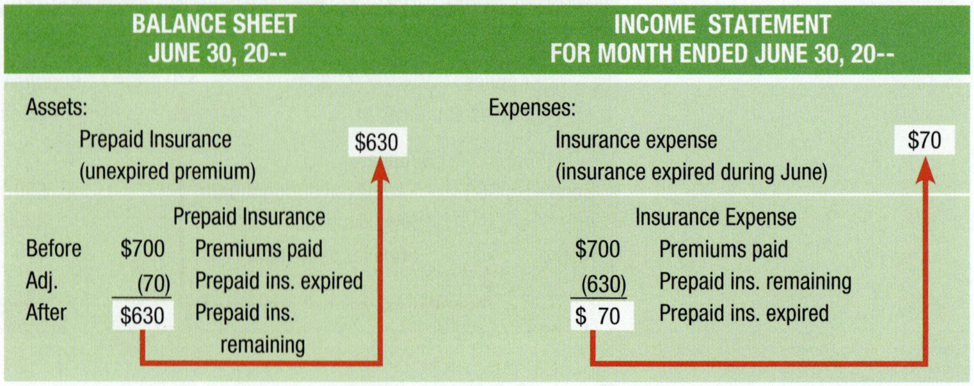

Wages Expense

Mitch paid his part-time employees $1,650 on June 27. Since then, they have earned an additional $400, but have not yet been paid. The additional wages expense must be recognized.

Since the employees have not been paid, Wages Payable, a liability, should be established. Thus, Wages Expense is debited and Wages Payable is credited for $400 in Figure 5-7. Note in Figure 5-8 that Wages Expense of $2,050 is reported on the income statement and Wages Payable of $400 is reported on the balance sheet.

FIGURE 5-7 Adjustment for Unpaid Wages

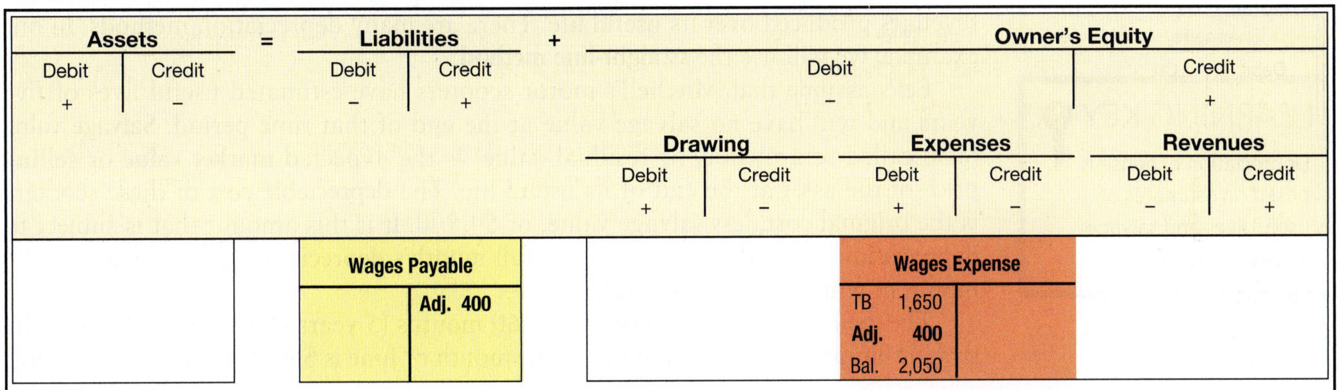

GENERAL JOURNAL PAGE 3

	DATE		DESCRIPTION	POST REF.	DEBIT	CREDIT	
1			Adjusting Entry				1
8			Wages Expense		400 00		8
9			Wages Payable			400 00	9
10							10

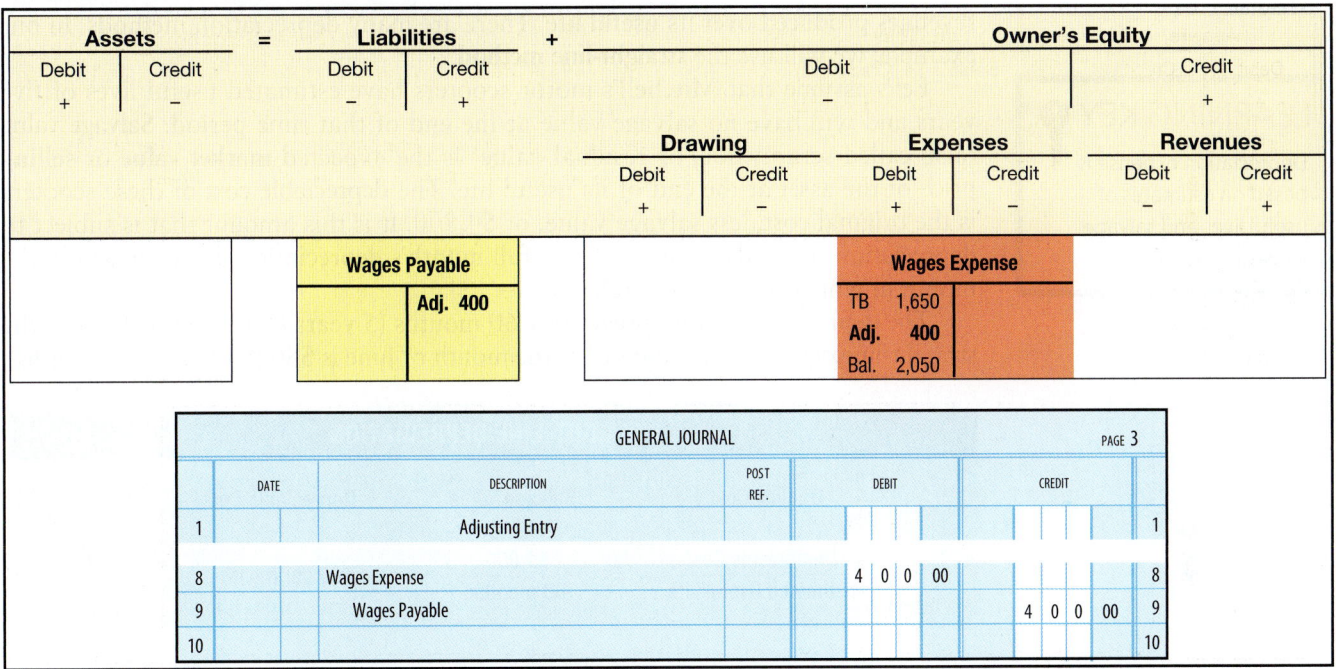

FIGURE 5-8 Effect of Adjusting Entry for Wages on Financial Statements

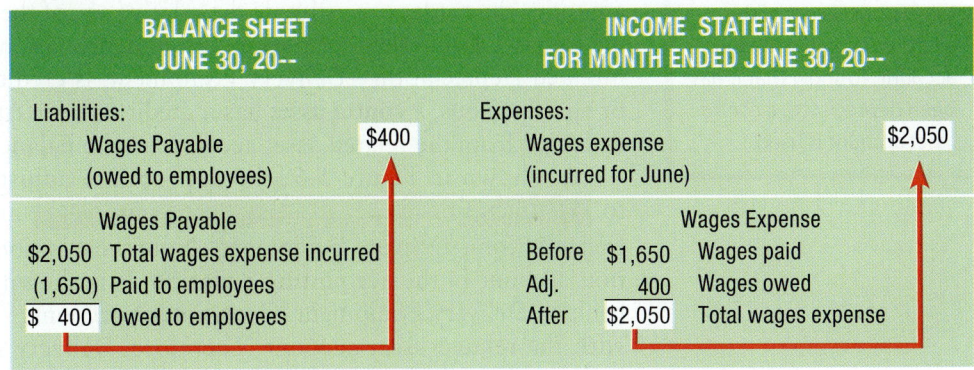

BALANCE SHEET JUNE 30, 20--			INCOME STATEMENT FOR MONTH ENDED JUNE 30, 20--		
Liabilities:			Expenses:		
	Wages Payable (owed to employees)	$400		Wages expense (incurred for June)	$2,050
	Wages Payable			Wages Expense	
$2,050	Total wages expense incurred		Before $1,650	Wages paid	
(1,650)	Paid to employees		Adj. 400	Wages owed	
$ 400	Owed to employees		After $2,050	Total wages expense	

LEARNING KEY

The historical cost principle is an important accounting concept. Many assets are recorded at their actual cost. This historical cost is not adjusted for changes in market values.

To learn about other depreciation methods, see the appendix to this chapter.

LEARNING KEY

Depreciation expense is based on estimates of useful lives and salvage values.

Depreciation Expense

During the month of June, Mitch purchased three motor scooters. Since the scooters will provide future benefits, they were recorded as assets in the delivery equipment account. Under the **historical cost principle**, many assets are required to be recorded at their actual cost, in this case $4,800. This cost remains on the books as long as the business owns the asset. No adjustments are made for changes in the market value of the asset. It does not matter whether the firm got a "good buy" or paid "too much" when the asset was purchased.

The period of time that an asset is expected to help produce revenues is called its **useful life**. The asset's useful life expires as a result of wear and tear or because it no longer satisfies the needs of the business. For example, as miles are added to the scooters, they will become less reliable and will eventually fail to run. As this happens, depreciation expense should be recognized and the value of the asset should be reduced. **Depreciation** is a method of *matching* an asset's original cost against the revenues produced over its useful life. There are many depreciation methods. In our example, we will use the **straight-line method**.

Let's assume that Mitchell's motor scooters have estimated useful lives of five years and will have no salvage value at the end of that time period. **Salvage value** (also called scrap value, or residual value) is the expected **market value** or selling price of the asset at the end of its useful life. The **depreciable cost** of these scooters is the original cost, less salvage value, or $4,800. It is this amount that is subject to depreciation. Let's also assume that a full month's depreciation is recognized in the month in which an asset is purchased.

The depreciable cost is spread over 60 months (5 years × 12 months). Thus, the straight-line depreciation expense for the month of June is $80 ($4,800 ÷ 60 months).

STRAIGHT-LINE DEPRECIATION

Original Cost − Salvage Value = Depreciable Cost

$$\frac{\text{Depreciable Cost}}{\text{Estimated Useful Life}} = \frac{\$4{,}800}{60\text{ months}} = \$80\text{ per month}$$

LEARNING KEY

Depreciable assets provide benefits over more than one year. Therefore, the historical cost of the asset remains in the asset account. To show that it has been depreciated, a *contra-asset* account is used.

When we made adjustments for supplies and prepaid insurance, the asset accounts were credited to show that they had been consumed. Assets of a durable nature that are expected to provide benefits over several years or more, called **plant assets**, require a different approach. The business maintains a record of the original cost and the amount of depreciation taken since the asset was acquired. By comparing these two amounts, the reader can estimate the relative age of the assets. Thus, instead of crediting Delivery Equipment for the amount of depreciation, a contra-asset account, Accumulated Depreciation—Delivery Equipment, is credited. "Contra" means opposite or against. Thus, a **contra-asset** has a credit balance (the opposite of an asset) and is deducted from the related asset account on the balance sheet.

As shown in Figure 5-9, the appropriate adjusting entry consists of a debit to Depreciation Expense—Delivery Equipment and a credit to Accumulated Depreciation—Delivery Equipment. Note the position of the accumulated depreciation account in the accounting equation. It is shown in the assets section, directly beneath Delivery Equipment. Contra-asset accounts should always be shown along with the related asset account. Therefore, Delivery Equipment and Accumulated Depreciation—Delivery Equipment are shown together.

FIGURE 5-9 Adjustment for Depreciation of Delivery Equipment

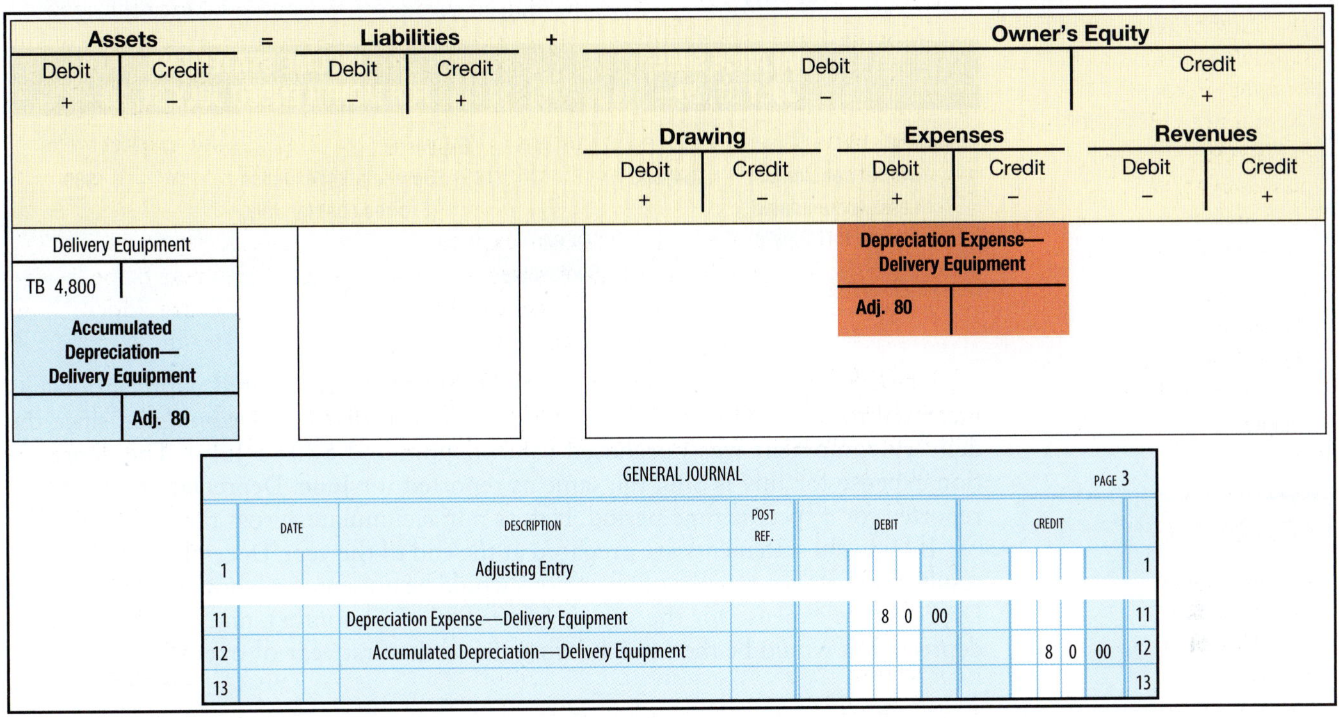
Assets = Liabilities + Owner's Equity
Debit + Credit −
Debit − Credit +
Debit −
Credit +
Drawing Debit + Credit −
Expenses Debit + Credit −
Revenues Debit − Credit +
Delivery Equipment
TB 4,800
Accumulated Depreciation—Delivery Equipment
Adj. 80
Depreciation Expense—Delivery Equipment
Adj. 80
GENERAL JOURNAL
PAGE 3
DATE DESCRIPTION POST REF. DEBIT CREDIT
1 Adjusting Entry 1
11 Depreciation Expense—Delivery Equipment 8 0 00 11
12 Accumulated Depreciation—Delivery Equipment 8 0 00 12
13 13

> **LEARNING KEY**
> There is no individual account that reports book value. It must be computed.
>
> Cost of Plant Assets
> − Accumulated Depreciation
> = Book Value

The same concept is used on the balance sheet. Note in Figure 5-10 that Accumulated Depreciation is reported immediately beneath Delivery Equipment as a deduction. The difference between these accounts is known as the **book value**, or **undepreciated cost**, of the delivery equipment. Book value simply means the value carried on the books or in the accounting records. It does *not* represent the market value, or selling price, of the asset.

FIGURE 5-10 Effect of Adjusting Entry for Depreciation on Financial Statements for June

BALANCE SHEET JUNE 30, 20--			INCOME STATEMENT FOR MONTH ENDED JUNE 30, 20--	
Assets:			Expenses:	
Delivery equipment	$4,800		Depreciation expense	$80
Less: Accumulated depreciation	80	$4,720 (Book value)	(Expired cost for June)	

If no delivery equipment is bought or sold during the next month, the same adjusting entry would be made at the end of July. If an income statement for the month of July and a balance sheet as of July 31 were prepared, the amounts shown in Figure 5-11 would be reported for the delivery equipment.

FIGURE 5-11 Effect of Adjusting Entry for Depreciation on Financial Statements for July

BALANCE SHEET JULY 31, 20--			INCOME STATEMENT FOR MONTH ENDED JULY 31, 20--	
Assets:			Expenses:	
Delivery equipment	$4,800		Depreciation expense	$80
Less: Accumulated depreciation	160	$4,640 (Book value)	(Expired cost for July)	

The cost ($4,800) remains unchanged, but the accumulated depreciation has increased to $160. This represents *the depreciation that has accumulated* since the delivery equipment was purchased ($80 in June and $80 in July). The depreciation expense for July is $80, the same as reported for June. Depreciation expense is reported for a specific time period. It does not accumulate across reporting periods.

If financial statements are prepared at the end of the year, December 31, 20--, the results for the seven months of operations would be presented as shown in Figure 5-12. Depreciation expense for the year is $560 ($80 × 7 months), and the accumulated depreciation would be the same because this is the first year of operation.

Cost / Useful life	$4,800 / 60 months	= $ 80
Dep./month		$ 80
Months in service		× 7
Dep. June–Dec.		$560

FIGURE 5-12 Straight-Line Depreciation for Seven Months

BALANCE SHEET DECEMBER 31, 20--			INCOME STATEMENT FOR YEAR ENDED DECEMBER 31, 20--	
Assets:			Expenses:	
Delivery equipment	$4,800		Depreciation expense	$560
Less: Accumulated depreciation	560	$4,240 (Book value)	(Expired cost for June through December)	

Expanded Chart of Accounts

CHECKPOINT

Complete Checkpoint-1 on page 158 to test your basic understanding of LO1.

Several new accounts were needed to make the adjusting entries. New accounts are easily added to the chart of accounts, as shown in Figure 5-13. Note the close relationship between assets and contra-assets in the numbering of the accounts. Contra-accounts carry the same number as the related asset account with a ".1" suffix. For example, Delivery Equipment is account number 185 and the contra-asset account, Accumulated Depreciation—Delivery Equipment, is account number 185.1.

LO2

Posting Adjusting Entries

Post adjusting entries to the general ledger.

Adjusting entries are posted to the general ledger in the same manner as all other entries, except that "*Adjusting*" is written in the Item column of the general ledger. Figure 5-14 shows the posting of the adjusting entries. The posting reference numbers are inserted as each entry is posted.

FIGURE 5-13 Expanded Chart of Accounts

MITCHELL'S CAMPUS DELIVERY
CHART OF ACCOUNTS

Assets		**Revenues**	
101	Cash	401	Delivery Fees
122	Accounts Receivable		
141	Supplies	**Expenses**	
145	Prepaid Insurance	511	Wages Expense
185	Delivery Equipment	521	Rent Expense
185.1	Accumulated Depr.—	523	Supplies Expense
	Delivery Equipment	525	Phone Expense
		535	Insurance Expense
Liabilities		541	Depr. Expense —
202	Accounts Payable		Delivery Equipment
219	Wages Payable		
Owner's Equity			
311	Mitchell Williams, Capital		
312	Mitchell Williams, Drawing		

FIGURE 5-14 Posting the Adjusting Entries

GENERAL JOURNAL PAGE 3

	DATE		DESCRIPTION	POST. REF.	DEBIT	CREDIT	
1			Adjusting Entries				1
2	20-- June	30	Supplies Expense	523	60 00		2
3			Supplies	141		60 00	3
4							4

(a)

GENERAL LEDGER

ACCOUNT: Supplies ACCOUNT NO. 141

DATE		ITEM	POST. REF.	DEBIT	CREDIT	BALANCE DEBIT	BALANCE CREDIT
20-- June	16		J1	80 00		80 00	
	30	Adjusting	J3		60 00	20 00	

ACCOUNT: Supplies Expense ACCOUNT NO. 523

DATE		ITEM	POST. REF.	DEBIT	CREDIT	BALANCE DEBIT	BALANCE CREDIT
20-- June	30	Adjusting	J3	60 00		60 00	

(b)

	DATE		DESCRIPTION	POST. REF.	DEBIT	CREDIT	
5		30	Insurance Expense	535	70 00		5
6			Prepaid Insurance	145		70 00	6
7							7

ACCOUNT: Prepaid Insurance ACCOUNT NO. 145

DATE		ITEM	POST. REF.	DEBIT	CREDIT	BALANCE DEBIT	BALANCE CREDIT
20-- June	18		J1	700 00		700 00	
	30	Adjusting	J3		70 00	630 00	

ACCOUNT: Insurance Expense ACCOUNT NO. 535

DATE		ITEM	POST. REF.	DEBIT	CREDIT	BALANCE DEBIT	BALANCE CREDIT
20-- June	30	Adjusting	J3	70 00		70 00	

(continued)

FIGURE 5-14 Posting the Adjusting Entries (*concluded*)

(c)

8	30	Wages Expense	511	4 0 0 00		8
9		Wages Payable	219		4 0 0 00	9
10						10

ACCOUNT: Wages Payable ACCOUNT NO. 219

DATE		ITEM	POST. REF.	DEBIT	CREDIT	BALANCE DEBIT	BALANCE CREDIT
20-- June	30	Adjusting	J3		4 0 0 00		4 0 0 00

ACCOUNT: Wages Expense ACCOUNT NO. 511

DATE		ITEM	POST. REF.	DEBIT	CREDIT	BALANCE DEBIT	BALANCE CREDIT
20-- June	27		J1	1 6 5 0 00		1 6 5 0 00	
	30	Adjusting	J3	4 0 0 00		2 0 5 0 00	

(d)

11	30	Depr. Expense — Delivery Equipment	541	8 0 00		11
12		Accum. Depr. — Delivery Equipment	185.1		8 0 00	12
13						

ACCOUNT: Accumulated Depreciation—Delivery Equipment ACCOUNT NO. 185.1

DATE		ITEM	POST. REF.	DEBIT	CREDIT	BALANCE DEBIT	BALANCE CREDIT
20-- June	30	Adjusting	J3		8 0 00		8 0 00

ACCOUNT: Depreciation Expense—Delivery Equipment ACCOUNT NO. 541

DATE		ITEM	POST. REF.	DEBIT	CREDIT	BALANCE DEBIT	BALANCE CREDIT
20-- June	30	Adjusting	J3	8 0 00		8 0 00	

CHECKPOINT

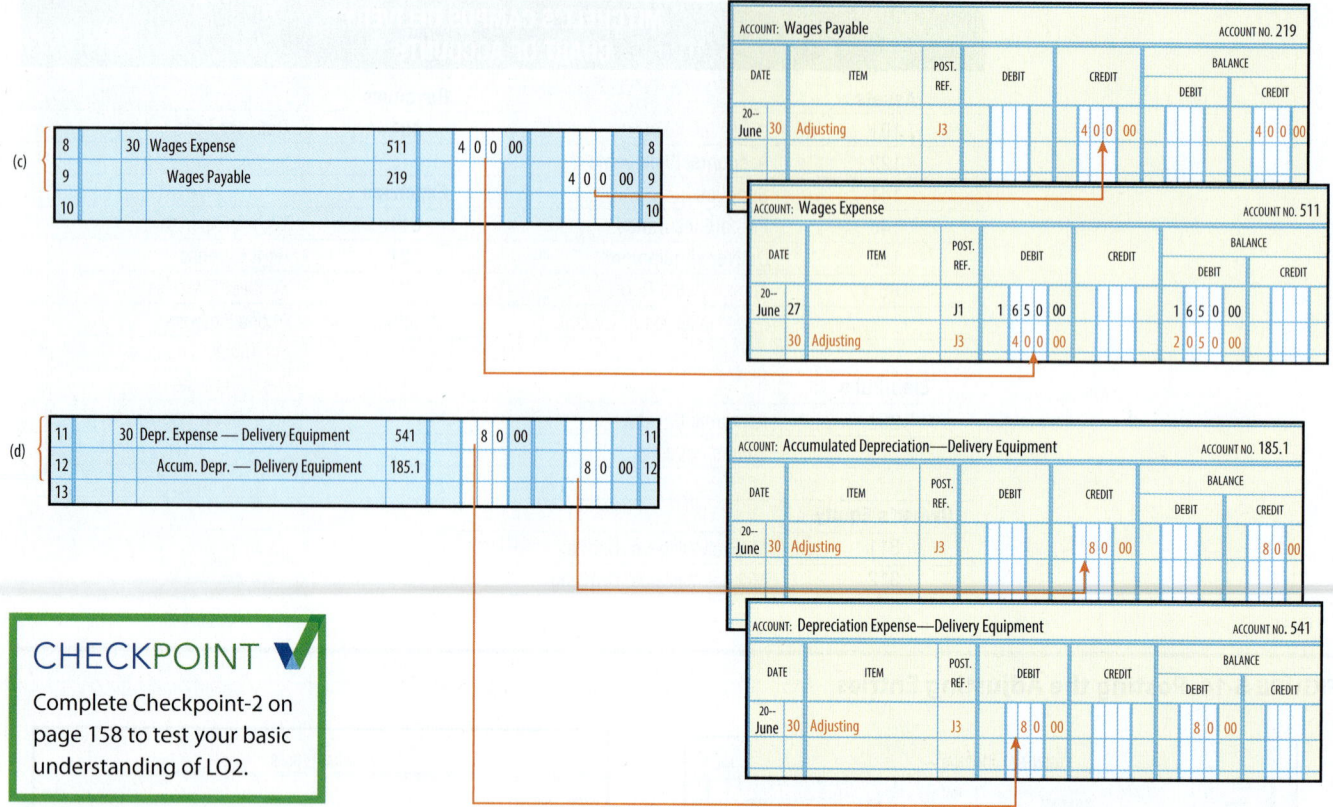

Complete Checkpoint-2 on page 158 to test your basic understanding of LO2.

LO3 The Work Sheet

Prepare a work sheet.

A **work sheet** pulls together all of the information needed to enter adjusting entries and prepare the financial statements. Work sheets are not financial statements, are not a formal part of the accounting system, and are not a required part of the accounting process. However, many accountants prepare them because they are very helpful in planning the adjustments and preparing the financial statements. Ordinarily, only the accountant uses a work sheet. For this reason, a work sheet is usually prepared as an Excel spreadsheet. When accounting software is used, a work sheet is not needed. We walk you through the manual creation of a work sheet in this section and throughout Chapter 6 to help you understand how work sheets are set up and used by accountants.

The 10-Column Work Sheet

Although a work sheet can take several forms, a common format has a column for account titles and 10 amount columns grouped into five pairs of debits and credits. The work sheet format and the five steps in preparing the work sheet are illustrated in Figure 5-15. As with financial statements, the work sheet has a heading consisting of the name of the company, name of the working paper, and the date of the accounting period just ended. The five major column headings for the work sheet are Trial Balance, Adjustments, Adjusted Trial Balance, Income Statement, and Balance Sheet.

FIGURE 5-15 Steps in Preparing the Work Sheet

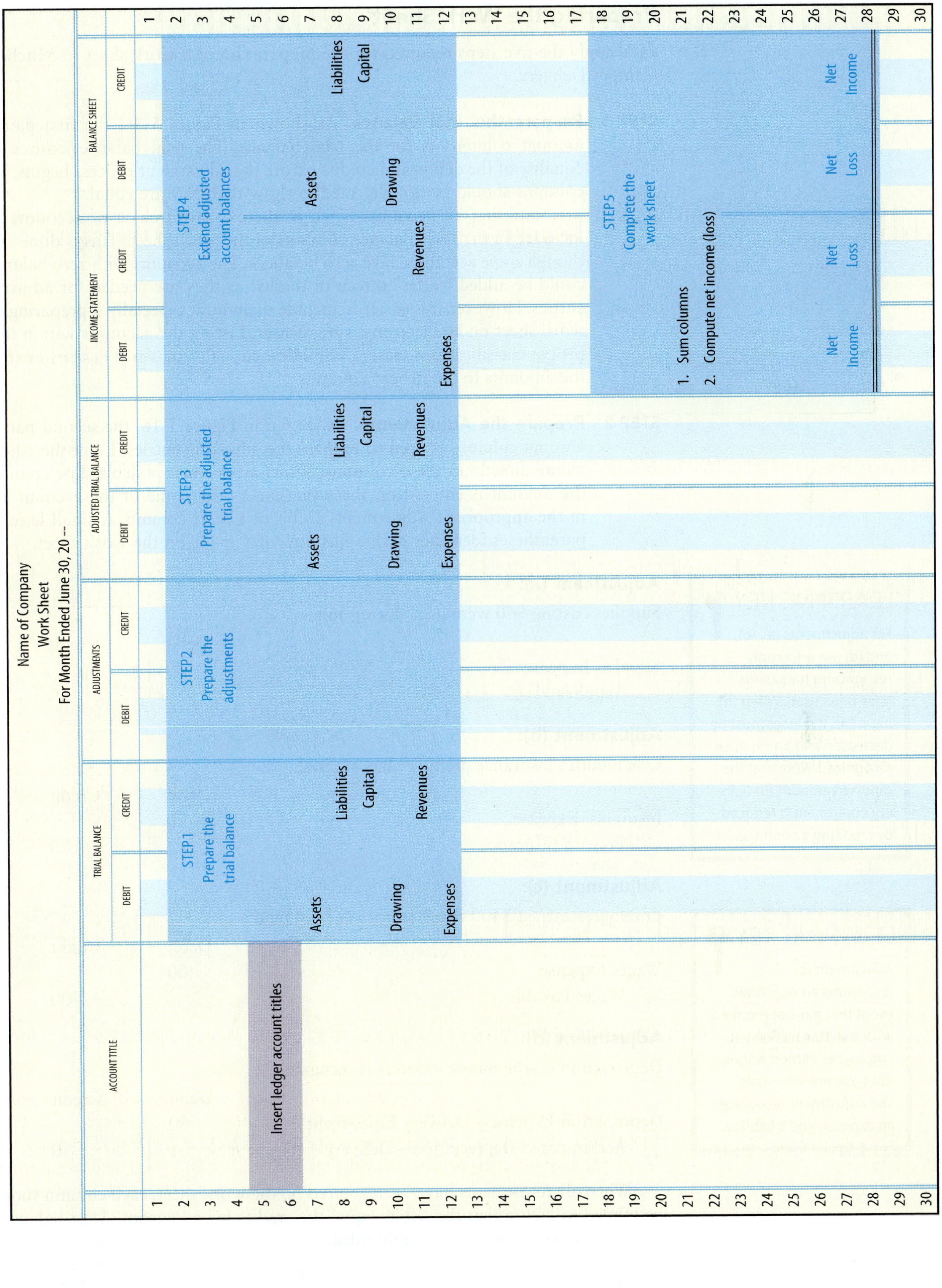
Name of Company
Work Sheet
For Month Ended June 30, 20 --
ACCOUNT TITLE
TRIAL BALANCE
DEBIT
CREDIT
ADJUSTMENTS
DEBIT
CREDIT
ADJUSTED TRIAL BALANCE
DEBIT
CREDIT
INCOME STATEMENT
DEBIT
CREDIT
BALANCE SHEET
DEBIT
CREDIT
Insert ledger account titles
STEP 1 Prepare the trial balance
Assets
Liabilities
Capital
Drawing
Revenues
Expenses
STEP 2 Prepare the adjustments
STEP 3 Prepare the adjusted trial balance
Assets
Liabilities
Capital
Drawing
Revenues
Expenses
Expenses
Revenues
STEP 4 Extend adjusted account balances
Assets
Drawing
Liabilities
Capital
STEP 5 Complete the work sheet
1. Sum columns
2. Compute net income (loss)
Net Income
Net Loss
Net Loss
Net Income

Preparing the Work Sheet

Let's apply the five steps required for the preparation of a work sheet to Mitchell's Campus Delivery.

STEP 1 **Prepare the Trial Balance.** As shown in Figure 5-16, the first pair of amount columns is for the trial balance. The trial balance assures the equality of the debits and credits before the adjustment process begins. The columns should be double ruled to show that they are equal.

Note that all accounts listed in the expanded chart of accounts are included in the Trial Balance columns of the work sheet. This is done even though some accounts have zero balances. The accounts with zero balances could be added to the bottom of the list as they are needed for adjusting entries. However, it is easier to include them now, especially if preparing the work sheet on an electronic spreadsheet. Listing the accounts within their proper classifications (assets, liabilities, etc.) also makes it easier to extend the amounts to the proper columns.

STEP 2 **Prepare the Adjustments.** As shown in Figure 5-16, the second pair of amount columns is used to prepare the adjusting entries. Enter the adjustments directly in these columns. When an account is debited or credited, the amount is entered on the same line as the name of the account and in the appropriate Adjustments Debit or Credit column. A small letter in parentheses identifies each adjusting entry made on the work sheet.

> **LEARNING KEY**
> For adjustments (a), (b), and (d), we are simply recognizing that assets have been used. When this happens, the asset must be decreased and an expense recognized. Note that the reported amount for delivery equipment is reduced by crediting a contra-asset.

Adjustment (a):

Supplies costing $60 were used during June.

	Debit	Credit
Supplies Expense	60	
Supplies		60

Adjustment (b):

One month's insurance premium has expired.

	Debit	Credit
Insurance Expense	70	
Prepaid Insurance		70

> **LEARNING KEY**
> Adjustment (c) recognizes an economic event that has not required an actual transaction yet. Employees earned wages, but have not been paid. The adjustment recognizes an expense and a liability.

Adjustment (c):

Employees earned $400 that has not yet been paid.

	Debit	Credit
Wages Expense	400	
Wages Payable		400

Adjustment (d):

Depreciation on the motor scooters is recognized.

	Debit	Credit
Depreciation Expense—Delivery Equipment	80	
Accumulated Depreciation—Delivery Equipment		80

When all adjustments have been entered on the work sheet, each column should be totaled to assure that the debits equal the credits for all entries. After balancing the columns, they should be double ruled.

FIGURE 5-16 Step 1: Prepare the Trial Balance; Step 2: Prepare the Adjustments

Mitchell's Campus Delivery
Work Sheet
For Month Ended June 30, 20 - -

	ACCOUNT TITLE	TRIAL BALANCE		ADJUSTMENT		ADJUSTED TRIAL BALANCE		INCOME STATEMENT		BALANCE SHEET		
		DEBIT	CREDIT	DEBIT	CREDIT	DEBIT	CREDIT	DEBIT	CREDIT	DEBIT	CREDIT	
1	Cash	470 00										1
2	Accounts Receivable	3,100 00										2
3	Supplies	80 00			(a) 60 00							3
4	Prepaid Insurance	700 00			(b) 70 00							4
5	Delivery Equipment	4,800 00										5
6	Accum. Depr.—Delivery Equipment				(d) 80 00							6
7	Accounts Payable		1,900 00									7
8	Wages Payable				(c) 400 00							8
9	Mitchell Williams, Capital		5,000 00									9
10	Mitchell Williams, Drawing	3,000 00										10
11	Delivery Fees		8,000 00									11
12	Wages Expense	1,650 00		(c) 400 00								12
13	Rent Expense	1,000 00										13
14	Supplies Expense			(a) 60 00								14
15	Phone Expense	100 00										15
16	Insurance Expense			(b) 70 00								16
17	Depr. Expense—Delivery Equipment			(d) 80 00								17
18		14,900 00	14,900 00	610 00	610 00							18
19	Net income											19
20		STEP 1		STEP 2								20
21												21
22												22
23												23
24												24
25												25
26												26
27												27
28												28
29												29
30												30

Step 1: Prepare the Trial Balance.
- Write the heading, account titles, and the debit and credit amounts from the general ledger.
- Place a single rule across the Trial Balance columns and total the debit and credit amounts.
- Place a double rule under the totals for each column.
- Total debits must equal total credits.

Step 2: Prepare the Adjustments.
- Record the adjustments.
  Hint: Make certain that each adjustment is on the same line as the account name and in the appropriate column.
  Hint: Identify each adjusting entry by a letter in parentheses.
- Rule the Adjustments columns.
- Total the Debit and Credit columns and double rule the columns.
- Total debits must equal total credits.

STEP 3 **Prepare the Adjusted Trial Balance.** As shown in Figure 5-17, the third pair of amount columns on the work sheet is the **Adjusted Trial Balance columns**.

- When an account balance is not affected by entries in the Adjustments columns, the amount in the Trial Balance columns is extended directly to the Adjusted Trial Balance columns.
- *When affected by an entry in the Adjustments columns, the account balance to be entered in the Adjusted Trial Balance columns increases or decreases by the amount of the adjusting entry.*

For example, in Mitchell's business, Supplies are listed in the Trial Balance Debit column as $80. Since the entry of $60 is in the Adjustments Credit column, the amount extended to the Adjusted Trial Balance Debit column is $20 ($80 – $60).

Wages Expense is listed in the Trial Balance Debit column as $1,650. Since $400 is in the Adjustments Debit column, the amount extended to the Adjusted Trial Balance Debit column is $2,050 ($1,650 + $400).

After all extensions have been made, the Adjusted Trial Balance columns are totaled to prove the equality of the debits and the credits. Once balanced, the columns are double ruled.

STEP 4 **Extend Adjusted Balances to the Income Statement and Balance Sheet Columns.** As shown in Figure 5-18, each account listed in the Adjusted Trial Balance must be extended to either the Income Statement or Balance Sheet columns. The **Income Statement columns** show the amounts that will be reported in the income statement. All revenue accounts are extended to the Income Statement Credit column and expense accounts are extended to the Income Statement Debit column.

The asset, liability, drawing, and capital accounts are extended to the **Balance Sheet columns**. Although called the Balance Sheet columns, these columns of the work sheet show the amounts that will be reported in the balance sheet and the statement of owner's equity. The asset and drawing accounts are extended to the Balance Sheet Debit column. The liability and owner's capital accounts are extended to the Balance Sheet Credit column.

> **LEARNING KEY**
> The Balance Sheet columns show the amounts for both the balance sheet and the statement of owner's equity.

STEP 5 **Complete the Work Sheet.** To complete the work sheet, first total the Income Statement columns. If the total of the credits (revenues) exceeds the total of the debits (expenses), the difference represents net income. If the total of the debits exceeds the total of the credits, the difference represents a net loss.

The Income Statement columns of Mitchell's work sheet in Figure 5-18 show total credits of $8,000 and total debits of $3,360. The difference, $4,640, is the net income for the month of June. This amount should be added to the Debit column to balance the Income Statement columns. "Net Income" should be written on the same line in the Account Title column. If the business had a net loss, the amount of the loss would be added to the Income Statement Credit column and the words "Net Loss" would be written in the Account Title column. Once balanced, the columns should be double ruled.

Finally, the Balance Sheet columns are totaled. The difference between the totals of these columns also is the amount of net income or net loss for the accounting period. If the total debits exceed the total credits, the difference is net income. If the total credits exceed the total debits, the difference is a net loss. This difference should be the same as the difference we found for the Income Statement columns.

> **LEARNING KEY**
> In the Balance Sheet columns of the work sheet, total debits minus total credits equals net *income* if greater than zero and equals net loss if less than zero.

FIGURE 5-17 Step 3: Prepare the Adjusted Trial Balance

Mitchell's Campus Delivery
Work Sheet
For Month Ended June 30, 20 - -

	ACCOUNT TITLE	TRIAL BALANCE		ADJUSTMENT		ADJUSTED TRIAL BALANCE		INCOME STATEMENT		BALANCE SHEET		
		DEBIT	CREDIT	DEBIT	CREDIT	DEBIT	CREDIT	DEBIT	CREDIT	DEBIT	CREDIT	
1	Cash	470 00				470 00						1
2	Accounts Receivable	3100 00				3100 00						2
3	Supplies	80 00			(a) 60 00	20 00						3
4	Prepaid Insurance	700 00			(b) 70 00	630 00						4
5	Delivery Equipment	4800 00				4800 00						5
6	Accum. Depr.—Delivery Equipment				(d) 80 00		80 00					6
7	Accounts Payable		1900 00				1900 00					7
8	Wages Payable				(c) 400 00		400 00					8
9	Mitchell Williams, Capital		5000 00				5000 00					9
10	Mitchell Williams, Drawing	3000 00				3000 00						10
11	Delivery Fees		8000 00				8000 00					11
12	Wages Expense	1650 00		(c) 400 00		2050 00						12
13	Rent Expense	1000 00				1000 00						13
14	Supplies Expense			(a) 60 00		60 00						14
15	Phone Expense	100 00				100 00						15
16	Insurance Expense			(b) 70 00		70 00						16
17	Depr. Expense—Delivery Equipment			(d) 80 00		80 00						17
18		14900 00	14900 00	610 00	610 00	15380 00	15380 00					18
19	Net income											19
20		STEP 1		STEP 2		STEP 3						20
21												21
22												22
23												23
24												24
25												25
26												26
27												27
28												28
29												29
30												30

No adjustment: simply extend balance to appropriate column.

A debit and a credit: subtract.

A single debit or credit: extend to appropriate column.

Two debits: add.

When columns are balanced, use double ruling.

Step 3: Prepare the Adjusted Trial Balance.

- Extend those debits and credits that are not adjusted directly to the appropriate Adjusted Trial Balance column.
- Enter the adjusted balances in the appropriate Adjusted Trial Balance column.

  Hint: If an account has a debit and a credit, subtract the adjustment. If an account has two debits or two credits, add the adjustment.
- Single rule the Adjusted Trial Balance columns. Total and double rule the Debit and Credit columns.
- Total debits must equal total credits.

FIGURE 5-18 **Step 4: Extend Adjusted Balances to the Inc. Stmt. & Balance Sheet Columns; Step 5: Complete the Work Sheet**

Mitchell's Campus Delivery
Work Sheet
For Month Ended June 30, 20 - -

	ACCOUNT TITLE	TRIAL BALANCE		ADJUSTMENT		ADJUSTED TRIAL BALANCE		INCOME STATEMENT		BALANCE SHEET		
		DEBIT	CREDIT	DEBIT	CREDIT	DEBIT	CREDIT	DEBIT	CREDIT	DEBIT	CREDIT	
1	Cash	470 00				470 00				470 00		1
2	Accounts Receivable	3100 00				3100 00				3100 00		2
3	Supplies	80 00			(a) 60 00	20 00				20 00		3
4	Prepaid Insurance	700 00			(b) 70 00	630 00				630 00		4
5	Delivery Equipment	4800 00				4800 00				4800 00		5
6	Accum. Depr.—Delivery Equipment				(d) 80 00		80 00				80 00	6
7	Accounts Payable		1900 00				1900 00				1900 00	7
8	Wages Payable				(c) 400 00		400 00				400 00	8
9	Mitchell Williams, Capital		5000 00				5000 00				5000 00	9
10	Mitchell Williams, Drawing	3000 00				3000 00				3000 00		10
11	Delivery Fees		8000 00				8000 00		8000 00			11
12	Wages Expense	1650 00		(c) 400 00		2050 00		2050 00				12
13	Rent Expense	1000 00				1000 00		1000 00				13
14	Supplies Expense			(a) 60 00		60 00		60 00				14
15	Phone Expense	100 00				100 00		100 00				15
16	Insurance Expense			(b) 70 00		70 00		70 00				16
17	Depr. Expense—Delivery Equipment			(d) 80 00		80 00		80 00				17
18		14900 00	14900 00	610 00	610 00	15380 00	15380 00	3360 00	8000 00	12020 00	7380 00	18
19	Net income							4640 00			4640 00	19
20								8000 00	8000 00	12020 00	12020 00	20
21												21
22												22

STEP 1 STEP 2 STEP 3 STEPS 4 AND 5

Step 4: Extend Adjusted Balances to the Income Statement and Balance Sheet Columns.
- Extend all revenue accounts to the Income Statement Credit column.
- Extend all expense accounts to the Income Statement Debit column.
- Extend the asset and drawing accounts to the Balance Sheet Debit column.
- Extend the liability and owner's capital accounts to the Balance Sheet Credit columns.

Step 5: Complete the Work Sheet.
- Rule and total the Income Statement and Balance Sheet columns.
- Calculate the difference between the Income Statement Debit and Credit columns.
- Calculate the difference between the Balance Sheet Debit and Credit columns.
  Hint: If the Income Statement credits exceed debits, net income has occurred; otherwise a net loss has occurred. If the Balance Sheet debits exceed the credits, the difference is net income; otherwise a net loss has occurred.
  Hint: The difference between the Balance Sheet columns should be the same as the difference between the Income Statement columns.
- Add the net income to the Income Statement Debit column or add the net loss to the Income Statement Credit column. Add the net income to the Balance Sheet credit column or the net loss to the Balance Sheet Debit column. Write "Net income" or "Net Loss" in the Account Title column.
- Total and double rule the columns.

The Balance Sheet columns of Mitchell's work sheet show total debits of $12,020 and total credits of $7,380. The difference of $4,640 represents the net income for the month. This amount is added to the Credit column to balance the Balance Sheet columns. If the business had a net loss, this amount would be added to the Balance Sheet Debit column. Once balanced, the columns should be double ruled.

A trick for remembering the appropriate placement of the net income and net loss is the following: Net Income *apart*; Net Loss *together*. Figure 5-19 illustrates this learning aid.

CHECKPOINT

Complete Checkpoint-3 on page 158 to test your basic understanding of LO3.

FIGURE 5-19 Net Income Apart, Net Loss Together

	INCOME STATEMENT		BALANCE SHEET	
	DEBIT	CREDIT	DEBIT	CREDIT
	1135 00	2000 00	4815 00	3950 00
Net Income	865 00			865 00
	2000 00	2000 00	4815 00	4815 00

Apart

	INCOME STATEMENT		BALANCE SHEET	
	DEBIT	CREDIT	DEBIT	CREDIT
	2500 00	2000 00	5015 00	5515 00
Net Loss		500 00	500 00	
	2500 00	2500 00	5515 00	5515 00

Together

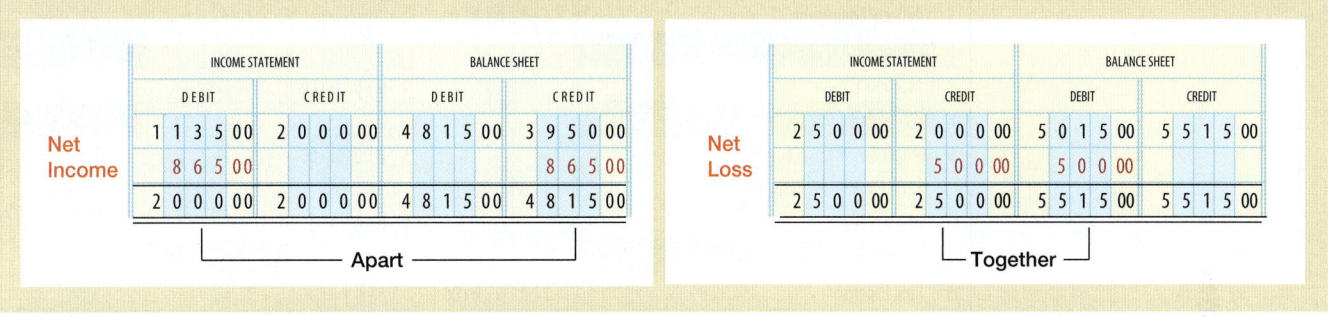

LO4 Finding Errors on the Work Sheet

Describe methods for finding errors on the work sheet.

If any of the columns on the work sheet do not balance, you must find the error before you continue. Once you are confident that the work sheet is accurate, you are ready to journalize the adjusting entries and prepare financial statements. Figure 5-20 offers tips for finding errors on the work sheet.

FIGURE 5-20 Finding Errors on the Work Sheet

TIPS FOR FINDING ERRORS ON THE WORK SHEET
1. Check the addition of all columns.
2. Check the addition and subtraction required when extending to the Adjusted Trial Balance columns.
3. Make sure the adjusted account balances have been extended to the appropriate columns.
4. Make sure that the net income or net loss has been added to the appropriate columns.

CHECKPOINT

Complete Checkpoint-4 on page 158 to test your basic understanding of LO4.

LO5 Journalizing Adjusting Entries from the Work Sheet

Journalize adjusting entries from the work sheet.

Keep in mind that the work sheet simply helps the accountant organize the end-of-period work. *Writing the adjustments on the work sheet has no effect on the ledger accounts in the accounting system. The only way to change the balance of a ledger account is to make a journal entry.* Once the work sheet has been completed, simply copy the adjustments from the work sheet to the journal, as shown in Figure 5-21.

FIGURE 5-21 Journalizing Adjusting Entries from the Work Sheet

Mitchell's Campus Delivery
Work Sheet (Partial)
For Month Ended June 30, 20--

	ACCOUNT TITLE	TRIAL BALANCE DEBIT	TRIAL BALANCE CREDIT	ADJUSTMENTS DEBIT	ADJUSTMENTS CREDIT
1	Cash	470 00			
2	Accounts Receivable	3100 00			
3	Supplies	80 00			(a) 60 00
4	Prepaid Insurance	700 00			(b) 70 00
5	Delivery Equipment	4800 00			
6	Accum. Depr.—Delivery Equipment				(d) 80 00
7	Accounts Payable		1900 00		
8	Wages Payable				(c) 400 00
9	Mitchell Williams, Capital		5000 00		
10	Mitchell Williams, Drawing	3000 00			
11	Delivery Fees		8000 00		
12	Wages Expense	1650 00		(c) 400 00	
13	Rent Expense	1000 00			
14	Supplies Expense			(a) 60 00	
15	Phone Expense	100 00			
16	Insurance Expense			(b) 70 00	
17	Depr. Expense—Delivery Equipment			(d) 80 00	
18		14900 00	14900 00	610 00	610 00

GENERAL JOURNAL PAGE 3

		DATE		DESCRIPTION	POST. REF.	DEBIT	CREDIT	
	1			Adjusting Entries				1
(a)	2	20-- June	30	Supplies Expense	523	60 00		2
	3			Supplies	141		60 00	3
	4							4
(b)	5		30	Insurance Expense	535	70 00		5
	6			Prepaid Insurance	145		70 00	6
	7							7
(c)	8		30	Wages Expense	511	400 00		8
	9			Wages Payable	219		400 00	9
	10							10
(d)	11		30	Depr. Expense—Delivery Equipment	541	80 00		11
	12			Accum. Depr.—Delivery Equipment	185.1		80 00	12

CHECKPOINT

Complete Checkpoint-5 on page 159 to test your basic understanding of LO5.

Mitchell's adjusting entries are illustrated in Figure 5-21 as they would appear in a general journal. Note that the last day of the accounting period, June 30, has been entered in the date column and "*Adjusting Entries*" is written in the Description column prior to the first adjusting entry. No explanation is required in the Description column for individual adjusting entries. We simply label them as adjusting entries.

LO6

Methods of Accounting: Cash, Modified Cash, and Accrual

Explain the cash, modified cash, and accrual bases of accounting.

The accrual basis of accounting offers the best matching of revenues and expenses and is required under generally accepted accounting principles. GAAP financial statements prepared using the accrual method are particularly important when major businesses want to raise large amounts of money. Investors and creditors expect GAAP financial statements and generally will not invest or make loans without them.

However, many small professional service organizations are not concerned with raising large amounts of money from investors and creditors. These organizations include CPAs, doctors, dentists, lawyers, engineers, and architects. Since these organizations do not need to prepare GAAP financial statements, they often use the cash or modified cash basis. If one of these organizations needs to borrow money from a bank that requires GAAP financial statements, an accountant can convert the financial statements to the accrual basis.

Under the **accrual basis of accounting**, revenues are recorded when earned. Revenues are considered earned when a service has been provided or a product has been sold, regardless of when cash is received from the customer. If cash is not received, a receivable is set up.

The accrual basis also assumes that expenses are recorded when incurred. Expenses are incurred when a service is received or an asset consumed in an effort to generate revenues. This is done regardless of when cash is paid. If cash is not paid when a service is received, a payable is set up. When assets are consumed, prepaid assets are decreased or long-term assets are depreciated. Since the accrual basis accounts for long-term assets, prepaid assets, receivables, and payables, it is the most comprehensive system and best method of measuring income for the vast majority of businesses.

LEARNING KEY

Accrual Basis

Accounting for: Revenues and Expenses	**Accounting for: Assets and Liabilities**	
Record revenue when earned.	Accounts receivable:	Yes
Record expenses when incurred.	Accounts payable:	Yes
	Prepaid assets:	Yes
	Long-term assets:	Yes

Under the **cash basis of accounting**, revenues are recorded when cash is received and expenses are recorded when cash is paid. This method will provide results that are similar to the accrual basis if there are few receivables, payables, and assets. However, as shown in Figure 5-22, the cash and accrual bases can result in very different measures of net income if a business has significant amounts of receivables, payables, and assets.

LEARNING KEY

Cash Basis

Accounting for: Revenues and Expenses	**Accounting for: Assets and Liabilities**	
Record revenue when cash is received.	Accounts receivable:	No
Record expenses when cash is paid.	Accounts payable:	No
	Prepaid assets:	No
	Long-term assets:	No

FIGURE 5-22 Cash versus Accrual Accounting

RECOGNITION OF REVENUES AND EXPENSES: ACCRUAL BASIS VS. CASH BASIS				
	Method of Accounting			
	Accrual Basis		Cash Basis	
Transaction	Expense	Revenue	Expense	Revenue
(a) Provided services on account, $600.		$600		
(b) Paid wages earned this period, $300	$300		$300	
(c) Received cash for services performed on account last month, $200				$ 200
(d) Received cleaning bill for month, $250	250			
(e) Paid on account for last month's advertising, $100			100	
(f) Purchase of supplies, $50			50	
(g) Supplies used during month, $40	40			
	$590	$600	$450	$ 200
Revenue		$600		$ 200
Expense		590		450
Net Income (Loss)		$ 10		$(250)
Revenues are recognized when:		earned		cash is received
Expenses are recognized when:		incurred		cash is paid

The modified cash basis is the same as the accrual basis, except receivables and payables are not recognized for revenues and operating expenses.

A third method of accounting combines aspects of the cash and accrual methods. With the **modified cash basis of accounting**, a business uses the cash basis for recording revenues and most expenses. Exceptions are made when cash is paid for assets with useful lives greater than one accounting period. For example, under a strict cash basis, if cash is paid for equipment, buildings, supplies, or insurance, the amount is immediately recorded as an expense. This approach could cause major distortions when measuring net income. Under the modified cash basis, cash payments like these are recorded as assets, and adjustments are made each period as under the accrual basis. Liabilities associated with the acquisition of these assets are also recognized.

Although similar to the accrual basis, the modified cash basis does not account for receivables or for payables for services received. Thus, the modified cash basis is a combination of the cash and accrual methods of accounting. The differences and similarities among the cash, modified cash, and accrual methods of accounting are demonstrated in Figure 5-23.

LEARNING KEY

Modified Cash Basis

Accounting for:
Revenues and Expenses

Record revenue when cash is received.

Record expenses when cash is paid, except for assets with useful lives greater than one accounting period. Accrual accounting is used for prepaid assets (insurance and supplies) and long-term assets.

Accounting for:
Assets and Liabilities

Accounts receivable:	No
Accounts payable	
for purchase of assets:	Yes
for services received:	No
Prepaid assets:	Yes
Long-term assets:	Yes

FIGURE 5-23 Comparison of Cash, Modified Cash, and Accrual Methods

ENTRIES MADE UNDER EACH ACCOUNTING METHOD			
Event	**Cash**	**Modified Cash**	**Accrual**
Revenues: Perform services for cash	Cash Professional Fees	Cash Professional Fees	Cash Professional Fees
Perform services on account	No entry	No entry	Accounts Receivable Professional Fees
Expenses: Pay cash for operating expenses: wages, advertising, rent, phone, etc.	Expense Cash	Expense Cash	Expense Cash
Pay cash for prepaid items: insurance, supplies, etc.	Expense Cash	Prepaid Asset Cash	Prepaid Asset Cash
Pay cash for property, plant, and equipment (PP&E)	Expense Cash	PP&E Asset Cash	PP&E Asset Cash
Receive bill for services received	No entry	No entry	Expense Accounts Payable
End-of-period adjustments: Wages earned by employees but not paid	No entry	No entry	Wages Expense Wages Payable
Prepaid items used	No entry	Expense Prepaid Asset	Expense Prepaid Asset
Depreciation on property, plant, and equipment	No entry	Depreciation Expense Accumulated Depreciation	Depreciation Expense Accumulated Depreciation
Other: Purchase of assets on account	No entry	Asset Accounts Payable	Asset Accounts Payable
Payments for assets purchased on account	Expense Cash	Accounts Payable Cash	Accounts Payable Cash

LEARNING KEY

The shaded areas in Figure 5-23 show that sometimes the modified cash basis is the same as the cash basis and sometimes it is the same as the accrual basis. For some transactions, all methods are the same.

CHECKPOINT

Complete Checkpoint-6 on page 159 to test your basic understanding of LO6.

If all businesses were the same, only one method of accounting would be needed. However, businesses vary in their need for major assets like buildings and equipment, the amount of customer receivables, and payables to suppliers. For example, if a business were rather small with no major assets, receivables, or payables, it would be simpler to use the cash basis of accounting. In addition, under these circumstances, the difference in net income under the accrual and cash bases of accounting would be small. Most individuals fit this description and use the cash basis on their tax returns.

Businesses with buildings and equipment, but few receivables and payables, might use the modified cash basis. Again, the accounting would be a little simpler and differences between net income computed under the modified cash and accrual bases would be small. Finally, businesses with buildings and equipment, and receivables and payables, should use the accrual basis of accounting to achieve the best matching of revenues and expenses.

SELF-STUDY

LEARNING OBJECTIVES		Key Points to Remember
LO1	**Prepare end-of-period adjustments.**	End-of-period adjustments are necessary to bring the general ledger accounts up to date prior to preparing financial statements. Reasons to adjust the trial balance are as follows: 1. To report all revenues earned during the accounting period. 2. To report all expenses incurred to produce the revenues during the accounting period. 3. To accurately report the assets on the balance sheet. Some assets may have expired, depreciated, or been used up during the accounting period. 4. To accurately report the liabilities on the balance sheet date. Expenses may have been incurred, but not yet paid.
LO2	**Post adjusting entries to the general ledger.**	Adjusting entries are posted to the general ledger in the same manner as all other entries, except that "Adjusting" is written in the Item column of the general ledger.
LO3	**Prepare a work sheet.**	Steps in preparing the work sheet are as follows: 1. Prepare the trial balance. 2. Prepare the adjustments. 3. Prepare the adjusted trial balance. 4. Extend the adjusted account balances to the Income Statement and Balance Sheet columns. 5. Total the Income Statement and Balance Sheet columns to compute the net income or net loss.
LO4	**Describe methods for finding errors on the work sheet.**	Tips for finding errors on the work sheet include the following: 1. Check the addition of all columns. 2. Check the addition and subtraction required when extending to the Adjusted Trial Balance columns. 3. Make sure the adjusted account balances have been extended to the appropriate columns. 4. Make sure that the net income or net loss has been added to the appropriate columns.
LO5	**Journalize adjusting entries from the work sheet.**	The adjustments are copied from the work sheet to the journal. The last day of the accounting period is entered in the Date column and "Adjusting Entries" is written in the Description column.
LO6	**Explain the cash, modified cash, and accrual bases of accounting.**	Cash Basis—Record revenues when cash is received and expenses when cash is paid. Accrual Basis—Record revenues when earned and expenses as incurred. Modified Cash Basis—Same as accrual, except no accounts receivable and no accounts payable for operating expenses.

DEMONSTRATION PROBLEM

Justin Park is a lawyer specializing in corporate tax law. He began his practice on January 1. A chart of accounts and trial balance taken on December 31, 20--, are provided below and on page 154.

Information for year-end adjustments is as follows:

(a) Office supplies on hand at year-end amounted to $300.

(b) On January 1, 20--, Park purchased office equipment costing $15,000 with an expected life of five years and no salvage value.

(c) Computer equipment costing $6,000 with an expected life of three years and no salvage value was purchased on July 1, 20--. Assume that Park computes depreciation to the nearest full month.

(d) A premium of $1,200 for a one-year insurance policy was paid on December 1, 20--.

(e) Wages earned by Park's part-time secretary, which have not yet been paid, amount to $300.

REQUIRED

1. Prepare the work sheet for the year ended December 31, 20--.
2. Prepare adjusting entries in a general journal.

JUSTIN PARK LEGAL SERVICES
CHART OF ACCOUNTS

Assets		**Revenue**	
101	Cash	401	Client Fees
142	Office Supplies		
145	Prepaid Insurance	**Expenses**	
181	Office Equipment	511	Wages Expense
181.1	Accumulated Depr.—	521	Rent Expense
	Office Equipment	523	Office Supplies Expense
187	Computer Equipment	525	Phone Expense
187.1	Accumulated Depr.—	533	Utilities Expense
	Computer Equipment	535	Insurance Expense
Liabilities		541	Depr. Expense—
201	Notes Payable		Office Equipment
202	Accounts Payable	542	Depr. Expense—
219	Wages Payable		Computer Equipment
Owner's Equity			
311	Justin Park, Capital		
312	Justin Park, Drawing		

(continued)

Justin Park Legal Services
Trial Balance
December 31, 20 --

ACCOUNT TITLE	ACCOUNT NO.	DEBIT BALANCE	CREDIT BALANCE
Cash	101	7,000.00	
Office Supplies	142	800.00	
Prepaid Insurance	145	1,200.00	
Office Equipment	181	15,000.00	
Computer Equipment	187	6,000.00	
Notes Payable	201		5,000.00
Accounts Payable	202		500.00
Justin Park, Capital	311		11,400.00
Justin Park, Drawing	312	5,000.00	
Client Fees	401		40,000.00
Wages Expense	511	12,000.00	
Rent Expense	521	5,000.00	
Phone Expense	525	1,000.00	
Utilities Expense	533	3,900.00	
		56,900.00	56,900.00

The solution to part (1) is found on page 155.

2.

GENERAL JOURNAL PAGE 11

	DATE		DESCRIPTION	POST. REF.	DEBIT	CREDIT	
1			Adjusting Entries				1
2	20-- Dec.	31	Office Supplies Expense		500.00		2
3			Office Supplies			500.00	3
4							4
5		31	Depr. Expense—Office Equipment		3,000.00		5
6			Accum. Depr.—Office Equipment			3,000.00	6
7							7
8		31	Depr. Expense—Computer Equipment		1,000.00		8
9			Accum. Depr.—Computer Equipment			1,000.00	9
10							10
11		31	Insurance Expense		100.00		11
12			Prepaid Insurance			100.00	12
13							13
14		31	Wages Expense		300.00		14
15			Wages Payable			300.00	15

SOLUTION 1.

Justin Park Legal Services
Work Sheet
For Year Ended December 31, 20--

	ACCOUNT TITLE	TRIAL BALANCE		ADJUSTMENTS		ADJUSTED TRIAL BALANCE		INCOME STATEMENT		BALANCE SHEET		
		DEBIT	CREDIT	DEBIT	CREDIT	DEBIT	CREDIT	DEBIT	CREDIT	DEBIT	CREDIT	
1	Cash	7000 00				7000 00				7000 00		1
2	Office Supplies	800 00			(a) 500 00	300 00				300 00		2
3	Prepaid Insurance	1200 00			(d) 100 00	1100 00				1100 00		3
4	Office Equipment	15000 00				15000 00				15000 00		4
5	Accum. Depr.—Office Equip.				(b) 3000 00		3000 00				3000 00	5
6	Computer Equipment	6000 00				6000 00				6000 00		6
7	Accum. Depr.—Computer Equip.				(c) 1000 00		1000 00				1000 00	7
8	Notes Payable		5000 00				5000 00				5000 00	8
9	Accounts Payable		500 00				500 00				500 00	9
10	Wages Payable				(e) 300 00		300 00				300 00	10
11	Justin Park, Capital		11400 00				11400 00				11400 00	11
12	Justin Park, Drawing	5000 00				5000 00				5000 00		12
13	Client Fees		40000 00				40000 00		40000 00			13
14	Wages Expense	12000 00		(e) 300 00		12300 00		12300 00				14
15	Rent Expense	5000 00				5000 00		5000 00				15
16	Office Supplies Expense			(a) 500 00		500 00		500 00				16
17	Phone Expense	1000 00				1000 00		1000 00				17
18	Utilities Expense	3900 00				3900 00		3900 00				18
19	Insurance Expense			(d) 100 00		100 00		100 00				19
20	Depr. Expense—Office Equip.			(b) 3000 00		3000 00		3000 00				20
21	Depr. Expense—Computer Equip.			(c) 1000 00		1000 00		1000 00				21
22		56900 00	56900 00	4900 00	4900 00	61200 00	61200 00	26800 00	40000 00	34400 00	21200 00	22
23	Net Income							13200 00			13200 00	23
24								40000 00	40000 00	34400 00	34400 00	24

KEY TERMS

accrual basis of accounting (149) A method of accounting under which revenues are recorded when earned and expenses are recorded when incurred.

Adjusted Trial Balance columns (144) The third pair of amount columns on the work sheet. They are used to prove the equality of the debits and credits in the general ledger accounts after making all end-of-period adjustments.

adjusting entries (131) Journal entries made at the end of an accounting period to reflect changes in account balances that are not the direct result of an exchange with an outside party.

Balance Sheet columns (144) The work sheet columns that show the amounts that will be reported in the balance sheet and the statement of owner's equity.

book value (137) The difference between the asset account and its related accumulated depreciation account. The value reflected by the accounting records.

cash basis of accounting (149) A method of accounting under which revenues are recorded when cash is received and expenses are recorded when cash is paid.

contra-asset (136) An account with a credit balance that is deducted from the related asset account on the balance sheet.

depreciable cost (136) The cost of an asset that is subject to depreciation.

depreciation (136) A method of matching an asset's original cost against the revenues produced over its useful life.

expense recognition principle (131) Expenses should be recognized when incurred, regardless of when cash is paid. Expenses are generally considered to be incurred when services are received or assets consumed.

fiscal year (131) A 12-month period for which financial reports are prepared.

historical cost principle (136) A principle that requires many assets to be recorded at their actual cost.

Income Statement columns (144) The work sheet columns that show the amounts that will be reported in the income statement.

market value (136) The amount an item can be sold for under normal economic conditions.

matching principle (131) The proper matching of revenues earned during an accounting period with the expenses incurred to produce the revenues is often referred to as the matching principle.

modified cash basis of accounting (150) A method of accounting that combines aspects of the cash and accrual methods. It uses the cash basis for recording revenues and most expenses. Exceptions are made when cash is paid for assets with useful lives greater than one accounting period.

plant assets (136) Assets of a durable nature that will be used for operations over several years. Examples include buildings and equipment.

revenue recognition principle (131) Revenues should be recognized when earned, regardless of when cash is received from the customer. Revenues are considered earned when a service has been provided or a product has been sold.

salvage value (136) The expected market value of an asset at the end of its useful life.

straight-line method (136) A depreciation method in which the depreciable cost is divided by the estimated useful life.

undepreciated cost (137) The difference between the asset account and its related accumulated depreciation account. Also known as book value.

useful life (136) The period of time that an asset is expected to help produce revenues.

work sheet (140) A form used to pull together all of the information needed to enter adjusting entries and prepare the financial statements.

SELF-STUDY TEST QUESTIONS

True/False

1. **LO1** The matching principle in accounting requires the matching of debits and credits.
2. **LO1** Adjusting entries are required at the end of the accounting period because of mistakes in the journal and ledger.
3. **LO1** As part of the adjustment of supplies, an expense account is debited and Supplies is credited for the amount of supplies used during the accounting period.
4. **LO1** Depreciable cost is the difference between the original cost of the asset and its accumulated depreciation.
5. **LO1** The purpose of depreciation is to record the asset's market value in the accounting records.

Multiple Choice

1. **LO1** The purpose of depreciation is to
   (a) spread the cost of an asset over its useful life.
   (b) show the current market value of an asset.
   (c) set up a reserve fund to purchase a new asset.
   (d) expense the asset in the year it was purchased.
2. **LO1** Depreciable cost is the
   (a) difference between original cost and accumulated depreciation.
   (b) difference in actual cost and true market value.
   (c) difference between original cost and estimated salvage value.
   (d) difference between estimated salvage value and actual salvage value.
3. **LO1** Book value is the
   (a) difference between market value and estimated value.
   (b) difference between market value and historical cost.
   (c) difference between original cost and salvage value.
   (d) difference between original cost and accumulated depreciation.
4. **LO1** The adjustment for wages earned by employees but not yet paid is
   (a) debit Wages Payable and credit Wages Expense.
   (b) debit Wages Expense and credit Cash.
   (c) debit Wages Expense and credit Wages Payable.
   (d) debit Wages Expense and credit Accounts Receivable.
5. **LO3** The first step in preparing a work sheet is to
   (a) prepare the trial balance.
   (b) prepare the adjustments.
   (c) prepare the adjusted trial balance.
   (d) extend the amounts from the Adjusted Trial Balance to the Income Statement and Balance Sheet columns.

CHECKPOINT ✓

Checkpoint Exercises

1. **LO1** On December 31, the trial balance indicates that the supplies account has a balance, prior to the adjusting entry, of $100. A physical count of the supplies inventory shows that $70 of supplies remain. What adjustment should be made to the supplies account?

2. **LO2** When posting adjusting entries to the general ledger, what is written in the Item column?

3. **LO3** Indicate the heading for the columns of the work sheet A through F below.

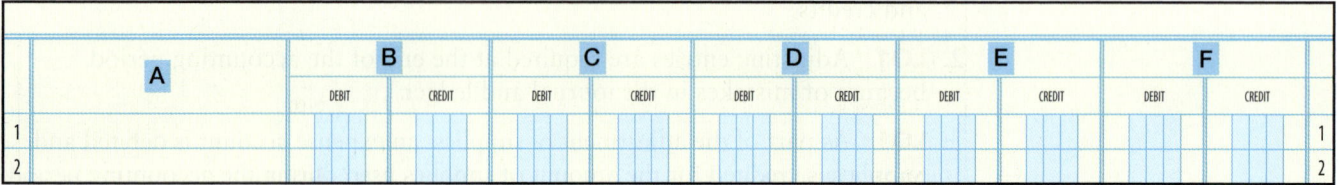

	A	B		C		D		E		F		
		DEBIT	CREDIT	DEBIT	CREDIT	DEBIT	CREDIT	DEBIT	CREDIT	DEBIT	CREDIT	
1												1
2												2

4. **LO4** Find the error(s) in the work sheet below.

	ACCOUNT TITLE	TRIAL BALANCE		ADJUSTMENTS		ADJUSTED TRIAL BALANCE		INCOME STATEMENT		BALANCE SHEET		
		DEBIT	CREDIT	DEBIT	CREDIT	DEBIT	CREDIT	DEBIT	CREDIT	DEBIT	CREDIT	
1	Cash	370 00				370 00				370 00		1
2	Accounts Receivable	650 00				650 00				650 00		2
3	Supplies	80 00			(a) 60 00	140 00				140 00		3
4	Prepaid Insurance	200 00			(b) 25 00	175 00				175 00		4
5	Delivery Equipment	3 600 00				3 600 00				3 600 00		5
6	Accum. Depr.—Delivery Equipment				(d) 100 00		100 00				100 00	6
7	Accounts Payable		1 800 00				1 800 00				1 800 00	7
8	Wages Payable				(c) 50 00		50 00				50 00	8
9	Mitchell Williams, Capital		2 000 00				2 000 00				2 000 00	9
10	Mitchell Williams, Drawing	150 00				150 00				150 00		10
11	Delivery Fees		2 150 00				2 150 00		2 150 00			11
12	Wages Expense	650 00		(c) 50 00		700 00		700 00				12
13	Rent Expense	200 00				200 00		200 00				13
14	Supplies Expense			(a) 60 00		60 00		60 00				14
15	Phone Expense	50 00				50 00		50 00				15
16	Insurance Expense			(b) 25 00		25 00		25 00				16
17	Depr. Expense—Delivery Equipment			(d) 100 00		100 00		100 00				17
18		5 950 00	5 950 00	235 00	235 00	6 220 00	6 100 00	1 135 00	2 150 00	5 085 00	3 950 00	18
19								1 015 00			1 135 00	19
20								2 150 00	2 150 00	5 085 00	5 085 00	20
21												21
22												22
23												23
24												24

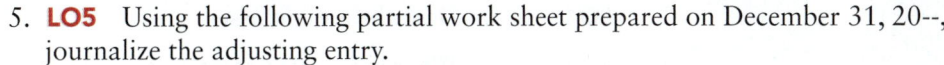

5. **LO5** Using the following partial work sheet prepared on December 31, 20--, journalize the adjusting entry.

	ACCOUNT TITLE	TRIAL BALANCE DEBIT	TRIAL BALANCE CREDIT	ADJUSTMENTS DEBIT	ADJUSTMENTS CREDIT
1	Cash	370 00			
2	Accounts Receivable	650 00			
3	Supplies	80 00			
4	Prepaid Insurance	200 00			(b) 50 00
5	Delivery Equipment	3600 00			
6	Accum. Depr.—Delivery Equipment				
7	Accounts Payable		1800 00		
8	Wages Payable				
9	Mitchell Williams, Capital		2000 00		
10	Mitchell Williams, Drawing	150 00			
11	Delivery Fees		2150 00		
12	Wages Expense	650 00			
13	Rent Expense	200 00			
14	Supplies Expense				
15	Phone Expense	50 00			
16	Insurance Expense			(b) 50 00	
17	Depr. Expense—Delivery Equipment				
18		5950 00	5950 00	50 00	50 00
19					

6. **LO6** Bill Roberts provided legal advice to a client for $500 on account. Roberts paid a legal assistant $50 for research on this engagement and used office supplies costing $10. If these are the only transactions for the period, compute net income under the cash, accrual, and modified cash bases.

The answers to the Self-Study Test Questions are at the end of the chapter (pages 177–178).

APPLYING YOUR KNOWLEDGE

CengageNowv2 provides "Show Me How" videos for selected exercises and problems. Additional resources, such as Excel templates for completing selected exercises and problems, are available for download from the companion website at Cengage.com.

REVIEW QUESTIONS

LO1 1. Explain the revenue recognition principle.

LO1 2. Explain the expense recognition principle.

LO1 3. Explain the matching principle.

LO1 4. Explain the historical cost principle.

LO1 5. Describe a plant asset.

LO1 6. What is a contra-asset?

LO1 7. What is the useful life of an asset?

LO1 8. What is the purpose of depreciation?

LO1 9. What is an asset's depreciable cost?

LO1 10. What is the book value of an asset?

LO3 11. Explain the purpose of the work sheet.

LO3 12. Identify the five major column headings on a work sheet.

LO3 13. List the five steps taken in preparing a work sheet.

LO4 14. Describe four tips for finding errors on the work sheet.

LO6 15. Explain when revenues are recorded under the cash basis, modified cash basis, and accrual basis of accounting.

LO6 16. Explain when expenses are recorded under the cash basis, modified cash basis, and accrual basis of accounting.

SERIES A EXERCISES

E 5-1A (LO1) ADJUSTMENT FOR SUPPLIES On December 31, the trial balance indicates that the supplies account has a balance, prior to the adjusting entry, of $320. A physical count of the supplies inventory shows that $90 of supplies remain. Analyze this adjustment for supplies using T accounts, and then formally enter this adjustment in the general journal.

E 5-2A (LO1) ADJUSTMENT FOR INSURANCE On December 1, a six-month liability insurance policy was purchased for $900. Analyze the required adjustment as of December 31 using T accounts, and then formally enter this adjustment in the general journal.

E 5-3A (LO1) ADJUSTMENT FOR WAGES On December 31, the trial balance shows wages expense of $600. An additional $200 of wages was earned by the employees, but has not yet been paid. Analyze this adjustment for wages using T accounts, and then formally enter this adjustment in the general journal.

E 5-4A (LO1) ADJUSTMENT FOR DEPRECIATION OF ASSET On December 1, delivery equipment was purchased for $7,200. The delivery equipment has an estimated useful life of four years (48 months) and no salvage value. Using the straight-line depreciation method, analyze the necessary adjusting entry as of December 31 (one month) using T accounts, and then formally enter this adjustment in the general journal.

E 5-5A (LO1) CALCULATION OF BOOK VALUE On June 1, 20--, a depreciable asset was acquired for $6,840. The asset has an estimated useful life of six years (72 months) and no salvage value. Using the straight-line depreciation method, calculate the book value as of December 31, 20--.

E 5-6A (LO1)

ANALYSIS OF ADJUSTING ENTRY FOR SUPPLIES Analyze each situation and indicate the correct dollar amount for the adjusting entry. (Trial balance is abbreviated as TB.)

1. Ending inventory of supplies is $260.

(Balance Sheet) Supplies

TB	580	
Bal. ______		

(Income Statement) Supplies Expense

2. Amount of supplies used is $230.

(Balance Sheet) Supplies

TB	435	
Bal. ______		

(Income Statement) Supplies Expense

E 5-7A (LO1)

ANALYSIS OF ADJUSTING ENTRY FOR INSURANCE Analyze each situation and indicate the correct dollar amount for the adjusting entry.

1. Amount of insurance expired is $970.

(Balance Sheet) Prepaid Insurance

TB	1,450	
Bal. ______		

(Income Statement) Insurance Expense

2. Amount of unexpired insurance is $565.

(Balance Sheet) Prepaid Insurance

TB	1,350	
Bal. ______		

(Income Statement) Insurance Expense

E 5-8A (LO2)

POSTING ADJUSTING ENTRIES Two adjusting entries are in the following general journal. Post these adjusting entries to the four general ledger accounts. The following account numbers were taken from the chart of accounts: 141, Supplies; 219, Wages Payable; 511, Wages Expense; and 523, Supplies Expense. If you are not using the working papers that accompany this text, enter the following balances before posting the entries: Supplies, $200 Debit; and Wages Expense, $1,200 Debit.

(continued)

GENERAL JOURNAL PAGE 9

	DATE		DESCRIPTION	POST. REF.	DEBIT	CREDIT	
1			Adjusting Entries				1
2	20-- Dec.	31	Supplies Expense		85 00		2
3			Supplies			85 00	3
4							4
5		31	Wages Expense		220 00		5
6			Wages Payable			220 00	6

E 5-9A (LO3)
✓ Adjustments col. total: $1,550

WORK SHEET AND ADJUSTING ENTRIES A partial work sheet for Jim Jacobs' Furniture Repair is shown as follows. Indicate by letters (a) through (d) the four adjustments in the Adjustments columns of the work sheet, properly matching each debit and credit. Complete the Adjustments columns.

Jim Jacobs' Furniture Repair
Work Sheet (Partial)
For Year Ended December 31, 20 - -

	ACCOUNT TITLE	TRIAL BALANCE		ADJUSTMENTS		ADJUSTED TRIAL BALANCE		
		DEBIT	CREDIT	DEBIT	CREDIT	DEBIT	CREDIT	
1	Cash	100 00				100 00		1
2	Supplies	850 00				200 00		2
3	Prepaid Insurance	900 00				300 00		3
4	Delivery Equipment	3600 00				3600 00		4
5	Accum. Depr.—Delivery Equipment		600 00				800 00	5
6	Wages Payable						100 00	6
7	Jim Jacobs, Capital		4000 00				4000 00	7
8	Repair Fees		1650 00				1650 00	8
9	Wages Expense	600 00				700 00		9
10	Advertising Expense	200 00				200 00		10
11	Supplies Expense					650 00		11
12	Insurance Expense					600 00		12
13	Depr. Expense—Delivery Equipment					200 00		13
14		6250 00	6250 00			6550 00	6550 00	14

E 5-10A (LO5)

JOURNALIZING ADJUSTING ENTRIES From the Adjustments columns in Exercise 5-9A, journalize the four adjusting entries, as of December 31, in proper general journal format.

E 5-11A (LO3)

EXTENDING ADJUSTED BALANCES TO THE INCOME STATEMENT AND BALANCE SHEET COLUMNS Indicate with an "X" whether each account total should be extended to the Income Statement Debit or Credit or to the Balance Sheet Debit or Credit columns on the work sheet.

	Income Statement		Balance Sheet	
	Debit	Credit	Debit	Credit
Cash	______	______	______	______
Accounts Receivable	______	______	______	______
Supplies	______	______	______	______
Prepaid Insurance	______	______	______	______
Delivery Equipment	______	______	______	______
Accum. Depr.—Delivery Equipment	______	______	______	______
Accounts Payable	______	______	______	______
Wages Payable	______	______	______	______
Owner, Capital	______	______	______	______
Owner, Drawing	______	______	______	______
Delivery Fees	______	______	______	______
Wages Expense	______	______	______	______
Rent Expense	______	______	______	______
Supplies Expense	______	______	______	______
Insurance Expense	______	______	______	______
Depr. Exp.—Delivery Equipment	______	______	______	______

E 5-12A (LO3)

ANALYSIS OF NET INCOME OR NET LOSS ON THE WORK SHEET Indicate with an "X" in which columns, Income Statement Debit or Credit or Balance Sheet Debit or Credit, a net income or a net loss would appear on a work sheet.

	Income Statement		Balance Sheet	
	Debit	Credit	Debit	Credit
Net Income	______	______	______	______
Net Loss	______	______	______	______

E 5-13A (LO6)

✓ See Figure 5-23 in text

CASH, MODIFIED CASH, AND ACCRUAL BASES OF ACCOUNTING Prepare the entry for each of the following transactions, using the (a) cash basis, (b) modified cash basis, and (c) accrual basis of accounting.

1. Purchase supplies on account.
2. Make payment on asset previously purchased.
3. Purchase supplies for cash.
4. Purchase insurance for cash.
5. Pay cash for wages.
6. Pay cash for phone expense.
7. Pay cash for new equipment.

End-of-Period Adjusting Entries:

8. Wages earned but not paid.
9. Prepaid item purchased, partly used.
10. Depreciation on long-term assets.

SERIES A PROBLEMS

P 5-14A (LO1/3)
✓ Adjustments col. total: $2,145
✓ Net income: $810

ADJUSTMENTS AND WORK SHEET SHOWING NET INCOME The trial balance after one month of operation for Mason's Delivery Service as of September 30, 20--, is shown below. Data to complete the adjustments are as follows:

(a) Supplies inventory as of September 30, $90.
(b) Insurance expired (used), $650.
(c) Depreciation on delivery equipment, $600.
(d) Wages earned by employees but not paid as of September 30, $350.

REQUIRED

1. Enter the adjustments in the Adjustments columns of the work sheet.
2. Complete the work sheet.

Mason's Delivery Service
Work Sheet (Partial)
For Month Ended September 30, 20 - -

	ACCOUNT TITLE	TRIAL BALANCE DEBIT	TRIAL BALANCE CREDIT	ADJUSTMENTS DEBIT	ADJUSTMENTS CREDIT	
1	Cash	1,600.00				1
2	Accounts Receivable	940.00				2
3	Supplies	635.00				3
4	Prepaid Insurance	1,200.00				4
5	Delivery Equipment	6,400.00				5
6	Accum. Depr.—Delivery Equipment					6
7	Accounts Payable		1,220.00			7
8	Wages Payable					8
9	Jill Mason, Capital		8,000.00			9
10	Jill Mason, Drawing	1,400.00				10
11	Delivery Fees		6,200.00			11
12	Wages Expense	1,500.00				12
13	Advertising Expense	460.00				13
14	Rent Expense	800.00				14
15	Supplies Expense					15
16	Phone Expense	165.00				16
17	Insurance Expense					17
18	Repair Expense	230.00				18
19	Oil and Gas Expense	90.00				19
20	Depr. Expense—Delivery Equipment					20
21		15,420.00	15,420.00			21

P 5-15A (LO1/3)
✓ Adjustments col. total: $1,380
✓ Net loss: $2,495

ADJUSTMENTS AND WORK SHEET SHOWING A NET LOSS Jason Armstrong started a business called Campus Delivery Service. After the first month of operations, the trial balance as of November 30, 20--, is as shown on the next page.

REQUIRED

1. Analyze the following adjustments and enter them on the work sheet.
   (a) Ending inventory of supplies on November 30, $185.
   (b) Unexpired (remaining) insurance as of November 30, $800.
   (c) Depreciation expense on van, $300.
   (d) Wages earned but not paid as of November 30, $190.
2. Complete the work sheet.

Campus Delivery Service
Work Sheet (Partial)
For Month Ended November 30, 20 - -

	Account Title	Trial Balance Debit	Trial Balance Credit	Adjustments Debit	Adjustments Credit	
1	Cash	980 00				1
2	Accounts Receivable	590 00				2
3	Supplies	575 00				3
4	Prepaid Insurance	1 300 00				4
5	Van	5 800 00				5
6	Accum. Depr.—Van					6
7	Accounts Payable		960 00			7
8	Wages Payable					8
9	Jason Armstrong, Capital		10 000 00			9
10	Jason Armstrong, Drawing	600 00				10
11	Delivery Fees		2 600 00			11
12	Wages Expense	1 800 00				12
13	Advertising Expense	380 00				13
14	Rent Expense	900 00				14
15	Supplies Expense					15
16	Phone Expense	220 00				16
17	Insurance Expense					17
18	Repair Expense	315 00				18
19	Oil and Gas Expense	100 00				19
20	Depr. Expense—Van					20
21		13 560 00	13 560 00			21

P 5-16A **(LO2/5)** JOURNALIZE AND POST ADJUSTING ENTRIES FROM THE WORK SHEET Refer to Problem 5-15A and the following additional information:

Account Name	Account Number	Balance in Account Before Adjusting Entry
Supplies	141	$ 575
Prepaid Insurance	145	1,300
Accum. Depr.—Van	185.1	0
Wages Payable	219	0
Wages Expense	511	1,800
Supplies Expense	523	0
Insurance Expense	535	0
Depr. Expense—Van	541	0

(*continued*)

REQUIRED

1. Journalize the adjusting entries on page 5 of the general journal.
2. Post the adjusting entries to the general ledger. (If you are not using the working papers that accompany this text, enter the balances provided in this problem before posting the adjusting entries.)

P 5-17A (LO4)
✓ Adjustments col. total: $1,160
✓ Net income: $1,575

CORRECTING WORK SHEET WITH ERRORS A beginning accounting student tried to complete a work sheet for Joyce Lee's Tax Service. The following adjusting entries were to have been analyzed and entered onto the work sheet. The work sheet is shown on page 167.

(a) Ending inventory of supplies as of March 31, $160.
(b) Unexpired insurance as of March 31, $520.
(c) Depreciation of office equipment, $275.
(d) Wages earned, but not paid as of March 31, $110.

REQUIRED

The accounting student made a number of errors. Review the work sheet for addition mistakes, transpositions, and other errors and make all necessary corrections.

SERIES B EXERCISES

E 5-1B (LO1)

ADJUSTMENT FOR SUPPLIES On July 31, the trial balance indicates that the supplies account has a balance, prior to the adjusting entry, of $430. A physical count of the supplies inventory shows that $120 of supplies remain. Analyze the adjustment for supplies using T accounts, and then formally enter this adjustment in the general journal.

E 5-2B (LO1)

ADJUSTMENT FOR INSURANCE On July 1, a six-month liability insurance policy was purchased for $750. Analyze the required adjustment as of July 31 using T accounts, and then formally enter this adjustment in the general journal.

E 5-3B (LO1)

ADJUSTMENT FOR WAGES On July 31, the trial balance shows wages expense of $800. An additional $150 of wages was earned by the employees but has not yet been paid. Analyze the required adjustment using T accounts, and then formally enter this adjustment in the general journal.

E 5-4B (LO1)

ADJUSTMENT FOR DEPRECIATION OF ASSET On July 1, delivery equipment was purchased for $4,320. The delivery equipment has an estimated useful life of three years (36 months) and no salvage value. Using the straight-line depreciation method, analyze the necessary adjusting entry as of July 31 (one month) using T accounts, and then formally enter this adjustment in the general journal.

E 5-5B (LO1)

CALCULATION OF BOOK VALUE On January 1, 20--, a depreciable asset was acquired for $5,760. The asset has an estimated useful life of four years (48 months) and no salvage value. Use the straight-line depreciation method to calculate the book value as of July 1, 20--.

PROBLEM 5-17A

Joyce Lee's Tax Service
Work Sheet
For Month Ended March 31, 20--

	ACCOUNT TITLE	TRIAL BALANCE		ADJUSTMENTS		ADJUSTED TRIAL BALANCE		INCOME STATEMENT		BALANCE SHEET		
		DEBIT	CREDIT	DEBIT	CREDIT	DEBIT	CREDIT	DEBIT	CREDIT	DEBIT	CREDIT	
1	Cash	1725 00				1725 00				1752 00		1
2	Accounts Receivable	960 00				960 00				96 00		2
3	Supplies	525 00			(a) 160 00	365 00				365 00		3
4	Prepaid Insurance	930 00			(b) 410 00	540 00				540 00		4
5	Office Equipment	5450 00			(c) 275 00	5175 00				5175 00		5
6	Accum. Depr.– Office Equipment											6
7	Accounts Payable		480 00				480 00				480 00	7
8	Wages Payable				(d) 110 00		110 00		110 00			8
9	Joyce Lee, Capital		7500 00				7500 00				7500 00	9
10	Joyce Lee, Drawing	1125 00				1125 00		1125 00				10
11	Professional Fees		5700 00				5700 00		5700 00			11
12	Wages Expense	1420 00		(d) 110 00		1420 00		1420 00			1580 00	12
13	Advertising Expense	350 00				350 00		350 00				13
14	Rent Expense	700 00				700 00		700 00				14
15	Supplies Expense			(a) 160 00		160 00		160 00				15
16	Phone Expense	130 00				130 00		130 00				16
17	Utilities Expense	190 00				190 00		190 00				17
18	Insurance Expense			(b) 410 00		410 00		41 00				18
19	Depr. Expense–Office Equipment			(c) 275 00		275 00		275 00				19
20	Miscellaneous Expense	175 00				175 00		175 00				20
21												21
22		13680 00	13680 00	955 00	955 00	13160 00	13790 00	4566 00	5810 00	9508 00	7980 00	22
23								1244 00			1528 00	23
24								5810 00	5810 00	9508 00	9508 00	24
25												25
26												26
27												27
28												28
29												29
30												30

Contains Errors

This work sheet contains errors.

E 5-6B (LO1)

ANALYSIS OF ADJUSTING ENTRY FOR SUPPLIES Analyze each situation and indicate the correct dollar amount for the adjusting entry.

1. Ending inventory of supplies is $95.

(Balance Sheet) Supplies

TB	540	
Bal. ________		

(Income Statement) Supplies Expense

2. Amount of supplies used is $280.

(Balance Sheet) Supplies

TB	330	
Bal. ________		

(Income Statement) Supplies Expense

E 5-7B (LO1)

ANALYSIS OF ADJUSTING ENTRY FOR INSURANCE Analyze each situation and indicate the correct dollar amount for the adjusting entry.

1. Amount of insurance expired (used) is $830.

(Balance Sheet) Prepaid Insurance

TB	960	
Bal. ________		

(Income Statement) Insurance Expense

2. Amount of unexpired (remaining) insurance is $340.

(Balance Sheet) Prepaid Insurance

TB	1,135	
Bal. ________		

(Income Statement) Insurance Expense

E 5-8B (LO2)

POSTING ADJUSTING ENTRIES Two adjusting entries are shown in the following general journal. Post these adjusting entries to the four general ledger accounts. The following account numbers were taken from the chart of accounts: 145, Prepaid Insurance; 183.1, Accumulated Depreciation—Cleaning Equipment; 541, Depreciation Expense—Cleaning Equipment; and 535, Insurance Expense. If you are not using the working papers that accompany this text, enter the following balances before posting the entries: Prepaid Insurance, $960 Debit; Accumulated Depreciation—Cleaning Equipment, $870 Credit.

GENERAL JOURNAL PAGE 7

	DATE		DESCRIPTION	POST. REF.	DEBIT	CREDIT	
1			Adjusting Entries				1
2	20-- July	31	Insurance Expense		320 00		2
3			Prepaid Insurance			320 00	3
4							4
5		31	Depr. Expense—Cleaning Equipment		145 00		5
6			Accum. Depr.—Cleaning Equipment			145 00	6

E 5-9B (LO3)
✓ Adjustments col. total: $1,530

WORK SHEET AND ADJUSTING ENTRIES A partial work sheet for Jasmine Kah's Auto Detailing is shown below. Indicate by letters (a) through (d) the four adjustments in the Adjustments columns of the work sheet, properly matching each debit and credit. Complete the Adjustments columns.

Jasmine Kah's Auto Detailing
Work Sheet (Partial)
For Month Ended June 30, 20 - -

	ACCOUNT TITLE	TRIAL BALANCE DEBIT	TRIAL BALANCE CREDIT	ADJUSTMENTS DEBIT	ADJUSTMENTS CREDIT	ADJUSTED TRIAL BALANCE DEBIT	ADJUSTED TRIAL BALANCE CREDIT	
1	Cash	150 00				150 00		1
2	Supplies	520 00				90 00		2
3	Prepaid Insurance	750 00				200 00		3
4	Cleaning Equipment	5,400 00				5,400 00		4
5	Accum. Depr.— Cleaning Equipment		850 00				1,150 00	5
6	Wages Payable						250 00	6
7	Jasmine Kah, Capital		4,600 00				4,600 00	7
8	Detailing Fees		2,220 00				2,220 00	8
9	Wages Expense	700 00				950 00		9
10	Advertising Expense	150 00				150 00		10
11	Supplies Expense					430 00		11
12	Insurance Expense					550 00		12
13	Depr. Expense—Cleaning Equipment					300 00		13
14		7,670 00	7,670 00			8,220 00	8,220 00	14

E 5-10B (LO5)

JOURNALIZING ADJUSTING ENTRIES From the Adjustments columns in Exercise 5-9B, journalize the four adjusting entries as of June 30, in proper general journal format.

E 5-11B (LO3)

EXTENDING ADJUSTED BALANCES TO THE INCOME STATEMENT AND BALANCE SHEET COLUMNS Indicate with an "X" whether each account total should be extended to the Income Statement Debit or Credit or to the Balance Sheet Debit or Credit columns on the work sheet.

(continued)

	Income Statement		Balance Sheet	
	Debit	Credit	Debit	Credit
Cash	______	______	______	______
Accounts Receivable	______	______	______	______
Supplies	______	______	______	______
Prepaid Insurance	______	______	______	______
Automobile	______	______	______	______
Accum. Depr.—Automobile	______	______	______	______
Accounts Payable	______	______	______	______
Wages Payable	______	______	______	______
Owner, Capital	______	______	______	______
Owner, Drawing	______	______	______	______
Service Fees	______	______	______	______
Wages Expense	______	______	______	______
Supplies Expense	______	______	______	______
Utilities Expense	______	______	______	______
Insurance Expense	______	______	______	______
Depr. Exp.—Automobile	______	______	______	______

E 5-12B (LO3)

ANALYSIS OF NET INCOME OR NET LOSS ON THE WORK SHEET Insert the dollar amounts where the net income or net loss would appear on the work sheet.

	Income Statement		Balance Sheet	
	Debit	Credit	Debit	Credit
Net Income: $2,500	______	______	______	______
Net Loss: $1,900	______	______	______	______

E 5-13B (LO6)

✓ See Figure 5-23 in text

CASH, MODIFIED CASH, AND ACCRUAL BASES OF ACCOUNTING For each journal entry shown below, indicate the accounting method(s) for which the entry would be appropriate. If the journal entry is not appropriate for a particular accounting method, explain the proper accounting treatment for that method.

1. Office Equipment
   Cash
      Purchased equipment for cash
2. Office Equipment
   Accounts Payable
      Purchased equipment on account
3. Cash
   Revenue
      Cash receipts for week
4. Accounts Receivable
   Revenue
      Services performed on account
5. Prepaid Insurance
   Cash
      Purchased prepaid asset
6. Supplies
   Accounts Payable
      Purchased prepaid asset

7. Phone Expense
   Cash
      Paid phone bill
8. Wages Expense
   Cash
      Paid wages for month
9. Accounts Payable
   Cash
      Made payment on account

Adjusting Entries:

10. Supplies Expense
    Supplies
11. Wages Expense
    Wages Payable
12. Depreciation Expense—Office Equipment
    Accumulated Depreciation—Office Equipment

SERIES B PROBLEMS

P 5-14B (LO1/3)
✓ Adjustments col. total: $805
✓ Net income: $2,410

ADJUSTMENTS AND WORK SHEET SHOWING NET INCOME Louie Long started a business called Louie's Lawn Service. The trial balance as of March 31, after the first month of operation, is as follows:

Louie's Lawn Service
Work Sheet
For Month Ended March 31, 20 --

	ACCOUNT TITLE	TRIAL BALANCE DEBIT	TRIAL BALANCE CREDIT	ADJUSTMENTS DEBIT	ADJUSTMENTS CREDIT	
1	Cash	1,375 00				1
2	Accounts Receivable	880 00				2
3	Supplies	490 00				3
4	Prepaid Insurance	800 00				4
5	Lawn Equipment	5,700 00				5
6	Accum. Depr.—Lawn Equipment					6
7	Accounts Payable		780 00			7
8	Wages Payable					8
9	Louie Long, Capital		6,500 00			9
10	Louie Long, Drawing	1,250 00				10
11	Lawn Service Fees		6,100 00			11
12	Wages Expense	1,145 00				12
13	Advertising Expense	540 00				13
14	Rent Expense	725 00				14
15	Supplies Expense					15
16	Phone Expense	160 00				16
17	Insurance Expense					17
18	Repair Expense	250 00				18
19	Depr. Expense—Lawn Equipment					19
20	Miscellaneous Expense	65 00				20
21		13,380 00	13,380 00			21

(*continued*)

REQUIRED

1. Analyze the following adjustments and enter them on a work sheet.
   (a) Ending supplies inventory as of March 31, $165.
   (b) Insurance expired (used), $100.
   (c) Depreciation of lawn equipment, $200.
   (d) Wages earned but not paid as of March 31, $180.
2. Complete the work sheet.

P 5-15B (LO1/3)
✓ Adjustments col. total: $990
✓ Net loss: $1,625

ADJUSTMENTS AND WORK SHEET SHOWING A NET LOSS Val Nolan started a business called Nolan's Home Appraisals. The trial balance as of October 31, after the first month of operations, is as follows:

Nolan's Home Appraisals
Work Sheet
For Month Ended October 31, 20 - -

	ACCOUNT TITLE	TRIAL BALANCE DEBIT	TRIAL BALANCE CREDIT	ADJUSTMENTS DEBIT	ADJUSTMENTS CREDIT	
1	Cash	830 00				1
2	Accounts Receivable	760 00				2
3	Supplies	625 00				3
4	Prepaid Insurance	950 00				4
5	Automobile	6,500 00				5
6	Accum. Depr.—Automobile					6
7	Accounts Payable		1,500 00			7
8	Wages Payable					8
9	Val Nolan, Capital		9,900 00			9
10	Val Nolan, Drawing	1,100 00				10
11	Appraisal Fees		3,000 00			11
12	Wages Expense	1,560 00				12
13	Advertising Expense	420 00				13
14	Rent Expense	1,050 00				14
15	Supplies Expense					15
16	Phone Expense	255 00				16
17	Insurance Expense					17
18	Repair Expense	270 00				18
19	Oil and Gas Expense	80 00				19
20	Depr. Expense—Automobile					20
21		14,400 00	14,400 00			21

REQUIRED

1. Analyze the following adjustments and enter them on the work sheet.
   (a) Supplies inventory as of October 31, $210.
   (b) Unexpired (remaining) insurance as of October 31, $800.
   (c) Depreciation of automobile, $250.
   (d) Wages earned but not paid as of October 31, $175.
2. Complete the work sheet.

P 5-16B (LO2/5)

JOURNALIZE AND POST ADJUSTING ENTRIES FROM THE WORK SHEET Refer to Problem 5-15B and the following additional information:

Account Name	Account Number	Balance in Account Before Adjusting Entry
Supplies	141	$ 625
Prepaid Insurance	145	950
Accum. Depr.—Automobile	185.1	0
Wages Payable	219	0
Wages Expense	511	1,560
Supplies Expense	523	0
Insurance Expense	535	0
Depr. Expense—Automobile	541	0

REQUIRED

1. Journalize the adjusting entries on page 3 of the general journal.
2. Post the adjusting entries to the general ledger. (If you are not using the working papers that accompany this text, enter the balances provided in this problem before posting the adjusting entries.)

P 5-17B (LO4)

✓ Adjustments col. total: $1,640
✓ Net income: $1,405

CORRECTING WORK SHEET WITH ERRORS A beginning accounting student tried to complete a work sheet for Dick Ady's Bookkeeping Service. The following adjusting entries were to have been analyzed and entered in the work sheet:

(a) Ending inventory of supplies on July 31, $130.
(b) Unexpired insurance on July 31, $420.
(c) Depreciation of office equipment, $325.
(d) Wages earned, but not paid as of July 31, $95.

REQUIRED

Review the work sheet shown on page 174 for addition mistakes, transpositions, and other errors and make all necessary corrections.

MANAGING YOUR WRITING

CHECK LIST
- ☐ Managing
- ☐ Planning
- ☐ Drafting
- ☐ Break
- ☐ Revising
- ☐ Managing

Delia Alvarez, owner of Delia's Lawn Service, wants to borrow money to buy new lawn equipment. A local bank has asked for financial statements. Alvarez has asked you to prepare financial statements for the year ended December 31, 20--. You have been given the unadjusted trial balance on page 175 and suspect that Alvarez expects you to base your statements on this information. You are concerned, however, that some of the account balances may need to be adjusted. Write a memo to Alvarez explaining what additional information you need before you can prepare the financial statements. Alvarez is not familiar with accounting issues. Therefore, explain in your memo why you need this information, the potential impact of this information on the financial statements, and the importance of making these adjustments before approaching the bank for a loan.

(*continued*)

PROBLEM 5-17B

Dick Ady's Bookkeeping Service
Work Sheet
For Month Ended July 31, 20--

	ACCOUNT TITLE	TRIAL BALANCE DEBIT	TRIAL BALANCE CREDIT	ADJUSTMENTS DEBIT	ADJUSTMENTS CREDIT	ADJUSTED TRIAL BALANCE DEBIT	ADJUSTED TRIAL BALANCE CREDIT	INCOME STATEMENT DEBIT	INCOME STATEMENT CREDIT	BALANCE SHEET DEBIT	BALANCE SHEET CREDIT	
1	Cash	1365 00				1365 00				1356 00		1
2	Accounts Receivable	845 00				845 00			845 00			2
3	Supplies	620 00			(a) 490 00	130 00				130 00		3
4	Prepaid Insurance	1150 00			(b) 420 00	730 00				730 00		4
5	Office Equipment	6400 00			(c) 325 00	6725 00				6725 00		5
6	Accum. Depr.—Office Equipment											6
7	Accounts Payable		735 00				735 00				735 00	7
8	Wages Payable				(d) 95 00		95 00				59 00	8
9	Dick Ady, Capital		7800 00				7800 00				7800 00	9
10	Dick Ady, Drawing	1200 00				1200 00				1200 00		10
11	Professional Fees		6350 00				6350 00		6350 00			11
12	Wages Expense	1495 00		(d) 95 00		1590 00		1590 00				12
13	Advertising Expense	380 00				380 00		380 00				13
14	Rent Expense	850 00				850 00		850 00				14
15	Supplies Expense			(a) 490 00		490 00		490 00				15
16	Phone Expense	205 00				205 00		250 00				16
17	Utilities Expense	285 00				285 00		285 00				17
18	Insurance Expense			(b) 420 00		420 00		420 00				18
19	Depr. Expense—Office Equipment			(c) 325 00		325 00		325 00				19
20	Miscellaneous Expense	90 00				90 00		90 00				20
21	Net Income	14885 00	14885 00	1330 00	1330 00	15630 00	14980 00	4880 00	7195 00	10141 00	8594 00	21
22								2315 00			1547 00	22
23								7195 00	7195 00	10141 00	10141 00	23
24												24
25												25
26												26
27												27
28												28
29												29
30												30

Contains Errors

This work sheet contains errors.

Delia's Lawn Service Trial Balance December 31, 20 - -			
ACCOUNT TITLE	ACCOUNT NO.	DEBIT BALANCE	CREDIT BALANCE
Cash	101	770 00	
Accounts Receivable	122	1 700 00	
Supplies	142	280 00	
Prepaid Insurance	145	400 00	
Lawn Equipment	183	13 800 00	
Accounts Payable	202		2 200 00
Delia Alvarez, Capital	311		3 000 00
Delia Alvarez, Drawing	312	350 00	
Lawn Cutting Fees	401		52 400 00
Wages Expense	511	35 850 00	
Rent Expense	521	1 200 00	
Gas and Oil Expense	538	3 250 00	
		57 600 00	57 600 00

MASTERY PROBLEM

✓ **Adjusted Trial Bal. total: $58,500**
✓ **Net income: $13,630**

Kristi Williams offers family counseling services specializing in financial and marital problems. A chart of accounts and a trial balance taken on December 31, 20--, follow.

KRISTI WILLIAMS FAMILY COUNSELING SERVICES CHART OF ACCOUNTS			
Assets		**Revenue**	
101	Cash	401	Client Fees
142	Office Supplies		
145	Prepaid Insurance	**Expenses**	
181	Office Equipment	511	Wages Expense
181.1	Accumulated Depr.—	521	Rent Expense
	Office Equipment	523	Office Supplies Expense
187	Computer Equipment	533	Utilities Expense
187.1	Accumulated Depr.—	535	Insurance Expense
	Computer Equipment	541	Depr. Expense—
Liabilities			Office Equipment
201	Notes Payable	542	Depr. Expense—
202	Accounts Payable		Computer Equipment
		549	Miscellaneous Expense
Owner's Equity			
311	Kristi Williams, Capital		
312	Kristi Williams, Drawing		

(continued)

Kristi Williams Family Counseling Services Trial Balance December 31, 20 - -			
ACCOUNT TITLE	ACCOUNT NO.	DEBIT BALANCE	CREDIT BALANCE
Cash	101	8 7 3 0 00	
Office Supplies	142	7 0 0 00	
Prepaid Insurance	145	6 0 0 00	
Office Equipment	181	18 0 0 0 00	
Computer Equipment	187	6 0 0 0 00	
Notes Payable	201		8 0 0 0 00
Accounts Payable	202		5 0 0 00
Kristi Williams, Capital	311		11 4 0 0 00
Kristi Williams, Drawing	312	3 0 0 0 00	
Client Fees	401		35 8 0 0 00
Wages Expense	511	9 5 0 0 00	
Rent Expense	521	6 0 0 0 00	
Utilities Expense	533	2 1 7 0 00	
Miscellaneous Expense	549	1 0 0 0 00	
		55 7 0 0 00	55 7 0 0 00

Information for year-end adjustments is as follows:

(a) Office supplies on hand at year-end amounted to $100.

(b) On January 1, 20--, Williams purchased office equipment that cost $18,000. It has an expected useful life of 10 years and no salvage value.

(c) On July 1, 20--, Williams purchased computer equipment costing $6,000. It has an expected useful life of three years and no salvage value. Assume that Williams computes depreciation to the nearest full month.

(d) On December 1, 20--, Williams paid a premium of $600 for a six-month insurance policy.

REQUIRED

1. Prepare the work sheet for the year ended December 31, 20--.
2. Prepare adjusting entries in a general journal.

CHALLENGE PROBLEM

This problem challenges you to apply your cumulative accounting knowledge to move a step beyond the material in the chapter.

Your friend, Diane Kiefner, teaches elementary school and operates her own wilderness kayaking tours in the summers. She thinks she has been doing fine financially, but has never really measured her profits. Until this year, her business has always had more money at the end of the summer than at the beginning. She enjoys kayaking and as long as she came out a little ahead, that was fine. Unfortunately, Diane had to dip into her savings to make up for "losses" on her kayaking tours this past summer. Hearing that you have been studying accounting, she brought a list of cash receipts and expenditures and would like you to try to figure out what happened.

Cash balance beginning of summer		$15,000
Cash receipts from kayakers over the summer	$10,000	
Cash expenditures over the summer	13,500	
Amount taken from savings		(3,500)
Cash balance end of summer		$11,500

When asked for more details on the expenditures and the kayaking gear that you saw in her garage, Diane provided the following information:

Expenditures were made on the following items:	
Brochures used to advertise her services (Diane only used about 1/4 of them and plans to use the remainder over the next three summers.)	$1,000
Food for trips (nothing left)	2,000
Rent on equipment used by kayakers on trips	3,000
Travel expenses	4,000
A new kayak and paddles (At the beginning of the summer, Diane bought a new kayak and paddles. Up to this time, she had always borrowed her father's. Diane expects to use the equipment for about five years. At that time, she expects it to have no value.)	3,500

A trial balance based on this information follows. As you will note, Diane's trial balance is not consistent with some of the concepts discussed in this chapter.

Diane Kiefner's Wilderness Kayaking Tours
Work Sheet
For Summer Ended 20 - -

	ACCOUNT TITLE	TRIAL BALANCE		ADJUSTMENTS		ADJUSTED TRIAL BALANCE		INCOME STATEMENT		BALANCE SHEET		
		DEBIT	CREDIT	DEBIT	CREDIT	DEBIT	CREDIT	DEBIT	CREDIT	DEBIT	CREDIT	
1	Cash	11 5 0 0 00										1
2	Diane Kiefner, Capital		15 0 0 0 00									2
3	Tour Revenue		10 0 0 0 00									3
4	Advertising Supplies Expense	1 0 0 0 00										4
5	Food Expense	2 0 0 0 00										5
6	Equipment Rental Expense	3 0 0 0 00										6
7	Travel Expense	4 0 0 0 00										7
8	Kayak Expense	3 5 0 0 00										8
9		25 0 0 0 00	25 0 0 0 00									9

REQUIRED

1. Complete Diane's work sheet by making appropriate adjustments and extensions. *Note*: (a) You may need to add new accounts. (b) Some of the adjustments you need to make are actually "corrections of errors" Diane has made in classifying certain items.
2. What is your best measure of Diane's net income for the summer of 20--?

ANSWERS TO SELF-STUDY TEST QUESTIONS

True/False

1. F (match revenues and expenses)
2. F (to bring accounts up to date)
3. T
4. F (depreciable cost = cost − salvage value)
5. F (to match cost of asset against revenues it will help generate)

Multiple Choice

1. a **2.** c **3.** d **4.** c **5.** a

Checkpoint Exercises

1. Supplies should be reduced (credited) for $30.
2. Adjusting.
3. A. Account Title
   B. Trial Balance
   C. Adjustments
   D. Adjusted Trial Balance
   E. Income Statement
   F. Balance Sheet
4. Errors are highlighted in yellow.

	ACCOUNT TITLE	TRIAL BALANCE DEBIT	TRIAL BALANCE CREDIT	ADJUSTMENTS DEBIT	ADJUSTMENTS CREDIT	ADJUSTED TRIAL BALANCE DEBIT	ADJUSTED TRIAL BALANCE CREDIT	INCOME STATEMENT DEBIT	INCOME STATEMENT CREDIT	BALANCE SHEET DEBIT	BALANCE SHEET CREDIT	
1	Cash	370 00				370 00				370 00		1
2	Accounts Receivable	650 00				650 00				650 00		2
3	Supplies	80 00			(a) 60 00	140 00				140 00		3
4	Prepaid Insurance	200 00			(b) 25 00	175 00				175 00		4
5	Delivery Equipment	3 600 00				3 600 00				3 600 00		5
6	Accum. Depr.—Delivery Equipment				(d) 100 00		100 00				100 00	6
7	Accounts Payable		1 800 00				1 800 00				1 800 00	7
8	Wages Payable				(c) 50 00		50 00				50 00	8
9	Mitchell Williams, Capital		2 000 00				2 000 00				2 000 00	9
10	Mitchell Williams, Drawing	150 00				150 00				150 00		10
11	Delivery Fees		2 150 00				2 150 00		2 150 00			11
12	Wages Expense	650 00		(c) 50 00		700 00		700 00				12
13	Rent Expense	200 00				200 00		200 00				13
14	Supplies Expense			(a) 60 00		60 00		60 00				14
15	Phone Expense	50 00				50 00		50 00				15
16	Insurance Expense			(b) 25 00		25 00		25 00				16
17	Depr. Expense—Delivery Equipment			(d) 100 00		100 00		100 00				17
18		5 950 00	5 950 00	235 00	235 00	6 220 00	6 100 00	1 135 00	2 150 00	5 085 00	3 950 00	18
19	Net Income							1 015 00			1 135 00	19
20								2 150 00	2 150 00	5 085 00	5 085 00	20
21												21

5.

	Adjusting Entry		
Dec. 31	Insurance Expense	50.00	
	Prepaid Insurance		50.00

6.

Transaction	Cash Basis	Accrual Basis	Modified Cash Basis
Services on account	$ —	$500	$ —
Payment for legal research assistance	(50)	(50)	(50)
Office supplies used		(10)	(10)
Net Income (Net Loss)	$(50)	$440	$(60)

CHAPTER 5 APPENDIX

Depreciation Methods

LEARNING OBJECTIVES

Careful study of this appendix should enable you to:

LO1 Prepare a depreciation schedule using the straight-line method.

LO2 Prepare a depreciation schedule using the sum-of-the-years'-digits method.

LO3 Prepare a depreciation schedule using the double-declining-balance method.

LO4 Prepare a depreciation schedule for tax purposes using the Modified Accelerated Cost Recovery System.

In Chapter 5, we introduced the straight-line method of depreciation. Here, we will review this method and illustrate three others: sum-of-the-years'-digits; double-declining-balance; and, for tax purposes, the Modified Accelerated Cost Recovery System. For all illustrations, we will assume that a delivery van was purchased for $40,000. It has a five-year useful life and salvage value of $4,000.

LO1 Straight-Line Method

Prepare a depreciation schedule using the straight-line method.

Under the **straight-line depreciation method**, an equal amount of depreciation will be taken each period. First, compute the depreciable cost by subtracting the salvage value from the cost of the asset. This is done because we expect to sell the asset for $4,000 at the end of its useful life. Thus, the total cost to be recognized as an expense over the five years is $36,000, not $40,000.

Cost	−	Salvage Value	=	Depreciable Cost
$40,000	−	$4,000	=	$36,000

Next, we divide the depreciable cost by the expected life of the asset, five years.

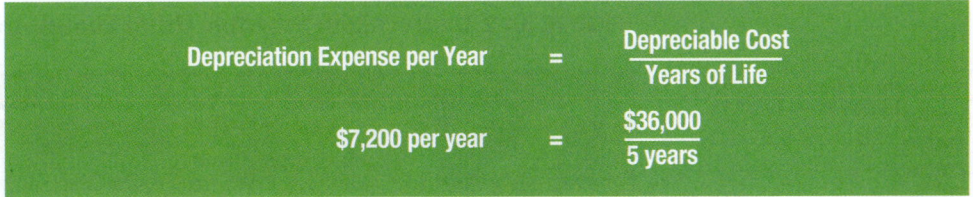

$$\text{Depreciation Expense per Year} = \frac{\text{Depreciable Cost}}{\text{Years of Life}}$$

$$\$7{,}200 \text{ per year} = \frac{\$36{,}000}{5 \text{ years}}$$

When preparing a depreciation schedule, it is often convenient to use a depreciation rate per year. In this case, it would be 20% (100% ÷ 5 years of life). Figure 5A-1 shows the depreciation expense, accumulated depreciation, and book value for each of the five years.

FIGURE 5A-1 Depreciation Schedule Using Straight-Line Method

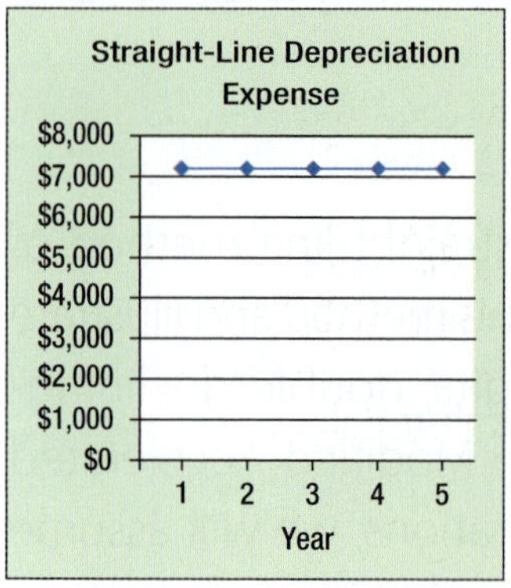

STRAIGHT-LINE DEPRECIATION

Year	Depreciable Cost	×	Rate	=	Depreciation Expense	Accumulated Depreciation (End of Year)	Book Value (End of Year)
1	$36,000		20%		$7,200	$ 7,200	$32,800
2	36,000		20%		7,200	14,400	25,600
3	36,000		20%		7,200	21,600	18,400
4	36,000		20%		7,200	28,800	11,200
5	36,000		20%		7,200	36,000	4,000

Cost	$40,000
– Salvage Value	4,000
Depreciable Cost	$36,000

100% / 5 Years = 20%

Same amount each year

Accum. Depr. increases by the same amount each year, $7,200.

Cost – Accum. Depr. = Book Value

LO2 Sum-of-the-Years'-Digits

Prepare a depreciation schedule using the sum-of-the-years'-digits method.

Under the sum-of-the-years'-digits depreciation method, depreciation is determined by multiplying the depreciable cost by a schedule of fractions. The numerator of the fraction for a specific year is the number of years of remaining useful life for the asset, measured from the beginning of the year. The denominator for all fractions is determined by adding the digits that represent the years of the estimated life of the asset. The calculation of the sum-of-the-years'-digits for our delivery van with a five-year useful life is shown below.

Sum-of-the-Years'-Digits = 5 + 4 + 3 + 2 + 1 = 15

A depreciation schedule using these fractions is shown in Figure 5A-2.

FIGURE 5A-2 Depreciation Schedule Using Sum-of-the-Years'-Digits Method

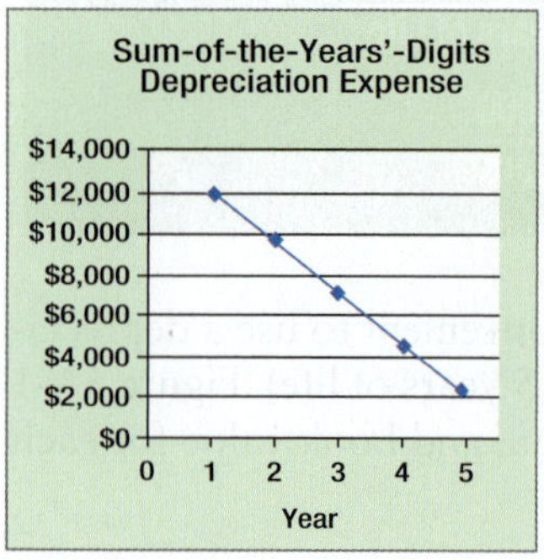

SUM-OF-THE-YEARS'-DIGITS

Year	Depreciable Cost	×	Rate	=	Depreciation Expense	Accumulated Depreciation (End of Year)	Book Value (End of Year)
1	$36,000		5/15		$12,000	$12,000	$28,000
2	36,000		4/15		9,600	21,600	18,400
3	36,000		3/15		7,200	28,800	11,200
4	36,000		2/15		4,800	33,600	6,400
5	36,000		1/15		2,400	36,000	4,000

Cost	$40,000
– Salvage Value	4,000
Depreciable Cost	$36,000

Remaining life from beginning of period / SYD

Expense gets smaller each year

Accum. Depr. increases by amount of current year's depreciation expense.

Cost – Accum. Depr. = Book Value

LO3 Double-Declining-Balance Method

Prepare a depreciation schedule using the double-declining-balance method.

Under the **double-declining-balance depreciation method**, the book value is multiplied by a fixed rate, often double the straight-line rate. The van has a five-year life, so the straight-line rate is 1 ÷ 5, or 20%. Double the straight-line rate is 2 × 20%, or 40%. The double-declining-balance depreciation schedule is shown in Figure 5A-3. Note that the rate is applied to the book value of the asset. Once the book value is reduced to the expected salvage value, $4,000, no more depreciation may be recognized.

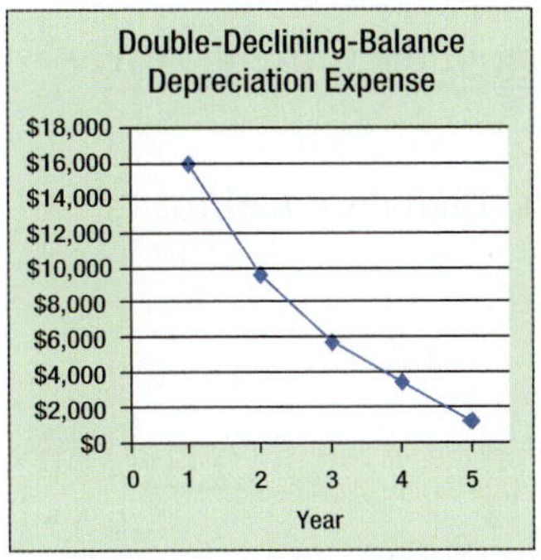

FIGURE 5A-3 Depreciation Schedule Using Double-Declining-Balance Method

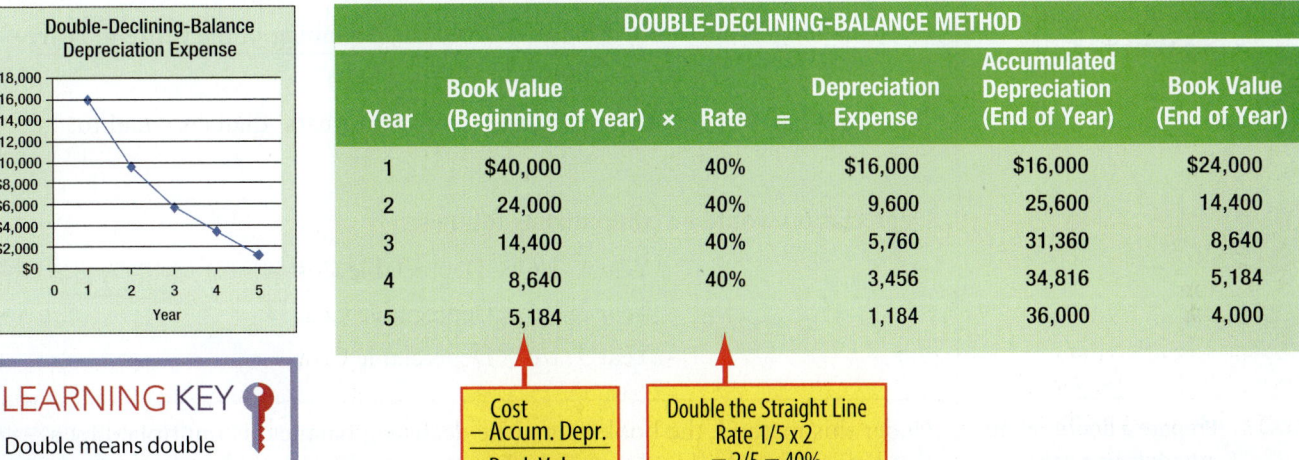

DOUBLE-DECLINING-BALANCE METHOD

Year	Book Value (Beginning of Year)	×	Rate	=	Depreciation Expense	Accumulated Depreciation (End of Year)	Book Value (End of Year)
1	$40,000		40%		$16,000	$16,000	$24,000
2	24,000		40%		9,600	25,600	14,400
3	14,400		40%		5,760	31,360	8,640
4	8,640		40%		3,456	34,816	5,184
5	5,184				1,184	36,000	4,000

Cost
– Accum. Depr.
Book Value

Double the Straight Line Rate 1/5 x 2 = 2/5 = 40%

LEARNING KEY

Double means double the straight-line rate. Declining-balance means that the rate is multiplied by the book value (not depreciable cost) at the beginning of each year. This amount is declining each year.

LO4 Modified Accelerated Cost Recovery System

Prepare a depreciation schedule for tax purposes using the Modified Accelerated Cost Recovery System.

For assets purchased since 1986, many firms use the **Modified Accelerated Cost Recovery System (MACRS)** for tax purposes. Under this method, the Internal Revenue Service (IRS) classifies various assets according to useful life and sets depreciation rates for each year of the asset's life. These rates are then multiplied by the cost of the asset. Even though the van is expected to have a useful life of five years, and a salvage value of $4,000, the IRS schedule, shown in Figure 5A-4, spreads the depreciation over a six-year period and assumes no salvage value.

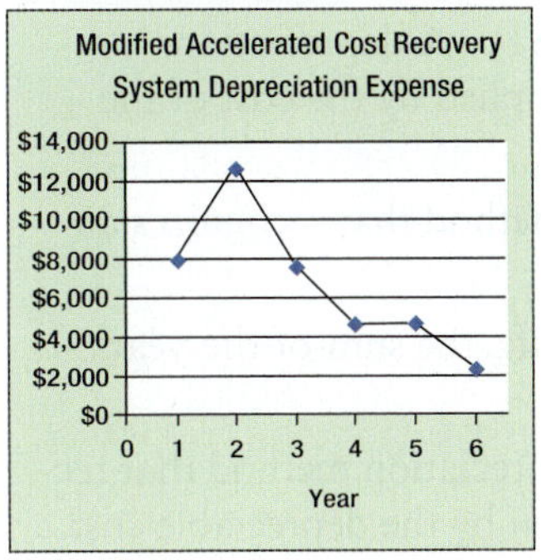

FIGURE 5A-4 Depreciation Schedule Using Modified Accelerated Cost Recovery System

MODIFIED ACCELERATED COST RECOVERY SYSTEM

Year	Cost	×	Rate	=	Depreciation Expense	Accumulated Depreciation (End of Year)	Book Value (End of Year)
1	$40,000		20.00%		$ 8,000	$ 8,000	$32,000
2	40,000		32.00%		12,800	20,800	19,200
3	40,000		19.20%		7,680	28,480	11,520
4	40,000		11.52%		4,608	33,088	6,912
5	40,000		11.52%		4,608	37,696	2,304
6	40,000		5.76%		2,304	40,000	0

Rate set by IRS

Cost
–Accum. Depr.
Book Value

LEARNING OBJECTIVES	Key Points to Remember
LO1 Prepare a depreciation schedule using the straight-line method.	Under straight-line depreciation, an equal amount of depreciation is taken each period. Depreciation expense for each year is computed as follows: Cost − Salvage Value = Depreciable Cost/Expected Years of Life = Depreciation Expense per Year
LO2 Prepare a depreciation schedule using the sum-of-the-years'-digits method.	Under the sum-of-the-years'-digits method, the depreciable cost is multiplied by a fraction. The fraction consists of the following: $\frac{\text{Remaining Years of Life Measured from the Beginning of the Current Year}}{\text{Sum-of-the-Years'-Digits}}$ If an asset has a life of three years, the sum-of-the-years'-digits is equal to: $3+2+1=6$ Depreciation would be computed as follows: Year 1: $3/6 \times$ Depreciable Cost Year 2: $2/6 \times$ Depreciable Cost Year 3: $1/6 \times$ Depreciable Cost
LO3 Prepare a depreciation schedule using the double-declining-balance method.	Under this method, the book value (the declining balance) is multiplied by a fixed rate, often double the straight-line rate.
LO4 Prepare a depreciation schedule for tax purposes using the Modified Accelerated Cost Recovery System.	Under this method, the IRS provides the depreciation rates to be applied to the cost of the asset. Simply multiply the rate provided by the IRS by the cost of the asset.

KEY TERMS

double-declining-balance depreciation method (181) A depreciation method that recognizes depreciation each year by multiplying a rate (typically double the straight-line rate) by the book value of the asset.

Modified Accelerated Cost Recovery System (MACRS) (181) A depreciation method in which rates determined by the IRS are multiplied by the cost of the asset to determine depreciation expense for the year.

straight-line depreciation method (179) A depreciation method that recognizes an equal amount of depreciation each year.

sum-of-the-years'-digits (180) If an asset has a five-year life, the sum-of-the-years'-digits is computed as follows: $5+4+3+2+1=15$.

sum-of-the-years'-digits depreciation method (180) A depreciation method that recognizes depreciation each year by multiplying a fraction by the depreciable cost. The numerator of the fraction is the remaining life of the asset, measured from the beginning of the year. The denominator is the sum-of-the-years'-digits.

REVIEW QUESTIONS

1. List three depreciation methods used for financial reporting.
2. Which depreciation method is used for tax purposes?

SERIES A EXERCISES

E 5Apx-1A (LO1)
✓ Accum. depr. end of Yr. 2: $10,000

STRAIGHT-LINE DEPRECIATION A small delivery truck was purchased on January 1 at a cost of $25,000. It has an estimated useful life of four years and an estimated salvage value of $5,000. Prepare a depreciation schedule showing the depreciation expense, accumulated depreciation, and book value for each year under the straight-line method.

E 5Apx-2A (LO2)
✓ Accum. depr. end of Yr. 2: $14,000

SUM-OF-THE-YEARS'-DIGITS DEPRECIATION Using the information given in Exercise 5Apx-1A, prepare a depreciation schedule showing the depreciation expense, accumulated depreciation, and book value for each year under the sum-of-the-years'-digits method.

E 5Apx-3A (LO3)
✓ Accum. depr. end of Yr. 2: $18,750

DOUBLE-DECLINING-BALANCE DEPRECIATION Using the information given in Exercise 5Apx-1A, prepare a depreciation schedule showing the depreciation expense, accumulated depreciation, and book value for each year under the double-declining-balance method.

E 5Apx-4A (LO4)
✓ Accum. depr. end of Yr. 2: $13,000

MODIFIED ACCELERATED COST RECOVERY SYSTEM Using the information given in Exercise 5Apx-1A and the rates shown in Figure 5A-4, prepare a depreciation schedule showing the depreciation expense, accumulated depreciation, and book value for each year under the Modified Accelerated Cost Recovery System. For tax purposes, assume that the truck has a useful life of five years. (The IRS schedule will spread depreciation over six years.)

SERIES B EXERCISES

E 5Apx-1B (LO1)
✓ Accum. depr. end of Yr. 2: $1,800

STRAIGHT-LINE DEPRECIATION A computer was purchased on January 1 at a cost of $5,000. It has an estimated useful life of five years and an estimated salvage value of $500. Prepare a depreciation schedule showing the depreciation expense, accumulated depreciation, and book value for each year under the straight-line method.

E 5Apx-2B (LO2)
✓ Accum. depr. end of Yr. 2: $2,700

SUM-OF-THE-YEARS'-DIGITS DEPRECIATION Using the information given in Exercise 5Apx-1B, prepare a depreciation schedule showing the depreciation expense, accumulated depreciation, and book value for each year under the sum-of-the-years'-digits method.

E 5Apx-3B (LO3)
✓ Accum. depr. end of Yr. 2: $3,200

DOUBLE-DECLINING-BALANCE DEPRECIATION Using the information given in Exercise 5Apx-1B, prepare a depreciation schedule showing the depreciation expense, accumulated depreciation, and book value for each year under the double-declining-balance method.

E 5Apx-4B (LO4)
✓ Accum. depr. end of Yr. 2: $2,600

MODIFIED ACCELERATED COST RECOVERY SYSTEM Using the information given in Exercise 5Apx-1B and the rates shown in Figure 5A-4, prepare a depreciation schedule showing the depreciation expense, accumulated depreciation, and book value for each year under the Modified Accelerated Cost Recovery System. For tax purposes, assume that the computer has a useful life of five years. (The IRS schedule will spread depreciation over six years.)

RICH MILLER

Chapter 6 Financial Statements and the Closing Process

LEARNING OBJECTIVES

Careful study of this chapter should enable you to:

LO1 **Prepare financial statements with the aid of a work sheet.**

LO2 **Journalize and post closing entries.**

LO3 **Prepare a post-closing trial balance.**

LO4 **List and describe the steps in the accounting cycle.**

Indy Express Band is central Indiana's premier variety band. It offers a popular mix of musical styles from Top 40 to Big Band. The eight-piece band is led by Greg Imboden, fronted by Cozette Myers, driven by a three-piece horn section, and backed by a tight rhythm section. The **Indy Express Band** is perfect for a wedding reception, corporate function, conference event, dinner dance, or charity ball. Members of **Indy Express Band** have provided music for entertainers such as Jay Leno, Rod Stewart, Natalie Cole, Dionne Warwick, and Al Jarreau.

In addition to playing at weddings and other events, the band generally performs on New Year's Eve, the same day many businesses prepare closing entries. In this chapter, we complete the accounting cycle by demonstrating how to make closing entries and prepare the post-closing trial balance.

The work sheet, introduced in Chapter 5, is used for three major end-of-period activities:

1. journalizing adjusting entries,
2. preparing financial statements, and
3. journalizing closing entries.

This chapter illustrates the use of the work sheet for preparing financial statements and closing entries. In addition, the post-closing trial balance is explained and illustrated. All of these activities take place at the end of the firm's fiscal year. However, to continue our illustration of Mitchell's Campus Delivery, we demonstrate these activities at the end of the first month of operations.

LO1 The Financial Statements

Prepare financial statements with the aid of a work sheet.

The work sheet prepared in Chapter 5 supplies most of the information needed to prepare an income statement, a statement of owner's equity, and a balance sheet. The statements and work sheet columns from which they are derived for Mitchell's Campus Delivery are shown in Figures 6-1 and 6-2.

As you refer to the financial statements in Figures 6-1 and 6-2, notice the placement of dollar signs, single rulings, and double rulings. Dollar signs are placed at the top of each column and beneath rulings. Single rulings indicate addition or subtraction, and double rulings are placed under totals. Notice that each statement heading contains three lines: (1) company name, (2) statement title, and (3) period ended or date.

The Income Statement

Multiple columns are used on the financial statements to make them easier to read. There are no debit or credit columns on the financial statements.

Figure 6-1 shows how the Income Statement columns of the work sheet provide the information needed to prepare an income statement. Revenue is shown first, followed by an itemized and totaled list of expenses. Then, net income is calculated to double check the accuracy of the work sheet. It is presented with a double ruling as the last item in the statement.

The expenses could be listed in the same order that they appear in the chart of accounts or in descending order by dollar amount. The second approach helps the reader identify the most important expenses.

The Statement of Owner's Equity

LEARNING KEY

The owner's capital account in the general ledger must be reviewed to determine if additional investments were made during the accounting period.

The Balance Sheet columns of the work sheet provide most of the information needed to prepare a statement of owner's equity. Figure 6-2 shows that Mitchell's capital account balance and the drawing account balance are in the Balance Sheet columns. Be careful, however, when using the capital account balance reported on the work sheet. This account balance is the beginning balance *plus any investments made during the period*. Recall that Mitchell's beginning capital balance was zero. During June, he made an investment of $5,000. Thus, as reported previously, the beginning balance on the statement of owner's equity must be zero with the $5,000 reported as an investment during June. The net income for the month can be found either on

FIGURE 6-1 Linkages Between the Work Sheet and Income Statement

Mitchell's Campus Delivery
Work Sheet (Partial)
For Month Ended June 30, 20 - -

	ACCOUNT TITLE	INCOME STATEMENT DEBIT	INCOME STATEMENT CREDIT
1	Cash		
2	Accounts Receivable		
3	Supplies		
4	Prepaid Insurance		
5	Delivery Equipment		
6	Accum. Depr.—Delivery Equipment		
7	Accounts Payable		
8	Wages Payable		
9	Mitchell Williams, Capital		
10	Mitchell Williams, Drawing		
11	Delivery Fees		8 0 0 0 00
12	Wages Expense	2 0 5 0 00	
13	Rent Expense	1 0 0 0 00	
14	Supplies Expense	6 0 00	
15	Phone Expense	1 0 0 00	
16	Insurance Expense	7 0 00	
17	Depr. Expense—Delivery Equipment	8 0 00	
18		3 3 6 0 00	8 0 0 0 00
19	Net Income	4 6 4 0 00	
20		8 0 0 0 00	8 0 0 0 00
21			
22			
23			

Formatting Reminders:
Statement Heading
Name of company
Title of statement
Accounting period ended
Revenues listed first
Expenses listed second by amount (largest to smallest), or in chart of accounts order. Amounts are itemized in left column, subtotaled in right column.

Prepare Income Statement First

Mitchell's Campus Delivery
Income Statement
For Month Ended June 30, 20 --

Revenue:		
Delivery fees		$8,000
Expenses:		
Wages expense	$2,050	
Rent expense	1,000	
Supplies expense	60	
Phone expense	100	
Insurance expense	70	
Depr. expense—delivery equip.	80	
Total expenses		3,360
Net income		$4,640

Dollar signs used at top of columns and under rulings.
Single rulings indicate addition or subtraction.
Double rulings indicate totals.

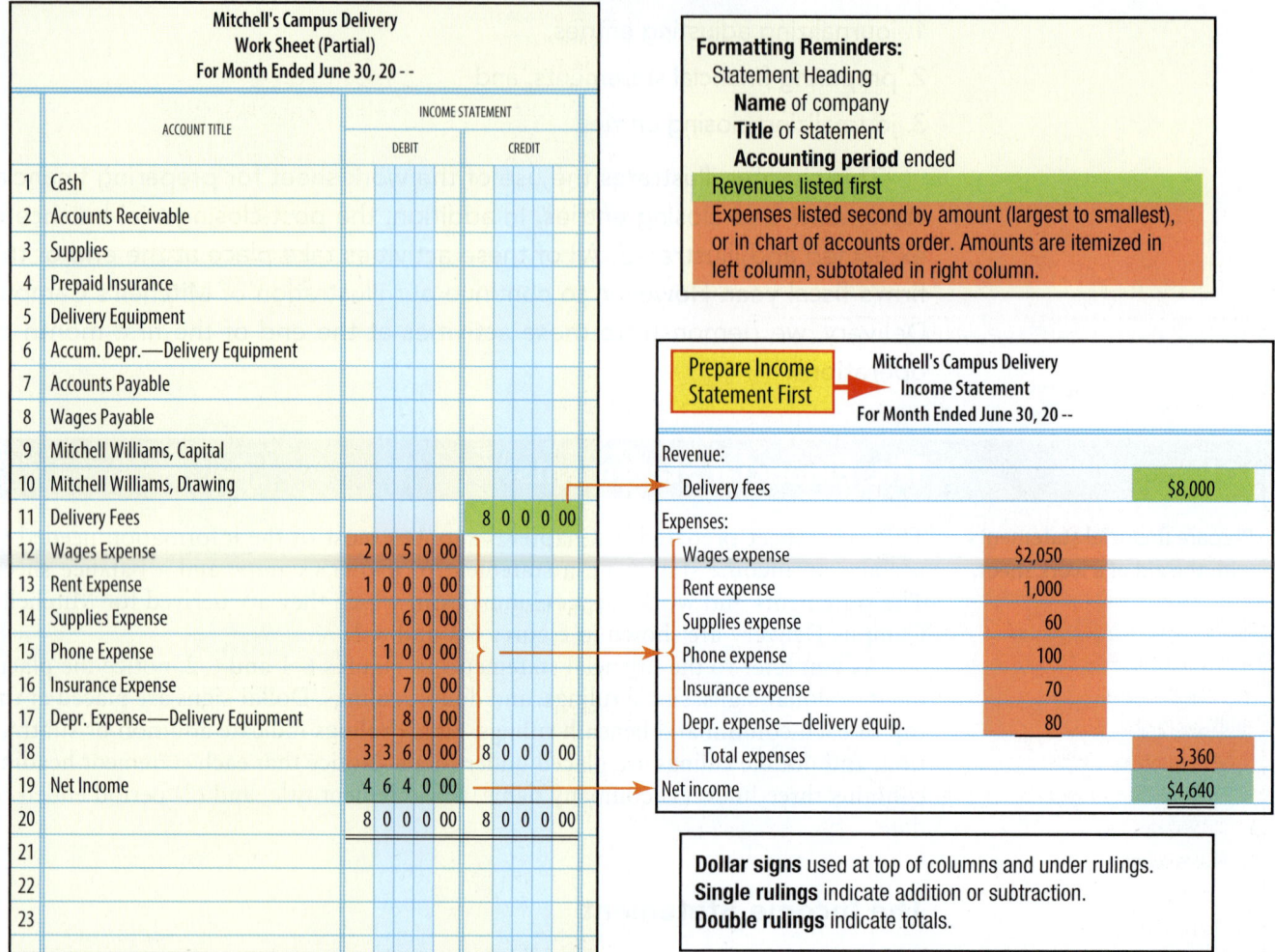

the work sheet at the bottom of the Income Statement (see Figure 6-1) and Balance Sheet columns or on the income statement itself. With these items of information, the statement of owner's equity can be prepared.

The Balance Sheet

As shown in Figure 6-2, the work sheet and the statement of owner's equity are used to prepare Mitchell's balance sheet. The asset and liability amounts can be found in the Balance Sheet columns of the work sheet. The ending balance in Mitchell Williams Capital has been computed on the statement of owner's equity. This amount should be copied from the statement of owner's equity to the balance sheet.

Two important features of the balance sheet in Figure 6-2 should be noted. First, it is a **report form of balance sheet**, which means that the liabilities and owner's equity sections are shown below the assets section. It differs from an **account form of balance sheet** in which the assets are on the left and the liabilities and owner's equity sections are on the right. (See Mitchell's balance sheet illustrated in Figure 2-2 on page 33 in Chapter 2.)

Second, it is a **classified balance sheet**, which means that similar items are grouped together on the balance sheet. Assets are classified as current assets and property, plant, and equipment. Similarly, liabilities are broken down into current and long-term sections. The following major balance sheet classifications are generally used.

FIGURE 6-2 Linkages Between the Work Sheet, Statement of Owner's Equity, and Balance Sheet

Statement Heading
Name of company
Title of statement
Date for BS and accounting period ended for SOE
Current assets: cash and items that will be converted to cash or consumed within a year.
Property, plant, and equipment: durable assets that will help produce revenues for several years.
Current liabilities: amounts owed that will be paid within a year (will require the use of current assets).

Note: The statement of owner's equity is prepared before the balance sheet. The S.O.E. is shown below the B.S. to enhance the illustration of the linkages between the work sheet and financial statements.

Mitchell's Campus Delivery
Work Sheet (Partial)
For Month Ended June 30, 20 - -

	ACCOUNT TITLE	BALANCE SHEET DEBIT	BALANCE SHEET CREDIT
1	Cash	470 00	
2	Accounts Receivable	3 100 00	
3	Supplies	20 00	
4	Prepaid Insurance	630 00	
5	Delivery Equipment	4 800 00	
6	Accum. Depr.—Delivery Equip.		80 00
7	Accounts Payable		1 900 00
8	Wages Payable		400 00
9	Mitchell Williams, Capital		5 000 00
10	Mitchell Williams, Drawing	3 000 00	
11	Delivery Fees		
12	Wages Expense		
13	Rent Expense		
14	Supplies Expense		
15	Phone Expense		
16	Insurance Expense		
17	Depr. Expense—Delivery Equip.		
18		12 020 00	7 380 00
19	Net Income		4 640 00
20		12 020 00	12 020 00
21			

Prepare BS Third

Mitchell's Campus Delivery
Balance Sheet
June 30, 20 --

Assets		
Current assets:		
Cash	$ 470	
Accounts receivable	3,100	
Supplies	20	
Prepaid insurance	630	
Total current assets		$4,220
Property, plant, and equipment:		
Delivery equipment	$4,800	
Less accumulated depreciation	80	4,720
Total assets		$8,940
Liabilities		
Current liabilities:		
Accounts payable	$1,900	
Wages payable	400	
Total current liabilities		$2,300
Owner's Equity		
Mitchell Williams, capital		6,640
Total liabilities and owner's equity		$8,940

Prepare SOE Second

Mitchell's Campus Delivery
Statement of Owner's Equity
For Month Ended June 30, 20 --

Mitchell Williams, capital, June 1, 20--		$ —
Investments during June		5,000
Total investment		$5,000
Net income for June	$4,640	
Less: withdrawals for June	3,000	
Increase in capital		1,640
Mitchell Williams, capital, June 30, 20--		$6,640

Ending capital is not taken from the work sheet. It is computed on the statement of owner's equity.
Dollar signs used at top of columns and under rulings.
Single rulings indicate addition or subtraction.
Double rulings indicate totals.

Current Assets

Current assets include cash and assets that will be converted into cash or consumed within either one year or the normal operating cycle of the business, whichever is longer. Examples include cash, accounts receivable, supplies, and prepaid insurance. As shown in Figure 6-3, an **operating cycle** is the period of time required to purchase supplies and services and convert them back into cash.

FIGURE 6-3 Operating Cycle

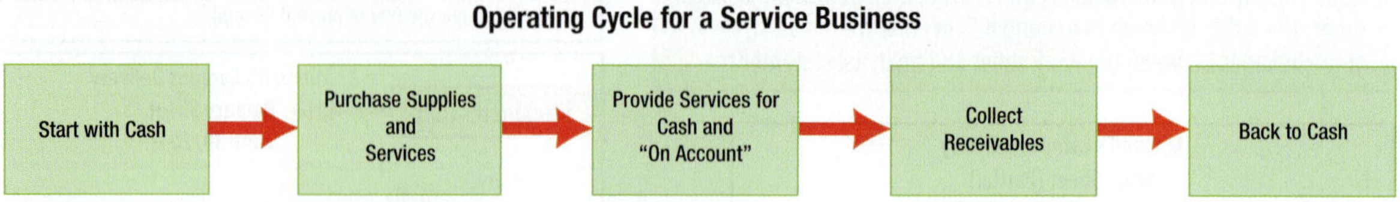

Property, Plant, and Equipment

Property, plant, and equipment, also called **plant assets** or **long-term assets**, represent assets that are expected to serve the business for many years. Examples include land, buildings, and equipment.

Current Liabilities

Current liabilities are due within either one year or the normal operating cycle of the business, whichever is longer. They will be paid out of current assets. Accounts payable and wages payable are classified as current liabilities.

Long-Term Liabilities

Long-term liabilities, or **long-term debt**, are obligations that are not expected to be paid within a year and do not require the use of current assets. A mortgage on an office building is an example of a long-term liability. Mitch has no long-term debts. If he did, they would be listed on the balance sheet in the long-term liabilities section immediately following the current liabilities.

Additional Investments by the Owner (Revisited)

If the owner of a business made additional investments during the accounting period, the owner's capital reported in the Balance Sheet columns of the work sheet represents the beginning balance plus any additional investments made during the accounting period. Thus, it may not represent the beginning balance of the capital account and should not be used to prepare the statements. If this amount were used as the beginning balance on the statement of owner's equity, it would not equal the ending balance from last period and would create confusion for those comparing the two statements. In addition, the statement would not reflect all of the activities affecting the owner's capital account during the period.

Therefore, we must also review the owner's capital account in the general ledger to get the information needed to prepare the statement of owner's equity. Figure 6-4 illustrates this situation for another business, Ramon's Shopping Service. The $5,000 balance of July 1, 20--, in Ramon Balboa's general ledger capital account is used as the beginning balance on the statement of owner's equity. Note that this is also the ending balance on June 30, 20--. The additional investment of $3,000 made on July 5 and posted to Balboa's general ledger capital account is reported by writing "Investments during period" on the line immediately after the beginning balance. The beginning balance plus investments during the period equals the total investment by the owner in the business and is the amount reported in the Balance Sheet columns of the work sheet. From this point, the preparation of the statement is the same as for businesses without additional investments.

FIGURE 6-4 Statement of Owner's Equity with Additional Investment

GENERAL LEDGER

ACCOUNT: Ramon Balboa, Capital ACCOUNT NO. 311

DATE		ITEM	POST. REF.	DEBIT	CREDIT	BALANCE DEBIT	BALANCE CREDIT
20-- July	1	Balance	J5		5 000 00		5 000 00
	5		J5		3 000 00		8 000 00

Additional investment

Amount reported on work sheet

Ramon's Shopping Service
Statement of Owner's Equity
For Months Ended June 30 and July 31, 20 - -

	June		July	
Ramon Balboa, beginning capital		$4,000		$5,000
Investments during period				3,000
Total investment				$8,000
Net income for the month	$1,500		$2,100	
Less withdrawals for the month	500		250	
Increase in capital		1,000		1,850
Ramon Balboa, ending capital		$5,000		$9,850

From general ledger

From work sheet

CHECKPOINT

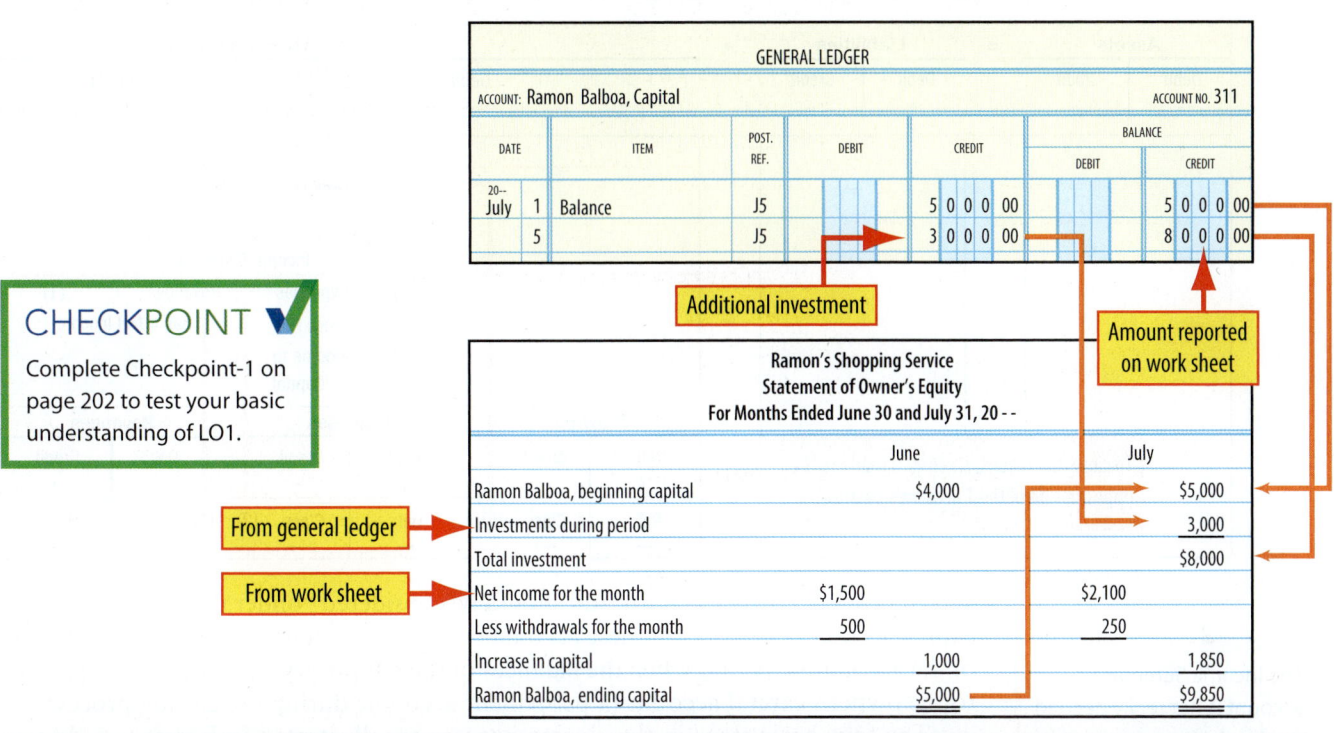

Complete Checkpoint-1 on page 202 to test your basic understanding of LO1.

LO2 The Closing Process

Journalize and post closing entries.

Assets, liabilities, and the owner's capital account accumulate information across accounting periods. For example, the cash balance at the end of one accounting period must be the same as the cash balance at the beginning of the next period. Thus, the balance reported for Cash is a result of all cash transactions since the business first opened. This is true for all accounts reported on the balance sheet. For this reason, they are called **permanent accounts**.

LEARNING KEY

Permanent accounts contain the results of all transactions since the business started. Their balances are carried forward to each new accounting period.

Revenue, expense, and drawing accounts accumulate information *for only a specific accounting period*. When preparing the financial statements, only revenues, expenses, and withdrawals for *this year* should be reported. Revenues, expenses, and withdrawals from prior years should not be included in *this year's* financial statements. Similarly, *this year's* revenues, expenses, and withdrawals should not be included in next year's financial statements. Thus, at the end of the fiscal year, these accounts must be *closed*. The **closing process** gives these accounts zero balances so they are prepared to accumulate new information for the next accounting period. Since these accounts are closed at the end of each period, they are called **temporary accounts**.

LEARNING KEY

Temporary accounts contain information for one accounting period. These accounts are closed at the end of each accounting period.

The accounting records are closed "as of" December 31, or another fiscal year-end chosen by the business. The actual adjusting entries, closing entries, and financial statements are generally prepared several weeks after the official closing date. However, it is important to include all transactions occurring prior to year-end in the *current* year's financial statements. Similarly, transactions taking place after year-end must be included in the *next* year's financial statements. Improper timing of the recognition of transactions taking place around the end of the year can have major effects on the reported profits. For example, some businesses have been found to "leave the books open" for a few days to include a major sale, or other profitable transactions, that actually took place after the end of the fiscal year. Thus, proper treatment of transactions taking place around the end of the year is carefully monitored by auditors.

The closing process is most clearly demonstrated by returning to the accounting equation and T accounts. As shown in Figure 6-5, revenue, expense, and drawing

FIGURE 6-5 The Closing Process

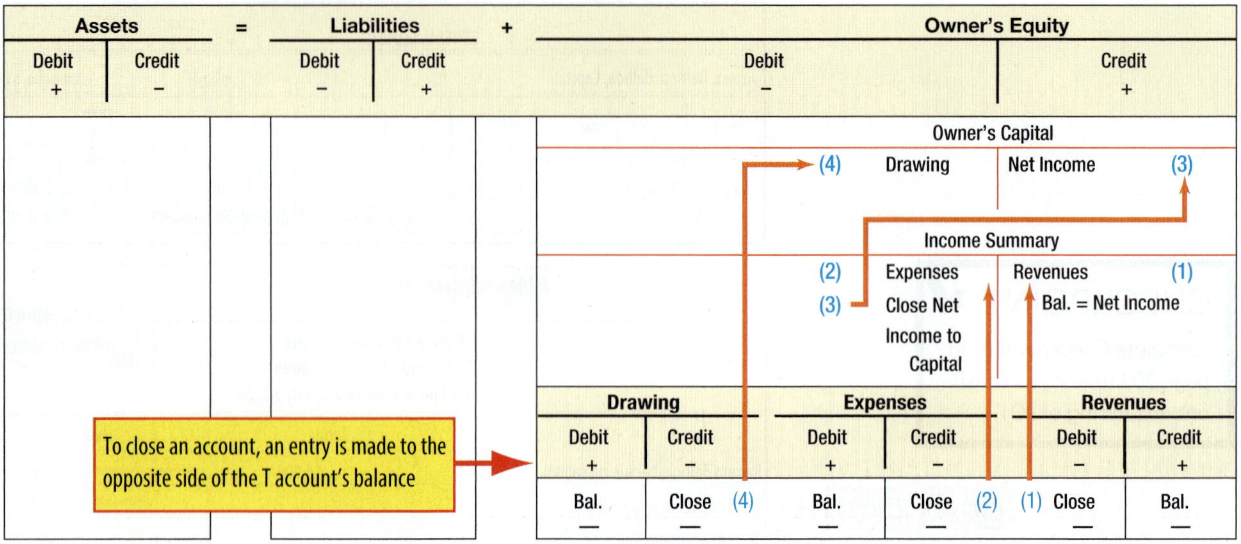

accounts impact owner's equity and should be considered "under the umbrella" of the capital account. The effect of these accounts on owner's equity is formalized at the end of the accounting period when the balances of the temporary accounts are transferred to the owner's capital account (a permanent account) during the closing process.

The Income Summary account is not really needed for the closing process. Revenue and expense accounts can be closed directly to the owner's capital account. One benefit of using the Income Summary account is that its balance before closing to the capital account equals the net income or net loss for the period. Thus, it can serve as a check of the accuracy of the closing entries for revenues and expenses.

The four basic steps in the closing process are illustrated in Figure 6-5. As you can see, a new account, **Income Summary**, is used in the closing process. This account may also be called *Expense and Revenue Summary*. This temporary account is used to close the revenue and expense accounts. After closing the revenues and expenses to Income Summary, the balance of this account is equal to the net income. This is why it is called Income Summary. Income Summary is opened during the closing process. Then it is closed to the owner's capital account. It does not appear on any financial statement. The four steps in the closing process are explained below.

Steps in the Closing Process

STEP 1 Close Revenue Accounts to Income Summary. Revenues have credit balances and increase owner's equity. Therefore, the revenue account is debited to create a zero balance. Income Summary is credited for the same amount.

STEP 2 Close Expense Accounts to Income Summary. Expenses have debit balances and reduce owner's equity. Therefore, the expense accounts are credited to create a zero balance. Income Summary must be debited for the total of the expenses.

STEP 3 Close Income Summary to the Owner's Capital Account. The balance in Income Summary represents the net income (credit balance) or net loss (debit balance). If net income has been earned, Income Summary is debited to create a zero balance, and the owner's capital account is credited. If a net loss has been incurred, the owner's capital account is debited and Income Summary is credited to create a zero balance. Figure 6-6 shows examples for closing net income and net loss.

STEP 4 Close Drawing to the Owner's Capital Account. Drawing has a debit balance and reduces owner's equity. Therefore, it is credited to create a zero balance. The owner's capital account is debited.

LEARNING KEY

The owner can make withdrawals from the business at any time, as long as the assets are available. These withdrawals have nothing to do with measuring the profitability of the firm. Thus, they are closed directly to the owner's capital account.

Upon completion of these four steps, all temporary accounts have zero balances. The earnings and withdrawals for the period have been transferred to the owner's capital account. Closing entries for Mitchell's Campus Delivery, in T account form, are illustrated in Figure 6-7.

FIGURE 6-6 Step 3: Closing Net Income and Closing Net Loss

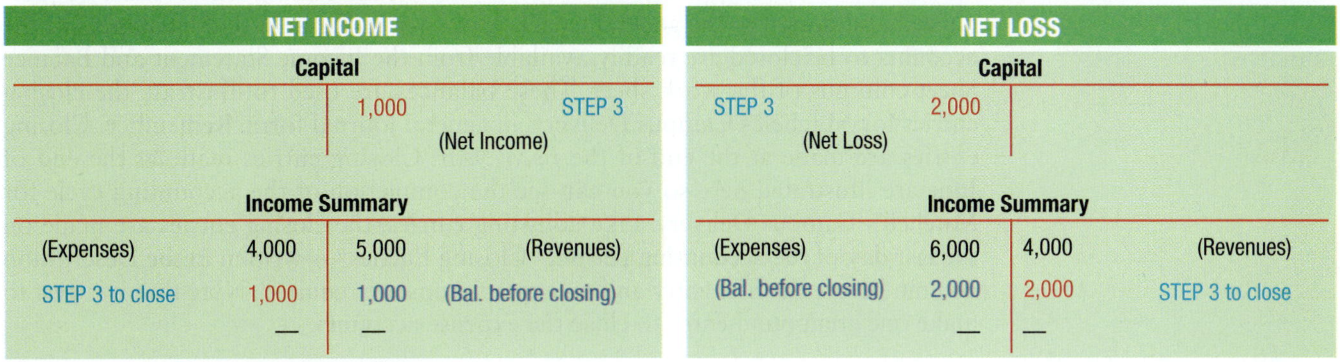

Dashes (—) in the T Accounts indicate zero balances

FIGURE 6-7 Closing Entries in T Account Form

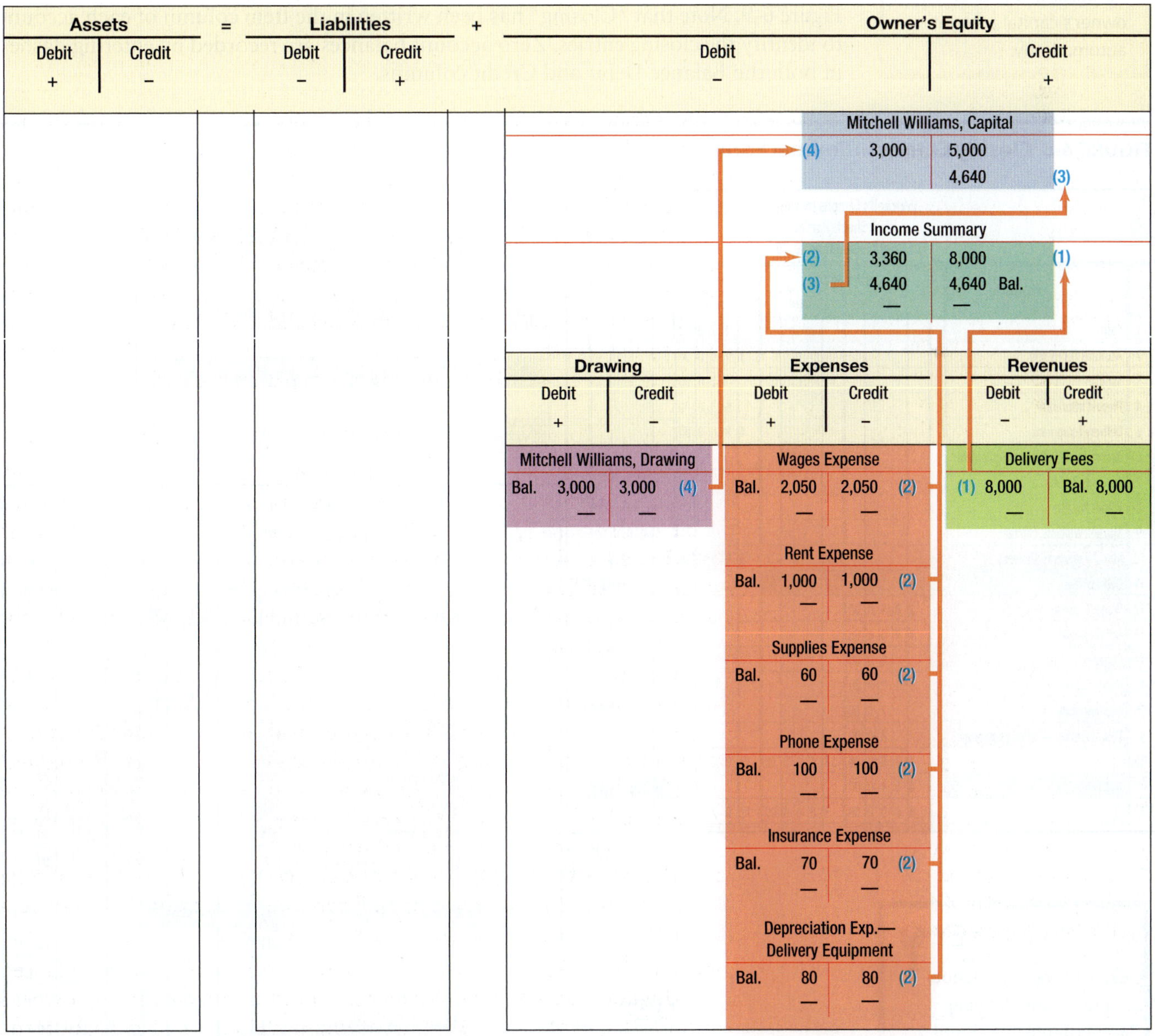

Dashes (—) in the T Accounts indicate zero balances

Journalize Closing Entries

Of course, to actually change the ledger accounts, the closing entries must be journalized and posted to the general ledger. As shown in Figure 6-8, the balances of the accounts to be closed are readily available from the Income Statement and Balance Sheet columns of the work sheet. These balances are used to illustrate the closing entries for Mitchell's Campus Delivery, in general journal form. Remember: Closing entries are made at the end of the *fiscal year*. Closing entries made at the end of June are illustrated here so you can see the completion of the accounting cycle for Mitchell's Campus Delivery. Like adjusting entries, the closing entries are made on the last day of the accounting period. "Closing Entries" is written in the Description column before the first entry and no explanations are required. Note that it is best to make one compound entry to close the expense accounts.

Computer programs post the closing entries to the owner's capital account automatically.

Post the Closing Entries

The account numbers have been entered in the Posting Reference column of the journal to show that the entries have been posted to the ledger accounts illustrated in Figure 6-9. Note that "Closing" has been written in the Item column of each account to identify the closing entries. Zero account balances are recorded by entering dashes in both the Balance Debit and Credit columns.

FIGURE 6-8 Closing Entries in Journal Form

Mitchell's Campus Delivery
Work Sheet (Partial)
For Month Ended June 30, 20 - -

	ACCOUNT TITLE	INCOME STATEMENT DEBIT	INCOME STATEMENT CREDIT	BALANCE SHEET DEBIT	BALANCE SHEET CREDIT
1	Cash			470 00	
2	Accounts Receivable			3100 00	
3	Supplies			20 00	
4	Prepaid Insurance			630 00	
5	Delivery Equipment			4800 00	
6	Accum. Depr.—Delivery Equipment				80 00
7	Accounts Payable				1900 00
8	Wages Payable				400 00
9	Mitchell Williams, Capital				5000 00
10	Mitchell Williams, Drawing			3000 00	
11	Delivery Fees		8000 00		
12	Wages Expense	2050 00			
13	Rent Expense	1000 00			
14	Supplies Expense	60 00			
15	Phone Expense	100 00			
16	Insurance Expense	70 00			
17	Depr. Expense—Delivery Equipment	80 00			
18		3360 00	8000 00	12020 00	7380 00
19	Net Income	4640 00			4640 00
20		8000 00	8000 00	12020 00	12020 00

STEP 1: Close revenue accounts to Income Summary.

STEP 2: Close expense accounts to Income Summary.

STEP 3: Close Income Summary to the owner's capital account.

STEP 4: Close Drawing to the owner's capital account.

GENERAL JOURNAL PAGE 4

DATE		DESCRIPTION	POST. REF.	DEBIT	CREDIT	
		Closing Entries				1
20-- June	30	Delivery Fees	401	8000 00		2
		Income Summary	313		8000 00	3
						4
	30	Income Summary	313	3360 00		5
		Wages Expense	511		2050 00	6
		Rent Expense	521		1000 00	7
		Supplies Expense	523		60 00	8
		Phone Expense	525		100 00	9
		Insurance Expense	535		70 00	10
		Depr. Expense—Delivery Equipment	541		80 00	11
						12
	30	Income Summary	313	4640 00		13
		Mitchell Williams, Capital	311		4640 00	14
						15
	30	Mitchell Williams, Capital	311	3000 00		16
		Mitchell Williams, Drawing	312		3000 00	17
						18

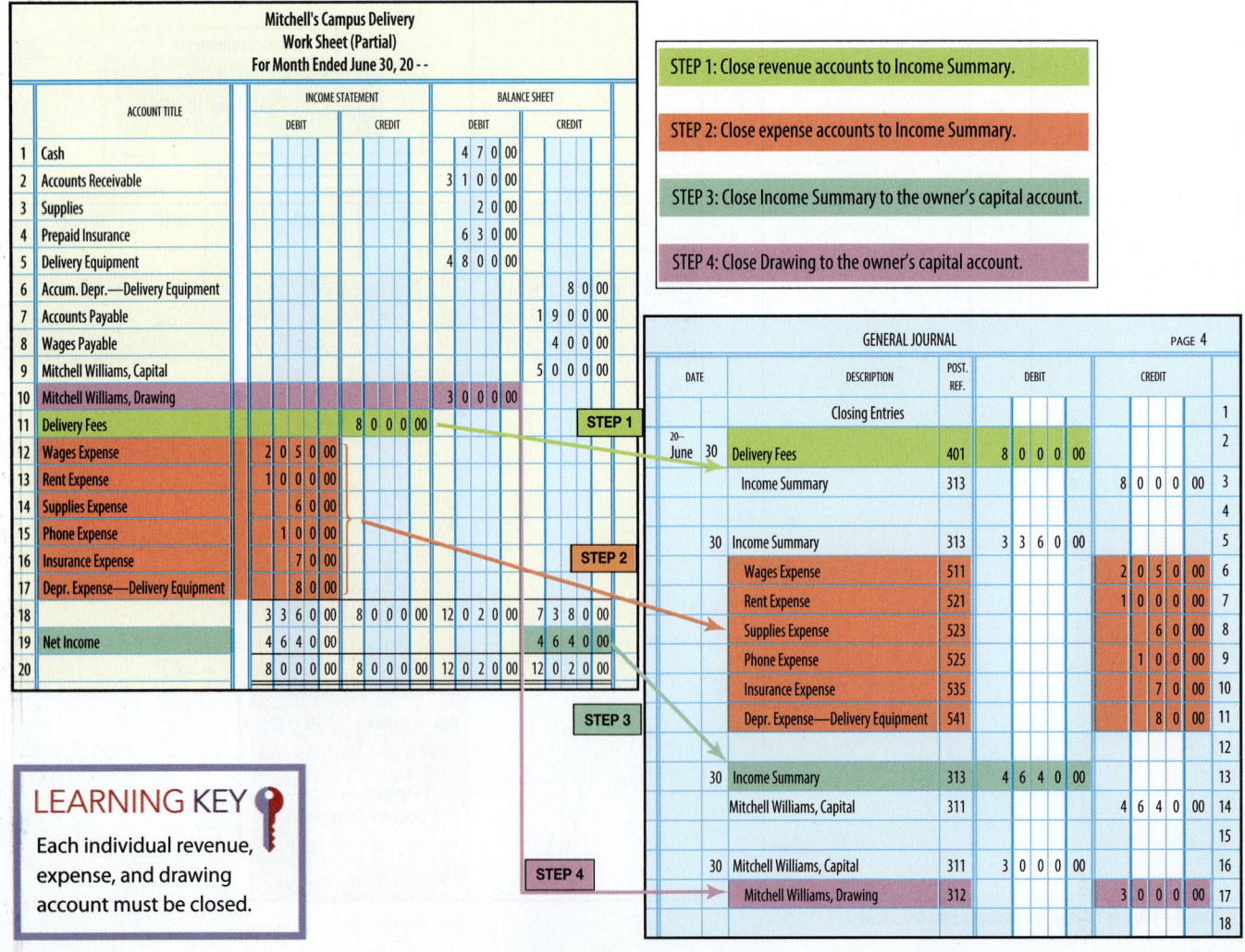

LEARNING KEY Each individual revenue, expense, and drawing account must be closed.

YOUR PERSPECTIVE

Bookkeeping, Accounting, and Auditing Clerks

Bookkeeping clerks are responsible for maintaining an organization's general ledger, recording transactions, and posting debits and credits. They produce the organization's financial statements, prepare bank deposits, and confirm account reconciliations. Other duties may include handling payroll, purchasing, and invoicing, and tracking overdue accounts. *Accounting clerks*, typically found in larger organizations, perform specialized duties and have titles such as accounts payable or accounts receivable clerk, which reflect the type of work they do. *Auditing clerks* check the accuracy of figures, posted transactions, and accounting reports. If small errors are found, the auditing clerk may make the corrections. However, in the case of major errors, senior management would be informed.

These jobs are extremely important because the financial information maintained is reported in the organization's financial statements. The information must be prepared accurately and in a timely manner because it is used to make critical business decisions.

FIGURE 6-9 Closing Entries Posted to the General Ledger

GENERAL LEDGER

ACCOUNT: Mitchell Williams, Capital — ACCOUNT NO. 311

DATE		ITEM	POST. REF.	DEBIT	CREDIT	BALANCE DEBIT	BALANCE CREDIT
20-- June	1		J1		5,000.00		5,000.00
	30	Closing	J4		4,640.00		9,640.00
	30	Closing	J4	3,000.00			6,640.00

ACCOUNT: Mitchell Williams, Drawing — ACCOUNT NO. 312

DATE		ITEM	POST. REF.	DEBIT	CREDIT	BALANCE DEBIT	BALANCE CREDIT
20-- June	30		J2	3,000.00		3,000.00	
	30	Closing	J4		3,000.00	—	—

ACCOUNT: Income Summary — ACCOUNT NO. 313

DATE		ITEM	POST. REF.	DEBIT	CREDIT	BALANCE DEBIT	BALANCE CREDIT
20-- June	30	Closing	J4		8,000.00		8,000.00
	30	Closing	J4	3,360.00			4,640.00
	30	Closing	J4	4,640.00		—	—

ACCOUNT: Delivery Fees — ACCOUNT NO. 401

DATE		ITEM	POST. REF.	DEBIT	CREDIT	BALANCE DEBIT	BALANCE CREDIT
20-- June	6		J1		2,100.00		2,100.00
	15		J1		2,400.00		4,500.00
	30		J2		3,500.00		8,000.00
	30	Closing	J4	8,000.00		—	—

(continued)

FIGURE 6-9 Closing Entries Posted to the General Ledger (*concluded*)

ACCOUNT: Wages Expense — ACCOUNT NO. 511

DATE		ITEM	POST. REF.	DEBIT	CREDIT	BALANCE DEBIT	BALANCE CREDIT
20-- June	27		J2	1,650.00		1,650.00	
	30	Adjusting	J3	400.00		2,050.00	
	30	Closing	J4		2,050.00	—	—

ACCOUNT: Rent Expense — ACCOUNT NO. 521

DATE		ITEM	POST REF.	DEBIT	CREDIT	BALANCE DEBIT	BALANCE CREDIT
20-- June	7		J1	1,000.00		1,000.00	
	30	Closing	J4		1,000.00	—	—

ACCOUNT: Supplies Expense — ACCOUNT NO. 523

DATE		ITEM	POST. REF.	DEBIT	CREDIT	BALANCE DEBIT	BALANCE CREDIT
20-- June	30	Adjusting	J3	60.00		60.00	
	30	Closing	J4		60.00	—	—

ACCOUNT: Phone Expense — ACCOUNT NO. 525

DATE		ITEM	POST. REF.	DEBIT	CREDIT	BALANCE DEBIT	BALANCE CREDIT
20-- June	15		J1	100.00		100.00	
	30	Closing	J4		100.00	—	—

ACCOUNT: Insurance Expense — ACCOUNT NO. 535

DATE		ITEM	POST. REF.	DEBIT	CREDIT	BALANCE DEBIT	BALANCE CREDIT
20-- June	30	Adjusting	J3	70.00		70.00	
	30	Closing	J4		70.00	—	—

ACCOUNT: Depreciation Expense—Delivery Equipment — ACCOUNT NO. 541

DATE		ITEM	POST. REF.	DEBIT	CREDIT	BALANCE DEBIT	BALANCE CREDIT
20-- June	30	Adjusting	J3	80.00		80.00	
	30	Closing	J4		80.00	—	—

CHECKPOINT

Complete Checkpoint-2 on page 202 to test your basic understanding of LO2.

LO3 Post-Closing Trial Balance

Prepare a post-closing trial balance.

After posting the closing entries, a **post-closing trial balance** should be prepared to prove the equality of the debit and credit balances in the general ledger accounts. The ending balance of each general ledger account that remains open at the end of the year is listed. Remember: Only the permanent accounts remain open after the closing process is completed. Figure 6-10 shows the post-closing trial balance for Mitchell's ledger.

Note that all amounts reflected on the post-closing trial balance are the same as reported in the Balance Sheet columns of the work sheet except Drawing and Owner's Capital. Drawing was closed. Owner's Capital was updated to reflect revenues, expenses, and drawing for the accounting period.

LEARNING KEY

Once the closing entries are posted, the general ledger capital account balance will agree with the amount reported on the balance sheet.

CHECKPOINT

Complete Checkpoint-3 on page 202 to test your basic understanding of LO3.

FIGURE 6-10 Post-Closing Trial Balance

Mitchell's Campus Delivery
Post-Closing Trial Balance
June 30, 20 - -

ACCOUNT TITLE	ACCOUNT NO.	DEBIT BALANCE	CREDIT BALANCE
Cash	101	470 00	
Accounts Receivable	122	3100 00	
Supplies	141	20 00	
Prepaid Insurance	145	630 00	
Delivery Equipment	185	4800 00	
Accumulated Depreciation—Delivery Equipment	185.1		80 00
Accounts Payable	202		1900 00
Wages Payable	219		400 00
Mitchell Williams, Capital	311		6640 00
		9020 00	9020 00

A BROADER VIEW

Importance of Earnings to the Stock Market

Investors in the stock market pay close attention to earnings reported on the income statement. If earnings are different from what investors are expecting, the price of the stock may go up or down. For example, AT&T's share prices dipped simply because they missed expected earnings by a penny per share.

ISTOCK.COM/MDDPHOTO

LO4 The Accounting Cycle

List and describe the steps in the accounting cycle.

The steps involved in accounting for all of the business activities during an accounting period are called the **accounting cycle**. The cycle begins with the analysis of source documents and ends with a post-closing trial balance. A brief summary of the steps in the cycle follows.

Steps in the Accounting Cycle

LEARNING KEY

Properly analyzing and journalizing transactions is very important. A mistake made in step 1 is carried through the entire accounting cycle.

During Accounting Period

STEP 1 Analyze source documents.

STEP 2 Journalize the transactions.

STEP 3 Post to the general ledger accounts.

End of Accounting Period

STEP 4 Prepare a trial balance.

STEP 5 Determine and prepare the needed adjustments on the work sheet.

STEP 6 Complete an end-of-period work sheet.

STEP 7 Journalize and post the adjusting entries.

STEP 8 Prepare an income statement, a statement of owner's equity, and a balance sheet.

STEP 9 Journalize and post the closing entries.

STEP 10 Prepare a post-closing trial balance.

Steps 4 through 10 in the preceding list are performed *as of* the last day of the accounting period. This does not mean that they are actually done on the last day. The accountant may not be able to do any of these things until the first few days (sometimes weeks) of the next period. Nevertheless, the work sheet, statements, and entries are prepared as of the closing date.

SELF-STUDY

LEARNING OBJECTIVES	Key Points to Remember
LO1 Prepare financial statements with the aid of a work sheet.	The work sheet is used as an aid in preparing 1. adjusting entries, 2. financial statements, and 3. closing entries. The following classifications are used for accounts reported on the balance sheet. • *Current assets* include cash and assets that will be converted into cash or consumed within either one year or the normal operating cycle of the business, whichever is longer. An *operating cycle* is the time required to purchase supplies and services and convert them back into cash. • *Property, plant, and equipment*, also called *plant assets* or *long-term assets*, represent assets that are expected to serve the business for many years. • *Current liabilities* are liabilities that are due within either one year or the normal operating cycle of the business, whichever is longer, and that are to be paid out of current assets. • *Long-term liabilities*, or *long-term debt*, are obligations that are not expected to be paid within a year and do not require the use of current assets.
LO2 Journalize and post closing entries.	Steps in the closing process are: 1. Close revenue accounts to Income Summary. 2. Close expense accounts to Income Summary. 3. Close Income Summary to the owner's capital account. 4. Close Drawing to the owner's capital account.

(continued)

LEARNING OBJECTIVES Key Points to Remember

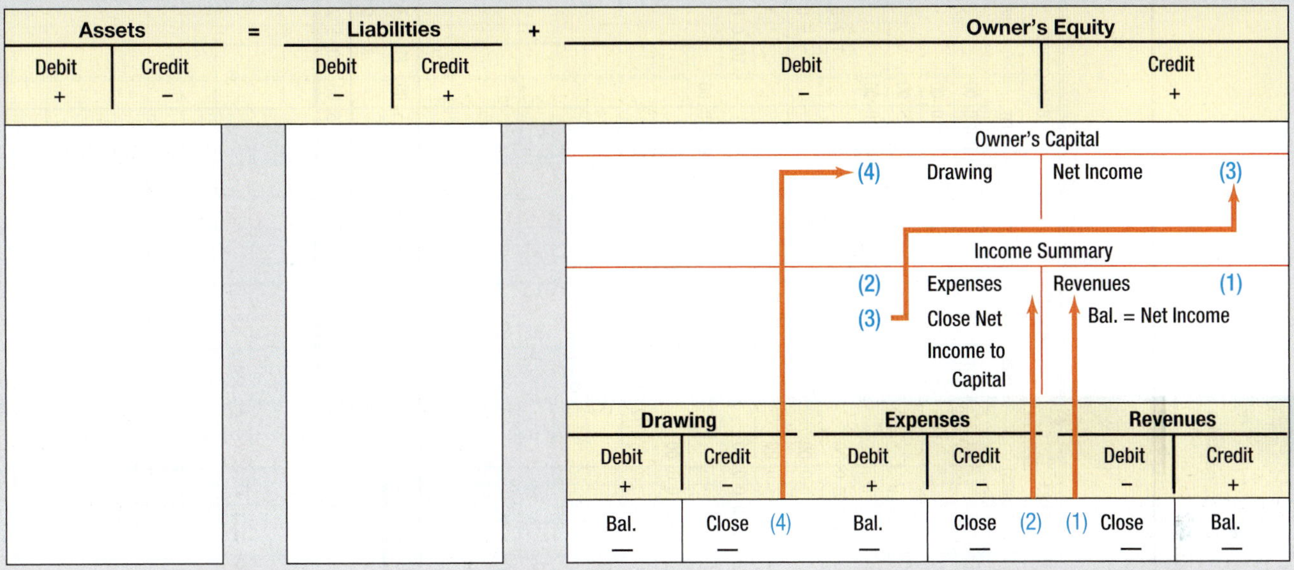

LO3	**Prepare a post-closing trial balance.**	After posting the closing entries, a post-closing trial balance should be prepared to prove the equality of the debit and credit balances in the general ledger accounts. The accounts shown in the post-closing trial balance are the permanent accounts.
LO4	**List and describe the steps in the accounting cycle.**	Steps in the accounting cycle are: *During Accounting Period* 1. Analyze source documents. 2. Journalize the transactions. 3. Post to the general ledger accounts. *End of Accounting Period* 4. Prepare a trial balance. 5. Determine and prepare the needed adjustments on the work sheet. 6. Complete an end-of-period work sheet. 7. Journalize and post the adjusting entries. 8. Prepare an income statement, a statement of owner's equity, and a balance sheet. 9. Journalize and post the closing entries. 10. Prepare a post-closing trial balance.

DEMONSTRATION PROBLEM

Timothy Chang owns and operates Hard Copy Printers. A work sheet for the year ended December 31, 20--, is provided on the next page. Chang made no additional investments during the year.

REQUIRED

1. Prepare financial statements.
2. Prepare closing entries.

Hard Copy Printers
Work Sheet
For Year Ended December 31, 20--

	ACCOUNT TITLE	TRIAL BALANCE		ADJUSTMENTS		ADJUSTED TRIAL BALANCE		INCOME STATEMENT		BALANCE SHEET		
		DEBIT	CREDIT	DEBIT	CREDIT	DEBIT	CREDIT	DEBIT	CREDIT	DEBIT	CREDIT	
1	Cash	1,180.00				1,180.00				1,180.00		1
2	Paper Supplies	3,600.00			(a) 3,550.00	50.00				50.00		2
3	Prepaid Insurance	1,000.00			(b) 505.00	495.00				495.00		3
4	Printing Equipment	5,800.00				5,800.00				5,800.00		4
5	Accum. Depr.—Printing Equipment				(d) 1,200.00		1,200.00				1,200.00	5
6	Accounts Payable		500.00				500.00				500.00	6
7	Wages Payable				(c) 30.00		30.00				30.00	7
8	Timothy Chang, Capital		10,000.00				10,000.00				10,000.00	8
9	Timothy Chang, Drawing	13,000.00				13,000.00				13,000.00		9
10	Printing Fees		35,100.00				35,100.00		35,100.00			10
11	Wages Expense	11,970.00		(c) 30.00		12,000.00		12,000.00				11
12	Rent Expense	7,500.00				7,500.00		7,500.00				12
13	Paper Supplies Expense			(a) 3,550.00		3,550.00		3,550.00				13
14	Phone Expense	550.00				550.00		550.00				14
15	Utilities Expense	1,000.00				1,000.00		1,000.00				15
16	Insurance Expense			(b) 505.00		505.00		505.00				16
17	Depr. Expense—Printing Equipment			(d) 1,200.00		1,200.00		1,200.00				17
18		45,600.00	45,600.00	5,285.00	5,285.00	46,830.00	46,830.00	26,305.00	35,100.00	20,525.00	11,730.00	18
19	Net Income							8,795.00			8,795.00	19
20								35,100.00	35,100.00	20,525.00	20,525.00	20
21												21
22												22
23												23
24												24
25												25
26												26
27												27
28												28
29												29
30												30

SOLUTION 1.

Hard Copy Printers
Income Statement
For Year Ended December 31, 20 --

Revenue:		
Printing fees		$35,100
Expenses:		
Wages expense	$12,000	
Rent expense	7,500	
Paper supplies expense	3,550	
Phone expense	550	
Utilities expense	1,000	
Insurance expense	505	
Depreciation expense—printing equipment	1,200	
Total expenses		26,305
Net income		$ 8,795

Hard Copy Printers
Statement of Owner's Equity
For Year Ended December 31, 20 --

Timothy Chang, capital, January 1, 20 --		$10,000
Net income for 20 --	$ 8,795	
Less withdrawals for 20 --	13,000	
Decrease in capital		(4,205)
Timothy Chang, capital, December 31, 20 --		$ 5,795

Hard Copy Printers
Balance Sheet
December 31, 20 - -

Assets		
Current assets:		
Cash	$ 1,180	
Paper supplies	50	
Prepaid insurance	495	
Total current assets		$ 1,725
Property, plant, and equipment:		
Printing equipment	$ 5,800	
Less accumulated depreciation	1,200	4,600
Total assets		$ 6,325
Liabilities		
Current liabilities:		
Accounts payable	$ 500	
Wages payable	30	
Total current liabilities		$ 530
Owner's Equity		
Timothy Chang, capital		5,795
Total liabilities and owner's equity		$ 6,325

SOLUTION 2.

GENERAL JOURNAL PAGE 4

	DATE		DESCRIPTION	POST. REF.	DEBIT	CREDIT	
1			Closing Entries				1
2	20-- Dec.	31	Printing Fees		35 1 0 0 00		2
3			Income Summary			35 1 0 0 00	3
4							4
5		31	Income Summary		26 3 0 5 00		5
6			Wages Expense			12 0 0 0 00	6
7			Rent Expense			7 5 0 0 00	7
8			Paper Supplies Expense			3 5 5 0 00	8
9			Phone Expense			5 5 0 00	9
10			Utilities Expense			1 0 0 0 00	10
11			Insurance Expense			5 0 5 00	11
12			Depr. Expense—Printing Equipment			1 2 0 0 00	12
13							13
14		31	Income Summary		8 7 9 5 00		14
15			Timothy Chang, Capital			8 7 9 5 00	15
16							16
17		31	Timothy Chang, Capital		13 0 0 0 00		17
18			Timothy Chang, Drawing			13 0 0 0 00	18
19							19

KEY TERMS

account form of balance sheet (186) A balance sheet in which the assets are on the left and the liabilities and the owner's equity sections are on the right.

accounting cycle (195) The steps involved in accounting for all of the business activities during an accounting period.

classified balance sheet (186) A balance sheet with separate categories for current assets; property, plant, and equipment; current liabilities; and long-term liabilities.

closing process (189) The process of giving zero balances to the temporary accounts so that they can accumulate information for the next accounting period.

current assets (188) Cash and assets that will be converted into cash or consumed within either one year or the normal operating cycle of the business, whichever is longer.

current liabilities (188) Liabilities that are due within either one year or the normal operating cycle of the business, whichever is longer, and that are to be paid out of current assets.

Income Summary (190) A temporary account used in the closing process to summarize the effects of all revenue and expense accounts.

long-term assets (188) See property, plant, and equipment.

long-term debt (188) See long-term liabilities.

long-term liabilities (188) Obligations that are not expected to be paid within a year and do not require the use of current assets. Also called long-term debt.

operating cycle (188) The period of time required to purchase supplies and services and convert them back into cash.

permanent accounts (189) Accounts that accumulate information across accounting periods; all accounts reported on the balance sheet.

plant assets (188) See property, plant, and equipment.

post-closing trial balance (194) Prepared after posting the closing entries to prove the equality of the debit and credit balances in the general ledger accounts.

property, plant, and equipment (188) Assets that are expected to serve the business for many years. Also called plant assets or long-term assets.

report form of balance sheet (186) A balance sheet in which the liabilities and the owner's equity sections are shown below the assets section.

temporary accounts (189) Accounts that do not accumulate information across accounting periods but are closed, such as the drawing account and all income statement accounts.

SELF-STUDY TEST QUESTIONS

True/False

1. **LO1** Expenses are listed on the income statement as they appear in the chart of accounts or in descending order (by dollar amount).
2. **LO1** Additional investments of capital during the month are not reported on the statement of owner's equity.
3. **LO1** The income statement cannot be prepared using the work sheet alone.
4. **LO1** A classified balance sheet groups similar items, such as current assets together.
5. **LO2** Temporary accounts are closed at the end of each accounting period.

Multiple Choice

1. **LO2** Which of these types of accounts is considered a "permanent" account?
   (a) Revenue (c) Drawing
   (b) Asset (d) Expense
2. **LO2** Which of these accounts is considered a "temporary" account?
   (a) Cash (c) J. Jones, Capital
   (b) Accounts Payable (d) J. Jones, Drawing
3. **LO2** Which of these is the first step in the closing process?
   (a) Close revenue account(s). (c) Close the Income Summary account.
   (b) Close expense accounts. (d) Close the drawing account.
4. **LO3** The ________ is prepared after closing entries are posted to prove the equality of debit and credit balances.
   (a) balance sheet (c) post-closing trial balance
   (b) income statement (d) statement of owner's equity
5. **LO4** Steps that begin with analyzing source documents and conclude with the post-closing trial balance are called the
   (a) closing process. (c) adjusting entries.
   (b) accounting cycle. (d) posting process.

CHECKPOINT

Checkpoint Exercises

1. **LO1** Joe Fisher operates Fisher Consulting. A partial work sheet for August 20-- is provided below. Fisher made no additional investments during the month. Prepare an income statement, statement of owner's equity, and balance sheet.

Fisher Consulting
Work Sheet (Partial)
For Month Ended August 31, 20--

	ACCOUNT TITLE	INCOME STATEMENT DEBIT	INCOME STATEMENT CREDIT	BALANCE SHEET DEBIT	BALANCE SHEET CREDIT	
1	Cash			2 500 00		1
2	Accounts Receivable			800 00		2
3	Equipment			3 800 00		3
4	Accum. Depr.— Equipment				200 00	4
5	Accounts Payable				1 000 00	5
6	Joe Fisher, Capital				3 000 00	6
7	Joe Fisher, Drawing			300 00		7
8	Professional Fees		5 000 00			8
9	Wages Expense	1 000 00				9
10	Rent Expense	700 00				10
11	Depreciation Expense	100 00				11
12		1 800 00	5 000 00	7 400 00	4 200 00	12
13	Net Income	3 200 00			3 200 00	13
14		5 000 00	5 000 00	7 400 00	7 400 00	14
15						15
16						16

2. **LO2** Using the work sheet provided in Checkpoint Exercise 1, prepare closing entries in general journal form.

3. **LO3** Using the work sheet provided in Checkpoint Exercise 1 and financial statements prepared for that exercise, prepare a post-closing trial balance.

The answers to the Self-Study Test Questions are at the end of the chapter (pages 215–217).

APPLYING YOUR KNOWLEDGE

REVIEW QUESTIONS

LO1 1. Identify the source of the information needed to prepare the income statement.

LO1 2. Describe two approaches to listing the expenses in the income statement.

LO1 3. Identify the sources of the information needed to prepare the statement of owner's equity.

CengageNowv2 provides "Show Me How" videos for selected exercises and problems. Additional resources, such as Excel templates for completing selected exercises and problems, are available for download from the companion website at Cengage.com.

LO1 4. If additional investments were made during the year, what information in addition to the work sheet would be needed to prepare the statement of owner's equity?

LO1 5. Identify the sources of the information needed to prepare the balance sheet.

LO2 6. What is a permanent account? On which financial statement are permanent accounts reported?

LO2 7. Name three types of temporary accounts.

LO2 8. List the four steps for closing the temporary accounts.

LO2 9. Describe the net effect of the four closing entries on the balance of the owner's capital account. Where else is this same amount calculated?

LO3 10. What is the purpose of the post-closing trial balance?

LO4 11. List the 10 steps in the accounting cycle.

SERIES A EXERCISES

E 6-1A (LO1)
✓ Net income: $2,220

INCOME STATEMENT From the partial work sheet for Major Advising below, prepare an income statement.

E 6-2A (LO1)
✓ Capital 1/31: $5,420

STATEMENT OF OWNER'S EQUITY From the partial work sheet below, prepare a statement of owner's equity, assuming no additional investment was made by the owner.

E 6-3A (LO1)
✓ Total assets: $6,720

BALANCE SHEET From the statement of owner's equity prepared in E 6-2A and the partial work sheet below, prepare a balance sheet.

(FOR EXERCISES 6-1A, 6-2A, 6-3A, AND 6-4A)

Major Advising
Work Sheet (Partial)
For Month Ended January 31, 20 - -

	ACCOUNT TITLE	INCOME STATEMENT DEBIT	INCOME STATEMENT CREDIT	BALANCE SHEET DEBIT	BALANCE SHEET CREDIT	
1	Cash			1,339 00		1
2	Accounts Receivable			935 00		2
3	Supplies			346 00		3
4	Prepaid Insurance			800 00		4
5	Office Equipment			3,500 00		5
6	Accum. Depr.—Office Equipment				200 00	6
7	Accounts Payable				1,000 00	7
8	Wages Payable				300 00	8
9	Ed Major, Capital				4,100 00	9
10	Ed Major, Drawing			900 00		10
11	Advising Fees		4,140 00			11
12	Wages Expense	700 00				12
13	Advertising Expense	90 00				13
14	Rent Expense	500 00				14
15	Supplies Expense	150 00				15
16	Phone Expense	67 00				16
17	Electricity Expense	48 00				17
18	Insurance Expense	89 00				18
19	Gas and Oil Expense	53 00				19
20	Depr. Expense—Office Equipment	200 00				20
21	Miscellaneous Expense	23 00				21
22		1,920 00	4,140 00	7,820 00	5,600 00	22
23	Net Income	2,220 00			2,220 00	23
24		4,140 00	4,140 00	7,820 00	7,820 00	24

E 6-4A (LO2)
✓ Capital 1/31: $5,420

CLOSING ENTRIES (NET INCOME) Set up T accounts for Major Advising based on the work sheet in Exercise 6-1A and the chart of accounts provided below. Enter the existing balance for each account. Prepare closing entries in general journal form. Then post the closing entries to the T accounts.

Chart of Accounts

Assets		Revenues	
101	Cash	401	Advising Fees
122	Accounts Receivable		
141	Supplies	**Expenses**	
145	Prepaid Insurance	511	Wages Expense
181	Office Equipment	512	Advertising Expense
181.1	Accum. Depr.—Office Equip.	521	Rent Expense
		524	Supplies Expense
Liabilities		525	Phone Expense
202	Accounts Payable	533	Electricity Expense
219	Wages Payable	535	Insurance Expense
		538	Gas and Oil Expense
Owner's Equity		541	Depr. Exp.—Office Equip.
311	Ed Major, Capital	549	Miscellaneous Expense
312	Ed Major, Drawing		
313	Income Summary		

E 6-5A (LO2)

CLOSING ENTRIES (NET INCOME) Using the following partial listing of T accounts, prepare closing entries in general journal form dated April 30, 20--. Then post the closing entries to the T accounts.

Cash 101

Bal. 500	

Accounts Receivable 122

Bal. 1,500	

Wages Payable 219

	Bal. 400

Chris Williams, Capital 311

	Bal. 9,000

Chris Williams, Drawing 312

Bal. 1,000	

Income Summary 313

Golf Instruction Fees 401

	Bal. 4,000

Wages Expense 511

Bal. 800	

Advertising Expense 512

Bal. 200	

Travel Expense 515

Bal. 600	

Supplies Expense 524

Bal. 500	

Insurance Expense 535

Bal 100	

Postage Expense 536

Bal. 50	

Gas and Oil Expense 538

Bal. 150	

Miscellaneous Expense 549

Bal. 80	

E 6-6A (LO2)
✓ Capital 1/31: $2,597

CLOSING ENTRIES (NET LOSS) Using the following partial listing of T accounts, prepare closing entries in general journal form dated January 31, 20--. Then post the closing entries to the T accounts.

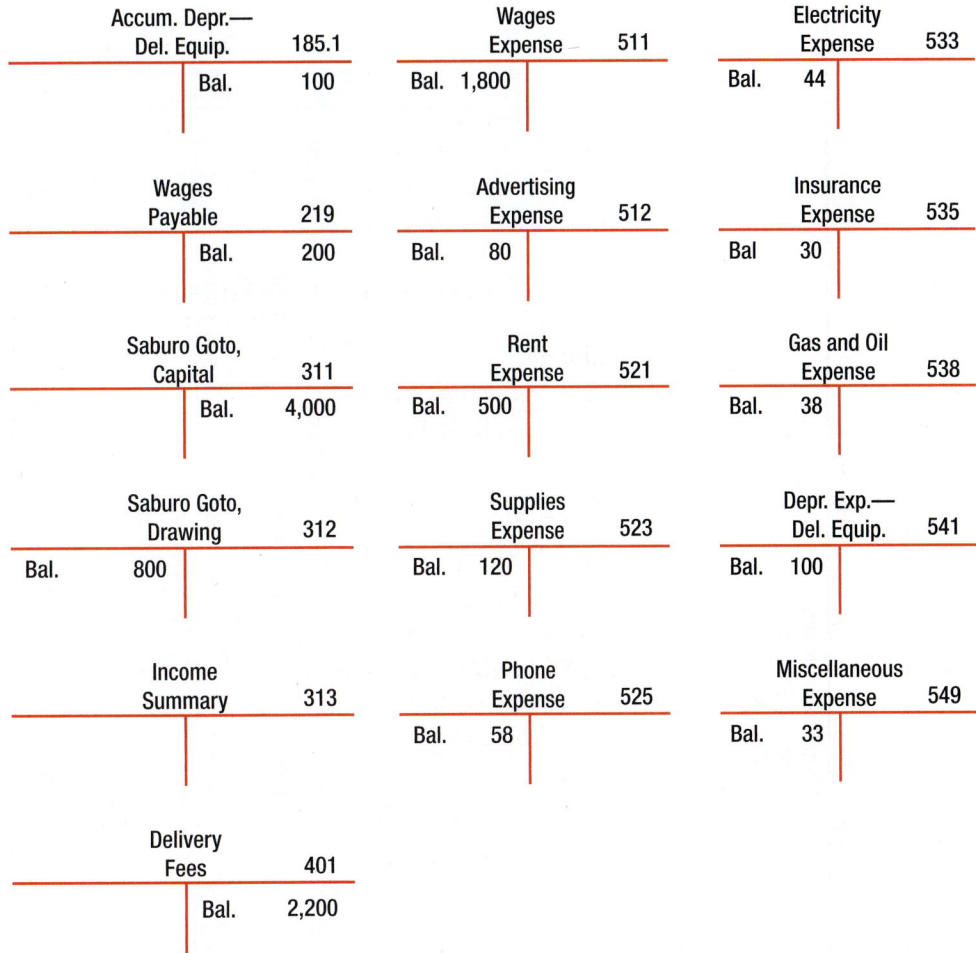

Accum. Depr.—Del. Equip. 185.1	
	Bal. 100

Wages Payable 219	
	Bal. 200

Saburo Goto, Capital 311	
	Bal. 4,000

Saburo Goto, Drawing 312	
Bal. 800	

Income Summary 313	

Delivery Fees 401	
	Bal. 2,200

Wages Expense 511	
Bal. 1,800	

Advertising Expense 512	
Bal. 80	

Rent Expense 521	
Bal. 500	

Supplies Expense 523	
Bal. 120	

Phone Expense 525	
Bal. 58	

Electricity Expense 533	
Bal. 44	

Insurance Expense 535	
Bal 30	

Gas and Oil Expense 538	
Bal. 38	

Depr. Exp.—Del. Equip. 541	
Bal. 100	

Miscellaneous Expense 549	
Bal. 33	

SERIES A PROBLEMS

P 6-7A (LO1)
✓ Net income: $838
✓ Capital 1/31: $7,738
✓ Total assets 1/31: $9,338

FINANCIAL STATEMENTS Page 206 shows a work sheet for Megaffin's Repairs. No additional investments were made by the owner during the month.

REQUIRED

1. Prepare an income statement.
2. Prepare a statement of owner's equity.
3. Prepare a balance sheet.

PROBLEM 6-7A

Megaffin's Repairs
Work Sheet
For Month Ended January 31, 20--

	ACCOUNT TITLE	TRIAL BALANCE DEBIT	TRIAL BALANCE CREDIT	ADJUSTMENTS DEBIT	ADJUSTMENTS CREDIT	ADJUSTED TRIAL BALANCE DEBIT	ADJUSTED TRIAL BALANCE CREDIT	INCOME STATEMENT DEBIT	INCOME STATEMENT CREDIT	BALANCE SHEET DEBIT	BALANCE SHEET CREDIT	
1	Cash	3,673.00				3,673.00				3,673.00		1
2	Accounts Receivable	1,450.00				1,450.00				1,450.00		2
3	Supplies	700.00			300.00	400.00				400.00		3
4	Prepaid Insurance	900.00			230.00	670.00				670.00		4
5	Delivery Equipment	3,200.00				3,200.00				3,200.00		5
6	Accum. Depr.—Delivery Equipment				55.00		55.00				55.00	6
7	Accounts Payable		1,200.00				1,200.00				1,200.00	7
8	Wages Payable				400.00		400.00				400.00	8
9	Don Megaffin, Capital		8,000.00				8,000.00				8,000.00	9
10	Don Megaffin, Drawing	1,100.00				1,100.00				1,100.00		10
11	Repair Fees		4,700.00				4,700.00		4,700.00			11
12	Wages Expense	1,750.00		400.00		2,150.00		2,150.00				12
13	Advertising Expense	200.00				200.00		200.00				13
14	Rent Expense	640.00				640.00		640.00				14
15	Supplies Expense			300.00		300.00		300.00				15
16	Phone Expense	50.00				50.00		50.00				16
17	Insurance Expense			230.00		230.00		230.00				17
18	Gas and Oil Expense	200.00				200.00		200.00				18
19	Depr. Expense—Delivery Equipment			55.00		55.00		55.00				19
20	Miscellaneous Expense	37.00				37.00		37.00				20
21		13,900.00	13,900.00	985.00	985.00	14,355.00	14,355.00	3,862.00	4,700.00	10,493.00	9,655.00	21
22	Net Income							838.00			838.00	22
23								4,700.00	4,700.00	10,493.00	10,493.00	23
24												24
25												25
26												26
27												27
28												28
29												29
30												30

P 6-8A (LO2/3)
✓ Capital 1/31: $7,738
✓ Post-closing trial balance total debits: $9,393

CLOSING ENTRIES AND POST-CLOSING TRIAL BALANCE Refer to the work sheet in Problem 6-7A for Megaffin's Repairs. The trial balance amounts (before adjustments) have been entered in the ledger accounts provided in the working papers. If you are not using the working papers that accompany this book, set up ledger accounts and enter these balances as of January 31, 20--. A chart of accounts is provided below.

Megaffin's Repairs
Chart of Accounts

Assets		Revenues	
101	Cash	401	Repair Fees
122	Accounts Receivable		
141	Supplies	Expenses	
145	Prepaid Insurance	511	Wages Expense
185	Delivery Equipment	512	Advertising Expense
185.1	Accum. Depr.—Delivery Equip.	521	Rent Expense
		523	Supplies Expense
Liabilities		525	Phone Expense
202	Accounts Payable	535	Insurance Expense
219	Wages Payable	538	Gas and Oil Expense
		541	Depr. Exp.—Delivery Equip.
Owner's Equity		549	Miscellaneous Expense
311	Don Megaffin, Capital		
312	Don Megaffin, Drawing		
313	Income Summary		

REQUIRED

1. Journalize (page 10) and post the adjusting entries.
2. Journalize (page 11) and post the closing entries.
3. Prepare a post-closing trial balance.

P 6-9A (LO1)
✓ Capital 1/31: $6,820

STATEMENT OF OWNER'S EQUITY The capital account for Autumn Chou, including an additional investment, and a partial work sheet are shown below and on page 208.

REQUIRED

Prepare a statement of owner's equity.

GENERAL LEDGER

ACCOUNT: Autumn Chou, Capital ACCOUNT NO. 311

DATE		ITEM	POST. REF.	DEBIT	CREDIT	BALANCE DEBIT	BALANCE CREDIT
20-- Jan.	1	Balance	✔				4 8 0 0 00
	18		J1		1 2 0 0 00		6 0 0 0 00

Autumn's Home Designs
Work Sheet (Partial)
For Month Ended January 31, 20 --

	ACCOUNT TITLE	INCOME STATEMENT		BALANCE SHEET		
		DEBIT	CREDIT	DEBIT	CREDIT	
1	Cash			3,200.00		1
2	Accounts Receivable			1,600.00		2
3	Supplies			800.00		3
4	Prepaid Insurance			900.00		4
5	Office Equipment			2,500.00		5
6	Accum. Depr.—Office Equipment				50.00	6
7	Accounts Payable				1,950.00	7
8	Wages Payable				180.00	8
9	Autumn Chou, Capital				6,000.00	9
10	Autumn Chou, Drawing			1,000.00		10
11	Design Fees		4,866.00			11
12	Wages Expense	1,900.00				12
13	Advertising Expense	21.00				13
14	Rent Expense	600.00				14
15	Supplies Expense	200.00				15
16	Phone Expense	85.00				16
17	Electricity Expense	48.00				17
18	Insurance Expense	60.00				18
19	Gas and Oil Expense	32.00				19
20	Depr. Expense—Office Equipment	50.00				20
21	Miscellaneous Expense	50.00				21
22		3,046.00	4,866.00	10,000.00	8,180.00	22
23	Net Income	1,820.00			1,820.00	23
24		4,866.00	4,866.00	10,000.00	10,000.00	24

SERIES B EXERCISES

E 6-1B (LO1)
✓ Net income: $1,826

INCOME STATEMENT From the partial work sheet for Adams' Shoe Shine on the next page, prepare an income statement.

E 6-2B (LO1)
✓ Capital 6/30: $5,826

STATEMENT OF OWNER'S EQUITY From the partial work sheet on the next page, prepare a statement of owner's equity, assuming no additional investment was made by the owner.

E 6-3B (LO1)
✓ Total assets: $7,936

BALANCE SHEET From the statement of owner's equity prepared in E 6-2B and the partial work sheet on the next page, prepare a balance sheet for Adams' Shoe Shine.

(FOR EXERCISES 6-1B, 6-2B, 6-3B, AND 6-4B)

Adams' Shoe Shine
Work Sheet (Partial)
For Month Ended June 30, 20 - -

	ACCOUNT TITLE	INCOME STATEMENT DEBIT	INCOME STATEMENT CREDIT	BALANCE SHEET DEBIT	BALANCE SHEET CREDIT	
1	Cash			3,262.00		1
2	Accounts Receivable			1,244.00		2
3	Supplies			800.00		3
4	Prepaid Insurance			640.00		4
5	Office Equipment			2,100.00		5
6	Accum. Depr.—Office Equipment				110.00	6
7	Accounts Payable				1,850.00	7
8	Wages Payable				260.00	8
9	Mary Adams, Capital				6,000.00	9
10	Mary Adams, Drawing			2,000.00		10
11	Service Fees		4,813.00			11
12	Wages Expense	1,080.00				12
13	Advertising Expense	34.00				13
14	Rent Expense	900.00				14
15	Supplies Expense	322.00				15
16	Phone Expense	133.00				16
17	Utilities Expense	102.00				17
18	Insurance Expense	120.00				18
19	Gas and Oil Expense	88.00				19
20	Depr. Expense—Office Equipment	110.00				20
21	Miscellaneous Expense	98.00				21
22		2,987.00	4,813.00	10,046.00	8,220.00	22
23	Net Income	1,826.00			1,826.00	23
24		4,813.00	4,813.00	10,046.00	10,046.00	24

E 6-4B (LO2)
✓ Capital 6/30: $5,826

CLOSING ENTRIES (NET INCOME) Set up T accounts for Adams' Shoe Shine based on the work sheet above and the chart of accounts provided below. Enter the existing balance for each account. Prepare closing entries in general journal form. Then post the closing entries to the T accounts.

Chart of Accounts

Assets
101 Cash
122 Accounts Receivable
141 Supplies
145 Prepaid Insurance
181 Office Equipment
181.1 Accum. Depr.—Office Equip.

Liabilities
202 Accounts Payable
219 Wages Payable

Owner's Equity
311 Mary Adams, Capital
312 Mary Adams, Drawing
313 Income Summary

Revenues
401 Service Fees

Expenses
511 Wages Expense
512 Advertising Expense
521 Rent Expense
523 Supplies Expense
525 Phone Expense
533 Utilities Expense
535 Insurance Expense
538 Gas and Oil Expense
542 Depr. Exp.—Office Equip.
549 Miscellaneous Expense

E 6-5B (LO2)

CLOSING ENTRIES (NET INCOME) Using the following partial listing of T accounts, prepare closing entries in general journal form dated May 31, 20--. Then post the closing entries to the T accounts.

Account	No.	Debit	Credit
Cash	101	Bal. 600	
Income Summary	313		
Supplies Expense	524	Bal. 900	
Accounts Receivable	122	Bal. 1,800	
Lawn Service Fees	401		Bal. 5,000
Insurance Expense	535	Bal. 300	
Wages Payable	219		Bal. 500
Wages Expense	511	Bal. 400	
Postage Expense	536	Bal. 40	
Mark Thrasher, Capital	311		Bal. 8,000
Advertising Expense	512	Bal. 600	
Gas and Oil Expense	538	Bal. 700	
Mark Thrasher, Drawing	312	Bal. 800	
Travel Expense	515	Bal. 100	
Miscellaneous Expense	549	Bal. 200	

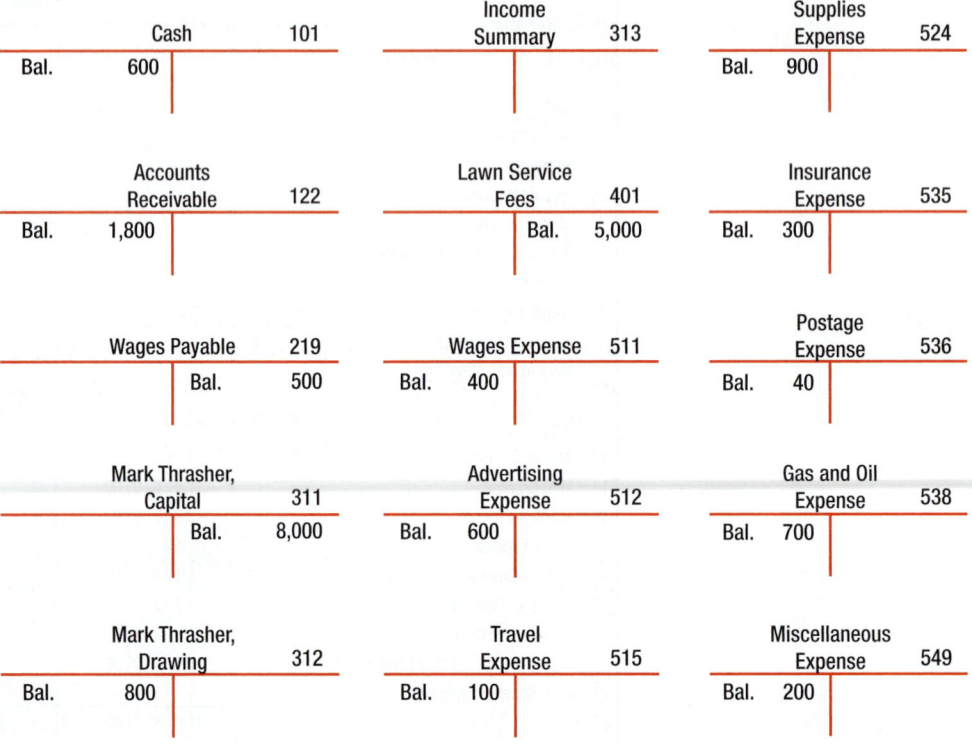

E 6-6B (LO2)
✓ Capital 6/30: $3,826

CLOSING ENTRIES (NET LOSS) Using the following partial listing of T accounts, prepare closing entries in general journal form dated June 30, 20--. Then post the closing entries to the T accounts.

Account	No.	Debit	Credit
Accum. Depr.—Office Equip.	181.1		Bal. 110
Wages Expense	511	Bal. 1,080	
Utilities Expense	533	Bal. 102	
Wages Payable	219		Bal. 260
Advertising Expense	512	Bal. 34	
Insurance Expense	535	Bal. 120	
Raquel Zapata, Capital	311		Bal. 6,000
Rent Expense	521	Bal. 900	
Gas and Oil Expense	538	Bal. 88	
Raquel Zapata, Drawing	312	Bal. 2,000	
Supplies Expense	523	Bal. 322	
Depr. Exp.—Office Equip.	541	Bal. 110	
Income Summary	313		
Phone Expense	525	Bal. 133	
Miscellaneous Expense	549	Bal. 98	
Referral Fees	401		Bal. 2,813

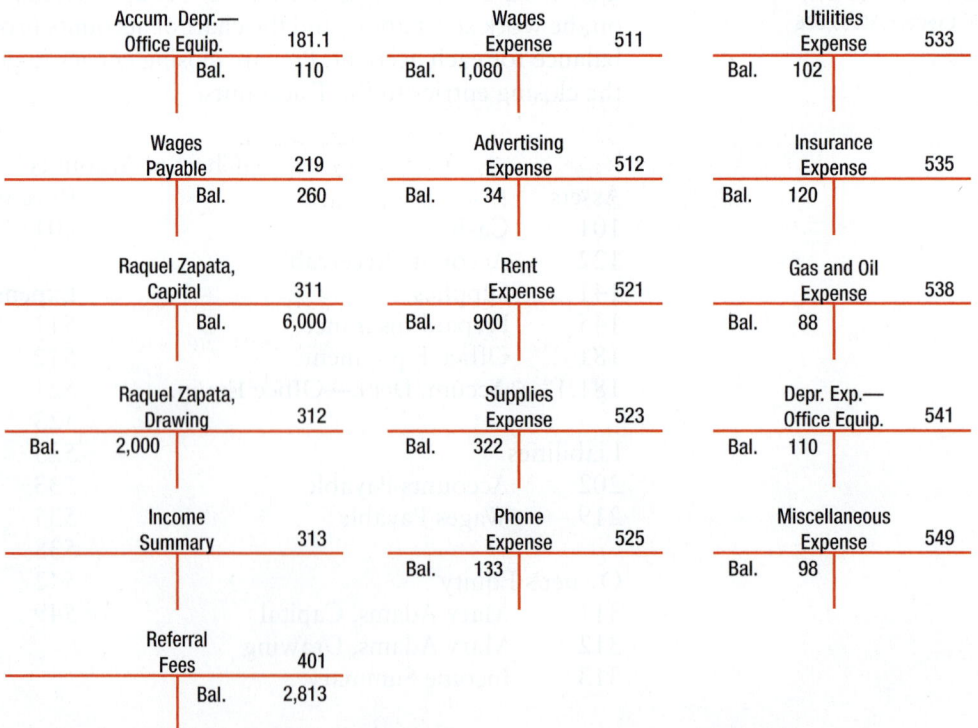

SERIES B PROBLEMS

P 6-7B (LO1)
✓ Net income: $1,450
✓ Capital 6/30: $7,650
✓ Total assets: $9,350

FINANCIAL STATEMENTS A work sheet for Juanita's Consulting is shown on the following page. There were no additional investments made by the owner during the month.

REQUIRED

1. Prepare an income statement.
2. Prepare a statement of owner's equity.
3. Prepare a balance sheet.

P 6-8B (LO2/3)
✓ Capital 6/30: $7,650
✓ Post-closing trial bal. total debits: $9,460

CLOSING ENTRIES AND POST-CLOSING TRIAL BALANCE Refer to the work sheet for Juanita's Consulting in Problem 6-7B. The trial balance amounts (before adjustments) have been entered in the ledger accounts provided in the working papers. If you are not using the working papers that accompany this book, set up ledger accounts and enter these balances as of June 30, 20--. A chart of accounts is provided below.

Juanita's Consulting
Chart of Accounts

Assets		**Revenues**	
101	Cash	401	Consulting Fees
122	Accounts Receivable		
141	Supplies	**Expenses**	
145	Prepaid Insurance	511	Wages Expense
181	Office Equipment	512	Advertising Expense
181.1	Accum. Depr.—Office Equip.	521	Rent Expense
		523	Supplies Expense
Liabilities		525	Phone Expense
202	Accounts Payable	533	Electricity Expense
219	Wages Payable	535	Insurance Expense
		538	Gas and Oil Expense
Owner's Equity		541	Depr. Exp.—Office Equip.
311	Juanita Alvarez, Capital	549	Miscellaneous Expense
312	Juanita Alvarez, Drawing		
313	Income Summary		

REQUIRED

1. Journalize (page 10) and post the adjusting entries.
2. Journalize (page 11) and post the closing entries.
3. Prepare a post-closing trial balance.

PROBLEM 6-7B

Juanita's Consulting
Work Sheet
For Month Ended June 30, 20--

	ACCOUNT TITLE	TRIAL BALANCE		ADJUSTMENTS		ADJUSTED TRIAL BALANCE		INCOME STATEMENT		BALANCE SHEET		
		DEBIT	CREDIT	DEBIT	CREDIT	DEBIT	CREDIT	DEBIT	CREDIT	DEBIT	CREDIT	
1	Cash	5,285.00				5,285.00				5,285.00		1
2	Accounts Receivable	1,075.00				1,075.00				1,075.00		2
3	Supplies	750.00			(a) 250.00	500.00				500.00		3
4	Prepaid Insurance	500.00			(b) 100.00	400.00				400.00		4
5	Office Equipment	2,200.00				2,200.00				2,200.00		5
6	Accum. Depr.—Office Equipment				(d) 110.00		110.00				110.00	6
7	Accounts Payable		1,500.00				1,500.00				1,500.00	7
8	Wages Payable				(c) 200.00		200.00				200.00	8
9	Juanita Alvarez, Capital		7,000.00				7,000.00				7,000.00	9
10	Juanita Alvarez, Drawing	800.00				800.00				800.00		10
11	Consulting Fees		4,204.00				4,204.00		4,204.00			11
12	Wages Expense	1,400.00		(c) 200.00		1,600.00		1,600.00				12
13	Advertising Expense	60.00				60.00		60.00				13
14	Rent Expense	500.00				500.00		500.00				14
15	Supplies Expense			(a) 250.00		250.00		250.00				15
16	Phone Expense	46.00				46.00		46.00				16
17	Electricity Expense	39.00				39.00		39.00				17
18	Insurance Expense			(b) 100.00		100.00		100.00				18
19	Gas and Oil Expense	28.00				28.00		28.00				19
20	Depr. Expense—Office Equipment			(d) 110.00		110.00		110.00				20
21	Miscellaneous Expense	21.00				21.00		21.00				21
22		12,704.00	12,704.00	660.00	660.00	13,014.00	13,014.00	2,754.00	4,204.00	10,260.00	8,810.00	22
23	Net Income							1,450.00			1,450.00	23
24								4,204.00	4,204.00	10,260.00	10,260.00	24
25												25
26												26
27												27
28												28
29												29
30												30

P 6-9B (LO1)
✓ Capital 1/31: $9,975

STATEMENT OF OWNER'S EQUITY The capital account for Minta's Editorial Services, including an additional investment, and a partial work sheet are shown below.

GENERAL LEDGER

ACCOUNT: Minta Berry, Capital — ACCOUNT NO. 311

DATE		ITEM	POST. REF.	DEBIT	CREDIT	BALANCE DEBIT	BALANCE CREDIT
20-- Jan.	1	Balance	✔				3,600.00
	22		J1		2,900.00		6,500.00

Minta's Editorial Services
Work Sheet (Partial)
For Month Ended January 31, 20 --

	ACCOUNT TITLE	INCOME STATEMENT DEBIT	INCOME STATEMENT CREDIT	BALANCE SHEET DEBIT	BALANCE SHEET CREDIT	
1	Cash			3,800.00		1
2	Accounts Receivable			2,200.00		2
3	Supplies			1,000.00		3
4	Prepaid Insurance			950.00		4
5	Computer Equipment			4,500.00		5
6	Accum. Depr.—Computer Equipment				225.00	6
7	Accounts Payable				2,100.00	7
8	Wages Payable				150.00	8
9	Minta Berry, Capital				6,500.00	9
10	Minta Berry, Drawing			1,700.00		10
11	Editing Fees		7,012.00			11
12	Wages Expense	600.00				12
13	Advertising Expense	49.00				13
14	Rent Expense	450.00				14
15	Supplies Expense	288.00				15
16	Phone Expense	44.00				16
17	Utilities Expense	38.00				17
18	Insurance Expense	125.00				18
19	Depr. Expense—Computer Equipment	225.00				19
20	Miscellaneous Expense	18.00				20
21		1,837.00	7,012.00	14,150.00	8,975.00	21
22	Net Income	5,175.00			5,175.00	22
23		7,012.00	7,012.00	14,150.00	14,150.00	23

REQUIRED

Prepare a statement of owner's equity.

MANAGING YOUR WRITING

CHECK LIST
- ☐ Managing
- ☐ Planning
- ☐ Drafting
- ☐ Break
- ☐ Revising
- ☐ Managing

At lunch, two bookkeepers got into a heated discussion about whether closing entries should be made before or after preparing the financial statements. They have come to you to resolve this issue and have agreed to accept your position. Write a memo explaining the purpose of closing entries and whether they should be made before or after preparing the financial statements.

MASTERY PROBLEM

✓ Total assets: $4,740
✓ E. Soltis, capital, Dec. 31: $4,475

Elizabeth Soltis owns and operates Aunt Ibby's Styling Salon. A year-end work sheet is provided on the next page. Using this information, prepare adjusting entries, financial statements, and closing entries. Soltis made no additional investments during the year.

MASTERY PROBLEM

Aunt Ibby's Styling Salon
Work Sheet
For Year Ended December 31, 20--

	ACCOUNT TITLE	TRIAL BALANCE DEBIT	TRIAL BALANCE CREDIT	ADJUSTMENTS DEBIT	ADJUSTMENTS CREDIT	ADJUSTED TRIAL BALANCE DEBIT	ADJUSTED TRIAL BALANCE CREDIT	INCOME STATEMENT DEBIT	INCOME STATEMENT CREDIT	BALANCE SHEET DEBIT	BALANCE SHEET CREDIT	
1	Cash	940 00				940 00				940 00		1
2	Styling Supplies	1500 00			(a) 1450 00	50 00				50 00		2
3	Prepaid Insurance	800 00			(b) 650 00	150 00				150 00		3
4	Salon Equipment	4500 00				4500 00				4500 00		4
5	Accum. Depr.—Salon Equipment				(d) 900 00		900 00				900 00	5
6	Accounts Payable		225 00				225 00				225 00	6
7	Wages Payable				(c) 40 00		40 00				40 00	7
8	Elizabeth Soltis, Capital		2765 00				2765 00				2765 00	8
9	Elizabeth Soltis, Drawing	12000 00				12000 00				12000 00		9
10	Styling Fees		32000 00				32000 00		32000 00			10
11	Wages Expense	8000 00		(c) 40 00		8040 00		8040 00				11
12	Rent Expense	6000 00				6000 00		6000 00				12
13	Styling Supplies Expense			(a) 1450 00		1450 00		1450 00				13
14	Phone Expense	450 00				450 00		450 00				14
15	Utilities Expense	800 00				800 00		800 00				15
16	Insurance Expense			(b) 650 00		650 00		650 00				16
17	Depr. Expense—Salon Equipment			(d) 900 00		900 00		900 00				17
18		34990 00	34990 00	3040 00	3040 00	35930 00	35930 00	18290 00	32000 00	17640 00	3930 00	18
19	Net Income							13710 00			13710 00	19
20								32000 00	32000 00	17640 00	17640 00	20
21												21
22												22
23												23
24												24
25												25
26												26
27												27
28												28
29												29
30												30

CHALLENGE PROBLEM

This problem challenges you to apply your cumulative accounting knowledge to move a step beyond the material in the chapter.

✓ Net loss: $2,100
✓ Capital, 1/31/20--: ($700)

Provided below is a partial work sheet for Ardery Advising.

Ardery Advising
Work Sheet (Partial)
For Month Ended January 31, 20 - -

	ACCOUNT TITLE	INCOME STATEMENT DEBIT	INCOME STATEMENT CREDIT	BALANCE SHEET DEBIT	BALANCE SHEET CREDIT	
1	Cash			2,412.00		1
2	Accounts Receivable			896.00		2
3	Supplies			482.00		3
4	Prepaid Insurance			900.00		4
5	Office Equipment			3,000.00		5
6	Accum. Depr.—Office Equipment				2,000.00	6
7	Accounts Payable				2,190.00	7
8	Wages Payable				1,200.00	8
9	Notes Payable				3,000.00	9
10	Sam Ardery, Capital				2,200.00	10
11	Sam Ardery, Drawing			800.00		11
12	Advising Fees		3,802.00			12
13	Wages Expense	1,800.00				13
14	Advertising Expense	400.00				14
15	Rent Expense	1,500.00				15
16	Supplies Expense	120.00				16
17	Phone Expense	300.00				17
18	Electricity Expense	44.00				18
19	Insurance Expense	200.00				19
20	Gas and Oil Expense	38.00				20
21	Depr. Expense—Office Equipment	1,000.00				21
22	Miscellaneous Expense	500.00				22
23		5,902.00	3,802.00	8,490.00	10,590.00	23
24	Net Loss		2,100.00	2,100.00		24
25		5,902.00	5,902.00	10,590.00	10,590.00	25

REQUIRED

During January, Ardery made an additional investment of $1,200. Prepare an income statement, statement of owner's equity, and balance sheet for Ardery Advising.

ANSWERS TO SELF-STUDY TEST QUESTIONS

True/False

1. T
2. F (additional investments are shown as an addition to the beginning balance)
3. F 4. T 5. T

Multiple Choice

1. b 2. d 3. a 4. c 5. b

CHECKPOINT

Checkpoint Exercises

1.

Fisher Consulting Income Statement For Month Ended August 31, 20 --		
Revenue:		
Professional fees		$5,000
Expenses:		
Wages expense	$1,000	
Rent expense	700	
Depreciation expense	100	
Total expenses		1,800
Net income		$3,200

Fisher Consulting Statement of Owner's Equity For Month Ended August 31, 20 --		
Joe Fisher, capital, August 1, 20 - -		$3,000
Net income for August	$3,200	
Less withdrawals for August	300	
Increase in capital		2,900
Joe Fisher, capital, August 31, 20 - -		$5,900

Fisher Consulting Balance Sheet August 31, 20 --		
Assets		
Current assets:		
Cash	$2,500	
Accounts receivable	800	
Total current assets		$3,300
Property, plant, and equipment:		
Equipment	$3,800	
Less accumulated depreciation	200	3,600
Total assets		$6,900
Liabilities		
Current liabilities:		
Accounts payable		$1,000
Owner's Equity		
Joe Fisher, capital, August 31, 20--		5,900
Total liabilities and owner's equity		$6,900

2.

DATE		DESCRIPTION	POST. REF.	DEBIT	CREDIT
		Closing Entries			
20-- Aug.	31	Professional Fees		5,000.00	
		Income Summary			5,000.00
	31	Income Summary		1,800.00	
		Wages Expense			1,000.00
		Rent Expense			700.00
		Depreciation Expense			100.00
	31	Income Summary		3,200.00	
		Joe Fisher, capital			3,200.00
	31	Joe Fisher, Capital		300.00	
		Joe Fisher, Drawing			300.00

3.

Joe Fisher, Consulting
Post-Closing Trial Balance
August 31, 20 - -

ACCOUNT TITLE	ACCOUNT NO	DEBIT BALANCE	CREDIT BALANCE
Cash		2,500.00	
Accounts Receivable		800.00	
Equipment		3,800.00	
Accumulated Depr.—Equipment			200.00
Accounts Payable			1,000.00
Joe Fisher, Capital			5,900.00
		7,100.00	7,100.00

CHAPTER 6 APPENDIX

Statement of Cash Flows

LEARNING OBJECTIVES

Careful study of this appendix should enable you to:

LO1 **Classify business transactions as operating, investing, or financing.**

LO2 **Prepare a statement of cash flows by analyzing and categorizing a series of business transactions.**

Thus far, we have discussed three financial statements: the income statement, the statement of owner's equity, and the balance sheet. A fourth statement, the statement of cash flows, is also very important. It explains what the business did to generate cash and how the cash was used. This is done by categorizing all cash transactions into three types of activities: operating, investing, and financing.

LO1 Types of Business Activities

Classify business transactions as operating, investing, or financing.

Cash flows from **operating activities** are related to the revenues and expenses reported on the income statement. Examples include cash received for services performed and the payment of cash for expenses.

Investing activities are those transactions involving the purchase and sale of long-term assets, lending money, and collecting the principal on the related loans.

Financing activities are those transactions dealing with the exchange of cash between the business and its owners and creditors. Examples include cash received from the owner to finance the operations and cash paid to the owner as withdrawals. Financing activities also include borrowing cash and repaying the loan principal.

Figure 6A-1 provides a review of the transactions for Mitchell's Campus Delivery for the month of June. The transactions are classified as operating, investing, or financing, and an explanation for the classification is provided.

LEARNING KEY

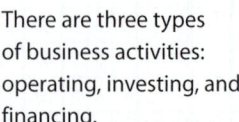

There are three types of business activities: operating, investing, and financing.

LEARNING KEY

Lending money to another entity is an outflow of cash from investing activities. The collection of the principal when the loan is due is an inflow of cash from investing activities. Borrowing cash is an inflow from financing activities. Repayment of the loan principal is an outflow from financing activities.

FIGURE 6A-1 Summary of Transactions for Mitchell's Campus Delivery

SUMMARY OF TRANSACTIONS FOR MITCHELL'S CAMPUS DELIVERY	TYPE OF TRANSACTION	EXPLANATION
(a) Mitchell Williams invested cash in his business, $5,000.	Financing	Cash received from the owner is an inflow from financing activities. Don't be fooled by the word "invested." From the company's point of view, this is a way to *finance* the business.
(b) Purchased delivery equipment for cash, $2,000.	Investing	Purchases of long-term assets are investments.
(c) Purchased delivery equipment on account from Big Red Scooters, $1,800. (*Note*: Big Red has loaned Mitch $1,800.)	No cash involved	This transaction will not affect the main sections of the statement of cash flows. (This is a noncash investing and financing activity.)
(d) Paid first installment to Big Red Scooters, $600. [See transaction (c).]	Financing	Repayments of loans are financing activities.
(e) Received cash for delivery services rendered, $2,100.	Operating	Cash received as a result of providing services is classified as an operating activity.
(f) Paid cash for June office rent, $1,000.	Operating	Cash payments for expenses are classified as operating activities.
(g) Paid phone bill, $100.	Operating	Cash payments for expenses are classified as operating activities.
(h) Made deliveries on account for a total of $2,400. $400 for the Library and $2,000 for the School of Music.	No cash involved	This transaction will not affect the statement of cash flows.
(i) Purchased supplies for cash, $80.	Operating	Cash payments for expenses are classified as operating activities. Most of these supplies were used up. Those that remain will be used in the near future. These are not long-term assets and, thus, do not qualify as investments.
(j) Received $1,900 in cash for services performed in transaction (h): $400 from the Library and $1,500 from the School of Music.	Operating	Cash received as a result of providing services is classified as an operating activity.
(k) Purchased a third scooter from Big Red Scooters, $1,000. A down payment of $300 was made with the remaining payments expected over the next four months.	Investing	Purchases of long-term assets are investments. Only the $300 cash paid will be reported on the statement of cash flows.
(l) Paid cash for a seven-month liability insurance policy, $700. Coverage began on June 1.	Operating	Cash payments for expenses are classified as operating activities. Prepaid Insurance is not considered a long-term asset and, thus, does not qualify as an investment.
(m) Paid wages of part-time employees, $1,650.	Operating	Cash payments for expenses are classified as operating activities.
(n) Earned delivery fees for the remainder of the month amounting to $3,500. $900 in cash and $2,600 on account. Deliveries on account: Library ($250) and Athletic Ticket Office ($2,350).	Operating	Cash received ($900) as a result of providing services is classified as an operating activity.
(o) Mitch withdrew cash for personal use, $3,000.	Financing	Cash payments to owners are classified as a financing activity.

LO2 Preparing the Statement of Cash Flows

Prepare a statement of cash flows by analyzing and categorizing a series of business transactions.

The classifications of the cash transactions for Mitchell's Campus Delivery are summarized in the expanded cash T account shown in Figure 6A-2. Using this information, we can prepare a statement of cash flows. As shown in Figure 6A-3, the heading is similar to that used for the income statement. Since the statement of cash flows reports on the flow of cash for a period of time, the statement is dated for the month ended June 30, 20--.

The main body of the statement is arranged in three sections: operating, investing, and financing activities. First, cash received from customers is listed under operating activities. Then, cash payments for operating activities are listed and totaled. The net amount is reported as net cash provided by operating activities. Since this is

FIGURE 6A-2 Cash T Account for Mitchell's Campus Delivery with Classifications of Cash Transactions

Event	Classification	Amount	Amount	Classification	Event	
		CASH				
(a) Investment by Mitch.	Financing	5,000	2,000	Investing	Purchased delivery equipment.	(b)
(e) Cash received for services.	Operating	2,100	600	Financing	Made payment on loan.	(d)
(j) Cash received for services.	Operating	1,900	1,000	Operating	Paid office rent.	(f)
(n) Cash received for services.	Operating	900	100	Operating	Paid phone bill.	(g)
		9,900	80	Operating	Purchased supplies.	(i)
			300	Investing	Purchased delivery equipment.	(k)
			700	Operating	Paid for insurance.	(l)
			1,650	Operating	Paid wages.	(m)
			3,000	Financing	Withdrawal by owner.	(o)
			9,430			
	Bal.	470				

FIGURE 6A-3 Statement of Cash Flows for Mitchell's Campus Delivery

Mitchell's Campus Delivery
Statement of Cash Flows
For Month Ended June 30, 20 - -

Cash flows from operating activities:		
Cash received from customers for delivery services		$4,900
Cash paid for wages	$ (1,650)	
Cash paid for rent	(1,000)	
Cash paid for supplies	(80)	
Cash paid for phone	(100)	
Cash paid for insurance	(700)	
Total cash paid for operations		(3,530)
Net cash provided by operating activities		$1,370
Cash flows from investing activities:		
Cash paid for delivery equipment	$ (2,300)	
Net cash used for investing activities		(2,300)
Cash flows from financing activities:		
Cash investment by owner	$ 5,000	
Cash withdrawal by owner	(3,000)	
Payment made on loan	(600)	
Net cash provided by financing activities		1,400
Net increase in cash		$ 470

the main purpose of the business, it is important to be able to generate positive cash flows from operating activities.

> **LEARNING KEY**
> To prove the accuracy of the statement of cash flows, compare the net increase or decrease reported on the statement with the change in the balance of the cash account.

The next two sections list the inflows and outflows from investing and financing activities. Debits to the cash account are inflows and credits are outflows. Note that there was an outflow, or net use of cash, from investing activities resulting from the purchase of the motor scooters. In addition, cash was provided from financing activities because Mitchell's initial investment more than covered his withdrawal and the payment on the loan. These investing and financing activities are typical for a new business.

The sum of the inflows and outflows from operating, investing, and financing activities equals the net increase (or decrease) in the cash account during the period. Since this is a new business, the cash account had a beginning balance of zero. The ending balance is $470. This agrees with the net increase in cash of $470 reported on the statement of cash flows.

This appendix introduces you to the purpose and format of the statement of cash flows. Here, we classified entries made to the cash account as operating, investing, or financing. These classifications were then used to prepare the statement. Businesses have thousands of entries to the cash account. Thus, this approach to preparing the statement is not really practical. Other approaches to preparing the statement will be discussed in Chapter 23. However, the purpose and format of the statements are the same.

LEARNING OBJECTIVES — Key Points to Remember

LO1 Classify business transactions as operating, investing, or financing.

The purpose of the statement of cash flows is to report what the firm did to generate cash and how the cash was used. Business transactions are classified as operating, investing, and financing activities.

Operating activities are those transactions related to the revenues and expenses reported on the income statement.

Investing activities are those transactions involving the purchase and sale of long-term assets, lending money, and collecting the principal on the related loans.

Financing activities are those transactions dealing with the exchange of cash between the business and its owners and creditors.

LO2 Prepare a statement of cash flows by analyzing and categorizing a series of business transactions.

The main body of the statement of cash flows consists of three sections: operating, investing, and financing activities.

Name of Business
Statement of Cash Flows
For Period Ended Date

Cash flows from operating activities:		
Cash received from customers		$ x,xxx
List cash paid for various expenses	$ (xxx)	
Total cash paid for operations		(x,xxx)
Net cash provided by (used for) operating activities		$ xxx
Cash flows from investing activities:		
List cash received from the sale of long-term assets and other investing activities	$ x,xxx	
List cash paid for the purchase of long-term assets and other investing activities	(x,xxx)	
Net cash provided by (used for) investing activities		x,xxx
Cash flows from financing activities:		
List cash received from owners and creditors	$ x,xxx	
List cash paid to owners and creditors	(xxx)	
Net cash provided by (used for) financing activities		x,xxx
Net increase (decrease) in cash		$ xxx

KEY TERMS

financing activities (218) Those transactions dealing with the exchange of cash between the business and its owners and creditors.

investing activities (218) Those transactions involving the purchase and sale of long-term assets, lending money, and collecting the principal on the related loans.

operating activities (218) Those transactions related to the revenues and expenses reported on the income statement.

REVIEW QUESTIONS

LO1 1. Explain the purpose of the statement of cash flows.

LO1 2. Define and provide examples of the three types of business activities.

SERIES A EXERCISE

E 6Apx-1A (LO1)

CLASSIFYING BUSINESS TRANSACTIONS Dolores Lopez opened a new consulting business. The following transactions occurred during January of the current year. Classify each transaction as an operating, an investing, or a financing activity.

(a) Invested cash in the business, $10,000.
(b) Paid office rent, $500.
(c) Purchased office equipment. Paid $1,500 cash and agreed to pay the balance of $2,000 in four monthly installments.
(d) Received cash for services rendered, $900.
(e) Paid phone bill, $65.
(f) Made payment on loan in transaction (c), $500.
(g) Paid wages to part-time employee, $500.
(h) Received cash for services rendered, $800.
(i) Paid electricity bill, $85.
(j) Withdrew cash for personal use, $100.
(k) Paid wages to part-time employee, $500.

SERIES A PROBLEM

P 6Apx-2A (LO2)
✓ Operating activities: $50
✓ Investing activities: ($1,500)
✓ Financing activities: $9,400

PREPARING A STATEMENT OF CASH FLOWS Prepare a statement of cash flows based on the transactions reported in Exercise 6Apx-1A.

SERIES B EXERCISE

E 6Apx-1B (LO1)

CLASSIFYING BUSINESS TRANSACTIONS Bob Jacobs opened an advertising agency. The following transactions occurred during January of the current year. Classify each transaction as an operating, an investing, or a financing activity.

(a) Invested cash in the business, $5,000.
(b) Purchased office equipment. Paid $2,500 cash and agreed to pay the balance of $2,000 in four monthly installments.
(c) Paid office rent, $400.
(d) Received cash for services rendered, $700.
(e) Paid phone bill, $95.
(f) Received cash for services rendered, $600.
(g) Made payment on loan in transaction (b), $500.
(h) Paid wages to part-time employee, $800.
(i) Paid electricity bill, $100.
(j) Withdrew cash for personal use, $500.
(k) Paid wages to part-time employee, $600.

SERIES B PROBLEM

P 6Apx-2B (LO2)
✓ Operating activities: ($695)
✓ Investing activities: ($2,500)
✓ Financing activities: $4,000

PREPARING A STATEMENT OF CASH FLOWS Prepare a statement of cash flows based on the transactions reported in Exercise 6Apx-1B.

COMPREHENSIVE PROBLEM 1:

The Accounting Cycle

This comprehensive problem is intended to serve as a mini-practice set without the source documents. As such, students should plan on about three to four hours to complete this problem.

Bob Night opened The General's Favorite Fishing Hole. The fishing camp is open from April through September and attracts many famous college basketball coaches during the off-season. Guests typically register for one week, arriving on Sunday afternoon and returning home the following Saturday afternoon. The registration fee includes room and board, the use of fishing boats, and professional instruction in fishing techniques. The chart of accounts for the camping operations is provided below.

The General's Favorite Fishing Hole
Chart of Accounts

Assets		**Revenues**	
101	Cash	401	Registration Fees
142	Office Supplies		
144	Food Supplies	**Expenses**	
145	Prepaid Insurance	511	Wages Expense
181	Fishing Boats	521	Rent Expense
181.1	Accum. Depr.—Fishing Boats	523	Office Supplies Expense
		524	Food Supplies Expense
Liabilities		525	Phone Expense
202	Accounts Payable	533	Utilities Expense
219	Wages Payable	535	Insurance Expense
		536	Postage Expense
Owner's Equity		542	Depr. Exp.—Fishing Boats
311	Bob Night, Capital		
312	Bob Night, Drawing		
313	Income Summary		

The following transactions took place during April 20--.

Apr.	1	Night invested cash in business, $90,000.
	1	Paid insurance premium for six-month camping season, $9,000.
	2	Paid rent for lodge and campgrounds for the month of April, $40,000.
	2	Deposited registration fees, $35,000.
	2	Purchased 10 fishing boats on account for $60,000. The boats have estimated useful lives of five years, at which time they will be donated to a local day camp. Arrangements were made to pay for the boats in July.
	3	Purchased food supplies from Acme Super Market on account, $7,000.
	5	Purchased office supplies from Gordon Office Supplies on account, $500.
	7	Deposited registration fees, $38,600.
	10	Purchased food supplies from Acme Super Market on account, $8,200.
	10	Paid wages to fishing guides, $10,000.
	14	Deposited registration fees, $30,500.

(continued)

Apr. 16	Purchased food supplies from Acme Super Market on account, $9,000.
17	Paid wages to fishing guides, $10,000.
18	Paid postage, $150.
21	Deposited registration fees, $35,600.
24	Purchased food supplies from Acme Super Market on account, $8,500.
24	Paid wages to fishing guides, $10,000.
28	Deposited registration fees, $32,000.
29	Paid wages to fishing guides, $10,000.
30	Purchased food supplies from Acme Super Market on account, $6,000.
30	Paid Acme Super Market on account, $32,700.
30	Paid utilities bill, $2,000.
30	Paid phone bill, $1,200.
30	Bob Night withdrew cash for personal use, $6,000.

Adjustment information for the end of April is provided below.

(a) Office supplies remaining on hand, $100.

(b) Food supplies remaining on hand, $8,000.

(c) Insurance expired during the month of April, $1,500.

(d) Depreciation on the fishing boats for the month of April, $1,000.

(e) Wages earned, but not yet paid, at the end of April, $500.

REQUIRED

1. Enter the transactions in a general journal. Enter transactions from April 1–5 on page 1, April 7–18 on page 2, April 21–29 and the first two entries for April 30 on page 3, and the remaining entries for April 30 on page 4.
2. Post the entries to the general ledger. (If you are not using the working papers that accompany this text, you will need to enter the account titles and account numbers in the general ledger accounts.)
3. Prepare a trial balance on a work sheet.
4. Complete the work sheet.
5. Journalize the adjusting entries (page 5).
6. Post the adjusting entries to the general ledger.
7. Prepare the income statement.
8. Prepare the statement of owner's equity.
9. Prepare the balance sheet.
10. Journalize the closing entries (pages 5 and 6).
11. Post the closing entries to the general ledger.
12. Prepare a post-closing trial balance.

COMPREHENSIVE PROBLEM 1, PERIOD 2:

The Accounting Cycle

This comprehensive problem is intended to serve as a mini-practice set without the source documents. As such, students should plan on about three to four hours to complete this problem.

During the month of May 20--, The General's Favorite Fishing Hole engaged in the following transactions. These transactions required an expansion of the chart of accounts as shown below.

Assets

101	Cash
122	Accounts Receivable
142	Office Supplies
144	Food Supplies
145	Prepaid Insurance
146	Prepaid Subscriptions
161	Land
171	Buildings
171.1	Accum. Depr.—Buildings
181	Fishing Boats
181.1	Accum. Depr.—Fishing Boats
182	Surround Sound System
182.1	Accum. Depr.—Surround Sound Sys.
183	Big Screen TV
183.1	Accum. Depr.—Big Screen TV

Liabilities

202	Accounts Payable
219	Wages Payable

Owner's Equity

311	Bob Night, Capital
312	Bob Night, Drawing
313	Income Summary

Revenues

401	Registration Fees
404	Vending Commission Revenue

Expenses

511	Wages Expense
512	Advertising Expense
521	Rent Expense
523	Office Supplies Expense
524	Food Supplies Expense
525	Phone Expense
533	Utilities Expense
535	Insurance Expense
536	Postage Expense
537	Repair Expense
540	Depr. Exp.—Buildings
541	Depr. Exp.—Surround Sound Sys.
542	Depr. Exp.—Fishing Boats
543	Depr. Exp.—Big Screen TV
546	Satellite Programming Exp.
548	Subscriptions Expense

May 1 In order to provide snacks for guests on a 24-hour basis, Night signed a contract with Snack Attack. Snack Attack will install vending machines with food and drinks and pay a 10% commission on all sales. Estimated payments are made at the beginning of each month. Night received a check for $200, the estimated commission on sales for May.

2 Night purchased a surround sound system and big screen TV with a digital satellite system for the guest lounge. The surround sound system cost $3,600 and has an estimated useful life of five years and no salvage value. The TV cost $8,000, has an estimated useful life of eight years, and has a salvage value of $800. Night paid cash for both items.

2 Paid for May's programming on the new digital satellite system, $125.

(*continued*)

May	3	Night's office manager returned $100 worth of office supplies to Gordon Office Supply. Night received a $100 reduction on the account.
	3	Deposited registration fees, $52,700.
	3	Paid rent for lodge and campgrounds for the month of May, $40,000.
	3	In preparation for the purchase of a nearby campground, Night invested an additional $600,000.
	4	Paid Gordon Office Supply on account, $400.
	4	Purchased the assets of a competing business and paid cash for the following: land, $100,000; lodge, $530,000; and fishing boats, $9,000. The lodge has a remaining useful life of 50 years and a $50,000 salvage value. The boats have remaining lives of five years and no salvage value.
	5	Paid May's insurance premium for the new camp, $1,000. (See above transaction.)
	5	Purchased food supplies from Acme Super Market on account, $22,950.
	5	Purchased office supplies from Gordon Office Supplies on account, $1,200.
	7	Night paid $40 each for one-year subscriptions to *Fishing Illustrated*, *Fishing Unlimited*, and *Fish Master*. The magazines are published monthly.
	10	Deposited registration fees, $62,750.
	13	Paid wages to fishing guides, $30,000. (Don't forget wages payable from prior month.)
	14	A guest became ill and was unable to stay for the entire week. A refund was issued in the amount of $1,000.
	17	Deposited registration fees, $63,000.
	19	Purchased food supplies from Acme Super Market on account, $18,400.
	21	Deposited registration fees, $63,400.
	23	Paid $2,500 for May's advertising spots on National Sports Talk Radio.
	25	Paid repair fee for damaged boat, $850.
	27	Paid wages to fishing guides, $30,000.
	28	Paid $1,800 for May's advertising spots on billboards.
	29	Purchased food supplies from Acme Super Market on account, $14,325.
	30	Paid utilities bill, $3,300.
	30	Paid phone bill, $1,800.
	30	Paid Acme Super Market on account, $47,350.
	31	Bob Night withdrew cash for personal use, $7,500.

Adjustment information at the end of May is provided below.

(a) Total vending machine sales were $2,300 for the month of May. A 10% commission is earned on these sales.

(b) Straight-line depreciation is used for the 10 boats purchased on April 2 for $60,000. The useful life for these assets is five years and there is no salvage value. A full month's depreciation was taken in April on these boats. Straight-line depreciation is also used for the two boats purchased in May. Make one adjusting entry for all depreciation on the boats.

(c) Straight-line depreciation is used to depreciate the surround sound system.

(d) Straight-line depreciation is used to depreciate the big screen TV.

(e) Straight-line depreciation is used for the building purchased in May.

(f) On April 2, Night paid $9,000 for insurance during the six-month camping season. May's portion of this premium was used up during this month.

(g) Night received his May issues of *Fishing Illustrated, Fishing Unlimited*, and *Fish Master*.

(h) Office supplies remaining on hand, $150.

(i) Food supplies remaining on hand, $5,925.

(j) Wages earned, but not yet paid, at the end of May, $6,000.

REQUIRED

1. Enter the transactions in a general journal. Enter transactions from May 1–4 on page 7, May 5–28 on page 8, and the remaining entries on page 9. To save time and space, don't enter descriptions for the journal entries.
2. Post the entries to the general ledger. (If you are not using the working papers that accompany this text, you will need to enter the account titles, account numbers, and balances from April 30 in the general ledger accounts.)
3. Prepare a trial balance on a work sheet.
4. Complete the work sheet.
5. Journalize the adjusting entries on page 10 of the general journal.
6. Post the adjusting entries to the general ledger.
7. Prepare the income statement.
8. Prepare the statement of owner's equity.
9. Prepare the balance sheet.
10. Journalize the closing entries on page 11 of the general journal.
11. Post the closing entries to the general ledger.
12. Prepare a post-closing trial balance.

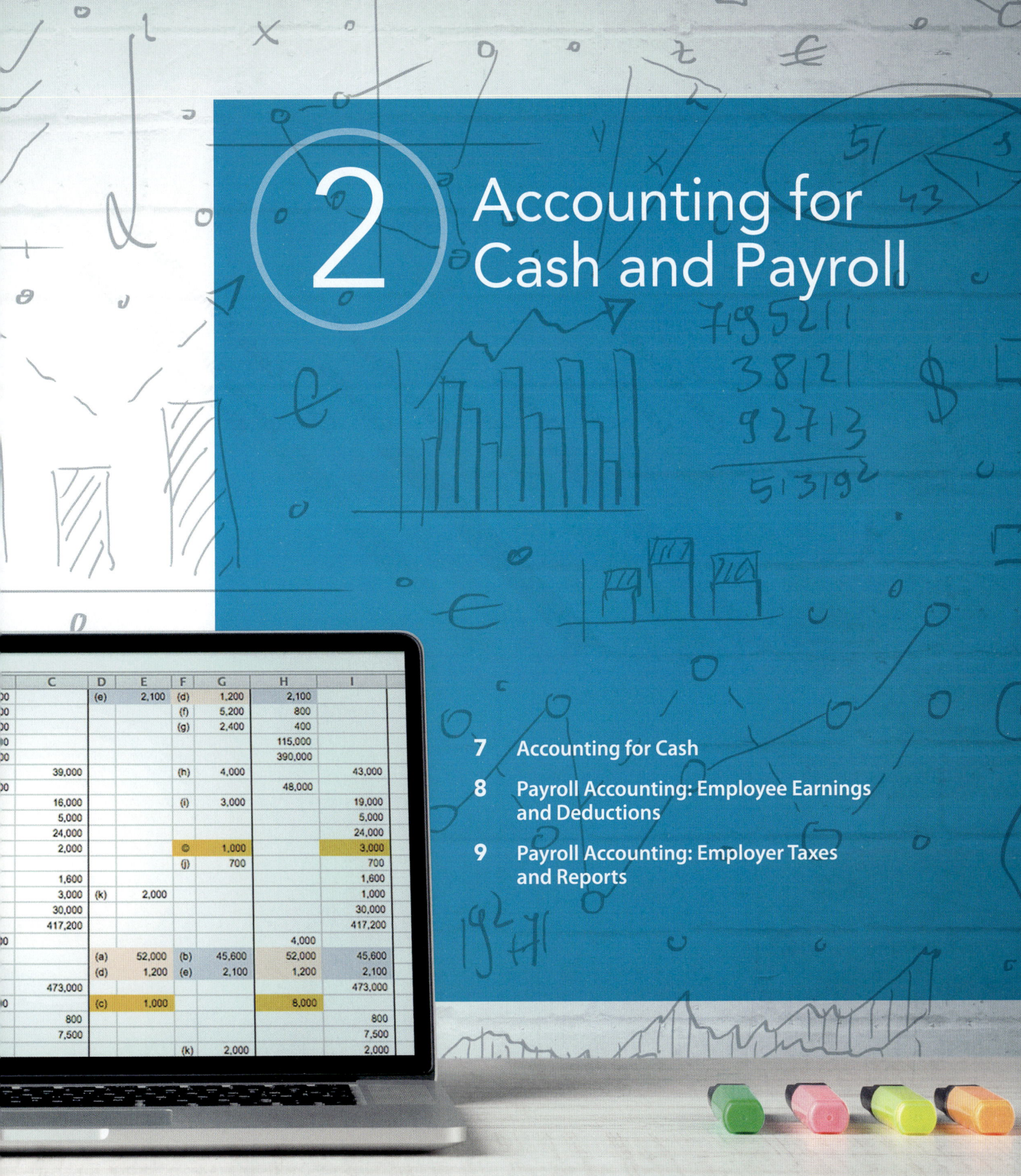

2 Accounting for Cash and Payroll

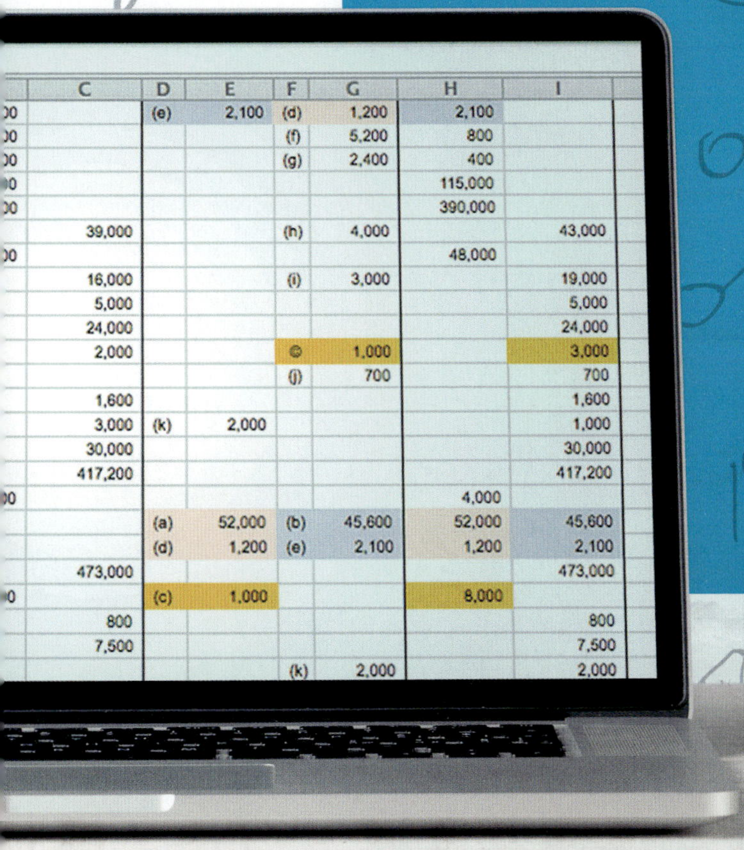

7 Accounting for Cash

8 Payroll Accounting: Employee Earnings and Deductions

9 Payroll Accounting: Employer Taxes and Reports

Add some color to your learning!

Throughout the text, you will be introduced to many important terms and types of accounts. To help you learn the different terms and types of accounts, we have coded many of them using the following color key in Part 2:

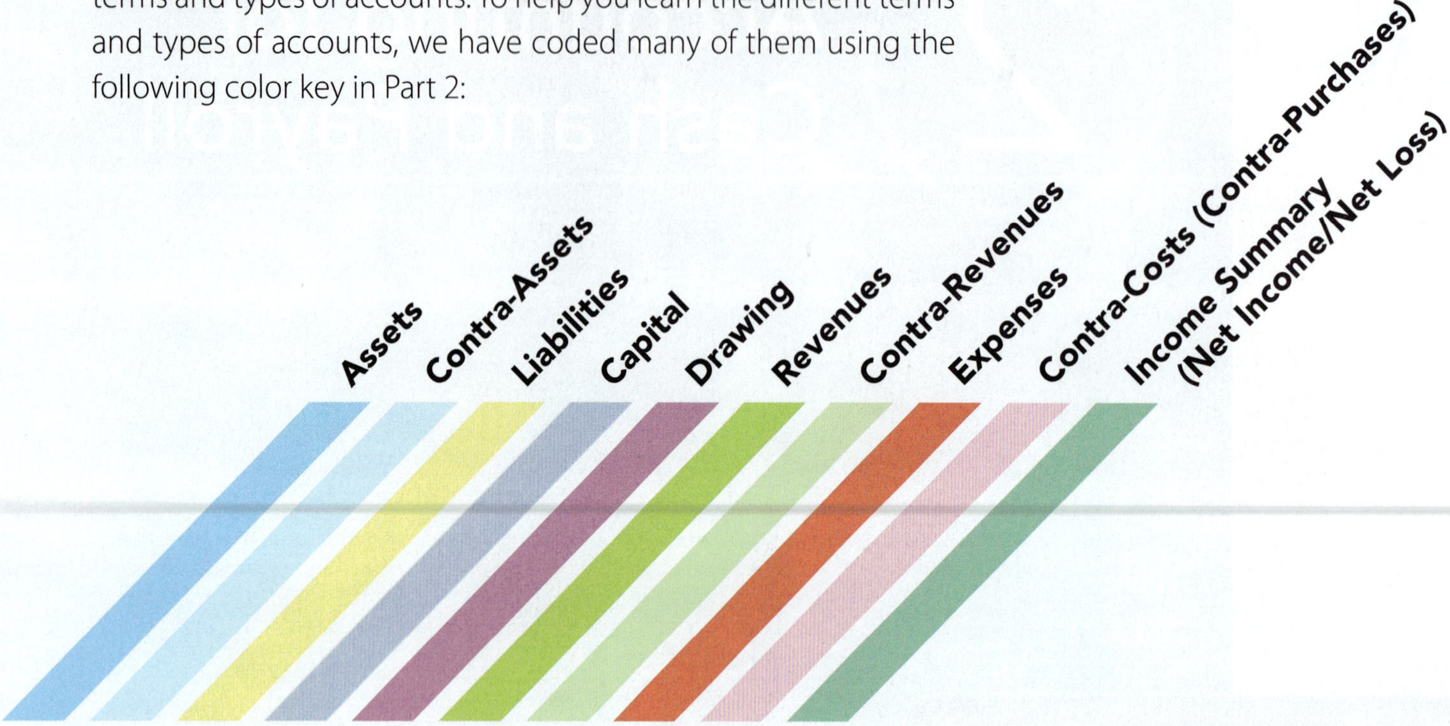

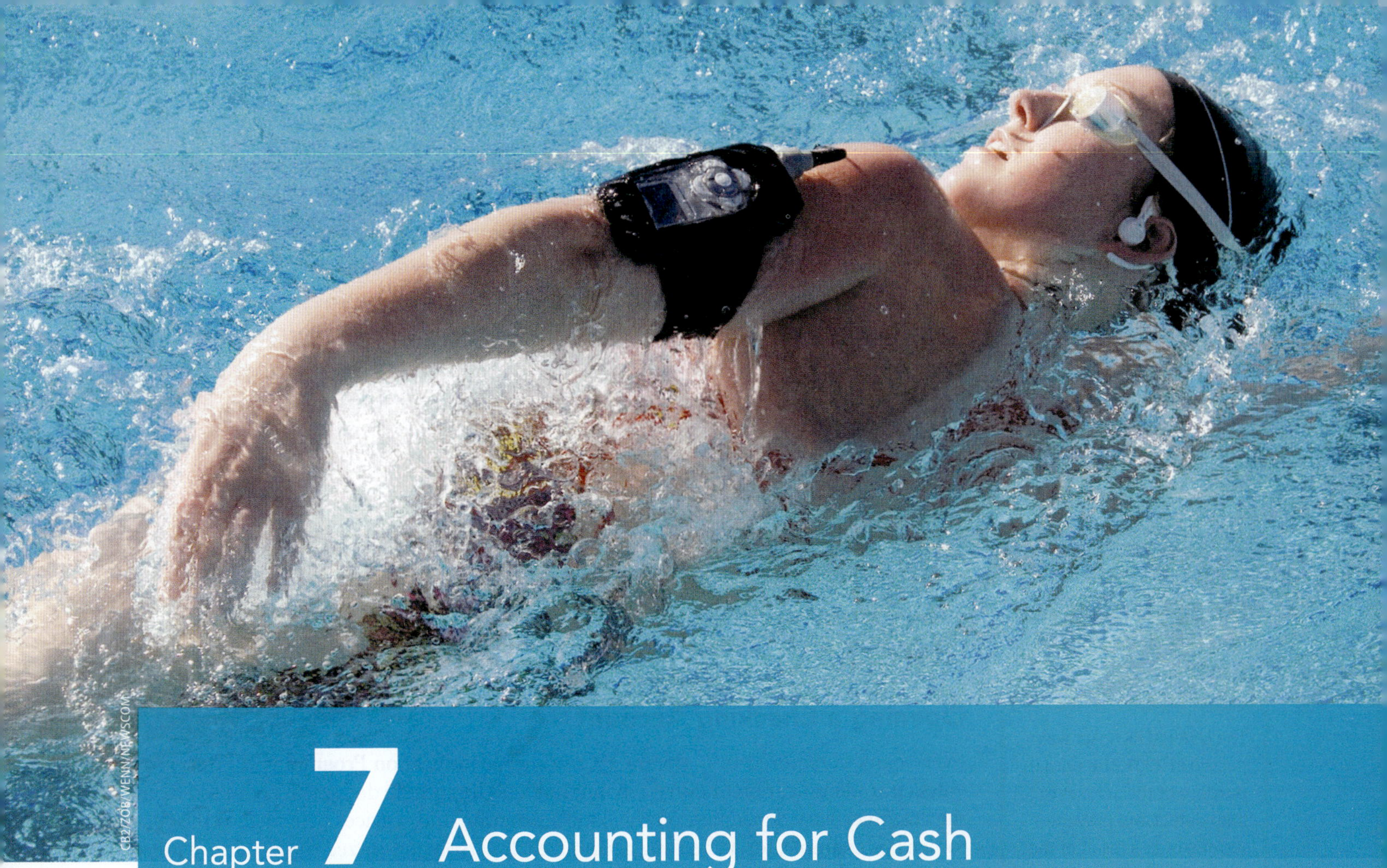
CB2/ZOB/WENN/NEWSCOM

Chapter 7 Accounting for Cash

H20 Audio was founded in 2003 with its home office in San Diego, California. Its key products include waterproof, weatherproof, and sweatproof audio equipment designed to enable athletes to use their electronics across virtually all sports, especially underwater. H20 Audio sells its merchandise online, in major electronics stores, in sports shops, and in other retailers throughout the United States and in more than 30 other countries. The company started quite small, but it grew rapidly. In one four-year period, its revenues increased more than 800%.

Two of the challenges for a company growing as fast as H20 Audio are managing and protecting its cash. H20 Audio has multiple checking accounts, receives cash receipts from multiple sources, and makes cash payments for many different bills. The company must have clear procedures and complete and accurate records in order to properly control cash and to plan for future needs. In this chapter, you will learn some of the ways to manage this critical business asset.

LEARNING OBJECTIVES

Careful study of this chapter should enable you to:

LO1 Describe how to open and use a checking account.

LO2 Prepare a bank reconciliation and related journal entries.

LO3 Establish and use a petty cash fund.

LO4 Establish a change fund and use the cash short and over account.

Cash is an asset that is quite familiar and important to all of us. We generally think of **cash** as the bills and coins in our pockets and the money we have in our checking accounts. To a business, cash also includes checks received from customers, money orders, and bank cashier's checks.

Because it plays such a central role in operating a business, cash must be carefully managed and controlled. A business should have a system of **internal control**—a set of policies and procedures designed to ensure proper accounting for transactions. For good internal control of cash transactions, all cash received should be deposited daily in a bank. All disbursements, except for payments from petty cash, should be made by check.

LO1

Checking Account

Describe how to open and use a checking account.

The key documents and forms required in opening and using a checking account are the signature card, deposit tickets, checks, and bank statements.

Opening a Checking Account

> The USA PATRIOT Act was passed in 2001. The primary purpose of the act was to help detect and prevent terrorism. As a result of the act, all banks must have a CIP that provides clear identification of every account holder of the bank.

Every bank is required to maintain a **Customer Identification Program (CIP)** that provides clear identification of every account holder. The specific documents required from the customer vary depending on the bank's program and services provided to the customer. For example, for a checking account, each person authorized to sign checks must complete and sign a **signature card** (Figure 7-1 on page 233). The bank can use this card to verify the depositor's signature on banking transactions. The taxpayer identification number (TIN) is the depositor's Social Security number or employer identification number (EIN). This number is shown on the card to identify the depositor for income tax purposes. An EIN can be obtained from the Internal Revenue Service.

Making Deposits

> Because of the high volume of transactions that they process, banks normally review signatures only on checks for large amounts and a sample of others. This makes it important for you to review your monthly bank statement.

A **deposit ticket** (Figure 7-2 on page 234) is a form showing a detailed listing of items being deposited. Bills, coins, and checks are listed separately. Each check can be identified by its **ABA (American Bankers Association) Number**. This number is the small fraction printed in the upper right-hand corner of each check (see Figure 7-4 on page 236). Part of this number also appears in a **magnetic ink character recognition (MICR) code** on the lower left side of the front of each check. The code is used to sort and route checks throughout the U.S. banking system. Normally, only the numerator of the fraction is used in identifying checks on the deposit ticket. Alternatively, the individual checks can be identified by the name of the writer of the check.

The depositor delivers or mails the deposit ticket and all items being deposited to the bank. The bank then gives or mails a receipt to the depositor. The deposit also can be made after business hours by using the night depository provided by most banks. The deposit is put in a locked bag, which is placed in a secure drawer or chute at the bank, for processing the following morning.

Deposits can also be made at ATMs and through mobile apps. These methods are discussed later in the chapter.

> When checks are deposited, there commonly is a delay before the funds are available for withdrawal. The delay can vary from one to eleven days, depending on the newness of the account, size and source of the checks, and many other factors.

Endorsements

Each check being deposited (or cashed) must be endorsed by the payee, the party to whom the check is payable. The **endorsement** consists of stamping or writing the

FIGURE 7-1 Signature Card

ACCOUNT NUMBER

ACCOUNT OWNER(S) NAME & ADDRESS

OWNERSHIP OF ACCOUNT - PERSONAL PURPOSE

☐ INDIVIDUAL ☐ ______________________

☐ JOINT - WITH SURVIVORSHIP (and not as tenants in common)

☐ JOINT - NO SURVIVORSHIP (as tenants in common)

☐ TRUST - SEPARATE AGREEMENT

____

☐ REVOCABLE TRUST OR ☐ PAY-ON-DEATH DESIGNATION AS DEFINED IN THIS AGREEMENT

Name and Address of Beneficiaries:

TYPE OF ACCOUNT

☐ NEW ☐ EXISTING

☐ CHECKING ☐ SAVINGS

☐ MONEY MARKET ☐ CERTIFICATE OF DEPOSIT

☐ NOW ☐ ______________

This is your (check one):

☐ Permanent ☐ Temporary account agreement

Number of signatures required for withdrawal ______________

FACSIMILE SIGNATURE(S) ALLOWED? ☐ YES ☐ NO

X ______________________________________

OWNERSHIP OF ACCOUNT - BUSINESS PURPOSE

☐ SOLE PROPRIETORSHIP

☐ CORPORATION: ☐ FOR PROFIT ☐ NOT FOR PROFIT

☐ PARTNERSHIP

☐ ______________________________

BUSINESS: ______________________________

COUNTRY & STATE OF ORGANIZATION: ______________________________

AUTHORIZATION DATED: ______________________________

SIGNATURE(S) - The undersigned certifies the accuracy of the information he/she has provided and acknowledges receipt of a completed copy of this form. The undersigned authorizes the financial institution to verify credit and employment history and/or have a credit reporting agency prepare a credit report on the undersigned, as individuals. The undersigned also acknowledge the receipt of a copy and agree to the terms of the following agreement(s) and/or disclosure(s):

☐ Terms & Conditions ☐ Truth in Savings ☐ Funds Availability

☐ Electronic Fund Transfers ☐ Privacy ☐ Substitute Checks

☐ Common Features ☐ ______________________

X ______________________________

I.D. # ______________ D.O.B. ______________

X ______________________________

I.D. # ______________ D.O.B. ______________

X ______________________________

I.D. # ______________ D.O.B. ______________

X ______________________________

I.D. # ______________ D.O.B. ______________

☐ Authorized Signer (Individual Accounts Only)

X ______________________________

I.D. # ______________ D.O.B. ______________

DATE OPENED ______________ BY ______________

INITIAL DEPOSIT $ ______________

☐ CASH ☐ CHECK ☐ ______________

HOME PHONE# ______________________________

BUSINESS PHONE# ______________________________

DRIVER'S LICENSE# ______________________________

E-MAIL ______________________________

EMPLOYER ______________________________

MOTHER'S MAIDEN NAME ______________________________

Name and address of someone who will always know your location: _____

____

____

BACKUP WITHHOLDING CERTIFICATIONS

TIN: ______________________________

☐ **TAXPAYER I.D. NUMBER -** The Taxpayer Identification Number shown above(TIN) is my correct taxpayer identification number.

☐ **BACKUP WITHHOLDING -** I am not subject to backup withholding either because I have not been notified that I am subject to backup withholding as a result of a failure to report all interest or dividends, or the Internal Revenue Service has notified me that I am no longer subject to backup withholding.

☐ **EXEMPT RECIPIENTS -** I am an exempt recipient under the Internal Revenue Service Regulations.

SIGNATURE: I certify under penalties of perjury the statements checked in this section and that I am a U.S. citizen or other U.S. person (as defined in the instructions).

X ______________________________________

(Date)

FIGURE 7-2 Deposit Ticket

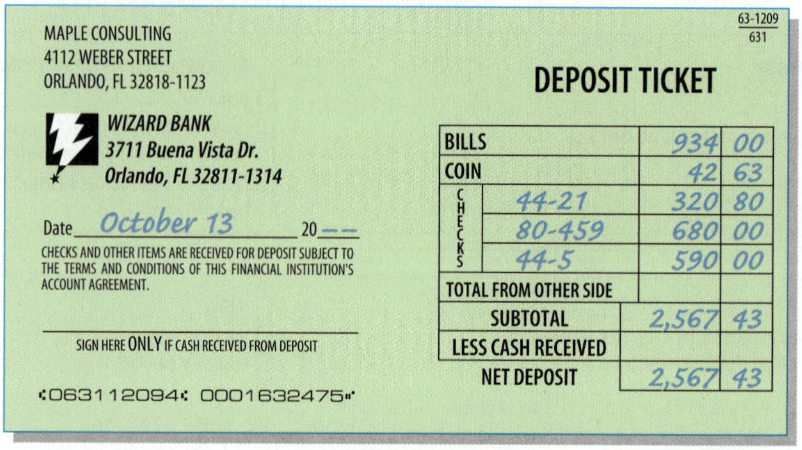

payee's name and sometimes other information on the back of the check, in the space provided near the left end. There are two basic types of endorsements.

1. **Blank endorsement**—the payee simply signs the back of the check. This makes the check payable to any bearer.
2. **Restrictive endorsement**—the payee adds words such as "Pay to the order of (specific) bank," or "Pay to Daryl Beck" to restrict the payment of the check to a specific party. By adding words such as "For deposit only," the payee can restrict the payment of the check for a specific purpose.

Businesses commonly use a rubber stamp to endorse checks for deposit. The check shown in Figure 7-3 has been stamped with a restrictive endorsement.

FIGURE 7-3 Restrictive Endorsement

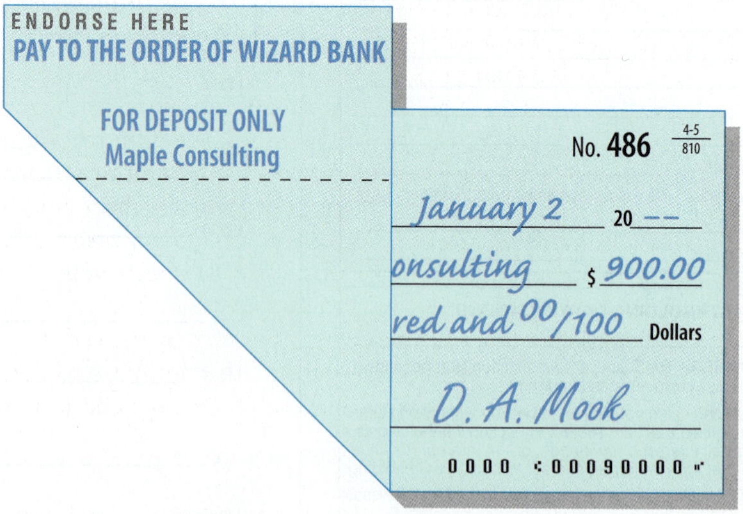

Automated Teller Machines

Postage stamps can be purchased at some ATMs. For deposits, some ATMs can provide an image of any checks being deposited.

Most banks now make **automated teller machines (ATMs)** available at all times to depositors for making deposits or withdrawals. Each depositor has a plastic card and a personal identification number (PIN). The depositor inserts the card, keys in the PIN, indicates whether the transaction is a withdrawal or a deposit, and enters the amount. The machine has a drawer or door for withdrawal or deposit.

Most ATMs are now on a system such as Cirrus that allows noncustomers to use other ATMs in both the United States and foreign countries. There are also "cash machines" that supply only cash and do not take deposits. These are often found at airports and convenience stores.

The convenience of ATMs and other forms of electronic banking discussed later in this chapter comes with a challenge: security. It is very important to keep PIN numbers and other forms of passwords safe, to protect your assets.

It is also important for the depositor to keep an accounting record of ATM withdrawals and deposits. This is done on the check stub or register described in the following section, and with an appropriate journal entry.

Writing Checks

A **check** is a document ordering a bank to pay cash from a depositor's account. There are three parties to every check.

1. **Drawer**—the depositor who orders the bank to pay the cash.
2. **Drawee**—the bank on which the check is drawn.
3. **Payee**—the party to whom the check is payable.

Checks used by businesses are usually bound in the form of a book. In some checkbooks, each check is attached to a **check stub** (Figure 7-4) that contains space to record all relevant information about the check. Other checkbooks are accompanied by a small register book in which the relevant information is noted. If a financial computer software package is used, both the check and the register can be prepared electronically.

When a check needs to be voided, follow these procedures: 1. tear off or completely cross out (deface) the signature, 2. write "Void" by the check number on the check stub or check register, and 3. file the voided check numerically with the other records of canceled checks.

Note that the check stubs in Figure 7-4 contain space to record amounts deposited. It generally is a good idea also to indicate the date of the deposit, as shown on check stub No. 108.

Use the following three steps in preparing a check:

STEP 1 Complete the check stub or register.

STEP 2 Enter the date, payee name, and amount on the check.

STEP 3 Sign the check.

The check stub is completed first so that the drawer retains a record of each check issued. This information is needed to determine the proper journal entry for the transaction.

The "payee's" name is entered on the first long line on the check, followed by the amount in figures. The amount in words is then entered on the second long line. If the amount in figures does not agree with the amount in words, the bank usually contacts the drawer for the correct amount or returns the check unpaid.

The most critical point in preparing a check is signing it, and this should be done last. The signature authorizes the bank to pay cash from the drawer's account. The check signer should make sure that all other aspects of the check are correct before signing it.

LEARNING KEY

The check should not be signed until the check signer has verified that all aspects of the check are correct.

The numbers at the bottom of the check are preprinted on every check. They indicate the bank routing number used by the Federal Reserve Bank, the bank account number, and the check number. This information and the code in the upper right-hand corner of the check are used to process the check through the banking system.

Bank Statement

A statement of account issued by a bank to each depositor once a month is called a **bank statement**. Banks prepare bank statements using various formats. Figure 7-5 is a simple bank statement for a checking account. The statement shows the following:

1. The balance at the beginning of the period.
2. Deposits and other amounts added during the period.
3. Checks and other amounts subtracted during the period.
4. Other electronic transactions.
5. The balance at the end of the period.

FIGURE 7-4 Checks and Check Stubs

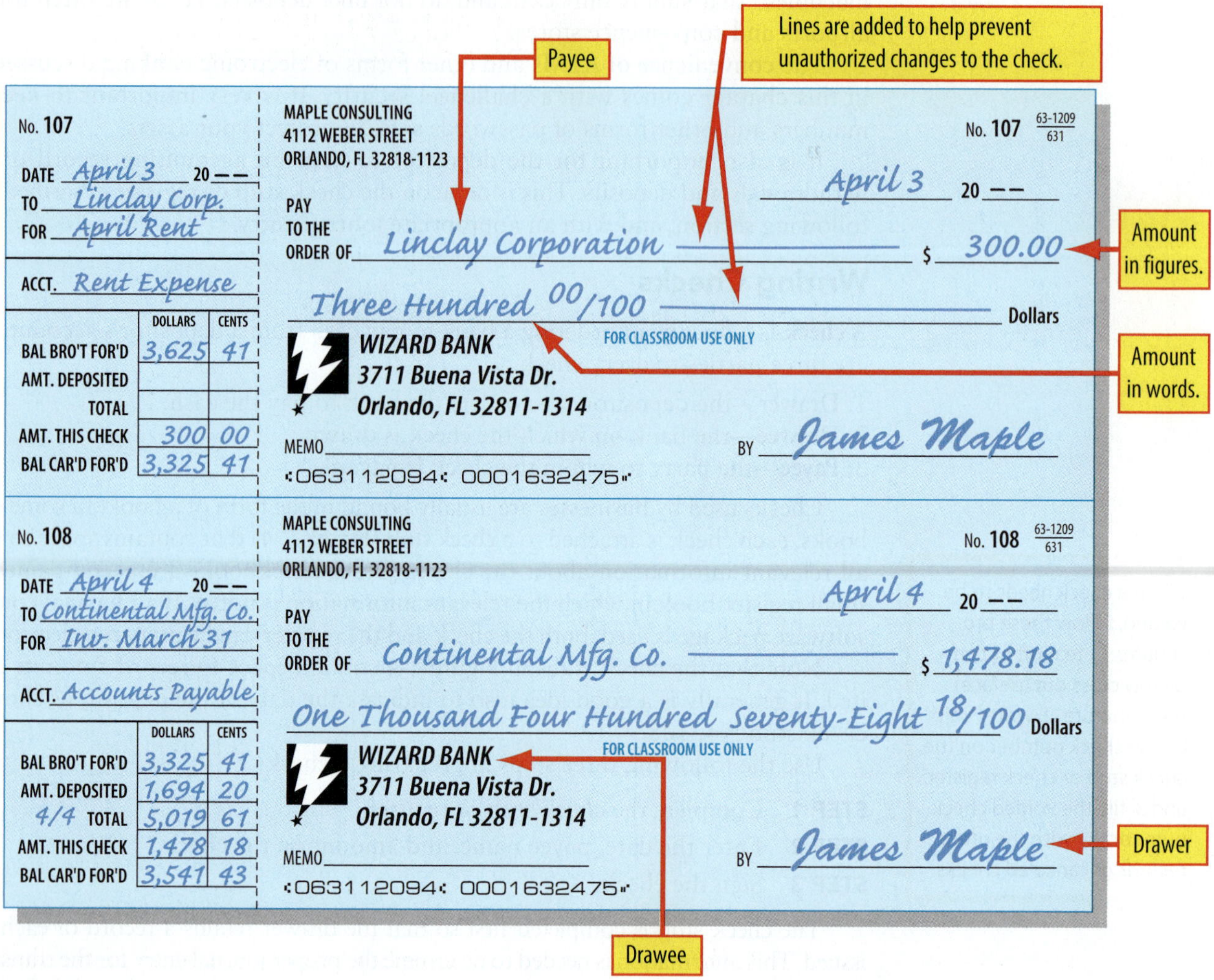

CHECKPOINT

Complete Checkpoint-1 on page 253 to test your basic understanding of LO1.

With the bank statement, the bank normally sends the following to the depositor:

1. Listing of **canceled checks**—a list of the depositor's checks paid by the bank during the period. The bank may send "imaged" sheets showing only the faces of the checks or the checks themselves, although this is increasingly uncommon today.
2. Any other forms representing items added to or subtracted from the account.

LO2 Reconciling the Bank Statement

Prepare a bank reconciliation and related journal entries.

On any given day, the balance in the cash account on the depositor's books (the book balance) is unlikely to be the same as that on the bank's books (the bank balance). This difference can be due to errors, but it usually is caused by timing. Transactions generally are recorded by the business at a time that is different from when the bank records them.

Deposits

Suppose there are cash receipts of $600 on April 30. These cash receipts would be recorded on the depositor's books on April 30, and a deposit of $600 would be transmitted to the bank. The deposit would not clear however, until at least the following

FIGURE 7-5 Bank Statement

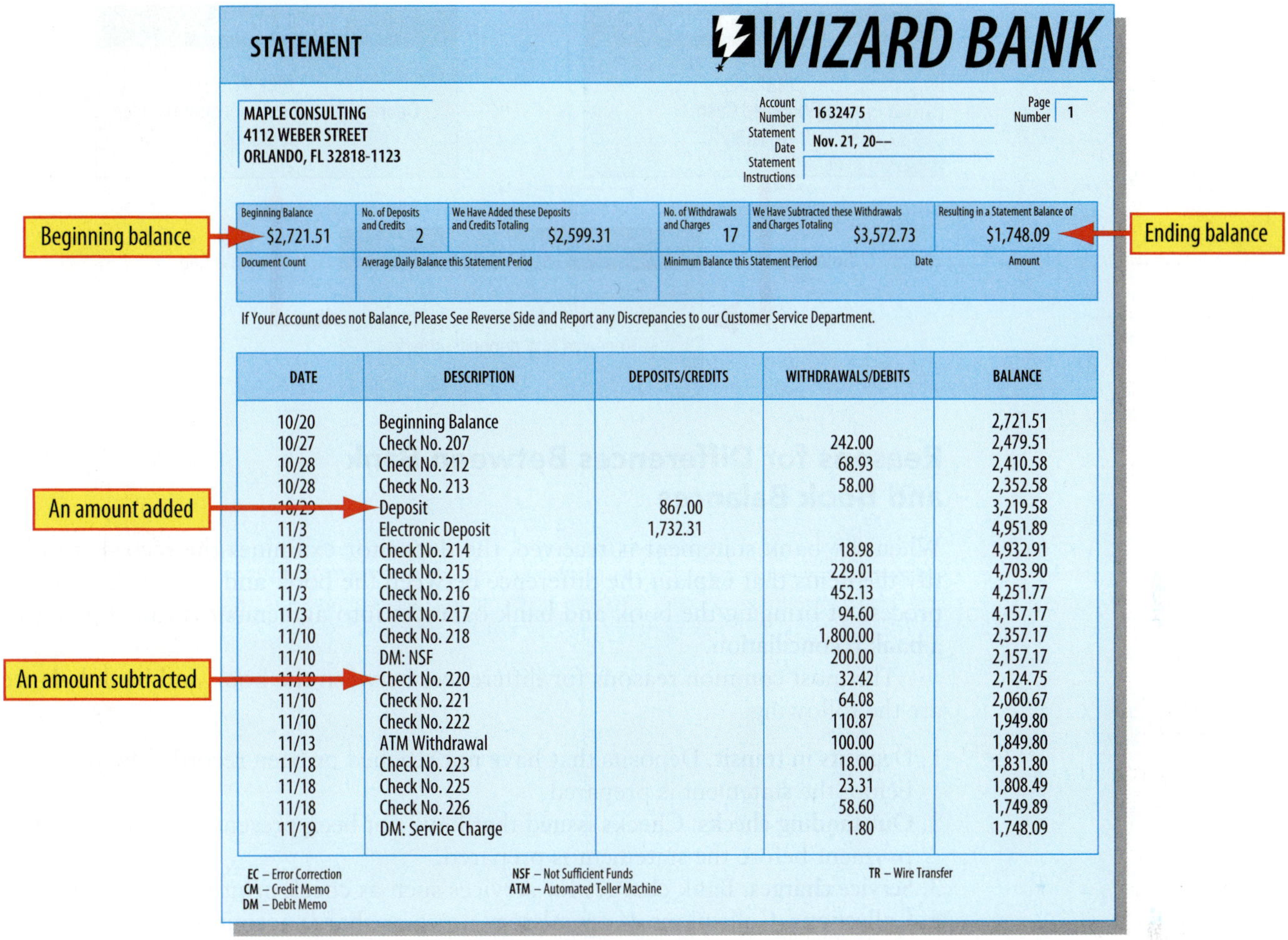

STATEMENT — WIZARD BANK

MAPLE CONSULTING
4112 WEBER STREET
ORLANDO, FL 32818-1123

Account Number: 16 3247 5 — Page Number: 1
Statement Date: Nov. 21, 20––
Statement Instructions:

Beginning Balance	No. of Deposits and Credits	We Have Added these Deposits and Credits Totaling	No. of Withdrawals and Charges	We Have Subtracted these Withdrawals and Charges Totaling	Resulting in a Statement Balance of
$2,721.51	2	$2,599.31	17	$3,572.73	$1,748.09

Document Count | Average Daily Balance this Statement Period | Minimum Balance this Statement Period | Date | Amount

If Your Account does not Balance, Please See Reverse Side and Report any Discrepancies to our Customer Service Department.

DATE	DESCRIPTION	DEPOSITS/CREDITS	WITHDRAWALS/DEBITS	BALANCE
10/20	Beginning Balance			2,721.51
10/27	Check No. 207		242.00	2,479.51
10/28	Check No. 212		68.93	2,410.58
10/28	Check No. 213		58.00	2,352.58
10/29	Deposit	867.00		3,219.58
11/3	Electronic Deposit	1,732.31		4,951.89
11/3	Check No. 214		18.98	4,932.91
11/3	Check No. 215		229.01	4,703.90
11/3	Check No. 216		452.13	4,251.77
11/3	Check No. 217		94.60	4,157.17
11/10	Check No. 218		1,800.00	2,357.17
11/10	DM: NSF		200.00	2,157.17
11/10	Check No. 220		32.42	2,124.75
11/10	Check No. 221		64.08	2,060.67
11/10	Check No. 222		110.87	1,949.80
11/13	ATM Withdrawal		100.00	1,849.80
11/18	Check No. 223		18.00	1,831.80
11/18	Check No. 225		23.31	1,808.49
11/18	Check No. 226		58.60	1,749.89
11/19	DM: Service Charge		1.80	1,748.09

EC – Error Correction
CM – Credit Memo
DM – Debit Memo
NSF – Not Sufficient Funds
ATM – Automated Teller Machine
TR – Wire Transfer

day, May 1. This timing difference in recording the $600 of cash receipts is illustrated in Figure 7-6. Notice that on April 30, the balances in the depositor's books and in the bank's books would be different. The depositor's book balance would be $600 more than the bank's book balance.

FIGURE 7-6 Depositor and Bank Records—Deposits

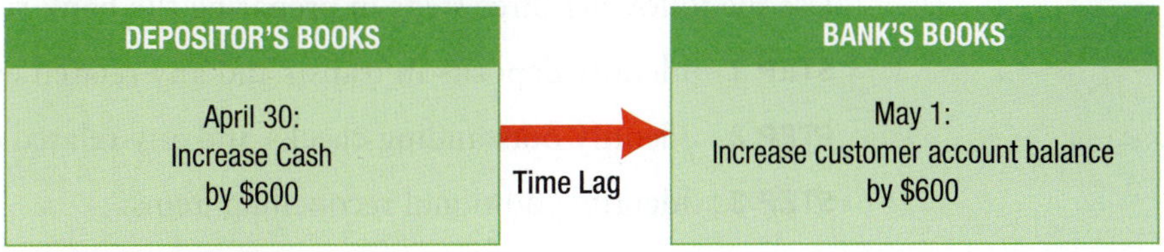

Cash Payments

Similar timing differences occur with cash payments. Suppose a check for $350 is written on April 30. This cash payment would be recorded on the depositor's books on April 30 and the check mailed to the payee. The check probably would not be received by the payee until May 3. If the payee deposited the check promptly, it still would not clear the bank until May 4. This timing difference in recording the $350 cash payment is illustrated in Figure 7-7. Notice once again that on April 30, the balances in the depositor's books and in the bank's books would be different. The depositor's book balance would be $350 less than the bank's book balance.

FIGURE 7-7 **Depositor and Bank Records—Cash Payments**

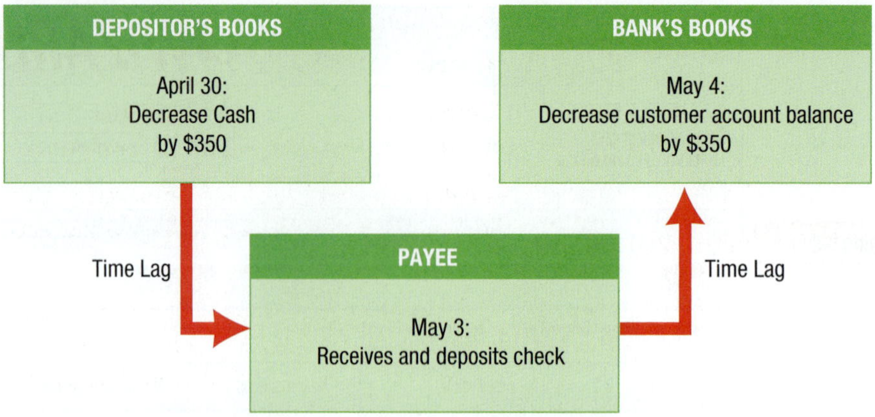

Reasons for Differences Between Bank and Book Balances

When the bank statement is received, the depositor examines the records to identify the items that explain the difference between the book and bank balances. This process of bringing the book and bank balances into agreement is called preparing a **bank reconciliation**.

The most common reasons for differences between the book and bank balances are the following:

1. **Deposits in transit**. Deposits that have not reached or been recorded by the bank before the statement is prepared.
2. **Outstanding checks**. Checks issued that have not been presented to the bank for payment before the statement is prepared.
3. **Service charges**. Bank charges for services such as check printing and processing.
4. **Collections**. Collections of promissory notes or charge accounts made by the bank on behalf of the depositor.
5. **Not sufficient funds (NSF) checks**. Checks deposited by the depositor that are not paid because the drawer did not have sufficient funds.
6. **Errors**. Errors made by the bank or the depositor in recording cash transactions.

Steps in Preparing the Bank Reconciliation

Use the following three steps in preparing the bank reconciliation:

STEP 1 Identify deposits in transit and any related errors.

STEP 2 Identify outstanding checks and any related errors.

STEP 3 Identify additional reconciling items.

Deposits in Transit and Related Errors

Follow these steps:

STEP 1 Compare deposits listed on the bank statement with deposits in transit on last month's bank reconciliation. All of last month's deposits in transit should appear on the current month's bank statement.

STEP 2 Compare the remaining deposits on the bank statement with deposits listed in the accounting records. Any deposits listed in the accounting records but not on the bank statement are deposits in transit on the current bank reconciliation.

STEP 3 Compare the individual deposit amounts on the bank statement and in the accounting records. If they differ, the error needs to be corrected.

Outstanding Checks and Related Errors

Follow these steps:

STEP 1 Compare canceled checks with the bank statement and the accounting records. If the amounts differ, the error needs to be corrected.

STEP 2 As each canceled check is compared with the accounting records, place a check mark on the check stub or other accounting record to indicate that the check has cleared.

STEP 3 Any checks written that have not been checked off represent outstanding checks on the bank reconciliation. This includes outstanding checks from last month's bank reconciliation that have not yet cleared.

Some banks pay interest on checking account balances. This reconciling item would be handled in the same manner as a bank credit memo.

Additional Reconciling Items

Compare any additions and deductions on the bank statement that are not deposits or checks with the accounting records. Items that the bank adds to the account are called **credit memos**. Items that the bank deducts from the account are called **debit memos**. Remember that a depositor's account is a liability to the bank. Thus, a credit memo increases this liability; a debit memo reduces the liability. Any of these items not appearing in the accounting records represent additional items on the bank reconciliation.

Illustration of a Bank Reconciliation

A general format for the bank reconciliation is shown in Figure 7-8. Not every item shown in this illustration would be in every bank reconciliation, but this format is helpful in determining where to put items. A bank reconciliation form also can be found on the back of most bank statements. Figure 7-9 is an example of such a form with instructions. Some banks also include a reconciliation form on their website.

To illustrate the preparation of a bank reconciliation, we will use the Maple Consulting bank statement shown in Figure 7-5. That statement shows a balance of $1,748.09 as of November 21. The balance in Maple's check stubs and general ledger

FIGURE 7-8 Bank Reconciliation Format

BANK RECONCILIATION		
Bank statement balance		$xxxx
Add: Deposits in transit	$xxxx	
Bank errors (that understate balance)	xxxx	xxxx
		$xxxx
Deduct: Outstanding checks	$xxxx	
Bank errors (that overstate balance)	xxxx	xxxx
Adjusted bank balance		$xxxx
Book balance		$xxxx
Add: Bank credit memos	$xxxx	
Book errors (that understate balance)	xxxx	xxxx
		$xxxx
Deduct: Bank debit memos	$xxxx	
Book errors (that overstate balance)	xxxx	xxxx
Adjusted book balance		$xxxx

FIGURE 7-9 Reconciliation Form From Bank Statement

Outstanding Deposits

Date	Amount
Total	$

Outstanding Withdrawals

Date	Amount
Total	$

1. List any deposits that do not appear on your statement in the Outstanding Deposits section at the left. Record the total.
2. Check off in your book register all checks, withdrawals (including Check Card and ATM) and automatic payments that appear on your statement. Withdrawals that are NOT checked off should be recorded in the Outstanding Withdrawals section at the left. Record the total.
3. Enter the ending balance shown on this statement. $__________
4. Enter the total deposits recorded in the Outstanding Deposits section. $__________
5. Total the amounts in steps 3 and 4. $__________
6. Enter the total withdrawals recorded in the Outstanding Withdrawals section. $__________
7. Subtract the amount in step 6 from the amount in step 5. This is your balance. $__________
8. Enter in your register and subtract from your register balance any checks, withdrawals, or other debits (including fees, if any) that appear on your statement but have not been recorded in your register.
9. Enter in your register and add to your register balance any deposits or other credits (including interest, if any) that appear in your statement but have not been recorded in your register.
10. The balance in your register should be the same as the balance shown in step 7. If it does not match, review and check all figures used, and check the addition and subtraction in your register. If necessary, review and balance your statement from the previous month.

FIGURE 7-10 Bank Reconciliation

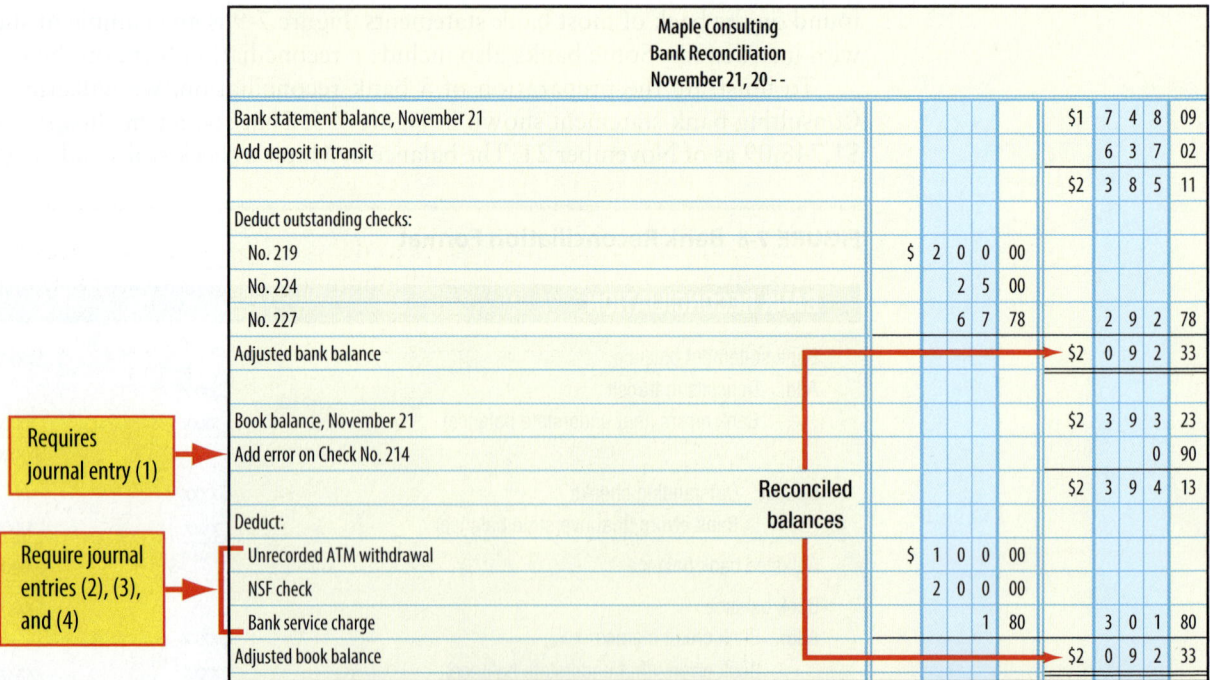

Maple Consulting
Bank Reconciliation
November 21, 20 - -

Bank statement balance, November 21		$1748 09
Add deposit in transit		637 02
		$2385 11
Deduct outstanding checks:		
No. 219	$200 00	
No. 224	25 00	
No. 227	67 78	292 78
Adjusted bank balance		$2092 33
Book balance, November 21		$2393 23
Add error on Check No. 214		0 90
		$2394 13
Deduct:		
Unrecorded ATM withdrawal	$100 00	
NSF check	200 00	
Bank service charge	1 80	301 80
Adjusted book balance		$2092 33

Requires journal entry (1) → Add error on Check No. 214

Require journal entries (2), (3), and (4) → Unrecorded ATM withdrawal, NSF check, Bank service charge

Reconciled balances → Adjusted bank balance, Adjusted book balance

cash account is $2,393.23. The three steps described on page 238 were used to identify the following items, and the reconciliation in Figure 7-10 was prepared.

1. A deposit of $637.02 recorded on November 21 had not been received by the bank. Maple has received the funds but the amount has not yet been counted by the bank. This deposit in transit is added to the bank statement balance.

2. Check numbers 219, 224, and 227 are outstanding. The funds have been disbursed by Maple but have not yet been paid out by the bank. The amount of these outstanding checks is subtracted from the bank statement balance.
3. Check number 214 was written for $18.98 but was entered on the check stub and on the books as $19.88. This $0.90 error is added to the book balance because $0.90 too much had been deducted from the book balance.
4. Maple made an ATM withdrawal of $100 on November 13 for personal use but did not record the withdrawal on the books. The bank has reduced Maple's balance by this amount. Thus, this amount is deducted from the book balance.
5. The bank returned an NSF check of $200. This was a check received by Maple from a customer. The bank has reduced Maple's balance by $200, but Maple has not yet recorded it. This amount is deducted from the book balance.
6. The bank service charge was $1.80. The bank has reduced Maple's balance by this amount, but Maple has not yet recorded it. This amount is deducted from the book balance.

LEARNING KEY

Journal entries are needed to correct errors in the books and to record bank additions and deductions that are not in the books.

Journal Entries

Only two kinds of items appearing on a bank reconciliation require journal entries.

1. Errors in the depositor's books.
2. Bank additions and deductions that do not already appear in the books.

Note the four items in the lower portion of the bank reconciliation in Figure 7-10. A journal entry always is required for each item in this book balance portion of the bank reconciliation. The four journal entries for Maple Consulting are shown below, using entry numbers matching those noted in Figure 7-10.

The $0.90 item is an error in the accounting records that occurred when the check amount was incorrectly entered. Assume that $18.98 was in payment of an account payable which had been incorrectly debited for $19.88. The entry to correct this error is as follows:

4		(1) Cash		0 90		4
5		Accounts Payable			0 90	5
6		Error in recording check				6

The $100 ATM withdrawal has been deducted from Maple's account by the bank. Maple has not yet recorded the withdrawal. Maple withdrew the funds for personal use, so the following journal entry is required:

8		(2) James Maple, Drawing		1 0 0 00		8
9		Cash			1 0 0 00	9
10		Unrecorded ATM withdrawal				10

The $200 NSF check is a deduction by the bank for a check deposited by Maple that proved to be worthless. This amount must be deducted from the book balance. Assuming that $200 was received from a customer on account, the following journal entry is required:

12		(3) Accounts Receivable		2 0 0 00		12
13		Cash			2 0 0 00	13
14		Unrecorded NSF check				14

The $1.80 bank service charge is a fee for bank services received by Maple. The bank has deducted this amount from Maple's account. Bank service charges are usually small and are charged to Miscellaneous Expense.

16	(4) Miscellaneous Expense	1 80		16
17	Cash		1 80	17
18	Bank service charge			18

Figure 7-11 contains a detailed list of items that require journal entries.

FIGURE 7-11 Bank Reconciliation Items that Require Journal Entries

ADDITIONS TO CASH BALANCE	DEDUCTIONS FROM CASH BALANCE
* Unrecorded deposits (including ATM) * Note collected by bank * Interest earned * Errors: 1. Added too little as a deposit 2. Deducted too much as a check	* Unrecorded ATM withdrawals * NSF checks * Bank service charges * Deposits recorded twice * Unrecorded checks * Loan payments * Interest payments * Errors: 1. Added too much as a deposit 2. Deducted too little as a check

Electronic Banking

Thus far in the chapter, we have explained and illustrated mainly a world of paper deposits, payments, and bank statements. Such a world still exists. But while many businesses and individuals still write and receive checks, the paper world of banking is shrinking rapidly. In fact, virtually every aspect of banking processes can be handled electronically.

Electronic Funds Transfer

Both deposits and payments can be made with **electronic funds transfer (EFT)**, using a computer rather than paper checks. Your net pay can be sent electronically by your employer to your bank, and you can review the summary of your compensation and various deductions on your computer. You can take a picture of a check with your smart phone and send it to the bank as a deposit. You can transfer funds between savings and checking accounts electronically. You can buy lunch or groceries, or withdraw money from a bank machine using your debit card. Payments on your credit card account or for utility bills can be made electronically. And your bank statement probably is sent to you electronically by your bank.

Businesses also are making increasing use of EFT in handling cash transactions. For example, as noted above, employee wages can be paid using EFT. Bills from suppliers also can be paid by EFT. Payments from customers frequently are in electronic form. And funds can be transferred electronically among multiple accounts at different banks.

Bank Reconciliations

Even the idea of the monthly bank reconciliation requires adjustment in an electronic banking world. In a paper world, you deposit paper checks, write paper checks, and keep paper records of your financial activities. Once a month, the bank sends you a bank statement and you "reconcile" your transactions and balance with the bank's records. In the electronic banking world, you can use your smartphone to regularly (daily?) view the effects of your transactions on your balance. There is no waiting until month-end to compare your records with the bank's. With fully electronic banking, the monthly reconciliation can be replaced by a regular "monitoring" of the account. If the bank's processing of a transaction is different from yours, you can

CHECKPOINT

Complete Checkpoint-2 on page 254 to test your basic understanding of LO2.

see it immediately and correct your records or contact the bank. There should be very little news in a monthly bank statement in an electronic banking world.

Heavy use of EFT will present record keeping challenges. Many of the documents handled in a purely manual environment disappear when EFT is used. Bank accounts are just one of many areas where computers require accountants to think in new ways. Regardless of what system is used, the key point to remember is that the accounting records must be correctly updated.

A BROADER VIEW

Fraud—A Real Threat to Small Business

Every two years, the Association of Certified Fraud Examiners (ACFE) surveys its members on the occupational fraud they have investigated during the preceding two years. The most recent survey showed that more than 30% of the frauds occurred in small businesses. In addition, the median loss suffered by small businesses was $150,000. The most commonly cited factor that allowed the fraud to occur was a lack of adequate internal control. And the majority of the asset misappropriation cases involved theft or misuse of cash.

These survey findings show the importance of the kinds of internal controls over cash described in this chapter and the appendix.

DON FARRALL/PHOTODISC/GETTY IMAGES

LO3 The Petty Cash Fund

Establish and use a petty cash fund.

For good control over cash, payments generally should be made by check. Unfortunately, payments of very small amounts by check can be both inconvenient and inefficient. For example, the time and cost required to write a check for $0.70 to mail a letter might be greater than the cost of the postage. Therefore, businesses customarily establish a **petty cash fund** to pay for small items with cash. "Petty" means small, and both the amount of the fund and the maximum amount of any bill that can be paid from the fund are small.

Establishing a Petty Cash Fund

To establish a petty cash fund, a check is written to the petty cash custodian for the amount to be set aside in the fund. The amount may be $50, $100, $200, or any amount considered necessary. The journal entry to establish a petty cash fund of $100 would be as follows:

4			Petty Cash		100 00		4
5			Cash			100 00	5
6			Establish petty cash fund				6

Petty Cash is an asset that is listed immediately below Cash on the balance sheet.

The custodian cashes the check and places the money in a petty cash box. For good control, the custodian should be the only person authorized to make payments from the fund. The custodian should be able to account for the full amount of the fund at any time.

Making Payments from a Petty Cash Fund

A receipt called a **petty cash voucher** (Figure 7-12) should be prepared for every payment from the fund. The voucher shows the name of the payee, the purpose of the payment, and the account to be charged for the payment. Each voucher should be signed by the custodian and by the person receiving the cash. The vouchers should be numbered consecutively so that all vouchers can be accounted for. At any time, the sum of the current vouchers and the unused cash should equal the original amount of the fund.

FIGURE 7-12 Petty Cash Voucher

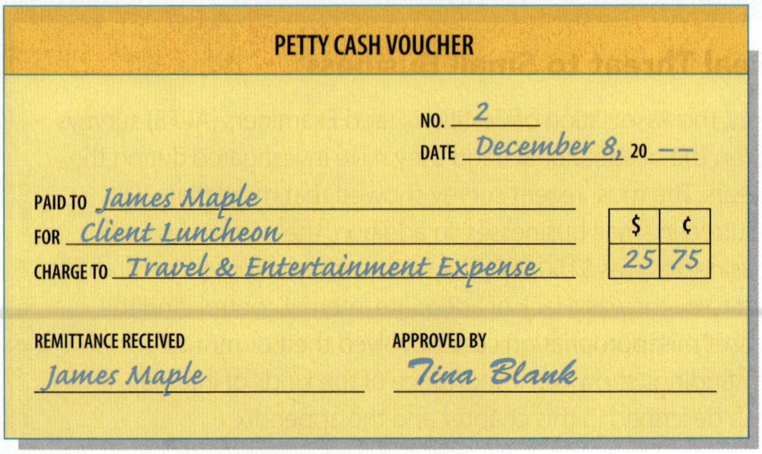
PETTY CASH VOUCHER

NO. 2
DATE December 8, 20 --

PAID TO James Maple
FOR Client Luncheon
CHARGE TO Travel & Entertainment Expense

$	¢
25	75

REMITTANCE RECEIVED James Maple
APPROVED BY Tina Blank

Petty Cash Payments Record

When a petty cash fund is maintained, a formal record is often kept of all payments from the fund. The **petty cash payments record** (Figure 7-13) is a special multi-column record that supplements the regular accounting records. It is not a journal. The headings of the Distribution of Payments columns may vary, depending upon the types of expenditures.

The petty cash payments record of Maple Consulting is shown in Figure 7-13. A narrative of the petty cash transactions shown in Figure 7-13 is as follows:

Dec. 1 Maple issued a check for $200 payable to Tina Blank, Petty Cash Custodian. Blank cashed the check and placed the money in a secure cash box.

A notation of the amount received is made in the Description column of the petty cash payments record. In addition, this transaction is entered in the journal as follows:

8	Dec. 1	Petty Cash		200 00		8
9		Cash			200 00	9
10		Establish petty cash fund				10

During the month of December, the following payments were made from the petty cash fund:

Dec. 5 Paid $32.80 to Jerry's Auto for servicing the company automobile. Voucher No. 1.

8 Reimbursed Maple $25.75 for the amount spent for lunch with a client. Voucher No. 2.

9 Gave Maple $30 for personal use. Voucher No. 3.

There is no special Distribution column for entering amounts withdrawn by the owner for personal use. Therefore, this payment is entered by writing the account name in the Account column and $30 in the Amount column at the extreme right of the petty cash payments record.

FIGURE 7-13 Maple Consulting's Petty Cash Payments Record

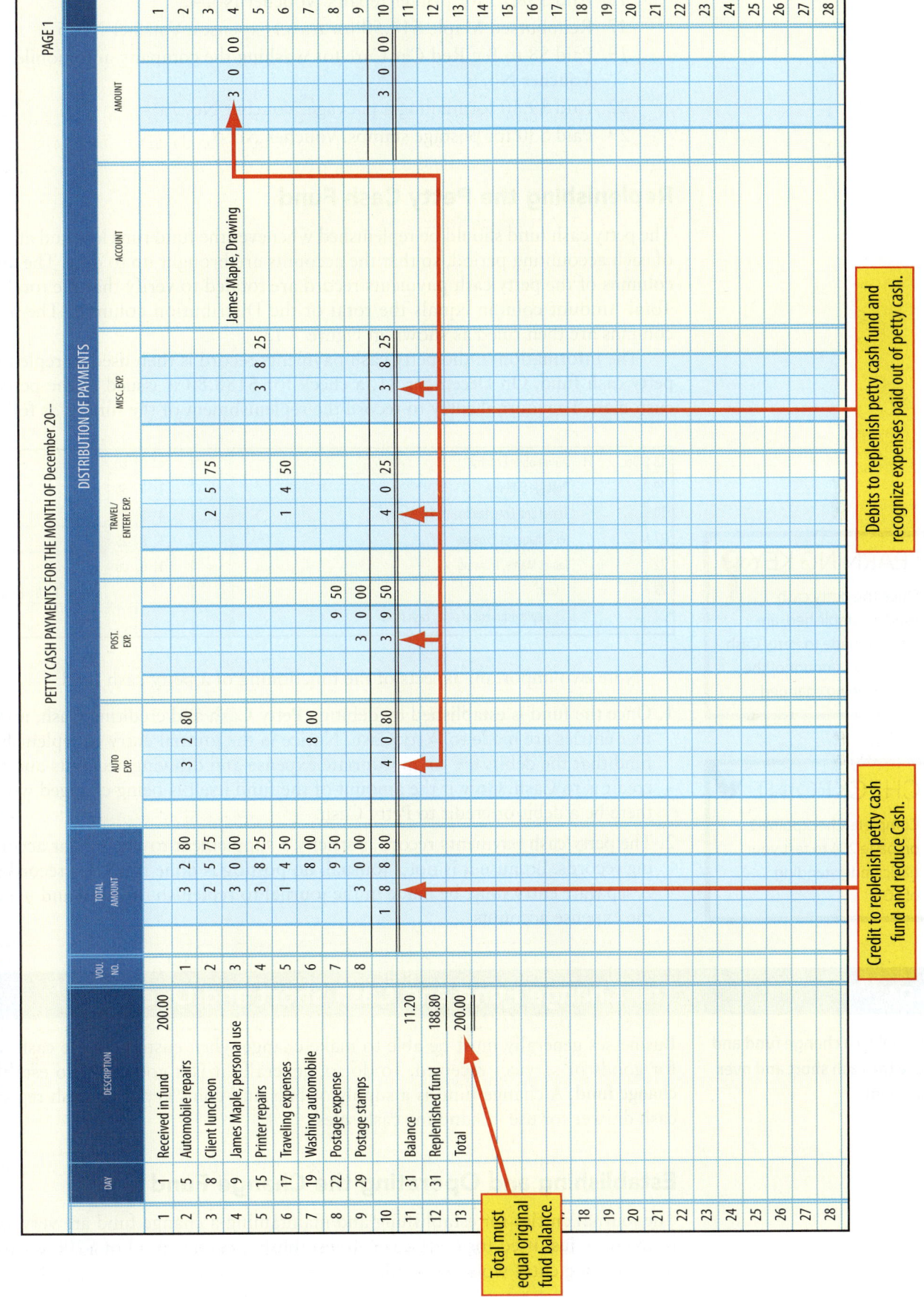

PETTY CASH PAYMENTS FOR THE MONTH OF December 20-- PAGE 1

DAY	DESCRIPTION		VOU. NO.	TOTAL AMOUNT	DISTRIBUTION OF PAYMENTS: AUTO EXP.	POST. EXP.	TRAVEL/ ENTERT. EXP.	MISC. EXP.	ACCOUNT	AMOUNT
1	Received in fund	200.00								
5	Automobile repairs		1	32 80	32 80					
8	Client luncheon		2	25 75			25 75			
9	James Maple, personal use		3	30 00					James Maple, Drawing	30 00
15	Printer repairs		4	38 25				38 25		
17	Traveling expenses		5	14 50			14 50			
19	Washing automobile		6	8 00	8 00					
22	Postage expense		7	9 50		9 50				
29	Postage stamps		8	30 00		30 00				
				188 80	40 80	39 50	40 25	38 25		30 00
31	Balance	11.20								
31	Replenished fund	188.80								
	Total	200.00								

Total must equal original fund balance.

Credit to replenish petty cash fund and reduce Cash.

Debits to replenish petty cash fund and recognize expenses paid out of petty cash.

15 Paid $38.25 for printer repairs. Voucher No. 4.
17 Reimbursed Maple $14.50 for travel expenses. Voucher No. 5.
19 Paid $8 to Big Red Car Care for washing the company automobile. Voucher No. 6.
22 Paid $9.50 for mailing a package. Voucher No. 7.
29 Paid $30 for postage stamps. Voucher No. 8.

Replenishing the Petty Cash Fund

The petty cash fund should be replenished whenever the fund runs low and at the end of each accounting period, so that the accounts are brought up to date. The amount columns of the petty cash payments record are totaled to verify that the total of the Total Amount column equals the total of the Distribution columns. The amount columns are then ruled as shown in Figure 7-13.

The information in the petty cash payments record is then used to replenish the petty cash fund. On December 31, a check for $188.80 is issued to the petty cash custodian. The journal entry to record the replenishment of the fund is as follows:

18	Dec.	31	Automobile Expense		40 80		18
19			Postage Expense		39 50		19
20			Travel and Entertainment Expense		40 25		20
21			Miscellaneous Expense		38 25		21
22			James Maple, Drawing		30 00		22
23			Cash			188 80	23
24			Replenishment of petty cash fund				24

LEARNING KEY
Once the petty cash fund is established, an entry is made to Petty Cash only if the amount of the fund is being changed.

CHECKPOINT
Complete Checkpoint-3 on page 254 to test your basic understanding of LO3.

Note two important aspects of the functioning of a petty cash fund.

1. Once the fund is established by debiting Petty Cash and crediting Cash, no further entries are made to Petty Cash. Notice in the journal entry to replenish the fund that the debits are to appropriate expense and drawing accounts and the credit is to Cash. Only if the amount of the fund itself is being changed would there be a debit or credit to Petty Cash.
2. The petty cash payments record is strictly a supplement to the regular accounting records. Because it is not a journal, no posting is done from this record. A separate entry must be made in the journal to replenish the fund and update the expense accounts.

LO4 The Change Fund and Cash Short and Over

Establish a change fund and use the cash short and over account.

Businesses generally must be able to make change when customers use cash to pay for goods or services received. To do so, generally it is a good idea to establish a **change fund**. A change fund is a supply of bills and coins kept in a cash register or cash drawer for use in handling cash sales.

Establishing and Operating the Change Fund

The journal entries for establishing and maintaining a change fund are very similar to the ones just used for petty cash. To establish a change fund of $200 on June 1, the following entry would be made:

8	June 1	Change Fund		2 0 0 00			8
9		Cash				2 0 0 00	9
10		Establish change fund					10

At the end of the day, cash received during the day is deposited, but the change fund is held back for use the following business day. For example, if cash of $1,250 was received on June 3 for services provided, the cash drawer would contain $1,450, as follows:

Change fund	$ 200
Cash sales	1,250
Total cash on hand	$1,450

The $1,250 would be deposited in the bank, and the following journal entry would be made:

12	June 3	Cash		1 2 5 0 00			12
13		Service Fees				1 2 5 0 00	13
14		Cash received for services					14

LEARNING KEY

Once the change fund is established, an entry is made to Change Fund only if the amount of the fund is being changed.

Notice the additional similarity between the change fund and the petty cash fund. Once the change fund is established by a debit to Change Fund and a credit to Cash, no further entries are made to the change fund. Only if the amount of the change fund itself is being changed would there be a debit or credit to Change Fund.

Cash Short and Over

An unavoidable part of the change-making process is that errors can occur. It is important to know whether such errors have occurred and how to account for them.

Businesses commonly use cash registers with tapes that accumulate a record of the day's receipts. The amount of cash according to the tapes plus the amount of the change fund can be compared with the amount of cash in the register to determine any error. For example, assume a cash shortage is identified for June 19.

Change fund	$ 200
Receipts per register tapes	963
Total	$1,163
Cash count	1,161
Cash shortage	$ 2

Similarly, assume a cash overage is identified for June 20.

Change fund	$ 200
Receipts per register tapes	814
Total	$1,014
Cash count	1,015
Cash overage	$ 1

We account for such errors by using an account called Cash Short and Over. In T account form, Cash Short and Over appears as follows:

Cash Short and Over	
Shortage (Expense)	Overage (Revenue)

The register tapes on June 19 showed receipts of $963 and the change fund was $200, but only $1,161 in cash was counted. The journal entry on June 19 to record the revenues and cash shortage (remember that we hold back the change fund) would be as follows:

18	June	19	Cash		961 00		18
19			Cash Short and Over		2 00		19
20			Service Fees			963 00	20
21			Record service fees and cash shortage				21

The entry on June 20 to record the revenues and cash overage (holding back the change fund) would be as follows:

23	June	20	Cash		815 00		23
24			Service Fees			814 00	24
25			Cash Short and Over			1 00	25
26			Record service fees and cash overage				26

CHECKPOINT

Complete Checkpoint-4 on page 254 to test your basic understanding of LO4.

The cash short and over account is used to accumulate cash shortages and overages throughout the accounting period. At the end of the period, a debit balance in the account (a net shortage) is treated as an expense. A credit balance in the account (a net overage) is treated as revenue.

YOUR PERSPECTIVE

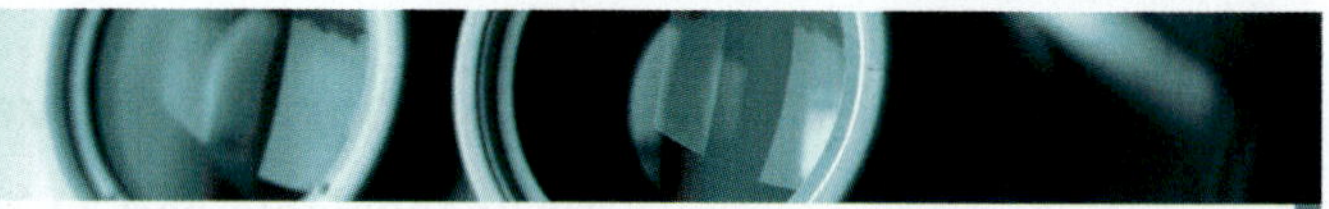

Cashier

Anyone who has ever worked in a retail environment knows that cash is a precious asset. *Cashiers* are responsible for safeguarding this cash in stores and restaurants. At the beginning of each shift, the cashier begins by counting the change fund in the assigned register. The change fund is a supply of currency and coins kept in a cash register or drawer used in handling cash sales. This is one way the business maintains control over cash. At the end of the shift, the cashier recounts the cash and compares it to the register tape to determine any shortages or overages. This is important because the business needs to know if errors have occurred and to decide how to account for them.

SELF-STUDY

LEARNING OBJECTIVES	Key Points to Remember
LO1 Describe how to open and use a checking account.	Three steps to follow in preparing a check are as follows: 1. Complete the check stub or register. 2. Enter the date, payee name, and amount on the check. 3. Sign the check.

LEARNING OBJECTIVES	Key Points to Remember
LO2 Prepare a bank reconciliation and related journal entries.	The most common reasons for differences between the book and bank cash balances are as follows: 1. Deposits in transit 2. Outstanding checks 3. Bank service charges 4. Bank collections for the depositor 5. NSF checks 6. Errors by the bank or the depositor Three steps to follow in preparing a bank reconciliation are as follows: 1. Identify deposits in transit and any related errors. 2. Identify outstanding checks and any related errors. 3. Identify additional reconciling items. Only two kinds of items on a bank reconciliation require journal entries. 1. Errors in the depositor's books. 2. Bank additions and deductions that do not already appear in the books.
LO3 Establish and use a petty cash fund.	Two important aspects of the functioning of a petty cash fund are as follows: 1. Once the fund is established, subsequent entries do not affect the petty cash account balance, unless the size of the fund itself is being changed. 2. The petty cash payments record is supplemental to the regular accounting records. No posting is done from this record.
LO4 Establish a change fund and use the cash short and over account.	A change fund is established by debiting Change Fund and crediting Cash. Cash shortages and overages are accounted for using the cash short and over account. A debit balance in this account represents expense; a credit balance represents revenue.

DEMONSTRATION PROBLEM

Jason Kuhn's check stubs indicated a balance of $4,565.12 for Kuhn's Wilderness Outfitters on March 31. This included a record of a deposit of $926.10 mailed to the bank on March 30, but not credited to Kuhn's account until April 1. In addition, the following checks were outstanding on March 31:

No. 462	$524.26
No. 465	$213.41
No. 473	$543.58
No. 476	$351.38
No. 477	$197.45

The bank statement showed a balance of $5,419 as of March 31. The bank statement included a service charge of $4.10 with the date of March 29. In matching the canceled checks and record of deposits with the stubs, it was discovered that

Check No. 456, a payment on account to Office Suppliers, Inc., for $39 was erroneously recorded on the stub as $93. This caused the bank balance on that stub and those following to be $54 too small. It was also discovered that an ATM withdrawal of $100 for personal use was not recorded on the books.

Kuhn maintains a $200 petty cash fund. His petty cash payments record showed the following totals at the end of March of the current year:

Automobile expense	$ 32.40
Postage expense	27.50
Charitable contributions expense	35.00
Phone expense	6.20
Travel and entertainment expense	38.60
Miscellaneous expense	17.75
Jason Kuhn, drawing	40.00
Total	$197.45

This left a balance of $2.55 in the petty cash fund, and the fund was replenished.

REQUIRED

1. Prepare a bank reconciliation for Jason Kuhn as of March 31, 20--.
2. Journalize the entries that should be made by Kuhn on his books as of March 31, 20--, (a) as a result of the bank reconciliation and (b) to replenish the petty cash fund.
3. Show proof that, after these entries, the total of the cash and petty cash account balances equals $4,715.02.

SOLUTION 1.

Kuhn's Wilderness Outfitters
Bank Reconciliation
March 31, 20 --

Bank statement balance, March 31		$5,419.00
Add deposit in transit		926.10
		$6,345.10
Deduct outstanding checks:		
No. 462	$524.26	
No. 465	213.41	
No. 473	543.58	
No. 476	351.38	
No. 477	197.45	1,830.08
Adjusted bank balance		$4,515.02
Book balance, March 31		$4,565.12
Add error on Check No. 456		54.00
		$4,619.12
Deduct: Bank service charge	$4.10	
Unrecorded ATM withdrawal	100.00	104.10
Adjusted book balance		$4,515.02

SOLUTION 2a.

3						3
4	Mar.	31	Miscellaneous Expense	4.10		4
5			Cash		4.10	5
6			Bank service charge			6
7						7
8			Cash	54.00		8
9			Accounts Payable—Office Suppliers, Inc.		54.00	9
10			Error on Check No. 456			10
11						11
12			Jason Kuhn, Drawing	100.00		12
13			Cash		100.00	13
14			Unrecorded ATM withdrawal			14
15						15
16		31	Automobile Expense	32.40		16
17			Postage Expense	27.50		17
18			Charitable Contributions Expense	35.00		18
19			Phone Expense	6.20		19
20			Travel and Entertainment Expense	38.60		20
21			Miscellaneous Expense	17.75		21
22			Jason Kuhn, Drawing	40.00		22
23			Cash		197.45	23
24			Replenishment of petty cash fund			24
25						25

b. (lines 16–24 above)

SOLUTION 3.

Cash in bank:		
Check stub balance, March 31	$4,565.12	
Plus error on Ck. No. 456	54.00	
Less bank charges	(104.10)	
Adjusted cash in bank		$4,515.02
Cash on hand:		
Petty cash fund	$ 2.55	
Add replenishment	197.45	
Adjusted cash on hand		200.00
Total cash in bank and petty cash on hand		$4,715.02

KEY TERMS

ABA (American Bankers Association) Number (232) The small fraction printed in the upper right-hand corner of each check.

automated teller machine (ATM) (234) A machine used by depositors to make withdrawals or deposits at any time.

bank reconciliation (238) A report used to bring the book and bank balances into agreement.

bank statement (235) A statement of account issued by a bank to each depositor once a month.

blank endorsement (234) An endorsement where the payee simply signs the back of the check, making the check payable to any bearer.

canceled check (236) A depositor's check paid by the bank during the bank statement period.

cash (232) To a business, cash includes bills, coins, checks received from customers, money orders, and bank cashier's checks.

change fund (246) A supply of bills and coins kept in a cash register or cash drawer for use in handling cash sales.

check (235) A document ordering a bank to pay cash from a depositor's account.

check stub (235) In some checkbooks, a document attached to a check that contains space for relevant information about the check.

collections (238) Collections of promissory notes or charge accounts made by the bank on behalf of the depositor.

credit memo (239) An item that the bank adds to the account.

Customer Identification Program (CIP) (232) A program every bank is required to maintain that provides clear identification of every account holder.

debit memo (239) An item that the bank deducts from the account.

deposit ticket (232) A form showing a detailed listing of items being deposited.

deposits in transit (238) Deposits that have not reached or been recorded by the bank before the bank statement is prepared.

drawee (235) The bank on which the check is drawn.

drawer (235) The depositor who orders the bank to pay the cash.

electronic funds transfer (EFT) (242) A process using a computer rather than paper checks to complete transactions with the bank.

endorsement (232) Stamping or writing the payee's name and sometimes other information on the back of the check.

errors (238) Errors made by the bank or the depositor in recording cash transactions.

internal control (232) A set of procedures designed to ensure proper accounting for transactions.

magnetic ink character recognition (MICR) code (232) The character code used to print identifying information on the lower left front side of each check.

not sufficient funds (NSF) check (238) A check deposited by the depositor that is not paid because the drawer did not have sufficient funds.

outstanding check (238) A check issued that has not been presented to the bank for payment before the statement is prepared.

payee (235) The person being paid the cash.

petty cash fund (243) A fund established to pay for small items with cash.

petty cash payments record (244) A special multi-column record that supplements the regular accounting records.

petty cash voucher (244) A receipt that is prepared for every payment from the petty cash fund.

restrictive endorsement (234) An endorsement where the payee adds words such as "Pay to the order of (specific) bank" or "For deposit only" to restrict the payment of the check.

service charge (238) A bank charge for services such as check printing and processing.

signature card (232) A card that is completed and signed by each person authorized to sign checks.

SELF-STUDY TEST QUESTIONS

True/False

1. **LO2** The primary purpose of a bank reconciliation is to detect and correct errors made by the bank in its records.
2. **LO2** NSF checks are subtracted from the bank statement balance on the bank reconciliation.
3. **LO2** The bank service charge requires a journal entry to record its effects on the cash account.
4. **LO2** Unrecorded ATM withdrawals are added to the book balance on the bank reconciliation.
5. **LO3** The petty cash record is a journal of original entry (entries are posted from it to the general ledger accounts).

Multiple Choice

1. **LO2** Which of these could be *added* to the ending book balance?
   (a) Service charges
   (b) NSF check
   (c) Checkbook errors that understate balance
   (d) Outstanding checks
2. **LO2** Which of these is *subtracted* from the ending book balance?
   (a) Deposits in transit
   (b) Service charges
   (c) Note collection
   (d) Bank errors
3. **LO2** Which of these is *added* to the ending bank statement balance?
   (a) Outstanding checks
   (b) Service charges
   (c) Checkbook errors
   (d) Deposits in transit
4. **LO3** To establish a petty cash fund, which account is debited?
   (a) Cash
   (b) Petty Cash
   (c) Miscellaneous Expense
   (d) Revenue
5. **LO4** When the cash short and over account has a debit balance at the end of the month, it is considered
   (a) an expense.
   (b) an asset.
   (c) revenue.
   (d) a liability.

CHECKPOINT

Checkpoint Exercises

1. **LO1** Match the following words with their definitions by entering the correct number in the spaces below.
   1. deposit ticket
   2. ATM
   3. check
   4. bank statement
   5. blank endorsement

   ____ a. A document ordering a bank to pay cash from a depositor's account.

   ____ b. An endorsement where the payee simply signs the back of the check, making the check payable to any bearer.

   ____ c. Automated teller machine—a machine used by depositors to make withdrawals or deposits at any time.

____ d. A statement of account issued by a bank to each depositor once a month.

____ e. A form showing a detailed listing of items being deposited.

2. **LO2** Indicate how each of the following items should be treated in a bank reconciliation by entering the correct letter in the spaces provided.

   a. Add to bank statement balance
   b. Subtract from bank statement balance
   c. Add to book balance
   d. Subtract from book balance

   ____ 1. Interest earned on checking account balance
   ____ 2. Error in checkbook whereby a check for $82 was entered in the checkbook as $28
   ____ 3. Deposit in transit
   ____ 4. Outstanding checks

3. **LO3** A petty cash fund established for $200 had the following cash payments during the month:

Phone expense	$23.50
Automobile expense	49.10
H. Appy, drawing	50.00

   Prepare the journal entry to replenish the petty cash fund at the end of the month.

4. **LO4** The cash register tape for June 30 showed cash receipts of $876, and the cash in the register drawer was $1,070. A change fund of $200 is maintained.

   Prepare the journal entry for service fees and cash short and over at June 30.

The answers to the Self-Study Test Questions are at the end of the chapter (page 266).

APPLYING YOUR KNOWLEDGE

CengageNowv2 provides "Show Me How" videos for selected exercises and problems. Additional resources, such as Excel templates for completing selected exercises and problems, are available for download from the companion website at Cengage.com.

REVIEW QUESTIONS

LO1 1. Why must a signature card be filled out and signed to open a checking account?

LO1 2. Explain the difference between a blank endorsement and a restrictive endorsement.

LO1 3. Who are the three parties to every check?

LO1 4. What are the three steps to follow in preparing a check?

LO2 5. What are the most common reasons for differences between the book and bank cash balances?

LO2 6. What are the three steps to follow in preparing a bank reconciliation?

LO2 7. What two kinds of items on a bank reconciliation require journal entries?

LO2 8. Name five common uses of electronic funds transfer.

LO3 9. What is the purpose of a petty cash fund?

LO3 10. What should be prepared every time a petty cash payment is made?

LO3 11. At what two times should the petty cash fund be replenished?

LO3 12. From what source is the information obtained for issuing a check to replenish the petty cash fund?

LO4 13. At what two times would an entry be made affecting the change fund?

LO4 14. What does a debit balance in the cash short and over account represent? What does a credit balance in this account represent?

SERIES A EXERCISES

E 7-1A **(LO1)**

CHECKING ACCOUNT TERMS Match the following words with their definitions:

1. An endorsement where the payee simply signs on the back of the check
2. An endorsement that contains words like "For Deposit Only" together with the signature
3. A card filled out and signed by each person authorized to sign checks on an account
4. The depositor who orders the bank to pay cash from the depositor's account
5. The bank on which the check is drawn
6. The person being paid the cash
7. A check that has been paid by the bank and is being returned to the depositor

a. signature card
b. canceled check
c. blank endorsement
d. drawer
e. restrictive endorsement
f. drawee
g. payee

E 7-2A **(LO1)**
✓ Net deposit: $962.20

PREPARE DEPOSIT TICKET Based on the following information, prepare a deposit ticket:

Date:		January 15, 20--
Bills:		$396.00
Coin:		23.20
Checks:	No. 4-12	372.00
	No. 80-318	127.00
	No. 3-8	44.00

E 7-3A (LO1)

PREPARE CHECK AND STUB Based on the following information, prepare a check and stub:

Date:	January 15, 20--
Balance brought forward:	$2,841.50
Deposit:	(from Exercise 7-2A)
Check to:	J. M. Suppliers
Amount:	$150.00
For:	Office Supplies
Signature:	Sign your name

E 7-4A (LO2)

BANK RECONCILIATION PROCEDURES In a format similar to the following, indicate whether the action at the left will result in an addition to (+) or subtraction from (−) the ending bank balance or the ending book balance.

	Ending Bank Balance	Ending Book Balance
1. Deposits in transit to the bank	________	________
2. Error in checkbook: check recorded as $32 but was actually for $23	________	________
3. Service fee charged by the bank	________	________
4. Outstanding checks	________	________
5. NSF check deposited earlier	________	________
6. Error in checkbook: check recorded as $22 but was actually for $220	________	________
7. Bank credit memo advising a note was collected for us	________	________

E 7-5A (LO2)

✓ NSF check: Dr. Accounts Receivable, $468

PREPARE JOURNAL ENTRIES FOR BANK RECONCILIATION Based on the following bank reconciliation, prepare the journal entries:

Carmen Lui Associates
Bank Reconciliation
July 31, 20 - -

Bank statement balance, July 31		$3,316.80
Add deposits in transit	$300.00	
	118.00	418.00
		$3,734.80
Deduct outstanding checks:		
No. 296	$424.20	
No. 299	22.60	
No. 301	39.90	486.70
Adjusted bank balance		$3,248.10
Book balance, July 31		$3,700.50
Add error on Check No. 291*		27.60
		$3,728.10
Deduct: NSF check	$468.00	
Bank service charge	12.00	480.00
Adjusted book balance		$3,248.10
*Accounts Payable was debited in original entry.		

E 7-6A (LO3)
✓ Replenishment: Cr. Cash, $228.10

PETTY CASH JOURNAL ENTRIES Based on the following petty cash information, prepare (a) the journal entry to establish a petty cash fund and (b) the journal entry to replenish the petty cash fund.

On January 1, 20--, a check was written in the amount of $300 to establish a petty cash fund. During January, the following vouchers were written for cash removed from the petty cash drawer:

Voucher No.	Account Debited	Amount
1	Phone Expense	$21.20
2	Automobile Expense	39.60
3	James Lucas, Drawing	85.00
4	Postage Expense	15.30
5	Charitable Contributions Expense	20.00
6	Miscellaneous Expense	47.00

E 7-7A (LO4)
✓ Apr. 16: Cr. Cash Short and Over, $1.75

CASH SHORT AND OVER ENTRIES Based on the following information, prepare the weekly entries for cash receipts from service fees and cash short and over. A change fund of $100 is maintained.

Date	Change Fund	Cash Register Receipt Amount	Actual Cash Counted
Apr. 2	$100	$268.50	$366.50
9	100	237.75	333.50
16	100	309.25	411.00
23	100	226.50	324.00
30	100	318.00	422.00

SERIES A PROBLEMS

P 7-8A (LO2)
✓ Adjusted book balance: $5,023

BANK RECONCILIATION AND RELATED JOURNAL ENTRIES The book balance in the checking account of Johnson Enterprises as of October 31 is $5,718. The bank statement shows an ending balance of $5,217. The following information is discovered by (1) comparing last month's deposits in transit and outstanding checks with this month's bank statement, (2) comparing deposits and checks written per books and per bank in the current month, and (3) noting service charges and other debit and credit memos shown on the bank statement.

Deposits in transit:	10/29	$210.00
	10/30	406.00
Outstanding checks:	No. 1635	56.40
	No. 1639	175.00
	No. 1641	135.50
	No. 1653	443.10
Unrecorded ATM withdrawal:*		200.00
Bank service charge:		37.00
NSF check:		476.00
Error on Check No. 1624	Checkbook shows it was for $75, but it was actually written for $57. Accounts Payable was debited.	

*Funds were withdrawn by Enoch Johnson for personal use.

(continued)

REQUIRED

1. Prepare a bank reconciliation as of October 31, 20--.
2. Prepare the required journal entries.

P 7-9A (LO2)
✓ Adjusted bank balance: $3,069.95

BANK RECONCILIATION AND RELATED JOURNAL ENTRIES The book balance in the checking account of Lyle's Salon as of November 30 is $3,282.95. The bank statement shows an ending balance of $2,127. By examining last month's bank reconciliation, comparing the deposits and checks written per books and per bank in November, and noting the service charges and other debit and credit memos shown on the bank statement, the following were found:

(a) An ATM withdrawal of $150 on November 18 by Lyle for personal use was not recorded on the books.
(b) A bank debit memo issued for an NSF check from a customer of $19.50.
(c) A bank credit memo issued for interest of $19 earned during the month.
(d) On November 30, a deposit of $1,177 was made, which is not shown on the bank statement.
(e) A bank debit memo issued for $17.50 for bank service charges.
(f) Checks No. 549, 561, and 562 for the amounts of $185, $21, and $9.40, respectively, were written during November but have not yet been received by the bank.
(g) The reconciliation from the previous month showed outstanding checks totaling $271.95. One of those checks, No. 471 for $18.65, has not yet been received by the bank.
(h) Check No. 523 written to a creditor in the amount of $372.90 was recorded in the books as $327.90.

REQUIRED

1. Prepare a bank reconciliation as of November 30.
2. Prepare the required journal entries.

P 7-10A (LO3)
✓ Replenishment: Cr. Cash, $149

PETTY CASH RECORD AND JOURNAL ENTRIES On May 1, a petty cash fund was established for $150. The following vouchers were issued during May:

Date	Voucher No.	Purpose	Amount
May 1	1	Postage due	$ 3.50
3	2	Office supplies	11.00
5	3	Auto repair (miscellaneous)	43.00
7	4	Drawing (Joy Adams)	25.00
11	5	Donation (Red Cross)	10.00
15	6	Travel expenses	28.00
22	7	Postage stamps	3.50
26	8	Phone call	5.00
30	9	Donation (Boy Scouts)	20.00

REQUIRED

1. Prepare the journal entry to establish the petty cash fund.
2. Record the vouchers in the petty cash record. Total and rule the petty cash record.
3. Prepare the journal entry to replenish the petty cash fund. Make the appropriate entry in the petty cash record.

P 7-11A (LO4)
✓ July 23: Dr. Cash Short and Over, $2.50

CASH SHORT AND OVER ENTRIES Listed below are the weekly cash register tape amounts for service fees and the related cash counts during the month of July. A change fund of $100 is maintained.

Date	Change Fund	Cash Register Receipt Amount	Actual Cash Counted
July 2	$100	$289.50	$387.00
9	100	311.50	411.50
16	100	306.00	408.50
23	100	317.50	415.00
30	100	296.00	399.50

REQUIRED

1. Prepare the journal entries to record the cash service fees and cash short and over for each of the five weeks.
2. Post to the cash short and over account (use Account No. 516).
3. Determine the ending balance of the cash short and over account. Does it represent an expense or revenue?

SERIES B EXERCISES

E 7-1B (LO1)

CHECKING ACCOUNT TERMS Match the following words with their definitions:

1. Banking number used to identify checks for deposit tickets
2. A card filled out to open a checking account
3. A machine from which withdrawals can be taken or deposits made to accounts
4. A place where relevant information is recorded about a check
5. A set of procedures designed to ensure proper accounting for transactions
6. A statement of account issued to each depositor once a month
7. A detailed listing of items being deposited to an account

a. bank statement
b. deposit ticket
c. signature card
d. internal control
e. check stub
f. ATM
g. ABA number

E 7-2B (LO1)
✓ Total deposit: $645

PREPARE DEPOSIT TICKET Based on the following information, prepare a deposit ticket:

Date: November 15, 20--

Bills:		$283
Coin:		19
Checks:	No. 3-22	201
	No. 19-366	114
	No. 3-2	28

(continued)

E 7-3B (LO1)

PREPARE CHECK AND STUB Based on the following information, prepare a check and stub:

Date:	November 15, 20--
Balance brought forward:	$3,181
Deposit:	(from Exercise 7-2B)
Check to:	R. J. Smith Co.
Amount:	$120
For:	Payment on account
Signature:	Sign your name

E 7-4B (LO2)

BANK RECONCILIATION PROCEDURES In a format similar to the following, indicate whether the action at the left will result in an addition to (+) or subtraction from (−) the ending bank balance or the ending book balance.

	Ending Bank Balance	Ending Book Balance
1. Service fee of $12 charged by the bank	________	________
2. Outstanding checks	________	________
3. Error in checkbook: check recorded as $36 was actually for $28	________	________
4. NSF check deposited earlier	________	________
5. Bank credit memo advising a note was collected for us	________	________
6. Deposits in transit to the bank	________	________
7. Error in checkbook: check recorded as $182 was actually for $218	________	________

E 7-5B (LO2)

✓ NSF check: Dr. Accounts Receivable, $66

PREPARE JOURNAL ENTRIES FOR BANK RECONCILIATION Based on the following bank reconciliation, prepare the journal entries:

Ruggero Celini Associates
Bank Reconciliation
July 31, 20--

Bank statement balance, July 31		$1,784.00
Add deposits in transit	$418.50	
	100.50	519.00
		$2,303.00
Deduct outstanding checks:		
No. 185	$206.50	
No. 203	317.40	
No. 210	56.10	580.00
Adjusted bank balance		$1,723.00
Book balance, July 31		$1,792.00
Add: Error on Check No. 191*	10.00	
Interest earned	2.00	12.00
		$1,804.00
Deduct: NSF check	$66.00	
Bank service charge	15.00	81.00
Adjusted book balance		$1,723.00

*Accounts Payable was debited in original entry.

E 7-6B (LO3)
✓ Replenishment: Cr. Cash, $190

PETTY CASH JOURNAL ENTRIES Based on the following petty cash information, prepare (a) the journal entry to establish a petty cash fund and (b) the journal entry to replenish the petty cash fund.

On October 1, 20--, a check was written in the amount of $200 to establish a petty cash fund. During October, the following vouchers were written for cash taken from the petty cash drawer:

Voucher No.	Account Debited	Amount
1	Postage Expense	$13
2	Miscellaneous Expense	17
3	John Flanagan, Drawing	45
4	Phone Expense	36
5	Charitable Contributions Expense	50
6	Automobile Expense	29

E 7-7B (LO4)
✓ June 15: Dr. Cash Short and Over, $2

CASH SHORT AND OVER ENTRIES Based on the following information, prepare the weekly entries for cash receipts from service fees and cash short and over. A change fund of $100 is maintained.

Date	Change Fund	Cash Register Receipt Amount	Actual Cash Counted
June 1	$100	$330.00	$433.00
8	100	297.00	400.00
15	100	233.00	331.00
22	100	302.00	396.50
29	100	316.00	412.00

SERIES B PROBLEMS

P 7-8B (LO2)
✓ Adjusted book balance: $2,674

BANK RECONCILIATION AND RELATED JOURNAL ENTRIES The book balance in the checking account of Kyri Enterprises as of November 30 is $2,964. The bank statement shows an ending balance of $2,525. The following information is discovered by (1) comparing last month's deposits in transit and outstanding checks with this month's bank statement, (2) comparing deposits and checks written per books and per bank in the current month, and (3) noting service charges and other debit and credit memos shown on the bank statement.

Deposits in transit:	11/29	$125
	11/30	200
Outstanding checks:	No. 322	17
	No. 324	105
	No. 327	54
Unrecorded ATM withdrawal:*		100
Bank service charge:		25
NSF check:		185

Error on Check No. 321 — Checkbook shows it was for $64, but it was actually written for $44. Accounts Payable was debited.

*Funds were withdrawn by Susan Kyri for personal use.

(continued)

REQUIRED

1. Prepare a bank reconciliation as of November 30, 20--.
2. Prepare the required journal entries.

P 7-9B (LO2)
✓ Adjusted bank balance: $4,518.70

BANK RECONCILIATION AND RELATED JOURNAL ENTRIES The book balance in the checking account of Tori's Health Center as of April 30 is $4,690.30. The bank statement shows an ending balance of $3,275.60. By examining last month's bank reconciliation, comparing the deposits and checks written per books and per bank in April, and noting the service charges and other debit and credit memos shown on the bank statement, the following were found:

(a) An ATM withdrawal of $200 on April 20 by Tori for personal use was not recorded on the books.
(b) A bank debit memo issued for an NSF check from a customer of $29.10.
(c) A bank credit memo issued for interest of $28 earned during the month.
(d) On April 30, a deposit of $1,592 was made, which is not shown on the bank statement.
(e) A bank debit memo issued for $24.50 for bank service charges.
(f) Checks No. 481, 493, and 494 for the amounts of $215, $71, and $24.30, respectively, were written during April but have not yet been received by the bank.
(g) The reconciliation from the previous month showed outstanding checks totaling $418.25. One of these checks, No. 397 for $38.60, has not yet been received by the bank.
(h) Check No. 422 written to a creditor in the amount of $217.90 was recorded in the books as $271.90.

REQUIRED

1. Prepare a bank reconciliation as of April 30.
2. Prepare the required journal entries.

P 7-10B (LO3)
✓ Replenishment: Cr. Cash, $87

PETTY CASH RECORD AND JOURNAL ENTRIES On July 1, a petty cash fund was established for $100. The following vouchers were issued during July:

Date	Voucher No.	Purpose	Amount
July 1	1	Office supplies	$ 3.00
3	2	Donation (Goodwill)	15.00
5	3	Travel expenses	5.00
7	4	Postage due	2.00
8	5	Office supplies	4.00
11	6	Postage due	3.50
15	7	Phone call	5.00
21	8	Travel expenses	11.00
25	9	Withdrawal by owner (L. Ortiz)	20.00
26	10	Copier repair (miscellaneous)	18.50

REQUIRED

1. Prepare the journal entry to establish the petty cash fund.
2. Record the vouchers in the petty cash record. Total and rule the petty cash record.
3. Prepare the journal entry to replenish the petty cash fund. Make the appropriate entry in the petty cash record.

P 7-11B (LO4)
✓ Aug. 8: Dr. Cash Short and Over, $3.50

CASH SHORT AND OVER ENTRIES Listed below are the weekly cash register tape amounts for service fees and the related cash counts during the month of July. A change fund of $200 is maintained.

Date	Change Fund	Cash Register Receipt Amount	Actual Cash Counted
Aug. 1	$200	$292.50	$495.00
8	200	305.00	501.50
15	200	286.00	486.00
22	200	330.25	532.75
29	200	299.20	495.00

REQUIRED

1. Prepare the journal entries to record the cash service fees and cash short and over for each of the five weeks.
2. Post to the cash short and over account (use Account No. 516).
3. Determine the ending balance of the cash short and over account. Does it represent an expense or revenue?

CHECK LIST
- ☐ Managing
- ☐ Planning
- ☐ Drafting
- ☐ Break
- ☐ Revising
- ☐ Managing

MANAGING YOUR WRITING

The current month's bank statement for your account arrives in the mail. In reviewing the statement, you notice a deposit listed for $400 that you did not make. It has been credited in error to your account.

Discuss whether you have an ethical or legal obligation to inform the bank of the error. What action should you take?

ETHICS

ETHICS CASE

Ben Thomas works as a teller for First National Bank. When he arrived at work on Friday, the branch manager, Frank Mills, asked him to get his cash drawer out early because the head teller, Naomi Ray, was conducting a surprise cash count for all the tellers. Surprise cash counts are usually done four or five times a year by the branch manager or the head teller and once or twice a year by internal auditors. Ben's drawer was $100 short and his reconciliation tape showed that he was in balance on Thursday night. Naomi asked Ben for an explanation, and Ben immediately took $100 out of his pocket and handed it to her. He went on to explain he needed the cash to buy prescriptions for his son and pay for groceries and intended to put the $100 back in his cash drawer on Monday, which was pay day. He also told Naomi that this was the first time he had ever "borrowed" money from his cash drawer and that he would never do it again.

1. What are the ethical considerations in this case from both Ben's and Naomi's perspectives?
2. What options does Naomi have to address this problem?
3. Assume Naomi chooses to inform the branch manager. Write a short incident report describing the findings.
4. In small groups, come up with as many ideas as possible on how to safeguard cash on hand in a bank (petty cash, teller drawer cash, and vault cash) from employee theft and mismanagement.

MASTERY PROBLEM

✓ Adjusted bank balance: $4,324.05

Turner Excavation maintains a checking account and has decided to open a petty cash fund. The following petty cash fund transactions occurred during July:

July	2	Established a petty cash fund by issuing Check No. 301 for $100.
	5	Paid $25 from the petty cash fund for postage. Voucher No. 1.
	7	Paid $30 from the petty cash fund for delivery of flowers (Miscellaneous Expense). Voucher No. 2.
	8	Paid $20 from the petty cash fund to repair a tire on the company truck. Voucher No. 3.
	12	Paid $22 from the petty cash fund for a newspaper advertisement. Voucher No. 4.
	13	Issued Check No. 303 to replenish the petty cash fund. (Total and rule the petty cash payments record. Record the balance and the amount needed to replenish the fund in the Description column of the petty cash payments record.)
	20	Paid $26 from the petty cash fund to reimburse an employee for expenses incurred to repair the company truck. Voucher No. 5.
	24	Paid $12.50 from the petty cash fund for phone calls made from a phone booth. Voucher No. 6.
	28	Paid $25 from the petty cash fund as a contribution to the YMCA. Voucher No. 7.
	31	Issued Check No. 308 to replenish the petty cash fund. (Total and rule the petty cash payments record. Record the balance and the amount needed to replenish the fund in the Description column of the petty cash payments record.)

The following additional transactions occurred during July:

July	5	Issued Check No. 302 to pay office rent, $650.
	15	Issued Check No. 304 for office equipment, $525.
	17	Issued Check No. 305 for the purchase of supplies, $133.
	18	Issued Check No. 306 to pay attorney fees, $1,000.
	30	Issued Check No. 307 to pay newspaper for an advertisement, $200.20.

REQUIRED

1. Record the petty cash transactions in a petty cash payments record.
2. Make all required general journal entries for the cash transactions. (*Note*: The petty cash fund was established and replenished twice during July.)
3. The bank statement on page 265 was received in the mail. Deposits were made on July 6 for $3,500 and on July 29 for $2,350. The book balance on July 31 is $4,331.55. Notice the discrepancy in Check No. 302 that cleared the bank for $655. This check was written on July 5 for rent expense, but was incorrectly entered on the check stub and in the journal as $650. Prepare a bank reconciliation and make any necessary journal entries as of July 31.

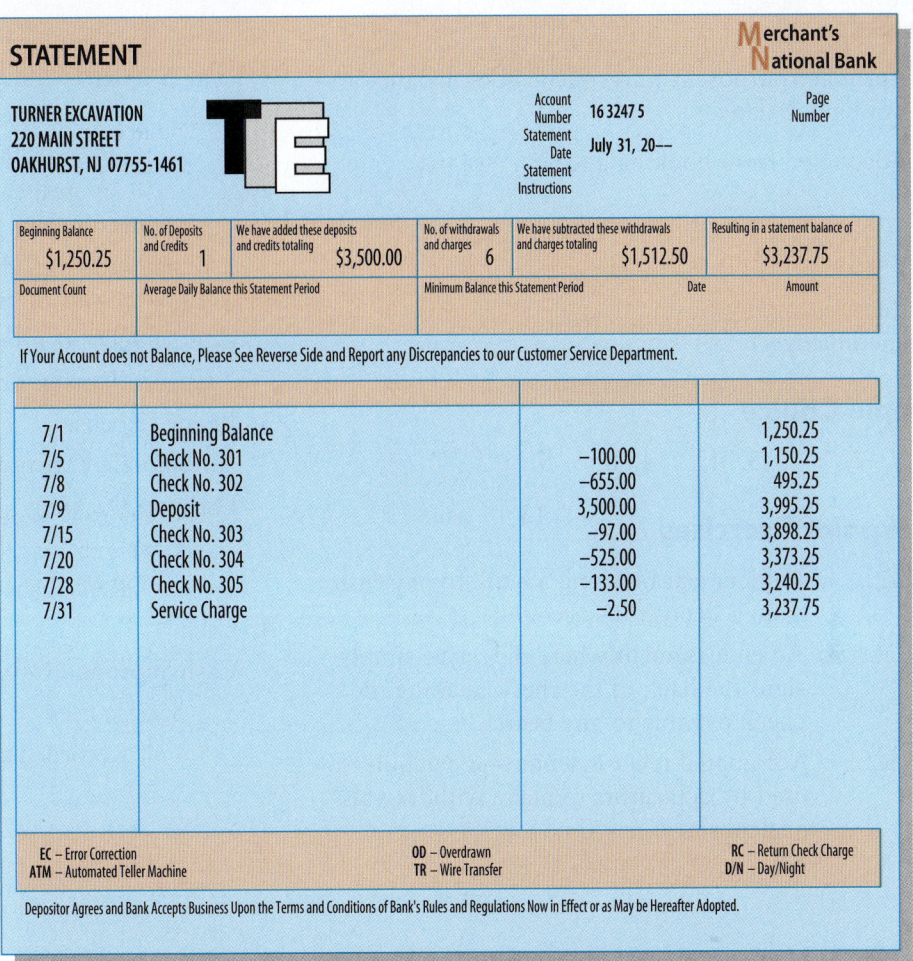

STATEMENT — Merchant's National Bank

TURNER EXCAVATION
220 MAIN STREET
OAKHURST, NJ 07755-1461

Account Number: 16 3247 5
Statement Date: July 31, 20--
Statement Instructions
Page Number

Beginning Balance	No. of Deposits and Credits	We have added these deposits and credits totaling	No. of withdrawals and charges	We have subtracted these withdrawals and charges totaling	Resulting in a statement balance of
$1,250.25	1	$3,500.00	6	$1,512.50	$3,237.75
Document Count	Average Daily Balance this Statement Period		Minimum Balance this Statement Period	Date	Amount

If Your Account does not Balance, Please See Reverse Side and Report any Discrepancies to our Customer Service Department.

7/1	Beginning Balance		1,250.25
7/5	Check No. 301	−100.00	1,150.25
7/8	Check No. 302	−655.00	495.25
7/9	Deposit	3,500.00	3,995.25
7/15	Check No. 303	−97.00	3,898.25
7/20	Check No. 304	−525.00	3,373.25
7/28	Check No. 305	−133.00	3,240.25
7/31	Service Charge	−2.50	3,237.75

EC – Error Correction
ATM – Automated Teller Machine
OD – Overdrawn
TR – Wire Transfer
RC – Return Check Charge
D/N – Day/Night

Depositor Agrees and Bank Accepts Business Upon the Terms and Conditions of Bank's Rules and Regulations Now in Effect or as May be Hereafter Adopted.

CHALLENGE PROBLEM

This problem challenges you to apply your cumulative accounting knowledge to move a step beyond the material in the chapter.

✓ 2. Item 4: Dr. Depositor Accounts, $350

Susan Panera is preparing the June 30 bank reconciliation for Panera Bakery. She discovers the following items that explain the difference between the cash balance on her books and the balance as reported by Lawrence Bank:

1. An ATM withdrawal of $200 for personal use was not recorded by Susan.
2. A deposit of $850 was recorded by Susan but has not been received by Lawrence Bank as of June 30.
3. A check written in payment on account to Jayhawk Supply for $340 was recorded by Susan as $430 and by Lawrence Bank as $530.
4. An ATM deposit of $350 was recorded twice by Lawrence Bank.
5. An electronic funds transfer of $260 to Sunflower Mills as a payment on account was not recorded by Susan.
6. Checks No. 103 for $235 and No. 110 for $127 had not cleared Lawrence Bank as of June 30.

REQUIRED

1. Prepare the journal entries required to correct Panera Bakery's books as of June 30.
2. Prepare the journal entries required to correct Lawrence Bank's books as of June 30.

ANSWERS TO SELF-STUDY TEST QUESTIONS

True/False

1. F (primary purpose is to reconcile book balance with bank balance)
2. F (deducted from book balance)
3. T
4. F (deducted from book balance)
5. F (entries are not posted from petty cash record to general ledger)

Multiple Choice

1. c 2. b 3. d 4. b 5. a

Checkpoint Exercises

1. __3__ a. A document ordering a bank to pay cash from a depositor's account.
   __5__ b. An endorsement where the payee simply signs the back of the check, making the check payable to any bearer.
   __2__ c. Automated teller machine—a machine used by depositors to make withdrawals or deposits at any time.
   __4__ d. A statement of account issued by a bank to each depositor once a month.
   __1__ e. A form showing a detailed listing of items being deposited.
2. __c__ 1. Interest earned on checking account balance
   __d__ 2. Error in checkbook whereby a check for $82 was entered in the checkbook as $28
   __a__ 3. Deposit in transit
   __b__ 4. Outstanding checks
3.

Phone Expense	23.50	
Automobile Expense	49.10	
H. Appy, Drawing	50.00	
Cash		122.60
Replenished petty cash fund		

4.

Cash	870.00	
Cash Short and Over	6.00	
Service Fees		876.00
Recorded service fees and cash shortage		

CHAPTER 7 APPENDIX

Internal Controls

LEARNING OBJECTIVES

Careful study of this appendix should enable you to:

LO1 **Explain the importance of internal control.**

LO2 **Define internal control and describe its key components.**

LO3 **Describe selected internal controls over cash receipts.**

LO4 **Describe selected internal controls over cash payments and the use of a voucher system.**

In Chapter 7, we introduced the concept of internal control and provided some examples of good internal control over cash transactions. Here, we examine internal control in greater depth.

We do the following:

1. Explain why internal control has achieved greater importance today.
2. Identify the key components of internal control.
3. Give examples of internal control over cash receipts.
4. Describe internal control of cash payments using a voucher system.

LO1 Importance of Internal Control

Explain the importance of internal control.

To be successful, management must have adequate control of the operations of the business. For example, the records of business activities must be reliable and timely, so that management has the information it needs to take necessary actions. The assets of the business must be known and protected. Employees must follow the rules and procedures defined by management. Accurate information must be available to report to owners, lenders, and regulatory bodies, such as the IRS. Without good internal control, it simply would not be possible to effectively and efficiently run a business.

The importance of strong internal control for managing a business has been known for years. But in 2002, the importance of internal control was raised to a whole new level. In July 2002, Congress passed the Sarbanes-Oxley Act (SOX). SOX applies to all **publicly held companies**—companies whose stock is traded on the major stock exchanges. Section 404 (a) of SOX requires these companies to report annually on the effectiveness of internal control over financial reporting. For decades, these corporations have been required to provide audited financial statements. Now, they must also report on the quality of their internal control system. Figure 7A-1 provides an example of management's Section 404 (a) report for Microsoft.

One of the interesting effects of SOX is how widely its rules are being felt. Officially, SOX applies to all publicly held companies and their external auditors. But SOX is causing many other companies and managements to look closely at the quality of their internal controls. The logic is simple: if internal controls are so important for publicly held companies, they probably deserve attention in other companies as well. Clearly, internal controls are a hot topic today.

FIGURE 7A-1 Section 404 Internal Control Report

REPORT OF MANAGEMENT ON INTERNAL CONTROL OVER FINANCIAL REPORTING

Our management [of Microsoft] is responsible for establishing and maintaining adequate internal control over financial reporting for the company. Internal control over financial reporting is a process to provide reasonable assurance regarding the reliability of our financial reporting for external purposes in accordance with accounting principles generally accepted in the United States of America. Internal control over financial reporting includes maintaining records that in reasonable detail accurately and fairly reflect our transactions; providing reasonable assurance that transactions are recorded as necessary for preparation of our financial statements; providing reasonable assurance that receipts and expenditures of company assets are made in accordance with management authorization; and providing reasonable assurance that unauthorized acquisition, use, or disposition of company assets that could have a material effect on our financial statements would be prevented or detected on a timely basis. Because of its inherent limitations, internal control over financial reporting is not intended to provide absolute assurance that a misstatement of our financial statements would be prevented or detected.

Management conducted an evaluation of the effectiveness of our internal control over financial reporting based on the framework in Internal Control—Integrated Framework issued by the Committee of Sponsoring Organizations (2013) of the Treadway Commission. Based on this evaluation, management concluded that the company's internal control over financial reporting was effective as of June 30, 2016. There were no changes in our internal control over financial reporting during the quarter ended June 30, 2016 that have materially affected, or are reasonably likely to materially affect, our internal control over financial reporting. Deloitte & Touche LLP has audited our internal control over financial reporting as of June 30, 2016; their report follows.

LO2

Key Components of Internal Control

Define internal control and describe its key components.

Internal control is really important. So what exactly do we mean by internal control? Both the concept and attempts to define it have existed for many years. For our purposes, the following is a good definition:

> Internal control is a system developed by a company to provide reasonable assurance of achieving (1) effective and efficient operations, (2) reliable financial reporting, and (3) compliance with laws and regulations.

Several internal control frameworks have been developed that are consistent with this definition. The most widely accepted framework in the United States contains the following five components:

- Control environment
- Risk assessment
- Control activities
- Information and communication system
- Monitoring processes

Control Environment

The control environment is the policies, procedures, and attitudes of the top management and owners of the business. It is often referred to as the "tone at the top." It includes the organization structure, management's philosophy and operating style, integrity and ethical values, and commitment to competent, trustworthy employees. The control environment provides the foundation for all other components of internal control.

Risk Assessment

Risk assessment is management's process for identifying, analyzing, and responding to its business risks. All businesses face various and changing risks from both external and internal sources. These risks include error and fraud. As part of the risk assessment component of internal control, management must deal with these risks. For example, if a business sells products like computers that are affected by rapid technology changes, its marketing and inventory plans should carefully guard against obsolete inventory. If a business has high employee turnover, its employee screening and training programs should be very thorough and up to date. If a business is growing rapidly, it should regularly review its internal controls to see that they fit the size and activities of the business.

Control Activities

Control activities are the policies and procedures established to help management meet its control objectives. Control activities can be classified in various ways. Four types of control activities are particularly important for our purposes.

1. Segregation of duties
2. Authorization procedures and related responsibilities
3. Adequate documents and records
4. Protection of assets and records

Segregation of duties means that:

1. Different employees should be responsible for different parts of a transaction and
2. Employees who account for transactions should not also have custody of the assets.

For example, one employee should be responsible for ordering goods and another employee should be responsible for issuing the check to pay for them. One employee should be responsible for recording the purchase of goods and another employee should be responsible for receiving and placing the goods in inventory. This segregation of duties provides a built-in check by one employee on another. One employee cannot obtain goods for personal use without being caught by another employee.

In computerized systems, programs and data files often combine the duties of several employees. For example, programs can order goods automatically at a preset level from approved vendors, and payments then can be made based on an electronic billing. This requires a different segregation of duties. Three functions must be segregated: (1) system design and programming, (2) system operations, and (3) data file and program storage.

Authorization procedures and related responsibilities means that every business activity should be properly authorized. In addition, it should be possible to identify who is responsible for every activity that has occurred. For example, to acquire new equipment, a signed document should authorize the purchase. After the purchase is made, this signed document shows who is responsible for the action.

In computerized systems, as noted above, the combination of processing programs and data files can initiate transactions. Therefore, special authorization procedures are needed. Once a program is operating, no changes should be allowed in that program without authorization. Similarly, no changes should be allowed in a data file without authorization. It is essential to protect both the programs and data files from unauthorized access.

Adequate documents and records means that accounting documents and records should be used so that all business transactions are recorded. For example, every purchase that occurs should be supported by a document. These documents should be:

- prenumbered,
- used in sequence, and
- subsequently accounted for.

In this way, the business can be sure that it has made a record of each transaction.

One of the benefits of a computerized system is that the programs can automatically account for the sequence of transactions or documents. Numbers and sequences of sales, purchases, employees for payroll, and payments can be accounted for. If there is any break in the proper numbering sequence, an error message is created.

A computerized system also requires additional documentation. For example, complete documentation is needed of all code, development, and testing of programs before they are put in operation.

Protection of assets and records means that assets and records should be physically and logically protected. For assets, this generally means physical protection. Some examples are vaults for cash, securities, and precious gems, or secure storage rooms for inventory. For records, this can mean storing journals, ledgers, and key documents in physically secure locations. In computerized systems, both physical and logical protection are needed. For example, an online retailer needs assurance that transactions are valid and accurate, customer credit card information is protected, and its website is secure. Passwords are a common form of logical protection of data files and processing programs.

Information and Communication System

The information and communication system is the set of procedures, processes, and records used to initiate, process, record, and report the business's transactions. In addition, the system accounts for the related assets and liabilities. Typically, the system has several subcomponents for different business processes, such as:

- sales,
- cash receipts,
- purchases, and
- cash payments.

The journals and ledgers we learned to use in the previous chapters would be part of an information and communication system.

A computerized system provides great opportunities in this area of internal control. Because of the power of the computer, data files can be compared across departments or other business units to identify problem areas. Data can be screened to ensure their quality, and input from customers and suppliers can be gathered and analyzed.

Monitoring Processes

Monitoring processes are the methods used by management to determine that the controls are operating properly, and that the controls are modified in response to changes in assessed risks. Figure 7A-2 provides some examples of such processes. Monitoring can be part of the ongoing activities of the business or a separate process. One ongoing activity could be comparisons of financial reports with expectations. If financial reports differ from expectations, it could indicate internal control failures. Follow-up on customer complaints regarding account balances might also uncover internal control weaknesses. The most common form of separate process is the work of the internal audit department. Internal auditors evaluate the design of the internal control system in light of the business risks. They also perform specific tests to determine whether internal controls are operating properly. If a business is not large enough to have an internal audit department, these responsibilities must be assumed by top management.

Computers also can help with the monitoring process. Large volumes of data can be analyzed at very low cost. For example, an entire data file of payment transactions can be examined to identify large amounts, duplicates, and unknown suppliers.

FIGURE 7A-2 Sample Monitoring Processes

- Comparison of results with expectations
- Review of customer correspondence
- Internal audit

LO3 Internal Controls Over Cash Receipts

Describe selected internal controls over cash receipts.

The main purposes of internal controls over cash receipts are to make sure that

- all cash received by the business is recorded in the accounts, and
- the cash is promptly deposited in the business bank account.

The exact form of some of these controls will vary depending on whether the cash is received directly from customers for sales, or is received by mail as a collection on account. Some of the key internal controls are shown in Figure 7A-3 and described in the following paragraphs.

FIGURE 7A-3 Sample Controls over Cash Receipts

Do these three amounts agree?

Cash receipts per register record	=	Cash receipts per register drawer	=	Cash receipts per bank deposit

Do these two amounts agree?

Cash receipts per remittance list	=	Cash receipts per bank deposit

Do transactions and balances per books and bank agree?

Monthly bank reconciliation

If cash is received directly from customers, the use of a cash register or terminal with a printed receipt is essential. Only authorized employees should be allowed to operate the register. The register should generate an internal record of all transactions entered, including a total of cash receipts. This amount should be reconciled with the actual cash (and checks) in the register drawer. Any differences greater than a small amount to allow for errors in making change should be investigated. All cash receipts should be deposited daily in the business bank account. The total deposited and the total cash receipts according to the register should be reconciled and any differences investigated.

If cash is received as collections on account, the mail room should be supervised and employees who handle the cash (checks) should have no access to the accounting records. One reason for separating the handling of cash from the accounting records is to prevent lapping. **Lapping** means stealing cash received on account from one customer and hiding the theft by applying the cash received on account from another customer to the first customer's account. For example, assume customer A sends a check for $500 as a payment on account and that the employee keeps the $500 for him/herself. This causes customer A's account to be in error by $500. So when customer B makes a $500 payment on account, the employee applies this cash receipt to customer A's account. The dishonest employee must continue lapping the accounts receivable in this manner to continue to conceal the theft.

When the mail is opened, a remittance list should be prepared showing all amounts received and from whom they are received. Checks should be immediately endorsed "For deposit" to the business bank account.

The remittance list is sent to the accounting department for use in recording the collections in the journal and ledgers. The cash is sent to the cash receipts department to deposit in the business bank account. The total of the remittance list and the amount of the bank deposit should be independently verified and any differences investigated.

An additional internal control common to both systems described above is the independent monthly preparation of a bank reconciliation. Procedures for preparing the bank reconciliation are described in Chapter 7. The cash receipts, cash payments, and beginning and ending balances per bank and per books must be reconciled. The reconciliation should be prepared by employees who have no access to cash. Any differences should be investigated.

Many businesses have multiple bank accounts and transfer cash among them. When there are multiple bank accounts, it is possible to overstate the cash balance by engaging in kiting. **Kiting** consists of recording a transfer of cash *into* one bank account in the current period, but not recording the transfer *out of* another bank account until the following period. For example, assume that a $1,000 check is written on bank account A on June 30, but not recorded as a cash payment until July 1. This check is deposited in bank account B and recorded as a cash receipt on June 30. By recording the transaction in this manner, the cash balance in both bank accounts includes the $1,000 at June 30. The total cash balance is thus overstated by $1,000 on June 30.

One of the reasons internal controls over cash are so important is that they help businesses manage their cash resources. Naturally, it is important to plan to have sufficient cash to meet current obligations. But it is also important not to allow too much cash to lie idle. Management should carefully monitor and plan for its cash needs. Strong internal controls help with this process.

LO4 Internal Controls Over Cash Payments

Describe selected internal controls over cash payments and the use of a voucher system.

The main purpose of internal controls over cash payments is to make sure cash is paid only for goods and services received by the business, consistent with its best interests. To achieve this objective, controls are needed from the beginning of the process of acquiring goods and services through the payment of cash for those goods and services. An effective way to do so is with a voucher system.

According to the 2016 ACFE Report, fraudulent disbursements are the most common form of asset misappropriation.

Voucher System

Three of the four control activities described above can be combined to control cash payments by using a **voucher system**. A voucher system is a control technique that requires every acquisition and subsequent payment to be supported by an approved voucher. A **voucher** is a document which shows that an acquisition is proper and that payment is authorized.

The Purchasing Process

Figure 7A-4 is a simplified illustration of how the purchasing portion of a voucher system operates. An authorized person or department prepares a purchase requisition to indicate the need for goods. The purchasing department reviews and approves the purchase requisition and prepares a purchase order to send to the supplier. When the goods are received, a receiving report is prepared. A copy of each of these documents is sent to the vouchers payable section in the accounting department.

When the purchase invoice arrives, it is compared with the purchase requisition, purchase order, and receiving report. If the purchase invoice is

- for the goods ordered (purchase requisition and purchase order),
- at the correct price (purchase order),
- and for the correct quantity (receiving report),

then a voucher like the one in Figure 7A-5 on page 274 is prepared. This is the first key control provided by the voucher system. If any aspect of the purchase is improper, it will be caught when the voucher is prepared.

FIGURE 7A-4 Voucher System—Purchasing Process

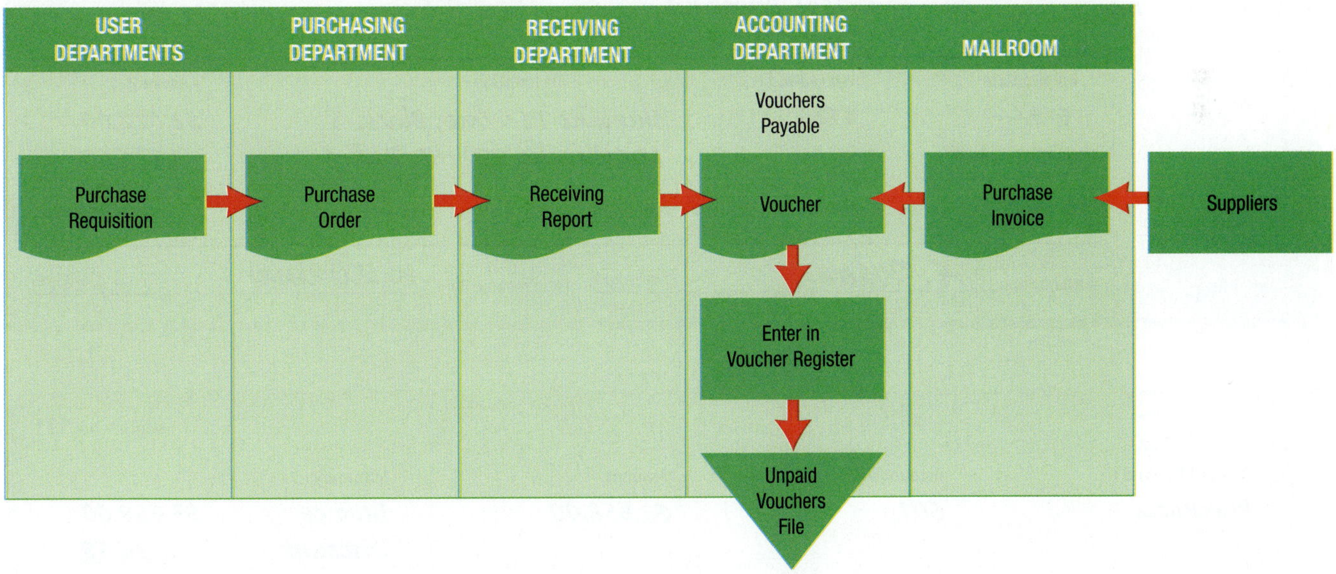

The front of the voucher usually shows the voucher number, date, supplier, and what was purchased. The back indicates the accounts to be debited and the payment date, check number, and amount.

After the voucher is prepared and approved, it is entered in a special journal called a **voucher register**. A voucher register is used to record purchases of all types of assets and services.

After the voucher is entered in the voucher register, the voucher and supporting documents (purchase requisition, purchase order, receiving report, and purchase invoice) are stapled together. This "voucher packet" is then filed in an **unpaid vouchers file**, normally by due date. Alternatively, vouchers can be filed by supplier name. Filing by due date is preferred because this helps management plan for cash needs. It also helps ensure that vouchers are paid on the due date and cash discounts are taken.

The completed voucher provides the basis for paying the supplier's invoice on the due date. This is the second key control provided by the voucher system. No payment may be made without an approved voucher.

Notice how three of the four control activities that are part of an internal control system can be seen in this system.

- *Duties are segregated* because different employees order, receive, and record the purchases.
- *Authorization* is required to order the goods and to prepare the voucher.
- The *documents and records* include purchase requisitions, purchase orders, receiving reports, and vouchers that are prenumbered and accounted for. This means that every recorded purchase is supported by the following five documents:

1. Voucher
2. Purchase invoice

> **LEARNING KEY**
> The voucher system contains elements of internal control such as segregation of duties, authorization to order the goods and prepare the voucher, and accounting procedures that require prenumbering and accounting for the supporting documents.

FIGURE 7A-5 Voucher

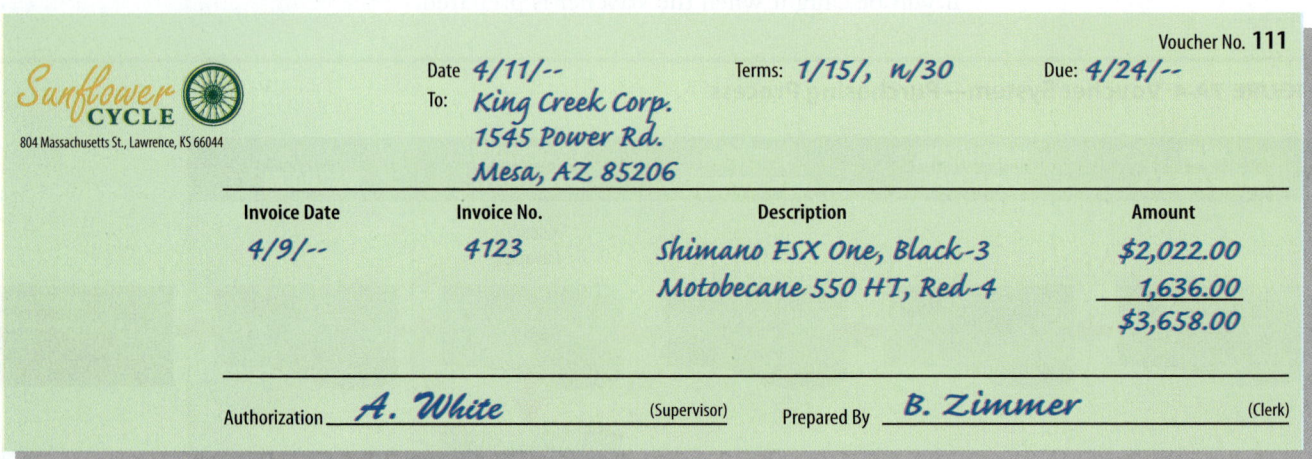

Sunflower CYCLE
804 Massachusetts St., Lawrence, KS 66044

Voucher No. **111**

Date 4/11/-- Terms: 1/15/, n/30 Due: 4/24/--

To: King Creek Corp.
1545 Power Rd.
Mesa, AZ 85206

Invoice Date	Invoice No.	Description	Amount
4/9/--	4123	Shimano FSX One, Black-3	$2,022.00
		Motobecane 550 HT, Red-4	1,636.00
			$3,658.00

Authorization A. White (Supervisor) Prepared By B. Zimmer (Clerk)

Voucher No. **111**

Account Debited	Account No.	Amount	Summary	
Purchases	501	$3,658.00	Invoice	$3,658.00
			Discount	36.58
			Net	$3,621.42

Payment Date 4/24/-- Check No. 331 Amount $3,621.42

Approved Distribution J. G. Payment

Back

3. Receiving report
4. Purchase order
5. Purchase requisition

This provides management with strong assurance that purchasing activities are properly controlled.

The Payment Process

Figure 7A-6 is a simplified illustration of the payment process when a voucher system is used. On the due date, the voucher is pulled from the unpaid vouchers file. The voucher is given to the person responsible for preparing and signing checks (the cashier in this illustration). The cashier reviews each voucher and supporting documents to see that the expenditure is proper. The cashier then prepares and signs the check and sends it to the supplier. It is important for internal control that no check be prepared without a supporting voucher and that the check be mailed as soon as it is signed.

Ordinary checks may be used to make payments, but under the voucher system, voucher checks often are used. A **voucher check** is a check with space for entering data about the voucher being paid. Figure 7A-7 on page 276 shows a voucher check used to pay Voucher No. 111 (Figure 7A-5).

The voucher check has two parts:

1. The check itself, which is similar to an ordinary check
2. An attached statement, which indicates the invoice being paid and any deductions

In addition, the voucher check stub identifies the voucher number being paid.

LEARNING KEY

For good internal control of cash payments, it is important for the check to be mailed as soon as it is signed.

FIGURE 7A-6 Voucher System—Payment Process

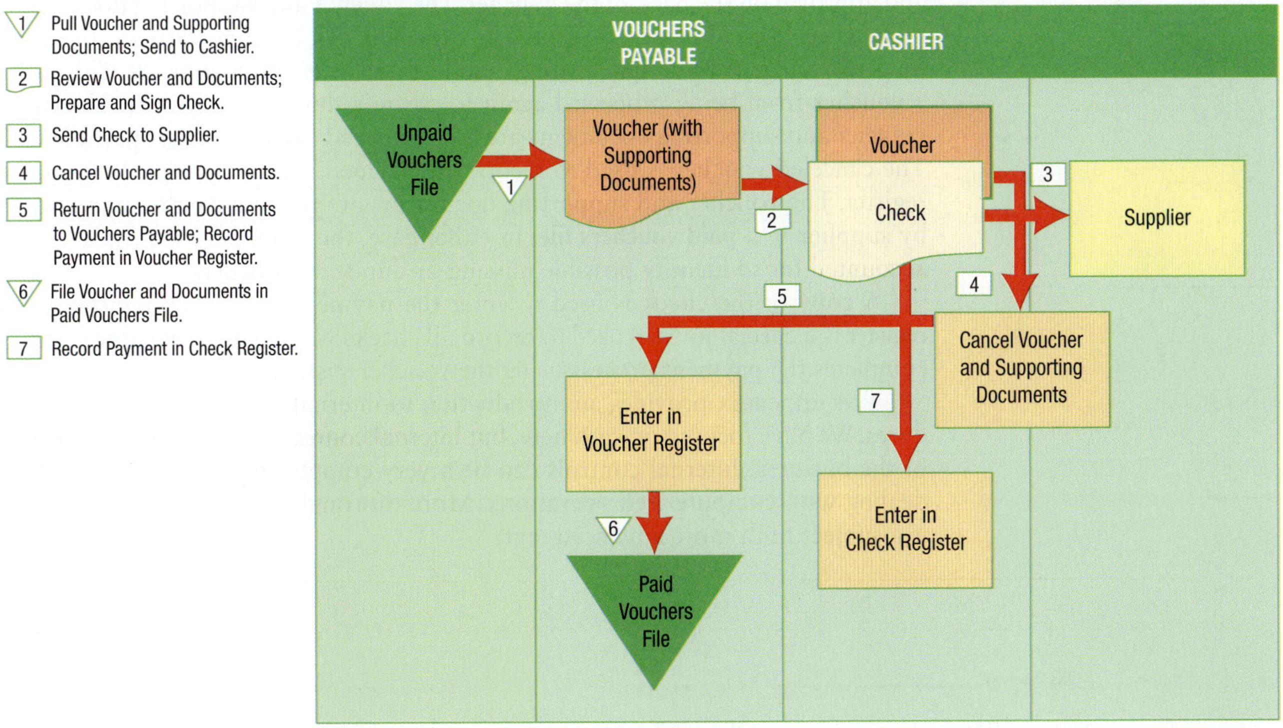
1 Pull Voucher and Supporting Documents; Send to Cashier.
2 Review Voucher and Documents; Prepare and Sign Check.
3 Send Check to Supplier.
4 Cancel Voucher and Documents.
5 Return Voucher and Documents to Vouchers Payable; Record Payment in Voucher Register.
6 File Voucher and Documents in Paid Vouchers File.
7 Record Payment in Check Register.
VOUCHERS PAYABLE
CASHIER
Unpaid Vouchers File
Voucher (with Supporting Documents)
Voucher
Check
Supplier
Cancel Voucher and Supporting Documents
Enter in Voucher Register
Enter in Check Register
Paid Vouchers File

FIGURE 7A-7 Voucher Check

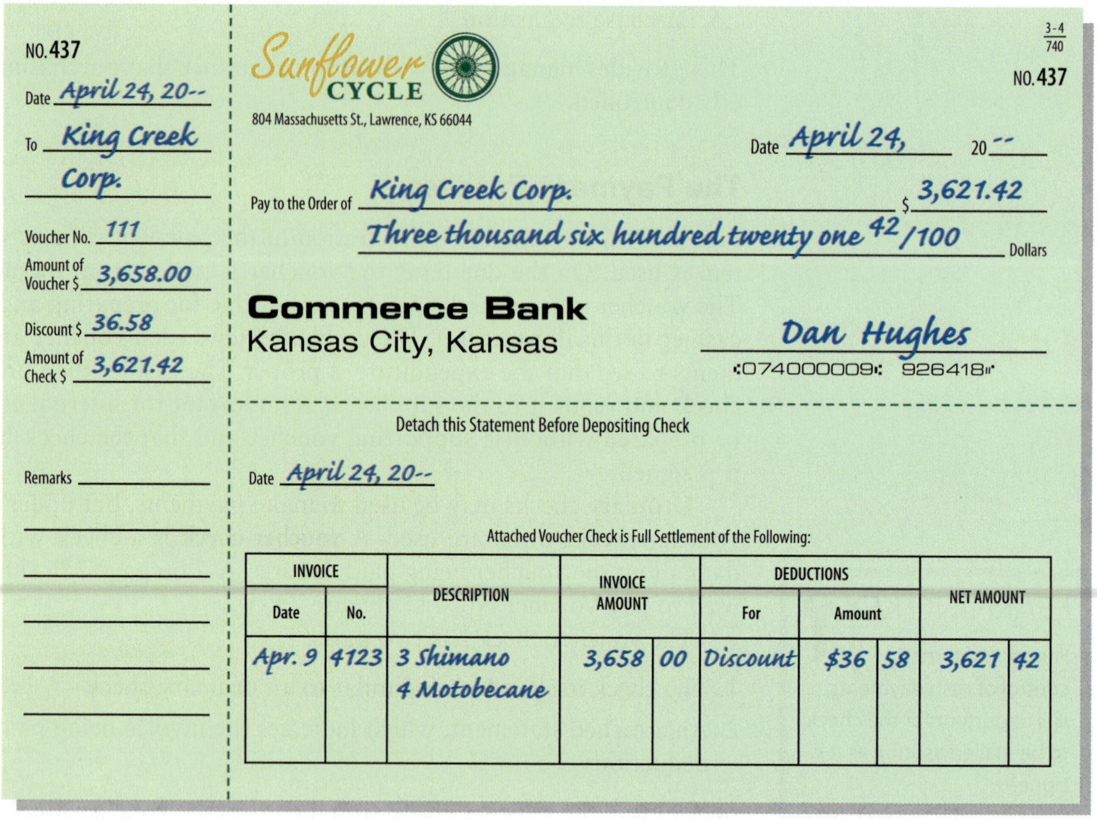

NO. 437
Date April 24, 20--
To King Creek Corp.
Voucher No. 111
Amount of Voucher $ 3,658.00
Discount $ 36.58
Amount of Check $ 3,621.42
Remarks

Sunflower CYCLE
804 Massachusetts St., Lawrence, KS 66044

3-4/740
NO. 437

Date April 24, 20--

Pay to the Order of King Creek Corp. $ 3,621.42
Three thousand six hundred twenty one 42/100 Dollars

Commerce Bank
Kansas City, Kansas

Dan Hughes

⑆074000009⑆ 926418⑈

Detach this Statement Before Depositing Check

Date April 24, 20--

Attached Voucher Check is Full Settlement of the Following:

INVOICE		DESCRIPTION	INVOICE AMOUNT		DEDUCTIONS			NET AMOUNT	
Date	No.				For	Amount			
Apr. 9	4123	3 Shimano 4 Motobecane	3,658	00	Discount	$36	58	3,621	42

After the voucher has been paid, the cashier completes the "Payment" information and approval on the back of the voucher. The voucher and supporting documents are then canceled to indicate payment. The canceling can be done with a rubber stamp, by perforating, or by simply writing "paid" on all relevant documents. This prevents a voucher from being processed again to create a duplicate payment. The canceled voucher and supporting documents are then returned to the vouchers payable section. The canceled voucher is used to record the payment of the voucher in the voucher register. The voucher and supporting documents are then filed either numerically or by supplier in a **paid vouchers file**. In either case, the numerical sequence should be accounted for to identify possible missing or duplicate vouchers.

A copy of the check is used to enter the payment in a check register. A **check register** is a special journal used to record all checks written in a voucher system. This completes the payment process using the voucher system.

This appendix provides an introduction to internal control concepts and procedures. We have focused on cash here, but internal controls are important in every area of the business. Internal controls can be a very complicated subject, particularly in dealing with computerized operations. More thorough analysis of internal controls is a subject for a more advanced text.

LEARNING OBJECTIVES	Key Points to Remember
LO1 **Explain the importance of internal control.**	Internal controls help assure management that it has reliable records to run the business and prepare needed reports. In addition, SOX requires publicly held companies to report annually on the quality of their internal control system.
LO2 **Define internal control and describe its key components.**	Internal control is a system developed by a company to provide reasonable assurance of achieving (1) effective and efficient operations, (2) reliable financial reporting, and (3) compliance with laws and regulations. The key components are as follows: • Control environment • Risk assessment • Control activities • Information and communication system • Monitoring processes
LO3 **Describe selected internal controls over cash receipts.**	If cash is received directly from customers, a cash register should be used. The record of cash receipts per the register should be reconciled with the actual cash in the drawer. If cash is received by mail, a remittance list should be prepared and sent to accounting. The checks should be endorsed immediately "For deposit" and sent to the cash receipts department for deposit in the bank. The remittance list and bank deposit should be independently reconciled.
LO4 **Describe selected internal controls over cash payments and the use of a voucher system.**	Every acquisition and subsequent payment should be supported by an approved voucher. The voucher should be supported by a purchase requisition, purchase order, receiving report, and purchase invoice. On the due date, checks are written only for approved vouchers, and vouchers and supporting documents are canceled to prevent reuse.

KEY TERMS

check register (276) A special journal used to record all checks written in a voucher system.

kiting (272) Recording a transfer of cash *into* one bank account in the current period, but not recording the transfer *out of* another bank account until the following period.

lapping (272) Stealing cash received on account from one customer and hiding the theft by applying the cash received on account from another customer to the first customer's account.

paid vouchers file (276) A file in which paid vouchers and supporting documents are placed, organized either numerically or by supplier.

publicly held companies (267) Companies whose stock is traded on the major stock exchanges.

unpaid vouchers file (274) A file in which unpaid voucher packets are placed, normally organized by due date.

voucher (273) A document that shows that an acquisition is proper and that payment is authorized.

voucher check (275) A check with space for entering data about the voucher being paid.

voucher register (273) A special journal used to record purchases of all types of assets and services.

voucher system (273) A control technique that requires that every acquisition and subsequent payment be supported by an approved voucher.

REVIEW QUESTIONS

LO1 1. What does Section 404 of the Sarbanes-Oxley Act require?

LO2 2. What is the meaning of internal control?

LO2 3. What are the five components of internal control?

LO2 4. What are the four types of control activities?

LO3 5. What are the main purposes of internal controls over cash receipts?

LO4 6. What is the main purpose of internal controls over cash payments?

LO4 7. What is a voucher system?

LO4 8. In a voucher system, each recorded purchase is supported by what five documents?

LO4 9. What is the purpose of canceling the voucher and supporting documents when a payment is made?

SERIES A EXERCISES

E 7Apx-1A (LO2)

INTERNAL CONTROL COMPONENTS The most widely accepted internal control framework in the United States contains the following five components. Describe each of them.

1. Control environment
2. Risk assessment
3. Control activities
4. Information and communication system
5. Monitoring processes

E 7Apx-2A (LO2)

INTERNAL CONTROL PROCEDURES AND PROCESSES In the left column below, five different internal control procedures and processes are described. In the right column, the five components of internal control are listed. Match the procedures and processes with the components by placing the letter of the appropriate component on the blank provided.

1. _____ A company publishes and uses a code of ethical conduct.
2. _____ The accounting system automatically generates monthly sales reports for each product line.
3. _____ A company has established an internal audit department.
4. _____ All purchases above $5,000 must be approved in writing by the head of the purchasing department.
5. _____ A company invests heavily in employee training programs because of the technical nature of its products.

a. Control environment
b. Risk assessment
c. Control activities
d. Information and communication system
e. Monitoring processes

E 7Apx-3A (LO4)

PURCHASING PROCESS USING A VOUCHER SYSTEM In the following flowchart, identify the documents, records, and procedures that illustrate the purchasing process in a voucher system.

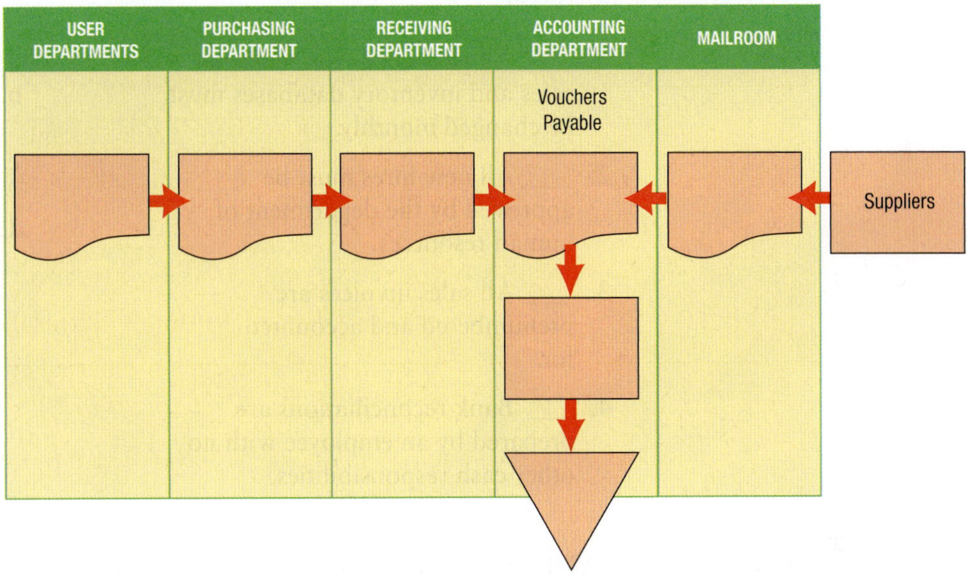

SERIES A PROBLEM

P 7Apx-4A (LO2/3/4)

USING INTERNAL CONTROLS TO PREVENT ERRORS The following misstatements occurred in the records of ICW Company. For each misstatement, suggest a control to prevent it from happening.

1. A bill from a supplier was paid even though the shipment was not received.
2. A supplier's bill was paid twice for the same purchase.
3. A plant employee increased his pay rate by entering the computer system using a plant terminal and altering the payroll records.
4. The cash receipts clerk kept a portion of the regular bank deposits for personal use and concealed the theft by manipulating the monthly bank reconciliation she prepared.

SERIES B EXERCISES

E 7Apx-1B (LO2)

INTERNAL CONTROL COMPONENTS Four types of internal control activities are listed below. Describe each of them.

1. Segregation of duties
2. Authorization procedures and related responsibilities
3. Adequate documents and records
4. Protection of assets and records

E 7Apx-2B (LO2) INTERNAL CONTROL PROCEDURES AND PROCESSES In the left column below, four different internal control procedures are described. In the right column, the four basic types of internal control activities are listed. Match the procedures with the activities by placing the letter of the appropriate activity on the blank provided.

1. ____ All passwords for access to sales and inventory databases must be changed monthly.
2. ____ All new hires must be approved by the department of human resources.
3. ____ All sales invoices are prenumbered and accounted for.
4. ____ Bank reconciliations are prepared by an employee with no other cash responsibilities.

a. Segregation of duties
b. Authorization procedures and related responsibilities
c. Adequate documents and records
d. Protection of assets and records

E 7Apx-3B (LO4) PAYMENT PROCESS USING A VOUCHER SYSTEM In the following flowchart, identify the documents, records, and procedures that illustrate the payment process using a voucher system.

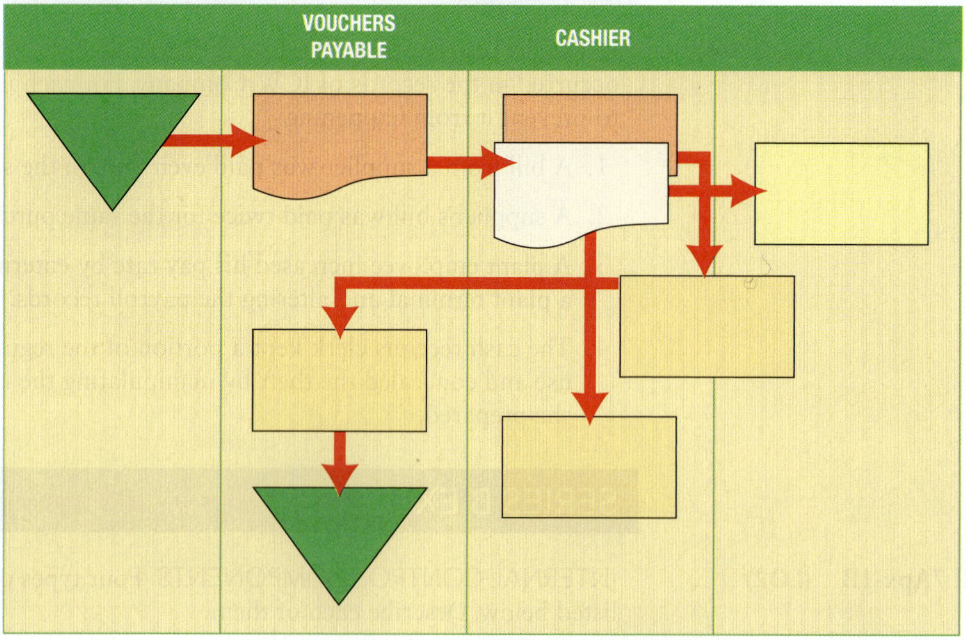

SERIES B PROBLEM

P 7Apx-4B **(LO2/3/4)**

USING INTERNAL CONTROLS TO PREVENT ERRORS The following misstatements occurred in the records of MW Company. For each misstatement, suggest a control to prevent it from happening.

1. A bill from a supplier was paid for goods that had not been ordered.
2. A supplier's bill for 50 boxes of materials was paid even though only 40 boxes were received.
3. Expensive product components were stolen by an employee from a loading dock area after hours.
4. No bill was sent to a customer for a shipment because the shipping document was lost after the shipment was made.

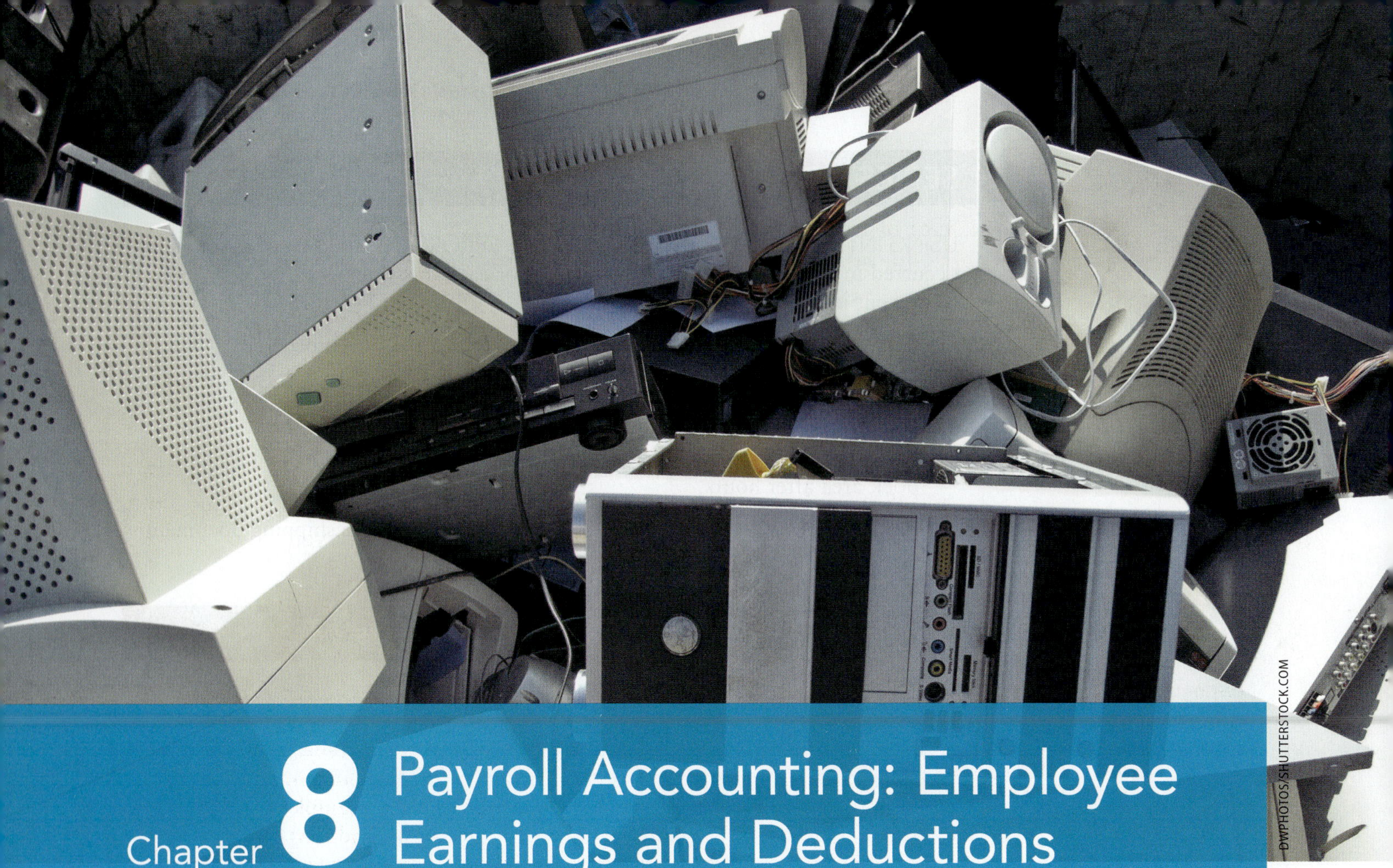
DWPHOTOS/SHUTTERSTOCK.COM

Chapter 8 Payroll Accounting: Employee Earnings and Deductions

LEARNING OBJECTIVES

Careful study of this chapter should enable you to:

LO1 Distinguish between employees and independent contractors.

LO2 Calculate employee earnings and deductions.

LO3 Describe and prepare payroll records.

LO4 Account for employee earnings and deductions.

LO5 Describe various payroll record-keeping methods.

When a company upgrades its computers and needs to dump its old ones, it might be time to call Intechra Group. Intechra Group provides computer hardware, software, and database disposal and recycling services nationwide. Founded in 1987, the company grew rapidly in response to environmental and privacy concerns about the use of IT assets. In 2010, Intechra was acquired by Arrow Electronics and now functions as a subsidiary of Arrow. Intechra is one of the largest electronics life-cycle management companies in the United States and currently processes more than ten million pounds of electronics annually. With more than 10,000 employees, it offers both on-site services and secure transport of assets to its locations. Consistent with environmental concerns, the entire recycling operation is performed under a zero-landfill policy for e-waste.

A company such as Intechra requires a variety of employees—from highly technical to basic materials handling staff—with very different rates of pay. For legal and operating efficiency reasons, a company must accurately track and control its payroll costs. It needs to know not only what to pay its people, but also what taxes to withhold from their wages. In this chapter, you will learn how to identify and account for payroll expenses for multiple employees.

Chapters 8 and 9 provide a basic introduction to payroll accounting. To assume responsibility for this area in a business, a full course in payroll accounting should be taken.

The only contact most of us have with payroll is receiving a paycheck. Few of us have seen the large amount of record keeping needed to produce that paycheck.

Employers maintain complete payroll accounting records for two reasons. First, payroll costs are major expenditures for most companies. Payroll accounting records provide data useful in analyzing and controlling these expenditures. Second, federal, state, and local laws require employers to keep payroll records. Companies must accumulate payroll data both for the business as a whole and for each employee.

There are two major types of payroll taxes: those paid by the employee and those paid by the employer. In this chapter, we discuss employee taxes. In Chapter 9, we address payroll taxes paid by the employer.

LO1

Employees and Independent Contractors

Distinguish between employees and independent contractors.

Not every person who performs services for a business is considered an employee. An **employee** works under the control and direction of an employer. Examples include secretaries, maintenance workers, salesclerks, and plant supervisors. In contrast, an **independent contractor** performs a service for a fee and does not work under the control and direction of the company paying for the service. Examples of independent contractors include public accountants, real estate agents, and lawyers.

The distinction between an employee and an independent contractor is important for payroll purposes. Government laws and regulations regarding payroll are much more complex for employees than for independent contractors. Employers must deduct certain taxes, maintain payroll records, and file numerous reports for all employees. Only one form (Form 1099) must be filed for independent contractors. The payroll accounting procedures described in this chapter apply only to employer/employee relationships.

LO2

Employee Earnings and Deductions

Calculate employee earnings and deductions.

Three steps are required to determine how much to pay an employee for a pay period:

1. Calculate total earnings.
2. Determine the amounts of deductions.
3. Subtract deductions from total earnings to compute net pay.

Salaries and Wages

Compensation for managerial or administrative services usually is called **salary**. A salary normally is expressed in biweekly (every two weeks), monthly, or annual terms. Compensation for skilled or unskilled labor usually is referred to as **wages**. Wages ordinarily are expressed in terms of hours, weeks, or units produced. The terms "salaries" and "wages" often are used interchangeably in practice.

The **Fair Labor Standards Act (FLSA)**, often called the Federal Wage and Hour Law, requires employers to pay overtime at 1½ times the regular rate to any hourly employee who works over 40 hours in a week. Some companies pay a higher rate for hours worked on Saturday or Sunday, but this is not required by the FLSA. Some salaried employees are exempt from the FLSA rules and are not paid overtime.

Computing Total Earnings

Compensation usually is based on the time worked during the payroll period. Sometimes it is based on sales or units of output during the period. When compensation is based on time, a record must be kept of the time worked by each employee. Time cards (Figure 8-1) are helpful for this purpose. In large businesses with computer-based timekeeping systems, plastic cards or badges with special magnetic strips or bar codes (Figure 8-2) can be used. Employees use the cards to clock in and out at terminals with card readers. For increased security, these terminals also are available with fingerprint readers.

FIGURE 8-1 Time Card

Westly, Inc.
Time Card — Hourly Payroll

Emp. Name Kuzmik, Helen   Base Dept.: Sales
Emp. ID: 359-47-1138   Pay Per. End: 12/19/20--

Date	Time In	Time Out	Time In	Time Out	HOURS Reg	OT	DT	Total
12/13	8:00	12:30	13:00	17:30	8	1		9
12/14	8:00	12:30	13:00	17:30	8	1		9
12/15	8:00	12:30	13:00	17:30	8	1		9
12/16	8:00	12:30	13:00	17:30	8	1		9
12/17	8:00	12:30	13:00	17:30	8	1		9
12/18	10:00	15:00				5		5
12/19	13:00	17:00					4	4
TOTAL					40	10	4	54

Remarks

Approval TM
Dept. Head

To illustrate the computation of total earnings, look at the time card of Helen Kuzmik in Figure 8-1. The card shows that Kuzmik worked 54 hours for the week.

Regular hours	40 hours
Overtime	10
Double time	4
Total hours worked	54 hours

Kuzmik's regular rate of pay is $14 per hour. She is paid 1½ times the regular rate for hours in excess of 8 on Monday through Friday and any hours worked on

FIGURE 8-2 Time Cards and Clock Terminal

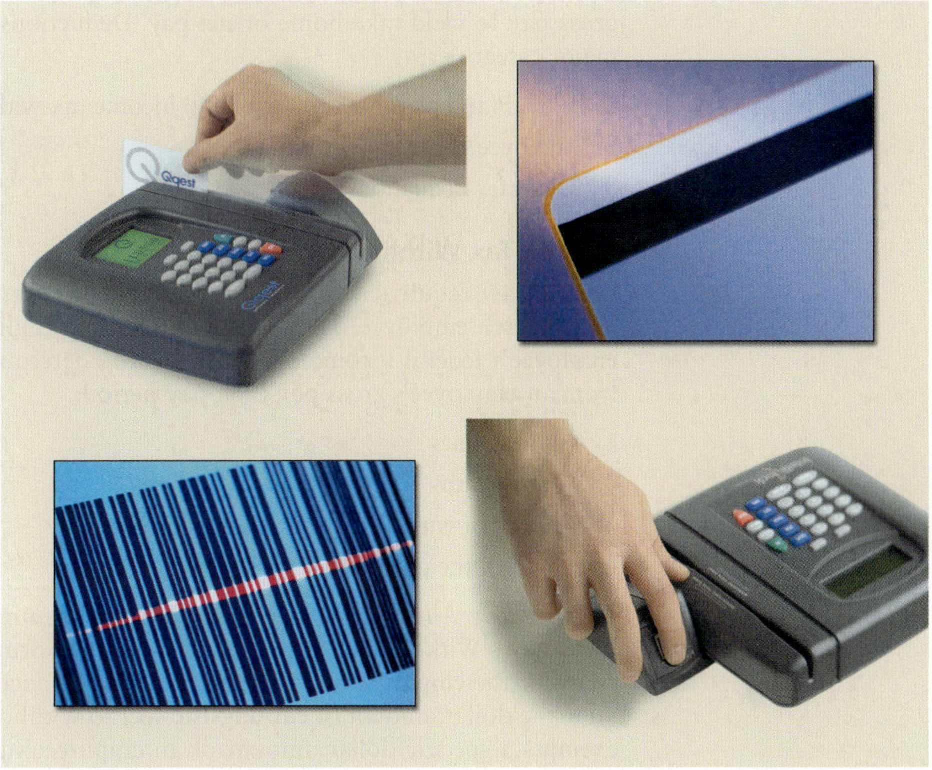

GETTY IMAGES/PHOTODISC, TIMECLOCK PHOTOS – COURTESY OF QQEST SOFTWARE; WWW.QQESTTIME.COM

Saturday, and twice the regular rate for hours on Sunday. Kuzmik's total earnings for the week ended December 19 are computed as follows:

40 hours × \$14	\$560
10 hours × \$21 (1½ × \$14 = \$21)	210
4 hours (on Sunday) × \$28 (2 × \$14 = \$28)	112
Total earnings for the week	\$882

There are 52 weeks in each year but not 4 weeks in each month. That is why monthly salaries must be annualized in order to determine the hourly rate.

Salaried employees who are not exempt from the FSLA rules may also be entitled to premium pay for overtime. If this is the case, it is necessary to compute the regular hourly rate of pay before computing the overtime rate. To illustrate, assume that Linda Swaney has a salary of \$2,600 a month plus 1½ times the regular hourly rate for hours in excess of 40 per week. Swaney's overtime rate of pay is computed as follows:

\$2,600 × 12 months	\$31,200 annual pay
\$31,200 ÷ 52 weeks	\$600.00 pay per week
\$600.00 ÷ 40 hours	\$15.00 pay per regular hour
\$15.00 × 1½	\$22.50 overtime pay per hour

If Swaney worked 50 hours during the week ended December 19, her total earnings for the week would be computed as follows:

40 hours × \$15.00	\$600.00
10 hours × \$22.50	225.00
Total earnings for the week	\$825.00

Deductions from Total Earnings

An employee's total earnings are called **gross pay**. Various deductions are made from gross pay to yield take-home or **net pay**. Deductions from gross pay fall into three major categories:

1. Federal (and possibly state and city) income tax withholding
2. Employee FICA tax withholding
3. Voluntary deductions

Income Tax Withholding

Federal law requires employers to withhold certain amounts from the total earnings of each employee. These withholdings are applied toward the payment of the employee's federal income tax. Four factors determine the amount to be withheld from an employee's gross pay each pay period:

1. Total earnings
2. Marital status
3. Number of withholding allowances claimed
4. Length of the pay period

Withholding Allowances. Each employee is required to furnish the employer an Employee's Withholding Allowance Certificate, Form W-4 (Figure 8-3). The marital status of the employee and the number of allowances claimed on Form W-4 determine the dollar amount of earnings subject to withholding. A **withholding allowance** exempts a specific dollar amount of an employee's gross pay from federal income tax withholding. In general, each employee is permitted one personal withholding allowance, one for a spouse who does not also claim an allowance, and one for each dependent.

FIGURE 8-3 Employee's Withholding Allowance Certificate (Form W-4)

Form **W-4**
Department of the Treasury
Internal Revenue Service

Employee's Withholding Allowance Certificate

▶ **Whether you are entitled to claim a certain number of allowances or exemption from withholding is subject to review by the IRS. Your employer may be required to send a copy of this form to the IRS.**

OMB No. 1545-0074
20--

1 Your first name and middle initial: Ken M. | Last name: Istone | 2 Your social security number: 393 58 8194

Home address (number and street or rural route): 1546 Swallow Drive

3 ☐ Single ☒ Married ☐ Married, but withhold at higher Single rate.
Note. *If married, but legally separated, or spouse is a nonresident alien, check the "Single" box.*

City or town, state, and ZIP code: St. Louis, MO 63144-4752

4 **If your last name differs from that shown on your social security card, check here. You must call 1-800-772-1213 for a replacement card.** ▶ ☐

5 Total number of allowances you are claiming (from line **H** above **or** from the applicable worksheet on page 2) . . . 5 | 4

6 Additional amount, if any, you want withheld from each paycheck . . . . 6 | $

7 I claim exemption from withholding for 20--, and I certify that I meet **both** of the following conditions for exemption.
- Last year I had a right to a refund of **all** federal income tax withheld because I had **no** tax liability **and**
- This year I expect a refund of **all** federal income tax withheld because I expect to have **no** tax liability.

If you meet both conditions, write "Exempt" here . . . . ▶ 7

Under penalties of perjury, I declare that I have examined this certificate and to the best of my knowledge and belief, it is true, correct, and complete.

Employee's signature
(Form is not valid unless you sign it.) ▶ Ken M. Istone   Date ▶ January 3, 20--

8 Employer's name and address (Employer: Complete lines 8 and 10 only if sending to the IRS.) | 9 Office code (optional) | 10 Employer identification number (EIN)

For Privacy Act and Paperwork Reduction Act Notice, see page 2. Cat. No. 10220Q Form **W-4** (20--)

A withholding certificate completed by Ken Istone is shown in Figure 8-3. Istone is married, has a spouse who does not claim an allowance, and has two dependent children. On line 5 of the W-4 form, Istone claims four allowances, calculated as follows:

Personal allowance	1
Spouse allowance	1
Allowances for dependents	2
Total withholding allowances	4

Circular E and many other IRS publications and forms can be found at the IRS Web site: www.irs.gov. These materials are essential for working in payroll accounting.

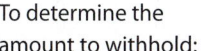

Wage-Bracket Method. Employers generally use the **wage-bracket method** or the **percentage method** to determine the amount of tax to be withheld from an employee's pay. We will illustrate the wage-bracket method here. The employee's gross pay for a specific time period is traced into the appropriate wage-bracket table provided by the Internal Revenue Service (IRS). These tables cover various time periods, and there are separate tables for single and married taxpayers. Copies are provided in *Circular E—Employer's Tax Guide*, also known as Publication 15, which may be obtained from any local IRS office or at the IRS Internet site.

Portions of weekly income tax wage-bracket withholding tables for single and married persons are illustrated in Figure 8-4. Assume that Ken Istone (who claims 4 allowances) had gross earnings of $640 for the week ending December 19, 20--. The amount to withhold for Istone is determined by using the following steps, as shown in Figure 8-4 for married persons (on page 289):

1. Find the row for wages of "at least $635, but less than $645."
2. Find the column headed "4 withholding allowances."
3. Where the row and column cross, $10 is given as the amount to be withheld.

LEARNING KEY

To determine the amount to withhold:

1. Find the row for wages.
2. Find the column for withholding allowances.
3. Find the amount where they cross.

For state or city income taxes, withholding generally is handled in one of two ways: (1) forms and tables similar to those provided by the IRS are used or (2) an amount equal to a percentage of the federal withholding amount is withheld.

Employee FICA Tax Withholding

An additional Medicare tax of 0.9% is imposed on employee earnings of more than $200,000 for single filers, and more than $250,000 for joint filers.

The Federal Insurance Contributions Act requires employers to withhold **FICA taxes** from employees' earnings. FICA taxes include amounts for both Social Security and Medicare programs. Social Security provides pensions and disability benefits. Medicare provides health insurance.

Congress has frequently changed the tax rates and the maximum amounts of earnings subject to FICA taxes. For this text, we assume the Social Security rate is 6.2% on maximum earnings of $128,400. The Medicare rate is 1.45% on all earnings; there is no maximum.

To illustrate the calculation of FICA taxes, assume the following earnings for Sarah Cadrain:

	Earnings	
Pay Period	Week	Year-to-Date
Dec. 6–12	$2,000	$127,340
Dec. 13–19	$2,060	$129,400

For the week of December 6–12, FICA taxes on Cadrain's earnings would be:

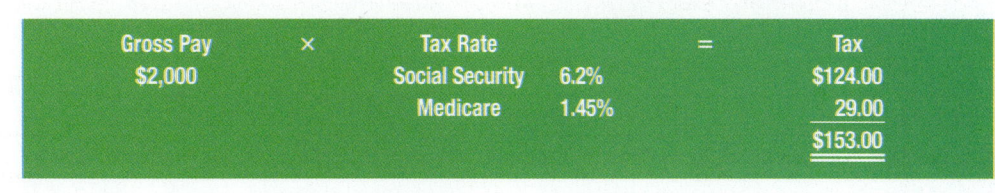

Gross Pay	×	Tax Rate		=	Tax
$2,000		Social Security	6.2%		$124.00
		Medicare	1.45%		29.00
					$153.00

FIGURE 8-4 Federal Withholding Tax Table: Single Persons

SINGLE Persons—WEEKLY Payroll Period

(For Wages Paid through December 31, 2018)

And the wages are–		And the number of withholding allowances claimed is—										
At least	But less than	0	1	2	3	4	5	6	7	8	9	10
		The amount of income tax to be withheld is—										
$360	$370	$32	$22	$13	$5	$0	$0	$0	$0	$0	$0	$0
370	380	33	23	14	6	0	0	0	0	0	0	0
380	390	34	24	15	7	0	0	0	0	0	0	0
390	400	35	26	16	8	0	0	0	0	0	0	0
400	410	36	27	17	9	1	0	0	0	0	0	0
410	420	38	28	18	10	2	0	0	0	0	0	0
420	430	39	29	20	11	3	0	0	0	0	0	0
430	440	40	30	21	12	4	0	0	0	0	0	0
440	450	41	32	22	13	5	0	0	0	0	0	0
450	460	42	33	23	14	6	0	0	0	0	0	0
460	470	44	34	24	15	7	0	0	0	0	0	0
470	480	45	35	26	16	8	0	0	0	0	0	0
480	490	46	36	27	17	9	1	0	0	0	0	0
490	500	47	38	28	18	10	2	0	0	0	0	0
500	510	48	39	29	20	11	3	0	0	0	0	0
510	520	50	40	30	21	12	4	0	0	0	0	0
520	530	51	41	32	22	13	5	0	0	0	0	0
530	540	52	42	33	23	14	6	0	0	0	0	0
540	550	53	44	34	24	15	7	0	0	0	0	0
550	560	54	45	35	26	16	8	1	0	0	0	0
560	570	56	46	36	27	17	9	2	0	0	0	0
570	580	57	47	38	28	18	10	3	0	0	0	0
580	590	58	48	39	29	20	11	4	0	0	0	0
590	600	59	50	40	30	21	12	5	0	0	0	0
600	610	60	51	41	32	22	13	6	0	0	0	0
610	620	62	52	42	33	23	14	7	0	0	0	0
620	630	63	53	44	34	24	15	8	0	0	0	0
630	640	64	54	45	35	26	16	9	1	0	0	0
640	650	65	56	46	36	27	17	10	2	0	0	0
650	660	66	57	47	38	28	19	11	3	0	0	0
660	670	68	58	48	39	29	20	12	4	0	0	0
670	680	69	59	50	40	30	21	13	5	0	0	0
680	690	70	60	51	41	32	22	14	6	0	0	0
690	700	71	62	52	42	33	23	15	7	0	0	0
700	710	72	63	53	44	34	25	16	8	0	0	0
710	720	74	64	54	45	35	26	17	9	1	0	0
720	730	75	65	56	46	36	27	18	10	2	0	0
730	740	76	66	57	47	38	28	19	11	3	0	0
740	750	77	68	58	48	39	29	20	12	4	0	0
750	760	78	69	59	50	40	31	21	13	5	0	0
760	770	80	70	60	51	41	32	22	14	6	0	0
770	780	81	71	62	52	42	33	23	15	7	0	0
780	790	82	72	63	53	44	34	25	16	8	0	0
790	800	83	74	64	54	45	35	26	17	9	1	0
800	810	84	75	65	56	46	37	27	18	10	2	0
810	820	86	76	66	57	47	38	28	19	11	3	0
820	830	88	77	68	58	48	39	29	20	12	4	0
830	840	90	78	69	59	50	40	31	21	13	5	0
840	850	92	80	70	60	51	41	32	22	14	6	0

FIGURE 8-4 Federal Withholding Tax Table: (*concluded*) Married Persons

MARRIED Persons—WEEKLY Payroll Period
(For Wages Paid through December 31, 2018)

And the wages are–		And the number of withholding allowances claimed is—										
At least	But less than	0	1	2	3	(2) 4	5	6	7	8	9	10
		The amount of income tax to be withheld is—										
$425	$435	$21	$13	$5	$0	$0	$0	$0	$0	$0	$0	$0
435	445	22	14	6	0	0	0	0	0	0	0	0
445	455	23	15	7	0	0	0	0	0	0	0	0
455	465	24	16	8	0	0	0	0	0	0	0	0
465	475	25	17	9	1	0	0	0	0	0	0	0
475	485	26	18	10	2	0	0	0	0	0	0	0
485	495	27	19	11	3	0	0	0	0	0	0	0
495	505	28	20	12	4	0	0	0	0	0	0	0
505	515	29	21	13	5	0	0	0	0	0	0	0
515	525	30	22	14	6	0	0	0	0	0	0	0
525	535	31	23	15	7	0	0	0	0	0	0	0
535	545	32	24	16	8	0	0	0	0	0	0	0
545	555	33	25	17	9	1	0	0	0	0	0	0
555	565	34	26	18	10	2	0	0	0	0	0	0
565	575	35	27	19	11	3	0	0	0	0	0	0
575	585	36	28	20	12	4	0	0	0	0	0	0
585	595	37	29	21	13	5	0	0	0	0	0	0
595	605	38	30	22	14	6	0	0	0	0	0	0
605	615	39	31	23	15	7	0	0	0	0	0	0
615	625	40	32	24	16	8	0	0	0	0	0	0
625	635	42	33	25	17	9	1	0	0	0	0	0
(1) 635	645	43	34	26	18	(3) 10	2	0	0	0	0	0
645	655	44	35	27	19	11	3	0	0	0	0	0
655	665	45	36	28	20	12	4	0	0	0	0	0
665	675	46	37	29	21	13	5	0	0	0	0	0
675	685	48	38	30	22	14	6	0	0	0	0	0
685	695	49	39	31	23	15	7	0	0	0	0	0
695	705	50	40	32	24	16	8	0	0	0	0	0
705	715	51	42	33	25	17	9	1	0	0	0	0
715	725	52	43	34	26	18	10	2	0	0	0	0
725	735	54	44	35	27	19	11	3	0	0	0	0
735	745	55	45	36	28	20	12	4	0	0	0	0
745	755	56	46	37	29	21	13	5	0	0	0	0
755	765	57	48	38	30	22	14	6	0	0	0	0
765	775	58	49	39	31	23	15	7	0	0	0	0
775	785	60	50	40	32	24	16	8	0	0	0	0
785	795	61	51	42	33	25	17	9	1	0	0	0
795	805	62	52	43	34	26	18	10	2	0	0	0
805	815	63	54	44	35	27	19	11	3	0	0	0
815	825	64	55	45	36	28	20	12	4	0	0	0
825	835	66	56	46	37	29	21	13	5	0	0	0
835	845	67	57	48	38	30	22	14	6	0	0	0
845	855	68	58	49	39	31	23	15	7	0	0	0
855	865	69	60	50	40	32	24	16	8	0	0	0
865	875	70	61	51	42	33	25	17	9	1	0	0
875	885	72	62	52	43	34	26	18	10	2	0	0
885	895	73	63	54	44	35	27	19	11	3	0	0
895	905	74	64	55	45	36	28	20	12	4	0	0
905	915	75	66	56	46	37	29	21	13	5	0	0
1,315	1,325	124	115	105	96	86	77	67	57	48	38	30
1,325	1,335	126	116	106	97	87	78	68	59	49	39	31
1,335	1,345	127	117	108	98	88	79	69	60	50	41	32
1,345	1,355	128	118	109	99	90	80	71	61	51	42	33
1,355	1,365	129	120	110	100	91	81	72	62	53	43	34
1,365	1,375	130	121	111	102	92	83	73	63	54	44	35
1,375	1,385	132	122	112	103	93	84	74	65	55	45	36
1,385	1,395	133	123	114	104	95	85	75	66	56	47	37
1,395	1,405	134	124	115	105	96	86	77	67	57	48	38
1,405	1,415	135	126	116	106	97	87	78	68	59	49	39
1,415	1,425	136	127	117	108	98	89	79	69	60	50	41
1,425	1,435	138	128	118	109	99	90	80	71	61	51	42
1,435	1,445	139	129	120	110	101	91	81	72	62	53	43
1,445	1,455	140	130	121	111	102	92	83	73	63	54	44
1,455	1,465	141	132	122	112	103	93	84	74	65	55	45
1,465	1,475	142	133	123	114	104	95	85	75	66	56	47
1,475	1,485	144	134	124	115	105	96	86	77	67	57	48
1,485	1,495	145	135	126	116	107	97	87	78	68	59	49
1,495	1,505	146	136	127	117	108	98	89	79	69	60	50
1,505	1,515	147	138	128	118	109	99	90	80	71	61	51

When the Social Security program was established in 1937, the tax was 1% on earnings up to $3,000 per year!

During the week of December 13–19, Cadrain's earnings for the calendar year went over the $128,400 Social Security maximum by $1,000 ($129,400 – $128,400). Therefore, $1,000 of her $2,060 earnings for the week would not be subject to the Social Security tax.

Year-to-date earnings	$129,400
Social Security maximum	128,400
Amount not subject to Social Security tax	$ 1,000

The Social Security tax on Cadrain's December 13–19 earnings would be:

Gross pay	$2,060.00
Amount not subject to Social Security tax	1,000.00
Amount subject to Social Security tax	$1,060.00
Tax rate	6.2%
Social Security tax	$ 65.72

Since there is no Medicare maximum, all of Cadrain's December 13–19 earnings would be subject to the Medicare tax.

Gross pay	$2,060.00
Tax rate	1.45%
Medicare tax	$ 29.87

The total FICA tax would be:

Social Security tax	$65.72
Medicare tax	29.87
Total FICA tax	95.59

For the rest of the calendar year through December 31, Cadrain's earnings would be subject only to Medicare taxes.

If you use Microsoft® Excel to create a payroll register, a column or row *may* be off by a few cents. This usually occurs in the Social Security and Medicare tax calculations because of rounding. To get an accurate number, use the "ROUND" function in any cell with more than two non-zero decimal places.

Voluntary Deductions

In addition to the mandatory deductions from employee earnings for income and FICA taxes, many other deductions are possible. These deductions are usually voluntary and depend on specific agreements between the employee and employer. Examples of voluntary deductions are:

1. U.S. savings bond purchases
2. Health insurance premiums
3. Credit union deposits
4. Pension plan payments
5. Charitable contributions

Computing Net Pay

To compute an employee's net pay for the period, subtract all tax withholdings and voluntary deductions from the gross pay. Ken Istone's net pay for the week ended December 19 would be calculated as follows:

Gross pay		$640.00
Deductions:		
Federal income tax withholding	$10.00	
Social Security tax withholding	39.68	
Medicare tax withholding	9.28	
Health insurance premiums	10.00	
Total deductions		68.96
Net pay		$571.04

CHECKPOINT

Complete Checkpoint-1 on page 305 to test your basic understanding of LO2.

LO3

Payroll Records

Describe and prepare payroll records.

Payroll records should provide the following information for each employee:

1. Name, address, occupation, Social Security number, marital status, and number of withholding allowances
2. Gross amount of earnings, date of payment, and period covered by each payroll
3. Gross amount of earnings accumulated for the year
4. Amounts of taxes and other items withheld

Three types of payroll records are used to accumulate this information:

1. The payroll register
2. The payroll check (or record of direct deposit) with earnings statement attached
3. The employee earnings record

These records can be prepared by either manual or automated methods. The illustrations in this chapter are based on a manual system. The forms and procedures illustrated are equally applicable to both manual and automated systems.

Payroll Register

A good example of a deduction column that could be added is State Income Tax. In the payroll register in Figure 8-5, the column could be inserted immediately after Federal Income Tax.

A **payroll register** is a form used to assemble the data required at the end of each payroll period. Figure 8-5 on pages 292 and 293 illustrates Westly, Inc.'s payroll register for the payroll period ended December 19, 20--. Detailed information on earnings, taxable earnings, deductions, and net pay is provided for each employee. Column headings for deductions may vary, depending on which deductions are commonly used by a particular business. The sources of key information in the register are indicated in Figure 8-5.

Note four important things about Westly's payroll register:

1. The first $128,400 of earnings of each employee is subject to Social Security tax. The Cumulative Total column, under the Earnings category, shows that Sarah Cadrain has exceeded this limit during the period. Thus, only $1,060 of her earnings for this pay period is subject to Social Security tax, as shown in the Taxable Earnings columns.
2. There are two Taxable Earnings columns: Unemployment Compensation and Social Security. Only one of these columns (Social Security) is needed to determine employee taxes. Both columns are shown here because they are a standard part of a payroll register. The Unemployment Compensation column is needed to determine this payroll tax on employers. The Social Security column is needed to determine both employee and employer Social Security taxes. The two employer taxes (Unemployment Compensation and Social Security) are discussed in Chapter 9.
3. Regular deductions are made from employee earnings for federal income tax and Social Security and Medicare taxes.
4. Voluntary deductions are made for health insurance and United Way contributions, based on agreements with individual employees.

FIGURE 8-5 Payroll Register (left side)

PAYROLL REGISTER

	NAME	ALLOWANCES	MARITAL STATUS	EARNINGS: REGULAR	EARNINGS: OVERTIME	EARNINGS: TOTAL	EARNINGS: CUMULATIVE TOTAL	TAXABLE EARNINGS: UNEMPLOYMENT COMPENSATION	TAXABLE EARNINGS: SOCIAL SECURITY
1	Cadrain, Sarah	4	M	2 000 00	60 00	2 060 00	129 400 00	0 00	1 060 00
2	Gruder, James	1	S	760 00	140 00	900 00	43 400 00	0 00	900 00
3	Istone, Ken	4	M	640 00		640 00	32 025 00	0 00	640 00
4	Kuzmik, Helen	2	M	560 00	322 00	882 00	34 000 00	0 00	882 00
5	Lee, Hoseoup	3	M	620 00		620 00	31 340 00	0 00	620 00
6	Swaney, Linda	2	S	600 00	225 00	825 00	30 500 00	0 00	825 00
7	Tucci, Paul	3	M	610 00		610 00	30 100 00	0 00	610 00
8	Wiles, Harry	1	S	360 00		360 00	6 300 00	360 00	360 00
9				6 150 00	747 00	6 897 00	337 065 00	360 00	5 897 00
10									

Time cards, pay rates

Prior period total + current period earnings

Current below $7,000 cumul. total

Current below $128,400 cumul. total

Discussed in Chapter 9

After the data for each employee have been entered, the amount columns in the payroll register should be totaled and the totals verified as follows:

Regular earnings		$6,150.00
Overtime earnings		747.00
Gross earnings		$6,897.00
Deductions:		
Federal income tax	$444.00	
Social Security tax	365.61	
Medicare tax	100.01	
Health insurance premiums	46.00	
United Way	40.00	995.62
Net amount of payroll		$5,901.38

In a computerized accounting system, the payroll software performs this proof. An error in the payroll register could cause the payment of an incorrect amount to an employee. It also could result in sending an incorrect amount to the government or other agencies for whom funds are withheld.

Paying Employees

Employees should be paid by check or by direct deposit. Data needed to prepare a paycheck for each employee are contained in the payroll register. In a computer-based system, the paychecks and payroll register normally are prepared at the same time. The employer furnishes an earnings statement to each employee along with each paycheck. Paychecks with detachable earnings statements, like the one for Ken Istone illustrated in Figure 8-6, are widely used for this purpose. Before the check is deposited or cashed, the employee should detach the stub and keep it for his records.

FIGURE 8-5 Payroll Register (right side)

—WEEK ENDED 12/19/--

DEDUCTIONS									
FEDERAL INCOME TAX	SOCIAL SECURITY TAX	MEDICARE TAX	HEALTH INSURANCE	UNITED WAY	OTHER	TOTAL	NET PAY	CHECK NO.	
175 00	65 72	29 87				270 59	1789 41	409	1
86 00	55 80	13 05		20 00		174 85	725 15	410	2
10 00	39 68	9 28	10 00			68 96	571 04	411	3
52 00	54 68	12 79	13 00	20 00		152 47	729 53	412	4
16 00	38 44	8 99	13 00			76 43	543 57	413	5
68 00	51 15	11 96				131 11	693 89	414	6
15 00	37 82	8 85	10 00			71 67	538 33	415	7
22 00	22 32	5 22				49 54	310 46	416	8
444 00	365 61	100 01	46 00	40 00	0 0 00	995 62	5901 38		9
									10

Withholding Tax Table (Federal Income Tax)

6.2% × Social Security taxable earnings (Social Security Tax)

1.45% × total earnings (Medicare Tax)

Specific employer–employee agreements (Health Insurance, United Way)

Total earnings – total deductions (Net Pay)

FIGURE 8-6 Paycheck and Earnings Statement

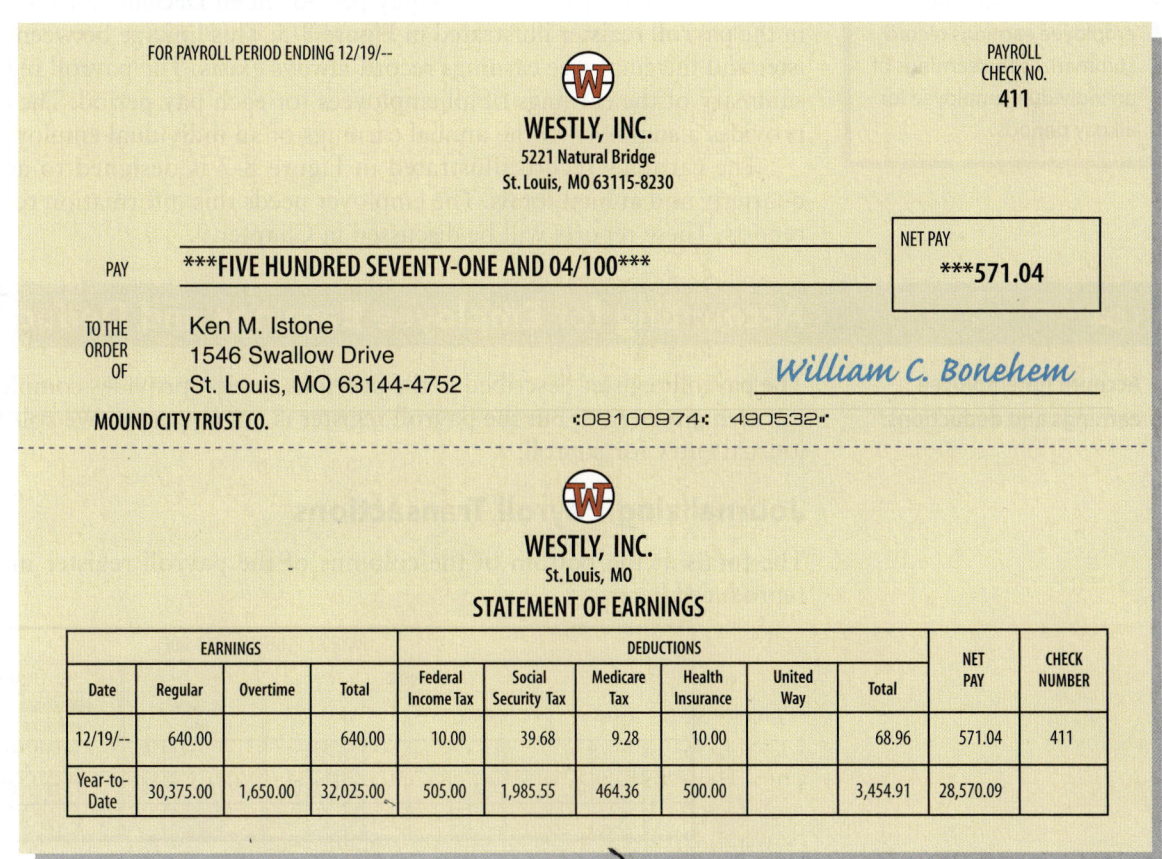

FOR PAYROLL PERIOD ENDING 12/19/--

PAYROLL CHECK NO. 411

WESTLY, INC.
5221 Natural Bridge
St. Louis, MO 63115-8230

PAY ***FIVE HUNDRED SEVENTY-ONE AND 04/100***

NET PAY ***571.04

TO THE ORDER OF
Ken M. Istone
1546 Swallow Drive
St. Louis, MO 63144-4752

William C. Bonehem

MOUND CITY TRUST CO.

⑆08100974⑆ 490532⑈

WESTLY, INC.
St. Louis, MO

STATEMENT OF EARNINGS

EARNINGS				DEDUCTIONS						NET PAY	CHECK NUMBER
Date	Regular	Overtime	Total	Federal Income Tax	Social Security Tax	Medicare Tax	Health Insurance	United Way	Total		
12/19/--	640.00		640.00	10.00	39.68	9.28	10.00		68.96	571.04	411
Year-to-Date	30,375.00	1,650.00	32,025.00	505.00	1,985.55	464.36	500.00		3,454.91	28,570.09	

FIGURE 8-7 Employee Earnings Record (left side)

EMPLOYEE EARNINGS RECORD

PERIOD ENDED	EARNINGS				TAXABLE EARNINGS	
	REGULAR	OVERTIME	TOTAL	CUMULATIVE TOTAL	UNEMPLOYMENT COMPENSATION	SOCIAL SECURITY
11/28	640 00		640 00	29 955 00		640 00
12/5	640 00	75 00	715 00	30 595 00		715 00
12/12	640 00	75 00	715 00	31 310 00		715 00
12/19	640 00		640 00	32 025 00		640 00

GENDER	DEPARTMENT	OCCUPATION	SOCIAL SECURITY NUMBER	MARITAL STATUS	ALLOWANCES
M ✔ F	Maintenance	Service	393-58-8194	M	4

When **direct deposit** is used, the employee does not even handle the paycheck. Rather, payment is deposited directly by the employer into the employee's bank account using an electronic funds transfer (EFT). The employee receives only the earnings statement from the check indicating the deposit has been made. Payment by check or direct deposit provides better internal accounting control than payment by cash.

Employee Earnings Record

> **LEARNING KEY**
>
> The payroll register and employee earnings record are linked. The payroll register shows the earnings of all employees for a single pay period. The employee earnings record summarizes the earnings of an individual employee for all pay periods.

A separate record of each employee's earnings is called an **employee earnings record**. An employee earnings record for Ken M. Istone for a portion of the last quarter of the calendar year is illustrated in Figure 8-7 above.

The information in this record is obtained from the payroll register. In a computer-based system, the employee earnings record can be updated at the same time the payroll register is prepared.

Istone's earnings for four weeks of the last quarter of the year are shown on this form. Note that the entry for the pay period ended December 19 is the same as that in the payroll register illustrated in Figure 8-5. This linkage between the payroll register and the employee earnings record always exists. The payroll register provides a summary of the earnings of all employees for each pay period. The earnings record provides a summary of the annual earnings of an individual employee.

The earnings record illustrated in Figure 8-7 is designed to accumulate both quarterly and annual totals. The employer needs this information to prepare several reports. These reports will be discussed in Chapter 9.

LO4 Accounting for Employee Earnings and Deductions

Account for employee earnings and deductions.

The payroll register described in the previous section provides complete payroll data for each pay period. But the payroll register is not a journal. We still need to make a journal entry for payroll.

Journalizing Payroll Transactions

The totals at the bottom of the columns of the payroll register in Figure 8-5 are reproduced here.

PAYROLL REGISTER (LEFT SIDE)

EARNINGS				TAXABLE EARNINGS	
REGULAR	OVERTIME	TOTAL	CUMULATIVE TOTAL	UNEMPLOYMENT COMPENSATION	SOCIAL SECURITY
6 150 00	747 00	6 897 00	337 065 00	360 00	5 897 00

(1)

FIGURE 8-7 Employee Earnings Record (right side)

FOR PERIOD ENDED 20--

DEDUCTIONS: FEDERAL INCOME TAX	SOCIAL SECURITY TAX	MEDICARE TAX	HEALTH INSURANCE	UNITED WAY	OTHER		TOTAL	CHECK NO.	AMOUNT
10 00	39 68	9 28	10 00				68 96	387	571 04
18 00	44 33	10 37	10 00				82 70	395	632 30
18 00	44 33	10 37	10 00				82 70	403	632 30
10 00	39 68	9 28	10 00				68 96	411	571 04

PAY RATE	DATE OF BIRTH	DATE HIRED	NAME/ADDRESS	EMPLOYEE NUMBER
$640/wk	8/17/64	1/3/87	Ken M. Istone 1546 Swallow Drive St. Louis, MO 63144-4752	3

A BROADER VIEW

Payroll Fraud—Paying for Ghosts

A supervisor at Haas Transfer Warehouse embezzled $12,000 from the company by collecting paychecks for former employees. When an employee left the company, the supervisor continued to submit a department time report for the employee. This caused a paycheck to be generated for the "ghost" employee. The supervisor then simply kept this paycheck when others were distributed to actual employees.

This fraud shows the importance of two procedures that appear in this chapter: (1) a time card, plastic card, or badge should be used for each employee to keep an accurate record of time worked and (2) payment by direct deposit or electronic funds transfer to the employee's bank is a good internal control.

PHOTOALTO/ALIX MINDE/JUPITER IMAGES

The numbered amounts in the payroll register column totals thus provide the basis for recording the payroll. If the employee paychecks are written from the regular bank account, the following journal entry is made:

PAYROLL REGISTER (RIGHT SIDE) 20--

DEDUCTIONS: FEDERAL INCOME TAX	SOCIAL SECURITY TAX	MEDICARE TAX	HEALTH INSURANCE	UNITED WAY	OTHER		TOTAL		NET PAY
444 00	365 61	100 01	46 00	40 00	0 00	0 00	995 62		5901 38
(2)	(3)	(4)	(5)	(6)					(7)

An alternative to crediting Cash immediately for the net amount due ($5,901.38) to employees is to credit this amount to Wages and Salaries Payable. Then Wages and Salaries Payable is debited and Cash is credited when the employees are paid.

		DATE		DESCRIPTION	POST REF.	DEBIT	CREDIT	
(1)	5	Dec.	19	Wages and Salaries Expense		6897 00		5
(2)	6			Employee Federal Income Tax Payable			444 00	6
(3)	7			Social Security Tax Payable			365 61	7
(4)	8			Medicare Tax Payable			100 01	8
(5)	9			Health Insurance Premiums Payable			46 00	9
(6)	10			United Way Contributions Payable			40 00	10
(7)	11			Cash			5901 38	11
	12			Payroll for week ended Dec. 19				12

Employee paychecks also can be written from a special payroll bank account. Large businesses with many employees commonly use a payroll bank account. If Westly used a payroll bank account, it first would have made the following entry on December 19 to transfer funds from the regular bank account to the payroll bank account:

	DATE		DESCRIPTION	POST REF.	DEBIT	CREDIT	
1	Dec.	19	Payroll Cash		5901 38		1
2			Cash			5901 38	2
3			Cash for Dec. 19 payroll				3

Then, the payroll entry shown above would be made, except that the credit of $5,901.38 would be to Payroll Cash rather than Cash.

If a payroll bank account is used, individual checks totaling $5,901.38 are written to the employees from that account. Otherwise, individual checks totaling that amount are written to the employees from the regular bank account.

Notice two important facts about the payroll entry. First, Wages and Salaries Expense is debited for the gross pay of the employees. The expense to the employer is the gross pay, not the employees' net pay after deductions. Second, a separate account is kept for each deduction.

The accounts needed in entering deductions depend upon the deductions involved. To understand the accounting for these deductions, consider what the employer is doing. By deducting amounts from employees' earnings, the employer is simply serving as an agent for the government and other groups. Amounts that are deducted from an employee's gross earnings must be paid by the employer to these groups. Therefore, a separate account should be kept for the liability for each type of deduction.

To help us understand the journal entry for payroll, let's use the accounting equation to examine the accounts involved. The seven accounts affected by the payroll entry above are shown in the accounting equation in Figure 8-8.

LEARNING KEY

Wages and Salaries Expense is debited for the gross pay. A separate account is kept for each earnings deduction. Cash is credited for the net pay.

FIGURE 8-8 Accounting for Payroll

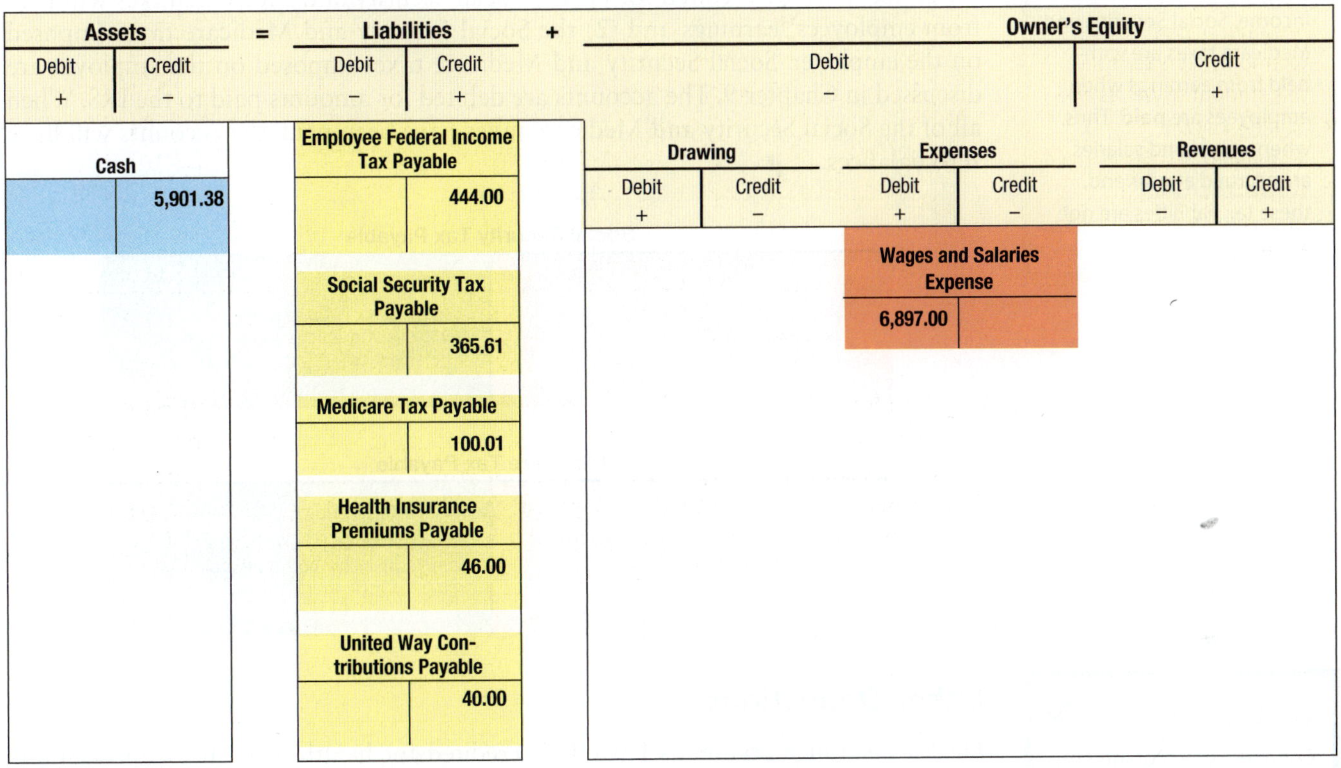

Wages and Salaries Expense

This account is debited for the gross pay of all employees for each pay period. Sometimes separate expense accounts are kept for the employees of different departments. Thus, separate accounts may be kept for Office Salaries Expense, Sales Salaries Expense, and Factory Wages Expense.

Wages and Salaries Expense

Debit	Credit
Gross pay of employees for each pay period	

Employee Federal Income Tax Payable

This account is credited for the total federal income tax withheld from employees' earnings. The account is debited for amounts paid to the IRS. When all of the income taxes withheld have been paid, the account will have a zero balance. A state or city income tax payable account is used in a similar manner.

Employee Federal Income Tax Payable

Debit	Credit
Payment of federal income tax previously withheld	Federal income tax withheld from employees' earnings

Social Security and Medicare Taxes Payable

> Income, Social Security, and Medicare taxes are withheld from earnings when employees are **paid**. Thus, when wages and salaries are accrued at year end, these tax liabilities are not accrued.

These accounts are credited for (1) the Social Security and Medicare taxes withheld from employees' earnings and (2) the Social Security and Medicare taxes imposed on the employer. Social Security and Medicare taxes imposed on the employer are discussed in Chapter 9. The accounts are debited for amounts paid to the IRS. When all of the Social Security and Medicare taxes have been paid, the accounts will have zero balances.

Social Security Tax Payable

Debit	Credit
Payment of Social Security tax previously withheld or imposed	Social Security taxes (1) withheld from employees' earnings and (2) imposed on the employer

Medicare Tax Payable

Debit	Credit
Payment of Medicare tax previously withheld or imposed	Medicare taxes (1) withheld from employees' earnings and (2) imposed on the employer

> CHECKPOINT
> Complete Checkpoint-2 on page 305 to test your basic understanding of LO4.

Other Deductions

Health Insurance Premiums Payable is credited for health insurance contributions deducted from an employee's pay. The account is debited for the subsequent payment of these amounts to the health insurer. United Way Contributions Payable is handled in a similar manner.

LO5 Payroll Record-Keeping Methods

Describe various payroll record-keeping methods.

You probably noticed that the same information appears in several places in the payroll records—in the payroll register, paycheck and stub, and employee earnings records. If all records are prepared by hand (a **manual system**), the same information would be recorded several times. Unless an employer has only a few employees, this can be very inefficient. Various approaches are available to make payroll accounting more efficient and accurate.

Both medium- and large-size businesses commonly use two approaches for payroll record keeping: payroll processing centers and electronic systems. A **payroll processing center** is a business that sells payroll record-keeping services. The employer provides the center with all basic employee data and each period's report of hours worked. The processing center maintains all payroll records and prepares each period's payroll checks. Payroll processing center fees tend to be much less than the cost to an employer of handling payroll internally.

An **electronic system** is a computer system based on a software package that performs all payroll record keeping and prepares payroll checks or EFT records. In this system, only the employee number and hours worked need to be entered into a computer each pay period, as shown in Figure 8-9. All other payroll data needed to prepare the payroll records can be stored in the computer. The computer uses the employee number and hours worked to determine the gross pay, deductions, and net pay. The payroll register, checks (or EFTs), and employee earnings records are provided as outputs.

FIGURE 8-9 Electronic Payroll System

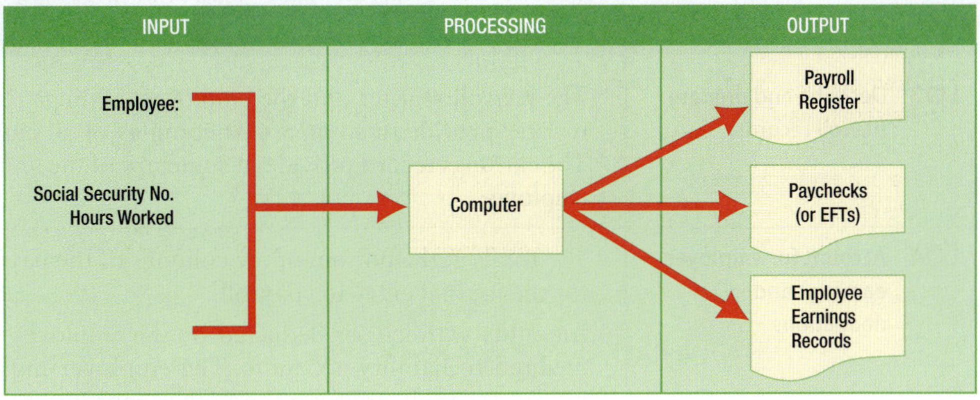

The same inputs and outputs are required in all payroll systems. Even with a computer, the data required for payroll processing have to be entered into the system at some point. The outputs—the payroll register, paychecks, and employee earnings records—are basically the same under each system.

SELF-STUDY

LEARNING OBJECTIVES	Key Points to Remember
LO1 Distinguish between employees and independent contractors.	Employees work under the control and direction of an employer. Independent contractors perform a service for a fee and do not work under the control and direction of the company paying for the service. Payroll accounting procedures apply only to employees, not to independent contractors.
LO2 Calculate employee earnings and deductions.	Three steps are required to determine how much to pay an employee for a pay period: 1. Calculate total earnings. 2. Determine the amounts of deductions. 3. Subtract deductions from total earnings to compute net pay. Deductions from gross pay fall into three categories: 1. Income tax withholding 2. Employee Social Security and Medicare taxes withholding 3. Voluntary deductions Four factors determine the amount to be withheld from an employee's gross pay each pay period: 1. Total earnings 2. Marital status 3. Number of withholding allowances claimed 4. Length of the pay period

(continued)

LEARNING OBJECTIVES	Key Points to Remember
LO3 Describe and prepare payroll records.	The payroll register and the employee earnings record are linked. The payroll register provides a summary of earnings of all employees for each pay period. The earnings record provides a summary of the annual earnings of an individual employee.
LO4 Account for employee earnings and deductions.	The totals at the bottom of the columns of the payroll register provide the basis for the journal entry for payroll. Amounts withheld or deducted by the employer from employee earnings are credited to liability accounts. The employer must pay these amounts to the proper government groups and other appropriate groups.
LO5 Describe various payroll record-keeping methods.	In a manual payroll system, the same information needs to be recorded several times. An electronic payroll system is much more efficient.

DEMONSTRATION PROBLEM

Carole Vohsen operates a pet grooming salon called Canine Coiffures. She has five employees, all of whom are paid on a weekly basis. Canine Coiffures uses a payroll register, individual employee earnings records, a journal, and a general ledger.

The payroll data for each employee for the week ended January 21, 20--, are given below. Employees are paid 1½ times the regular rate for work over 40 hours a week.

Name	Employee No.	No. of Allowances	Marital Status	Total Hours Worked Jan. 15–21	Rate	Total Earnings Jan. 1–14
DeNourie, Katie	1	2	S	44	$14.50	$1,218.00
Garriott, Pete	2	1	M	40	15.00	1,260.00
Martinez, Sheila	3	3	M	40	15.50	1,302.00
Parker, Nancy	4	2	M	42	14.00	1,176.00
Shapiro, John	5	2	S	40	14.50	1,190.00

Sheila Martinez is the manager of the Shampooing Department. Her Social Security number is 500-88-4189, and she was born April 12, 1969. She lives at 46 Darling Crossing, Norwich, CT, 06360. Martinez was hired September 1 of last year.

Canine Coiffures uses a federal income tax withholding table. A portion of this weekly table is provided in Figure 8-4 on pages 288 and 289. Social Security tax is withheld at the rate of 6.2% of the first $128,400 earned. Medicare tax is withheld at the rate of 1.45%, and city earnings tax at the rate of 1%, both applied to gross pay. Garriott and Parker each have $14 and DeNourie and Martinez each have $10 withheld for health insurance. DeNourie, Martinez, and Shapiro each have $15 withheld to be invested in the groomers' credit union. Garriott and Shapiro each have $18.75 withheld under a savings bond purchase plan.

Canine Coiffures' payroll is met by drawing checks on its regular bank account. This week, the checks were issued in sequence, beginning with No. 811.

REQUIRED

1. Prepare a payroll register for Canine Coiffures for the week ended January 21, 20--. (In the Taxable Earnings/Unemployment Compensation column, enter the same amounts as in the Social Security column.) Total the amount columns, verify the totals, and rule with single and double lines.
2. Prepare an employee earnings record for Sheila Martinez for the week ended January 21, 20--.
3. Assuming that the wages for the week ended January 21 were paid on January 23, prepare the journal entry for the payment of this payroll.
4. Post the entry in requirement (3) to the affected accounts in the ledger of Canine Coiffures. Do not enter any amounts in the Balance columns. Use account numbers as follows: Cash—101; Employee Federal Income Tax Payable—211; Social Security Tax Payable—212; Medicare Tax Payable—213; City Earnings Tax Payable—215; Health Insurance Premiums Payable—216; Credit Union Payable—217; Savings Bond Deductions Payable—218; Wages and Salaries Expense—511.

SOLUTION 1.

PAYROLL REGISTER

					EARNINGS				TAXABLE EARNINGS	
	NAME	EMPLOYEE NO.	ALLOWANCES	MARITAL STATUS	REGULAR	OVERTIME	TOTAL	CUMULATIVE TOTAL	UNEMPLOYMENT COMPENSATION	SOCIAL SECURITY
1	DeNourie, Katie	1	2	S	580 00	87 00	667 00	1885 00	667 00	667 00
2	Garriott, Pete	2	1	M	600 00		600 00	1860 00	600 00	600 00
3	Martinez, Sheila	3	3	M	620 00		620 00	1922 00	620 00	620 00
4	Parker, Nancy	4	2	M	560 00	42 00	602 00	1778 00	602 00	602 00
5	Shapiro, John	5	2	S	580 00		580 00	1770 00	580 00	580 00
6					2940 00	129 00	3069 00	9215 00	3069 00	3069 00
7										
8										
9										
10										

—WEEK ENDED 12/19/--

DEDUCTIONS										
FEDERAL INCOME TAX	SOCIAL SECURITY TAX	MEDICARE TAX	CITY TAX	HEALTH INSURANCE	CREDIT UNION	OTHER	TOTAL	NET PAY	CHECK NO.	
48 00	41 35	9 67	6 67	10 00	15 00		130 69	536 31	811	1
30 00	37 20	8 70	6 00	14 00		18 75	114 65	485 35	812	2
16 00	38 44	8 99	6 20	10 00	15 00		94 63	525 37	813	3
22 00	37 32	8 73	6 02	14 00			88 07	513 93	814	4
39 00	35 96	8 41	5 80		15 00	18 75	122 92	457 08	815	5
155 00	190 27	44 50	30 69	48 00	45 00	37 50	550 96	2518 04		6
										7
										8
										9
										10

SOLUTION 2.

EMPLOYEE EARNINGS RECORD

20-- PERIOD ENDED	EARNINGS: REGULAR	EARNINGS: OVERTIME	EARNINGS: TOTAL	EARNINGS: CUMULATIVE TOTAL	TAXABLE EARNINGS: UNEMPLOYMENT COMPENSATION	TAXABLE EARNINGS: SOCIAL SECURITY
1/7						
1/14						
1/21	620 00		620 00	1922 00	620 00	620 00
1/28						

GENDER	DEPARTMENT	OCCUPATION	SOCIAL SECURITY NUMBER	MARITAL STATUS	ALLOWANCES
M ☐ F ✔	Shampooing	Manager	500-88-4189	M	3

FOR PERIOD ENDED 20--

DEDUCTIONS: FEDERAL INCOME TAX	SOCIAL SECURITY TAX	MEDICARE TAX	CITY TAX	HEALTH INSURANCE	CREDIT UNION	OTHER	TOTAL	CHECK NO.	AMOUNT
16 00	38 44	8 99	6 20	10 00	15 00		94 63	813	525 37

PAY RATE	DATE OF BIRTH	DATE HIRED	NAME/ADDRESS	EMPLOYEE NUMBER
$15.50	4/12/69	9/1/--	Sheila Martinez 46 Darling Crossing Norwich, CT 06360	3

SOLUTION 3.

GENERAL JOURNAL PAGE 1

	DATE		DESCRIPTION	POST. REF.	DEBIT	CREDIT	
1	20-- Jan.	23	Wages and Salaries Expense	511	3,069 00		1
2			Employee Federal Income Tax Payable	211		155 00	2
3			Social Security Tax Payable	212		190 27	3
4			Medicare Tax Payable	213		44 50	4
5			City Earnings Tax Payable	215		30 69	5
6			Health Insurance Premiums Payable	216		48 00	6
7			Credit Union Payable	217		45 00	7
8			Savings Bond Deductions Payable	218		37 50	8
9			Cash	101		2,518 04	9
10			Payroll for week ended Jan. 21				10

SOLUTION 4.

GENERAL LEDGER

ACCOUNT: Cash — ACCOUNT NO. 101

DATE		ITEM	POST. REF.	DEBIT	CREDIT	BALANCE DEBIT	BALANCE CREDIT
20-- Jan.	23		J1		2,518.04		

ACCOUNT: Employee Federal Income Tax Payable — ACCOUNT NO. 211

DATE		ITEM	POST. REF.	DEBIT	CREDIT	BALANCE DEBIT	BALANCE CREDIT
20-- Jan.	23		J1		155.00		

ACCOUNT: Social Security Tax Payable — ACCOUNT NO. 212

DATE		ITEM	POST. REF.	DEBIT	CREDIT	BALANCE DEBIT	BALANCE CREDIT
20-- Jan.	23		J1		190.27		

ACCOUNT: Medicare Tax Payable — ACCOUNT NO. 213

DATE		ITEM	POST. REF.	DEBIT	CREDIT	BALANCE DEBIT	BALANCE CREDIT
20-- Jan.	23		J1		44.50		

ACCOUNT: City Earnings Tax Payable — ACCOUNT NO. 215

DATE		ITEM	POST. REF.	DEBIT	CREDIT	BALANCE DEBIT	BALANCE CREDIT
20-- Jan.	23		J1		30.69		

ACCOUNT: Health Insurance Premiums Payable — ACCOUNT NO. 216

DATE		ITEM	POST. REF.	DEBIT	CREDIT	BALANCE DEBIT	BALANCE CREDIT
20-- Jan.	23		J1		48.00		

ACCOUNT: Credit Union Payable — ACCOUNT NO. 217

DATE		ITEM	POST. REF.	DEBIT	CREDIT	BALANCE DEBIT	BALANCE CREDIT
20-- Jan.	23		J1		45.00		

ACCOUNT: Savings Bond Deductions Payable — ACCOUNT NO. 218

DATE		ITEM	POST. REF.	DEBIT	CREDIT	BALANCE DEBIT	BALANCE CREDIT
20-- Jan.	23		J1		37.50		

ACCOUNT: Wages and Salaries Expense — ACCOUNT NO. 511

DATE		ITEM	POST. REF.	DEBIT	CREDIT	BALANCE DEBIT	BALANCE CREDIT
20-- Jan.	23		J1	3,069.00			

KEY TERMS

direct deposit (294) A payroll method in which the employee does not handle the paycheck; payment is made by the employer directly to the employee's bank account using EFT.

electronic system (298) A computer system based on a software package that performs all payroll record keeping and prepares payroll checks.

employee (283) Someone who works under the control and direction of an employer.

employee earnings record (294) A separate record of each employee's earnings.

Fair Labor Standards Act (FLSA) (283) A law that requires employers to pay overtime at 1½ times the regular rate to any hourly employee who works over 40 hours in a week.

FICA taxes (287) Payroll taxes withheld to provide Social Security and Medicare benefits.

gross pay (286) An employee's total earnings.

independent contractor (283) Someone who performs a service for a fee and does not work under the control and direction of the company paying for the service.

manual system (298) Payroll system in which all records are prepared by hand.

net pay (286) Gross pay less mandatory and voluntary deductions.

payroll processing center (298) A business that sells payroll record-keeping services.

payroll register (291) A form used to assemble the data required at the end of each payroll period.

percentage method (287) A method of determining the amount to withhold from an employee's gross pay for a specific period.

salary (283) Compensation for managerial or administrative services.

wage-bracket method (287) A method of determining the amount to withhold from an employee's gross pay for a specific time period. Wage-bracket tables are provided by the Internal Revenue Service.

wages (283) Compensation for skilled or unskilled labor.

withholding allowance (286) A specific dollar amount of an employee's gross pay that is exempt from federal income tax withholding.

SELF-STUDY TEST QUESTIONS

True/False

1. **LO1** An independent contractor is one who works under the control and direction of an employer.
2. **LO1** Government laws and regulations regarding payroll are more complex for employees than for independent contractors.
3. **LO2** Compensation for skilled or unskilled labor expressed in terms of hours, weeks, or units is called salary.
4. **LO2** An employee's total earnings is called gross pay.
5. **LO3** A payroll register is a multi-column form used to assemble the data required at the end of each payroll period.

Multiple Choice

1. **LO2** Jack Smith is married, has a spouse who is not employed and has five dependent children. How many withholding allowances is Smith entitled to?
   (a) 5 (c) 7
   (b) 6 (d) 8

2. **LO2** Nancy Summers worked 44 hours during the past week. She is entitled to 1½ times her regular pay for all hours worked in excess of 40 during the week. Her regular rate of pay is $15.00. Social Security tax is withheld at the rate of 6.2% and Medicare tax is withheld at the rate of 1.45%; federal income tax withheld is $39; and $5 of union dues are withheld. Her net pay for the week is
   (a) $593.21. (c) $690.
   (b) $651. (d) $637.22.

3. **LO2** Which of the following is *not* a factor that determines the amount of federal income tax to be withheld from an employee's gross pay?
   (a) marital status (c) total earnings
   (b) number of withholding allowances claimed (d) age of employee

4. **LO3** A separate record of each employee's earnings is called a(n)
   (a) payroll register. (c) W-4.
   (b) employee earnings record. (d) earnings statement.

5. **LO4** Social Security Tax Payable and Medicare Tax Payable are classified as
   (a) liabilities. (c) owner's equity.
   (b) assets. (d) expenses.

CHECKPOINT ✓

Checkpoint Exercises

1. **LO2** Qian Wang is paid a regular rate of $14 per hour and 1½ times the regular rate for hours worked over 40 in a week. During the past week, Qian worked 45 hours.
   (a) Compute Qian's gross pay for the week.
   (b) Assume Qian is married and claims two withholding allowances. Compute the amount of federal income tax her employer should withhold for the week.

2. **LO4** The column totals from the payroll register of Jawhawk Supplies for the week ended February 9 were as follows:

Total earnings	$4,600.00
Federal income tax	417.00
Social Security tax	285.20
Medicare tax	66.70
State income tax	46.00
Health insurance	181.00

   Prepare the journal entry to record the payroll, crediting Cash for the net pay.

The answers to the Self-Study Test Questions are at the end of the chapter (page 316).

APPLYING YOUR KNOWLEDGE

CengageNowv2 provides "Show Me How" videos for selected exercises and problems. Additional resources, such as Excel templates for completing selected exercises and problems, are available for download from the companion website at Cengage.com.

REVIEW QUESTIONS

LO1 1. Why is it important for payroll accounting purposes to distinguish between an employee and an independent contractor?

LO2 2. Name three major categories of deductions from an employee's gross pay.

LO2 3. Identify the four factors that determine the amount of federal income tax that is withheld from an employee's pay each pay period.

LO2 4. In general, an employee is entitled to withholding allowances for what purposes?

LO3 5. Identify the three payroll records usually needed by an employer.

LO3 6. Describe the information contained in the payroll register.

LO3 7. Why is it important to total and verify the totals of the payroll register after the data for each employee have been entered?

LO3 8. Distinguish between the payroll register and the employee earnings record.

LO4 9. Explain what an employer does with the amounts withheld from an employee's pay.

LO5 10. Explain why payroll processing centers and electronic systems are commonly used in payroll accounting.

SERIES A EXERCISES

E 8-1A (LO2)
✓ Gross pay: $795

COMPUTING WEEKLY GROSS PAY Ryan Lawrence's regular hourly rate is $15. He receives 1½ times the regular rate for any hours worked over 40 a week and double the rate for work on Sunday. During the past week, Lawrence worked 8 hours each day Monday through Thursday, 10 hours on Friday, and 5 hours on Sunday. Compute Lawrence's gross pay for the past week.

E 8-2A (LO2)
✓ b: $712.50

COMPUTING OVERTIME RATE OF PAY AND GROSS WEEKLY PAY Rebecca Huang receives a regular salary of $2,600 a month and is paid 1½ times the regular hourly rate for hours worked in excess of 40 per week.

(a) Calculate Huang's overtime rate of pay.

(b) Calculate Huang's total gross weekly pay if she works 45 hours during the week.

E 8-3A (LO2)
✓ e:$7

COMPUTING FEDERAL INCOME TAX Using the table in Figure 8-4 on pages 288 and 289, determine the amount of federal income tax an employer should withhold weekly for employees with the following marital status, earnings, and withholding allowances:

	Marital Status	Total Weekly Earnings	Number of Allowances	Amount of Withholding
(a)	S	$447.60	2	________
(b)	S	451.50	1	________
(c)	M	481.15	3	________
(d)	S	490.52	0	________
(e)	M	691.89	5	________

E 8-4A (LO2)
✓ 3d row, Soc. Sec. tax: $161.20

CALCULATING SOCIAL SECURITY AND MEDICARE TAXES Assume a Social Security tax rate of 6.2% is applied to maximum earnings of $128,400 and a Medicare tax rate of 1.45% is applied to all earnings. Calculate the Social Security and Medicare taxes for the following situations:

Cumul. Pay Before Current Weekly Payroll	Current Gross Pay	Year-to-Date Earnings	Soc. Sec. Maximum	Amount Over Max. Soc. Sec.	Amount Subject to Soc. Sec.	Soc. Sec. Tax Withheld	Medicare Tax Withheld
$ 22,000	$1,700	________	$128,400	________	________	________	________
54,000	4,200	________	128,400	________	________	________	________
125,800	3,925	________	128,400	________	________	________	________
127,800	4,600	________	128,400	________	________	________	________

E 8-5A (LO2)
✓ Net pay: $639.15

COMPUTING NET PAY Mary Sue Guild works for a company that pays its employees 1½ times the regular rate for all hours worked in excess of 40 per week. Guild's pay rate is $14.50 per hour. Her wages are subject to deductions for federal income tax, Social Security tax, and Medicare tax. She is married and claims four withholding allowances. Guild has a ½-hour lunch break during an 8½-hour day. Her time card is shown below.

Name Mary Sue Guild

Week Ending March 30, 20--

Day	In	Out	In	Out	Hours Worked: Regular	Hours Worked: Overtime
M	7:57	12:05	12:35	4:33	8	
T	7:52	12:09	12:39	5:05	8	½
W	7:59	12:15	12:45	5:30	8	1
T	8:00	12:01	12:30	6:31	8	2
F	7:56	12:05	12:34	4:30	8	
S	8:00	10:31				2½

(continued)

Complete the following for the week:

(a) _________ regular hours × \$14.50 per hour	\$_________
(b) _________ overtime hours × \$21.75 per hour	\$_________
(c) Total gross wages	\$_________
(d) Federal income tax withholding (from tax tables in Figure 8-4, pages 288 and 289)	\$_________
(e) Social Security withholding at 6.2%	\$_________
(f) Medicare withholding at 1.45%	\$_________
(g) Total withholding	\$_________
(h) Net pay	\$_________

E 8-6A (LO4)
✓ Med. tax: \$126.15

JOURNALIZING PAYROLL TRANSACTIONS On December 31, the payroll register of Hamstreet Associates indicated the following information:

Wages and Salaries Expense	\$8,700.00
Employee Federal Income Tax Payable	920.00
United Way Contributions Payable	200.00
Earnings subject to Social Security tax	8,000.00

Determine the amount of Social Security and Medicare taxes to be withheld and record the journal entry for the payroll, crediting Cash for the net pay.

E 8-7A (LO4)
✓ Cr. Cash: \$4,932.37

PAYROLL JOURNAL ENTRY Journalize the following data taken from the payroll register of CopyMasters as of April 15, 20—:

Regular earnings	\$5,715.00
Overtime earnings	790.00
Deductions:	
Federal income tax	625.00
Social Security tax	403.31
Medicare tax	94.32
Pension plan	80.00
Health insurance premiums	270.00
United Way contributions	100.00

SERIES A PROBLEMS

P 8-8A (LO2/4)
✓ Net pay: \$425.30

GROSS PAY, DEDUCTIONS, AND NET PAY Donald Chin works for Northwest Supplies. His rate of pay is \$14.00 per hour, and he is paid 1½ times the regular rate for all hours worked in excess of 40 per week. During the last week of January of the current year, he worked 48 hours. Chin is married and claims three withholding allowances on his W-4 form. His weekly wages are subject to the following deductions:

(a) Employee federal income tax (use Figure 8-4 on pages 288 and 289)
(b) Social Security tax at 6.2%
(c) Medicare tax at 1.45%
(d) Health insurance premium, \$85

(e) Credit union, $125

(f) United Way contribution, $10

REQUIRED

1. Compute Chin's regular pay, overtime pay, gross pay, and net pay.
2. Journalize the payment of his wages for the week ended January 31, crediting Cash for the net amount.

P 8-9A (LO2/3/4)
✓ Cr. Cash: $2,410.41

PAYROLL REGISTER AND PAYROLL JOURNAL ENTRY Mary Losch operates a travel agency called Mary's Luxury Travel. She has five employees, all of whom are paid on a weekly basis. The travel agency uses a payroll register, individual employee earnings records, and a general journal.

Mary's Luxury Travel uses a weekly federal income tax withholding table like the one in Figure 8-4 on pages 288 and 289. The payroll data for each employee for the week ended March 22, 20—, are given below. Employees are paid 1½ times the regular rate for working over 40 hours a week.

Name	No. of Allowances	Marital Status	Total Hours Worked Mar. 16–22	Rate	Total Earnings Jan. 1–Mar. 15
Bacon, Andrea	4	M	44	$14.00	$6,300.00
Cole, Andrew	1	S	40	15.00	6,150.00
Hicks, Melvin	3	M	44	13.50	5,805.00
Leung, Cara	1	S	36	14.00	5,600.00
Melling, Melissa	2	M	40	14.50	5,945.00

Social Security tax is withheld from the first $128,400 of earnings at the rate of 6.2%. Medicare tax is withheld at the rate of 1.45%, and city earnings tax at the rate of 1%, both applied to gross pay. Bacon and Leung have $15 withheld and Cole and Hicks have $10 withheld for health insurance. Bacon and Leung have $20 withheld to be invested in the travel agency's credit union. Cole has $38.75 withheld and Hicks has $18.75 withheld under a savings bond purchase plan.

Mary's Luxury Travel's payroll is met by drawing checks on its regular bank account. The checks were issued in sequence, beginning with Check No. 423.

REQUIRED

1. Prepare a payroll register for Mary's Luxury Travel for the week ended March 22, 20--. (In the Taxable Earnings/Unemployment Compensation column, enter the same amounts as in the Social Security column.) Total the amount columns, verify the totals, and rule with single and double lines.
2. Assuming that the wages for the week ended March 22 were paid on March 24, prepare the journal entry for the payment of the payroll.

P 8-10A (LO3)
✓ Soc. Sec. tax: $37.20

EMPLOYEE EARNINGS RECORD Mary's Luxury Travel in Problem 8-9A keeps employee earnings records. Andrew Cole, employee number 62, is employed as a manager in the ticket sales department. He was born on May 8, 1986, and was hired on June 1 of last year. His Social Security number is 544-67-1283. He lives at 28 Quarry Drive, Vernon, CT, 06066.

REQUIRED

For the week ended March 22, complete an employee earnings record for Andrew Cole. (Insert earnings data only for the week of March 22.)

SERIES B EXERCISES

E 8-1B (LO2)
✓ Gross pay: $678

COMPUTING WEEKLY GROSS PAY Manuel Soto's regular hourly rate is $12. He receives 1½ times the regular rate for hours worked in excess of 40 a week and double the rate for work on Sunday. During the past week, Soto worked 8 hours each day Monday through Thursday, 11 hours on Friday, and 6 hours on Sunday. Compute Soto's gross pay for the past week.

E 8-2B (LO2)
✓ b: $918.75

COMPUTING OVERTIME RATE OF PAY AND GROSS WEEKLY PAY Mike Fritz receives a regular salary of $3,120 a month and is paid 1½ times the regular hourly rate for hours worked in excess of 40 per week.

(a) Calculate Fritz's overtime rate of pay. (Compute to the nearest half cent.)
(b) Calculate Fritz's total gross weekly pay if he works 46 hours during the week.

E 8-3B (LO2)
✓ e: $62

COMPUTING FEDERAL INCOME TAX Using the table in Figure 8-4 on pages 288 and 289, determine the amount of federal income tax an employer should withhold weekly for employees with the following marital status, earnings, and withholding allowances:

	Marital Status	Total Weekly Earnings	Number of Allowances	Amount of Withholding
(a)	M	$546.00	3	________
(b)	M	490.00	1	________
(c)	S	461.39	2	________
(d)	M	522.88	2	________
(e)	S	612.00	0	________

E 8-4B (LO2)
✓ 3rd row, Soc. Sec. tax: $179.80

CALCULATING SOCIAL SECURITY AND MEDICARE TAXES Assume a Social Security tax rate of 6.2% is applied to maximum earnings of $128,400 and a Medicare tax rate of 1.45% is applied to all earnings. Calculate the Social Security and Medicare taxes for the following situations:

Cumul. Pay Before Current Weekly Payroll	Current Gross Pay	Year-to-Date Earnings	Soc. Sec. Maximum	Amount Over Max. Soc. Sec.	Amount Subject to Soc. Sec.	Soc. Sec. Tax Withheld	Medicare Tax Withheld
$ 31,000	$1,500	________	$128,400	________	________	________	________
53,000	2,860	________	128,400	________	________	________	________
125,500	3,140	________	128,400	________	________	________	________
127,600	2,920	________	128,400	________	________	________	________

E 8-5B (LO2)
✓ Net pay: $658.39

COMPUTING NET PAY Tom Hallinan works for a company that pays its employees 1½ times the regular rate for all hours worked in excess of 40 per week. Hallinan's pay rate is $15 per hour. His wages are subject to deductions for federal income tax, Social Security tax, and Medicare tax. He is married and claims five withholding allowances. Hallinan has a ½-hour lunch break during an 8½-hour day. His time card is on next page.

Name	Tom Hallinan					
Week Ending	March 30, 20--					
Day	In	Out	In	Out	Hours Worked	
					Regular	Overtime
M	7:55	12:02	12:32	5:33	8	1
T	7:59	12:04	12:34	6:05	8	1½
W	7:59	12:05	12:35	4:30	8	
T	8:00	12:01	12:30	5:01	8	½
F	7:58	12:02	12:31	5:33	8	1
S	7:59	9:33				1½

Complete the following for the week:

(a) _________ regular hours × $15 per hour $_________

(b) _________ overtime hours × $22.50 per hour $_________

(c) Total gross wages $_________

(d) Federal income tax withholding (from tax tables in Figure 8-4, pages 288 and 289) $_________

(e) Social Security withholding at 6.2% $_________

(f) Medicare withholding at 1.45% $_________

(g) Total withholding $_________

(h) Net pay $_________

E 8-6B (LO4)
✓ Med. tax: $136.30

JOURNALIZING PAYROLL TRANSACTIONS On November 30, the payroll register of Webster & Smith indicated the following information:

Wages and Salaries Expense	$9,400.00
Employee Federal Income Tax Payable	985.00
United Way Contributions Payable	200.00
Earnings subject to Social Security tax	9,400.00

Determine the amount of Social Security and Medicare taxes to be withheld and record the journal entry for the payroll, crediting Cash for the net pay.

E 8-7B (LO4)
✓ Cr. Cash: $5,696.54

PAYROLL JOURNAL ENTRY Journalize the following data taken from the payroll register of Himes Bakery as of June 12, 20--:

Regular earnings	$6,520.00
Overtime earnings	950.00
Deductions:	
Federal income tax	782.00
Social Security tax	463.14
Medicare tax	108.32
Pension plan	80.00
Health insurance premiums	190.00
United Way contributions	150.00

SERIES B PROBLEMS

P 8-8B (LO2/4)
✓ Net pay: $416.15

GROSS PAY, DEDUCTIONS, AND NET PAY Elyse Lin works for Columbia Industries. Her rate of pay is $14.50 per hour, and she is paid 1½ times the regular rate for all hours worked in excess of 40 per week. During the last week of January of the current year, she worked 46 hours. Lin is married and claims two withholding allowances on her W-4 form. Her weekly wages are subject to the following deductions:

(a) Employee federal income tax (use Figure 8-4 on pages 288 and 289)
(b) Social Security tax at 6.2%
(c) Medicare tax at 1.45%
(d) Health insurance premium, $92
(e) Credit union, $110
(f) United Way contribution, $5

REQUIRED

1. Compute Lin's regular pay, overtime pay, gross pay, and net pay.
2. Journalize the payment of her wages for the week ended January 31, crediting Cash for the net amount.

P 8-9B (LO2/3/4)
✓ Cr. Cash: $2,374.27

PAYROLL REGISTER AND PAYROLL JOURNAL ENTRY Karen Jolly operates a bakery called Karen's Cupcakes. She has five employees, all of whom are paid on a weekly basis. Karen's Cupcakes uses a payroll register, individual employee earnings records, and a general journal.

Karen's Cupcakes uses a weekly federal income tax withholding table like the one in Figure 8-4 on pages 288 and 289. The payroll data for each employee for the week ended February 15, 20--, are given below. Employees are paid 1½ times the regular rate for working over 40 hours a week.

Name	No. of Allowances	Marital Status	Total Hours Worked Feb. 9–15	Rate	Total Earnings Jan. 1–Feb. 8
Barone, William	1	S	40	$14.00	$3,360.00
Hastings, Gene	4	M	45	15.00	3,870.00
Nitobe, Isako	3	M	46	12.00	3,168.00
Smith, Judy	2	M	42	13.00	3,276.00
Tarshis, Dolores	1	S	39	14.50	3,480.00

Social Security tax is withheld from the first $128,400 of earnings at the rate of 6.2%. Medicare tax is withheld at the rate of 1.45%, and city earnings tax at the rate of 1%, both applied to gross pay. Hastings and Smith have $35 withheld and Nitobe and Tarshis have $15 withheld for health insurance. Nitobe and Tarshis have $25 withheld to be invested in the bakers' credit union. Hastings has $18.75 withheld and Smith has $43.75 withheld under a savings bond purchase plan.

Karen's Cupcakes' payroll is met by drawing checks on its regular bank account. The checks were issued in sequence, beginning with No. 365.

REQUIRED

1. Prepare a payroll register for Karen's Cupcakes for the week ended February 15, 20--. (In the Taxable Earnings/Unemployment Compensation column, enter the same amounts as in the Social Security column.) Total the amount columns, verify the totals, and rule with single and double lines.
2. Assuming that the wages for the week ended February 15 were paid on February 17, prepare the journal entry for the payment of this payroll.

P 8-10B (LO3)
✓ Soc. Sec. tax: $34.72

EMPLOYEE EARNINGS RECORD Karen's Cupcakes in Problem 8-9B keeps employee earnings records. William Barone, employee number 19, is employed as a baker in the desserts department. He was born on August 26, 1979, and was hired on October 1 of last year. His Social Security number is 342-73-4681. He lives at 30 Timber Lane, Willington, CT, 06279.

REQUIRED

For the week ended February 15, complete an employee earnings record for William Barone. (Insert earnings data only for the week of February 15.)

CHECK LIST
- ☐ Managing
- ☐ Planning
- ☐ Drafting
- ☐ Break
- ☐ Revising
- ☐ Managing

MANAGING YOUR WRITING

The federal minimum wage originally was only 25 cents an hour. Today it is $7.25 an hour and many states have minimum wage rates much higher. Assume that Congress is considering raising the minimum wage again and your U.S. representative is asking for public opinion on this issue. Write a letter to your representative with arguments for and against a higher minimum wage.

ETHICS

ETHICS CASE

Maura Lowe is a payroll accountant for N & L Company. She prepares and processes the company's payroll on a weekly basis and has been at N & L for only three months. All employees are paid on Friday. On Wednesday afternoon, Simon Lentz, one of the company's top sales associates, asks Maura to not take out any payroll deductions from his pay this week. He explains that he is short of cash and needs the full amount of his gross salary just to put food on the table and make his past-due car payment. He promises Maura that she can catch up on the deductions over the next month. The deductions include employee income tax, Social Security tax, Medicare tax, and health insurance premiums.

1. Is Simon's request of Maura ethical? Why or why not?
2. If this were the first pay period of the year and Maura agreed not to take out deductions from Simon's pay, what effect would this have on the liabilities section of the balance sheet?
3. Write a short paragraph from Maura to Simon explaining how omitting deductions from a pay period will cause errors in the company's financial statements.
4. In small groups, discuss what action Maura should take regarding Simon's request.

MASTERY PROBLEM

✓ Cr. Cash: $4,824.92

Abigail Trenkamp owns and operates the Trenkamp Collection Agency. Listed below are the name, number of allowances claimed, marital status, information from time cards on hours worked each day, and the hourly rate of each employee. All hours worked in excess of 40 hours for Monday through Friday are paid at 1½ times the regular rate. All weekend hours are paid at double the regular rate.

Trenkamp uses a weekly federal income tax withholding table (see Figure 8-4 on pages 288 and 289). Social Security tax is withheld at the rate of 6.2% for the first $128,400 earned. Medicare tax is withheld at 1.45% and state income tax at 3.5%. Each employee has $12 withheld for health insurance. All employees use payroll deduction to the credit union for varying amounts as listed.

Trenkamp Collection Agency
Payroll Information for the Week Ended November 18, 20--

Name	Employee No.	No of Allow.	Marital Status	Hours Worked S	S	M	T	W	T	F	Hourly Rate	Credit Union Deposit	Total Earnings 1/1–11/11
Berling, James	1	3	M	2	2	9	8	8	9	10	$12	$149.60	$ 24,525
Merz, Linda	2	4	M	0	0	8	8	8	8	10	15	117.00	30,480
Goetz, Ken	3	2	M	0	0	6	7	8	9	10	13	91.30	23,400
Menick, Judd	4	2	S	8	8	0	0	8	8	9	13	126.50	26,325
Morales, Eva	5	3	M	0	0	8	8	8	6	8	13	117.05	24,730
Heimbrock, Jacob	6	5	M	0	0	8	8	8	8	4	42	154.25	127,440
Townsley, Sarah	7	2	M	4	0	6	6	6	6	4	12	83.05	21,425
Salzman, Beth	8	2	M	6	2	8	8	6	6	6	11	130.00	6,635
Layton, Esther	9	3	M	0	0	8	8	8	8	8	11	88.00	5,635
Thompson, David	10	5	M	0	2	10	9	7	7	10	14	128.90	25,830
Vadillo, Carmen	11	2	S	8	0	4	8	8	8	9	13	139.11	24,115

The Trenkamp Collection Agency follows the practice of drawing a single check for the net amount of the payroll and depositing the check in a special payroll account at the bank. Individual checks issued were numbered consecutively, beginning with No. 331.

REQUIRED

1. Prepare a payroll register for Trenkamp Collection Agency for the week ended November 18, 20--. (In the Taxable Earnings/Unemployment Compensation column, enter $365 for Salzman and $440 for Layton. Leave this column blank for all other employees.) Total the amount columns, verify the totals, and rule with single and double lines.
2. Assuming that the wages for the week ended November 18 were paid on November 21, prepare the journal entry for the payment of this payroll.

3. The current employee earnings record for Beth Salzman is provided in the working papers. Update Salzman's earnings record to reflect the November 18 payroll. Although this information should have been entered earlier, complete the required information on the earnings record. The necessary information is as follows:

Name	Beth F. Salzman
Address	12 Windmill Lane Trumbull, CT 06611
Employee No.	8
Gender	Female
Department	Administration
Occupation	Office Assistant
Social Security No.	446-46-6321
Marital Status	Married
Allowances	2
Pay Rate	$11.00 per hour
Date of Birth	4/5/84
Date Hired	7/22/--

CHALLENGE PROBLEM

This problem challenges you to apply your cumulative accounting knowledge to move a step beyond the material in the chapter.

✓ **Dr. Wages and Salaries Expense: $1,596**

Irina Company pays its employees weekly. The last pay period for 20-1 was on December 28. From December 28 through December 31, the employees earned $1,754, so the following adjusting entry was made:

	Date		Description		Debit	Credit	
5	20-1 Dec	31	Wages and Salaries Expense		1 7 5 4 00		5
6			Wages and Salaries Payable			1 7 5 4 00	6
7			To record accrued wages and salaries				7

The first pay period in 20-2 was on January 4. The totals line from Irina Company's payroll register for the week ended January 4, 20-2, was as follows:

PAYROLL REGISTER—WEEK ENDED January 4, 20-2

		Earnings: Regular	Earnings: Overtime	Earnings: Total	Cumulative Total	Taxable Earnings: Unemployment Compensation	Taxable Earnings: Social Security
1	Totals	3 3 5 0 00		3 3 5 0 00	3 3 5 0 00	3 3 5 0 00	3 3 5 0 00

Deductions: Federal Income Tax	Social Security Tax	Medicare Tax	Health Insurance	United Way	Other	Total	Net Pay	
2 4 2 00	2 0 7 70	4 8 58	5 0 00	8 0 00		6 2 8 28	2 7 2 1 72	1

REQUIRED

1. Prepare the journal entry for the payment of the payroll on January 4, 20-2.
2. Prepare T accounts for Wages and Salaries Expense and Wages and Salaries Payable showing the beginning balance, January 4, 20-2, entry, and ending balance as of January 4, 20-2.

ANSWERS TO SELF-STUDY TEST QUESTIONS

True/False

1. F (does *not* work under control and direction)
2. T
3. F (is called wages)
4. T
5. T

Multiple Choice

1. c   2. a   3. d   4. b   5. a

Checkpoint Exercises

1.

(a)

40 × $14	=	$560
5 × $14 × 1.5	=	105
Gross pay		$665

(b) $29

2.

Wages and Salaries Expense	4,600.00	
Employee Federal Income Tax Payable		417.00
Social Security Tax Payable		285.20
Medicare Tax Payable		66.70
State Income Tax Payable		46.00
Health Insurance Premiums Payable		181.00
Cash		3,604.10

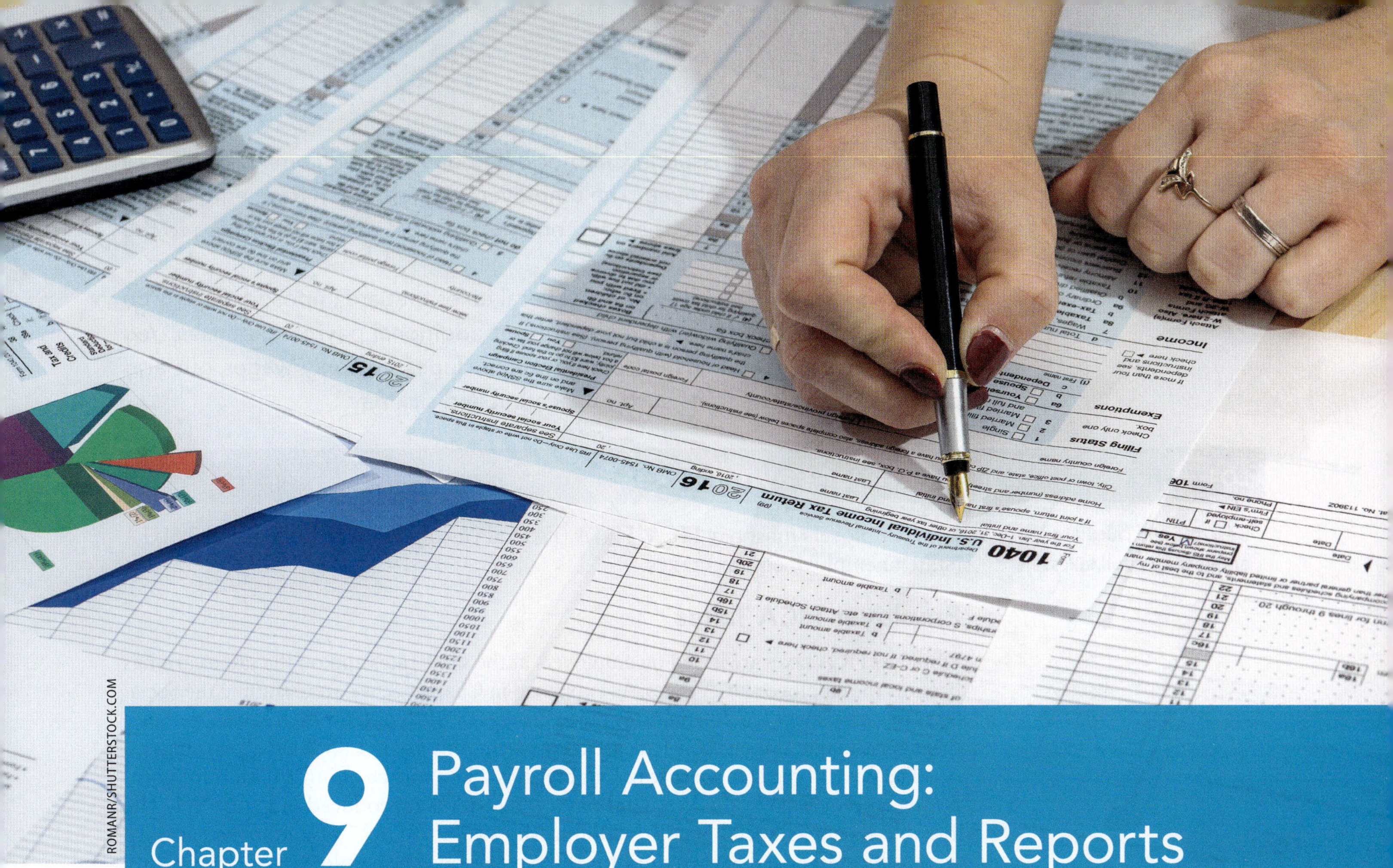

ROMANR/SHUTTERSTOCK.COM

Chapter 9 Payroll Accounting: Employer Taxes and Reports

As competition has become more global, many challenges to businesses have developed. Learning how to function in many different languages and cultures is one of these challenges. LinguaLinx is a full-service translation company that offers help with language issues. Founded in 2002, LinguaLinx has offices in the United States and the United Kingdom. It employs more than 5,000 native-speaking linguists with skills tailored to provide services in more than 100 languages. Some examples of its capabilities include simple text translation, simultaneous interpretation, sign language, copywriting, and even Braille production. It can also provide on-site language instruction classes.

LinguaLinx faces the same kinds of payroll issues as Intechra, the company described in the introduction to Chapter 8. But LinguaLinx would face the added challenge of employees in multiple countries, so it would need to know the regulations in each location. In addition, you will learn in this chapter that employers must account for not just ***employee*** wages and taxes but also ***employer*** taxes. The complexity of payroll accounting is a major reason why many businesses hire an outside company to manage their payroll. You will also learn about two of these payroll service companies in this chapter's "A Broader View."

LEARNING OBJECTIVES

Careful study of this chapter should enable you to:

LO1 Describe and calculate employer payroll taxes.

LO2 Account for employer payroll taxes expense.

LO3 Describe employer reporting and payment responsibilities.

LO4 Describe and account for workers' compensation insurance.

The taxes we discussed in Chapter 8 had one thing in common—they all were levied on the employee. The employer withheld them from employees' earnings and paid them to the government. They did not add anything to the employer's payroll expenses.

In this chapter, we will examine several taxes that are imposed directly on the employer. All of these taxes represent additional payroll expenses. You will see that the total cost of employees includes not only wages but also payroll taxes and benefits such as vacation and sick pay.

LO1

Employer Payroll Taxes

Describe and calculate employer payroll taxes.

Most employers must pay FICA, FUTA (Federal Unemployment Tax Act), and SUTA (state unemployment tax) taxes.

Employer FICA Taxes

Employer FICA taxes are levied on employers at the same rates and on the same earnings bases as the employee FICA taxes. As explained in Chapter 8, we are assuming the Social Security component is 6.2% on maximum earnings of $128,400 for each employee. Since there is no maximum on the Medicare component, this tax is 1.45% on all earnings.

The payroll register we saw in Chapter 8 is a key source of information for computing employer payroll taxes. That payroll register is reproduced in Figure 9-1. The Taxable Earnings Social Security column shows that $5,897 of employee earnings were subject to Social Security tax for the pay period. The employer's Social Security tax on these earnings is computed as follows:

FIGURE 9-1 Payroll Register (left side)

PAYROLL REGISTER

				EARNINGS				TAXABLE EARNINGS	
	NAME	ALLOWANCES	MARITAL STATUS	REGULAR	OVERTIME	TOTAL	CUMULATIVE TOTAL	UNEMPLOYMENT COMPENSATION	SOCIAL SECURITY
1	Cadrain, Sarah	4	M	2000 00	60 00	2060 00	129400 00	0 00	1060 00
2	Gruder, James	1	S	760 00	140 00	900 00	43400 00	0 00	900 00
3	Istone, Ken	4	M	640 00		640 00	32025 00	0 00	640 00
4	Kuzmik, Helen	2	M	560 00	322 00	882 00	34000 00	0 00	882 00
5	Lee, Hoseoup	3	M	620 00		620 00	31340 00	0 00	620 00
6	Swaney, Linda	2	S	600 00	225 00	825 00	30500 00	0 00	825 00
7	Tucci, Paul	3	M	610 00		610 00	30100 00	0 00	610 00
8	Wiles, Harry	1	S	360 00		360 00	6300 00	360 00	360 00
9				6150 00	747 00	6897 00	337065 00	360 00	5897 00
10									

Time cards, pay rates

Prior period total + current period earnings

Current below $7,000 cumul. total

Current below $128,400 cumul. total

Discussed in Chapter 9

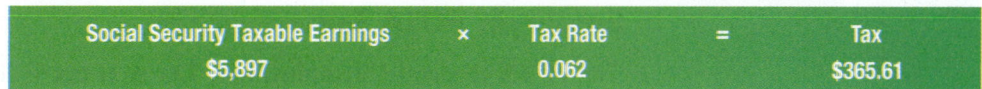

Social Security Taxable Earnings	×	Tax Rate	=	Tax
$5,897		0.062		$365.61

LEARNING KEY

Use the information in the payroll register to compute employer payroll taxes.

The Medicare tax applies to the total earnings of $6,897. The employer's Medicare tax on these earnings is computed as follows:

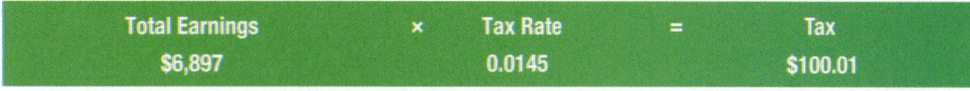

Total Earnings	×	Tax Rate	=	Tax
$6,897		0.0145		$100.01

These amounts plus the employees' Social Security and Medicare taxes withheld must be paid by the employer to the Internal Revenue Service (IRS).

Self-Employment Tax

Individuals who own and run their own business are considered self-employed. These individuals can be viewed as both employer and employee. They do not receive salary or wages from the business, but they do have earnings in the form of the business net income. **Self-employment income** is the net income of a trade or business run by an individual. The **Self-Employment Contributions Act (SECA)** requires self-employed individuals earning net self-employment income of $400 or more to pay a **self-employment tax**. Self-employment tax is a contribution to the FICA program. The tax rates are double the Social Security and Medicare rates (12.4% + 2.9% = 15.3% total). They are applied to the same income bases as those used for the Social Security and Medicare taxes. *Publication 334, Tax Guide for Small Business*, contains helpful information for self-employed persons.

The self-employment tax rate is double the employee and employer Social Security and Medicare rates because the self-employed person is considered both the employer and employee.

FIGURE 9-1 Payroll Register (right side)

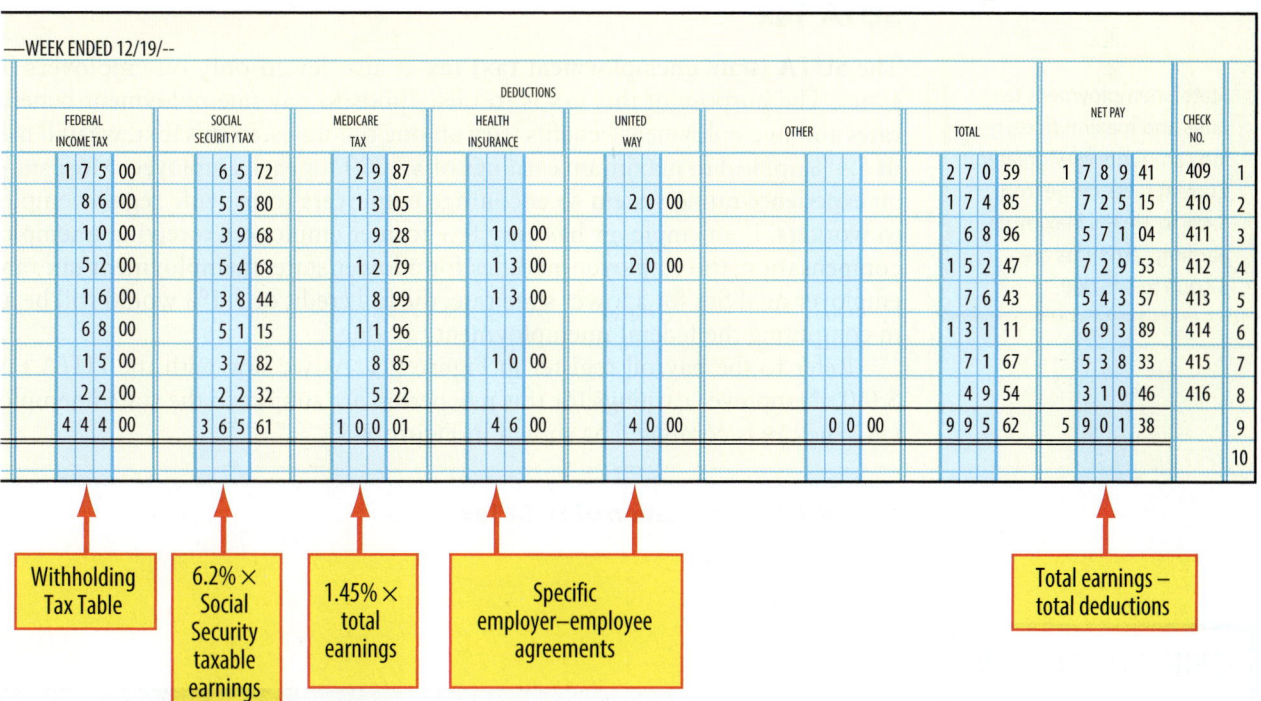

—WEEK ENDED 12/19/--

DEDUCTIONS: FEDERAL INCOME TAX	SOCIAL SECURITY TAX	MEDICARE TAX	HEALTH INSURANCE	UNITED WAY	OTHER	TOTAL	NET PAY	CHECK NO.	
175.00	65.72	29.87				270.59	1,789.41	409	1
86.00	55.80	13.05		20.00		174.85	725.15	410	2
10.00	39.68	9.28	10.00			68.96	571.04	411	3
52.00	54.68	12.79	13.00	20.00		152.47	729.53	412	4
16.00	38.44	8.99	13.00			76.43	543.57	413	5
68.00	51.15	11.96				131.11	693.89	414	6
15.00	37.82	8.85	10.00			71.67	538.33	415	7
22.00	22.32	5.22				49.54	310.46	416	8
444.00	365.61	100.01	46.00	40.00	00.00	995.62	5,901.38		9
									10

Withholding Tax Table (Federal Income Tax)

6.2% × Social Security taxable earnings (Social Security Tax)

1.45% × total earnings (Medicare Tax)

Specific employer–employee agreements (Health Insurance; United Way)

Total earnings – total deductions (Net Pay)

Employer FUTA Tax

The **FUTA (Federal Unemployment Tax Act) tax** is levied only on employers. It is not deducted from employees' earnings. The purpose of this tax is to raise funds to administer the combined federal/state unemployment compensation program. The maximum amount of earnings subject to the FUTA tax and the tax rate can be changed by Congress. The current rate is 6.0% applied to maximum earnings of $7,000 for each employee, but employers are allowed a credit of up to 5.4% for participation in state unemployment programs. Thus, the effective federal rate is commonly 0.6%.

Gross FUTA rate	6.0%
Credit for state unemployment taxes	5.4%
Net FUTA rate	0.6%

To illustrate the computation of the FUTA tax, refer to Figure 9-1. The Taxable Earnings Unemployment Compensation column shows that only $360 of employee earnings were subject to the FUTA tax. This amount is low because the payroll period is late in the calendar year (December 19, 20--). It is common for most employees to exceed the $7,000 earnings limit by this time. The FUTA tax is computed as shown in Figure 9-2.

FIGURE 9-2 Computation of FUTA Tax

	UNEMPLOYMENT COMPENSATION
5	
6	
7	
8	360 00
9	360 00

FUTA Taxable Earnings	×	Tax Rate	=	Tax
$360		0.006		$2.16

SUTA Tax

State unemployment tax rates and maximum earnings amounts vary greatly. Current rates range from 5.4% to 14.3%. Maximum earnings amounts are $7,000 to $45,000.

The **SUTA (state unemployment tax) tax** is also levied only on employers in most states. The purpose of this tax is to raise funds to pay unemployment benefits. Tax rates and unemployment benefits vary among the states. In this text, we will use a rate of 5.4% applied to maximum earnings of $7,000 for each employee. Most states have an **experience-rating system** to encourage employers to provide regular employment to workers. If an employer has very few former employees receiving unemployment compensation, the employer qualifies for a lower state unemployment tax rate. If an employer qualifies for a lower state rate, the full credit of 5.4% would still be allowed in computing the federal unemployment tax due.

Refer to the payroll register in Figure 9-1. As we saw with the FUTA tax, only $360 of employee earnings for this pay period are subject to the state unemployment tax. The tax is computed as shown in Figure 9-3.

FIGURE 9-3 Computation of SUTA Tax

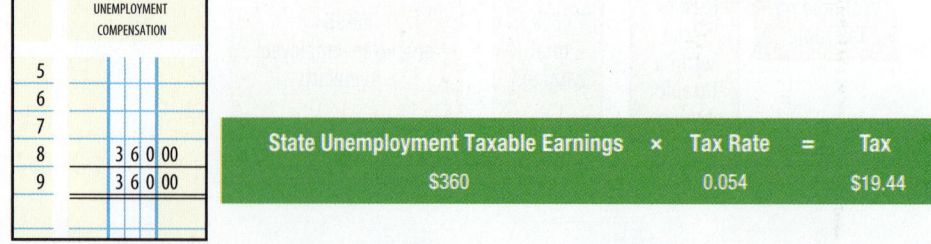

	UNEMPLOYMENT COMPENSATION
5	
6	
7	
8	360 00
9	360 00

State Unemployment Taxable Earnings	×	Tax Rate	=	Tax
$360		0.054		$19.44

CHECKPOINT

Complete Checkpoint-1 on page 340 to test your basic understanding of LO1.

LO2 Accounting for Employer Payroll Taxes

Account for employer payroll taxes expense.

Now that we have computed the employer payroll taxes, we need to journalize them. It is common to debit all employer payroll taxes to a single account—Payroll Taxes Expense. However, we usually credit separate liability accounts for Social Security, Medicare, FUTA, and SUTA taxes payable.

Journalizing Employer Payroll Taxes

The employer payroll taxes computed in the previous section can be summarized as follows:

Employer's Social Security tax	$365.61
Employer's Medicare tax	100.01
FUTA tax	2.16
SUTA tax	19.44
Total employer payroll taxes	$487.22

These amounts provide the basis for the following journal entry:

5	Dec.	19	Payroll Taxes Expense		487 22		5
6			Social Security Tax Payable			365 61	6
7			Medicare Tax Payable			100 01	7
8			FUTA Tax Payable			2 16	8
9			SUTA Tax Payable			19 44	9
10			Employer payroll taxes for week ended Dec. 19				10

The steps needed to prepare this journal entry for employer payroll taxes are as follows:

STEP 1 Obtain the total earnings and taxable earnings amounts from the Earnings—Total and Taxable Earnings columns of the payroll register. In this case, total earnings were $6,897; Social Security taxable earnings were $5,897; and Unemployment Compensation taxable earnings were $360.

STEP 2 Compute the amount of employer Social Security tax by multiplying the Social Security taxable earnings by 6.2%.

STEP 3 Compute the amount of employer Medicare tax by multiplying total earnings by 1.45%.

STEP 4 Compute the amount of FUTA tax by multiplying the Unemployment Taxable earnings by 0.6%.

STEP 5 Compute the amount of SUTA tax by multiplying the Unemployment Taxable earnings by 5.4%.

STEP 6 Prepare the appropriate journal entry using the amounts computed in steps 2–5.

To understand the journal entry for employer payroll taxes, let's use the accounting equation to examine the accounts involved. The five accounts affected by the payroll taxes entry above are shown in the accounting equation in Figure 9-4.

FIGURE 9-4 Accounting for Payroll Taxes

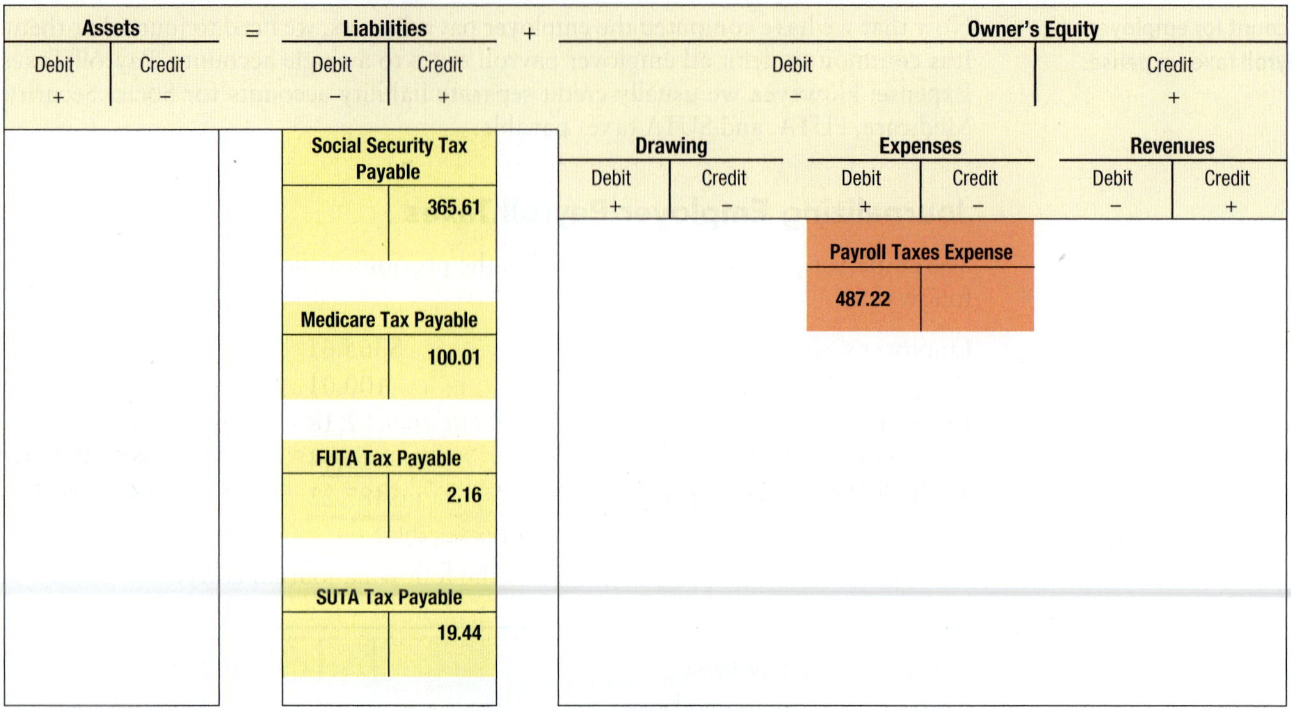

Payroll Taxes Expense

The Social Security, Medicare, FUTA, and SUTA taxes imposed on the employer are expenses of doing business. Each of the employer taxes is debited to Payroll Taxes Expense.

Payroll Taxes Expense

Debit	Credit
Social Security, Medicare, FUTA, and SUTA taxes imposed on the employer	

Social Security and Medicare Taxes Payable

These are the same liability accounts used in Chapter 8 to record the Social Security and Medicare taxes withheld from employees' earnings. The accounts are credited to enter the Social Security and Medicare taxes imposed on the employer. They are debited when the taxes are paid to the IRS. When all of the Social Security and Medicare taxes have been paid, the accounts will have zero balances.

Social Security Tax Payable

Debit	Credit
Payment of Social Security tax	Social Security taxes (1) withheld from employees' earnings and (2) imposed on the employer

Medicare Tax Payable

Debit	Credit
Payment of Medicare tax	Medicare taxes (1) withheld from employees' earnings and (2) imposed on the employer

> **LEARNING KEY**
> Employer and employee Social Security and Medicare taxes are credited to the same liability accounts because both of these taxes are due and will be paid to the IRS.

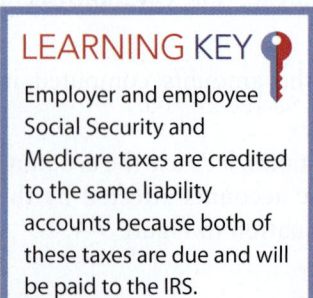

FUTA Tax Payable

A separate liability account entitled FUTA Tax Payable is kept for the employer's FUTA tax. This account is credited for the tax imposed on employers under the Federal Unemployment Tax Act. The account is debited when this tax is paid. When all of the FUTA taxes have been paid, the account will have a zero balance.

FUTA Tax Payable

Debit	Credit
Payment of FUTA tax	FUTA tax imposed on the employer

SUTA Tax Payable

A separate liability account entitled SUTA Tax Payable is kept for the state unemployment tax. This account is credited for the tax imposed on employers under the state unemployment compensation laws. The account is debited when this tax is paid. When all of the state unemployment taxes have been paid, the account will have a zero balance.

SUTA Tax Payable

Debit	Credit
Payment of SUTA tax	SUTA tax imposed on the employer

Total Payroll Cost of an Employee

It is interesting to note what it really costs to employ a person. The employer must, of course, pay the gross wages of an employee. In addition, the employer must pay payroll taxes on employee earnings up to certain dollar limits.

To illustrate, assume that an employee earns $26,000 a year. The total cost of this employee to the employer is calculated as follows:

Gross wages	$26,000
Employer Social Security tax, 6.2% of $26,000	1,612
Employer Medicare tax, 1.45% of $26,000	377
State unemployment tax, 5.4% of $7,000	378
FUTA tax, 0.6% of $7,000	42
	$28,409

CHECKPOINT

Complete Checkpoint-2 on page 340 to test your basic understanding of LO2.

Thus, the total payroll cost of employing a person whose stated compensation is $26,000 is $28,409. Employer payroll taxes clearly are a significant cost of doing business. Employer-paid medical insurance and pension plans can further increase total payroll costs.

LO3 Reporting and Payment Responsibilities

Describe employer reporting and payment responsibilities.

Employer payroll reporting and payment responsibilities fall into six areas:

1. Federal income tax withholding and Social Security and Medicare taxes
2. FUTA taxes
3. SUTA taxes
4. Employee Wage and Tax Statement (Form W-2)
5. Summary of employee wages and taxes (Form W-3)
6. Employment eligibility verification (Form I-9)

Federal Income Tax Withholding and Social Security and Medicare Taxes

Three important aspects of employer reporting and payment responsibilities for federal income tax withholding and Social Security and Medicare taxes are as follows:

1. Determining when payments are due
2. Use of electronic funds transfer to make federal tax deposits
3. Use of Form 941, Employer's Quarterly Federal Tax Return

When Payments Are Due

The date by which federal income tax withholding and Social Security and Medicare taxes must be paid depends on the amount of these taxes. Figure 9-5 summarizes the deposit rules stated in *Circular E—Employer's Tax Guide*. In general, the larger the amount that needs to be deposited, the more frequently payments must be made. For simplicity, we will assume that deposits must be made 15 days after the end of each month.

FIGURE 9-5 Summary of Deposit Rules

ACCUMULATED TAX LIABILITY	DEPOSIT DUE
1. Less than $2,500 at the end of the current quarter	1. Pay with Form 941 at end of the month following end of the quarter
2. $2,500 or more at the end of the current quarter and $50,000 or less in total during the lookback period	2. Deposit 15 days after end of the month
3. $2,500 or more at the end of the current quarter and more than $50,000 in total during the lookback period	3. Deposit every Wednesday or Friday, depending on day of the week payroll payments are made
4. $100,000 or more on any day during the current quarter	4. Deposit by the end of the next banking day

The "lookback period" identified in Figure 9-5 is the four quarters beginning July 1, two years ago, and ending June 30, one year ago. For example, the lookback period for calendar year 2019 is illustrated in Figure 9-6. The four-quarter lookback period begins July 1, 2017 ("two years ago") and ends June 30, 2018 ("one year ago").

FIGURE 9-6 Lookback Period for 2019

		JAN. 1, 2018			JAN. 1, 2019
July 1, 2017 through Sept. 30, 2017	Oct. 1, 2017 through Dec. 31, 2017	Jan. 1, 2018 through Mar. 31, 2018	Apr. 1, 2018 through June 30, 2018	July 1, 2018 through Sept. 30, 2018	Oct. 1, 2018 through Dec. 31, 2018
Quarter 1	Quarter 2	Quarter 3	Quarter 4		

The IRS strongly encourages businesses to both file and pay electronically. To file: go to www.IRS.gov/EmploymentEFile for additional information. To pay: go to www.EFTPS.gov.

Making Federal Tax Deposits

Deposits of employee federal income tax withheld, and Social Security and Medicare taxes must be made using electronic funds transfer. Generally, the **Electronic Federal Tax Payment System (EFTPS)** is used. The EFTPS is an electronic funds transfer system designed for making federal tax deposits.

On February 15, Westly, Inc., used the EFTPS to deposit $6,325.70 for the following taxes on wages paid in January:

Employees' income tax withheld from wages		$2,042.00
Social Security tax:		
Withheld from employees' wages	$1,681.80	
Imposed on employer	1,681.80	3,363.60
Medicare tax:		
Withheld from employees' wages	$ 460.05	
Imposed on employer	460.05	920.10
Amount of check		$6,325.70

The journal entry for this deposit would be as follows:

5	Feb.	15	Employee Federal Income Tax Payable		2 0 4 2 00		5
6			Social Security Tax Payable		3 3 6 3 60		6
7			Medicare Tax Payable		9 2 0 10		7
8			Cash			6 3 2 5 70	8
9			Deposit of employee federal income tax and				9
10			Social Security and Medicare taxes				10

Form 941

If the total tax liability for federal income taxes, Social Security, and Medicare taxes is less than $1,000, Form 944, Employer's Annual Federal Tax Return, may be used. Permission to do so must be obtained from the IRS, and the form must be filed by January 31.

Form 941, Employer's Quarterly Federal Tax Return, must be filed with the IRS at the end of the month following each calendar quarter. This form reports the following taxes for the quarter:

1. Employee federal income tax withheld
2. Employee Social Security and Medicare taxes withheld
3. Employer Social Security and Medicare taxes

If the total amount of taxes due is less than $2,500, payment may be made with Form 941, using Form 941-V.

A completed Form 941 for Westly, Inc., for the first quarter of the calendar year is shown in Figure 9-7. Westly had made its monthly tax deposits using EFTPS. Instructions for completing the form are provided with the form and in *Circular E*.

FUTA Taxes

Federal unemployment taxes must be calculated on a quarterly basis. If the accumulated liability exceeds $500, the total must be deposited by the end of the month following the close of the quarter. If the liability is $500 or less, no deposit is necessary. The amount is simply added to the amount to be deposited for the next quarter. FUTA taxes are deposited using an electronic funds transfer, usually EFTPS.

Assume that an employer's accumulated FUTA tax liability for the first quarter of the calendar year is $508. The employer would deposit this amount on April 30. The journal entry for this transaction would be as follows:

15	Apr.	30	FUTA Tax Payable		5 0 8 00		15
16			Cash			5 0 8 00	16
17			Deposit of federal unemployment tax				17

FIGURE 9-7 Employer's Quarterly Federal Tax Return (Form 941)

Form **941 for 20--: Employer's QUARTERLY Federal Tax Return** 950117
(Rev. January 2018) Department of the Treasury — Internal Revenue Service OMB No. 1545-0029

Employer identification number (EIN) 4 3 – 0 2 1 1 6 3 0

Name *(not your trade name)*

Trade name *(if any)* Westly, Inc.

Address 5221 Natural Bridge
Number Street Suite or room number

St. Louis MO 63115-8230
City State ZIP code

Foreign country name Foreign province/county Foreign postal code

Report for this Quarter of 2018
(Check one.)

- [X] **1:** January, February, March
- [ ] **2:** April, May, June
- [ ] **3:** July, August, September
- [ ] **4:** October, November, December

Go to *www.irs.gov/Form941* for instructions and the latest information.

Read the separate instructions before you complete Form 941. Type or print within the boxes.

Part 1: Answer these questions for this quarter.

		Column 1		Column 2		
1	Number of employees who received wages, tips, or other compensation for the pay period including: *Mar. 12* (Quarter 1), *June 12* (Quarter 2), *Sept. 12* (Quarter 3), or *Dec. 12* (Quarter 4)				1	8
2	Wages, tips, and other compensation				2	81,900.00
3	Federal income tax withheld from wages, tips, and other compensation				3	6,552.00
4	If no wages, tips, and other compensation are subject to social security or Medicare tax					☐ Check and go to line 6.
5a	Taxable social security wages	81,900.00	× 0.124 =	10,155.60		
5b	Taxable social security tips	.	× 0.124 =	.		
5c	Taxable Medicare wages & tips	81,900.00	× 0.029 =	2,375.10		
5d	Taxable wages & tips subject to Additional Medicare Tax withholding	.	× 0.009 =	.		
5e	Add Column 2 from lines 5a, 5b, 5c, and 5d				5e	12,530.70
5f	Section 3121(q) Notice and Demand—Tax due on unreported tips (see instructions)				5f	.
6	**Total taxes before adjustments.** Add lines 3, 5e, and 5f				6	19,082.70
7	Current quarter's adjustment for fractions of cents				7	.
8	Current quarter's adjustment for sick pay				8	.
9	Current quarter's adjustments for tips and group-term life insurance				9	.
10	**Total taxes after adjustments.** Combine lines 6 through 9				10	19,082.70
11	**Qualified small business payroll tax credit for increasing research activities.** Attach Form 8974				11	19,082.70
12	**Total taxes after adjustments and credits.** Subtract line 11 from line 10				12	.
13	**Total deposits for this quarter, including overpayment applied from a prior quarter and overpayments applied from Form 941-X, 941-X (PR), 944-X, or 944-X (SP) filed in the current quarter**				13	.
14	**Balance due.** If line 12 is more than line 13, enter the difference and see instructions				14	.
15	**Overpayment.** If line 13 is more than line 12, enter the difference	.		Check one: ☐ Apply to next return. ☐ Send a refund.		

Employee federal income tax withheld

Employee and employer Social Security taxes

Employee and employer Medicare taxes

► **You MUST complete both pages of Form 941 and SIGN it.** Next ➡

For Privacy Act and Paperwork Reduction Act Notice, see the back of the Payment Voucher. Cat. No. 17001Z Form **941** (Rev. 1-20--)

FIGURE 9-7 Employer's Quarterly Federal Tax Return (Form 941) (concluded)

950217

Name *(not your trade name)*	Employer identification number (EIN)

Part 2: Tell us about your deposit schedule and tax liability for this quarter.

If you are unsure about whether you are a monthly schedule depositor or a semiweekly schedule depositor, see section 11 of Pub. 15.

16 Check one: ☐ **Line 12 on this return is less than $2,500 or line 12 on the return for the prior quarter was less than $2,500, and you didn't incur a $100,000 next-day deposit obligation during the current quarter.** If line 12 for the prior quarter was less than $2,500 but line 12 on this return is $100,000 or more, you must provide a record of your federal tax liability. If you are a monthly schedule depositor, complete the deposit schedule below; if you are a semiweekly schedule depositor, attach Schedule B (Form 941). Go to Part 3.

☒ **You were a monthly schedule depositor for the entire quarter.** Enter your tax liability for each month and total liability for the quarter, then go to Part 3.

Tax liability: Month 1	6,325.70	
Month 2	5,900.20	
Month 3	6,856.80	
Total liability for quarter	19,082.70	**Total must equal line 12.**

☐ **You were a semiweekly schedule depositor for any part of this quarter.** Complete Schedule B (Form 941), Report of Tax Liability for Semiweekly Schedule Depositors, and attach it to Form 941.

Part 3: Tell us about your business. If a question does NOT apply to your business, leave it blank.

17 If your business has closed or you stopped paying wages . . . . ☐ Check here, and

enter the final date you paid wages [/ /].

18 If you are a seasonal employer and you don't have to file a return for every quarter of the year . . ☐ Check here.

Part 4: May we speak with your third-party designee?

Do you want to allow an employee, a paid tax preparer, or another person to discuss this return with the IRS? See the instructions for details.

☐ Yes. Designee's name and phone number [ ] [ ]

Select a 5-digit Personal Identification Number (PIN) to use when talking to the IRS. ☐☐☐☐☐

☒ No.

Part 5: Sign here. You MUST complete both pages of Form 941 and SIGN it.

Under penalties of perjury, I declare that I have examined this return, including accompanying schedules and statements, and to the best of my knowledge and belief, it is true, correct, and complete. Declaration of preparer (other than taxpayer) is based on all information of which preparer has any knowledge.

X Sign your name here	*William P. Jones*	Print your name here	*William P Jones*
		Print your title here	*Treasurer*
Date	*4/30/ --*	Best daytime phone	

Paid Preparer Use Only Check if you are self-employed . . . ☐

Preparer's name		PTIN	
Preparer's signature		Date	/ /
Firm's name (or yours if self-employed)		EIN	
Address		Phone	
City	State	ZIP code	

Form 940

In addition to making quarterly deposits, employers are required to file an annual report of federal unemployment tax using Form 940 (Figure 9-8). If all quarterly deposits have been made, this form must be filed with the IRS by the beginning of the second week of February. Otherwise, it must be filed by January 31. Figure 9-8 shows a completed

FIGURE 9-8 Employer's Annual Federal Unemployment (FUTA) Tax Return (Form 940)

Form **940 for 20--: Employer's Annual Federal Unemployment (FUTA) Tax Return** 850113

Department of the Treasury — Internal Revenue Service OMB No. 1545-0028

Employer identification number (EIN) 4 3 – 0 2 1 1 6 3 0

Name *(not your trade name)*

Trade name *(if any)* Westly, Inc.

Address 5221 Natural Bridge
Number Street Suite or room number

St. Louis MO 63115-8230
City State ZIP code

Foreign country name Foreign province/county Foreign postal code

Type of Return
(Check all that apply.)

- ☐ **a.** Amended
- ☐ **b.** Successor employer
- ☐ **c.** No payments to employees in 2014
- ☐ **d.** Final: Business closed or stopped paying wages

Instructions and prior-year forms are available at *www.irs.gov/form940.*

Read the separate instructions before you complete this form. Please type or print within the boxes.

Part 1: Tell us about your return. If any line does NOT apply, leave it blank.

1a	**If you had to pay state unemployment tax in one state only, enter the state abbreviation** .	1a	M O
1b	**If you had to pay state unemployment tax in more than one state, you are a multi-state employer** . . .	1b	☐ Check here. Complete Schedule A (Form 940).
2	**If you paid wages in a state that is subject to CREDIT REDUCTION** . . .	2	☐ Check here. Complete Schedule A (Form 940).

Part 2: Determine your FUTA tax before adjustments for 2014. If any line does NOT apply, leave it blank.

3	**Total payments to all employees** . . .	3	343,400.00
4	**Payments exempt from FUTA tax** . . . 4		
	Check all that apply: 4a ☐ Fringe benefits; 4b ☐ Group-term life insurance; 4c ☐ Retirement/Pension; 4d ☐ Dependent care; 4e ☐ Other		
5	**Total of payments made to each employee in excess of $7,000** . . . 5 — 280,820.00		
6	**Subtotal** (line 4 + line 5 = line 6) . . .	6	280,820.00
7	**Total taxable FUTA wages** (line 3 – line 6 = line 7) (see instructions) . . .	7	62,580.00
8	**FUTA tax before adjustments** (line 7 x .006 = line 8) . . .	8	375.48

FUTA taxable wages

Part 3: Determine your adjustments. If any line does NOT apply, leave it blank.

9	**If ALL of the taxable FUTA wages you paid were excluded from state unemployment tax, multiply line 7 by .054** (line 7 × .054 = line 9). Go to line 12 . . .	9	.
10	**If SOME of the taxable FUTA wages you paid were excluded from state unemployment tax, OR you paid ANY state unemployment tax late** (after the due date for filing Form 940), complete the worksheet in the instructions. Enter the amount from line 7 of the worksheet . .	10	.
11	**If credit reduction applies,** enter the total from Schedule A (Form 940) . . .	11	.

Part 4: Determine your FUTA tax and balance due or overpayment for 2014. If any line does NOT apply, leave it blank.

12	**Total FUTA tax after adjustments** (lines 8 + 9 + 10 + 11 = line 12) . . .	12	375.48
13	**FUTA tax deposited for the year, including any overpayment applied from a prior year** .	13	.
14	**Balance due** (If line 12 is more than line 13, enter the excess on line 14.) • If line 14 is more than $500, you must deposit your tax. • If line 14 is $500 or less, you may pay with this return. (see instructions) . . .	14	375.48
15	**Overpayment** (If line 13 is more than line 12, enter the excess on line 15 and check a box below.) . . .	15	.

FUTA tax

FUTA tax paid

FUTA tax due

► You **MUST** complete both pages of this form and **SIGN** it. Check one: ☐ Apply to next return. ☐ Send a refund.

Next ►

For Privacy Act and Paperwork Reduction Act Notice, see the back of Form 940-V, Payment Voucher. Cat. No. 112340 Form **940** (20--)

Form 940 for Westly, Inc. Instructions for completing the form are provided with the form and in *Circular E*. If a balance is due, it may be paid using EFTPS, or Form 940-V if the amount due is $500 or less. Figure 9-9 shows a completed Form 940-V for Westly.

SUTA Taxes

Deposit rules and forms for state unemployment taxes vary among the states. Deposits usually are required on a quarterly basis. Assume that Westly's accumulated state

FIGURE 9-8 Employer's Annual Federal Unemployment (FUTA) Tax Return (Form 940) (*concluded*)

850212

Name *(not your trade name)* | **Employer identification number (EIN)**

Part 5: Report your FUTA tax liability by quarter only if line 12 is more than $500. If not, go to Part 6.

16 Report the amount of your FUTA tax liability for each quarter; do NOT enter the amount you deposited. If you had no liability for a quarter, leave the line blank.

16a	**1st quarter** (January 1 – March 31)	**16a**	.
16b	**2nd quarter** (April 1 – June 30)	**16b**	.
16c	**3rd quarter** (July 1 – September 30)	**16c**	.
16d	**4th quarter** (October 1 – December 31)	**16d**	.

17 Total tax liability for the year (lines 16a + 16b + 16c + 16d = line 17) **17** . **Total must equal line 12.**

Part 6: May we speak with your third-party designee?

Do you want to allow an employee, a paid tax preparer, or another person to discuss this return with the IRS? See the instructions for details.

☐ **Yes.** Designee's name and phone number

Select a 5-digit Personal Identification Number (PIN) to use when talking to IRS

☐ **No.**

Part 7: Sign here. You MUST complete both pages of this form and SIGN it.

Under penalties of perjury, I declare that I have examined this return, including accompanying schedules and statements, and to the best of my knowledge and belief, it is true, correct, and complete, and that no part of any payment made to a state unemployment fund claimed as a credit was, or is to be, deducted from the payments made to employees. Declaration of preparer (other than taxpayer) is based on all information of which preparer has any knowledge.

✗ Sign your name here *William P. Jones*

Print your name here: WILLIAM P. JONES

Print your title here: TREASURER

Date: 1 / 31 / --

Best daytime phone

Paid Preparer Use Only

Check if you are self-employed . ☐

Preparer's name | PTIN

Preparer's signature | Date / /

Firm's name (or yours if self-employed) | EIN

Address | Phone ( ) –

City | State | ZIP code

Page **2** Form **940** (20--)

FIGURE 9-9 Payment Voucher (Form 940-V)

Form **940-V**
Department of the Treasury
Internal Revenue Service

Payment Voucher
▶ Do not staple or attach this voucher to your payment.

OMB No. 1545-0028
20--

1 Enter your employer identification number (EIN).
43 0211630

2 **Enter the amount of your payment.** ▶
Make your check or money order payable to **"United States Treasury"**

Dollars	Cents
375	48

3 Enter your business name (individual name if sole proprietor).
Westly, Inc.
Enter your address.
5221 Natural Bridge
Enter your city, state, and ZIP code or your city, foreign country name, foreign province/county, and foreign postal code.
St. Louis, MO 63115-8230

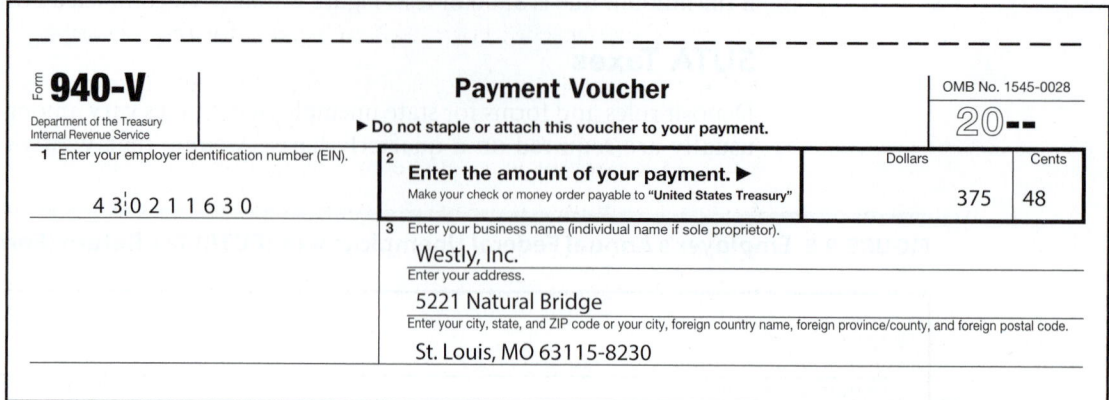

unemployment liability for the first quarter of the calendar year is $3,240. The journal entry for the deposit of this amount with the state on April 30 would be as follows:

19	Apr.	30	SUTA Tax Payable		3,240.00		19
20			Cash			3,240.00	20
21			Deposit of state unemployment tax				21

Employee Wage and Tax Statement

By January 31 of each year, employers must furnish each employee with a Wage and Tax Statement, Form W-2 (Figure 9-10). This form shows the total amount of wages

FIGURE 9-10 Wage and Tax Statement (Form W-2)

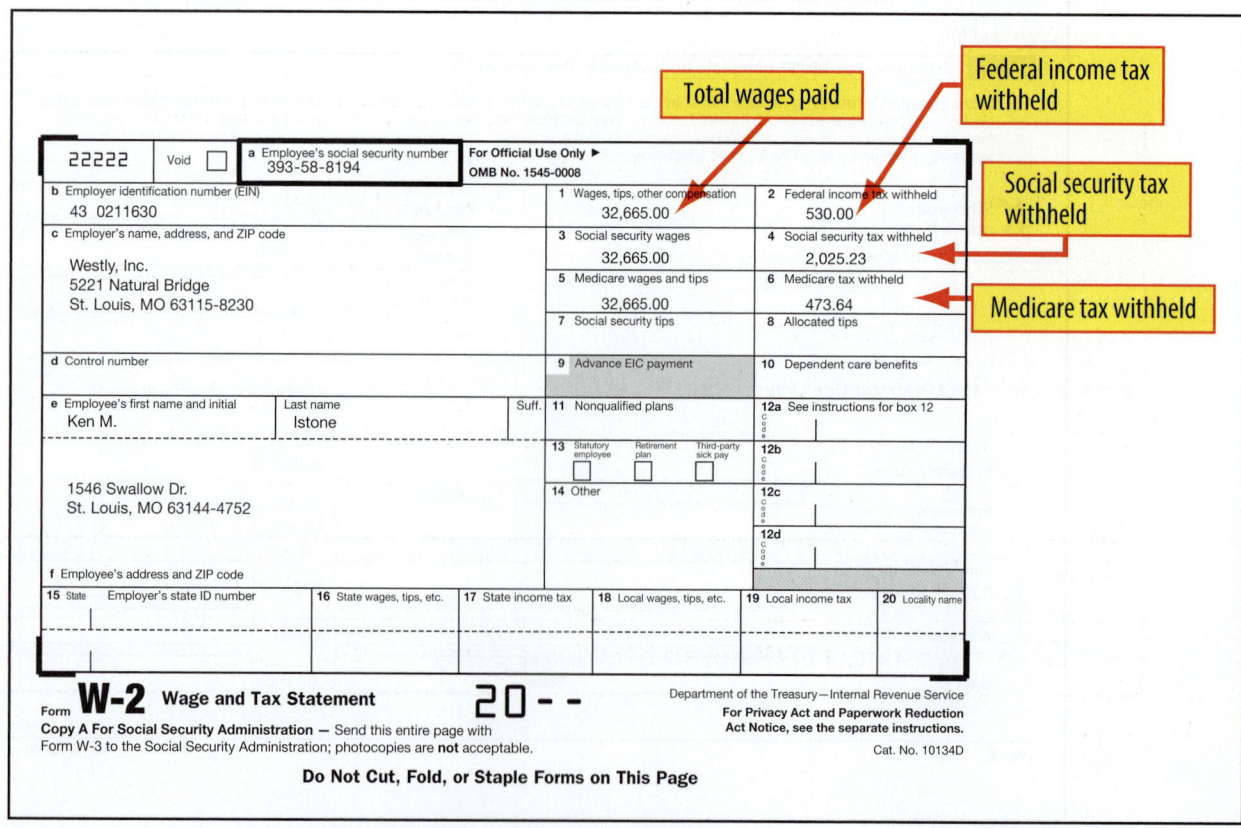

Total wages paid

Federal income tax withheld

Social security tax withheld

Medicare tax withheld

22222 Void ☐

a Employee's social security number 393-58-8194

For Official Use Only ▶
OMB No. 1545-0008

b Employer identification number (EIN)
43 0211630

c Employer's name, address, and ZIP code
Westly, Inc.
5221 Natural Bridge
St. Louis, MO 63115-8230

1 Wages, tips, other compensation 32,665.00	2 Federal income tax withheld 530.00
3 Social security wages 32,665.00	4 Social security tax withheld 2,025.23
5 Medicare wages and tips 32,665.00	6 Medicare tax withheld 473.64
7 Social security tips	8 Allocated tips
9 Advance EIC payment	10 Dependent care benefits
11 Nonqualified plans	12a See instructions for box 12
13 Statutory employee ☐ Retirement plan ☐ Third-party sick pay ☐	12b
14 Other	12c
	12d

d Control number

e Employee's first name and initial Ken M. Last name Istone Suff.

1546 Swallow Dr.
St. Louis, MO 63144-4752

f Employee's address and ZIP code

15 State Employer's state ID number	16 State wages, tips, etc.	17 State income tax	18 Local wages, tips, etc.	19 Local income tax	20 Locality name

Form **W-2** Wage and Tax Statement 20--

Department of the Treasury—Internal Revenue Service
For Privacy Act and Paperwork Reduction Act Notice, see the separate instructions.
Cat. No. 10134D

Copy A For Social Security Administration — Send this entire page with Form W-3 to the Social Security Administration; photocopies are **not** acceptable.

Do Not Cut, Fold, or Staple Forms on This Page

paid to the employee and the amounts of taxes withheld during the preceding taxable year. The employee earnings record contains the information needed to complete this form.

Multiple copies of Form W-2 are needed for the following purposes:

- Copy A—Employer sends to Social Security Administration
- Copy B—Employee files with federal income tax return
- Copy C—Employee retains for his or her own records
- Copy D—Employer retains for business records
- Copy 1—Employer sends to state, city, or local tax department
- Copy 2—Employee files with state, city, or local income tax return

The Social Security Administration is encouraging employers to file Form W-3 and Forms W-2 electronically instead of on paper.

Summary of Employee Wages and Taxes

Employers send Form W-3, Transmittal of Wage and Tax Statements (Figure 9-11), with Copy A of Forms W-2 to the Social Security Administration. Form W-3 must be filed by January 31 following the end of each taxable year. This form summarizes

FIGURE 9-11 Transmittal of Wage and Tax Statements (Form W-3)

DO NOT STAPLE

33333	a Control number	For Official Use Only ▶ OMB No. 1545-0008

b Kind of Payer (Check one): ☐ 941 ☐ Military ☐ 943 ☐ 944 ☐ CT-1 ☐ Hshld. emp. ☐ Medicare govt. emp.

Kind of Employer (Check one): ☐ None apply ☐ 501c non-govt. ☐ State/local non-501c ☐ State/local 501c ☐ Federal govt.

Third-party sick pay (Check if applicable) ☐

c Total number of Forms W-2 8	d Establishment number	1 Wages, tips, other compensation 343,400.00	2 Federal income tax withheld 27,432.00
e Employer identification number (EIN) 43 0211630		3 Social security wages 340,400.00	4 Social security tax withheld 21,104.80
f Employer's name Westly, Inc.		5 Medicare wages and tips 343,400.00	6 Medicare tax withheld 4,979.30
5221 Natural Bridge St.Louis, MO 63115-8230 g Employer's address and ZIP code		7 Social security tips	8 Allocated tips
		9	10 Dependent care benefits
		11 Nonqualified plans	12a Deferred compensation
h Other EIN used this year		13 For third-party sick pay use only	12b
15 State MO | Employer's state ID number 21686001		14 Income tax withheld by payer of third-party sick pay	
16 State wages, tips, etc. 307,828.00	17 State income tax	18 Local wages, tips, etc.	19 Local income tax
Employer's contact person		Employer's telephone number	For Official Use Only
Employer's fax number		Employer's email address	

Under penalties of perjury, I declare that I have examined this return and accompanying documents and, to the best of my knowledge and belief, they are true, correct, and complete.

Signature ▶ Title ▶ Date ▶

Form **W-3 Transmittal of Wage and Tax Statements** 20-- Department of the Treasury Internal Revenue Service

the employee earnings and tax information presented on Forms W-2 for the year. Information needed to complete Form W-3 is contained in the employee earnings records.

Employment Eligibility Verification

Every employee hired after November 6, 1986, must complete Form I-9, Employment Eligibility Verification. The purpose of this form is to document that each employee is authorized to work in the United States. The employee completes Section 1 of the form and provides the employer with evidence of the employee's identity and authorization to work. The employer completes Section 2 of the form indicating what evidence the employer examined.

Form I-9 is not filed with any government agency. Instead, it must be retained by the employer and made available for inspection if requested by the Department of Homeland Security or the Department of Labor.

Summary of Taxes, Reports, and Payments

Keeping track of the many payroll taxes can be a challenge for an employer. Figure 9-12 summarizes the various employee and employer taxes we have discussed in Chapters 8 and 9. Figure 9-13 shows a calendar that highlights the due dates for the various reports and deposits. The calendar assumes the following for an employer:

1. Undeposited FIT (federal income tax) and Social Security and Medicare taxes of $2,500 at the end of each quarter and less than $50,000 during the lookback period
2. Undeposited FUTA taxes of more than $500 at the end of each quarter
3. SUTA taxes deposited quarterly

The combination of payroll taxes, reports, deposit rules, and due dates can make payroll accounting rather complex. In fact, this is a major reason why small businesses often hire an accountant or an outside company to handle payroll.

FIGURE 9-12 Summary of Employee and Employer Taxes

	TAX APPLIES TO	
TAX	EMPLOYEE	EMPLOYER
Federal income tax	X	
State income tax	X	
Social Security	X	X
Medicare	X	X
FUTA		X
SUTA		X*

*Also applies to employees in some states.

CHECKPOINT

Complete Checkpoint-3 on page 341 to test your basic understanding of LO3.

FIGURE 9-13 Payroll Calendar

- File Forms 940, 941, W-3, and state unemployment tax report, and send W-2 to employees.
- File Form 940
- File Form 941 and make FUTA and SUTA tax deposits.
- Deposit FIT and Social Security and Medicare taxes from previous month.

January

S	M	T	W	T	F	S
			1	2	3	4
5	6	7	8	9	10	11
12	13	14	**15**	16	17	18
19	20	21	22	23	24	25
26	27	28	29	30	**31**	

February

S	M	T	W	T	F	S
						1
2	3	4	5	6	7	8
9	**10**	11	12	13	14	15
16	**17**	18	19	20	21	22
23	24	25	26	27	28	29

March

S	M	T	W	T	F	S
1	2	3	4	5	6	7
8	9	10	11	12	13	14
15	**16**	17	18	19	20	21
22	23	24	25	26	27	28
29	30	31				

April

S	M	T	W	T	F	S
			1	2	3	4
5	6	7	8	9	10	11
12	13	14	**15**	16	17	18
19	20	21	22	23	24	25
26	27	28	29	**30**		

May

S	M	T	W	T	F	S
					1	2
3	4	5	6	7	8	9
10	11	12	13	14	**15**	16
17	18	19	20	21	22	23
24	25	26	27	28	29	30
31						

June

S	M	T	W	T	F	S
	1	2	3	4	5	6
7	8	9	10	11	12	13
14	**15**	16	17	18	19	20
21	22	23	24	25	26	27
28	29	30				

July

S	M	T	W	T	F	S
			1	2	3	4
5	6	7	8	9	10	11
12	13	14	**15**	16	17	18
19	20	21	22	23	24	25
26	27	28	29	30	**31**	

August

S	M	T	W	T	F	S
						1
2	3	4	5	6	7	8
9	10	11	12	13	14	15
16	**17**	18	19	20	21	22
23	24	25	26	27	28	29
30	31					

September

S	M	T	W	T	F	S
		1	2	3	4	5
6	7	8	9	10	11	12
13	14	**15**	16	17	18	19
20	21	22	23	24	25	26
27	28	29	30			

October

S	M	T	W	T	F	S
				1	2	3
4	5	6	7	8	9	10
11	12	13	14	**15**	16	17
18	19	20	21	22	23	24
25	26	27	28	29	30	31

November

S	M	T	W	T	F	S
1	**2**	3	4	5	6	7
8	9	10	11	12	13	14
15	**16**	17	18	19	20	21
22	23	24	25	26	27	28
29	30					

December

S	M	T	W	T	F	S
		1	2	3	4	5
6	7	8	9	10	11	12
13	14	**15**	16	17	18	19
20	21	22	23	24	25	26
27	28	29	30	31		

LO4 Workers' Compensation Insurance

Describe and account for workers' compensation insurance.

Most states require employers to carry workers' compensation insurance. **Workers' compensation insurance** provides insurance for employees who suffer a work-related illness or injury.

The employer usually pays the entire cost of workers' compensation insurance. The cost of the insurance depends on the number of employees, riskiness of the job, and the company's accident history. For example, the insurance premium for workers in a chemical plant could be higher than for office workers. Employers generally obtain the insurance either from the state in which they operate or from a private insurance company.

The employer usually pays the premium at the beginning of the year, based on the estimated payroll for the year. At the end of the year, after the actual amount of payroll is known, an adjustment is made. If the employer has overpaid, a credit is received from the state or insurance company. If the employer has underpaid, an additional premium is paid.

A BROADER VIEW

Dealing with Payroll Complexity—Let Someone Else Do It

A common way for both small and large businesses to deal with the complexity of payroll reports, deposit rules, and due dates is to hire an outside company to handle the payroll. Payroll processing companies have combined payroll expertise with the power of computers to create a major business enterprise based on the efficient and effective provision of payroll services.

The extent to which businesses use outside companies to handle payroll can be seen in two of the largest payroll processing companies: Automatic Data Processing, Inc. (ADP) and Paychex, Inc. ADP has operations in the United States, Canada, Europe, South America, Africa, the Mid-East, Australia, and Asia; provides payroll services to 650,000 clients; and has revenues of over $12.5 billion. Paychex has more than 100 locations nationwide, provides services to 605,000 clients, and has revenues of $3.2 billion. These companies prepare employee paychecks, journals, and summary reports; collect and remit funds for federal, and local payroll taxes; and file all required forms with government taxing authorities.

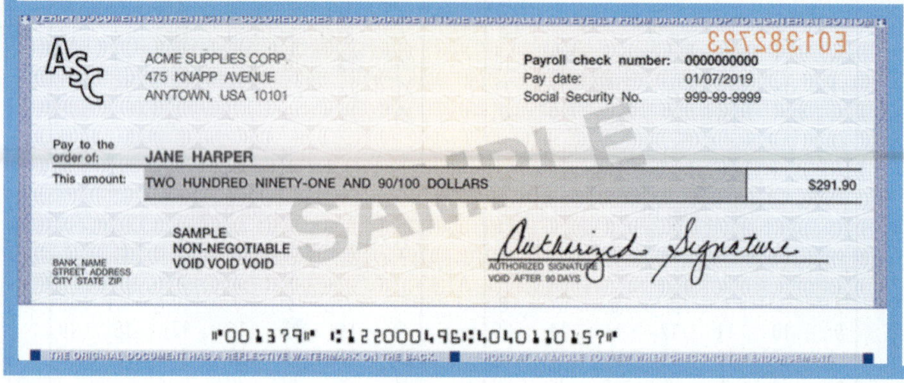

ADP, INC.

To illustrate the accounting for workers' compensation insurance, assume that Lockwood Co. expects its payroll for the year to be $210,000. If Lockwood's insurance premium rate is 0.2%, its payment for workers' compensation insurance at the beginning of the year would be $420.

Estimated Payroll	×	Rate	=	Estimated Insurance Premium
$210,000		0.002		$420.00

The journal entry for the payment of this $420 premium would be as follows:

7	Jan.	2	Workers' Compensation Insurance Expense		420 00		7
8			Cash			420 00	8
9			Paid insurance premium				9

If Lockwood's actual payroll for the year is $220,000, Lockwood would owe an additional premium of $20 at year-end.

Actual Payroll	×	Rate	=	Insurance Premium
$220,000		0.002		$440.00
Less premium paid				420.00
Additional premium due				$ 20.00

The adjusting entry at year-end for this additional expense would be as follows:

11	Dec.	31	Workers' Compensation Insurance Expense		20 00		11
12			Workers' Compensation Insurance Payable			20 00	12
13			Adjustment for insurance premium				13

In T account form, the total Workers' Compensation Insurance Expense of $440.00 would look like this:

Workers' Compensation Insurance Expense

Debit	Credit
420.00	
20.00	
440.00	

If Lockwood's actual payroll for the year is only $205,000, Lockwood would be due a refund of $10.

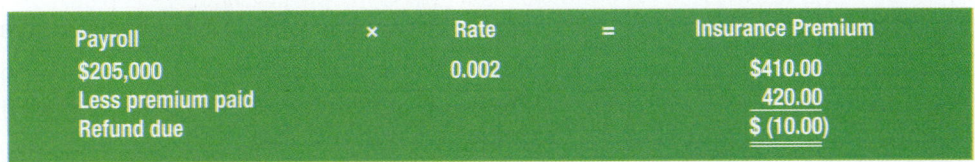

Payroll	×	Rate	=	Insurance Premium
$205,000		0.002		$410.00
Less premium paid				420.00
Refund due				$ (10.00)

The adjusting entry at year-end for this refund due would be as follows:

16	Dec.	31	Insurance Refund Receivable		10 00		16
17			Workers' Compensation Insurance Expense			10 00	17
18			Adjustment for insurance premium				18

In T account form, the total Workers' Compensation Insurance Expense of $410 would look like this:

Workers' Compensation Insurance Expense

Debit	Credit
420.00	10.00
410.00	

CHECKPOINT

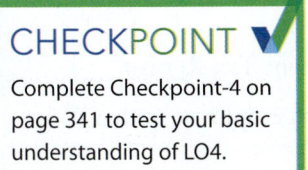

Complete Checkpoint-4 on page 341 to test your basic understanding of LO4.

SELF-STUDY

LEARNING OBJECTIVES	Key Points to Remember
LO1 Describe and calculate employer payroll taxes. **LO2** Account for employer payroll taxes expense.	Employer payroll taxes include FICA, FUTA, and SUTA taxes. These taxes represent additional payroll expenses of the employer. The journal entry for payroll taxes is as follows:

8	Payroll Taxes Expense	x x x xx			8
9	Social Security Tax Payable			x x x xx	9
10	Medicare Tax Payable			x x x xx	10
11	FUTA Tax Payable			x x x xx	11
12	SUTA Tax Payable			x x x xx	12

The steps to be followed in preparing this journal entry are as follows:

1. Obtain the total earnings and taxable earnings amounts from the Earnings—Total and Taxable Earnings columns of the payroll register.
2. Compute the amount of employer Social Security tax by multiplying the Social Security taxable earnings by 6.2%.
3. Compute the amount of employer Medicare tax by multiplying total earnings by 1.45%.
4. Compute the amount of FUTA tax by multiplying the Unemployment Taxable earnings by 0.6%.
5. Compute the amount of SUTA tax by multiplying the Unemployment Taxable earnings by 5.4%.
6. Prepare the appropriate journal entry using the amounts computed in steps 2–5.

LO3 Describe employer reporting and payment responsibilities.

Employer payroll reporting and payment responsibilities fall into six areas:

1. Federal income tax withholding and Social Security and Medicare taxes
2. FUTA taxes
3. SUTA taxes
4. Employee Wage and Tax Statement (Form W-2)
5. Summary of employee wages and taxes (Form W-3)
6. Employment eligibility verification (Form I-9)

Most federal tax deposits are made using the EFTPS. In addition, two forms are needed in reporting and paying employer payroll taxes:

1. Form 941, Employer's Quarterly Federal Tax Return
2. Form 940, Employer's Annual Federal Unemployment Tax Return

By January 31 of each year, employers must provide each employee with a Wage and Tax Statement, Form W-2.
By January 31 of each year, employers must file Form W-3 and Copy A of Forms W-2 with the Social Security Administration.

LEARNING OBJECTIVES	Key Points to Remember
LO4 Describe and account for workers' compensation insurance.	Workers' compensation insurance provides insurance for employees who suffer a work-related illness or injury. Employers generally are required to carry and pay the entire cost of this insurance.

DEMONSTRATION PROBLEM

The Totals line from Hart Company's payroll register for the week ended December 31, 20--, is as follows:

(left side) PAYROLL REGISTER

	NAME	EMPLOYEE NUMBER	ALLOWANCES	MARITAL STATUS	EARNINGS: REGULAR	EARNINGS: OVERTIME	EARNINGS: TOTAL	EARNINGS: CUMULATIVE TOTAL	TAXABLE EARNINGS: UNEMPLOYMENT COMPENSATION	TAXABLE EARNINGS: SOCIAL SECURITY
21	Totals				3 5 0 0 00	3 0 0 00	3 8 0 0 00	197 6 0 0 00	4 0 0 00	3 8 0 0 00

—PERIOD ENDED December 31, 20-- (right side)

DEDUCTIONS: FEDERAL INCOME TAX	DEDUCTIONS: SOCIAL SECURITY TAX	DEDUCTIONS: MEDICARE TAX	DEDUCTIONS: HEALTH INSURANCE	DEDUCTIONS: UNITED WAY	DEDUCTIONS: OTHER	DEDUCTIONS: TOTAL	NET PAY	CHECK NO.	
3 8 0 00	2 3 5 60	5 5 10	5 0 00	1 0 0 00		8 2 0 70	2 9 7 9 30		21

Payroll taxes are imposed as follows: Social Security, 6.2%; Medicare, 1.45%; FUTA, 0.6%; and SUTA, 5.4%.

REQUIRED

1. a. Prepare the journal entry for payment of this payroll on December 31, 20--.
   b. Prepare the journal entry for the employer's payroll taxes for the period ended December 31, 20--.
2. Hart Company had the following balances in its general ledger *after* the entries for requirement (1) were made:

Employee Federal Income Tax Payable	$1,620.00
Social Security Tax Payable	1,847.00
Medicare Tax Payable	433.00
FUTA Tax Payable	27.20
SUTA Tax Payable	183.60

   a. Prepare the journal entry for payment of the liabilities for employee federal income taxes and Social Security and Medicare taxes on January 15, 20--.
   b. Prepare the journal entry for payment of the liability for FUTA tax on January 31, 20--.
   c. Prepare the journal entry for payment of the liability for SUTA tax on January 31, 20--.

3. Hart Company paid a premium of $280 for workers' compensation insurance based on estimated payroll as of the beginning of the year. Based on actual payroll as of the end of the year, the premium is $298. Prepare the adjusting entry on December 31 for the additional workers' compensation insurance premium.

SOLUTION 1.

GENERAL JOURNAL PAGE 1

	DATE		DESCRIPTION	POST. REF.	DEBIT	CREDIT	
	20--						
1	Dec.	31	Wages and Salaries Expense		3800 00		1
2			Employee Federal Income Tax Payable			380 00	2
3			Social Security Tax Payable			235 60	3
4			Medicare Tax Payable			55 10	4
5			Health Insurance Premiums Payable			50 00	5
6			United Way Contributions Payable			100 00	6
7			Cash			2979 30	7
8			To record Dec. 31 payroll				8
9							9
10		31	Payroll Taxes Expense		314 70		10
11			Social Security Tax Payable			235 60	11
12			Medicare Tax Payable			55 10	12
13			FUTA Tax Payable			2 40	13
14			SUTA Tax Payable			21 60	14
15			Employer payroll taxes for week ended Dec. 31				15

SOLUTION 2. and 3.

18	Jan.	15	Employee Federal Income Tax Payable		1620 00		18
19			Social Security Tax Payable		1847 00		19
20			Medicare Tax Payable		433 00		20
21			Cash			3900 00	21
22			Deposit of employee federal income tax and				22
23			Social Security and Medicare taxes				23
24							24
25		31	FUTA Tax Payable		27 20		25
26			Cash			27 20	26
27			Paid FUTA tax				27
28							28
29		31	SUTA Tax Payable		183 60		29
30			Cash			183 60	30
31			Paid SUTA tax				31
32							32
33	Dec.	31	Workers' Compensation Insurance Expense		18 00		33
34			Workers' Compensation Insurance Payable			18 00	34
35			Adjustment for insurance premium				35

KEY TERMS

Electronic Federal Tax Payment System (EFTPS) (324) An electronic funds transfer system for making federal tax deposits.

employer FICA taxes (318) Taxes levied on employers at the same rates and on the same earnings bases as the employee FICA taxes.

experience-rating system (320) A system to encourage employers to provide regular employment to workers.

FUTA (Federal Unemployment Tax Act) tax (320) A tax levied on employers to raise funds to administer the federal/state unemployment compensation program.

Self-Employment Contributions Act (SECA) (319) A government Act that requires self-employed individuals to pay tax on net self-employment income.

self-employment income (319) The net income of a trade or business run by an individual.

self-employment tax (319) A tax on the earnings of a self-employed person at double the Social Security and Medicare rates.

SUTA (state unemployment tax) tax (320) A tax levied on employers to raise funds to pay unemployment benefits.

workers' compensation insurance (333) Insurance carried by employers for employees who suffer a work-related illness or injury.

SELF-STUDY TEST QUESTIONS

True/False

1. **LO1** Employer payroll taxes are deducted from the employee's pay.
2. **LO1** The payroll register is a key source of information for computing employer payroll taxes.
3. **LO1** Self-employment income is the net income of a trade or business owned and run by an individual.
4. **LO1** The FUTA tax is levied only on the employees.
5. **LO3** The W-4, which shows total annual earnings and deductions for federal and state income taxes, must be completed by the employer and given to the employee by January 31.

Multiple Choice

1. **LO2** The general ledger accounts commonly used to record the employer's Social Security, Medicare, FUTA, and SUTA taxes are classified as
   (a) assets.
   (b) liabilities.
   (c) expenses.
   (d) owner's equity.

2. **LO2** Joyce Lee earns $30,000 a year. Her employer pays a matching Social Security tax of 6.2% on the first $128,400 in earnings, a Medicare tax of 1.45% on gross earnings, and a FUTA tax of 0.6% and a SUTA tax of 5.4%, both on the first $7,000 in earnings. What is the total cost of Joyce Lee to her employer?
   (a) $32,295 (c) $30,420
   (b) $30,000 (d) $32,715

3. **LO3** The Form 941 tax deposit includes which of the following types of taxes withheld from the employee and paid by the employer?
   (a) Federal income tax and FUTA tax
   (b) Federal income tax and Social Security and Medicare taxes
   (c) Social Security and Medicare taxes and SUTA tax
   (d) FUTA tax and SUTA tax

4. **LO4** Workers' compensation provides insurance for employees who
   (a) are unemployed due to a layoff.
   (b) are unemployed due to a plant closing.
   (c) are underemployed and need additional compensation.
   (d) suffer a work-related illness or injury.

5. **LO4** The journal entry at the end of the year that recognizes an additional premium owed under workers' compensation insurance will include a
   (a) debit to Workers' Compensation Insurance Expense.
   (b) debit to Cash.
   (c) debit to Workers' Compensation Insurance Payable.
   (d) credit to Workers' Compensation Insurance Expense.

CHECKPOINT

Checkpoint Exercises

1. **LO1** Total earnings for the employees of Gary's Grill for the week ended January 14, 20--, were $6,400. The following payroll taxes were levied on these earnings:

Social Security	6.2%
Medicare	1.45%
FUTA	0.6%
SUTA	5.4%

   Calculate Gary's payroll taxes expense for the week ended January 14, 20--.

2. **LO2** Liu's Lounge had the following payroll taxes expense for the week ended February 10, 20--:

Social Security	$595.20
Medicare	139.20
FUTA	76.80
SUTA	518.40

   Prepare the journal entry for these payroll taxes.

3. **LO3** ARC Co. owes the following amounts for payroll taxes and employees' withholding of Social Security, Medicare, and federal income tax as of April 15:

Social Security Tax Payable	$6,750.00
Medicare Tax Payable	1,575.00
FUTA Tax Payable	360.00
SUTA Tax Payable	2,646.00
Employee Federal Income Tax Payable	4,095.00

Prepare the journal entries for:

(a) Deposit of the employees' federal income taxes and the Social Security and Medicare taxes on April 15.

(b) Deposits of the FUTA and SUTA taxes on April 30.

4. **LO4** LC Co. estimates that its total payroll for the year will be $260,000. LC's workers' compensation insurance premium rate is 0.22%. Calculate LC's estimated workers' compensation insurance premium and prepare the journal entry for the payment of this amount.

The answers to the Self-Study Test Questions are at the end of the chapter (pages 351–352).

APPLYING YOUR KNOWLEDGE

CengageNowv2 provides "Show Me How" videos for selected exercises and problems. Additional resources, such as Excel templates for completing selected exercises and problems, are available for download from the companion website at Cengage.com.

REVIEW QUESTIONS

LO1 1. Why do employer payroll taxes represent an additional expense to the employer, whereas the various employee payroll taxes do not?

LO1 2. At what rate and on what earnings base is the employer's Social Security tax levied?

LO1 3. What is the purpose of the FUTA tax, and who must pay it?

LO1 4. What is the purpose of the state unemployment tax, and who must pay it?

LO2 5. What accounts are affected when employer payroll tax expenses are properly recorded?

LO2 6. Identify all items that are debited or credited to Social Security Tax Payable and to Medicare Tax Payable.

LO2 7. Explain why an employee whose gross salary is $20,000 costs an employer more than $20,000 to employ.

LO3 8. What is the purpose of the EFTPS?

LO3 9. What is the purpose of Form 941, Employer's Quarterly Federal Tax Return?

LO3 10. What is the purpose of Form 940, Employer's Annual Federal Unemployment Tax Return?

LO3 11. What information appears on Form W-2, the employee's Wage and Tax Statement?

LO3 12. What is the purpose of Form I-9, Employment Eligibility Verification?

LO4 13. What is the purpose of workers' compensation insurance, and who must pay for it?

SERIES A EXERCISES

E 9-1A (LO1/2)
✓ SUTA tax: $567

CALCULATION AND JOURNAL ENTRY FOR EMPLOYER PAYROLL TAXES Portions of the payroll register for Barney's Bagels for the week ended July 15 are shown below. The SUTA tax rate is 5.4%, and the FUTA tax rate is 0.6%, both of which are levied on the first $7,000 of earnings. The Social Security tax rate is 6.2% on the first $128,400 of earnings. The Medicare rate is 1.45% on gross earnings.

Barney's Bagels
Payroll Register

	Total Taxable Earnings of All Employees	
Total Earnings	**Unemployment Compensation**	**Social Security**
$12,200	$10,500	$12,200

Calculate the employer's payroll taxes expense and prepare the journal entry to record the employer's payroll taxes expense for the week ended July 15 of the current year.

E 9-2A (LO1/2)
✓ Medicare tax: $58

CALCULATION AND JOURNAL ENTRY FOR EMPLOYER PAYROLL TAXES Earnings for several employees for the week ended March 12, 20--, are as follows:

		Taxable Earnings	
Employee Name	**Current Earnings**	**Unemployment Compensation**	**Social Security**
Aus, Glenn E.	$ 700	$200	$ 700
Diaz, Charles K.	350	350	350
Knapp, Carol S.	1,200	—	1,200
Mueller, Deborah F.	830	125	830
Yeager, Jackie R.	920	35	920

Calculate the employer's payroll taxes expense and prepare the journal entry as of March 12, 20--, assuming that FUTA tax is 0.6%, SUTA tax is 5.4%, Social Security tax is 6.2%, and Medicare tax is 1.45%.

E 9-3A (LO1/2)
✓ Soc. Sec. tax: $672.70

CALCULATION OF TAXABLE EARNINGS AND EMPLOYER PAYROLL TAXES AND PREPARATION OF JOURNAL ENTRY Selected information from the payroll register of Joanie's Boutique for the week ended September 14, 20--, is as follows: Social Security tax is 6.2% on the first $128,400 of earnings for each employee. Medicare tax is 1.45% of gross earnings. FUTA tax is 0.6% and SUTA tax is 5.4% on the first $7,000 of earnings.

			Taxable Earnings	
Employee Name	Cumulative Pay Before Current Earnings	Current Gross Pay	Unemployment Compensation	Social Security
Jordahl, Stephanie	$ 6,600	$1,190		
Keesling, Emily	6,150	1,070		
Palmer, Stefan	55,200	2,410		
Soltis, Robin	54,300	2,280		
Stout, Hannah	29,050	2,030		
Xia, Xu	126,530	2,850		

Calculate the amount of taxable earnings for unemployment, Social Security, and Medicare taxes, and prepare the journal entry to record the employer's payroll taxes as of September 14, 20--.

E 9-4A (LO1/2)
✓ Soc. Sec. Tax: $2,170

TOTAL COST OF EMPLOYEE Mandy Feng employs Jay Johnson at a salary of $35,000 a year. Feng is subject to employer Social Security taxes at a rate of 6.2% and Medicare taxes at a rate of 1.45% on Johnson's salary. In addition, Feng must pay SUTA tax at a rate of 5.4% and FUTA tax at a rate of 0.6% on the first $7,000 of Johnson's salary.

Compute the total cost to Feng of employing Johnson for the year.

E 9-5A (LO3)
✓ 941 deposit: $19,735

JOURNAL ENTRIES FOR PAYMENT OF EMPLOYER PAYROLL TAXES Angel Ruiz owns a business called Ruiz Construction Co. He does his banking at Citizens National Bank in Portland, Oregon. The amounts in his general ledger for payroll taxes and the employees' withholding of Social Security, Medicare, and federal income tax payable as of April 15 of the current year are as follows:

Social Security tax payable (includes both employer and employee)	$11,250
Medicare tax payable (includes both employer and employee)	2,625
FUTA tax payable	600
SUTA tax payable	4,050
Employee income tax payable	5,860

Journalize the quarterly payment of the employee federal income taxes and Social Security and Medicare taxes on April 15, 20--, and the payments of the FUTA and SUTA taxes on April 30, 20--.

E 9-6A (LO4)
✓ 2. Additional premium due: $12

WORKERS' COMPENSATION INSURANCE AND ADJUSTMENT Specialty Manufacturing estimated that its total payroll for the coming year would be $450,000. The workers' compensation insurance premium rate is 0.2%.

REQUIRED

1. Calculate the estimated workers' compensation insurance premium and prepare the journal entry for the payment as of January 2, 20--.
2. Assume that Specialty Manufacturing's actual payroll for the year is $456,000. Calculate the total insurance premium owed and prepare a journal entry as of December 31, 20--, to record the adjustment for the underpayment. The actual payment of the additional premium will take place in January of the next year.

SERIES A PROBLEMS

P 9-7A (LO1/2)
✓ Soc. Sec. tax: $455.08

CALCULATING PAYROLL TAXES EXPENSE AND PREPARING JOURNAL ENTRY Selected information from the payroll register of Ebeling's Dairy for the week ended July 7, 20--, is shown below. The SUTA tax rate is 5.4%, and the FUTA tax rate is 0.6%, both on the first $7,000 of earnings. Social Security tax on the employer is 6.2% on the first $128,400 of earnings, and Medicare tax is 1.45% on gross earnings.

			Taxable Earnings	
Employee Name	Cumulative Pay Before Current Earnings	Current Weekly Earnings	Unemployment Compensation	Social Security
Click, Katelyn	$ 6,650	$ 800		
Coombs, Michelle	6,370	720		
Fauss, Erin	33,460	1,200		
Lenihan, Marcus	6,930	900		
McMahon, Drew	127,050	4,440		
Newell, Marg	35,470	1,110		
Stevens, Matt	38,675	1,260		

REQUIRED

1. Calculate the total employer payroll taxes for these employees.
2. Prepare the journal entry to record the employer payroll taxes as of July 7, 20--.

P 9-8A (LO2/3)
✓ Payroll taxes expense: $3,864

JOURNALIZING AND POSTING PAYROLL ENTRIES Cascade Company has four employees. All are paid on a monthly basis. The fiscal year of the business is June 1 to May 31.

The accounts kept by Cascade include the following:

Account Number	Title	Balance on June 1
101	Cash	$70,200
211	Employee Federal Income Tax Payable	3,553
212	Social Security Tax Payable	5,103
213	Medicare Tax Payable	1,197
218	Savings Bond Deductions Payable	1,225
221	FUTA Tax Payable	574
222	SUTA Tax Payable	2,835
511	Wages and Salaries Expense	0
530	Payroll Taxes Expense	0

The following transactions relating to payrolls and payroll taxes occurred during June and July:

June 15	Paid $9,853 covering the following May taxes:		
	Social Security tax		$5,103
	Medicare tax		1,197
	Employee federal income tax withheld		3,553
	Total		$9,853
30	June payroll:		
	Total wages and salaries expense		$42,000
	Less amounts withheld:		
	Social Security tax	$2,604	
	Medicare tax	609	
	Employee federal income tax	3,570	
	Savings bond deductions	1,225	8,008
	Net amount paid		$33,992
30	Purchased savings bonds for employees, $2,450		
30	Employer payroll taxes expenses for June were:		
	Social Security		$2,604
	Medicare		609
	FUTA		84
	SUTA		567
	Total		$3,864
July 15	Paid $9,996 covering the following June taxes:		
	Social Security tax		$5,208
	Medicare tax		1,218
	Employee federal income tax withheld		3,570
	Total		$9,996
31	Paid SUTA tax for the quarter, $3,402		
31	Paid FUTA tax, $658		

REQUIRED

1. Journalize the preceding transactions using a general journal.
2. Open T accounts for the payroll expenses and liabilities. Enter the beginning balances and post the transactions recorded in the journal.

P 9-9A (LO4)
✓ 3. Refund due: $48

WORKERS' COMPENSATION INSURANCE AND ADJUSTMENT Willamette Manufacturing estimated that its total payroll for the coming year would be $650,000. The workers' compensation insurance premium rate is 0.3%.

REQUIRED

1. Calculate the estimated workers' compensation insurance premium and prepare the journal entry for the payment as of January 2, 20--.
2. Assume that Willamette Manufacturing's actual payroll for the year was $672,000. Calculate the total insurance premium owed and prepare a journal entry as of December 31, 20--, to record the adjustment for the underpayment. The actual payment of the additional premium will take place in January of the next year.
3. Assume instead that Willamette Manufacturing's actual payroll for the year was $634,000. Prepare a journal entry as of December 31, 20--, for the total amount that should be refunded. The refund will not be received until the next year.

SERIES B EXERCISES

E 9-1B (LO1/2)
✓ SUTA tax: $664.74

CALCULATION AND JOURNAL ENTRY FOR EMPLOYER PAYROLL TAXES Portions of the payroll register for Kathy's Cupcakes for the week ended June 21 are shown below. The SUTA tax rate is 5.4%, and the FUTA tax rate is 0.6%, both on the first $7,000 of earnings. The Social Security tax rate is 6.2% on the first $128,400 of earnings. The Medicare rate is 1.45% on gross earnings.

Kathy's Cupcakes
Payroll Register

	Total Taxable Earnings of All Employees	
Total Earnings	Unemployment Compensation	Social Security
$15,680	$12,310	$15,680

Calculate the employer's payroll taxes expense and prepare the journal entry to record the employer's payroll taxes expense for the week ended June 21 of the current year.

E 9-2B (LO1/2)
✓ Medicare tax: $79.24

CALCULATION AND JOURNAL ENTRY FOR EMPLOYER PAYROLL TAXES Earnings for several employees for the week ended April 7, 20--, are as follows:

		Taxable Earnings	
Employee Name	Current Earnings	Unemployment Compensation	Social Security
Boyd, Glenda L.	$ 850	$300	$ 850
Evans, Sheryl N.	970	225	970
Fox, Howard J.	830	830	830
Jacobs, Phyllis J.	1,825	—	1,825
Roh, William R.	990	25	990

Calculate the employer's payroll taxes expense and prepare the journal entry as of April 7, 20--, assuming that FUTA tax is 0.6%, SUTA tax is 5.4%, Social Security tax is 6.2%, and Medicare tax is 1.45%.

E 9-3B (LO1/2)
✓ Soc. Sec. tax: $569.16

CALCULATION OF TAXABLE EARNINGS AND EMPLOYER PAYROLL TAXES, AND PREPARATION OF JOURNAL ENTRY Selected information from the payroll register of Howard's Cutlery for the week ended October 7, 20--, is presented below. Social Security tax is 6.2% on the first $128,400 of earnings for each employee. Medicare tax is 1.45% on gross earnings. FUTA tax is 0.6% and SUTA tax is 5.4% on the first $7,000 of earnings.

			Taxable Earnings	
Employee Name	Cumulative Pay Before Current Earnings	Current Gross Pay	Unemployment Compensation	Social Security
Carlson, David J.	$ 6,635	$ 950		
Delgado, Luisa	6,150	1,215		
Lewis, Arlene S.	54,375	2,415		
Nixon, Robert R.	53,870	1,750		
Shippe, Lance W.	24,830	1,450		
Watts, Brandon Q.	127,000	3,120		

Calculate the amount of taxable earnings for unemployment, Social Security, and Medicare taxes, and prepare the journal entry to record the employer's payroll taxes as of October 7, 20--.

E 9-4B (LO1/2)
✓ Soc. Sec. tax: $2,852

TOTAL COST OF EMPLOYEE B. F. Goodson employs Eduardo Gonzales at a salary of $46,000 a year. Goodson is subject to employer Social Security taxes at a rate of 6.2% and Medicare taxes at a rate of 1.45% on Gonzales's salary. In addition, Goodson must pay SUTA tax at a rate of 5.4% and FUTA tax at a rate of 0.6% on the first $7,000 of Gonzales's salary.

Compute the total cost to Goodson of employing Gonzales for the year.

E 9-5B (LO3)
✓ 941 deposit: $17,073

JOURNAL ENTRIES FOR PAYMENT OF EMPLOYER PAYROLL TAXES Francis Baker owns a business called Baker Construction Co. She does her banking at the American National Bank in Seattle, Washington. The amounts in her general ledger for payroll taxes and employees' withholding of Social Security, Medicare, and federal income tax payable as of July 15 of the current year are as follows:

Social Security tax payable (includes both employer and employee)	$9,563
Medicare tax payable (includes both employer and employee)	2,250
FUTA tax payable	504
SUTA tax payable	3,402
Employee federal income tax payable	5,260

Journalize the quarterly payment of the employee federal income taxes and Social Security and Medicare taxes on July 15, 20--, and the payments of the FUTA and SUTA taxes on July 31, 20--.

E 9-6B (LO4)
✓ 2. Additional premium due: $22

WORKERS' COMPENSATION INSURANCE AND ADJUSTMENT Columbia Industries estimated that its total payroll for the coming year would be $385,000. The workers' compensation insurance premium rate is 0.2%.

REQUIRED

1. Calculate the estimated workers' compensation insurance premium and prepare the journal entry for the payment as of January 2, 20--.
2. Assume that Columbia Industries' actual payroll for the year is $396,000. Calculate the total insurance premium owed and prepare a journal entry as of December 31, 20--, to record the adjustment for the underpayment. The actual payment of the additional premium will take place in January of the next year.

SERIES B PROBLEMS

P 9-7B (LO1/2)
✓ Soc. Sec. tax: $543.74

CALCULATING PAYROLL TAXES EXPENSE AND PREPARING JOURNAL ENTRY Selected information from the payroll register of Wray's Drug Store for the week ended July 14, 20--, is shown below. The SUTA tax rate is 5.4% and the FUTA tax rate is 0.6%, both on the first $7,000 of earnings. Social Security tax on the employer is 6.2% on the first $128,400 of earnings, and Medicare tax is 1.45% on gross earnings.

(continued)

Employee Name	Cumulative Pay Before Current Earnings	Current Weekly Earnings	Taxable Earnings: Unemployment Compensation	Taxable Earnings: Social Security
Ackers, Alice	$ 6,460	$ 645		
Conley, Dorothy	27,560	1,025		
Davis, James	6,850	565		
Lawrence, Kevin	62,850	2,875		
Rawlings, Judy	26,350	985		
Tanaka, Sumio	22,320	835		
Vadillo, Raynette	126,560	3,540		

REQUIRED

1. Calculate the total employer payroll taxes for these employees.
2. Prepare the journal entry to record the employer payroll taxes as of July 14, 20--.

P 9-8B (LO2/3)
✓ Payroll taxes expense: $2,105.33

JOURNALIZING AND POSTING PAYROLL ENTRIES Oxford Company has five employees. All are paid on a monthly basis. The fiscal year of the business is June 1 to May 31.

The accounts kept by Oxford Company include the following:

Account Number	Title	Balance on June 1
101	Cash	$69,500.00
211	Employee Federal Income Tax Payable	2,018.00
212	Social Security Tax Payable	2,735.00
213	Medicare Tax Payable	641.00
218	Savings Bond Deductions Payable	787.50
221	FUTA Tax Payable	540.00
222	SUTA Tax Payable	1,380.00
511	Wages and Salaries Expense	0.00
530	Payroll Taxes Expense	0.00

The following transactions relating to payrolls and payroll taxes occurred during June and July:

June 15	Paid $5,394.00 covering the following May taxes:		
	Social Security tax		$2,735.00
	Medicare tax		641.00
	Employee federal income tax withheld		2,018.00
	Total		$5,394.00
30	June payroll:		
	Total wages and salaries expense		$22,050.00
	Less amounts withheld:		
	Social Security tax	$1,367.10	
	Medicare tax	319.73	
	Employee federal income tax	1,920.00	
	Savings bond deductions	787.50	4,394.33
	Net amount paid		$17,655.67
30	Purchased savings bonds for employees, $1,575.00		

30	Employer payroll taxes expenses for June were:	
	Social Security	$1,367.10
	Medicare	319.73
	FUTA	54.00
	SUTA	364.50
	Total	$2,105.33
July 15	Paid $5,293.66 covering the following June taxes:	
	Social Security tax	$2,734.20
	Medicare tax	639.46
	Employee federal income tax withheld	1,920.00
	Total	$5,293.66
31	Paid SUTA tax for the quarter, $1,744.50	
31	Paid FUTA tax, $594.00	

REQUIRED

1. Journalize the preceding transactions using a general journal.
2. Open T accounts for the payroll expenses and liabilities. Enter the beginning balances and post the transactions recorded in the journal.

P 9-9B (LO4)
✓ 3. Refund due: $16

WORKERS' COMPENSATION INSURANCE AND ADJUSTMENT Multnomah Manufacturing estimated that its total payroll for the coming year would be $540,000. The workers' compensation insurance premium rate is 0.2%.

REQUIRED

1. Calculate the estimated workers' compensation insurance premium and prepare the journal entry for the payment as of January 2, 20--.
2. Assume that Multnomah Manufacturing's actual payroll for the year was $562,000. Calculate the total insurance premium owed and prepare a journal entry as of December 31, 20--, to record the adjustment for the underpayment. The actual payment of the additional premium will take place in January of the next year.
3. Assume instead that Multnomah Manufacturing's actual payroll for the year was $532,000. Prepare a journal entry as of December 31, 20--, for the total amount that should be refunded. The refund will not be received until the next year.

CHECK LIST
- ☐ Managing
- ☐ Planning
- ☐ Drafting
- ☐ Break
- ☐ Revising
- ☐ Managing

MANAGING YOUR WRITING

The director of the art department at an advertising company, Wilson Watson, wants to hire new office staff. His boss tells him that to do so he must find in his budget not only the base salary for this position but an additional 30% for "fringe benefits." Wilson explodes: "How in the world can there be 30% in fringe benefits?" Write a memo to Wilson Watson explaining the costs that probably make up these fringe benefits.

ETHICS

ETHICS CASE

Bob Estes works at Cliffrock Company in the central receiving department. He unpacks incoming shipments and verifies quantities of goods received. Over the weekend, Bob pulled a muscle in his back while playing basketball. When he came to work on Monday and started unpacking shipments, his back started to hurt again. Bob called the human resources department and told them he hurt his back lifting a package at work. He was told to fill out an accident report and sent to an orthopedic clinic with a workers' compensation form. The doctor at the clinic told Bob not to lift anything heavy for two weeks and to stay home from work for at least one week.

1. Is Bob entitled to workers' compensation? Why or why not?
2. What effect will Bob's claim have on Cliffrock Company's workers' compensation insurance premium?
3. Write a short memo from the human resources department to Cliffrock Company's employees explaining the purpose of workers' compensation.
4. In small groups, discuss the job-related illness or injury risks of a computer input operator and measures an employer might take to minimize these risks.

MASTERY PROBLEM

✓ **Payroll taxes expense: $720.75**

The totals line from Nix Company's payroll register for the week ended March 31, 20--, is as follows:

(left side) PAYROLL REGISTER

	NAME	EMPLOYEE NUMBER	ALLOWANCES	MARITAL STATUS	EARNINGS: REGULAR	EARNINGS: OVERTIME	EARNINGS: TOTAL	EARNINGS: CUMULATIVE TOTAL	TAXABLE EARNINGS: UNEMPLOYMENT COMPENSATION	TAXABLE EARNINGS: SOCIAL SECURITY
21	Totals				5,400.00	100.00	5,500.00	71,500.00	5,000.00	5,500.00

—PERIOD ENDED March 31, 20-- (right side)

DEDUCTIONS: FEDERAL INCOME TAX	DEDUCTIONS: SOCIAL SECURITY TAX	DEDUCTIONS: MEDICARE TAX	DEDUCTIONS: HEALTH INSURANCE	DEDUCTIONS: LIFE INSURANCE	DEDUCTIONS: OTHER	DEDUCTIONS: TOTAL	NET PAY	CHECK NO.	
500.00	341.00	79.75	165.00	200.00		1,285.75	4,214.25		21

Payroll taxes are imposed as follows: Social Security tax, 6.2%; Medicare tax, 1.45%; FUTA tax, 0.6%; and SUTA tax, 5.4%.

REQUIRED

1. a. Prepare the journal entry for payment of this payroll on March 31, 20--.
   b. Prepare the journal entry for the employer's payroll taxes for the period ended March 31, 20--.
2. Nix Company had the following balances in its general ledger before the entries for requirement (1) were made:

Employee federal income tax payable	$2,500
Social Security tax payable	2,008
Medicare tax payable	470
FUTA tax payable	520
SUTA tax payable	4,510

a. Prepare the journal entry for payment of the liabilities for federal income taxes and Social Security and Medicare taxes on April 15, 20--.
b. Prepare the journal entry for payment of the liability for FUTA tax on April 30, 20--.
c. Prepare the journal entry for payment of the liability for SUTA tax on April 30, 20--.

3. Nix Company paid a premium of $420 for workers' compensation insurance based on the estimated payroll as of the beginning of the year. Based on actual payroll as of the end of the year, the premium is only $400. Prepare the adjusting entry to reflect the overpayment of the insurance premium at the end of the year (December 31, 20--).

CHALLENGE PROBLEM

This problem challenges you to apply your cumulative accounting knowledge to move a step beyond the material in the chapter.

✓ Payroll taxes expense: $1,281.25

Payrex Co. has six employees. All are paid on a weekly basis. For the payroll period ending January 7, total employee earnings were $12,500, all of which were subject to SUTA, FUTA, Social Security, and Medicare taxes. The SUTA tax rate in Payrex's state is 5.4%, but Payrex qualifies for a rate of 2.0% because of its good record of providing regular employment to its employees. Other employer payroll taxes are at the rates described in the chapter.

REQUIRED

1. Calculate Payrex's FUTA, SUTA, Social Security, and Medicare taxes for the week ended January 7.
2. Prepare the journal entry for Payrex's payroll taxes for the week ended January 7.
3. What amount of payroll taxes did Payrex save because of its good employment record?

ANSWERS TO SELF-STUDY TEST QUESTIONS

True/False

1. F (these taxes are paid by the employer)
2. T
3. T
4. F (FUTA tax is levied on employers)
5. F (this Form is W-2)

Multiple Choice

1. b 2. d 3. b 4. d 5. a

Checkpoint Exercises

1.

Social Security	$396.80
Medicare	92.80
FUTA	38.40
SUTA	345.60
Total	$873.60

2. Payroll Taxes Expense	1,329.60	
Social Security Tax Payable		595.20
Medicare Tax Payable		139.20
FUTA Tax Payable		76.80
SUTA Tax Payable		518.40
Employer payroll taxes for week ended Feb. 10		
3. (a) Social Security Tax Payable	6,750.00	
Medicare Tax Payable	1,575.00	
Employee Federal Income Tax Payable	4,095.00	
Cash		12,420.00
Deposit of employee federal income tax and Social Security and Medicare taxes		
(b) FUTA Tax Payable		
Cash	360.00	
Paid FUTA tax		360.00
SUTA Tax Payable		
Cash	2,646.00	
Paid SUTA tax		2,646.00
4. Workers' Compensation Insurance Expense		
Cash	572.00	
Paid insurance premium		572.00

3 Accounting for a Merchandising Business

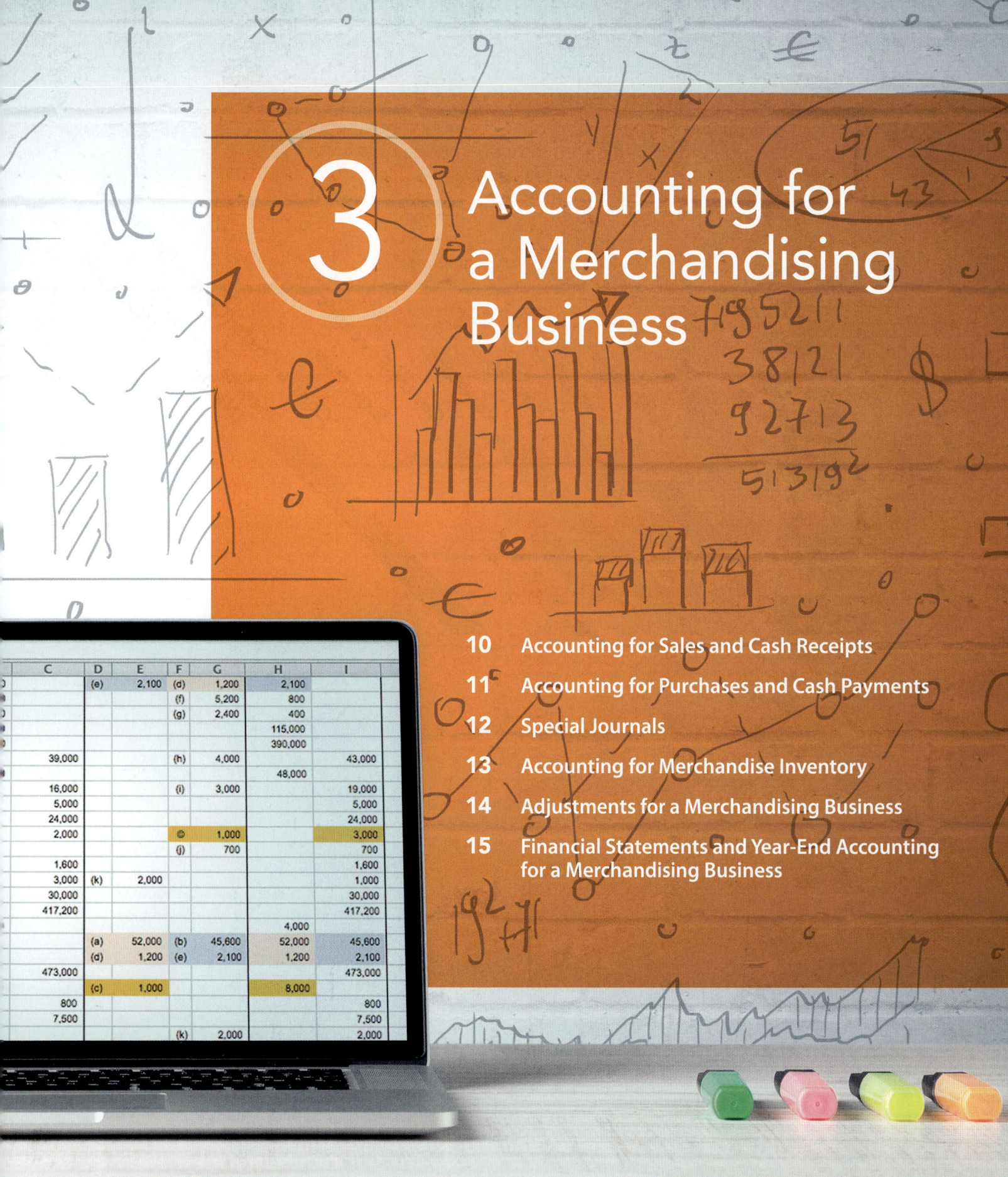

10 Accounting for Sales and Cash Receipts

11 Accounting for Purchases and Cash Payments

12 Special Journals

13 Accounting for Merchandise Inventory

14 Adjustments for a Merchandising Business

15 Financial Statements and Year-End Accounting for a Merchandising Business

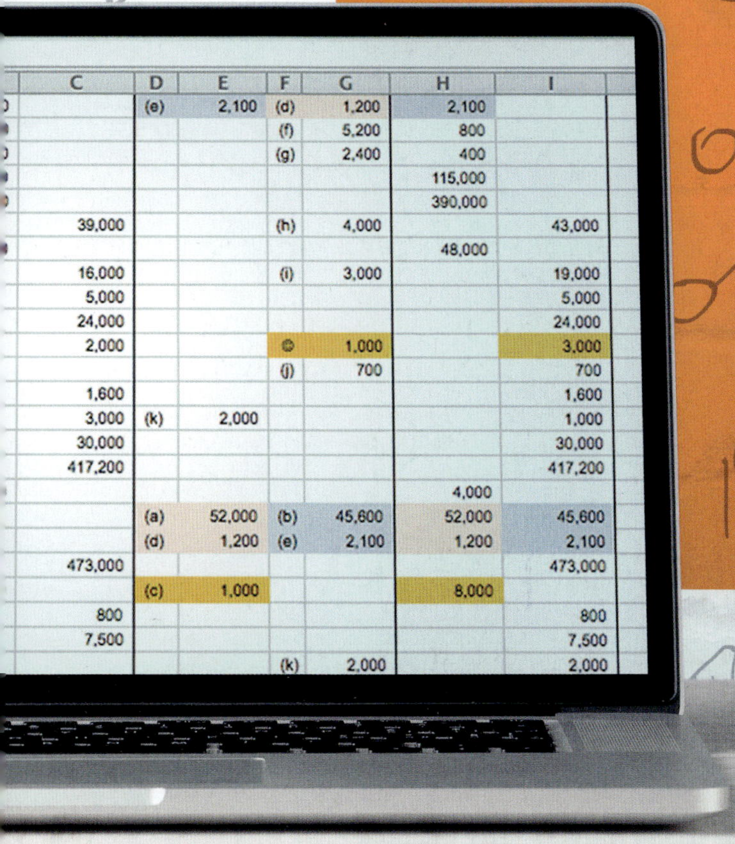

Add some color to your learning!

Throughout the text, you will be introduced to many important terms and types of accounts. To help you learn the different terms and types of accounts, we have coded many of them using the following color key in Part 3:

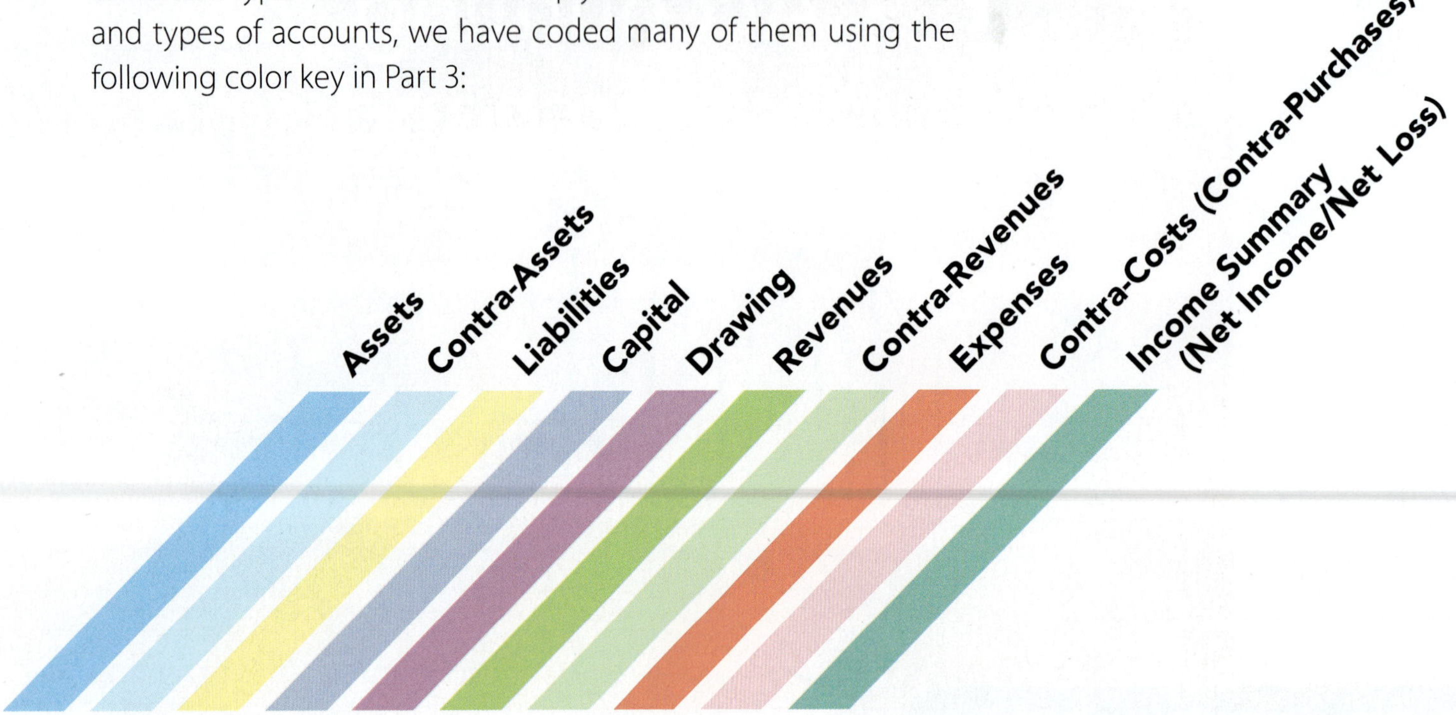

SOURCE: EARTHBRANDS.COM

Chapter 10 Accounting for Sales and Cash Receipts

In recent years, we have seen increasing concern about how our actions affect the environment. Kalso Earth Shoes is an example of a company whose business reflects this concern. Kalso Earth Shoes is a storefront and online shoe retailer specializing in eco-friendly shoes. Its shoes use less-toxic, water-based rather than solvent- or oil-based, adhesives. All leathers are tanned using a vegetable-tanning process, which uses tannic acids found in plants. Even its shoe boxes are glue-free.

Kalso Earth Shoes began as one small store in Copenhagen, Denmark, in 1960. By the late 1960's, it expanded beyond Denmark, and to the United States in 1970. It surged in popularity, experiencing growth so strong that it was unable to keep up with demand. At one point, franchise owners sued the United States distributor for lack of product. Today Kalso Earth Shoes has operations in many countries, selling both from storefronts and online. The company has learned that it needs a good system to manage and account for its high volume of sales, including cash, on account, and by credit card. In this chapter, you will learn how to account for these different kinds of sales transactions.

LEARNING OBJECTIVES

Careful study of this chapter should enable you to:

LO1 **Describe merchandise sales transactions.**

LO2 **Describe and use merchandise sales accounts.**

LO3 **Describe and use the accounts receivable ledger.**

LO4 **Prepare a schedule of accounts receivable.**

Over the last nine chapters, we have learned how to account for a service business. We are now ready to consider accounting for a different kind of business—merchandising. A **merchandising business** purchases merchandise such as clothing, furniture, or computers, and sells that merchandise to customers. For example, some large shoe and department stores buy shoes from Kalso Earth Shoes and sell them to their customers.

This chapter examines how to account for the sale of merchandise using the accrual basis of accounting. We will learn how to use five new accounts and a subsidiary ledger.

LO1 Merchandise Sales Transactions

Describe merchandise sales transactions.

A **sale** is a transfer of merchandise from one business or individual to another in exchange for cash or a promise to pay cash. Sales procedures and documents vary greatly, depending on the nature and size of the business.

> A company such as Kalso Earth Shoes makes some sales online. For Web-based transactions, companies use electronic forms that are similar to the paper documents described in this chapter.

Retailer

Retail businesses generally sell to customers who enter the store, select the merchandise they want, and bring it to a salesclerk. The salesclerk enters the sale in some type of electronic cash register that generates a receipt for the customer. A copy of the receipt is retained in the register. Most registers can print a summary of the day's sales activity, like the one in Figure 10-1. This summary can be sent to accounting and used to journalize sales in the accounting records.

FIGURE 10-1 Cash Register Tape Summary

```
    (1)
CASH SALES        327.79 *
    (3)
MCARD/VISA        550.62 *
    (6)
LAYAWAY            79.50 *
TOTAL CASH        957.91 *
    (2)
CHARGE SALES      543.84 *
    (5)
APPROVAL          126.58 *
TOTAL CHARGE      670.42 *

TOTAL SALES     1,628.33 G*
SALES TAX          81.42 *
                   81.42 *

REC'D ON ACCT.    324.51 *
                  324.51 *

PAID OUT           76.51 *
                   76.51 *

NO SALE             0.00 *
                    0.00 *

*     SUB-TOTAL
G*   GRAND TOTAL
```

An additional document often created as evidence of a sale in a retail business is a **sales ticket** (Figure 10-2). One copy of the sales ticket is given to the customer and the other copy is sent to accounting.

FIGURE 10-2 Sales Ticket

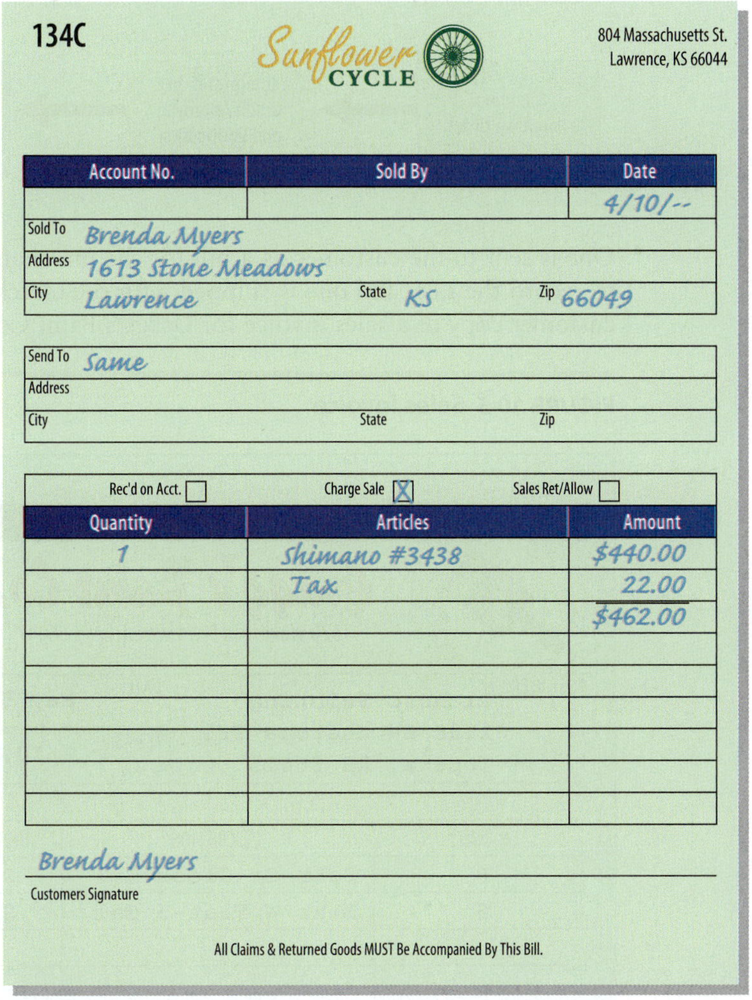

134C

Sunflower CYCLE

804 Massachusetts St.
Lawrence, KS 66044

Account No.	Sold By	Date
		4/10/--

Sold To Brenda Myers
Address 1613 Stone Meadows
City Lawrence State KS Zip 66049

Send To Same
Address
City State Zip

Rec'd on Acct. ☐ Charge Sale ☒ Sales Ret/Allow ☐

Quantity	Articles	Amount
1	Shimano #3438	$440.00
	Tax	22.00
		$462.00

Brenda Myers
Customers Signature

All Claims & Returned Goods MUST Be Accompanied By This Bill.

Wholesaler

Figure 10-3 shows how the wholesaler plays a different role than the retailer in the marketing chain. Retailers usually sell to final consumers, whereas wholesalers tend to sell to retailers. This causes the wholesale sales transaction process to differ, as shown in Figure 10-4.

FIGURE 10-3 Marketing Chain

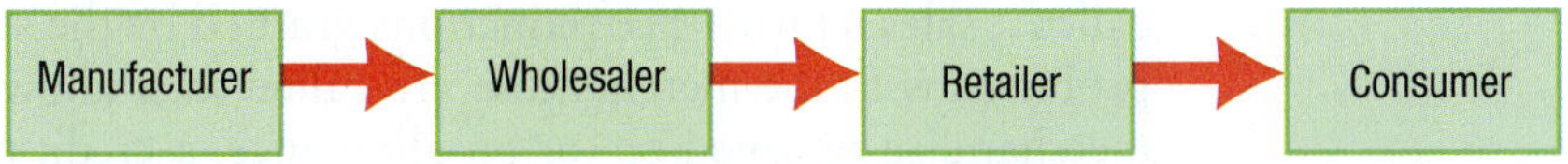

In a computerized system, customer orders can be submitted electronically. Even the credit approval can be processed electronically.

Customers commonly mail, fax, or send electronic orders to buy merchandise from wholesalers. When the customer purchase order arrives, the customer name and items being ordered are determined. Since wholesalers typically make sales on account, credit approval is needed. Three copies of a **sales invoice** are then generated.

FIGURE 10-4 Wholesale Sales Transaction Process

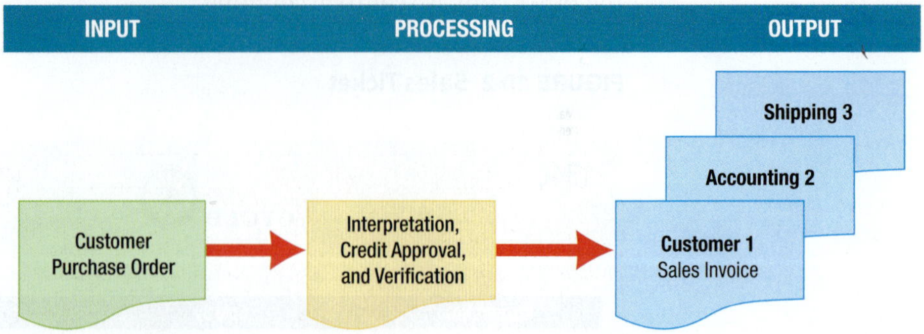

One is sent to the customer as a bill for the merchandise, one is sent to accounting to record the sale, and one is shipped with the merchandise. Figure 10-5 shows the customer copy of a sales invoice for Gragg's Paint Company.

FIGURE 10-5 Sales Invoice

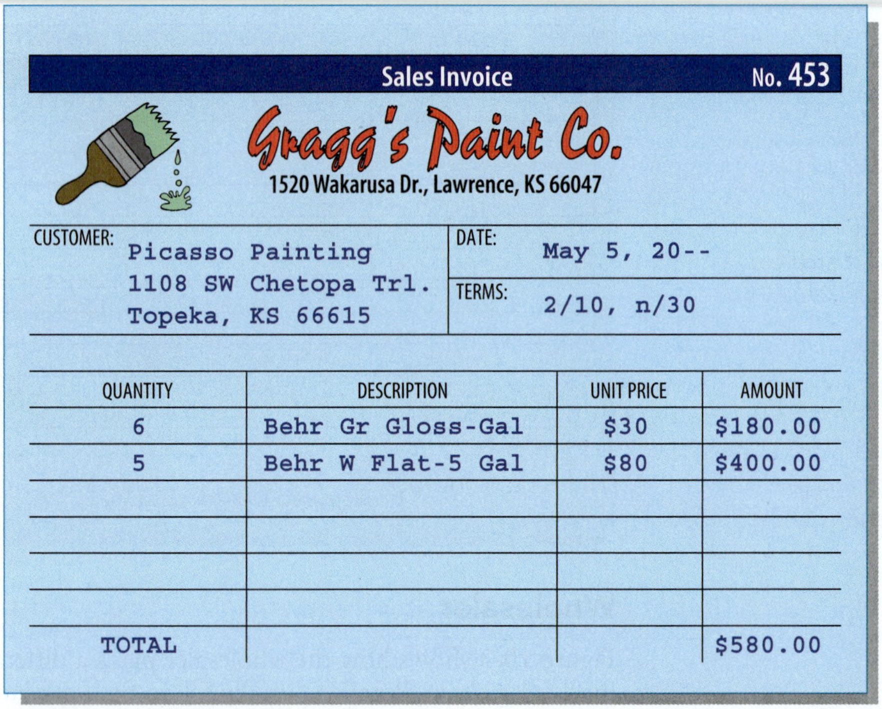

Sales Invoice No. 453

Gragg's Paint Co.
1520 Wakarusa Dr., Lawrence, KS 66047

CUSTOMER: Picasso Painting
1108 SW Chetopa Trl.
Topeka, KS 66615

DATE: May 5, 20--

TERMS: 2/10, n/30

QUANTITY	DESCRIPTION	UNIT PRICE	AMOUNT
6	Behr Gr Gloss-Gal	$30	$180.00
5	Behr W Flat-5 Gal	$80	$400.00
TOTAL			$580.00

Credit Memorandum

Both retailers and wholesalers sometimes have customers return goods or seek price reductions for damaged goods. Merchandise returned by a customer for a refund is called a **sales return**. Price reductions granted by the seller because of defects or other problems with the merchandise are called **sales allowances**. When credit is given for merchandise returned or for an allowance, a **credit memo** is issued for the amount involved. This document gets its name from the same debit and credit concepts you learned in Chapter 3. It is called a credit memo because the customer's account receivable is *credited* to reduce the amount the customer owes. One copy of the credit memo is given to the customer and one copy is sent to accounting. Figure 10-6 shows a credit memo issued by Sunflower Cycle for merchandise returned by a customer.

FIGURE 10-6 Credit Memo

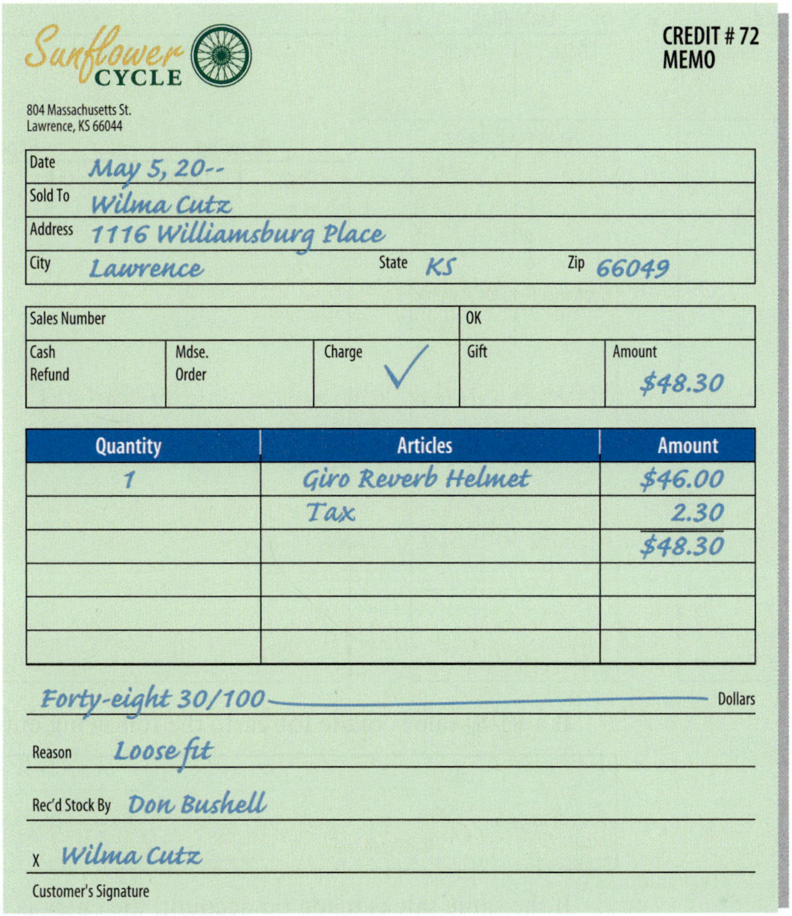

Sunflower CYCLE

804 Massachusetts St.
Lawrence, KS 66044

CREDIT # 72
MEMO

Date May 5, 20--
Sold To Wilma Cutz
Address 1116 Williamsburg Place
City Lawrence State KS Zip 66049

Sales Number			OK	
Cash Refund	Mdse. Order	Charge ✓	Gift	Amount $48.30

Quantity	Articles	Amount
1	Giro Reverb Helmet	$46.00
	Tax	2.30
		$48.30

Forty-eight 30/100 Dollars

Reason Loose fit

Rec'd Stock By Don Bushell

X Wilma Cutz
Customer's Signature

CHECKPOINT

Complete Checkpoint-1 on page 383 to test your basic understanding of LO1.

LO2 Merchandise Sales Accounts

Describe and use merchandise sales accounts.

To account for merchandise sales transactions, we will use five new accounts:

1. Sales
2. Sales Tax Payable
3. Sales Returns and Allowances
4. Customer Refunds Payable
5. Sales Discounts

The position of these accounts in the accounting equation and their normal balances are shown in Figure 10-7.

Sales Account

The sales account is a revenue account used to record sales of merchandise. The account is credited for the selling price of merchandise sold during the period.

Sales

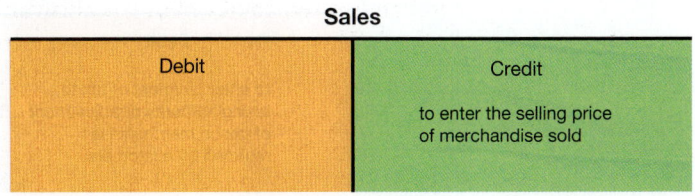

Debit	Credit
	to enter the selling price of merchandise sold

FIGURE 10-7 Accounting for Merchandise Sales Transactions

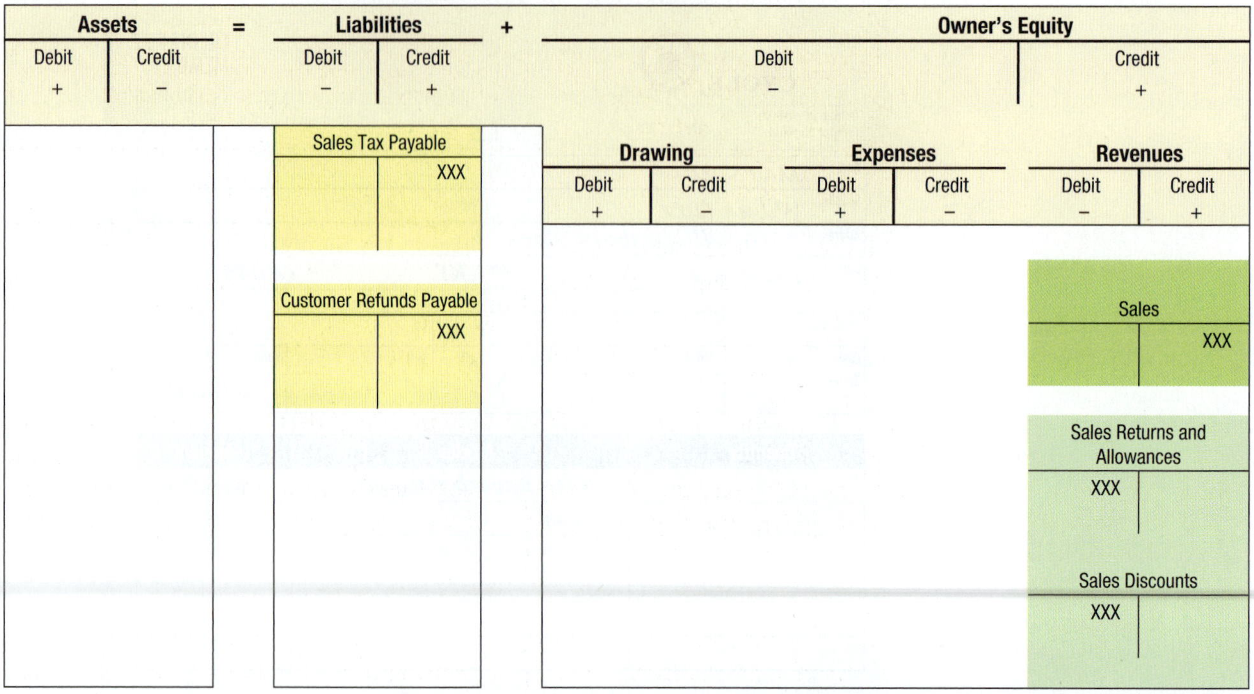

If a $100 sale is made for cash, the following entry is made:

5	Cash	1 0 0 00		5
6	Sales		1 0 0 00	6
7	Made cash sale			7

If the same sale is made on account, the entry is as follows:

The customer's name is placed after Accounts Receivable

5	Accounts Receivable/Customer	1 0 0 00		5
6	Sales		1 0 0 00	6
7	Made credit sale			7

Accounts Receivable is followed by a slash (/) and the name of the specific customer who owes the money. Accounts Receivable is the same account we first saw in Chapter 2. It is a general ledger account. The "Customer" name is for the customer's account in the accounts receivable ledger. This ledger is explained later in this chapter.

Sales Tax Payable Account

Most states require retailers to collect sales tax on sales to final consumers. When sales tax is imposed on merchandise sold, a separate account for Sales Tax Payable is kept. This is a liability account that is credited for the taxes imposed on sales. The account is debited for sales taxes paid to the proper taxing authority or for sales taxes on merchandise returned by customers. A credit balance in the account indicates the amount owed to the taxing authority for taxes collected.

Sales Tax Payable

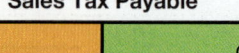

Debit	Credit
to enter payment of tax to taxing authority or adjustment of tax on merchandise returned by customers	to enter tax imposed on sales

If a cash sale for $100 plus 5% sales tax (5% × $100 = $5) occurs, the following entry is made:

10	Cash	105 00		10
11	Sales		100 00	11
12	Sales Tax Payable		5 00	12
13	Made cash sale			13

If the same sale is made on account, the entry is as follows:

10	Accounts Receivable/Customer	105 00		10
11	Sales		100 00	11
12	Sales Tax Payable		5 00	12
13	Made credit sale			13

The debit to Accounts Receivable indicates that the amount owed by customers to the business has increased. Since the buyer has accepted the merchandise and promised to pay for it, revenue is recognized by crediting Sales. Sales Tax Payable is credited because the amount of sales tax owed to the taxing authority has increased.

Sales Returns and Allowances Account

Sales Returns and Allowances is a **contra-revenue account**, which has a debit balance and is deducted from the related revenue account. Sales returns and sales allowances are debited to this account. As shown in Figure 10-8, this account is reported as a deduction from Sales on the income statement. Returns and allowances are debited to a separate account rather than directly to Sales so that the business can more readily keep track of this activity.

Sales Returns and Allowances

Debit	Credit
to enter returns and allowances	

Look at the credit memo in Figure 10-6 on page 359. The entry for the return of the riding helmet by Wilma Cutz would be as follows:

19	Sales Returns and Allowances	46 00		19
20	Sales Tax Payable	2 30		20
21	Accounts Receivable/Wilma Cutz		48 30	21
22	Returned merchandise—Credit Memo #72			22

FIGURE 10-8 Sales Returns and Allowances on the Income Statement

Sales	$38,500	
Less sales returns and allowances	200	
Net sales		$38,300

Note carefully the parts of this entry. Sales Returns and Allowances is debited for the amount of the sale, *excluding* the sales tax. Sales Tax Payable is debited separately for the sales tax on the original sale amount. Accounts Receivable is credited for the total amount originally billed to Cutz.

End-of-Period Adjustment

In addition to the sales returns and allowances that occurred during the current year, other returns and allowances will happen in the following year on sales that occurred in the current year. To account for these later returns and allowances in the correct time period, an adjusting entry is needed as follows:

23		Sales Returns and Allowances		x x x		23
24		Customer Refunds Payable			x x x	24
25		Estimated returns and allowances				25

LEARNING KEY

To record returns and allowances, debit Sales Returns and Allowances for the amount of the sale excluding the sales tax.

First, Sales Returns and Allowances is debited for the estimated amount of current year sales that will be returned in the following year. Then, Customer Refunds Payable is credited for the estimated amount of current year sales that will be refunded in the following year. Customer Refunds Payable is a current liability reported with liabilities on the balance sheet, as shown in Figure 10-9.

FIGURE 10-9 Customer Refunds Payable on the Balance Sheet

Current Liabilities	
Accounts payable	xxxx
Customer Refunds Payable	xxxx

Sales Discounts Account

Another type of discount sometimes offered between businesses is a trade discount. This discount is explained in Chapter 11.

Some businesses offer **cash discounts** to encourage prompt payment by customers who buy merchandise on account. When credit is tight and businesses are short of cash, it is particularly important to convert accounts receivable into cash as soon as possible. Prompt collection of accounts receivable also reduces the risk that those receivables will become uncollectible. Some possible credit terms are shown in Figure 10-10.

FIGURE 10-10 Credit Terms

TERMS	MEANING
2/10, n/30*	2% discount off sales price if paid within 10 days Total amount due within 30 days
1/10, n/30	Same as 2/10, n/30, except 1% discount instead of 2%
2/eom, n/60	2% discount if paid before end of month Total amount due within 60 days
3/10 eom, n/60	3% discount if paid within 10 days after end of month Total amount due within 60 days

*See Figure 10-5. A discount of $11.60 (2% × $580) is allowed if this invoice is paid by May 15 (invoice date of May 5 + 10 days).

To the seller, cash discounts are considered **sales discounts**. Sales Discounts is a contra-revenue account to which cash discounts allowed are debited. Like Sales Returns and Allowances, this account is reported as a deduction from Sales on the income statement, as shown in Figure 10-11.

Sales Discounts

Debit	Credit
to enter cash discounts	

FIGURE 10-11 Sales Discounts on the Income Statement

Sales		$38,500	
Less: Sales returns and allowances	$200		
Sales discounts	140	340	
Net sales			$38,160

If merchandise is sold for $100 with credit terms of 2/10, n/30, and cash is received within the discount period, two entries are made.

At time of sale:

26		Accounts Receivable/Customer	1 0 0 00		26
27		Sales		1 0 0 00	27
28		Made sale on account			28

At time of collection:

30		Cash	9 8 00		30
31		Sales Discounts	2 00		31
32		Accounts Receivable/Customer		1 0 0 00	32
33		Received cash on account			33

Figure 10-12 shows how (1) a sale on account followed by (2) collection with a cash discount affects the accounts receivable, sales, cash, and sales discounts accounts.

FIGURE 10-12 Sales on Account → Collection with Cash Discount

	(1) Credit Sale	−	2% Cash Discount	=	(2) Cash Collection
Net Sales =	$100	−	$2	=	$98

(1)

ENTRY FOR CREDIT SALE		
Accounts Receivable	1 0 0 00	
Sales		1 0 0 00

(2)

ENTRY FOR CASH COLLECTION		
Cash	9 8 00	
Sales Discounts	2 00	
Accounts Receivable		1 0 0 00

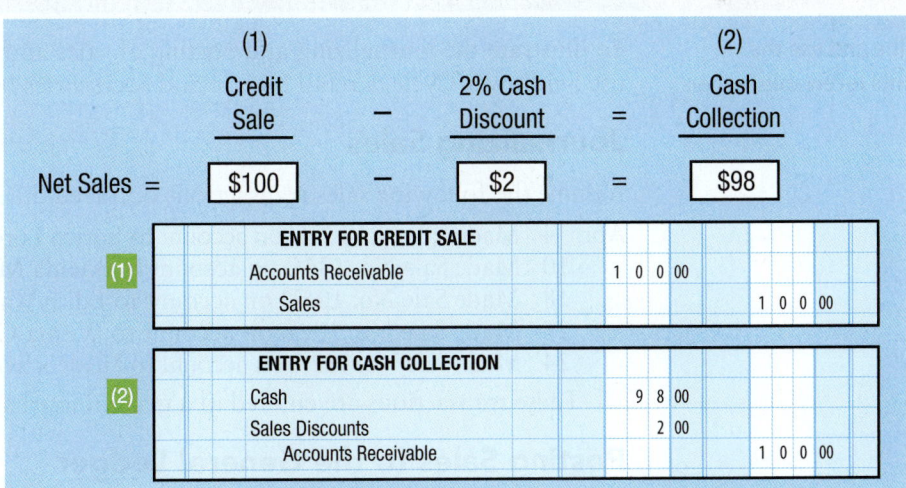

If any merchandise has been returned, the sales discount is calculated on the sale amount after deducting the return. For the above sale for $100, if $30 of merchandise is returned, the following entry is made:

5		Sales Returns and Allowances	3 0 00		5
6		Accounts Receivable		3 0 00	6
7		Returned merchandise			7

The discount on the remaining \$70 collection then would be 2% × \$70 = \$1.40. The journal entry for the collection is:

9		Cash		68.60		9
10		Sales Discount		1.40		10
11		Accounts Receivable			70.00	11
12		Received cash on account				12

If there is a sales tax, the discount is calculated on the sale amount excluding the sales tax. Assume merchandise is sold for \$100 plus 5% sales tax (5% × \$100 = \$5), with credit terms of 2/10, n/30. At the time of the sale, the following entry is made:

1		Accounts Receivable		105.00		1
2		Sales			100.00	2
3		Sales Tax Payable			5.00	3
4		Made sale on account				4

If cash is received within the discount period, the discount is 2% × \$100 = \$2, and the entry is:

6		Cash		103.00		6
7		Sales Discounts		2.00		7
8		Accounts Receivable			105.00	8
9		Received cash on account				9

CHECKPOINT

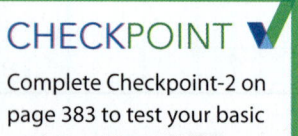

Complete Checkpoint-2 on page 383 to test your basic understanding of LO2.

Note that this entry does not affect Sales Tax Payable. The sales tax is based on the amount of the sale, which is not affected by the timing of the collection on account.

LO3

Journalizing and Posting Sales and Cash Receipts Transactions

Describe and use the accounts receivable ledger.

To illustrate the journalizing and posting of sales and cash receipts transactions, we use Sunflower Cycle, a retail bicycle and accessories business.

Journalizing Sales

Assume the following sales transactions occurred during April 20--:

Apr. 4 Made Sale No. 133C on account to Enrico Lorenzo, \$1,520 plus \$76 sales tax.
10 Made Sale No. 134C on account to Brenda Myers, \$440 plus \$22 sales tax.
18 Made Sale No. 105D on account to Edith Walton, \$980 plus \$49 sales tax.
21 Made Sale No. 202B on account to Wilma Cutz, \$620 plus \$31 sales tax.
24 Made Sale No. 162A on account to Heidi Schwitzer, \$1,600 plus \$80 sales tax.

These transactions are entered in a general journal, as shown in Figure 10-13.

Posting Sales to the General Ledger

Sales transactions are posted from the general journal to the general ledger in the same manner as was illustrated in Chapter 4. Several steps are used, as indicated in Figure 10-14, for Sunflower Cycle's April 4 and 10 sales transactions.

In the general ledger account:

STEP 1 Enter the date of the transaction in the Date column.

STEP 2 Enter the amount of the debit or credit in the Debit or Credit column.

STEP 3 Enter the new balance in the Balance columns under Debit or Credit.

STEP 4 Enter the journal page number from which each transaction is posted in the Posting Reference column.

FIGURE 10-13 Sales Entered in General Journal

4	Apr.	4	Accounts Receivable/E. Lorenzo		1596 00		4
5			Sales			1520 00	5
6			Sales Tax Payable			76 00	6
7			Sale No. 133C				7
8							8
9		10	Accounts Receivable/B. Myers		462 00		9
10			Sales			440 00	10
11			Sales Tax Payable			22 00	11
12			Sale No. 134C				12
13							13
14		18	Accounts Receivable/E. Walton		1029 00		14
15			Sales			980 00	15
16			Sales Tax Payable			49 00	16
17			Sale No. 105D				17
18							18
19		21	Accounts Receivable/W. Cutz		651 00		19
20			Sales			620 00	20
21			Sales Tax Payable			31 00	21
22			Sale No. 202B				22
23							23
24		24	Accounts Receivable/H. Schwitzer		1680 00		24
25			Sales			1600 00	25
26			Sales Tax Payable			80 00	26
27			Sale No. 162A				27

In the journal:

STEP 5 Enter the ledger account number in the Posting Reference column of the journal for each transaction that is posted.

Other sales transactions would be posted in the same manner.

Posting Sales to the Accounts Receivable Ledger

After all posting to the general ledger is completed, the accounts receivable, sales tax payable, and sales accounts in the general ledger are up to date. But at this point, Sunflower Cycle has no complete record of the account receivable from *individual customers*. To run the business properly, Sunflower Cycle needs this information.

A common approach to keeping a record of each customer's account receivable is to use an **accounts receivable ledger**. This is a separate ledger containing an individual account receivable for each customer. It is called a **subsidiary ledger**. A summary accounts receivable account called a **controlling account** is still maintained in the general ledger. The accounts receivable ledger is "subsidiary" to this account. If there are many customer accounts, it is good practice to assign each customer an account number. The subsidiary ledger accounts are kept in either alphabetical or numerical order, depending on whether customer accounts are identified by number. Figure 10-15 shows part of the accounts receivable ledger for Sunflower Cycle.

Figure 10-15 illustrates the use of the accounts receivable ledger for Sunflower Cycle's April 4 and 10 sales transactions. The accounts receivable ledger is posted from the journal *daily* so that current information is available for each customer at

FIGURE 10-14 Posting Sales to the General Ledger

GENERAL JOURNAL (Partial) Page 8

Date		Description	Post. Ref.	Debit	Credit
20--					
Apr.	4	Accounts Receivable/E. Lorenzo	122	1,596.00	
		Sales 5	401		1,520.00
		Sales Tax Payable	231		76.00
		Sale No.133C			
	10	Accounts Receivable/B. Myers	122	462.00	
		Sales 5	401		440.00
		Sales Tax Payable	231		22.00
		Sale No.134C			

2

GENERAL LEDGER (Partial)

ACCOUNT Accounts Receivable ACCOUNT NO.122

Date		Item	Post. Ref.	Debit	Credit	Balance Debit	Balance Credit
20--							
Apr.	1	Bal.	✓			12,000.00	
1	4	4	J8	1,596.00		13,596.00	
	10		J8	462.00		14,058.00	
						3	

ACCOUNT Sales Tax Payable ACCOUNT NO.231

Date		Item	Post. Ref.	Debit	Credit	Balance Debit	Balance Credit
20--							
Apr. 1	4	4	J8		76.00		76.00
	10		J8		22.00		98.00
							3

ACCOUNT Sales ACCOUNT NO. 401

Date		Item	Post. Ref.	Debit	Credit	Balance Debit	Balance Credit
20--							
Apr.	1	Bal.	✓				67,000.00
1	4	4	J8		1,520.00		68,520.00
	10		J8		440.00		68,960.00
							3

LEARNING KEY

When an accounts receivable ledger is used, the Posting Reference column in the general journal serves two purposes. (1) The account number is inserted to indicate the general ledger account has been posted. (2) A slash (/) and a check mark (✓) are inserted to indicate the accounts receivable ledger account has been posted.

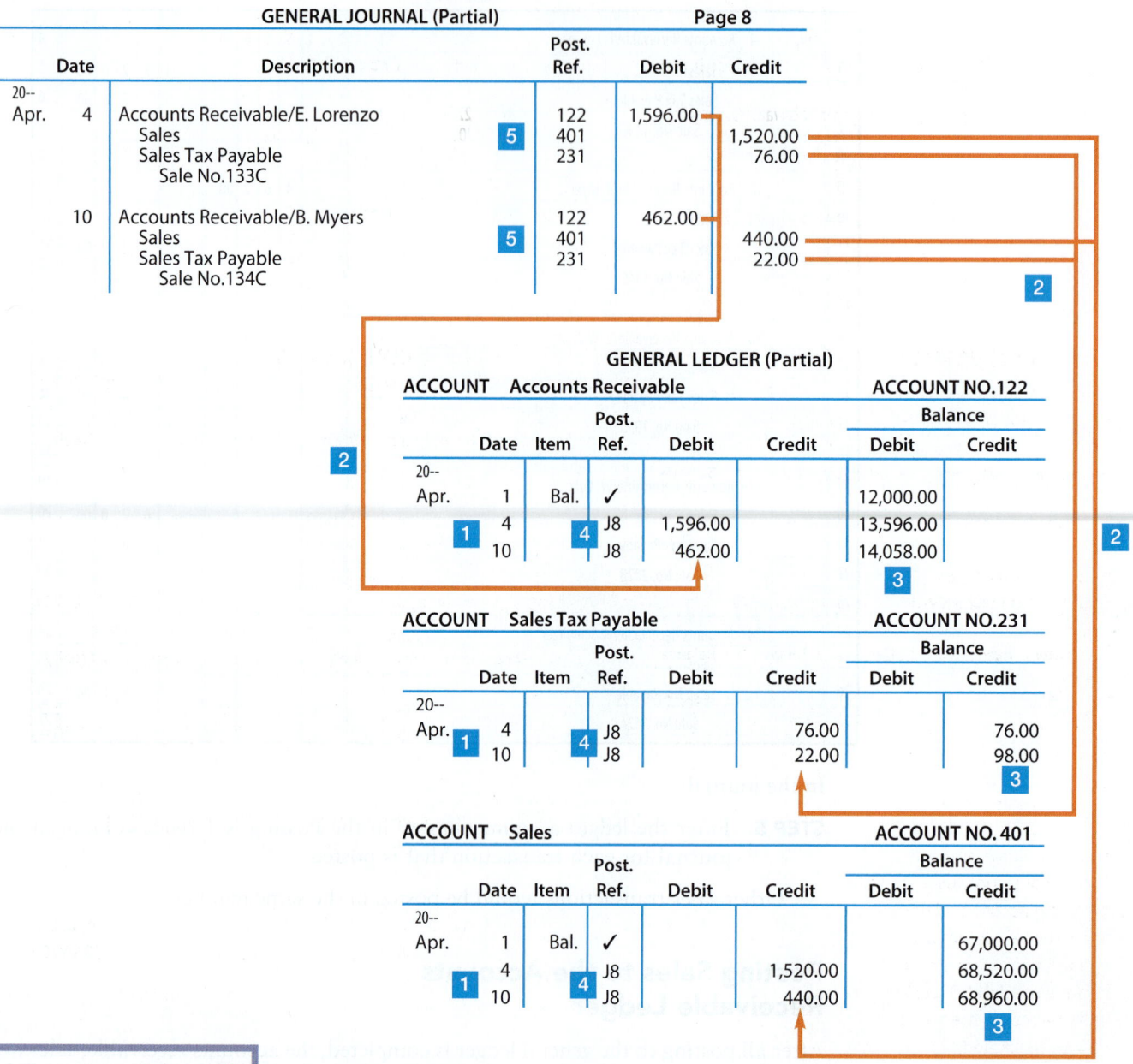

all times. Note that including the individual customer name after Accounts Receivable in each journal entry helps in the posting process. Several steps are used to post from the general journal to the accounts receivable ledger, as shown in Figure 10-15.

In the accounts receivable ledger account:

STEP 1 Enter the date of the transaction in the Date column.

STEP 2 Enter the amount of the debit or credit in the Debit or Credit column.

STEP 3 Enter the new balance in the Balance column.

STEP 4 Enter the journal page number from which each transaction is posted in the Posting Reference column.

In the journal:

STEP 5 Enter a slash (/) followed by a check mark (✓) in the Posting Reference column of the journal for each transaction that is posted.

FIGURE 10-15 Posting Sales to the Accounts Receivable Ledger

GENERAL JOURNAL (Partial) Page 8

Date		Description	Post. Ref.	Debit	Credit
20--					
Apr.	4	Accounts Receivable/E. Lorenzo	5 122/✓	1,596.00	
		Sales	401		1,520.00
		Sales Tax Payable	231		76.00
		Sale No.133C			
	10	Accounts Receivable/B. Myers	5 122/✓	462.00	
		Sales	401		440.00
		Sales Tax Payable	231		22.00
		Sale No.134C			

2

ACCOUNTS RECEIVABLE LEDGER (Partial)

NAME Enrico Lorenzo
ADDRESS 1827 N. 100 Rd., Baldwin City, KS 66006

Date		Item	Post. Ref.	Debit	Credit	Balance
20--						
Apr.	1 4		4 J8	1,596.00		1,596.00 3

NAME Brenda Myers
ADDRESS 1613 Stone Meadows, Lawrence, KS 66049

Date		Item	Post. Ref.	Debit	Credit	Balance
20--						
Apr.	1 10		4 J8	462.00		462.00 3

GENERAL LEDGER (Partial)

ACCOUNT Accounts Receivable ACCOUNT NO. 122

Date		Item	Post. Ref.	Debit	Credit	Balance Debit	Balance Credit
20--							
Apr.	1	Bal.	✓			12,000.00	
	4		J8	1,596.00		13,596.00	
	10		J8	462.00		14,058.00	

ACCOUNT Sales Tax Payable ACCOUNT NO. 231

Date		Item	Post. Ref.	Debit	Credit	Balance Debit	Balance Credit
20--							
Apr.	4		J8		76.00		76.00
	10		J8		22.00		98.00

ACCOUNT Sales ACCOUNT NO. 401

Date		Item	Post. Ref.	Debit	Credit	Balance Debit	Balance Credit
20--							
Apr.	1	Bal.	✓				67,000.00
	4		J8		1,520.00		68,520.00
	10		J8		440.00		68,960.00

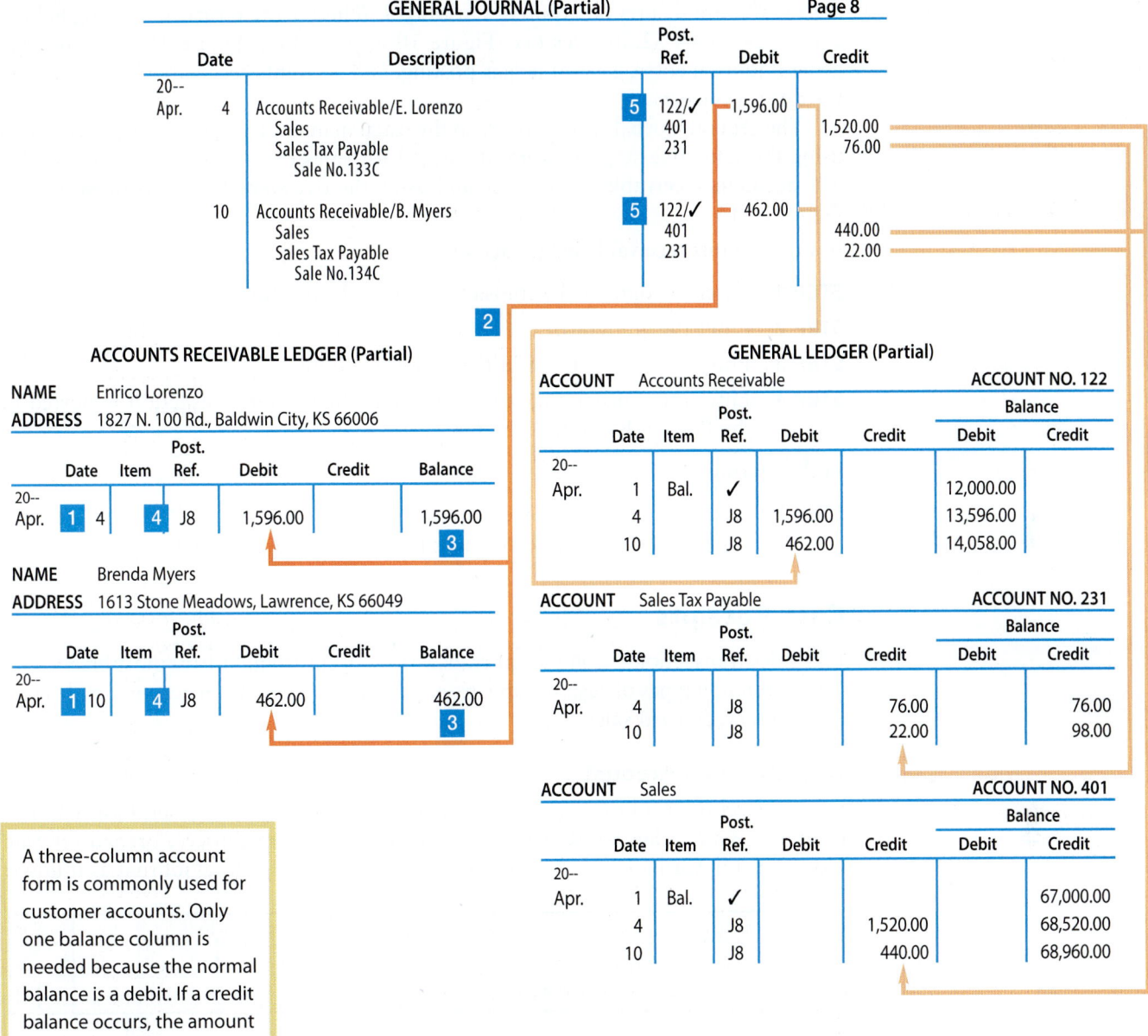

A three-column account form is commonly used for customer accounts. Only one balance column is needed because the normal balance is a debit. If a credit balance occurs, the amount may be bracketed.

The accounts receivable ledger also can be posted from the source document used to make the general journal entry. For example, Sales Ticket No. 134C (see Figure 10-2) could be used to post that sale to Brenda Myers' account in the accounts receivable ledger. In this case, 134C would be inserted in the Posting Reference column of her account. In addition, a slash and check mark would be entered in the Posting Reference column of the journal.

LEARNING KEY

The total of the accounts receivable ledger balances must equal the Accounts Receivable balance in the general ledger.

Note the relationship between the general journal, accounts receivable ledger, and general ledger. Entries in the general journal are posted to the general ledger and accounts receivable ledger. After the posting of the accounts receivable ledger and the general ledger is completed, the total of the accounts receivable ledger balances should equal the Accounts Receivable balance in the general ledger. Remember, the accounts receivable ledger is simply a detailed listing of the same information that is summarized in Accounts Receivable in the general ledger.

Sales Returns and Allowances

If a customer returns merchandise or is given an allowance for damaged merchandise, a general journal entry is required. On May 5, Wilma Cutz returned a riding helmet costing $46 plus $2.30 sales tax (Figure 10-6, page 359). Figure 10-16 shows the general journal entry, general ledger posting, and accounts receivable ledger posting for this transaction.

The general journal entry is made in the usual manner. The general ledger is posted using the same five steps as were illustrated for sales transactions in Figure 10-14. The accounts receivable ledger is posted using the five steps below, as illustrated in Figure 10-16.

In the accounts receivable ledger account:

STEP 1 Enter the date of the transaction in the Date column.

STEP 2 Enter the amount of the debit or credit in the Debit or Credit column.

STEP 3 Enter the new balance in the Balance column.

STEP 4 Enter the journal page number from which each transaction is posted in the Posting Reference column.

In the journal:

STEP 5 Enter a slash (/) followed by a check mark (✓) in the Posting Reference column of the journal for each transaction that is posted.

Cash Receipts

Like sales transactions, cash receipt transactions occur frequently in most businesses. Three common types of cash receipts from sales are collections on account, cash sales, and bank credit card sales.

Collections on Account

Sales on account lead to cash receipts, which are entered in the general journal. For example, assume that Sunflower Cycle receives cash from Enrico Lorenzo for Sale No. 133C on April 14. The transaction is recorded in the general journal as follows:

25	Apr.	14	Cash		1 5 9 6 00		25
26			Accounts Receivable/E. Lorenzo			1 5 9 6 00	26
27			Received cash on account				27

YOUR PERSPECTIVE

Financial Clerk

Financial clerks are found in many organizations including retail businesses, medical offices, banks, and government agencies. Some financial clerks, such as *billing* and *posting clerks*, prepare and send invoices to customers after reviewing documents such as purchase orders, sales tickets, and charge slips. These clerks also interact with customers to get or give account information. Some financial clerks specialize as *credit authorizers and checkers*, reviewing a business's or individual customer's credit history to aid in determining creditworthiness. Other types of financial clerks include *brokerage clerks, loan interviewers, new account clerks*, and *insurance claims and policy-processing clerks*.

FIGURE 10-16 Accounting for Sales Returns and Allowances

GENERAL JOURNAL (Partial) **Page 9**

Date		Description	Post. Ref.	Debit	Credit
20--					
May	5	Sales Returns and Allowances	401.1	46.00	
		Sales Tax Payable	231	2.30	
		Accounts Receivable/W. Cutz	5 122/✓		48.30
		Returned merchandise—Credit Memo #72			

ACCOUNTS RECEIVABLE LEDGER (Partial)

NAME Wilma Cutz
ADDRESS 1116 Williamsburg Place, Lawrence, KS 66049

Date		Item	Post. Ref.	Debit	Credit	Balance
20--						
May	1	Bal.	✓			651.00
1	5	4	J9		48.30	602.70
						3

2

GENERAL LEDGER (Partial)

ACCOUNT Accounts Receivable ACCOUNT NO. 122

Date		Item	Post. Ref.	Debit	Credit	Balance Debit	Balance Credit
20--							
May	1	Bal.	✓			14,331.00	
	5		J9		48.30	14,282.70	

ACCOUNT Sales Tax Payable ACCOUNT NO. 231

Date		Item	Post. Ref.	Debit	Credit	Balance Debit	Balance Credit
20--							
May	1	Bal.	✓				563.00
	5		J9	2.30			560.70

ACCOUNT Sales Returns and Allowances ACCOUNT NO. 401.1

Date		Item	Post. Ref.	Debit	Credit	Balance Debit	Balance Credit
20--							
May	1	Bal.	✓			274.00	
	5		J9	46.00		320.00	

Cash Sales

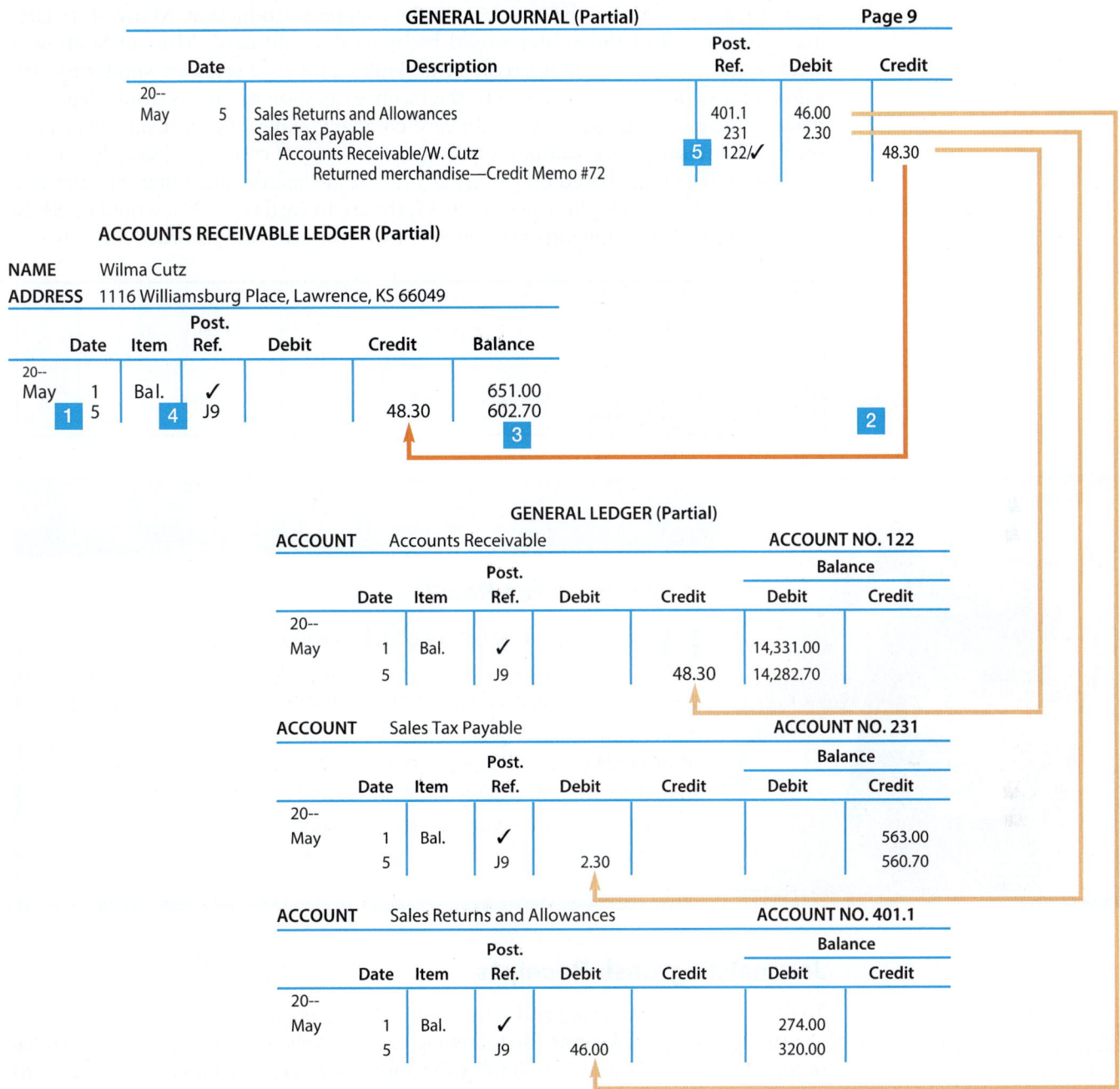

Most businesses also regularly make cash sales. The following entry shows a cash sale of \$500 plus sales tax of \$25 (5% × \$500) recorded in the general journal on May 5:

3	May	5	Cash		525 00		3
4			Sales			500 00	4
5			Sales Tax Payable			25 00	5
6			Made cash sale				6

Bank Credit Card Sales

An increasing amount of sales today are made using bank credit cards. In fact, consider Kalso Earth Shoes, the company in the chapter introduction. Many of its sales are online, so all of these sales would be by bank credit card. Most of Sunflower Cycle's sales also are by bank credit card. Bank credit card sales are similar to cash sales because the cash is available to the business as soon as an electronic deposit is made at the end of the day. The credit card company makes the electronic deposit to the merchandiser's bank account for the gross amount of credit card sales less a processing fee. The fee is based on the gross amount of the sale, including the sales tax. Thus, on a sale of \$100 plus sales tax of \$5, the credit card fee at 4% would be \$4.20 (4% × \$105). The following entry shows this credit card sale recorded on May 6:

8	May	6	Cash		100 80		8
9			Bank Credit Card Expense		4 20		9
10			Sales			100 00	10
11			Sales Tax Payable			5 00	11
12			Made credit card sale				12

AASTOCK/SHUTTERSTOCK.COM

A BROADER VIEW

Is This Sale for Real?

U.S. businesses lose billions of dollars annually because of credit card fraud and bad checks. To reduce credit card fraud, cashiers should do two things: (1) Watch the customer sign the credit card slip and match it to the signature on the card. (2) Obtain an approval code on all credit card transactions. To reduce bad check losses, cashiers should accept only a driver's license as identification. They should compare the picture with the customer, watch the check being signed, and match the check signature with that on the driver's license.

Journalizing Cash Receipts

To illustrate the journalizing and posting of cash receipts transactions, we continue to use Sunflower Cycle. Assume the following cash receipts transactions related to sales occurred during April 20--. (To simplify the illustration, cash sales and bank credit card sales for the month are summarized as single transactions at the end of the month.)

Apr.	14	Received cash on account from Enrico Lorenzo for Sale No. 133C, \$1,596.
	20	Received cash on account from Brenda Myers for Sale No. 134C, \$462.
	28	Received cash on account from Edith Walton for Sale No. 105D, \$1,029.
	30	Cash sales for the month are \$3,600 plus tax of \$180.
	30	Bank credit card sales for the month are \$22,500 plus tax of \$1,125. Bank credit card expenses on these sales are \$900.

These transactions are entered in a general journal as shown in Figure 10-17.

FIGURE 10-17 Cash Receipts Entered in General Journal

4	Apr.	14	Cash		1,596.00		4
5			Accounts Receivable/E. Lorenzo			1,596.00	5
6			Received cash on account				6
7							7
8		20	Cash		462.00		8
9			Accounts Receivable/B. Myers			462.00	9
10			Received cash on account				10
11							11
12		28	Cash		1,029.00		12
13			Accounts Receivable/E. Walton			1,029.00	13
14			Received cash on account				14
15							15
16		30	Cash		3,780.00		16
17			Sales			3,600.00	17
18			Sales Tax Payable			180.00	18
19			Made cash sales				19
20							20
21		30	Cash		22,725.00		21
22			Bank Credit Card Expense		900.00		22
23			Sales			22,500.00	23
24			Sales Tax Payable			1,125.00	24
25			Made credit card sales				25

Posting Cash Receipts to the General Ledger and Accounts Receivable Ledger

Cash receipts transactions are posted to the general ledger in the same manner as was illustrated for sales transactions in Figure 10-14. To post cash receipts to the accounts receivable ledger, the steps below are used, as illustrated in Figure 10-18 for Sunflower Cycle's April 14 and 20 cash receipts transactions.

In the accounts receivable ledger account:

STEP 1 Enter the date of the transaction in the Date column.

STEP 2 Enter the amount of the debit or credit in the Debit or Credit column.

STEP 3 Enter the new balance in the Balance column.

STEP 4 Enter the journal page number from which each transaction is posted in the Posting Reference column.

In the journal:

STEP 5 Enter a slash (/) followed by a check mark (✓) in the Posting Reference column of the journal for each transaction that is posted.

CHECKPOINT

Complete Checkpoint-3 on page 383 to test your basic understanding of LO3.

FIGURE 10-18 Posting Cash Receipts to the General Ledger and Accounts Receivable Ledger

GENERAL JOURNAL (Partial) Page 8

Date		Description	Post. Ref.	Debit	Credit
20--					
Apr.	14	Cash	101	1,596.00	
		Accounts Receivable/E. Lorenzo	5 122/ ✓		1,596.00
		Received cash on account			
	20	Cash	101	462.00	
		Accounts Receivable/B. Myers	5 122/ ✓		462.00
		Received cash on account			

2

ACCOUNTS RECEIVABLE LEDGER (Partial)

NAME Enrico Lorenzo
ADDRESS 1827 N. 100 Rd., Baldwin City, KS 66006

Date		Item	Post. Ref.	Debit	Credit	Balance
20--						
Apr. 1	4	4	J8	1,596.00		1,596.00
	14		J8		1,596.00	0 3

NAME Brenda Myers
ADDRESS 1613 Stone Meadows, Lawrence, KS 66049

Date		Item	Post. Ref.	Debit	Credit	Balance
20--						
Apr. 1	10	4	J8	462.00		462.00
	20		J8		462.00	0 3

GENERAL LEDGER (Partial)

ACCOUNT Cash ACCOUNT NO. 101

Date		Item	Post. Ref.	Debit	Credit	Balance Debit	Balance Credit
20--							
Apr.	1	Bal.	✓			20,000.00	
	14		J8	1,596.00		21,596.00	
	20		J8	462.00		22,058.00	

ACCOUNT Accounts Receivable ACCOUNT NO. 122

Date		Item	Post. Ref.	Debit	Credit	Balance Debit	Balance Credit
20--							
Apr.	1	Bal.	✓			12,000.00	
	4		J8	1,596.00		13,596.00	
	10		J8	462.00		14,058.00	
	14		J8		1,596.00	12,462.00	
	18		J8	1,029.00		13,491.00	
	20		J8		462.00	13,029.00	

LO4 Schedule of Accounts Receivable

Prepare a schedule of accounts receivable.

At the end of the month, all postings to Accounts Receivable in the general ledger and to the accounts receivable ledger should be complete, as shown in Figure 10-19. At this point, the Accounts Receivable balance in the general ledger should equal the sum of the customer balances in the accounts receivable ledger.

To verify that the sum of the accounts receivable ledger balances equals the Accounts Receivable balance, a **schedule of accounts receivable** is prepared. This is an alphabetical or numerical listing of customer accounts and balances, usually prepared at the end of the month. Note that customers whose account balance is zero are not included. The schedule of accounts receivable for Sunflower Cycle as of April 30 is illustrated in Figure 10-20.

This schedule is prepared from the list of customer accounts in the accounts receivable ledger. The total calculated in the schedule is compared with the balance in Accounts Receivable in the general ledger. Note that the $14,331 total listed in the schedule equals the Accounts Receivable balance shown in Figure 10-19. If the schedule total and the Accounts Receivable balance do not agree, the error must be located and corrected. To find the error, use the following procedures:

STEP 1 Verify the total of the schedule.

STEP 2 Verify the postings to the accounts receivable ledger.

STEP 3 Verify the postings to Accounts Receivable in the general ledger.

FIGURE 10-19 General Ledger and Accounts Receivable Ledger after Posting

ACCOUNTS RECEIVABLE LEDGER

NAME Helen Avery
ADDRESS 308 Devon Ave, Overbrook, KS 66524

Date		Item	Post. Ref.	Debit	Credit	Balance
20– Apr.	1	Bal.	✓			2,302.00

NAME Wilma Cutz
ADDRESS 1116 Williamsburg Place, Lawrence, KS 66049

Date		Item	Post. Ref.	Debit	Credit	Balance
20– Apr.	21		J9	651.00		651.00

NAME Enrico Lorenzo
ADDRESS 1827 N. 100 Rd., Baldwin City, KS 66006

Date		Item	Post. Ref.	Debit	Credit	Balance
20– Apr.	4		J8	1,596.00		1,596.00
	14		J8		1,596.00	0

NAME Brenda Myers
ADDRESS 1613 Stone Meadows, Lawrence, KS 66049

Date		Item	Post. Ref.	Debit	Credit	Balance
20– Apr.	10		J8	462.00		462.00
	20		J8		462.00	0

NAME Heidi Schwitzer
ADDRESS 13913 Nicklaus Dr., Overland Park, KS 66223

Date		Item	Post. Ref.	Debit	Credit	Balance
20– Apr.	1	Bal.	✓			1,883.00
	24		J9	1,680.00		3,563.00

ACCOUNTS RECEIVABLE LEDGER (Continued)

NAME Ken Ulmet
ADDRESS 2616 Sawgrass Dr., Lawrence, KS 66047

Date		Item	Post. Ref.	Debit	Credit	Balance
20-- Apr.	1	Bal.	✓			3,315.00

NAME Edith Walton
ADDRESS 1418 N. 600 Rd., Baldwin, KS 66006

Date		Item	Post. Ref.	Debit	Credit	Balance
20-- Apr.	18		J8	1,029.00		1,029.00
	28		J9		1,029.00	0

NAME Vivian Winston
ADDRESS 1613 Alvamar Dr., Lawrence, KS 66047

Date		Item	Post. Ref.	Debit	Credit	Balance
20-- Apr.	1	Bal.	✓			4,500.00

GENERAL LEDGER (Partial)

ACCOUNT Accounts Receivable ACCOUNT NO. 122

Date		Item	Post. Ref.	Debit	Credit	Balance Debit	Balance Credit
20-- Apr.	1	Bal.	✓			12,000.00	
	4		J8	1,596.00		13,596.00	
	10		J8	462.00		14,058.00	
	14		J8		1,596.00	12,462.00	
	18		J8	1,029.00		13,491.00	
	20		J8		462.00	13,029.00	
	21		J9	651.00		13,680.00	
	24		J9	1,680.00		15,360.00	
	28		J9		1,029.00	14,331.00	

FIGURE 10-20 Schedule of Accounts Receivable

Sunflower Cycle
Schedule of Accounts Receivable
April 30, 20--

Helen Avery	$ 2 3 0 2 00
Wilma Cutz	6 5 1 00
Heidi Schwitzer	3 5 6 3 00
Ken Ulmet	3 3 1 5 00
Vivian Winston	4 5 0 0 00
Total	$14 3 3 1 00

CHECKPOINT

Complete Checkpoint-4 on pages 383–384 to test your basic understanding of LO4.

SELF-STUDY

LEARNING OBJECTIVES	Key Points to Remember
LO1 Describe merchandise sales transactions.	A merchandising business buys and sells merchandise. Retailers generally make sales in the store. Important accounting documents are cash register tapes and sales tickets. Wholesalers generally ship merchandise to retailers. A key accounting document is the sales invoice. When customers return merchandise or obtain price adjustments, a credit memo is issued.
LO2 Describe and use merchandise sales accounts.	Five accounts are used in accounting for merchandise sales transactions. 1. Sales 2. Sales Tax Payable 3. Sales Returns and Allowances 4. Customer Refunds Payable 5. Sales Discounts
LO3 Describe and use the accounts receivable ledger.	To post sales transactions to the general ledger, use these five steps. **In the general ledger account:** **STEP 1** Enter the date of the transaction in the Date column. **STEP 2** Enter the amount of the debit or credit in the Debit or Credit column. **STEP 3** Enter the new balance in the Balance columns under Debit or Credit. **STEP 4** Enter the journal page number from which each transaction is posted in the Posting Reference column. **In the journal:** **STEP 5** Enter the ledger account number in the Posting Reference column of the journal for each transaction that is posted. An accounts receivable ledger is a separate ledger containing an individual account receivable for each customer. To post sales transactions to the accounts receivable ledger, use these five steps. **In the accounts receivable ledger account:** **STEP 1** Enter the date of the transaction in the Date column. **STEP 2** Enter the amount of the debit or credit in the Debit or Credit column. **STEP 3** Enter the new balance in the Balance column. **STEP 4** Enter the journal page number from which each transaction is posted in the Posting Reference column. **In the journal:** **STEP 5** Enter a slash (/) followed by a check mark (✓) in the Posting Reference column of the journal for each transaction that is posted. To post cash receipts transactions to the general ledger, use these five steps. **In the general ledger account:** **STEP 1** Enter the date of the transaction in the Date column. **STEP 2** Enter the amount of the debit or credit in the Debit or Credit column.

LEARNING OBJECTIVES	Key Points to Remember
LO3 (concluded)	**STEP 3** Enter the new balance in the Balance columns under Debit or Credit. **STEP 4** Enter the journal page number from which each transaction is posted in the Posting Reference column. **In the journal:** **STEP 5** Enter the ledger account number in the Posting Reference column of the journal for each transaction that is posted. To post cash receipts transactions to the accounts receivable ledger, use these five steps. **In the accounts receivable ledger account:** **STEP 1** Enter the date of the transaction in the Date column. **STEP 2** Enter the amount of the debit or credit in the Debit or Credit column. **STEP 3** Enter the new balance in the Balance column. **STEP 4** Enter the journal page number from which each transaction is posted in the Posting Reference column. **In the journal:** **STEP 5** Enter a slash (/) followed by a check mark (✓) in the Posting Reference column of the journal for each transaction that is posted.
LO4 **Prepare a schedule of accounts receivable.**	The schedule of accounts receivable is used to verify that the sum of the accounts receivable ledger balances equals the Accounts Receivable balance.

DEMONSTRATION PROBLEM

Karen Hunt operates Hunt's Audio-Video Store. The books include a general journal, general ledger, and accounts receivable ledger. The following transactions related to sales on account and cash receipts occurred during April 20--:

Apr.	3	Sold merchandise on account to Susan Haberman, \$159.50 plus tax of \$11.17. Sale No. 41.
	4	Sold merchandise on account to Goro Kimura, \$299.95 plus tax of \$21. Sale No. 42.
	6	Received payment from Tera Scherrer on account, \$69.50.
	7	Issued Credit Memo No. 48 to Kenneth Watt for merchandise returned that had been sold on account, \$42.75 including tax of \$2.80.
	10	Received payment from Kellie Cokley on account, \$99.95.
	11	Sold merchandise on account to Victor Cardona, \$499.95 plus tax of \$35. Sale No. 43.
	14	Received payment from Kenneth Watt in full settlement of account, \$157.
	17	Sold merchandise on account to Susan Haberman, \$379.95 plus tax of \$26.60. Sale No. 44.

(continued)

Apr.	19	Sold merchandise on account to Tera Scherrer, $59.95 plus tax of $4.20. Sale No. 45.
	21	Issued Credit Memo No. 49 to Goro Kimura for merchandise returned that had been sold on account, $53.45 including tax of $3.50.
	24	Received payment from Victor Cardona on account, $299.95.
	25	Sold merchandise on account to Kellie Cokley, $179.50 plus tax of $12.57. Sale No. 46.
	26	Received payment from Susan Haberman on account, $250.65.
	28	Sold merchandise on account to Kenneth Watt, $49.95 plus tax of $3.50. Sale No. 47.
	30	Bank credit card sales for the month were $1,220 plus tax of $85.40. Bank credit card expense on these sales was $65.27.
	30	Cash sales for the month were $2,000 plus tax of $140.

Hunt had the following general ledger account balances as of April 1:

Account Title	Account No.	General Ledger Balance on April 1
Cash	101	$5,000.00
Accounts Receivable	122	1,208.63
Sales Tax Payable	231	72.52
Sales	401	8,421.49
Sales Returns and Allowances	401.1	168.43
Bank Credit Card Expense	513	215.00

Hunt also had the following accounts receivable ledger account balances as of April 1:

Customer	Accounts Receivable Balance
Victor Cardona 6300 Washington Blvd. St. Louis, MO 63130-9523	$299.95
Kellie Cokley 4220 Kingsbury Blvd. St. Louis, MO 63130-1645	$99.95
Susan Haberman 9421 Garden Ct. Kirkwood, MO 63122-1878	$79.98
Goro Kimura 6612 Arundel Pl. Clayton, MO 63150-9266	$379.50
Tera Scherrer 315 W. Linden St. Webster Groves, MO 63119-9881	$149.50
Kenneth Watt 11742 Fawnridge Dr. St. Louis, MO 63131-1726	$199.75

REQUIRED

1. Open general ledger accounts and three-column accounts receivable ledger accounts for Hunt's Audio-Video Store as of April 1, 20--. Enter the April 1 balance in each of the accounts.
2. Enter each transaction in a general journal (beginning on page 7).
3. Post directly from the journal to the proper customers' accounts in the accounts receivable ledger. Each subsidiary ledger account should show the initial "J," followed by the appropriate journal page number as a posting reference for each transaction.
4. Post from the journal to the proper general ledger accounts. Each general ledger account should show the initial "J," followed by the appropriate journal page number as a posting reference for each transaction.
5. Prove the balance of the summary accounts receivable account by preparing a schedule of accounts receivable as of April 30, based on the accounts receivable ledger.

SOLUTION 1. and 3.

ACCOUNTS RECEIVABLE LEDGER

NAME: Victor Cardona

DATE		ITEM	POST. REF.	DEBIT	CREDIT	BALANCE
20--						
Apr.	1	Balance	✓			299.95
	11		J7	534.95		834.90
	24		J8		299.95	534.95

NAME: Kellie Cokley

DATE		ITEM	POST. REF.	DEBIT	CREDIT	BALANCE
20--						
Apr.	1	Balance	✓			99.95
	10		J7		99.95	—
	25		J8	192.07		192.07

NAME: Susan Haberman

DATE		ITEM	POST. REF.	DEBIT	CREDIT	BALANCE
20--						
Apr.	1	Balance	✓			79.98
	3		J7	170.67		250.65
	17		J7	406.55		657.20
	26		J8		250.65	406.55

NAME: Goro Kimura

DATE		ITEM	POST REF.	DEBIT	CREDIT	BALANCE
20--						
Apr.	1	Balance	✓			379.50
	4		J7	320.95		700.45
	21		J8		53.45	647.00

(continued)

NAME: Tera Scherrer

DATE		ITEM	POST. REF.	DEBIT	CREDIT	BALANCE
20-- Apr.	1	Balance	✓			149.50
	6		J7		69.50	80.00
	19		J8	64.15		144.15

NAME: Kenneth Watt

DATE		ITEM	POST. REF.	DEBIT	CREDIT	BALANCE
20-- Apr.	1	Balance	✓			199.75
	7		J7		42.75	157.00
	14		J7		157.00	—
	28		J8	53.45		53.45

SOLUTION 2., 3., and 4.

GENERAL JOURNAL PAGE 7

	DATE		DESCRIPTION	POST. REF.	DEBIT	CREDIT	
1	20-- Apr.	3	Accounts Receivable/Susan Haberman	122/✓	170.67		1
2			Sales	401		159.50	2
3			Sales Tax Payable	231		11.17	3
4			Sale No. 41				4
5							5
6		4	Accounts Receivable/Goro Kimura	122/✓	320.95		6
7			Sales	401		299.95	7
8			Sales Tax Payable	231		21.00	8
9			Sale No. 42				9
10							10
11		6	Cash	101	69.50		11
12			Accounts Receivable/Tera Scherrer	122/✓		69.50	12
13			Received cash on account				13
14							14
15		7	Sales Returns and Allowances	401.1	39.95		15
16			Sales Tax Payable	231	2.80		16
17			Accounts Receivable/Kenneth Watt	122/✓		42.75	17
18			Returned merchandise				18
19							19
20		10	Cash	101	99.95		20
21			Accounts Receivable/Kellie Cokley	122/✓		99.95	21
22			Received cash on account				22
23							23
24		11	Accounts Receivable/Victor Cardona	122/✓	534.95		24
25			Sales	401		499.95	25
26			Sales Tax Payable	231		35.00	26
27			Sale No. 43				27
28							28
29		14	Cash	101	157.00		29
30			Accounts Receivable/Kenneth Watt	122/✓		157.00	30
31			Received cash on account				31
32							32
33		17	Accounts Receivable/Susan Haberman	122/✓	406.55		33
34			Sales	401		379.95	34
35			Sales Tax Payable	231		26.60	35
36			Sale No. 44				36

SOLUTION 2., 3., and 4.

GENERAL JOURNAL PAGE 8

	DATE		DESCRIPTION	POST. REF.	DEBIT	CREDIT	
1	20-- Apr.	19	Accounts Receivable/Tera Scherrer	122/✓	64.15		1
2			Sales	401		59.95	2
3			Sales Tax Payable	231		4.20	3
4			Sale No. 45				4
5							5
6		21	Sales Returns and Allowances	401.1	49.95		6
7			Sales Tax Payable	231	3.50		7
8			Accounts Receivable/Goro Kimura	122/✓		53.45	8
9			Returned merchandise—Credit Memo #49				9
10							10
11		24	Cash	101	299.95		11
12			Accounts Receivable/Victor Cardona	122/✓		299.95	12
13			Received cash on account				13
14							14
15		25	Accounts Receivable/Kellie Cokley	122/✓	192.07		15
16			Sales	401		179.50	16
17			Sales Tax Payable	231		12.57	17
18			Sale No. 46				18
19							19
20		26	Cash	101	250.65		20
21			Accounts Receivable/Susan Haberman	122/✓		250.65	21
22			Received cash on account				22
23							23
24		28	Accounts Receivable/Kenneth Watt	122/✓	53.45		24
25			Sales	401		49.95	25
26			Sales Tax Payable	231		3.50	26
27			Sale No. 47				27
28							28
29		30	Cash	101	1240.13		29
30			Bank Credit Card Expense	513	65.27		30
31			Sales	401		1220.00	31
32			Sales Tax Payable	231		85.40	32
33			Credit card sales				33
34							34
35		30	Cash	101	2140.00		35
36			Sales	401		2000.00	36
37			Sales Tax Payable	231		140.00	37
38			Made cash sales				38

SOLUTION 1. and 4.

GENERAL LEDGER (PARTIAL)

ACCOUNT: Cash ACCOUNT NO. 101

DATE		ITEM	POST. REF.	DEBIT	CREDIT	BALANCE DEBIT	BALANCE CREDIT
20-- Apr.	1	Balance	✓			5000.00	
	6		J7	69.50		5069.50	
	10		J7	99.95		5169.45	
	14		J7	157.00		5326.45	
	24		J8	299.95		5626.40	
	26		J8	250.65		5877.05	
	30		J8	1240.13		7117.18	
	30		J8	2140.00		9257.18	

(continued)

SOLUTION 1. and 4.

ACCOUNT: Accounts Receivable — ACCOUNT NO. 122

DATE		ITEM	POST. REF.	DEBIT	CREDIT	BALANCE DEBIT	BALANCE CREDIT
20-- Apr.	1	Balance	✓			1208 63	
	3		J7	170 67		1379 30	
	4		J7	320 95		1700 25	
	6		J7		69 50	1630 75	
	7		J7		42 75	1588 00	
	10		J7		99 95	1488 05	
	11		J7	534 95		2023 00	
	14		J7		157 00	1866 00	
	17		J7	406 55		2272 55	
	19		J8	64 15		2336 70	
	21		J8		53 45	2283 25	
	24		J8		299 95	1983 30	
	25		J8	192 07		2175 37	
	26		J8		250 65	1924 72	
	28		J8	53 45		1978 17	

ACCOUNT: Sales Tax Payable — ACCOUNT NO. 231

DATE		ITEM	POST. REF.	DEBIT	CREDIT	BALANCE DEBIT	BALANCE CREDIT
20-- Apr.	1	Balance	✓				72 52
	3		J7		11 17		83 69
	4		J7		21 00		104 69
	7		J7	2 80			101 89
	11		J7		35 00		136 89
	17		J7		26 60		163 49
	19		J8		4 20		167 69
	21		J8	3 50			164 19
	25		J8		12 57		176 76
	28		J8		3 50		180 26
	30		J8		85 40		265 66
	30		J8		140 00		405 66

ACCOUNT: Sales — ACCOUNT NO. 401

DATE		ITEM	POST. REF.	DEBIT	CREDIT	BALANCE DEBIT	BALANCE CREDIT
20-- Apr.	1	Balance	✓				8421 49
	3		J7		159 50		8580 99
	4		J7		299 95		8880 94
	11		J7		499 95		9380 89
	17		J7		379 95		9760 84
	19		J8		59 95		9820 79
	25		J8		179 50		10000 29
	28		J8		49 95		10050 24
	30		J8		1220 00		11270 24
	30		J8		2000 00		13270 24

SOLUTION 1. and 4.

ACCOUNT: Sales Returns and Allowances ACCOUNT NO. 401.1

DATE		ITEM	POST. REF.	DEBIT	CREDIT	BALANCE DEBIT	BALANCE CREDIT
20-- Apr.	1	Balance	✓			168.43	
	7		J7	39.95		208.38	
	21		J8	49.95		258.33	

ACCOUNT: Bank Credit Card Expense ACCOUNT NO. 513

DATE		ITEM	POST. REF.	DEBIT	CREDIT	BALANCE DEBIT	BALANCE CREDIT
20-- Apr.	1	Balance	✓			215.00	
	30		J8	65.27		280.27	

SOLUTION 5.

Hunt's Audio-Video Store
Schedule of Accounts Receivable
April 30, 20--

Victor Cardona		534.95
Kellie Cokley		192.07
Susan Haberman		406.55
Goro Kimura		647.00
Tera Scherrer		144.15
Kenneth Watt		53.45
Total	1,978.17	

KEY TERMS

accounts receivable ledger (365) A separate ledger containing an individual account receivable for each customer, kept in either alphabetical or numerical order.

cash discounts (362) Discounts to encourage prompt payment by customers who buy merchandise on account.

contra-revenue account (361) An account with a debit balance that is deducted from the related revenue account.

controlling account (365) A summary account maintained in the general ledger with a subsidiary ledger (for example, the accounts receivable ledger).

credit memo (358) A document issued when credit is given for merchandise returned or for an allowance.

merchandising business (356) A business that purchases merchandise such as clothing, furniture, or computers, and sells that merchandise to its customers.

sale (356) A transfer of merchandise from one business or individual to another in exchange for cash or a promise to pay cash.

sales allowances (358) Reductions in the price of merchandise granted by the seller because of defects or other problems with the merchandise.

sales discounts (362) To the seller, cash discounts are considered sales discounts.

sales invoice (357) A document that is generated to bill the customer to whom the sale was made.

sales return (358) Merchandise returned by a customer for a refund.

sales ticket (357) A document created as evidence of a sale in a retail business.

schedule of accounts receivable (372) An alphabetical or numerical listing of customer accounts and balances, usually prepared at the end of the month.

subsidiary ledger (365) A separate ledger made up of individual accounts that contain the detail for a controlling account.

SELF-STUDY TEST QUESTIONS

True/False

1. **LO1** Reductions in the price of merchandise granted by the seller because of defects or other problems with the merchandise are called sales allowances.
2. **LO2** All sales, for cash or on credit, can be recorded in the general journal.
3. **LO2** Sales Tax Payable is a liability account that is credited for the amount of tax imposed on sales.
4. **LO2** Sales Returns and Allowances is debited for the amount of the sale, including the sales tax on that amount.
5. **LO2** Cash discounts are offered to encourage prompt payment by customers who buy on account.

Multiple Choice

1. **LO2** A credit sale of $250 plus a 6% sales tax would require a debit to Accounts Receivable of
   (a) $15. (c) $30.
   (b) $280. (d) $265.
2. **LO2** When $25 of merchandise is returned for a credit on account, what is the amount of the credit to Accounts Receivable, assuming a 6% sales tax rate?
   (a) $1.50 (c) $26.50
   (b) $25.00 (d) $31.00
3. **LO3** When $300 plus sales tax of 6% is received for an amount previously owed, Cash is debited for what amount?
   (a) $18 (c) $300
   (b) $318 (d) $282
4. **LO3** When credit sales are $325 plus sales tax of 5%, and there is a bank credit card fee of 3%, what is the debit to Bank Credit Card Expense?
   (a) $16.25 (c) $341.25
   (b) $10.24 (d) $331.01
5. **LO3** Cash receipts should
   (a) be posted to customer accounts daily.
   (b) be posted to customer accounts weekly.
   (c) be posted to customer accounts at the end of the month.
   (d) not be posted.

CHECKPOINT

Checkpoint Exercises

1. **LO1** The sales transaction process for a wholesale business is shown below.

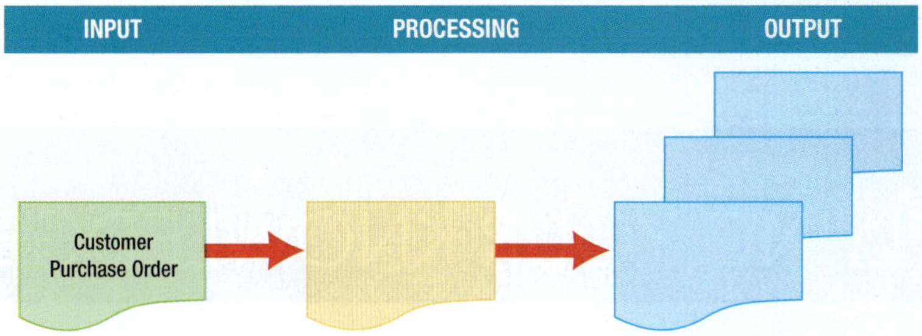

Complete the illustration by providing the missing information in the blank symbols.

2. **LO2** Prepare journal entries for the following sales and cash receipts transactions.

   (a) Merchandise is sold on account for \$300 plus 3% sales tax, with 2/10, n/30 cash discount terms.
   (b) Part of the merchandise sold in transaction (a) for \$70 plus sales tax is returned for credit.
   (c) The balance on account for the merchandise sold in transaction (a) is paid in cash within the discount period.

3. **LO3** The following journal entries are for current sales and cash receipts transactions. Using T accounts, post these transactions to Cash, Accounts Receivable, Sales, Sales Returns and Allowances, and Sales Tax Payable in the general ledger, and to the customer account in the accounts receivable ledger.

	Description	Debit	Credit
(a)	Accounts Receivable/M. Schapiro	288 40	
	Sales		280 00
	Sales Tax Payable		8 40
	Made sale on account		

	Description	Debit	Credit
(b)	Sales Returns and Allowances	60 00	
	Sales Tax Payable	1 80	
	Accounts Receivable/M. Shapiro		61 80
	Returned merchandise		

	Description	Debit	Credit
(c)	Cash	226 60	
	Accounts Receivable/M. Shapiro		226 60
	Received on account		

4. **LO4** On March 24, MS Company's Accounts Receivable consisted of the following customer balances:

S. Burton	\$310
A. Tangier	240
J. Holmes	504
F. Fullman	110
P. Molty	90

(continued)

During the following week, MS made a sale of $104 to Molty and collected cash on account of $207 from Burton and $360 from Holmes. Prepare a schedule of accounts receivable for MS at March 31, 20--.

The answers to the Self-Study Test Questions are at the end of the chapter (pages 397–398).

APPLYING YOUR KNOWLEDGE

CengageNowv2 provides "Show Me How" videos for selected exercises and problems. Additional resources, such as Excel templates for completing selected exercises and problems, are available for download from the companion website at Cengage.com.

REVIEW QUESTIONS

LO1 1. Identify the sales documents commonly used in retail and wholesale businesses.

LO1 2. What is the purpose of a credit memo?

LO2 3. Describe how each of the following accounts is used: (1) Sales, (2) Sales Tax Payable, (3) Sales Returns and Allowances, (4) Customer Refunds Payable, and (5) Sales Discounts.

LO3 4. What steps are followed in posting sales from the general journal to the general ledger?

LO3 5. What steps are followed in posting sales from the general journal to the accounts receivable ledger?

LO3 6. What steps are followed in posting sales returns and allowances from the general journal to the general ledger and accounts receivable ledger?

LO3 7. What steps are followed in posting cash receipts from the general journal to the general ledger?

LO3 8. What steps are followed in posting cash receipts from the general journal to the accounts receivable ledger?

LO4 9. If the total of the schedule of accounts receivable does not agree with the Accounts Receivable balance, what procedures should be used to search for the error?

SERIES A EXERCISES

E 10-1A (LO1)

SALES DOCUMENTS For each document or procedure listed below, indicate whether it would be used for a retail business or a wholesale business, as described in the chapter.

1. sales ticket
2. sales invoice
3. credit approval
4. cash register tape summary
5. credit memo
6. customer purchase order

E 10-2A (LO2)

✓ 3(d):

Sales Ret. & Allow.	25	
Accts. Rec.		25

SALES TRANSACTIONS AND T ACCOUNTS Using T accounts for Cash, Accounts Receivable, Sales Tax Payable, Sales, Sales Returns and Allowances, and Sales Discounts, enter the following sales transactions. Use a new set of accounts for each part, 1–5.

1. No sales tax.
   (a) Merchandise is sold for $320 cash.
   (b) Merchandise is sold on account for $385.
   (c) Payment is received for merchandise sold on account.
2. 5% sales tax.
   (a) Merchandise is sold for $320 cash plus sales tax.
   (b) Merchandise is sold on account for $385 plus sales tax.
   (c) Payment is received for merchandise sold on account.
3. Cash and credit sales, with returned merchandise.
   (a) Merchandise is sold for $340 cash.
   (b) $30 of merchandise sold for $340 is returned for refund.
   (c) Merchandise is sold on account for $280.
   (d) $25 of merchandise sold for $280 is returned for a credit.
   (e) Payment is received for balance owed on merchandise sold on account.
4. 5% sales tax, with returned merchandise.
   (a) Merchandise is sold on account for $400 plus sales tax.
   (b) Merchandise sold on account for $60 plus sales tax is returned for a credit.
   (c) Balance on account is received in cash.
   (d) Merchandise is sold for $260 cash plus sales tax.
   (e) $40 of merchandise sold for $260 cash plus sales tax is returned for a refund.
5. Sales on account, with 2/10, n/30 cash discount terms.
   (a) Merchandise is sold on account for $450.
   (b) The balance is paid within the discount period.
   (c) Merchandise is sold on account for $280.
   (d) The balance is paid after the discount period.

E 10-3A (LO2)

✓ Net sales: $3,370

COMPUTING NET SALES Based on the following information, compute net sales.

Gross sales	$3,860
Sales returns and allowances	410
Sales discounts	80

E 10-4A (LO2)

SALES RETURNS AND ALLOWANCES ADJUSTMENT At the end of year 1, JC's estimates that $2,000 of the current year's sales will be returned in year 2. Prepare the adjusting entry at the end of year 1 to record the estimated sales returns and allowances and customer refunds payable for this $2,000. Use accounts as illustrated in the chapter.

E 10-5A (LO2)

✓ Aug 20:

Cash	176.80	
Accts Rec/K. Krtek		176.80

JOURNALIZING SALES, SALES RETURNS AND ALLOWANCES, AND CASH RECEIPTS Prepare journal entries for the following transactions.

Aug.	4	Sold merchandise on account to S. Miller for $320 plus sales tax of 4%, with 2/10, n/30 cash discount terms.
	6	Sold merchandise on account to K. Krtek for $210 plus sales tax of 4%.
	10	S. Miller returned merchandise purchased on August 4 for $20 plus sales tax for credit.

(continued)

Aug. 13 S. Miller paid the balance due on her account.
15 K. Krtek returned merchandise purchased on August 6 for $40 plus sales tax for credit.
20 K. Krtek paid the balance due on his account.

E 10-6A (LO3)
✓ May 1:
A/R–J. Adams 2,120
Sales 2,000
Sales Tax Payable 120

JOURNALIZING SALES TRANSACTIONS Enter the following transactions in a general journal. Use a 6% sales tax rate.

May 1 Sold merchandise on account to J. Adams, $2,000 plus sales tax. Sale No. 488.
4 Sold merchandise on account to B. Clark, $1,800 plus sales tax. Sale No. 489.
8 Sold merchandise on account to A. Duck, $1,500 plus sales tax. Sale No. 490.
11 Sold merchandise on account to E. Hill, $1,950 plus sales tax. Sale No. 491.

E 10-7A (LO3)
✓ Ending Accts. Rec. balance: $4,059

JOURNALIZING SALES RETURNS AND ALLOWANCES Enter the following transactions starting on page 60 of a general journal and post them to the appropriate general ledger and accounts receivable ledger accounts. Use account numbers as shown in the chapter. Beginning balance in Accounts Receivable is $4,200. Beginning balances in selected customer accounts are Abramowitz, $850; Gruder, $428; and Perez, $1,018.

June 1 John B. Abramowitz returned merchandise previously purchased on account (Sale No. 329), $73.
6 Marie L. Perez returned merchandise previously purchased on account (Sale No. 321), $44.
8 L. B. Gruder returned merchandise previously purchased on account (Sale No. 299), $24.

E 10-8A (LO3)
✓ July 6:
Cash 643
A/R–J. Adler 643

JOURNALIZING CASH RECEIPTS Enter the following transactions in a general journal:

July 6 James Adler made payment on account, $643.
10 Cash sales for the week were $2,320.
14 Betty Havel made payment on account, $430.
15 J. L. Borg made payment on account, $117.
17 Cash sales for the week were $2,237.

E 10-9A (LO4)
✓ Accts. Rec. balance: $4,586

SCHEDULE OF ACCOUNTS RECEIVABLE From the accounts receivable ledger shown, prepare a schedule of accounts receivable for Pheng Co. as of August 31, 20--.

ACCOUNTS RECEIVABLE LEDGER

NAME B & G Distributors

ADDRESS 2628 Burlington Avenue, Chicago, IL 60604-1329

DATE		ITEM	POST. REF.	DEBIT	CREDIT	BALANCE
20-- Aug.	3		J1	1 3 8 0 00		1 3 8 0 00
	8		J1		1 4 0 00	1 2 4 0 00

NAME M. Chang
ADDRESS 1422 SW Pacific, Chicago, IL 60603-8596

DATE		ITEM	POST. REF.	DEBIT	CREDIT	BALANCE
20-- Aug.	5		J1	2,136.00		2,136.00
	11		J2		2,136.00	—

NAME B. J. Hinschliff & Co.
ADDRESS 133 College Blvd., Des Plaines, IL 60611-4431

DATE		ITEM	POST. REF.	DEBIT	CREDIT	BALANCE
20-- Aug.	15		J2	1,106.00		1,106.00
	21		J3	384.00		1,490.00

NAME Sally M. Pitts
ADDRESS 213 East 29th Place, Chicago, IL 60601-6287

DATE		ITEM	POST. REF.	DEBIT	CREDIT	BALANCE
20-- Aug.	21		J3	838.00		838.00

NAME Trendsetters, Inc.
ADDRESS 29 Industrial Way, Chicago, IL 60600-5918

DATE		ITEM	POST. REF.	DEBIT	CREDIT	BALANCE
20-- Aug.	28		J4	1,018.00		1,018.00

SERIES A PROBLEMS

P 10-10A (LO2/3)
✓ Accts. Rec. balance: $16,345.20

SALES TRANSACTIONS J. K. Bijan owns a retail business and made the following sales on account during the month of August 20--. There is a 6% sales tax on all sales.

Aug. 1 Sale No. 213 to Jung Manufacturing Co., $1,200 plus sales tax.
3 Sale No. 214 to Hassad Co., $3,600 plus sales tax.
7 Sale No. 215 to Helsinki, Inc., $1,400 plus sales tax. (Open a new account for this customer. Address is 125 Fishers Dr., Noblesville, IN 47870-8867.)
11 Sale No. 216 to Ardis Myler, $1,280 plus sales tax.
18 Sale No. 217 to Hassad Co., $4,330 plus sales tax.
22 Sale No. 218 to Jung Manufacturing Co., $2,000 plus sales tax.
30 Sale No. 219 to Ardis Myler, $1,610 plus sales tax.

REQUIRED

1. Record the transactions starting on page 15 of a general journal.
2. Post from the journal to the general ledger and accounts receivable ledger accounts. Use account numbers as shown in the chapter.

P 10-11A (LO2/3)
✓ Accts. Rec. balance: $3,533.08

CASH RECEIPTS TRANSACTIONS Zebra Imaginarium, a retail business, had the following cash receipts during December 20--. The sales tax is 6%.

Dec.	1	Received payment on account from Michael Anderson, $1,360.
	2	Received payment on account from Ansel Manufacturing, $382.
	7	Cash sales for the week were $3,160 plus tax. Bank credit card sales for the week were $1,000 plus tax. Bank credit card fee is 3%.
	8	Received payment on account from J. Gorbea, $880.
	11	Michael Anderson returned merchandise for a credit, $60 plus tax.
	14	Cash sales for the week were $2,800 plus tax. Bank credit card sales for the week were $800 plus tax. Bank credit card fee is 3%.
	20	Received payment on account from Tom Wilson, $1,110.
	21	Ansel Manufacturing returned merchandise for a credit, $22 plus tax.
	21	Cash sales for the week were $3,200 plus tax.
	24	Received payment on account from Rachel Carson, $2,000.

Beginning general ledger account balances were:

Cash	$9,862
Accounts Receivable	9,352

Beginning customer account balances were:

M. Anderson	$2,480
Ansel Manufacturing	982
J. Gorbea	880
R. Carson	3,200
T. Wilson	1,810

REQUIRED

1. Record the transactions starting on page 20 of a general journal.
2. Post from the journal to the general ledger and accounts receivable ledger accounts. Use account numbers as shown in the chapter.

P 10-12A (LO2/3)
✓ Accts. Rec. balance: $8,208.80

SALES AND CASH RECEIPTS TRANSACTIONS Sourk Distributors is a retail business. The following sales, returns, and cash receipts occurred during March 20--. There is an 8% sales tax. Beginning general ledger account balances were Cash, $9,586; and Accounts Receivable, $1,016. Beginning customer account balances included Whitaker Group, $1,016.

Mar.	1	Sale on account No. 33C to Donachie & Co., $1,700 plus sales tax.
	3	Sale on account No. 33D to R. J. Kibubu, Inc., $2,190 plus sales tax.
	5	Donachie & Co. returned merchandise from Sale No. 33C for a credit (Credit Memo No. 66), $40 plus sales tax.
	7	Cash sales for the week were $3,140 plus sales tax.
	10	Received payment from Donachie & Co. for Sale No. 33C less Credit Memo No. 66.
	11	Sale on account No. 33E to Eck Bakery, $1,230 plus sales tax.
	13	Received payment from R. J. Kibubu for Sale No. 33D.
	14	Cash sales for the week were $4,100 plus sales tax.

Mar. 16 Eck Bakery returned merchandise from Sale No. 33E for a credit (Credit Memo No. 67), $34 plus sales tax.
18 Sale on account No. 33F to R. J. Kibubu, Inc., $2,580 plus sales tax.
20 Received payment from Eck Bakery for Sale No. 33E less Credit Memo No. 67.
21 Cash sales for the week were $2,510 plus sales tax.
25 Sale on account No. 33G to Eck Bakery, $2,010 plus sales tax.
27 Sale on account No. 33H to Whitaker Group, $2,070 plus sales tax.
28 Cash sales for the week were $3,420 plus sales tax.

REQUIRED

1. Record the transactions starting on page 7 of a general journal.
2. Post from the journal to the general ledger and accounts receivable ledger accounts. Use account numbers as shown in the chapter.

P 10-13A (LO4)
✓ Accts. Rec. balance, Whitaker Group: $3,251.60

SCHEDULE OF ACCOUNTS RECEIVABLE Based on the information provided in Problem 10-12A, prepare a schedule of accounts receivable for Sourk Distributors as of March 31, 20--. Verify that the accounts receivable account balance in the general ledger agrees with the schedule of accounts receivable total.

SERIES B EXERCISES

E 10-1B (LO1)

SALES DOCUMENTS Indicate whether each of the following documents or procedures is for a retail business or for a wholesale business, as described in the chapter.

1. A cash register receipt is given to the customer.
2. Credit approval is required since sales are almost always "on account."
3. Three copies of the sales invoice are prepared: one for shipping, one for the customer (as a bill), and one for accounting.
4. A sales ticket is given to a customer and another copy is sent to accounting.
5. The sales process begins with a customer purchase order.
6. The sales invoice itemizes what is sold, its cost, and the total amount owed.

E 10-2B (LO2)
✓ 3(d):
Sales Ret. & Allow. 24
Accts. Rec. 24

SALES TRANSACTIONS AND T ACCOUNTS Using T accounts for Cash, Accounts Receivable, Sales Tax Payable, Sales, Sales Returns and Allowances, and Sales Discounts, enter the following sales transactions. Use a new set of accounts for each part, 1–5.

1. No sales tax.
   (a) Merchandise is sold for $250 cash.
   (b) Merchandise is sold on account for $225.
   (c) Payment is received for merchandise sold on account.
2. 6% sales tax.
   (a) Merchandise is sold for $250 cash plus sales tax.
   (b) Merchandise is sold on account for $225 plus sales tax.
   (c) Payment is received for merchandise sold on account.

(continued)

3. Cash and credit sales, with returned merchandise.
   (a) Merchandise is sold for $481 cash.
   (b) $18 of merchandise sold for $481 is returned for a refund.
   (c) Merchandise is sold on account for $388.
   (d) $24 of merchandise sold for $388 is returned for a credit.
   (e) Payment is received for balance owed on merchandise sold on account.
4. 6% sales tax, with returned merchandise.
   (a) Merchandise is sold on account for $480 plus sales tax.
   (b) Merchandise sold on account for $30 plus sales tax is returned.
   (c) The balance on the account is received in cash.
   (d) Merchandise is sold for $300 cash plus sales tax.
   (e) $30 of merchandise sold for $300 cash plus sales tax is returned for a refund.
5. Sales on account, with 2/10, n/30 cash discount terms.
   (a) Merchandise is sold on account for $280.
   (b) The balance is paid within the discount period.
   (c) Merchandise is sold on account for $203.
   (d) The balance is paid after the discount period.

E 10-3B (LO2)
✓ Net sales: $2,502

COMPUTING NET SALES Based on the following information, compute net sales:

Gross sales	$2,880
Sales returns and allowances	322
Sales discounts	56

E 10-4B (LO2)

SALES RETURNS AND ALLOWANCES ADJUSTMENT At the end of year 1, MC's estimates that $2,400 of the current year's sales will be returned in year 2. Prepare the adjusting entry at the end of year 1 to record the estimated sales returns and allowances and customer refunds payable for this $2,400. Use accounts as illustrated in the chapter.

E 10-5B (LO2)
✓ Oct. 20:

Cash	228.80	
Accts Rec/B. Farnsby		228.80

JOURNALIZING SALES, SALES RETURNS AND ALLOWANCES, AND CASH RECEIPTS Prepare journal entries for the following transactions.

Oct. 5 Sold merchandise on account to B. Farnsby for $280 plus sales tax of 4%.
8 Sold merchandise on account to F. Preetee for $240 plus sales tax of 4%, with 2/10, n/30 cash discount terms.
11 F. Preetee returned merchandise purchased on October 8 for $50 plus sales tax for credit.
17 F. Preetee paid the balance due on her account.
18 B. Farnsby returned merchandise purchased on October 5 for $60 plus sales tax for credit.
20 B. Farnsby paid the balance due on his account.

E 10-6B (LO3)
✓ Sept. 1:

A/R–K. Smith	1,890	
Sales		1800
Sales Tax Payable		90

JOURNALIZING SALES TRANSACTIONS Enter the following transactions in a general journal. Use a 5% sales tax rate.

Sept. 1 Sold merchandise on account to K. Smith, $1,800 plus sales tax. Sale No. 228.
3 Sold merchandise on account to J. Arnes, $3,100 plus sales tax. Sale No. 229.
5 Sold merchandise on account to M. Denison, $2,800 plus sales tax. Sale No. 230.
7 Sold merchandise on account to B. Marshall, $1,900 plus sales tax. Sale No. 231.

E 10-7B (LO3)
✓ Ending Accts. Rec. balance: $3,777

JOURNALIZING SALES RETURNS AND ALLOWANCES Enter the following transactions starting on page 60 of a general journal and post them to the appropriate general ledger and accounts receivable ledger accounts. Use account numbers as shown in the chapter. Beginning balance in Accounts Receivable is $3,900. Beginning balances in selected customer accounts are Adams, $850; Greene, $428; and Phillips, $1,018.

June 1 Marie L. Phillips returned merchandise previously purchased on account (Sale No. 33), $43.
11 John B. Adams returned merchandise previously purchased on account (Sale No. 34), $59.
15 L. B. Greene returned merchandise previously purchased on account (Sale No. 35), $21.

E 10-8B (LO3)
✓ Nov. 1:
Cash 750
A/R–J. Haghighat 750

JOURNALIZING CASH RECEIPTS Enter the following transactions in a general journal:

Nov. 1 Jean Haghighat made payment on account, $750.
12 Marc Antonoff made payment on account, $464.
15 Cash sales were $3,763.
18 Will Mossein made payment on account, $241.
25 Cash sales were $2,648.

E 10-9B (LO4)
✓ Accts. Rec. balance: $6,402

SCHEDULE OF ACCOUNTS RECEIVABLE From the accounts receivable ledger shown, prepare a schedule of accounts receivable for Gelph Co. as of November 30, 20--.

ACCOUNTS RECEIVABLE LEDGER

NAME James L. Adams Co.
ADDRESS 24481 McAdams Road, Dallas, TX 77001-3465

DATE		ITEM	POST. REF.	DEBIT	CREDIT	BALANCE
20--						
Nov.	1		J1	3 1 8 0 00		3 1 8 0 00
	5		J1		1 8 0 00	3 0 0 0 00
	7		J2	2 0 0 00		3 2 0 0 00

NAME Trish Berens
ADDRESS 34 West 55th Avenue, Fort Worth, TX 76310-8182

DATE		ITEM	POST. REF.	DEBIT	CREDIT	BALANCE
20--						
Nov.	3		J1	1 3 6 0 00		1 3 6 0 00

NAME M and T Jenkins, Inc.
ADDRESS 100 NW Richfield, Austin, TX 78481-3791

DATE		ITEM	POST. REF.	DEBIT	CREDIT	BALANCE
20--						
Nov.	5		J1	2 6 2 8 00		2 6 2 8 00
	12		J2		2 6 2 8 00	—

(continued)

NAME R & J Travis

ADDRESS 288 Beacon Street, Dallas, TX 79301-6642

DATE		ITEM	POST. REF.	DEBIT	CREDIT	BALANCE
20-- Nov.	22		J3	1 8 4 2 00		1 8 4 2 00

SERIES B PROBLEMS

P 10-10B (LO2/3)
✓ Accts. Rec. balance: $13,072.50

SALES TRANSACTIONS T. M. Maxwell owns a retail business and made the following sales on account during the month of July 20--. There is a 5% sales tax on all sales.

July	1	Sale No. 101 to Saga, Inc., $1,200 plus sales tax.
	8	Sale No. 102 to Vinnie Ward, $2,100 plus sales tax.
	15	Sale No. 103 to Dvorak Manufacturing, $4,300 plus sales tax.
	21	Sale No. 104 to Vinnie Ward, $1,800 plus sales tax.
	24	Sale No. 105 to Zapata Co., $1,600 plus sales tax. (Open a new account for this customer. Address is 789 N. Stafford Dr., Bloomington, IN 47401-6201.)
	29	Sale No. 106 to Saga, Inc., $1,450 plus sales tax.

REQUIRED

1. Record the transactions starting on page 15 of a general journal.
2. Post from the journal to the general ledger and accounts receivable ledger accounts. Use account numbers as shown in the chapter.

P 10-11B (LO2/3)
✓ Accts. Rec. balance: $2,744.45

CASH RECEIPTS TRANSACTIONS Color Florists, a retail business, had the following cash receipts during January 20--. The sales tax is 5%.

Jan.	1	Received payment on account from Ray Boyd, $880.
	3	Received payment on account from Clint Hassell, $271.
	5	Cash sales for the week were $2,800 plus tax. Bank credit card sales for the week were $1,200 plus tax. Bank credit card fee is 3%.
	8	Received payment on account from Jan Sowada, $912.
	11	Ray Boyd returned merchandise for a credit, $40 plus tax.
	12	Cash sales for the week were $3,100 plus tax. Bank credit card sales for the week were $1,900 plus tax. Bank credit card fee is 3%.
	15	Received payment on account from Robert Zehnle, $1,100.
	18	Robert Zehnle returned merchandise for a credit, $31 plus tax.
	19	Cash sales for the week were $2,230 plus tax.
	25	Received payment on account from Dazai Manufacturing, $318.

Beginning general ledger account balances were:

Cash	$2,890.75
Accounts Receivable	6,300.00

Beginning customer account balances were:

R. Boyd	$1,400
Dazai Manufacturing	318
C. Hassell	815
J. Sowada	1,481
R. Zehnle	2,286

REQUIRED

1. Record the transactions starting on page 20 of a general journal.
2. Post from the journal to the general ledger and accounts receivable ledger accounts. Use account numbers as shown in the chapter.

P 10-12B (LO2/3)
✓ Accts. Rec. balance: $6,104.25

SALES AND CASH RECEIPTS TRANSACTIONS Paul Jackson owns a retail business. The following sales, returns, and cash receipts are for April 20--. There is a 7% sales tax.

Apr.	1	Sale on account No. 111 to O. L. Meyers, $2,100 plus sales tax.
	3	Sale on account No. 112 to Andrew Plaa, $1,000 plus sales tax.
	6	O. L. Meyers returned merchandise from Sale No. 111 for a credit (Credit Memo No. 42), $50 plus sales tax.
	7	Cash sales for the week were $3,240 plus sales tax.
	9	Received payment from O. L. Meyers for Sale No. 111 less Credit Memo No. 42.
	12	Sale on account No. 113 to Melissa Richfield, $980 plus sales tax.
	14	Cash sales for the week were $2,180 plus sales tax.
	17	Melissa Richfield returned merchandise from Sale No. 113 for a credit (Credit Memo No. 43), $40 plus sales tax.
	19	Sale on account No. 114 to Kelsay Munkres, $1,020 plus sales tax.
	21	Cash sales for the week were $2,600 plus sales tax.
	24	Sale on account No. 115 to O. L. Meyers, $920 plus sales tax.
	27	Sale on account No. 116 to Andrew Plaa, $1,320 plus sales tax.
	28	Cash sales for the week were $2,800 plus sales tax.
	29	Received payment from Melissa Richfield for $2,186.

Beginning general ledger account balances were:

Cash	$2,864.54
Accounts Receivable	2,726.25

Beginning customer account balances were:

K. Munkres	$ 482.00
M. Richfield	2,244.25

REQUIRED

1. Record the transactions starting on page 7 of a general journal.
2. Post from the journal to the general ledger and accounts receivable ledger accounts. Use account numbers as shown in the chapter.

P 10-13B (LO4)
✓ Accts. Rec. balance, Melissa Richfield: $1,064.05

SCHEDULE OF ACCOUNTS RECEIVABLE Based on the information provided in Problem 10-12B, prepare a schedule of accounts receivable for Paul Jackson as of April 30, 20--. Verify that the accounts receivable account balance in the general ledger agrees with the schedule of accounts receivable total.

CHECK LIST
- ☐ Managing
- ☐ Planning
- ☐ Drafting
- ☐ Break
- ☐ Revising
- ☐ Managing

MANAGING YOUR WRITING

You and your spouse have separate charge accounts at a local department store. When you tried to use your card last week, you were told that you were over your credit limit. This puzzled you because you had paid the entire account balance several weeks ago. When the monthly statements arrived yesterday, the error was clear. The store had credited your payment to your spouse's account.

Your account was treated as over the limit, and the store charged you interest on the unpaid balance. You suspect that part of the problem is that you and your spouse use the same last name (Morales) and have similar first names (Carmen and Carmelo).

Write a letter to the store requesting correction of your accounts and suggesting a way to identify your accounts so that this error does not happen again.

ETHICS

ETHICS CASE

Wholesale Health Supply sells a variety of medical equipment and supplies to retailers. When a new retailer is approved for credit, one of the criteria is that the retailer must have been in business for at least six months. Good Earth Foods placed a large order with Wholesale Health Supply and requested credit terms. Wholesale Health Supply faxed a credit request form to Good Earth Foods, and the buyer at Good Earth Foods faxed the completed form back to Wholesale Health Supply. Robin Sylvester, the sales manager at Wholesale Health Supply, saw the credit application and noticed Good Earth Foods had only been in business for two months. Thinking she might lose the order if Good Earth Foods wasn't extended credit, Robin authorized the shipment. She figured by the time the credit department rejected the application, Good Earth Foods would have received the order and the vice president would override the rejection to keep a new customer. Robin was sure that everything would turn out alright.

1. Do you think Robin's decision to ship the order was unethical? Why or why not?
2. What would you have done if you were in Robin's position?
3. Write a memo from the credit department manager to Robin Sylvester explaining the reasoning behind requiring a new credit customer to be in business for at least six months.
4. In small groups, discuss ways to prevent a situation like this from happening.

MASTERY PROBLEM

✓ Accts. Rec. balance: $1,900.54

Geoff and Sandy Harland own and operate Wayward Kennel and Pet Supply. Their motto is, "If your pet is not becoming to you, he should be coming to us." The Harlands maintain a sales tax payable account throughout the month to account for the 6% sales tax. They use a general journal, general ledger, and accounts receivable ledger. The following sales and cash collections took place during the month of September:

Sept.	2	Sold a fish aquarium on account to Ken Shank, $125 plus tax of $7.50, terms n/30. Sale No. 101.
	3	Sold dog food on account to Nancy Truelove, $68.25 plus tax of $4.10, terms n/30. Sale No. 102.
	5	Sold a bird cage on account to Jean Warkentin, $43.95 plus tax of $2.64, terms n/30. Sale No. 103.
	8	Cash sales for the week were $2,332.45 plus tax of $139.95.
	10	Received cash for boarding and grooming services, $625 plus tax of $37.50.
	11	Jean Warkentin stopped by the store to point out a minor defect in the bird cage purchased in Sale No. 103. The Harlands offered a sales allowance of $10 plus tax on the price of the cage which satisfied Warkentin.
	12	Sold a cockatoo on account to Tully Shaw, $1,200 plus tax of $72, terms n/30. Sale No. 104.
	14	Received cash on account from Rosa Alanso, $256.
	15	Rosa Alanso returned merchandise, $93.28 including tax of $5.28.
	15	Cash sales for the week were $2,656.85 plus tax of $159.41.
	16	Received cash on account from Nancy Truelove, $58.25.
	18	Received cash for boarding and grooming services, $535 plus tax of $32.10.
	19	Received cash on account from Ed Cochran, $63.25.
	20	Sold pet supplies on account to Susan Hays, $83.33 plus tax of $5, terms n/30. Sale No. 105.
	21	Sold three Labrador Retriever puppies to All American Day Camp, $375 plus tax of $22.50, terms n/30. Sale No. 106.
	22	Cash sales for the week were $3,122.45 plus tax of $187.35.
	23	Received cash for boarding and grooming services, $515 plus tax of $30.90.
	25	Received cash on account from Ken Shank, $132.50.
	26	Received cash on account from Nancy Truelove, $72.35.
	27	Received cash on account from Joe Gloy, $273.25.
	28	Borrowed cash to purchase a pet limousine, $11,000.
	29	Cash sales for the week were $2,835.45 plus tax of $170.13.
	30	Received cash for boarding and grooming services, $488 plus tax of $29.28.

(continued)

Wayward had the following general ledger account balances as of September 1:

Account Title	Account No.	General Ledger Balance on Sept. 1
Cash	101	$23,500.25
Accounts Receivable	122	850.75
Notes Payable	201	2,500.00
Sales Tax Payable	231	909.90
Sales	401	13,050.48
Sales Returns and Allowances	401.1	86.00
Boarding and Grooming Revenue	402	2,115.00

Wayward also had the following accounts receivable ledger balances as of September 1:

Customer	Accounts Receivable Balance
Rosa Alanso 2541 East 2nd Street Bloomington, IN 47401-5356	$456.00
Ed Cochran 2669 Windcrest Drive Bloomington, IN 47401-5446	$ 63.25
Joe Gloy 1458 Parnell Avenue Muncie, IN 47304-2682	$273.25
Nancy Truelove 2300 E. National Road Cumberland, IN 46229-4824	$ 58.25

New customers opening accounts during September were as follows:

All American Day Camp
3025 Old Mill Run
Bloomington, IN 47408-1080

Susan Hays
1424 Jackson Creek Road
Nashville, IN 47448-2245

Ken Shank
6422 E. Bender Road
Bloomington, IN 47401-7756

Tully Shaw
3315 Longview Avenue
Bloomington, IN 47401-7223

Jean Warkentin
1813 Deep Well Court
Bloomington, IN 47401-5124

REQUIRED

1. Enter the transactions for the month of September in a general journal. (Begin with page 7.)
2. Post the entries to the general and subsidiary ledgers. Open new accounts for any customers who did not have a balance as of September 1.
3. Prepare a schedule of accounts receivable.
4. Compute the net sales for the month of September.

This problem challenges you to apply your cumulative accounting knowledge to move a step beyond the material in the chapter.

✓ June 14: Dr. Sales Discount, $12

CHALLENGE PROBLEM

Enter the following transactions in a general journal:

June	4	Sold merchandise on account to T. Allen, $1,500 plus 6% sales tax, with 1/10, n/30 cash discount terms.
	7	Sold merchandise on account to K. Bryant, $1,800 plus 6% sales tax, with 1/10, n/30 cash discount terms.
	11	T. Allen returned merchandise totaling $300 from the June 4 sale, for credit.
	14	T. Allen paid the balance due from the June 4 sale, less discount.
	17	K. Bryant paid the balance due from the June 7 sale, less discount.

ANSWERS TO SELF-STUDY TEST QUESTIONS

True/False

1. T
2. T
3. T
4. F (the debit *excludes* the sales tax)
5. T

Multiple Choice

1. d **2.** c **3.** b **4.** b **5.** a

Checkpoint Exercises

1.

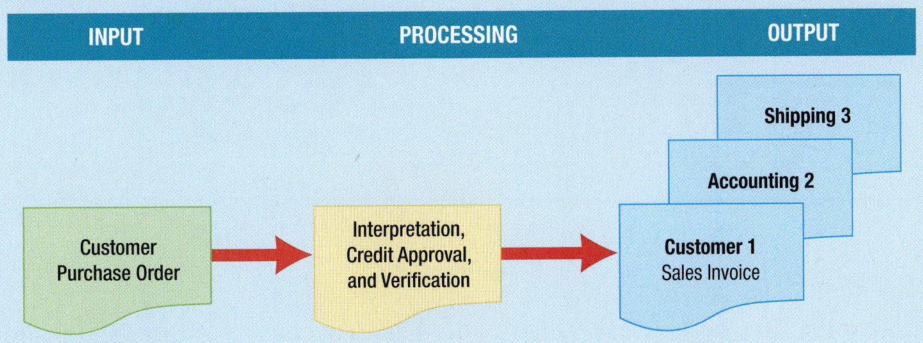

2.

(a)		Accounts Receivable		309 00	
		Sales			300 00
		Sales Tax Payable			9 00
		Made credit sale			

(b)		Sales Returns and Allowances		70 00	
		Sales Tax Payable		2 10	
		Accounts Receivable			72 10
		Returned merchandise			

(c)		Cash		232 30	
		Sales Discounts		4 60	
		Accounts Receivable			236 90
		Received cash on account			

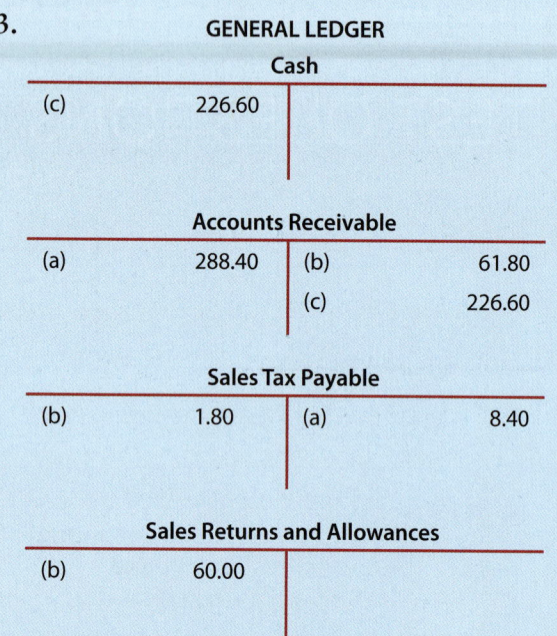

3. GENERAL LEDGER

Cash

(c)	226.60		

Accounts Receivable

(a)	288.40	(b)	61.80
		(c)	226.60

Sales Tax Payable

(b)	1.80	(a)	8.40

Sales Returns and Allowances

(b)	60.00		

Sales

		(a)	280.00

Accounts Receivable Ledger
M. Schapiro

(a)	288.40	(b)	61.80
		(c)	226.60

4. Schedule of Accounts Receivable
March 31, 20--

S. Burton	$103
A. Tangier	240
J. Holmes	144
F. Fullman	110
P. Molty	194
Total	$791

Chapter 11 Accounting for Purchases and Cash Payments

In Chapter 10, we heard about Kalso Earth Shoes, the company whose eco-friendly shoes reflect a concern about the environment. Innovar Environmental is a different kind of company that addresses environmental issues in a totally different way. Innovar provides services to enable government and businesses to become green through environmental consulting, construction, and renovation. Its projects include lead paint, asbestos, and mold abatement; facilities demolition; site enhancements; green construction; natural disaster recovery; storage tank removal; and more.

Innovar was founded in 2000 and is based in Denver, Colorado. It has benefited from the nationwide interest in going green, increasing its revenues in one three-year period by 200%, to $12.2 million. You might recall that one of Kalso Earth Shoes' biggest challenges was accounting for its high volume of sales activity. In contrast, Innovar has far fewer but larger sales transactions. Its challenge is accounting for the many purchases of items used in its major construction and renovation projects. In this chapter, you will learn how to account for purchases transactions, including various discounts, freight charges, and the return of items to the manufacturer.

LEARNING OBJECTIVES

Careful study of this chapter should enable you to:

LO1 **Describe merchandise purchases transactions.**

LO2 **Describe and use merchandise purchases accounts and compute gross profit.**

LO3 **Describe and use the accounts payable ledger.**

LO4 **Prepare a schedule of accounts payable.**

Chapter 10 demonstrated how to account for sales in a merchandising business. This chapter continues the study of the merchandising business by examining how to account for merchandise purchases. We will learn how to use four new accounts and another subsidiary ledger.

LO1 Merchandise Purchases Transactions

Describe merchandise purchases transactions.

In everyday language, purchases can refer to almost anything we have bought. For a merchandising business, however, **purchases** refer to merchandise acquired for resale. These are goods a business buys for the sole purpose of selling them to its customers.

Purchasing procedures and documents vary, depending on the nature and size of a business. For example, in a small business, the owner or an employee might do the buying on a part-time basis. In a large business, there might be a separate purchasing department with a full-time manager and staff. In addition, the procedures and documents used can be affected by whether purchases are made on account or for cash.

Figure 11-1 shows some of the major documents used in the purchasing process of a merchandising business. In discussing the purchasing process, we will assume that the business makes purchases on account and has a purchasing department.

FIGURE 11-1 Purchasing Process Documents (Flowchart)

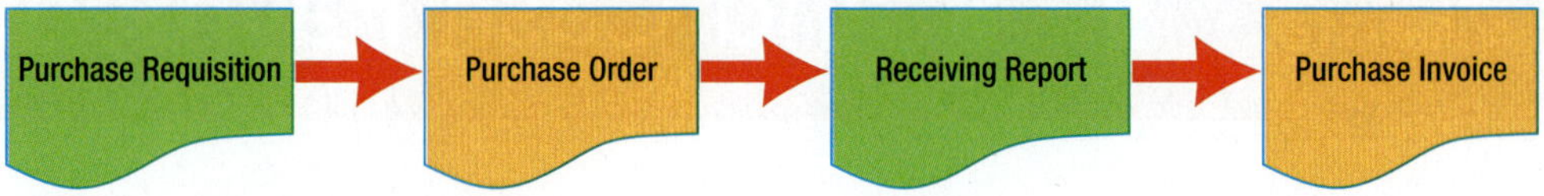

Purchase Requisition

Electronic forms used in a computerized system are similar to the paper documents described in this chapter.

A **purchase requisition** is an internal form sent to the purchasing department to request the purchase of merchandise or other property. Any authorized person or department can prepare this form and submit it to the purchasing department. Figure 11-2 shows a purchase requisition used by Sunflower Cycle. One copy of this form is sent to the purchasing department, one goes to the accounting department, and one is kept by the department that prepared the requisition.

Purchase Order

When electronic purchase orders are used, the information is sent to the vendor and the accounting and purchasing departments at the same time.

The purchasing department reviews and approves the purchase requisition and prepares a purchase order. A **purchase order** is a written order to buy goods from a specific vendor (supplier). Figure 11-3 shows a purchase order prepared by Sunflower Cycle based on the purchase requisition in Figure 11-2. One copy of the purchase order is sent to the vendor to order the goods, one goes to the accounting department, and one copy is kept in the purchasing department. Other copies may be sent to the department that prepared the purchase requisition and to the receiving area.

Receiving Report and Purchase Invoice

When the merchandise is received, a **receiving report** indicating what has been received is prepared. The receiving report can be a separate form, such as a copy of the purchase order received from the purchasing department, or one can be created from

FIGURE 11-2 Purchase Requisition

Sunflower CYCLE
804 Massachusetts St., Lawrence, KS 66044

PURCHASE REQUISITION NO. A-106

Date Issued February 24, 20--	Order From Quality Bike Products 6400 W. 105th St. Bloomington, MN 55438
Date Required March 12, 20--	
Required For Department Parts	
Deliver To Sam Tangari	

Quantity	Description
3	SRAM Apex Double Tap Right Lever
3	SRAM PG-1070 10-speed 11-28
2	Campagnolo Big Corkscrew

Purchasing Department Memorandum

Placed By *Emily Green*	Date February 26, 20--
Approved By *Dan Hughes*	Issued To Quality Bike Products 6400 W. 105th St. Bloomington, MN 55438
Purchase Order No. 312	

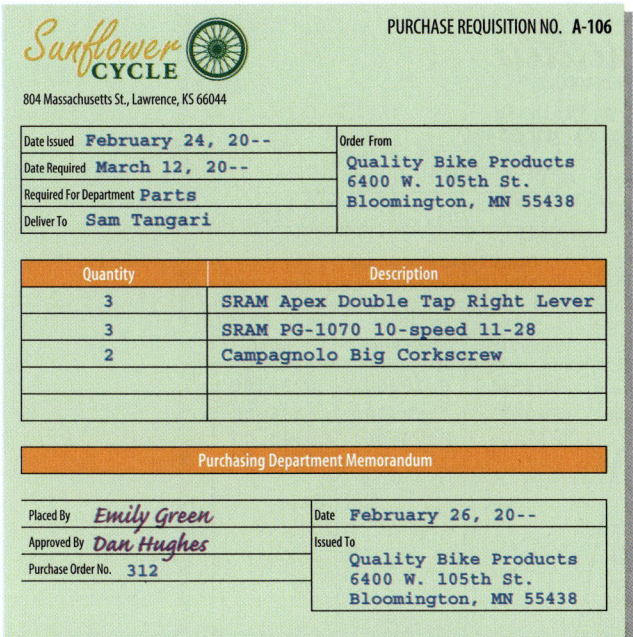

FIGURE 11-3 Purchase Order

Sunflower CYCLE
804 Massachusetts St., Lawrence, KS 66044

PURCHASE ORDER NO. 312

Date February 26, 20--	Order From Quality Bike Products 6400 W. 105th St. Bloomington, MN 55438
Deliver By March 12, 20--	
Ship By UPS Ground	
FOB Bloomington	

Quantity	Description	Unit Price	Total
3	SRAM Apex Double Tap Right Lever	$ 78.00	$234.00
3	SRAM PG-1070 10-speed 11-28	62.00	186.00
2	Campagnolo Big Corkscrew	170.00	340.00
	Total		$760.00

Dan Hughes

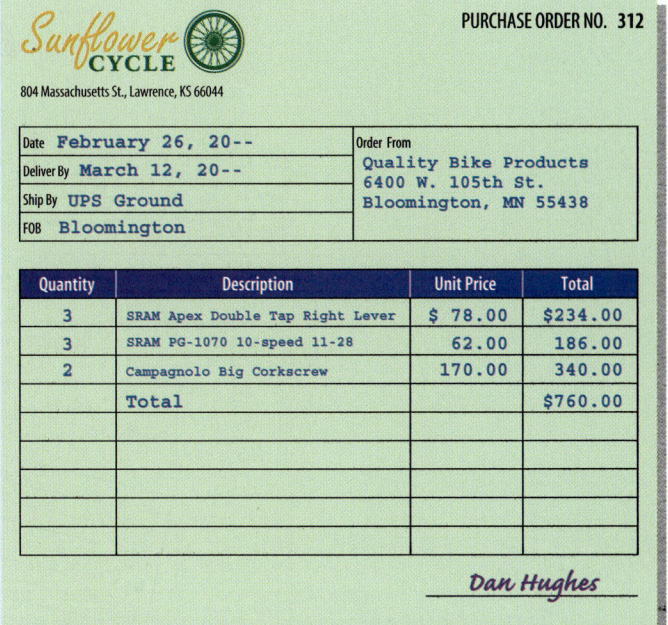

YOUR PERSPECTIVE

Procurement Clerk

In many large businesses the task of keeping track of purchases and supplies is done by a *procurement clerk.* Procurement clerks compile requests for materials and prepare purchase orders. They also handle questions concerning orders as well as order changes or cancelations. They make sure the purchases arrive on time and that the items meet the required specifications. Upon receiving an order, procurement clerks prepare a receiving report or stamp the vendor's invoice to show that the item has been received. As this chapter explains, the receiving report is an important part of good internal control over purchases and payments.

the vendor's purchase invoice. Figure 11-4 shows a vendor invoice on which a rubber stamp has been used to imprint a type of receiving report. The receiving clerk has indicated on the form the date and condition of the goods received.

An **invoice** is a document prepared by the seller (vendor) as a bill for the merchandise shipped. To the seller, this is a sales invoice, as explained in Chapter 10. To the buyer, this is a **purchase invoice**. Figure 11-4 shows an invoice sent by Quality Bike Products to Sunflower Cycle for the goods ordered with the purchase order in Figure 11-3.

The accounting department compares the purchase invoice with the purchase requisition, purchase order, and receiving report. If the invoice is for the goods ordered and received and the correct price, the invoice is paid by the due date.

This is an example of good internal control. The procedure helps ensure that the business pays only for goods it ordered and received, and at the correct price.

FIGURE 11-4 Purchase Invoice

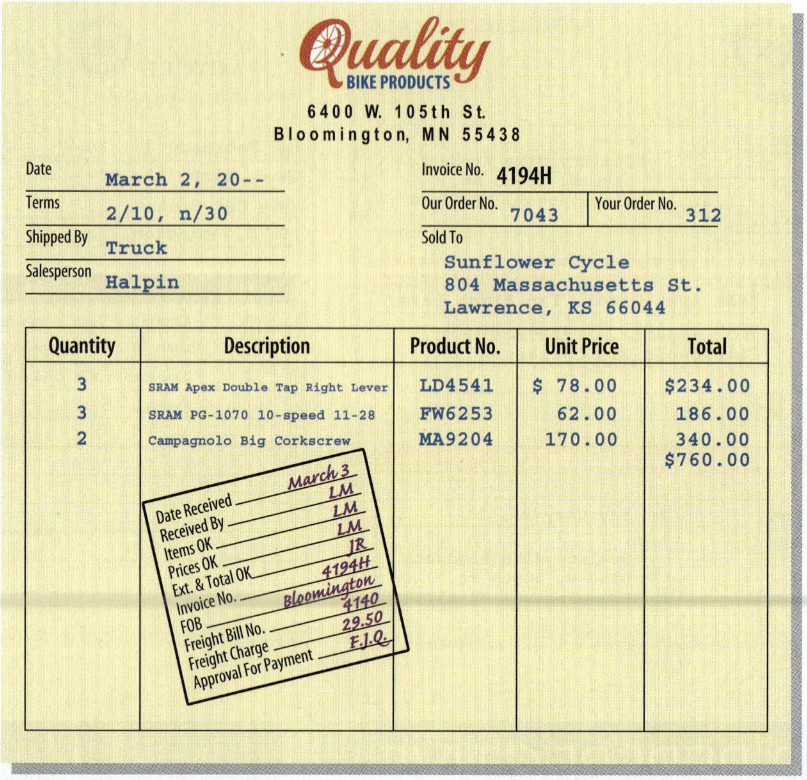

Quality BIKE PRODUCTS
6400 W. 105th St.
Bloomington, MN 55438

Date March 2, 20--
Terms 2/10, n/30
Shipped By Truck
Salesperson Halpin

Invoice No. 4194H
Our Order No. 7043 Your Order No. 312
Sold To Sunflower Cycle
804 Massachusetts St.
Lawrence, KS 66044

Quantity	Description	Product No.	Unit Price	Total
3	SRAM Apex Double Tap Right Lever	LD4541	$ 78.00	$234.00
3	SRAM PG-1070 10-speed 11-28	FW6253	62.00	186.00
2	Campagnolo Big Corkscrew	MA9204	170.00	340.00
				$760.00

Date Received March 3
Received By LM
Items OK LM
Prices OK LM
Ext. & Total OK JR
Invoice No. 4194H
FOB Bloomington
Freight Bill No. 4140
Freight Charge 29.50
Approval For Payment F.J.Q.

Voucher System

Internal control over purchases and cash payments can be strengthened further by using a voucher system, as described in the Appendix to Chapter 7. Recall that a **voucher** is a document which shows that an acquisition is proper and that payment is authorized. A **voucher system** is a control technique that requires every acquisition and subsequent payment to be supported by an approved voucher.

Figure 11-5 is a copy of Figure 7A-5, a voucher used by Sunflower Cycle. The voucher is prepared in the accounting department based on the purchase requisition, purchase order, receiving report, and purchase invoice. The completed and signed voucher provides the support for paying the purchase invoice. The voucher in Figure 11-5 represents the basis on which a payment of $3,621.42 would be made to King Creek Corporation. The voucher system is a key internal control to see that all purchases and payments are properly authorized.

Cash and Trade Discounts

Notice that the invoice in Figure 11-5 shows terms of 1/15, n/30. These are the same credit terms discussed in Chapter 10. A discount is available if the bill is paid within the discount period. The only difference is that we are now looking from the buyer's point of view rather than the seller's. We will see how to account for these discounts later in this chapter.

Another type of discount, called a **trade discount**, is often offered by manufacturers and wholesalers. This discount is a reduction from the list or catalog price offered to different classes of customers. By simply adjusting the trade discount percentages,

FIGURE 11-5 Voucher

Sunflower CYCLE
804 Massachusetts St., Lawrence, KS 66044

Voucher No. **111**

Date 4/11/-- Terms: 1/15/, n/30 Due: 4/24/--

To: King Creek Corp.
1545 Power Rd.
Mesa, AZ 85206

Invoice Date	Invoice No.	Description	Amount
4/9/--	4123	Shimano FSX One, Black-3	$2,022.00
		Motobecane 550 HT, Red-4	1,636.00
			$3,658.00

Authorization A. White (Supervisor) Prepared By B. Zimmer (Clerk)

Front

Voucher No. **111**

Account Debited	Account No.	Amount	Summary	
Purchases	501	$3,658.00	Invoice	$3,658.00
			Discount	36.58
			Net	$3,621.42

Payment Date 4/24/-- Check No. 331 Amount $3,621.42

Approved Distribution J. G. Payment

Back

companies can avoid the cost of reprinting catalogs every time there is a change in prices. Trade discounts are usually shown as a deduction from the total amount of the invoice. For example, the invoice in Figure 11-6 includes a trade discount of 10%. The amount to be entered in the accounting records for this invoice is $684, the net amount after deducting the trade discount of $76. Trade discounts represent a reduction in the price of the merchandise and should not be entered in the accounts of either the seller or the buyer.

LEARNING KEY

Purchases and sales subject to trade discounts should be recorded in the accounting records at the *net amount* after deducting the trade discounts.

We need to be careful in computing the cash discount when an invoice has both cash and trade discounts. The cash discount applies to the *net amount* after deducting the trade discount. For example, the cash discount and amount to be paid on the invoice in Figure 11-6 would be calculated as follows:

Gross amount	$760.00
Less 10% trade discount	76.00
Net amount	$684.00
Less 2% cash discount	13.68
Amount to be paid	$670.32

CHECKPOINT

Complete Checkpoint-1 on page 423 to test your basic understanding of LO1.

FIGURE 11-6 Purchase Invoice with Trade Discount

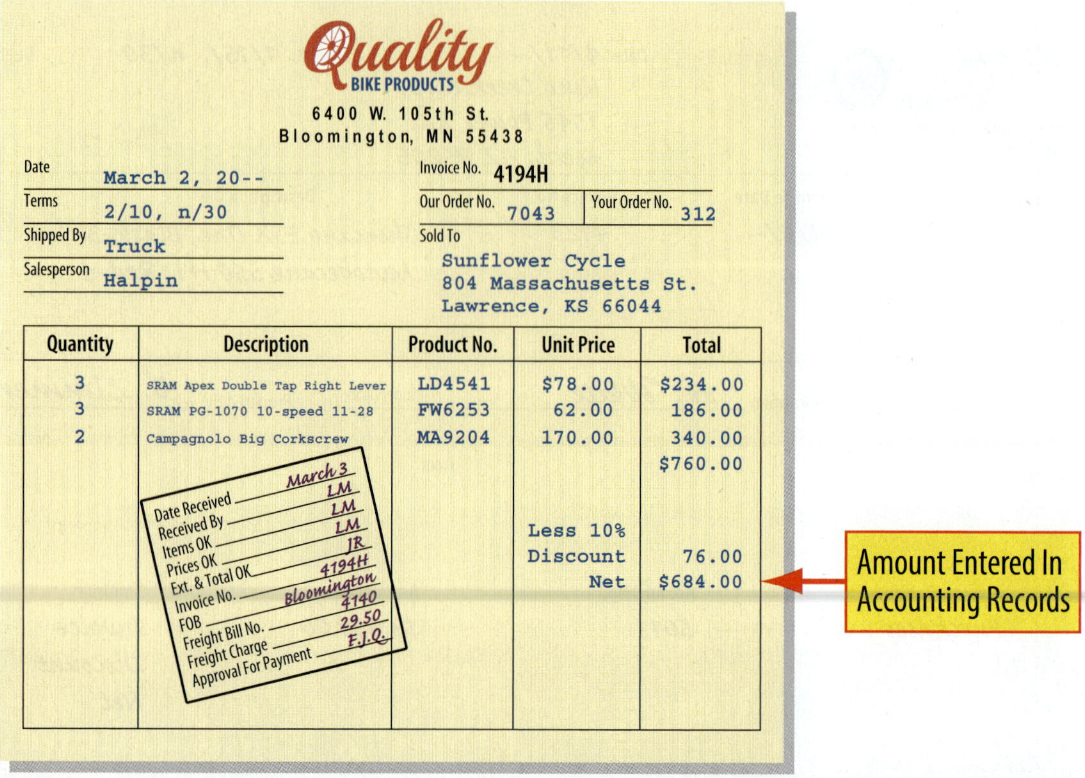
Quality BIKE PRODUCTS
6400 W. 105th St.
Bloomington, MN 55438

Date March 2, 20--
Terms 2/10, n/30
Shipped By Truck
Salesperson Halpin

Invoice No. 4194H
Our Order No. 7043 Your Order No. 312
Sold To
Sunflower Cycle
804 Massachusetts St.
Lawrence, KS 66044

Quantity	Description	Product No.	Unit Price	Total
3	SRAM Apex Double Tap Right Lever	LD4541	$78.00	$234.00
3	SRAM PG-1070 10-speed 11-28	FW6253	62.00	186.00
2	Campagnolo Big Corkscrew	MA9204	170.00	340.00
				$760.00
			Less 10% Discount	76.00
			Net	$684.00

LO2 Merchandise Purchases Accounts

Describe and use merchandise purchases accounts and compute gross profit.

To account for merchandise purchases transactions, we will use four new accounts.

1. Purchases
2. Purchases Returns and Allowances
3. Purchases Discounts
4. Freight-In

The position of these accounts in the accounting equation and their normal balances are shown in Figure 11-7.

Purchases Account

The purchases account is used to record the cost of merchandise purchased.

The approach to accounting for merchandise purchases shown in this chapter is known as the periodic method. Other inventory methods are covered in Chapter 13.

Purchases

Debit	Credit
to enter the cost of merchandise purchased	

If a $100 purchase is made for cash, the following entry is made:

5			Purchases		1 0 0 00		5
6			Cash			1 0 0 00	6
7			Made cash purchase				7

FIGURE 11-7 Accounting for Merchandise Purchases Transactions

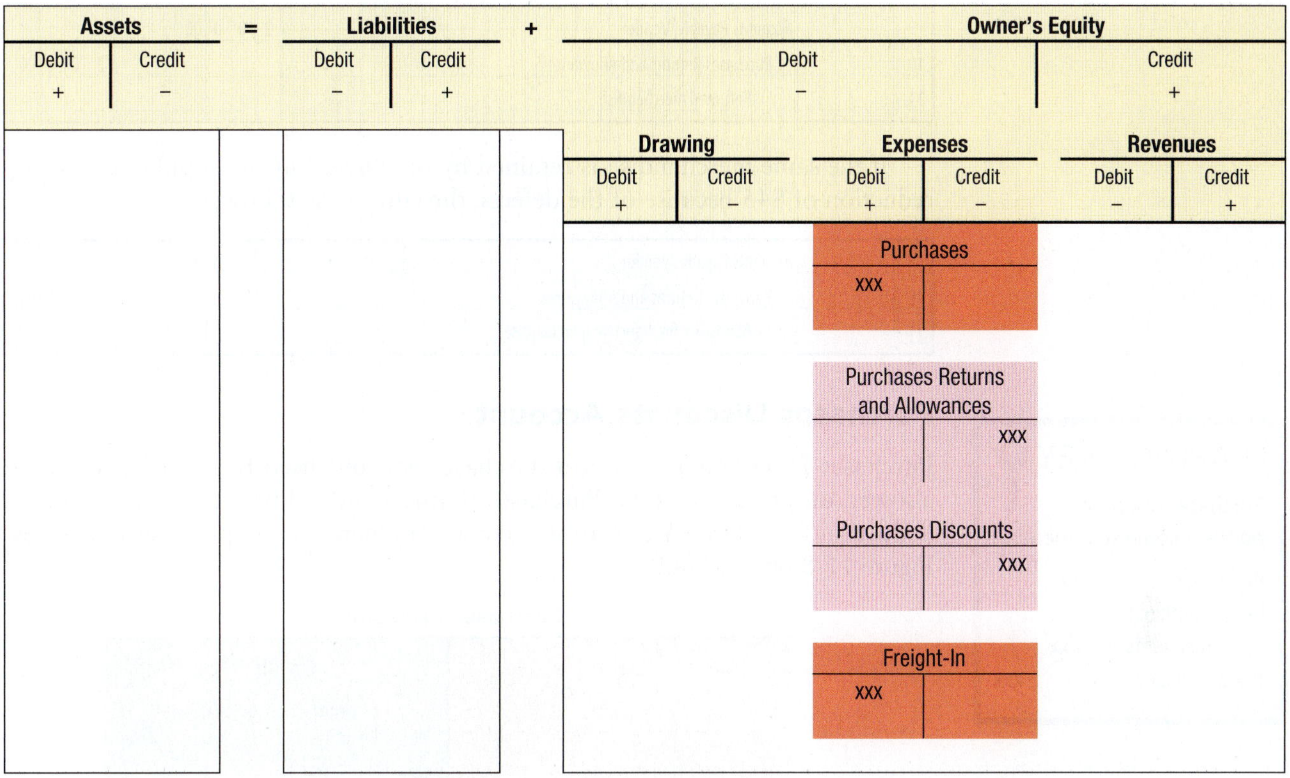

If the same purchase is made on account, the entry is as follows:

The vendor's name is placed after Accounts Payable.

5		Purchases	1 0 0 00		5
6		Accounts Payable/Vendor		1 0 0 00	6
7		Made purchase on account			7

Accounts Payable is followed by a slash (/) and the name of the specific vendor to whom the purchaser owes money. The vendor name is for the vendor's account in the accounts payable ledger. This ledger is explained later in this chapter.

> **LEARNING KEY**
>
> Purchases returns and allowances on the income statement:
>
> | | | |
> |---|---|---|
> | Purchases | XXX | |
> | Less: Purch. ret. & all. | XX | |
> | Net purchases | | XXX |

Purchases Returns and Allowances Account

Purchases Returns and Allowances is a **contra-cost** (or **contra-purchases**) **account**, which has a credit balance and is deducted from the related cost account. Purchases returns and purchases allowances are credited to this account. It is reported as a deduction from Purchases on the income statement to compute net purchases (see Figure 11-8 on page 409).

Purchases returns and allowances are similar to the sales returns and allowances we discussed in Chapter 10. We are simply looking at returns and allowances from the buyer's point of view. If merchandise is returned to a supplier, or the supplier grants a price reduction because of defects or other problems with merchandise purchased, Purchases Returns and Allowances is credited.

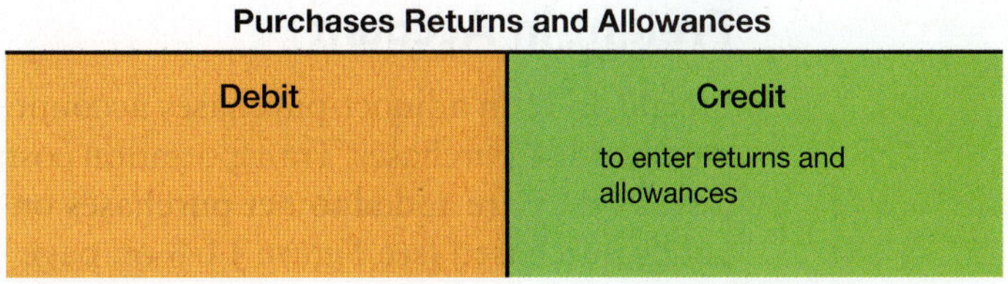

If merchandise that was purchased on account for $200 is defective and is returned to the supplier, the following entry is made:

		Debit	Credit	
9	Accounts Payable/Vendor	200 00		9
10	Purchases Returns and Allowances		200 00	10
11	Returned merchandise			11

If the same merchandise is retained by the buyer but the supplier grants a price reduction of $45 because of the defects, the entry is as follows:

		Debit	Credit	
9	Accounts Payable/Vendor	45 00		9
10	Purchases Returns and Allowances		45 00	10
11	Allowance for defective merchandise			11

Purchases Discounts Account

LEARNING KEY

Purchases discounts on the income statement:

Purchases	xxx	
Less: Purchases discounts	xx	
Net purchases		xxx

Purchases Discounts is a contra-purchases account used to record cash discounts allowed on purchases. Like Purchases Returns and Allowances, it is reported as a deduction from Purchases on the income statement to compute net purchases (see Figure 11-8 on page 409).

Purchases Discounts

Debit	Credit
	to enter cash discounts taken

If merchandise is purchased for $100 on account, with credit terms of 2/10, n/30, the following entry is made:

		Debit	Credit	
14	Purchases	100 00		14
15	Accounts Payable/Vendor		100 00	15
16	Made purchase on account			16

If payment for the merchandise is then made within the discount period, the entry is as follows:

		Debit	Credit	
18	Accounts Payable/Vendor	100 00		18
19	Cash		98 00	19
20	Purchases Discounts		2 00	20
21	Made payment on account			21

This approach to accounting for purchases discounts is known as the "gross-price method." The "net-price method" is described in the appendix.

Note the parts of this entry. Accounts Payable is debited for $100, the full amount of the invoice, because the entire debt has been satisfied. Cash is credited for only $98 because that is all that was required to pay the debt. The difference of $2 ($100 – $98) is credited to Purchases Discounts, which represents a reduction in the purchase price of the merchandise. That is why Purchases Discounts is deducted from Purchases on the income statement.

Freight-In Account

Freight-In is an adjunct-purchases account used to record transportation charges on merchandise purchases. Transportation costs are part of the total cost of the merchandise, so they are added to net purchases on the income statement to compute cost of goods purchased (see Figure 11-8 on page 409).

A BROADER VIEW

Cash Management—Those Discounts Matter

If a business makes a $2,000 purchase on account, with terms of 2/10, n/30, the available discount is only $40 ($2,000 × 0.02). On the surface, this seems unimportant, like "small change." But take a closer look. If the business does not pay $1,960 ($2,000 – $40) within 10 days, it must pay $2,000 within 30 days. This means that the business would pay $40 for the use of $1,960 for 20 more days. If we assume a 360-day year, the approximate annual interest rate for using the $1,960 for 20 days is 36%. (In Chapter 17 you will learn to compute the exact interest rate.)

The innocent looking 2% cash discount represents a very high rate of interest. If a business regularly misses cash discount opportunities, the annual dollar cost can be substantial. For sound cash management, take advantage of discounts.

MARMADUKE ST. JOHN/ALAMY STOCK PHOTO

LEARNING KEY

Freight-in on the income statement:

Net purchases	xxx	
Add freight-in		
Cost of goods purchased	xx	xxx

Freight-In

Debit	Credit
to enter transportation charges on merchandise purchases	

Transportation charges are expressed in FOB (free on board) terms that indicate who is responsible for paying the freight costs. **FOB shipping point** means that transportation charges are paid by the buyer. The buyer records these costs in a freight-in account. **FOB destination** means that transportation charges are paid by the seller. The seller records these costs in a freight-out or delivery expense account. FOB terms also tell us who owns the inventory and who should count it in their inventory account. Under FOB shipping point, the buyer owns the inventory as soon as it is shipped and should count it in inventory. Under FOB destination, the seller owns the inventory until it is delivered to the buyer and the seller should count it in inventory.

When the terms are FOB shipping point, either the freight charges will be listed separately on the purchase invoice or a separate freight bill will be sent. Assume Sunflower Cycle receives an invoice for $400 plus freight charges of $38. The entry for this purchase is as follows:

25		Purchases	400.00		25
26		Freight-In	38.00		26
27		Accounts Payable/Vendor		438.00	27
28		Made purchase on account			28

Assume instead that Sunflower Cycle receives an invoice for $400 for the same merchandise, shipped FOB shipping point. Sunflower Cycle then receives a separate bill from the transportation company for $38. These two transactions are entered as follows:

30		Purchases		400 00		30
31		Accounts Payable/Vendor			400 00	31
32		Made purchase on account				32
33						33
34		Freight-In		38 00		34
35		Accounts Payable/Vendor			38 00	35
36		Freight charges on merchandise purchase				36

When the terms are FOB destination, generally no freight charges appear on the purchase invoice. The buyer simply records the purchase at the amount of the invoice. The freight-in account is not used in recording this purchase.

Computation of Gross Profit

An important step in determining net income for a merchandising business is the calculation of its gross profit. **Gross profit** (also called **gross margin**) is the difference between net sales and cost of goods sold. **Cost of goods sold** (also called **cost of merchandise sold**) is the difference between the goods available for sale and the ending inventory. It indicates the cost of the goods sold during the period. Gross profit provides very important information. It tells management the amount of sales dollars available to cover expenses, after covering the cost of the goods sold.

As a simple example, gross profit is computed as follows:

Net sales	$8,400
Cost of goods sold	5,300
Gross profit	$3,100

In a more realistic situation, we must compute net sales and cost of goods sold, in order to compute gross profit. Multiple steps are involved. To illustrate, we use three of the four new accounts described in Chapter 10, the four new accounts described in this chapter, and the merchandise inventory balances. Assume that a company has the following sales, purchases, and merchandise inventory balances for the year ended December 31, 20--:

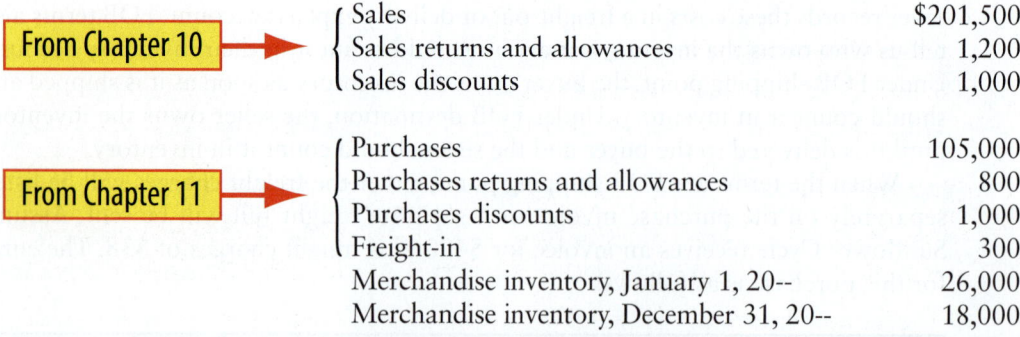

From Chapter 10 →	Sales	$201,500
	Sales returns and allowances	1,200
	Sales discounts	1,000
From Chapter 11 →	Purchases	105,000
	Purchases returns and allowances	800
	Purchases discounts	1,000
	Freight-in	300
	Merchandise inventory, January 1, 20--	26,000
	Merchandise inventory, December 31, 20--	18,000

Figure 11-8 uses these balances to compute net sales, net purchases, cost of goods sold, and gross profit. The following four steps in computing gross profit are labeled in the figure:

STEP 1 Compute net sales.

(Sales − Sales Returns and Allowances − Sales Discounts)

STEP 2 Compute goods available for sale.

(Beginning Inventory + Cost of Goods Purchased)

Merchandise inventory is discussed more fully in Chapters 14-15, including explanation of an additional component of inventory.

STEP 3 Compute cost of goods sold.
(Goods Available for Sale – Ending Inventory)

STEP 4 Compute gross profit.
(Net Sales – Cost of Goods Sold)

FIGURE 11-8 Computation of Gross Profit on a Partial Income Statement

Income Statement (partial)

	Revenue from sales:				
	Sales			$201,500	
	Less: Sales returns and allowances		$ 1,200		
	Sales discounts		1,000	2,200	
Step 1	**Net sales**				$ 199,300
	Cost of goods sold:				
	Merchandise inventory, Jan. 1			$ 26,000	
	Purchases		$105,000		
	Less: Purchases returns and allowances	$ 800			
	Purchases discounts	1,000	1,800		
	Net purchases		$103,200		
	Add freight-in		300		
	Cost of goods purchased			103,500	
Step 2	**Goods available for sale**			$ 129,500	
	Less merchandise inventory, Dec. 31			18,000	
Step 3	**Cost of goods sold**				111,500
Step 4	**Gross profit**				$ 87,800

CHECKPOINT

Complete Checkpoint-2 on page 424 to test your basic understanding of LO2.

LEARNING KEY

Cost of Goods Sold = Beginning Inventory + Net Purchases + Freight-In − Ending Inventory

Gross Profit = Net Sales − Cost of Goods Sold

LO3 Journalizing and Posting Purchases and Cash Payments Transactions

Describe and use the accounts payable ledger.

To illustrate the journalizing and posting of purchases transactions, we will continue with the transactions of Sunflower Cycle.

Purchases

Assume the following purchases on account occurred during the month of April:

Apr. 4 Purchased merchandise from Bilenky Cycle Works, $3,300. Invoice No. 631, dated April 2, terms, n/30.

8 Purchased merchandise from Ellsworth, $2,500. Invoice No. 927D, dated April 6, terms, n/30.

(continued)

Apr. 11 Purchased merchandise from Gunnar Cycles, $8,700.
Invoice No. 804, dated April 9, terms, 1/15, n/30.

17 Purchased merchandise from Milwaukee Cycle Co., $800.
Invoice No. 611, dated April 16, terms, n/30.

23 Purchased merchandise from Rans Designs, Inc., $5,300.
Invoice No. 1465, dated April 22, terms, 1/10, n/30.

These transactions are entered in a general journal as shown in Figure 11-9.

FIGURE 11-9 Purchases Entered in General Journal

GENERAL JOURNAL — PAGE 6

	DATE		DESCRIPTION	POST. REF.	DEBIT	CREDIT	
1	20-- Apr.	4	Purchases		3 3 0 0 00		1
2			Accounts Payable/Bilenky Cycle Works			3 3 0 0 00	2
3			Invoice No. 631				3
4							4
5		8	Purchases		2 5 0 0 00		5
6			Accounts Payable/Ellsworth			2 5 0 0 00	6
7			Invoice No. 927D				7
8							8
9		11	Purchases		8 7 0 0 00		9
10			Accounts Payable/Gunnar Cycles			8 7 0 0 00	10
11			Invoice No. 804				11
12							12
13		17	Purchases		8 0 0 00		13
14			Accounts Payable/Milwaukee Cycle Co.			8 0 0 00	14
15			Invoice No. 611				15
16							16
17		23	Purchases		5 3 0 0 00		17
18			Accounts Payable/Rans Designs, Inc.			5 3 0 0 00	18
19			Invoice No. 1465				19

Posting Purchases to the General Ledger

Purchases transactions are posted from the general journal to the general ledger in the same manner as was illustrated for sales in Chapter 10. The following steps are used, as indicated in Figure 11-10 for Sunflower Cycle's April 4 and 8 purchases transactions:

In the general ledger account:

STEP 1 Enter the date of the transaction in the Date column.

STEP 2 Enter the amount of the debit or credit in the Debit or Credit column.

STEP 3 Enter the new balance in the Balance columns under Debit or Credit.

STEP 4 Enter the journal page number from which each transaction is posted in the Posting Reference column.

In the journal:

STEP 5 Enter the ledger account number in the Posting Reference column of the journal for each transaction that is posted.

Other purchases transactions would be posted in the same manner.

FIGURE 11-10 Posting Purchases to the General Ledger

GENERAL JOURNAL (Partial) Page 6

Date		Description	Post. Ref.	Debit	Credit
20--					
Apr.	4	Purchases	501	3,300.00	
		Accounts Payable/Bilenky Cycle Works	202		3,300.00
		Invoice No. 631			
	8	Purchases	501	2,500.00	
		Accounts Payable/Ellsworth	202		2,500.00
		Invoice No. 927D			

GENERAL LEDGER (Partial)

ACCOUNT Accounts Payable ACCOUNT NO. 202

Date		Item	Post. Ref.	Debit	Credit	Balance Debit	Balance Credit
20--							
Apr.	1	Bal.	✓				4,800.00
	4		J6		3,300.00		8,100.00
	8		J6		2,500.00		10,600.00

ACCOUNT Purchases ACCOUNT NO. 501

Date		Item	Post. Ref.	Debit	Credit	Balance Debit	Balance Credit
20--							
Apr.	1	Bal.	✓			37,400.00	
	4		J6	3,300.00		40,700.00	
	8		J6	2,500.00		43,200.00	

A three-column account form is commonly used for supplier accounts. Only one balance column is needed because the normal balance is a credit. If a debit balance occurs, the amount may be bracketed.

LEARNING KEY

When an accounts payable ledger is used, the Posting Reference column in the general journal serves two purposes. (1) The account number is inserted to indicate the general ledger account has been posted. (2) A slash (/) and a check mark (✓) are inserted to indicate the accounts payable ledger account has been posted.

Posting Purchases to the Accounts Payable Ledger

The Purchases and Accounts Payable resulting from merchandise purchases on account are now up to date in the general ledger. A record can be kept of the amount owed to each supplier by using an **accounts payable ledger**. This is a separate ledger containing an individual account payable for each supplier. It is similar to the accounts receivable ledger we saw in Chapter 10. A summary accounts payable account called a controlling account is maintained in the general ledger. The accounts payable ledger is "subsidiary" to this account. If there are many supplier accounts, it is a good practice to assign each supplier an account number. The subsidiary ledger accounts are kept in either alphabetical or numerical order, depending on whether the supplier accounts are identified by number.

Figure 11-11 illustrates the use of the accounts payable ledger for Sunflower Cycle's April 4 and 8 purchases transactions. Note that the individual vendor name follows accounts payable in each journal entry affecting Accounts Payable. The following steps are used to post from the general journal to the accounts payable ledger, as shown in Figure 11-11:

In the accounts payable ledger account:

STEP 1 Enter the date of the transaction in the Date column.

STEP 2 Enter the amount of the debit or credit in the Debit or Credit column.

FIGURE 11-11 Posting Purchases to the Accounts Payable Ledger

GENERAL JOURNAL (Partial) — Page 6

Date		Description	Post. Ref.	Debit	Credit
20--					
Apr.	4	Purchases	501	3,300.00	
		Accounts Payable/Bilenky Cycle Works	5 202/✓		3,300.00
		Invoice No. 631			
	8	Purchases	501	2,500.00	
		Accounts Payable/Ellsworth	5 202/✓		2,500.00
		Invoice No. 927D			

2

ACCOUNTS PAYABLE LEDGER (Partial)

NAME Bilenky Cycle Works
ADDRESS 5319 N. 2nd. St., Philadelphia, PA 19120

Date		Item	Post. Ref.	Debit	Credit	Balance
20--						
Apr. 1	4		4 J6		3,300.00	3,300.00 3

NAME Ellsworth
ADDRESS 16275 Technology Dr., San Diego, CA 92127

Date		Item	Post. Ref.	Debit	Credit	Balance
20--						
Apr. 1	8		4 J6		2,500.00	2,500.00 3

GENERAL LEDGER (Partial)

ACCOUNT Accounts Payable — ACCOUNT NO. 202

Date		Item	Post. Ref.	Debit	Credit	Balance Debit	Balance Credit
20--							
Apr.	1	Bal.	✓				4,800.00
	4		J6		3,300.00		8,100.00
	8		J6		2,500.00		10,600.00

ACCOUNT Purchases — ACCOUNT NO. 501

Date		Item	Post. Ref.	Debit	Credit	Balance Debit	Balance Credit
20--							
Apr.	1	Bal.	✓			37,400	
	4		J6	3,300.00		40,700	
	8		J6	2,500.00		43,200	

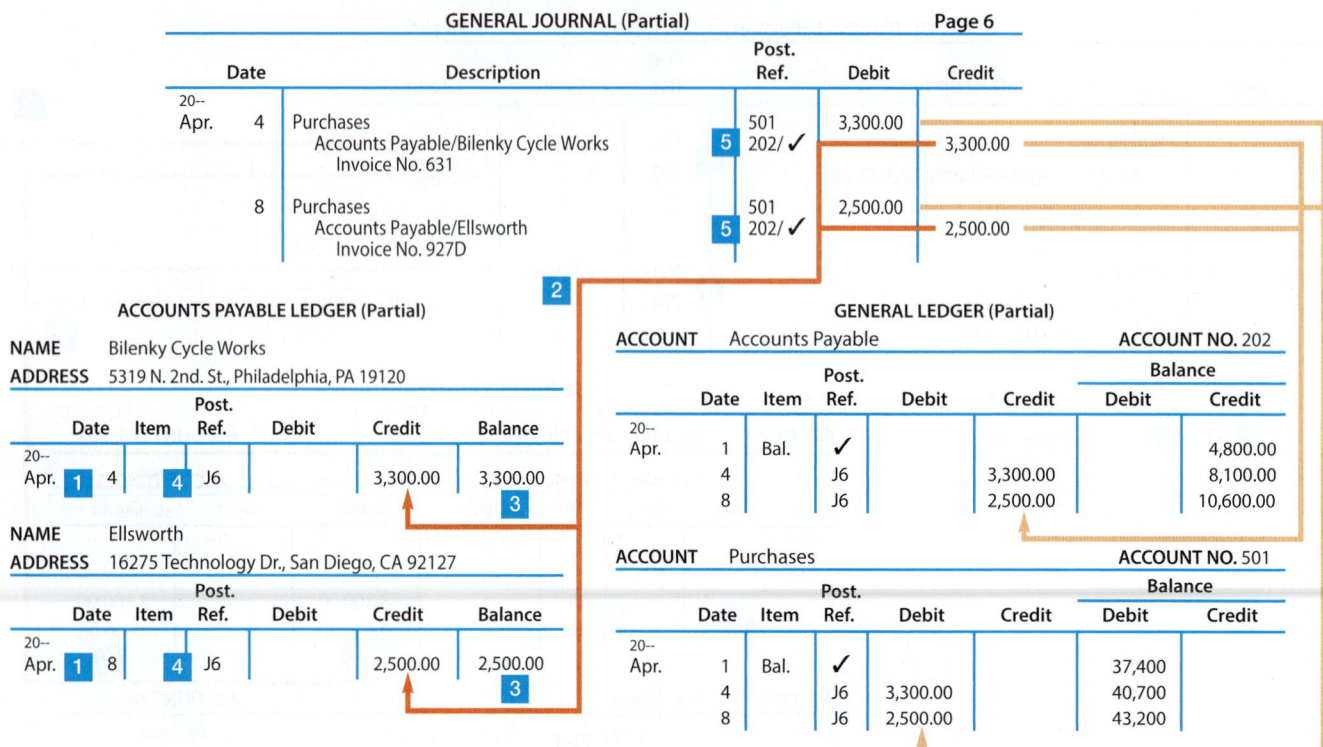

STEP 3 Enter the new balance in the Balance column.

STEP 4 Enter the journal page number from which each transaction is posted in the Posting Reference column.

In the journal:

STEP 5 Enter a slash (/) followed by a check mark (✓) in the Posting Reference column of the journal for each transaction that is posted.

> **LEARNING KEY**
> The total of the accounts payable ledger balances must equal the Accounts Payable balance in the general ledger.

Note the relationship between the general journal, accounts payable ledger, and general ledger. All general journal entries are posted to both the general ledger and the accounts payable ledger. After the posting of the accounts payable ledger and general ledger is completed, the total of the accounts payable ledger balances should equal the Accounts Payable balance in the general ledger.

Purchases Returns and Allowances

If a buyer returns merchandise or is given an allowance for damaged merchandise, a general journal entry is required. Assume that on May 4, Sunflower Cycle returns $200 of merchandise to Rans Designs, Inc. These goods were part of a purchase made on April 23. Figure 11-12 shows the general journal entry, general ledger posting, and accounts payable ledger posting for this transaction.

The general journal entry is made in the usual manner. The general ledger is posted using the same five steps as were illustrated for purchases transactions in Figure 11-10. The accounts payable ledger is posted using the following five steps, as illustrated in Figure 11-12:

In the accounts payable ledger account:

STEP 1 Enter the date of the transaction in the Date column.

STEP 2 Enter the amount of the debit or credit in the Debit or Credit column.

FIGURE 11-12 Accounting for Purchases Returns and Allowances

GENERAL JOURNAL (Partial) Page 8

Date		Description	Post. Ref.	Debit	Credit
20--					
May	4	Accounts Payable/Rans Designs, Inc.	5 202/ ✓	200.00	
		Purchases Returns and Allowances	501.1		200.00
		Returned merchandise			

ACCOUNTS PAYABLE LEDGER (Partial)

NAME Rans Designs, Inc.
ADDRESS 4600 Highway 183, Hays, KS 67601

Date		Item	Post. Ref.	Debit	Credit	Balance
20--						
May	1	Bal.				5,300.00
1	4	4	J8	200.00		5,100.00 3

2 GENERAL LEDGER (Partial)

ACCOUNT Accounts Payable ACCOUNT NO. 202

Date		Item	Post. Ref.	Debit	Credit	Balance Debit	Balance Credit
20--							
May	1	Bal.	✓				11,900.00
	4		J8	200.00			11,700.00

ACCOUNT Purchases Returns and Allowances ACCOUNT NO. 501.1

Date		Item	Post. Ref.	Debit	Credit	Balance Debit	Balance Credit
20--							
May	1	Bal.	✓				370.00
	4		J8		200.00		570.00

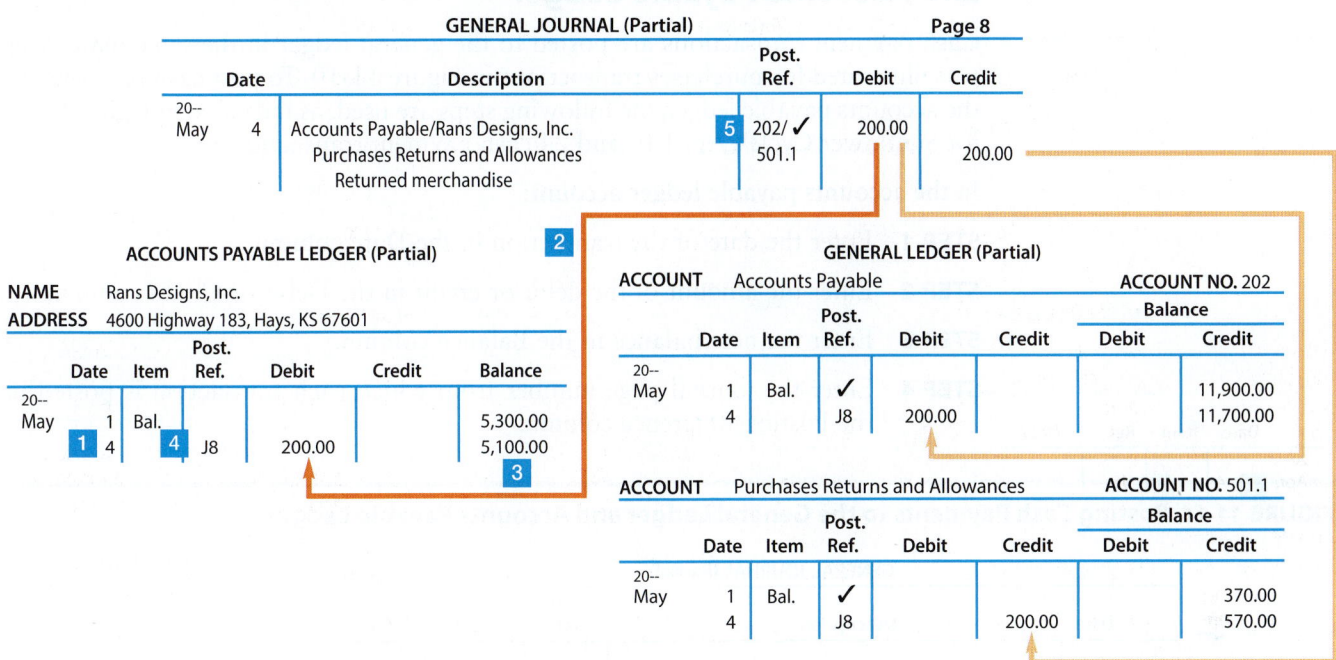

STEP 3 Enter the new balance in the Balance column.

STEP 4 Enter the journal page number from which each transaction is posted in the Posting Reference column.

In the journal:

STEP 5 Enter a slash (/) followed by a check mark (✓) in the Posting Reference column of the journal for each transaction that is posted.

Cash Payments

To illustrate the journalizing and posting of cash payments, we will use Sunflower Cycle's cash payment transactions. Assume Sunflower Cycle made the following two payments on account during the month of April:

Apr. 10 Paid Ace Wheelworks $4,800 for purchases made on account.
24 Paid Gunnar Cycles $8,700 less discount of 1% for purchases made on account.

These transactions are entered in a general journal as shown in Figure 11-13.

FIGURE 11-13 Cash Payments Entered in a General Journal

30	Apr.	10	Accounts Payable/Ace Wheelworks		4 8 0 0 00		30
31			Cash			4 8 0 0 00	31
32			Made payment on account				32
33							33
34		24	Accounts Payable/Gunnar Cycles		8 7 0 0 00		34
35			Cash			8 6 1 3 00	35
36			Purchases Discounts			8 7 00	36
37			Made payment less discount on account				37

Posting Cash Payments to the General Ledger and Accounts Payable Ledger

Cash payment transactions are posted to the general ledger in the same manner as was illustrated for purchases transactions in Figure 11-10. To post cash payments to the accounts payable ledger, the following steps are used, as indicated in Figure 11-14 for Sunflower Cycle's April 10 and 24 cash payment transactions:

In the accounts payable ledger account:

STEP 1 Enter the date of the transaction in the Date column.

STEP 2 Enter the amount of the debit or credit in the Debit or Credit column.

STEP 3 Enter the new balance in the Balance column.

STEP 4 Enter the journal page number from which each transaction is posted in the Posting Reference column.

FIGURE 11-14 Posting Cash Payments to the General Ledger and Accounts Payable Ledger

GENERAL JOURNAL (Partial) — Page 6

Date		Description	Post. Ref.	Debit	Credit
20--					
Apr.	10	Accounts Payable/Ace Wheelworks	[5] 202/ ✓	4,800.00	
		Cash	101		4,800.00
		Made payment on account			
	24	Accounts Payable/Gunnar Cycles	[5] 202/ ✓	8,700.00	
		Cash	101		8,613.00
		Purchases Discounts	501.2		87.00
		Made payment less discount on account			

[2]

ACCOUNTS PAYABLE LEDGER (Partial)

NAME Ace Wheelworks
ADDRESS 145 Elm St., Somerville, MA 02144

Date		Item	Post. Ref.	Debit	Credit	Balance
20--						
Apr.	1	Bal.	✓			4,800.00
	[1] 10		[4] J6	4,800.00		— [3]

NAME Gunnar Cycles
ADDRESS 816 W. Bakke Ave, Waterford, WI 53185

Date		Item	Post. Ref.	Debit	Credit	Balance
20--						
Apr.	11		J6		8,700.00	8,700.00
	[1] 24		[4] J6	8,700.00		— [3]

GENERAL LEDGER (Partial)

ACCOUNT Cash — ACCOUNT NO. 101

Date		Item	Post. Ref.	Debit	Credit	Balance Debit	Balance Credit
20--							
Apr.	1	Bal.	✓			20,000.00	
	10		J6		4,800.00	15,200.00	
	24		J6		8,613.00	6,587.00	

ACCOUNT Accounts Payable — ACCOUNT NO. 202

Date		Item	Post. Ref.	Debit	Credit	Balance Debit	Balance Credit
20--							
Apr.	1	Bal.	✓				4,800.00
	4		J6		3,300.00		8,100.00
	8		J6		2,500.00		10,600.00
	10		J6	4,800.00			5,800.00
	11		J6		8,700.00		14,500.00
	17		J6		800.00		15,300.00
	23		J6		5,300.00		20,600.00
	24		J6	8,700.00			11,900.00

ACCOUNT Purchases Discounts — ACCOUNT NO. 501. 2

Date		Item	Post. Ref.	Debit	Credit	Balance Debit	Balance Credit
20--							
Apr.	1	Bal.	✓				330.00
	24		J6		87.00		417.00

CHECKPOINT

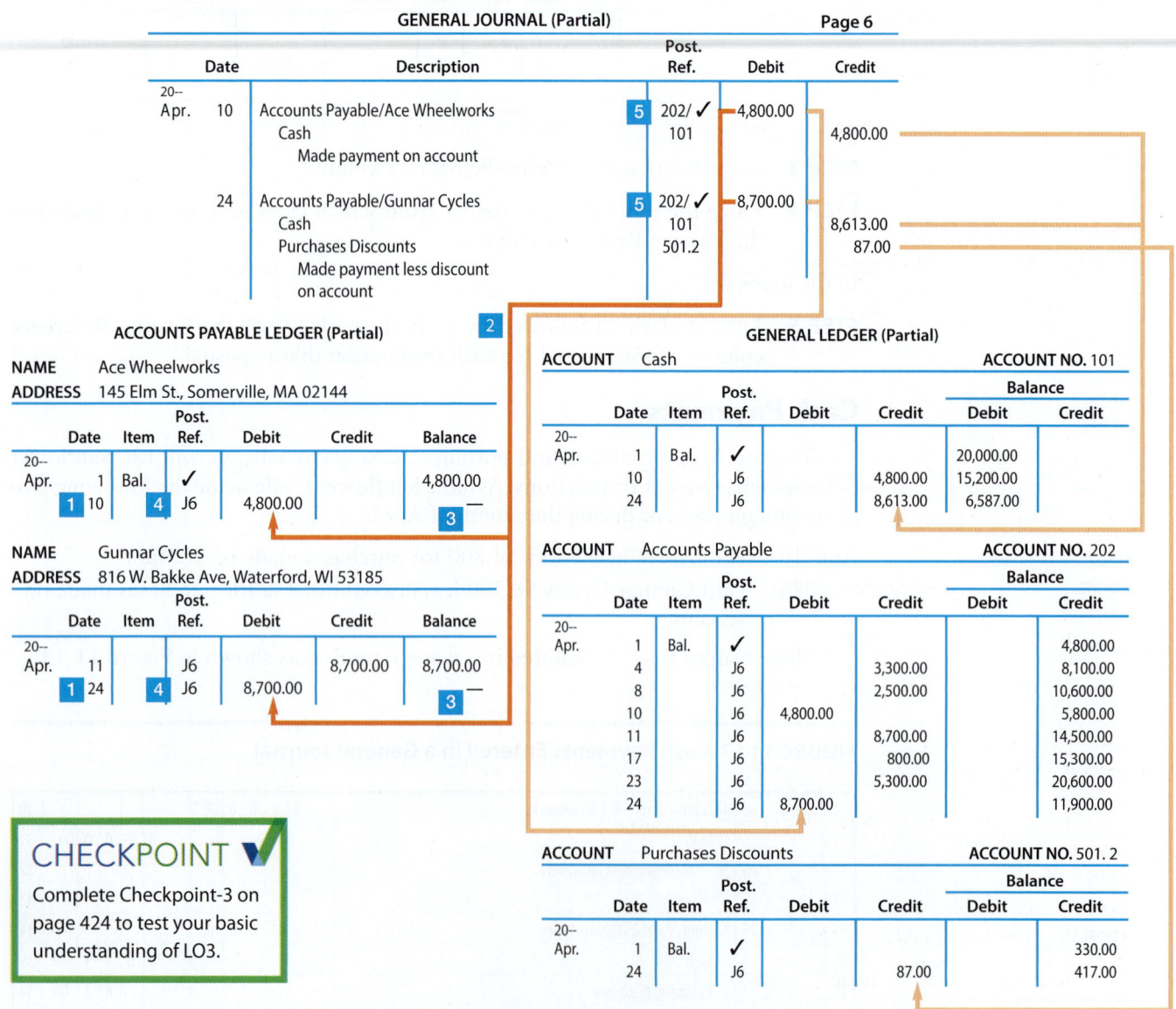

Complete Checkpoint-3 on page 424 to test your basic understanding of LO3.

In the journal:

STEP 5 Enter a slash (/) followed by a check mark (✓) in the Posting Reference column of the journal for each transaction that is posted.

LO4 Schedule of Accounts Payable

Prepare a schedule of accounts payable.

At the end of the month, all postings to Accounts Payable in the general ledger and to the accounts payable ledger should be complete, as shown in Figure 11-15. At this point, the Accounts Payable balance in the general ledger should equal the sum of the supplier balances in the accounts payable ledger.

To verify that the sum of the accounts payable ledger balances equals the Accounts Payable balance, a **schedule of accounts payable** is prepared. This is an alphabetical or numerical listing of supplier accounts and balances, usually prepared at the end of the month. Figure 11-16 shows the schedule of accounts payable for Sunflower Cycle as of April 30. Note that suppliers whose account balance is zero are not included.

FIGURE 11-15 General Ledger and Accounts Payable Ledger after Posting

ACCOUNTS PAYABLE LEDGER

NAME Ace Wheelworks
ADDRESS 145 Elm St., Somerville, MA 02144

Date		Item	Post. Ref.	Debit	Credit	Balance
20--						
Apr.	1	Bal.	✓			4,800.00
	10		J6	4,800.00		—

NAME Bilenky Cycle Works
ADDRESS 5319 N. 2nd. St., Philadelphia, PA 19120

Date		Item	Post. Ref.	Debit	Credit	Balance
20--						
Apr.	4		J6		3,300.00	3,300.00

NAME Ellsworth
ADDRESS 16275 Technology Dr., San Diego, CA 92127

Date		Item	Post. Ref.	Debit	Credit	Balance
20--						
Apr.	8		J6		2,500.00	2,500.00

NAME Gunnar Cycles
ADDRESS 816 W. Bakke Ave, Waterford, WI 53185

Date		Item	Post. Ref.	Debit	Credit	Balance
20--						
Apr.	11		J6		8,700.00	8,700.00
	24		J6	8,700.00		—

NAME Milwaukee Cycle Co.
ADDRESS 1018 W. Lincoln Ave, Milwaukee, WI 53215

Date		Item	Post. Ref.	Debit	Credit	Balance
20--						
Apr.	17		J6		800.00	800.00

NAME Rans Designs, Inc.
ADDRESS 4600 Highway 183, Hays, KS 67601

Date		Item	Post. Ref.	Debit	Credit	Balance
20--						
Apr.	23		J6		5,300.00	5,300.00

GENERAL LEDGER (Partial)

ACCOUNT Accounts Payable ACCOUNT NO. 202

Date		Item	Post. Ref.	Debit	Credit	Balance Debit	Balance Credit
20--							
Apr.	1	Bal.	✓				4,800.00
	4		J6		3,300.00		8,100.00
	8		J6		2,500.00		10,600.00
	10		J6	4,800.00			5,800.00
	11		J6		8,700.00		14,500.00
	17		J6		800.00		15,300.00
	23		J6		5,300.00		20,600.00
	24		J6	8,700.00			11,900.00

FIGURE 11-16 Schedule of Accounts Payable

Sunflower Cycle Schedule of Accounts Payable April 30, 20--	
Bilenky Cycle Works	$ 3,300.00
Ellsworth	2,500.00
Milwaukee Cycle Co.	800.00
Rans Designs, Inc.	5,300.00
	$11,900.00

This schedule is prepared from the supplier accounts in the accounts payable ledger. The total calculated in the schedule is compared with the balance in Accounts Payable in the general ledger. Note that the $11,900 total listed in the schedule equals the Accounts Payable balance shown in Figure 11-15. If the schedule total and the Accounts Payable balance do not agree, the error must be located and corrected. To find the error, use the following procedures:

STEP 1 Verify the total of the schedule.

STEP 2 Verify the postings to the accounts payable ledger.

STEP 3 Verify the postings to Accounts Payable in the general ledger.

CHECKPOINT

Complete Checkpoint-4 on page 424 to test your basic understanding of LO4.

SELF-STUDY

LEARNING OBJECTIVES		Key Points to Remember
LO1	**Describe merchandise purchases transactions.**	For a merchandising business, purchases refers to merchandise acquired for resale. Major documents used in the purchasing process are the purchase requisition, purchase order, receiving report, and purchase invoice.
LO2	**Describe and use merchandise purchases accounts and compute gross profit.**	Four accounts are used in accounting for merchandise purchases transactions. 1. Purchases 2. Purchases Returns and Allowances 3. Purchases Discounts 4. Freight-In Cost of Goods Sold = Beginning Inventory + Net Purchases + Freight-In − Ending Inventory Gross Profit = Net Sales − Cost of Goods Sold
LO3	**Describe and use the accounts payable ledger.**	To post purchases transactions to the general ledger: **In the general ledger account:** **STEP 1** Enter the date of the transaction in the Date column. **STEP 2** Enter the amount of the debit or credit in the Debit or Credit column. **STEP 3** Enter the new balance in the Balance columns under Debit or Credit. **STEP 4** Enter the journal page number from which each transaction is posted in the Posting Reference column.

LEARNING OBJECTIVES	Key Points to Remember
LO3 (concluded)	**In the journal:** **STEP 5** Enter the ledger account number in the Posting Reference column of the journal for each transaction that is posted. An accounts payable ledger is a separate ledger containing an individual account payable for each supplier. To post from the general journal to the accounts payable ledger: **In the accounts payable ledger account:** **STEP 1** Enter the date of the transaction in the Date column. **STEP 2** Enter the amount of the debit or credit in the Debit or Credit column. **STEP 3** Enter the new balance in the Balance column. **STEP 4** Enter the journal page number from which each transaction is posted in the Posting Reference column. **In the journal:** **STEP 5** Enter a slash (/) followed by a check mark (✓) in the Posting Reference column of the journal for each transaction that is posted. To post cash payments transactions to the general ledger: **In the general ledger account:** **STEP 1** Enter the date of the transaction in the Date column. **STEP 2** Enter the amount of the debit or credit in the Debit or Credit column. **STEP 3** Enter the new balance in the Balance columns under Debit or Credit. **STEP 4** Enter the journal page number from which each transaction is posted in the Posting Reference column. **In the journal:** **STEP 5** Enter the ledger account number in the Posting Reference column of the journal for each transaction that is posted. To post cash payments transactions to the accounts payable ledger: **In the accounts payable ledger account:** **STEP 1** Enter the date of the transaction in the Date column. **STEP 2** Enter the amount of the debit or credit in the Debit or Credit column. **STEP 3** Enter the new balance in the Balance column. **STEP 4** Enter the journal page number from which each transaction is posted in the Posting Reference column. **In the journal:** **STEP 5** Enter a slash (/) followed by a check mark (✓) in the Posting Reference column of the journal for each transaction that is posted.
LO4 Prepare a schedule of accounts payable.	The schedule of accounts payable is used to verify that the sum of the accounts payable ledger balances equals the Accounts Payable balance.

DEMONSTRATION PROBLEM

Jodi Rutman operates a retail pharmacy called Rutman Pharmacy. The books include a general journal, a general ledger, and an accounts payable ledger. The following transactions are related to purchases and cash payments for the month of June 20--:

June	1	Purchased merchandise from Sullivan Co. on account, $234.20. Invoice No. 71, dated June 1, terms 2/10, n/30.
	2	Issued Check No. 536 for payment of June rent (Rent Expense), $1,000.
	5	Purchased merchandise from Amfac Drug Supply on account, $562.40. Invoice No. 196, dated June 2, terms 1/15, n/30.
	7	Purchased merchandise from University Drug Co. on account, $367.35. Invoice No. 914A, dated June 5, terms 3/10 eom, n/30.
	9	Issued Check No. 537 to Sullivan Co. in payment of Invoice No. 71 less 2% discount.
	12	Received a credit memo from Amfac Drug Supply for merchandise returned that was purchased on June 5, $46.20.
	14	Purchased merchandise from Mutual Drug Co. on account, $479.40. Invoice No. 745, dated June 14, terms 2/10, n/30.
	15	Received a credit memo from University Drug Co. for merchandise returned that was purchased on June 7, $53.70.
	16	Issued Check No. 538 to Amfac Drug Supply in payment of Invoice No. 196 less the credit memo of June 12 and less 1% discount.
	23	Issued Check No. 539 to Mutual Drug Co. in payment of Invoice No. 745 less 2% discount.
	27	Purchased merchandise from Flites Pharmaceuticals on account, $638.47. Invoice No. 675, dated June 27, terms 2/10 eom, n/30.
	29	Issued Check No. 540 to Dolgin Candy Co. for a cash purchase of merchandise, $270.20.
	30	Issued Check No. 541 to Vashon Medical Supply in payment of Invoice No. 416, $1,217.69. No discount allowed.

REQUIRED

1. Enter the transactions in a general journal (start with page 7).
2. Post from the journal to the general ledger accounts and the accounts payable ledger. Account numbers and June 1 balances are as indicated in the accounts presented below. Then, update the account balances.
3. Prepare a schedule of accounts payable from the accounts payable ledger in the problem. Verify that the total of accounts payable in the schedule equals the June 30 balance of Accounts Payable in the general ledger.

SOLUTION 1.

GENERAL JOURNAL — Page 7

	DATE		DESCRIPTION	POST. REF.	DEBIT	CREDIT	
1	20-- June	1	Purchases	501	234 20		1
2			Accounts Payable/Sullivan Co.	202/✓		234 20	2
3			Invoice No. 71				3
4							4
5		2	Rent Expense	521	1000 00		5
6			Cash	101		1000 00	6
7			Check No. 536				7
8							8
9		5	Purchases	501	562 40		9
10			Accounts Payable/Amfac Drug Supply	202/✓		562 40	10
11			Invoice No. 196				11
12							12
13		7	Purchases	501	367 35		13
14			Accounts Payable/University Drug Co.	202/✓		367 35	14
15			Invoice No. 914A				15
16							16
17		9	Accounts Payable/Sullivan Co.	202/✓	234 20		17
18			Cash	101		229 52	18
19			Purchases Discounts	501.2		4 68	19
20			Check No. 537				20
21							21
22		12	Accounts Payable/Amfac Drug Supply	202/✓	46 20		22
23			Purchases Returns and Allowances	501.1		46 20	23
24			Returned merchandise				24
25							25
26		14	Purchases	501	479 40		26
27			Accounts Payable/Mutual Drug Co.	202/✓		479 40	27
28			Invoice No. 745				28

GENERAL JOURNAL — Page 8

	DATE		DESCRIPTION	POST. REF.	DEBIT	CREDIT	
1	20-- June	15	Accounts Payable/University Drug Co.	202/✓	53 70		1
2			Purchases Returns and Allowances	501.1		53 70	2
3			Returned merchandise				3
4							4
5		16	Accounts Payable/Amfac Drug Supply	202/✓	516 20		5
6			Cash	101		511 04	6
7			Purchases Discounts	501.2		5 16	7
8			Check No. 538				8
9							9
10		23	Accounts Payable/Mutual Drug Co.	202/✓	479 40		10
11			Cash	101		469 81	11
12			Purchases Discounts	501.2		9 59	12
13			Check No. 539				13
14							14
15		27	Purchases	501	638 47		15
16			Accounts Payable/Flites Pharmaceuticals	202/✓		638 47	16
17			Invoice No. 675				17
18							18
19		29	Purchases	501	270 20		19
20			Cash	101		270 20	20
21			Check No. 540				21
22							22
23		30	Accounts Payable/Vashon Medical Supply	202/✓	1217 69		23
24			Cash	101		1217 69	24
25			Check No. 541				25

(continued)

SOLUTION 2.

ACCOUNT: Cash — ACCOUNT NO. 101

DATE		ITEM	POST. REF.	DEBIT	CREDIT	BALANCE DEBIT	BALANCE CREDIT
20-- June	1	Balance	✓			9,180.00	
	2		J7		1,000.00	8,180.00	
	9		J7		229.52	7,950.48	
	16		J8		511.04	7,439.44	
	23		J8		469.81	6,969.63	
	29		J8		270.20	6,699.43	
	30		J8		1,217.69	5,481.74	

ACCOUNT: Accounts Payable — ACCOUNT NO. 202

DATE		ITEM	POST. REF.	DEBIT	CREDIT	BALANCE DEBIT	BALANCE CREDIT
20-- June	1	Balance	✓				1,217.69
	1		J7		234.20		1,451.89
	5		J7		562.40		2,014.29
	7		J7		367.35		2,381.64
	9		J7	234.20			2,147.44
	12		J7	46.20			2,101.24
	14		J7		479.40		2,580.64
	15		J8	53.70			2,526.94
	16		J8	516.20			2,010.74
	23		J8	479.40			1,531.34
	27		J8		638.47		2,169.81
	30		J8	1,217.69			952.12

ACCOUNT: Purchases — ACCOUNT NO. 501

DATE		ITEM	POST. REF.	DEBIT	CREDIT	BALANCE DEBIT	BALANCE CREDIT
20-- June	1	Balance	✓			13,826.25	
	1		J7	234.20		14,060.45	
	5		J7	562.40		14,622.85	
	7		J7	367.35		14,990.20	
	14		J7	479.40		15,469.60	
	27		J8	638.47		16,108.07	
	29		J8	270.20		16,378.27	

ACCOUNT: Purchases Returns and Allowances — ACCOUNT NO. 501.1

DATE		ITEM	POST. REF.	DEBIT	CREDIT	BALANCE DEBIT	BALANCE CREDIT
20-- June	1	Balance	✓				312.63
	12		J7		46.20		358.83
	15		J8		53.70		412.53

ACCOUNT: Purchases Discounts ACCOUNT NO. 501.2

DATE		ITEM	POST. REF.	DEBIT	CREDIT	BALANCE DEBIT	BALANCE CREDIT
20-- June	1	Balance	✓				211 45
	9		J7		4 68		216 13
	16		J8		5 16		221 29
	23		J8		9 59		230 88

ACCOUNT: Rent Expense ACCOUNT NO. 521

DATE		ITEM	POST. REF.	DEBIT	CREDIT	BALANCE DEBIT	BALANCE CREDIT
20-- June	1	Balance	✓			5000 00	
	2		J7	1000 00		6000 00	

ACCOUNTS PAYABLE LEDGER

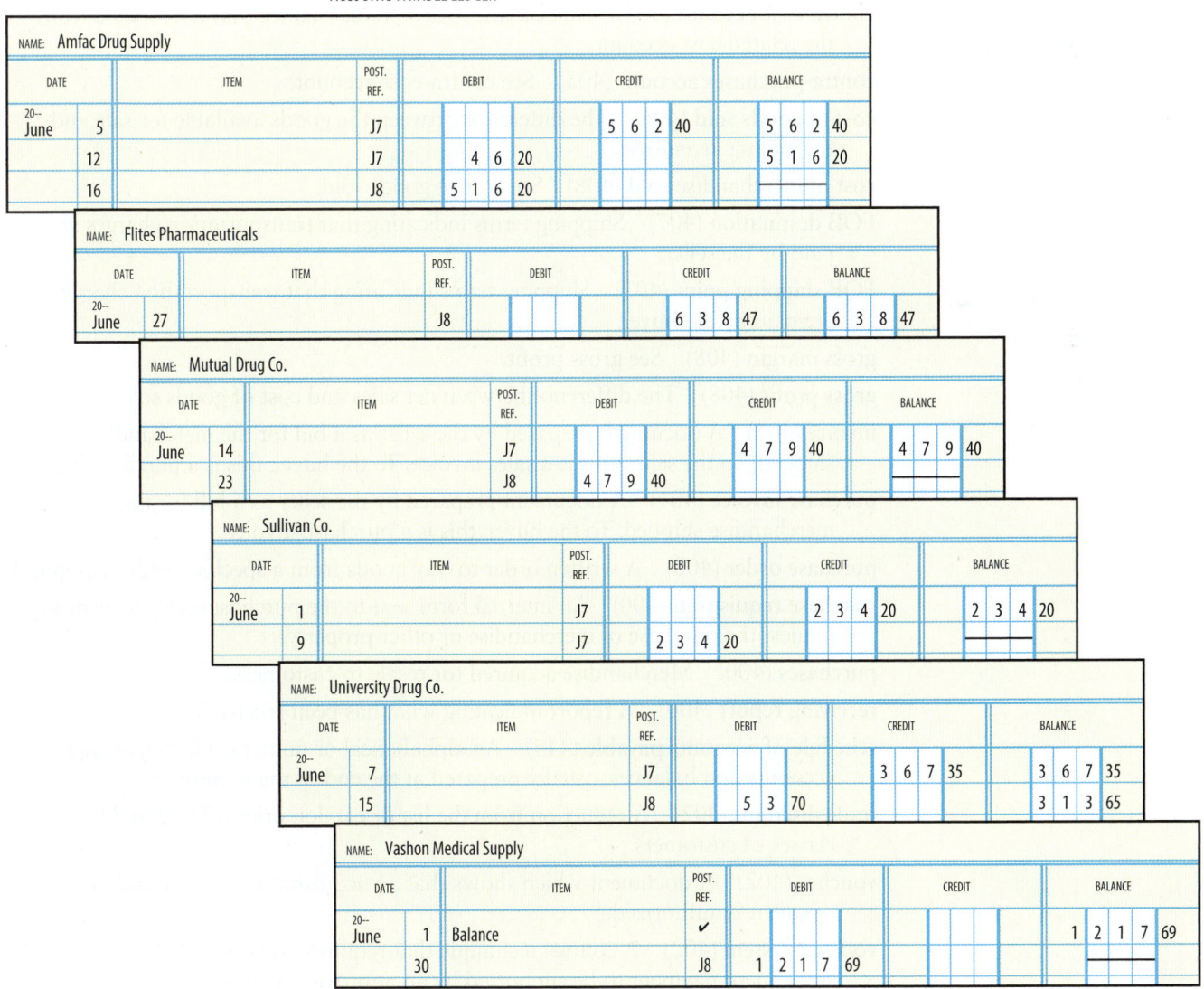

NAME: Amfac Drug Supply

DATE		ITEM	POST. REF.	DEBIT	CREDIT	BALANCE
20-- June	5		J7		562 40	562 40
	12		J7	46 20		516 20
	16		J8	516 20		—

NAME: Flites Pharmaceuticals

DATE		ITEM	POST. REF.	DEBIT	CREDIT	BALANCE
20-- June	27		J8		638 47	638 47

NAME: Mutual Drug Co.

DATE		ITEM	POST. REF.	DEBIT	CREDIT	BALANCE
20-- June	14		J7		479 40	479 40
	23		J8	479 40		—

NAME: Sullivan Co.

DATE		ITEM	POST. REF.	DEBIT	CREDIT	BALANCE
20-- June	1		J7		234 20	234 20
	9		J7	234 20		—

NAME: University Drug Co.

DATE		ITEM	POST. REF.	DEBIT	CREDIT	BALANCE
20-- June	7		J7		367 35	367 35
	15		J8	53 70		313 65

NAME: Vashon Medical Supply

DATE		ITEM	POST. REF.	DEBIT	CREDIT	BALANCE
20-- June	1	Balance	✓			1217 69
	30		J8	1217 69		—

(continued)

SOLUTION 3.

Rutman Pharmacy Schedule of Accounts Payable June 30, 20--	
Flites Pharmaceuticals	$ 6,388.47
University Drug Co.	3,133.65
	$ 9,522.12
Proof	
Balance of Accounts Payable, June 30	$ 9,522.12

KEY TERMS

accounts payable ledger (411) A separate ledger containing an individual account payable for each supplier.

contra-cost account (405) An account with a credit balance that is deducted from the related cost account.

contra-purchases account (405) See contra-cost account.

cost of goods sold (408) The difference between the goods available for sale and the ending inventory.

cost of merchandise sold (408) See cost of goods sold.

FOB destination (407) Shipping terms indicating that transportation charges are paid by the seller.

FOB shipping point (407) Shipping terms indicating that transportation charges are paid by the buyer.

gross margin (408) See gross profit.

gross profit (408) The difference between net sales and cost of goods sold.

invoice (401) A document prepared by the seller as a bill for the merchandise shipped. To the seller, this is a sales invoice. To the buyer, this is a purchase invoice.

purchase invoice (401) A document prepared by the seller as a bill for the merchandise shipped. To the buyer, this is a purchase invoice.

purchase order (400) A written order to buy goods from a specific vendor (supplier).

purchase requisition (400) An internal form sent to the purchasing department to request the purchase of merchandise or other property.

purchases (400) Merchandise acquired for resale to customers.

receiving report (400) A report indicating what has been received.

schedule of accounts payable (415) An alphabetical or numerical listing of supplier accounts and balances, usually prepared at the end of the month.

trade discount (402) A reduction from the list or catalog price offered to different classes of customers.

voucher (402) A document which shows that an acquisition is proper and that payment is authorized.

voucher system (402) A control technique that requires every acquisition and subsequent payment to be supported by an approved voucher.

SELF-STUDY TEST QUESTIONS

True/False

1. **LO1** In the purchasing process, the purchase invoice is the first document prepared.
2. **LO1** A sales invoice prepared by the seller is called a purchase invoice by the buyer.
3. **LO1** A trade discount is a reduction from the list or catalog price offered to different classes of customers.
4. **LO2** Purchases Returns and Allowances is debited when merchandise is returned for credit.
5. **LO2** FOB shipping point means that transportation charges are paid by the seller.

Multiple Choice

1. **LO1** A purchase of merchandise for $300 with a trade discount of 10% would require a debit to Purchases of
   (a) $330.
   (b) $300.
   (c) $297.
   (d) $270.
2. **LO2** In the income statement, Freight-In is
   (a) added to purchases.
   (b) subtracted from purchases.
   (c) added to sales.
   (d) subtracted from cost of goods sold.
3. **LO2** The difference between net sales and cost of goods sold is called
   (a) gross profit.
   (b) net purchases.
   (c) goods available for sale.
   (d) the bottom line.
4. **LO2** The difference between merchandise available for sale and the end-of-period merchandise inventory is called
   (a) gross profit.
   (b) net purchases.
   (c) net sales.
   (d) cost of goods sold.
5. **LO2** A purchase invoice for $1,200 with credit terms 2/10, n/30, and a return of $300 received by the seller prior to payment, is paid within the discount period. A check should be sent for
   (a) $1,200.
   (b) $882.
   (c) $900.
   (d) $810.

CHECKPOINT ✓

Checkpoint Exercises

1. **LO1** Deering Housewares purchased merchandise for $1,200 less a 10% trade discount with credit terms of 1/10, n/30.
   a. Compute the trade discount.
   b. Compute the amount at which to record this purchase.
   c. Compute the cash discount if the payment for the merchandise is made within the discount period.

2. **LO2** Based on the following data for Dave's Supply House, determine the gross profit.

Net sales	$92,000
Merchandise inventory, January 1, 20--	27,000
Purchases during the year	60,800
Purchases returns and allowances during the year	3,100
Purchases discounts during the year	1,300
Merchandise inventory, December 31, 20--	24,000

3. **LO3** The following journal entries are for current purchases and cash payments transactions. Using T accounts, post these transactions to Cash, Accounts Payable, Purchases, Purchases Returns and Allowances, and Purchases Discounts in the general ledger, and the vendor account in the accounts payable ledger.

a. Purchases	350.00	
Accounts Payable/J. Bedas		350.00
b. Accounts Payable/J. Bedas	70.00	
Purchases Returns and Allowances		70.00
c. Accounts Payable/J. Bedas	280.00	
Cash		274.40
Purchases Discounts		5.60

4. **LO4** On June 23, Felini Plumbing's accounts payable consisted of the following vendor balances:

B. Sutton	$245
A. Gagne	703
L. Mohler	410
P. Luffman	190
Z. Quary	263

During the following week, Felini Plumbing made a purchase of $180 from Mohler and made cash payments on account of $375 to Gagne and $110 to Quary. Prepare a schedule of accounts payable for Felini Plumbing at June 30, 20--.

The answers to the Self-Study Test Questions are at the end of the chapter (pages 436–437).

APPLYING YOUR KNOWLEDGE

REVIEW QUESTIONS

LO1 1. Identify the major documents commonly used in the purchasing process.

LO1 2. Distinguish between a cash discount and a trade discount.

LO1 3. What is a voucher system?

LO1 4. In a voucher system, a payment is supported by what five documents?

CengageNowv2 provides "Show Me How" videos for selected exercises and problems. Additional resources, such as Excel templates for completing selected exercises and problems, are available for download from the companion website at Cengage.com.

LO2 5. Describe how each of the following accounts is used: (1) Purchases, (2) Purchases Returns and Allowances, (3) Purchases Discounts, and (4) Freight-In.

LO2 6. How are cost of goods sold and gross profit computed?

LO3 7. What steps are followed in posting purchases from the general journal to the general ledger?

LO3 8. What steps are followed in posting purchases from the general journal to the accounts payable ledger?

LO3 9. What steps are followed in posting purchases returns and allowances from the general journal to the general ledger and accounts payable ledger?

LO3 10. What steps are followed in posting cash payments from the general journal to the general ledger?

LO3 11. What steps are followed in posting cash payments from the general journal to the accounts payable ledger?

LO4 12. If the total of the schedule of accounts payable does not agree with the Accounts Payable balance, what procedures should be used to search for the error?

SERIES A EXERCISES

E 11-1A (LO1)

PURCHASING DOCUMENTS AND FLOWCHART LABELING A partially completed flowchart showing some of the major documents commonly used in the purchasing function of a merchandise business is presented below. Identify documents 1, 3, and 4.

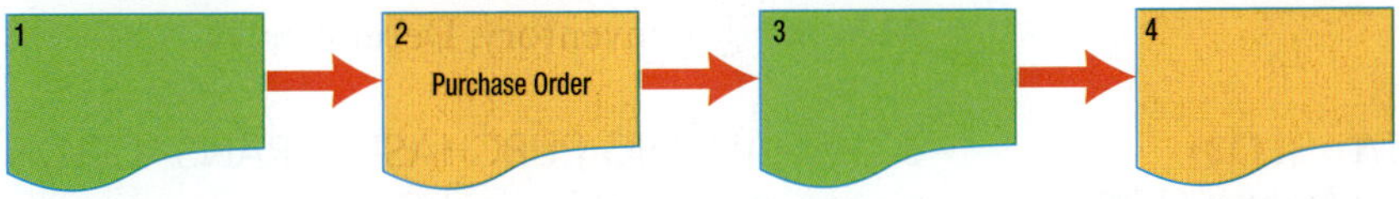

E 11-2A (LO1/2)
✓ 2: $1,764

TRADE DISCOUNT AND CASH DISCOUNTS Merchandise was purchased on account from Jacob's Distributors on May 17. The purchase price was $2,000, less a 10% trade discount and credit terms of 2/10, n/30.

1. Calculate the net amount to record the invoice, less the 10% trade discount.
2. Calculate the amount to be paid on this invoice within the discount period.
3. Journalize the purchase of the merchandise on May 17 in a general journal. Journalize the payment on May 27 (within the discount period).

E 11-3A (LO2)
✓ 3(c): Purchases Discounts: $70

PURCHASE TRANSACTIONS AND T ACCOUNTS Using T accounts for Cash, Accounts Payable, Purchases, Purchases Returns and Allowances, Purchases Discounts, and Freight-In, enter the following purchase transactions. Identify each transaction with its corresponding letter. Use a new set of T accounts for each set of transactions, 1–4.

1. Purchase of merchandise with cash.
   (a) Merchandise is purchased for cash, $1,500.
   (b) Merchandise listed at $3,500, less a trade discount of 15%, is purchased for cash.

(continued)

2. Purchase of merchandise on account with credit terms.
   (a) Merchandise is purchased on account, credit terms 2/10, n/30, $2,000.
   (b) Merchandise is purchased on account, credit terms 3/10, n/30, $1,200.
   (c) Payment is made on invoice (a) within the discount period.
   (d) Payment is made on invoice (b) too late to receive the cash discount.
3. Purchase of merchandise on account with return of merchandise.
   (a) Merchandise is purchased on account, credit terms 2/10, n/30, $4,000.
   (b) Merchandise is returned for credit before payment is made, $500.
   (c) Payment is made within the discount period.
4. Purchase of merchandise with freight-in.
   (a) Merchandise is purchased on account, $2,500 plus freight charges of $100. Terms of the sale were FOB shipping point.
   (b) Payment is made for the cost of merchandise and the freight charge.

E 11-4A (LO2)
✓ Cost of goods sold: $43,000

COMPUTING GROSS PROFIT The following data were taken from the accounts of Fluter Hardware, a small retail business. Determine the gross profit.

Sales	$120,000
Sales returns and allowances	900
Sales discounts	650
Merchandise inventory, January 1	35,000
Purchases during the period	77,600
Purchases returns and allowances during the period	4,100
Purchases discounts taken during the period	2,300
Freight-in on merchandise purchased during the period	1,250
Merchandise inventory, December 31	32,000

E 11-5A (LO3)
✓ May 9: Dr. Purchases, $2,500

JOURNALIZING PURCHASES TRANSACTIONS Journalize the following transactions in a general journal:

May	3	Purchased merchandise from Reed, $6,100. Invoice No. 321, dated May 1, terms n/30.
	9	Purchased merchandise from Omana, $2,500. Invoice No. 614, dated May 8, terms 2/10, n/30.
	18	Purchased merchandise from Yao Distributors, $2,200. Invoice No. 180, dated May 15, terms 1/15, n/30.
	23	Purchased merchandise from Brown, $5,300. Invoice No. 913, dated May 22, terms 1/10, n/30.

E 11-6A (LO3)
✓ Ending Accounts Payable balance: $8,600

JOURNALIZING PURCHASES RETURNS AND ALLOWANCES AND POSTING TO GENERAL LEDGER AND ACCOUNTS PAYABLE LEDGER Using page 3 of a general journal and the following general ledger and accounts payable ledger accounts, journalize and post the following transactions:

July	7	Returned merchandise to Starcraft Industries, $700.
	15	Returned merchandise to XYZ, Inc., $450.
	27	Returned merchandise to Datamagic, $900.

General Ledger

Account No.	Account	Balance July 1, 20--
202	Accounts Payable	$10,650
501.1	Purchases Returns and Allowances	---

Accounts Payable Ledger

Name	Balance July 1, 20--
Datamagic	$2,600
Starcraft Industries	4,300
XYZ, Inc.	3,750

E 11-7A (LO3)
✓ Sept. 12: Cr. Cash, $8,019

JOURNALIZING CASH PAYMENTS TRANSACTIONS Enter the following cash payments transactions in a general journal:

Sept. 5 Issued Check No. 318 to Whittle Corp. for merchandise purchased August 28, $5,000, terms 2/10, n/30. Payment is made within the discount period.

12 Issued Check No. 319 to Martin Company for merchandise purchased September 2, $8,500, terms 1/10, n/30. A credit memo had been received on September 8 from Martin Company for merchandise returned, $400. Payment is made within the discount period after deduction for the return dated September 8.

19 Issued Check No. 320 to Cloud Systems for merchandise purchased August 20, $6,100, terms n/30.

27 Issued Check No. 321 to Dynamic Data for merchandise purchased September 17, $7,000, terms 2/10, n/30. Payment is made within the discount period.

E 11-8A (LO4)
✓ Total Accounts Payable: $14,370

SCHEDULE OF ACCOUNTS PAYABLE Ryan's Express, a retail business, had the following beginning balances and purchases and payments activity in its accounts payable ledger during October. Prepare a schedule of accounts payable for Ryan's Express as of October 31, 20--.

Accounts Payable Ledger

Name	Balance Oct. 1, 20--	Purchases	Payments
Columbia Products	$4,350	$3,060	$2,060
Favorite Fashions	4,910	1,970	2,600
Rustic Legends	5,130	2,625	3,015

SERIES A PROBLEMS

P 11-9A (LO2/3)
✓ Purchases balance: $20,790

PURCHASES TRANSACTIONS J. B. Speck, owner of Speck's Galleria, made the following purchases of merchandise on account during the month of September:

Sept. 3 Purchase Invoice No. 415, $2,650, from Smith Distributors.

8 Purchase Invoice No. 132, $3,830, from Michaels Wholesaler.

11 Purchase Invoice No. 614, $3,140, from J. B. Sanders & Co.

18 Purchase Invoice No. 329, $2,250, from Bateman & Jones, Inc.

(continued)

Sept. 23 Purchase Invoice No. 767, $4,160, from Smith Distributors.
27 Purchase Invoice No. 744, $1,980, from Anderson Company.
30 Purchase Invoice No. 652, $2,780, from Michaels Wholesaler.

REQUIRED

1. Record the transactions starting with page 16 of a general journal.
2. Post from the general journal to the general ledger accounts and to the accounts payable ledger accounts. Use general ledger account numbers as shown in the chapter.

P 11-10A (LO2/3)
✓ Accounts Payable balance: $1,900

CASH PAYMENTS TRANSACTIONS Sam Santiago operates a retail variety store. The books include a general journal and an accounts payable ledger. Selected account balances on May 1 are as follows:

General Ledger	
Cash	$40,000
Accounts Payable	20,000

Accounts Payable Ledger	
Fantastic Toys	$ 5,200
Goya Outlet	3,800
Mueller's Distributors	3,600
Van Kooning	7,400

The following are the transactions related to cash payments for the month of May:

May 1 Issued Check No. 426 in payment of May rent (Rent Expense), $2,400.
3 Issued Check No. 427 to Mueller's Distributors in payment of merchandise purchased on account, $3,600, less a 3% discount. Check was written for $3,492.
7 Issued Check No. 428 to Van Kooning in partial payment of merchandise purchased on account, $5,500. A cash discount was not allowed.
12 Issued Check No. 429 to Fantastic Toys for merchandise purchased on account, $5,200, less a 1% discount. Check was written for $5,148.
15 Issued Check No. 430 to City Power and Light (Utilities Expense), $1,720.
18 Issued Check No. 431 to A-1 Warehouse for a cash purchase of merchandise, $4,800.
26 Issued Check No. 432 to Goya Outlet for merchandise purchased on account, $3,800, less a 2% discount. Check was written for $3,724.
30 Issued Check No. 433 to Mercury Transit Company for freight charges on merchandise purchased (Freight-In), $1,200.
31 Issued Check No. 434 to Town Merchants for a cash purchase of merchandise, $3,000.

REQUIRED

1. Enter the transactions starting with page 9 of a general journal.
2. Post from the general journal to the general ledger and the accounts payable ledger. Use general ledger account numbers as shown in the chapter.

P 11-11A (LO2/3)
✓ Cash balance: $10,284

PURCHASES AND CASH PAYMENTS TRANSACTIONS Emily Frank owns a small retail business called Frank's Fantasy. The cash account has a balance of $21,000 on July 1. The following transactions occurred during July:

July	1	Issued Check No. 414 in payment of July rent, $2,500.
	1	Purchased merchandise on account from Tilly's Toys, Invoice No. 311, $2,800, terms 2/10, n/30.
	3	Purchased merchandise on account from Scheer & Company, Invoice No. 812, $3,300, terms 1/10, n/30.
	5	Returned merchandise purchased from Tilly's Toys, receiving a credit memo on the amount owed, $300.
	8	Purchased merchandise on account from Donna's Dolls, Invoice No. 139, $2,900, terms 2/10, n/30.
	11	Issued Check No. 415 to Tilly's Toys for merchandise purchased on account, less return of July 5 and less 2% discount.
	13	Issued Check No. 416 to Scheer & Company for merchandise purchased on account, less 1% discount.
	15	Returned merchandise purchased from Donna's Dolls, receiving a credit memo on the amount owed, $350.
	18	Issued Check No. 417 to Donna's Dolls for merchandise purchased on account, less return of July 15 and less 2% discount.
	25	Purchased merchandise on account from Applied Business, Invoice No. 489, $2,650, terms n/30.
	26	Purchased merchandise on account from Tilly's Toys, Invoice No. 375, $2,180, terms 2/10, n/30.
	29	Purchased merchandise on account from Scheer & Company, Invoice No. 883, $3,560, terms 1/10, n/30.

REQUIRED

1. Enter the transactions starting with page 16 of a general journal.
2. Post from the journal to the general ledger and accounts payable ledger accounts. Use general ledger account numbers as shown in the chapter.

P 11-12A (LO4)
✓ Accounts Payable balance, Tilly's Toys: $2,180

SCHEDULE OF ACCOUNTS PAYABLE Based on the information provided in Problem 11-11A, prepare a schedule of accounts payable for Frank's Fantasy as of July 31, 20--. Verify that the accounts payable account balance in the general ledger agrees with the schedule of accounts payable total.

SERIES B EXERCISES

E 11-1B (LO1)

PURCHASING DOCUMENTS AND FLOWCHART LABELING A flowchart showing some of the major documents commonly used in the purchasing function of a merchandise business is presented below. Briefly describe each document.

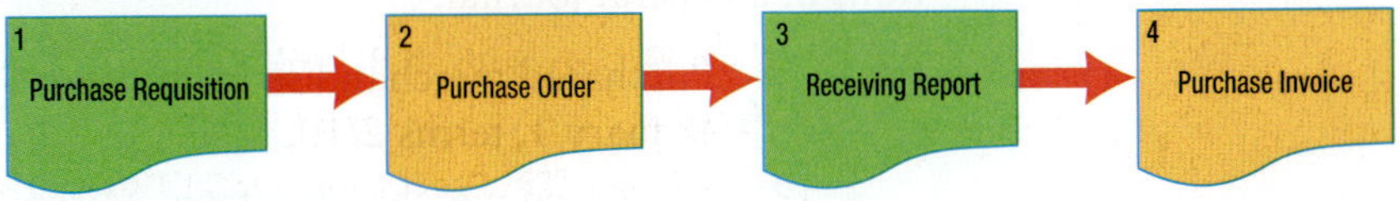

E 11-2B (LO1/2)
✓ 2: $4,365

TRADE DISCOUNT AND CASH DISCOUNTS Merchandise was purchased on account from Grant's Distributors on June 12. The purchase price was $5,000, less a 10% trade discount and credit terms of 3/10, n/30.

1. Calculate the net amount to record the invoice, less the 10% trade discount.
2. Calculate the amount to be paid on this invoice within the discount period.
3. Journalize the purchase of the merchandise on June 12 and the payment on June 22 (within the discount period) in a general journal.

E 11-3B (LO2)
✓ 3(c): Purchases Discounts, $100

PURCHASE TRANSACTIONS AND T ACCOUNTS Using T accounts for Cash, Accounts Payable, Purchases, Purchases Returns and Allowances, Purchases Discounts, and Freight-In, enter the following purchase transactions. Identify each transaction with its corresponding letter. Use a new set of T accounts for each set of transactions, 1–4.

1. Purchase of merchandise with cash.
   (a) Merchandise is purchased for cash, $2,300.
   (b) Merchandise listed at $4,000, less a trade discount of 10%, is purchased for cash.
2. Purchase of merchandise on account with credit terms.
   (a) Merchandise is purchased on account, credit terms 2/10, n/30, $4,000.
   (b) Merchandise is purchased on account, credit terms 3/10, n/30, $2,800.
   (c) Payment is made on invoice (a) within the discount period.
   (d) Payment is made on invoice (b) too late to receive the cash discount.
3. Purchase of merchandise on account with return of merchandise.
   (a) Merchandise is purchased on account, credit terms 2/10, n/30, $5,600.
   (b) Merchandise is returned for credit before payment is made, $600.
   (c) Payment is made within the discount period.
4. Purchase of merchandise with freight-in.
   (a) Merchandise is purchased on account, $3,800 plus freight charges of $200. Terms of the sale were FOB shipping point.
   (b) Payment is made for the cost of merchandise and the freight charge.

E 11-4B (LO2)
✓ Cost of goods sold: $76,700

COMPUTING GROSS PROFIT The following data were taken from the accounts of Burnside Bedknobs, a retail business. Determine the gross profit.

Sales	$116,900
Sales returns and allowances	1,100
Sales discounts	400
Merchandise inventory, January 1	30,000
Purchases during the period	100,000
Purchases returns and allowances during the period	2,000
Purchases discounts taken during the period	2,800
Freight-in on merchandise purchased during the period	1,500
Merchandise inventory, December 31	50,000

E 11-5B (LO3)
✓ Jan. 12: Dr. Purchases, $9,000

JOURNALIZING PURCHASES TRANSACTIONS Journalize the following transactions in a general journal:

Jan.	3	Purchased merchandise from Feng, $6,000. Invoice No. 416, dated January 1, terms 2/10, n/30.
	12	Purchased merchandise from Miranda, $9,000. Invoice No. 624, dated January 10, terms n/30.

Jan. 19 Purchased merchandise from J. B. Barba, $6,400. Invoice No. 190, dated January 18, terms 1/10, n/30.

26 Purchased merchandise from Ramirez, $3,700. Invoice No. 923, dated January 25, terms 1/15, n/30.

E 11-6B (LO3)
✓ Ending Accounts Payable balance: $6,950

JOURNALIZING PURCHASES RETURNS AND ALLOWANCES AND POSTING TO GENERAL LEDGER AND ACCOUNTS PAYABLE LEDGER Using page 3 of a general journal and the following general ledger accounts and accounts payable ledger accounts, journalize and post the following transactions:

Mar. 5 Returned merchandise to Tower Industries, $500.

11 Returned merchandise to A & D Arms, $625.

23 Returned merchandise to Mighty Mansion, $275.

General Ledger

Account No.	Account	Balance Mar. 1, 20--
202	Accounts Payable	$8,350
501.1	Purchases Returns and Allowances	---

Accounts Payable Ledger

Name	Balance Mar. 1, 20--
A & D Arms	$2,300
Mighty Mansion	1,450
Tower Industries	4,600

E 11-7B (LO3)
✓ Apr. 19: Cr. Cash, $4,950

JOURNALIZING CASH PAYMENTS TRANSACTIONS Enter the following cash payments transactions in a general journal:

Apr. 5 Issued Check No. 429 to Standard Industries for merchandise purchased March 27, $8,000, terms 2/10, n/30. Payment is made within the discount period.

19 Issued Check No. 430 to Finest Company for merchandise purchased April 10, $5,300, terms 1/10, n/30. A credit memo had been received on April 12 from Finest Company for merchandise returned, $300. Payment is made within the discount period after deduction for the return dated April 12.

21 Issued Check No. 431 to Funny Follies for merchandise purchased March 22, $3,250, terms n/30.

29 Issued Check No. 432 to Classic Data for merchandise purchased April 20, $7,000, terms 2/10, n/30. Payment is made within the discount period.

E 11-8B (LO4)
✓ Total accounts payable: $10,565

SCHEDULE OF ACCOUNTS PAYABLE Crystal's Candles, a retail business, had the following balances and purchases and payments activity in its accounts payable ledger during November. Prepare a schedule of accounts payable for Crystal's Candles as of November 30, 20--.

Accounts Payable Ledger

Name	Balance Nov. 1, 20--	Purchases	Payments
Carl's Candle Wax	$4,135	$ 955	$1,610
Handy Supplies	3,490	1,320	1,850
Wishy Wicks	3,300	1,905	1,080

SERIES B PROBLEMS

P 11-9B (LO2/3)
✓ Purchases balance: $18,515

PURCHASES TRANSACTIONS Ann Benton, owner of Benton's Galleria, made the following purchases of merchandise on account during the month of October:

Oct.	2	Purchase Invoice No. 321, $1,950, from Boggs Distributors.
	7	Purchase Invoice No. 152, $2,915, from Wolfs Wholesaler.
	10	Purchase Invoice No. 634, $3,565, from Komuro & Co.
	16	Purchase Invoice No. 349, $2,845, from Fritz & McCord, Inc.
	24	Purchase Invoice No. 587, $3,370, from Boggs Distributors.
	26	Purchase Invoice No. 764, $2,240, from Sanderson Company.
	31	Purchase Invoice No. 672, $1,630, from Wolfs Wholesaler.

REQUIRED

1. Record the transactions starting with page 16 of a general journal.
2. Post from the general journal to the general ledger accounts and to the accounts payable ledger accounts. Use general ledger account numbers as shown in the chapter.

P 11-10B (LO2/3)
✓ Accounts Payable balance: $600

CASH PAYMENTS TRANSACTIONS Kay Zembrowski operates a retail variety store. The books include a general journal and an accounts payable ledger. Selected account balances on May 1 are as follows:

General Ledger	
Cash	$40,000
Accounts Payable	20,000
Accounts Payable Ledger	
Cortez Distributors	$ 4,200
Indra & Velga	6,800
Toy Corner	4,600
Troutman Outlet	4,400

The following transactions are related to cash payments for the month of May:

May	1	Issued Check No. 326 in payment of May rent (Rent Expense), $2,600.
	4	Issued Check No. 327 to Cortez Distributors in payment of merchandise purchased on account, $4,200, less a 3% discount. Check was written for $4,074.
	7	Issued Check No. 328 to Indra & Velga in partial payment of merchandise purchased on account, $6,200. A cash discount was not allowed.
	11	Issued Check No. 329 to Toy Corner for merchandise purchased on account, $4,600, less a 1% discount. Check was written for $4,554.
	15	Issued Check No. 330 to County Power and Light (Utilities Expense), $1,500.
	19	Issued Check No. 331 to Builders Warehouse for a cash purchase of merchandise, $3,500.
	25	Issued Check No. 332 to Troutman Outlet for merchandise purchased on account, $4,400, less a 2% discount. Check was written for $4,312.

May 30 Issued Check No. 333 to Rapid Transit Company for freight charges on merchandise purchased (Freight-In), $800.

31 Issued Check No. 334 to City Merchants for a cash purchase of merchandise, $2,350.

REQUIRED

1. Enter the transactions starting with page 9 of a general journal.
2. Post from the general journal to the general ledger and the accounts payable ledger. Use general ledger account numbers as shown in the chapter.

P 11-11B (LO2/3)
✓ Cash balance: $12,790

PURCHASES AND CASH PAYMENTS TRANSACTIONS Debbie Mueller owns a small retail business called Debbie's Doll House. The cash account has a balance of $20,000 on July 1. The following transactions occurred during July:

July 1 Issued Check No. 314 for July rent, $1,400.

1 Purchased merchandise on account from Topper's Toys, Invoice No. 211, $2,500, terms 2/10, n/30.

3 Purchased merchandise on account from Jones & Company, Invoice No. 812, $2,800, terms 1/10, n/30.

5 Returned merchandise purchased from Topper's Toys receiving a credit memo on the amount owed, $400.

8 Purchased merchandise on account from Downtown Merchants, Invoice No. 159, $1,600, terms 2/10, n/30.

11 Issued Check No. 315 to Topper's Toys for merchandise purchased on account, less return of July 5 and less 2% discount.

13 Issued Check No. 316 to Jones & Company for merchandise purchased on account, less 1% discount.

15 Returned merchandise purchased from Downtown Merchants receiving a credit memo on the amount owed, $600.

18 Issued Check No. 317 to Downtown Merchants for merchandise purchased on account, less return of July 15 and less 2% discount.

25 Purchased merchandise on account from Columbia Products, Invoice No. 468, $3,200, terms n/30.

26 Purchased merchandise on account from Topper's Toys, Invoice No. 395, $1,430, terms 2/10, n/30.

29 Purchased merchandise on account from Jones & Company, Invoice No. 853, $2,970, terms 1/10, n/30.

REQUIRED

1. Enter the transactions starting with page 16 of a general journal.
2. Post from the journal to the general ledger and accounts payable ledger accounts. Use general ledger account numbers as shown in the chapter.

P 11-12B (LO4)
✓ Accounts Payable balance, Topper's Toys: $1,430

SCHEDULE OF ACCOUNTS PAYABLE Based on the information provided in Problem 11-11B, prepare a schedule of accounts payable for Debbie's Doll House as of July 31, 20--. Verify that the accounts payable account balance in the general ledger agrees with the schedule of accounts payable total.

CHECK LIST
- ☐ Managing
- ☐ Planning
- ☐ Drafting
- ☐ Break
- ☐ Revising
- ☐ Managing

MANAGING YOUR WRITING

You are working as a summer intern at a rapidly growing organic food distributor. Part of your responsibility is to assist in the accounts payable department. You notice that most bills from suppliers are not paid within the discount period. The manager of accounts payable says the bills are organized by vendor, like the accounts payable ledger, and she is too busy to keep track of the discount periods. Besides, the owner has told her that the 1% and 2% discounts available are not worth worrying about.

Write a memo to the owner explaining why it is expensive not to take advantage of cash discounts on credit purchases. In addition, suggest a way to file (organize) supplier invoices so that they are paid within the discount period.

ETHICS

ETHICS CASE

Bob's Discount Auto Parts receives a cash discount of 2% from Auto Warehouse if it pays an invoice within 10 days. Bob, the owner, consistently sends payments 15 to 20 days after receiving the invoice and still deducts the amount of the discount. Last week, Bob received a call from Auto Warehouse reminding him that in order to get the discount, an invoice must be paid within 10 days. When Bob received the next invoice, he dated the check exactly 10 days from the date of the invoice but didn't mail the check for another week. The receivables manager from Auto Warehouse called Bob and again reminded him that the check should be mailed by the 10th day in order to receive the 2% discount. When Bob received the next invoice, he mailed it on time but post-dated the check for the following week.

1. Are Bob's attempts to extend the discount period unethical?
2. What alternatives can Auto Warehouse take to prevent Bob's Discount Auto Parts from stretching the discount period?
3. Write a short note from Auto Warehouse to Bob's Discount Auto Parts explaining cash discounts and credit terms.
4. In small groups, make a list of the advantages and disadvantages of offering cash discounts.

MASTERY PROBLEM

✓ Accounts Payable balance: $10,000

Michelle French owns and operates Books and More, a retail book store. Selected account balances on June 1 are as follows:

General Ledger	
Cash	$32,200.00
Accounts Payable	2,000.00
M. French, Drawing	18,000.00
Purchases	67,021.66
Purchases Returns and Allowances	2,315.23
Purchases Discounts	905.00
Freight-In	522.60
Rent Expense	3,125.00
Utilities Expense	1,522.87

Accounts Payable Ledger	
Northeastern Publishing Co.	$ 2,000.00

The following purchases and cash payments transactions took place during the month of June:

June 1 Purchased books on account from Irving Publishing Company, $2,100. Invoice No. 101, terms 2/10, n/30, FOB destination.

2 Issued Check No. 300 to Northeastern Publishing Co. for goods purchased on May 23, terms 2/10, n/30, $1,960 (the $2,000 invoice amount less the 2% discount).

3 Purchased books on account from Broadway Publishing, Inc., $2,880. Invoice No. 711, less a 20% trade discount, and invoice terms of 3/10, n/30, FOB shipping point.

3 Issued Check No. 301 to Mayday Shipping for delivery from Broadway Publishing, Inc., $250.

4 Issued Check No. 302 for June rent, $625.

8 Purchased books on account from Northeastern Publishing Co., $5,825. Invoice No. 268, terms 2/eom, n/60, FOB destination.

10 Received a credit memo from Irving Publishing Company, $550. Books had been returned because the covers were on upside down.

13 Issued Check No. 304 to Broadway Publishing, Inc., for the purchase made on June 3. (Check No. 303 was voided because an error was made in preparing it.)

28 Made the following purchases:

Invoice No.	Company	Amount	Terms
579	Broadway Publishing, Inc.	$2,350	2/10, n/30, FOB destination
406	Northeastern Publishing Co.	4,200	2/eom, n/60, FOB destination
964	Riley Publishing Co.	3,450	3/10, n/30, FOB destination

30 Issued Check No. 305 to Taylor County Utility Co. for June utilities, $325.

30 French withdrew cash for personal use, $4,500. Issued Check No. 306.

30 Issued Check No. 307 to Irving Publishing Company for purchase made on June 1 less returns made on June 10.

30 Issued Check No. 308 to Northeastern Publishing Co. for purchase made on June 8.

30 Issued Check No. 309 for books purchased at an auction, $1,328.

REQUIRED

1. Enter the transactions in a general journal (start with page 16).
2. Post from the journal to the general ledger accounts and the accounts payable ledger. Use general ledger account numbers as indicated in the chapter.
3. Prepare a schedule of accounts payable.
4. If merchandise inventory was $35,523 on January 1 and $42,100 as of June 30, prepare the cost of goods sold section of the income statement for the six months ended June 30, 20--.

CHALLENGE PROBLEM

This problem challenges you to apply your cumulative accounting knowledge to move a step beyond the material in the chapter.

✓ May 14: Cr. Purchases Discounts, $9

Record the following transactions in a general journal:

May	4	Merchandise listed at $2,900, less a trade discount of 10%, is purchased on account, credit terms of 1/10, n/30, shipping terms FOB destination.
	8	Merchandise purchased on May 4, listed at $520, is returned for credit.
	14	Partial payment is made for the merchandise purchased on May 4, listed at $1,000, less 1% discount.
June	3	Payment is made of the balance due on the May 4 purchase.

ANSWERS TO SELF-STUDY TEST QUESTIONS

True/False

1. F (purchase requisition)
2. T
3. T
4. F (credited)
5. F (buyer)

Multiple Choice

1. d **2.** a **3.** a **4.** d **5.** b

Checkpoint Exercises

1. a. $\$1,200 \times 10\% = \$120$
   b. $\$1,200 - \$120 = \$1,080$
   c. $\$1,200 - \$120 = \$1,080 \times 1\% = \$10.80$
2. Net sales

Net sales				$92,000
Cost of goods sold:				
Merchandise inventory, Jan. 1			$27,000	
Purchases		$60,800		
Less: Purchases returns and allowances	$3,100			
Purchases discounts	1,300	4,400		
Cost of goods purchased			56,400	
Goods available for sale			$83,400	
Less merchandise inventory, Dec. 31			24,000	
Cost of goods sold				59,400
Gross profit				$32,600

3. **GENERAL LEDGER**

Cash

		(c)	274.40

Accounts Payable

(b)	70.00	(a)	350.00
(c)	280.00		

Purchases

(a)	350.00		

Purchases Returns and Allowances

		(b)	70.00

Purchases Discounts

		(c)	5.60

Accounts Payable Ledger

J. Bedas

(b)	70.00	(a)	350.00
(c)	280.00		

4. Felini Plumbing
Schedule of Accounts Payable
June 30, 20--

B. Sutton	$ 245
A. Gagne	328
L. Mohler	590
P. Luffman	190
Z. Quary	153
Total	$1,506

CHAPTER 11 APPENDIX

The Net-Price Method of Recording Purchases

LEARNING OBJECTIVES

Careful study of this appendix should enable you to:

LO1 Describe the net-price method of recording purchases.

LO2 Record purchases and cash payments using the net-price method.

LO1

Net-Price Method

Describe the net-price method of recording purchases.

In this chapter, purchases were recorded using the **gross-price method**. Under this method, purchases are recorded at the gross amount, regardless of available cash discounts. An alternative approach to accounting for purchases is the **net-price method**. Under this method, purchases are recorded at the net amount, assuming that all available cash discounts will be taken.

LO2

Recording with the Net-Price Method

Record purchases and cash payments using the net-price method.

To compare the gross-price and net-price methods, reconsider the purchase for $100 on account, with credit terms of 2/10, n/30, on page 405. At the time of the purchase, the following entries are made under the two methods:

Gross-Price			Net-Price		
Purchases	100.00		Purchases	98.00*	
Accounts Payable		100.00	Accounts Payable		98.00

*$100—$2 (2% cash discount)

If the payment for the merchandise is made within the discount period, the entries are as follows:

Gross-Price			Net-Price		
Accounts Payable	100.00		Accounts Payable	98.00	
Cash		98.00	Cash		98.00
Purchases Discounts		2.00			

If payment for the merchandise is not made until after the discount period, the entries are as follows:

Gross-Price			Net-Price		
Accounts Payable	100.00		Accounts Payable	98.00	
Cash		100.00	Purchases Discounts Lost	2.00	
			Cash		100.00

Note that under the net-price method a new account, Purchases Discounts Lost, is used. Purchases Discounts Lost is a temporary owner's equity account used to record cash discounts lost on purchases. It is reported as an expense on the income statement.

Purchases Discounts Lost

Debit	Credit
to enter discounts lost because of late payment of invoices	

Purchases Discounts Lost represents a finance charge for postponing the payment for merchandise. If the balance in this account is large relative to the amount of gross purchases, management should review its cash payment procedures.

LEARNING OBJECTIVES		Key Points to Remember
LO1	**Describe the net-price method of recording purchases.**	Under the net-price method, purchases are recorded at the net amount, assuming all available cash discounts will be taken.
LO2	**Record purchases and cash payments using the net-price method.**	Assume a purchase is made for \$100 on account, with credit terms of 2/10, n/30. Under the net-price method, the entry at the time of purchase is as follows: Purchases 98 Accounts Payable 98 If payment is made within the discount period, the entry is as follows: Accounts Payable 98 Cash 98 If payment is not made until after the discount period, the entry is as follows: Accounts Payable 98 Purchases Discounts Lost 2 Cash 100

KEY TERMS

gross-price method (438) Under this method, purchases are recorded at the gross amount.

net-price method (438) Under this method, purchases are recorded at the net amount, assuming all available cash discounts are taken.

REVIEW QUESTIONS

LO1 1. At what amount are purchases recorded under the net-price method?

LO2 2. Under the net-price method, if payment for merchandise is not made within the discount period, what accounts are debited when the payment is made?

LO2 3. (a) What kind of an account is Purchases Discounts Lost?
(b) How is this item reported on the income statement?

SERIES A EXERCISE

E 11Apx-1A (LO2)
✓ 1. Apr. 11: Cr. Purchases Discounts, $20

PURCHASES TRANSACTIONS—GROSS-PRICE AND NET-PRICE METHODS
Romero's Heating and Cooling had the following transactions during April:

Apr.	2	Purchased merchandise on account from Alanon Valve for $1,000, terms 2/10, n/30.
	5	Purchased merchandise on account from Leon's Garage for $1,400, terms 1/10, n/30.
	11	Paid the amount due to Alanon Valve for the purchase on April 2.
	25	Paid the amount due to Leon's Garage for the purchase on April 5.

1. Prepare general journal entries for these transactions using the gross-price method.
2. Prepare general journal entries for these transactions using the net-price method.

SERIES B EXERCISE

E 11Apx-1B (LO2)
✓ 2. May 27: Dr. Purchases Discounts Lost, $12

PURCHASES TRANSACTIONS—GROSS-PRICE AND NET-PRICE METHODS
Gloria's Repair Shop had the following transactions during May:

May	2	Purchased merchandise on account from Delgado's Supply for $900, terms 2/10, n/30.
	6	Purchased merchandise on account from Goro's Auto Care for $1,200, terms 1/10, n/30.
	11	Paid the amount due to Delgado's Supply for the purchase on May 2.
	27	Paid the amount due to Goro's Auto Care for the purchase on May 6.

1. Prepare general journal entries for these transactions using the gross-price method.
2. Prepare general journal entries for these transactions using the net-price method.

ISTOCK.COM/KUPICOO

Chapter 12 Special Journals

If you are an active health and fitness enthusiast, you might already know of NutraPlanet, perhaps through its nutraplanet.com Web sites. NutraPlanet was founded in 2004 and is headquartered in Graham, North Carolina. After a slow start, it has grown into one of the world's top Web sites for sports and nutrition supplements.

NutraPlanet sells a wide array of health supplements. Many are targeted at bodybuilding, but its product categories include amino acids, carbohydrates, cardiovascular support, fat burners, herbs, joint support, and many others. Its products tend to be priced in the $13–$70 range. Most of the sales for a company like this probably would be for relatively small dollar amounts. This means the volume of transactions to generate annual sales in the millions would be huge. NutraPlanet would need a way to record all of this activity that is more efficient than the methods we have seen in Chapters 10 and 11. In Chapter 12, you will learn about a more efficient way to record transactions. In the "A Broader View" feature, you will see how computer software can add even greater efficiency.

LEARNING OBJECTIVES

Careful study of this chapter should enable you to:

LO1 **Describe, explain the purpose of, and identify transactions recorded in special journals.**

LO2 **Describe and use the sales journal.**

LO3 **Describe and use the cash receipts journal.**

LO4 **Describe and use the purchases journal.**

LO5 **Describe and use the cash payments journal.**

Chapters 10 and 11 demonstrated how to account for sales, cash receipts, purchases, and cash payments in a merchandising business. We also saw how to use accounts receivable and accounts payable ledgers to keep track of individual customer and supplier accounts. In this chapter, we continue to study how to account for sales, cash receipts, purchases, and cash payments, but our objective is to find a way to be more efficient. We will learn how to use four special journals that enable us to achieve this objective.

LO1

Special Journals

Describe, explain the purpose of, and identify transactions recorded in special journals.

A **special journal** is a journal designed for recording only certain kinds of transactions. A special journal can be created for almost any kind of transaction. The types of special journals a business uses should depend on the types of transactions that occur most frequently for a business. The more transactions of a specific type that occur, the more likely a special journal of that type would be useful for the business.

The primary purpose of using special journals is to save time journalizing and posting transactions. In a general journal, we recorded transactions by writing the account names, debit and credit amounts, and an explanation for each transaction on several lines in the journal. In contrast, most transactions are entered in a special journal on a single line, with the debit and credit amounts indicated in special columns provided for each account. This enables substantial time saving. The posting process also is more efficient. Using the general journal, each transaction is posted separately to the appropriate general ledger accounts. With a special journal, summary postings of column totals are made to appropriate accounts on a periodic basis.

Of course, even if a business uses special journals, there still is a need for a general journal. For example, transactions that occur infrequently, and adjusting and closing entries, usually are recorded in the general journal.

The following four special journals are commonly used by businesses:

- Sales journal
- Cash receipts journal
- Purchases journal
- Cash payments journal

LEARNING KEY

The special journals and general journal are books of original entry. Each transaction is recorded in only one of these journals.

Figure 12-1 identifies the types of transactions recorded in each of the four special journals and the general journal. You might find it helpful to refer back to Figure 12-1 as the four special journals are introduced in this chapter.

FIGURE 12-1 Types of Journals and Transactions

TYPE OF JOURNAL	TYPE OF TRANSACTIONS RECORDED
Sales journal	All sales of merchandise on account
Cash receipts journal	All cash receipts
Purchases journal	All purchases of merchandise on account
Cash payments journal	All cash payments
General journal	All other transactions

In the following sections, we will examine the journalizing and posting process using each of the four special journals.

LO2 Sales Journal

Describe and use the sales journal.

A sales journal is a special journal used to record only sales of merchandise on account. To illustrate the journalizing and posting of sales transactions in the sales journal, we use the following five sales transactions for Sunflower Cycle from Chapter 10.

LEARNING KEY Use a sales journal only for recording sales of merchandise on account.

Apr. 4 Made Sale No. 133C on account to Enrico Lorenzo, $1,520, plus $76 sales tax.

10 Made Sale No. 134C on account to Brenda Myers, $440, plus $22 sales tax.

18 Made Sale No. 105D on account to Edith Walton, $980, plus $49 sales tax.

21 Made Sale No. 202B on account to Wilma Cutz, $620, plus $31 sales tax.

24 Made Sale No. 162A on account to Heidi Schwitzer, $1,600, plus $80 sales tax.

The general journal entries for these five transactions are shown in Figure 12-2.

FIGURE 12-2 Sales Entered in General Journal

4	Apr.	4	Accounts Receivable/E. Lorenzo		1,596.00		4
5			Sales			1,520.00	5
6			Sales Tax Payable			76.00	6
7			Sale No. 133C				7
8							8
9		10	Accounts Receivable/B. Myers		462.00		9
10			Sales			440.00	10
11			Sales Tax Payable			22.00	11
12			Sale No. 134C				12
13							13
14		18	Accounts Receivable/E. Walton		1,029.00		14
15			Sales			980.00	15
16			Sales Tax Payable			49.00	16
17			Sale No. 105D				17
18							18
19		21	Accounts Receivable/W. Cutz		651.00		19
20			Sales			620.00	20
21			Sales Tax Payable			31.00	21
22			Sale No. 202B				22
23							23
24		24	Accounts Receivable/H. Schwitzer		1,680.00		24
25			Sales			1,600.00	25
26			Sales Tax Payable			80.00	26
27			Sale No. 162A				27

Notice that each of these five entries involved the same three accounts. The same account titles were recorded five times. Similarly, to post these entries to the general ledger, five separate postings would be made to each of the three accounts, a total of 15 postings.

These transactions can be recorded more efficiently by using a sales journal. To illustrate, reconsider the five sales made on account by Sunflower Cycle. They are entered in the sales journal in Figure 12-3. The sales journal provides separate columns for Accounts Receivable Debit, Sales Credit, and Sales Tax Payable Credit, the

> Remember that sales returns and allowances are recorded in the general journal, as illustrated in Chapter 10, not in the sales journal.

three accounts used repeatedly in the general journal in Figure 12-2. A sale is recorded in the sales journal by entering the following information:

1. Date
2. Sale number
3. Customer (to whom sold)
4. Dollar amounts

There is no need to enter any general ledger account titles, since they appear in the column headings.

FIGURE 12-3 Sunflower Cycle Sales Journal

SALES JOURNAL — PAGE 6

	DATE		SALE NO.	TO WHOM SOLD	POST. REF.	ACCOUNTS RECEIVABLE DEBIT	SALES CREDIT	SALES TAX PAYABLE CREDIT	
	20--								
1	Apr.	4	133C	Enrico Lorenzo		1 5 9 6 00	1 5 2 0 00	7 6 00	1
2		10	134C	Brenda Myers		4 6 2 00	4 4 0 00	2 2 00	2
3		18	105D	Edith Walton		1 0 2 9 00	9 8 0 00	4 9 00	3
4		21	202B	Wilma Cutz		6 5 1 00	6 2 0 00	3 1 00	4
5		24	162A	Heidi Schwitzer		1 6 8 0 00	1 6 0 0 00	8 0 00	5

> This chapter illustrates a manual accounting system. With a computerized system, journals/ledgers are updated simultaneously when a transaction is entered, and there is no need for special journals (see A Broader View on page 452).

The sales journal in Figure 12-3 is designed for a company, like Sunflower Cycle, that charges sales tax. For a wholesaler or any other company that does not charge sales tax, a sales journal like that in Figure 12-4 would be sufficient. In this case, there is only a single amount column headed Accounts Receivable Debit/Sales Credit. With no sales tax, the Accounts Receivable Debit and Sales Credit amounts are identical for each sale. Thus, only a single column is needed.

FIGURE 12-4 Sales Journal Without Sales Tax

SALES JOURNAL — PAGE 1

DATE		SALE NO.	TO WHOM SOLD	POST. REF.	ACCOUNTS RECEIVABLE DEBIT/ SALES CREDIT

Posting from the Sales Journal

Posting from the sales journal also is very efficient. Each general ledger account used in the sales journal requires only one posting each period. Figure 12-5 illustrates the general ledger posting process for Sunflower Cycle's sales journal for the month of April.

The following steps are used to post from the sales journal to the general ledger at the end of each month, as indicated in Figure 12-5:

> Step 1 is the main difference in posting the sales journal to the general ledger. Steps 2–6 are essentially the same as steps 1–5 used to post from the general journal.

In the sales journal:

STEP 1 Total the amount columns, verify that the total of the debit column equals the total of the credit columns, and rule the columns.

In the ledger account:

STEP 2 Enter the date of the transaction in the Date column.

STEP 3 Enter the amount of the debit or credit in the Debit or Credit column.

FIGURE 12-5 Posting the Sales Journal to the General Ledger

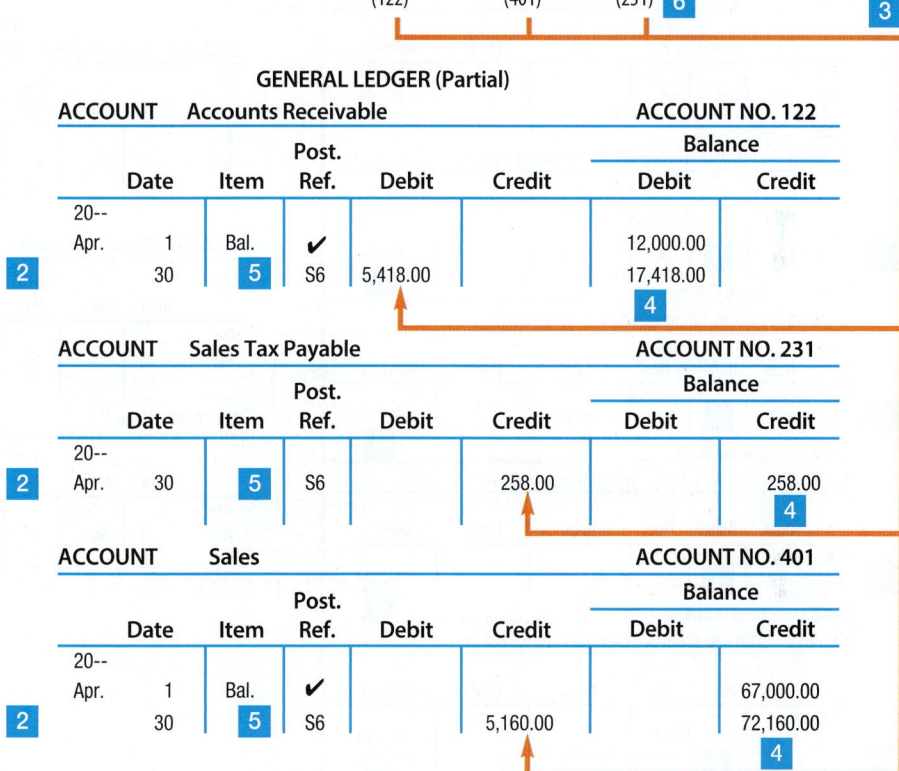

SALES JOURNAL — Page 6

Date		Sale No.	To Whom Sold	Post. Ref.	Accounts Receivable Debit	Sales Credit	Sales Tax Payable Credit
20--							
Apr.	4	133C	Enrico Lorenzo		1,596.00	1,520.00	76.00
	10	134C	Brenda Myers		462.00	440.00	22.00
	18	105D	Edith Walton		1,029.00	980.00	49.00
	21	202B	Wilma Cutz		651.00	620.00	31.00
	24	162A	Heidi Schwitzer		1,680.00	1,600.00	80.00
					5,418.00	5,160.00	258.00 1
					(122)	(401)	(231) 6

3

1 Debit total: $5,418

Credit total: $5,160
258
$5,418

GENERAL LEDGER (Partial)

ACCOUNT Accounts Receivable — ACCOUNT NO. 122

	Date		Item	Post. Ref.	Debit	Credit	Balance Debit	Balance Credit
	20--							
	Apr.	1	Bal.	✔			12,000.00	
2		30	5	S6	5,418.00		17,418.00 4	

ACCOUNT Sales Tax Payable — ACCOUNT NO. 231

	Date		Item	Post. Ref.	Debit	Credit	Balance Debit	Balance Credit
	20--							
2	Apr.	30	5	S6		258.00		258.00 4

ACCOUNT Sales — ACCOUNT NO. 401

	Date		Item	Post. Ref.	Debit	Credit	Balance Debit	Balance Credit
	20--							
	Apr.	1	Bal.	✔				67,000.00
2		30	5	S6		5,160.00		72,160.00 4

LEARNING KEY

All special journal entries are posted to the general and subsidiary ledger accounts, *not* to the general journal.

If the accounts receivable ledger is posted daily and the general ledger is posted at the end of the month, the accounts receivable ledger total will equal the general ledger Accounts Receivable total only at the end of the month.

STEP 4 Enter the new balance in the Balance columns under Debit or Credit.

STEP 5 Enter the initial "S" and the journal page number in the Posting Reference column.

In the sales journal:

STEP 6 Enter the ledger account number immediately below the column totals for each account that is posted.

As we saw in Chapter 10, Sunflower Cycle also needs a record of the accounts receivable from *individual customers*. Figure 12-6 illustrates the use of the accounts receivable ledger. The accounts receivable ledger is posted *daily* so that current information is available for each customer at all times. The following steps are used to post the sales journal to the accounts receivable ledger, as shown in Figure 12-6:

FIGURE 12-6 Posting from the Sales Journal to the Accounts Receivable Ledger

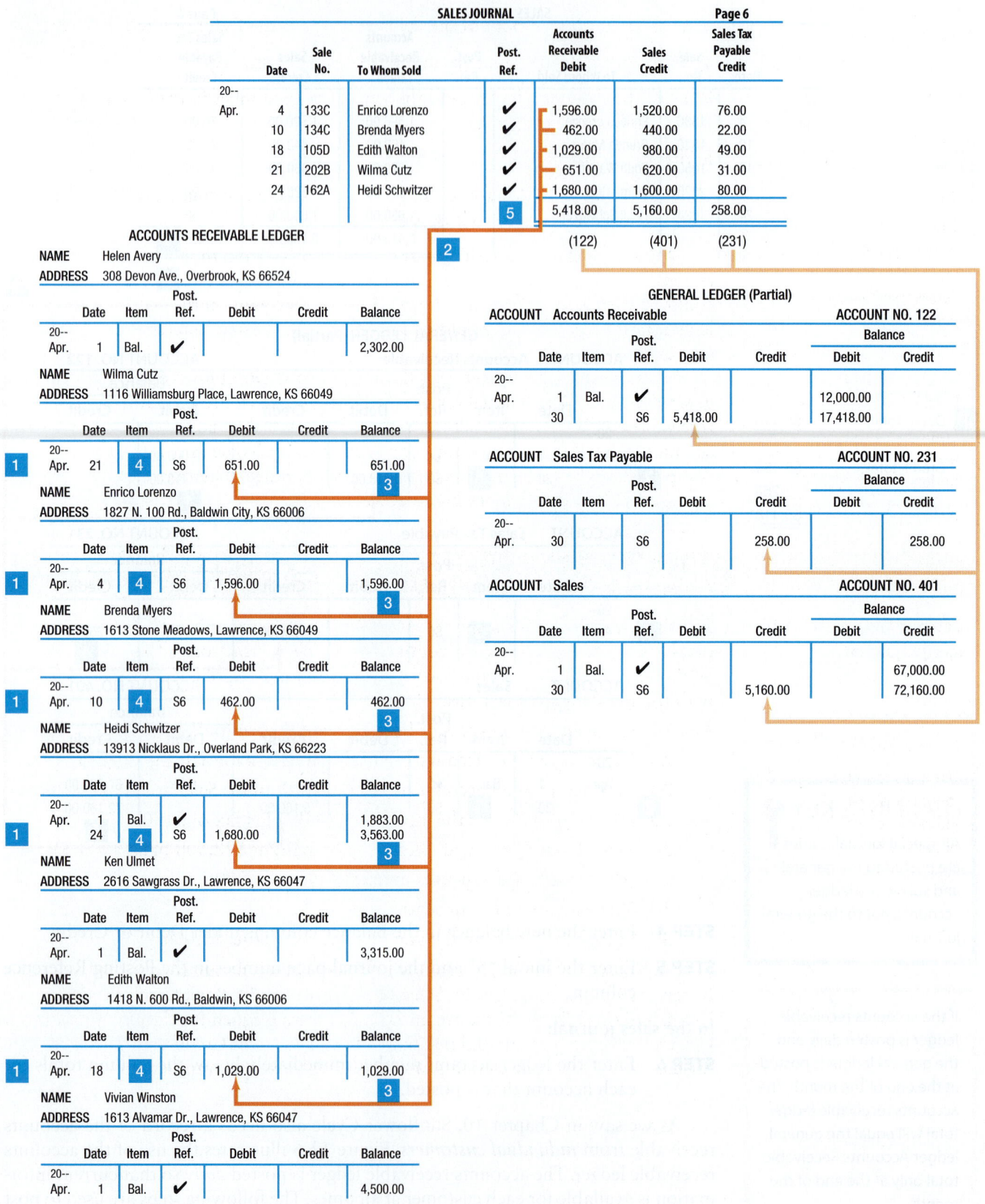

SALES JOURNAL — Page 6

Date		Sale No.	To Whom Sold	Post. Ref.	Accounts Receivable Debit	Sales Credit	Sales Tax Payable Credit
20--							
Apr.	4	133C	Enrico Lorenzo	✔	1,596.00	1,520.00	76.00
	10	134C	Brenda Myers	✔	462.00	440.00	22.00
	18	105D	Edith Walton	✔	1,029.00	980.00	49.00
	21	202B	Wilma Cutz	✔	651.00	620.00	31.00
	24	162A	Heidi Schwitzer	✔	1,680.00	1,600.00	80.00
				5	5,418.00	5,160.00	258.00
					(122)	(401)	(231)

2

ACCOUNTS RECEIVABLE LEDGER

NAME Helen Avery
ADDRESS 308 Devon Ave., Overbrook, KS 66524

Date		Item	Post. Ref.	Debit	Credit	Balance
20--						
Apr.	1	Bal.	✔			2,302.00

NAME Wilma Cutz
ADDRESS 1116 Williamsburg Place, Lawrence, KS 66049

Date		Item	Post. Ref.	Debit	Credit	Balance
20--						
1 Apr.	21	4	S6	651.00		651.00 3

NAME Enrico Lorenzo
ADDRESS 1827 N. 100 Rd., Baldwin City, KS 66006

Date		Item	Post. Ref.	Debit	Credit	Balance
20--						
1 Apr.	4	4	S6	1,596.00		1,596.00 3

NAME Brenda Myers
ADDRESS 1613 Stone Meadows, Lawrence, KS 66049

Date		Item	Post. Ref.	Debit	Credit	Balance
20--						
1 Apr.	10	4	S6	462.00		462.00 3

NAME Heidi Schwitzer
ADDRESS 13913 Nicklaus Dr., Overland Park, KS 66223

Date		Item	Post. Ref.	Debit	Credit	Balance
20--						
Apr.	1	Bal.	✔			1,883.00
1	24	4	S6	1,680.00		3,563.00 3

NAME Ken Ulmet
ADDRESS 2616 Sawgrass Dr., Lawrence, KS 66047

Date		Item	Post. Ref.	Debit	Credit	Balance
20--						
Apr.	1	Bal.	✔			3,315.00

NAME Edith Walton
ADDRESS 1418 N. 600 Rd., Baldwin, KS 66006

Date		Item	Post. Ref.	Debit	Credit	Balance
20--						
1 Apr.	18	4	S6	1,029.00		1,029.00 3

NAME Vivian Winston
ADDRESS 1613 Alvamar Dr., Lawrence, KS 66047

Date		Item	Post. Ref.	Debit	Credit	Balance
20--						
Apr.	1	Bal.	✔			4,500.00

GENERAL LEDGER (Partial)

ACCOUNT Accounts Receivable — ACCOUNT NO. 122

Date		Item	Post. Ref.	Debit	Credit	Balance Debit	Balance Credit
20--							
Apr.	1	Bal.	✔			12,000.00	
	30		S6	5,418.00		17,418.00	

ACCOUNT Sales Tax Payable — ACCOUNT NO. 231

Date		Item	Post. Ref.	Debit	Credit	Balance Debit	Balance Credit
20--							
Apr.	30		S6		258.00		258.00

ACCOUNT Sales — ACCOUNT NO. 401

Date		Item	Post. Ref.	Debit	Credit	Balance Debit	Balance Credit
20--							
Apr.	1	Bal.	✔				67,000.00
	30		S6		5,160.00		72,160.00

In the accounts receivable ledger account:

STEP 1 Enter the date of the transaction in the Date column.

STEP 2 Enter the amount of the debit or credit in the Debit or Credit column.

STEP 3 Enter the new balance in the Balance column.

STEP 4 Enter the initial "S" and the journal page number in the Posting Reference column.

In the sales journal:

STEP 5 Enter a check mark (✓) in the Posting Reference column of the journal for each transaction that is posted.

LEARNING KEY

The total of the accounts receivable ledger balances must equal the Accounts Receivable balance in the general ledger.

The accounts receivable ledger also can be posted from the source document used to make the sales journal entry. For example, sales ticket #134C (see Figure 10-2) could be used to post that sale to Brenda Myers' account in the accounts receivable ledger. In this case, 134C would be inserted in the Posting Reference column of her account.

Note the relationship between the sales journal, accounts receivable ledger, and general ledger. All individual entries in the sales journal are posted to the accounts receivable ledger. The totals of all entries in the sales journal are posted to the general ledger accounts. After the posting of the accounts receivable ledger and the general ledger is completed, the total of the accounts receivable ledger balances should equal the Accounts Receivable balance in the general ledger.

CHECKPOINT

Complete Checkpoint-1 on page 470 to test your basic understanding of LO2.

LO3 Cash Receipts Journal

Describe and use the cash receipts journal.

A **cash receipts journal** is a special journal used to record only cash receipts transactions. To illustrate its use, we continue with the transactions of Sunflower Cycle. Sunflower Cycle's cash receipts journal for the month of April is shown in Figure 12-7, with the following transactions:

LEARNING KEY

Use a cash receipts journal to streamline journalizing and posting of cash receipts.

Apr. 14 Received cash on account from Enrico Lorenzo for Sale No. 133C, $1,596.
20 Received cash on account from Brenda Myers for Sale No. 134C, $462.
28 Received cash on account from Edith Walton for Sale No. 105D, $1,029.
30 Made cash sales for the month of $3,600 plus tax of $180.
30 Made bank credit card sales for the month of $22,500 plus tax of $1,125. Bank credit card expenses on these sales are $900.
30 Received cash for rent revenue, $600.
30 Borrowed cash from the bank by signing a note, $3,000.

Sunflower Cycle's cash receipts journal provides separate columns for Accounts Receivable Credit, Sales Credit, Sales Tax Payable Credit, Bank Credit Card Expense Debit, and Cash Debit. These are the accounts most frequently affected by Sunflower Cycle's cash receipts transactions. In addition, a General Credit column is provided for credits to any other accounts affected by cash receipts transactions.

FIGURE 12-7 Sunflower Cycle Cash Receipts Journal

CASH RECEIPTS JOURNAL PAGE 7

	DATE		ACCOUNT CREDITED	POST. REF.	GENERAL CREDIT	ACCOUNTS RECEIVABLE CREDIT	SALES CREDIT	SALES TAX PAYABLE CREDIT	BANK CREDIT CARD EXPENSE DEBIT	CASH DEBIT	
	20--										
1	Apr.	14	Enrico Lorenzo			1596 00				1596 00	1
2		20	Brenda Myers			462 00				462 00	2
3		28	Edith Walton			1029 00				1029 00	3
4		30					3600 00	180 00		3780 00	4
5		30					22500 00	1125 00	900 00	22725 00	5
6		30	Rent Revenue		600 00					600 00	6
7		30	Notes Payable		3000 00					3000 00	7
8											8

A cash receipt is recorded in the cash receipts journal by entering the following information:

1. Date
2. Account credited (if applicable)
3. Dollar amounts

The Account Credited column is used for two purposes.

1. To identify the customer name for any collection on account. This column is used whenever the Accounts Receivable Credit column is used.
2. To enter the appropriate account name whenever the General Credit column is used.

The Account Credited column is left blank if the entry is for cash sales or bank credit card sales.

The cash receipts journal in Figure 12-7 is designed for a company like Sunflower Cycle, which charges sales tax, makes bank credit card sales, and offers no cash discounts. For a wholesaler that does not charge sales tax, makes no bank credit card sales, and offers cash discounts, a cash receipts journal like the one in Figure 12-8 would be used. Recall that a special journal should be designed with column headings for frequently used accounts. Thus, the cash receipts journal in Figure 12-8 has no Sales Tax Payable Credit or Bank Credit Card Expense Debit column. Instead, a Sales Discounts Debit column is provided. In this way, the common cash receipts transactions of the wholesaler can be easily and efficiently recorded.

FIGURE 12-8 Cash Receipts Journal Without Sales Tax

CASH RECEIPTS JOURNAL PAGE 1

	DATE	ACCOUNT CREDITED	POST. REF.	GENERAL CREDIT	ACCOUNTS RECEIVABLE CREDIT	SALES CREDIT	SALES DISCOUNTS DEBIT	CASH DEBIT	
1									1

Posting from the Cash Receipts Journal

The cash receipts journal is posted to the general ledger in two stages, as illustrated in Figure 12-9. First, on a daily basis, the individual amounts in the General Credit column are posted. Second, at the end of the month, the totals of each of the other amount columns are posted.

FIGURE 12-9 Posting from the Cash Receipts Journal to the General Ledger

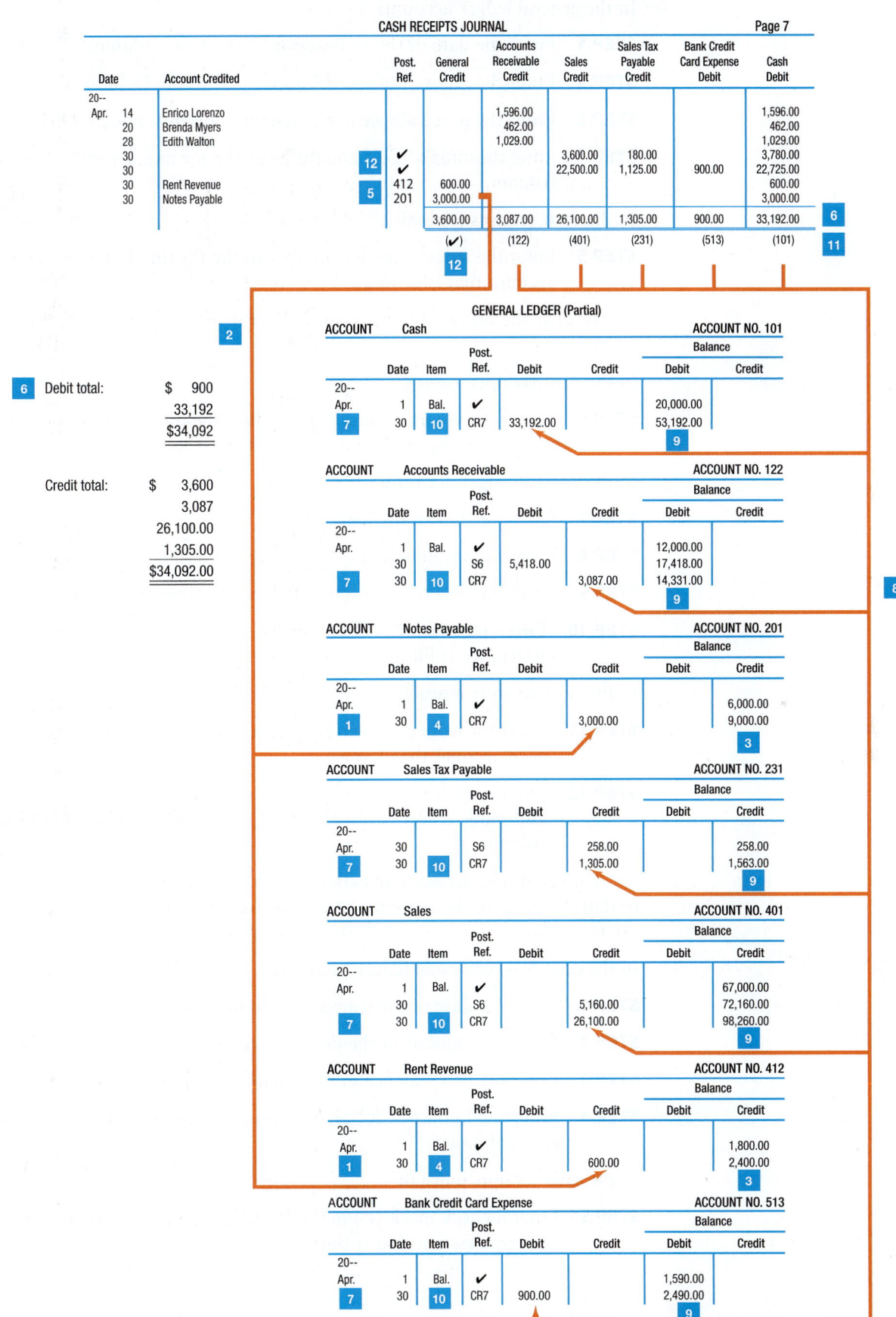

CASH RECEIPTS JOURNAL — Page 7

Date		Account Credited	Post. Ref.	General Credit	Accounts Receivable Credit	Sales Credit	Sales Tax Payable Credit	Bank Credit Card Expense Debit	Cash Debit	
20--										
Apr.	14	Enrico Lorenzo			1,596.00				1,596.00	
	20	Brenda Myers			462.00				462.00	
	28	Edith Walton			1,029.00				1,029.00	
	30		12 ✔			3,600.00	180.00		3,780.00	
	30		✔			22,500.00	1,125.00	900.00	22,725.00	
	30	Rent Revenue	5 412	600.00					600.00	
	30	Notes Payable	201	3,000.00					3,000.00	
				3,600.00	3,087.00	26,100.00	1,305.00	900.00	33,192.00	6
				(✔) 12	(122)	(401)	(231)	(513)	(101)	11

6 Debit total:

$ 900	
33,192	
$34,092	

Credit total:

$ 3,600	
3,087	
26,100.00	
1,305.00	
$34,092.00	

GENERAL LEDGER (Partial) 2 8

ACCOUNT Cash — ACCOUNT NO. 101

	Date	Item	Post. Ref.	Debit	Credit	Balance Debit	Balance Credit
20--							
Apr.	1	Bal.	✔			20,000.00	
7	30	10	CR7	33,192.00		53,192.00 9	

ACCOUNT Accounts Receivable — ACCOUNT NO. 122

	Date	Item	Post. Ref.	Debit	Credit	Balance Debit	Balance Credit
20--							
Apr.	1	Bal.	✔			12,000.00	
	30		S6	5,418.00		17,418.00	
7	30	10	CR7		3,087.00	14,331.00 9	

ACCOUNT Notes Payable — ACCOUNT NO. 201

	Date	Item	Post. Ref.	Debit	Credit	Balance Debit	Balance Credit
20--							
Apr.	1	Bal.	✔				6,000.00
1	30	4	CR7		3,000.00		9,000.00 3

ACCOUNT Sales Tax Payable — ACCOUNT NO. 231

	Date	Item	Post. Ref.	Debit	Credit	Balance Debit	Balance Credit
20--							
Apr.	30		S6		258.00		258.00
7	30	10	CR7		1,305.00		1,563.00 9

ACCOUNT Sales — ACCOUNT NO. 401

	Date	Item	Post. Ref.	Debit	Credit	Balance Debit	Balance Credit
20--							
Apr.	1	Bal.	✔				67,000.00
	30		S6		5,160.00		72,160.00
7	30	10	CR7		26,100.00		98,260.00 9

ACCOUNT Rent Revenue — ACCOUNT NO. 412

	Date	Item	Post. Ref.	Debit	Credit	Balance Debit	Balance Credit
20--							
Apr.	1	Bal.	✔				1,800.00
1	30	4	CR7		600.00		2,400.00 3

ACCOUNT Bank Credit Card Expense — ACCOUNT NO. 513

	Date	Item	Post. Ref.	Debit	Credit	Balance Debit	Balance Credit
20--							
Apr.	1	Bal.	✔			1,590.00	
7	30	10	CR7	900.00		2,490.00 9	

To post the General Credit column, on a daily basis, use the following steps:

In the general ledger account:

STEP 1 Enter the date of the transaction in the Date column.

STEP 2 Enter the amount of the debit or credit in the Debit or Credit column.

STEP 3 Enter the new balance in the Balance columns under Debit or Credit.

STEP 4 Enter the initials "CR" and the journal page number in the Posting Reference column.

In the cash receipts journal:

STEP 5 Enter the ledger account number in the Posting Reference column for each account that is posted.

To post the other amount columns, at the end of the month, use the following steps:

In the cash receipts journal:

STEP 6 Total the amount columns, verify that the total of the debit columns equals the total of the credit columns, and rule the columns.

In the general ledger account:

STEP 7 Enter the date in the Date column.

STEP 8 Enter the amount of the debit or credit in the Debit or Credit column.

STEP 9 Enter the new balance in the Balance columns under Debit or Credit.

STEP 10 Enter the initials "CR" and the journal page number in the Posting Reference column.

In the cash receipts journal:

STEP 11 Enter the ledger account number immediately below the column totals for each account that is posted.

STEP 12 Enter a check mark (✓) in the Posting Reference column for the cash sales and bank credit card sales, and immediately below the General Credit column.

The general ledger accounts affected by the cash receipts transactions are now up to date. Postings to the accounts receivable ledger also must be made. These postings are made daily. Figure 12-10 illustrates the posting procedures, as follows:

In the accounts receivable ledger account:

STEP 1 Enter the date of the transaction in the Date column.

STEP 2 Enter the amount of the debit or credit in the Debit or Credit column.

STEP 3 Enter the new balance in the Balance column.

STEP 4 Enter the initials "CR" and the journal page number in the Posting Reference column.

In the cash receipts journal:

STEP 5 Enter a check mark (✓) in the Posting Reference column of the journal for each transaction that is posted.

FIGURE 12-10 Posting from the Cash Receipts Journal to the Accounts Receivable Ledger

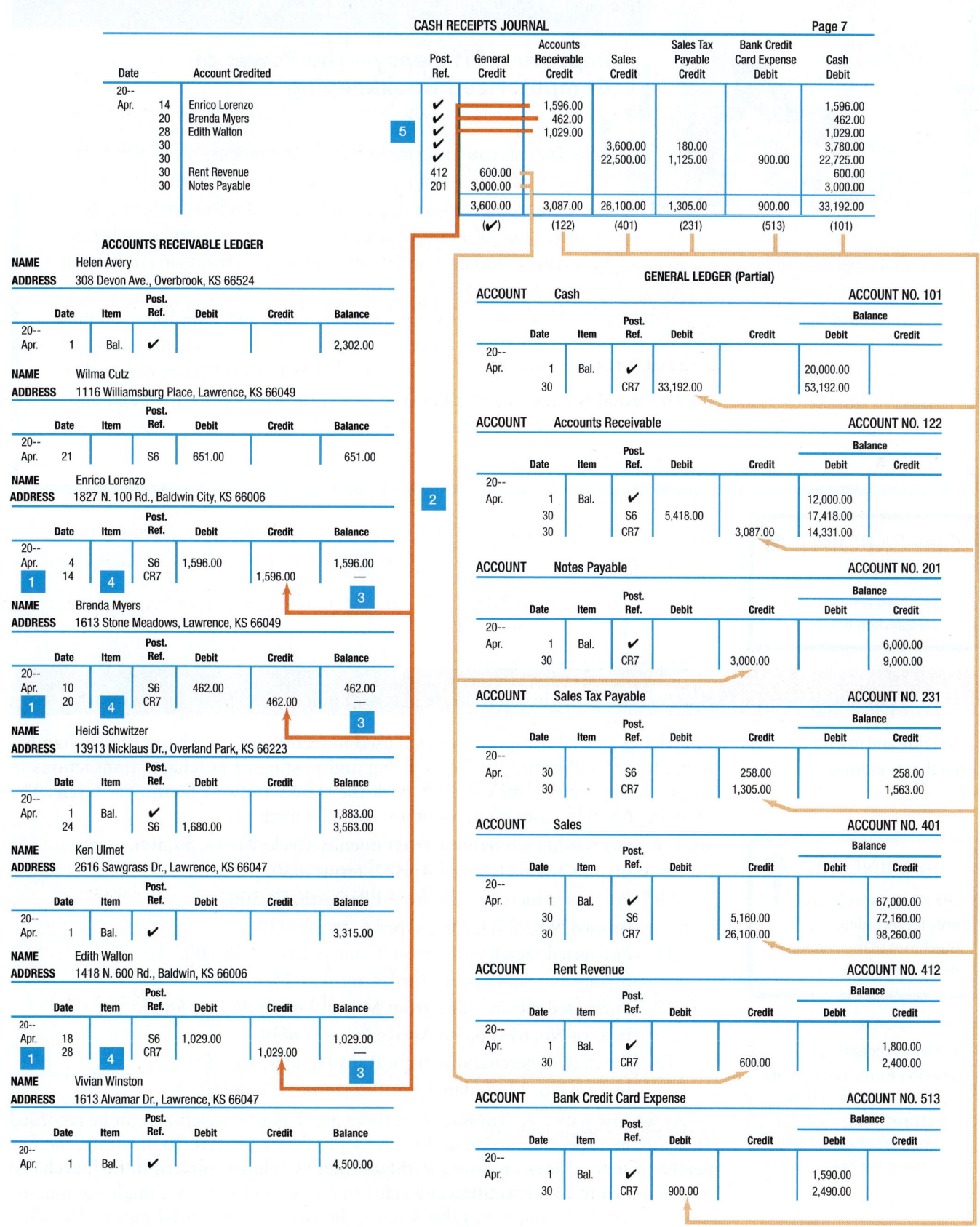

CASH RECEIPTS JOURNAL — Page 7

Date		Account Credited	Post. Ref.	General Credit	Accounts Receivable Credit	Sales Credit	Sales Tax Payable Credit	Bank Credit Card Expense Debit	Cash Debit
20--									
Apr.	14	Enrico Lorenzo	✔		1,596.00				1,596.00
	20	Brenda Myers	✔		462.00				462.00
	28	Edith Walton	✔		1,029.00				1,029.00
	30		✔			3,600.00	180.00		3,780.00
	30		✔			22,500.00	1,125.00	900.00	22,725.00
	30	Rent Revenue	412	600.00					600.00
	30	Notes Payable	201	3,000.00					3,000.00
				3,600.00	3,087.00	26,100.00	1,305.00	900.00	33,192.00
				(✔)	(122)	(401)	(231)	(513)	(101)

ACCOUNTS RECEIVABLE LEDGER

NAME Helen Avery
ADDRESS 308 Devon Ave., Overbrook, KS 66524

Date		Item	Post. Ref.	Debit	Credit	Balance
20--						
Apr.	1	Bal.	✔			2,302.00

NAME Wilma Cutz
ADDRESS 1116 Williamsburg Place, Lawrence, KS 66049

Date		Item	Post. Ref.	Debit	Credit	Balance
20--						
Apr.	21		S6	651.00		651.00

NAME Enrico Lorenzo
ADDRESS 1827 N. 100 Rd., Baldwin City, KS 66006

Date		Item	Post. Ref.	Debit	Credit	Balance
20--						
Apr.	4		S6	1,596.00		1,596.00
	14		CR7		1,596.00	—

NAME Brenda Myers
ADDRESS 1613 Stone Meadows, Lawrence, KS 66049

Date		Item	Post. Ref.	Debit	Credit	Balance
20--						
Apr.	10		S6	462.00		462.00
	20		CR7		462.00	—

NAME Heidi Schwitzer
ADDRESS 13913 Nicklaus Dr., Overland Park, KS 66223

Date		Item	Post. Ref.	Debit	Credit	Balance
20--						
Apr.	1	Bal.	✔			1,883.00
	24		S6	1,680.00		3,563.00

NAME Ken Ulmet
ADDRESS 2616 Sawgrass Dr., Lawrence, KS 66047

Date		Item	Post. Ref.	Debit	Credit	Balance
20--						
Apr.	1	Bal.	✔			3,315.00

NAME Edith Walton
ADDRESS 1418 N. 600 Rd., Baldwin, KS 66006

Date		Item	Post. Ref.	Debit	Credit	Balance
20--						
Apr.	18		S6	1,029.00		1,029.00
	28		CR7		1,029.00	—

NAME Vivian Winston
ADDRESS 1613 Alvamar Dr., Lawrence, KS 66047

Date		Item	Post. Ref.	Debit	Credit	Balance
20--						
Apr.	1	Bal.	✔			4,500.00

GENERAL LEDGER (Partial)

ACCOUNT Cash — ACCOUNT NO. 101

Date		Item	Post. Ref.	Debit	Credit	Balance Debit	Balance Credit
20--							
Apr.	1	Bal.	✔			20,000.00	
	30		CR7	33,192.00		53,192.00	

ACCOUNT Accounts Receivable — ACCOUNT NO. 122

Date		Item	Post. Ref.	Debit	Credit	Balance Debit	Balance Credit
20--							
Apr.	1	Bal.	✔			12,000.00	
	30		S6	5,418.00		17,418.00	
	30		CR7		3,087.00	14,331.00	

ACCOUNT Notes Payable — ACCOUNT NO. 201

Date		Item	Post. Ref.	Debit	Credit	Balance Debit	Balance Credit
20--							
Apr.	1	Bal.	✔				6,000.00
	30		CR7		3,000.00		9,000.00

ACCOUNT Sales Tax Payable — ACCOUNT NO. 231

Date		Item	Post. Ref.	Debit	Credit	Balance Debit	Balance Credit
20--							
Apr.	30		S6		258.00		258.00
	30		CR7		1,305.00		1,563.00

ACCOUNT Sales — ACCOUNT NO. 401

Date		Item	Post. Ref.	Debit	Credit	Balance Debit	Balance Credit
20--							
Apr.	1	Bal.	✔				67,000.00
	30		S6		5,160.00		72,160.00
	30		CR7		26,100.00		98,260.00

ACCOUNT Rent Revenue — ACCOUNT NO. 412

Date		Item	Post. Ref.	Debit	Credit	Balance Debit	Balance Credit
20--							
Apr.	1	Bal.	✔				1,800.00
	30		CR7		600.00		2,400.00

ACCOUNT Bank Credit Card Expense — ACCOUNT NO. 513

Date		Item	Post. Ref.	Debit	Credit	Balance Debit	Balance Credit
20--							
Apr.	1	Bal.	✔			1,590.00	
	30		CR7	900.00		2,490.00	

KURHAN/SHUTTERSTOCK.COM

A BROADER VIEW

Improving Efficiency—The Power of Computerized Bookkeeping

In this chapter, we see many examples of the ways in which special journals can make the bookkeeping process more efficient. Yet, these efficiency gains pale by comparison with the power of computerized bookkeeping. By means of a single keyboard entry, journals, general and subsidiary ledgers, customer and supplier accounts, periodic financial reports, and more can be updated, and there is no need to maintain special journals. You can even pay bills when due electronically as part of the system.

Some good examples of computerized bookkeeping software are QuickBooks® and Sage 50 Accounting. Both of these software packages utilize the one entry-many reports feature. The user makes entries using the keyboard; then the system tracks the effects on the financial status of the business. The software can analyze accounts receivable and accounts payable, process payroll, print checks, and track expenses by vendor and revenues by customer. It can also produce income statements and balance sheets. It is even possible to customize the programs to match different business types.

CHECKPOINT

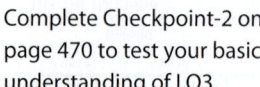

Complete Checkpoint-2 on page 470 to test your basic understanding of LO3.

LO4 Purchases Journal

Describe and use the purchases journal.

A **purchases journal** is a special journal used to record only purchases of merchandise on account. To illustrate the journalizing and posting of purchases transactions in the purchases journal, we continue with the transactions of Sunflower Cycle. The following five purchases on account are from Chapter 11:

Apr. 4 Purchased merchandise from Bilenky Cycle Works, $3,300. Invoice No. 631, dated April 2, terms n/30.
8 Purchased merchandise from Ellsworth, $2,500. Invoice No. 927D, dated April 6, terms n/30.
11 Purchased merchandise from Gunnar Cycles, $8,700. Invoice No. 804, dated April 9, terms 1/15, n/30.
17 Purchased merchandise from Milwaukee Cycle Co., $800. Invoice No. 611, dated April 16, terms n/30.
23 Purchased merchandise from Rans Designs, Inc., $5,300. Invoice No. 1465, dated April 22, terms 1/10, n/30.

LEARNING KEY

Use a purchases journal only for recording purchases of merchandise on account.

In some accounting systems, a purchases journal can be used to record all purchases on account. For example, see Figure 12-13.

As we saw with sales transactions, these purchases transactions can be recorded efficiently in a special journal, in this case a purchases journal. To illustrate, the five merchandise purchases on account of Sunflower Cycle are entered in the purchases journal in Figure 12-11. Sunflower Cycle's purchases journal has a single column for Purchases Debit/Accounts Payable Credit, the two accounts used repeatedly when these transactions are recorded in a general journal. A purchase is recorded in the purchases journal by entering the following information:

FIGURE 12-11 Sunflower Cycle Purchases Journal

PURCHASES JOURNAL PAGE 8

	DATE		INVOICE NO.	FROM WHOM PURCHASED	POST. REF.	PURCHASES DEBIT/ ACCOUNTS PAYABLE CREDIT	
	20--						
1	Apr.	4	631	Bilenky Cycle Works		3 3 0 0 00	1
2		8	927D	Ellsworth		2 5 0 0 00	2
3		11	804	Gunnar Cycles		8 7 0 0 00	3
4		17	611	Milwaukee Cycle Co.		8 0 0 00	4
5		23	1465	Rans Designs, Inc.		5 3 0 0 00	5
6						20 6 0 0 00	6

Remember that purchases returns and allowances are recorded in the general journal, as illustrated in Chapter 11, not in the purchases journal.

1. Date
2. Invoice number
3. Supplier (from whom purchased)
4. Dollar amount

There is no need to enter any general ledger account titles, since they appear in the column heading.

The purchases journal in Figure 12-11 is designed for a company like Sunflower Cycle, whose suppliers generally pay freight charges. For a company that frequently pays freight charges as part of the purchase price of merchandise, a purchases journal like the one in Figure 12-12 would be used. In this case, there are three columns: (1) Purchases Debit, (2) Freight-In Debit, and (3) Accounts Payable Credit.

FIGURE 12-12 Purchases Journal with Freight-In Column

PURCHASES JOURNAL

DATE	INVOICE NO.	FROM WHOM PURCHASED	POST. REF.	PURCHASES DEBIT	FREIGHT-IN DEBIT	ACCOUNTS PAYABLE CREDIT

If a company uses a purchases journal to record all purchases on account, including merchandise purchases, a purchases journal like the one in Figure 12-13 could be used.

FIGURE 12-13 Purchases Journal for All Purchases on Account

PURCHASES JOURNAL

DATE	INVOICE NO.	FROM WHOM PURCHASED	POST. REF.	MERCH. PURCHASES DEBIT	SUPPLIES DEBIT	COMPUTER EQUIP. DEBIT	OTHER ACCOUNTS DEBIT	ACCOUNTS PAYABLE CREDIT

Posting from the Purchases Journal

Step 1 is the main difference in posting the purchases journal to the general ledger. Steps 2–6 are essentially the same as steps 1–5 used to post the general journal.

Each general ledger account used in the purchases journal requires only one posting each period. Figure 12-14 illustrates the general ledger posting process for Sunflower Cycle's purchases journal for the month of April.

The following steps are used to post from the purchases journal to the general ledger at the end of each month, as indicated in Figure 12-14:

In the purchases journal:

STEP 1 Total and rule the amount column.

FIGURE 12-14 Posting from the Purchases Journal to the General Ledger

PURCHASES JOURNAL — Page 8

Date		Invoice No.	From Whom Purchased	Post. Ref.	Purchases Debit/ Accounts Payable Credit	
20--						
Apr.	4	631	Bilenky Cycle Works		3,300.00	
	8	927D	Ellsworth		2,500.00	
	11	804	Gunnar Cycles		8,700.00	
	17	611	Milwaukee Cycle Co.		800.00	
	23	1465	Rans Designs, Inc.		5,300.00	
					20,600.00	1
					(501) (202)	6

3

GENERAL LEDGER (Partial)

ACCOUNT Accounts Payable — ACCOUNT NO. 202

Date		Item	Post. Ref.	Debit	Credit	Balance Debit	Balance Credit
20--							
Apr.	1	Bal	✔				4,800.00
2	30	5	P8		20,600.00		25,400.00
							4

ACCOUNT Purchases — ACCOUNT NO.501

Date		Item	Post. Ref.	Debit	Credit	Balance Debit	Balance Credit
20--							
Apr.	1	Bal	✔			37,400.00	
2	30	5	P8	20,600.00		58,000.00	
						4	

In the general ledger account:

STEP 2 Enter the date in the Date column.

STEP 3 Enter the amount of the debit or credit in the Debit or Credit column.

STEP 4 Enter the new balance in the Balance columns under Debit or Credit.

STEP 5 Enter the initial "P" and the journal page number in the Posting Reference column.

In the purchases journal:

STEP 6 Enter the Purchases and Accounts Payable account numbers immediately below the column total.

> If the accounts payable ledger is posted daily and the general ledger is posted at the end of the month, the accounts payable ledger total will equal the general ledger Accounts Payable total only at the end of the month.

To maintain a record of the amount owed to each supplier, an accounts payable ledger is used. Figure 12-15 illustrates the use of the accounts payable ledger. The following steps are used to post from the purchases journal to the accounts payable ledger daily, as shown in Figure 12-15:

In the accounts payable ledger account:

STEP 1 Enter the date of the transaction in the Date column.

STEP 2 Enter the amount of the debit or credit in the Debit or Credit column.

STEP 3 Enter the new balance in the Balance column.

STEP 4 Enter the initial "P" and the journal page number in the Posting Reference column.

In the purchases journal:

STEP 5 Enter a check mark (✓) in the Posting Reference column of the journal for each transaction that is posted.

> **CHECKPOINT ✓**
>
> Complete Checkpoint-3 on page 471 to test your basic understanding of LO4.

After the posting of the accounts payable ledger and general ledger is completed, the total of the accounts payable ledger balances should equal the Accounts Payable balance in the general ledger.

FIGURE 12-15 Posting from the Purchases Journal to the Accounts Payable Ledger

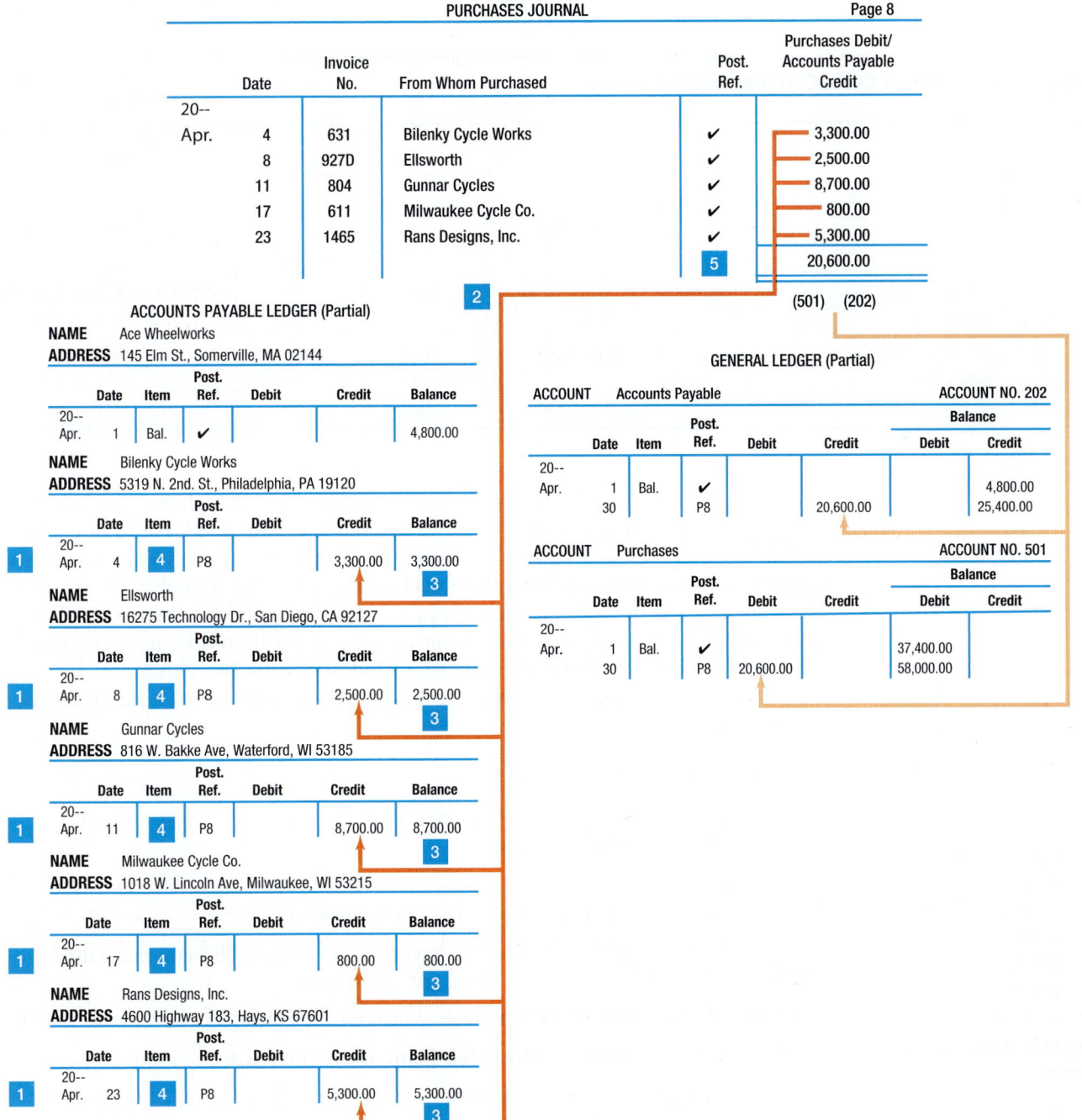

PURCHASES JOURNAL — Page 8

Date		Invoice No.	From Whom Purchased	Post. Ref.	Purchases Debit/ Accounts Payable Credit
20--					
Apr.	4	631	Bilenky Cycle Works	✓	3,300.00
	8	927D	Ellsworth	✓	2,500.00
	11	804	Gunnar Cycles	✓	8,700.00
	17	611	Milwaukee Cycle Co.	✓	800.00
	23	1465	Rans Designs, Inc.	✓	5,300.00
				5	20,600.00
					(501) (202)

2

ACCOUNTS PAYABLE LEDGER (Partial)

NAME Ace Wheelworks
ADDRESS 145 Elm St., Somerville, MA 02144

Date		Item	Post. Ref.	Debit	Credit	Balance
20--						
Apr.	1	Bal.	✓			4,800.00

NAME Bilenky Cycle Works
ADDRESS 5319 N. 2nd. St., Philadelphia, PA 19120

Date		Item	Post. Ref.	Debit	Credit	Balance
20--						
1 Apr.	4	4	P8		3,300.00	3,300.00 3

NAME Ellsworth
ADDRESS 16275 Technology Dr., San Diego, CA 92127

Date		Item	Post. Ref.	Debit	Credit	Balance
20--						
1 Apr.	8	4	P8		2,500.00	2,500.00 3

NAME Gunnar Cycles
ADDRESS 816 W. Bakke Ave, Waterford, WI 53185

Date		Item	Post. Ref.	Debit	Credit	Balance
20--						
1 Apr.	11	4	P8		8,700.00	8,700.00 3

NAME Milwaukee Cycle Co.
ADDRESS 1018 W. Lincoln Ave, Milwaukee, WI 53215

Date		Item	Post. Ref.	Debit	Credit	Balance
20--						
1 Apr.	17	4	P8		800.00	800.00 3

NAME Rans Designs, Inc.
ADDRESS 4600 Highway 183, Hays, KS 67601

Date		Item	Post. Ref.	Debit	Credit	Balance
20--						
1 Apr.	23	4	P8		5,300.00	5,300.00 3

GENERAL LEDGER (Partial)

ACCOUNT Accounts Payable — ACCOUNT NO. 202

Date		Item	Post. Ref.	Debit	Credit	Balance Debit	Balance Credit
20--							
Apr.	1	Bal.	✓				4,800.00
	30		P8		20,600.00		25,400.00

ACCOUNT Purchases — ACCOUNT NO. 501

Date		Item	Post. Ref.	Debit	Credit	Balance Debit	Balance Credit
20--							
Apr.	1	Bal.	✓			37,400.00	
	30		P8	20,600.00		58,000.00	

LO5 Cash Payments Journal

Describe and use the cash payments journal.

A **cash payments journal** is a special journal used to record only cash payments transactions. To illustrate its use, we will record the cash payments transactions of Sunflower Cycle. Sunflower Cycle's cash payments journal for the month of April is shown in Figure 12-16. Five types of cash payments transactions are shown as follows:

1. Payment of an expense (April 2)
2. Cash purchase (April 4)
3. Payment of an account payable (April 10 and 24)
4. Payment of a note payable (April 14)
5. Withdrawal by the owner (April 22)

LEARNING KEY Use a cash payments journal to streamline journalizing and posting of cash payments.

FIGURE 12-16 Sunflower Cycle Cash Payments Journal

CASH PAYMENTS JOURNAL

	DATE		CK. NO.	ACCOUNT DEBITED	POST. REF.	GENERAL DEBIT	ACCOUNTS PAYABLE DEBIT	PURCHASES DEBIT	PURCHASES DISCOUNTS CREDIT	CASH CREDIT	
1	Apr.	2	307	Rent Expense		1,200.00				1,200.00	1
2		4	308					1,400.00		1,400.00	2
3		10	309	Ace Wheelworks			4,800.00			4,800.00	3
4		14	310	Notes Payable		2,000.00				2,000.00	4
5		22	311	Sam Tangari, Drawing		1,600.00				1,600.00	5
6		24	312	Gunnar Cycles			8,700.00		87.00	8,613.00	6
7						4,800.00	13,500.00	1,400.00	87.00	19,613.00	7

Sunflower Cycle's cash payments journal provides separate columns for Accounts Payable Debit, Purchases Debit, Purchases Discounts Credit, and Cash Credit. These are the accounts most frequently affected by Sunflower Cycle's cash payments transactions. In addition, a General Debit column is provided for debits to any other accounts affected by cash payments transactions. For good internal control over cash payments, all payments (except out of petty cash) should be made by check. Therefore, the cash payments journal also includes a Check No. column.

A cash payment is recorded in the cash payments journal by entering the following information:

1. Date
2. Check number
3. Account debited (if applicable)
4. Dollar amounts

The Account Debited column is used for two purposes:

1. To identify the supplier name for any payment on account. This column is used whenever the Accounts Payable Debit column is used.
2. To enter the appropriate account name whenever the General Debit column is used.

The Account Debited column is left blank if the entry is for cash purchases.

Posting from the Cash Payments Journal

The cash payments journal is posted to the general ledger in two stages, as illustrated in Figure 12-17. First, on a daily basis, the individual amounts in the General Debit column are posted. Second, at the end of the month, the totals of each of the other amount columns are posted.

To post the General Debit column, on a daily basis, the following steps are used:

In the general ledger account:

STEP 1 Enter the date of the transaction in the Date column.

STEP 2 Enter the amount of the debit or credit in the Debit or Credit column.

STEP 3 Enter the new balance in the Balance columns under Debit or Credit.

STEP 4 Enter the initials "CP" and the journal page number in the Posting Reference column.

In the cash payments journal:

STEP 5 Enter the ledger account number in the Posting Reference column for each account that is posted.

To post the other amount columns, at the end of the month, the following steps are used:

In the cash payments journal:

STEP 6 Total the amount columns, verify that the total of the debit columns equals the total of the credit columns, and rule the columns.

In the general ledger account:

STEP 7 Enter the date in the Date column.

STEP 8 Enter the amount of the debit or credit in the Debit or Credit column.

STEP 9 Enter the new balance in the Balance columns under Debit or Credit.

STEP 10 Enter the initials "CP" and the journal page number in the Posting Reference column.

In the cash payments journal:

STEP 11 Enter the ledger account number immediately below the column totals for each account that is posted.

STEP 12 Enter a check mark (✓) in the Posting Reference column for the cash purchases, and immediately below the General Debit column.

Postings from the cash payments journal to the accounts payable ledger also must be made. These postings are made daily. Posting procedures are as follows, as shown in Figure 12-18:

In the accounts payable ledger account:

STEP 1 Enter the date of the transaction in the Date column.

STEP 2 Enter the amount of the debit or credit in the Debit or Credit column.

STEP 3 Enter the new balance in the Balance column.

STEP 4 Enter the initials "CP" and the journal page number in the Posting Reference column.

In the cash payments journal:

STEP 5 Enter a check mark (✓) in the Posting Reference column of the journal for each transaction that is posted.

FIGURE 12-17 Posting from the Cash Payments Journal to the General Ledger

CASH PAYMENTS JOURNAL Page 12

Date	Check No.	Account Debited		Post. Ref.	General Debit	Accounts Payable Debit	Purchases Debit	Purchases Discounts Credit	Cash Credit
20-- Apr. 2	307	Rent Expense	5	521	1,200.00				1,200.00
4	308		12	✔			1,400.00		1,400.00
10	309	Ace Wheelworks				4,800.00			4,800.00
14	310	Notes Payable	5	201	2,000.00				2,000.00
22	311	Sam Tangari, Drawing	5	312	1,600.00				1,600.00
24	312	Gunnar Cycles				8,700.00		87.00	8,613.00
					4,800.00	13,500.00	1,400.00	87.00	19,613.00 [6]
					(✔) [12]	(202)	(501)	(501.2)	(101) [11]

[8] [2]

[6] Debit total:

Debit total:	$ 4,800.00
	13,500
	1,400
	$19,700.00
Credit total:	$ 87
	19,613.00
	$19,700.00

GENERAL LEDGER (Partial)

ACCOUNT Cash — ACCOUNT NO. 101

Date	Item	Post. Ref.	Debit	Credit	Balance Debit	Balance Credit
20-- Apr. 1	Bal.	✔			20,000.00	
30		CR7	12,992.00		32,992.00	
[7] 30	[10]	CP12		19,613.00	13,379.00 [9]	

ACCOUNT Notes Payable — ACCOUNT NO. 201

Date	Item	Post. Ref.	Debit	Credit	Balance Debit	Balance Credit
20-- Apr. 1	Bal.	✔				6,000.00
[1] 14	[4]	CP12	2,000.00			4,000.00 [3]

ACCOUNT Accounts Payable — ACCOUNT NO. 202

Date	Item	Post. Ref.	Debit	Credit	Balance Debit	Balance Credit
20-- Apr. 1	Bal.	✔				4,800.00
30		P8		20,600.00		25,400.00
[7] 30	[10]	CP12	13,500.00			11,900.00 [9]

ACCOUNT Sam Tangari, Drawing — ACCOUNT NO. 312

Date	Item	Post. Ref.	Debit	Credit	Balance Debit	Balance Credit
20-- Apr. 1	Bal.	✔			1,500.00	
[1] 22	[4]	CP12	1,600.00		3,100.00 [3]	

ACCOUNT Purchases — ACCOUNT NO. 501

Date	Item	Post. Ref.	Debit	Credit	Balance Debit	Balance Credit
20-- Apr. 1	Bal.	✔			37,400.00	
30		P8	20,600.00		58,000.00	
[7] 30	[10]	CP12	1,400.00		59,400.00 [9]	

ACCOUNT Purchases Discounts — ACCOUNT NO. 501.2

Date	Item	Post. Ref.	Debit	Credit	Balance Debit	Balance Credit
20-- Apr. 1	Bal.	✔				330.00
[7] 30	[10]	CP12		87.00		417.00 [9]

ACCOUNT Rent Expense — ACCOUNT NO. 521

Date	Item	Post. Ref.	Debit	Credit	Balance Debit	Balance Credit
20-- Apr. 1	Bal.	✔			3,600.00	
[1] 2	[4]	CP12	1,200.00		4,800.00 [3]	

FIGURE 12-18 Posting from the Cash Payments Journal to the Accounts Payable Ledger

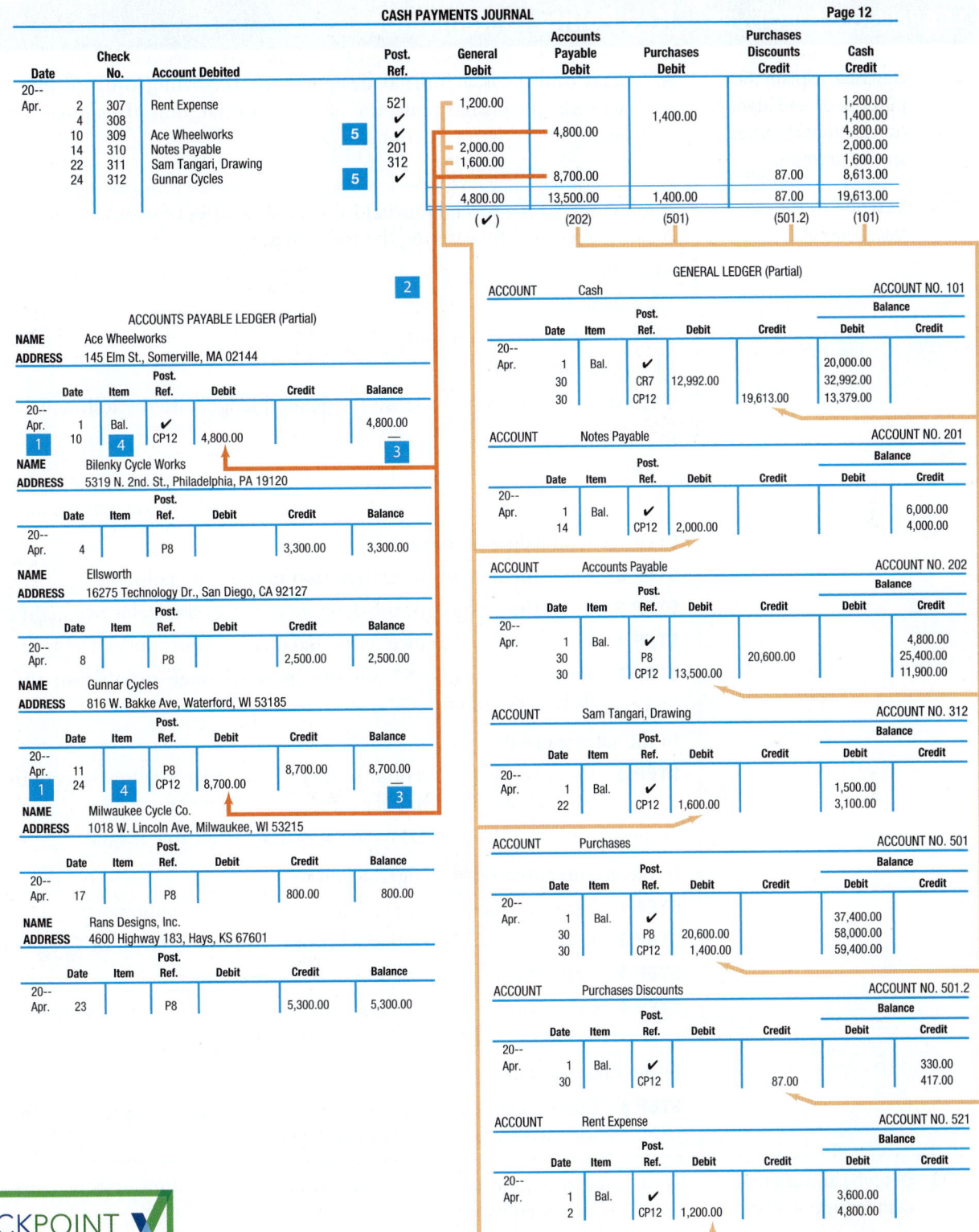

CASH PAYMENTS JOURNAL Page 12

Date		Check No.	Account Debited	Post. Ref.	General Debit	Accounts Payable Debit	Purchases Debit	Purchases Discounts Credit	Cash Credit
20--									
Apr.	2	307	Rent Expense	521	1,200.00				1,200.00
	4	308		✔			1,400.00		1,400.00
	10	309	Ace Wheelworks	5 ✔		4,800.00			4,800.00
	14	310	Notes Payable	201	2,000.00				2,000.00
	22	311	Sam Tangari, Drawing	312	1,600.00				1,600.00
	24	312	Gunnar Cycles	5 ✔		8,700.00		87.00	8,613.00
					4,800.00	13,500.00	1,400.00	87.00	19,613.00
					(✔)	(202)	(501)	(501.2)	(101)

2

ACCOUNTS PAYABLE LEDGER (Partial)

NAME Ace Wheelworks
ADDRESS 145 Elm St., Somerville, MA 02144

Date		Item	Post. Ref.	Debit	Credit	Balance
20--						
Apr.	1	Bal.	✔			4,800.00
1	10	4	CP12	4,800.00		— 3

NAME Bilenky Cycle Works
ADDRESS 5319 N. 2nd. St., Philadelphia, PA 19120

Date		Item	Post. Ref.	Debit	Credit	Balance
20--						
Apr.	4		P8		3,300.00	3,300.00

NAME Ellsworth
ADDRESS 16275 Technology Dr., San Diego, CA 92127

Date		Item	Post. Ref.	Debit	Credit	Balance
20--						
Apr.	8		P8		2,500.00	2,500.00

NAME Gunnar Cycles
ADDRESS 816 W. Bakke Ave, Waterford, WI 53185

Date		Item	Post. Ref.	Debit	Credit	Balance
20--						
Apr.	11		P8		8,700.00	8,700.00
1	24	4	CP12	8,700.00		— 3

NAME Milwaukee Cycle Co.
ADDRESS 1018 W. Lincoln Ave, Milwaukee, WI 53215

Date		Item	Post. Ref.	Debit	Credit	Balance
20--						
Apr.	17		P8		800.00	800.00

NAME Rans Designs, Inc.
ADDRESS 4600 Highway 183, Hays, KS 67601

Date		Item	Post. Ref.	Debit	Credit	Balance
20--						
Apr.	23		P8		5,300.00	5,300.00

GENERAL LEDGER (Partial)

ACCOUNT Cash — ACCOUNT NO. 101

Date		Item	Post. Ref.	Debit	Credit	Balance Debit	Balance Credit
20--							
Apr.	1	Bal.	✔			20,000.00	
	30		CR7	12,992.00		32,992.00	
	30		CP12		19,613.00	13,379.00	

ACCOUNT Notes Payable — ACCOUNT NO. 201

Date		Item	Post. Ref.	Debit	Credit	Balance Debit	Balance Credit
20--							
Apr.	1	Bal.	✔				6,000.00
	14		CP12	2,000.00			4,000.00

ACCOUNT Accounts Payable — ACCOUNT NO. 202

Date		Item	Post. Ref.	Debit	Credit	Balance Debit	Balance Credit
20--							
Apr.	1	Bal.	✔				4,800.00
	30		P8		20,600.00		25,400.00
	30		CP12	13,500.00			11,900.00

ACCOUNT Sam Tangari, Drawing — ACCOUNT NO. 312

Date		Item	Post. Ref.	Debit	Credit	Balance Debit	Balance Credit
20--							
Apr.	1	Bal.	✔			1,500.00	
	22		CP12	1,600.00		3,100.00	

ACCOUNT Purchases — ACCOUNT NO. 501

Date		Item	Post. Ref.	Debit	Credit	Balance Debit	Balance Credit
20--							
Apr.	1	Bal.	✔			37,400.00	
	30		P8	20,600.00		58,000.00	
	30		CP12	1,400.00		59,400.00	

ACCOUNT Purchases Discounts — ACCOUNT NO. 501.2

Date		Item	Post. Ref.	Debit	Credit	Balance Debit	Balance Credit
20--							
Apr.	1	Bal.	✔				330.00
	30		CP12		87.00		417.00

ACCOUNT Rent Expense — ACCOUNT NO. 521

Date		Item	Post. Ref.	Debit	Credit	Balance Debit	Balance Credit
20--							
Apr.	1	Bal.	✔			3,600.00	
	2		CP12	1,200.00		4,800.00	

CHECKPOINT

Complete Checkpoint-4 on page 471 to test your basic understanding of LO5.

SELF-STUDY

LEARNING OBJECTIVES	Key Points to Remember
LO1 Describe, explain the purpose of, and identify transactions recorded in special journals.	A special journal is a journal designed for recording only certain kinds of transactions. The primary purpose of using special journals is to save time journalizing and posting transactions.
LO2 Describe and use the sales journal.	A sales journal is a special journal for recording sales of merchandise on account. A sale is recorded by entering the following: 1. Date 2. Sale number 3. Customer (to whom sold) 4. Dollar amounts To post from the sales journal to the general ledger, use the following steps: **In the sales journal:** **STEP 1** Total the amount columns, verify that the total of the debit column equals the total of the credit columns, and rule the columns. **In the general ledger account:** **STEP 2** Enter the date of the transaction in the Date column. **STEP 3** Enter the amount of the debit or credit in the Debit or Credit column. **STEP 4** Enter the new balance in the Balance columns under Debit or Credit. **STEP 5** Enter the initial "S" and the journal page number in the Posting Reference column. **In the sales journal:** **STEP 6** Enter the ledger account number immediately below the column totals for each account that is posted. To post from the sales journal to the accounts receivable ledger: **In the accounts receivable ledger account:** **STEP 1** Enter the date of the transaction in the Date column. **STEP 2** Enter the amount of the debit or credit in the Debit or Credit column. **STEP 3** Enter the new balance in the Balance column. **STEP 4** Enter the initial "S" and the journal page number in the Posting Reference column. **In the sales journal:** **STEP 5** Enter a check mark (✓) in the Posting Reference column of the journal for each transaction that is posted.
LO3 Describe and use the cash receipts journal.	A cash receipts journal is a special journal for recording cash receipts. A cash receipt is recorded by entering the following: 1. Date 2. Account credited (if applicable) 3. Dollar amounts

LEARNING OBJECTIVES	Key Points to Remember
LO3 **(continued)**	To post from the cash receipts journal to the general ledger: To post the General Credit column, on a daily basis, use the following steps: **In the general ledger account:** **STEP 1** Enter the date of the transaction in the Date column. **STEP 2** Enter the amount of the debit or credit in the Debit or Credit column. **STEP 3** Enter the new balance in the Balance columns under Debit or Credit. **STEP 4** Enter the initials "CR" and the journal page number in the Posting Reference column. **In the cash receipts journal:** **STEP 5** Enter the ledger account number in the Posting Reference column for each account that is posted. To post the other amount columns, at the end of the month, use the following steps: **In the cash receipts journal:** **STEP 6** Total the amount columns, verify that the total of the debit columns equals the total of the credit columns, and rule the columns. **In the general ledger account:** **STEP 7** Enter the date in the Date column. **STEP 8** Enter the amount of the debit or credit in the Debit or Credit column. **STEP 9** Enter the new balance in the Balance columns under Debit or Credit. **STEP 10** Enter the initials "CR" and the journal page number in the Posting Reference column. **In the cash receipts journal:** **STEP 11** Enter the ledger account number immediately below the column totals for each account that is posted. **STEP 12** Enter a check mark (✓) in the Posting Reference column for the cash sales and bank credit card sales, and immediately below the General Credit column. To post from the cash receipts journal to the accounts receivable ledger, use the following steps: **In the accounts receivable ledger account:** **STEP 1** Enter the date of the transaction in the Date column. **STEP 2** Enter the amount of the debit or credit in the Debit or Credit column. **STEP 3** Enter the new balance in the Balance column. **STEP 4** Enter the initials "CR" and the journal page number in the Posting Reference column. **In the cash receipts journal:** **STEP 5** Enter a check mark (✓) in the Posting Reference column of the journal for each transaction that is posted.

(continued)

LEARNING OBJECTIVES	Key Points to Remember
LO4 Describe and use the purchases journal.	A purchases journal is a special journal for recording purchases of merchandise on account. A purchase is recorded by entering the following: 1. Date 2. Invoice number 3. Supplier (from whom purchased) 4. Dollar amount To post from the purchases journal to the general ledger, use the following steps: **In the purchases journal:** **STEP 1** Total and rule the amount column. **In the general ledger account:** **STEP 2** Enter the date in the Date column. **STEP 3** Enter the amount of the debit or credit in the Debit or Credit column. **STEP 4** Enter the new balance in the Balance columns under Debit or Credit. **STEP 5** Enter the initial "P" and the journal page number in the Posting Reference column. **In the purchases journal:** **STEP 6** Enter the Purchases and Accounts Payable account numbers immediately below the column total. To post from the purchases journal to the accounts payable ledger, use the following steps: **In the accounts payable ledger account:** **STEP 1** Enter the date of the transaction in the Date column. **STEP 2** Enter the amount of the debit or credit in the Debit or Credit column. **STEP 3** Enter the new balance in the Balance column. **STEP 4** Enter the initial "P" and the journal page number in the Posting Reference column. **In the purchases journal:** **STEP 5** Enter a check mark (✓) in the Posting Reference column of the journal for each transaction that is posted.
LO5 Describe and use the cash payments journal.	A cash payments journal is a special journal for recording cash payments. A cash payment is recorded by entering the following: 1. Date 2. Check number 3. Account debited (if applicable) 4. Dollar amounts

LEARNING OBJECTIVES	Key Points to Remember

LO5 (concluded)

To post from the cash payments journal to the general ledger:

To post the General Debit column, on a daily basis, use the following steps:

In the general ledger account:

STEP 1 Enter the date of the transaction in the Date column.

STEP 2 Enter the amount of the debit or credit in the Debit or Credit column.

STEP 3 Enter the new balance in the Balance columns under Debit or Credit.

STEP 4 Enter the initials "CP" and the journal page number in the Posting Reference column.

In the cash payments journal:

STEP 5 Enter the ledger account number in the Posting Reference column for each account that is posted.

To post the other amount columns, at the end of the month, use the following steps:

In the cash payments journal:

STEP 6 Total the amount columns, verify that the total of the debit columns equals the total of the credit columns, and rule the columns.

In the general ledger account:

STEP 7 Enter the date in the Date column.

STEP 8 Enter the amount of the debit or credit in the Debit or Credit column.

STEP 9 Enter the new balance in the Balance columns under Debit or Credit.

STEP 10 Enter the initials "CP" and the journal page number in the Posting Reference column.

In the cash payments journal:

STEP 11 Enter the ledger account number immediately below the column totals for each account that is posted.

STEP 12 Enter a check mark (✓) in the Posting Reference column for the cash purchases, and immediately below the General Debit column.

To post from the cash payments journal to the accounts payable ledger, use the following steps:

In the accounts payable ledger account:

STEP 1 Enter the date of the transaction in the Date column.

STEP 2 Enter the amount of the debit or credit in the Debit or Credit column.

STEP 3 Enter the new balance in the Balance column.

STEP 4 Enter the initials "CP" and the journal page number in the Posting Reference column.

In the cash payments journal:

STEP 5 Enter a check mark (✓) in the Posting Reference column of the journal for each transaction that is posted.

DEMONSTRATION PROBLEM

During the month of May 20--, David's Specialty Shop engaged in the following transactions:

May	1	Sold merchandise on account to Molly Mac, $2,000, plus tax of $100. Sale No. 533.
	2	Issued Check No. 750 to Kari Co. in partial payment of May 1 balance, $800, less 2% discount.
	3	Purchased merchandise on account from Scanlan Wholesalers, $2,000. Invoice No. 621, dated May 3, terms 2/10, n/30.
	4	Purchased merchandise on account from Simpson Enterprises, $1,500. Invoice No. 767, dated May 4, terms 2/15, n/30.
	4	Issued Check No. 751 in payment of phone expense for the month of April, $200.
	8	Sold merchandise for cash, $3,600, plus tax of $180.
	9	Received payment from Cody Slaton in full settlement of account, $2,500.
	10	Issued Check No. 752 to Scanlan Wholesalers in payment of May 1 balance of $1,200.
	12	Sold merchandise on account to Cody Slaton, $3,000, plus tax of $150. Sale No. 534.
	12	Received payment from Kori Reynolds on account, $2,100.
	13	Issued Check No. 753 to Simpson Enterprises in payment of May 4 purchase. Invoice No. 767, less 2% discount.
	13	Cody Slaton returned merchandise for a credit, $1,000, plus sales tax of $50.
	17	Returned merchandise to Johnson Essentials for credit, $500.
	22	Received payment from Natalie Gabbert on account, $1,555.
	27	Sold merchandise on account to Natalie Gabbert, $2,000, plus tax of $100. Sale No. 535.
	29	Issued Check No. 754 in payment of wages (Wages Expense) for the four-week period ending May 30, $1,100.

Selected account balances as of May 1 were as follows:

Account	Account No.	Debit	Credit
Cash	101	$10,050	
Accounts Receivable	122	6,900	
Accounts Payable	202		$4,550

David's also had the following subsidiary ledger balances as of May 1:

Accounts Receivable:

Customer	Accounts Receivable Balance
Natalie Gabbert 12 Jude Lane Hartford, CT 06117	$1,821
Molly Mac 52 Juniper Road Hartford, CT 06118	279
Kori Reynolds 700 Hobbes Dr. Avon, CT 06108	2,300
Cody Slaton 5200 Hamilton Ave. Hartford, CT 06111	2,500

Accounts Payable:

Vendor	Accounts Payable Balance
Johnson Essentials 34 Harry Ave. East Hartford, CT 05234	$2,350
Kari Co. 1009 Drake Rd. Farmington, CT 06082	1,000
Scanlan Wholesalers 43 Lucky Lane Bristol, CT 06007	1,200
Simpson Enterprises 888 Anders Street Newington, CT 06789	—

When the general journal and multiple special journals are used, post to the ledger in the following sequence:
- General Journal
- Sales Journal
- Cash Receipts Journal
- Purchases Journal
- Cash Payments Journal

REQUIRED

1. Record the transactions in the sales journal, cash receipts journal, purchases journal, cash payments journal, and general journal. Total, verify, and rule the columns where appropriate at the end of the month.
2. Post from the journals to the general ledger, accounts receivable ledger, and accounts payable ledger accounts. Use account numbers as shown in the chapter.

SOLUTION 1.

SALES JOURNAL — PAGE 7

	DATE		SALE NO.	TO WHOM SOLD	POST. REF.	ACCOUNTS RECEIVABLE DEBIT	SALES CREDIT	SALES TAX PAYABLE CREDIT	
1	20-- May	1	533	Molly Mac	✔	2,100.00	2,000.00	100.00	1
2		12	534	Cody Slaton	✔	3,150.00	3,000.00	150.00	2
3		27	535	Natalie Gabbert	✔	2,100.00	2,000.00	100.00	3
4						7,350.00	7,000.00	350.00	4
5						(122)	(401)	(231)	5

(continued)

PURCHASES JOURNAL PAGE 6

	DATE		INVOICE NO.	FROM WHOM PURCHASED	POST. REF.	PURCHASES DEBIT/ ACCOUNTS PAYABLE CREDIT	
1	20-- May	3	621	Scanlan Wholesalers	✔	2,000.00	1
2		4	767	Simpson Enterprises	✔	1,500.00	2
3						3,500.00	3
4						(501) (202)	4

GENERAL JOURNAL PAGE 5

	DATE		DESCRIPTION	POST. REF.	DEBIT	CREDIT	
1	20-- May	13	Sales Returns and Allowances	401.1	1,000.00		1
2			Sales Tax Payable	231	50.00		2
3			Accounts Receivable/Cody Slaton	122/✔		1,050.00	3
4			Accepted returned merchandise				4
5							5
6		17	Accounts Payable/Johnson Essentials	202/✔	500.00		6
7			Purchases Returns and Allowances	501.1		500.00	7
8			Returned merchandise				8
9							9

CASH PAYMENTS JOURNAL PAGE 11

	DATE		CK. NO.	ACCOUNT DEBITED	POST. REF.	GENERAL DEBIT	ACCOUNTS PAYABLE DEBIT	PURCHASES DEBIT	PURCHASES DISCOUNTS CREDIT	CASH CREDIT	
1	20-- May	2	750	Kari Co.	✔		800.00		16.00	784.00	1
2		4	751	Phone Expense	525	200.00				200.00	2
3		10	752	Scanlan Wholesalers	✔		1,200.00			1,200.00	3
4		13	753	Simpson Enterprises	✔		1,500.00		30.00	1,470.00	4
5		29	754	Wages Expense	511	1,100.00				1,100.00	5
6						1,300.00	3,500.00		46.00	4,754.00	6
7						(✓)	(202)		(501.2)	(101)	7

CASH RECEIPTS JOURNAL PAGE 10

	DATE		ACCOUNT CREDITED	POST. REF.	GENERAL CREDIT	ACCOUNTS RECEIVABLE CREDIT	SALES CREDIT	SALES TAX PAYABLE CREDIT	CASH DEBIT	
1	20-- May	8		✔			3,600.00	180.00	3,780.00	1
2		9	C. Slaton	✔		2,500.00			2,500.00	2
3		12	K. Reynolds	✔		2,100.00			2,100.00	3
4		22	N. Gabbert	✔		1,555.00			1,555.00	4
5						6,155.00	3,600.00	180.00	9,935.00	5
6						(122)	(401)	(231)	(101)	6

SOLUTION 2.

GENERAL LEDGER

ACCOUNT: Cash ACCOUNT NO. 101

DATE		ITEM	POST. REF.	DEBIT	CREDIT	BALANCE DEBIT	BALANCE CREDIT
20-- May	1	Balance	✔			10,050.00	
	31		CR10	9,935.00		19,985.00	
	31		CP11		4,754.00	15,231.00	

ACCOUNT: Accounts Receivable ACCOUNT NO. 122

DATE		ITEM	POST. REF.	DEBIT	CREDIT	BALANCE DEBIT	BALANCE CREDIT
20-- May	1	Balance	✔			6,900.00	
	13		J5		1,050.00	5,850.00	
	31		S7	7,350.00		13,200.00	
	31		CR10		6,155.00	7,045.00	

ACCOUNT: Accounts Payable ACCOUNT NO. 202

DATE		ITEM	POST. REF.	DEBIT	CREDIT	BALANCE DEBIT	BALANCE CREDIT
20-- May	1	Balance	✔				4,550.00
	17		J5	500.00			4,050.00
	31		P6		3,500.00		7,550.00
	31		CP11	3,500.00			4,050.00

ACCOUNT: Sales Tax Payable ACCOUNT NO. 231

DATE		ITEM	POST. REF.	DEBIT	CREDIT	BALANCE DEBIT	BALANCE CREDIT
20-- May	13		J5	50.00		50.00	
	31		S7		350.00		300.00
	31		CR10		180.00		480.00

ACCOUNT: Sales ACCOUNT NO. 401

DATE		ITEM	POST. REF.	DEBIT	CREDIT	BALANCE DEBIT	BALANCE CREDIT
20-- May	31		S7		7,000.00		7,000.00
	31		CR10		3,600.00		10,600.00

ACCOUNT: Sales Returns and Allowances ACCOUNT NO. 401.1

DATE		ITEM	POST. REF.	DEBIT	CREDIT	BALANCE DEBIT	BALANCE CREDIT
20-- May	13		J5	1,000.00		1,000.00	

ACCOUNT: Purchases ACCOUNT NO. 501

DATE		ITEM	POST. REF.	DEBIT	CREDIT	BALANCE DEBIT	BALANCE CREDIT
20-- May	31		P6	3,500.00		3,500.00	

ACCOUNT: Purchases Returns and Allowances ACCOUNT NO. 501.1

DATE		ITEM	POST. REF.	DEBIT	CREDIT	BALANCE DEBIT	BALANCE CREDIT
20-- May	17		J5		500.00		500.00

(continued)

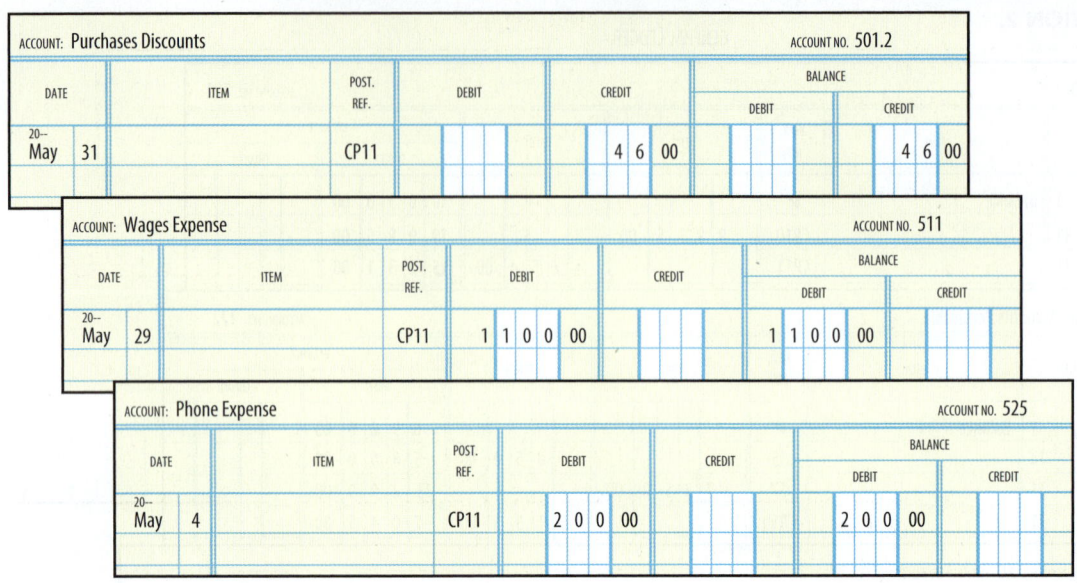

ACCOUNT: Purchases Discounts ACCOUNT NO. 501.2

DATE		ITEM	POST. REF.	DEBIT	CREDIT	BALANCE DEBIT	BALANCE CREDIT
20-- May	31		CP11		46 00		46 00

ACCOUNT: Wages Expense ACCOUNT NO. 511

DATE		ITEM	POST. REF.	DEBIT	CREDIT	BALANCE DEBIT	BALANCE CREDIT
20-- May	29		CP11	1100 00		1100 00	

ACCOUNT: Phone Expense ACCOUNT NO. 525

DATE		ITEM	POST. REF.	DEBIT	CREDIT	BALANCE DEBIT	BALANCE CREDIT
20-- May	4		CP11	200 00		200 00	

ACCOUNTS RECEIVABLE LEDGER

NAME: Natalie Gabbert
ADDRESS: 12 Jude Lane, Hartford, CT 06117

DATE		ITEM	POST. REF.	DEBIT	CREDIT	BALANCE
20-- May	1	Balance	✔			1821 00
	22		CR10		1555 00	266 00
	27		S7	2100 00		2366 00

NAME: Molly Mac
ADDRESS: 52 Juniper Road, Hartford, CT 06118

DATE		ITEM	POST. REF.	DEBIT	CREDIT	BALANCE
20-- May	1	Balance	✔			279 00
	1		S7	2100 00		2379 00

NAME: Kori Reynolds
ADDRESS: 700 Hobbes Dr., Avon, CT 06108

DATE		ITEM	POST. REF.	DEBIT	CREDIT	BALANCE
20-- May	1	Balance	✔			2300 00
	12		CR10		2100 00	200 00

NAME: Cody Slaton
ADDRESS: 5200 Hamilton Ave., Hartford, CT 06111

DATE		ITEM	POST. REF.	DEBIT	CREDIT	BALANCE
20-- May	1	Balance	✔			2500 00
	9		CR10		2500 00	—
	12		S7	3150 00		3150 00
	13		J5		1050 00	2100 00

ACCOUNTS PAYABLE LEDGER

NAME: Johnson Essentials
ADDRESS: 34 Harry Ave., East Hartford, CT 05234

DATE		ITEM	POST. REF.	DEBIT	CREDIT	BALANCE
20-- May	1	Balance	✔			2,350.00
	17		J5	500.00		1,850.00

NAME: Kari Co.
ADDRESS: 1009 Drake Rd., Farmington, CT 06082

DATE		ITEM	POST. REF.	DEBIT	CREDIT	BALANCE
20-- May	1	Balance	✔			1,000.00
	2		CP11	800.00		200.00

NAME: Scanlan Wholesalers
ADDRESS: 43 Lucky Lane, Bristol, CT 06007

DATE		ITEM	POST. REF.	DEBIT	CREDIT	BALANCE
20-- May	1	Balance	✔			1,200.00
	3		P6		2,000.00	3,200.00
	10		CP11	1,200.00		2,000.00

NAME: Simpson Enterprises
ADDRESS: 888 Anders Street, Newington, CT 06789

DATE		ITEM	POST. REF.	DEBIT	CREDIT	BALANCE
20-- May	1	Balance	✔			—
	4		P6		1,500.00	1,500.00
	13		CP11	1,500.00		—

KEY TERMS

cash payments journal (456) A special journal used to record only cash payments transactions.

cash receipts journal (447) A special journal used to record only cash receipts transactions.

purchases journal (452) A special journal used to record only purchases of merchandise on account. (Or in some systems, to record all purchases on account.)

sales journal (443) A special journal used to record only sales of merchandise on account.

special journal (442) A journal designed for recording only certain kinds of transactions.

SELF-STUDY TEST QUESTIONS

True/False

1. **LO1** The types of special journals a business uses should depend on the types of transactions it has most frequently.
2. **LO1** If a business uses special journals, it generally will not need a general journal.
3. **LO2** All sales, for cash or on credit, are recorded in the sales journal.
4. **LO3** A cash receipts journal is used to record all cash receipts transactions.
5. **LO4** Purchases returns and allowances are recorded in the general journal.

Multiple Choice

1. **LO2** The first step in posting the sales journal to the general ledger is to
   (a) total and verify the equality of the amount columns.
   (b) enter the date in the Date column of the ledger account.
   (c) enter the new balance in the Balance columns of the ledger account.
   (d) enter the ledger account number below the column totals in the journal.
2. **LO3** In the cash receipts journal, each amount in the General Credit column is posted
   (a) daily.
   (b) weekly.
   (c) at the end of the month.
   (d) at the end of the year.
3. **LO4** The journal that should be used to record the return of merchandise for credit is the
   (a) purchases journal.
   (b) cash payments journal.
   (c) general journal.
   (d) accounts payable journal.
4. **LO4** A purchases journal usually is used to record all
   (a) purchases.
   (b) cash purchases.
   (c) purchases of merchandise on account.
   (d) purchases returns and allowances.
5. **LO5** In the cash payments journal, each amount in the General Debit column is posted
   (a) daily.
   (b) weekly.
   (c) at the end of the month.
   (d) at the end of the year.

CHECKPOINT

Checkpoint Exercises

1. **LO2** Enter the following transaction in a sales journal like the one illustrated in the chapter:

   June 1 Made Sale No. 214 on account to Erin Lucas, $840, plus $42 sales tax.

2. **LO3** Enter the following transactions in a cash receipts journal like the one illustrated in the chapter:

   June 7 Received cash on account from Erin Lucas, $882.
   30 Made cash sales for the month of $2,150, plus sales tax of $107.50.
   30 Received cash for rent revenue, $750.

3. **LO4** Enter the following transaction in a purchases journal like the one illustrated in the chapter:

Apr. 6 Purchased merchandise from Clever, $1,680. Invoice No. 131, dated April 6, terms n/30.

4. **LO5** Enter the following transactions in a cash payments journal like the one illustrated in the chapter:

Aug. 2 Issued Check No. 193 in payment of August rent (Rent Expense), $2,200.

6 Issued Check No. 194 to Mason Hardware in payment of merchandise purchased on account, $1,700, less 2% discount. The check was written for $1,666.

10 Issued Check No. 195 to Augie's Wholesale for cash purchase of merchandise, $2,730.

The answers to the Self-Study Test Questions are at the end of the chapter (pages 486–487).

APPLYING YOUR KNOWLEDGE

CengageNowv2 provides "Show Me How" videos for selected exercises and problems. Additional resources, such as Excel templates for completing selected exercises and problems, are available for download from the companion website at Cengage.com.

REVIEW QUESTIONS

LO1 1. What is the primary purpose of using special journals?

LO2 2. List four items of information about each sale entered in the sales journal.

LO2 3. What steps are followed in posting from the sales journal to the general ledger?

LO2 4. What steps are followed in posting from the sales journal to the accounts receivable ledger?

LO3 5. List three items of information about each cash receipt entered in the cash receipts journal.

LO3 6. What steps are followed in posting from the cash receipts journal to the general ledger?

LO3 7. What steps are followed in posting from the cash receipts journal to the accounts receivable ledger?

LO4 8. List four items of information about each purchase entered in the purchases journal.

LO4 9. What steps are followed in posting from the purchases journal to the general ledger?

LO4 10. What steps are followed in posting from the purchases journal to the accounts payable ledger?

LO5 11. List four items of information about each cash payment entered in the cash payments journal.

LO5 12. What steps are followed in posting from the cash payments journal to the general ledger?

LO5 13. What steps are followed in posting from the cash payments journal to the accounts payable ledger?

SERIES A EXERCISES

E 12-1A (LO1)

RECORDING TRANSACTIONS IN THE PROPER JOURNAL Identify the journal (sales, cash receipts, purchases, cash payments, or general) in which each of the following transactions should be recorded:

(a) Sold merchandise on account.
(b) Purchased delivery truck on account for use in the business.
(c) Received payment from customer on account.
(d) Purchased merchandise on account.
(e) Issued check in payment of electric bill.
(f) Recorded depreciation on factory building.

E 12-2A (LO2)
✓ May 1: Dr. Accounts Receivable/ J. Adams, $2,120

JOURNALIZING SALES TRANSACTIONS Enter the following transactions in a sales journal. Use a 6% sales tax rate.

May 1 Sold merchandise on account to J. Adams, $2,000, plus sales tax. Sale No. 488.
4 Sold merchandise on account to B. Clark, $1,800, plus sales tax. Sale No. 489.
8 Sold merchandise on account to A. Duck, $1,500, plus sales tax. Sale No. 490.
11 Sold merchandise on account to E. Hill, $1,950, plus sales tax. Sale No. 491.

E 12-3A (LO3)
✓ July 6: Cr. Accounts Receivable/ Daren Chesbrough, $527

JOURNALIZING CASH RECEIPTS Enter the following transactions in a cash receipts journal:

July 6 Daren Chesbrough made payment on account, $527.
10 Made cash sales for the week, $2,470.
14 Adam Casady made payment on account, $394.
15 Yue Zou made payment on account, $203.
17 Made cash sales for the week, $2,360.

E 12-4A (LO4)
✓ May 9: Purchases Dr./Accounts Payable Cr., $3,100

JOURNALIZING PURCHASES TRANSACTIONS Enter the following transactions in a purchases journal like the one below:

May 3 Purchased merchandise from Climen, $7,200. Invoice No. 321, dated May 1, terms n/30.
9 Purchased merchandise from Misho, $3,100. Invoice No. 614, dated May 8, terms 2/10, n/30.
18 Purchased merchandise from Alelu Distributors, $4,700. Invoice No. 180, dated May 15, terms 1/15, n/30.
23 Purchased merchandise from Saltex, $5,900. Invoice No. 913, dated May 22, terms 1/10, n/30.

PURCHASES JOURNAL				PAGE
DATE	INVOICE NO.	FROM WHOM PURCHASED	POST. REF.	PURCHASES DEBIT/ ACCOUNTS PAYABLE CREDIT

E 12-5A (LO5)
✓ Sept. 12: Cash Cr., $7,920

JOURNALIZING CASH PAYMENTS Lakeview Industries uses a cash payments journal. Prepare a cash payments journal using the same format and account titles as illustrated in the chapter. Record the following payments for merchandise purchased:

Sept. 5 Issued Check No. 318 to Clausen Corp. for merchandise purchased August 28, $5,000, terms 2/10, n/30. Payment is made within the discount period.

12 Issued Check No. 319 to McGonigle Co. for merchandise purchased September 2, $8,400, terms 1/10, n/30. A credit memo had previously been received from McGonigle Co. for merchandise returned, $400. Payment is made within the discount period after deduction for the return dated September 8.

19 Issued Check No. 320 to Elite Systems for merchandise purchased August 19, $4,600, terms n/30.

27 Issued Check No. 321 to Glenn Falls for merchandise purchased September 17, $7,000, terms 2/10, n/30. Payment is made within the discount period.

SERIES A PROBLEMS

P 12-6A (LO2)
✓ Total Accounts Receivable Dr.: $16,599.60

SALES JOURNAL Futi Ishanyan owns a retail business and made the following sales during the month of August 20--. There is a 6% sales tax on all sales.

Aug. 1 Sale No. 213 to Jeter Manufacturing Co., $1,300, plus sales tax.

3 Sale No. 214 to Hassan Co., $2,600, plus sales tax.

7 Sale No. 215 to Habrock, Inc., $1,700, plus sales tax. (Open a new account for this customer. Address is 125 Fishers Dr., Noblesville, IN 47870–8867.)

11 Sale No. 216 to Seth Mowbray, $1,400, plus sales tax.

18 Sale No. 217 to Hassan Co., $3,960, plus sales tax.

22 Sale No. 218 to Jeter Manufacturing Co., $2,800, plus sales tax.

30 Sale No. 219 to Seth Mowbray, $1,900, plus sales tax.

REQUIRED

1. Record the transactions in the sales journal starting with page 8. Total and verify the column totals and rule the columns.
2. Post from the sales journal to the general ledger and accounts receivable ledger accounts. Use account numbers as shown in the chapter.

P 12-7A (LO3)
✓ Total Accounts Receivable Cr.: $5,732

CASH RECEIPTS JOURNAL Zebra Imaginarium, a retail business, had the following cash receipts during December 20--. The sales tax is 6%.

Dec. 1 Received payment on account from Michael Anderson, $1,360.

2 Received payment on account from Ansel Manufacturing, $382.

7 Made cash sales for the week, $3,160, plus tax. Bank credit card sales for the week, $1,000, plus tax. Bank credit card fee is 3%.

(continued)

Dec. 8 Received payment on account from J. Gorbea, $880.

11 Michael Anderson returned merchandise for a credit, $60, plus tax.

14 Made cash sales for the week, $2,800, plus tax. Bank credit card sales for the week, $800, plus tax. Bank credit card fee is 3%.

20 Received payment on account from Tom Wilson, $1,110.

21 Ansel Manufacturing returned merchandise for a credit, $22, plus tax.

21 Made cash sales for the week, $3,200, plus tax.

24 Received payment on account from Rachel Carson, $2,000.

Beginning general ledger account balances were as follows:

Cash	$9,862
Accounts Receivable	9,352

Beginning customer account balances were as follows:

M. Anderson	$2,480
Ansel Manufacturing	982
J. Gorbea	880
R. Carson	3,200
T. Wilson	1,810

REQUIRED

1. Record the transactions in the cash receipts journal. Total and verify column totals and rule the columns. Use the general journal to record sales returns and allowances.
2. Post from the journals to the general ledger and accounts receivable ledger accounts. Use account numbers as shown in the chapter.

P 12-8A (LO2/3)
✓ **Total Accounts Receivable Dr.: $12,745.08**

SALES JOURNAL, CASH RECEIPTS JOURNAL, AND GENERAL JOURNAL Owens Distributors is a retail business. The following sales, returns, and cash receipts occurred during March 20--. There is an 8% sales tax. Beginning general ledger account balances were Cash, $9,741; and Accounts Receivable, $1,058.25. Beginning customer account balances were Thompson Group, $1,058.25.

Mar. 1 Sold merchandise to Able & Co., $1,800, plus sales tax. Sale No. 33C.

3 Sold merchandise to R. J. Kalas, Inc., $2,240, plus sales tax. Sale No. 33D.

5 Able & Co. returned merchandise from Sale No. 33C for a credit (Credit Memo No. 66), $30, plus sales tax.

7 Made cash sales for the week, $3,160, plus sales tax.

10 Received payment from Able & Co. for Sale No. 33C less Credit Memo No. 66.

11 Sold merchandise to Blevins Bakery, $1,210, plus sales tax. Sale No. 33E.

13 Received payment from R. J. Kalas for Sale No. 33D.

14 Made cash sales for the week, $4,200, plus sales tax.

16 Blevins Bakery returned merchandise from Sale No. 33E for a credit (Credit Memo No. 67), $44, plus sales tax.

18 Sold merchandise to R. J. Kalas, Inc., $2,620, plus sales tax. Sale No. 33F.

20 Received payment from Blevins Bakery for Sale No. 33E less Credit Memo No. 67.

Mar. 21 Made cash sales for the week, $2,400, plus sales tax.
25 Sold merchandise to Blevins Bakery, $1,915, plus sales tax. Sale No. 33G.
27 Sold merchandise to Thompson Group, $2,016, plus sales tax. Sale No. 33H.
28 Made cash sales for the week, $3,500, plus sales tax.

REQUIRED

1. Record the transactions in the sales journal, cash receipts journal, and general journal. Total, verify, and rule the columns where appropriate at the end of the month.
2. Post from the journals to the general ledger and accounts receivable ledger accounts. Use account numbers as shown in the chapter.

P 12-9A (LO4)
✓ Total Purchases Dr.: $20,790

PURCHASES JOURNAL J. B. Speck, owner of Speck's Galleria, made the following purchases of merchandise on account during the month of September:

Sept. 3 Purchase Invoice No. 415, $2,650, from Smith Distributors.
8 Purchase Invoice No. 132, $3,830, from Michaels Wholesaler.
11 Purchase Invoice No. 614, $3,140, from J. B. Sanders & Co.
18 Purchase Invoice No. 329, $2,250, from Bateman & Jones, Inc.
23 Purchase Invoice No. 867, $4,160, from Smith Distributors.
27 Purchase Invoice No. 744, $1,980, from Anderson Company.
30 Purchase Invoice No. 652, $2,780, from Michaels Wholesaler.

REQUIRED

1. Record the transactions in the purchases journal. Total and rule the journal.
2. Post from the purchases journal to the general ledger and accounts payable ledger accounts. Use account numbers as shown in the chapter.

P 12-10A (LO4)
✓ Helmut's Hair Supply account balance: $4,240

PURCHASES JOURNAL, GENERAL LEDGER, AND ACCOUNTS PAYABLE LEDGER The purchases journal of Kevin's Kettle, a small retail business, is as follows:

PURCHASES JOURNAL PAGE 1

	DATE		INVOICE NO.	FROM WHOM PURCHASED	POST. REF.	PURCHASES DEBIT/ ACCOUNTS PAYABLE CREDIT	
	20--						
1	Jan.	2	101	Ruiz Imports		3,000.00	1
2		3	621	Helmut's Hair Supply		2,480.00	2
3		7	195	Viola's Boutique		4,360.00	3
4		12	267	Royal Flush		1,950.00	4
5		18	903	Maria's Melodies		4,700.00	5
6		25	680	Helmut's Hair Supply		1,760.00	6
7						18,250.00	7

REQUIRED

1. Post the total of the purchases journal to the appropriate general ledger accounts. Use account numbers as shown in the chapter.
2. Post the individual purchase amounts to the accounts payable ledger.

P 12-11A (LO5)
✓ Total Cash Cr.: $30,984

CASH PAYMENTS JOURNAL Sam Santiago operates a retail variety store. The books include a cash payments journal and an accounts payable ledger. All cash payments (except petty cash) are entered in the cash payments journal.

Selected account balances on May 1 are as follows:

General Ledger	
Cash	$40,000
Accounts Payable	20,000

Accounts Payable Ledger	
Fantastic Toys	$5,200
Goya Outlet	3,800
Mueller's Distributors	3,600
Van Kooning	7,400

The following are the transactions related to cash payments for the month of May:

May 1 Issued Check No. 426 in payment of May rent (Rent Expense), $2,400.

3 Issued Check No. 427 to Mueller's Distributors in payment of merchandise purchased on account, $3,600, less a 3% discount. Check was written for $3,492.

7 Issued Check No. 428 to Van Kooning in partial payment of merchandise purchased on account, $5,500. A cash discount was not allowed.

12 Issued Check No. 429 to Fantastic Toys for merchandise purchased on account, $5,200, less a 1% discount. Check was written for $5,148.

15 Issued Check No. 430 to City Power and Light (Utilities Expense), $1,720.

18 Issued Check No. 431 to A-1 Warehouse for a cash purchase of merchandise, $4,800.

26 Issued Check No. 432 to Goya Outlet for merchandise purchased on account, $3,800, less a 2% discount. Check was written for $3,724.

30 Issued Check No. 433 to Mercury Transit Company for freight charges on merchandise purchased (Freight-In), $1,200.

31 Issued Check No. 434 to Town Merchants for a cash purchase of merchandise, $3,000.

REQUIRED

1. Enter the transactions in a cash payments journal. Total, rule, and prove the cash payments journal.
2. Post from the cash payments journal to the general ledger and accounts payable ledger. Use general ledger account numbers as shown in the chapter.

P 12-12A (LO4/5)
✓ Total Cash Cr.: $11,170

PURCHASES JOURNAL, CASH PAYMENTS JOURNAL, AND GENERAL JOURNAL Freddy Flint owns a small retail business called Flint's Fantasy. The cash account has a balance of $20,000 on July 1. The following transactions occurred during July:

July 1 Issued Check No. 414 in payment of July rent, $1,500.

1 Purchased merchandise on account from Tang's Toys, Invoice No. 311, $2,700, terms 2/10, n/30.

July 3 Purchased merchandise on account from Sillas & Company, Invoice No. 812, $3,100, terms 1/10, n/30.

5 Returned merchandise purchased from Tang's Toys, receiving a credit memo on the amount owed, $500.

8 Purchased merchandise on account from Daisy's Dolls, Invoice No. 139, $1,900, terms 2/10, n/30.

11 Issued Check No. 415 to Tang's Toys for merchandise purchased on account, less return of July 5 and less 2% discount.

13 Issued Check No. 416 to Sillas & Company for merchandise purchased on account, less 1% discount.

15 Returned merchandise purchased from Daisy's Dolls, receiving a credit memo on the amount owed, $400.

18 Issued Check No. 417 to Daisy's Dolls for merchandise purchased on account, less return of July 15 and less 2% discount.

25 Purchased merchandise on account from Allied Business, Invoice No. 489, $2,450, terms n/30.

26 Purchased merchandise on account from Tang's Toys, Invoice No. 375, $1,980, terms 2/10, n/30.

29 Purchased merchandise on account from Sillas & Company, Invoice No. 883, $3,460, terms 1/10, n/30.

31 Freddy Flint withdrew cash for personal use, $2,000. Issued Check No. 418.

31 Issued Check No. 419 to Glisan Distributors for a cash purchase of merchandise, $975.

REQUIRED

1. Record the transactions in the purchases journal, cash payments journal, and general journal. Total and rule the purchases and cash payments journals. Prove the cash payments journal.
2. Post from the journals to the general ledger and accounts payable ledger accounts. Use general ledger account numbers as shown in the chapter.

SERIES B EXERCISES

E 12-1B (LO1)

RECORDING TRANSACTIONS IN THE PROPER JOURNAL Identify the journal (sales, cash receipts, purchases, cash payments, or general) in which each of the following transactions should be recorded:

(a) Issued credit memo to customer for merchandise returned.
(b) Sold merchandise for cash.
(c) Purchased merchandise on account.
(d) Issued checks to employees in payment of wages.
(e) Purchased factory supplies on account.
(f) Sold merchandise on account.

E 12-2B (LO2)
✓ Sept. 1: Dr. Accounts Receivable/K. Smith, $1,890

JOURNALIZING SALES TRANSACTIONS Enter the following transactions in a sales journal. Use a 5% sales tax rate.

(continued)

Sept. 1 Sold merchandise on account to K. Smith, $1,800, plus sales tax. Sale No. 228.

3 Sold merchandise on account to J. Arnes, $3,100, plus sales tax. Sale No. 229.

5 Sold merchandise on account to M. Denison, $2,800, plus sales tax. Sale No. 230.

7 Sold merchandise on account to B. Marshall, $1,900, plus sales tax. Sale No. 231.

E 12-3B (LO3)

✓ Nov. 1: Cr. Accounts Receivable/Jean Haghighat, $750

JOURNALIZING CASH RECEIPTS Enter the following transactions in a cash receipts journal:

Nov. 1 Jean Haghighat made payment on account, $750.

12 Marc Antonoff made payment on account, $464.

15 Made cash sales, $3,763.

18 Will Mossein made payment on account, $241.

25 Made cash sales, $2,648.

E 12-4B (LO4)

✓ Jan. 3: Purchases Dr./Accounts Payable Cr., $6,000

JOURNALIZING PURCHASES TRANSACTIONS Enter the following transactions in a purchases journal like the one below:

Jan. 3 Purchased merchandise from Feng, $6,000. Invoice No. 416, dated January 1, terms 2/10, n/30.

12 Purchased merchandise from Miranda, $9,000. Invoice No. 624, dated January 10, terms n/30.

19 Purchased merchandise from J. B. Barba, $6,400. Invoice No. 190, dated January 18, terms 1/10, n/30.

26 Purchased merchandise from Ramirez, $3,700. Invoice No. 923, dated January 25, terms 1/15, n/30.

PURCHASES JOURNAL PAGE

DATE	INVOICE NO.	FROM WHOM PURCHASED	POST. REF.	PURCHASES DEBIT/ ACCOUNTS PAYABLE CREDIT

E 12-5B (LO5)

✓ Apr. 19: Cash Cr., $4,950

JOURNALIZING CASH PAYMENTS Sandcastles Northwest uses a cash payments journal. Prepare a cash payments journal using the same format and account titles as illustrated in the chapter. Record the following payments for merchandise purchased:

Apr. 5 Issued Check No. 429 to Standard Industries for merchandise purchased April 3, $8,000, terms 2/10, n/30. Payment is made within the discount period.

19 Issued Check No. 430 to Finest Company for merchandise purchased April 10, $5,300, terms 1/10, n/30. A credit memo had previously been received from Finest Company for merchandise returned, $300. Payment is made within the discount period after deduction for the return dated April 12.

21 Issued Check No. 431 to Funny Follies for merchandise purchased March 21, $3,250, terms n/30.

29 Issued Check No. 432 to Classic Data for merchandise purchased April 20, $7,000, terms 2/10, n/30. Payment is made within the discount period.

SERIES B PROBLEMS

P 12-6B (LO2)
✓ Total Accounts Receivable Dr.: $13,072.50

SALES JOURNAL T. M. Maxwell owns a retail business and made the following sales during the month of July 20--. There is a 5% sales tax on all sales.

July 1 Sale No. 101 to Saga, Inc., $1,200, plus sales tax.
8 Sale No. 102 to Vinnie Ward, $2,100, plus sales tax.
15 Sale No. 103 to Dvorak Manufacturing, $4,300, plus sales tax.
21 Sale No. 104 to Vinnie Ward, $1,800, plus sales tax.
24 Sale No. 105 to Zapata Co., $1,600, plus sales tax. (Open a new account for this customer. Address is 789 N. Stafford Dr., Bloomington, IN 47401–6201.)
29 Sale No. 106 to Saga, Inc., $1,450, plus sales tax.

REQUIRED

1. Record the transactions in the sales journal. Total and verify the column totals and rule the columns.
2. Post the sales journal to the general ledger and accounts receivable ledger accounts. Use account numbers as shown in the chapter.

P 12-7B (LO3)
✓ Total Accounts Receivable Cr.: $3,481

CASH RECEIPTS JOURNAL Color Florists, a retail business, had the following cash receipts during January 20--. The sales tax is 5%.

Jan. 1 Received payment on account from Ray Boyd, $880.
3 Received payment on account from Clint Hassell, $271.
5 Made cash sales for the week, $2,800, plus tax. Bank credit card sales for the week, $1,200, plus tax. Bank credit card fee is 3%.
8 Received payment on account from Jan Sowada, $912.
11 Ray Boyd returned merchandise for a credit, $40, plus tax.
12 Made cash sales for the week, $3,100, plus tax. Bank credit card sales for the week, $1,900, plus tax. Bank credit card fee is 3%.
15 Received payment on account from Robert Zehnle, $1,100.
18 Robert Zehnle returned merchandise for a credit, $31, plus tax.
19 Made cash sales for the week, $2,230, plus tax.
25 Received payment on account from Dazai Manufacturing, $318.

Beginning general ledger account balances were as follows:

Cash	$2,890.75
Accounts Receivable	6,300.00

Beginning customer account balances were as follows:

R. Boyd	$1,400
Dazai Manufacturing	318
C. Hassell	815
J. Sowada	1,481
R. Zehnle	2,286

(*continued*)

REQUIRED

1. Record the transactions in the cash receipts journal. Total and verify the column totals and rule the columns. Use the general journal to record sales returns and allowances.
2. Post from the journals to the general ledger and accounts receivable ledger accounts. Use account numbers as shown in the chapter.

P 12-8B (LO2/3)
✓ Total Accounts Receivable Dr.: $7,853.80

SALES JOURNAL, CASH RECEIPTS JOURNAL, AND GENERAL JOURNAL Paul Jackson owns a retail business. The following sales, returns, and cash receipts are for April 20--. There is a 7% sales tax.

Apr.	1	Sold merchandise to O. L. Meyers, $2,100, plus sales tax. Sale No. 111.
	3	Sold merchandise to Andrew Plaa, $1,000, plus sales tax. Sale No. 112.
	6	O. L. Meyers returned merchandise from Sale No. 111 for a credit (Credit Memo No. 42), $50, plus sales tax.
	7	Made cash sales for the week, $3,240, plus sales tax.
	9	Received payment from O. L. Meyers for Sale No. 111, less Credit Memo No. 42.
	12	Sold merchandise to Melissa Richfield, $980, plus sales tax. Sale No. 113.
	14	Made cash sales for the week, $2,180, plus sales tax.
	17	Melissa Richfield returned merchandise from Sale No. 113 for a credit (Credit Memo No. 43), $40, plus sales tax.
	19	Sold merchandise to Kelsay Munkres, $1,020, plus sales tax. Sale No. 114.
	21	Made cash sales for the week, $2,600, plus sales tax.
	24	Sold merchandise to O. L. Meyers, $920, plus sales tax. Sale No. 115.
	27	Sold merchandise to Andrew Plaa, $1,320, plus sales tax. Sale No. 116.
	28	Made cash sales for the week, $2,800, plus sales tax.

Beginning general ledger account balances were as follows:

Cash	$2,864.54
Accounts Receivable	2,726.25

Beginning customer account balances were as follows:

O. L. Meyers	$2,186.00
K. Munkres	482.00
M. Richfield	58.25

REQUIRED

1. Record the transactions in the sales journal, cash receipts journal, and general journal. Total, verify, and rule the columns where appropriate at the end of the month.
2. Post from the journals to the general ledger and accounts receivable ledger accounts. Use account numbers as shown in the chapter.

P 12-9B (LO4)
✓ Total Purchases Dr.: $18,515

PURCHASES JOURNAL Ann Benton, owner of Benton's Galleria, made the following purchases of merchandise on account during the month of October:

Oct.	2	Purchase Invoice No. 321, $1,950, from Boggs Distributors.
	7	Purchase Invoice No. 152, $2,915, from Wolfs Wholesaler.
	10	Purchase Invoice No. 634, $3,565, from Komuro & Co.
	16	Purchase Invoice No. 349, $2,845, from Fritz & McCord, Inc.
	24	Purchase Invoice No. 587, $3,370, from Boggs Distributors.
	26	Purchase Invoice No. 764, $2,240, from Sanderson Company.
	31	Purchase Invoice No. 672, $1,630, from Wolfs Wholesaler.

REQUIRED

1. Record the transactions in the purchases journal. Total and rule the journal.
2. Post from the purchases journal to the general ledger and accounts payable ledger accounts. Use account numbers as shown in the chapter.

P 12-10B (LO4)
✓ Amelia & Vincente account balance: $7,810

PURCHASES JOURNAL, GENERAL LEDGER, AND ACCOUNTS PAYABLE LEDGER The purchases journal of Ryan's Rats Nest, a small retail business, is as follows:

PURCHASES JOURNAL — PAGE 1

	DATE		INVOICE NO.	FROM WHOM PURCHASED	POST. REF.	PURCHASES DEBIT/ ACCOUNTS PAYABLE CREDIT	
	20--						
1	Jan.	3	121	Sandra's Sweets		4 4 9 0 00	1
2		5	641	Amelia & Vincente		5 9 2 0 00	2
3		9	215	Nobuko's Nature Store		2 6 8 0 00	3
4		15	227	Smith and Johnson Company		6 5 6 0 00	4
5		21	933	Hidemi, Inc.		1 3 0 0 00	5
6		30	650	Amelia & Vincente		1 8 9 0 00	6
7						22 8 4 0 00	7

REQUIRED

1. Post the total of the purchases journal to the appropriate general ledger accounts. Use account numbers as shown in the chapter.
2. Post the individual purchase amounts to the accounts payable ledger.

P 12-11B (LO5)
✓ Total Cash Cr.: $29,890

CASH PAYMENTS JOURNAL Kay Zembrowski operates a retail variety store. The books include a cash payments journal and an accounts payable ledger. All cash payments (except petty cash) are entered in the cash payments journal. Selected account balances on May 1 are as follows:

General Ledger

Cash	$40,000
Accounts Payable	20,000

Accounts Payable Ledger

Cortez Distributors	$4,200
Indra & Velga	6,800
Toy Corner	4,600
Troutman Outlet	4,400

(continued)

The following transactions are related to cash payments for the month of May:

May 1 Issued Check No. 326 in payment of May rent (Rent Expense), $2,600.

4 Issued Check No. 327 to Cortez Distributors in payment of merchandise purchased on account, $4,200, less a 3% discount. Check was written for $4,074.

7 Issued Check No. 328 to Indra & Velga in partial payment of merchandise purchased on account, $6,200. A cash discount was not allowed.

11 Issued Check No. 329 to Toy Corner for merchandise purchased on account, $4,600, less a 1% discount. Check was written for $4,554.

15 Issued Check No. 330 to County Power and Light (Utilities Expense), $1,500.

19 Issued Check No. 331 to Builders Warehouse for a cash purchase of merchandise, $3,500.

25 Issued Check No. 332 to Troutman Outlet for merchandise purchased on account, $4,400, less a 2% discount. Check was written for $4,312.

30 Issued Check No. 333 to Rapid Transit Company for freight charges on merchandise purchased (Freight-In), $800.

31 Issued Check No. 334 to City Merchants for a cash purchase of merchandise, $2,350.

REQUIRED

1. Enter the transactions in a cash payments journal. Total, rule, and prove the cash payments journal.
2. Post from the cash payments journal to the general ledger and accounts payable ledger. Use general ledger account numbers as shown in the chapter.

P 12-12B (LO4/5)
✓ Total Cash Cr.: $10,760

PURCHASES JOURNAL, CASH PAYMENTS JOURNAL, AND GENERAL JOURNAL

Debbie Mueller owns a small retail business called Debbie's Doll House. The cash account has a balance of $20,000 on July 1. The following transactions occurred during July:

July 1 Issued Check No. 314 for July rent, $1,400.

1 Purchased merchandise on account from Topper's Toys, Invoice No. 211, $2,500, terms 2/10, n/30.

3 Purchased merchandise on account from Jones & Company, Invoice No. 812, $2,800, terms 1/10, n/30.

5 Returned merchandise purchased from Topper's Toys receiving a credit memo on the amount owed, $400.

8 Purchased merchandise on account from Downtown Merchants, Invoice No. 159, $1,600, terms 2/10, n/30.

11 Issued Check No. 315 to Topper's Toys for merchandise purchased on account, less return of July 5 and less 2% discount.

13 Issued Check No. 316 to Jones & Company for merchandise purchased on account, less 1% discount.

15 Returned merchandise purchased from Downtown Merchants receiving a credit memo on the amount owed, $600.

July 18 Issued Check No. 317 to Downtown Merchants for merchandise purchased on account, less return of July 15 and less 2% discount.

25 Purchased merchandise on account from Columbia Products, Invoice No. 468, $3,200, terms n/30.

26 Purchased merchandise on account from Topper's Toys, Invoice No. 395, $1,430, terms 2/10, n/30.

29 Purchased merchandise on account from Jones & Company, Invoice No. 853, $2,970, terms 1/10, n/30.

31 Mueller withdrew cash for personal use, $2,500. Issued Check No. 318.

31 Issued Check No. 319 to Burnside Warehouse for a cash purchase of merchandise, $1,050.

REQUIRED

1. Record the transactions in the purchases journal, cash payments journal, and general journal. Total and rule the purchases and cash payments journals. Prove the cash payments journal.
2. Post from the journals to the general ledger and accounts payable ledger accounts. Use general ledger account numbers as shown in the chapter.

CHECK LIST
- ☐ **Managing**
- ☐ **Planning**
- ☐ **Drafting**
- ☐ **Break**
- ☐ **Revising**
- ☐ **Managing**

MANAGING YOUR WRITING

You have a part-time job as a bookkeeper at a local office supply store. The accounting records consist of a general journal and general ledger. The manager is concerned about efficiency and feels that too much time is spent recording transactions. In addition, there sometimes is difficulty determining the amount owed to specific suppliers. The manager knows you are an accounting student and asks for your suggestions to improve the accounting function.

Write a memo to the manager describing how to increase efficiency and accuracy by using different accounting records.

ETHICS

ETHICS CASE

Judy Baresford, the store manager of Comfort Futons, noticed that the amount of time the two bookkeepers were spending on accounts receivable, accounts payable, and cash receipts was increasing due to the store's increase in sales. A friend of Judy's who is also a store manager suggested that she might want to have some special journals designed that would reduce the amount of work involved in the day-to-day bookkeeping at her store. Judy approached Jon Fortner and Sue Stavio, the bookkeepers, and asked them to come up with a proposal for special journals. During lunch, Jon told Sue he thought designing special journals would be a lot of work and it was not in his job description. Sue told him not to worry because she would just copy pages of special journals from her accounting textbook and they could submit these journals as their own design. Jon liked the idea and they agreed to meet the next night, scan the journals into Word, and submit them to Judy the following morning.

1. Do you think Sue's suggestion is unethical? Why or why not?
2. In using the generic special journals from Sue's accounting textbook, what possible problems can you foresee?
3. If you were Judy, how would you respond to Sue and Jon's "plan"?

MASTERY PROBLEM

✓ Total Accounts Receivable Cr.: $7,235

During the month of October 20--, The Pink Petal flower shop engaged in the following transactions:

Oct. 1 Sold merchandise on account to Elizabeth Shoemaker, $1,000, plus tax of $50. Sale No. 222.
2 Issued Check No. 190 to Jill Hand in payment of October 1 balance of $500, less 2% discount.
2 Purchased merchandise on account from Flower Wholesalers, $4,000. Invoice No. 500, dated October 2, terms 2/10, n/30.
4 Purchased merchandise on account from Seidl Enterprises, $700. Invoice No. 527, dated October 4, terms 2/15, n/30.
5 Issued Check No. 191 in payment of phone expense for the month of September, $150.
7 Sold merchandise for cash, $3,500, plus tax of $175.
9 Received payment from Leigh Summers in full settlement of account, $2,000.
11 Issued Check No. 192 to Flower Wholesalers in payment of October 1 balance of $1,500.
12 Sold merchandise on account to Leigh Summers, $2,000, plus tax of $100. Sale No. 223.
12 Received payment from Meg Johnson on account, $3,100.
13 Issued Check No. 193 to Seidl Enterprises in payment of October 4 purchase. Invoice No. 527, less 2% discount.
14 Meg Johnson returned merchandise for a credit, $300, plus sales tax of $15.
17 Returned merchandise to Vases Etc. for credit, $900.
24 Received payment from David's Decorating on account, $2,135.
27 Sold merchandise on account to David's Decorating, $3,000, plus tax of $150. Sale No. 224.
29 Issued Check No. 194 in payment of wages (Wages Expense) for the four-week period ending October 30, $900.

Selected account balances as of October 1 were as follows:

Account	Account No.	Debit	Credit
Cash	101	$18,225	
Accounts Receivable	122	9,619	
Accounts Payable	202		$5,120

The Pink Petal also had the following subsidiary ledger balances as of October 1:

Accounts Receivable:

Customer	Accounts Receivable Balance
David's Decorating 12 Jude Lane Hartford, CT 06117	$3,340

Elizabeth Shoemaker 52 Juniper Road Hartford, CT 06118	$ 279
Meg Johnson 700 Hobbes Dr. Avon, CT 06108	4,000
Leigh Summers 5200 Hamilton Ave. Hartford, CT 06111	2,000

Accounts Payable:

Vendor	Accounts Payable Balance
Vases Etc. 34 Harry Ave. East Hartford, CT 05234	$3,120
Jill Hand 1009 Drake Rd. Farmington, CT 06082	500
Flower Wholesalers 43 Lucky Lane Bristol, CT 06007	1,500
Seidl Enterprises 888 Anders Street Newington, CT 06789	—

REQUIRED

1. Record the transactions in a sales journal (page 7), cash receipts journal (page 10), purchases journal (page 6), cash payments journal (page 11), and general journal (page 5). Total, verify, and rule the columns where appropriate at the end of the month.
2. Post from the journals to the general ledger, accounts receivable ledger, and accounts payable ledger accounts. Use account numbers as shown in the chapter.

CHALLENGE PROBLEM

This problem challenges you to apply your cumulative accounting knowledge to move a step beyond the material in the chapter.

✓ **June 3: Cr. City Sales Tax Payable, $4.22**

Screpcap Co. had the following transactions during the first week of June:

June 1 Purchased merchandise on account from Acme Supply, $2,700, plus freight charges of $160.

1 Issued Check No. 219 to Denver Wholesalers for merchandise purchased on account, $720, less 1% discount.

1 Sold merchandise on account to F. Colby, $246, plus 5% state sales tax plus 2% city sales tax.

(*continued*)

June 2 Received cash on account from N. Dunlop, $315.

2 Made cash sale of $413 plus 5% state sales tax plus 2% city sales tax.

2 Purchased merchandise on account from Permon Co., $3,200, plus freight charges of $190.

3 Sold merchandise on account to F. Ayres, $211, plus 5% state sales tax plus 2% city sales tax.

3 Issued Check No. 220 to Ellis Co. for merchandise purchased on account, $847, less 1% discount.

3 Received cash on account from F. Graves, $463.

4 Issued Check No. 221 to Penguin Warehouse for merchandise purchased on account, $950, less 1% discount.

4 Sold merchandise on account to K. Stanga, $318, plus 5% state sales tax plus 2% city sales tax.

4 Purchased merchandise on account from Mason Milling, $1,630, plus freight charges of $90.

4 Received cash on account from O. Alston, $381.

5 Made cash sale of $319 plus 5% state sales tax plus 2% city sales tax.

5 Issued Check No. 222 to Acme Supply for merchandise purchased on account, $980, less 1% discount.

REQUIRED

1. Record the transactions in a general journal.
2. Assuming these are the types of transactions Screpcap Co. experiences on a regular basis, design the following special journals for Screpcap:
   (a) Sales journal
   (b) Cash receipts journal
   (c) Purchases journal
   (d) Cash payments journal

ANSWERS TO SELF-STUDY TEST QUESTIONS

True/False

1. T
2. F (general journal is still needed)
3. F (only credit sales)
4. T
5. T

Multiple Choice

1. a 2. a 3. c 4. c 5. a

Checkpoint Exercises

1.

SALES JOURNAL — PAGE 7

	DATE		SALE NO.	TO WHOM SOLD	POST. REF.	ACCOUNT RECEIVABLE DEBIT	SALES CREDIT	SALES TAX PAYABLE CREDIT	
1	June	1	214	Erin Lucas		882 00	840 00	42 00	1

2.

CASH RECEIPTS JOURNAL — PAGE

	DATE			ACCOUNT CREDITED	POST. REF.	GENERAL CREDIT	ACCOUNTS RECEIVABLE CREDIT	SALES CREDIT	SALES TAX PAYABLE CREDIT	CASH DEBIT	
1	June	7		Erin Lucas			882 00			882 00	1
2		30						2 150 00	107 50	2 257 50	2
3		30		Rent Revenue		750 00				750 00	3
4											4

3.

PURCHASES JOURNAL — PAGE

	DATE		INVOICE NO.	FROM WHOM PURCHASED	POST. REF.	PURCHASES DEBIT/ ACCOUNTS PAYABLE CREDIT	
1	Apr.	6	131	Clever		1 680 00	1
2							2

4.

CASH PAYMENTS JOURNAL — PAGE

	DATE		CK NO.	ACCOUNT DEBITED	POST. REF.	GENERAL DEBIT	ACCOUNTS PAYABLE DEBIT	PURCHASES DEBIT	PURCHASES DISCOUNTS CREDIT	CASH CREDIT	
1	Aug.	2	193	Rent Expense		2 200 00				2 200 00	1
2		6	194	Mason Hardware			1 700 00		34 00	1 666 00	2
3		10	195					2 730 00		2 730 00	3
4											4

Chapter 13 Accounting for Merchandise Inventory

LEARNING OBJECTIVES

Careful study of this chapter should enable you to:

LO1 **Explain the impact of merchandise inventory on the financial statements.**

LO2 **Describe the two principal systems of accounting for merchandise inventory—the periodic system and the perpetual system.**

LO3 **Compute the costs allocated to the ending inventory and cost of goods sold using different inventory methods.**

LO4 **Estimate the ending inventory and cost of goods sold by using the gross profit and retail inventory methods.**

"Be particular. Never sell anything you would not want yourself." That was Barney Kroger's motto in 1883 when he invested his life savings of $372 to open a grocery store at 66 Pearl Street in downtown Cincinnati. With nearly 2,800 stores in 35 states and annual sales of more than $115.3 billion, Kroger today ranks as one of the world's largest retailers. In addition, they operate over 700 convenience stores, 300 jewelry stores, just under 1,500 supermarket fuel centers and about 2,000 pharmacies.

As you walk through a grocery store, have you ever wondered what the store paid for each item? It would be nice to know which items are "good buys" and which are "overpriced." What happens when management pays different amounts for identical products on the shelf? In this chapter, you will learn how merchandising firms determine which items were sold and which remain. That is, how they determine the cost of the goods sold and the cost of the goods remaining on the shelves at the end of the year.

In Chapters 10 and 11, you learned how to account for the purchase and sale of merchandise. One of the major reasons for keeping accounting records is to determine the net income (or net loss) of a business. A major component of net income is the gross profit. In Chapter 11, you learned how to compute gross profit. An abbreviated form of this calculation is shown below.

Calculation of Gross Profit		
Net sales		$110
Cost of goods sold		
Merchandise inventory, Jan. 1	$ 20	
Purchases	80	
Cost of goods available for sale	$100	
Less merchandise inventory, Dec. 31	30	
Cost of goods sold		70
Gross profit		$ 40

The terms *goods* and *merchandise* mean the same thing and are used interchangeably.

For a merchandising business, the cost of goods available for sale ($100) during the accounting period must be divided between cost of goods sold ($70) and ending merchandise inventory ($30). In Chapter 11, the costs assigned to these accounts were provided. In this chapter, you will learn how to determine the dollar amounts assigned to cost of goods sold and ending merchandise inventory. In Chapter 14, we will illustrate the end-of-period adjustments required to bring the cost of goods sold and merchandise inventory accounts up to date to reflect their proper balances.

LO1

The Impact of Merchandise Inventory on Financial Statements

Explain the impact of merchandise inventory on the financial statements.

This year's ending inventory becomes next year's beginning inventory.

LEARNING KEY

If the ending inventory for 20-1 is understated, net income for 20-1 is understated and net income for 20-2 is overstated.

LEARNING KEY

If the ending inventory for 20-1 is overstated, net income for 20-1 is overstated and net income for 20-2 is understated.

A company's ending inventory must be reported accurately. An error in the reported inventory will cause errors on the income statement, statement of owner's equity, and balance sheet. In addition, since this year's ending inventory becomes next year's beginning inventory, financial statements for the following year will also contain errors.

Figure 13-1 illustrates the impact of an error in the *ending inventory*. The first pair of columns presents partial financial statements when the ending inventory is correct. For this illustration, sales, cost of goods sold, and operating expenses are assumed to be the same for 20-1 and 20-2. Thus, the same net income of $30 and beginning and ending merchandise inventories of $20 are reported for both years.

The second pair of columns in Figure 13-1 illustrates the effects of understating the ending inventory. Understating the ending inventory for 20-1 by $5 causes the cost of goods sold to be overstated by $5 and net income to be understated by $5. Since net income is reported on the statement of owner's equity, Erv Bultman's capital on December 31 is understated by $5. The understated capital also appears in the owner's equity section of the balance sheet. The understated ending inventory is reported in the current assets section of the balance sheet.

Even if the ending inventory for 20-2 is accurately reported, we still have a problem with the income statement. Since the ending inventory for 20-1 was understated, the beginning inventory for 20-2 is understated also ($15 instead of $20). This error causes cost of goods sold to be understated by $5 and net income to be overstated by $5.

At this point, we can see that this inventory error "washes out" over the two-year period. The understated net income for 20-1 is offset by overstated net income in 20-2. Thus, Bultman's capital account as of December 31, 20-2, is reported accurately on the statement of owner's equity and balance sheet at $160. Assuming no future inventory errors, the financial statements for 20-3 and thereafter will be correct.

FIGURE 13-1 Effect of Inventory Errors on Net Income

FINANCIAL STATEMENTS	ENDING INVENTORY FOR 20-1 IS CORRECT				ENDING INVENTORY FOR 20-1 IS UNDERSTATED				ENDING INVENTORY FOR 20-1 IS OVERSTATED			
	20-1		20-2		20-1		20-2		20-1		20-2	
Income Statement												
Sales		80		80		80		80		80		80
Cost of goods sold:												
Beginning merchandise inventory	20		**20**		20		**15**		20		**25**	
Add purchases (net)	40		40		40		40		40		40	
Cost of goods available for sale	60		60		60		55		60		65	
Less ending merchandise inventory	**(20)**		(20)		**(15)**		(20)		**(25)**		(20)	
Cost of goods sold		(40)		(40)		(45)		(35)		(35)		(45)
Gross profit		40		40		35		45		45		35
Operating expenses		(10)		(10)		(10)		(10)		(10)		(10)
Net income		30		30		25		35		35		25
Statement of Owner's Equity												
Erv Bultman, capital, January 1	100		130		100		125		100		135	
Net income	30		30		25		35		35		25	
Erv Bultman, capital, December 31		130		160		125		160		135		160
Balance Sheet (Partial)												
Current assets:												
Merchandise inventory		20		20		15		20		25		20
Owner's equity:												
Erv Bultman, capital		130		160		125		160		135		160

The third pair of columns in Figure 13-1 illustrates the effects of overstating the ending inventory in 20-1. This causes net income to be overstated in 20-1 and understated in 20-2. As previously discussed, these errors "wash out" by the end of 20-2. Thus, Bultman's capital account is correct in the 20-2 financial statements.

It is very important to have an accurate count and valuation for the ending inventory. Since errors in the ending inventory have a direct effect on net income for the period, managers may be tempted to manipulate this amount to achieve a desired result: to either increase net income to make the company look good, or decrease net income to reduce taxes or smooth earnings. For this reason, observing and verifying the ending inventory is an important aspect of an external auditor's job.

CHECKPOINT

Complete Checkpoint-1 on page 508 to test your basic understanding of LO1.

YOUR PERSPECTIVE

Material Recording Clerk – Part 1

Material recording clerks track the shipment, receipt, or movement of items within a business. They use computers, tablets, or other electronic devices to keep an accurate record of the organization's inventory and compile reports on the organization's inventory. Sensors and tags allow the devices to detect movement of the inventory items, which enables the clerks to update reports without having to count the items manually. Information material recording clerks collect helps managers to know the cost of goods sold to date and the inventory on hand. Managers use this information to make important operating decisions.

LO2

Types of Inventory Systems: Periodic and Perpetual

Describe the two principal systems of accounting for merchandise inventory—the periodic system and the perpetual system.

The two principal systems of accounting for merchandise inventory are the periodic and the perpetual systems. Entries made for inventory transactions under these systems are illustrated in Figure 13-2. Chapter 11 illustrated the periodic inventory system. As shown in Figure 13-2, under the **periodic inventory system**, no entries are made to the merchandise inventory or cost of goods sold account during the year. Thus, the balance in the merchandise inventory account is based on the physical count of inventory taken at the end of the last accounting period. The merchandise inventory and the cost of goods sold for the current period are not determined until the end of the current accounting period, when a physical inventory is taken. At that time, the following formula is applied to calculate cost of goods sold:

Beginning Inventory (based on last year's ending physical count)
\+ Net Purchases (account balance at end of this year)
= Cost of Goods Available for Sale
− Ending Inventory (based on this year's ending physical count)
= Cost of Goods Sold (for this year)

Adjusting entries are needed at the end of the fiscal year to update the merchandise inventory account and cost of goods sold. These entries are illustrated in Chapter 14.

As shown in Figure 13-2, under the **perpetual inventory system**, entries are made to the merchandise inventory and cost of goods sold accounts as transactions take place during the accounting period. The merchandise inventory account is debited for the cost of all goods purchased, including freight charges, and credited for the cost of all goods sold. In addition, this account is debited when customers return merchandise and is credited when suppliers grant returns, allowances, and discounts. Thus, the balance of the account represents the cost of goods on hand at all times. The cost of goods sold account is debited when merchandise is sold and credited when customers return merchandise. Thus, the balance of the account reflects the cost of goods sold at any point during the accounting period. No year-end adjusting entry is necessary as long as the physical inventory agrees with the amount reported in the merchandise inventory account. In Chapter 14, we will illustrate the proper adjustments if this is not true and an additional adjustment for inventory expected to be returned in the next accounting period.

LEARNING KEY
Under the periodic inventory system, the ending inventory and cost of goods sold are determined at the end of the accounting period, when a physical inventory is taken.

LEARNING KEY
Under the perpetual inventory system, cost of goods sold and the amount of merchandise inventory on hand are continually updated as merchandise is bought and sold.

CHECKPOINT
Complete Checkpoint-2 on page 508 to test your basic understanding of LO2.

FIGURE 13-2 Entries for Periodic and Perpetual Inventory Systems

TRANSACTION	PERIODIC SYSTEM			PERPETUAL SYSTEM		
1. Purchased merchandise on account, $100.	Purchases	100		Merchandise Inventory	100	
	Accounts Payable		100	Accounts Payable		100
2. Paid freight charge, $30.	Freight-In	30		Merchandise Inventory	30	
	Cash		30	Cash		30
3. Sold merchandise on account, $80. The cost of the merchandise was $50.	Accounts Receivable	80		Accounts Receivable	80	
	Sales		80	Sales		80
				Cost of Goods Sold	50	
				Merchandise Inventory		50
4. Merchandise costing $10 was returned to the supplier.	Accounts Payable	10		Accounts Payable	10	
	Purchases Ret. & Allow.		10	Merchandise Inventory		10
5. Customers returned merchandise sold for $20. The cost of the merchandise was $15.	Sales Ret. and Allow.	20		Sales Ret. and Allow.	20	
	Accounts Receivable		20	Accounts Receivable		20
				Merchandise Inventory	15	
				Cost of Goods Sold		15
6. Paid for merchandise costing $100. The supplier granted a 2% discount for prompt payment.	Accounts Payable	100		Accounts Payable	100	
	Purchases Discounts		2	Merchandise Inventory		2
	Cash		98	Cash		98

LO3 Assigning Costs to Inventory and Cost of Goods Sold

Compute the costs allocated to the ending inventory and cost of goods sold using different inventory methods.

To determine the cost of goods sold and ending inventory, it is important to understand:

1. the purpose of a physical inventory,
2. the specific calculations used under the periodic and perpetual systems, and
3. the role of the lower-of-cost-or-market rule.

Taking a Physical Inventory

Under the periodic system, the goods on hand at the end of the period are counted to allocate merchandise costs between sold and unsold goods. This process is called taking a **physical inventory**. A physical inventory is also important under the perpetual system. It verifies that the amount of merchandise actually held agrees with what is reported in the accounting records.

Even under the perpetual inventory system, there will be differences between the actual inventory on the floor and the amount on the books. These differences are the result of breakage, spoilage, and theft. Thieves rarely yell "Debit Loss Due to Theft and credit Merchandise Inventory" as they attempt to leave the store with merchandise under their coats.

Taking a physical inventory can be a sizable task. Frequently, it is done after regular business hours. Some companies even close for a few days to take inventory. The ideal time to count the goods is when the quantity on hand is at its lowest level. A fiscal year that starts and ends at the time the stock of goods is normally at its lowest level is known as a **natural business year**. Such a year is used by many businesses for accounting purposes.

Various procedures are followed in taking an inventory to be sure that no items are missed and that no items are included more than once. Frequently, persons taking inventory work in pairs: one counts the items and the other records the information. Usually, this information is entered on a special form called an **inventory sheet**, like the one illustrated in Figure 13-3. The inventory sheet has columns for recording the description of each item, the quantity on hand, the cost per unit, and the extension.

FIGURE 13-3 Inventory Sheet

INVENTORY Aug. 31 20-- Page 1

Sheet No. 1 | Called by L.M.M. | Entered by K.N.

Department A | Location Storeroom

Costed by C.M.H. | Extended by C.M.H. | Examined by C.J.C.

Description	Quantity	Unit	Unit Cost	Extensions	
Table Lamp	20	ea.	62.80	1,256.00	
Wall Rack	18	ea.	19.70	354.60	
Bookcase	7	ea.	88.10	616.70	
End Table	13	ea.	53.20	691.60	
Desk	6	ea.	158.30	949.80	
Total					6,465.10

A BROADER VIEW

All Kinds of Businesses Need Accounting Systems

MARC F. HENNING/ALAMY STOCK PHOTO

At any given time, a typical Wal-Mart discount store has more than 120,000 standard items in stock. Every item must be inventoried and replenished in a timely way to avoid having too much or too little stock. Wal-Mart associates have the aid of RFDI (radio frequency identification) tags to track pallets of products through their supply chain. These tags can be read by a handheld computer, linked by a radio-frequency network to in-store terminals. These high-tech devices provide up-to-the-minute information on inventory on hand, upcoming deliveries, and stock at Wal-Mart distribution centers.

Only goods that are the property of the company should be included in a physical inventory. Two special situations that require care to determine ownership are (1) goods held for sale on **consignment** and (2) goods **in transit**. Sometimes one business will try to sell merchandise for another business or individual on a commission basis. This is called selling goods on consignment. Goods held on consignment remain the property of the shipper (**consignor**). They should not be included in the inventory of the company holding the goods (**consignee**).

To determine whether goods in transit at year-end should be included in inventory, we must know the FOB (free on board) terms. If goods are shipped FOB shipping point, the buyer pays for shipping and the goods belong to the buyer as soon as they are shipped. If goods are shipped FOB destination, the seller pays for shipping and the goods belong to the seller until they are received by the buyer.

After calculating the quantities of goods owned at the end of the period, the proper cost must be assigned to the inventory. In addition to the purchase price, we include delivery costs (freight-in), insurance, and, occasionally, storage fees. Therefore, cost means all necessary and reasonable costs incurred to get the goods to the buyer's place of business.

If all purchases of the same item were made at the same price per unit, computing the cost of the ending inventory would be simple. We would multiply the number of units by the cost per unit. In a world of changing prices, however, identical items are purchased at different times and at different costs per unit. Of the goods available for sale, how do we decide which units were sold and which units remain on the shelf? As shown in Figure 13-4, this decision affects the income statement and balance sheet. The following four inventory methods have become generally accepted for answering this question:

1. Specific identification
2. First-in, first-out (FIFO)
3. Weighted-average
4. Last-in, first-out (LIFO)

These methods may be applied under the periodic or perpetual inventory systems.

Use of Inventory Methods

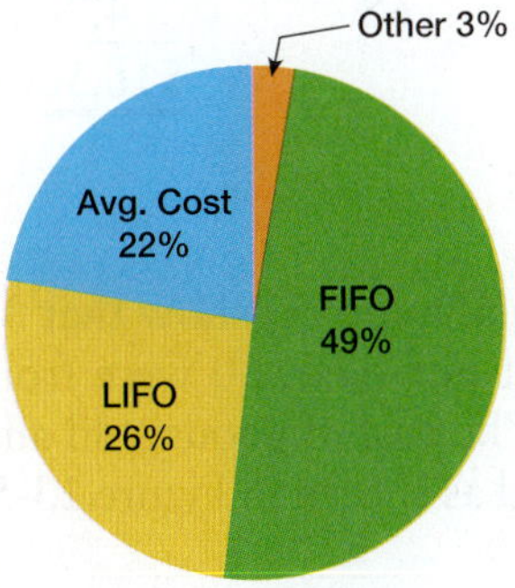

Pie chart is based on a recent survey of 500 companies listed with the SEC published in the AICPA's *Accounting Trends and Techniques*.

FIGURE 13-4 Allocation of Goods Available for Sale to Cost of Goods Sold and Ending Inventory

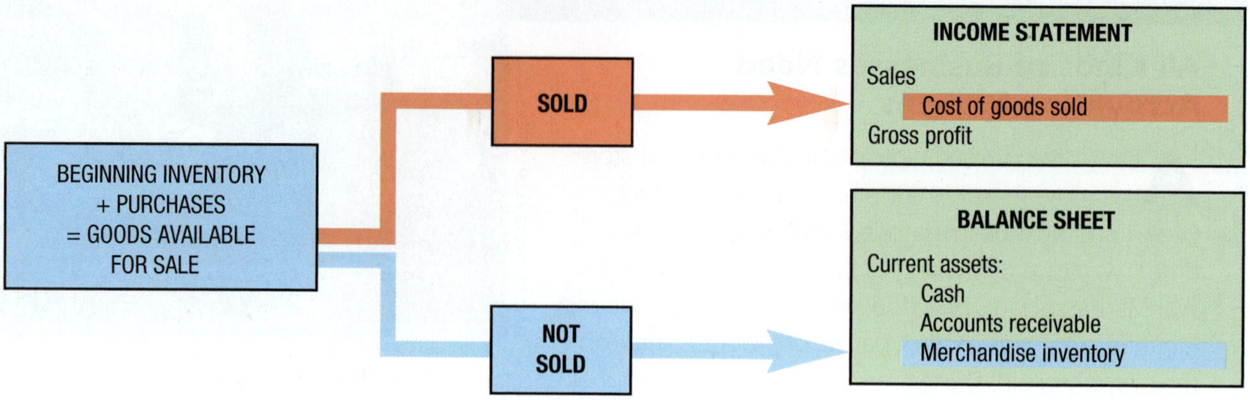

The Periodic Inventory System

LEARNING KEY The specific identification method requires that each inventory item have a distinguishing feature or marking to assure proper identification.

Specific Identification Method

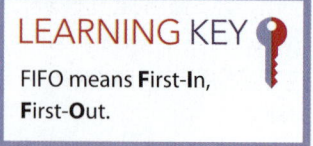

When each unit of inventory can be specifically identified, the **specific identification method** can be used. To use this method, inventory items must be physically different from each other, or they must have serial numbers. Examples include cars, motorcycles, furniture, appliances, and fine jewelry. When a unit is sold, its cost is determined from the supplier's invoice. Unless computerized, this method is practical only for businesses in which sales volume is relatively low and inventory unit value is relatively high. Otherwise, record keeping becomes expensive and time consuming.

To illustrate how specific identification costing works, assume the following data for an inventory of one specific model of color printers:

Color Printers (Model AP 4500)

	Units	Unit Price	Total Cost
On hand at start of period	40	$62	$ 2,480
Purchased during period:			
1st purchase	60	65	3,900
2nd purchase	80	67	5,360
3rd purchase	70	68	4,760
Number of units available for sale	250		$16,500
On hand at end of period	50		
Number of units sold during period	200		

Of the 200 units sold during the period, the printer serial numbers show that 30 were from the beginning inventory, 50 were from the first purchase, 60 were from the second purchase, and 60 were from the last purchase. The cost of goods sold and the cost of inventory at the end of the period are determined as shown in Figure 13-5.

LEARNING KEY FIFO means **F**irst-**I**n, **F**irst-**O**ut.

First-In, First-Out (FIFO) Method

Another widely used method of allocating merchandise cost is called the **first-in, first-out**, or **FIFO, method**. This costing method assumes that the first goods purchased were the first goods sold. Therefore, the latest goods purchased remain in inventory.

Whenever possible, a business will attempt to sell the older goods first. This is particularly true of businesses that sell perishable items or merchandise that may become obsolete. Grocery stores, fresh fruit stands, and computer software businesses

FIGURE 13-5 Specific Identification Inventory Method

BEGINNING INVENTORY AND PURCHASES	COST OF GOODS SOLD			COST OF ENDING INVENTORY		
	Units	Unit Price	Total	Units	Unit Price	Total
Beginning inventory	30	$62	$ 1,860	10	$62	$ 620
1st purchase	50	65	3,250	10	65	650
2nd purchase	60	67	4,020	20	67	1,340
3rd purchase	60	68	4,080	10	68	680
Total	200		$13,210	50		$ 3,290
Alternative calculation if given goods available for sale and cost of goods sold or ending inventory.	Cost of goods available for sale Less cost of ending inventory Cost of goods sold		$16,500 (3,290) $13,210	Cost of goods available for sale Less cost of goods sold Cost of ending inventory		$16,500 (13,210) $ 3,290

are good examples. These businesses must rotate their stock forward. They pull the oldest bread, milk, fruit, and vegetables to the front of the shelves and try to sell all copies of the current software before a new version arrives. FIFO costing is, therefore, widely used because it often follows the actual movement of goods. It assumes that the oldest units have been sold and the newest or freshest units are in the ending inventory.

Applying FIFO to the printer inventory data, the cost of goods sold and the cost of inventory at the end of the period are determined as shown in Figure 13-6.

FIGURE 13-6 FIFO Inventory Method

BEGINNING INVENTORY AND PURCHASES	COST OF GOODS SOLD			COST OF ENDING INVENTORY		
	Units	Unit Price	Total	Units	Unit Price	Total
Beginning inventory	40	$62	$ 2,480		$62	$ 0
1st purchase	60	65	3,900		65	0
2nd purchase	80	67	5,360		67	0
3rd purchase	20	68	1,360	50	68	3,400
Total	200		$13,100	50		$ 3,400
Alternative calculation if given goods available for sale and cost of goods sold or ending inventory.	Cost of goods available for sale Less cost of ending inventory Cost of goods sold		$16,500 (3,400) $13,100	Cost of goods available for sale Less cost of goods sold Cost of ending inventory		$16,500 (13,100) $ 3,400

Note that the 50 items on hand at the end of the period are considered to be those most recently purchased.

FIFO costing is widely used because businesses have used this method for a long time. Accountants are reluctant to change a long-followed method of accounting when such a change would affect the comparability of their income calculations over a period of years. **Consistency** based on comparability is an important accounting principle.

> **LEARNING KEY**
> The consistency principle of accounting suggests that a business should use the same accounting techniques from year to year.

Weighted-Average Method

Another method of allocating merchandise cost is called the **weighted-average method**, or **average cost method**. This costing method is based on the average cost of identical units.

Consider the printer inventory data again. The average cost of identical units is determined by dividing the total cost of units available for sale ($16,500) by the total number of units available for sale (250).

$$\frac{\$16{,}500\text{ (cost of units available for sale)}}{250\text{ (units available for sale)}} = \$66\text{ weighted-average cost per unit}$$

The cost of goods sold and the cost of the end-of-period inventory are calculated as follows:

Cost of goods sold	200 units @ $66	=	$13,200
Cost of ending inventory	50 units @ $66	=	3,300
Total	250 units		$16,500

There is a logical appeal to the weighted-average method of allocating cost between goods sold and goods on hand. In this example, one-fifth (50) of the total units available (250) were unsold. The weighted-average method assigns one-fifth ($3,300) of the total cost ($16,500) to these goods.

LEARNING KEY

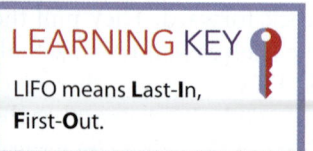

LIFO means **L**ast-**In**, **F**irst-**O**ut.

Last-In, First-Out (LIFO) Method

A fourth method of allocating merchandise cost is called the **last-in, first-out**, or **LIFO, method**. It assumes that the sales in the period were made from the most recently purchased goods. Therefore, the earliest goods purchased remain in inventory.

This physical flow is associated with businesses selling products that are not perishable or likely to become obsolete, and may be difficult to handle. Imagine a large barrel of nails at a lumberyard. Customers take nails from the top of the barrel. When the supply gets low, new nails are simply piled on top of the old ones. There is no need to rotate the nails from the bottom to the top of the barrel.

Applying LIFO to the printer inventory data, the cost of goods sold and the cost of inventory at the end of the period are determined as shown in Figure 13-7.

FIGURE 13-7 LIFO Inventory Method

BEGINNING INVENTORY AND PURCHASES	COST OF GOODS SOLD			COST OF ENDING INVENTORY		
	Units	Unit Price	Total	Units	Unit Price	Total
Beginning inventory		$62	$ 0	40	$62	$ 2,480
1st purchase	50	65	3,250	10	65	650
2nd purchase	80	67	5,360		67	0
3rd purchase	70	68	4,760	—	68	0
Total	200		$13,370	50		$ 3,130
Alternative calculation if given goods available for sale and cost of goods sold or ending inventory.	Cost of goods available for sale Less cost of ending inventory Cost of goods sold		$16,500 (3,130) $13,370	Cost of goods available for sale Less cost of goods sold Cost of ending inventory		$ 16,500 (13,370) $ 3,130

Note that the 50 units on hand at the end of the period are considered to be the 40 units in the beginning inventory plus 10 of the units from the first purchase.

The LIFO method has been justified on the grounds that the physical movement of goods in some businesses is actually last-in, first-out. This is rarely the case, but the method has become popular for other reasons. One persuasive argument for the use of the LIFO method is that it matches the most current cost of items purchased

Although LIFO is acceptable under U.S. GAAP and many U.S. companies use this method for financial reporting and tax purposes, it is not permitted under International Financial Reporting Standards (IFRS).

against the current sales revenue. When the most current costs of purchases are subtracted from sales revenue, the impact of changing prices on the resulting gross profit figure is minimized. In the opinion of many accountants, this is proper and desirable.

Another reason for the popularity of the LIFO method is its effect on income taxes. When prices are rising, net income calculated under the LIFO method is less than net income calculated under either the FIFO or the weighted-average method. Since the net income amount under LIFO is less, the related income tax will be less. The reverse would be true if prices were falling. However, periods of falling prices over the past two centuries have been few and brief.

Opponents of the LIFO method contend that its use causes old, out-of-date inventory costs to be shown on the balance sheet. The theoretical and practical merits of FIFO versus LIFO are the subject of much professional debate.

LEARNING KEY

The inventory method used does not have to match the physical flow of goods.

Physical Flows and Cost Flows

Of the four inventory costing methods described, only the specific identification costing method will necessarily reflect cost flows that match physical flows of goods. Each of the other three methods—FIFO, weighted-average, and LIFO—is based on assumed cost flows. The assumed cost flows *are not required to reflect the actual physical movement of goods* within the company. Any one of the three assumed cost flow methods could be used under any set of physical flow conditions. For example, a fresh fruit stand with an actual FIFO flow of inventory may use LIFO for accounting purposes. Similarly, a supplier of building materials that sells nails, lumber, and sand off the top of the pile may use FIFO even though the physical flow of goods is LIFO.

Comparison of Methods

To compare the results of the four inventory methods, let's assume that the 200 printers in our example were sold for $18,000. Figure 13-8 contrasts the ending inventory, cost of goods sold, and gross profit under each of the four methods.

FIGURE 13-8 Comparison of Inventory Methods

PARTIAL INCOME STATEMENT	SPECIFIC IDENTIFICATION		FIFO		WEIGHTED AVERAGE		LIFO	
Sales		$18,000		$18,000		$18,000		$18,000
Cost of goods sold:								
Beginning inventory	$ 2,480		$ 2,480		$ 2,480		$ 2,480	
Purchases	14,020		14,020		14,020		14,020	
Goods available for sale	$16,500		$16,500		$16,500		$16,500	
Less ending inventory	3,290		3,400		3,300		3,130	
Cost of goods sold		13,210		13,100		13,200		13,370
Gross profit		$ 4,790		$ 4,900		$ 4,800		$ 4,630

During periods of rising prices, we can observe the following: LIFO generally produces the highest cost of goods sold, lowest gross profit, and lowest ending inventory. Since the most recent units purchased are assumed to have been sold, the most recent costs are matched against revenues and this provides the best measure of gross profit and net income. After all, the units sold must be replaced at current prices. However, under LIFO, the first units purchased are assumed to remain in inventory. This means that units purchased many years ago may remain in the ending inventory. These dollar amounts are likely to have little meaning when measuring the firm's assets, performance, or financial health.

LIFO is sometimes referred to as FISH: First In, Still Here.

LEARNING KEY

In periods of rising prices, LIFO produces the lowest net income and FIFO produces the highest net income.

FIFO is sometimes referred to as LISH: Last In, Still Here.

FIFO generally produces the lowest cost of goods sold, highest gross profit, and highest ending inventory. Since the last units purchased are assumed to be in ending inventory, these most recent costs provide the best inventory measure on the balance sheet. However, under FIFO, the first units purchased are assumed to have been sold. This means that somewhat older prices are used to compute cost of goods sold and gross profit than under LIFO. Thus, these measures are somewhat less useful than those computed under LIFO.

The weighted-average inventory method produces measures between LIFO and FIFO. The specific identification method will produce measures based on the actual units sold.

The Internal Revenue Service requires the use of the same inventory method for tax and financial reporting purposes. Since LIFO generally produces the highest cost of goods sold, lowest gross profit, and lowest tax liability, many firms use the LIFO inventory method to minimize federal income taxes. The tax dollars saved are then available for other purposes.

As discussed earlier, keep the following in mind when selecting the inventory method to be used by a business:

1. The physical flow of the inventory does not need to match the flow assumed by the inventory method.
2. The consistency principle requires that the same accounting methods be followed from period to period. Although it is acceptable to make changes, it is not appropriate to switch back and forth from FIFO to LIFO based on the desire to maximize or minimize earnings for a given year.

The Perpetual Inventory System

Under the perpetual inventory system, a continuous record is maintained for the quantities and costs of goods on hand at all times. The general ledger account for Merchandise Inventory under such a system is somewhat like the account for Cash. It provides a day-by-day record of each addition (purchase) and subtraction (sale). The balance of the account at any time shows the cost of goods that should be on hand.

LEARNING KEY

A controlling account and subsidiary ledger are maintained for inventory in much the same way as for accounts receivable and accounts payable.

When perpetual inventory records are kept, the merchandise inventory account in the general ledger is usually a controlling account. A subsidiary ledger is maintained with an account for each type of merchandise. These accounts are often recorded on cards or, more likely, in computer files. As shown in Figure 13-9, the subsidiary accounts are designed to handle additions and subtractions and determine the new balance after each change. Goods sold usually are assigned cost on either a FIFO, moving-average, or LIFO basis. Procedures for applying the FIFO method in a perpetual inventory system are similar to those illustrated for a periodic system. The first units purchased are treated as the first units sold. The illustration in Figure 13-9 is based on the FIFO method. The specific techniques used to apply the moving-average and LIFO methods in a perpetual system are more complicated. They are illustrated in the chapter appendix.

Lower-of-Cost-or-Market Method of Inventory Valuation

Lower-of-cost-or-market may not be used with LIFO costing for tax purposes.

If the value of inventory declines while it is being held, the loss should be recognized in the period of the decline. The purpose of the **lower-of-cost-or-market method** is to recognize such losses on the income statement and to report the lower inventory valuation on the balance sheet.

FIGURE 13-9 Perpetual Inventory Record: FIFO Method

DATE	PURCHASES			COST OF GOODS SOLD				INVENTORY ON HAND				
	Units	Cost/ Unit	Total	Units	Cost/ Unit	CGS	Cumulative CGS	Layer	Units	Cost/ Unit	Layer Cost	Total
Jan. 1 (BI)								(1)	40	$62	$2,480	$2,480
Feb. 15				30	$62	$ 1,860	$ 1,860	(1)	10	$62	$ 620	$ 620
Mar. 1								(1)	10	$62	$ 620	
	60	$65	$3,900	→				(2)	60	65	3,900	$4,520
Apr. 1				10	$62	$ 620		(2)	30	$65	$1,950	
				30	$65	1,950	$ 4,430					$1,950
May 15								(2)	30	$65	$1,950	
	80	$67	$5,360	→				(3)	80	67	5,360	$7,310
June 30				30	$65	$ 1,950		(3)	20	$67	$1,340	
				60	67	4,020	$10,400					$1,340
Aug. 28								(3)	20	$67	$1,340	
	70	$68	$4,760	→				(4)	70	68	4,760	$6,100
Oct. 30				20	$67	$ 1,340		(4)	50	$68	$3,400	
				20	68	1,360	$13,100					$3,400
Cost of Goods Sold during 20--							$13,100					
BI: Beginning Inventory												

In applying the lower-of-cost-or-market method, "**cost**" means the dollar amount calculated using one of the four inventory costing methods. "**Market**" means the cost to replace the inventory. It is the price in the market in which goods are purchased by the business—not the price in the market in which they are normally sold by the business. The lower-of-cost-or-market method assumes that a decline in the purchase (replacement) price of inventory is accompanied by a decline in the selling price. In this sense, a decline in the purchase (replacement) price signals a decline in the value of the inventory.

To illustrate the lower-of-cost-or-market method, assume the following end-of-period inventory data for three items:

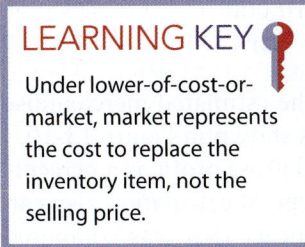

> **LEARNING KEY**
> Under lower-of-cost-or-market, market represents the cost to replace the inventory item, not the selling price.

Item	Recorded Purchase Cost	End-of-Period Market Value	Lower-of-Cost-or-Market
1	$ 8,000	$ 7,000	$ 7,000
2	9,000	10,000	9,000
3	7,000	6,500	6,500
	$24,000	$23,500	$22,500

The illustration shows two ways to calculate the lower-of-cost-or-market. First, the lower-of-cost-or-market method can be applied to the total inventory. This involves comparing the $24,000 total cost with the $23,500 *total end-of-period market value*. Under the second approach, the method is applied to each item in inventory. This involves comparing the $24,000 total cost with the

$22,500 lower-of-cost-or-market value determined by comparing cost with market value for *each item*. Either approach is acceptable, but the one chosen should be applied consistently across periods.

The difference between the cost and market value is considered a loss due to holding inventory. Normally, it is charged to an account such as **Loss on Write-Down of Inventory**. For example, based on application of the method to the total inventory in the previous illustration, a $500 loss ($24,000 – $23,500) is recognized as follows:

14			Loss on Write-Down of Inventory	500 00		14
15			Merchandise Inventory		500 00	15
16			To recognize loss in value of inventory held			16

CHECKPOINT

Complete Checkpoint-3 on page 508 to test your basic understanding of LO3.

The loss due to write-down of inventory should be reported on the income statement as an expense. Although not a preferred treatment, some businesses include it in cost of goods sold if the amounts are small.

LO4 Estimating Ending Inventory and Cost of Goods Sold

Estimate the ending inventory and cost of goods sold by using the gross profit and retail inventory methods.

Many businesses prepare monthly or quarterly financial statements. To do this, the business must estimate the inventory at the end of the month or quarter and the cost of goods sold for the period. This is not a problem for businesses using the perpetual inventory method. Although these amounts need to be verified by a physical inventory at the end of the year, the unverified amounts are generally reliable estimates and can be used for these "interim" statements.

Businesses using the periodic inventory method must use other methods to estimate the ending inventory and cost of goods sold. Two generally accepted methods are the gross profit method and the retail inventory method.

Gross Profit Method of Estimating Inventory

Under the **gross profit method**, a business's normal gross profit (net sales – cost of goods sold) is used to estimate the cost of goods sold and ending inventory. To illustrate the gross profit method, assume the following data with respect to Groomer Company:

Inventory, start of period	$ 80,000
Net purchases, first month	$ 70,000
Net sales, first month	$110,000
Normal gross profit as a percentage of sales	40%

The estimated cost of goods sold for the month and the estimated merchandise inventory at the end of the month would be determined as shown in Figure 13-10.

This calculation is appropriate only if the firm's normal gross profit as a percentage of net sales has been relatively stable over time. This type of calculation also can be used to test the reasonableness of the amount of inventory that was computed on the basis of a physical count. A large difference between the two amounts might indicate a mistake in the count, a mistake in the costing of the items, or a marked change in the gross profit rate. The gross profit procedure also can be used to estimate the cost of an inventory that was destroyed by fire or other casualty.

FIGURE 13-10 Steps for the Gross Profit Method

STEP 1	Compute the cost of goods available for sale.	Cost of goods available for sale:		
		Inventory, start of period	$ 80,000	
		Net purchases, first month	70,000	
		Cost of goods available for sale:		$150,000
STEP 2	Estimate cost of goods sold by deducting the normal gross profit from net sales.	Estimated cost of goods sold:		
		Net sales	$110,000	
		Normal gross profit ($110,000 × 40%)	44,000	
		Estimated cost of goods sold		66,000
STEP 3	Estimate the ending inventory by deducting cost of goods sold from the cost of goods available for sale.	Estimated end-of-month inventory		$ 84,000

Retail Method of Estimating Inventory

Many retail businesses, such as department and clothing stores, use a variation of the gross profit method to calculate cost of goods sold and ending inventory. The procedure used, called the **retail method** of inventory, requires keeping records of both the cost and selling (retail) prices of all goods purchased. This information can be used to estimate cost of goods sold and ending inventory, as shown in Figure 13-11.

FIGURE 13-11 Steps in the Retail Inventory Method

			COST	RETAIL
STEP 1	Compute the cost of goods available for sale at cost and retail.	Inventory, start of period	$ 60,000	$ 85,000
		Net purchases during period	126,000	163,000
		Goods available for sale	$186,000	$248,000
STEP 2	Compute the ending inventory at retail by subtracting sales at retail from goods available for sale at retail.	Less net sales for period		180,000
		Inventory, end of period, at retail		$ 68,000
STEP 3	Compute the cost-to-retail ratio by dividing the cost of goods available for sale by the retail value of the goods available for sale.	Ratio of cost-to-retail prices of goods available for sale ($186,000 ÷ $248,000)		75%
STEP 4	Estimate the cost of the ending inventory by multiplying the ending inventory at retail (step 2) by the cost-to-retail ratio.	Inventory, end of period, at estimated cost (75% of $68,000)	(51,000)	
STEP 5	Estimate cost of goods sold by a. Subtracting the estimated ending inventory from the cost of goods available for sale, or	Estimated cost of goods sold	$135,000	
	b. Multiplying sales at retail by the cost-to-retail ratio.	Sales of $180,000 × 75% = $135,000		

CHECKPOINT

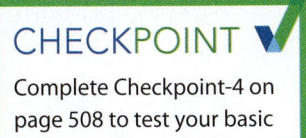

Complete Checkpoint-4 on page 508 to test your basic understanding of LO4.

LEARNING OBJECTIVES	Key Points to Remember
LO1 Explain the impact of merchandise inventory on the financial statements.	The cost of goods available for sale during the accounting period must be divided between the cost of goods sold and the ending merchandise inventory. Cost of goods sold is reported on the income statement and used to determine the gross profit for the period. The ending merchandise inventory is reported as a current asset on the balance sheet. Figure 13-12 illustrates the allocation of cost of goods available for sale into cost of goods sold and ending inventory.

FIGURE 13-12 Allocation of Goods Available for Sale to Cost of Goods Sold and Ending Inventory

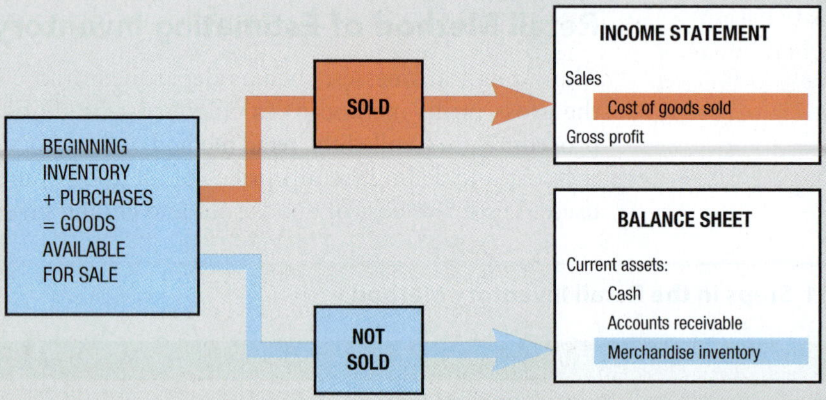

LO2 Describe the two principal systems of accounting for merchandise inventory—the periodic system and the perpetual system.

There are two systems of accounting for merchandise.

Periodic Inventory System

1. The purchases account is debited for the cost of all goods purchased.
2. The sales account is credited for the selling prices of all goods sold.
3. At the end of the accounting period, a physical inventory is taken, and the following formula is applied to calculate cost of goods sold:

Beginning Inventory (last year's ending physical count)
\+ Net Purchases (account balance at end of this year)
= Cost of Goods Available for Sale
− Ending Inventory (this year's ending physical count)
= Cost of Goods Sold (for this year)

Perpetual Inventory System

1. The merchandise inventory account is debited for all purchases.
2. The cost of goods sold account is debited, and the merchandise inventory account is credited for all sales.
3. Thus, the merchandise inventory account provides a running balance of the goods on hand.

LEARNING OBJECTIVES	Key Points to Remember
LO3 **Compute the costs allocated to the ending inventory and cost of goods sold using different inventory methods.**	One of the following four inventory methods is generally used to determine the costs assigned to the goods sold and ending inventory: • Specific identification • FIFO: first-in, first-out • Weighted-average • LIFO: last-in, first-out The actual physical flow of inventory does not have to match the method used. During periods of rising prices, LIFO produces the lowest net income, and FIFO produces the highest net income.
LO4 **Estimate the ending inventory and cost of goods sold by using the gross profit and retail inventory methods.**	Firms using the periodic inventory method often need to estimate their inventory. Two methods are used for this purpose. • **Gross Profit Method**—The firm's normal gross profit as a percentage of net sales is used to estimate cost of goods sold and ending inventory in three steps: 1. Compute the cost of goods available for sale. 2. Estimate cost of goods sold by deducting the normal gross profit (net sales × normal gross profit as percentage of net sales) from net sales. 3. Estimate the ending inventory by deducting cost of goods sold from the cost of goods available for sale. • **Retail Inventory Method**—The firm's ratio of cost-to-retail prices of goods available for sale is used to estimate ending inventory and cost of goods sold in five basic steps: 1. Compute the cost of goods available for sale at cost and retail. 2. Compute the ending inventory at retail by subtracting sales at retail from goods available for sale at retail. 3. Compute the cost-to-retail ratio by dividing the cost of goods available for sale by the retail value of the goods available for sale. 4. Estimate the cost of ending inventory by multiplying the ending inventory at retail (step 2) by the cost-to-retail ratio. 5. Estimate cost of goods sold by: a. subtracting the estimated ending inventory from the cost of goods available for sale, or b. multiplying sales at retail by the cost-to-retail ratio.

DEMONSTRATION PROBLEM

Fialka Company's beginning inventory and purchases during the fiscal year ended October 31, 20-2, were as follows:

		Units	Unit Price	Total Cost
November 1, 20-1	Beginning inventory	500	$25.00	$ 12,500
November 12, 20-1	1st purchase	600	26.25	15,750
December 28, 20-1	2nd purchase	400	27.50	11,000

(continued)

		Units	Unit Price	Total Cost
March 29, 20-2	3rd purchase	1,000	28.00	28,000
May 31, 20-2	4th purchase	750	28.50	21,375
July 29, 20-2	5th purchase	350	29.00	10,150
August 30, 20-2	6th purchase	675	30.00	20,250
October 21, 20-2	7th purchase	225	31.00	6,975
		4,500		$126,000

There are 1,600 units of inventory on hand on October 31, 20-2.

REQUIRED

1. Calculate the total amount to be assigned to cost of goods sold for the fiscal year and ending inventory on October 31, 20-2, under each of the following periodic inventory methods:
   (a) FIFO
   (b) LIFO
   (c) Weighted-average cost (round calculations to two decimal places)
2. Assume that the market price per unit (cost to replace) of Fialka's inventory on October 31, 20-2, was $29. Calculate the total amount to be assigned to the ending inventory on October 31, 20-2, under each of the following methods:
   (a) FIFO lower-of-cost-or-market
   (b) Weighted-average lower-of-cost-or-market
3. Prepare required entries to apply:
   (a) FIFO lower-of-cost-or-market
   (b) Weighted-average lower-of-cost-or-market
4. Assume that a fire destroyed Fialka's store and all inventory on October 31, just prior to taking a physical inventory. Thus, Fialka must estimate the ending inventory and cost of goods sold. During the fiscal year ended October 31, 20-2, net sales of $134,000 were made. The normal gross profit rate is 40%. Use the gross profit method to estimate the cost of goods sold for the fiscal year ended October 31, 20-2, and the inventory on October 31, 20-2.

SOLUTION 1a.

DATE		FIFO INVENTORY METHOD Cost of Goods Sold			COST OF ENDING INVENTORY		
20-1/-2		Units	Unit Price	Total	Units	Unit Price	Total
Nov. 1	Beginning inventory	500	$25.00	$ 12,500		$25.00	$ 0
Nov. 12	1st purchase	600	26.25	15,750		26.25	0
Dec. 28	2nd purchase	400	27.50	11,000		27.50	0
Mar. 29	3rd purchase	1,000	28.00	28,000		28.00	0
May 31	4th purchase	400	28.50	11,400	350	28.50	9,975
July 29	5th purchase		29.00	0	350	29.00	10,150
Aug. 30	6th purchase		30.00	0	675	30.00	20,250
Oct. 21	7th purchase		31.00	0	225	31.00	6,975
	Total	2,900		$ 78,650	1,600		$ 47,350
Alternative calculation if given goods available for sale and cost of goods sold or ending inventory.		Cost of goods available for sale Less cost of ending inventory Cost of goods sold		$126,000 (47,350) $ 78,650	Cost of goods available for sale Less cost of goods sold Cost of ending inventory		$126,000 (78,650) $ 47,350

SOLUTION 1b.

DATE		LIFO INVENTORY METHOD Cost of Goods Sold			COST OF ENDING INVENTORY		
20-1/-2		Units	Unit Price	Total	Units	Unit Price	Total
Nov. 1	Beginning inventory		$25.00	$ 0	500	$25.00	$ 12,500
Nov. 12	1st purchase		26.25	0	600	26.25	15,750
Dec. 28	2nd purchase		27.50	0	400	27.50	11,000
Mar. 29	3rd purchase	900	28.00	25,200	100	28.00	2,800
May 31	4th purchase	750	28.50	21,375		28.50	0
July 29	5th purchase	350	29.00	10,150		29.00	0
Aug. 30	6th purchase	675	30.00	20,250		30.00	0
Oct. 21	7th purchase	225	31.00	6,975		31.00	0
	Total	2,900		$ 83,950	1,600		$ 42,050
Alternative calculation if given goods available for sale and cost of goods sold or ending inventory.		Cost of goods available for sale Less cost of ending inventory Cost of goods sold		$126,000 (42,050) $ 83,950	Cost of goods available for sale Less cost of goods sold Cost of ending inventory		$126,000 (83,950) $ 42,050

SOLUTION 1c.	Weighted-average method:		
	Average cost per unit: $126,000 ÷ 4,500 units = $28		
	Inventory, October 31, 20-2:		
	1,600 units @ $28 =	$ 44,800	
	Cost of goods sold for 20-1/-2:		
	2,900 units @ $28 =	$ 81,200	
SOLUTION 2a.	FIFO lower-of-cost-or-market:		
	FIFO cost	$ 47,350	
	Market 1,600 units @ $29	46,400	
	Choose market	46,400	
SOLUTION 2b.	Weighted-average lower-of-cost-or-market:		
	Weighted-average cost	$ 44,800	
	Market 1,600 units @ $29	46,400	
	Choose weighted-average cost	44,800	
SOLUTION 3a.	Loss on Write-Down of Inventory	950	
	Merchandise Inventory		950
SOLUTION 3b.	No entry required.		
SOLUTION 4.	Estimated inventory on October 31, 20-2:		
	Inventory, November 1, 20-1	$ 12,500	
	Net purchases, November 1, 20-1 through October 31, 20-2	113,500	
	Cost of goods available for sale		$126,000
	Estimated cost of goods sold:		
	Net sales	$134,000	
	Normal gross profit ($134,000 × 40%)	53,600	
	Estimated cost of goods sold		80,400
	Estimated inventory on October 31, 20-2		$ 45,600

KEY TERMS

average cost method (495) See weighted-average method.

consignee (493) The company holding the merchandise of another business to be sold.

consignment (493) Goods that are held by one business for sale but that are owned by another business.

consignor (493) The owner of the merchandise that is held by another business.

consistency (495) The principle that states that a business should use the same accounting methods from period to period. This improves the comparability of the financial statements over time.

cost (499) In applying the lower-of-cost-or-market method, cost means the dollar amount calculated using one of the four inventory costing methods.

first-in, first-out (FIFO) method (494) A method of allocating merchandise cost which assumes that the first goods purchased were the first goods sold and, therefore, that the latest goods purchased remain in inventory.

gross profit method (500) A method of estimating inventory in which a business's normal gross profit percentage is used to estimate the cost of goods sold and ending inventory.

in transit (493) Goods that are in the process of being shipped between the seller and the buyer.

inventory sheet (492) A form used for recording inventory items. It has columns for recording the description of each item, the quantity on hand, the cost per unit, and the extension.

last-in, first-out (LIFO) method (496) A method of allocating merchandise cost which assumes that the sales in the period were made from the most recently purchased goods. Therefore, the earliest goods purchased remain in inventory.

Loss on Write-Down of Inventory (500) This account is debited when the market value (replacement cost) of the inventory is below cost when applying the lower-of-cost-or-market method of inventory valuation. It is reported on the income statement as an expense.

lower-of-cost-or-market method (498) An inventory valuation method under which inventory is valued at the lower-of-cost-or-market value (replacement cost).

market (499) In applying the lower-of-cost-or-market method, market means the cost to replace the inventory. It is the prevailing price in the market in which goods are purchased—not the prevailing price in the market in which they are normally sold.

natural business year (492) A fiscal year that starts and ends at the time the stock of goods is normally at its lowest level.

periodic inventory system (491) Under this system, the ending inventory and cost of goods sold are determined at the end of the accounting period, when a physical inventory is taken.

perpetual inventory system (491) Under this system, the merchandise inventory and cost of goods sold accounts are updated when merchandise is bought and sold.

physical inventory (492) A physical count of the goods on hand.

retail method (501) A variation of the gross profit method that is used by many retail businesses, such as department and clothing stores, to estimate the cost of goods sold and ending inventory.

specific identification method (494) A method of allocating merchandise cost in which each unit of inventory is specifically identified.

weighted-average method (495) A method of allocating merchandise cost based on the average cost of identical units. The average cost of identical units is determined by dividing the total cost of units available for sale by the total number of units available for sale.

SELF-STUDY TEST QUESTIONS

True/False

1. **LO1** An overstatement of ending inventory in the year 20-1 will cause net income to be overstated in the year 20-1.
2. **LO1** An understatement of ending inventory in the year 20-1 will cause net income to be overstated in the year 20-2, assuming no other errors.
3. **LO2** Under the perpetual system of accounting for inventory, the current merchandise inventory and the cost of goods sold are not determined until the end of the accounting period when a physical inventory is taken.
4. **LO3** A fiscal year that starts and ends at the time the stock of goods is normally at its lowest level is known as a natural business year.
5. **LO3** If goods are shipped FOB shipping point, the seller pays for the shipping costs.

Multiple Choice

1. **LO1** An understatement of ending inventory in the year 20-1 will cause the owner's equity account at the end of the year 20-2, assuming no other errors, to be
   (a) understated. (c) overstated.
   (b) correctly stated. (d) none of the above.
2. **LO3** Goods held on consignment remain the property of the
   (a) consignee. (c) buyer.
   (b) consignor. (d) seller.
3. **LO3** In times of rising prices, the inventory cost method that will yield the lowest net income is
   (a) FIFO. (c) LIFO.
   (b) weighted-average. (d) none of the above.

4. **LO3** In times of rising prices, the inventory cost method that will yield the highest cost of goods sold is
   (a) LIFO. (c) FIFO.
   (b) weighted-average. (d) none of the above.
5. **LO3** In the application of "lower-of-cost-or-market," market is the
   (a) lowest sales price. (c) replacement cost.
   (b) highest sales price. (d) average sales price.

CHECKPOINT

Checkpoint Exercises

1. **LO1** If the ending inventory is overstated by $10,000, indicate what, if anything, is incorrect about the following:

Cost of goods sold	__________
Gross profit	__________
Net income	__________
Ending owner's capital	__________

2. **LO2** Using the following information, compute the ending balance of the merchandise inventory account under the perpetual inventory system.

a.	Merchandise inventory, beginning balance	$ 20,000
b.	Purchased merchandise on account	200,000
c.	Sold merchandise on account	240,000
d.	Cost of merchandise sold in (c)	120,000
e.	Freight charges paid on inventory delivered to showroom	1,000
f.	Refund provided to customers for merchandise returned	800
g.	Cost of merchandise returned by customers	500

3. **LO3** Use the following information to compute cost of goods sold under the FIFO and LIFO inventory methods. The firm sold 200 units.

	Units	Unit Price	Total
Beginning inventory	50	$ 5	$ 250
1st purchase	100	8	800
2nd purchase	150	10	1,500

4. **LO4** Kulsrud Company would like to estimate the current inventory level. Using the gross profit method and the following information, estimate the current inventory level for Kulsrud Company.

Goods available for sale	$100,000
Net sales	150,000
Normal gross profit as a percent of sales	40%

The answers to the Self-Study Test Questions are at the end of the chapter (pages 518–519).

APPLYING YOUR KNOWLEDGE

CengageNowv2 provides "Show Me How" videos for selected exercises and problems. Additional resources, such as Excel templates for completing selected exercises and problems, are available for download from the companion website at Cengage.com.

REVIEW QUESTIONS

LO1 1. What financial statements are affected by an error in the ending inventory?

LO2 2. What is the main difference between the periodic system of accounting for inventory and the perpetual system of accounting for inventory?

LO3 3. Is a physical inventory necessary under the periodic system? Why or why not?

LO3 4. Is a physical inventory necessary under the perpetual system? Why or why not?

LO3 5. In a period of rising prices, which inventory method will result in:

(a) the highest cost of goods sold?
(b) the lowest cost of goods sold?
(c) the highest ending inventory?
(d) the lowest ending inventory?
(e) the highest gross profit?
(f) the lowest gross profit?

LO3 6. What two factors are taken into account by the weighted-average method of merchandise cost allocation?

LO3 7. Which inventory method always follows the actual physical flow of merchandise?

LO3 8. When lower-of-cost-or-market is assigned to the items that comprise the ending merchandise inventory, what does "cost" mean? What does "market" mean?

LO4 9. List the three steps followed under the gross profit method of estimating inventory.

LO4 10. List the five steps followed under the retail method of estimating inventory.

SERIES A EXERCISES

E 13-1A **(LO1)**

INVENTORY ERRORS Assume that in year 1, the ending merchandise inventory is overstated by $50,000. If this is the only error in years 1 and 2, indicate which items will be understated, overstated, or correctly stated for years 1 and 2.

	Year 1	Year 2
Ending merchandise inventory	______	______
Beginning merchandise inventory	______	______
Cost of goods sold	______	______
Gross profit	______	______
Net income	______	______
Ending owner's capital	______	______

E 13-2A (LO2)

JOURNAL ENTRIES—PERIODIC INVENTORY Paul Nasipak owns a business called Diamond Distributors. The following transactions took place during January of the current year. Journalize the transactions in a general journal using the periodic inventory method.

Jan.	5	Purchased merchandise on account from Prestigious Jewelers, $3,300.
	8	Paid freight charge on merchandise purchased, $300.
	12	Sold merchandise on account to Diamonds Unlimited, $4,500.
	15	Received a credit memo from Prestigious Jewelers for merchandise returned, $700.
	22	Issued a credit memo to Diamonds Unlimited for merchandise returned, $900.

E 13-3A (LO2)

JOURNAL ENTRIES—PERPETUAL INVENTORY Joan Ziemba owns a small variety store. The following transactions took place during March of the current year. Journalize the transactions in a general journal using the perpetual inventory method.

Mar.	3	Purchased merchandise on account from City Galleria, $2,900.
	7	Paid freight charge on merchandise purchased, $225.
	13	Sold merchandise on account to Amber Specialties, $3,400. The cost of the merchandise was $2,200.
	18	Received a credit memo from City Galleria for merchandise returned, $650.
	22	Issued a credit memo to Amber Specialties for merchandise returned, $600. The cost of the merchandise was $320.

E 13-4A (LO3)
✓ End. inv.: $52,000

ENDING INVENTORY COSTS Sandy Chen owns a small specialty store, named Chen's Chattel, whose year-end is June 30. Determine the total amount that should be included in Chen's Chattel's year-end inventory. A physical inventory taken on June 30 reveals the following:

Cost of merchandise on the showroom floor and in the warehouse	$43,600
Goods held on consignment (consignor is National Manufacturer)	6,400
Goods that Chen's Chattel, as the consignor, has for sale at the location of the Grand Avenue Vista	4,400
Sales invoices indicate that merchandise was shipped on June 29, terms FOB shipping point, delivered at buyer's receiving dock on July 3	3,800
Sales invoices indicate that merchandise was shipped on June 25, terms FOB destination, delivered at buyer's receiving dock on July 5	4,000

E 13-5A (LO3)
✓ 1. End. inv., FIFO: $300.00
✓ Weighted-avg.: $242.50

LOWER-OF-COST-OR-MARKET Stalberg Company's beginning inventory and purchases during the fiscal year ended December 31, 20--, were as follows:

		Units	Unit Price	Total Cost
Jan. 1	Beginning inventory	10	$20	$200
Mar. 5	1st purchase	10	22	220
Sept. 9	2nd purchase	10	25	250
Dec. 8	3rd purchase	10	30	300
		40		$970

There are 10 units of inventory on hand on December 31.

1. Calculate the total amount to be assigned to the ending inventory under each of the following periodic inventory methods:
   (a) FIFO
   (b) Weighted-average (round calculations to two decimal places)
2. Assume that the market price per unit (cost to replace) of Stalberg's inventory on December 31, 20--, was $26. Calculate the total amount to be assigned to the ending inventory on December 31 under each of the following methods:
   (a) FIFO lower-of-cost-or-market
   (b) Weighted-average lower-of-cost-or-market
3. What journal entry would be made under lower-of-cost-or-market for parts 2(a) and (b) above?

SERIES A PROBLEMS

P 13-6A (LO3)
✓ Cost of goods sold, FIFO: 61,500
✓ LIFO: 68,450
✓ Weighted-avg.: 64,530
✓ Specific I.D.: 63,200

SPECIFIC IDENTIFICATION, FIFO, LIFO, AND WEIGHTED-AVERAGE Swing Company's beginning inventory and purchases during the fiscal year ended September 30, 20-2, were as follows:

		Units	Unit Price	Total Cost
October 1, 20-1	Beginning inventory	400	$20.00	$ 8,000
October 18	1st purchase	500	20.50	10,250
November 25	2nd purchase	200	21.50	4,300
January 12, 20-2	3rd purchase	300	23.00	6,900
March 17	4th purchase	900	24.50	22,050
June 2	5th purchase	800	25.00	20,000
August 21	6th purchase	200	26.00	5,200
September 27	7th purchase	700	27.00	18,900
		4,000		$95,600

Use the following information for the specific identification method.

There are 1,300 units of inventory on hand on September 30, 20-2. Of these 1,300 units:

100 are from October 18, 20-1	1st purchase
200 are from January 12, 20-2	3rd purchase
100 are from March 17	4th purchase
400 are from June 2	5th purchase
200 are from August 21	6th purchase
300 are from September 27	7th purchase

(continued)

REQUIRED

Calculate the total amount to be assigned to cost of goods sold for the fiscal year ended September 30, 20-2, and ending inventory on September 30, 20-2, under each of the following periodic inventory methods:

1. FIFO
2. LIFO
3. Weighted-average (round calculations to two decimal places)
4. Specific identification

P 13-7A (LO3)
✓ 1. Ending inv., FIFO: $13,825
✓ LIFO: $8,000
✓ Weighted-avg.: $10,500

COST ALLOCATION AND LOWER-OF-COST-OR-MARKET Douglas Company's beginning inventory and purchases during the fiscal year ended December 31, 20--, were as follows:

		Units	Unit Price	Total Cost
January 1, 20--	Beginning inventory	1,100	$ 8.00	$ 8,800
March 5	1st purchase	900	9.00	8,100
April 16	2nd purchase	400	9.50	3,800
June 3	3rd purchase	700	10.25	7,175
August 18	4th purchase	600	11.00	6,600
September 13	5th purchase	800	12.00	9,600
November 14	6th purchase	400	14.00	5,600
December 3	7th purchase	500	14.05	7,025
		5,400		$56,700

There are 1,000 units of inventory on hand on December 31.

REQUIRED

1. Calculate the total amount to be assigned to the ending inventory and cost of goods sold on December 31 under each of the following methods:
   (a) FIFO
   (b) LIFO
   (c) Weighted-average (round calculations to two decimal places)
2. Assume that the market price per unit (cost to replace) of Douglas's inventory on December 31 was $13. Calculate the total amount to be assigned to the ending inventory on December 31 under each of the following methods:
   (a) FIFO lower-of-cost-or-market
   (b) Weighted-average lower-of-cost-or-market
3. Prepare required entries to apply:
   (a) FIFO lower-of-cost-or-market
   (b) Weighted-average lower-of-cost-or-market

P 13-8A (LO4)
✓ Est. ending inv.: $80,800

GROSS PROFIT METHOD A fire completely destroyed all the inventory of Glisan Lumber Yard on August 5, 20--. Fortunately, the accounting records were not destroyed in the fire. The following information is provided by Glisan Lumber Yard for the time period January 1 through August 5:

Beginning inventory, January 1, 20--	$100,000
Net purchases, January 1 through August 5	420,000
Net sales, January 1 through August 5	732,000
Normal gross profit as a percentage of sales	40%

REQUIRED

Estimate the amount of merchandise inventory destroyed in the fire on August 5 using the gross profit method.

P 13-9A (LO4)
✓ Est. ending inv.: $39,000

RETAIL INVENTORY METHOD The following information is provided by Raynette's Pharmacy for the last quarter of its fiscal year ending on March 31, 20--:

	Cost	Retail
Inventory, start of period, January 1, 20--	$ 32,000	$ 52,000
Net purchases during the period	176,000	268,000
Net sales for the period		260,000

REQUIRED

1. Estimate the ending inventory as of March 31 using the retail inventory method.
2. Estimate the cost of goods sold for the time period January 1 through March 31 using the retail inventory method.

SERIES B EXERCISES

E 13-1B (LO1)

INVENTORY ERRORS Assume that in year 1, the ending merchandise inventory is understated by $40,000. If this is the only error in years 1 and 2, indicate which items will be understated, overstated, or correctly stated for years 1 and 2.

	Year 1	Year 2
Ending merchandise inventory	______	______
Beginning merchandise inventory	______	______
Cost of goods sold	______	______
Gross profit	______	______
Net income	______	______
Ending owner's capital	______	______

E 13-2B (LO2)

JOURNAL ENTRIES—PERIODIC INVENTORY Amy Douglas owns a business called Douglas Distributors. The following transactions took place during January of the current year. Journalize the transactions in a general journal using the periodic inventory method.

Jan.	5	Purchased merchandise on account from Elite Warehouse, $4,100.
	8	Paid freight charge on merchandise purchased, $300.
	12	Sold merchandise on account to Memories Unlimited, $5,200.
	15	Received a credit memo from Elite Warehouse for merchandise returned, $700.
	22	Issued a credit memo to Memories Unlimited for merchandise returned, $400.

(*continued*)

E 13-3B (LO2)

JOURNAL ENTRIES—PERPETUAL INVENTORY Doreen Woods owns a small variety store. The following transactions took place during March of the current year. Journalize the transactions in a general journal using the perpetual inventory method.

Mar.	3	Purchased merchandise on account from Corner Galleria, $3,500.
	7	Paid freight charge on merchandise purchased, $200.
	13	Sold merchandise on account to Sonya Specialties, $4,250. The cost of the merchandise was $2,550.
	18	Received a credit memo from Corner Galleria for merchandise returned, $900.
	22	Issued a credit memo to Sonya Specialties for merchandise returned, $500. The cost of the merchandise was $300.

E 13-4B (LO3)
✓ Ending inv.: $53,700

ENDING INVENTORY COSTS Danny Steele owns a small specialty store, named Steele's Storeroom, whose year-end is June 30. Determine the total amount that should be included in Steele's Storeroom's year-end inventory. A physical inventory taken on June 30 reveals the following:

Cost of merchandise on the showroom floor and in the warehouse	$42,600
Goods held on consignment (consignor is Quality Manufacturer)	7,600
Goods that Steele's Storeroom, as the consignor, has for sale at the location of Midtown Galleria	8,300
Sales invoices indicate that merchandise was shipped on June 28, terms FOB shipping point, delivered at buyer's receiving dock on July 6	4,350
Sales invoices indicate that merchandise was shipped on June 26, terms FOB destination, delivered at buyer's receiving dock on July 1	2,800

E 13-5B (LO3)
✓ 1. Ending inv., FIFO: $800
✓ Weighted-avg.: $697.20

LOWER-OF-COST-OR-MARKET Bouie Company's beginning inventory and purchases during the fiscal year ended December 31, 20--, were as follows:

		Units	Unit Price	Total Cost
Jan. 1	Beginning inventory	20	$30	$ 600
Mar. 5	1st purchase	22	34	748
Sept. 9	2nd purchase	24	35	840
Dec. 8	3rd purchase	22	40	880
		88		$3,068

There are 20 units of inventory on hand on December 31.

1. Calculate the total amount to be assigned to the ending inventory under each of the following periodic inventory methods:
   (a) FIFO
   (b) Weighted-average (round calculations to two decimal places)
2. Assume that the market price per unit (cost to replace) of Bouie's inventory on December 31, 20--, was $39. Calculate the total amount to be assigned to the ending inventory on December 31 under each of the following methods:
   (a) FIFO lower-of-cost-or-market
   (b) Weighted-average lower-of-cost-or-market
3. What journal entry would be made under lower-of-cost-or-market for parts 2(a) and (b) above?

SERIES B PROBLEMS

P 13-6B (LO3)
✓ Ending inv., FIFO: $19,075
✓ LIFO: $14,350
✓ Weighted-avg.: $16,290
✓ Specific I.D.: $17,000

SPECIFIC IDENTIFICATION, FIFO, LIFO, AND WEIGHTED-AVERAGE Boyce Company's beginning inventory and purchases during the fiscal year ended September 30, 20-2, were as follows:

		Units	Unit Price	Total Cost
October 1, 20-1	Beginning inventory	400	$15.00	$ 6,000
October 18	1st purchase	300	16.50	4,950
November 25	2nd purchase	600	17.00	10,200
January 12, 20-2	3rd purchase	700	17.25	12,075
March 17	4th purchase	800	18.00	14,400
June 2	5th purchase	400	19.00	7,600
August 21	6th purchase	300	21.00	6,300
September 27	7th purchase	500	21.75	10,875
		4,000		$72,400

Use the following information for the specific identification method.

There are 900 units of inventory on hand on September 30, 20-2. Of these 900 units:

50 are from October 18, 20-1	1st purchase
300 are from January 12, 20-2	3rd purchase
100 are from March 17	4th purchase
200 are from June 2	5th purchase
50 are from August 21	6th purchase
200 are from September 27	7th purchase

REQUIRED

Calculate the total amount to be assigned to the cost of goods sold for the fiscal year ended September 30, 20-2, and ending inventory on September 30, 20-2, under each of the following periodic inventory methods:

1. FIFO
2. LIFO
3. Weighted-average (round calculations to two decimal places)
4. Specific identification

P 13-7B (LO3)
✓ 1. Cost of goods sold, FIFO: $55,950
✓ LIFO: $64,300
✓ Weighted avg.: $60,475

COST ALLOCATION AND LOWER-OF-COST-OR-MARKET Hall Company's beginning inventory and purchases during the fiscal year ended December 31, 20--, were as follows:

		Units	Unit Price	Total Cost
January 1	Beginning inventory	800	$11.00	$ 8,800
March 5	1st purchase	600	12.00	7,200
April 16	2nd purchase	500	12.50	6,250
June 3	3rd purchase	700	14.00	9,800
August 18	4th purchase	800	15.00	12,000
September 13	5th purchase	900	17.00	15,300
November 14	6th purchase	400	18.00	7,200
December 3	7th purchase	500	20.30	10,150
		5,200		$76,700

There are 1,100 units of inventory on hand on December 31.

(continued)

REQUIRED

1. Calculate the total amount to be assigned to the ending inventory and cost of goods sold on December 31 under each of the following methods:
   (a) FIFO
   (b) LIFO
   (c) Weighted-average (round calculations to two decimal places)
2. Assume that the market price per unit (cost to replace) of Hall's inventory on December 31 was $16. Calculate the total amount to be assigned to the ending inventory on December 31 under each of the following methods:
   (a) FIFO lower-of-cost-or-market
   (b) Weighted-average lower-of-cost-or-market
3. Prepare required entries to apply:
   (a) FIFO lower-of-cost-or-market
   (b) Weighted-average lower-of-cost-or-market

P 13-8B (LO4)
✓ Est. inv.: $82,500

GROSS PROFIT METHOD A flood completely destroyed all the inventory of Bayside Waterworks Company on July 1, 20--. Fortunately, the accounting records were not destroyed in the flood. The following information is provided by Bayside Waterworks for the time period January 1 through July 1, 20--:

Beginning inventory, January 1, 20--	$ 60,000
Net purchases, January 1 through July 1	380,000
Net sales, January 1 through July 1	650,000
Normal gross profit as a percentage of sales	45%

REQUIRED

Estimate the amount of merchandise inventory destroyed in the flood on July 1 using the gross profit method.

P 13-9B (LO4)
✓ Est. cost of goods sold: $193,750

RETAIL INVENTORY METHOD The following information is provided by Beverly's Basket Corner for the last quarter of its fiscal year ending on March 31, 20--:

	Cost	Retail
Inventory, start of period, January 1, 20--	$ 50,000	$ 80,000
Net purchases during the period	220,000	352,000
Net sales for the period		310,000

REQUIRED

1. Estimate the ending inventory as of March 31 using the retail inventory method.
2. Estimate the cost of goods sold for the time period January 1 through March 31 using the retail inventory method.

CHECK LIST
☐ Managing
☐ Planning
☐ Drafting
☐ Break
☐ Revising
☐ Managing

MANAGING YOUR WRITING

Most major grocery chains have optical scanning devices at the checkout stands and they certainly reduce the time required to check out. What benefits do they provide to the business? Next time you go to the grocery store, take a few minutes to chat with the manager. Ask the manager to describe the benefits of the scanning devices over the old machines that required the clerk to key in each purchase. Pay particular attention to the linkage between the scanning devices and the inventory systems. Be sure to ask whether the grocery store is on a periodic or perpetual system.

After your visit, write a memo to your instructor describing the benefits of the scanning devices and how they are linked with the inventory system.

ETHICS

ETHICS CASE

Electronics, Inc. is a high-volume, wholesale merchandising company. Most of its inventory turns over four or five times a year. The company has had 50 units of a particular brand of computers on hand for over a year. These computers have not sold and probably will not sell unless they are discounted 60 to 70%. The accountant is carrying them on the books at cost and intends to recognize the loss when they are sold. This way, she can avoid a significant write-down in inventory on the current year's financial statements.

1. Is the accountant correct in her treatment of the inventory? Why or why not?
2. If the computers cost $1,000 each and their market value is 40% of their cost, journalize the entry necessary for the write-down.
3. In groups of three or four, make a list of reasons why inventories of electronic equipment might have to be written down.

MASTERY PROBLEM

✓ **1. Cost of goods sold, FIFO: $64,250**
✓ **LIFO: $75,000**
✓ **Weighted-avg.: $69,600**
✓ **2. Ending inv., FIFO LCM: $21,600**
✓ **Weighted-avg. LCM: $17,400**
✓ **3. Estimated inv.: $22,000**

Hurst Company's beginning inventory and purchases during the fiscal year ended December 31, 20-2, were as follows:

		Units	Unit Price	Total Cost
January 1, 20-2	Beginning inventory	1,500	$10.00	$15,000
January 12	1st purchase	500	11.50	5,750
February 28	2nd purchase	600	14.50	8,700
June 29	3rd purchase	1,200	15.00	18,000
August 31	4th purchase	800	16.50	13,200
October 29	5th purchase	300	18.00	5,400
November 30	6th purchase	700	18.50	12,950
December 21	7th purchase	400	20.00	8,000
		6,000		$87,000

There are 1,200 units of inventory on hand on December 31, 20-2.

REQUIRED

1. Calculate the total amount to be assigned to the cost of goods sold for 20-2 and ending inventory on December 31 under each of the following periodic inventory methods:
   (a) FIFO
   (b) LIFO
   (c) Weighted-average (round calculations to two decimal places)

(continued)

2. Assume that the market price per unit (cost to replace) of Hurst's inventory on December 31 was $18. Calculate the total amount to be assigned to the ending inventory on December 31 under each of the following methods:
   (a) FIFO lower-of-cost-or-market
   (b) Weighted-average lower-of-cost-or-market
3. In addition to taking a physical inventory on December 31, Hurst decides to estimate the ending inventory and cost of goods sold. During the fiscal year ended December 31, 20-2, net sales of $100,000 were made at a normal gross profit rate of 35%. Use the gross profit method to estimate the cost of goods sold for the fiscal year ended December 31 and the inventory on December 31.

CHALLENGE PROBLEM

This problem challenges you to apply your cumulative accounting knowledge to move a step beyond the material in the chapter.

✓ FIFO CGS 20-2: $4,250
✓ LIFO CGS 20-2: $4,200

Bhushan Company has been using LIFO for inventory purposes because it would prefer to keep gross profits low for tax purposes. In its second year of operation (20-2), the controller pointed out that this strategy did not appear to work and suggested that FIFO cost of goods sold would have been higher than LIFO cost of goods sold for 20-2. Is this possible?

20-1	Units	Cost/Unit
Purchase 1	100	$1.00
Purchase 2	200	2.00
Purchase 3	300	3.00
Ending inventory	200	

20-2	Units	Cost/Unit
Beginning inventory	200	
Purchase 4	150	$4.00
Purchase 5	250	5.00
Purchase 6	350	6.00
Ending inventory	50	

REQUIRED

Using the information provided, compute the cost of goods sold for 20-1 and 20-2 comparing the LIFO and FIFO methods.

ANSWERS TO SELF-STUDY TEST QUESTIONS

True/False

1. T
2. T
3. F (this is true for the periodic method)
4. T
5. F (the buyer pays)

Multiple Choice

1. b 2. b 3. c 4. a 5. c

Checkpoint Exercises

1.

Cost of goods sold	Understated by $10,000
Gross profit	Overstated by $10,000
Net income	Overstated by $10,000
Ending owner's capital	Overstated by $10,000

2. Beginning inventory

Merchandise inventory, beginning balance	$ 20,000
Purchased merchandise on account	200,000
Cost of merchandise sold	(120,000)
Freight charges paid on inventory delivered to showroom	1,000
Cost of merchandise returned by customers	500
Ending inventory	$101,500

3. FIFO cost of goods sold:

50 units @ $ 5 =	$ 250
100 units @ $ 8 =	800
50 units @ $10 =	500
FIFO cost of goods sold	$1,550

LIFO cost of goods sold:

150 units @ $10 =	$1,500
50 units @ $ 8 =	400
LIFO cost of goods sold	$1,900

4. Estimated inventory using the gross profit method:

Cost of goods available for sale		$100,000
Net sales	$150,000	
Normal gross profit	60,000	
($150,000 × 40% = $60,000)		
Estimated cost of goods sold		90,000
Estimated inventory		$ 10,000

CHAPTER 13 APPENDIX

Perpetual Inventory Method: LIFO and Moving-Average Methods

LEARNING OBJECTIVES

Careful study of this appendix should enable you to:

LO1 **Compute the costs allocated to the ending inventory and cost of goods sold using the perpetual LIFO inventory method.**

LO2 **Compute the costs allocated to the ending inventory and cost of goods sold using the perpetual moving-average inventory method.**

In Chapter 13, you learned how to apply the LIFO and weighted-average inventory methods under the periodic inventory system. Recall that all calculations under the periodic system are done at the end of the accounting period. Under the perpetual system, costs are computed every time merchandise is purchased and sold. These costs are used to maintain a running record of the cost of goods sold to date and the balance of inventory on hand.

LO1 Perpetual LIFO

Compute the costs allocated to the ending inventory and cost of goods sold using the perpetual LIFO inventory method.

When using the **perpetual LIFO inventory method**, every time inventory is purchased a new layer is formed. When inventory is sold, we assume that the most recently purchased layer is sold first. As those units are used up, units are taken from the next most recently purchased layer. To illustrate, let's assume that Phaler's Fishing Supplies has the following beginning inventory, purchases, and sales of one type of bobber during the month of June. Note that the beginning inventory also has layers based on the prices paid in earlier periods.

Date	Beginning Inventory and Purchases		Sales
	Units	Cost/Unit	Units
June 1 (BI)	20	$0.80	
	160	1.00	
	20	1.20	
June 4	300	1.50	
June 20			400
June 30	100	1.80	

BI: Beginning Inventory

As shown in Figure 13A-1, the beginning inventory of 200 units forms Phaler's first three layers of inventory. The purchase on June 4 forms a fourth layer (300 units @ $1.50 = $450). At this point, Phaler has a total of 500 units at a total cost of $650. On June 20, Phaler sells 400 units. Under perpetual LIFO, we assume that the 300 units purchased on June 4 are sold first, followed by 20 that cost $1.20 each and 80 units that cost $1.00 each from the beginning inventory. The cost of goods sold on June 20 is $554. The cost of the inventory on hand is $96. At this point, Phaler has 100 units remaining from the beginning inventory.

FIGURE 13A-1 Perpetual LIFO Inventory System

DATE	PURCHASES			COST OF GOODS SOLD				INVENTORY ON HAND				
	Units	Cost/ Unit	Total	Units	Cost/ Unit	CGS	Cumulative CGS	Layer	Units	Cost/ Unit	Layer Cost	Total
June 1 (BI)								(1)	20	$0.80	$ 16.00	
								(2)	160	1.00	160.00	
								(3)	20	1.20	24.00	$200.00
June 4								(1)	20	$0.80	$ 16.00	
								(2)	160	1.00	160.00	
								(3)	20	1.20	24.00	
	300	$1.50	$450.00	→				(4)	300	1.50	450.00	$650.00
June. 20				300	$1.50	$450.00		(1)	20	$0.80	$ 16.00	
				20	1.20	24.00		(2)	80	1.00	80.00	$ 96.00
				80	1.00	80.00	$554.00					
June 30								(1)	20	$0.80	$ 16.00	
								(2)	80	1.00	80.00	
	100	$1.80	$180.00	→				(5)	100	1.80	180.00	$276.00
Cost of Goods Sold for June							$554.00					

BI: Beginning Inventory

On June 30, Phaler purchases 100 units at $1.80 each. This forms a new fifth layer (100 @ $1.80 = $180). This layer is added to the two layers remaining from the beginning inventory for a total of 200 units at a total cost of $276 of inventory on hand on June 30. Note that the third ($1.20 layer) and fourth ($1.50 layer) layers of inventory are gone. They will never reappear. If Phaler makes additional sales before buying more inventory, they will come from the fifth layer at $1.80 each, followed by units from the second ($1.00) and then the first ($0.80) layers.

LO2 Perpetual Moving-Average

Compute the costs allocated to the ending inventory and cost of goods sold using the perpetual moving-average inventory method.

When using the **perpetual moving-average inventory method**, every time inventory is purchased a new average cost per unit is calculated. When inventory is sold, the most recent average cost is used to measure cost of goods sold and the remaining inventory on hand. To illustrate, let's look again at the purchases and sales of Phaler's Fishing Supplies for the month of June.

Date	Beginning Inventory and Purchases		Sales
	Units	Cost/Unit	Units
June 1 (BI)	20	$0.80	
	160	1.00	
	20	1.20	
June 4	300	1.50	
June 20			400
June 30	100	1.80	

BI: Beginning Inventory

When using the moving average inventory method, it is best to do the calculations on a calculator or computer spreadsheet. Carry each calculation out to the number of decimal places allowed by the technology used. This will reduce rounding errors.

As shown in Figure 13A-2, a new average cost is calculated each time a purchase is made. The average cost of the June 1 beginning inventory is shown as $1 ($200 cost/200 units). To compute the average cost after buying more inventory on June 4, we take the cost of the inventory on hand ($200 + $450 = $650) and divide by the number of units on hand (200 + 300 = 500). Thus, the average cost of the inventory on hand on June 4 is $1.30 per unit. To compute the cost of the 400 units sold on June 20, multiply the 400 units by $1.30 to get the cost of goods sold of $520. The remaining cost of the inventory on hand is $130 ($650 − $520). The number of units on hand is reduced to 100 (500 − 400).

On June 30, 100 additional units are purchased. This increases the units on hand to 200 (100 + 100) and the cost of the inventory on hand to $310 ($130 + $180). Dividing the cost of the inventory on hand by the number of units on hand provides a new moving-average cost of $1.55 ($310 ÷ 200). If Phaler makes another sale before buying additional units, this average cost will be used to compute the cost of goods sold and determine the cost of the inventory remaining on hand. Note that selling inventory does not change the moving-average cost. This is because the units are being removed at the most recent average cost.

FIGURE 13A-2 Perpetual Moving-Average Inventory System

DATE	PURCHASES			COST OF GOODS SOLD				INVENTORY ON HAND AND AVG. COST/UNIT			
	Units	Cost/ Unit	Total	Units	Cost/ Unit	CGS	Cumulative CGS	Cost of Purchase or (Sale)	Cost of Inventory on Hand	Units on Hand	AVG. Cost/Unit
June 1 (BI)									$200.00	200.00	$1.0000
June 4	300.00	$1.50	$450.00					$ 450.00	650.00	500.00	1.3000
June 20				400.00	$1.30	$520.00	$520.00	(520.00)	130.00	100.00	1.3000
June 30	100.00	$1.80	$180.00					180.00	310.00	200.00	1.5500
Cost of Goods Sold during June							$520.00				
BI: Beginning Inventory											

LEARNING OBJECTIVES	Key Points to Remember
LO1 Compute the costs allocated to the ending inventory and cost of goods sold using the perpetual LIFO inventory method.	When using the perpetual LIFO inventory method, every time inventory is purchased, a new layer is formed. When inventory is sold, we assume the units were sold out of the most recent layer. As those units are used up, additional sales are taken from the next most recently purchased layer.
LO2 Compute the costs allocated to the ending inventory and cost of goods sold using the perpetual moving-average inventory method.	When using the perpetual moving-average inventory method, every time inventory is purchased, a new average cost per unit is calculated. When inventory is sold, the most recent average cost is used to measure cost of goods sold and the remaining inventory on hand.

KEY TERMS

perpetual LIFO inventory method (520) A method of allocating merchandise cost which assumes that every time inventory is purchased, a new layer is formed. When inventory is sold, units are sold out of the most recent layer. As those units are used up, additional sales are taken from the next most recently purchased layer.

perpetual moving-average inventory method (521) A method of allocating merchandise cost which assumes that every time inventory is purchased, a new average cost per unit is calculated. When inventory is sold, the most recent average cost is used to measure cost of goods sold and the remaining inventory on hand.

REVIEW QUESTION

LO1

1. Explain the primary difference between the periodic and perpetual inventory systems when calculating cost of goods sold and merchandise inventory.

SERIES A EXERCISE

E 13Apx-1A (LO1/2)
✓ CGS under perpetual LIFO: $3,345
✓ CGS under perpetual moving-average: $3,250

PERPETUAL: LIFO AND MOVING-AVERAGE The beginning inventory, purchases, and sales for Myrl Sign Company for the month of April follow.

Date	Beginning Inventory and Purchases		Sales
	Units	Cost/Unit	Units
April 1 (BI)	100	$4.30	
	100	4.50	
	200	4.60	
April 20	400	5.50	
April 30			650

BI: Beginning Inventory

REQUIRED

Calculate the total amount to be assigned to cost of goods sold for April and the ending inventory on April 30, under each of the following methods:

1. Perpetual LIFO inventory method.
2. Perpetual moving-average inventory method.

SERIES A PROBLEM

P 13Apx-2A (LO1/2)
✓ CGS under perpetual LIFO: $1,900
✓ CGS under perpetual moving-average: $1,856.64

PERPETUAL: LIFO AND MOVING-AVERAGE Kelley Company began business on January 1, 20-1. Purchases and sales during the month of January follow.

Date	Purchases		Sales
	Units	Cost/Unit	Units
Jan. 1	100	$1.00	
Jan. 4	400	1.10	
Jan. 5			300
Jan. 10	300	1.30	
Jan. 12			200
Jan. 15	200	1.35	
Jan. 18	500	1.60	
Jan. 22			800
Jan. 27			100
Jan. 31	300	1.80	

(continued)

REQUIRED

Calculate the total amount to be assigned to cost of goods sold for January and the ending inventory on January 31, under each of the following methods:

1. Perpetual LIFO inventory method.
2. Perpetual moving-average inventory method.

SERIES B EXERCISE

E 13Apx-1B (LO1/2)
✓ CGS under perpetual LIFO: $5,435
✓ CGS under perpetual moving-average: $5,395

PERPETUAL: LIFO AND MOVING-AVERAGE The beginning inventory, purchases, and sales for Harrington Equipment Company for the month of August follow.

Date	Beginning Inventory and Purchases		Sales
	Units	Cost/Unit	Units
Aug. 1 (BI)	100	$8.00	
	150	8.10	
	250	8.30	
Aug. 15	300	8.50	
Aug. 31			650

BI: Beginning Inventory

REQUIRED

Calculate the total amount to be assigned to cost of goods sold for August and the ending inventory on August 31, under each of the following methods:

1. Perpetual LIFO inventory method.
2. Perpetual moving-average inventory method.

SERIES B PROBLEM

P 13Apx-2B (LO1/2)
✓ CGS under perpetual LIFO: $3,720
✓ CGS under perpetual moving-average: $3,665.25

PERPETUAL: LIFO AND MOVING-AVERAGE Vozniak Company began business on January 1, 20-1. Purchases and sales during the month of January follow.

Date	Purchases		Sales
	Units	Cost/Unit	Units
Jan. 1	100	$2.00	
Jan. 5	500	2.30	
Jan. 7			300
Jan. 12	300	2.40	
Jan. 15			300
Jan. 17	200	2.50	
Jan. 19	500	2.70	
Jan. 24			800
Jan. 28			100
Jan. 31	200	2.90	

REQUIRED

Calculate the total amount to be assigned to cost of goods sold for January and the ending inventory on January 31, under each of the following methods:

1. Perpetual LIFO inventory method.
2. Perpetual moving-average inventory method.

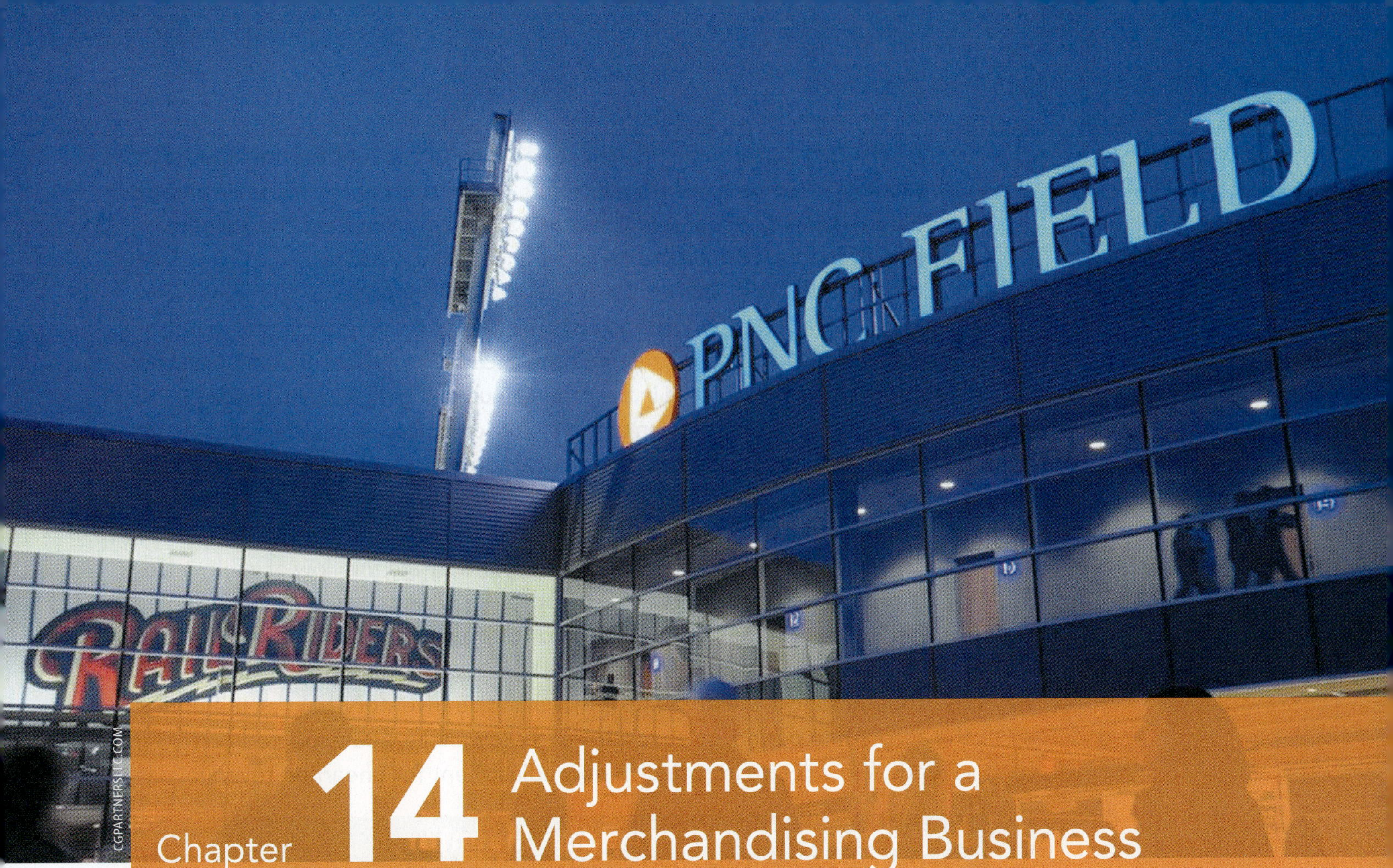

CGPARTNERSLLC.COM

Chapter 14 Adjustments for a Merchandising Business

The Scranton/Wilkes-Barre (PA) RailRiders are the Class AAA affiliate of the New York Yankees. They play in the North Division of the International League with the Buffalo Bisons, Lehigh Valley IronPigs, Pawtucket Red Sox, Rochester Red Wings, and Syracuse Chiefs. The franchise was founded in 1989 when the Maine Guides moved to Pennsylvania. From 1989 to 2006, the team was the Class AAA International League affiliate of the Philadelphia Phillies known as the Red Barons.

The RailRiders play at PNC Field, which was built on Montage Mountain between Scranton and Wilkes-Barre and has a capacity of 10,300, including luxury suites with indoor and outdoor seating. It opened in 1989 and was completely rebuilt for the 2013 season.

Often, we are expected to pay in advance for goods and services. This is true for season tickets for sporting events like the Scranton/Wilkes-Barre RailRiders, magazine subscriptions, or tickets for popular operas or rock concerts. In return, we expect to receive the goods or services. In this chapter, you will learn proper accounting for cash receipts received in advance, which are known as unearned revenues.

LEARNING OBJECTIVES

Careful study of this chapter should enable you to:

LO1 Prepare adjustments for merchandise inventory using the periodic inventory system.

LO2 Prepare an adjustment for unearned revenue.

LO3 Prepare adjustments for a merchandising business.

LO4 Journalize adjusting entries for a merchandising business.

LO5 Prepare adjustments for merchandise inventory using the perpetual inventory system.

In Chapters 10 through 13, we learned how to account for the day-to-day transactions of a merchandising business. In this chapter, we focus on end-of-period adjustments. Finally, in Chapter 15, we will complete the accounting cycle by preparing financial statements and closing entries.

In Chapter 5 we illustrated the preparation of a traditional 10-column work sheet that was used to prepare adjusting entries and the financial statements in Chapter 6. With the use of computers and accounting software, traditional work sheets are not as prevalent as in the past. The updating of accounts (posting) and the preparation of financial statements are often computer driven. Nevertheless, we believe spreadsheets that capture the adjusting process and organize the accounts for the preparation of the financial statements are beneficial when learning about the flow of accounting information. Thus, we will use an abbreviated, six column, work sheet (spreadsheet) in this chapter to help illustrate this flow of information.

This spreadsheet is used to prepare adjustments for supplies, prepaid insurance, wages earned but not paid, depreciation, and other necessary year-end adjustments. A merchandising business must also make adjustments to properly report the amount of merchandise inventory held at the end of the accounting period, sales returns and allowances, and expected customer refunds. We will also introduce a new adjustment for unearned revenue.

LO1

Adjustments for Merchandise Inventory: Periodic Inventory System

Prepare adjustments for merchandise inventory using the periodic inventory system.

As discussed in Chapter 13, under the periodic inventory system when merchandise inventory is purchased, the purchases account is debited and Cash or Accounts Payable is credited. When inventory is sold, Cash or Accounts Receivable is debited and Sales is credited. Figure 14-1 provides a review of these entries.

FIGURE 14-1 Review of Entries for Purchase and Sale of Merchandise

TRANSACTION	ENTRY		
Purchase of merchandise	Purchases	XXX	
	Accounts Payable or Cash		XXX
Sale of merchandise	Accounts Receivable or Cash	XXX	
	Sales		XXX

Note that the merchandise inventory account is not debited or credited in either of these entries. Since sales, purchases, sales returns, and purchases returns have taken place during the year and have not been entered in the merchandise inventory account, the beginning balance of the merchandise inventory account no longer provides an accurate measure of the inventory held at the end of the year. Thus, adjustments must be made. For other assets, like prepaid insurance, we would simply make an adjustment for the change in the asset account. *We do not follow this procedure for merchandise inventory.*

The adjustment for merchandise inventory is done in two steps.

Periodic Inventory Adjustments:
1. Take out the old.
2. Bring in the new.

1. Remove the beginning inventory from the merchandise inventory account by making the following entry:

Income Summary	old	
Merchandise Inventory		old

2. Enter the ending inventory in the merchandise inventory account by making the following entry:

Merchandise Inventory	new	
Income Summary		new

As discussed in Chapter 13, the quantity of inventory on hand at the end of the accounting period is determined by taking a physical count of the goods on hand. The cost of these goods is determined by using FIFO, LIFO, or another inventory method. Of course, this year's ending inventory becomes next year's beginning inventory.

To illustrate the adjustment for merchandise inventory, let's assume that Andy's Auto Parts had a beginning merchandise inventory of $23,000. During the year, the entries shown in Figure 14-1 were made as merchandise was purchased and sold. At the end of the accounting period, a physical inventory of the merchandise determined that merchandise costing $27,000 was still on hand.

To appreciate the reason for the different adjustment process, recall the discussion in Chapter 13 of how the beginning and ending inventories are used when computing cost of goods sold. As shown in the bottom portion of Figure 14-2, the beginning

FIGURE 14-2 Calculation of Cost of Goods Sold

	A	B	C	D	E	F	G
1	Andy's Auto Part's						
2	End-of-Period Spreadsheet						
3	For Year Ended December 31, 20--						
4	ACCOUNT TITLE	TRIAL BALANCE		ADJUSTMENTS		ADJUSTED TRIAL BALANCE	
5		DEBIT	CREDIT	DEBIT	CREDIT	DEBIT	CREDIT
6						Beginning Inventory	Ending Inventory
7							
8	Merchandise Inventory	23,000.00		27,000.00	23,000.00	27,000.00	
9	Estimated Returns Inventory	2,000.00		3,000.00	2,000.00	3,000.00	
10	Customer Refunds Payable		2,600.00		1,400.00		4,000.00
11	Income Summary			23,000.00	27,000.00	23,000.00	27,000.00
12				2,000.00	3,000.00	2,000.00	3,000.00
13	Sales		145,000.00				145,000.00
14	Sales Returns and Allowances	8,400.00		1,400.00		9,800.00	
15	Purchases	80,000.00				80,000.00	
16	Purchases Returns and Allowances		1,000.00				1,000.00
17	Purchases Discounts		500.00				500.00
18	Freight-In	700.00				700.00	
19							

Step 1: Remove Beginning Inventory	Income Summary	23,000.00	
	Merchandise Inventory		23,000.00
Step 2: Enter Ending Inventory	Merchandise Inventory	27,000.00	
	Income Summary		27,000.00
Step 3: Update for New Estimate of Customer Refunds Payable	Sales Returns and Allowances	1,400.00	
	Customer Refunds Payable		1,400.00
Step 4: Remove Beginning Estimated Returns Inventory	Income Summary	2,000.00	
	Estimated Returns Inventory		2,000.00
Step 5: Enter Ending Estimated Returns Inventory	Estimated Returns Inventory	3,000.00	
	Income Summary		3,000.00

Sales			$ 145,000.00	
Less: Sales Returns and Allowances			9,800.00	$ 135,200.00
Cost of goods sold:				
Merchandise Inventory, January 1		$ 23,000.00		
Estimated Returns Inventory, January 1		2,000.00	$ 25,000.00	
Purchases		$ 80,000.00		
Less: Purchases Returns and Allowances	$ 1,000.00			
Purchases Discounts	500.00	1,500.00		
Net Purchases		$ 78,500.00		
Add freight-in		700.00		
Cost of goods purchased			79,200.00	
Goods available for sale			$ 104,200.00	
Less: Merchandise inventory, December 31		$ 27,000.00		
Estimated Returns Inventory, December 31		3,000.00	30,000.00	
Cost of goods sold				74,200.00

YOUR PERSPECTIVE

Store Merchandiser

Some *material recording clerks*—such as shipping clerks, stock clerks, expediting clerks, and material and product inspecting clerks—have specialized responsibilities. *Shipping clerks* process shipment orders, compute freight costs, and prepare invoices. *Stock clerks* receive shipments and put products on shelves. *Expediting clerks* work with vendors to ensure that supplies are shipped on time. *Material and product inspecting clerks* both record the quantity of products that come into a store or warehouse and inspect for damaged goods. Because the perpetual inventory system is continuously updated, inventory must be verified to determine shrinkage due to theft, breakage, or spoilage. Material recording clerks take physical inventory counts on a regular basis enabling journal entries to be adjusted.

inventory is added to purchases to compute cost of goods available for sale. The ending inventory is subtracted from cost of goods available for sale to compute cost of goods sold.

Many firms use a spreadsheet to prepare financial statements. Thus, all of the information needed to compute cost of goods sold should be readily available in the Adjusted Trial Balance columns of the spreadsheet. To provide this information, we need an adjustment technique that results in the beginning inventory being extended into the Adjusted Trial Balance *Debit* column so it can be *added* to purchases. Further, we need the ending inventory extended into the Adjusted Trial Balance *Credit* column so it will be *subtracted* when computing cost of goods sold. As shown in Figure 14-2, this can be accomplished in two steps by using the income summary account.

LEARNING KEY

Both the debit and credit amounts on the income summary line are extended to the Adjusted Trial Balance columns.

STEP 1 The beginning inventory ($23,000) is removed by crediting Merchandise Inventory. Income Summary is debited because this amount is used in the calculation of cost of goods sold and net income.

STEP 2 The ending inventory ($27,000) is entered by debiting Merchandise Inventory. Income Summary is credited because this amount is also used in the calculation of cost of goods sold and net income.

Note that the debit *and* credit adjustments made to Income Summary are extended into the Adjusted Trial Balance columns. This is done because the individual amounts are needed for the calculation of cost of goods sold on the income statement (beginning inventory + purchases − ending inventory = cost of goods sold).

STEPS 3–5 Steps 3–5 in the inventory adjustment process address issues related to customers returning inventory. Recall from Chapters 10 and 13, that in a merchandising business, it is likely that customers will return some of the merchandise that was purchased. The entry made when merchandise is returned during the current period is as follows:

Merchandise Returns Throughout the Year →

Sales Returns and Allowances	xxx	
Accounts Receivable (or Cash)		xxx

Under the periodic method, the returned inventory is not debited to the merchandise inventory account. Instead, it will be captured in the physical count of the ending inventory, if not sold by the end of the year.

It is also important to recognize that some of the inventory sold this year is likely to be returned next year. To properly measure assets, liabilities, and related revenues and expenses, we must make adjusting entries at the end of the period. Let's assume Andy's estimates that customers will be granted $4,000 in refunds of this year's sales next year and the merchandise expected to be returned will have a cost of $3,000. Thus, as discussed in Chapter 10, **Customer Refunds Payable** must be adjusted to equal the estimated $4,000 liability. As shown in Figures 14-2 and 14-3, the Trial Balance reflects a balance of $2,600 before adjustment. Therefore, we must make the following adjusting entry.

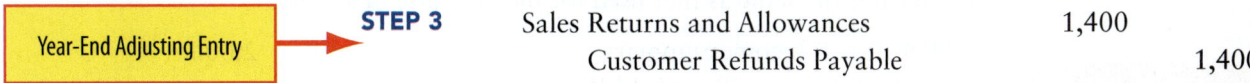

Year-End Adjusting Entry

STEP 3	Sales Returns and Allowances	1,400	
	Customer Refunds Payable		1,400

As shown in Figure 14-3, Sales Returns and Allowances is a contra-revenue account subtracted from the Sales account on the income statement when computing net sales. Customer Refunds Payable is a current liability account. It will be adjusted at the end of each accounting period to properly reflect the amount of refunds expected to be paid next period as a result of sales in the current period.

FIGURE 14-3 Adjustments for Sales Returns and Allowances

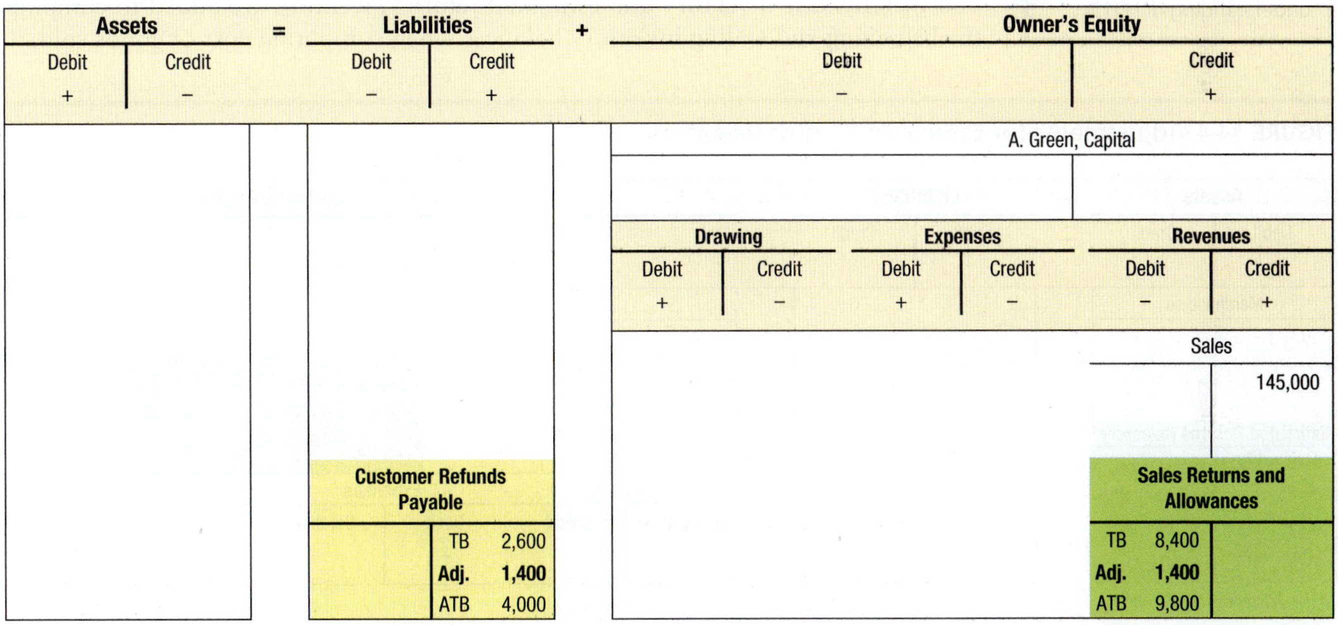

ATB: Adjusted Trial Balance

When customers return merchandise purchased this year, or last year, we assume Sales Returns and Allowances is debited and Accounts Receivable (or Cash) is credited. As with Merchandise Inventory under the periodic method, no entries are made to Customer Refunds Payable during the year. At the end of each year, Customer Refunds Payable is adjusted to reflect estimated refunds to be paid next year as a result of this year's sales. This adjustment may increase or decrease the balance in Customer Refunds Payable and, as a result, Sales Returns and Allowances.

In **STEPS 4 AND 5**, we adjust for the estimated inventory to be returned next year. **Estimated Returns Inventory** is an asset account that represents the estimated cost of merchandise inventory sold this year, but expected to be returned next year. This account is reported as a current asset on the Balance Sheet and is often combined with Merchandise Inventory. Since it is a new account, we will report it separately here and in Chapter 15. Keep in mind, however, both accounts are used to measure the beginning and ending inventory on the balance sheet and when calculating cost of goods sold on the income statement. As with the Merchandise Inventory account, under the periodic inventory system, no entries will be made to this account during the year. This account will be adjusted at the end of each period to properly reflect the cost of merchandise sold this period, but expected to be returned next period.

As shown in Figures 14-2 and 14-4, Estimated Returns Inventory has a trial balance of $2,000 before adjustment. The adjustment to properly reflect the required $3,000 balance, the cost of the expected returns, will be done in two steps. This approach is the same as that used for merchandise inventory.

Year End Adjusting Entries

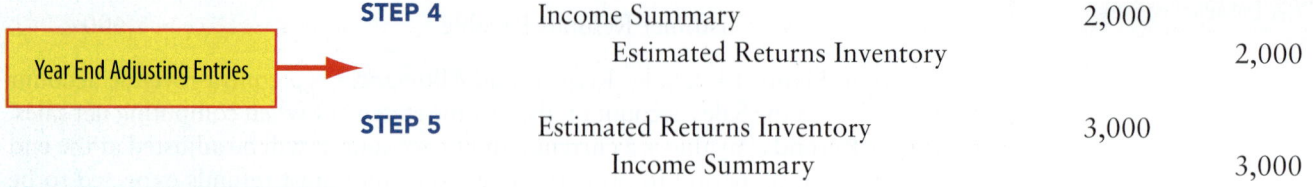

STEP 4	Income Summary	2,000	
	Estimated Returns Inventory		2,000
STEP 5	Estimated Returns Inventory	3,000	
	Income Summary		3,000

CHECKPOINT

Complete Checkpoint-1 on page 546 to test your basic understanding of LO1.

Note in Figure 14-2, the adjustment and extensions of the Estimated Returns Inventory account are treated the same as Merchandise Inventory. The adjustments are done in two steps and the debits and credits to Income Summary are extended to the Adjusted Trial Balance columns. Note also in the lower portion of Figure 14-2 that merchandise inventory and estimated returns inventory are added to compute the beginning and ending inventory balances when computing cost of goods sold.

FIGURE 14-4 Adjustments for Estimated Returns Inventory

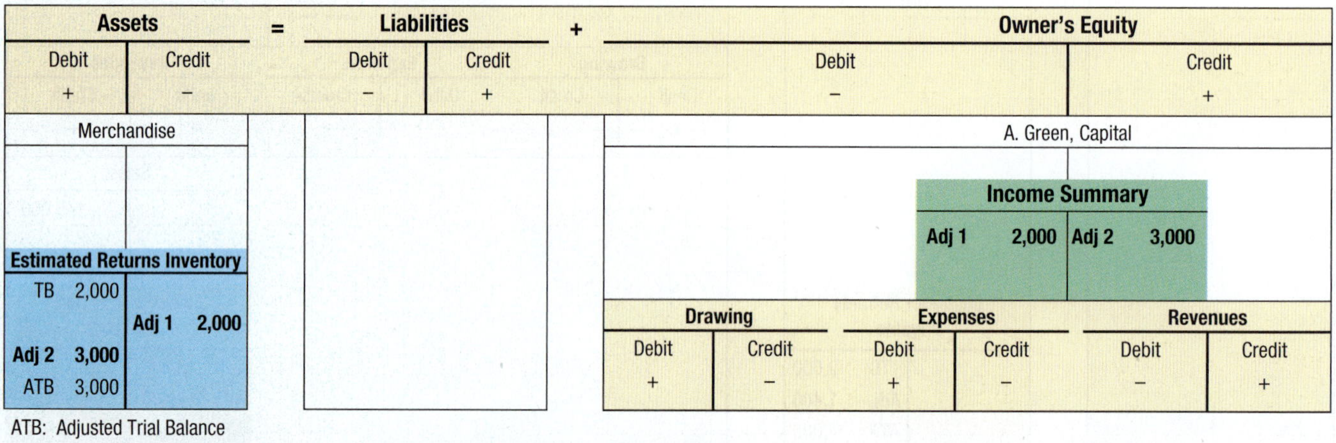

LO2 Adjustment for Unearned Revenue

Prepare an adjustment for unearned revenue.

Unearned revenue and customer refunds payable are similar liabilities. In both cases, the customer has paid for a product or service with the promise of a refund if not satisfied.

Some businesses require payment before delivering a product or performing a service. Examples include insurance companies, magazine publishers, apartment complexes, college food services, and professional sports and theater companies that sell season tickets. The cash received in advance is called **unearned revenue**. Since the cash has been received in advance, the company owes the customers the product or service, or must refund their money. Thus, unearned revenue is reported as a *liability* on the balance sheet.

To illustrate, let's assume that Brown County Playhouse sells season tickets for five plays produced throughout the year. Tickets sell for $10 for each play ($50 for a season ticket) and a maximum of 1,000 seats can be sold for each play. For simplicity, let's assume that all shows sell out during the first week that season tickets are

> **LEARNING KEY**
> Remember, under the accrual basis of accounting, revenue is recorded when *earned* (when the performance obligation has been satisfied) regardless of when cash is received.

available for sale. As shown below and in Figure 14-5, the sale of the tickets would be recorded as follows:

8		(1) Cash		50 0 0 0 00		8
9		Unearned Ticket Revenue			50 0 0 0 00	9
10		Season ticket sales				10
11		($10 × 1,000 seats × 5 shows)				11

To prepare financial statements following production of the third show, an adjusting entry is needed to recognize that $30,000 ($10 × 1,000 seats × 3 shows) in ticket revenue has been earned. To do this, the following adjusting entry is made:

13		Adjusting Entries				13
14		Unearned Ticket Revenue		30 0 0 0 00		14
15		Ticket Revenue			30 0 0 0 00	15

The remaining balance of $20,000 in Unearned Ticket Revenue is reported as a current liability on the balance sheet.

FIGURE 14-5 Entries for Unearned Revenue

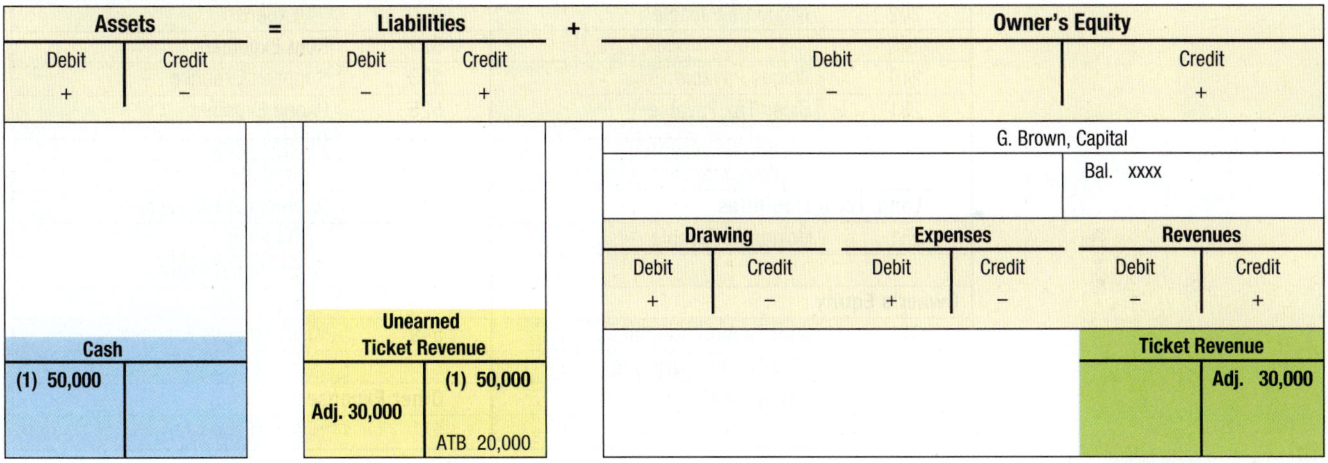

Expanded Chart of Accounts

Let's take a look at where the new accounts for a merchandising business fit into a chart of accounts. Recall that the chart of accounts follows the form of the accounting equation (assets = liabilities + owner's equity + revenues − expenses). A chart of accounts for Sunflower Cycle is provided in Figure 14-6. Note the classification of the new accounts introduced in Chapters 10 and 11 for a merchandising firm.

Merchandise Inventory and Estimated Returns Inventory are listed as current assets. Since Sunflower Cycle sells subscriptions to a computer magazine that it produces, Unearned Subscriptions Revenue is listed as a current liability, and Subscriptions Revenue is listed as a revenue. Customer Refunds Payable is also listed as a current liability. Sales Returns and Allowances and Sales Discounts are contra-revenue accounts. Recall, however, that Sunflower Cycle does not offer sales discounts.

FIGURE 14-6 Chart of Accounts for Sunflower Cycle

SUNFLOWER CYCLE CHART OF ACCOUNTS			
Assets		**Revenue**	
Current Assets		401	Sales
101	Cash	401.1	Sales Returns and Allowances
122	Accounts Receivable	**Other Revenue**	
131	Merchandise Inventory	411	Interest Revenue
135	Estimated Returns Inventory	412	Rent Revenue
141	Supplies	413	Subscriptions Revenue
145	Prepaid Insurance	**Expenses**	
Property, Plant, and Equipment		**Cost of Goods Sold**	
161	Land	501	Purchases
171	Building	501.1	Purchases Returns and Allowances
171.1	Accumulated Depreciation—Building	501.2	Purchases Discounts
181	Equipment	502	Freight-In
181.1	Accumulated Depreciation—Equipment	**Operating Expenses**	
Liabilities		511	Wages Expense
Current Liabilities		512	Advertising Expense
201	Notes Payable	513	Bank Credit Card Expense
202	Accounts Payable	521	Rent Expense
203	Customer Refunds Payable	523	Supplies Expense
219	Wages Payable	525	Phone Expense
231	Sales Tax Payable	533	Utilities Expense
241	Unearned Subscriptions Revenue	535	Insurance Expense
Long-Term Liabilities		540	Depreciation Expense—Building
251	Mortgage Payable	541	Depreciation Expense—Equipment
Owner's Equity		549	Miscellaneous Expense
311	Sam Tangari, Capital		
312	Sam Tangari, Drawing	**Other Expenses**	
313	Income Summary	551	Interest Expense

Purchases, Purchases Returns and Allowances, Purchases Discounts, and Freight-In are used to compute cost of goods sold. Thus, they are listed under this heading. Purchases Returns and Allowances and Purchases Discounts are often called contra-cost accounts or contra-purchases accounts.

Interest Expense is classified as "Other Expenses" instead of being listed under Operating Expenses. This is because it represents the expense of obtaining money to do business, rather than an expense directly associated with operating the business.

CHECKPOINT

Complete Checkpoint-2 on page 546 to test your basic understanding of LO2.

A BROADER VIEW

The Importance of Inventory

BALCERZAK/SHUTTERSTOCK.COM

Note the important role of the ending inventory in the calculation of cost of goods sold in Figure 14-2. If the ending inventory is overstated for any reason, net income will also be overstated. Given this important relationship, auditors observe and verify the accuracy of the physical inventory. However, unethical managers, desperate to improve profits, have on occasion found ways to mislead auditors.

In one case, managers overstated inventory counts for items that the auditors had not physically verified. In another case, auditors found a barrel whose contents had been valued by management at thousands of dollars. It actually contained floor sweepings. Finally, there was a case where management called the auditor, the day after the inventory audit, to report that additional inventory had arrived and should be included in the inventory count. The auditor never verified that the inventory was real. It turned out to be a scam that helped the company double its reported profits for the year. These unfortunate events highlight the reason auditors must exercise great care when conducting an inventory audit.

LO3

Adjustments for a Merchandising Business

Prepare adjustments for a merchandising business.

Let's first look at the preparation of adjustments for a merchandising business using T accounts. Figure 14-7 provides year-end adjustment information for Sunflower Cycle. Figure 14-8 shows adjusting entries based on this information. The unadjusted balances for these accounts were taken from Sunflower Cycle's trial balance.

FIGURE 14-7 Year-End Adjustment Data for Sunflower Cycle

YEAR-END ADJUSTMENT DATA FOR SUNFLOWER CYCLE	
(a, b)	A physical count showed that merchandise inventory costing $45,600 is on hand as of December 31.
(c, d, e)	It is estimated that $3,000 in this year's sales will be returned by customers next year. The cost of the merchandise expected to be returned is estimated to be $2,100.
(f)	Supplies remaining at the end of the year, $800.
(g)	Unexpired insurance on December 31, $400.
(h)	Depreciation expense on the building for the year, $4,000.
(i)	Depreciation expense on the equipment for the year, $3,000.
(j)	Wages earned but not paid as of December 31, $700.
(k)	Sunflower Cycle publishes a cycling magazine. Subscribers pay in advance. Unearned subscriptions revenue as of December 31, $1,000.

FIGURE 14-8 Adjusting Entries for Sunflower Cycle

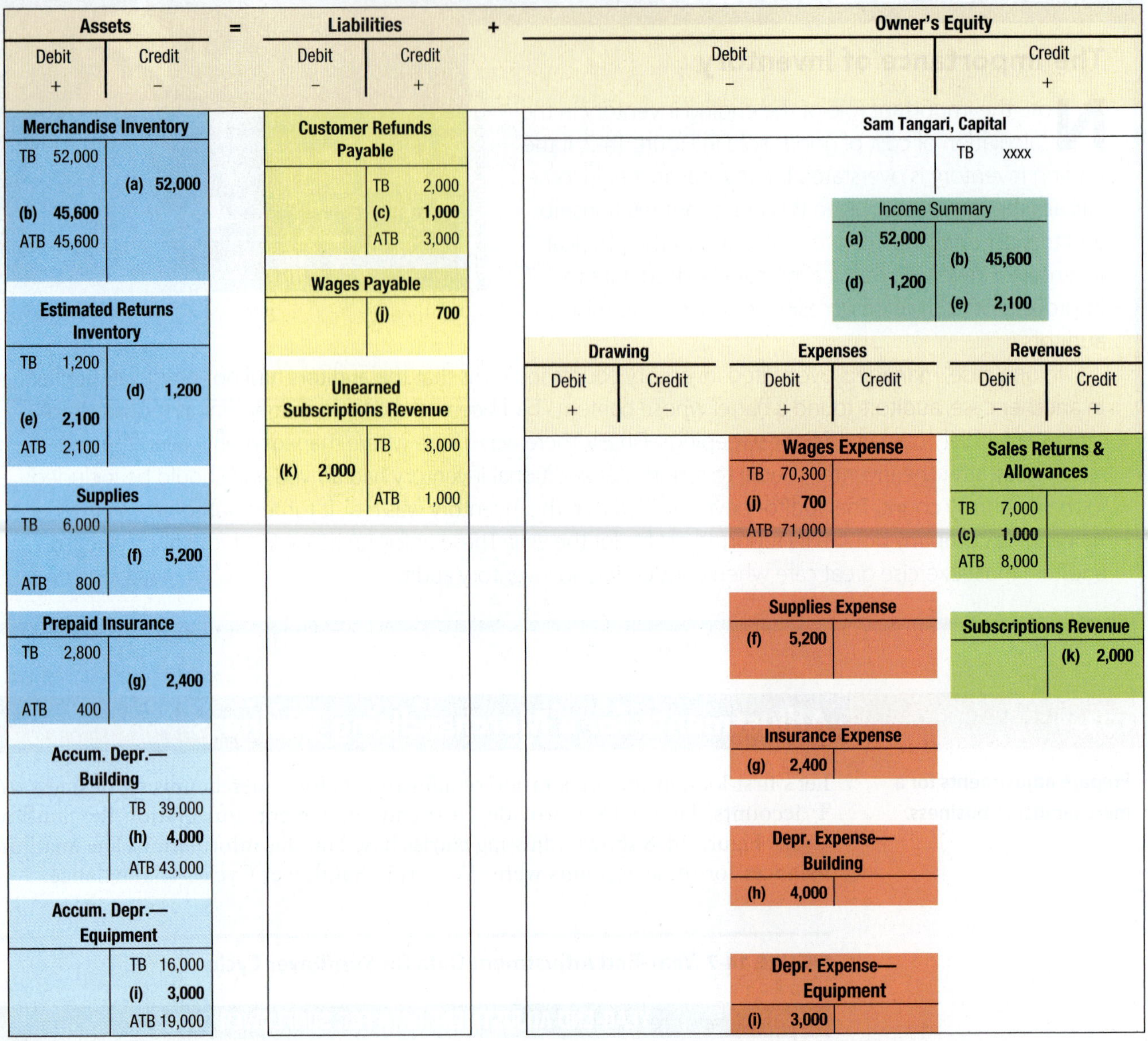

Adjustments may also be planned using an end-of-period spreadsheet. A spreadsheet for Sunflower Cycle is provided in Figure 14-9. It is prepared in four basic steps.

STEP 1 The Trial Balance columns are completed by copying the balances of all accounts from the general ledger (not shown).

STEP 2 Adjustments are entered. These entries are exactly the same as those made in T account form in Figure 14-8.

STEP 3 Extensions are made to the Adjusted Trial Balance columns. Note that all debit and credit amounts for Income Summary are extended.

STEP 4 By using a spreadsheet it is easy to compute net income for the period. Simply add all of the income statement accounts listed in the Adjusted Trial Balance columns. The income statement accounts are grouped together and include all accounts from Income Summary to the bottom of the columns. Those with credit balances total $533,000 and represent revenues and other accounts that increase net income. Those with debit balances total $432,600 and represent expenses and other accounts that reduce net income. Since the credits are greater than the debits, the difference of $100,400 equals net income for the period. If the debits exceed the credits, we would have a net loss.

FIGURE 14-9 Year End Spreadsheet for Sunflower Cycle

	A	B	C	D	E	F	G	H	I
1				Sunflower Cycle					
2				End-of-Period Spreadsheet					
3				For the Year Ended December 31, 20--					
4	ACCOUNT TITLE	TRIAL BALANCE		ADJUSTMENTS				ADJUSTED TRIAL BALANCE	
5		DEBIT	CREDIT	DEBIT		CREDIT		DEBIT	CREDIT
6	Cash	26,000.00						26,000.00	
7	Accounts Receivable	13,000.00						13,000.00	
8	Merchandise Inventory	52,000.00		(b)	45,600.00	(a)	52,000.00	45,600.00	
9	Estimated Returns Inventory	1,200.00		(e)	2,100.00	(d)	1,200.00	2,100.00	
10	Supplies	6,000.00				(f)	5,200.00	800.00	
11	Prepaid Insurance	2,800.00				(g)	2,400.00	400.00	
12	Land	115,000.00						115,000.00	
13	Building	390,000.00						390,000.00	
14	Accum. Depr.—Building		39,000.00			(h)	4,000.00		43,000.00
15	Equipment	48,000.00						48,000.00	
16	Accum. Depr.—Equipment		16,000.00			(i)	3,000.00		19,000.00
17	Notes Payable		5,000.00						5,000.00
18	Accounts Payable		24,000.00						24,000.00
19	Customer Refunds Payable		2,000.00			(c)	1,000.00		3,000.00
20	Wages Payable					(j)	700.00		700.00
21	Sales Tax Payable		1,600.00						1,600.00
22	Unearned Subscriptions Revenue		3,000.00	(k)	2,000.00				1,000.00
23	Mortgage Payable		30,000.00						30,000.00
24	Sam Tangari, Capital		417,200.00						417,200.00
25	Sam Tangari, Drawing	4,000.00						4,000.00	
26	Income Summary			(a)	52,000.00	(b)	45,600.00	52,000.00	45,600.00
27				(d)	1,200.00	(e)	2,100.00	1,200.00	2,100.00
28	Sales		473,000.00						473,000.00
29	Sales Returns and Allowances	7,000.00		(c)	1,000.00			8,000.00	
30	Interest Revenue		800.00						800.00
31	Rent Revenue		7,500.00						7,500.00
32	Subscriptions Revenue					(k)	2,000.00		2,000.00
33	Purchases	239,600.00						239,600.00	
34	Purchases Returns and Allowances		1,100.00						1,100.00
35	Purchases Discounts		900.00						900.00
36	Freight-In	1,300.00						1,300.00	
37	Wages Expense	70,300.00		(j)	700.00			71,000.00	
38	Advertising Expense	10,200.00						10,200.00	
39	Bank Credit Card Expense	8,100.00						8,100.00	
40	Rent Expense	14,000.00						14,000.00	
41	Supplies Expense			(f)	5,200.00			5,200.00	
42	Phone Expense	1,800.00						1,800.00	
43	Utilities Expense	7,500.00						7,500.00	
44	Insurance Expense			(g)	2,400.00			2,400.00	
45	Depr. Expense—Building			(h)	4,000.00			4,000.00	
46	Depr. Expense—Equipment			(i)	3,000.00			3,000.00	
47	Miscellaneous Expense	1,700.00						1,700.00	
48	Interest Expense	1,600.00						1,600.00	
49		1,021,100.00	1,021,100.00		119,200.00		119,200.00	1,077,500.00	1,077,500.00
50		STEP 1		STEP 2				STEP 3	
51	STEP 4							$ 432,600.00	$ 533,000.00
52	Net Income							100,400.00	

LO4 Adjusting Entries

Journalize adjusting entries for a merchandising business.

Adjustments on a spreadsheet have no effect on the actual accounts in the general ledger. Journal entries must be made to enter the adjustments into the accounting system. Figure 14-10 shows the adjusting entries for Sunflower Cycle.

LEARNING KEY

Recall that the spreadsheet is just a planning tool. The adjusting entries must be entered in the general journal.

FIGURE 14-10 Adjusting Entries for Sunflower Cycle

GENERAL JOURNAL PAGE 3

	DATE		DESCRIPTION	POST. REF.	DEBIT	CREDIT	
1			Adjusting Entries				1
2	20-- Dec.	31	Income Summary		52,000.00		2
3			Merchandise Inventory			52,000.00	3
4							4
5		31	Merchandise Inventory		45,600.00		5
6			Income Summary			45,600.00	6
7							7
8		31	Sales Returns and Allowances		1,000.00		8
9			Customer Refunds Payable			1,000.00	9
10							10
11		31	Income Summary		1,200.00		11
12			Estimated Returns Inventory			1,200.00	12
13							13
14		31	Estimated Returns Inventory		2,100.00		14
15			Income Summary			2,100.00	15
16							16
17		31	Supplies Expense		5,200.00		17
18			Supplies			5,200.00	18
19							19
20		31	Insurance Expense		2,400.00		20
21			Prepaid Insurance			2,400.00	21
22							22
23		31	Depr. Expense—Building		4,000.00		23
24			Accumulated Depr.—Building			4,000.00	24
25							25
26		31	Depr. Expense—Equipment		3,000.00		26
27			Accumulated Depr.—Equipment			3,000.00	27
28							28
29		31	Wages Expense		700.00		29
30			Wages Payable			700.00	30
31							31
32		31	Unearned Subscriptions Revenue		2,000.00		32
33			Subscriptions Revenue			2,000.00	33
34							34

CHECKPOINT

Complete Checkpoint-4 on page 547 to test your basic understanding of LO4.

LO5 Adjusting Entries Under the Perpetual Inventory System

Prepare adjustments for merchandise inventory using the perpetual inventory system.

Under the perpetual inventory system, the merchandise inventory, estimated returns inventory, cost of goods sold, and customer refunds payable accounts are continually updated throughout the year to reflect inventory purchases, sales, returns by customers, and returns to suppliers. Figure 14-11 illustrates the entries made for these transactions under the periodic and perpetual inventory systems. In addition, it illustrates year-end adjusting entries under both systems. Many of these entries are provided as review. Complete discussions of new entries for expected sales returns and allowances and inventory shrinkage under the perpetual inventory system follow the figure.

FIGURE 14-11 Entries for Periodic and Perpetual Inventory Systems

TRANSACTION	PERIODIC SYSTEM			PERPETUAL SYSTEM		
Purchased merchandise on account, $800	Purchases	800		Merchandise Inventory	800	
	Accounts Payable		800	Accounts Payable		800
Sold merchandise on account, $400. The cost of the merchandise sold was $300	Accounts Receivable	400		Accounts Receivable	400	
	Sales		400	Sales		400
				Cost of Goods Sold	300	
				Merchandise Inventory		300
Returned merchandise to supplier. Cost was $100.	Accounts Payable	100		Accounts Payable	100	
	Purchases Returns and Allowances		100	Merchandise Inventory		100
Customer returns merchandise sold in the <u>current</u> period for a refund of $50, cost was $40.	Sales Returns and Allowances	50		Sales Returns and Allowances	50	
	Accounts Receivable or Cash		50	Accounts Receivable or Cash		50
				Merchandise Inventory	40	
				Cost of Goods Sold		40
Customer returns merchandise sold in the <u>prior</u> period for a refund of $60, cost was $48.	Sales Returns and Allowances	60		Customer Refunds Payable	60	
	Accounts Receivable or Cash		60	Accounts Receivable or Cash		60
				Merchandise Inventory	48	
				Estimated Returns Inventory		48
YEAR-END ADJUSTMENTS	**PERIODIC SYSTEM**			**PERPETUAL SYSTEM**		
Adjustment for Merchandise Inventory	Income Summary	XX		Inventory Short and Over	XX	
	Merchandise Inventory		XX	Merchandise Inventory		XX
	Merchandise Inventory	XX				
	Income Summary		XX			
Adjustment for Estimated Returns Inventory: Sales made this year, but expected to be returned next year.	Income Summary	XX		Estimated Returns Inventory	XX	
	Estimated Returns Inventory		XX	Cost of Goods Sold		XX
	Estimated Returns Inventory	XX				
	Income Summary		XX			
Adjustment for Sales Returns and Allowances: Sales made this year, but expected to be returned next year.	Sales Returns and Allowances	XX		Sales Returns and Allowances	XX	
	Customer Refunds Payable		XX	Customer Refunds Payable		XX

Adjustments for Expected Sales Returns and Allowances

At the end of each period, it is important to adjust for merchandise sold this accounting period, but expected to be returned in the next period. As shown below, the adjusting entries for the perpetual inventory system are similar to the periodic system. But there are important differences.

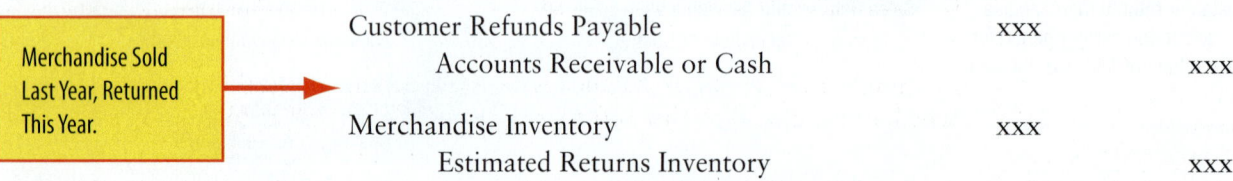

Year End Adjusting Entries

Sales Returns and Allowances	xxx	
Customer Refunds Payable		xxx
Estimated Returns Inventory	xxx	
Cost of Goods Sold		xxx

Since the business has the ability to track the details of inventory transactions, Merchandise Inventory, Estimated Returns Inventory, Cost of Goods Sold, and Customer Refunds Payable are updated throughout the year, and adjusted at year-end for next year's estimates.

To illustrate the underlying accounting let's assume facts similar to those used in Figure 14-2 for Andy's Auto Parts. Andy's estimates that customers will be granted $4,000 in refunds of this year's sales next year and the merchandise expected to be returned will have a cost of $3,000. Thus, Customer Refunds Payable and Estimated Returns Inventory must be adjusted to equal these amounts. This is the same process as followed under the periodic system. However, the dollar amounts for these adjustments will be different under the perpetual inventory system. This is because of the entries made during the year. As shown in Figure 14-11, when a customer returns merchandise purchased in the prior year, the following entries are made under the perpetual system.

Merchandise Sold Last Year, Returned This Year.

Customer Refunds Payable	xxx	
Accounts Receivable or Cash		xxx
Merchandise Inventory	xxx	
Estimated Returns Inventory		xxx

> It is preferable to debit Returned Merchandise Inventory instead of Merchandise Inventory to maintain a distinction between inventory that is brand new and inventory that has been returned and may need to be discounted. We will leave this distinction to more advanced texts.

Thus, if last year's estimates for refunds and returns inventory were accurate, the ending balances of these accounts should approach zero. Let's assume these unadjusted balances are as follows:

	A	B	C
1		TRIAL BALANCE	
2		DEBIT	CREDIT
3	Estimated Returns Inventory	300.00	
4	Customer Refunds Payable		400.00
5			

Therefore, under the perpetual inventory system, we must make the following adjusting entries at year-end:

Year-End Adjusting Entries (See Fig. 14-11.)

Sales Returns and Allowances	3,600	
Customer Refunds Payable		3,600
(4,000 − 400 = 3,600)		
Estimated Returns Inventory	2,700	
Cost of Goods Sold		2,700
(3,000 − 300 = 2,700)		

Adjustments for Inventory Shrinkage

As discussed in Chapter 13, the perpetual inventory system does not eliminate the need for taking physical inventories. The perpetual records must be compared with the physical inventory to discover and correct any errors or losses of merchandise from theft, breakage, or spoilage. This is known as **inventory shrinkage**. If a difference is found between the physical count and the amount in the perpetual inventory records, the records must be corrected by an adjusting entry. Some firms use Cost of Goods Sold to make this adjustment. A preferable approach is to use an account called **Inventory Short and Over**. For example, if the book balance is $3,840 and the physical count shows $3,710 worth of merchandise, the $130 shortage would be entered as follows:

3			Adjusting Entries			3
4			Inventory Short and Over		130 00		4
5			Merchandise Inventory			130 00	5
6			To adjust inventory per physical count				6

Similarly, if the book balance is $3,840 and the physical count shows $3,900 worth of merchandise, this $60 overage would be entered as follows:

3			Adjusting Entries				3
4			Merchandise Inventory		60 00		4
5			Inventory Short and Over			60 00	5
6			To adjust inventory per physical count				6

LEARNING KEY

A physical inventory is still important under the perpetual inventory system. It is used to verify the accuracy of the inventory records.

If Inventory Short and Over has a debit balance, the account is listed with other expenses on the income statement. If it has a credit balance, the account is listed with other revenues on the income statement.

Using a separate account, Inventory Short and Over, makes it easier for management to track inventory problems associated with errors, theft, breakage, and spoilage. Further, it removes these items from the calculation of cost of goods sold and provides a better measure of the gross profit on sales.

A business that sells a wide selection of low-cost goods may not find it practical to keep a perpetual inventory. In contrast, a business that sells a few high-cost items (cars, fine jewelry, stereo equipment) can maintain such a record without incurring excessive processing costs. The increasing use of computers and optical scanning devices at the point of sale has enabled more and more businesses to switch from the periodic to the perpetual inventory system.

CHECKPOINT

Complete Checkpoint-5 on page 547 to test your basic understanding of LO5.

SELF-STUDY

LEARNING OBJECTIVES — Key Points to Remember

LO1 Prepare adjustments for merchandise inventory using the periodic inventory system.

Extra care is required for the end-of-period adjustment for merchandise inventory and the related extensions on a spreadsheet. The five-step adjustment process used on a spreadsheet is shown below. This technique is used so that all of the information required to compute cost of goods sold on the income statement is provided in the Adjusted Trial Balance columns of the spreadsheet.

	A	B	C	D	E	F	G
1	ACCOUNT TITLE	TRIAL BALANCE		ADJUSTMENTS		ADJUSTED TRIAL BALANCE	
2		DEBIT	CREDIT	DEBIT	CREDIT	DEBIT	CREDIT
3							
4							
5	Merchandise Inventory	23,000.00		27,000.00	23,000.00	27,000.00	
6	Estimated Returns Inventory	2,000.00		3,000.00	2,000.00	3,000.00	
7	Customer Refunds Payable		2,600.00		1,400.00		4,000.00
8	Income Summary			23,000.00	27,000.00	23,000.00	27,000.00
9				2,000.00	3,000.00	2,000.00	3,000.00
10	Sales		145,000.00				145,000.00
11	Sales Returns and Allowances	8,400.00		1,400.00		9,800.00	
12	Purchases	80,000.00				80,000.00	
13							

Step 1: Remove Beginning Inventory	Income Summary	23,000.00	
	Merchandise Inventory		23,000.00
Step 2: Enter Ending Inventory	Merchandise Inventory	27,000.00	
	Income Summary		27,000.00
Step 3: Update for New Estimate of Customer Refunds Payable	Sales Returns and Allowances	1,400.00	
	Customer Refunds Payable		1,400.00
Step 4: Remove Beginning Estimated Returns Inventory	Income Summary	2,000.00	
	Estimated Returns Inventory		2,000.00
Step 5: Enter Ending Estimated Returns Inventory	Estimated Returns Inventory	3,000.00	
	Income Summary		3,000.00

Cost of goods sold:			
Merchandise Inventory, January 1	$ 23,000.00		
Estimated returns inventory, January 1	2,000.00	$ 25,000.00	
Purchases		80,000.00	
Goods available for sale		$ 105,000.00	
Less: Merchandise inventory, December 31	$ 27,000.00		
Estimated returns inventory, December 31	3,000.00	30,000.00	
Cost of goods sold			75,000.00

LO2 Prepare an adjustment for unearned revenue.

Some firms receive cash before providing a service or selling a product. The cash received in advance is considered a liability, unearned revenue, until earned. The adjusting entry to recognize that unearned revenue has become earned is as follows:

Unearned Revenue	xxx	
Revenue		xxx

LO3 Prepare adjustments for a merchandising business.

Adjustments can be prepared electronically using accounting software, with T accounts, or on a spreadsheet. Steps to follow when using a spreadsheet are as follows:

1. Prepare the trial balance.
2. Prepare the adjustments.
3. Prepare the adjusted trial balance.
4. Compute net income using the income statement accounts in the adjusted trial balance columns.

LEARNING OBJECTIVES	Key Points to Remember
LO4 **Journalize adjusting entries for a merchandising business.**	A spreadsheet is a useful tool when preparing end-of-period adjustments and financial statements. Adjustments made on a spreadsheet must be entered in a journal and posted to the ledger.

LO5 **Prepare adjustments for merchandise inventory using the perpetual inventory system.**	At the end of each period, it is important to adjust for merchandise sold this accounting period, but expected to be returned in the next period. As shown below, the adjusting entries for the perpetual inventory system are similar to the periodic system. However, since these accounts are updated throughout the year, the dollar amounts for the adjustment will be quite different.
	
	Sales Returns and Allowances xxx
	    Customer Refunds Payable xxx
	Estimated Returns Inventory xxx
	    Cost of Goods Sold xxx
	
	Since the business has the ability to track the details of inventory transactions, Merchandise Inventory, is updated throughout the year for all transactions affecting this account. Thus, the firm knows how much inventory should be on hand at any given point in time. However, the balance of the merchandise inventory account must be verified with an actual physical count of the inventory before issuing financial statements. If there is a difference, an adjusting entry is made. If the balance in the inventory account is greater than the physical count, the following entry is made:
	
	Inventory Short and Over xxx
	    Merchandise Inventory xxx
	
	If the balance in the inventory account is less than the physical count, the following entry is made:
	
	Merchandise Inventory xxx
	    Inventory Short and Over xxx

DEMONSTRATION PROBLEM

Aaron Patton owns and operates Patton's Bait Shop. A year-end trial balance is shown on page 542.

Patton uses the periodic inventory system. Year-end adjustment data are as follows:

(a, b) A physical count shows that merchandise inventory costing $53,000 is on hand as of December 31, 20--.

(c, d, e) Patton estimates that customers will be granted $5,000 in refunds of this year's sales next year and the merchandise expected to be returned will have a cost of $2,800.

(f) Supplies remaining at the end of the year, $200.

(continued)

(g) Unexpired insurance on December 31, $300.
(h) Depreciation expense on the building for 20--, $2,000.
(i) Depreciation expense on the equipment for 20--, $1,500.
(j) Wages earned but not paid as of December 31, $1,200.
(k) Patton also offers guided tours which clients pay for in advance. Unearned tour guide revenue as of December 31, $5,000.

REQUIRED

1. Prepare a year-end spreadsheet.
2. Journalize the adjusting entries.
3. Compute cost of goods sold using the spreadsheet prepared for part (1).

	A	B	C
1	**Patton's Bait Shop**		
2	**Trial Balance**		
3	**For the Year Ended December 31, 20--**		
4	ACCOUNT TITLE	DEBIT BALANCE	CREDIT BALANCE
5			
6	Cash	40,400.00	
7	Accounts Receivable	7,500.00	
8	Merchandise Inventory	47,400.00	
9	Estimated Returns Inventory	2,500.00	
10	Supplies	900.00	
11	Prepaid Insurance	1,200.00	
12	Land	85,000.00	
13	Building	45,000.00	
14	Accumulated Depreciation—Building		8,000.00
15	Equipment	25,000.00	
16	Accumulated Depreciation—Equipment		7,500.00
17	Accounts Payable		5,000.00
18	Customer Refunds Payable		3,000.00
19	Wages Payable		
20	Unearned Tour Guide Revenue		30,000.00
21	Aaron Patton, Capital		174,900.00
22	Aaron Patton, Drawing	10,000.00	
23	Income Summary		
24			
25	Sales		222,750.00
26	Sales Returns and Allowances	12,000.00	
27	Tour Guide Revenue		
28	Purchases	102,500.00	
29	Purchases Returns and Allowances		400.00
30	Purchases Discounts		500.00
31	Freight-In	150.00	
32	Wages Expense	61,000.00	
33	Advertising Expense	3,750.00	
34	Supplies Expense		
35	Phone Expense	1,750.00	
36	Utilities Expense	6,000.00	
37	Insurance Expense		
38	Depreciation Expense—Building		
39	Depreciation Expense—Equipment		
40		452,050.00	452,050.00
41			

SOLUTION 1.

	A	B	C	D	E	F	G	H	I
1	Patton's Bait Shop								
2	End-of-Period Spreadsheet								
3	For the Year Ended December 31, 20--								
4	ACCOUNT TITLE	TRIAL BALANCE		ADJUSTMENTS				ADJUSTED TRIAL BALANCE	
5		DEBIT	CREDIT		DEBIT		CREDIT	DEBIT	CREDIT
6	Cash	40,400.00						40,400.00	
7	Accounts Receivable	7,500.00						7,500.00	
8	Merchandise Inventory	47,400.00		(b)	53,000.00	(a)	47,400.00	53,000.00	
9	Estimated Returns Inventory	2,500.00		(e)	2,800.00	(d)	2,500.00	2,800.00	
10	Supplies	900.00				(f)	700.00	200.00	
11	Prepaid Insurance	1,200.00				(g)	900.00	300.00	
12	Land	85,000.00						85,000.00	
13	Building	45,000.00						45,000.00	
14	Accum. Depr.—Building		8,000.00			(h)	2,000.00		10,000.00
15	Equipment	25,000.00						25,000.00	
16	Accum. Depr.—Equipment		7,500.00			(i)	1,500.00		9,000.00
17	Accounts Payable		5,000.00						5,000.00
18	Customer Refunds Payable		3,000.00			(c)	2,000.00		5,000.00
19	Wages Payable					(j)	1,200.00		1,200.00
20	Unearned Tour Guide Revenue		30,000.00	(k)	25,000.00				5,000.00
21	Aaron Patton, Capital		174,900.00						174,900.00
22	Aaron Patton, Drawing	10,000.00						10,000.00	
23	Income Summary			(a)	47,400.00	(b)	53,000.00	47,400.00	53,000.00
24				(d)	2,500.00	(e)	2,800.00	2,500.00	2,800.00
25	Sales		222,750.00						222,750.00
26	Sales Returns and Allowances	12,000.00		(c)	2,000.00			14,000.00	
27	Tour Guide Revenue					(k)	25,000.00		25,000.00
28	Purchases	102,500.00						102,500.00	
29	Purchases Returns and Allowances		400.00						400.00
30	Purchases Discounts		500.00						500.00
31	Freight-In	150.00						150.00	
32	Wages Expense	61,000.00		(j)	1,200.00			62,200.00	
33	Advertising Expense	3,750.00						3,750.00	
34	Supplies Expense			(f)	700.00			700.00	
35	Phone Expense	1,750.00						1,750.00	
36	Utilities Expense	6,000.00						6,000.00	
37	Insurance Expense			(g)	900.00			900.00	
38	Depr. Expense—Building			(h)	2,000.00			2,000.00	
39	Depr. Expense—Equipment			(i)	1,500.00			1,500.00	
40		452,050.00	452,050.00		139,000.00		139,000.00	514,550.00	514,550.00
41								245,350.00	304,450.00
42	Net Income							59,100.00	
43									

SOLUTION 2.

GENERAL JOURNAL PAGE 3

	DATE		DESCRIPTION	POST REF.	DEBIT	CREDIT	
1			Adjusting Entries				1
2	20-- Dec.	31	Income Summary		47,400.00		2
3			Merchandise Inventory			47,400.00	3
4							4
5		31	Merchandise Inventory		53,000.00		5
6			Income Summary			53,000.00	6
7							7
8		31	Sales Returns and Allowances		2,000.00		8
9			Customer Refunds Payable			2,000.00	9
10							10
11		31	Income Summary		2,500.00		11
12			Estimated Returns Inventory			2,500.00	12
13							13
14		31	Estimated Returns Inventory		2,800.00		14
15			Income Summary			2,800.00	15
16							16
17		31	Supplies Expense		700.00		17
18			Supplies			700.00	18
19							19
20		31	Insurance Expense		900.00		20
21			Prepaid Insurance			900.00	21
22							22
23		31	Depreciation Expense—Building		2,000.00		23
24			Accumulated Depreciation—Building			2,000.00	24
25							25
23		31	Depreciation Expense—Equipment		1,500.00		23
24			Accumulated Depreciation—Equipment			1,500.00	24
25							25
26		31	Wages Expense		1,200.00		26
27			Wages Payable			1,200.00	27
28							28
29		31	Unearned Tour Guide Revenue		25,000.00		29
30			Tour Guide Revenue			25,000.00	30

SOLUTION 3.

Cost of goods sold:				
Merchandise inventory, January 1		$ 47,400		
Estimated returns inventory, January 1		2,500	$ 49,900	
Purchases		$102,500		
Less: Purchases returns and allowances	$400			
Purchases discounts	500	900		
Net purchases		$101,600		
Add freight-in		150		
Cost of goods purchased			101,750	
Goods available for sale			$151,650	
Less: Merchandise inventory, December 31		$ 53,000		
Estimated returns inventory, December 31		2,800	55,800	
Cost of goods sold				95,850

KEY TERMS

Customer Refunds Payable (529) A liability account used to report the estimated refunds to be paid to customers next year as a result of returning merchandise sold this year.

Estimated Returns Inventory (529) An asset-account that represents the estimated cost of merchandise inventory sold this year, but expected to be returned next year.

inventory shrinkage (539) Losses of merchandise from theft, breakage, or spoilage.

Inventory Short and Over (539) An account used to adjust the perpetual inventory records when a difference exists between the physical count and the amount in the perpetual inventory records.

unearned revenue (530) Cash received in advance of delivering a product or performing a service.

SELF-STUDY TEST QUESTIONS

True/False

1. **LO1** Under the periodic inventory system, the beginning inventory is removed from the merchandise inventory account with a credit to Merchandise Inventory and a debit to Income Summary.
2. **LO1** Under the periodic inventory system, the ending inventory is entered by debiting Merchandise Inventory and crediting Income Summary.
3. **LO2** The cash received in advance before delivering a product or performing a service is called unearned revenue.
4. **LO2** Unearned revenue is adjusted into an expense account at the end of the accounting period.
5. **LO1/2** Sales Returns and Allowances is classified as a contra-cost account on the income statement.

Multiple Choice

1. **LO1** Under the periodic inventory system, what account is credited when an estimate is made for sales made this year, but expected to be returned next year?
   (a) Merchandise Inventory
   (b) Customer Refunds Payable
   (c) Sales
   (d) Sales Returns and Allowances
2. **LO1** Under the periodic inventory system, what account is debited when an estimate is made for sales made this year, but expected to be returned next year?
   (a) Sales Returns and Allowances
   (b) Merchandise Inventory
   (c) Customer Refunds Payable
   (d) Sales

3. **LO1** Under the periodic inventory system, what account is debited when an estimate is made for the cost of merchandise inventory sold this year, but expected to be returned next year?
   (a) Estimated Returns Inventory
   (b) Sales Returns and Allowances
   (c) Merchandise Inventory
   (d) Customer Refunds Payable

4. **LO2** Unearned revenue is classified as what type of account?
   (a) Asset
   (b) Liability
   (c) Owner's Equity
   (d) Revenue
   (e) Expense

5. **LO5** Under the perpetual inventory method, what account is credited when adjusting for the estimated cost of the merchandise sold this period, but expected to be returned next period?
   (a) Merchandise Inventory
   (b) Cost of Goods Sold
   (c) Customer Refunds Payable
   (d) Sales Returns and Allowances

CHECKPOINT

Checkpoint Exercises

1. **LO1** Prepare the cost of goods sold section for Joseph's Gift Shop. The following amounts are known:

Beginning merchandise inventory	$ 20,000
Ending merchandise inventory	15,000
Purchases	171,000

2. **LO2** The Venice Theatre sold and collected cash of $45,000 for season tickets. Upon collection of cash, Unearned Ticket Revenue was credited. At the end of the accounting period, $15,000 had been earned. Make the appropriate adjusting entry.

3. **LO3** Information relating to inventory for Janie Par Gifts is provided below.

Beginning merchandise inventory	$120,000
Ending merchandise inventory	90,000
Purchases	250,000

   1. Set up a spreadsheet similar to the one provided below.
   2. Enter the appropriate information from above into the Trial Balance columns.
   3. Prepare appropriate adjustments and extensions to the Adjusted Trial Balance columns.

	A	B	C	D	E	F	G
1	ACCOUNT TITLE	TRIAL BALANCE		ADJUSTMENTS		ADJUSTED TRIAL BALANCE	
2		DEBIT	CREDIT	DEBIT	CREDIT	DEBIT	CREDIT
3	Merchandise Inventory						
4	Income Summary						
5	Purchases						
6							

4. **LO4** Using the spreadsheet provided below, prepare the adjusting entries for merchandise inventory.

	A	B	C	D	E	F	G
1	ACCOUNT TITLE	TRIAL BALANCE		ADJUSTMENTS			
2		DEBIT	CREDIT		DEBIT		CREDIT
3	Merchandise Inventory	50,000.00		(b)	60,000.00	(a)	50,000.00
4	Income Summary			(a)	50,000.00	(b)	60,000.00
5	Purchases	80,000.00					
6							

5. **LO5** The following information is provided by Koffi Products:

Ending balance of merchandise inventory account	$50,000
Physical count of ending merchandise inventory	48,000

Prepare the appropriate adjusting entry under the perpetual inventory system.

The answers to the Self-Study Test Questions are at the end of the chapter (page 562).

APPLYING YOUR KNOWLEDGE

CengageNowv2 provides "Show Me How" videos for selected exercises and problems. Additional resources, such as Excel templates for completing selected exercises and problems, are available for download from the companion website at Cengage.com.

REVIEW QUESTIONS

LO1 1. A firm is preparing to make adjusting entries at the end of the accounting period. The balance of the merchandise inventory account is $200,000. If the firm is using the periodic inventory system, what does this balance represent?

LO1 2. What spreadsheet amounts are used to compute cost of goods sold?

LO1 3. Why are both the debit and credit amounts in the Adjustments columns on the Income Summary line of the spreadsheet extended to the Adjusted Trial Balance columns?

LO2 4. What is an unearned revenue?

LO2 5. Give three examples of unearned revenue.

LO3 6. List the four steps taken to prepare an end-of-period spreadsheet.

LO1/5 7. Why is it important to make end-of-period adjustments for merchandise sold this year, but expected to be returned next period?

LO5 8. A firm is preparing to make adjusting entries at the end of the accounting period. The balance of the merchandise inventory account is $100,000. If the firm is using the perpetual inventory system, what does this balance represent?

SERIES A EXERCISES

E 14-1A (LO1)

ADJUSTMENT FOR MERCHANDISE INVENTORY USING T ACCOUNTS: PERIODIC INVENTORY SYSTEM Ibby Smith owns and operates Ibby's Ice Cream Cones. Her beginning inventory as of January 1, 20--, was $45,000, and her ending inventory as of December 31, 20--, was $57,000. Set up T accounts for Merchandise Inventory and Income Summary and perform the year-end adjustment for Merchandise Inventory.

E 14-2A (LO1)
✓ Sales R&A end bal.: $21,000

ADJUSTMENT FOR MERCHANDISE INVENTORY USING T ACCOUNTS: PERIODIC INVENTORY SYSTEM WITH SALES RETURNS AND ALLOWANCES Sam Edwards owns a business called Sam's Stuff. A physical count determined his ending inventory as of December 31, 20-- was $72,000. Based on past experience, Sam estimates that $5,000 of sales from this year will be returned next year. The cost of the merchandise expected to be returned is $3,000. Using the partial Trial Balance provided below, set up T accounts for Merchandise Inventory, Estimated Returns Inventory, Customer Refunds Payable, Sales Returns and Allowances, and Income Summary and prepare the year-end adjustments for Merchandise Inventory and related accounts.

	A	B	C
1		TRIAL BALANCE	
2		(PARTIAL)	
3	Merchandise Inventory	60,000.00	
4	Estimated Returns Inventory	2,500.00	
6	Customer Refunds Payable		4,000.00
7	Sales Returns and Allowances	20,000.00	
8	Income Summary		
9			

E-14-3A (LO1)
✓ Cost of goods sold: $73,450

CALCULATION OF COST OF GOODS SOLD: PERIODIC INVENTORY SYSTEM Prepare the cost of goods sold section for Adams Gift Shop. The following amounts are known:

Beginning merchandise inventory	$27,000
Ending merchandise inventory	22,000
Purchases	78,000
Purchases returns and allowances	3,900
Purchases discounts	6,000
Freight-in	350

E 14-4A (LO1)
✓ Cost of goods sold: $73,850

CALCULATION OF COST OF GOODS SOLD: PERIODIC INVENTORY SYSTEM WITH SALES RETURNS AND ALLOWANCES Use the same information as provided in Exercise 14-3A, but assume the business makes estimates for sales returns and allowances at year-end. The balances for estimated returns inventory are provided below. Prepare the cost of goods sold section of the income statement.

Beginning estimated returns inventory	$2,000
Ending estimated returns inventory	1,600

E 14-5A (LO2)

ADJUSTMENT FOR UNEARNED REVENUES USING T ACCOUNTS Set up T accounts for Cash, Unearned Ticket Revenue, and Ticket Revenue. Post the following two transactions to the appropriate accounts, indicating each transaction by letter:

(a) Sold 1,200 season tickets at $400 each, receiving cash of $480,000.

(b) An end-of-period adjustment is needed to recognize that $120,000 in ticket revenue has been earned.

E 14-6A (LO3)
✓ Cost of goods sold: $188, 900

MERCHANDISE INVENTORY ADJUSTMENTS: PERIODIC INVENTORY SYSTEM WITH SALES RETURNS AND ALLOWANCES Use the information provided below to prepare a partial end-of-period spreadsheet for Karen's Gift Shop for the year ended December 31, 20--. The ending merchandise inventory is $60,000. Karen estimates that customers will be granted $15,000 in refunds next year for merchandise sold this year. The estimated cost of the returned inventory is $10,000.

	A	B	C
1	Karen's Gift Shop		
2	Partial Trial Balance		
3	For Year Ended December 31, 20--		
4–5	ACCOUNT TITLE	DEBIT BALANCE	CREDIT BALANCE
6	Merchandise Inventory	55,000.00	
7	Estimated Returns Inventory	8,000.00	
8	Customer Refunds Payable		12,000.00
9	Income Summary		
10			
11	Sales		280,000.00
12	Sales Returns and Allowances	18,000.00	
13	Purchases	200,000.00	
14	Purchases Returns and Allowances		3,000.00
15	Purchases Discounts		2,500.00
16	Freight-In	1,400.00	
17			

1. Complete the Adjustments columns for Merchandise Inventory and related accounts.
2. Extend all accounts to the Adjusted Trial Balance columns.
3. Prepare the cost of goods sold section from the spreadsheet.

E 14-7A (LO3)
✓ Beg. inv.: $60,500

DETERMINING THE BEGINNING AND ENDING INVENTORY FROM A PARTIAL SPREADSHEET: PERIODIC INVENTORY SYSTEM From the following partial spreadsheet, indicate the dollar amount of beginning and ending merchandise inventory to be used to compute cost of goods sold.

	A	B	C	D	E
1	ACCOUNT TITLE	ADJUSTMENTS		ADJUSTED TRIAL BALANCE	
2		DEBIT	CREDIT	DEBIT	CREDIT
3	Merchandise Inventory	60,000.00	55,000.00	60,000.00	
4	Estimated Returns Inventory	6,000.00	5,500.00	6,000.00	
5	Supplies		4,700.00	3,300.00	
6	Prepaid Insurance		1,600.00	3,800.00	
7	Customer Refunds Payable		2,200.00		7,200.00
8	Income Summary	55,000.00	60,000.00	55,000.00	60,000.00
9		5,500.00	6,000.00	5,500.00	6,000.00
10	Sales				525,140.00
11	Sales Returns and Allowances	2,200.00		16,700.00	
12					

E 14-8A (LO4)
✓ (a)
Inc. Sum. 45,000
Mdse. Inv. 45,000

JOURNALIZE ADJUSTING ENTRIES FOR A MERCHANDISING BUSINESS The following partial spreadsheet is taken from the books of Vinnie's Vegetable Market, for the year ended December 31, 20--. Journalize the adjustments in a general journal.

	A	B	C	D	E	F	G
1	**Vinnie's Vegetable Market**						
2	**End-of-Period Spreadsheet (Partial)**						
3	**For Year Ended December 31, 20--**						
4	ACCOUNT TITLE	TRIAL BALANCE		ADJUSTMENTS			
5		DEBIT	CREDIT	DEBIT		CREDIT	
6	Merchandise Inventory	45,000.00		(b)	50,000.00	(a)	45,000.00
7	Supplies	10,000.00				(d)	7,000.00
8	Building	60,000.00					
9	Accum. Depr.—Building		15,000.00			(e)	5,000.00
10	Wages Payable					(f)	1,200.00
11	Unearned Membership Fees		3,000.00	(c)	2,000.00		
12	Income Summary			(a)	45,000.00	(b)	50,000.00
13	Membership Fees		20,000.00			(c)	2,000.00
14	Wages Expense	37,000.00		(f)	1,200.00		
15	Supplies Expense			(d)	7,000.00		
16	Depr. Expense—Building			(e)	5,000.00		
17					110,200.00		110,200.00
18							

E 14-9A (LO5)

JOURNAL ENTRIES UNDER THE PERPETUAL INVENTORY SYSTEM Bhushan Building Supplies entered into the following transactions. Prepare journal entries under the perpetual inventory system.

June 1 Purchased merchandise on account from Brij Builder's Materials, $500,000.

3 Purchased merchandise for cash, $400,000.

5 Sold merchandise on account to Champa Construction for $20,000. The merchandise cost $15,000.

E 14-10A (LO5)
✓ Cost of goods sold: $282,600

ADJUSTMENTS FOR A MERCHANDISING BUSINESS: PERPETUAL INVENTORY SYSTEM WITH SALES RETURNS AND ALLOWANCES A partial Trial Balance for Curless Company as of December 31, 20-- is provided below.

	A	B	C
1	**Curless Company**		
2	**Partial Trial Balance**		
3	**For Year Ended December 31, 20--**		
4–5	ACCOUNT TITLE	DEBIT BALANCE	CREDIT BALANCE
6	Merchandise Inventory	150,000.00	
7	Estimated Returns Inventory	500.00	
8	Customer Refunds Payable		650.00
9	Sales		425,000.00
10	Sales Returns and Allowances	18,000.00	
11	Cost of Goods Sold	288,000.00	
12			

Curless has made the following estimates for next year:

1. Sales made this year of $7,800 will be returned next year and customers will be granted full refunds.
2. The estimated cost of the inventory sold this year and expected to be returned by customers next year is $5,900.

Open T accounts and enter the balances for the above accounts. Make appropriate adjustments to the T accounts.

E 14-11A (LO5)

JOURNALIZE ADJUSTING ENTRY FOR INVENTORY SHRINKAGE: PERPETUAL INVENTORY SYSTEM On December 31, Anup Enterprises completed a physical count of its inventory. Although the merchandise inventory account shows a balance of $350,000, the physical count comes to $325,000. Prepare the appropriate adjusting entry under the perpetual inventory system.

SERIES A PROBLEMS

P 14-12A (LO1/2/3/4)
✓ Adj. col. total: $201,400
✓ Adj. Trial Bal. total: $1,093,050

PREPARATION OF ADJUSTMENTS ON A SPREADSHEET FOR A MERCHANDISING BUSINESS: PERIODIC METHOD The trial balance for the Venice Beach Kite Shop, a business owned by Molly Young is shown on page 552. Year-end adjustment information is as follows:

(a, b) A physical count shows that merchandise inventory costing $85,000 is on hand as of December 31, 20--.

(c, d, e) Young estimates that customers will be granted $5,700 in refunds of this year's sales next year and the merchandise expected to be returned will have a cost of $4,300.

(f) Supplies remaining at the end of the year, $3,300.

(g) Unexpired insurance on December 31, $3,800.

(h) Depreciation expense on the building for 20--, $12,500.

(i) Depreciation expense on the store equipment for 20--, $5,000.

(j) Unearned rent revenue as of December 31, $4,500.

(k) Wages earned but not paid as of December 31, $3,500.

REQUIRED

1. Complete the Adjustments columns, identifying each adjustment with its corresponding letter.
2. Complete the spreadsheet.
3. Enter the adjustments in a general journal.

(continued)

	A	B	C
1	**Venice Beach Kite Shop**		
2	**Trial Balance**		
3	**For the Year Ended December 31, 20--**		
4	ACCOUNT TITLE	DEBIT BALANCE	CREDIT BALANCE
5			
6	Cash	20,000.00	
7	Accounts Receivable	14,000.00	
8	Merchandise Inventory	75,000.00	
9	Estimated Returns Inventory	3,200.00	
10	Supplies	8,000.00	
11	Prepaid Insurance	5,400.00	
12	Land	130,000.00	
13	Building	250,000.00	
14	Accumulated Depreciation—Building		100,000.00
15	Store Equipment	100,000.00	
16	Accumulated Depreciation—Equipment		40,000.00
17	Accounts Payable		9,600.00
18	Customer Refunds Payable		3,500.00
19	Wages Payable		
20	Sales Tax Payable		5,900.00
21	Unearned Rent Revenue		8,900.00
22	M. Young, Capital		284,310.00
23	M. Young, Drawing	26,000.00	
24	Income Summary		
25			
26	Sales		525,140.00
27	Sales Returns and Allowances	14,500.00	
28	Rent Revenue		
29	Purchases	125,000.00	
30	Purchases Returns and Allowances		1,400.00
31	Purchases Discounts		1,800.00
32	Freight-In	2,100.00	
33	Wages Expense	125,000.00	
34	Advertising Expense	13,000.00	
35	Supplies Expense		
36	Phone Expense	1,350.00	
37	Utilities Expense	8,000.00	
38	Insurance Expense		
39	Depreciation Expense—Building		
40	Depreciation Expense—Equipment		
41	Rent Expense	60,000.00	
42		980,550.00	980,550.00
43			

P 14-13A (LO1/2/4)
✓ Adj. col. total: $221,540

WORKING BACKWARD FROM ADJUSTED TRIAL BALANCE TO DETERMINE ADJUSTING ENTRIES The partial spreadsheet shown below is taken from the books of Sunstate Computer Supply, a business owned by Michelle Thibeault, for the year ended December 31, 20--. Sunstate is on the periodic inventory system.

REQUIRED

1. Determine the adjusting entries by analyzing the difference between the adjusted trial balance and the trial balance.
2. Journalize the adjusting entries in a general journal.

	A	B	C	D	E	F	G
1	**Sunstate Computer Supply**						
2	**End-of-Period Spreadsheet**						
3	**For the Year Ended December 31, 20--**						
4	ACCOUNT TITLE	TRIAL BALANCE		ADJUSTMENTS		ADJUSTED TRIAL BALANCE	
5		DEBIT	CREDIT	DEBIT	CREDIT	DEBIT	CREDIT
6	Cash	22,000.00				22,000.00	
7	Accounts Receivable	15,400.00				15,400.00	
8	Merchandise Inventory	82,500.00				93,500.00	
9	Estimated Returns Inventory	3,520.00				4,730.00	
10	Supplies	8,800.00				3,630.00	
11	Prepaid Insurance	5,940.00				4,180.00	
12	Land	143,000.00				143,000.00	
13	Building	275,000.00				275,000.00	
14	Accum. Depr.—Building		110,000.00				123,750.00
15	Store Equipment	110,000.00				110,000.00	
16	Accum. Depr.—Store Equipment		44,000.00				49,500.00
17	Accounts Payable		10,560.00				10,560.00
18	Customer Refunds Payable		3,850.00				6,270.00
19	Wages Payable						3,850.00
20	Sales Tax Payable		6,490.00				6,490.00
21	Unearned Rent Revenue		9,790.00				4,950.00
22	M. Thibeault, Capital		312,741.00				312,741.00
23	M. Thibeault, Drawing	28,600.00				28,600.00	
24	Income Summary					82,500.00	93,500.00
25						3,520.00	4,730.00
26	Sales		577,654.00				577,654.00
27	Sales Returns and Allowances	15,950.00				18,370.00	
28	Rent Revenue						4,840.00
29	Purchases	137,500.00				137,500.00	
30	Purchases Returns and Allowances		1,540.00				1,540.00
31	Purchases Discounts		1,980.00				1,980.00
32	Freight-In	2,310.00				2,310.00	
33	Wages Expense	137,500.00				141,350.00	
34	Advertising Expense	14,300.00				14,300.00	
35	Supplies Expense					5,170.00	
36	Phone Expense	1,485.00				1,485.00	
37	Utilities Expense	8,800.00				8,800.00	
38	Insurance Expense					1,760.00	
39	Depr. Expense—Building					13,750.00	
40	Depr. Expense—Store Equipment					5,500.00	
41	Rent Expense	66,000.00				66,000.00	
42		1078,605.00	1078,605.00			1202,355.00	1202,355.00
43		**STEP 1**		**STEP 2**		**STEP 3**	
44	**STEP 4**					502,315.00	684,244.00
45	Net Income					181,929.00	
46							

SERIES B EXERCISES

E 14-1B (LO1)

ADJUSTMENT FOR MERCHANDISE INVENTORY USING T ACCOUNTS: PERIODIC INVENTORY SYSTEM Doran May owns and operates the Chocolate Moose Ice Cream stand. His beginning inventory as of January 1, 20--, was $33,000, and his ending inventory as of December 31, 20--, was $36,000. Set up T accounts for Merchandise Inventory and Income Summary and perform the year-end adjustment for Merchandise Inventory.

E 14-2B (LO1)
✓ Sales R&A end bal.: $16,500

ADJUSTMENT FOR MERCHANDISE INVENTORY USING T ACCOUNTS: PERIODIC INVENTORY SYSTEM WITH SALES RETURNS AND ALLOWANCES Ronica Kluge owns a business called Roni's Rummage. A physical count determined the ending inventory as of December 31, 20-- was $80,000. Based on past experience, Roni estimates that $6,000 of sales from this year will be refunded next year. The cost of the merchandise expected to be returned is $4,000. Using the partial Trial Balance provided below, set up T accounts for Merchandise Inventory, Estimated Returns Inventory, Customer Refunds Payable, Sales Returns and Allowances, and Income Summary and prepare the year-end adjustments for Merchandise Inventory and related accounts.

	A	B	C
1		TRIAL BALANCE	
2			
3	Merchandise Inventory	75,000.00	
4	Estimated Returns Inventory	3,000.00	
5	Customer Refunds Payable		4,500.00
6	Sales Returns and Allowances	15,000.00	
7	Income Summary		
8			

E 14-3B (LO1)
✓ Cost of goods sold: $58,100

CALCULATION OF COST OF GOODS SOLD: PERIODIC INVENTORY SYSTEM Prepare the cost of goods sold section for Havens Gift Shop. The following amounts are known:

Beginning merchandise inventory	$29,000
Ending merchandise inventory	27,000
Purchases	62,000
Purchases returns and allowances	2,800
Purchases discounts	3,400
Freight-in	300

E 14-4B (LO1)
✓ Cost of goods sold: $57,200

CALCULATION OF COST OF GOODS SOLD: PERIODIC INVENTORY SYSTEM WITH SALES RETURNS AND ALLOWANCES Use the same information as provided in Exercise 14-3B, but assume the business makes estimates for sales returns and allowances at year end. The balances for estimated returns inventory are provided below. Prepare the cost of goods sold section of the income statement.

Beginning estimated returns inventory	$2,600
Ending estimated returns inventory	3,500

E 14-5B (LO2)

ADJUSTMENT FOR UNEARNED REVENUES USING T ACCOUNTS Set up T accounts for Cash, Unearned Ticket Revenue, and Ticket Revenue. Post the following two transactions to the appropriate accounts, indicating each transaction by letter:

(a) Sold 1,200 season tickets at $20 each, receiving cash of $24,000.

(b) An end-of-period adjustment is needed to recognize that $19,000 in ticket revenue has been earned.

E 14-6B (LO3)
✓ Cost of goods sold: $112,400

MERCHANDISE INVENTORY ADJUSTMENTS: PERIODIC INVENTORY SYSTEM WITH SALES RETURNS AND ALLOWANCES Use the information provided below to prepare a partial end-of-period spreadsheet for Nick's Gift Shop for the year ended December 31, 20--. The ending merchandise inventory is $45,000. Nick estimates that customers will be granted $5,500, in refunds next year for merchandise sold this year. The estimated cost of the returned inventory is $3,500.

	A	B	C
1	**Nick's Gift Shop**		
2	**Partial Trial Balance**		
3	**For Year Ended December 31, 20--**		
4	ACCOUNT TITLE	DEBIT BALANCE	CREDIT BALANCE
5			
6	Merchandise Inventory	40,000.00	
7	Estimated Returns Inventory	2,500.00	
8	Customer Refunds Payable		5,000.00
9	Income Summary		
10			
11	Sales		175,000.00
12	Sales Returns and Allowances	13,000.00	
13	Purchases	120,000.00	
14	Purchases Returns and Allowances		1,400.00
15	Purchases Discounts		1,000.00
16	Freight-In	800.00	
17			

1. Complete the Adjustments columns for Merchandise Inventory and related accounts.
2. Extend all accounts to the Adjusted Trial Balance columns.
3. Prepare the cost of goods sold section from the spreadsheet.

E 14-7B (LO3)
✓ Beg.inv.: $49,000

DETERMINING THE BEGINNING AND ENDING INVENTORY FROM A PARTIAL SPREADSHEET: PERIODIC INVENTORY SYSTEM From the following partial spreadsheet, indicate the dollar amount of beginning and ending merchandise inventory to be used to compute cost of goods sold.

	A	B	C	D	E
1	ACCOUNT TITLE	ADJUSTMENTS		ADJUSTED TRIAL BALANCE	
2		DEBIT	CREDIT	DEBIT	CREDIT
3	Merchandise Inventory	40,000.00	45,000.00	40,000.00	
4	Estimated Returns Inventory	5,000.00	4,000.00	5,000.00	
5	Supplies		4,700.00	3,300.00	
6	Prepaid Insurance		1,600.00	3,800.00	
7	Customer Refunds Payable		2,200.00		6,000.00
8	Income Summary	45,000.00	40,000.00	45,000.00	40,000.00
9		4,000.00	5,000.00	4,000.00	5,000.00
10	Sales				525,140.00
11	Sales Returns and Allowances	2,200.00		16,700.00	
12					

E 14-8B (LO4)
✓ (b)
Mdse. Inv. 30,000
Inc. Sum. 30,000

JOURNALIZE ADJUSTING ENTRIES FOR A MERCHANDISING BUSINESS The following partial spreadsheet is taken from the books of the Venice Vegetable Market, for the year ended December 31, 20--. Journalize the adjustments in a general journal.

	A	B	C	D	E	F	G
1	**Venice Vegetable Market**						
2	**Spreadsheet (Partial)**						
3	**For Year Ended December 31, 20--**						
4	ACCOUNT TITLE	TRIAL BALANCE		ADJUSTMENTS			
5		DEBIT	CREDIT		DEBIT		CREDIT
6	Merchandise Inventory	35,000.00		(b)	30,000.00	(a)	35,000.00
7	Supplies	4,500.00				(d)	3,100.00
8	Building	50,000.00					
9	Accum. Depr.—Building		23,000.00			(e)	6,000.00
10	Wages Payable					(f)	1,300.00
11	Unearned Membership Revenue		7,000.00	(c)	5,500.00		
12	Income Summary			(a)	35,000.00	(b)	30,000.00
13	Membership Revenue		24,000.00			(c)	5,500.00
14	Wages Expense	41,000.00		(f)	1,300.00		
15	Supplies Expense			(d)	3,100.00		
16	Depr. Expense—Building			(e)	6,000.00		
17					80,900.00		80,900.00
18							

E 14-9B (LO5)

JOURNAL ENTRIES UNDER THE PERPETUAL INVENTORY SYSTEM Sunita Computer Supplies entered into the following transactions. Prepare journal entries under the perpetual inventory system.

May 1 Purchased merchandise on account from Anju Enterprises, $200,000.
8 Purchased merchandise for cash, $100,000.
15 Sold merchandise on account to Salil's Pharmacy for $8,000. The merchandise cost $5,000.

E 14-10B (LO5)
✓ Sales R&A end. bal.: $24,400

ADJUSTMENTS FOR A MERCHANDISING BUSINESS: PERPETUAL INVENTORY SYSTEM WITH SALES RETURNS AND ALLOWANCES A partial Trial Balance for Coleman Company as of December 31, 20-- is provided below.

	A	B	C
1	**Coleman Company**		
2	**Partial Trial Balance**		
3	**For Year Ended December 31, 20--**		
4	ACCOUNT TITLE	DEBIT BALANCE	CREDIT BALANCE
5			
6	Merchandise Inventory	165,000.00	
7	Estimated Returns Inventory	600.00	
8	Customer Refunds Payable		825.00
9	Sales		450,000.00
10	Sales Returns and Allowances	16,000.00	
11	Cost of Goods Sold	255,000.00	
12			

Coleman has made the following estimates for next year:

1. Sales made this year of $8,800 will be returned next year and customers will be granted full refunds.
2. The estimated cost of the inventory sold this year and expected to be returned by customers next year is $6,400.

Open T accounts and enter the balances for the above accounts. Make appropriate adjustments to the T accounts.

E 14-11B (LO5)

JOURNALIZE ADJUSTING ENTRY FOR INVENTORY SHRINKAGE: PERPETUAL INVENTORY SYSTEM On December 31, Anup Enterprises completed a physical count of its inventory. Although the merchandise inventory account shows a balance of $200,000, the physical count comes to $210,000. Prepare the appropriate adjusting entry under the perpetual inventory system.

SERIES B PROBLEMS

P 14-12B (LO1/2/3/4)

✓ Adj. col. total: $241,680
✓ Adj. Trial Bal. total: $1,311,660

PREPARATION OF ADJUSTMENTS ON A SPREADSHEET FOR A MERCHANDISING BUSINESS: PERIODIC METHOD The trial balance for the Basket Corner, a business owned by Linda Palermo is shown on page 558. Year-end adjustment information is as follows:

(a, b)	A physical count shows that merchandise inventory costing $102,000 is on hand as of December 31, 20--.
(c, d, e)	Palermo estimates that customers will be granted $6,840 in refunds of this year's sales next year and the merchandise expected to be returned will have a cost of $5,160.
(f)	Supplies remaining at the end of the year, $3,960.
(g)	Unexpired insurance on December 31, $4,560.
(h)	Depreciation expense on the building for 20--, $15,000.
(i)	Depreciation expense on the store equipment for 20--, $6,000.
(j)	Unearned rent revenue as of December 31, $5,400.
(k)	Wages earned but not paid as of December 31, $4,200.

REQUIRED

1. Complete the Adjustments columns, identifying each adjustment with its corresponding letter.
2. Complete the spreadsheet.
3. Enter the adjustments in a general journal.

(continued)

	A	B	C
1	Basket Corner		
2	Trial Balance		
3	For the Year Ended December 31, 20--		
4	ACCOUNT TITLE	DEBIT BALANCE	CREDIT BALANCE
5			
6	Cash	24,000.00	
7	Accounts Receivable	16,800.00	
8	Merchandise Inventory	90,000.00	
9	Estimated Returns Inventory	3,840.00	
10	Supplies	9,600.00	
11	Prepaid Insurance	6,480.00	
12	Land	156,000.00	
13	Building	300,000.00	
14	Accumulated Depreciation—Building		120,000.00
15	Store Equipment	120,000.00	
16	Accumulated Depreciation—Store Equipment		48,000.00
17	Accounts Payable		11,520.00
18	Customer Refunds Payable		4,200.00
19	Wages Payable		
20	Sales Tax Payable		7,080.00
21	Unearned Rent Revenue		10,680.00
22	L. Palermo, Capital		341,172.00
23	L. Palermo, Drawing	31,200.00	
24	Income Summary		
25			
26	Sales		630,168.00
27	Sales Returns and Allowances	17,400.00	
28	Rent Revenue		
29	Purchases	150,000.00	
30	Purchases Returns and Allowances		1,680.00
31	Purchases Discounts		2,160.00
32	Freight-In	2,520.00	
33	Wages Expense	150,000.00	
34	Advertising Expense	15,600.00	
35	Supplies Expense		
36	Phone Expense	1,620.00	
37	Utilities Expense	9,600.00	
38	Insurance Expense		
39	Depreciation Expense—Building		
40	Depreciation Expense—Store Equipment		
41	Rent Expense	72,000.00	
42		1,176,660.00	1,176,660.00
43			

P 14-13B **(LO1/2/4)**
✓ Adj. col. total: $261,820

WORKING BACKWARD FROM ADJUSTED TRIAL BALANCE TO DETERMINE ADJUSTING ENTRIES The partial spreadsheet shown below is taken from the books of Albers Pet Supply, a business owned by Carm Albers, for the year ended December 31, 20--. Albers is on the periodic inventory system.

REQUIRED

1. Determine the adjusting entries by analyzing the difference between the adjusted trial balance and the trial balance.
2. Journalize the adjusting entries in a general journal.

	A	B	C	D	E	F	G
1	**Albers Pet Supply**						
2	**End-of-Period Spreadsheet**						
3	**For the Year Ended December 31, 20--**						
4	ACCOUNT TITLE	TRIAL BALANCE		ADJUSTMENTS		ADJUSTED TRIAL BALANCE	
5		DEBIT	CREDIT	DEBIT	CREDIT	DEBIT	CREDIT
6	Cash	26,000.00				26,000.00	
7	Accounts Receivable	18,200.00				18,200.00	
8	Merchandise Inventory	97,500.00				110,500.00	
9	Estimated Returns Inventory	4,160.00				5,590.00	
10	Supplies	10,400.00				4,290.00	
11	Prepaid Insurance	7,020.00				4,940.00	
12	Land	169,000.00				169,000.00	
13	Building	325,000.00				325,000.00	
14	Accum. Depr.—Building		130,000.00				146,250.00
15	Store Equipment	130,000.00				130,000.00	
16	Accum. Depr.—Store Equipment		52,000.00				58,500.00
17	Accounts Payable		12,480.00				12,480.00
18	Customer Refunds Payable		4,550.00				7,410.00
19	Wages Payable						4,550.00
20	Sales Tax Payable		7,670.00				7,670.00
21	Unearned Rent Revenue		11,570.00				5,850.00
22	C. Albers, Capital		369,603.00				369,603.00
23	C. Albers, Drawing	33,800.00				33,800.00	
24	Income Summary					97,500.00	110,500.00
25						4,160.00	5,590.00
26	Sales		682,682.00				682,682.00
27	Sales Returns and Allowances	18,850.00				21,710.00	
28	Rent Revenue						5,720.00
29	Purchases	162,500.00				162,500.00	
30	Purchases Returns and Allowances		1,820.00				1,820.00
31	Purchases Discounts		2,340.00				2,340.00
32	Freight-In	2,730.00				2,730.00	
33	Wages Expense	162,500.00				167,050.00	
34	Advertising Expense	16,900.00				16,900.00	
35	Supplies Expense					6,110.00	
36	Phone Expense	1,755.00				1,755.00	
37	Utilities Expense	10,400.00				10,400.00	
38	Insurance Expense					2,080.00	
39	Depr. Expense—Building					16,250.00	
40	Depr. Expense—Store Equipment					6,500.00	
41	Rent Expense	78,000.00				78,000.00	
42		1,274,715.00	1,274,715.00			1,420,965.00	1,420,965.00
43						593,645.00	808,652.00
44	Net Income					215,007.00	
45							

CHECK LIST
- ☐ Managing
- ☐ Planning
- ☐ Drafting
- ☐ Break
- ☐ Revising
- ☐ Managing

MANAGING YOUR WRITING

A friend of yours recently opened Abracadabra, a sportswear shop specializing in monogrammed athletic gear. Most merchandise is special ordered for customers. However, a small inventory is on hand. Your friend does not understand why a physical inventory is necessary before preparing the financial statements. She knows how much she paid for all merchandise purchased. Why not simply use this amount for cost of goods sold? After all, it has been paid for. Write a brief memo explaining the purpose of the physical inventory and why she should not use the cost of purchases as cost of goods sold.

ETHICS

ETHICS CASE

Jason Tierro, an inventory clerk at Lexmar Company, is responsible for taking a physical count of the goods on hand at the end of the year. He has been performing this duty for several years. This year, Jason was very busy due to a shortage of personnel at the company, so he decided to just estimate the amount of ending inventory instead of doing an accurate count. He reasoned that he could come very close to the true amount because of his past experience working with inventory. Besides, he was sure that the sophisticated computer program that Lexmar had just invested in kept an accurate record of inventory on hand.

1. What is your opinion of Jason's reasoning?
2. If Jason underestimates the dollar amount of ending inventory, what effect will it have on net income for the current accounting period?
3. Write a short paragraph explaining why a physical inventory should be taken at least once a year.
4. In groups of three or four, make a list of possible reasons that the actual ending inventory might not agree with the ending inventory according to a computer system.

MASTERY PROBLEM

✓ Adj. Trial Bal. total: $153,800
✓ Cost of goods sold: $159,475

John Neff owns and operates Waikiki Surf Shop. A year-end trial balance is provided on page 561. Year-end adjustment data for the Waikiki Surf Shop are shown below.

Neff uses the periodic inventory system. Year-end adjustment data are as follows:

(a, b) A physical count shows that merchandise inventory costing $51,800 is on hand as of December 31, 20--.

(c, d, e) Neff estimates that customers will be granted $2,000 in refunds of this year's sales next year and the merchandise expected to be returned will have a cost of $1,200.

(f) Supplies remaining at the end of the year, $600.

(g) Unexpired insurance on December 31, $2,600.

(h) Depreciation expense on the building for 20--, $5,000.

(i) Depreciation expense on the store equipment for 20--, $3,000.

(j) Wages earned but not paid as of December 31, $1,800.

(k) Neff also offers boat rentals which clients pay for in advance. Unearned boat rental revenue as of December 31 is $3,000.

REQUIRED

1. Prepare a year-end spreadsheet.
2. Journalize the adjusting entries.
3. Compute cost of goods sold using the spreadsheet prepared for part (1).

	A	B	C
1	Waikiki Surf Shop		
2	Trial Balance		
3	For the Year Ended December 31, 20--		
4	ACCOUNT TITLE	DEBIT BALANCE	CREDIT BALANCE
5			
6	Cash	30,000.00	
7	Accounts Receivable	22,500.00	
8	Merchandise Inventory	56,200.00	
9	Estimated Returns Inventory	800.00	
10	Supplies	2,700.00	
11	Prepaid Insurance	3,600.00	
12	Land	115,000.00	
13	Building	135,000.00	
14	Accumulated Depreciation—Building		24,000.00
15	Store Equipment	75,000.00	
16	Accumulated Depreciation—Store Equipment		22,500.00
17	Accounts Payable		15,000.00
18	Customer Refunds Payable		1,100.00
19	Wages Payable		
20	Unearned Boat Rent Revenue		33,000.00
21	J. Neff, Capital		240,100.00
22	J. Neff, Drawing	40,875.00	
23	Income Summary		
24			
25	Sales		404,950.00
26	Sales Returns and Allowances	6,000.00	
27	Boat Rental Revenue		
28	Purchases	157,500.00	
29	Purchases Returns and Allowances		1,200.00
30	Purchases Discounts		1,500.00
31	Freight-In	675.00	
32	Wages Expense	63,000.00	
33	Advertising Expense	11,250.00	
34	Supplies Expense		
35	Phone Expense	5,250.00	
36	Utilities Expense	18,000.00	
37	Insurance Expense		
38	Depreciation Expense—Building		
39	Depreciation Expense—Equipment		
40		743,350.00	743,350.00
41			

CHALLENGE PROBLEM

This problem challenges you to apply your cumulative accounting knowledge to move a step beyond the material in the chapter.

✓ Net purchases in 20-1: $410,000

Block Foods, a retail grocery store, has agreed to purchase all of its merchandise from Square Wholesalers. In return, Block receives a special discount on purchases. Over recent months, Square noticed that purchases by Block had been falling off. At first, Square simply thought that business might be down for Block and was hopeful that their purchases would pick up. When business with Block did not return to a normal level, Square requested financial statements from Block. Square's records indicate that Block purchased $300,000 worth of merchandise during 20-1, the most recent year.

(continued)

Selected information taken from Block's financial statements is as follows:

Balance Sheet	**12/31/-1**	**12/31/-0**
Inventory	$30,000	$20,000
Income Statement		
Cost of goods sold	$400,000	

REQUIRED

Compute net purchases made by Block during 20-1. Does it appear that Block violated the agreement?

ANSWERS TO SELF-STUDY TEST QUESTIONS

True/False

1. T 2. T 3. T 4. F (revenue is recognized) 5. F (contra-revenue account)

Multiple Choice

1. b 2. a 3. a 4. b 5. b

Checkpoint Exercises

1.

Beginning merchandise inventory	$ 20,000
Purchases	171,000
Goods available for sale	$191,000
Less ending inventory	15,000
Cost of goods sold	$176,000

2.

Unearned Ticket Revenue	15,000	
Ticket Revenue		15,000

3.

	A	B	C	D	E	F	G
1	ACCOUNT TITLE	TRIAL BALANCE		ADJUSTMENTS		ADJUSTED TRIAL BALANCE	
2		DEBIT	CREDIT	DEBIT	CREDIT	DEBIT	CREDIT
3	Merchandise Inventory	120,000.00		(b) 90,000.00	(a) 120,000.00	90,000.00	
4	Income Summary			(a) 120,000.00	(b) 90,000.00	120,000.00	90,000.00
5	Purchases	250,000.00				250,000.00	
6							
7							
8							

4.

10		Income Summary	50,000.00		10
11		Merchandise Inventory		50,000.00	11
12		Merchandise Inventory	60,000.00		12
13		Income Summary		60,000.00	13

5.

8		Inventory Short and Over	2,000.00		8
9		Merchandise Inventory		2,000.00	9
10					10

Expense Method of Accounting for Prepaid Expenses

LEARNING OBJECTIVES

Careful study of this appendix should enable you to:

LO1 Use the expense method of accounting for prepaid expenses.

LO2 Make the appropriate adjusting entries when the expense method is used for prepaid expenses.

LO1 The Expense Method

Use the expense method of accounting for prepaid expenses.

Under the **expense method** of accounting for prepaid expenses, supplies and other prepaid items are entered as expenses when purchased. Under this method, we must adjust the accounts at the end of each accounting period to record the unused portions as assets. To illustrate, let's assume that the following entry was made when office supplies were purchased:

4			Office Supplies Expense		425.00		4
5			Cash			425.00	5
6			Purchased office supplies				6

In the next section, we will illustrate the proper adjusting entry when using the expense method.

LO2 Adjusting Entries Under the Expense Method

Make the appropriate adjusting entries when the expense method is used for prepaid expenses.

Office Supplies Expense was debited for a total of $425 during the period. An inventory taken at the end of the period shows that supplies on hand amounted to $150. The following adjusting entry is made for supplies on hand:

8			Office Supplies		150.00		8
9			Office Supplies Expense			150.00	9
10							10

As shown in the T accounts below, after this entry is posted, the office supplies expense account has a debit balance of $275. This amount is reported on the income statement as an operating expense. The office supplies account has a debit balance of $150. It is reported on the balance sheet as a current asset.

Office Supplies

Debit		Credit	
Adj.	150		

Office Supplies Expense

Debit		Credit	
	425	Adj.	150
Bal.	275		

Let's consider another example of the use of the expense method. The following entry was made for the payment of $6,000 for a three-year insurance policy:

11		Insurance Expense	6 0 0 0 00		11
12		Cash		6 0 0 0 00	12
13		Paid insurance premium			13

At the end of the first year, one-third of the premium has expired and two-thirds remains. Thus, $2,000 for insurance expense should be reported on the income statement and $4,000 in prepaid insurance should be reported on the balance sheet. The following adjusting entry is made:

15		Prepaid Insurance	4 0 0 0 00		15
16		Insurance Expense		4 0 0 0 00	16
17					17

As shown in the T accounts below, after this entry is posted, the prepaid insurance account has a debit balance of $4,000. The insurance expense account has a debit balance of $2,000.

Prepaid Insurance

Debit		Credit	
Adj.	4,000		

Insurance Expense

Debit		Credit	
	6,000	Adj.	4,000
Bal.	2,000		

The asset and expense methods of accounting for prepaid expenses give the same final result. In the **asset method**, the prepaid item is first debited to an asset account. At the end of each period, the amount consumed is debited to an expense account. In the expense method, the original amount is debited to an expense account. At the end of each accounting period, the portion not consumed is debited to an asset account.

LEARNING OBJECTIVES	Key Points to Remember
LO1 Use the expense method of accounting for prepaid expenses.	Under the expense method, an expense account is debited when prepaid items are acquired.
LO2 Make the appropriate adjusting entries when the expense method is used for prepaid expenses.	At the end of the accounting period, an asset must be recognized for the amount of the prepaid item remaining. The expense account must be credited so that the ending balance represents the amount of the item consumed.

KEY TERMS

asset method (564) Under this method, the acquisition of a prepaid item is debited to an asset account.

expense method (563) Under this method, the acquisition of a prepaid item is debited to an expense account.

SERIES A EXERCISE

E 14Apx-1A (LO1/2)

EXPENSE METHOD OF ACCOUNTING FOR PREPAID EXPENSES Davidson's Food Mart paid $1,200 in advance to the local newspaper for advertisements that will appear monthly. The following entry was made:

4		Advertising Expense		1 2 0 0 00		4
5		Cash			1 2 0 0 00	5
6		Paid prepaid advertising				6

At the end of the year, December 31, 20--, Davidson received notification that advertisements costing $800 had been run. Prepare the adjusting entry.

SERIES B EXERCISE

E 14Apx-1B (LO1/2)

EXPENSE METHOD OF ACCOUNTING FOR PREPAID EXPENSES Ryan's Fish House purchased supplies costing $3,000 for cash. This amount was debited to the supplies expense account. At the end of the year, December 31, 20--, an inventory showed that supplies costing $500 remained. Prepare the adjusting entry.

SOURCE: WOOT.COM

Chapter 15 Financial Statements and Year-End Accounting for a Merchandising Business

LEARNING OBJECTIVES

Careful study of this chapter should enable you to:

- **LO1** Prepare a single-step and multiple-step income statement for a merchandising business.
- **LO2** Prepare a statement of owner's equity.
- **LO3** Prepare a classified balance sheet.
- **LO4** Compute standard financial ratios.
- **LO5** Prepare closing entries for a merchandising business.
- **LO6** Prepare reversing entries.

"Woot" was originally a truncated expression commonly used by players of Dungeons and Dragons for "Wow, loot!" Woot, Inc. is an online store, founded in 2004, that focuses on "selling cool stuff cheap." The company is known for its honest item descriptions and limited customer service. For example, the website explains that the company doesn't take calls because its employees are busy finding new products and shipping orders. Further, don't try to return something until all other options have been exhausted. If you want cheap prices, don't expect great service. This candor is refreshing, but we suspect they will help you out if you need it. Early on, the company claimed profitability was anticipated by 2043. "By then we should be retired; someone smarter might take over and jack up the prices." Clever, but they must have been doing something right. Woot was acquired by Amazon for $110 million, though it does not appear that prices have increased. Originally, the most unique characteristic of this merchandiser was that it sold only one product each day. It was available from 12:00 A.M. until sold out, or 11:59 P.M., when a different product was posted. Missed a cool product? Too bad. You couldn't buy yesterday's item. More recently, Woot has been offering multiple products including electronics **woot!**, computers **woot!**, home **woot!**, **woot!** Tools & Gardens, sport **woot!**, **woot!** Accessories & Watches, kids **woot!**, shirt **woot!**, wine **woot!**, and sellout **woot!**. And, of course, there is Today's Woot, the featured deal of the day. This is the best deal Woot has to offer, at the lowest price you will find on the Web. But if you miss it, you are out of luck.

Though clearly unique, this business must perform year-end accounting in the same manner as other retailers. In this chapter, you will learn how Woot and other merchandising firms prepare financial statements, compute financial ratios to evaluate performance, and prepare closing and reversing entries. No matter how unique, businesses must follow similar accounting procedures so that profitability and financial health can be compared across years and with other companies.

The first six chapters of this text illustrated the accounting cycle for a service business. In this chapter, we complete the accounting cycle for a merchandising business.

In Chapter 14, we prepared the end-of-period spreadsheet and adjusting entries for Sunflower Cycle. In this chapter, we will prepare financial statements, look briefly at financial statement analysis, and demonstrate closing and reversing entries.

LO1

The Income Statement

Prepare a single-step and multiple-step income statement for a merchandising business.

As you know, a primary purpose of the spreadsheet is to serve as an aid in preparing the financial statements. Figure 15-1 shows the completed spreadsheet for Sunflower Cycle. We will use it to prepare financial statements.

The purpose of an income statement is to summarize the results of operations during an accounting period. The income statement shows the sources of revenue, types of expenses, and the amount of the net income or net loss for the period. Two forms of the income statement commonly used are the single step and the multiple step. The **single-step income statement** lists all revenue items and their total first, followed by all expense items and their total. The difference, which is either net income or net loss, is then calculated. A single-step income statement for Sunflower Cycle is illustrated in Figure 15-2.

The use of the spreadsheet to prepare a **multiple-step income statement** is illustrated in Figure 15-3. This type of income statement is commonly used for merchandising businesses. The term "multiple-step" is used because the final net income is calculated on a step-by-step basis. Gross sales is shown first, less sales returns and allowances and sales discounts. This difference is called **net sales**. (Many published income statements begin with the amount of net sales.) Cost of goods sold is subtracted next to arrive at **gross profit** (sometimes called **gross margin**).

Operating expenses are then listed and subtracted from the gross profit to compute **income from operations** (sometimes called **operating income**). Operating expenses are directly associated with providing the primary goods and services of the business. Some companies divide operating expenses into the following subcategories:

Selling expenses. These expenses are directly associated with selling activities. Examples include:

- Sales Salaries Expense
- Sales Commissions Expense
- Advertising Expense
- Bank Credit Card Expense
- Delivery Expense
- Depreciation Expense—Store Equipment and Fixtures

FIGURE 15-1 Sunflower Cycle Spreadsheet

	A	B	C	D	E	F	G	H	I
1	**Sunflower Cycle**								
2	**End-of-Period Spreadsheet**								
3	**For the Year Ended December 31, 20--**								
4	ACCOUNT TITLE	TRIAL BALANCE		ADJUSTMENTS				ADJUSTED TRIAL BALANCE	
5		DEBIT	CREDIT		DEBIT		CREDIT	DEBIT	CREDIT
6	Cash	26,000.00						26,000.00	
7	Accounts Receivable	13,000.00						13,000.00	
8	Merchandise Inventory	52,000.00		(b)	45,600.00	(a)	52,000.00	45,600.00	
9	Estimated Returns Inventory	1,200.00		(e)	2,100.00	(d)	1,200.00	2,100.00	
10	Supplies	6,000.00				(f)	5,200.00	800.00	
11	Prepaid Insurance	2,800.00				(g)	2,400.00	400.00	
12	Land	115,000.00						115,000.00	
13	Building	390,000.00						390,000.00	
14	Accum. Depr.—Building		39,000.00			(h)	4,000.00		43,000.00
15	Equipment	48,000.00						48,000.00	
16	Accum. Depr.—Equipment		16,000.00			(i)	3,000.00		19,000.00
17	Notes Payable		5,000.00						5,000.00
18	Accounts Payable		24,000.00						24,000.00
19	Customer Refunds Payable		2,000.00			(c)	1,000.00		3,000.00
20	Wages Payable					(j)	700.00		700.00
21	Sales Tax Payable		1,600.00						1,600.00
22	Unearned Subscriptions Revenue		3,000.00						1,000.00
23	Mortgage Payable		30,000.00	(k)	2,000.00				30,000.00
24	Sam Tangari, Capital		417,200.00						417,200.00
25	Sam Tangari, Drawing	4,000.00						4,000.00	
26	Income Summary			(a)	52,000.00	(b)	45,600.00	52,000.00	45,600.00
27				(d)	1,200.00	(e)	2,100.00	1,200.00	2,100.00
28	Sales		473,000.00						473,000.00
29	Sales Returns and Allowances	7,000.00		(c)	1,000.00			8,000.00	
30	Interest Revenue		800.00						800.00
31	Rent Revenue		7,500.00						7,500.00
32	Subscriptions Revenue					(k)	2,000.00		2,000.00
33	Purchases	239,600.00						239,600.00	
34	Purchases Returns and Allowances		1,100.00						1,100.00
35	Purchases Discounts		900.00						900,00
36	Freight-in	1,300.00						1,300.00	
37	Wages Expense	70,300.00		(j)	700.00			71,000.00	
38	Advertising Expense	10,200.00						10,200.00	
39	Bank Credit Card Expense	8,100.00						8,100.00	
40	Rent Expense	14,000.00						14,000.00	
41	Supplies Expense			(f)	5,200.00			5,200.00	
42	Phone Expense	1,800.00						1,800.00	
43	Utilities Expense	7,500.00						7,500.00	
44	Insurance Expense			(g)	2,400.00			2,400.00	
45	Depr. Expense—Building			(h)	4,000.00			4,000.00	
46	Depr. Expense—Equipment			(i)	3,000.00			3,000.00	
47	Miscellaneous Expense	1,700.00						1,700.00	
48	Interest Expense	1,600.00						1,600.00	
49		1,021,100.00	1,021,100.00		119,200.00		119,200.00	1,077,500.00	1,077,500.00
50								432,600.00	533,000.00
51	Net Income							100,400.00	
52									

FIGURE 15-2 Single-Step Income Statement

Sunflower Cycle Income Statement For Year Ended December 31, 20--		
Revenues:		
Net sales	$465,000	
Interest revenue	800	
Rent revenue	7,500	
Subscriptions revenue	2,000	
Total revenues		$475,300
Expenses:		
Cost of goods sold	$244,400	
Wages expense	71,000	
Advertising expense	10,200	
Bank credit card expense	8,100	
Rent expense	14,000	
Supplies expense	5,200	
Phone expense	1,800	
Utilities expense	7,500	
Insurance expense	2,400	
Depreciation expense—building	4,000	
Depreciation expense—equipment	3,000	
Miscellaneous expense	1,700	
Interest expense	1,600	
Total expenses		374,900
Net income		$100,400

LEARNING KEY Although the formats for the single-step and multiple-step income statements are different, the reported net income is the same.

By showing other revenues and other expenses separately, it is possible to show income from operations. This makes it easier for the reader to see how the business is doing in its main activity.

General expenses. These expenses are associated with administrative, office, or general operating activities. Examples include:

- Rent Expense
- Office Salaries Expense
- Office Supplies Expense
- Phone Expense
- Utilities Expense
- Insurance Expense
- Depreciation Expense—Office Equipment

Finally, other revenues are added and other expenses are subtracted to arrive at net income (or net loss). Note that the operating expenses are arranged according to the order given in the chart of accounts. They could also be listed by descending amount, with Miscellaneous Expense last.

FIGURE 15-3 Using a Spreadsheet to Prepare a Multiple-Step Income Statement

	A	B	C
1	Sunflower Cycle		
2	End-of-Period Spreadsheet (Partial)		
3	For the Year Ended December 31, 20--		
4	ACCOUNT TITLE	ADJUSTED TRIAL BALANCE	
5		DEBIT	CREDIT
6			
7			
17			
18	Income Summary	52,000.00	45,600.00
19		1,200.00	2,100.00
20	Sales		473,000.00
21	Sales Returns and Allowances	8,000.00	
22	Interest Revenue		800.00
23	Rent Revenue		7,500.00
24	Subscriptions Revenue		2,000.00
25	Purchases	239,600.00	
26	Purchases Returns and Allowances		1,100.00
27	Purchases Discounts		900.00
28	Freight-In	1,300.00	
29	Wages Expense	71,000.00	
30	Advertising Expense	10,200.00	
31	Bank Credit Card Expense	8,100.00	
32	Rent Expense	14,000.00	
33	Supplies Expense	5,200.00	
34	Phone Expense	1,800.00	
35	Utilities Expense	7,500.00	
36	Insurance Expense	2,400.00	
37	Depr. Expense—Building	4,000.00	
38	Depr. Expense—Equipment	3,000.00	
39	Miscellaneous Expense	1,700.00	
40	Interest Expense	1,600.00	
41		1,077,500.00	1,077,500.00
42		432,600.00	533,000.00
43	Net Income	100,400.00	
44			

Sunflower Cycle
Income Statement
For Year Ended December 31, 20--

Revenue from sales:				
Sales			$473,000	
Less sales returns and allowances			8,000	
Net sales				$465,000
Cost of goods sold:				
Merchandise inventory, January 1, 20--		$ 52,000		
Estimated returns inventory, January 1, 20--		1,200	$ 53,200	
Purchases		$239,600		
Less: Purchases returns and allowances	$1,100			
Purchases discounts	900	2,000		
Net purchases		$237,600		
Add freight-in		1,300		
Cost of goods purchased			238,900	
Goods available for sale			$292,100	
Less: Merchandise inventory, December 31, 20--		$ 45,600		
Estimated returns inventory, December 31, 20--		2,100	47,700	
Cost of goods sold				244,300
Gross profit				$220,600
Operating expenses:				
Wages expense			$ 71,000	
Advertising expense			10,200	
Bank credit card expense			8,100	
Rent expense			14,000	
Supplies expense			5,200	
Phone expense			1,800	
Utilities expense			7,500	
Insurance expense			2,400	
Depreciation expense—building			4,000	
Depreciation expense—equipment			3,000	
Miscellaneous expense			1,700	
Total operating expenses				128,900
Income from operations				$ 91,700
Other revenues:				
Interest revenue			$ 800	
Rent revenue			7,500	
Subscriptions revenue			2,000	
Total other revenues				10,300
Other expenses:				
Interest expense				1,600
Net income				$100,400

CHECKPOINT

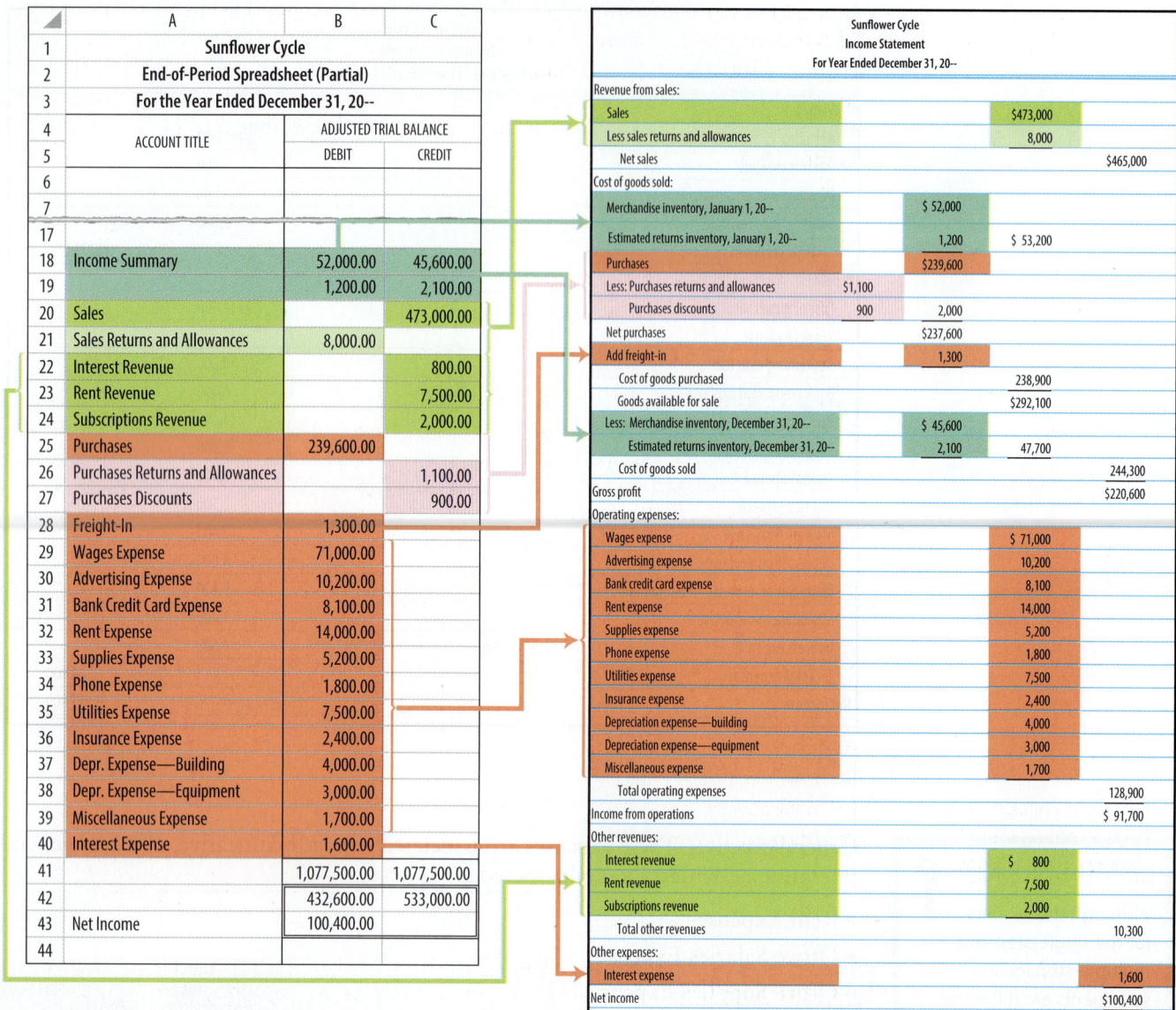

Complete Checkpoint-1 on page 592 to test your basic understanding of LO1.

LO2 The Statement of Owner's Equity

Prepare a statement of owner's equity.

The statement of owner's equity summarizes all changes in the owner's equity during the period. It includes the net income or loss and any additional investments or withdrawals by the owner. These changes result in the end-of-period balance shown on this statement and the balance sheet.

To prepare the statement of owner's equity for Sunflower Cycle, two sources of information are needed: (1) the spreadsheet and (2) Sam Tangari's capital account (no. 311) in the general ledger. The spreadsheet (Figure 15-1) shows net income of $100,400 and withdrawals of $4,000 during the year. Tangari's capital account (Figure 15-4) shows a beginning balance of $407,200. An additional $10,000 was invested in the business in February of the current year. The statement of owner's equity for Sunflower Cycle for the year ended December 31, 20--, is shown in Figure 15-5.

FIGURE 15-4 Capital Account for Sam Tangari

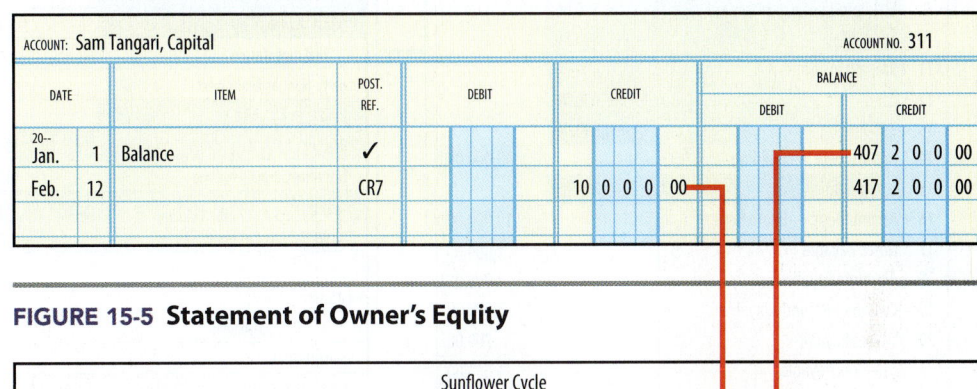

ACCOUNT: Sam Tangari, Capital ACCOUNT NO. 311

DATE		ITEM	POST. REF.	DEBIT	CREDIT	BALANCE DEBIT	BALANCE CREDIT
20-- Jan.	1	Balance	✓				407 2 0 0 00
Feb.	12		CR7		10 0 0 0 00		417 2 0 0 00

FIGURE 15-5 Statement of Owner's Equity

Sunflower Cycle
Statement of Owner's Equity
For Year Ended December 31, 20--

Sam Tangari, capital, January 1, 20 --		$407,200
Add additional investments		10,000
Total investment		$417,200
Net income for the year	$100,400	
Less withdrawals for the year	4,000	
Increase in capital		96,400
Sam Tangari, capital, December 31, 20--		$513,600

The statement of owner's equity is the same for a service business and a merchandising business.

CHECKPOINT

Complete Checkpoint-2 on page 592 to test your basic understanding of LO2.

LO3 Balance Sheet

Prepare a classified balance sheet.

The use of the spreadsheet to prepare a report form classified balance sheet is illustrated in Figure 15-6. The balance sheet classifications used by Sunflower Cycle are explained below.

LEARNING KEY

Note the use of the ending balance for merchandise inventory. It is reported on the income statement as part of the calculation of cost of goods sold. It also is reported on the balance sheet as a current asset.

Current Assets

Current assets include cash and all other assets expected to be converted into cash or consumed within one year or the normal operating cycle of the business, whichever is longer. The **operating cycle** is the length of time generally required for a business to buy inventory, sell it, and collect the cash. This time period is generally less than a year. Thus, most firms use one year for classifying current assets. In a merchandising business, the current assets usually include cash, receivables (such as accounts receivable and notes receivable), merchandise inventory, and estimated returns inventory. Since prepaid expenses, such as unused supplies and unexpired insurance, are likely to be consumed within a year, and they also are reported as current assets.

FIGURE 15-6 Using a Spreadsheet to Prepare a Report Form Classified Balance Sheet

	A	B	C
1	Sunflower Cycle		
2	End-of-Period Spreadsheet (Partial)		
3	For the Year Ended December 31, 20--		
4	ACCOUNT TITLE	ADJUSTED TRIAL BALANCE	
5		DEBIT	CREDIT
6	Cash	26,000.00	
7	Accounts Receivable	13,000.00	
8	Merchandise Inventory	45,600.00	
9	Estimated Returns Inventory	2,100.00	
10	Supplies	800.00	
11	Prepaid Insurance	400.00	
12	Land	115,000.00	
13	Building	390,000.00	
14	Accum. Depr.—Building		43,000.00
15	Equipment	48,000.00	
16	Accum. Depr.—Equipment		19,000.00
17	Notes Payable		5,000.00
18	Accounts Payable		24,000.00
19	Customer Refunds Payable		3,000.00
20	Wages Payable		700.00
21	Sales Tax Payable		1,600.00
22	Unearned Subscriptions Revenue		1,000.00
23	Mortgage Payable		30,000.00
24	Sam Tangari, Capital		417,200.00
25	Sam Tangari, Drawing	4,000.00	
26			
43			

Sunflower Cycle Balance Sheet December 31, 20--			
Assets			
Current assets:			
Cash		$ 26,000	
Accounts receivable		13,000	
Merchandise inventory		45,600	
Estimated returns inventory		2,100	
Supplies		800	
Prepaid insurance		400	
Total current assets			$ 87,900
Property, plant, and equipment:			
Land		$115,000	
Building	$ 390,000		
Less accum. depr.—building	43,000	347,000	
Equipment	$ 48,000		
Less accum. depr.—equip.	19,000	29,000	491,900
Total assets			$578,900
Liabilities			
Current liabilities:			
Notes payable	$ 5,000		
Accounts payable	24,000		
Customer refunds payable	3,000		
Wages payable	700		
Sales tax payable	1,600		
Unearned subscriptions revenue	1,000		
Mortgage payable (current portion)	500		
Total current liabilities		$ 35,800	
Long-term liabilities:			
Mortgage payable (current portion)	$ 30,000		
Less current portion	500	29,500	
Total liabilities			$ 65,300
Owner's Equity			
Sam Tangari, capital			513,600
Total liabilities and owner's equity			$578,900

*From statement of owner's equity.

Current assets are listed on the balance sheet from the most liquid to least liquid. **Liquidity** refers to the speed with which the company can convert the asset to cash. Cash is the most liquid asset and is always listed first. Notes Receivable, Accounts Receivable, Merchandise Inventory, and Estimated Returns Inventory often follow it on the balance sheet.

Property, Plant, and Equipment

Assets that are expected to be used for more than one year in the operation of a business are called **property, plant, and equipment**. Examples include land, buildings, office equipment, store equipment, and delivery equipment. Of these assets, only land is permanent; however, all of these assets have useful lives that are comparatively long. Typically, assets with longer useful lives are listed first.

The balance sheet of Sunflower Cycle shows Land, Building, and Equipment. Land is not depreciated. Accumulated depreciation amounts are shown as deductions from the costs of the building and equipment. The difference represents the **undepreciated cost**, or **book value**, of the assets. This amount less any salvage value will be written off as depreciation expense in future periods.

The current portion of long-term debt, the amount due within one year, is reported as a current liability. The remainder, the amount not due for more than one year, is reported under long-term liabilities.

Current Liabilities

Current liabilities include those obligations that are due within one year or the normal operating cycle of the business, whichever is longer, and will require the use of current assets. As of December 31, the current liabilities of Sunflower Cycle consist of Notes Payable, Accounts Payable, Customer Refunds Payable, Wages Payable, Sales Tax Payable, Unearned Subscriptions Revenue, and the portion of Mortgage Payable that is due within the next year.

Long-Term Liabilities

Long-term liabilities include those obligations that will extend beyond one year or the normal operating cycle, whichever is longer. A common long-term liability is a mortgage payable.

A **mortgage** is a written agreement specifying that if the borrower does not repay a debt, the lender has the right to take over specific property to satisfy the debt. When the debt is paid, the mortgage becomes void. **Mortgage Payable** is an account that is used to reflect an obligation that is secured by a mortgage on certain property.

Owner's Equity

CHECKPOINT

Complete Checkpoint-3 on page 592 to test your basic understanding of LO3.

The permanent owner's equity accounts reported on the balance sheet are determined by the type of organization. The accounts for a sole proprietorship, a partnership, and a corporation differ. Sunflower Cycle is a sole proprietorship and reports one owner's equity account, Sam Tangari, Capital. The balance of this account is taken from the statement of owner's equity. Partnerships are illustrated in Chapter 19 and corporations are discussed in Chapters 20 and 21.

LO4 Financial Statement Analysis

Compute standard financial ratios.

Both management and creditors are interested in using the financial statements to evaluate the financial condition and profitability of the firm. This can be done by making a few simple calculations.

Balance Sheet Analysis

Recall the following:

1. Current assets include cash, items that will be converted to cash, and items that will be consumed within one year.
2. Current liabilities are obligations that will require the use of current assets.

Thus, the difference between current assets and current liabilities represents the amount of capital the business has available for current operations. This is called **working capital**.

Working Capital = Current Assets − Current Liabilities

The balance sheet in Figure 15-6 shows that Sunflower Cycle has current assets of $87,900 and current liabilities of $35,800. Thus, the working capital at year end is $52,100 ($87,900 − $35,800). This amount should be more than adequate to satisfy current operating requirements.

Two measures of the firm's ability to pay its current liabilities are the **current ratio** and **quick ratio**. The formulas for calculating these ratios are as follows:

> **LEARNING KEY**
> Ratio analysis is most informative when the ratios are compared with past performance and with those of similar businesses.

				Sunflower Cycle		
Current Ratio	=	$\dfrac{\text{Current Assets}}{\text{Current Liabilities}}$	=	$\dfrac{\$87{,}900}{\$35{,}800}$	=	2.5 to 1
Quick Ratio	=	$\dfrac{\text{Quick Assets}}{\text{Current Liabilities}}$	=	$\dfrac{\$39{,}000}{\$35{,}800}$	=	1.1 to 1

Sunflower Cycle's current ratio of 2.5 to 1 is a little high which indicates a favorable financial position. The traditional "rule of thumb" has been that a current ratio should be about 2 to 1, but many businesses operate successfully on a current ratio of 1.5 to 1. Although a rule of thumb is helpful, it is better to compare an individual company to industry averages, which are available on the Internet.

> Information on industry averages is available in various publications from Dun & Bradstreet, Standard & Poor's, and Moody's.

Quick assets include cash and all other current assets that can be converted into cash quickly, such as accounts receivable and temporary investments. Temporary investments are discussed in more advanced textbooks. The balance sheet in Figure 15-6 shows total quick assets of $39,000 ($26,000 in cash + $13,000 in accounts receivable). This produces a quick ratio of 1.1 to 1. Quick assets appear to be more than adequate to meet current obligations. The traditional rule of thumb has been that a quick ratio should be about 1 to 1, but many businesses operate successfully on a quick ratio of 0.6 to 1.

Interstatement Analysis

Interstatement analysis provides a comparison of the relationships between selected income statement and balance sheet amounts. A good example of interstatement analysis is the ratio of net income to owner's equity in the business. This ratio is known as **return on owner's equity**.

Sunflower Cycle

$$\frac{\text{Return on}}{\text{Owner's Equity}} = \frac{\text{Net Income}}{\text{Average Owner's Equity}} = \frac{\$100{,}400}{(\$407{,}200 + \$513{,}600) \div 2}$$

$$= \frac{\$100{,}400}{\$460{,}400}$$

$$= 21.8\%$$

The statement of owner's equity in Figure 15-5 shows that the owner's equity of Sunflower Cycle was $407,200 on January 1 and $513,600 on December 31. The net income for the year of $100,400 is 21.8% of the average owner's equity. A comparison of this ratio with the return on owner's equity in prior years should be of interest to the owner. It may also be of interest to compare the return on owner's equity of Sunflower Cycle with the same ratio for other businesses of comparable nature and size. In general, however, this is considered an excellent rate of return.

A second ratio involving both income statement and balance sheet accounts is a measure of the time required to collect cash from credit customers. This financial measure is often computed in two ways. The **accounts receivable turnover** is the number of times the accounts receivable "turned over," or were collected, during the

Net credit sales is generally not reported in the financial statements. Use net sales, instead. As long as the proportion of cash and credit sales is reasonably stable over time, this ratio will provide a reasonable measure of the business's ability to collect receivables in a timely manner from year to year.

accounting period. Of course, a higher number indicates that cash is collected more quickly. This ratio is calculated as follows:

$$\text{Accounts Receivable Turnover} = \frac{\text{Net Credit Sales for the Period}}{\text{Average Accounts Receivable}}$$

The accounts receivable turnover for Sunflower Cycle for the year ended December 31 is computed as follows:

Net credit sales for the year (determined from the accounting records)	$110,000
Accounts receivable balance, January 1, 20-- (taken from last year's balance sheet)	10,000
Accounts receivable balance, December 31, 20--	13,000

Sunflower Cycle

$$\text{Average Accounts Receivable} = \frac{\text{Beginning Balance} + \text{Ending Balance}}{2} = \frac{\$10{,}000 + \$13{,}000}{2} = \$11{,}500$$

$$\text{Accounts Receivable Turnover} = \frac{\text{Net Credit Sales for the Period}}{\text{Average Accounts Receivable}} = \frac{\$110{,}000}{\$11{,}500} = 9.6$$

The **average collection period** is calculated by dividing the number of days in the year (365) by the rate of turnover to determine the number of days credit customers take to pay for their purchases. Sunflower Cycle's customers are taking about 38 days.

$$365 \text{ days} \div 9.6 = 38.2 \text{ days}$$

Comparing the average collection period with a business's credit terms offers an indication of whether customers are paying within the terms. If Sunflower Cycle allows credit terms of n/45, an average collection period of 38 days would suggest that customers are paying on a timely basis.

A third ratio involving both income statement and balance sheet accounts is the rate of **inventory turnover**. This is the number of times the merchandise inventory turned over, or was sold, during the accounting period. This ratio is calculated as follows:

$$\text{Inventory Turnover} = \frac{\text{Cost of Goods Sold for the Period}}{\text{Average Inventory}}$$

If inventory is taken only at the end of each accounting period, the average inventory for the period can be calculated by adding the beginning and ending inventories (including estimated returns inventory) and dividing their sum by two. Sunflower Cycle's turnover for the year ended December 31 is computed as follows:

Cost of goods sold for the period	$244,400
Beginning inventory	53,200
Ending inventory	47,700

Sunflower Cycle

$$\text{Average Inventory} = \frac{\text{Beginning Inventory} + \text{Ending Inventory}}{2} = \frac{\$53{,}200 + \$47{,}700}{2} = \$50{,}450$$

$$\text{Inventory Turnover} = \frac{\text{Cost of Goods Sold for the Period}}{\text{Average Inventory}} = \frac{\$244{,}400}{\$50{,}450} = 4.8$$

The **average days to sell inventory** can be computed by dividing the number of days in the year (365) by the inventory turnover. For Sunflower Cycle, it takes about two and one half months.

365 days ÷ 4.8 = 76 days

The higher the rate of inventory turnover, the smaller the profit required on each dollar of sales to produce a satisfactory gross profit. This is because the increase in the number of units sold offsets the smaller amount of gross profit earned per unit. For example, grocery stores have a very small gross profit on each item sold, but make up for this with a rapid inventory turnover. Other types of businesses, jewelers for example, need a high gross profit on each item because their inventory turnover is quite slow. Evaluations of Sunflower Cycle's rate of inventory turnover would require comparison with prior years, other companies, or its industry.

CHECKPOINT

Complete Checkpoint-4 on pages 592–593 to test your basic understanding of LO4.

LO5 Closing Entries

Prepare closing entries for a merchandising business.

Closing entries for a service business were illustrated in Chapter 6. The process is essentially the same for a merchandising business. All revenues and expenses reported on the income statement must be closed to Income Summary. Then, the income summary and drawing accounts are closed to the owner's capital account. Keep in mind, however, that a few new accounts were needed for a merchandising business. These include Sales Returns and Allowances, Sales Discounts, Purchases Returns and Allowances, and Purchases Discounts. Since these are temporary accounts reported on the income statement, they also must be closed. The easiest way to complete the closing process is by using the spreadsheet to prepare the closing entries in four basic steps, as illustrated in Figures 15-7 and 15-8.

FIGURE 15-7 The Closing Process

THE CLOSING PROCESS FOR A MERCHANDISING BUSINESS

STEP 1 All income statement accounts with credit balances are debited, with an offsetting credit to Income Summary.

STEP 2 All income statement accounts with debit balances are credited, with an offsetting debit to Income Summary.

STEP 3 The resulting balance in Income Summary, which is the net income or loss for the period, is transferred to the owner's capital account.

ACCOUNT: Income Summary — ACCOUNT NO. 331

DATE		ITEM	POST. REF.	DEBIT	CREDIT	BALANCE DEBIT	BALANCE CREDIT	Adjustments to:
20-- Dec.	31	Adjusting	J5	52,000.00		52,000.00		Remove Beg. Inventory
	31	Adjusting	J5		45,600.00	6,400.00		Enter End. Inventory
	31	Adjusting	J5	1,200.00		7,600.00		Remove Beg. Est. Ret. Inv.
	31	Adjusting	J5		2,100.00	5,500.00		Enter End. Est. Ret. Inv.
	31	Closing	J6		485,300.00		479,800.00	Closing step 1
	31	Closing	J6	379,400.00			100,400.00	Closing step 2
	31	Closing	J6	100,400.00		—	—	Closing step 3

STEP 4 The balance in the owner's drawing account is transferred to the owner's capital account.

FIGURE 15-8 Closing Entries for a Merchandising Business

	A	B	C
1	Sunflower Cycle		
2	End-of-Period Spreadsheet (Partial)		
3	For Year Ended December 31, 20--		
4	ACCOUNT TITLE	ADJUSTED TRIAL BALANCE	
5		DEBIT	CREDIT
6	Sam Tangari, Capital		417,200.00
7	Sam Tangari, Drawing	4,000.00	
8	Income Summary	52,000.00	45,600.00
9		1,200.00	2,100.00
10	Sales		473,000.00
11	Sales Returns and Allowances	8,000.00	
12	Interest Revenue		800.00
13	Rent Revenue		7,500.00
14	Subscriptions Revenue		2,000.00
15	Purchases	239,600.00	
16	Purchases Returns and Allow.		1,100.00
17	Purchases Discounts		900.00
18	Freight-In	1,300.00	
19	Wages Expense	71,000.00	
20	Advertising Expense	10,200.00	
21	Bank Credit Card Expense	8,100.00	
22	Rent Expense	14,000.00	
23	Supplies Expense	5,200.00	
24	Phone Expense	1,800.00	
25	Utilities Expense	7,500.00	
26	Insurance Expense	2,400.00	
27	Depr. Expense—Building	4,000.00	
28	Depr. Expense—Equipment	3,000.00	
29	Miscellaneous Expense	1,700.00	
30	Interest Expense	1,600.00	
31			

1 2 3

GENERAL JOURNAL PAGE 6

	DATE		DESCRIPTION	POST. REF.	DEBIT	CREDIT	
1	20--		Closing Entries				1
2	Dec.	31	Sales		473 000 00		2
3			Interest Revenue		800 00		3
4			Rent Revenue		7 500 00		4
5			Subscriptions Revenue		2 000 00		5
6			Purchases Returns and Allowances		1 100 00		6
7			Purchases Discounts		900 00		7
8			Income Summary			485 300 00	8
9							9
10		31	Income Summary		379 400 00		10
11			Sales Returns and Allowances			8 000 00	11
12			Purchases			239 600 00	12
13			Freight-In			1 300 00	13
14			Wages Expense			71 000 00	14
15			Advertising Expense			10 200 00	15
16			Bank Credit Card Expense			8 100 00	16
17			Rent Expense			14 000 00	17
18			Supplies Expense			5 200 00	18
19			Phone Expense			1 800 00	19
20			Utilities Expense			7 500 00	20
21			Insurance Expense			2 400 00	21
22			Depreciation Exp.—Building			4 000 00	22
23			Depreciation Exp.—Equip.			3 000 00	23
24			Miscellaneous Expense			1 700 00	24
25			Interest Expense			1 600 00	25
26							26
27		31	Income Summary		100 400 00		27
28			Sam Tangari, Capital			100 400 00	28
29							29
30		31	Sam Tangari, Capital		4 000 00		30
31			Sam Tangari, Drawing			4 000 00	31
32							32

Post-Closing Trial Balance

A trial balance of the general ledger accounts taken after the temporary owner's equity accounts have been closed is called a **post-closing trial balance**. The purpose of the post-closing trial balance is to prove that the general ledger is in balance at the beginning of a new accounting period, before any transactions for the new accounting period are entered. It should also confirm that all temporary accounts have zero balances. Figure 15-9 shows a post-closing trial balance for Sunflower Cycle.

The post-closing trial balance must be prepared by taking the balances from the general ledger accounts. It should not be prepared from the balances on the spreadsheet. Using the general ledger accounts helps ensure that all temporary accounts have been closed properly.

FIGURE 15-9 Post-Closing Trial Balance

	A	B	C	D
1	Sunflower Cycle			
2	Post-Closing Trial Balance			
3	For the Year Ended December 31, 20--			
4–5	ACCOUNT TITLE	ACCOUNT NO.	DEBIT BALANCE	CREDIT BALANCE
6	Cash	101	26,000.00	
7	Accounts Receivable	122	13,000.00	
8	Merchandise Inventory	131	45,600.00	
9	Estimated Returns Inventory	135	2,100.00	
10	Supplies	141	800.00	
11	Prepaid Insurance	145	400.00	
12	Land	161	115,000.00	
13	Building	171	390,000.00	
14	Accumulated Depreciation—Building	171.1		43,000.00
15	Equipment	181	48,000.00	
16	Accumulated Depreciation—Equipment	181.1		19,000.00
17	Notes Payable	201		5,000.00
18	Accounts Payable	202		24,000.00
19	Customer Refunds Payable	203		3,000.00
20	Wages Payable	219		700.00
21	Sales Tax Payable	231		1,600.00
22	Unearned Subscriptions Revenue	241		1,000.00
23	Mortgage Payable	251		30,000.00
24	Sam Tangari, Capital	311		513,600.00
25			640,900.00	640,900.00
26				

CHECKPOINT ✓

Complete Checkpoint-5 on page 594 to test your basic understanding of LO5.

VOLODYMYR KRASYUK/SHUTTERSTOCK.COM

A BROADER VIEW

Who Cares About Tracking Financial Ratios?

Tracking a business's average collection period for receivables can help investors avoid making poor investments. Take the case of Kendall Square, a supercomputer maker. In an effort to increase sales and profits, Kendall Square recognized large amounts of revenues that had not actually been earned. Since no cash was received for these sales, accounts receivable increased dramatically (by 57%). Similarly, the average collection period increased to 157 days. Large increases in the average collection period should warn potential investors that something might be wrong. What happened at Kendall Square? Over $10 million of sales on account was never collected. This was equal to almost half of the revenues reported for the year. When eventually discovered, Kendall Square's stock price fell from $24.25 to $2.28 a share.

LO6 Reversing Entries

Prepare reversing entries.

Numerous adjusting entries are needed at the end of the accounting period to bring the account balances up to date for presentation in the financial statements. Although not required, some of these adjusting entries should be reversed at the beginning of the next accounting period. This is done to simplify the recording of transactions in the new accounting period. As its name implies, a **reversing entry** is the reverse or opposite of the adjusting entry.

ADJUSTING ENTRY

4	Dec.	31	Wages Expense	7 0 0 00		4
5			Wages Payable		7 0 0 00	5

REVERSING ENTRY (OPPOSITE)

7	Jan.	1	Wages Payable	7 0 0 00		7
8			Wages Expense		7 0 0 00	8

To see the advantage of using reversing entries, let's consider the effect of reversing Sunflower Cycle's adjusting entry for wages earned, but not paid, at the end of the year. Figure 15-10 shows that accrued wages on December 31 were $700. These wages are for work performed by the employees on the last three days of the accounting period ($200 + $200 + $300 = $700). The employees will be paid on Friday, January 2, the normal payday.

Note that the adjusting and closing entries are the same, regardless of whether a reversing entry is made. However, the reversing entry on January 1 has an impact on the entry made when the employees are paid. **Without** a reversing entry, the payment on January 2, 20-2, must be split between reduction of the wages payable account for wages earned in 20-1 and Wages Expense for wages earned in 20-2. **With** a reversing entry, the bookkeeper simply debits Wages Expense and credits Cash, as is done on every other payday. Thus, the likelihood of error is reduced. Reversing entries are particularly important in large businesses where the individual recording the entry for wages may not even know what adjusting entries were made.

Not all adjusting entries should be reversed. To determine which adjusting entries to reverse, follow this rule: *Except for the first year of operations, reverse all adjusting entries that increase an asset or liability account from a zero balance.*

> **LEARNING KEY**
> Reverse all adjusting entries that increase an asset or liability account from a zero balance.

Except for the first year of operation, merchandise inventory, and contra-assets like accumulated depreciation, will have existing balances. Thus, they should never be reversed. The adjusting entries for Sunflower Cycle are shown in Figure 15-11. Note that only the adjustment for accrued wages is reversed in Figure 15-12.

FIGURE 15-10 Adjusting, Closing, and Reversing Entries for Wages

	20-1 12/29/-1 Monday	20-1 12/30/-1 Tuesday	20-1 12/31/-1 Wednesday	20-2 1/1/-2 Thursday	20-2 1/2/-2 Friday
Wages Earned	200	200	300	200	200
Wages Paid	0	0	0	0	1,100
Total Earned			700		400
Total Paid			0		1,100
Accrued Wages on 12/31/-1			700		

Date	Without Reversing Entry			With Reversing Entry		
12/31/-1 Adj. Entry	Wages Expense	700		Wages Expense	700	
	Wages Payable		700	Wages Payable		700
12/31/-1 Closing Entry	Income Summary	71,000		Income Summary	71,000	
	Wages Expense		71,000	Wages Expense		71,000
1/1/-2 Rev. Entry	No Entry			Wages Payable	700	
				Wages Expense		700
1/2/-2 Payment of Payroll	Wages Expense	400		Wages Expense	1,100	
	Wages Payable	700		Cash		1,100
	Cash		1,100			

Without Reversing Entry

Wages Expense

Description	Debit	Credit	Description
Bal.	70,300		
12/31/-1 Adj.	700		
		71,000	12/31/-1 Close
1/2/-2 Payroll	400		

Wages Payable

Description	Debit	Credit	Description
		700	12/31/-1 Adj.
1/2/-2 Payroll	700		

Cash

Description	Debit	Credit	Description
		1,100	1/2/-2 Payroll

With Reversing Entry

Wages Expense

Description	Debit	Credit	Description
Bal.	70,300		
12/31/-1 Adj.	700		
		71,000	12/31/-1 Close
		700	1/1/-2 Reversing
1/2/-2 Payroll	1,100		
Bal.	400		

Wages Payable

Description	Debit	Credit	Description
		700	12/31/-1 Adj.
1/1/-2 Reverse	700		

Cash

Description	Debit	Credit	Description
		1,100	1/2/-2 Payroll

FIGURE 15-11 Which Adjusting Entries to Reverse?

GENERAL JOURNAL PAGE 5

	DATE		DESCRIPTION	POST. REF.	DEBIT	CREDIT		SHOULD THE ADJUSTMENT BE REVERSED?
1			Adjusting Entries				1	
2	20-- Dec.	31	Income Summary		52 0 0 0 00		2	Never reverse adjustments for merchandise inventory.
3			Merchandise Inventory			52 0 0 0 00	3	
4							4	
5		31	Merchandise Inventory		45 6 0 0 00		5	Never reverse adjustments for merchandise inventory.
6			Income Summary			45 6 0 0 00	6	
7							7	
8		31	Sales Returns and Allowances		1 0 0 0 00		8	No. No asset or liability with a zero balance has been increased.
9			Customer Refunds Payable			1 0 0 0 00	9	
10							10	
11		31	Income Summary		1 2 0 0 00		11	Never reverse adjustments for merchandise inventory.
12			Estimated Returns Inventory			1 2 0 0 00	12	
13							13	
14		31	Estimated Returns Inventory		2 1 0 0 00		14	Never reverse adjustments for merchandise inventory.
15			Income Summary			2 1 0 0 00	15	
16							16	
17		31	Supplies Expense		5 2 0 0 00		17	No. No asset or liability with a zero balance has been increased.
18			Supplies			5 2 0 0 00	18	
19							19	
20		31	Insurance Expense		2 4 0 0 00		20	No. No asset or liability with a zero balance has been increased.
21			Prepaid Insurance			2 4 0 0 00	21	
22							22	
23		31	Depr. Expense—Building		4 0 0 0 00		23	Never reverse adjustments for depreciation.
24			Accum. Depr.—Building			4 0 0 0 00	24	
25							25	
26		31	Depr. Expense—Equipment		3 0 0 0 00		26	Never reverse adjustments for depreciation.
27			Accum. Depr.—Equipment			3 0 0 0 00	27	
28							28	
29		31	Wages Expense		7 0 0 00		29	Yes. A liability account with a zero balance has been increased.
30			Wages Payable			7 0 0 00	30	
31							31	
32		31	Unearned Subscriptions Revenue		2 0 0 0 00		32	No. No asset or liability with a zero balance has been increased.
33			Subscriptions Revenue			2 0 0 0 00	33	
34							34	

FIGURE 15-12 Reversing Entry for Sunflower Cycle

GENERAL JOURNAL PAGE 7

	DATE		DESCRIPTION	POST. REF.	DEBIT	CREDIT	
1			Reversing Entries				1
2	20-- Jan.	1	Wages Payable		7 0 0 00		2
3			Wages Expense			7 0 0 00	3
4							4
5							5

CHECKPOINT

Complete Checkpoint-6 on page 594 to test your basic understanding of LO6.

SELF-STUDY

LEARNING OBJECTIVES	Key Points to Remember
LO1 **Prepare a single-step and multiple-step income statement for a merchandising business.**	The general formats for a single-step and multiple-step income statement are shown below.

Single-Step
Income Statement
For Year Ended December 31, 20--

Revenues:		
List all revenues	$xxx	
Total revenues		$xxx
Expenses:		
Cost of goods sold	$xxx	
List all other expenses	xxx	
Total expenses		xxx
Net income		$xxx

Multiple-Step
Income Statement
For Year Ended December 31, 20--

Revenue from sales:		
Sales	$xxx	
Less sales returns and allowances	xxx	
Net sales		$xxx
Cost of goods sold		xxx
Gross profit		$xxx
Operating expenses:		
List all operating expenses	$xxx	
Total operating expenses		xxx
Income from operations		$xxx
Other revenue:		
List all other revenue	$xxx	
Total other revenue		xxx
Other expenses:		
List all other expenses	$xxx	
Total other expenses		xxx
Net income		$xxx

LO2 **Prepare a statement of owner's equity.**

A statement of owner's equity has the following format:

Business Name
Statement of Owner's Equity
For Year Ended December 31, 20--

Capital, January 1, 20--		$xxx
Add additional investments		xxx
Total investment		$xxx
Net income for the year	$xxx	
Less withdrawals	xxx	
Increase in capital		xxx
Capital, December 31, 20--		$xxx

LEARNING OBJECTIVES	Key Points to Remember
LO3 Prepare a classified balance sheet.	A classified balance sheet has the following major headings:

Business Name
Balance Sheet
December 31, 20--

Assets			
Current assets:			
List all current assets		$xxx	
Total current assets			$xxx
Property, plant, and equipment:			
List all property, plant, and equipment	$xxx		
Less accumulated depreciation (if appropriate)	xxx	$xxx	
Total property, plant, and equipment			xxx
Total assets			$xxx
Liabilities			
Current liabilities:			
List all current liabilities	$xxx		
Total current liabilities		$xxx	
Long-term liabilities:			
List all long-term liabilities	$xxx		
Total long-term liabilities		xxx	
Total liabilities			$xxx
Owner's Equity			
Owner's capital			xxx
Total liabilities and owner's equity			$xxx

LO4 Compute standard financial ratios.

The following measures of financial condition may be computed from financial statement information:

Working Capital = Current Assets − Current Liabilities

Current Ratio = Current Assets ÷ Current Liabilities

Quick Ratio = Quick Assets ÷ Current Liabilities

Return on Owner's Equity = Net Income ÷ Average Owner's Equity

$$\text{Accounts Receivable Turnover} = \frac{\text{Net Credit Sales for the Period}}{\text{Average Accounts Receivable}}$$

$$\text{Average Collection Period} = \frac{365}{\text{Accounts Receivable Turnover}}$$

$$\text{Inventory Turnover} = \frac{\text{Cost of Goods Sold for the Period}}{\text{Average Inventory}}$$

$$\text{Average Days to Sell Inventory} = \frac{365}{\text{Inventory Turnover}}$$

(continued)

LEARNING OBJECTIVES	Key Points to Remember
LO5 Prepare closing entries for a merchandising business.	The four steps in the closing process for a merchandising business are as follows: **STEP 1** All income statement accounts with credit balances are debited, with an offsetting credit to Income Summary. **STEP 2** All income statement accounts with debit balances are credited, with offsetting debit to Income Summary. **STEP 3** The resulting balance in Income Summary, which is the net income or loss for the period, is transferred to the owner's capital account. **STEP 4** The balance in the owner's drawing account is transferred to the owner's capital account.
LO6 Prepare reversing entries.	Use the following rule to determine which adjusting entries to reverse: Except for the first year of operations, reverse all adjusting entries that increase an asset or liability account from a zero balance.

DEMONSTRATION PROBLEM

Sara Wilson owns and operates Home Electronics. She has a store where she sells and repairs televisions and stereo equipment. A completed spreadsheet for 20-1 is provided on page 585. Sara made a $20,000 additional investment during 20-1. The current portion of Mortgage Payable is $1,000. Net credit sales for 20-1 were $200,000, and the balance of Accounts Receivable on January 1 was $26,000.

REQUIRED

1. Prepare a multiple-step income statement.
2. Prepare a statement of owner's equity.
3. Prepare a balance sheet.
4. Compute the following measures of performance and financial condition for 20-1:
   (a) Current ratio
   (b) Quick ratio
   (c) Working capital
   (d) Return on owner's equity
   (e) Accounts receivable turnover and the average number of days required to collect receivables
   (f) Inventory turnover and the average number of days required to sell inventory
5. Prepare adjusting entries and indicate which should be reversed and why.
6. Prepare closing entries.
7. Prepare reversing entries for the adjustments where appropriate.

	A	B	C	D	E	F	G	H	I
1	**Home Electronics**								
2	**End-of-Period Spreadsheet**								
3	**For the Year Ended December 31, 20--**								
4	ACCOUNT TITLE	TRIAL BALANCE		ADJUSTMENTS				ADJUSTED TRIAL BALANCE	
5		DEBIT	CREDIT		DEBIT		CREDIT	DEBIT	CREDIT
6	Cash	10,000.00						10,000.00	
7	Accounts Receivable	22,500.00						22,500.00	
8	Merchandise Inventory	37,400.00		(b)	44,400.00	(a)	37,400.00	44,400.00	
9	Estimated Returns Inventory	1,600.00		(e)	1,200.00	(d)	1,600.00	1,200.00	
10	Supplies	2,700.00				(f)	2,100.00	600.00	
11	Prepaid Insurance	3,600.00				(g)	2,700.00	900.00	
12	Land	15,000.00						15,000.00	
13	Building	135,000.00						135,000.00	
14	Accum. Depr.—Building		24,000.00			(h)	6,000.00		30,000.00
15	Store Equipment	75,000.00						75,000.00	
16	Accum. Depr.—Store Equipment		22,500.00			(i)	4,500.00		27,000.00
17	Notes Payable		7,500.00						7,500.00
18	Accounts Payable		15,000.00						15,000.00
19	Customer Refunds Payable		1,000.00			(c)	500.00		1,500.00
20	Wages Payable					(j)	675.00		675.00
21	Sales Tax Payable		2,250.00						2,250.00
22	Unearned Repair Revenue		18,000.00	(k)	15,000.00				3,000.00
23	Mortgage Payable		45,000.00						45,000.00
24	Sara Wilson, Capital		158,600.00						158,600.00
25	Sara Wilson, Drawing	30,000.00						30,000.00	
26	Income Summary			(a)	37,400.00	(b)	44,400.00	37,400.00	44,400.00
27				(d)	1,600.00	(e)	1,200.00	1,600.00	1,200.00
28	Sales		300,750.00						300,750.00
29	Sales Returns and Allowances	9,000.00		(c)	500.00			9,500.00	
30	Sales discounts	800.00						800.00	
31	Repair Fees						15,000.00		15,000.00
32	Interest Revenue		1,350.00						1,350.00
33	Purchases	157,500.00						157,500.00	
34	Purchases Returns and Allowances		1,200.00						1,200.00
35	Purchases Discounts		1,500.00						1,500.00
36	Freight-In	450.00						450.00	
37	Wages Expense	63,500.00		(j)	675.00			63,675.00	
38	Advertising Expense	3,750.00						3,750.00	
39	Supplies Expense			(f)	2,100.00			2,100.00	
40	Phone Expense	5,250.00						5,250.00	
41	Utilities Expense	18,000.00						18,000.00	
42	Insurance Expense			(g)	2,700.00			2,700.00	
43	Depr. Expense—Building			(h)	6,000.00			6,000.00	
44	Depr. Expense—Store Equipment			(i)	4,500.00			4,500.00	
45	Miscellaneous Expense	3,375.00						3,375.00	
46	Interest Expense	4,725.00						4,725.00	
47		598,650.00	598,650.00		116,075.00		116,075.00	655,925.00	655,925.00
48								321,325.00	365,400.00
49	Net Income							44,075.00	
50									

(continued)

SOLUTION 1.

Home Electronics
Income Statement
For Year Ended December 31, 20-1

Revenue from sales:				
Sales			$300,750	
Less: Sales returns and allowances		$ 9,500		
Sales discounts		800	10,300	
Net sales				$290,450
Cost of goods sold:				
Merchandise inventory, January 1, 20--		$ 37,400		
Estimated returns inventory		1,600	$ 39,000	
Purchases		$157,500		
Less: Purchases returns and allowances	$1,200			
Purchases discounts	1,500	2,700		
Net purchases		$154,800		
Add freight-in		450		
Cost of goods purchased			155,250	
Goods available for sale			$194,250	
Less: Merchandise inventory, December 31, 20--		$ 44,400		
Estimated returns inventory		1,200	45,600	
Cost of goods sold				148,650
Gross profit				$141,800
Operating expenses:				
Wages expense			$ 63,675	
Advertising expense			3,750	
Supplies expense			2,100	
Phone expense			5,250	
Utilities expense			18,000	
Insurance expense			2,700	
Depreciation expense—building			6,000	
Depreciation expense—store equipment			4,500	
Miscellaneous expense			3,375	
Total operating expenses				109,350
Income from operations				$ 32,450
Other revenues:				
Interest revenue			$ 1,350	
Repair fees			15,000	
Total other revenues				16,350
Other expenses:				
Interest expense				4,725
Net income				$ 44,075

SOLUTION 2.

Home Electronics
Statement of Owner's Equity
For Year Ended December 31, 20-1

S. Wilson, capital, January 1, 20--		$138,600
Add additional investments		20,000
Total investment		$158,600
Net income for the year	$44,075	
Less withdrawals for the year	30,000	
Increase in capital		14,075
S. Wilson, capital, December 31, 20--		$172,675

SOLUTION 3.

Home Electronics Balance Sheet December 31, 20-1			
Assets			
Current assets:			
Cash		$ 10,000	
Accounts receivable		22,500	
Merchandise inventory		44,400	
Estimated returns inventory		1,200	
Supplies		600	
Prepaid insurance		900	
Total current assets			$ 79,600
Property, plant, and equipment:			
Land		$ 15,000	
Building	$ 135,000		
Less accumulated depreciation	30,000	105,000	
Equipment	$ 75,000		
Less accumulated depreciation	27,000	48,000	168,000
Total assets			$247,600
Liabilities			
Current liabilities:			
Notes payable	$ 7,500		
Accounts payable	15,000		
Customer refunds payable	1,500		
Wages payable	675		
Sales tax payable	2,250		
Unearned repair fees	3,000		
Mortgage payable (current portion)	1,000		
Total current liabilities		$ 30,925	
Long-term liabilities:			
Mortgage payable	$ 45,000		
Less current portion	1,000	44,000	
Total liabilities			$ 74,925
Owner's Equity			
Sara Wilson, capital			172,675
Total liabilities and owner's equity			$247,600

SOLUTION 4.

(a) **Current Ratio**

$$\frac{\text{Current Assets}}{\text{Current Liabilities}} = \frac{\$79{,}600}{\$30{,}925} = 2.6 \text{ to } 1$$

(b) **Quick Ratio**

$$\frac{\text{Quick Assets}}{\text{Current Liabilities}} = \frac{\$32{,}500}{\$30{,}925} = 1.1 \text{ to } 1$$

Cash	$10,000
Accts. Rec.	22,500
	$32,500

(c) **Working Capital** = Current Assets − Current Liabilities

$$\$79{,}600 - \$30{,}925 = \$48{,}675$$

(d) **Return on Owner's Equity**

$$\frac{\text{Net Income}}{\text{Average Owner's Equity}} = \frac{\$44{,}075}{\$155{,}638} = 28.3\%$$

(continued)

Jan. 1	$138,600
Dec. 31	$172,675
Average	$155,638

(e) **Accounts Receivable Turnover**

$$\frac{\text{Net Credit Sales for the Period}}{\text{Average Accounts Receivable}} = \frac{\$200{,}000}{\$24{,}250} = 8.25 \quad \frac{365}{8.25} = 44.3 \text{ days to collect}$$

A/R 1-1	$26,000
A/R 12-31	$25,500
Average	$24,250

(f) **Inventory Turnover**

$$\frac{\text{CGS}}{\text{Average Inventory}} = \frac{\$148{,}650}{42{,}300} = 3.51 \quad \frac{365}{3.51} = 103.9 \text{ days to sell}$$

Inv. 1-1	$39,000
Inv. 12-31	$45,600
Average	$42,300

SOLUTION 5.

GENERAL JOURNAL PAGE 3

	DATE		DESCRIPTION	POST. REF.	DEBIT	CREDIT	
1			Adjusting Entries				1
2	20-1 Dec.	31	Income Summary		37,400.00		2
3			Merchandise Inventory			37,400.00	3
4							4
5		31	Merchandise Inventory		44,400.00		5
6			Income Summary			44,400.00	6
7							7
8		31	Sales Returns and Allowances		500.00		8
9			Customer Refunds Payable			500.00	9
10							10
11		31	Income Summary		1,600.00		11
12			Estimated Returns Inventory			1,600.00	12
13							13
14		31	Estimated Returns Inventory		1,200.00		14
15			Income Summary			1,200.00	15
16							16
17		31	Supplies Expense		2,100.00		17
18			Supplies			2,100.00	18
19							19
20		31	Insurance Expense		2,700.00		20
21			Prepaid Insurance			2,700.00	21
22							22
23		31	Depr. Expense—Building		6,000.00		23
24			Accum. Depr.—Building			6,000.00	24
25							25
26		31	Depr. Expense—Store Equipment		4,500.00		26
27			Accum. Depr.—Store Equipment			4,500.00	27
28							28
29		31	Wages Expense		675.00		29
30			Wages Payable			675.00	30
31							31
32		31	Unearned Repair Fees		15,000.00		32
33			Repair Fees			15,000.00	33
34							34

SHOULD THE ADJUSTMENT BE REVERSED?

Never reverse adjustments for merchandise inventory.

Never reverse adjustments for merchandise inventory.

No. No asset or liability with a zero balance has been increased.

Never reverse adjustments for merchandise inventory.

Never reverse adjustments for merchandise inventory.

No. No asset or liability with a zero balance has been increased.

No. No asset or liability with a zero balance has been increased.

Never reverse adjustments for depreciation.

Never reverse adjustments for depreciation.

Yes. A liability account with a zero balance has been increased.

No. No asset or liability with a zero balance has been increased.

SOLUTION 6.

GENERAL JOURNAL PAGE 4

	DATE		DESCRIPTION	POST. REF.	DEBIT	CREDIT	
1			Closing Entries				1
2	20-1 Dec.	31	Repair Fees		15,000.00		2
3			Sales		300,750.00		3
4			Interest Revenue		1,350.00		4
5			Purchases Returns and Allowances		1,200.00		5
6			Purchases Discounts		1,500.00		6
7			Income Summary			319,800.00	7
8							8
9		31	Income Summary		282,325.00		9
10			Sales Returns and Allowances			9,500.00	10
11			Sales Discounts			800.00	11
12			Purchases			157,500.00	12
13			Freight-In			450.00	13
14			Wages Expense			63,675.00	14
15			Advertising Expense			3,750.00	15
16			Supplies Expense			2,100.00	16
17			Phone Expense			5,250.00	17
18			Utilities Expense			18,000.00	18
19			Insurance Expense			2,700.00	19
20			Depr. Expense—Building			6,000.00	20
21			Depr. Expense—Store Equipment			4,500.00	21
22			Miscellaneous Expense			3,375.00	22
23			Interest Expense			4,725.00	23
24							24
25		31	Income Summary		44,075.00		25
26			Sara Wilson, Capital			44,075.00	26
27							27
28		31	Sara Wilson, Capital		30,000.00		28
29			Sara Wilson, Drawing			30,000.00	29
30							30

> Recall, four adjusting entries have already been made to Income Summary.

ACCOUNT: Income Summary ACCOUNT NO. 331

DATE		ITEM	POST. REF.	DEBIT	CREDIT	BALANCE DEBIT	BALANCE CREDIT	
20-- Dec.	31	Adjusting		37,400.00		37,400.00		Remove Beg. Inv.
	31	Adjusting			44,400.00		7,000.00	Enter End. Inv.
	31	Adjusting		1,600.00			5,400.00	Remove Beg. Est. Ret. Inv.
	31	Adjusting			1,200.00		6,600.00	Enter End. Est. Ret. Inv.
	31	Closing			319,800.00		326,400.00	Closing step 1
	31	Closing		282,325.00			44,075.00	Closing step 2
	31	Closing		44,075.00				Closing step 3

SOLUTION 7.

GENERAL JOURNAL PAGE 5

	DATE		DESCRIPTION	POST. REF.	DEBIT	CREDIT	
1			Reversing Entries				1
2	20-2 Jan.	1	Wages Payable		675 00		2
3			Wages Expense			675 00	3
4							4

KEY TERMS

accounts receivable turnover (574) The number of times the accounts receivable turned over, or were collected, during the accounting period. When 365 is divided by the turnover, this measure can be expressed in terms of the average number of days required to collect receivables.

average collection period (575) The number of days in the year (365) divided by the accounts receivable turnover. Provides an indication of the number of days credit customers take to pay for their purchases.

average days to sell inventory (576) The number of days in the year (365) divided by the inventory turnover. Provides an indication of the average number of days required to sell inventory.

book value (573) See undepreciated cost.

current assets (571) Cash and all other assets expected to be converted into cash or consumed within one year or the normal operating cycle of the business, whichever is longer.

current liabilities (573) Those obligations that are due within one year or the normal operating cycle of the business, whichever is longer, and will require the use of current assets.

current ratio (574) Current assets divided by current liabilities.

general expenses (569) Those expenses associated with administrative, office, or general operating activities.

gross margin (567) See gross profit.

gross profit (567) Net sales minus cost of goods sold.

income from operations (567) Gross profit minus operating expenses on a multiple-step income statement.

interstatement analysis (574) Compares the relationship between certain amounts in the income statement and balance sheet.

inventory turnover (575) The number of times the merchandise inventory turned over, or was sold, during the accounting period. When 365 is divided by the turnover, this measure can be expressed in terms of the average number of days required to sell inventory.

liquidity (572) Refers to the speed with which an asset can be converted to cash.

long-term liabilities (573) Those obligations that will extend beyond one year or the normal operating cycle, whichever is longer.

mortgage (573) A written agreement specifying that if the borrower does not repay a debt, the lender has the right to take over specific property to satisfy the debt.

Mortgage Payable (573) An account that is used to reflect an obligation that is secured by a mortgage on certain property.

multiple-step income statement (567) This statement shows a step-by-step calculation of net sales, cost of goods sold, gross profit, operating expenses, income from operations, other revenues and expenses, and net income.

net sales (567) Gross sales less sales returns and allowances and less sales discounts.

operating cycle (571) The length of time generally required for a business to buy inventory, sell it, and collect the cash.

operating income (567) See income from operations.

post-closing trial balance (577) A trial balance taken after the temporary owner's equity accounts have been closed.

property, plant, and equipment (572) Assets that are expected to be used for more than one year in the operation of a business.

quick assets (574) Cash and all other current assets that can be converted into cash quickly, such as accounts receivable and temporary investments.

quick ratio (574) Quick assets divided by current liabilities.

return on owner's equity (574) Net income divided by average owner's equity.

reversing entry (579) The opposite of the adjusting entry. It is made on the first day of the next accounting period and simplifies recording transactions in the new period.

selling expenses (567) Those expenses directly associated with selling activities.

single-step income statement (567) This statement lists all revenue items and their total first, followed by all expense items and their total.

undepreciated cost (573) Cost of plant and equipment less the accumulated depreciation amounts. Also called book value.

working capital (573) The difference between current assets and current liabilities, which represents the amount of capital the business has available for current operations.

SELF-STUDY TEST QUESTIONS

True/False

1. **LO1** A multiple-step form of income statement calculates gross profit, before subtracting operating expenses.
2. **LO3** Current assets include cash, items expected to convert into cash, and items that will be consumed during a year or the normal operating cycle, whichever is shorter.
3. **LO3** Current assets are listed on the balance sheet in order of liquidity.
4. **LO4** Working capital is the difference between current assets and current liabilities.
5. **LO4** Accounts receivable turnover is the number of times merchandise inventory turned over or was sold during the accounting period.

Multiple Choice

1. **LO3** Which of these assets is *not* a current asset?
   (a) Cash
   (b) Accounts Receivable
   (c) Office Equipment
   (d) Merchandise Inventory
2. **LO3** Which of these would be listed *first* on a balance sheet?
   (a) Accounts Receivable
   (b) Delivery Equipment
   (c) Accounts Payable
   (d) Prepaid Insurance

3. **LO4** Which of these is considered a *quick asset*?
   (a) Merchandise Inventory (c) Office Equipment
   (b) Accounts Receivable (d) Prepaid Insurance
4. **LO4** To calculate the accounts receivable turnover ratio, ______ is divided by average accounts receivable.
   (a) Net sales (c) Total sales
   (b) Cost of goods sold (d) Net credit sales
5. **LO4** Inventory turnover is calculated by dividing cost of goods sold by
   (a) average accounts receivable. (c) average inventory.
   (b) average owner's equity. (d) accounts receivable turnover.

CHECKPOINT

Checkpoint Exercises

Use the following spreadsheet for Yoder's Cool Stuff for Checkpoint Exercises 1, 2, and 3.

	A	B	C	D	E	F	G	H	I
1	**Yoder's Cool Stuff**								
2	**End-of-Period Spreadsheet**								
3	**For the Year Ended December 31, 20--**								
4	ACCOUNT TITLE	TRIAL BALANCE		ADJUSTMENTS				ADJUSTED TRIAL BALANCE	
5		DEBIT	CREDIT		DEBIT		CREDIT	DEBIT	CREDIT
6	Cash	7,400.00						7,400.00	
7	Accounts Receivable	13,000.00						13,000.00	
8	Merchandise Inventory	36,000.00		(b)	75,000.00	(a)	36,000.00	75,000.00	
9	Estimated Returns Inventory	4,000.00		(e)	5,000.00		4,000.00	5,000.00	
10	Supplies	1,600.00				(f)	1,200.00	400.00	
11	Prepaid Insurance	4,000.00				(g)	500.00	3,500.00	
12	Delivery Equipment	160,000.00						160,000.00	
13	Accum. Depr.—Delivery Equipment		40,000.00			(i)	20,000.00		60,000.00
14	Accounts Payable		30,000.00						30,000.00
15	Customer Refunds Payable		6,000.00			(c)	3,000.00		9,000.00
16	Wages Payable					(j)	1,000.00		1,000.00
17	Pete Yoder, Capital		88,000.00						88,000.00
18	Pete Yoder, Drawing	3,000.00						3,000.00	
19	Income Summary			(a)	36,000.00	(b)	75,000.00	36,000.00	75,000.00
20				(d)	4,000.00	(e)	5,000.00	4,000.00	5,000.00
21	Sales		261,000.00						261,000.00
22	Sales Returns and Allowances	18,000.00		(c)	3,000.00			21,000.00	
23	Purchases	160,000.00						160,000.00	
24	Wages Expense	13,000.00		(j)	1,000.00			14,000.00	
25	Rent Expense	4,000.00						4,000.00	
26	Supplies Expense			(f)	1,200.00			1,200.00	
27	Phone Expense	1,000.00						1,000.00	
28	Insurance Expense			(g)	500.00			500.00	
29	Depr. Expense—Delivery Equipment			(i)	20,000.00			20,000.00	
30		425,000.00	425,000.00		145,700.00		145,700.00	529,000.00	529,000.00
31								261,700.00	341,000.00
32	Net Income							79,300.00	
33									

1. **LO1** Prepare a multiple-step income statement for Yoder's Cool Stuff.
2. **LO2** Prepare a statement of owner's equity for Yoder's Cool Stuff. Assume the beginning balance of Yoder's capital account was $88,000.
3. **LO3** Prepare a balance sheet for Yoder's Cool Stuff.
4. **LO4** Using the financial statements for Herman's Parts provided on page 593, compute the following ratios:
   (a) Working capital (c) Return on owner's equity
   (b) Current ratio (d) Inventory turnover

Herman's Parts
Income Statement
For Month Ended May 31, 20--

Revenue from sales:			
Sales		$28,000	
Less sales returns and allowances		500	
Net sales			$27,500
Cost of goods sold:			
Merchandise inventory, May 1, 20--	$3,800		
Estimated returns inventory, May 1, 20--	200	$ 4,000	
Purchases		18,000	
Goods available for sale		$22,000	
Less: Merchandise inventory May 31, 20--	$5,700		
Estimated returns inventory, May 31, 20--	300	6,000	
Cost of goods sold			16,000
Gross profit			$11,500
Operating expenses:			
Wages expense		$ 7,800	
Rent Expense		300	
Supplies expense		100	
Phone expense		80	
Insurance expense		50	
Depreciation expense—delivery equipment		1,000	
Total operating expenses			9,330
Net income			$ 2,170

Herman's Parts
Statement of Owner's Equity
For Month Ended May 31, 20--

Herman Gillespie, capital, May 1, 20--		$5,000
Add additional investment		1,000
Total investment		$6,000
Net income for the month	$2,170	
Less withdrawals for the month	1,000	
Increase in capital		1,170
Herman Gillespie, capital, May 31, 20--		$7,170

Herman's Parts
Balance Sheet
May 31, 20--

Assets		
Current assets:		
Cash	$ 500	
Accounts receivable	1,920	
Merchandise inventory	5,700	
Estimated returns inventory	300	
Supplies	200	
Prepaid insurance	400	
Total current assets		$ 9,020
Property, plant, and equipment:		
Delivery equipment	$6,000	
Less accumulated depreciation	3,000	3,000
Total assets		$12,020
Liabilities		
Current liabilities:		
Accounts payable	$3,300	
Customer refunds payable	500	
Wages payable	1,050	
Total current liabilities		$ 4,850
Owner's Equity		
Herman Gillespie, capital		7,170
Total liabilities and owner's equity		$12,020

5. **LO5** Using the spreadsheet provided on page 594 for Yoder's Cool Stuff, prepare the closing entries.

6. **LO6** Pinto Company made the following adjusting entries at the end of the year. It is Pinto's fifth year in operation. Prepare the appropriate reversing entry(ies).

Depreciation Expense—Delivery Equipment	500.00	
Accumulated Depreciation—Delivery Equipment		500.00
Interest Expense	1,000.00	
Interest Payable		1,000.00

The answers to the Self-Study Test Questions are at the end of the chapter (pages 611–613).

APPLYING YOUR KNOWLEDGE

CengageNowv2 provides "Show Me How" videos for selected exercises and problems. Additional resources, such as Excel templates for completing selected exercises and problems, are available for download from the companion website at Cengage.com.

REVIEW QUESTIONS

LO1 1. Describe the nature of the two forms of an income statement.

LO4 2. Name and describe the calculation of two measures that provide an indication of a business's ability to pay current obligations.

LO4 3. Describe how to calculate the following ratios:
(a) Return on owner's equity
(b) Accounts receivable turnover
(c) Inventory turnover

LO5 4. Where is the information obtained that is needed in journalizing the closing entries?

LO5 5. Explain the function of each of the four closing entries made by Sunflower Cycle.

LO5 6. What is the purpose of a post-closing trial balance?

LO6 7. What is the primary purpose of reversing entries?

LO6 8. What is the customary date for reversing entries?

LO6 9. What adjusting entries should be reversed?

SERIES A EXERCISES

E 15-1A (LO1)
✓ Net sales: $140,600

REVENUE SECTION, MULTIPLE-STEP INCOME STATEMENT Based on the information that follows, prepare the revenue section of a multiple-step income statement.

Sales	$150,000
Sales Returns and Allowances	6,000
Sales Discounts	3,400

E 15-2A (LO1)
✓ Cost of goods sold: $103,670

COST OF GOODS SOLD SECTION, MULTIPLE-STEP INCOME STATEMENT Based on the information that follows, prepare the cost of goods sold section of a multiple-step income statement.

Merchandise Inventory, January 1, 20--	$ 35,000
Estimated Returns Inventory, January 1,20--	2,000
Purchases	106,000
Purchases Returns and Allowances	5,800
Purchases Discounts	3,230
Freight-In	700
Merchandise Inventory, December 31, 20--	29,500
Estimated Returns Inventory, December 31, 20--	1,500

E 15-3A (LO1)
✓ Cost of goods sold: $101,145
✓ Net income: $1,463

MULTIPLE-STEP INCOME STATEMENT Use the following information to prepare a multiple-step income statement, including the revenue section and the cost of goods sold section, for Sauter Office Supplies for the year ended December 31, 20--.

Sales	$156,300
Sales Returns and Allowances	2,360
Sales Discounts	4,167
Interest Revenue	425
Merchandise Inventory, January 1, 20--	29,000
Estimated Returns Inventory, January 1, 20--	600
Purchases	112,000
Purchases Returns and Allowances	5,640
Purchases Discounts	2,690
Freight-In	875
Merchandise Inventory, December 31, 20--	32,000
Estimated Returns Inventory, December 31, 20--	1,000
Wages Expense	27,600
Supplies Expense	700
Phone Expense	900
Utilities Expense	8,000
Insurance Expense	1,300
Depreciation Expense—Equipment	3,800
Miscellaneous Expense	590
Interest Expense	4,700

E 15-4A (LO4)
✓ Current ratio: 4.64 to 1
✓ Return on owner's equity: 28.9%
✓ Inventory turnover: 3.13

FINANCIAL RATIOS Based on the financial statements for Jackson Enterprises (income statement, statement of owner's equity, and balance sheet) shown on pages 596–597, prepare the following financial ratios. All sales are credit sales. The Accounts Receivable balance on January 1, 20--, was $21,600.

1. Working capital
2. Current ratio
3. Quick ratio
4. Return on owner's equity
5. Accounts receivable turnover and average number of days required to collect receivables
6. Inventory turnover and average number of days required to sell inventory

(continued)

Jackson Enterprises
Income Statement
For Year Ended December 31, 20--

Revenue from sales:				
Sales			$184,200	
Less sales returns and allowances			2,100	
Net sales				$182,100
Cost of goods sold:				
Merchandise Inventory, January 1, 20--		$30,000		
Estimated Returns Inventory, January 1, 20--		1,300	$ 31,300	
Purchases		$92,800		
Less: Purchases returns and allowances	$1,800			
Purchases discounts	1,856	3,656		
Net purchases		$89,144		
Add freight-in		933		
Cost of goods purchased			90,077	
Goods available for sale			$121,377	
Less: Merchandise inventory, Dec. 31, 20--		$27,000		
Estimated returns inventory, Dec. 31, 20--		1,177	28,177	
Cost of goods sold				93,200
Gross profit				$ 88,900
Operating expenses:				
Wages expense			$ 38,000	
Advertising expense			1,180	
Supplies expense			380	
Phone expense			2,210	
Utilities expense			11,000	
Insurance expense			900	
Depreciation expense—building			4,000	
Depreciation expense—equipment			3,800	
Miscellaneous expense			530	
Total operating expenses				62,000
Income from operations				$ 26,900
Other revenues:				
Interest revenue			$ 1,800	
Other expenses:				
Interest expense			900	900
Net income				$ 27,800

Jackson Enterprises
Statement of Owner's Equity
For Year Ended December 31, 20--

J. B. Gray, capital, January 1, 20--		$ 88,000
Net income for the year	$27,800	
Less withdrawals for the year	11,600	
Increase in capital		16,200
J. B. Gray, capital, December 31, 20--		$104,200

Jackson Enterprises Balance Sheet December 31, 20--			
Assets			
Current assets:			
Cash		$20,800	
Accounts receivable		18,900	
Merchandise inventory, Dec. 31, 20--	$27,000		
Estimated returns inventory, Dec. 31, 20--	1,177	28,177	
Supplies		1,323	
Prepaid insurance		900	
Total current assets			$ 70,100
Property, plant, and equipment:			
Building	$90,000		
Less accumulated depreciation—building	28,000	$62,000	
Equipment	$33,000		
Less accumulated depreciation—equipment	7,500	25,500	
Total property, plant, and equipment			87,500
Total assets			$157,600
Liabilities			
Current liabilities:			
Accounts payable	$11,100		
Customer refunds payable	1,500		
Wages payable	500		
Sales tax payable	1,200		
Mortgage payable (current portion)	800		
Total current liabilities		$15,100	
Long-term liabilities:			
Mortgage payable	$39,100		
Less current portion	800	38,300	
Total liabilities			$ 53,400
Owner's Equity			
J. B. Gray, capital			104,200
Total liabilities and owner's equity			$157,600

E 15-5A (LO5)

CLOSING ENTRIES Using the spreadsheet and partially completed Income Summary Account on page 598, prepare the following:

1. Closing entries for Gimbel's Gifts and Gadgets in a general journal.
2. A post-closing trial balance.

E 15-6A (LO6)

REVERSING ENTRIES From the spreadsheet used in Exercise 15-5A, identify the adjusting entry(ies) that should be reversed and prepare the reversing entry(ies).

E 15-7A (LO5/6)

ADJUSTING, CLOSING, AND REVERSING ENTRIES Prepare entries for (a), (b), and (c) listed below using two methods. First, prepare the entries without making a reversing entry. Second, prepare the entries with the use of a reversing entry. Use T-accounts to assist your analysis.

(a) Wages paid during 20-1 are $20,800.

(b) Wages earned but not paid (accrued) as of December 31, 20-1, are $300.

(c) On January 3, 20-2, payroll of $800 is paid, which includes the $300 of wages earned but not paid in December.

EXERCISE 15-5A

	A	B	C	D	E	F	G	H	I
1	Gimbles Gifts and Gadgets								
2	End-of-Period Spreadsheet								
3	For the Year Ended December 31, 20-1								
4	ACCOUNT TITLE	TRIAL BALANCE		ADJUSTMENTS				ADJUSTED TRIAL BALANCE	
5		DEBIT	CREDIT		DEBIT		CREDIT	DEBIT	CREDIT
6	Cash	16,000.00						16,000.00	
7	Accounts Receivable	11,200.00						11,200.00	
8	Merchandise Inventory	60,000.00		(b)	68,000.00	(a)	60,000.00	68,000.00	
9	Estimated Returns Inventory	2,560.00		(e)	3,440.00	(d)	2,560.00	3,440.00	
10	Supplies	6,400.00				(f)	3,760.00	2,640.00	
11	Prepaid Insurance	4,320.00				(g)	1,280.00	3,040.00	
12	Land	104,000.00						104,000.00	
13	Building	200,000.00						200,000.00	
14	Accum. Depr.—Building		80,000.00			(h)	10,000.00		90,000.00
15	Store Equipment	80,000.00						80,000.00	
16	Accum. Depr.—Store Equipment		32,000.00			(i)	4,000.00		36,000.00
17	Accounts Payable		7,680.00						7,680.00
18	Customer Refunds Payable		2,800.00			(c)	1,760.00		4,560.00
19	Wages Payable					(j)	2,800.00		2,800.00
20	Sales Tax Payable		4,720.00						4,720.00
21	Unearned Subscriptions Revenue		7,120.00	(k)	3,520.00				3,600.00
22	J.M. Gimble, Capital		227,448.00						227,448.00
23	J.M. Gimble, Drawing	20,800.00						20,800.00	
24	Income Summary			(a)	60,000.00	(b)	68,000.00	60,000.00	68,000.00
25				(d)	2,560.00	(e)	3,440.00	2,560.00	3,440.00
26	Sales		420,112.00						420,112.00
27	Sales Returns and Allowances	11,600.00		(c)	1,760.00			13,360.00	
28	Rent Revenue					(k)	3,520.00		3,520.00
29	Purchases	100,000.00						100,000.00	
30	Purchases Returns and Allowances		1,120.00						1,120.00
31	Purchases Discounts		1,440.00						1,440.00
32	Freight-In	1,680.00						1,680.00	
33	Wages Expense	100,000.00		(j)	2,800.00			102,800.00	
34	Advertising Expense	10,400.00						10,400.00	
35	Supplies Expense			(f)	3,760.00			3,760.00	
36	Phone Expense	1,080.00						1,080.00	
37	Utilities Expense	6,400.00						6,400.00	
38	Insurance Expense			(g)	1,280.00			1,280.00	
39	Depr. Expense—Building			(h)	10,000.00			10,000.00	
40	Depr. Expense—Store Equipment			(f)	4,000.00			4,000.00	
41	Rent Expense	48,000.00						48,000.00	
42		784,440.00	784,440.00		161,120.00		161,120.00	874,440.00	874,440.00
43								365,320.00	497,632.00
44	Net Income							132,312.00	
45									

ACCOUNT: Income Summary — ACCOUNT NO. 331

DATE		ITEM	POST. REF.	DEBIT	CREDIT	BALANCE DEBIT	BALANCE CREDIT
20-1 Dec.	31	Adjusting		60 0 0 0 00		60 0 0 0 00	
	31	Adjusting			68 0 0 0 00		8 0 0 0 00
	31	Adjusting		2 5 6 0 00			5 4 4 0 00
	31	Adjusting			3 4 4 0 00		8 8 8 0 00

SERIES A PROBLEMS

P 15-8A (LO1/2/3)
✓ Cost of goods sold: $150,960
✓ Total assets: $639,400

INCOME STATEMENT, STATEMENT OF OWNER'S EQUITY, AND BALANCE SHEET Paulson's Pet Store completed the Adjusted Trial Balance on page 600 for the year ended December 31, 20--. Owner's equity as of January 1, 20--, was $504,320. The current portion of Note Payable is $2,000.

REQUIRED

1. Prepare a multiple-step income statement.
2. Prepare a statement of owner's equity.
3. Prepare a balance sheet.

P 15-9A (LO4)
✓ Working capital: $85,200
✓ Quick ratio: 1.8 to 1
✓ Accts. receivable turnover: 32.8

FINANCIAL RATIOS Use the spreadsheet and financial statements prepared in Problem 15-8A. All sales are credit sales. The Accounts Receivable balance on January 1, 20--, was $10,200.

REQUIRED

Prepare the following financial ratios:

(a) Current ratio
(b) Quick ratio
(c) Working capital
(d) Return on owner's equity
(e) Accounts receivable turnover and average number of days required to collect receivables
(f) Inventory turnover and average number of days required to sell inventory

P 15-10A (LO5/6)
✓ Net income: $123,300
✓ Post-closing trial bal. col. totals: $687,150

END-OF-PERIOD SPREADSHEET, ADJUSTING, CLOSING, AND REVERSING ENTRIES Vicki's Fabric Store shows the trial balance on page 601 as of December 31, 20-1.

At the end of the year, the following adjustments need to be made:

(a, b) Merchandise inventory as of December 31, $31,600.
(c, d, e) Vicki estimates that customers will be granted $2,500 in refunds of this year's sales next year and the merchandise expected to be returned will have a cost of $1,800.
(f) Unused supplies on hand, $350.
(g) Insurance expired, $2,400.
(h) Depreciation expense for the year on building, $20,000.
(i) Depreciation expense for the year on equipment, $4,000.
(j) Wages earned but not paid (Wages Payable), $520.
(k) Unearned revenue on December 31, 20-1, $1,200.

(continued)

PROBLEM 15-8A

	A	B	C
1	Paulson's Pet Store		
2	End-of-Period Spreadsheet (Partial)		
3	December 31, 20--		
4	ACCOUNT TITLE	ADJUSTED TRIAL BALANCE	
5		DEBIT	CREDIT
6	Cash	23,440.00	
7	Accounts Receivable	9,360.00	
8	Merchandise Inventory	64,800.00	
9	Estimated Returns Inventory	1,200.00	
10	Supplies	2,400.00	
11	Prepaid Insurance	1,800.00	
12	Land	90,000.00	
13	Building	350,000.00	
14	Accum. Depr.—Building		20,000.00
15	Store Equipment	120,000.00	
16	Accum. Depr.—Store Equipment		3,600.00
17	Accounts Payable		9,560.00
18	Customer Refunds Payable		1,600.00
19	Wages Payable		1,200.00
20	Sales Tax Payable		3,440.00
21	Note Payable		16,000.00
22	B. Paulson, Capital		534,320.00
23	B. Paulson, Drawing	4,800.00	
24	Income Summary	59,200.00	64,800.00
25		800.00	1,200.00
26	Sales		326,040.00
27	Sales Returns and Allowances	5,360.00	
28	Purchases	162,640.00	
29	Purchases Returns and Allowances		4,080.00
30	Purchases Discounts		3,200.00
31	Freight-In	1,600.00	
32	Wages Expense	69,400.00	
33	Advertising Expense	1,200.00	
34	Supplies Expense	800.00	
35	Phone Expense	2,736.00	
36	Utilities Expense	2,864.00	
37	Insurance Expense	1,600.00	
38	Depr. Expense—Building	10,000.00	
39	Depr. Expense—Equipment	1,800.00	
40	Miscellaneous Expense	600.00	
41	Interest Expense	640.00	
42		989,040.00	989,040.00
43		321,240.00	399,320.00
44	Net Income	78,080.00	
45			

PROBLEM 15-10A CONT.

	A	B	C
1	**Vicki's Fabric Store**		
2	**Trial Balance**		
3	**For the Year Ended December 31, 20-1**		
4	ACCOUNT TITLE	DEBIT	CREDIT
5			
6	Cash	28,000.00	
7	Accounts Receivable	14,200.00	
8	Merchandise Inventory	30,000.00	
9	Estimated Returns Inventory	3,000.00	
10	Supplies	1,600.00	
11	Prepaid Insurance	3,600.00	
12	Land	120,000.00	
13	Building	400,000.00	
14	Accum. Depr.—Building		60,000.00
15	Equipment	90,000.00	
16	Accumulated Depr.—Equipment		12,000.00
17	Accounts Payable		11,420.00
18	Customer Refunds Payable		4,200.00
19	Wages Payable		
20	Sales Tax Payable		2,000.00
21	Unearned Costume Design Revenue		5,000.00
22	Note Payable		80,000.00
23	Vicki Roberts, Capital		387,620.00
24	Vicki Roberts, Drawing	21,610.00	
25	Income Summary		
26			
27	Sales		374,500.00
28	Sales Returns and Allowances	12,800.00	
29	Costume Design Revenue		1,200.00
30	Purchases	141,500.00	
31	Purchases Returns and Allowances		1,800.00
32	Purchases Discounts		830.00
33	Freight-In	800.00	
34	Wages Expense	65,000.00	
35	Advertising Expense	810.00	
36	Supplies Expense		
37	Phone Expense	1,210.00	
38	Utilities Expense	3,240.00	
39	Insurance Expense		
40	Depreciation Expense—Building		
41	Depreciation Expense—Equip.		
42	Interest Expense	3,200.00	
43		940,570.00	940,570.00
44			

(continued)

REQUIRED

1. Prepare an end-of-period spreadsheet.
2. Prepare adjusting entries and post adjusting entries to an Income Summary T account.
3. Prepare closing entries and post to a Capital T account. There were no additional investments this year.
4. Prepare a post-closing trial balance.
5. Prepare reversing entry(ies).

SERIES B EXERCISES

E 15-1B (LO1)
✓ Net sales: $82,196

REVENUE SECTION, MULTIPLE-STEP INCOME STATEMENT Based on the information that follows, prepare the revenue section of a multiple-step income statement.

Sales	$86,200
Sales Returns and Allowances	2,280
Sales Discounts	1,724

E 15-2B (LO1)
✓ Cost of goods sold: $59,442

COST OF GOODS SOLD SECTION, MULTIPLE-STEP INCOME STATEMENT Based on the information that follows, prepare the cost of goods sold section of a multiple-step income statement.

Merchandise Inventory, January 1, 20--	$13,000
Estimated Returns Inventory, January 1, 20--	800
Purchases	71,300
Purchases Returns and Allowances	3,188
Purchases Discounts	1,460
Freight-In	390
Merchandise Inventory, December 31, 20--	20,000
Estimated Returns Inventory, December 31, 20--	1,400

E 15-3B (LO1)
✓ Cost of goods sold: $109,714
✓ Net income: $12,040

MULTIPLE-STEP INCOME STATEMENT Use the following information to prepare a multiple-step income statement, including the revenue section and the cost of goods sold section, for Aeito's Plumbing Supplies for the year ended December 31, 20--.

Sales	$166,000
Sales Returns and Allowances	1,620
Sales Discounts	3,320
Interest Revenue	3,184
Merchandise Inventory, January 1, 20--	32,600
Estimated Returns Inventory, January 1, 20--	600
Purchases	111,300
Purchases Returns and Allowances	3,600
Purchases Discounts	2,226
Freight-In	640
Merchandise Inventory, December 31, 20--	29,200
Estimated Returns Inventory, December 31, 20--	400
Wages Expense	22,000
Supplies Expense	650
Phone Expense	1,100
Utilities Expense	9,000
Insurance Expense	1,000
Depreciation Expense—Building	4,600
Depreciation Expense—Equipment	2,800
Miscellaneous Expense	214
Interest Expense	1,126

E 15-4B (LO4)
✓ Current ratio: 3.68 to 1
✓ Return on owner's equity: 42.6%
✓ Inventory turnover: 3.42

FINANCIAL RATIOS Based on the financial statements, shown on pages 603–604, for McDonald Carpeting Co. (income statement, statement of owner's equity, and balance sheet), prepare the following financial ratios. All sales are credit sales. The balance of Accounts Receivable on January 1, 20--, was $6,800.

1. Working capital
2. Current ratio
3. Quick ratio
4. Return on owner's equity
5. Accounts receivable turnover and the average number of days required to collect receivables
6. Inventory turnover and the average number of days required to sell inventory

McDonald Carpeting Co.
Income Statement
For Year Ended December 31, 20--

Revenue from sales:				
Sales			$122,800	
Less sales returns and allowances			1,100	
Net sales				$121,700
Cost of goods sold:				
Merchandise Inventory, January 1, 20--		$18,000		
Estimated Returns Inventory, January 1, 20--		1,300	$ 19,300	
Purchases		$62,800		
Less: Purchases returns and allowances	$2,800			
Purchases discounts	1,944	4,744		
Net purchases		$58,056		
Add freight-in		944		
Cost of goods purchased			59,000	
Goods available for sale			$ 78,300	
Less: Merchandise inventory, December 31, 20--		$16,000		
Estimated returns inventory, December 31, 20--		700	16,700	
Cost of goods sold				61,600
Gross profit				$ 60,100
Operating expenses:				
Wages expense			$ 18,000	
Advertising expense			980	
Supplies expense			320	
Phone expense			1,200	
Utilities expense			8,000	
Insurance expense			800	
Depreciation expense—building			3,500	
Depreciation expense—equipment			2,500	
Miscellaneous expense			200	
Total operating expenses				35,500
Income from operations				$ 24,600
Other revenues:				
Interest revenue			$ 2,800	
Other expenses:				
Interest expense			2,100	700
Net income				$ 25,300

(continued)

McDonald Carpeting Co. Statement of Owner's Equity For Year Ended December 31, 20--		
C. S. McDonald, capital, January 1, 20--		$52,000
Net income for the year	$25,300	
Less withdrawals for the year	10,400	
Increase in capital		14,900
C. S. McDonald, capital, December 31, 20--		$66,900

McDonald Carpeting Co. Balance Sheet December 31, 20--			
Assets			
Current assets:			
Cash		$10,400	
Accounts receivable		8,900	
Merchandise inventory, December 31, 20--	$16,000		
Estimated returns inventory, December 31, 20--	700	16,700	
Supplies		1,200	
Prepaid insurance		700	
Total current assets			$37,900
Property, plant, and equipment:			
Building	$60,000		
Less accumulated depreciation—building	18,000	$42,000	
Equipment	$22,000		
Less accumulated depreciation—equipment	6,200	15,800	
Total property, plant, and equipment			57,800
Total assets			$95,700
Liabilities			
Current liabilities:			
Accounts payable	$ 7,500		
Customer refunds payable	900		
Wages payable	300		
Sales tax payable	1,000		
Mortgage payable (current portion)	600		
Total current liabilities		$10,300	
Long-term liabilities:			
Mortgage payable	$19,100		
Less current portion	600	18,500	
Total liabilities			$28,800
Owner's Equity			
C. S. McDonald, capital			66,900
Total liabilities and owner's equity			$95,700

E 15-5B (LO5) CLOSING ENTRIES Using the spreadsheet and partially completed Income Summary Account on page 605 prepare the following:

1. Closing entries for Balloons and Baubbles in a general journal.
2. A post-closing trial balance.

E 15-6B (LO6) REVERSING ENTRIES From the spreadsheet in Exercise 15-5B, identify the adjusting entry(ies) that should be reversed and prepare the reversing entry(ies).

E 15-7A (LO5/6) ADJUSTING, CLOSING, AND REVERSING ENTRIES Prepare entries for (a), (b), and (c) listed below using two methods. First, prepare the entries without making a reversing entry. Second, prepare the entries with the use of a reversing entry. Use T-accounts to assist your analysis.

(a) Wages paid during 20-1 are $20,080.

(b) Wages earned but not paid (accrued) as of December 31, 20-1, are $280.

(c) On January 3, 20-2, payroll of $840 is paid, which includes the $280 of wages earned but not paid in December.

EXERCISE 15-5B

	A	B	C	D	E	F	G	H	I
1	Balloons and Baubbles								
2	End-of-Period Spreadsheet								
3	For the Year Ended December 31, 20-1								
4	ACCOUNT TITLE	TRIAL BALANCE		ADJUSTMENTS				ADJUSTED TRIAL BALANCE	
5		DEBIT	CREDIT		DEBIT		CREDIT	DEBIT	CREDIT
6	Cash	18,000.00						18,000.00	
7	Accounts Receivable	12,600.00						12,600.00	
8	Merchandise Inventory	67,500.00		(b)	76,500.00	(a)	67,500.00	76,500.00	
9	Estimated Returns Inventory	2,880.00		(e)	3,870.00	(d)	2,880.00	3,870.00	
10	Supplies	7,200.00				(f)	4,230.00	2,970.00	
11	Prepaid Insurance	4,860.00				(g)	1,440.00	3,420.00	
12	Land	117,000.00						117,000.00	
13	Building	225,000.00						225,000.00	
14	Accum. Depr.—Building		90,000.00			(h)	11,250.00		101,250.00
15	Store Equipment	90,000.00						90,000.00	
16	Accum. Depr.—Store Equipment		36,000.00			(i)	4,500.00		40,500.00
17	Accounts Payable		8,640.00						8,640.00
18	Customer Refunds Payable		3,150.00			(c)	1,980.00		5,130.00
19	Wages Payable					(j)	3,150.00		3,150.00
20	Sales Tax Payable		5,310.00						5,310.00
21	Unearned Repair Revenue		8,010.00	(k)	3,960.00				4,050.00
22	L. Marlow, Capital		255,879.00						255,879.00
23	L. Marlow, Drawing	23,400.00						23,400.00	
24	Income Summary			(a)	67,500.00	(b)	76,500.00	67,500.00	76,500.00
25				(d)	2,880.00	(e)	3,870.00	2,880.00	3,870.00
26	Sales		472,626.00						427,626.00
27	Sales Returns and Allowances	13,050.00		(c)	1,980.00			15,030.00	
28	Rent Revenue					(k)	3,960.00		3,960.00
29	Purchases	112,500.00						112,500.00	
30	Purchases Returns and Allowances		1,260.00						1,260.00
31	Purchases Discounts		1,620.00						1,620.00
32	Freight-In	1,890.00						1,890.00	
33	Wages Expense	112,500.00		(j)	3,150.00			115,650.00	
34	Advertising Expense	11,700.00						11,700.00	
35	Supplies Expense			(f)	4,230.00			4,230.00	
36	Phone Expense	1,215.00						1,215.00	
37	Utilities Expense	7,200.00						7,200.00	
38	Insurance Expense			(g)	1,440.00			1,440.00	
39	Depr. Expense—Building			(h)	11,250.00			11,250.00	
40	Depr. Expense—Store Equipment			(i)	4,500.00			4,500.00	
41	Rent Expense	54,000.00						54,000.00	
42		882,495.00	882,495.00		181,260.00		181,260.00	983,745.00	983,745.00
43								410,985.00	559,836.00
44	Net Income							148,851.00	
45									

(continued)

EXERCISE 15-5B (Concluded)

ACCOUNT: Income Summary — ACCOUNT NO. 331

DATE		ITEM	POST. REF.	DEBIT	CREDIT	BALANCE DEBIT	BALANCE CREDIT
20-1 Dec.	31	Adjusting		67,500.00		67,500.00	
	31	Adjusting			76,500.00		9,000.00
	31	Adjusting		2,880.00			6,120.00
	31	Adjusting			3,870.00		9,990.00

SERIES B PROBLEMS

P 15-8B (LO1/2/3)
✓ Cost of goods sold: $166,056
✓ Total assets: $703,340

INCOME STATEMENT, STATEMENT OF OWNER'S EQUITY, AND BALANCE SHEET Backlund Farm Supply completed the Adjusted Trial Balance on page 607 for the year ended December 31, 20--. Owner's equity as of January 1, 20--, was $507,752. The current portion of Note Payable is $3,000.

REQUIRED

1. Prepare a multiple-step income statement.
2. Prepare a statement of owner's equity.
3. Prepare a balance sheet.

P 15-9B (LO4)
✓ Working capital: $92,920
✓ Quick ratio: 1.8 to 1
✓ Accts. receivable turnover: 20.9

FINANCIAL RATIOS Use the spreadsheet and financial statements prepared in Problem 15-8B. Net credit sales were $210,000. The Accounts Receivable balance on January 1 was $9,800.

REQUIRED

Prepare the following financial ratios:

(a) Current ratio
(b) Quick ratio
(c) Working capital
(d) Return on owner's equity
(e) Accounts receivable turnover and the average number of days required to collect receivables
(f) Inventory turnover and the average number of days required to sell inventory

P 15-10B (LO5/6)
✓ Net income: $147,960
✓ Post-closing trial bal. columns: $824,580

END-OF-PERIOD SPREADSHEET, ADJUSTING, CLOSING, AND REVERSING ENTRIES The trial balance for Danbury Kite Shop as of December 31, 20-1, is shown on page 608.

At the end of the year, the following adjustments need to be made:

(a, b) Merchandise inventory as of December 31, $37,920.
(c, d, e) Bill Danbury estimates that customers will be granted $3,000 in refunds of this year's sales next year and the merchandise expected to be returned will have a cost of $2,160.
(f) Unused supplies on hand, $420.
(g) Insurance expired, $2,880.
(h) Depreciation expense for the year on building, $24,000.
(i) Depreciation expense for the year on equipment, $4,800.
(j) Wages earned but not paid (Wages Payable), $624.
(k) Unearned repair revenue on December 31, 20-1, $1,440.

REQUIRED

1. Prepare an end-of-period spreadsheet.
2. Prepare adjusting entries and post adjusting entries to an Income Summary T account.
3. Prepare closing entries and post to a Capital T account. There were no additional investments this year.
4. Prepare a post-closing trial balance.
5. Prepare reversing entry(ies).

PROBLEM 15-8B

	A	B	C
1	**Backlund Farm Supply**		
2	**End-of-Period Spreadsheet (Partial)**		
3	**December 31, 20--**		
4	ACCOUNT TITLE	ADJUSTED TRIAL BALANCE	
5		DEBIT	CREDIT
6	Cash	25,784.00	
7	Accounts Receivable	10,296.00	
8	Merchandise Inventory	71,280.00	
9	Estimated Returns Inventory	1,320.00	
10	Supplies	2,640.00	
11	Prepaid Insurance	1,980.00	
12	Land	99,000.00	
13	Building	385,000.00	
14	Accum. Depr.—Building		22,000.00
15	Store Equipment	132,000.00	
16	Accum. Depr.—Store Equipment		3,960.00
17	Accounts Payable		10,516.00
18	Customer Refunds Payable		1,760.00
19	Wages Payable		1,320.00
20	Sales Tax Payable		3,784.00
21	Note Payable		17,600.00
22	J. Buckland, Capital		587,752.00
23	J. Buckland, Drawing	5,280.00	
24	Income Summary	65,120.00	71,280.00
25		880.00	1,320.00
26	Sales		358,644.00
27	Sales Returns and Allowances	5,896.00	
28	Purchases	178,904.00	
29	Purchases Returns and Allowances		4,488.00
30	Purchases Discounts		3,520.00
31	Freight-In	1,760.00	
32	Wages Expense	76,340.00	
33	Advertising Expense	1,320.00	
34	Supplies Expense	880.00	
35	Phone Expense	3,010.00	
36	Utilities Expense	3,150.00	
37	Insurance Expense	1,760.00	
38	Depr. Expense—Building	11,000.00	
39	Depr. Expense—Store Equipment	1,980.00	
40	Miscellaneous Expense	660.00	
41	Interest Expense	704.00	
42		1,087,944.00	1,087,944.00
43		353,364.00	439,252.00
44	Net Income	85,888.00	
45			

PROBLEM 15-10B

	A	B	C
1	Danbury Kite Shop		
2	Trial Balance		
3	For the Year Ended December 31, 20-1		
4	ACCOUNT TITLE	DEBIT	CREDIT
5			
6	Cash	33,600.00	
7	Accounts Receivable	17,040.00	
8	Merchandise Inventory	36,000.00	
9	Estimated Returns Inventory	3,600.00	
10	Supplies	1,920.00	
11	Prepaid Insurance	4,320.00	
12	Land	144,000.00	
13	Building	480,000.00	
14	Accum. Depr.—Building		72,000.00
15	Equipment	108,000.00	
16	Accumulated Depr.—Equipment		14,400.00
17	Accounts Payable		13,744.00
18	Customer Refunds Payable		5,000.00
19	Wages Payable		
20	Sales Tax Payable		2,400.00
21	Unearned Repair Revenue		6,000.00
22	Note Payable		96,000.00
23	W. Danbury, Capital		465,144.00
24	W. Danbury, Drawing	25,932.00	
25	Income Summary		
26			
27	Sales		449,400.00
28	Sales Returns and Allowances	15,360.00	
29	Repair Revenue		1,440.00
30	Purchases	169,800.00	
31	Purchases Returns and Allowances		2,160.00
32	Purchases Discounts		996.00
33	Freight-In	960.00	
34	Wages Expense	78,000.00	
35	Advertising Expense	972.00	
36	Supplies Expense		
37	Phone Expense	1,452.00	
38	Utilities Expense	3,888.00	
39	Insurance Expense		
40	Depreciation Expense—Building		
41	Depreciation Expense—Equip.		
42	Interest Expense	3,840.00	
43		1,128,684.00	1,128,684.00
44			

CHECK LIST

- ☐ Managing
- ☐ Planning
- ☐ Drafting
- ☐ Break
- ☐ Revising
- ☐ Managing

MANAGING YOUR WRITING

A friend of yours has the opportunity to invest in a small business. She has come to you for advice on how she might determine whether this would be a good investment. In particular, she is concerned about how long it takes to sell the merchandise and collect receivables. Draft a memo suggesting various ratios that should be computed to evaluate the business's profitability, ability to pay its current obligations, and time required to sell inventory and collect receivables.

ETHICS

ETHICS CASE

Brian Marlow recently was hired to prepare Louise Michener Consulting's year-end financial statements. Brian just earned his CPA certificate, and Louise Michener was one of his first clients. Louise employs a bookkeeper, Martha Halling, who does the daily journal entries and prepares a year-to-date trial balance at the end of each month. Martha gives the December 31 trial balance to a CPA to make the adjustments and generate the financial statements. As Brian was looking through Louise Michener's books, he noticed two things. First, in each of the last three years, a different CPA had prepared the financial statements. Second, the amount shown on the December 31 trial balance for miscellaneous expense was quite high this year compared to prior years. Brian called Martha to find out if she knew why miscellaneous expense had such a high balance. Martha's response was "I just do what Louise tells me to do. If she wants to charge personal expenses to the company, it's none of my business."

1. What should Brian do?
2. How might Brian's decision affect Martha? Has Martha done anything unethical?
3. Write a short letter from Brian to Louise explaining why personal items should not be charged to a business.
4. In small groups, discuss the ethical responsibilities of an accountant relating to a client's books.

MASTERY PROBLEM

✓ **Net income: $25,650**
✓ **Total assets: $125,000**
✓ **Current ratio: 3.4 to 1**
✓ **Return on owner's equity: 26.1%**

Dominique Fouque owns and operates Dominique's Doll House. She has a small shop in which she sells new and antique dolls. She is particularly well known for her collection of antique Ken and Barbie dolls. A completed spreadsheet for 20-3 is shown on page 610. Fouque made no additional investments during the year and the long-term note payable is due in 20-9. No portion of the long-term note is due within the next year. Net credit sales for 20-3 were $38,000, and receivables on January 1 were $3,000.

REQUIRED

1. Prepare a multiple-step income statement.
2. Prepare a statement of owner's equity.
3. Prepare a balance sheet.
4. Compute the following measures of performance and financial condition for 20-3:
   (a) Current ratio
   (b) Quick ratio
   (c) Working capital
   (d) Return on owner's equity
   (e) Accounts receivable turnover and average number of days required to collect receivables
   (f) Inventory turnover and the average number of days required to sell inventory
5. Prepare adjusting entries and indicate which should be reversed and why.
6. Open an Income Summary account. Post adjusting and closing entries (prepared in 7) to this account.
7. Prepare closing entries.
8. Prepare reversing entries for the adjustments where appropriate.

(continued)

MASTERY PROBLEM

	A	B	C	D	E	F	G	H	I
1	Dominique's Doll House								
2	End-of-Period Spreadsheet								
3	For the Year Ended December 31, 20-3								
4	ACCOUNT TITLE	TRIAL BALANCE		ADJUSTMENTS				ADJUSTED TRIAL BALANCE	
5		DEBIT	CREDIT		DEBIT		CREDIT	DEBIT	CREDIT
6	Cash	16,700.00						16,700.00	
7	Accounts Receivable	3,200.00						3,200.00	
8	Merchandise Inventory	31,300.00		(b)	28,000.00	(a)	31,300.00	28,000.00	
9	Estimated Returns Inventory	1,000.00		(e)	1,100.00	(d)	1,000.00	1,100.00	
10	Office Supplies	800.00				(f)	600.00	200.00	
11	Prepaid Insurance	1,200.00				(g)	400.00	800.00	
12	Store Equipment	95,000.00						95,000.00	
13	Accum. Depr.—Store Equipment		15,000.00			(h)	5,000.00		20,000.00
14	Notes Payable		6,000.00						6,000.00
15	Accounts Payable		5,500.00						5,500.00
16	Customer Refunds Payable		1,500.00			(c)	200.00		1,700.00
17	Wages Payable					(i)	200.00		200.00
18	Sales Tax Payable		850.00						850.00
19	Unearned Show Revenue		1,000.00	(j)	700.00				300.00
20	Long-term Note Payable		10,000.00						10,000.00
21	Dominique Fouque, Capital		95,800.00						95,800.00
22	Dominique Fouque, Drawing	21,000.00						21,000.00	
23	Income Summary			(a)	31,300.00	(b)	28,000.00	31,300.00	28,000.00
24				(d)	1,000.00	(e)	1,100.00	1,000.00	1,100.00
25	Sales		201,500.00						201,500.00
26	Sales Returns and Allowances	5,900.00		(c)	200.00			6,100.00	
27	Rent Revenue		5,000.00			(j)	700.00		5,700.00
28	Purchases	72,000.00						72,000.00	
29	Purchases Returns and Allowances		750.00						750.00
30	Freight-In	1,200.00						1,200.00	
31	Wages Expense	42,000.00		(i)	200.00			42,200.00	
32	Rent Expense	42,000.00						42,000.00	
33	Office Supplies Expense			(f)	600.00			600.00	
34	Phone Expense	1,500.00						1,500.00	
35	Utilities Expense	7,600.00						7,600.00	
36	Insurance Expense			(g)	400.00			400.00	
37	Depr. Expense—Store Equipment			(h)	5,000.00			5,000.00	
38	Interest Expense	500.00						500.00	
39		342,900.00	342,900.00		68,500.00		68,500.00	377,400.00	377,400.00
40								211,400.00	237,050.00
41	Net Income							25,650.00	
42									

CHALLENGE PROBLEM

This problem challenges you to apply your cumulative accounting knowledge to move a step beyond the material in the chapter.

✓ **Average days to convert inventory to cash: 45.0 days**

John Byers owns and operates Byers Building Supplies. The following information was taken from his financial statements:

Balance Sheet	12/31/-2	12/31/-1
Accounts Receivable	$700	$500
Inventory	300	100

Income Statement	
Net Credit Sales	$7,200
Cost of Goods Sold	5,000

All sales are made on account.

REQUIRED

Based on the above information, on average, approximately how many days pass from the time Byers purchases inventory until he receives cash from customers?

ANSWERS TO SELF-STUDY TEST QUESTIONS

True/False

1. T
2. F (whichever is longer)
3. T
4. T
5. F (number of times accounts receivable turned over)

Multiple Choice

1. c
2. a
3. b
4. d
5. c

Checkpoint Exercises

1.

Yoder's Cool Stuff
Income Statement
For Year Ended December 31, 20--

Revenue from sales:			
Sales		$261,000	
Less: sales returns and allowances		21,000	
Net sales			$240,000
Cost of goods sold:			
Merchandise inventory, January 1, 20--	$36,000		
Estimated returns inventory, January 1, 20--	4,000	$ 40,000	
Purchases		160,000	
Goods available for sale		$200,000	
Less: Merchandise inventory, December 31, 20--	$75,000		
Estimated returns inventory, December 31, 20--	5,000	80,000	
Cost of goods sold			120,000
Gross profit			$120,000
Operating expenses:			
Wages expense		$ 14,000	
Rent expense		4,000	
Supplies expense		1,200	
Phone expense		1,000	
Insurance expense		500	
Depr. expense—delivery equipment		20,000	
Total operating expenses			40,700
Net income			$ 79,300

2.

Yoder's Cool Stuff
Statement of Owner's Equity
For Year Ended December 31, 20--

P. Yoder, capital, January 1, 20--		$ 88,000
Net income for the year	$79,300	
Less withdrawals for the year	3,000	
Increase in capital		76,300
P. Yoder, capital, December 31, 20--		$164,300

3.

Yoder's Cool Stuff
Balance Sheet
December 31, 20--

Assets		
Current assets:		
Cash	$ 7,400	
Accounts receivable	13,000	
Merchandise inventory	75,000	
Estimated returns inventory	5,000	
Supplies	400	
Prepaid insurance	3,500	
Total current assets		$104,300
Property, plant, and equipment:		
Delivery equipment	$160,000	
Less accumulated depreciation—delivery equipment	60,000	100,000
Total assets		$204,300
Liabilities		
Current liabilities:		
Accounts payable	$ 30,000	
Customer refunds payable	9,000	
Wages payable	1,000	
Total current liabilities		$ 40,000
Owner's Equity		
Pete Yoder, capital		164,300
Total liabilities and owner's equity		$204,300

4. a. Working capital:

Current assets	$9,020
– Current liabilities	4,850
	$4,170

b. Current ratio:

$$\frac{\text{Current Assets}}{\text{Current Liabilities}} = \frac{\$9{,}020}{\$4{,}850} = 1.86 \text{ to } 1$$

c. Return on owner's equity:

$$\frac{\text{Net Income}}{\text{Average Owner's Equity}} = \frac{\$2{,}170}{(\$5{,}000 + \$7{,}170)/2} = \frac{\$2{,}170}{\$6{,}085} = 35.7\%$$

d. Inventory turnover:

$$\frac{\text{Cost of Goods Sold}}{\text{Average Inventory}} = \frac{\$16{,}000}{(\$4{,}000 + \$6{,}000)/2} = \frac{\$16{,}000}{\$5{,}000} = 3.2$$

5.

	DATE		DESCRIPTION	POST. REF.	DEBIT		CREDIT		
1	20--		Closing Entries						1
2	Dec.	31	Sales		261 000	00			2
3			Income Summary				261 000	00	3
4									4
5		31	Income Summary		221 700	00			5
6			Sales Returns and Allowances				21 000	00	6
7			Purchases				160 000	00	7
8			Wages Expense				14 000	00	8
9			Rent Expense				4 000	00	9
10			Supplies Expense				1 200	00	10
11			Phone Expense				1 000	00	11
12			Insurance Expense				500	00	12
13			Depr. Expense—Delivery Equipment				20 000	00	13
14									14
15		31	Income Summary		79 300	00			15
16			Pete Yoder, Capital				79 300	00	16
17									17
18		31	Pete Yoder, Capital		3 000	00			18
19			Pete Yoder, Drawing				3 000	00	19
20									20

Income Summary

	Debit	Credit	
BI	36,000.00	75,000.00	EI
B-ERI	4,000.00	5,000.00	E-ERI
		261,000.00	Rev.
Exp	221,700.00		
NI	79,300.00		

Pete Yoder, Capital

	Debit	Credit	
		88,000.00	ATB
Drawing	3,000.00	79,300.00	Net Income
		164,300.00	Bal.

ERI: Estimated Returns Inventory

6.

Interest Payable	1,000.00	
Interest Expense		1,000.00

Do not reverse the adjustment for depreciation expense. The adjusting entry does not increase an asset or liability from a zero balance and does not make the subsequent entry easier.

Accounting Cycle with Subsidiary Ledgers, Part 1

CengageNowv2 provides "Show Me How" videos for selected exercises and problems. Additional resources, such as Excel templates for completing selected exercises and problems, are available for download from the companion website at Cengage.com.

During the second half of December 20-1, TJ's Specialty Shop engaged in the following transactions:

Dec.	16	Received payment from Lucy Greene on account, $1,960.
	16	Sold merchandise on account to Kim Fields, $160, plus sales tax of $8. Sale No. 640.
	17	Returned merchandise to Evans Essentials for credit, $150.
	18	Issued Check No. 813 to Evans Essentials in payment of December 1 balance of $1,250, less the credit received on December 17.
	19	Sold merchandise on account to Lucy Greene, $620, plus tax of $31. Sale No. 641.
	22	Received payment from John Dempsey on account, $1,560.
	23	Issued Check No. 814 for the purchase of supplies, $120. (Debit Supplies)
	24	Purchased merchandise on account from West Wholesalers, $1,200. Invoice No. 465, dated December 24, terms n/30.
	26	Purchased merchandise on account from Nathen Co., $800. Invoice No. 817, dated December 26, terms 2/10, n/30.
	27	Issued Check No. 815 to KC Power & Light (Utilities Expense) for the month of December, $630.
	27	Sold merchandise on account to John Dempsey, $2,020, plus tax of $101. Sale No. 642.
	29	Received payment from Martha Boyle on account, $2,473.
	29	Issued Check No. 816 in payment of wages (Wages Expense) for the two-week period ending December 28, $1,100.
	30	Issued Check No. 817 to Meyers Trophy Shop for a cash purchase of merchandise, $200.

As of December 16, TJ's account balances were as follows:

Account	Account No.	Debit	Credit
Cash	101	$ 9,705	
Accounts Receivable	122	10,256	
Merchandise Inventory	131	21,800	
Estimated Returns Inventory	135	250	
Supplies	141	1,035	
Prepaid Insurance	145	1,380	
Land	161	8,750	
Building	171	52,000	
Accum. Depr.—Building	171.1		$ 9,200
Store Equipment	181	28,750	
Accum. Depr.—Store Equipment	181.1		9,300
Accounts Payable	202		3,600
Customer Refunds Payable	203		300

Wages Payable	219		
Sales Tax Payable	231		1,378
Mortgage Payable	251		12,525
Tom Jones, Capital	311		90,000
Tom Jones, Drawing	312	8,500	
Income Summary	313		
Sales	401		124,900
Sales Returns and Allowances	401.1	1,430	
Purchases	501	64,400	
Purchases Returns and Allowances	501.1		460
Purchases Discounts	501.2		698
Freight-In	502	175	
Wages Expense	511	26,100	
Advertising Expense	512	4,700	
Supplies Expense	524		
Phone Expense	525	2,180	
Utilities Expense	533	6,900	
Insurance Expense	535		
Depr. Expense—Building	540		
Depr. Expense—Store Equipment	541		
Miscellaneous Expense	549	2,700	
Interest Expense	551	1,350	
		$252,361	$252,361

TJ's also had the following subsidiary ledger balances as of December 16:

Accounts Receivable Ledger

Customer	Balance
Martha Boyle 12 Jude Lane Hartford, CT 06117	$3,796
Anne Clark 52 Juniper Road Hartford, CT 06118	2,100
John Dempsey 700 Hobbes Dr. Avon, CT 06108	1,560
Kim Fields 5200 Hamilton Ave. Hartford, CT 06117	—
Lucy Greene 236 Bally Lane Simsbury, CT 06123	2,800

Accounts Payable Ledger

Vendor	Balance
Evans Essentials 34 Harry Ave. East Hartford, CT 05234	$3,600
Nathen Co. 1009 Drake Rd. Farmington, CT 06082	—
Owen Enterprises 43 Lucky Lane Bristol, CT 06007	—
West Wholesalers 888 Anders Street Newington, CT 06789	—

(*continued*)

At the end of the year, the following adjustments (a)–(j) need to be made:

(a, b) Merchandise inventory as of December 31, $19,700.

(c, d, e) Jones estimates that customers will be granted $400 in refunds of this year's sales next year, and the merchandise expected to be returned will have a cost of $300.

(f) Unused supplies on hand, $525.

(g) Unexpired insurance on December 31, $1,000.

(h) Depreciation expense on the building for the year, $800.

(i) Depreciation expense on the store equipment for the year, $450.

(j) Wages earned but not paid as of December 31, $330.

REQUIRED

For those not using working papers:

1. If you are not using the working papers, open a general ledger, an accounts receivable ledger, and an accounts payable ledger as of December 16. Enter the December 16 balance of each of the accounts, with a check mark in the Posting Reference column.

For working paper users and nonusers:

2. Enter transactions for the second half of December in the general journal. Post immediately to the accounts receivable and accounts payable ledgers.
3. Post from the journal to the general ledger.
4. Prepare schedules of accounts receivable and accounts payable.
5. Prepare a year-end spreadsheet, an income statement, a statement of owner's equity, and a balance sheet. The mortgage payable includes $600 that is due within one year.
6. Journalize and post adjusting entries.
7. Journalize and post closing entries. (*Hint*: Close all expense and revenue account balances. Then, close Income Summary and Tom Jones, Drawing to Tom Jones, Capital.)
8. Prepare a post-closing trial balance.
9. Journalize and post reversing entries for the adjustments where appropriate, as of January 1, 20-2.

COMPREHENSIVE PROBLEM 2:

Accounting Cycle with Subsidiary Ledgers, Part 2

During the month of January 20-2, TJ's Specialty Shop engaged in the following transactions:

Jan. 1 Sold merchandise on account to Anne Clark, $3,000, plus tax of $150. Sale No. 643.

2 Issued Check No. 818 to Nathen Co. in payment of January 1 balance of $800, less 2% discount.

(*continued*)

Jan.	3	Purchased merchandise on account from West Wholesalers, $1,500. Invoice No. 678, dated January 3, terms 2/15, n/30.
	4	Purchased merchandise on account from Owen Enterprises, $2,000. Invoice No. 767, dated January 4, terms 2/10, n/30.
	4	Issued Check No. 819 in payment of phone expense for the month of January, $180.
	8	Sold merchandise for cash, $3,600, plus tax of $180.
	9	Received payment from Lucy Greene in full settlement of account, $1,491.
	10	Issued Check No. 820 to West Wholesalers in payment of January 1 balance of $1,200.
	12	Sold merchandise on account to Martha Boyle, $1,000, plus tax of $50. Sale No. 644.
	12	Received payment from Anne Clark on account, $2,100.
	12	Issued Check No. 821 in payment of wages (Wages Expense) for the two-week period ending January 11, $1,100.
	13	Issued Check No. 822 to Owen Enterprises in payment of January 4 purchase. Invoice No. 767, less 2% discount.
	13	Martha Boyle returned merchandise for a credit, $800, plus sales tax of $40.
	17	Returned merchandise to Evans Essentials for credit, $300.
	22	Received payment from John Dempsey on account, $2,121.
	26	Issued Check No. 823 in payment of wages (Wages Expense) for the two-week period ending January 25, $1,100.
	27	Issued Check No. 824 to KC Power & Light (Utilities Expense) for the month of January, $630.
	27	Sold merchandise on account to John Dempsey, $2,000, plus tax of $100. Sale No. 645.

Late in January, TJ's agreed to sell the business to a competitor. To agree on a selling price, financial statements are needed as of January 31 and for the month of January 20-2. To prepare these financial statements, TJ's must perform the same procedures it normally does at year-end.

At the end of January, the following adjustments (a)–(j) need to be made:

(a, b) Merchandise inventory as of January 31, $19,000.

(c, d, e) Jones estimates that customers will be granted $500 in refunds of this month's sales in subsequent months, and the merchandise expected to be returned will have a cost of $360.

(f) Unused supplies on hand, $115.

(g) Unexpired insurance on January 31, $968.

(h) Depreciation expense on the building for the month, $67.

(i) Depreciation expense on the store equipment for the month, $38.

(j) Wages earned but not paid as of January 31, $330.

REQUIRED

For those not using working papers:

1. If you are not using the working papers, open a general ledger, an accounts receivable ledger, and an accounts payable ledger as of January 1. Enter the January 1 balance of each of the accounts, with a check mark in the Posting Reference column. The beginning balances for Part 2 are the same as the balances from your solution to Part 1 of Comprehensive Problem 2.

For working paper users and nonusers:

2. Enter transactions for the month of January in the general journal. Post immediately to the accounts receivable and accounts payable ledgers.
3. Post from the journal to the general ledger.
4. Prepare schedules of accounts receivable and accounts payable.
5. Prepare a month-end spreadsheet income statement, statement of owner's equity, and balance sheet. The mortgage payable includes $600 that is due within one year.
6. Journalize and post adjusting entries.
7. Journalize and post closing entries. (*Hint*: Close all expense and revenue account balances. Then close Income Summary and Tom Jones, Drawing to Tom Jones, Capital.)
8. Prepare a post-closing trial balance.

*Page references in **bold** indicate defined terms.

A

AAA (American Accounting Association), 6
ABA Number, **232**
accountants, 8–10
account form of balance sheet, **186**
accounting, **4**
    careers opportunities in, 8–15, *fig.* 8
    job opportunities in, 10, *fig. 11–13*
    methods of, 149–151, *fig.* 150, *fig.* 151
    process of, 4–5, *fig. 5*
    process of, overview of, 35, *fig.* 35
    purpose of, 4
accounting clerks, **8**, 193
    job opportunities and salaries for, *fig.* 12
accounting cycle, **195–196**
    comprehensive problem on, 223–227
    with subsidiary ledgers, 614–618
accounting equation, **22–23**
    effect of transactions on, 23–31
    expanding, 25–26
accounting information, users of, *fig.* 4
accounting information systems, **10**
accounting period concept, **26**
Accounting Standards Update, **6**
accounts, **23**
    chart of, **88**, *fig.* 88
    general ledger, **94–95**
    permanent, **189**
    temporary, **189**
accounts payable, **21**
    schedule of, **415–416**, *fig.* 416
accounts payable ledger, **411**
    posting cash payments to, 414–415, *fig.* 414, *fig.* 415
    posting from the cash payments journal to, 457, *fig.* 459
    posting from the purchases journal to, 454–455, *fig.* 455
    posting purchases to, 411–412, *fig.* 412
    purchases returns and allowances in, 412–413, *fig.* 413
accounts payable manager, *fig.* 13
accounts receivable, **21**
    for merchandise sales, 359–360, *fig.* 360
    schedule of, **372**, *fig.* 373
accounts receivable ledger, **365–367**, *fig.* 367
    after posting, *fig.* 373
    posting cash receipts to, 371, *fig.* 372
    posting from the cash receipts journal to, 450, *fig.* 451
    posting from the sales journal to, 445–447, *fig.* 446
    sales returns and allowances in, 368, *fig.* 369
accounts receivable turnover, **574–575**
account titles, **23**
accrual basis of accounting, 130, **149–151**, *fig.* 150, *fig.* 151
ACFE (Association of Certified Fraud Examiners), 243
adequate documents and records, 270
adjusted trial balance, *fig.* 145
Adjusted Trial Balance columns, **144**
adjusting entries, 130–183
    defined, **131**
    depreciation expense, **136–138**, *fig.* 137, *fig.* 138
    end-of-period adjustments, 131–138, 362, *fig.* 362
    under the expense method, 563–565
    for inventory shrinkage, **539**
    journalizing, 536, *fig.* 536
    journalizing from the work sheet, 147–148, *fig.* 148
    for merchandising businesses, 525–565
    methods of accounting and, 149–151
    periodic inventory system, 526–530, *fig.* 537
    perpetual inventory system, 537–539, *fig.* 537
    posting, 138, *fig.* 139–140
    reversing entries, **579**, *fig.* 580–581
    for unearned revenue, 530–532
    workers' compensation insurance, 335
    the work sheet and, **140–148**
ADP (Automatic Data Processing, Inc.), 334
AICPA (American Institute of Certified Public Accountants), 6
American Accounting Association (AAA), 6
American Bankers Association, 232
American Institute of Certified Public Accountants (AICPA), 6
analyzing, **5**
    transactions (*see* transaction analysis)
AppRiver, 50
Arrow Electronics, 282
asset accounts, debits and credits in, 55–57
asset method, **564**
assets, **21**, 52
    in the accounting equation, 22–23
    cost of products and, 22
    current, **188**
Association of Certified Fraud Examiners (ACFE), 243
ATMs (automated teller machines), **234–235**
AT&T, 22, 195
auditing, **9**
    job opportunities and salaries in, *fig.* 13
auditing clerks, 193
authorization procedures and related responsibilities, 269–270
automated teller machines (ATMs), **234–235**
Automatic Data Processing, Inc. (ADP), 334
average collection period, **575**
average cost method. *see* weighted-average method
average days to sell inventory, **576**

B

bad checks, 370
balance, **51**
  credit, **54**
  debit, **54**
  normal, **54**
balance sheet, **34**, 186–188, *fig.* 33, *fig.* 187
  analysis of, 573–574
  linkages between work sheet and, *fig.* 187
  for merchandising businesses, 571–573, *fig.* 572
Balance Sheet columns, **144**
bank credit card sales, 370
bank reconciliation, **238**
  electronic banking and, **242**–243
  illustration of, 239–241, *fig.* 239–240
  journal entries, 241–242, *fig.* 242
bank statements, **235**–**236**
  reconciling, 236–243
"Big Four," 9
billing clerks, 368
blank endorsement, **234**
bookkeepers, **8**
  job opportunities and salaries for, *fig.* 12
bookkeeping, computerized, 452
bookkeeping clerks, 193
book of original entry, **89**
book value, **573**
brokerage clerks, 368
budget analysts, job opportunities and salaries for, *fig.* 12
budgeting, **10**
business activities, types of, 218–219
business entity, **21**
business entity concept, **21**
businesses, types of, 7, *fig.* 7
business transactions, **23**. *see also* transaction analysis

C

Campus Advantages, 85
canceled checks, **236**
capital, **21**
cash, **232**
  cash short and over, 247–248
  change fund, **246**–247
  checking accounts, 232–236
  petty cash fund, **243**–246
  reconciling bank statements, 236–243
  T account, *fig.* 52
cash basis of accounting, **149**–151, *fig.* 150, *fig.* 151
cash discounts, 362, 402
  cash management and, 407
cashiers, 248
cash management, 407
cash payments, 237, *fig.* 238
  internal controls over, 272–276
  journalizing and posting, 413–415, *fig.* 413, *fig.* 414
cash payments journal, 442, **456**, *fig.* 442, *fig.* 456
  posting from, 457, *fig.* 458–459
cash receipts, 368–371
  internal controls over, 271–272, *fig.* 271
cash receipts journal, **447**–451, *fig.* 448
  posting from, 448–450, *fig.* 449, *fig.* 451
cash register tape summary, 356, *fig.* 356
cash sales, 369
cash short and over account, 247–248
cash receipts journal, 442, *fig.* 442
Certified Fraud Examiner (CFE), **9**
Certified Internal Auditor (CIA), **10**
Certified Management Accountant (CMA), **10**
Certified Public Accountant (CPA), **9**
CFE (Certified Fraud Examiner), **9**
change fund, **246**–248
chart of accounts, **88**, *fig.* 88
  expanded, 138, 531–532, *fig.* 139, *fig.* 532
checking accounts, 232–236
  automated teller machines, 234–235
  bank statements, reconciling, 236–243
  electronic banking, 242–243
  endorsements, 232, 234
  fraud and, 370
  making deposits, 232, *fig.* 234
  opening, 232
  writing checks, 235
check registers, **276**
checks, **235**
  outstanding, **238**, 239
check stub, **235**, *fig.* 236
CIA (Certified Internal Auditor), **10**
CIP (Customer Identification Program), **232**
Circular E—Employer's Tax Guide, 287, 324
classified balance sheet, **186**
classifying, **5**
closing entries, 576–578, *fig.* 577
closing process, **189**–**194**
  accounting cycle and, **195**–**196**
  journalizing closing entries, 192, *fig.* 192
  for merchandising businesses, 576–578, *fig.* 576
  post-closing trial balance and, 194–195
  posting closing entries, 192, *fig.* 193–194
  steps in, 190, *fig.* 191
CMA (Certified Management Accountant), **10**
collections, **238**
  on account, 368
computerized bookkeeping, 452
computer skills, 10
consignee, **493**
consignment, **493**
consignor, **493**
consistency, **495**, 498
contra-asset, **136**
contra-cost accounts, **405**
contra-purchases accounts, **405**
contra-revenue accounts, **361**–**362**, *fig.* 361, *fig.* 362
control activities, 269–270
control environment, 268–269

controller, **10**
  job opportunities and salary for, *fig.* 13
controlling accounts, **366**
corporation, **7**, *fig.* 6
correcting entry, **102–103**, *fig.* 103. *see also* adjusting entries; errors
cost, **499**
cost accounting, **10**
cost flows, 497
cost of goods sold, **408**
  allocation of goods available for sale to, *fig.* 494
  assigning cost to, 492–500
  calculation of, *fig.* 527
  importance of inventory in, 533
cost of merchandise sold, **408**
CPA (Certified Public Accountant), **9**
credit authorizers and checkers, 368
credit balances, **54**
credit card sales, 370
credit memos, **239**, **358**, *fig.* 359
credits, **52–54**
  posting, *fig.* 96
credit terms, 362, *fig.* 362
current assets, **188**, **571–572**
current liabilities, **188**, **573**
current ratio, **574**
Customer Identification Program (CIP), **232**
Customer Refunds Payable, **529**

D

data flow, 86
Davis, Kenneth W., 13–15
debit balances, **54**
debit memos, 238–239
debits, **52–54**
  posting, *fig.* 95
deductions
  from employee earnings, 286–290
  voluntary, 290
Deloitte, 9
deposits
  making in checking accounts, 232, *fig.* 234
  reconciling bank statements, 237–238
deposits in transit, **238–239**
deposit tickets, **232**, *fig.* 234
depreciable cost, **136**
depreciation, **136**
depreciation expense, 136–138, *fig.* 137, *fig.* 138
depreciation methods, 179–183, 690–697
direct deposit, **294**
double-declining-balance method, **181**
double-entry accounting, 50–84
  debits and credits in, 52–54
  defined, **51**
  T account in, 50–52
  transaction analysis and, 54–66
  trial balance and, 66–67, *fig.* 67–68
drawee, **235**
drawer, **235**
drawing, **26**, 54
  debits and credits including, 57–65

E

earnings
  deductions from total, 286–290
  employee, 283–286
  importance of to the stock market, 195
EFT (electronic funds transfer), **242–243**
EFT (electronic funds transfers), 294
EFTPS (Electronic Federal Tax Payment System), **324–325**
EIN (employer identification number), 232
electronic banking, 242–243
Electronic Federal Tax Payment System (EFTPS), **324–325**
electronic funds transfers (EFT), **242–243**, 294
electronic system, 298–299, *fig.* 299
employee earnings record, 294, *fig.* 293–294
employee federal income tax payable, 297
employees, **283**
  earnings, 283–285
  paying, 292–294, *fig.* 293
  payroll records, 291–294
Employee's Withholding Allowance Certificate, Form W-4, 286–287, *fig.* 286
employer FICA taxes, **318–319**
employer identification number (EIN), 232
Employer's Annual Federal Unemployment (FUTA) Tax Return, 328–329, *fig.* 328–329
Employer's Quarterly Federal Tax Return, 325, *fig.* 326–327
employer taxes and reports, 317–352
  accounting for payroll, 321–323
  FICA, 318–319
  FUTA, **320**
  reporting and payment responsibilities, 323–333
  self-employment, 319
  summary of, 332, *fig.* 332
  workers' compensation insurance, 333–335
Employment Eligibility Verification, 332
ending inventory
  allocation of goods available for sale to cost of goods sold and, *fig.* 494
  cost of goods sold and, 533
end-of-period adjustments, 131–138, 362, 534–535, *fig.* 362, *fig.* 535
endorsements, **232**, 234
Ernst & Young, 9
errors
  in bank reconciliation, 238–239
  in inventory, 489–490, *fig.* 490
  in trial balance, 102–103
  on the work sheet, 147, *fig.* 147
Estimated Returns Inventory, **529**–530, *fig.* 530
expanded chart of accounts, 138, 531–532, *fig.* 139, *fig.* 532
Expense and Revenue Summary, 190

expense method, **563–565**
expense recognition principle, **131**
expenses, **25–26**, 54
  debits and credits including, 57–65
  depreciation, 136–138, *fig.* 137, *fig.* 138
  effect of transaction on the accounting equation, 26–31
  expense method of accounting for prepaid, **563–565**
experience-rating system, **320**
Exposure Draft, **6**

F

Fair Labor Standards Act (FLSA), **283**, 285
FASB (Financial Accounting Standards Board), 5–6
Federal Insurance Contributions Act (FICA), 287
Federal Unemployment Tax Act (FUTA) tax, **320**
FICA (Federal Insurance Contributions Act), 287
FICA taxes, **287**, 290
  employer, **318–319**
FIFO (first-in, first-out) method, **494–495**, 497–498, *fig.* 495, *fig.* 497, *fig.* 499
financial accounting, **10**
Financial Accounting Standards Board (FASB), 5–6
Financial Accounting Standards Board Accounting Standards Codification, **6**
financial clerks, 368
Financial Executives International (FEI), 6
financial ratios, 578
financial statement analysis, 573–576
financial statements, 32–34, 184–222, *fig.* 33
  adjusting entry for supplies on, *fig.* 133
  impact of merchandise inventory on, 489–490
  spreadsheets in preparing, 528
  trial balance linkages with, *fig.* 67–68
financing activities, **218**
first-in, first-out (FIFO) method, **494–495**, 497–498, *fig.* 495, *fig.* 497, *fig.* 499
fiscal year, **26**, **131**
Floyd's 99 Barbershop, 130
FLSA (Fair Labor Standards Act), **283**, 285
FOB destination, **407–408**
FOB shipping point, **407–408**
footings, **51**
forensic accounting, **9**
Form 940, 328–329, *fig.* 328–329
Form 940-V, *fig.* 330
Form 941, 325, *fig.* 326–327
Form 944, 325
Form 1099, 283
Form I-9, 332
Form W-2, 330–331, *fig.* 330
Form W-3, 331–332, *fig.* 331
Form W-4, 286–287, *fig.* 286
Fortune 500, 7
fraud, 243
  credit card, 370
  payroll, 295
free on board. *see* FOB destination
freight-in accounts, 406–407, *fig.* 409
FUTA (Federal Unemployment Tax Act) taxes, **320**, 323
  calculation and payment, 325–329, *fig.* 326–327, *fig.* 328
FUTA Tax Payable, 323

G

GAAP. *see* generally accepted accounting principles (GAAP)
general expenses, **569**
general journal, **89**–93
  after posting, *fig.* 97–98
  cash receipts in, 370, *fig.* 371
  entries, *fig.* 92–93
  posting cash payments from, 414, *fig.* 413
  purchases in, 409–410, *fig.* 410
  types of transactions in, *fig.* 442
general ledger, 93–101
  after posting, *fig.* 99–100, *fig.* 373
  closing entries posted to, *fig.* 193–194
  defined, **94**
  posting cash payments to, 414, *fig.* 414, *fig.* 415
  posting cash receipts in, 371, *fig.* 372
  posting from the cash payments journal to, 457, *fig.* 458
  posting from the cash receipts journal to, 448–450, *fig.* 449
  posting from the purchases journal to, 453–454, *fig.* 454
  posting from the sales journal to, 444–446, *fig.* 445
  posting purchases to, 410, *fig.* 411
  posting sales to, 364–365, *fig.* 365, *fig.* 366
  posting to, 95–97, *fig.* 97–100
general ledger account, **94–95**
generally accepted accounting principles (GAAP), **5–6**
General's Favorite Fishing Hole, The, 223–227
ghost employees, 295
governmental accounting, 10
gross margin, **408**, **567**
gross pay, **286**
gross-price method, **438**
gross profit, **408**, **567**
  computation of, 408–409, 489, *fig.* 409
gross profit method, **500**, *fig.* 501

H

H2O Audio, 231
Haas Transfer Warehouse, 295
Health Insurance Premiums Payable, 298
historical cost principle, **136**

I

IASB (International Accounting Standards Board), 6
IFRS (International Financial Reporting Standards), 6
IMA (Institute of Management Accountants), 6
income from operations, **567**
income statement, **32**, 34, 185, 567–570
  computation of gross profit on, *fig.* 409
  multiple-step, **567**, *fig.* 570
  single-step, **567**, *fig.* 569

Income Statement columns, **144**
Income Summary, **190**
income taxes
 state, 291
 withholding table for, *fig.* 288–289
income tax withholding, 286–287, *fig.* 288–289
 employer reporting and payments, 324–325
independent contractors, **283**
industrial engineering technician, 12
Indy Express Band, 184
information and communication systems, 270
Innovar, 399
input, **35**, *fig.* 35
Institute of Management Accountants (IMA), 6
insurance
 prepaid, 133–134, *fig.* 134
 workers' compensation, **333–335**
insurance claims and policy-processing clerks, 368
Intechra Group, 282
internal auditing, **10**
internal control, **232**, 401
 importance of, 267–268
 key components of, 268–271
 over cash receipts, 271–272
internal controls
 over cash payments, 272–276
Internal Revenue Service (IRS), 287, 498
International Accounting Standards Board (IASB), 6
International Financial Reporting Standards (IFRS), 6
interpreting, **5**
interstatement analysis, **574–576**
in transit, **493**
inventory, 488–524
 adjustments for under periodic inventory system, 526–530
 assigning cost to and cost of goods sold, 492–500
 average days to sell, **576**
 errors in, 489–490, *fig.* 490
 estimating ending, and cost of goods sold, 500–501
 impact of on financial statements, 489–490
 importance of, 533
 perpetual LIFO (last-in, first-out) method, **520–521**, *fig.* 521
 perpetual moving-average method, **521–522**, *fig.* 522
 turnover, **575**
 types of systems for, 491, *fig.* 491
 valuation, *498–500*
inventory sheet, **492**, *fig.* 492
Inventory Short and Over account, **539**
inventory shrinkage, **539**
inventory systems, 491, *fig.* 491
inventory turnover, **575**
investing activities, **218**
invoices, **401**
 purchase, **401**, *fig.* 402

J

Jets.com, 3
job opportunities, 10, *fig. 11–13*
journalizing, 85–129
 adjusting entries for merchandising businesses, 536, *fig.* 536
 adjusting entries from the work sheet, 147–148, *fig.* 148
 in bank reconciliation, 241–242, *fig.* 242
 cash receipts, 370, *fig.* 371
 chart of accounts and, **88**, *fig.* 88
 closing entries, 192, *fig.* 192
 closing process and, **189–194**
 correcting entries in, **102**–103, *fig.* 103
 defined, **89**
 employer payroll taxes, 321–322
 finding and correcting errors in the trial balance, 102–103, *fig.* 103
 flow of data and, 86
 general journal, 89–93
 general ledger, 93–101
 payroll transactions, 294–296, *fig.* 297
 posting to the general ledger, 95–100
 sales and cash receipts transactions, 364–372
 source documents and, 86, *fig.* 87
 trial balance and, **101**, *fig.* 101
journals, **89**
 cash payments, 442, **447–451**, *fig.* 442
 cash receipts, **447–451**
 purchases, **452–455**, *fig.* 453
 sales, 442, **443–447**, *fig.* 442
 special, **442–443**
 types of, 442, *fig.* 442

K

Kalso Earth Shoes, 355, 399
Kendall Square, 578
kiting, **272**
KPMG, 9
Kroger, 488
Kroger, Barney, 488

L

lapping, **272**
last-in, first-out (LIFO) method, **496–498**, *fig.* 496, *fig.* 497
 perpetual, **520–521**
liabilities, **21**, 53
 in the accounting equation, 22–23
 current, **188**
 long-term, **188**
liability accounts, debits and credits in, 55–57
LIFO (last-in, first-out) method, **496–498**, *fig.* 496, *fig.* 497
 perpetual, **520–521**
LinguaLinx, 317
liquidity, **572**
loan interviewers, 368
long-term assets, **188**
long-term debt, **188**
long-term liabilities, **188**, **573**

lookback period, 324
Loss on Write-Down of Inventory, **500**
lower-of-cost-or-market method, **498–500**

M

MACRS (Modified Accelerated Cost Recovery System), **181**, *fig.* 181
magnetic ink character recognition (MICR) code, **232**
management advisory services, **9**
managerial accounting, 10
manual system, 298
manufacturing businesses, 7, *fig.* 7
market, **499**
marketing chain, 357, *fig.* 357
matching principle, **131**
material recording clerks, 490
Mattel, Inc., 132
Medicare taxes, 287, 290, 298, 319, 322
  payments, 324–325
merchandising businesses, **7**, **356**, *fig.* 7
  adjustments for, 525–565
  closing entries for, 576–578
  financial statements for, 566–576
  inventory, 488–524
  journalizing and posting purchases and cash payments transactions, 409–415
  journalizing and posting sales and cash receipts transactions, 364–372
  merchandise purchases accounts, 404–409
  merchandise purchases transactions, 400–404
  reversing entries for, **579**, *fig.* 580–581
  sales accounts, 359–364
  sales transactions, 356–359
  schedule of accounts payable, **415–416**, *fig.* 416
  schedule of accounts receivable, 372, *fig.* 373
MICR (magnetic ink character recognition) code, **232**
Modified Accelerated Cost Recovery System (MACRS), **181**, *fig.* 181
modified cash basis of accounting, **150–151**, *fig.* 150, *fig.* 151
monitoring processes, 270–271
mortgage, **573**
Mortgage Payable account, **573**
moving-average method, **521–522**, *fig.* 522
multiple-step income statement, **567**, *fig.* 570

N

natural business year, **492**
net income, **26**, 147, *fig.* 147
  closing, *fig.* 191
net loss, **26**, 147, *fig.* 147
  closing, *fig.* 191
net pay, **286**
  computing, 290
net-price method, **438**
  recording with, 438
net sales, **567**
net worth, **21**
new account clerks, 368
Night, Bob, 223–227
normal balances, **54**
notes payable, **21**
not-for-profit accounting, 10
not sufficient funds (NSF) checks, **238**
NutraPlanet, 441

O

operating activities, **218**
operating cycle, **188**, **571**, *fig.* 188
operating income, **567**
operating statement, **32**, 34
output, **35**, *fig.* 35
outstanding checks, **238**, 239
overtime, 284
owner's capital, 53, *fig.* 53
owner's equity, **21**, 573
  in the accounting equation, 22–23
  accounts, debits and credits on, 55–57
  statement of, **34**, 185–186, *fig.* 187
  umbrella, 53, *fig.* 53
ownership structures, 6–7, *fig.* 6

P

paid vouchers file, **276**
para-accountants, **8**
partnership, **7**, *fig.* 6
paychecks, 292, *fig.* 293
Paychex, Inc., 334
payee, **235**
payment process, voucher system for, 275–276, *fig.* 275, *fig.* 276
payroll accounting, 282–316, *fig.* 297
  employee earnings and deductions, 283–290
  for employee earnings and deductions, 294–298
  for employees vs independent contractors, 283
  employer payroll taxes, 318–323
  employer taxes and reports, 317–352
  record-keeping methods, 298–299
  records in, 291–294
payroll calendar, 332, *fig.* 333
payroll fraud, 295
payroll processing center, 298, 334
payroll register, **291–292**, *fig.* 292, *fig.* 293, *fig.* 318–319
payroll taxes expense, 322
PCAOB (Public Company Accounting Oversight Board), 9
percentage method, **287**
periodic inventory system, **491**, 494–498, *fig.* 491
  adjustments in, 526–530
permanent accounts, **189**
perpetual inventory system, **491**, 498, *fig.* 491, *fig.* 499
  adjusting entries under, 537–539, *fig.* 537
  LIFO, 520–521

perpetual LIFO (last-in, first-out) method, **520–521**, *fig.* 521
perpetual moving-average method inventory method, **521–522**, *fig.* 522
personal identification numbers (PINs), 234
petty cash fund, **243–246**
  replenishing, 246
petty cash payments record, **244**, 246, *fig.* 245
petty cash voucher, **244**, *fig.* 244
physical flows of goods, 497
physical inventory, **492–493**, *fig.* 494
plant assets, **188**
PNC Field, 525
post-closing trial balance, **194**, **577**, *fig.* 195, *fig.* 578
posting, **95**
  adjusting entries, 138, *fig.* 139–140
  closing entries, 192, *fig.* 193–194
  to the general ledger, 95–97, *fig.* 97–100
posting clerks, 368
Preliminary Views, **5**
prepaid expenses, **563–565**
prepaid insurance, 133–134
PricewaterhouseCoopers, 9
private accounting, 10
processing, **35**, *fig.* 35
procurement clerks, 401
profit and loss statement, **32**, 34
property, plant, and equipment, **188**, **572–573**
protection of assets and records, 270
public accounting, 9
Publication 15, 287
Publication 334, Tax Guide for Small Business, 319
Public Company Accounting Oversight Board (PCAOB), 9
public hearings, **5**
publicly held companies, **267**
purchase invoices, **401**, *fig.* 402
purchase orders, **400**, *fig.* 401
purchase requisitions, **400**, *fig.* 401
purchases, **400**
  journalizing and posting, 409–415, *fig.* 410, *fig.* 411, *fig.* 3412, *fig.* 3413, *fig.* 3414
  merchandise accounts, 404–409
  merchandise transactions, 400–404
  returns and allowances, 412–413, *fig.* 413
purchases account, 404–405
purchases discounts accounts, 406, *fig.* 409
purchases journal, 442, **452–455**, *fig.* 442, *fig.* 453
  posting from, 453–455, *fig.* 454, *fig.* 455
purchases returns and allowances, 412–413, *fig.* 413
purchases returns and allowances account, 405–406
purchasing process, 273–274, *fig.* 273
  documents, *fig.* 400
  net-price method in, **438–440**
  voucher system for, 273–275, *fig.* 273

Q

quick assets, **574**
QuickBooks, 20, 452

R

RailRiders, 525
receiving reports, **400–401**
recording, **5**
record-keeping methods, 298–299
report form of balance sheet, **186**
reporting, **5**
residual value, **136**
restrictive endorsement, **234**, *fig.* 234
retailer, 356–357
retail method of inventory, **501**, *fig.* 501
return on owner's equity, **574**
revenue recognition principle, **131**
revenues, **25**, 53
  debits and credits including, 57–65
  effect of transaction on the accounting equation, 26–31
reversing entries, **579**, *fig.* 580–581
RFDI (radio frequency identification) tags, 493
risk assessment, 269
Rob's Bike Courier Service, 20

S

Sage 50 Accounting, 452
salaries expense, 297
salary, **283–284**
Salary.com, *fig.* 12–13
sales, **356**
  retail, 356–357
sales accounts, 359–364
sales allowances, **358**
  adjustments for, 529, *fig.* 529
sales discounts, 362, *fig.* 363
sales discounts account, 362–364, *fig.* 362, *fig.* 363
sales invoices, **357–358**, *fig.* 358
sales journal, 442, **443–447**, *fig.* 442, *fig.* 443
  posting from, 444–447, *fig.* 445, *fig.* 446
sales returns, **358**, 368
  adjustments for, 529, 538–539, *fig.* 529
sales returns and allowances account, 361–362, *fig.* 361, *fig.* 362
  adjustments in, 529, *fig.* 529
  posting to, 368, *fig.* 369
sales tax payable account, 360–361
sales tickets, **357**, *fig.* 357
sales transactions, in merchandising businesses, 356–359
salvage value, **136**
Sarbanes-Oxley Act (SOX), **9**, 267
schedule of accounts payable, **415–416**, *fig.* 416
schedule of accounts receivable, **372**, *fig.* 373
Scranton/Wilkes-Barre RailRiders, 525
scrap value, **136**
SEC. *see* Securities and Exchange Commission (SEC)
SECA (Self-Employment Contributions Act), **319**
Section 404 reports, 267, *fig.* 268
Securities and Exchange Commission (SEC), 5
segregation of duties, 269
Self-Employment Contributions Act (SECA), **319**

self-employment income, **319**
self-employment tax, **319**
selling expenses, **567**
service businesses, **7**, *fig.* 7
service charges, **238**
shrinkage, inventory, **539**
signature cards, **232**, *fig.* 233
single-step income statement, **567**, *fig.* 569
slide errors, *fig.* 102
Social Security taxes, 287, 290, 298, 318–319, 322
    payments, 324–325
sole proprietorship, **6**, *fig.* 6
source documents, **86**, *fig.* 87
    electronic, 87
    flow of data from, *fig.* 86
special journals, **442–443**
specific identification method, 493, **494**, 497–498, *fig.* 495, *fig.* 497
spreadsheets, 528
    end-of-period, 534–535, *fig.* 535
statement of cash flows, 218–222
    preparing, 219–221
statement of earnings, employee, *fig.* 293–294
statement of financial condition, **34**
statement of financial position, **34**
statement of owner's equity, **34**, 185–186, *fig.* 34
    additional investments by the owner and, 188, *fig.* 189
    linkages between work sheet and, *fig.* 187
    for merchandising businesses, 570–571, *fig.* 571
stock market, importance of earnings to, 195
straight-line method, **136**, **179**–180, *fig.* 138, *fig.* 180
subsidiary ledgers, **366**
    accounting cycle with, 614–618
summarizing, **5**
sum-of-the-years'-digits, **180**
sum-of-the-years'-digits method, **180**, *fig.* 180
supplies
    adjusting entries for, 132–133, *fig.* 133
    as asset or expense, 61
SUTA (state unemployment tax), **320**, 329–330, *fig.* 320
SUTA Tax Payable, 323

T

T account, 51
    balancing, 51–52
    cash, *fig.* 51
    closing entries in, *fig.* 191
    compared to general ledger account, *fig.* 94–95
    transaction analysis with, 54–66
tax accounting, **10**
taxation, **9**
taxes
    deposit rules summary, *fig.* 324
    EFTPS for, **324–325**
    employee, 287–290, 331–332
    employer payroll, 317–323, *fig.* 322
    sales, 360–361
    self-employment, **319**
    unemployment, 320
taxpayer identification number (TIN), 232
temporary accounts, **189**
time cards, 284–285, *fig.* 284, *fig.* 285
TIN (taxpayer identification number), 232
TJ's Specialty Shop, 614–618
total end-of-period market value, 499
trade discounts, **402–403**, *fig.* 404
transaction analysis, 20–49
    accounting elements in, 21–22
    accounting equation in, 22–23, 23–31
    of business transactions, 23
    financial statements and, 32–34
    steps in, *fig.* 55
    T account for, 54–66
transactions
    effect of on the accounting equation, 26–31
    summary of, 65, *fig.* 66, *fig.* 90
Transmittal of Wage and Tax Statements, 331–332, *fig.* 331
transportation charges, 407
transposition error, *fig.* 102
trial balance, 66–**67**, *fig.* 67–68
    adjusted, *fig.* 145
    adjustments to, 533–534, *fig.* 534
    finding and correcting errors in, 102–103, *fig.* 103
    flow of data to, *fig.* 86
    in ledger accounts, **101**, *fig.* 101
    post-closing, **194**, 577, *fig.* 195, *fig.* 578
    reasons to adjust, *fig.* 131
two-column general journal, **89**

U

undepreciated cost, **573**
unearned revenue, **530–532**, *fig.* 531
unemployment taxes, 320
United Technologies Corporation, 15
United Way Contributions Payable, 298
unpaid vouchers file, **274**
USA PATRIOT Act, 232
useful life, **136**

V

voluntary deductions, 290
voucher checks, 275–276, *fig.* 276
voucher register, **274–275**
vouchers, **402**, *fig.* 403
    petty cash, **244**, *fig.* 244
voucher systems, **273–275**, **402**, *fig.* 273

W

Wage and Tax Statement, 330–331, *fig.* 330
wage-bracket method, **287**
wages
    adjusting, closing, and reversing entries for, *fig.* 580
    job opportunities and, *fig.* 12–13

wages expense, 135, **283–284**, 297, *fig.* 135
Wal-Mart, 493
Walt Disney Company, 132
weighted-average method, **495–496**, 497–498, *fig.* 497
wholesalers, 357–358, *fig.* 357
withdrawals, **26**, 54. *see also* drawing
effect of transaction on the accounting equation, 26–31
withholding allowance, **286**
Woot, Inc., 566
workers' compensation insurance, **333–335**
working capital, **573–574**
work sheet, **140–148**
end-of period activities using, 185
finding errors on the, 147, *fig.* 147
journalizing adjusting entries from, 147–148, *fig.* 148
linkages with income statement, *fig.* 186
linkages with statement of owner's equity, *fig.* 187
preparing, 142–147, *fig.* 141, *fig.* 143
10-column, 140
writing skills, 13–15

COLLEGE ACCOUNTING
ACCOUNTING CYCLE FOR PROPRIETORSHIP (CHAPTERS 1–6)—QUICK REFERENCE

THE ACCOUNTING EQUATION

Assets = Liabilities + Owner's Equity

FINANCIAL STATEMENTS

Income Statement	**Revenues − Expenses = Net Income or Loss**
Statement of Owner's Equity	**Beginning Capital + Investments + Net Income − Withdrawals = Ending Capital**
Balance Sheet	**Assets = Liabilities + Owner's Equity**

T ACCOUNT

Title	
Debit = Left	Credit = Right

EXPANDED ACCOUNTING EQUATION SHOWING RULES OF DEBIT AND CREDIT

Assets		=	Liabilities		+	Owner's Equity	
Dr.	Cr.		Dr.	Cr.		Dr.	Cr.
+	−		−	+		−	+

Drawing		Expenses		Revenue	
Dr.	Cr.	Dr.	Cr.	Dr.	Cr.
+	−	+	−	−	+

STEPS IN MAJOR ACCOUNTING PROCESSES

Steps in Journalizing a Transaction

1. Enter the date.
2. Enter the account title and debit amount.
3. Enter the account title and credit amount.
4. Enter the explanation.

Steps in Posting from the Journal to the Ledger

In the ledger:

1. Enter the date in the Date column.
2. Enter the amount of each transaction in the Debit or Credit column.
3. Enter the new balance in the Balance column under Debit or Credit.
4. Enter the page number of the journal from which each transaction is posted in the Posting Reference column.

In the journal:

5. Enter the ledger account number in the Posting Reference column in the journal.

Steps in Preparing the Work Sheet

1. Prepare the trial balance.
2. Prepare the adjustments.
3. Prepare the adjusted trial balance.
4. Extend adjusted balances to the Income Statement and Balance Sheet columns.
5. Complete the work sheet.

Steps in the Closing Process

1. Close the revenue accounts to Income Summary.
2. Close the expense accounts to Income Summary.
3. Close Income Summary to the owner's capital account.
4. Close the drawing account to the owner's capital account.

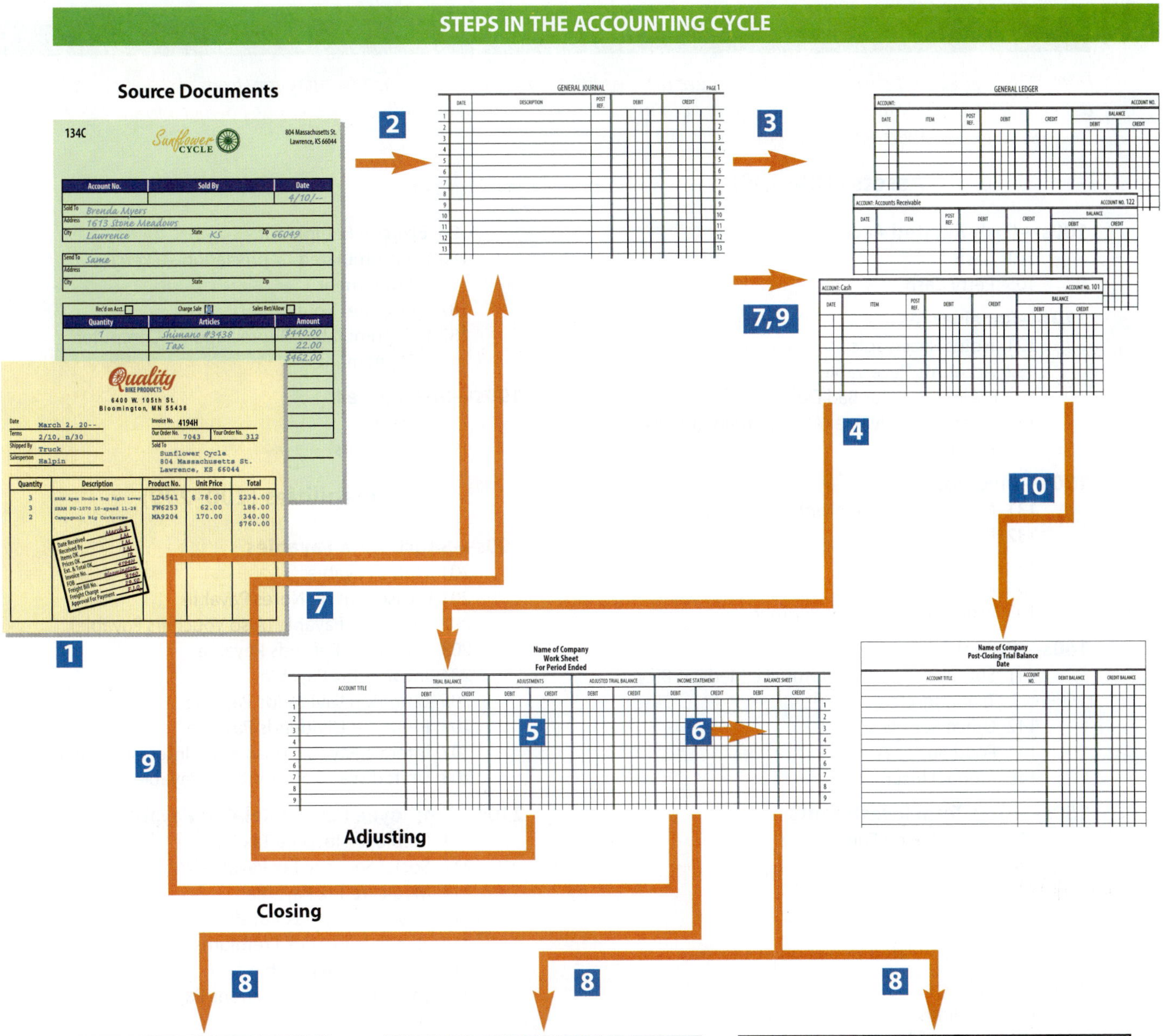

Mitchell's Campus Delivery Income Statement For Month Ended June 30, 20 --		
Revenues:		
Delivery fees		$2,150
Expenses:		
Wages expense	$650	
Rent expense	200	
Phone expense	50	
Total expenses		900
Net income		$1,250

Mitchell's Campus Delivery Statement of Owner's Equity For Month Ended June 30, 20 --		
Mitchell Williams, capital, June 1, 20--		$ —
Investments during June		2,000
Total investment		$2,000
Net income for June	$1,250	
Less: withdrawals for June	150	
Increase in capital		1,100
Mitchell Williams, capital, June 30, 20--		$3,100

Mitchell's Campus Delivery Balance Sheet June 30, 20 --			
Assets		Liabilities	
Cash	$ 370	Accounts payable	$1,800
Accounts receivable	650		
Supplies	80	Owner's Equity	
Prepaid insurance	200	Mitchell Williams, capital	3,100
Delivery equipment	3,600		
		Total liabilities and	
Total assets	$4,900	owner's equity	$4,900

Steps in the Accounting Cycle

During Accounting Period:

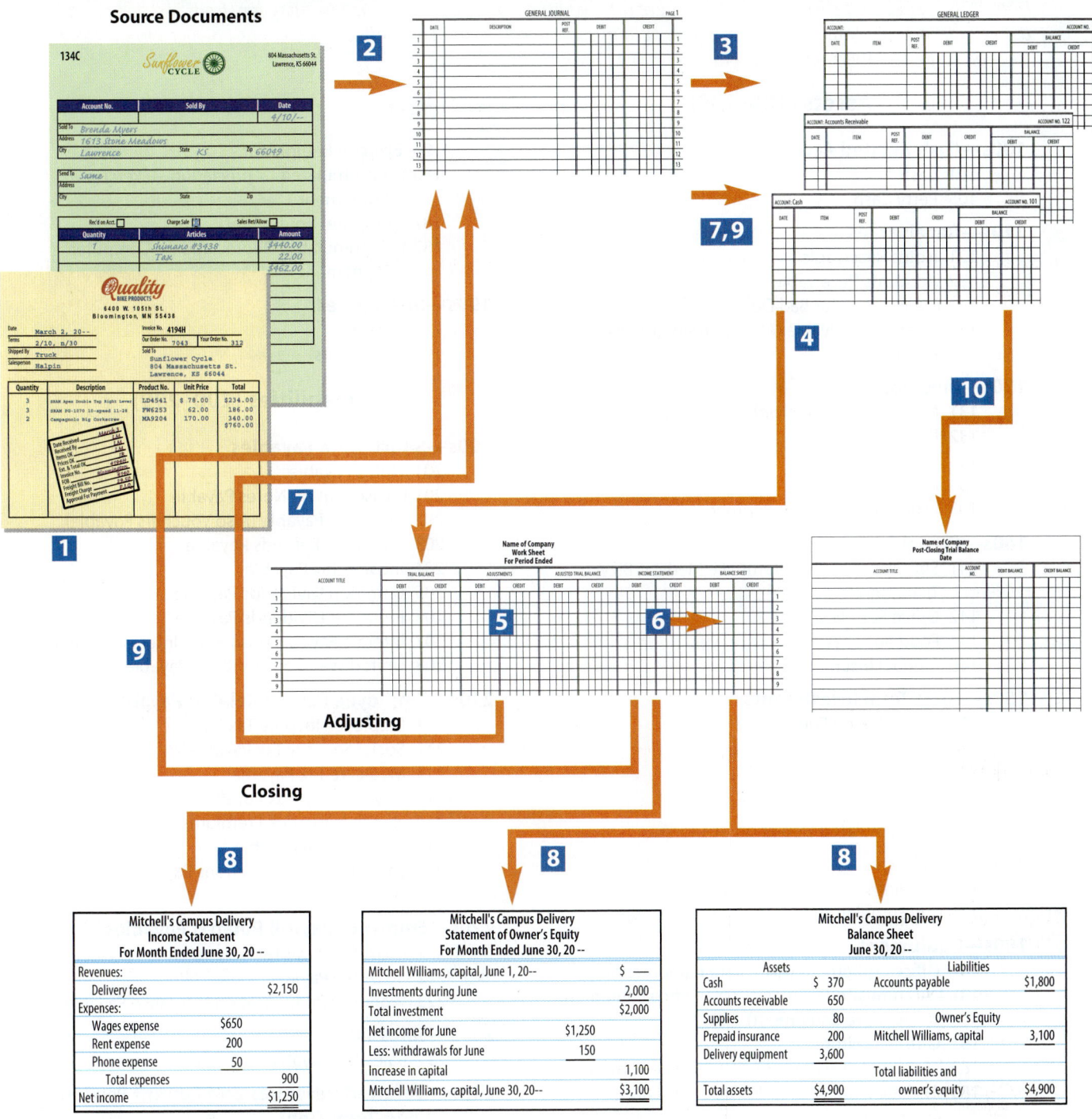

1. Analyze source documents.
2. Journalize the transactions.
3. Post to the ledger accounts.

End of Accounting Period:

4. Prepare a trial balance.
5. Determine and prepare the needed adjustments on the work sheet.
6. Complete an end-of-period work sheet.
7. Journalize and post the adjusting entries.
8. Prepare an income statement, statement of owner's equity, and balance sheet.
9. Journalize and post the closing entries.
10. Prepare a post-closing trial balance.

CHART OF ACCOUNTS

Note: While for a specific company each account number used would have only one title, titles vary from company to company as needed. Particularly for the Owner's Equity accounts, the accounts used depend on the company ownership structure (proprietorship, partnership, or corporation).

Assets (100–199)

100s—Cash Related Accounts
- 101 Cash
- 105 Petty Cash

120s—Receivables
- 121 Notes Receivable
- 122 Accounts Receivable
- 122.1 Allowance for Bad Debts
- 123 Interest Receivable (Also Accrued Interest Receivable)

130s—Inventories
- 131 Merchandise Inventory
- 132 Raw Materials
- 133 Work in Process
- 134 Finished Goods
- 135 Estimated Returns Inventory

140s—Prepaid Items
- 141 Supplies (Specialty items like Medical, Bicycle, Tailoring, etc.)
- 142 Office Supplies
- 144 Food Supplies
- 145 Prepaid Insurance

150s—Long-Term Investments
- 153 Bond Sinking Fund

160s—Land
- 161 Land
- 162 Natural Resources
- 162.1 Accumulated Depletion

170s—Buildings
- 171 Buildings
- 171.1 Accumulated Depreciation—Buildings

180s—Equipment
- 181 Office Equipment (Also Store Equipment)
- 181.1 Accumulated Depreciation—Office Equipment (Also Store Equipment)
- 182 Office Furniture
- 182.1 Accumulated Depreciation—Office Furniture
- 183 Athletic Equipment (Also Tailoring, Lawn, Cleaning)
- 183.1 Accumulated Depreciation—Athletic Equipment (Also Tailoring, Lawn, Cleaning)
- 184 Tennis Facilities (Also Basketball Facilities)
- 184.1 Accumulated Depreciation—Tennis Facilities (Also Basketball Facilities)
- 185 Delivery Equipment (Also Medical, Van)
- 185.1 Accumulated Depreciation—Delivery Equipment (Also Medical, Van)
- 186 Exercise Equipment
- 186.1 Accumulated Depreciation—Exercise Equipment
- 187 Computer Equipment
- 187.1 Accumulated Depreciation—Computer Equipment

190s—Intangibles
- 191 Patents
- 192 Copyrights

Liabilities (200–299)

200s—Short-Term Payables
- 201 Notes Payable
- 201.1 Discount on Notes Payable
- 202 Accounts Payable (Also Vouchers Payable)
- 203 Customer Refunds Payable
- 204 Income Tax Payable
- 205 Common Dividends Payable
- 206 Preferred Dividends Payable
- 207 Interest Payable (Also Bond Interest Payable)
- 208 United Way Contributions Payable

210s—Employee Payroll Related Payables
- 211 Employee Income Tax Payable
- 212 Social Security Tax Payable
- 213 Medicare Tax Payable
- 215 City Earnings Tax Payable
- 216 Health Insurance Premiums Payable
- 217 Credit Union Payable
- 218 Savings Bond Deductions Payable
- 219 Wages Payable

220s—Employer Payroll Related Payables
- 221 FUTA Tax Payable
- 222 SUTA Tax Payable
- 223 Workers' Compensation Insurance Payable

230s—Sales Tax
- 231 Sales Tax Payable

240s—Deferred Revenues and Current Portion of Long-Term Debt
- 241 Unearned Subscription Revenue (Also Unearned Ticket Revenue, Unearned Repair Fees)
- 242 Current Portion of Mortgage Payable

250s—Long-Term Liabilities
- 251 Mortgage Payable
- 252 Bonds Payable
- 252.1 Discount on Bonds Payable
- 253 Premium on Bonds Payable

Owner's Equity (300–399)

311 Rohan Macsen, Capital
312 Rohan Macsen, Drawing
313 Income Summary
321 Common Stock
321.1 Common Treasury Stock
322 Paid in Capital in Excess of Par/Stated Value—Common Stock
323 Preferred Stock
323.1 Preferred Treasury Stock
324 Paid in Capital in Excess of Par/Stated Value—Preferred Stock
327 Common Stock Subscribed
327.1 Common Stock Subscriptions Receivable
328 Preferred Stock Subscribed
328.1 Preferred Stock Subscriptions Receivable
329 Paid in Capital from Sale of Treasury Stock
331 Retained Earnings
332 Retained Earnings Appropriated for...
333 Cash Dividends
334 Stock Dividends

Revenues (400–499)

400s—Operating Revenues

401 Delivery Fees
401 Appraisal Fees
401 Medical Fees
401 Service Fees
401 Repair Fees
401 Sales
401.1 Sales Returns and Allowances
401.2 Sales Discounts
402 Boarding and Grooming Revenue
403 Subscriptions Revenue (if main line of business)

410s—Other Revenues

411 Interest Revenue
412 Rent Revenue
413 Subscriptions Revenue (if not main line of business)
414 Sinking Fund Earnings
415 Uncollectible Accounts Recovered
416 Gain on Sale/Exchange of Equipment
417 Gain on Bonds Redeemed

Operating Expenses (500–599)

500s—Cost of Goods Sold

501 Purchases
501.1 Purchases Returns and Allowances
501.2 Purchases Discounts
502 Freight-In
504 Overhead
505 Cost of Goods Sold

510s—Selling Expenses

511 Wages Expense (Also Wages and Salaries Expense)
512 Advertising Expense
513 Bank Credit Card Expense
514 Store Supplies Expense
515 Travel and Entertainment Expense
516 Cash Short and Over
519 Depreciation Expense—Store Equipment and Fixtures

520s–40s—General and Administrative Expenses

521 Rent Expense
522 Office Salaries Expense
523 Office Supplies Expense (Also Medical)
524 Other Supplies: Food Supplies Expense (Also Medical)
525 Phone Expense
526 Transportation/Automobile Expense (Also Laboratory, Travel)
527 Collection Expense
528 Inventory Short and Over
529 Loss on Write Down of Inventory
530 Payroll Taxes Expense
531 Workers' Compensation Insurance Expense
532 Bad Debt Expense
533 Electricity Expense, Utilities Expense
534 Charitable Contributions Expense
535 Insurance Expense
536 Postage Expense
537 Repair Expense
538 Oil and Gas Expense (Also Automobile Expense)
540 Depreciation Expense—Building
541 Depreciation Expense—Equipment (Also Tennis Facilities, Delivery Equipment, Office Equipment, Furniture)
542 Depreciation Expense—Other Equipment (Medical Equipment, Exercise Equipment, Computer Equipment)
543 Depletion Expense
544 Patent Amortization
545 Organization Expense
549 Miscellaneous Expense

550s—Other Expenses

551 Interest Expense (Also Bond Interest Expense)
552 Loss on Discarded Equipment
553 Loss on Sale/Exchange of Equipment
554 Loss on Bonds Redeemed
555 Income Tax Expense